Problem Solving in C
Including Breadth
and Laboratories

D1369263

Angela B. Shiflet
Wofford College

with contributions from
Robert Martin

WEST PUBLISHING COMPANY
Minneapolis / St. Paul   New York   Los Angeles   San Francisco

PRODUCTION CREDITS

Copyediting: Margaret C. Monahan

Design: John Rokusek

Composition: Carlisle Communications

Cover Image: FPG International Corp.

Photo Credits: **2**, Telegraph Colour Library/FPG International Corp.; **7 (top)**, Vannucci Foto-Services/FPG International Corp.; **7 (bottom)**, Victor Scocozza/FPG International Corp.; **12 (left & right)**, Courtesy of International Business Machines Corporation; **15 (top)**, ISU Photo Service; **15 (bottom)**, Courtesy of International Business Machines Corporation; **16 (top)**, Courtesy of International Business Machines Corporation; **16 (bottom)**, Historical Pictures/Stock Montage Inc.; **19**, Courtesy of International Business Machines Corporation; **21**, AT&T Archives; **30**, UPI/Bettmann; **43 (top)**, Freelance Photographer's Guild/FPG International Corp.; **43 (bottom left)**, Universal Pictures Shooting Star International; **43 (bottom right)**, S.S. Shooting Star; **58**, UPI/Bettmann; **80**, Photo courtesy of The Jet Propulsion Laboratory; **180**, Historical Pictures/Stock Montage; **342**, Ken Sherman/Phototake NYC; **399**, Historical Pictures/Stock Montage Inc.; **425**, Courtesy James E. Stoots, Jr., Lawrence Livermore National Laboratory. Run by The University of California for the Department of Energy. Printed with Permission of Cray Research, Inc.; **482**, Courtesy of International Business Machines Corporation; **506** Eric Kamp/Phototake NYC; **608**, UPI/Bettmann; **680**, Michael Freeman/Phototake NYC; **730**, Courtesy of International Business Machines Corporation; **909**, Courtesy of James E. Stoots, Lawrence Livermore National Laboratories.

WEST'S COMMITMENT TO THE ENVIRONMENT

In 1906, West Publishing Company began recycling materials left over from the production of books. This began a tradition of efficient and responsible use of resources. Today, up to 95 percent of our legal books and 70 percent of our college and school texts are printed on recycled, acid-free stock. West also recycles nearly 22 million pounds of scrap paper annually–the equivalent of 181,717 trees. Since the 1960s, West has devised ways to capture and recycle waste inks, solvents, oils, and vapors created in the printing process. We also recycle plastics of all kinds, wood, glass, corrugated cardboard, and batteries, and have eliminated the use of Styrofoam book packaging. We at West are proud of the longevity and the scope of our commitment to the environment.

Production, Prepress, Printing and Binding by West Publishing Company.

 TEXT IS PRINTED ON 10% POST CONSUMER RECYCLED PAPER PRINTED WITH SOY INK

British Library Cataloguing-in-Publication Data. A catalogue record for this book is available from the British Library.

COPYRIGHT © 1995   By WEST PUBLISHING COMPANY
610 Opperman Drive
P.O. Box 64526
St. Paul, MN 55164-0526

02 01 00 99 98 97 96 95   8 7 6 5 4 3 2 1 0

Library of Congress Cataloging-in-Publication Data

Shiflet, Angela B.
   Problem solving in C including breadth and laboratories / Angela
B. Shiflet.
      p.   cm.
   Includes index.
   ISBN 0-314-04554-6 (soft)
   1. C (Computer program language)   2. Problem solving--Data
processing.   I. Title.
QA76.73.C15S474 1995
005.13'3--dc20   94-37379
                                                           CIP

Dedicated to my husband,
George,
and my parents,
Isabell and Carroll Buzzett

Contents

6 Counter-Controlled Loops, 317

7 Characters, 359

9 Pointers, 493

12 Levels of Programming Abstraction, 705

13 Recursion, 781

Appendices

Preface

Problem Solving in C, Including Breadth and Laboratories introduces the beginning computer science student to the analysis, design, implementation, testing, and debugging of programs using ANSI C and to the breadth and richness of the computer science discipline. The text has a top-down approach to programming and presents material in a clear, visual manner with ample use of examples and figures. Instructors can tailor their courses in a variety of ways using this flexible text.

The student is introduced to functions in Chapter 1 and the *if* and *switch* statements in Chapter 3. This early coverage allows programs with some "meat" to be introduced fairly early in the term. Moreover, the separation of the discussions of integers (Chapter 2), floating point numbers (Chapter 4), and characters (Chapter 7) allows the student to focus on fewer concepts at a time. This organization holds the complexity to a minimum. The typical treatment of including all types in one chapter is like watering a lawn. After a while, the water simply runs off and is wasted. This text's organization allows maximum absorption of the material and concepts. The early presentation of functions and the gradual introduction of data types and syntax allow programming principles and problem solving to evolve as the language constructs are developed. The text emphasizes problem solving throughout, with several sections focusing on this topic. Moreover, a clear, straight-forward presentation of all topics is included, with good separation between each.

Each chapter concludes with a laboratory section that is truly integrated with the topics in the text. The laboratories give a wonderful hands-on introduction to many features of problem solving with C. Students can work through one or all laboratory exercises in a self-paced fashion or in a closed laboratory environment. Each laboratory moves through the chapter concepts, easing a student into writing and debugging programs. For example, the laboratory for Chapter 3 teaches the student how to write programs with stubs. The student uses a program from the laboratory disk, which is simply a program with a set of stub functions. The laboratory gives the student directions for fleshing out and then testing the functions—one function at a time—exactly as it would be done in the real world. When the laboratory is complete, the student has a program that he or she has put together using stubs. Such a laboratory builds programming confidence. The laboratory breaks the work into simple tasks that ensure student success. Hands-on computer work makes a student more confident and adventurous with a language. Program templates in several laboratories promote good design. Moreover, experimentation is encouraged, and several laboratories in later chapters (Chapters 10, 11, 14, and 15) have a teamwork component. (The *Instructor's Manual* has suggestions for individual assignments as alternatives to the team assignments.) Most laboratories have several exercises with multiple parts. Thus, to meet individual time requirements and needs, an instructor can assign one or all these exercises. Programming segments and data files to accompany the laboratories are on a disk included with the text. The instructor's disk contains answers to laboratory exercises.

A professor can cover all or some of a variety of breadth sections. This material presents a broad range of topics from the discipline of computer science. For example, breadth material includes such topics as the object-oriented paradigm, intellectual property, invention of the first computers, logic, color in computer graphics, machine and assembler languages, external storage, formal grammars, memory, and databases. The text disk includes the source code for a CPU simulator program, which executes the example machine language of Section 12.7. A computer graphics package on the disk accompanies Section 11.7. The package contains files of device-dependent and independent routines and device drivers (files of device-dependent routines) for Turbo C and Think C. Moreover, an outline of a generic driver can be used to develop drivers for other systems. The Learning Features section below contains a complete list of the 26 breadth sections. These breadth sections enhance the subject material, help place topics in perspective, and give students a preview of the discipline of computer science. Students like to see the relevance of the subject and what is ahead for them, and these sections give a good taste of the future.

The style of writing in the breadth material, laboratories, and text material is clear, direct, and readable. Students love examples, and there are many in the text. Large "case studies," as well as shorter examples, are developed in a top-down fashion and described with structure charts, pseudocode, and pre- and postconditions. Concrete examples make abstract concepts come alive.

Numerous figures accompany the examples and explanations. These figures help today's visually oriented students to "see" what happens inside the computer as each instruction executes. A number of figures show the movement of data and the effects of certain instructions on storage locations. For example, Figure 2.15 of Section 2.9 follows each change in memory with each line of the program. Color highlights changes in the figures and important segments of code. This visual orientation of the code and figures is even more important as students move to more abstract ideas.

Figures and examples help to explain the material, but students learn by doing. Each section has a number of exercises that correlate directly to the material. Answers to problems with numbers in color are located in Appendix J. Some exercises—such as those related to searching and sorting—have the students perform the task by hand before coding it. This kind of drill makes abstract concepts more concrete. The exercises are complete and thorough and have a good mix of easy and challenging questions. The text also includes questions from Graduate Record Computer Science Examinations. The *Instructor's Manual* contains answers to the remaining exercises. The C code in the text, the manual, and the disk has been computer tested.

Besides exercises, most sections contain programming projects, which range in difficulty and topics. These projects provide an additional source of applications. Some projects involve revising earlier projects, and several projects are from the Programming Contest sponsored by Fairleigh Dickinson University.

Along with programming projects and exercises, numerous features help students concentrate on important concepts. Each chapter begins with an introduction and list of goals. Programming and debugging hints at the end of each chapter cover such topics as walkthrough technique, clarity of user interface, debugging techniques, some errors C compilers do not flag, and mistaken operator symbols. Appendix H contains a summary of the UNIX dbx, Turbo C, and Think C debuggers.

The closing material of each chapter contains key terms, a summary, and review questions. The list of key terms includes page numbers, which make this feature useful for reviewing. The chapter summary helps to focus the reader on important points. Review questions and answers are a tremendous study aid.

Appendices include an ASCII table, keywords, operator precedence, conversion specifications, summary of file I/O, random number generators, contents of text disk, debugging on different systems, a Glossary, answers to selected exercises, and answers to review questions.

Learning Features

Breadth Material

At least one section in each chapter covers the breadth of computer science. These topics mesh with the chapter's material. The professor can cover all, some, or none of these topics. As the following list reveals, the 26 breadth sections complement the chapters in which they occur.

1 The Fundamentals of Computer Science
  1.2 The Discipline of Computer Science
  1.4 Invention of the First Computers
  1.6 The History of C

2 Integer Variables, Expressions, and Functions
  2.4 Storage of Integers in the Computer
  2.5 Integer Arithmetic in the Computer

3 Making Decisions
  3.5 Logic

4 Additional Numeric Types
  4.2 Storage of Floating Point Numbers

5 Looping
  5.6 Computer Time
  5.7 Truncation Error in Loops

6 Counter-Controlled Loops
  6.3 A Technique of Numerical Computing
  6.4 Intellectual Property

7 Characters
  7.4 Octal and Hexadecimal Number Systems

8 Arrays
  8.6 Color in Computer Graphics

9 Pointers
  9.2 Memory

10 Strings and String Functions
  10.7 Software Life Cycle for Large Systems

11 Structures and User-Defined Types
  11.3 Databases
  11.7 A Computer Graphics Package (accompanying software on text disk)

12 Levels of Programming Abstraction
  12.4 Some Operating System Features
  12.5 The Object-Oriented Paradigm
  12.6 C++: Object-Oriented Programming
  12.7 Machine and Assembler Languages (accompanying software on text disk)

13 Recursion
  13.3 Formal Grammars

Laboratories   Each chapter has a laboratory module with accompanying code on a disk. Some laboratories involve experimental methods. Others explore alternative implementations. All reinforce the material in the text. For example, the laboratory in the chapter on recursion has the student perform an experiment to compare the efficiency of the three summation algorithms, one nonrecursive and two recursive solutions. The following four laboratories employ the team approach:

Chapter 10   Develop a command-driven, line-oriented text editor
Chapter 11   Develop a stock portfolio program
Chapter 14   Maintain a program
Chapter 15   Formulate external documentation

The *Instructor's Manual* suggests variations for instructors who prefer individual to team assignments. Moreover, the instructor can use a laboratory in a scheduled, supervised environment or can assign parts of the laboratory for independent exploration by the student.

Example Operations and Applications   The text is example-driven. Most sections start with careful detailed discussions and simple examples to illustrate each new concept and end with a longer example illustrating analysis, design, and implementation. The level slowly increases as the reader progresses through the text. The organized approach to examples—particularly with accompanying diagrams—aids understanding of the subject.

Numerous Diagrams Highlighted with Color   Diagrams help students visualize the actions of operations and algorithms. Color emphasizes changes. For example, figures in Section 9.1 on The Concept of Pointers help to illuminate this challenging topic.

Section Exercises   Exercises appear at the end of each section, not just at the end of the chapter. These include short answer problems, diagrams of the execution of segments, design and coding of functions, applications, and questions from the Graduate Record Computer Science Examination. The text contains more than 1000 exercises in all.

Answers to Exercises   Answers to some exercises (those with numbers in color) appear in Appendix J which allows students to check their work for immediate reinforcement. The *Instructor's Manual* contains answers to the remaining exercises. Answers involving C code have been computer tested.

Programming Projects	An average of 15 programming projects are included per chapter. These major assignments allow students to design, code, and test. By completing such a project, the student enhances his or her understanding of the material and abilities in software development. For ease of assignment, projects are listed at the ends of the sections.
Historical Anecdotes	Such anecdotes add interest to the text and make computer science history more real. For example, Chapter 1's Programming and Debugging Hints contains the story of Grace Murray Hopper finding a "bug" in the computer. Moreover, the historical anecdotes often present material that a computer science major should know about the history of the discipline.
Chapter Introductions	An introduction at the beginning of each chapter gives an overview of the material in the chapter.
Chapter Goals	A list of study goals for the chapter follows the introduction.
Programming and Debugging Hints	Because students spend much time debugging programs, the hints sections are very useful.
Key Terms	Using the Key Terms section, students can test their knowledge of the important terms in the chapter. Because page numbers accompany the terms, students can readily check their answers or consult the text to refresh their memories.
Summary	The Summary presents a concise overview of chapter material.
Chapter Review Questions	For self-examination, each chapter also contains a list of review questions. Answers are in Appendix K.

Supplementary Materials

Instructor's Manual	An *Instructor's Manual* contains solutions to text exercises, answers to at least one project per chapter, additional test problems with answers, laboratory code answers, transparency masters, and suggestions for lectures. The accompanying disk has examples from the text, data files, laboratory exercises, and their answers. Code in the *Instructor's Manual* and on the disk have been computer tested.
Test Bank	A *Test Bank* on disk and in the *Instructor's Manual* contains test questions and answers for each chapter.

Laboratory Manual	A *Laboratory Manual* with disk contains the chapter laboratories. The manual has additional room for a student's notes and answers.
Text Disk	Included with the text is a disk of laboratory programs, program examples from the text, and data files in ANSI C.
Overhead Transparency Masters	Transparency masters of key figures, algorithms, and programs are available in the *Instructor's Manual*.

Testing of Code

The source code appearing in this textbook, *Instructor's Manual*, and the accompanying diskette was prepared and tested on a Macintosh 840 AV using Symantec's THINK C or Symantec C++ compiler, Version 6.0, and on a Mitsuba 80386 MS-DOS PC using Borland's C++ compiler, Versions 3.1 and 4.0. Every effort was made to ensure ANSI compliance and thus provide the student with portable example programs and code fragments. In all cases, the target execution environment is MS-DOS. These programs are not designed to be compiled or executed as MS Windows applications. Although these programs can be compiled using a Windows-based compiler or integrated development environment—such as Borland's C++ for Windows—the student must correctly specify the target environment and run the resulting programs within an MS-DOS shell.

Acknowledgments

Any project of this magnitude requires the cooperation and support of many people. The author gratefully acknowledges the many friends, colleagues and students for their help in the completion of this work. For his ideas and contributions to programming and problem solving, thanks go to Robert Martin. William Campbell and Jason Womick have been of enormous help—William through the manuscript preparation, text disk production, and glossary compilation; Jason in generating solutions for the exercises. Christine Clawson helped in checking the art and compiling the index. Helen Thomas gave much proofreading assistance.

At West Publishing, Peter Gordon has been a wonderful editor, giving valuable direction, imagination and encouragement. Michelle McAnelly, the production editor, did a fantastic job orchestrating the production phase of the project. Thanks also go to Peggy Monohan for her accurate copy editing, and to John Rokusek for the attractive design.

It is impossible to thank adequately John Hinkel, my friend and former colleague at Lander University. Not only has John been a source of many valuable ideas and insights, but also he has provided tremendous encouragement and enthusiasm throughout this project.

I would also like to acknowledge the administration of Wofford College, particularly Dan Maultsby, who provided encouragement and a reduced teaching load to write this book.

Some of the programming problems were contributed by faculty, staff, and students of the Department of Mathematics and Computer Science at Fairleigh Dickinson University, Madison New Jersey. These problems were compiled from those used in the University's annual programming contest over the last eight years. Particular thanks go to Dr. Peter Falley, Dr. Phil Laplante, and Ralph Knapp.

GRE test questions were selected from *The Graduate Record Examinations Descriptive Booklet 1991–93,* 1991 and *Practicing to Take the GRE Computer Science Test, 2nd Edition,* 1992, Educational Testing Service. Reprinted by permission of Educational Testing Service. Permission to reprint GRE materials does not constitute review or endorsement by Educational Testing Service of this publication as a whole or of any other testing information it may contain.

Borland Corp. contributed copies of Turbo C and Symantec Corp. donated Symantec C++ for use in the project.

I am grateful to the following reviewers who offered many valuable constructive criticisms:

John Lowther
 Michigan Technological University
E. Terry Magel
 Kentucky State University
Matthew Dickerson
 Middlebury College
Ronald A. Mann
 University of Louisville
Bill Stockwell
 University of Central Oklahoma
Marguerite K. Summers
 Sangamon State University
Sharon Underwood
 Livingston University
Sanjay Jain
 National University of Singapore
 (previously of University of Delaware)
Paul Morneau
 Adirondack Community College
Robert Geitz
 Oberlin College
Stephen P. Leach
 Florida State University
Grace Anne Crowder
 Towson State University
Peg Eaton
 Plymouth State College
Lorraine Callahan
 Northern Arizona University
Jeffrey A. Slomka
 Southwest Texas State University
Tim Davis
 University of Florida, Gainesville

Margaret Anne Pierce
 Georgia Southern University
Ronald J. Gould
 Emory University
Neil R. Sorensen
 Weber State University
John Carroll
 San Diego State University
Nathaniel G. Martin
 University of Rochester
Mike Michaelson
 Palomar College
Reggie Kwan
 Montana College of Mineral Science and Technology
James M. Frazier
 University of North Carolina at Charlotte
Stephen J. Allan
 Utah State University
A. M. Fayek
 California State University, Chico
Brian Malloy
 Clemson University
Richard J. Botting
 California State University, San Bernardino
Peter J. Gingo
 University of Akron
Dwayne A. McCalister
 California State University, Fresno
Marty J. Wolf
 Mankato State University
Susan M. Simons
 Memphis State University

My husband, George W. Shiflet, Jr., has encouraged me throughout this project and has done so much to make it possible for me to have the time to write. George and my parents, Isabell and Carroll Buzzett, have given me boundless love and support. It is to these three wonderful people that I dedicate this book.

The Fundamentals of Computer Science

Introduction

The steps in problem solving are an indication that computer science involves more than simply programming. Computer science is a mathematical, scientific, and engineering discipline with three major working methodologies—theory, abstraction, and design. The text begins your exploration of this rich discipline with practical tools—computers and software. Although you will spend much time working with these tools, their mastery is merely a means to an end, not the ultimate objective of this text.

This chapter begins with a discussion that continues throughout the text: How we effectively solve problems using the computer as a tool. Problem solving involves careful analysis to discover the nature of the problem. Problem solving also includes development of a logical process, or design of a solution, before approaching a

1

computer. Once our solution is implemented on a computer, real problem solving requires that we fully test our work.

To gain an appreciation of the computing environment, this chapter examines a model of a computer system and the steps for executing software on that computer. Several simple programs illustrate the implementation of a problem solution design in the computer language C. The top-down design method of problem solving and computer program writing is tied to a feature of many programming languages—the function.

Each chapter in the text contains breadth sections. These optional topics introduce you to material that should increase your understanding of the computer science field. At the end of each chapter, a laboratory helps you understand chapter material. The laboratories give a hands-on introduction to many features of problem solving with C. Software to accompany the laboratories is included on a disk available with the text.

Goals

To study

- The definition of computer science
- The three processes of computer science—theory, abstraction, and design
- A model of a computer system
- The history of computers
- The steps to execution of a computer program
- The history of the C programming language
- Several programs in C
- Top-down design and functions
- An overview of the computer science discipline

Section 1.1 **Solving Problems with the Computer**

We benefit from computer science applications every day. Cars have built-in computer monitoring of gas consumption and engine performance. This system informs the driver of the estimated number of miles before running out of gas and gives a mechanic detailed diagnostic information. Embedded computers in VCRs allow us to tape specific TV programs. "Smart" thermostats are computer controlled to regulate temperature and humidity in homes and buildings.

Many business transactions directly or indirectly involve computers. Bank automated teller machines (ATMs) are computer controlled to recognize valid users, transfer money between accounts, accept deposits, allow withdrawals, and give account balances. Moreover, through computerized hookup with the telephone system, facsimile (fax) machines can be used to transfer copies of documents all over the world.

Space exploration would be impossible without computers. Sectional pictures of the human body are made clearer with the aid of computers. In many situations, computers allow quick access to huge amounts of information. In seconds, a gas station attendant debits a credit card account. The school registrar quickly accesses a student's record. With a few keystrokes, a librarian can find the book we need at a library across the country.

Computers are not smart. They do precisely what we tell them to do—no more, no less. However, computers are very fast and accurate and are excellent at performing repetitive tasks. For example, a computer can perform millions, even billions, of additions in a fraction of a second.

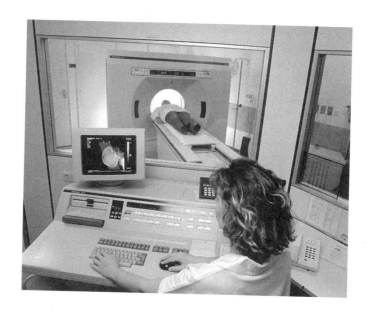

A sequence of instructions that tells the computer what to do is called a **program**. Many programs require certain **data** or values in a form that the computer can use for processing. The term **software** refers to the programs and data, and the term **hardware** refers to the computer itself and such associated equipment as printers and keyboards.

Definitions   A **program** is a sequence of instructions to the computer. **Data** are values in a form that the computer can use for processing. Programs and data are **software**. The equipment or physical components of a computer system are **hardware**.

Just as people use many languages to communicate with one another, many computer languages also exist. Each language has a distinct character with a special utility for solving certain classes of problems. An estimated 90% of all commercial programs are written in C. In this text, we use the C language to solve problems and explore computer science.

An Overview of Problem Solving

As with starting to write a major term paper, the first step to writing an effective program is proper thought and preparation. For a term paper, we identify the topic (problem) and analyze what we must do to write the paper. We read and collect references and develop a detailed outline of the paper with major topics and subtopics. We then write a draft, proofread, and revise the manuscript. At any stage, we may realize that we should cycle back to an earlier phase. For example, we might discover a major omission while outlining. As a result, we must rethink our analysis, collect additional references, and revise the outline. Preparation of a program follows a similar track. The steps to solving a problem with a computer are as follows:

1. **Analysis**
2. **Design**
3. **Implementation**
4. **Testing**

Analyzing the Problem

The careful solution to any problem begins with an analysis phase, in which we study the problem. The problem under analysis could be a scientific calculation or the processing of transactions at a bank's ATM. We must determine precise objectives of the solution to our problem, whether an estimate of fuel consumption or cash.

The material that the program generates is called **output.** For example, the output from an ATM includes instructions on a screen, a receipt, and, in certain cases, money. One output from a credit card transaction is a verification number. Moreover, a new customer's credit limit must be posted to the file of customer information. A **file,** which is stored by name, is a collection of information. A file may contain data, a program, or some other document.

Definitions The information that a computer program produces is **output.** A **file,** which is stored by name, is a collection of information.

After deciding upon the output, we determine the information that is needed to meet those objectives. These data are called the **input.** For example, the ATM requires the user to insert an ATM card, enter a password, and press certain buttons in response to questions. For a credit card transaction, input includes information from the customer's credit card, the amount of the purchase, and the customer's credit limit.

Definition The data that a program requires to produce its results are called **input.**

After identifying the output and input, we determine the major steps required for processing the input to produce the output. A **process** is a mechanism for converting input to output. We are considering the flow of data. In a picture of the data flow, a processing component is depicted as a rectangle having rounded corners, called a **black box.** At this stage, we do not attempt to determine how a process accomplishes its task. Arrows into the black box are labeled with the input data, and arrows coming out are marked with the output. Figure 1.1 illustrates such a black-box diagram for a credit card transaction system. The process box can be further broken down into more detailed process boxes, with data flowing into and out of each. This endeavor is similar to developing subtopics for the term paper's outline. Each black box represents a **module** or major task of the program.

Figure 1.1
Black-box diagram for a credit card transaction system

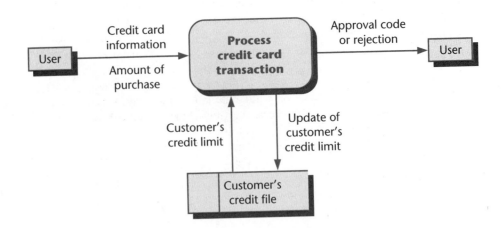

Definitions   A **process** is a mechanism for converting input to output. A **module** is a major task of a program or process.

Designing a Solution

Using the analysis, we design the solution. One pictorial technique to help us in the design is a **structure chart**, or **hierarchy diagram**, which is a diagram of the major tasks or functions of the program and their relation to one another. The diagram's shape is similar to an upside-down family tree. Figure 1.2 depicts a possible structure chart for the credit card transaction system in Figure 1.1. The chart indicates that the program has eight modules. The main module, to process the credit card transaction, calls on four other modules to perform subtasks: Read credit card identification data; read amount of purchase; update customer's credit file; and send approval code or rejection for the transaction. We then consider each submodule to determine if we should subdivide it. For example, updating the customer's credit file can involve several major tasks, such as finding the credit card number in the file, verifying that the card is valid, and adjusting the customer's credit limit. In Figure 1.2, these tasks are represented in boxes connected to the update-customer's-credit-file box. We then consider each of these modules. If each module represents a single task that needs no further subdivision, the structure chart design of the program is finished, and we can develop the logic for each module.

Definition   A **structure chart** or **hierarchy diagram** is a tree diagram of the major tasks of a program and their relation to one another. Modules are shown as rectangles. If a line connects module A at one level with module B at the next lower level, then B is a submodule of A.

The technique we have just illustrated is called **top-down design**. Top-down design incorporates **modular programming**, a process of developing programs with subprograms or modules. **Stepwise refinement** is central to top-down design and is widely employed in many disciplines. We start with the most general and work our way to the

Figure 1.2
Structure chart for a credit card verification program

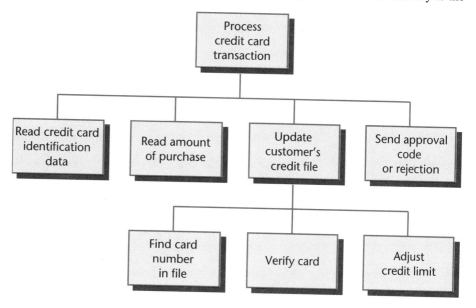

specific. Decomposition is based on functionality. We break down or decompose the task into simpler, more manageable, and generally smaller operational units. Ultimately, there is a collection of modules that we do not decompose further because we can implement them readily. At this stage, to prevent being overwhelmed by a project, we focus our attention on the analysis rather than on the details of how to implement any module in a programming language. Otherwise, we might produce a disorganized program that is difficult to write and correct. With proper analysis and design, implementation and testing go much smoother and faster.

Definitions   **Modular programming** is a process of developing programs with subprograms or modules. In the **stepwise refinement** method of problem solving, we start with the most general and work our way to the specific. **Top-down design** (with modular programming and stepwise refinement) is a design technique in which we divide a problem solution into more manageable tasks (modules). We can then divide each submodule in the same manner.

After breaking down the project into modules and submodules, we can design each module. We must decide on the structures in which to store the data. Consider the task of moving back to school. Your clothes and other belongings are analogous to the data. In planning the move, you have to decide whether to pack your things in suitcases or boxes.

While determining the **data structures**, or the frameworks for storing data, we also develop an **algorithm**. An algorithm contains the logic of the module or the step-by-step method of completing the module's task in a finite amount of time. An algorithm for solving a problem has the following characteristics:

1. Accomplishes the task
2. Gives step-by-step instructions on completing the task
3. Is not ambiguous
4. Finishes in a finite amount of time

Definitions   A **data structure** is a framework for storing data and the algorithms that implement and perform operations on the structure. An **algorithm** is a precise, unambiguous, step-by-step method of doing a task in a finite amount of time.

An algorithm for moving back to school is as follows:

Algorithm for moving back to school:

Get out suitcases
Pack clothes and toiletries in suitcases
As long as there is room in car, move suitcases and other personal items that are
    going to school into car
Say good-bye to family
Get gas
Drive to school
Move all items from car to dorm room
Unpack suitcases

Performance of this algorithm accomplishes the task of moving back to school. The steps are sequential. For example, we want to pack the suitcases before we move them to the car. The algorithm is clear and unambiguous. Following it, we can move back to school in a finite amount of time. The following recipe to fix spaghetti and sauce is another example of an algorithm:

Algorithm for fixing spaghetti and sauce:

Bring two quarts of water to a boil
Add 1 tsp salt to water
Add 1 lb package of spaghetti noodles to water
Open can of spaghetti sauce
Heat sauce
After noodles have been in water for 10 minutes, drain noodles
Put noodles in serving bowl
Pour sauce over noodles

Any set of directions for assembling an item, such as a stereo stand or a toy, should be an algorithm. We all know a person who has sworn that toy assembly directions were not correct; probably the directions did not form a step-by-step method of completing the task successfully in a finite amount of time.

In developing a design, we might realize that an error exists in the analysis. Such a discovery warrants a careful reconsideration of the analysis and a subsequent revision of the design.

Imple-menting the Design

After designing a solution to the problem, we are ready to translate the design into a programming language. This design implementation is also called coding, and all or part of the program is called code. Along with converting the design into instructions that a computer can understand, we include comments strictly for people. With these comments, or documentation, anyone can more easily figure out a program. Documentation makes it much easier even for the person who wrote the program to read and interpret the meaning of the code.

Definitions   The process of writing computer instructions in a programming language is called coding, and all or part of the program is called code.

Testing the Code

Testing a problem solution on the computer overlaps with the design implementation phase. When the computer follows the instructions in a program, we say the machine executes or runs the program. A sound technique involves implementing and testing modules one at a time. Thus, if an error exists, we can quickly and easily trace the source of the difficulty. We should carefully select test data for the program to cover as many situations as possible. For example, in the credit card verification program (Figure 1.1), we should make sure that the program handles incorrect data—such as negative numbers, zero, or extremely large charges—as well as valid data. Should we discover a fundamental error, we would return to an earlier phase, such as the design phase. After revising the design, we would cycle through the subsequent steps of the problem solving process.

Definition   A computer executes or runs a program when the machine is following the instructions in the program.

Maintaining the Product

Although most of the programs we develop in this course will be used only once and not revised, professional programs often go through a series of improvements. The activities after product delivery, in which a program is corrected, adapted, and improved, are called maintenance. An estimated 50–70% of all professional programming involves maintenance.

Definition   The activities after product delivery, in which a program is corrected, adapted, and improved, are called maintenance.

Summary

Throughout this text, we revisit the stages of problem solving. In a number of examples, we analyze a problem, design a solution, implement the solution in the C programming language, and test the program by executing it with test data. We will develop analytical skills and techniques. The text contains a number of algorithms for solving problems. An algorithm for solving one problem can often lead to the design of another solution. We will learn many features of C, so that we can implement our design in this programming language. We will also study how to test a program in an organized, module-by-module fashion.

We summarize the steps for solving a problem with a computer as follows:

1. **Analysis**
   a. Determine the output desired.
   b. Determine the input needed.
   c. Identify the processing required.
   d. Carefully state the objectives of each module.
2. **Design**
   a. Diagram a structure chart.
   b. Select appropriate data structures.
   c. Develop the logic of each module in an algorithm.
3. **Implementation**
   a. Code the solution.
   b. Provide documentation.
4. **Testing**
   a. Select test data.
   b. Test each module.
   c. Test the program as a whole.

Section 1.1 Exercises

1. List three applications of computer science other than those mentioned in this section.
2. Draw a black-box diagram for the task of writing a term paper.
3. Draw a structure chart for the task of writing a term paper.
4. Draw a structure chart for the operations of a soft drink vending machine.
5. Write an algorithm for brushing your teeth.
6.* Which of the following are algorithms?
   a. Directions on a box for preparing one bowl of oatmeal
   b. List of nutrients in the oatmeal
   c. List of health recommendations for a long life
   d. Directions for filling out a preregistration form
   e. Rules for dividing one number by another

Section 1.2 Breadth: The Discipline of Computer Science

Computer science involves more than just coding; writing instructions to tell the computer what to do is only one part of the subject. In 1989, the Task Force on the Core of Computer Science for the Association for Computing Machinery (ACM) gave the following definition of **computer science:**

---

*All numbers in color illustrate that the answer appears in the answer key in Appendix J.

Definition	The discipline of computing is the systematic study of algorithmic processes that describe and transform information: their theory, analysis, design, efficiency, implementation, and application. The fundamental question underlying all of computing is, "What can be (efficiently) automated?"*

Computer science is a mathematical, scientific, and engineering discipline. The subject uses paradigms that are characteristic of each area of the discipline. A **paradigm** is a working methodology, a process, or a technique for approaching a subject. The three basic paradigms of computer science—**theory, abstraction,** and **design**—are fundamental paradigms in mathematics, science, and engineering, respectively.

Definition	A paradigm is a working methodology, a process, or a technique for approaching a subject.

Theory Paradigm

Logic is part of a theoretical component that provides the mathematical underpinnings of the discipline. The design of a computer, the manipulation of data and programs in the computer, and the logic of programs all have mathematics as their basis. One area of computer science research that depends heavily on logic is the development of methods to prove that programs are correct and that they do exactly what they are supposed to do. The Federal Systems Division of IBM has used such methodologies to complete large projects ahead of schedule and under budget. *Computing Curricula 1991, Report of the ACM/IEEE-CS Joint Curriculum Task Force* gives the following elements of the theory paradigm common to mathematics and computer science:

1. Definitions and axioms
2. Theorems
3. Proofs
4. Interpretation of results

Abstraction Paradigm

The process of making and testing hypotheses about models and then revising designs or theories has its foundation in the experimental sciences. For example, we might run experiments to determine which of two data search methods is faster. Deriving a model of a computer is another example of abstraction. Such a model helps to explain how the various components of a computer work together. *Computing Curricula 1991* lists the following components of the abstraction paradigm that are common to the sciences and computer science:

1. Data collection and hypothesis formation
2. Modeling and prediction
3. Design of an experiment
4. Analysis of results

---

*Peter J. Denning et al., "Computing as a Discipline," *Communications of the ACM* 32 (1): 9-23, January 1989, pp. 9–23.

Design Paradigm

The design process used to develop a program or piece of computer equipment from analysis through maintenance is based in engineering. The previous section introduced the process of problem solving with a computer. Professionals who employ this method to create computer programs are called **software engineers**. The computer scientist who develops a hardware device to solve a specific problem uses these same steps. *Computing Curricula 1991* presents the following elements of the design paradigm:

1. Requirements
2. Specifications
3. Design and implementation
4. Testing and analysis

Section 1.3 **Model of a Computer System**

In Section 1.1, we considered problem solving with implementation on a computer. Through sound problem-solving techniques, we can create quality software. A **computer system**, however, consists of both software and hardware. In this section, we turn our attention to hardware.

Definition   A **computer system** consists of both software and hardware.

A computer system has the following five major hardware components:

1. **Input unit**
2. **Output unit**
3. **Secondary storage**
4. **Central processing unit (CPU)**
5. **Main memory** or **primary storage**

Figure 1.3 is a diagram of these components. Arrows indicate the flow of information, which includes data and program instructions.

Input and Output Devices

There are many input devices for entering data and programs into a computer. The most common input device is the **keyboard**, on which the user types information. Another popular input device is the mouse. As the user moves the **mouse** over a flat surface, an arrow or other indicator moves across the screen. By clicking a button on the mouse, the user issues commands. Most department stores use another input device, a **wand reader**. Attached to a computer, the wand reader scans the magnetically encoded product information on price tags. Many grocery stores have a similar input device—a **bar code reader**. These readers scan a product's bar code, the zebra-striped symbol, to obtain product information.

Some typical output devices are printers, speakers, and screens. Other names for "screen" are **monitor**, **CRT (cathode ray tube)**, and **VDT (video display terminal)**.

Secondary Storage

Information is stored in secondary storage on a semipermanent basis. The most common media are **magnetic disk** and **magnetic tape**. These media can store data and programs so that we only need to enter the material once. At any time, we can retrieve

Figure 1.3
Hardware
components of
a computer

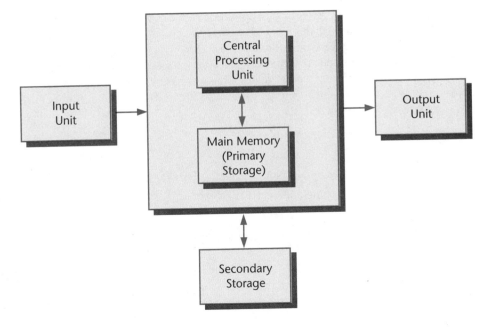

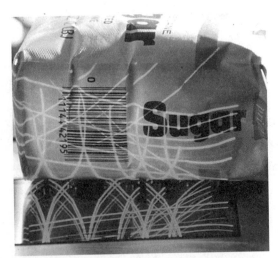

Bar code reader being used

Speakers and computer screen

information from secondary storage. A **disk drive** writes to and reads from the most common secondary storage media, **disks**. Information on a disk is accessed directly; that is, the disk drive can go immediately to the desired data. A **tape drive**, which is similar to a tape recorder, writes to and reads from **tapes**. Access to information on a tape is sequential. For instance, to find something in the middle of a tape, the computer must move past all the earlier data. Information access is faster on a disk, but tapes are inexpensive and can store huge amounts of data.

Definition   The **secondary storage unit**, which is a major hardware component of a computer system, stores information on a semipermanent basis.

Central Processing Unit

The input, output, and secondary storage devices attached to the computer are called **peripheral equipment**. The middle box in Figure 1.3 represents the heart of the computer—the CPU and main memory. Usually, these units are housed together in some type of box.

Definition   The input, and output, and secondary storage devices attached to the computer are called **peripheral equipment**.

As the name implies, the CPU is in charge of processing for the computer. Figure 1.4 represents the CPU with its two major components, the **arithmetic/logic unit (ALU)** and the **control unit**. The ALU performs all arithmetic operations (such as addition or multiplication) and logic operations (such as comparing two items or testing the truth of a condition). The control unit directs all the devices in the computer system.

Definitions   The **central processing unit (CPU)**, which is a major hardware component of a computer system, is in charge of processing for the computer. The CPU has two major components, the **arithmetic/logic unit (ALU)**, which performs all arithmetic and logic, and the **control unit**, which is in charge of directing all the devices in the computer system.

The control unit regulates main memory as well as the peripheral devices. Before program execution, the control unit directs that the program be brought into memory in a process called program **loading**. To execute a program, the computer performs the **fetch/execute cycle**. In this cycle, the control unit orders main memory to send an instruction to the CPU, which interprets the meaning of the instruction. Then, the control unit orders the appropriate unit to execute the instruction. For example, the control unit might direct the ALU to add one to a number, or it might command a disk drive to read data from a disk into memory. After the computer executes an instruction, the process starts over with the next instruction. This cycle continues until the program ends.

Definition   The **fetch/execute cycle** is the process performed by the computer while executing a program. As long as instructions remain, the control unit **fetches** or retrieves the next instruction from main memory; the CPU decodes the instruction; and the control unit commands the appropriate unit to execute the instruction.

Figure 1.4
Model of the CPU

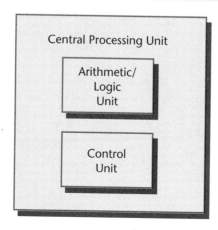

Figure 1.5
A model of main memory using campus post office boxes

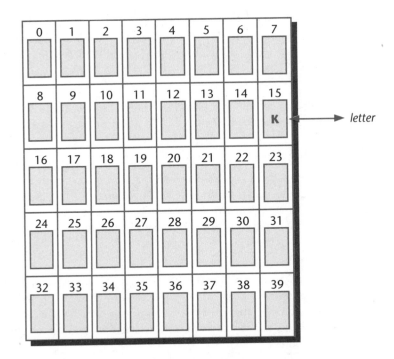

Note that the computer model we are developing is a single CPU computer, or a **sequential computer**. As the fetch/execute cycle indicates, the machine executes instructions in sequence, one after another. Other types of computers, called **parallel computers**, have more than one CPU. In a parallel computer, all CPUs can work simultaneously on one program.

Main Memory

Main memory holds data and programs. Memory consists of a sequence of locations or cells, each with its own **address**. The addresses start with zero and increase sequentially. Each location can store information. In Figure 1.5, suppose the cell with address 15 contains the letter K. A program might refer to the data item using the name *letter*, but the computer recognizes *letter* as the contents of cell 15, or K. We refer to a name, such as *letter*, in a program as an **identifier**.

Definitions   The **address** of a memory location is a number associated with that location. Addresses are sequential (0, 1, 2, etc.). An **identifier** is the name of something in a program.

Main memory is analogous to a bank of mail boxes in the campus post office, as in Figure 1.5. Suppose Marty Jones has mail box 15. Someone working in the post office might ask, "What is in box 15?" However, a friend of Marty's might wonder, "What does Marty have in his mail box?" We can refer to the box by its number (address) or its associated name. A student's mail box can change from semester to semester. Similarly, the location associated with *letter* can change from one program execution to another. By using an identifier, the programmer does not need to know the address.

Section 1.3 Exercises

1. List each peripheral device in your computer system and indicate whether it is an input, output, or secondary storage device.

2. What are the input and output devices associated with an ATM?
3. **a.** What are the input and output devices associated with the credit card transaction system of Section 1.1 (see Figure 1.1)?
   b. What is stored on secondary storage?
   c. Would this secondary storage medium be disk or tape? Why?

Section 1.4 Breadth: Invention of the First Computers

John V. Atanasoff

In the late 1930s, **John V. Atanasoff**, a professor at Iowa State College (which is now Iowa State University), was frustrated by the length of time it took him and his graduate students to solve tedious problems. For example, it could take months to solve one system of 29 equations in 29 unknowns; and the likelihood of errors was high. Atanasoff and his assistant **Clifford Berry** decided to design an electronic digital computer that would solve their special-purpose problems. The experience was frustrating for the inventors. Exasperated after grappling with such problems as how to represent numbers and characters in the computer, Atanasoff got into his car late one night and raced to nowhere on the lonely highways of Iowa. After several hours of dazed driving, he stopped at a roadside cafe on the Iowa–Illinois border. As he relaxed, insight suddenly came to him about several things, including the idea to represent everything in the computer with strings of zeros and ones. Two things are much easier to represent electronically than 10; a voltage of 0– 2.3 can represent 0; and a voltage of 2.3 or greater can indicate 1. As often happens after intense, lengthy concentration, the leap to understanding occurred unexpectedly. Atanasoff and Berry completed a prototype in 1939 and finished the **Atanasoff-Berry Computer**, or **ABC**, in 1941. However, with the onset of World War II, Atanasoff went off to help in the war effort, and others dismantled the ABC.

During the war, a serious need arose for computing shell trajectories for new weapons. Teams of women, called "computers," would perform the tedious, time-consuming calculations for the trajectory tables. In fact, one of the earliest definitions of "computer" is "one who computes." Under the direction of **J. Presper Eckert, Jr.,** and **John Mauchly,** scientists at the University of Pennsylvania started to build the **ENIAC** (Electronic Numerator, Integrator, Analyzer and Computer). This computer, which they did not complete until after the war in 1946, was the first general-purpose, electronic digital computer. It could solve a variety of scientific problems, not just systems of equations. The ENIAC could compute in 20 seconds a trajectory that would take a person two days to calculate. The machine was massive, and the story goes that turning on its 18,000 vacuum tubes would cause all the lights in West Philadel-

Punched card

phia to dim. Input and output were on punched cards, with the positions of holes in the cards representing the data. The input rate was 125 cards per minute. Moreover, for the ENIAC to solve a new problem, scientists had to rewire it. Imagine the difficulty we would have today if we had to alter the wiring in the computer every time we wanted to change from using a word processor to a spreadsheet!

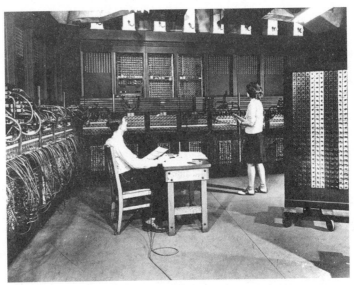

ENIAC

The solution to this tedious task of rewiring is attributed to **John von Neumann**, who determined that programs as well as data could be stored in computer memory. When we run our word processor, main memory contains the word processing software as well as our writing. When we want to switch to a spreadsheet, the computer loads that software into its memory. Most modern computers use **von Neumann architecture**.

Born in Budapest, Hungary, in 1903, von Neumann received his Ph.D. in mathematics at the age of 22. He contributed significantly to a variety of areas—the mathematical foundation of quantum theory, logic, the theory of games, economics, nuclear weapons, meteorology, as well as theory and applications in early computer science. Many stories tell of his phenomenal memory, reasoning ability, and computational speed. He could memorize a column of the telephone book at a glance, and he had mastered calculus by age 8. Halmos wrote in *Legend of John von Neumann*, "When his electronic computer was ready for its first preliminary test, someone suggested a relatively simple problem involving powers of 2. (It was something of this kind: what is the smallest power of 2 with the property that its decimal digit fourth from the right is 7? This is a completely trivial problem for a present-day computer: it takes only a fraction of a second of machine time.) The machine and Johnny started at the same time, and Johnny finished first."*

John von Neumann

Before leaving the topic of early computers, we should mention the controversy surrounding who invented the first computer. In 1964, the U.S. Patent Office issued Eckert and Mauchly a patent for their invention. Sperry Rand, which had purchased

*Halmos, P.R. "Legend of John von Neumann." *American Mathematical Monthly*. 80: 382–398, 1973.

the rights to the ENIAC, sued other computer companies that refused to pay patent royalties. In 1967, Honeywell countersued Sperry Rand, saying the patent was fraudulent. Mauchly had visited Atanasoff's laboratory, and many of the ABC's technical innovations were in the ENIAC. In 1974, the court ruled that Atanasoff had invented the modern computer. Nevertheless, the ABC was a specialized computer, whereas the ENIAC was a general-purpose digital computer. In 1980, the Association for Computing Machinery honored Eckert and Mauchly as the "Founders of Modern Computing."

Section 1.4 Exercises

Write a two-page, typed, double-spaced essay with references on one of the following topics:

1. John V. Atanasoff and the ABC
2. J. Presper Eckert, John Mauchly, and the ENIAC
3. John von Neumann
4. Honeywell's lawsuit against Sperry Rand

Section 1.5 Steps to Execution

Section 1.1 is an overview of problem solving with a computer, and Section 1.3 considers a model of a computer. In this section, we discuss what happens after we have designed a program and wish to implement it on a computer.

Editor

We start by typing the C program into the computer, probably using a **text editor**, or **editor**, which is a specialized word processor. With an editor, we can use the computer as a sophisticated typewriter having additional features that make it easy for us to enter and to edit or make changes to our program. The entered code is called the **source code** or **source program**. We save the source code, usually on a disk.

Definitions

A program typed into the computer is called the **source code** or **source program**. An **editor** is a specialized word processor to create and edit source code and data.

Preprocessor

When we issue an appropriate command, another program, called a **preprocessor**, automatically modifies the C source program according to our directions. The preprocessor does not change the program file, but instead creates a new file that contains the processed version of the program. For example, each program in the text contains the following line:

```
#include <stdio.h>
```

The pound sign in column 1 followed immediately by a word ("include") indicates that this line is a **preprocessor directive**, or an instruction to the preprocessor. In this case, we instruct the preprocessor to replace the directive with the contents of the file *stdio.h*. This file and its associated library make standard input and output (I/O) available to us. A **library** is a collection of implementations of useful tasks. For example, *printf* provides a way of printing. If a C program has the statement,

```
printf("Steps to Execution");
```

then execution of this line in the program causes

```
Steps to Execution
```

to appear on the screen.

Another directive, which we discuss fully in a later chapter, defines constants. For example, if a program contains the directive

```
#define MAXNUM 100
```

the preprocessor replaces every occurrence of the identifier *MAXNUM* with 100. Thus, the preprocessor converts the statement

```
x = MAXNUM;
```

to the statement

```
x = 100;
```

The new file created by the preprocessor no longer contains any preprocessor directives but has the appropriately substituted text. The preprocessor also can add or delete C program statements. Moreover, the preprocessor removes all comments, which help people understand the code but are not useful to the computer.

Definitions   A **preprocessor** is a program that removes all comments and modifies source code according to directives supplied in the program. A **preprocessor directive**, which begins with #, is an instruction to the preprocessor.

Compiler

Preprocessed code is sent to the **compiler**. Like the preprocessor, the compiler for C is a program. This program translates preprocessed source code into machine language, which is specific for each type of computer. Machine language consists only of strings or sequences of zeros and ones. We call 0 and 1 **binary digits**, or **bits**. Programmers of the earliest computers in the late 1940s had to write their programs in machine language, a tedious task to say the least. Soon, people started using **assembler languages**, which provide mnemonic abbreviations for the machine language instructions. For example, in a machine's language, the addition command might be 0110, but an assembler language might use the mnemonic ADD. Because machine language is different for each type of computer, assembler languages are different for each computer. A program written for one computer must be rewritten to run on a different type of computer. The code is **machine dependent**. Moreover, programming is tedious as these **low-level languages** are so closely associated with the underlying machine. (In a breadth section of Chapter 12, we examine an assembler language.)

Definitions   A **compiler** is a program that translates preprocessed source code into machine language. The **binary digits**, or **bits**, are 0 and 1. An **assembler language** is a computer language that provides mnemonic abbreviations for the machine language instructions. **Machine-dependent** code varies depending on the particular machine on which it runs.

In the mid-1950s, **John Backus** headed a team that created the first major high-level computer language—FORTRAN (FORmula TRANslator). The language is  **high-level**, not because it is more difficult than machine or assembler languages, but because it can express algorithms on a higher level of abstraction. One FORTRAN statement can replace many machine language instructions. A high-level language is more like English and, hence, easier to use. At first, people resisted using FORTRAN, thinking that programs written in FORTRAN would not run as fast as those written in an assembler language. Other people resented making the computer more accessible to those who were not professional programmers. Backus' team, however, did an excellent job, not only in designing the language, but also in creating a compiler that produced efficient machine code. Programmers discovered that they could spend less time writing and correcting code that ran at comparable times to assembler programs. Moreover, once language standards were established, the programmer could write **portable code**; the same program could run without modification on a different machine just by compiling it with the appropriate compiler. Today, hundreds of computer languages have been developed, each with its own compiler(s). Because each type of computer has its own machine language, a machine-specific compiler must exist for each language. Moreover, several different compilers for a popular language may be available on a widely used computer. For example, Microsoft C, Borland's Turbo C, and other C compilers are available for IBM PC compatible machines.

John Backus

Definitions   A **low-level language**, such as an assembler language or machine language, is closely associated with the underlying machine. A **high-level language**, such as FORTRAN or C, can express algorithms on a higher level of abstraction. A program is **portable** if it can run without modification on different machines just by compiling it with the appropriate compilers.

Besides allowing us to write programs that are portable and closer to our own language, another advantage of compilers is that they can alert us to syntax errors. A **syntax error** or **compile-time error** is a violation of the **syntax** or rules of a language. For example, we might forget to include a left parenthesis, such as

```
printf "<<<<Notice the left parenthesis is missing");
```

(Throughout the text, we use color for emphasis in program statements.) After detecting the syntax error, the compiler prints a diagnostic message, often giving the name of the file we are compiling, such as *testing.c*; the line number of the error, such as line 5; and a brief description of the problem.

```
File "testing.c"; Line 5
Error:  syntax error
```

After the compiler finds an error, compilation may continue in order to detect further errors, but the computer does not produce a compiled program.

Definitions   The **syntax** of a programming language is the set of rules for forming valid instructions. A **syntax error** or **compile-time error** violates the syntax of a language.

Perhaps the most frustrating syntax errors in C are those which occur when the programmer omits a semicolon or right parenthesis. The compiler flags such errors, but the line identified in the error message may not be the one in which the omission occurred. The reason is that the compiler may not detect the missing symbol until one or more lines past the point of the error. The error message may also be misleading or uninformative. For example, consider the following code on lines 5 and 6 of a program:

```
printf ("Notice the right parenthesis and semicolon >>>>>>"
printf ("are missing");
```

Alerted to the problem, we can easily spot the error: The right parenthesis and semicolon that should terminate the statement on line 5 are missing. The compiler, however, does not detect this omission on line 5 until encountering the *printf* on line 6 and is likely to display an error message associated with the second line instead of the first.

```
File "testing.c"; Line 6
Error:  syntax error
```

On occasion, the compiler displays a **warning message** to advise the programmer that a statement is technically acceptable but is unusual enough to constitute a potential error. For example, the statement

```
5;
```

does nothing. Consequently, a compiler might print the warning

```
File "testing.c"; Line 7
Warning:  code has no effect
```

A warning does not prevent a compiled program from being produced, whereas an error does.

Definition   A **warning message** from a compiler advises the programmer that a statement is technically acceptable but is unusual enough to constitute a potential error.

Linker   If the compiler does not detect any syntax errors, then it produces a file of **object code**, which is the machine language version of the source code.* The computer, however, is still not ready to execute the program. Often a program is so large that it is convenient to break it down into smaller units, with each part stored in a separate file. Moreover, our program might use features like *printf* that are defined elsewhere, perhaps in a C library. After compilation of our program files, the computer must somehow link these separate pieces to form a single **executable program**. This linking is usually

---

*On a UNIX system, the compiler produces assembly code, and another program, called an assembler, produces object code.

Figure 1.6 Steps to program execution

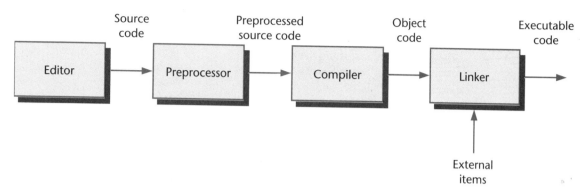

accomplished by a program called a **linker**, or **linkage editor**, which is often run automatically when a program is compiled. Figure 1.6 displays a diagram of the steps leading to program execution. The boxes contain the system programs and the arrows indicate their products.

> **Definition** A **linker** or **linkage editor** is a program that combines all the object code of a program with necessary external items to form an executable program.

Section 1.5 Exercises

1. Suppose a program contains the following code:

```
#define TAX_RATE   .06
#define NUM_ITEMS 50
⋮
tax = NUM_ITEMS * TAX_RATE * price;
```

Give the preprocessed code.

Section 1.6 Breadth: The History of C

Dennis Ritchie

The powerful C programming language has been applied to a variety of problems, especially in commercial software. For example, many computer graphics applications and the graphical computer algebra system *Mathematica* are written in C. (For more information about *Mathematica*, see Numerical and Symbolic Computation, Section 1.9.) One reason for this popularity is C's portability. We can easily transfer a program written in C from one computer to another with few or no changes. Another reason the language is desirable is that C programs can be faster and more efficient than comparable programs in most other high-level languages. The flexibility of C, however, is one of the strongest reasons for its popularity. The C language is often described as a "middle-level" language. C permits us to write programs in much the same style as that of most modern high-level languages, such as Pascal or FORTRAN. However, C permits close interaction with the inner workings of the computer. It is analogous to a car that provides automatic transmission, but allows the driver the option of shifting manually. With C, we can deal with the machine at a fairly low level. C is a general-purpose structured programming language. It is concise and extremely powerful.

An ancestor of C is BCPL, the Basic Combined Programming Language. **Ken Thompson**, a Bell Laboratories computer scientist, developed a version of BCPL, which he called B. **Dennis Ritchie**, another computer scientist at Bell Laboratories, modified and improved BCPL in the early 1970s. He chose the second letter of BCPL—C—to represent the new version. It is merely a coincidence that the letters B and C are in alphabetical order. Ritchie originally wrote the language for programming under the UNIX® operating system.* (An operating system is a set of programs that enables the user to interact with the hardware components of a computer system.) Later, Bell Laboratories rewrote UNIX itself almost entirely in C. Part of the motivation for creating BCPL, B, and C was to develop languages that were useful in systems programming, or programming on the operating system level.

Historically, C is a small language, with few names that are part of the language and no inherent I/O support. I/O support is provided in the form of a library of object code that can be linked with the user's program. In the 1970s and 1980s, many organizations wrote and implemented C compilers, which differed from one another in their requirements and libraries. One type of machine might even have several different compilers. To establish uniformity and facilitate portability, in 1989 the **American National Standards Institute** (ANSI) approved standards for the language as well as the required libraries. For example, ANSI specifies the standard I/O library, including *stdio.h*. The present text uses the standardized version of C, called **ANSI C**. In a later chapter, we discuss an extension to C, C++ (pronounced C plus plus). **Bjarne Stroustrup** of Bell Laboratories developed C++ in the early 1980s to provide a powerful form of programming, called **object-oriented programming**, that contains C as a subset.

Section 1.7 Implementation of the Design

In problem solving, we analyze the meaning of a problem, design a solution, implement the solution in a programming language, and test. At any stage, we may return to an earlier phase to revise the solution. In this section, we discuss the third phase of problem solving—implementation.

You may have seen long lines of printed computer programs or code. Have you stopped to consider that computer code, like a well-written business letter, has a very specific structure? In the following pages, we show several examples of short C language programs and the form and structure of those programs. The words and the structure with which they are written make up the language's syntax. Although the primary focus of this book is problem solving using computer programs, learning good programming syntax allows us to solve the problems more efficiently. At a number of points throughout the book, we discuss good programming style and structure.

---

*UNIX is a trademark of UNIX Systems Laboratories, which Novell Corp. now owns.

A Program to Display a Message

After analysis and design, we use an editor to type a program and save the implementation in a file. Figure 1.7 pictures an editing window, or enclosed area on the screen, containing a program. The program has been saved in a file named *welcome.c*. Other systems have different screen displays, but the C program is the same for each. In this section, we examine the different components of the following C program:

```
/* File: welcome.c - Program to print a welcoming message */
#include <stdio.h>
main()
{
    printf("Welcome to Computer Science!\n");
}
```

Execution of the program displays the following message on the screen welcoming the user to the discipline:

```
Welcome to Computer Science!
```

Figure 1.8 shows the output window that results from executing the program.

Comments

In discussing the implementation phase of problem solving in Section 1.1, we emphasized the importance of documentation inside a program to enhance readability. The opening line of the above program exhibits such internal documentation in the form of a **comment** that gives the name of the file storing the program and a description of the function of the program. The comment begins with the two characters /* and ends with */, with no space between the two characters. Between /* and */, we can include any uppercase or lowercase characters. The only restriction is that a comment cannot contain */ as part of its text. The preprocessor removes all comments, so they do not affect the way the program runs.

Definitions   A **comment** inside a program is documentation for people. The compiler ignores comments. In a C program, a comment begins with /* and ends with */. These symbols, /* and */, are called **delimiters** of the comment; */ is the **terminating delimiter**.

Figure 1.7   Editing window containing a program

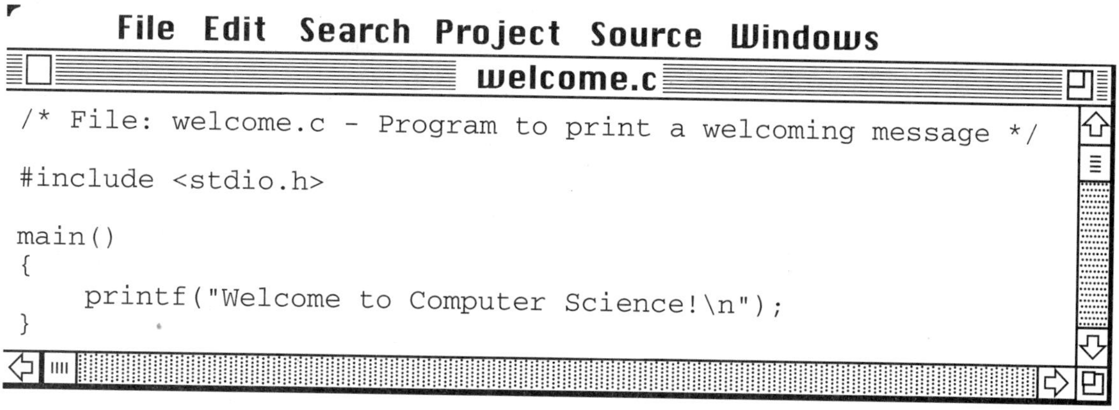

```
 File  Edit  Search  Project  Source  Windows
╔══════════════════════════════ welcome.c ══════════════════════════╗
 /* File: welcome.c - Program to print a welcoming message */

 #include <stdio.h>

 main()
 {
     printf("Welcome to Computer Science!\n");
 }
```

Figure 1.8   Output window that results from executing the program in Figure 1.7

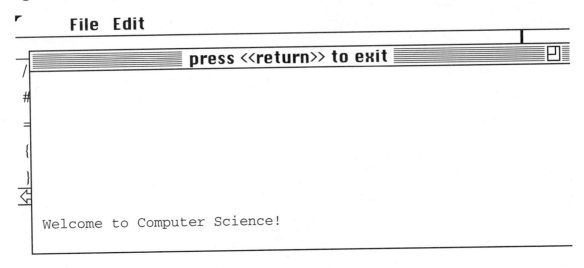

Comments may appear anywhere, except between quotation marks, and they can be of any length. A comment can start on the same line as other code or on a line of its own. If we place the terminating delimiter (*/) at the appropriate point, the comment can also extend over any number of lines. If we forget that delimiter, the rest of the program becomes one long comment, and compilation ends in a syntax error.

We usually place a general comment, such as one describing the role of the entire program or of a segment, on a line by itself. If the comment refers to a particular line only, we often include the documentation to the right on the same line.

Comments are important. Any program, no matter how well written, may at some time be amended to improve it, to allow for changing conditions, or to accommodate a governmental directive. The original author of the program may not be present or may not remember the logic of the program that he or she wrote several months or years earlier. To lessen the burden on the person who must amend a program, we should include ample comments when writing the program. Even in the midst of implementing and testing, it is amazingly easy to forget what was done only a few hours earlier. The task of including comments is tedious, and we may be tempted to postpone this obligation until the program is complete. However, by then, it may be hard to remember the program logic. It takes far less time to enter the comments as we type the program than to figure out the code later. Even on a small program, such as the one above, the comment helps the program reader save time when viewing the code by explaining immediately the purpose of the program. A descriptive software engineering phrase is "Write once, read many times."

Some programmers think C is such a concise language that a comment should accompany every line of code. Too many comments, however, can reduce the readability of the program. Even so, having too may comments is better than having too few.

Inclusion of
stdio.h

In order to make full use of such I/O operations as *printf*, we must include certain definitions in the program. The programmer should write the following line after the opening comment of the program:*

---

*Some compilers do not require this preprocessor directive for screen display.

```
#include <stdio.h>
```

The pound sign at the beginning indicates that this line is a preprocessor directive. Any directive must appear on a line by itself. When the preprocessor detects this directive, it inserts the contents of the file *stdio.h* into the source code. ANSI C specifies the contents of *stdio.h* and its supporting standard I/O library. The *.h* suffix indicates that the file is a **header file** or **header**. We include such a file at the head of a program to define certain values, symbols, and operations. The file name is inside angle brackets to indicate that it is in a special location on the disk.

Definition A **header file** or **header** defines certain values, symbols, and operations. Typically, files include such a header file to obtain access to its contents.

main

The program in Figure 1.7 specifies a group of **statements** or program instructions collectively called *main*. The system under which C runs recognizes this special name. It indicates the precise place in the program where execution begins. Every C program must have a *main*. Moreover, the word *main* must be in lowercase. C is **case sensitive**—the language "knows" the difference between uppercase and lowercase letters. Thus, *main, Main,* and *MAIN* are different file identifiers.

Definitions A **statement** in a program is a programming language instruction to the computer. A programming language is **case sensitive** if the language considers two identifiers different if they consist of the same characters in the same order except for variations in upper- and lowercase.

A pair of parentheses follow the word *main*. In the example, nothing is enclosed within the parentheses. We explain the significance of any information within these parentheses later.

Next comes the { symbol, called the **left** or **opening brace**. It matches the right brace, which is at the end. The braces enclose the **body** of *main*, including all of its statements. In this case, the body consists of only one statement, beginning with *printf*. A C program may include many statements between the two braces.

Definitions { is the **left** or **opening brace**, while } is the **right** or **closing brace**. The **body** of *main* consists of all its statements between the first left brace and last right brace.

printf

We use *printf* to display a message on the screen (the letter f in *printf* stands for "formatted"). We can also redirect this output to a printer. (The method of printing output depends on the system.) As the name implies, we often refer to *printf* causing the computer to "print" a message. The statement between the braces in the program in Figure 1.7 calls *printf* into action. In this example, *printf* has a single **string constant** or **string literal** value on which it operates. The computer prints the contents of this string constant, which is the sequence of characters within quotation marks (Welcome to Computer Science!). The quotation marks are not part of the string, but mark its beginning and end. A string after *printf* (is called the **control string** of *printf*. (We discuss how to employ the control string to produce formatted output in a later section.)

Definitions A **string constant** or **string literal** is a sequence of characters between quotation marks. The string immediately following *printf(* is a **control string**.

In this program, the control string ends with the symbols \n. These two adjacent symbols—the **backslash** (\) and n—together represent the **newline character**. (We refer to \n as the newline character. Strictly speaking, however, the character and its representation are not the same thing.) Even though the newline character is composed of two separate symbols, the compiler translates the pair into a single character.

The newline is analogous to a typewriter's carriage return, which advances the print head to the beginning of the next line. The newline character instructs the computer to advance to the next new line before printing subsequent information. Each time the computer finds \n within a control string, the output skips to a new line. If \n appears at the beginning of the string, the computer goes to a new line before printing the rest of the string. If the newline character occurs at the end of the control string, the computer prints the first part of the string and then advances to a new line.

Definition The **newline character** is \n. When processing \n in a control string of *printf,* the computer advances to the next new line before printing subsequent information.

What do you think would be the result of having a succession of \n characters?

```
printf("Welcome to Computer Science!\n\n");
printf("Again, welcome to Computer Science!\n");
```

In this example, the two newline characters together cause a blank line to appear in the output, as shown below:

```
Welcome to Computer Science!

Again, welcome to Computer Science!
```

Semicolon All C statements end with a **semicolon**. Notice the semicolon at the end of the statement containing *printf.* Novices to C frequently forget to add the semicolon, so be on your guard! The preprocessor directive

```
#include <stdio.h>
```

is not formally a part of C, and so does not end with a semicolon.

Style The closing brace marks the end of the program and matches the earlier opening brace. C program instructions are **free format**; they may appear anywhere. In Figure 1.7, the braces line up with the letter m of the word *main*. This alignment is not strictly necessary, but positioning the braces in this way makes the program more readable.

Definition A language has **free format** if statements may appear anywhere on one or several lines.

Indenting the statements in the body of *main* also makes the program more readable. Once again, the arrangement makes no difference to the compiler, but it helps program readers.

Spacing between instructions is of no consequence in C, nor does the language have many restrictions on where to end a line. Written in a compressed fashion, however, the program is difficult to read. The program in Figure 1.7 contains blank lines between the opening comment and the preprocessor directive and between this directive and *main*. Although the compiler ignores blank lines, spacing can separate tasks and improve readability.

Example 1.1

The following C program contains two statements with *printf*, but the control string of the first *printf* does not have a newline character:

```
/* Program to print part of a song */

#include <stdio.h>

main()
{
   printf("Give me land, lots of land");
   printf("And the starry skies above...\n");
}
```

Because the control string does not end with \n in the first *printf*, the computer does not move to a new line after the last word ("land"). Instead, it prints the first word in the second *printf* ("And") on the same line with the results of the first *printf*.

```
Give me land, lots of landAnd the starry skies above. . .
```

In the absence of \n, the computer assumes that it should print the next piece of information immediately after the first. To avoid this problem, we rewrite the first line as follows:

```
printf("Give me land, lots of land\n");
```

An alternative is to place the newline character at the beginning of the control string in the second *printf*. If this is done, the newline is effected before rest of the second string is printed.

```
printf("Give me land, lots of land");
printf("\nAnd the starry skies above. . .\n");
```

File *LAB011.c* on the disk that accompanies your text contains this program, and Exercises 1 and 2 of the laboratory at the end of this chapter pertain to this example. Working through the laboratory exercises shoud accelerate and deepen your understanding of the material.

Section 1.7 Exercises

1. Modify the program in Example 1.1 to double-space the output.

2. Find the syntax errors in the following compiler directive:

   ```
   #include stdio.h;
   ```

3. Find the syntax errors in the following program:

   ```
   /* This program has errors
   #include <stdio.h>

   main;
   (
      printf ('To err is human, ');
      printf ('to forgive divine./n')
   )
   ```

4. Describe the output of the following lines:

   ```
   printf("Well begun is half done.\n");
   printf("Well begun is half done.");
   printf("\n");
   ```

5. Give the output of the following program:

   ```
   /* This program prints several lines. */

   #include <stdio.h>

   main()
   {
      printf(" He who\n");
      printf("laughs last\nlasts\n");
      printf("last.\n");
   }
   ```

6. Give the output of the following program:

   ```
   /* This program produces some typewriter art. */

   #include <stdio.h>

   main()
   {
      printf("*\n**\n");
      printf("***\n****");
      printf("\n***");
      printf("**\n******\n");
   }
   ```

7. What is the effect of executing the following statement?

   ```
   printf("alpha\n\nbeta\n\ngamma\n");
   ```

8. What is printed by the following segments of C code?

  a. `printf("Going, one, \ntwo,\nthree.\n");`

  b. `printf("An apple a day keeps the doctor\n");`
     `printf("\n\n\n     away.\n");`

9. Identify the syntax errors in the following code?

```
mane{} \* this is one grait program; stand buy. . . /*
     (
        print('I think I am getting the hang of it./n')
```

10. Identify the syntax errors in the following code:

```
/* This program has some errors. . ./*

#include <stdio.h>;

main();
{
 print("When you get this output, you are through!\n")
}
```

Compile the program and identify the error messages given by your compiler. Correct these errors, and execute the program.

Section 1.7 Programming Projects

1. Write a program that prints your name and address.

2. Write a program that prints the following excerpt with credits and appropriate spacing:

```
The grey-ey'd morn smiles on the frowning night,
Chequering the eastern clouds with streaks of light.

    Shakespeare
    Romeo and Juliet
```

3. Using "typewriter art," write a program consisting of a series of *printf* instructions to draw the following picture of the Big Dipper:

        ★   ★   ★

    ★   ★   ★

  ★

Section 1.8 **Top-Down Design and Functions**

Grace Murray Hopper

Grace Murray Hopper, who was instrumental in the development of computer science, has described the early days of computers in the 1940s and early 1950s, when few programming language features existed. At that time, programmers discovered that they used certain tasks more than once, such as taking the square root of a number. To reuse the code, however, programmers had to copy their own or someone else's work. Invariably, they made transcription mistakes. Paper tape with holes punched in it to encode the data was used then as the input medium. Programmers hung the tape for common tasks on a clothes line in the computer room. If someone needed a routine—for example, to take the square root of a number—he or she would get the appropriate stream of paper tape from the clothes line to feed into the computer. Unfortunately, the tape was not very reliable because it broke frequently. Having a method of reusing the definitions of common tasks, however, was helpful.

Using Library Functions

In high-level languages, we have more sophisticated and easier methods of defining and implementing tasks. In C, a **function** is a subprogram that implements a task. A system supplies many functions, constants, and symbols in **libraries**. For example, *printf* is a function in the standard I/O library. We obtain access to this library by including its header file in our program

```
#include <stdio.h>
```

and linking the standard I/O object library with the object code of our program. The header file of source code contains information that allows the preprocessor and compiler to translate our source code program properly. The object library contains the definitions of the functions in object code.

> **Definitions**   A **function** is a subprogram that implements a task. A **library** includes a collection of implementations of useful tasks. In C, a library is composed of a header file and an object file. The header file in source code contains the interface to the library. The object file in object code contains function definitions.

To use the *printf* function from the standard I/O library, we specify the name of the function and have in parentheses the data that the function needs to perform its task. In other words, we **call** or **invoke** the function. The datum in parentheses is an **argument** or **actual parameter** to the function. The following statement contains a call to the *printf* function with an argument of "Here is the datum printf needs.\n":

```
printf("Here is the datum printf needs.\n");
```

This call to *printf* results in the output

```
Here is the datum printf needs.
```

The *printf* function also returns the number of output characters. Many functions return a value that the programmer uses. For example, the square root function (*sqrt*) in the math library returns the square root of its argument.

Definitions   An **argument** or **actual parameter** to a function is a datum passed to the function at the time the function is used. To **call** or **invoke** a function means to use it. A **call** or **invocation** of a function in a program causes the computer to interrupt execution of the routine containing the call in order to execute the function. In C, we call a function by giving its name and a list of its arguments, separated by commas and enclosed in parentheses. The format of a function call is

function_name(argument1, argument2,..., argumentn)

Connecting Functions to Top-Down Design

On the highest level, a function can be thought of as a way to extend a programming language. However, we are not dependent on libraries as the sole source of functions. We can write our own.

Functions are the mechanism by which we implement modules in a top-down design. Recall from Section 1.1 that in the top-down design of a problem solution, the analyst/designer begins by dividing the problem into manageable subtasks or modules. He or she then decomposes each subproblem into additional modules, each performing its own task. The process continues until the module needs no further decomposition, and we can define the module's task in a straightforward manner with program statements. A structure chart, such as the one in Figure 1.9 (for convenience repeated from Figure 1.2 of Section 1.1) for a credit card verification program, illustrates top-down design. The chart diagrams the problem modules and their relation to one another.

The implementation of this top-down solution to a problem uses a function to represent each module. We implement the module at the top of the structure chart as *main*, which is itself a function. As the chart indicates, *main* calls four other functions. Undoubtedly, *main* also contains C statements besides these calls. The function that performs the task of updating the customer's credit file also calls other functions to handle major components of its duties. Other than "Process credit card transaction"

Figure 1.9
Structure chart for a credit card verification program (repeated from Figure 1.2)

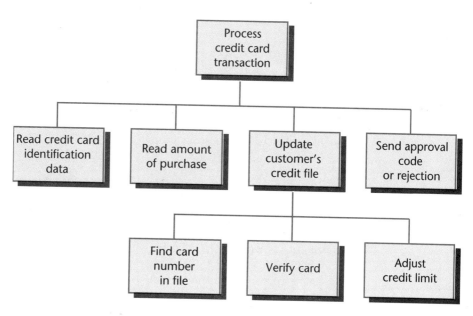

and "Update customer's credit file," the modules are implemented as functions that are composed of C statements that do not call any user-defined functions.

Problem and function decomposition are usually based on one or more of the following:

1. **Complexity.** Complex functions usually involve a large number of operations. We can describe such functions as a series of statements and calls to simpler functions.

2. **Recurrence of a given logic sequence.** Many operations are performed repeatedly or used in several different locations in a program. We can isolate such operations in a function that we can call as needed. We simplify design, implementation, and testing, because we design and implement the module only once. The function can be tested as a stand-alone unit rather than in every location where it is used.

3. **Generalization.** Many operations are performed frequently using different sets of similar data elements, such as alphabetizing a list of names. We can code these operations into reusable functions.

4. **Implementation hiding.** It is often useful to isolate certain operations so that a user of the operation knows nothing of the code. By isolating the operation in a function, the function developer can choose and redefine the implementation without affecting other parts of the user's program.

5. **Error finding and testing.** Simple functions are easily tested and verified. When a problem occurs in an uncomplicated function, we can usually isolate the error quickly. Complex functions are easier to test when they are composed of a series of pretested, simple functions. Furthermore, when we isolate an error in a single function, repairing the program amounts to correcting the offending module.

Once we perform the stepwise refinement of the problem, we use pseudocode to design each module. **Pseudocode** is a sequence of statements that are close to C, but more English-like, sometimes more general, and without the syntax requirements of a formal computer language. In pseudocode, we present the algorithm or method for doing the task. For example, the design for function *PrintHopper* to print the full name and title of Grace Murray Hopper (who was a Navy Rear Admiral and had a Ph.D. in mathematics) follows:

PrintHopper

Function to print the full name and title of Grace Murray Hopper

Algorithm:

print Hopper's name and title

Certainly, for this small problem, the algorithm is trivial. However, the design of *PrintHopper* does illustrate an organization we use in an enhanced form throughout the text. We give the name of the module, its purpose, and the algorithm in pseudocode. The pseudocode indicates what needs to be done but is not burdened with the syntactical demands of C. Moreover, we can use a phrase in pseudocode to represent several statements in C, such as "find the largest number in the list."

Definition **Pseudocode** is a sequence of statements that are close to C, but more English-like, sometimes more general, and without the syntax requirements of a formal computer language.

Function Definition

We saw in the last section that the function *main*, which is part of every program, has the following form:

```
main()
{
    statement(s)
}
```

A function that only displays has a similar form for its definition.

```
void function_name(void)
{
    statement(s)
}
```

The word *void* before the function's name indicates that the routine does not return a value. In the next chapter, we discuss functions that do return values, such as the square root function. The *void* in parentheses indicates that the function expects no data. The calling function cannot send an argument to this routine.

The function name *main* is mandatory, but we choose the names of the other user-defined functions, such as *PrintHopper*. The rules for naming functions are the same as those for naming any identifier in C:

1. The name must begin with a letter or underscore (_).

2. Any combination of letters, digits, and underscores can follow.

3. The name cannot be one of the keywords or reserved names in C. (Appendix B lists the keywords in C.)

Some compilers also limit the length of the name. Because the system uses function names that begin with an underscore, you should avoid such names for user-defined functions. Also, by convention, constants are usually in all capital letters. For example, the following preprocessor directive establishes *UPPER_BOUND* as the constant 10.

```
#define UPPER_BOUND 10
```

For clarity, the name should represent the action performed by the function.

Definition A **keyword** in C is a reserved name that cannot be used for a user-defined identifier.

The definition of *PrintHopper* is as follows:

```
/* Function to print the name and title of Grace Hopper */

void PrintHopper(void)
{
    printf("Rear Admiral Grace Murray Hopper, U.S.N., Ph.D.");
}
```

We can define functions in any order. Usually, programmers define the *main* function first or last in the file. In this text, modeling the top-down design, we define *main* and then the other functions as follows:

```
     ⋮
main()
{
    statement(s)
}

/* . . . */
void function_name1(void)
{
    statement(s)
}

/* . . . */
void function_name2(void)
{
    statement(s)
}
     ⋮
```

C does not permit the programmer to define a function within the braces of another function.

Calling a Function

Once we define a function to play a particular role in a program, we can call it repeatedly throughout that program. When we call or invoke a function the computer executes the body of the function. We call the function *PrintHopper* when we mention its name in another function. In the invocation, *PrintHopper* must be followed by a pair of empty parentheses to indicate no arguments. The invocation for *PrintHopper* is as follows:

```
PrintHopper();
```

A semicolon must be present to indicate the end of the statement containing the call. Upon encountering this invocation, the computer executes the body of *PrintHopper*, returning to *main* when finished. Figure 1.10 shows this transfer of control from *main* to *PrintHopper* and back. The computer executes a function only if another function invokes it. Even though the *PrintHopper* function is defined in the program, its

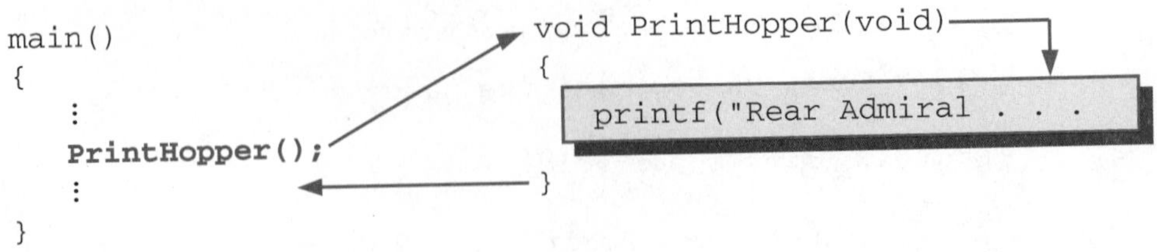

Figure 1.10   Transfer of control from *main* to *PrintHopper* and back

statements are never executed if another function does not invoke *PrintHopper*. Moreover, we can call a function any number of times; the computer dutifully executes the function's statements each time.

We might wonder how the *main* function is executed, because it is not formally invoked in the program. The **operating system**, or programs that help to control the computer's operations, automatically calls the *main* function on execution of the program. For this reason, a *main* must always be present; otherwise, the program cannot run.

Definition　An **operating system** is a collection of programs that enable a user to interact with computer system resources efficiently.

Function Prototype

We must **declare** or provide certain information about a function before we can define or use it. The function declaration is called a **function prototype**. The prototype defines the kind of value the function returns, the kinds of arguments it expects, and the function's name. Because *PrintHopper* does not return a value, *void* appears before the function's name. Moreover, because the function does not need any information from the calling routine, *void* appears in parentheses following its name. The function prototype for *PrintHopper* is as follows:

Thus, this prototype is identical to the first line of the function's definition, except for the presence of a semicolon. The prototype is a complete **declaration statement**, and it must end in a semicolon. However, the first line of the definition of a function, such as *main* or *PrintHopper*, is not a complete statement and does not have a semicolon.

Definition　A **function prototype** or **function declaration statement** provides information about the kind of value the function returns (if any), the kinds of arguments it expects (if any), and the function's name.

In most programs in the text, we place function prototype before the definition of *main*, as shown below:

```
/* . . . */

#include <stdio.h>

void PrintHopper(void);       /* function prototype-declaration */
```

```
main()
{
    ⋮
    PrintHopper();              /* call to function */
    ⋮
}

/* Function to print the name and title of Grace Hopper */

void PrintHopper(void)      /* start of function definition */
{
    printf("Rear Admiral Grace Murray Hopper, U.S.N., Ph.D.");
}
```

In the next chapter, we discuss alternatives for placement of prototypes.

A function prototype is an example of a **nonexecutable statement** that the compiler uses during compilation. An **executable statement**, or execution-time instruction, is an instruction for the computer to take some action during execution. A statement containing a call to *printf* or another function is an example of an executable statement. Any executable statement not within *main* must be part of some other function. Prototypes, however, do not need to appear in a function definition.

Definitions An **executable statement** is an execution-time instruction for the computer to follow during execution. A **nonexecutable statement** gives instructions to the compiler.

ANSI C Libraries

An ANSI C header file contains the prototypes for the functions defined in the corresponding object library. Thus, *stdio.h* contains the prototype for *printf*, and the standard I/O object file defines *printf*. With the prototype information in the header file, the compiler can determine the proper format of a call to *printf*. When we place the preprocessor directive to include *stdio.h* at the beginning of our program, we have the prototypes available throughout the program file.

Example 1.2

In this example, we write a program to print the following song:

```
This old man, he played one,
He played knick-knack on my thumb,
    With a knick-knack-paddy-whack,⎫
    Give the dog a bone,            ⎬ chorus
    This old man went rolling home. ⎭

This old man, he played two,
He played knick-knack on my shoe,
    With a knick-knack-paddy-whack,⎫
    Give the dog a bone,            ⎬ chorus
    This old man went rolling home. ⎭
```

```
This old man, he played three,
He played knick-knack on my knee,
    With a knick-knack-paddy-whack,
    Give the dog a bone,                     } chorus
    This old man went rolling home.
```

The problem of printing this song decomposes into tasks of printing each of three verses and the chorus. Figure 1.11 presents a structure chart for this design.

The *main* function calls the *FirstVerse, SecondVerse*, and *ThirdVerse* functions to display the verses and calls the *chorus* function to display the chorus. Thus, we write the calls to *printf* for the chorus only once. The following is pseudocode for the function *main*. Because the other functions involve straightforward printing, we do not include their pseudocode.

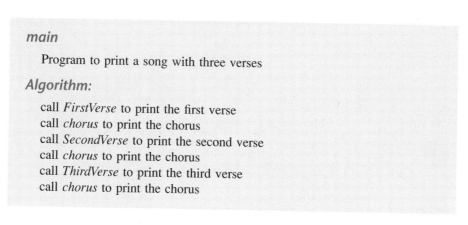

main

Program to print a song with three verses

Algorithm:

call *FirstVerse* to print the first verse
call *chorus* to print the chorus
call *SecondVerse* to print the second verse
call *chorus* to print the chorus
call *ThirdVerse* to print the third verse
call *chorus* to print the chorus

Figure 1.11
Structure chart
of "This Old
Man" program,
Example 1.2

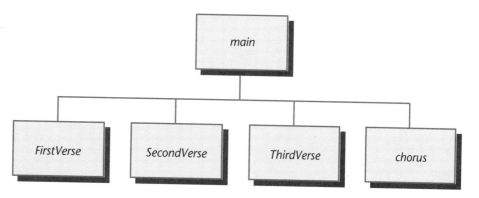

We now write the C code for the program.*

```c
/* Program to print "This Old Man" */

#include <stdio.h>

void chorus(void);
void FirstVerse(void);
void SecondVerse(void);
void ThirdVerse(void);

main()
{
    FirstVerse();
    chorus();

    SecondVerse();
    chorus();

    ThirdVerse();
    chorus();
}

/* Function to print the chorus */

void chorus(void)
{
    printf("   With a knick-knack-paddy-whack,\n");
    printf("   Give the dog a bone,\n");
    printf("   This old man went rolling home.\n\n");
}

/* Function to print the first verse */

void FirstVerse(void)
{
    printf("This old man, he played one,\n");
    printf("He played knick-knack on my thumb,\n");
}
```

---

*When compiling this program, some compilers issue a warning message such as the following:

```
Warning: Function should return a value
```

This message can be ignored. You may, however, be able to set the warning level on your compiler so that it does not issue such a message. Alternatively, you can add the following as the last statement in every *main* body:

```
return 0;
```

We discuss *return* statements in the next chapter.

```
/* Function to print the second verse */

void SecondVerse(void)
{
    printf("This old man, he played two,\n");
    printf("He played knick-knack on my shoe,\n");
}

/* Function to print the third verse */

void ThirdVerse(void)
{
    printf("This old man, he played three,\n");
    printf("He played knick-knack on my knee,\n");
}
```

The order in which we place the prototypes is irrelevant. Similarly, as long as prototypes precede them, the order of the function definitions also does not matter.

Section 1.8 Exercises

1. **a.** Define a function to print your name without the newline character.

   b. Give a prototype for this function.

   c. Write *main* to display several sentences that contain your name. Call the function from Part a as needed.

2. Find the errors in the following function definition:

   ```
   /* Function with errors */
   void fun;
   (
       printf("Does this line have an error?\n")
   )
   ```

3. Find the errors in the following function prototype:

   ```
   void fnc[void]
   ```

Section 1.8 Programming Projects

1. Design a structure chart and write a program to print several verses of "Mac-Donald's Farm." The program should print a title at the top and should use function calls in place of the repetitive material. The first verse is as follows:

   Old MacDonald had a farm, Ee-i, ee-i-o,
   And on this farm he had a duck, Ee-i, ee-i-o,
   With a quack quack here and a quack quack there,
   Here a quack, there a quack, everywhere a quack quack,
   Old MacDonald had a farm, Ee-i, ee-i-o

   The second verse uses "pig" and "oink" in place of "duck" and "quack," respectively. The third verse uses "cow" and "moo."

2. Design a structure chart and write a program that has two functions besides *main*, called *name* and *blanks*. The *name* function should print your name and advance to a new line, and *blanks* should produce five blanks without advancing to a new line. The output of the program should have your name appearing on each of six lines, five spaces to the right of its appearance on the previous line. A sample output for John Backus follows:

```
John Backus
        John Backus
                John Backus
                        John Backus
                                John Backus
                                        John Backus
```

3. Design a structure chart and write a program that has two functions besides *main*, called *LetterW* and *LetterO*. The *LetterW* function should print a large W and *LetterO* should print a large O in block letters. For example, *LetterW* should produce output similar to the following:

```
    x               x
     x             x
       x   x   x
        x x x x
          x   x
```

Use these functions to print WOW down the page.

4. Design a structure chart and write a program that prints the title and chorus of "Jingle Bells" twice. One chorus is as follows:

```
Jingle Bells
Jingle Bells
Jingle all the way
Oh, what fun it is to ride
In a one-horse open sleigh!
```

The *main* function should call a *chorus* function; *main* and *chorus* should both call a *title* function that prints the title.

Section 1.9 Breadth: Subject Areas of Computer Science

Computer science is a far-reaching discipline. Few people have mastered the entire scope of the discipline, including hardware, software, and theory. At elementary levels, a person sometimes has difficulty seeing beyond the chore of learning the concepts, jargon, and programming language syntax. A committee of the Association for Computing Machinery (ACM), the oldest and largest professional society of computer scientists, has recommended that students be exposed to the nine subject areas of the discipline discussed in the following paragraphs. These areas are central to your study of computer science in this and subsequent courses.

Algorithms and data structures

The definition of computer science in Section 1.2 begins, "The discipline of computing is the systematic study of algorithmic processes. . . ." In the last section, we described some algorithms for achieving a task. Part of computer science is not only discovering ways but of finding *optimal* ways of performing tasks. For example, one common task is sorting, such as arranging a list of names in alphabetical order. In many industrial computing centers, 30% of total computer time may be devoted to sorting data. Thus, it is very important for a sorting algorithm to perform this task as efficiently as possible. To illustrate, one poorly designed commercial program took two hours to sort a list of names, while another took less than one second.

Sorted dated are usually stored in a particular data structure, the array, which is built into the C language. An array is a sequence of items, such as a list of names. A data structure not only consists of the physical data storage but of the operations that manipulate the structures and algorithms that use these operations. For example, one operation on an array involves storing a value in a particular place in the sequence. To maintain alphabetization in a class roll, a professor might need to insert a new student's name in the fifth position, as shown below:

> Adams, Clarence
> Blackwell, Henry
> Davis, Susan
> Hinkel, Chris   ⟵————— Jordan, Mandi
> Patterson, Lynn
> Shaffer, Melony
> Williams, George

We consider the array and other built-in data structures in later chapters. We also develop a number of algorithms, such as a method of sorting an array. The area of algorithms and data structures is central to problem solving with the computer.

Architecture

Architecture involves ways of arranging efficient and dependable computer systems. A computer system consists of both software and hardware. About 30 years ago it was estimated that approximately every $1\frac{1}{2}$ years the speed and storage amount for a computer would double, while the price of that computer would remain about the same. Remarkably, this prediction has been fairly accurate.

Today, users hope that parallel computers can achieve even more remarkable speeds. A parallel computer has several main processing components instead of just one, all of which can work simultaneously on a program. For example, the Connection Machine has 64,000 of these components. Consider the task of cleaning a house, which takes quite a while for one person. If eight friends each clean a different room simultaneously, the job is completed much faster. Serious problems must be overcome, such as two people wanting to sweep with a single broom. Computer scientists must consider analogous problems in parallel processing.

Implementation of communications among computers is also part of architecture. Ironically, in the infancy of computers, Thomas Watson, Sr., then Chairman of the Board of IBM, thought that the world market would never be more than about five computers. The large number of computers today demands reliable communication among them. A computer network consists of computers and communication links between these systems. Internet is a worldwide interconnection of computer networks. With electronic mail, we can communicate over this network with people here and in foreign countries.

Artificial Intelligence and Robotics

Artificial intelligence (AI) is having computers do tasks, such that if a human did those tasks, we would say the person exhibited intelligence. The first applications of AI were in playing games, such as chess—a problem that still poses challenges in AI. Some programs now play at the master level. Each year, the Association for Computing Machinery's Computer Science Conference holds an international computer chess championship in which the best chess programs compete.

One aspect of AI with an increasing number of business applications allows computers to act as experts in certain areas. One such expert system can help a doctor make a medical diagnosis; another can help a geologist evaluate a mineral site.

An area that overlaps with AI and already has tremendous commercial applications is **robotics**. A **robot** is a programmed machine that can mechanically manipulate objects. Automobile manufacturers use robots to assemble vehicles. Robots can do jobs hazardous to humans, such as handling nuclear materials. Moreover, they can perform tasks that require a high degree of precision or a sterile environment. Robots that use AI might respond to voice commands, view a scene and interpret what it "sees," or detect shape and texture to handle delicate objects.

Database and Information Retrieval

A **database** is an integrated collection of files. Much data are placed in a database only once. However, the information in a database can be retrieved in many different forms. For example, a database for student use may provide information about possible careers. The student enters a number of his or her interests and characteristics. From these entries, the database provides a matching list of possible occupations. The student can also ask for a description of a particular occupation, including the skills and education required. Through another search, addresses of testing programs are available.

Part of this subject area involves the responsibility of the computer professional for the security and protection of information. One aborted joint venture between a credit bureau and a software developer had the potential of invading privacy on a grand scale. The companies were planning to sell a compact disk-read only memory (CD-ROM) with the names, approximate incomes, marital status, buying habits, and other personal information for 120 million U.S. consumers. There would be no way of correcting inaccuracies or of updating data on this permanent medium other than replacing the CD-ROM. Fortunately, public opinion killed the project.

Human-Computer Communication

This subject area involves efficient communication between people and computers. A primary advantage of modern computers is their ability to communicate with the user during program execution. Such programs are called **interactive**. Informative instructions and prompts that appear on the screen are essential to the utility of any interactive program. An explanation of what the program does and a menu of clear choices is far more instructive than just a question mark on the screen waiting for a user's response. As an example of the importance of careful communication, in 1987, Payroll Systems, Inc. (PSI) assumed management of employee benefits for Theron Corporation. PSI sent questionnaires to all Theron employees asking how to distribute their retirement assets between a stock fund and a fixed income fund, and personnel entered all the answers into the computer. Unfortunately, the locations for the responses on the screen were opposite of the order on the printed questionnaire, and the instructions on the screen were so terse that no one discovered the switch. All the data were entered in the

wrong order. The error was not discovered until after the 1987 stock market crash, when almost $200,000 was lost in retirement benefits. PSI accepted responsibility and their insurance company reimbursed employees.

Communications between human and machine might be verbal instead of written. A computer might announce that some task, such as printing, is complete or accept voice commands from the user. Programs that read documents aloud are especially beneficial to the visually handicapped. With the ambiguity of English, however, such programs can mispronounce words like "read," which has two pronunciations. The problems of the machine understanding the human are more significant. Computer scientists in the area of **natural language processing** must write algorithms for the computer to learn to understand an individual's accent and language ambiguity. For example, "write" and "right" have the same pronunciation but completely different meanings. Consequently, such systems usually recognize only a limited vocabulary with specific grammar rules.

Interactive programs can involve pictures instead of written and spoken words. For example, video games are interactive. They pose situations, the player responds with various moves, and the game reacts. Popular games are not only exciting but are easily understood and have good graphics. Many special effects we see in movies and commercials are also created with computer graphics. Computer scientists develop sophisticated graphics packages which artists use to generate realistic images.

Computer graphics from Jurassic Park

Computer graphics from Terminator II

Numerical and Symbolic Computation

Some computer scientists develop algorithms to solve equations in **mathematical modeling**, which is the study of methods to analyze complex, real-world problems in order to predict what might happen with some course of action. When experiments are too difficult, time consuming, costly, or dangerous to perform, a modeler might resort to **computer simulation**, or having a computer program imitate reality. For example, scientists have developed a simulation with graphics to help them understand and illustrate the formation of acid rain.

Computer scientists also create sophisticated mathematical software packages, such as *Mathematica*, which is a graphical computer algebra system written in C. The package can work with symbols and solve problems in virtually all areas of mathematics, including algebra and calculus. Consider how long it would take to solve the following system of equations by hand:

$$\begin{cases} x + y + z = \dfrac{29}{30} \\[2mm] 3x + y + 2z = \dfrac{31}{10} \\[2mm] 7x + 6y - z = \dfrac{13}{15} \end{cases}$$

With *Mathematica*, we can issue the command *Solve*, as follows:

```
Solve[{ x + y + z == 29/30,
        3x + y + 2z == 31/10,
        7x + 6y - z == 13/15}, {x, y, z}]
```

and obtain the answer in less than a second.

```
          2           1           4
{{x -> - -, y -> -(-), z -> -}}
          3           2           5
```

With *Mathematica*, the user can also generate impressive animations and three-dimensional graphics, as shown in Figure 1.12.

Operating Systems

An **operating system (OS)** is a collection of programs that enables the user to interact with computer system resources efficiently. An OS allows many people to use a large computer at the same time. For any computer, the OS manages all computer resources, such as printers and keyboards, and helps the computer recover from error conditions. The operating system to a large extent defines the character of the computer. For example, the user interface of an IBM PC with a DOS operating system is quite different from an Apple Macintosh running the MacOS operating system. The former is **command driven**, in which the user types commands in order to execute a program. MacOS has a **graphical user interface**, or **GUI** (pronounced gooey), in which the user makes choices with a mouse from menus or visual cues on the screen. To run a program, the Macintosh user clicks twice on an icon or picture representing the program.

Programming Languages

The machine language of a computer consists of sequences of zeros and ones, such as 1111001000011011101. Giving instructions to a computer in machine language is an extremely tedious and error-prone task for humans. Consequently, hundreds of

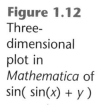

Figure 1.12
Three-
dimensional
plot in
Mathematica of
sin(sin(x) + y)

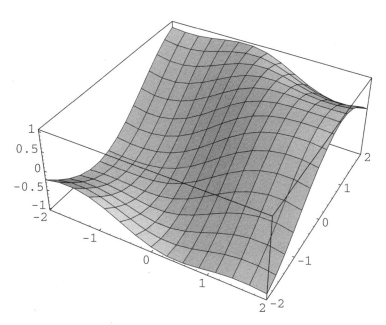

programming languages have been developed that are much closer to English and much easier for people to use. Certain languages are suited to business applications, others to science, some to AI, and others for work on parallel computers. In this text, we study one particular language in depth—C. However, this area of computer science involves much more than the elements of writing programs in one language.

Just as English has a grammar, so do programming languages. A grammar consists of a set of symbols and rules for combining those symbols. Unlike English, a programming language grammar must be unambiguous. Only one interpretation of a program must exist in order to automate the translation of that program into machine language. Those who create any programming language carefully develop its grammar and the meanings of certain symbol combinations so that the language is unambiguous. The choices of language developers give a language its own unique character. Many issues and techniques are involved in efficiently and correctly translating programs written in one particular language to machine language.

Software Methodology and Engineering

In the first section of the text, we discussed problem-solving concepts and the development process for programs. Throughout the text, we examine how to analyze, design, implement, and test programs effectively. Unfortunately, program errors are prevalent, even in commercially produced software. One leader in the computer science field reported on an important system he developed. He noted that, on the average, the compiler did not detect 40 errors per 1000 lines. Twelve bugs were not even discovered by any testing before release. Such mistakes can produce erroneous results and cost time, money, and even lives. Part of this area of computer science is to develop techniques to discover and correct errors and to prove that programs are correct.

Social, Ethical, and Professional Issues

Besides the previous nine subject areas and the three paradigms of theory, abstraction, and design, *Computing Curricula 1991* noted that we need to view the discipline in a social and professional context. Part of the social context of computer science is its history. The first computer was not built until the middle of the twentieth century, but many achievements important to this young discipline predate its development. For example, computational logic, which provides the basis for how computers and programs work, was formalized by a mathematician in the middle of the nineteenth century.

Ethical issues in computer science involve such considerations as the legal rights of software vendors. The copyright law originally applied to written works, but in 1980 Congress amended it to cover software as well.

Sensitivity to ethical issues is part of the professional responsibilities of a computer scientist. The **ACM Code of Ethics and Professional Conduct**, adopted in 1992, is intended to help computing specialists make ethical decisions in their work. The Code presents general moral imperatives, specific professional responsibilities, organizational leadership imperatives, and imperatives concerning compliance with the Code. Although many issues are involved, the Code states, "Excellence is perhaps the most important obligation of a professional."

Programming and Debugging Hints

Debugging Knowing the syntax of a language is not the same as knowing how to program in that language. Programming is a skill that people can obtain only through study and experience. The newcomer to C or to programming in general must recognize the fact that errors occur. In programming circles, errors are known as **bugs**, and the process of finding and eliminating bugs is known as **debugging**.

The term "bug" originates with the first electromechanical, general-purpose computer, the Mark I, completed during World War II. The lack of air conditioning meant that windows were left open on hot summer days. On one such day, the computer malfunctioned, and after hours of testing, laboratory workers walked into the machine and found the problem. A moth lodged on the contacts was preventing the flow of electricity. Carefully removing the insect and pasting it into the log book, Grace Murray Hopper wrote that they had found a "bug" in the computer. This famous bug is now on display at the Smithsonian Institute. Throughout the text, Programming and Debugging Hints will present ideas to help prevent or eliminate the inevitable program bugs.

In Section 1.5, we defined a **syntax error** or **compile-time error** as one that violates the syntax or rules of a language. The computer might compile a program but still detect an error during execution. Such a **run-time error** or **execution-time error** results in an error message and an abnormal end to program execution. One example of a run-time error on many systems is an attempt to divide a number by zero, which is an impossible task. The compiler does not discover such an error while it is compiling because no syntax violation occurs. Nevertheless, execution usually cannot continue with this computation.*

A **logic error** can cause more harm than a syntax or run-time error. The compiler flags syntax errors and the computer locates run-time errors, so the programmer can generally eliminate them from the program quickly. Logic errors, however, usually permit the program to run and produce incorrect results. Because such errors do not violate the rules of the language, the compiler cannot detect them. Often an incorrect algorithm produces the logic error. Another cause might be a mistyped statement that obeys the syntax of the language but performs an unintended computation.

---

*In IEEE arithmetic, the result of division by zero is NaN, Not a Number. In some situations, such a result is reasonable, and execution can continue. Many versions of C, however, abort execution when an attempt is made to divide by zero.

Sometimes it is frustrating for the programmer to find logic errors. In most programs, the final output is the result of many calculations performed by many statements. It can be difficult to trace the cause of an error if the programmer only uses the final output of the program. Throughout the text we study techniques that help in eliminating syntax, run-time, and logic errors.

Walkthrough Technique

Using the **walkthrough** technique, we can debug the design of a program in a modular fashion (module by module) before coding. In a walkthrough, a programmer—preferably someone other than the original author—mentally executes the pseudocode as though he or she were the computer. When a team works on a large project, formal walkthroughs often involve a group of participants. Such a review helps to ensure that program logic satisfies the requirements, is sound, and covers all possibilities. In Chapter 10, we discuss this technique in greater detail.

Modular Programming

Modular programming, or top-down design, is one technique that can help eliminate logic errors at an early stage in the development of a program. With modular programming a function performs each individual subtask of a programming problem. We want to maximize cohesion, with each function being devoted to a single task. In modular programming, most functions consist of calls to other functions. The statements of the main function are almost entirely calls to other functions, which in turn may call still other functions. Structure charts introduced in Section 1.1 depict a hierarchy diagram of such an arrangement. Only functions on the lowest level do not call other functions. These functions perform relatively simple tasks that the higher level functions use.

With modular programming, we can isolate and test individually each small, manageable subtask of a program. Moreover, we can easily find and modify each subtask. It is easier to identify the part of a program that is responsible for a particular error when we have clearly defined and separated each part of the program. Furthermore, modular programming makes it easier to amend the program or add new code at some later stage.

≋ Key Terms

The following are key terms from the non-breadth sections in Chapter 1. Write out the definition of a term immediately to check your answer. If you do not remember the definition or make an error, write the definition again. Repeat this process until you can give a correct definition without looking at the description in the text. Mark any terms that give you difficulty. After going through all the definitions, return to the terms that you have marked for further practice.

\n 26
address 14
algorithm 6
ALU 13
analysis 3
argument 31
arithmetic/logic unit 13
assembler language 19
binary digit 19
bit 19
black box 4
body 25
bug 46
call 31
case sensitive 25

central processing unit 11, 13
code 8
coding 8
comment 24
compile-time error 20, 46
compiler 19
computer system 11
control string 26
control unit 13
CPU 11, 13
data 3
data structure 6
debug 46
declaration statement 35
declare 35

Summary

A central theme throughout the text is problem solving with the computer. These steps are as follows:

1. Analysis. Determine output, input, and processing; state the objectives of each module.

2. Design. Diagram a structure chart, select the data structures, and develop the logic of each module.

3. Implementation. Code the solution and provide documentation.

4. Testing. Select test data, perform testing of each module, and test the program as a whole.

A computer system has the following five major hardware components:

1. Input unit

2. Output unit

3. Secondary storage

4. Central processing unit (CPU), which consists of the arithmetic/logic unit (ALU) and control unit

5. Main memory, which consists of memory locations, each having its own address (0, 1, 2, etc.)

To execute a program, a computer performs the fetch/execute cycle: As long as instructions remain, the control unit fetches or retrieves the next instruction from main memory; the CPU decodes the instruction; and the control unit commands the appropriate unit to execute the instruction.

To implement a program on the computer, we type it in, usually using an editor, to create a source program. A preprocessor program automatically removes comments and modifies the C source program according to our directions. If possible, a compiler translates the preprocessed source code into object code, a machine language version of the program. The compiler also locates syntax errors, which violate the syntax or rules of the language. A linker program combines all the object code of the program with necessary external items to form an executable program.

Any C program should contain ample comments for documentation. The form of a comment is

```
/* comment */
```

To make full use of such input and output operations as *printf*, the program must include the header file *stdio.h*.

```
#include <stdio.h>
```

Every C program contains a group of statements, called *main*, of the following form:

```
main()
{
    statement(s)
}
```

To print a sequence of characters, called a control string, we write

```
printf("sequence_of_characters");
```

A newline character (\n) in the control string causes the computer to advance to the beginning of the next line before displaying the remainder of the control string. A semicolon terminates each statement in a program.

A function is a subprogram that implements a task. Problem and function decomposition are usually based on one or more of the following: complexity, recurrence of a given logic sequence, generalization, implementation hiding, error finding and testing. Once we have performed the stepwise refinement of a problem, we use pseudocode to design each module. A function that only displays has the following form for its definition:

```
void function_name(void)
{
    statement(s)
}
```

An identifier, such as a function name, in C contains any combination of letters, digits, and underscores, but must begin with a letter or underscore (_) and cannot be a keyword. We can define functions in any order. The statement to call a function that only displays has the form

```
function_name();
```

The prototype or declaration for such a function is

```
void function_name(void);
```

Review Questions

This text feature is intended to help you study the nonbreadth material. Answers are in Appendix K. A useful way to practice with this section is to write answers to the questions and then to mark incorrect responses. Continue writing a response to a question until you can write a correct answer without looking at the text.

1. List the steps for solving a problem using a computer.
2. What is a structure chart?
3. What is an algorithm?
4. Name the five major hardware components of a computer system.
5. Give the two major components of the CPU.
6. Give the name of the process performed by the computer while executing a program.
7. What is an identifier?
8. What is an address of a memory location?
9. What is the name of the specialized word processor for entering programs?
10. List the steps to execution of a program.
11. What is the C preprocessor?
12. Give the preprocessor directive to define the value of π as a constant 3.14159.
13. Name the delimiters that are used to specify the beginning and end of a string constant (character string) in C.
14. What is the character string in a call to *printf* usually called?
15. What symbol terminates every C statement?
16. Name the delimiters that are used to specify the beginning and end of a group of instructions to be executed.
17. How is the newline character formed?
18. What symbols are used to specify a comment?
19. What function do you call to print a string constant?
20. What is the purpose of including comments in a program?
21. May comments extend beyond a single line?
22. What is a function argument?
23. Distinguish between a user-defined function and one supplied in the C library.
24. In what sense does the user-defined function feature of C extend the language?
25. Name a common function supplied in the standard I/O library.
26. What is a function prototype?
27. Give a statement that calls the function *chorus*.
28. Why should you use functions when programming in C?
29. What is the meaning of debugging?
30. What is a module? What is an example in C?
31. What are the rules regarding the naming of a function?
32. How often can a function be called?
33. What is meant by top-down design?

34. What symbols are used to encompass the body of a function?

35. Is the location of *main* important?

36. How is the *main* function normally invoked?

Laboratory

Each chapter contains a laboratory section. A disk included with the text has programming segments and data files to accompany the laboratories. You should work with this material at the computer. Various laboratories relate principles covered in the text to software and hardware, emphasize sound programming practices, and introduce experimental methods. Regardless of the format, working through the material will deepen your understanding of problem solving with the computer, C, and the discipline of computer science.

Obtain information from your professor or lab assistant on how to use the editor and how to compile, link, and execute a program on your computer system.

1. The goal of this exercise is to examine various components of a program. We make additions and changes to the final version of the program in Example 1.1 in Section 1.7 and observe their effects.

   a. Save a copy of the file *LAB011.c*, which is on the disk that accompanies the text, onto your own disk. Save your work frequently, at least every 15 minutes, and before you print or make global changes, such as replacing one word with another throughout the program.

   b. Compile, link, and execute *LAB011.c*.

   c. Insert a comment after the header comment that gives your name and the date. Rerun the program. Did the output change?

   d. Change the header comment to state the following:

```
Program to print part of "Don't Fence Me In"
```

   Run the program. Did the output change?

   e. In the second call to *printf*, change "And the" to "Under" and the ellipses (three continuation dots) to a period. Describe any change in the printout.

   f. Add another call to *printf* at the end of *main* that displays

```
Don't fence me in.
```

   g. Add another call to *printf* at the beginning of *main* that displays the title

```
Don't Fence Me In
```

   Have the computer print a few spaces before the title and a blank line before the words of the song.

   h. Add other calls to *printf* to display another verse after a blank line. Do not retype the last line, but use your editor to make a copy of this line from the first verse.

```
Let me roam in the wide
Open country that I love.
Don't fence me in.
```

i. When your program is working properly, print the listing (the code of the program). Print the output from a run.

j. By removing the proper \n for each verse, make changes so that the computer prints the first two lines of each verse on one line with the proper capitalization as follows:

```
                    Don't Fence Me In


    Give me land, lots of land under starry skies above.
    Don't fence me in.

    Let me roam in the wide open country that I love.
    Don't fence me in.
```

2. The aim of this exercise is to observe the messages from various errors. Make the change for each error listed below in the program file *LAB011.c* on your disk. Execute the program with the error, and write the error message or a description of the effect of the error. Then, correct the error and rerun the program to verify that the program is running correctly in preparation for the next part. Some compilers may not flag a particular change as an error. If your system does not indicate an error for a part, write a statement to that effect.

a. Delete the closing, */, of the comment.

b. Delete the opening, /*, of the comment.

c. Remove the preprocessor directive

```
#include <stdio.h>
```

With some compilers, removal of this directive does not cause an error when using *printf* for screen display. Does removal of the directive cause an error on your system?

d. Remove the angle brackets around *stdio.h* in the preprocessor directive.

e. Put a semicolon at the end of the preprocessor directive.

f. Misspell *stdio.h* by dropping the *d.*

g. Insert a semicolon after *main*().

h. Delete the parentheses in *main*().

i. Remove the braces in the program.

j. Place a semicolon after the closing brace.

k. Delete the semicolon from the last call to *printf.*

l. Misspell *printf* by dropping the *f.*

m. Use apostrophes instead of quotation marks in the first call to *printf.*

n. Exchange the two calls to *printf.* The other errors in this exercise are syntax errors violating the syntax of the language; the compiler should catch these mistakes. The error in this part is a logic error leading to incorrect results. We detect these errors by examining the output closely.

3. The purpose of this exercise is to practice with functions. We use the file *LAB013.c*, which contains the program from Example 1.2 of Section 1.8.

a. Save the program on your data disk.

b. Compile, link, and execute *LAB013.c.*

c. Using a call to *chorus*, have your program print the chorus twice at the end.

d. The call to *printf*

```
printf("This old man, he played one,\n");
```

can be split into two statements as follows:

```
printf("This old man, he played ");
printf("one,\n");
```

For the first line in each verse, convert the one call of *printf* to two cells, as shown above. Execute this variation to see that it works properly.

e. In the *printf* for the first line of each verse, change "played" to "sang." Notice there are three places to make identical adjustments.

f. Define a function *FirstLine* that prints "This old man, he played "; have a prototype for the function; and call this function from *FirstVerse*, *SecondVerse*, and *ThirdVerse* instead of *printf* in each.

g. By adjusting *FirstLine*, change the first line of each verse to "sang" instead of "played." Unlike Part e, only one modification is needed in the function to obtain three changes in the printout.

h. As in part d with the first line of each verse, print the second line of each verse with two calls to *printf*. The first *printf* should print "He played knick-knack on my".

i. Replace the *printf* from part h that prints "He played knick-knack on my" with a call to the function *SecondLine*. Do not define this function. What error message does the compiler give?

j. Introduce a prototype for the function in Part h. Do you still get the same error message?

k. Define the function *SecondLine* from Part i.

l. Print a listing and a run of the program.

2

Integer Variables, Expressions, and Functions

Introduction

Frequently, a problem solution on the computer involves numeric data as well as character strings. Computers are renowned for their ability to calculate accurately and at phenomenal speeds. They handle arithmetic calculations so efficiently that we often refer to computers as "number crunchers."

In this chapter, we learn how the computer manages integer numeric data (..., -3, -2, -1, 0, 1, 2, 3, ...). We see how, following the program's directions, the computer associates the name of a variable with a location in memory. So that the computer can allocate the correct amount of space, the program must designate the type of the data—such as integer information—that the location can hold. We also examine how long the relationship between a variable and a memory location lasts. During program execution, the computer can store an integer in such a variable's memory location by assigning or reading a value for the variable.

One way to read such a value is from keyboard input. We often find it convenient to write programs so that they interact with the user through the screen and keyboard. We have seen how a program can display messages to the user. Now, we discover that this communication can be two-way.

After input of data or assignment, the program can combine those values in expressions involving such operations as addition, subtraction, multiplication, division, and modulo arithmetic. In two breadth sections, we examine how the computer stores these integer values and how the machine performs addition and subtraction on integers.

Solution of a problem may require numerous computations. Continuing the discussion of problem solving and top-down design, we see that modules can do more than just display constant character strings. We consider functions that carry out tasks requiring integer input. These functions perform computations, and often they return integer results. Enhancing the design and implementation phases, we learn to consider the state of the system when the module finishes execution and the conditions that must be true for the function to perform its task.

Goals

To study

- The integer type and variables of that type
- Assignment of a value to a variable
- Arithmetic with integers
- How the computer stores integers
- How the computer performs integer arithmetic
- Interactive programs with integer input
- Functions that accept integer arguments or return integer values
- Program design, preconditions, and postconditions
- The range within a program over which a variable has meaning
- Pass by value

Section 2.1 **Integer Data**

C deals with several different kinds of numbers, and the integer is a basic data type. An integer, or whole number, does not have either a decimal point or a fractional portion. Some examples of integer numbers are 123, −34, 0, 345, −57, and 98. When we write a number in a program, we must not include a comma, because certain statements use commas to separate values. Therefore, we record thirty-thousand as 30000, not 30,000.

Definition   In mathematics, the **set of integers** is $\{...,-3, -2, -1, 0, 1, 2, 3, ...\}$.

On the computer, a number such as 13.6 is not an integer, because it contains a decimal point. Such a number is a floating point or real number, which we cover in Chapter 4. A number such as 15. or 15.0 is also a floating point number, even though its fractional part is zero. The critical consideration is whether the number contains a decimal point, regardless of what follows it.

Definition   A **floating point number** is a number stored in the computer with a decimal reference point.

Variables

The computer can store strings and numeric values in its memory for subsequent recall. To do so, the program must assign a unique **variable** name to each such area in memory. Once the location contains a data item, if an expression in the program uses the variable, the computer substitutes the value from memory.

Definition   A **variable** is a program's name for a memory location.

In order to appreciate the significance of variables, consider the following instruction:

```
printf("%d", 23 + 17);
```

When this instruction is executed, the sum of 23 and 17 is calculated and displayed. The %d within the control string is a **conversion specification** indicating that the number should be converted to decimal notation before printing. (We discuss this topic in the next section.) Once the sum is printed, it is lost from the computer's memory because the %d does not store the value. Should the need arise to evaluate this expression again, programming the expression once more would waste both human effort and computer time. A better approach is to store the result in the computer's memory. Most programs use many memory locations, represented by variable names, for precisely this reason.

Definition   A **conversion specification** specifies to what notation the computer should convert a value for input or output operations.

Variable Declaration

In C, a program must **declare** each variable. The program must contain a statement specifying precisely the kind of information the variable should contain. This rule applies to every variable in the program, regardless of the type. The compiler uses this **variable declaration**, which indicates the variable name and the data **type**, to allocate an appropriate amount of space for the variable. For example, on many computers, a floating point number consumes twice as much space as an integer.

Definitions   The **type** of a variable is the kind of data it can store. A **variable declaration** is a statement that indicates the variable's name and type.

If we wish to use the variable *number* to store an integer value, we must declare *number* to be of the type *int*. The abbreviation *int* is one of about 30 keywords in C. Keywords are reserved names in lowercase that we can never use as variable or function names. Appendix B contains a complete list of these words.

We write the keyword *int* as shown in the following example:

```
int number;
```

The full spelling, integer, is not a substitute and causes an error. In this example, *number* is the name of the variable that we declare to be of type *int*. Such a declaration usually occurs after the opening brace of *main* or of a function that uses the variable. In future chapters, we study data types other than integer.

We must declare all variables in C before using them. FORTRAN and several other programming languages do not have this requirement. Instead, FORTRAN variables that begin with the letters i through n are integer variables, whereas those beginning with other letters are floating point number variables. Such default declarations can result in costly errors. For example, the following FORTRAN statement

```
DO  7  I = 1, 3
```

instructs the computer to perform the statements from this point down to statement number 7 three times, with *I* having the value 1, then 2, and finally 3. Suppose the programmer types a period instead of a comma.

```
DO  7  I = 1. 3
```

In trying to decipher the statement, the FORTRAN compiler, which ignores blanks, considers the statement to be

```
DO7I = 1.3
```

This variation instructs the computer to do something entirely different from what the programmer intended. Using the default declaration, the compiler considers *DO7I* a floating point variable. During program execution, the computer places 1.3 in the memory location for *DO7I*. This particular error caused the first U.S. probe to Venus to be lost—a small error, but a multimillion dollar one!

Designers of C required explicit declaration of variables to assist the programmer in the following several ways:

1. If a variable is incorrectly spelled at some point in the program, the undeclared spelling is flagged as an error by the compiler. The programmer can quickly find and correct the misspelling. Otherwise, he or she might never be aware of the

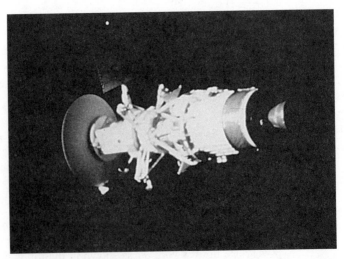

Venus probe

problem, and the program could produce incorrect results, such as with the probe to Venus.

2. Often, we arrange declarations of all the variables that are in a module in one place, so that a reader can see the module's ingredients at a glance.

3. Requiring declaration of the variables may encourage the programmer to refine his or her thinking about the program's logic.

Naming of Variables

We use the same rules for naming variables as we do for other identifiers, such as function names, as follows:

1. Identifiers must begin with a letter of the alphabet or an underscore (_). It is legal to start an identifier with an underscore, but most programmers avoid doing so to prevent possible conflict with special system names that begin with the underscore.

2. Any combination of letters, digits, and underscores can follow. Variable names consisting of just one letter are permissible but in most cases are discouraged.

3. The compiler is case sensitive—C regards uppercase and lowercase letters as different. Therefore, the variable names *NET, net,* and *Net* are three separate variables in C. Usually, however, identifiers in C are entirely in lowercase, such as *net_income,* or in mixed cases, such as *NetIncome.* Preprocessor constants, such as *MAX* in the following definition, are usually in all capitals:

```
#define MAX 35
```

4. The name cannot be a keyword, which the compiler reserves for specific purposes. Thus, we cannot give a variable a reserved name such as *int* (see Appendix B).

   A variable or other programmer-selected name may contain a keyword. For example, *integer* is a valid variable name, even though it contains the keyword *int.* As long as the C compiler can distinguish between the variable name and the keyword, no conflict exists.

   Certain other important words, such as *main* and *printf,* are not keywords. The *printf* function is a prewritten module that is part of the ANSI C standard libraries and not part of the language proper. Naming a variable *printf* does not cause the compiler to flag an error, but it prevents us from using the *printf* function for its normal purpose. We can use any name for only one specific task at a time, so naming a variable *printf* prevents the C compiler from recognizing the word as the name of the standard printing function. The name *main* is even more crucial in C. A program can start only at the section of code labeled *main.* Therefore, a program that does not contain this name does not link properly. The linker generates a link failure message like the following:

```
Link Failed
undefined: main
```

   All keywords in C are in lowercase. Consequently, the variable *Int* is valid even though *int* is a keyword. Because C is case sensitive, the capital letter prevents the compiler from confusing the two names. A conflict occurs only when the name of a variable exactly matches a keyword. It can be confusing to humans to use a variable name that looks like a keyword. Therefore, we should avoid using identifiers that are similar to keywords or that match other important features of the language.

5. At least the first 31 characters are significant.

Some examples of valid variable names are *count, total, GrossPay, i, quarter2, top_value*. Here are some invalid identifiers:

Variable	Why It Is Invalid
int	keyword
1998TAX	begins with a numeric character
#profit	must begin with an alphabetic character or underscore
period.	contains a period
bad name	contains a space

The identifier for a variable or function name should be descriptive of the role of the variable or function, respectively. For example, if a variable is to contain the result of adding two values, we might use the identifier *sum*. This name is **self-documenting** because it is descriptive like a comment. The identifier *s*, however, could stand for just about anything. A variable name should transmit as much information as possible to a reader of the program, so that he or she can more easily correct and change the code.

> **Definition** An identifier is **self-documenting** if the name is descriptive of the role of the item.

In this text, we use lowercase for one-word identifier names, such as *average*. A compound identifier, such as *TaxRate*, has the first letter of each word capitalized. If the compound identifier contains a name that should be in lowercase, such as *int*, we use an underscore to compound the identifier—for example, *random_int*. Preprocessor constants like *MAXNUM* defined with

```
#define MAXNUM 100
```

are in uppercase to avoid confusion with variable names.

You might choose another convention. Each programmer develops his or her own style over time. The main criterion should be that the system enhances program readability.

Section 2.1 Exercises

1. Which of the following are integers in C?

   a. 934   **b.** 56.0   **c.** 728.5   **d.** −77

   e. 49.   **f.** 3,599   **g.** −9738.0   **h.** 0

2. Which of the following are legal identifier names in C? For those that are not legal, explain why.

   a. *myWord!*   **b.** *figure*   **c.** *fig2.3*   **d.** *sec_2_1*

   e. *_out*   **f.** *Total*   **g.** *int*   **h.** *Tax Rate*

   i. *Tax_Rate*   **j.** *Tax-Rate*   **k.** *A*   **l.** *2Times*

Section 2.2 **The Assignment Statement**

In this section, we consider one of the ways for the program to instruct the computer to place a value in the memory location associated with a variable—the assignment statement.

The program in Example 2.1 declares the variable *NumberOfDays* to be of type *int,* as follows:

```
int NumberOfDays;
```

As Figure 2.1 shows, when the compiler encounters the declaration, it sets aside enough room in memory to store an integer and associates the identifier *NumberOf-Days* with that location. The compiler, however, does not place a value in the cell. The program assigns the number 7 to *NumberOfDays.*

```
NumberOfDays = 7;
```

This **assignment statement** causes the computer to store the integer 7 in main memory under the symbolic name *NumberOfDays.* Because an assignment statement causes the computer to take some action during program execution, the instruction is an **executable statement**. Figure 2.1 displays the effect of this statement at run time.

Definition   An **executable statement** causes the computer to take some action during program execution.

The assignment statement, which is one of the basic building blocks of C, has the following general format:

```
variable = expression;
```

Figure 2.1
The effect on memory of a declaration and assignment

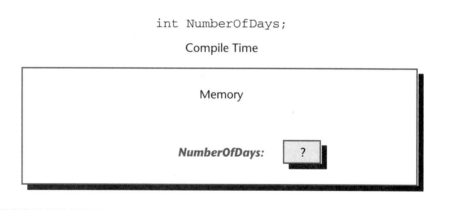

An expression may be a constant, such as 7; a variable; or a combination of constants and variables, such as *NumberOfWeekdays* + 2. We consider expressions in more detail in the next section. The variable getting the value of the expression appears on the left of the **assignment operator**, or the equal sign. Because an assignment changes the value of a variable, an assignment statement is a dynamic instruction, not a simple algebraic statement of equality. The statement instructs the computer to store the value of the right side of the equal sign (7) in the variable specified on the left side of the equal sign (*NumberOfDays*).

Definitions   An **assignment statement**, which has the form

```
variable = expression;
```

stores the value of the expression (the right side of the statement) in the memory location for the variable (the left side of the statement). The **assignment operator** is the equal sign.

Lvalues and Rvalues

The following pair of assignments is also legal for the integer variables *NumberOf-Weekdays* and *NumberOfDays:*

```
NumberOfWeekdays = 5;
NumberOfDays     = NumberOfWeekdays + 2;
}
```

Upon execution of the first statement, the computer stores 5 in the memory location for *NumberOfWeekdays*. Before making the second assignment, the computer obtains the value of *NumberOfWeekdays* from memory and evaluates the expression, *NumberOf-Weekdays* + 2. After evaluating this expression, the computer stores the result (7) in the variable *NumberOfDays*. Only one variable name can appear to the left of the equal sign. A statement such as

```
a + b = c
```

makes good sense in algebra, but is unacceptable in C.

Any value that can legally appear on the left-hand side of an assignment statement is an **lvalue**, and one that we can place on the right-hand side is an **rvalue**. A variable like *NumberOfDays* can appear on either side of an assignment statement. Thus, all variables are lvalues and rvalues. We cannot, however, reassign a value to the constant 7 or the expression *NumberOfWeekdays* + 2. They are rvalues but not lvalues.

Definitions   An **lvalue** can legally appear on the left-hand side of an assignment statement. An **rvalue** can legally appear on the right-hand side.

Example 2.1

This example presents a program that stores the number of days in a week in the variable *NumberOfDays* and then prints this value.

```
/* Declare, assign, and print an integer variable */

#include <stdio.h>

main()
{
    int NumberOfDays;              /* number of days in week */

    NumberOfDays = 7;
    printf("There are %d days in a week.\n", NumberOfDays);
}
```

After the opening brace, we declare the variable *NumberOfDays* to be of type *int*. Like other statements in C, the declaration statement terminates with a semicolon. The subsequent comment only describes the variable *NumberOfDays,* so it appears at the end of that line. We leave a blank line so that the program listing is more legible. C allows the use of white space—such as blank lines, tabs, and blanks—to highlight specific parts of a program and its output, as well as to enhance its appearance and readability. Moreover, white space delimits (immediately precedes and follows) keywords and identifiers.

Definition   **White space** in a program listing or output is a blank line, tab, blank, or form feed.

The second statement in the body of the main function is the assignment statement, which assigns the integer 7 to *NumberOfDays*. Next comes the familiar call to *printf,* which contains the characters %d. We mentioned in the previous section that this symbol is a **conversion specification**, which specifies how to convert a value's internal format in memory to an external format for output. In this case, the number is converted to the decimal integer or base 10 number. As Figure 2.2 indicates, at the position within the control string where %d appears, the computer is to insert the decimal integer value of *NumberOfDays,* which appears after the comma. With this substitution we obtain the following output:

```
There are 7 days in a week.
```

Figure 2.2
Output resulting from *printf* with conversion specification %d

```
                                    7

    printf("There are %d days in a week.\n", NumberOfDays);


            There are 7 days in a week.
```

Example 2.2

In this example, we have the computer calculate and print the number of units in 17 dozen. Pseudocode does not include declarations but may mention variable names. The following is pseudocode for the program:

> *main( )*
>
>   Program to calculate and print the number of units in 17 dozen
>
> *Algorithm:*
>
>   assign a value to the number of dozens, *NumberOfDozens*
>   calculate the number of units, *units*
>   print the result

The program is as follows:

```
/* Example 2.2. Program to print the number of units in 17 dozen */

#include <stdio.h>

#define DOZEN 12

main()
{
    int NumberOfDozens,      /* number of dozens */
        units;               /* number of units */

    NumberOfDozens = 17;
    units = NumberOfDozens * DOZEN;

    printf("%d dozen contain %d units.\n",
            NumberOfDozens, units);
}
```

The output is as follows:

```
17 dozen contain 204 units.
```

The number of units in a dozen does not change. Therefore, we define the preprocessor constant *DOZEN* as 12. This descriptive word makes the code more readable. The preprocessor replaces every occurrence of *DOZEN* with 12 before compilation begins.

In order to declare the variables *NumberOfDozens* and *units* to be integers, we can write two separate declarations or just one. The program has a single declaration, with a comma separating the two variables. We write the variables on separate lines so that we can easily include comments; the list of variables is more readable; and we can more quickly make editing changes. Alternatively, we could use two declarations, as shown here:

```
int NumberOfDozens;      /* number of dozens */
int units;               /* number of units */
```

Immediately after the declarations, we assign 17, the number of dozens, to the variable *NumberOfDozens*. The computer then stores 17 in the memory location for *NumberOfDozens*. The computation of the number of units (*units*) involves multiplying *DOZEN* (12) by this number of dozens. The asterisk (*) represents multiplication in C, so the assignment statement for *units* is as follows:

```
units = NumberOfDozens * DOZEN;
```

The common usage in algebra of implied multiplication, such as *xy* for the product of *x* and *y*, is not available in C. We must explicitly write the multiplication operator (*).

As Figure 2.3 pictures, the computer obtains the value of *NumberOfDozens* from memory, multiplies this value by *DOZEN* (12), and stores the result in the memory location for *units*. Clearly, before the computation, *NumberOfDozens* must have a value. For any expression, such as *NumberOfDozens * DOZEN*, there must be a value for each operand, such as *NumberOfDozens* and *DOZEN*.

Because we want to print the values of two variables (*NumberOfDozens* and *units*), the call to *printf* contains two conversion specifications within the control string. Moreover, the *printf* must list both identifiers at the end with comma separators. As Figure 2.4 illustrates, the first listed variable name (*NumberOfDozens*) is associated with the first %d and is therefore printed at the beginning of the line. The value of the second variable (*units*) is inserted in the position of the second conversion specification. A one-to-one correspondence exists between conversion specifications and identifiers.

Labeled Output

The programmer can use to great advantage the ability to combine text and variable values in a line of output. The text should clearly describe the meanings of the displayed values. A program that spews out many numbers with no explanation is

Figure 2.3
Changes in memory during execution of assignment

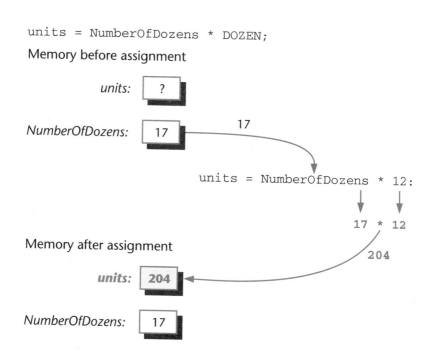

```
units = NumberOfDozens * DOZEN;
```
Memory before assignment

units: [?]

NumberOfDozens: [17]   17

```
units = NumberOfDozens * 12:
```
                                17 * 12

                                   204
Memory after assignment

units: [204]

NumberOfDozens: [17]

Figure 2.4   Output resulting from *printf* with two conversion specifications

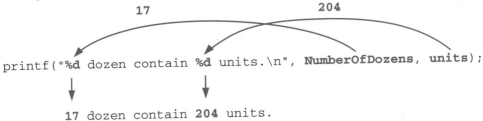

rarely of any use. Even the author of the program may forget the meaning of each number. In Section 2.6 concerning interactive programs, we see the necessity for clearly displayed instructions.

Not an Algebraic Formula

The assignment statement

```
units = NumberOfDozens * DOZEN;
```

is not an algebraic formula. An illustration of the difference between an algebraic equality and a programming assignment is the program segment

```
count = 5;
count = count + 1;
```

The last statement does **not** say that *count* is one more than itself. When the computer encounters the second statement at run time, it looks up the present value of *count* (5), evaluates the expression *count* + 1 (6), and stores the result of the computation in *count*. As Figure 2.5 demonstrates, the effect of the statement is to **increment** *count* by 1, from 5 to 6. We see later that incrementing by 1 is important when we need to count.

Figure 2.5 Changes in memory during execution of assignment

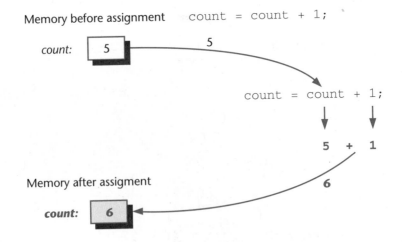

In many situations, we need an old value of a variable to compute the new value of the same variable.

Declaration-Initialization

In an interactive program, we usually obtain most of the data from the user. In the last section, we **initialized** a variable or assigned a value to a variable early in each program. C provides a way to combine a declaration with an assignment. For example, in the program in Example 2.2, we have the declaration and initialization of *NumberOfDozens* in separate statements.

```
int NumberOfDozens,      /* number of dozens */
     units;              /* number of units */

NumberOfDozens = 17;
units = NumberOfDozens * DOZEN;
```

We can combine these statements into an equivalent single statement, as follows:

```
int NumberOfDozens = 17,   /* number of dozens */
     units;                /* number of units */

units = NumberOfDozens * DOZEN;
```

Even though we can declare and initialize in one step, we should use this feature sparingly, primarily with constant values like 17. Separating a computation, such as *units = NumberOfDozens * DOZEN*, from the main body of executable statements into a declaration-initialization statement can be confusing to the reader, who might miss the initialization. In this case it is better only to have a combined declaration-initialization for *NumberOfDozens*.

Section 2.2 Exercises

1. **a.** Declare *tax* to be an integer variable.
   b. Assume *tax* has a value, and write a call to *printf* to display its value.
2. **a.** Declare *radius* and *circumference* to be integer variables.
   b. Assume both variables have values, and write a *printf* to display their values.
3. Which of the following are legal assignment statements? For those that are not, state why.

   a. x = 3;   **b.** 3 = x;   **c.** x = y + z;
   d. x = 5   **e.** 5x = 2x + 3x; **f.** amount = amount + 2;

4. Indicate whether each expression is an lvalue and/or an rvalue or neither.

   a. x   **b.** 567   **c.** 3 * y + z;
   d. 3 + y   **e.** int

5. What output is produced by the following program segment?

```
int x;
x = 1;
x = 2;
x = 3;
printf("%d %d %d\n", x, x, x);
```

6. What is printed by the following program?

```
#include <stdio.h>
main()
{
    int a, b, c;
    a = 4;
    b = a * 7;
    c = a + b;
    printf("a = %d, b = %d, c = %d\n", a, b, c);
}
```

7. Write a declaration-initialization of integer variable *month* with initial value 1.

8. Write a declaration-initialization of integer variable *count* with initial value 0.

9. Write a statement to assign 8 to variable *time*.

10. Write a statement to assign the product of variables *rate* and *time* to *distance*.

11. Write a statement to double the value of the variable *tax*.

12. Write a statement to subtract *discount* from *price*.

13. Suppose *age* = 10 and *grade* = 5. Give the output of the following:

```
printf("Mary is %d years old and in grade %d.\n",
        age, grade);
```

14. Suppose *radius* = 10, *height* = 4, and *volume* = 1256. Give the output of the following:

```
printf("The cylinder has the following dimensions:\n");
printf("radius = %d in, height = %d in, volume = %d in^3.\n",
        radius, height, volume);
```

Section 2.2 Programming Projects

For each of the following assignments, follow the problem-solving approach. Analyze the problem, and design a solution using a structure chart and pseudocode for each module. In the code, be sure to label all output and supply ample comments. Test thoroughly.

1. Write a program that converts an integer measurement in feet to inches.

2. Write a program that computes the number of hours and minutes in a month.

Section 2.3 Integer Arithmetic

Four Binary Operators

The four major arithmetic operations in C are **addition** (+), **subtraction** (−), **multiplication** (*), and **division** (/). This slash is not the same symbol as in the newline character (\n), which is a backslash. The asterisk represents multiplication because the letter x looks like a variable x, and the period indicates a decimal point. Each operation is a **binary operator**, because it works with two operands or terms at a time. C has no symbol for exponentiation or raising something to a power, such as x^2. The math library, however, has a power function (*pow*) which we discuss in Section 4.5.

Definition   A **binary operator** performs operations on two operands (terms).

In C, an **expression** involving these operators and only integer constants and variables has an integer value. Certainly, we expect $7 + 2$, $7 - 2$, and $7 * 2$ to be integers, but the result of integer division can be surprising. For example, with an integer dividend and divisor, the expression $7 / 2$ returns an integer in C. On a calculator, dividing 2 into 7 gives 3.5. In C, however, the computer **truncates** or chops off the decimal places, leaving the integer part, 3. Another way to consider the problem is that C takes the integer quotient 3 and ignores the integer remainder of 1.

$$\begin{array}{r} 3 \\ 2\overline{)7} \\ \underline{6} \\ 1 \end{array}$$

Definition   To **truncate** a real number means to chop off the value to the integer part.

Arithmetic Operations	Operator in C	Example with Integer Operands
addition	+	7 + 2 is 9
subtraction	−	7 − 2 is 5
multiplication	*	7 * 2 is 14
division	/	7 / 2 is 3

Example 2.3

In this example, we observe the effect of several integer divisions. Suppose a program declares integer variables *numerator*, *denominator*, and *quotient*, as follows:

```
int numerator,       /* numerator in computation   */
    denominator,     /* denominator in computation */
    quotient;        /* numerator / denominator    */
```

The assignments and *printf*

```
numerator   = 10;
denominator = 2;
quotient    = numerator / denominator;
printf("%d/%d is %d\n", numerator, denominator, quotient);
```

yield the expected output

```
10/2 is 5
```

A change in the initial assignments, however, can produce some surprising results.

```
numerator   = 26;
denominator = 4;
quotient    = numerator / denominator;
printf("%d/%d is %d\n", numerator, denominator, quotient);
```

Execution of these statements results in the unexpected output

```
26/4 is 6
```

C takes the integer quotient 6, ignoring the integer remainder of 2.

$$\begin{array}{r} 6 \\ 4\overline{)26} \\ \underline{24} \\ 2 \end{array}$$

When both operands (such as 26 and 4) are integers, the result is an integer.
The answer can be even more surprising when the quotient is zero.

```
numerator   = 2;
denominator = 3;
quotient    = numerator / denominator;
printf("%d/%d is %d\n", numerator, denominator, quotient);
```

This code generates the output

```
2/3 is 0
```

because

$$\begin{array}{r} 0 \\ 3\overline{)2} \\ \underline{0} \\ 2 \end{array}$$

Ignoring the integer remainder, the computer returns the quotient of 0.

Example 2.4

A programmer should be especially careful of such a truncation when an integer expression occurs in a sequence of computations. An earlier discard of a fractional part could produce horrendous errors. For example, suppose an item is on sale for two-thirds its normal price. Because of truncation, the following segment indicates the sale item is free:

```
/*
 * Segment to compute and print 2/3 of the sale price
 * But there is an ERROR
 */

int     percent = 2/3, /* ERROR - int division 2/3 is 0 */
        price = 30000; /* price of item */

printf("Original price = %d, sale price = %d\n",
       price, percent * price);
```

The output is as follows:

```
Original price = 30000, sale price = 0
```

As noted earlier, we cannot use a comma in writing numbers. Therefore, the declaration-initialization of *price* assigns 30000 (not 30,000) to the variable.

Because the statement involving *printf* is long, we split the statement at a comma that is not in the control string. We indent the continued portion for readability. In this program, the indented line contains a variable, *price,* and an expression, *percent * price*. Instead of storing the product *percent * price* in a temporary variable, *printf* displays the value of the expression directly.

Although truncation was detrimental in Example 2.4, it can also be helpful. For instance, given a two-digit number, such as 38, suppose we want to extract the most significant digit, in this case 3. The following integer division (38 / 10) produces 3:

$$
\begin{array}{r}
3 \\
10\overline{)38} \\
\underline{30} \\
8
\end{array}
$$

Modulus Operator

Whereas the division operator yields the quotient, the **modulus operator** (%) gives the remainder. Because 4 divides into 19 with a remainder of 3,

```
printf("The remainder of 19 divided by 4 is %d.\n", 19 % 4);
```

prints

```
The remainder of 19 divided by 4 is 3.
```

We read "19 % 4" as "19 **modulo** 4" or "19 **mod** 4." Unlike the division operator, the modulus operator must have integer operands; 19.3 % 4.6 is meaningless.

Definition The **modulus operator** (%) applied to two integer operands gives the remainder of the first operand divided by the second; *n* % *m* is the remainder in the division of *m* into *n*.

Arithmetic Operation	Operator in C	Example
modulus	%	7 % 2 is 1

To determine if an integer is odd or even, programmers usually employ the modulus operator. When we divide an even integer by 2, the remainder is always 0, whereas the remainder from dividing 2 into an odd integer is 1. For example, when we divide 2 into the even integer 14, the remainder is 0 (14 % 2 is 0). Dividing 2 into the odd integer 15 yields a remainder of 1 (15 % 2 is 1). In general, if *a* % *b* is 0, then *b* divides evenly into *a*.

Another application of modulus is to extract the least significant digit in a positive integer. For example, 10 divided into 38 has a quotient of 3, the most significant digit, and a remainder of 8, the least significant digit (38 % 10 is 8). Therefore, if *TwoDigits* is a two-digit integer, the following segment prints the digits separately:

```
printf("Most  significant digit = %d\n", TwoDigits / 10);
printf("Least significant digit = %d\n", TwoDigits % 10);
```

For *TwoDigits* = 38, the output is

```
Most   significant digit = 3
Least significant digit = 8
```

Example 2.5 _____

In this example, we automate the conversion of an inches measurement to an equivalent one in yards, feet, and inches. For example, 158 inches equal 4 yards, 1 foot, and 2 inches. Pseudocode at a higher level is as follows:

> *main( )*
>
>   Program to convert a measurement in inches to yards, feet, and inches
>
> *Algorithm:*
>
>   assign a value for the total number of inches
>   calculate the number of yards, feet, and inches
>   print the answer

The assignment and printing are no problem, but the calculation requires further thought. As with any program design, we must determine how we would solve the problem by hand before we can instruct a computer what to do. The computer is dumb, but it follows our instructions precisely and quickly.

A hand/calculator computation can also be useful in testing our program. It is a wonderful feeling to obtain a compiled program that executes, and we might be tempted to accept the output from the printer without really looking at the results. We could have a run-time error. The programmer should always execute a program several times with well-chosen test data and determine if the output for each run is correct. We must understand what to expect for each test case and verify that the results match our expectations.

Our approach for this problem is similar to our computations to obtain the most and least significant digits using the division and modulus operators. Of the three units of measure, inch is the smallest and yard is the largest. Starting at the lower end, we can obtain the total number of feet (ignoring yards) in the length using the fact that 12 inches are in a foot. The following computation with cancellation of the unit inches in the numerator (off to the side) and denominator indicates we should divide the length by 12.

$$158 \text{ inches} \times \frac{1 \text{ foot}}{12 \text{ inches}} = 13\frac{2}{12} \text{ feet}$$

Integer division shows that there are 13 feet in the 158 inches. The remainder of this division (158 % 12 is 2) gives the number of inches left—158 inches is 13 feet and 2 inches.

We now convert the 13 feet into yards and feet. Using the fact that 3 feet are in a yard, we have

$$13 \text{ feet} \times \frac{1 \text{ yard}}{3 \text{ feet}} = 4\frac{1}{3} \text{ yards}$$

and

$$13 \% 3 = 1$$

Thus, 13 feet contain 4 yards and 1 foot. Putting all the computations together, 158 inches = 4 yards, 1 foot, and 2 inches. The program below uses these computations:

```
/*
 * Example 2.5. Program to convert a measurement in inches
 * to yards, feet, and inches
 */

#include <stdio.h>

main()
{
    int TotalNumInches = 158, /* total length in inches    */
        yards,                /* # yards  in TotalNumInches */
        feet,                 /* # feet   in TotalNumInches */
        inches;               /* # inches in TotalNumInches */

    feet    = TotalNumInches / 12;
    inches = TotalNumInches % 12;

    yards   = feet / 3;
    feet    = feet % 3;

    printf("In %d inches there are ", TotalNumInches);
    printf("%d yard(s), %d foot(feet), and %d inch(es)\n",
            yards, feet, inches);
}
```

Execution produces the following output:

```
In 158 inches there are 4 yard(s), 1 foot(feet), and 2 inch(es)
```

In the program, we assign the integer *TotalNumInches* / 12 to *feet,* giving *feet* the value 13. This number, which is the total number of feet in 158 inches, is an intermediate result. Once we factor out the number of yards in the 13 feet with

```
yards = feet / 3;
```

we can compute the number of feet remaining with

```
feet = feet % 3;
```

Because we are using *feet* on the right side of two assignment statements and changing the value of *feet,* the order in which the computer performs these last two calculations is important. (Until *feet* is used on the left of the assignment, its value is not changed.) Should we reverse these statements in error, the assignment

```
feet   =  feet % 3;
```

would change the value of *feet* from 13 to 1. The subsequent integer division by 3 to obtain *yards* would yield the incorrect answer of 0. The order of the first two assignment statements, however, is irrelevant, because we are not changing the value of *TotalNumInches*. *TotalNumInches* never appears on the left of the assignment statement.

If we discover an error in the output, we should examine the logic of the program. However, we should not spend a long time doing so. A programmer who spends many minutes or hours staring at a program is being unproductive. Instead, we should use debugging techniques. Many C compilers have built-in **debuggers** that enable us to trace execution one statement at a time or to observe intermediate results, such as the early value of *feet*. In Chapter 6, we discuss debuggers in greater detail. Appendix H summarizes the operation of several debuggers. Even without a debugger, we can obtain valuable information with **diagnostic prints** of intermediate results. For example, suppose we did reverse the last two assignments by mistake and the output is

```
In 158 inches there are 0 yard(s), 1 foot(feet), and 2 inch(es)
```

The number of inches is correct, but the other two measurements are not. A *printf* of *feet* between the two pairs of computations can help us to locate the problem. To read the output clearly, we label the value in the *printf*. Also, we do not indent the *printf* so that later we can find it easily for deletion. The segment in question now reads

```
        feet    = TotalNumInches / 12;
        inches  = TotalNumInches % 12;

printf("*** feet = %d\n", feet);

        feet    = feet % 3;
        yards   = feet / 3;
```

Subsequent program execution produces

```
*** feet = 13
In 158 inches there are 0 yard(s), 1 foot(feet), and 2 inch(es)
```

We see that the intermediate result of 13 for *feet* is correct. We can immediately focus our attention on the last two assignment statements. If we still do not discover the problem, we could use another diagnostic print between the last two assignment statements.

ANSI C does not dictate the results of *numerator / denominator* and *numerator % denominator* when the integer *numerator* or *denominator* is negative. The answers vary from machine to machine. Some computers evaluate −15 / 4 as −4, others as −3. Similarly, −15 % 4 could be 1 or −3, depending on the result of the division. Because these operations are not portable with a negative operand, we should avoid such computations.

Printing %   Because % is also part of conversion specifications, such as %d, C requires two adjacent percent signs in the control string to print the symbol %. The following call to *printf*

```
printf("15 %% 2 is %d.\n", 15 % 2);
```

Figure 2.6
Printing of %

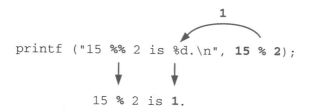

$$15 \text{ \% } 2 \text{ is } 1.$$

produces

```
15 % 2 is 1.
```

Inside the control string, we need two percent signs to print %. Outside the control string, the expression 15 % 2 evaluates the remainder. Figure 2.6 emphasizes this substitution.

Unary Minus

Besides the previous five binary operations, another common operator is the **unary minus**. We apply this operation to one operand to change its sign, as in the following:

```
flip = -net;
```

If *net* is 45, *flip* is −45; if *net* is −7, *flip* is −1 × −7 = 7.

Arithmetic Operation	Operator in C	Example
unary minus	−	−(−7) is 7

Operator Precedence

When several operations are present in an expression, a priority determines the operation that the computer calculates first. C adopts the same **priority** or **operator precedence** as mathematics. Understanding this precedence is important, because an incorrectly written expression can cause output errors, which are difficult to find. Worse yet, the error may go undetected while someone makes decisions based on the incorrect information.

Definition   **Operator precedence** or **priority** designates the order in which the computer performs operations in an expression.

The operator precedence in C for the operations considered so far appears in Table 2.1. As in mathematics, parentheses can override this precedence. We update this table as we discuss additional operators. Appendix C contains a complete list of the precedence of C operators.

Table 2.1 Operator precedence in C

Priority	Operation
1	unary minus
2	*, /, %
3	+, −

When two binary operations of equal priority are encountered in an expression—such as * and / or two pluses—they are evaluated from left to right. For example,

60 / 5 * 4 = (60 / 5) * 4 = 12 * 4 = 48

We use parentheses to multiply before dividing, as follows:

60 / (5 * 4) = 60 / 20 = 3

Example 2.6

Using C's operator precedence, let us evaluate the integer variable *ans*.

```
ans  =  14 - 10  /  2 + 8;
```

The appearance is deceptive, but because division has a higher priority than addition or subtraction, the computer calculates 10 / 2 first, as shown:

```
14 - (10 / 2) + 8
```

Thus, *ans* becomes $14 - 5 + 8 = (14 - 5) + 8 = 9 + 8 = \mathbf{17}$.
We use parentheses if we want to perform the subtraction first.

```
ans  =  (14 - 10) / 2 + 8;
```

In this case, the computer assigns $4 / 2 + 8 = 2 + 8 = \mathbf{10}$ to *ans*.
To perform the addition first, we again employ parentheses.

```
ans  =  14 - 10 / (2 + 8);
```

Thus, *ans* obtains the value **13**, which is $14 - 10 / 10 = 14 - 1$.

Example 2.7

We must be especially careful when translating into C a mathematical expression that uses stacked notation for fractions with the numerator appearing directly over the denominator. To write the following expression in C

$$\frac{x + y}{z + w}$$

we surround the numerator and the denominator with parentheses.

```
(x + y) / (z + w)
```

With integer division having a truncating effect, the assignment

```
ans  =  (14 - 10) / (2 + 8);
```

stores 0 (integer 4 / 10) in the memory location for *ans*. Comparing this result with those of the previous example, we see that parentheses cause entirely different answers.

Example 2.8

Using operator priority, let us determine the output from the following program segment:

```
int a = 74,
    b = 10,
    c = 2,
    d = 5,
    ans;

ans = a / b % c * d - b % (d - 1);
printf("ans = %d\n", ans);
```

The following are the steps in evaluating *ans* with the operation having the highest priority in color:

$$
\begin{aligned}
a\,/\,b\,\%\,c\,*\,d\,-\,b\,\%\,(d-1) &= 74\,/\,10\,\%\,2\,*\,5\,-\,10\,\%\,(5-1) \\
&= 74\,/\,10\,\%\,2\,*\,5\,-\,10\,\%\,4 \\
&= 7\,\%\,2\,*\,5\,-\,10\,\%\,4 \\
&= 1\,*\,5\,-\,10\,\%\,4 \\
&= 5\,-\,10\,\%\,4 \\
&= 5\,-\,2 \\
&= 3
\end{aligned}
$$

Thus, output from this segment is

```
ans = 3
```

Section 2.3 Exercises

Suppose a program segment has the following declaration-initializations:

```
int x = 5,
    y = 9,
    z = 2,
    w = 3,
    v = 6;
```

Calculate the C integer expressions for Exercises 1–24.

1. x + y / z	2. (x + y) / z	3. x / z + y
4. y + x / z + w	5. y + x / (z + w)	6. (x + y) / z + w
7. y % v	8. v % y	9. (x * y) % v
10. x * y % v	11. v * x / z	12. (x * v) / z
13. v / z * w	14. v / (z * w)	15. x / z * v
16. x / (z * v)	17. w + x % z	18. x % z * z % w
19. v / x * (y - 4)	20. -y - x	21. z / v * w
22. w * z / v	23. x - y - z	24. x - (y - z)

25. Using multiplication to square, write a C statement to evaluate

$$\frac{x^2}{y+3}\,z$$

26. Write a C statement to evaluate

$$\frac{y}{z^3}\,\frac{4y^2}{y-1}$$

27. Using the arithmetic operators provided in C, write a program that declares and assigns values to variables a, b, and c, and then does the following:

a. Halves the value of a

b. Doubles b

c. Multiplies c by itself

d. Prints the results of the preceding operations

28. The following program computes the perimeter of a rectangle. Add appropriate comments.

```
#include <stdio.h>
main()
{
    int length,
        width,
        perimeter;

    length = 13;
    width = 52;
    perimeter = 2 * length + 2 * width;

    printf("The perimeter of a rectangle with\n");
    printf(" length = %d and width = %d is %d\n",
            length, width, perimeter);
}
```

29. Write a statement to print the least significant digit of an integer variable *num*.

Section 2.3 **Programming Projects**

For each of the following assignments, follow the problem-solving approach. Analyze the problem, and design a solution using a structure chart and pseudocode for each module. In the code, be sure to label all output and supply ample comments. Test thoroughly.

1. Develop a program to take the dimensions of a box in inches and calculate and print the volume of a box in cubic inches. (The volume of a box is the product of its length, width, and height.)

2. Develop a program to convert a certain number of days to hours and to minutes.

3. Develop a program to initialize a variable to a three-digit integer and to print the hundreds, tens, and units digits of the variable. For example, suppose a variable is initialized to be 849. The output of the program should be as follows:

```
For the number 849, the hundreds digit is 8,
the tens digit is 4, and the units digit is 9.
```

4. Develop a program to convert a given number of days to a measure of time given in years, weeks, and days. For example, 375 days equals 1 year, 1 week, and 3 days. (Ignore leap years in this program.)

5. Develop a program to convert a given number of seconds to a measure of time given in hours, minutes, and seconds. For example, 18,618 seconds equals 5 hours, 10 minutes, and 18 seconds.

6. Develop a program to convert a number of cents into quarters, dimes, nickels, and pennies. For example, 92¢ equals 3 quarters, 1 dime, 1 nickel, and 2 pennies.

7. We can easily calculate the day of the week on which a given date falls if we know the Julian day for that date. For example, January 1 is always Julian day 1, because it is the first day of the year, whereas December 31 is day 365 in a nonleap year or day 366 in a leap year. The day of the week is calculated as follows:

year = year in question (all four digits)
JulianDay = Julian day of date in question (1 to 366)
fours = integer portion of (year − 1) / 4
hundreds = integer portion of (year − 1) / 100
FourHundreds = integer portion of (year − 1) / 400
DayOfTheWeek = (*year* + *JulianDay* + *fours* − *hundreds* + *FourHundreds*) % 7
where:

Result	Meaning
0	Saturday
1	Sunday
2	Monday
3	Tuesday
4	Wednesday
5	Thursday
6	Friday

Develop a program to calculate the day of the week. Verify its correctness by testing several dates.

Section 2.4 Breadth: Storage of Integers in the Computer

Binary Representation of Integers

The computer stores numbers using the **binary** or **base 2 number system**, which has only two digits, 0 and 1. By contrast, the decimal or base 10 number system that we use every day has 10 digits, 0–9. To understand binary representation, let us first consider the decimal number 5863, five thousand eight hundred sixty-three. The number consists of 5 thousands, 8 hundreds, 6 tens, and 3 ones. In expanded form, we have the following:

$$5863 = 5 \times 1000 + 8 \times 100 + 6 \times 10 + 3 \times 1$$

Notice that 1, 10, 100, and 1000 are all powers of 10—10^0, 10^1, 10^2, 10^3, respectively. Thus, we could write

$$5863 = 5 \times 10^3 + 8 \times 10^2 + 6 \times 10^1 + 3 \times 10^0$$

We represent numbers in base 2 similarly. However, base 2 has only 2 digits (0 and 1), and the expansion is in powers of 2, not 10. Hence, in the binary number 1101, the rightmost 1 indicates the number of ones; the 0 to the left indicates the number of twos; the next 1 represents the number of fours (2^2); and the leftmost 1 gives the number of eights (2^3). The expansion reveals the decimal or base 10 representation of the number.

$$1 \times 2^3 + 1 \times 2^2 + 0 \times 2^1 + 1 \times 2^0$$
$$= 1 \times 8 \ + 1 \times 4 \ + 0 \times 2 \ + 1$$
$$= 8 \qquad + 4 \qquad + 0 \qquad + 1$$
$$= 13$$

Thus, 1101 in binary is 13 in decimal. When confusion is possible, we write the base as a subscript to the number, such as 1101_2 and 13_{10}.

Definition   The **binary** or **base 2 number system** has two digits, 0 and 1. Reading a binary integer from right to left, the bit gives the number of units (2^0), twos (2^1), fours (2^2), eights (2^3), ...

Example 2.9

The following is the decimal number that 10110_2 represents:

$$1 \times 2^4 + 0 \times 2^3 + 1 \times 2^2 + 1 \times 2^1 + 0 \times 2^0$$
$$= 16 \qquad\qquad\qquad + 4 \qquad + 2$$
$$= 22$$

Notice with each position advanced to the left, the value is doubled: 1, 2, 4, 8, 16, 32, and so on.

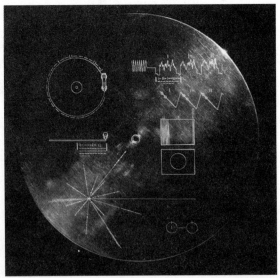

Cover of Voyager Record. A record of our civilization for extra terrestrial beings is attached to the exterior of the Voyager Spacecraft. How to play the record and the solar system's location are displayed using the binary number system with "—" meaning "0" and "|" indicating "1".

Example 2.10

The rightmost bit indicates the number of ones. The value of each successive position is double the value of the previous position. Thus, the values of the positions from right to left are the powers of two—1, 2, 4, 8, 16, 32, 64, 128, 256, 512, 1024, ...

To evaluate 1001100111_2 in base 10, we move from right to left, adding together the values of the positions that have ones in the binary number.

Value of position	512	256	128	64	32	16	8	4	2	1
Binary number	1	0	0	1	1	0	0	1	1	1
Decimal equivalent	512		+	64 + 32		+		4 + 2 + 1		= 615

Counting

We count in the decimal system without thinking, but analysis of the process can help us count in the binary system. Base 10 has 10 digits, 0–9. For incrementing a position when we reach the largest digit 9, we put 0 in that position and carry a 1 to the left. Thus, 10 follows 9. The number after 29 is 30.

$$29 + 1 = (2 \times 10 + 9) + 1$$
$$= 2 \times 10 + (9 + 1)$$
$$= 2 \times 10 + 1 \times 10 = 3 \times 10 = 30$$

As shown below, the number after 5999 is 6000, and 10,000 follows 9999:

$$5999 + 1 \rightarrow 5\ 9\ 9\ 9 \rightarrow 5\ 9\ 9\ 9 \rightarrow 5\ 9\ 9\ 9 = 6000$$

$$9999 + 1 \rightarrow 1\ 9\ 9\ 9\ 9 = 10,000$$

In the binary system, we run out of digits in a position quickly because we have only two—0 and 1. So in this number system, $0 + 1 = 1$, but $1 + 1$ cannot be 2, because the digit 2 does not exist in base 2. We make the rightmost or least significant position 0 and carry a 1 to the left to obtain $10_2 = 2_{10}$. Adding two bits in the binary number system gives only the following four possible outcomes:

```
   0        1        0        1
 + 0      + 0      + 1      + 1
 ---      ---      ---     ----
   0        1        1      1 0
```

0 carry 1

Continuing counting, $2 + 1 = 10_2 + 1_2 = 11_2 = 3_{10}$. What comes after 11_2?

$$11 + 1 \rightarrow 1\,\overset{1}{\underset{0}{1}} \rightarrow \overset{1}{\underset{0\;\;0}{1\;1}} \rightarrow 100$$

Example 2.11

Counting from 0 to 20 in the binary number system displays this carrying.

Decimal	Binary	Decimal	Binary	Decimal	Binary
0	0	7	111	14	1110
1	1	8	1000	15	1111
2	10	9	1001	16	10000
3	11	10	1010	17	10001
4	100	11	1011	18	10010
5	101	12	1100	19	10011
6	110	13	1101	20	10100

Decrementing by 1

Finding the next smallest integer or decrementing by 1 follows the reverse algorithm to addition.

> *Algorithm 2.1. Subtract 1 from an Integer:*
>
> if the least significant (rightmost) digit is greater than 0, then
>   subtract 1 from the least significant digit
> else
>   replace it with the largest digit in that base (9 in base 10, 1 in base 2)
>   subtract 1 from the integer to the left of the digit

Thus, $623_{10} - 1 = 622$, but $630 - 1 = 629$. Similarly, $10111_2 - 1 = 10110_2$, and $10110_2 - 1 = 10101_2$. Repeated application of this process yields, $3000 - 1 = \mathbf{2999}$ in the decimal system and $1000_2 - 1 = \mathbf{111_2}$ in the binary system.

Example 2.12

We illustrate the process by decrementing the following binary numbers by 1: 100010011, 1011100, 1000000.

$$
\begin{aligned}
10001\ 0011 - 1 &= 1\ 0001\ 0010 \\
101\ 1100 - 1 &= 101\ 1011 \\
100\ 0000 - 1 &= 11\ 1111
\end{aligned}
$$

Range of Unsigned Integers in a Computer

Subtraction can help us figure out the largest integer that a particular computer can represent. An **unsigned number** does not have a plus or minus. For example, what is the largest unsigned integer we can represent in 8 bits? We can easily write it in binary notation, $1111\ 1111_2$, but what is the equivalent decimal value? Instead of adding a long string of powers of 2, we notice that this binary number is one less than $1\ 0000\ 0000_2$. Remembering that the least significant position indicates the number of ones

(2^0), we see that the 1 is in the position of 2^8. Since $2^8 = 256$, $1111\ 1111_2 = 256_{10} - 1 = 255_{10}$. The smallest unsigned integer that can be represented with 8 bits is $0000\ 0000 = 0$. Thus, in 8 bits, we can represent 256 integers, from 0 to 255.

Many computers use 8 bits in a byte. A **byte** is a sequence of bits that can encode a character, such as 'A' or '%'. Interestingly, the term "byte" was coined in the late 1950s from "bite," but the spelling was changed to avoid an accidental drop of an "e" that would convert the word to "bit." Some people had resisted use of the term "bit" 10 years earlier, branding the acronym for "binary digit" as an "irresponsible vulgarity."

Definition A **byte** is a sequence of bits that can encode a character.

We can use the operator *sizeof* in C to determine the number of bytes of storage consumed by an integer or any other item on a particular computer. As illustrated in the following code segment, we can employ this operator several ways:

```
int intvar,
    SizeOfInt;

SizeOfInt = sizeof(intvar);
printf("An integer variable uses %d bytes\n", SizeOfInt);
SizeOfInt = sizeof(35);
printf("An integer constant uses %d bytes\n", SizeOfInt);
SizeOfInt = sizeof(int);
printf("A variable of type int uses %d bytes\n",
        SizeOfInt);
```

The three answers agree, because they all determine the number of bytes needed to store an integer value in the computer on which the code is running. According to the ANSI C standard, *sizeof(int)* is 2 or 4, depending on the particular implementation. The operand can be a variable, such as *intvar*; a constant, such as 35; or a type, such as *int*.

The syntax of *sizeof* is the same as that of a function, but it is an operator. Part of the C language, *sizeof* is not a library function. Moreover, *sizeof* is a keyword, so we cannot use the name as an identifier. Its returned value is determined at compilation time, even before the program is executed. Thus, we do not need to assign a value to *intvar* before determining the amount of space set aside for this variable.

Example 2.13

Some microcomputers store integers in 16 bits. In these machines, the largest possible unsigned integer is $1111\ 1111\ 1111\ 1111_2$ and the smallest is 0. In all, the computer can store $1\ 0000\ 0000\ 0000\ 0000_2 = 2^{16} = 65{,}536$ different unsigned integers.

Conversion of a Decimal Integer to Binary

We have seen how to convert a base 2 integer to base 10, but how do we do the reverse operation? Suppose we wish to convert 13 to the binary system. We must determine the number of ones, twos, fours, eights, and so on, that are in the number. We accomplish this task by repeatedly dividing by the base, 2. The base (2) goes into 13 six times with a remainder of 1, or

$$13 = 6 \times 2 + 1 = 6 \times 2^1 + 1 \times 2^0$$

Consequently, 13 has one unit (2^0). We repeat the process with the quotient, 6. Two divides evenly into 6

$$6 = 3 \times 2 + 0 = 3 \times 2^1 + 0 \times 2^0$$

Substituting back into the expansion of 13, we have

$$
\begin{aligned}
13 &= 6 \times 2^1 + 1 \times 2^0 \\
&= (3 \times 2^1 + 0 \times 2^0) \times 2^1 + 1 \times 2^0 \\
&= 3 \times 2^2 + 0 \times 2^1 + 1 \times 2^0
\end{aligned}
$$

Thus, there are 0 units (2^0) in 6 and, equivalently, 0 twos in 13. Continuing by dividing 2 into the former quotient of 3, we obtain

$$3 = 1 \times 2 + 1 = 1 \times 2^1 + 1 \times 2^0$$

Substituting this expansion for 3 into what we have for 13 so far, we obtain

$$
\begin{aligned}
13 &= 3 \times 2^2 + 0 \times 2^1 + 1 \times 2^0 \\
&= (1 \times 2^1 + 1 \times 2^0) \times 2^2 + 0 \times 2^1 + 1 \times 2^0 \\
&= 1 \times 2^3 + 1 \times 2^2 + 0 \times 2^1 + 1 \times 2^0
\end{aligned}
$$

Thus, 13 has one eight (2^3), one four (2^2), no twos (2^1), and one unit (2^0). The expansion of 13_{10} in the binary system is 1101_2. We repeatedly divided the quotient by 2, taking the remainders for the binary digits. Notice when we divide by 2, we obtain a remainder less than 2, a bit. We stop the process when we arrive at a quotient of zero. To make the process easier to see in large problems, we write the quotient below instead of above the dividend and write the remainder to the side. The expansion consists of the remainders taken in reverse order, from bottom to top, as shown below:

Remainders

2	13	
	6	1
	3	0
	1	1
	0	1

Algorithm 2.2. Convert a Base 10 Representation (Q) of an Integer to a Base 2 Representation:

repeat until Q is zero:
    record the remainder of the division of 2 into Q
    Q is the integer quotient of Q / 2
the base 2 number has the remainders in reverse order of discovery

Example 2.14

In this example, we convert the decimal number 186 to binary using Algorithm 2.2. Repeatedly dividing by 2, we obtain

<pre>
         Remainders

2 | 186
  | 93   0   ↑
  | 46   1
  | 23   0
  | 11   1
  | 5   1
  | 2   1
  | 1   0
  | 0   1
</pre>

Thus, $186_{10} = 10111010_2$.

Section 2.4 Exercises

Express the binary numbers in Exercises 1–9 in the decimal number system.

1. 111   **2.** 1011   **3.** 1000

4. 1111   **5.** 10010   **6.** 110001

7. 111101   **8.** 1000000   **9.** 10011010

Express the base 10 numbers in Exercises 10–17 in base 2.

10. 4   **11.** 7   **12.** 11   **13.** 15

14. 3   **15.** 19   **16.** 25   **17.** 10

18. Count from 21 to 45 in the binary number system.

Increment and decrement by 1 each binary number in Exercises 19–22.

19. 11001   **20.** 1011   **21.** 1000   **22.** 11100

Find the smallest and largest unsigned integers that can be expressed in the number of bits in Exercises 23–25.

23. 4   **24.** 7   **25.** 32

26. Consider the following sequence of binary numbers:
1, 10, 100, 1000, 10000, 100000

a. Describe the change in position of the 1 in reading the sequence from left to right, from one number to the next?

b. What happens to the decimal values of these numbers in reading the sequence?

c. Do your observations still hold for the following sequence: 101, 1010, 10100, 101000

d. Based on your observation, double 101110.

e. Check your work for Part d by converting the binary number to base 10.

f. Reading the sequences in Parts a and c from right to left, what happens to the values?

Convert the decimal numbers in Exercises 27–30 to equivalent binary numbers.

27. 23   **28.** 56   **29.** 87   **30.** 291

31. The following appeared in the sample questions of *Practicing to Take the GRE Computer Science Test, 2nd Edition:*

The number of 1's in the binary representation of

$$13 \cdot 16^3 + 11 \cdot 16^2 + 9 \cdot 16 + 3$$

is which of the following?

(A) 7   (B) 8   (C) 9   (D) 10   (E) 12

Section 2.4 Programming Projects

For each of the following programs, label all output and supply ample comments.

1. Develop a program to print the number of bits needed to store an integer on your computer. Assume 8 bits to a byte.

2. Develop a program to initialize a variable to a 3-digit number, and print its expansion in base 10. For example, for the number 937, the output would be

```
937 = 7 * 1 + 3 * 10 + 9 * 100
```

To extract the 3, we obtain 93 through integer division by 10, and then use modulo 10 on the result.

Section 2.5 Breadth: Integer Arithmetic in the Computer

Signed-Magnitude Representation

We must be able to represent negative integers in the computer. Several methods have been used, but the most obvious way is to convert the number to binary and stick on another bit to indicate sign—0 for positive and 1 for negative. Suppose integers are stored using this **signed-magnitude** technique in 8 bits, so that the leftmost or most significant bit holds the sign while the remaining bits represent the magnitude. Consequently, $0010\ 1001_2$ represents $+41_{10}$.

```
0 0 1 0   1 0 0 1
    32  + 8  + 1
```

+   41

With the leftmost bit being 1, $1010\ 1001_2$ represents -41_{10}.

```
1 0 1 0   1 0 0 1
    32  + 8  + 1
```

−   41

Early computers used signed-magnitude, but the circuitry for arithmetic was complicated, and the mapping from the signed-magnitude representation to decimal integers was not one-to-one. For example, representing zero as all zeros, (0000 0000) seems natural, but that represents +0. The bit string 1000 0000 indicates −0. Thus, to determine if a variable had a value of zero, the programmer had to check if the variable was $+0$ or -0.

Two's Complement Represen- tation

A method of representing numbers that avoids this problem and simplifies the arithmetic and circuitry is called **two's complement notation**. We can still determine the sign by looking at the most significant bit. Positive integers have a most significant bit of 0, whereas this bit for negative integers is 1. Moreover, the two's complement notation for a positive integer is identical to its signed-magnitude representation. For negative numbers, however, the sequence of bits after the most significant bit of 1 is not the magnitude in base 2.

Let us consider the process of obtaining the two's complement representation of a negative integer, -41. We first convert the absolute value or magnitude of 41 to binary.

$41_{10} = 0010\ 1001_2$

Then we take the **complement** of each bit, which is its opposite value. Consequently, ones become zeros, and zeros become ones. This number, $1101\ 0110_2$, is called the **one's complement** of 41.

Notice that even the sign bit changes.

Another way to take the one's complement that is helpful when considering other bases is to subtract the number from all ones. After all, $1 - 0 = 1$ and $1 - 1 = 0$. Thus,

$$\begin{array}{r} 1111\ 1111 \\ -\ 0010\ 1001 \\ \hline 1101\ 0110 \end{array}$$

To complete the process of deriving the **two's complement**, we increment or add one to this one's complement.

$-41_{10} = 1101\ 0111_2$

Algorithm 2.3. Compute the Two's Complement of a Binary Integer:

find the one's complement by complementing each bit, $0 \leftrightarrow 1$
increment the result by 1

The two's complement representation of a nonnegative integer (such as 41) is its representation in the binary number system (such as $0010\ 1001_2$). To express a negative integer (such as -41) in two's complement representation, we express the corresponding positive integer (41) in the binary number system ($0010\ 1001_2$), take the one's complement of that binary integer ($1101\ 0110_2$), and add 1 to the result ($1101\ 0111_2$).

Example 2.15

Let us go through this process to express the decimal integers 104 and -104 in 8 bits with two's complement representation. The initial step is to convert 104 to binary.

```
                     Remainders

       2 | 104
         |  52       0        ↑
         |  26       0        |
         |  13       0        |
         |   6       1        |
         |   3       0        |
         |   1       1        |
         |   0       1
```

We place a zero bit at the beginning to show the sign (positive) for the 8-bit number and obtain $104_{10} = 0110\ 1000_2$. For -104, we complement each bit and then add 1, as shown:

Step 1
```
0 1 1 0   1 0 0 0
↓ ↓ ↓ ↓   ↓ ↓ ↓ ↓
1 0 0 1   0 1 1 1
```

Step 2
```
1 0 0 1   0 1 1 1
+                1
─────────────────
1 0 0 1   1 0 0 0
```

Thus, $-104_{10} = 1001\ 1000_2$.

If the computer stores integers using 16 bits, we take the two's complement of $0000\ 0000\ 0110\ 1000_2$, yielding $1111\ 1111\ 1001\ 1000_2$.

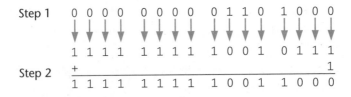

Step 1
```
0 0 0 0   0 0 0 0   0 1 1 0   1 0 0 0
↓ ↓ ↓ ↓   ↓ ↓ ↓ ↓   ↓ ↓ ↓ ↓   ↓ ↓ ↓ ↓
1 1 1 1   1 1 1 1   1 0 0 1   0 1 1 1
```
Step 2
```
+                                    1
─────────────────────────────────────
1 1 1 1   1 1 1 1   1 0 0 1   1 0 0 0
```

One trick of taking the two's complement of a binary number like $0110\ 1000_2$ is to start at the left, complementing every bit down to, but not including, the rightmost 1. Thus, the four leftmost bits of $0110\ 1000_2$ are each complemented, while those on the right are not.

```
0 1 1 0   1 0 0 0
↓ ↓ ↓ ↓   ← ← ← ←
1 0 0 1   1 0 0 0
```

Note that if we take the two's complement of this representation ($1001\ 1000_2 = -104_{10}$), we return to its positive counterpart ($0110\ 1000_2 = +104_{10}$). In general, the two's complement of the two's complement is the original number, just as taking the negative of a negative is positive. Two's complement representation not only agrees with this property of numbers, but it is easy to implement in the circuitry of the computer; and there is only one representation for zero.

Example 2.16

Assume a computer uses 8-bit, two's complement representation for integers. Let us determine the decimal numbers that the following two's complement integers represent: a. 0000 0101   b. 1111 1011   c. 0111 1111   d. 1000 0000   e. 1111 1111

a. The leading 0 indicates that 0000 0101 is a positive integer, so we can determine immediately that it represents $4 + 1 = +5$.

b. With the most significant bit being 1, 1111 1011 represents a negative integer. To determine the magnitude, we take the two's complement by complementing all bits up to but not including the rightmost 1 (or by subtracting the number from 1111 1111 and then adding 1)—0000 0101. Consequently, 1111 1011 is the representation for -5.

c. 0111 1111 represents a positive integer that is one less than the unsigned binary integer $1000\ 0000 = 128_{10}$. Thus, our original number is 127.

d. 1000 0000 represents a negative integer. To determine the magnitude of the number, we determine the decimal equivalent of its two's complement. The two's complement of this number, however, is also 1000 0000, which represents 128 in base 2. Therefore, the sequence of bits in two's complement notation represents -128_{10}. Moreover, this number is the smallest integer that can be expressed in 8-bit, two's complement representation. Thus, the range of 8-bit signed integers is from -128_{10} to 127_{10}, and we have one more negative integer than positive.

e. The two's complement of $1111\ 1111_2$ is $0000\ 0001_2$, indicating that the original number represents the largest negative integer, -1_{10}.

Example 2.17

Following the same procedure as in Parts c and d of the last example, let us find the range of the decimal integers using 16-bit, two's complement representation. The largest positive integer is

$$0111\ 1111\ 1111\ 1111 = 32{,}767$$

which is one less than the unsigned integer $1000\ 0000\ 0000\ 0000 = 2^{15} = 32{,}768$. The smallest negative integer is 1000 0000 0000 0000 in two's complement notation. As in Part d above, this integer is its own two's complement. Therefore, $-32{,}768$ is the smallest negative integer. Many microcomputers store integers in 16 bits, so that the range of number of type *int* is from $-32{,}768$ to $32{,}767$.

Addition

We did a limited amount of addition using a carry as we counted in base 2. Recall that if the digit to which we are adding 1 is the largest in that base, we write 0 and carry 1. The carry is added to the next position, such as in the following examples:

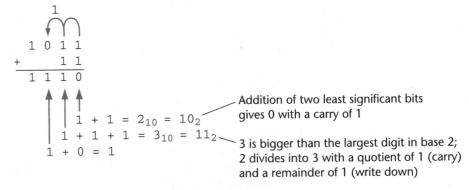

Base 10   Base 2

```
   1                 1
  ∩                 ⌢⌢⌢
 3 9         1 0 0 1 1 1
+ 1         +           1
─────       ─────────────
 4 0         1 0 1 0 0 0
```

Notice how the carry occurs in each problem, as follows:

$$39 + 1 = (3 \times 10 + 9) + 1 = 3 \times 10 + 1 \times 10 = 4 \times 10$$
$$100111 + 1 = (2^5 + 2^2 + 2 + 1)_{10} + 1$$
$$= 2^5 + 2^2 + 2 + 2$$
$$= 2^5 + 2^2 + 2 \times 2$$
$$= 2^5 + 2^2 + 2^2$$
$$= 2^5 + 2 \times 2^2$$
$$= 2^5 + 2^3 = 101000_2$$

Adding numbers other than 1 is similar. Consider the binary sum $1011 + 11$.

```
        1
       ⌢⌢⌢
    1 0 1 1
 +      1 1
 ──────────
    1 1 1 0
    ↑ ↑ ↑
```

$1 + 1 = 2_{10} = 10_2$ Addition of two least significant bits gives 0 with a carry of 1

$1 + 1 + 1 = 3_{10} = 11_2$ 3 is bigger than the largest digit in base 2; 2 divides into 3 with a quotient of 1 (carry) and a remainder of 1 (write down)

$1 + 0 = 1$

A big advantage of two's complement arithmetic is that we can use the same circuitry for adding positive or negative numbers. Consider the following sum:

		Unsigned	*Signed*
1011 1110	=	190	−66
+0010 1101	=	+45	+45
1110 1011	=	235	−21

As unsigned integers, $1011\ 1110_2$ and $0010\ 1101_2$ are 190 and 45, respectively. Their sum is $1110\ 1011_2$ or 235. As an 8-bit, two's complement integer, $1011\ 1110$ represents -66. The sum, which is now -21, is still correct.

Example 2.18

Suppose we are working on a microcomputer with 16-bit integers, and we have the following statements for *int* variable *i*:

```
i = 20480;
i = i + 16384;
printf("%d\n", i);
```

Surprisingly, the value printed is -28672 instead of the correct answer of 36864.

$$
\begin{array}{rcl}
0101\ 0000\ 0000\ 0000 & = & 20{,}480 \\
+0100\ 0000\ 0000\ 0000 & = & +16{,}384 \\
\hline
1001\ 0000\ 0000\ 0000_2 & = & -28{,}672
\end{array}
$$

The problem arises when the leftmost bit, the sign bit, gets the carry from the addition of 1 and 1, converting the result to a negative number. There simply are not enough bits to express the answer, so the final answer has the wrong sign. We must be conscious of this problem, called **overflow**, on any computer, but overflow is more likely to occur on microcomputers because they often use fewer bytes to hold numbers than larger computers. Overflow also happens when we add two negative integers and get a positive result. For example, if 8 bits store an integer, addition of -128 and -128 ends in an overflow value of 0.

$$
\begin{array}{rcl}
1000\ 0000 & = & -128 \\
+1000\ 0000 & = & -128 \\
\hline
0000\ 0000 & = & 0
\end{array}
$$

Definition   **Overflow** is an error condition that occurs when there are not enough bits to express a value.

Subtraction

Subtraction in different bases parallels subtraction in the decimal number system. To subtract y from x in base 10, we change the sign of y and add. For example, $10 - (-7) = 10 + (+7) = 17$ or $35 - 6 = 35 + (-6) = 29$. Similarly, when using two's complement representation, to subtract y from x, we take the two's complement of the code for y and add.

Example 2.19

Let us perform the following subtraction using 8-bit, two's complement integers:

$$
\begin{array}{ccccc}
 & & & & \text{Check in base 10} \\
0011\ 1011 & & 0011\ 1011 & = & 59 \\
-1110\ 1001 & \longrightarrow & +0001\ 0111 & = & -(-23) \\
\cline{3-3}
 & & 0101\ 0010_2 & = & 82_{10}
\end{array}
$$

Multiplication and Division by Two

We do not cover multiplication or division here except by powers of 2. To perform multiplication and division by 2^n, computers use a technique called **shifting**. Chapter 15 discusses the operations in C of (logical) shifting the value in a cell to the left or right. In shifting a fixed-length representation for an integer, one bit falls off the end and a 0 appears at the other end. Notice what happens to the value stored in an 8-bit cell (9_{10}) as the contents are shifted several times to the left, as follows:

$$
\begin{array}{rll}
 & 0000\ 1001 \leftarrow 0 & 9 \\
0 \leftarrow & 0001\ 0010 \leftarrow 0 & 18 \\
0 \leftarrow & 0010\ 0100 \leftarrow 0 & 36 \\
0 \leftarrow & 0100\ 1000 & 72
\end{array}
$$

If the number is a signed integer, shifting again results in code representing a negative number and overflow. If the number is an unsigned integer, we can have one more shift before that most significant 1 falls off the end. The reason shifting to the left causes doubling goes back to our representation of numbers. Consider what happens in binary if we double 9_{10}:

$$9 \quad = 1001_2 = 2^3 + 1$$
$$2 \cdot 9 = 2(2^3 + 1)$$
$$= 2^4 + 2^1$$
$$= 10010_2 = 18$$

Shifting to the right results in an integral halving of the unsigned integer, as shown below:

$$0 \longrightarrow 0000\ 1001 \qquad 9$$
$$0 \longrightarrow 0000\ 0100 \longrightarrow 1 \quad 4$$
$$0 \longrightarrow 0000\ 0010 \longrightarrow 0 \quad 2$$
$$0 \longrightarrow 0000\ 0001 \longrightarrow 0 \quad 1$$

Of course, division by 2 must be integer division so that 9/2 results in 4 instead of 4.5.

A basic understanding of how numbers are stored and manipulated helps us to gain insight into some of the features of a programming language and some of the problems we might encounter.

Section 2.5 Exercises

Express each decimal number in Exercises 1–8 in 8-bit, two's complement representation.

1. 91   **2.** −91   **3.** 115   **4.** −37

5. −64   **6.** −151   **7.** 128   **8.** −6

Express each decimal number in Exercises 9–11 in 16-bit, two's complement representation.

9. 91   **10.** −91   **11.** −151

12. Find the range of decimal integers that can be expressed with two's complement representation

  a. with 32 bits

  b. with 64 bits

The numbers in Exercises 13–15 are expressed in two's complement representation. In each case, give the larger of the two signed integers.

13. 0111 1100, 0011 1010   **14.** 0011 1111, 1100 0000

15. 1111 1111, 1001 0011

Find the sums of the unsigned numbers in base 2 in Exercises 16 and 17.

16. 11 1110 1111 + 10 1101   **17.** 1111 + 1001 + 1 1011 + 101

For Exercises 18–21, perform the indicated operations on the 8-bit, two's complement representations for integers. Convert to base 10 to check your answer.

18.   1001 1100   **19.**   0010 1011   **20.**   1110 0000   **21.**   0011 0110
      + 0111 0100   + 0101 1101   + 1001 1100   − 1111 0110

22. Suppose $0011\ 1010_2$ is the unsigned 8-bit binary representation for an integer. Double the number, expressing the answer in bases 2 and 10. Halve the number, expressing the answer in bases 2 and 10.

23. Repeat Exercise 22 for $1001\ 1101_2$.

24. The following appeared in the sample questions of *Practicing to Take the GRE Computer Science Test, 2nd Edition:*
    Which of the following pairs of 8-bit, two's-complement numbers will result in overflow when the members of the pairs are added?
    (A) 11111111, 00000001
    (B) 00000001, 10000000
    (C) 11111111, 10000001
    (D) 10000001, 10101010
    (E) 00111111, 00111111

Section 2.5 Programming Project

Write a program using *sizeof* to determine the number of bytes to store an integer on your computer. From this result, find the range of integers that your computer can store. Revise the program to print the largest and smallest integers. Add 1 to the largest integer, subtract 1 from the smallest, and print the results. Be sure to label your output well. Write an explanation of the results using calculations similar to those in this section.

Section 2.6 Interactive Programs

Interactive versus Batch Programs

One primary advantage of modern computers is their ability to communicate with the user during program execution. This feature enables the programmer to enter values into variables on demand, without having to change the program itself. With an **interactive program**, execution pauses each time the program needs an input value from the user. Once the user enters the required value and presses the return or enter key, execution resumes. For example, an airline reservation system is interactive. On a screen, the computer displays directions and asks the user for certain data. The travel or ticket agent responds, requesting flight information and reservations. In turn, the computer takes actions based on the user's input. In this section, we learn how to write interactive programs in C.

Definition An **interactive program** converses with the user and obtains data during program execution.

Interactive programming is not convenient for a large amount of data. In such situations, data are stored in a file, usually on disk or tape. A **batch program**, which obtains its data from files, runs without interactive communication with the user. The user obtains the output at the end of execution. For example, a program to produce semester grade reports would be a batch program. In Section 7.5, we consider input and output involving files.

> **Definition**   A **batch program** does not converse with the user during program execution. Instead, data are obtained from files.

Interactive Programs in C

In C, the function *scanf* ("scan formatted") in the standard input/output (I/O) library permits program interruption during execution to read required values into variables. The following is a call to *scanf* to obtain a value for integer variable *n:*

```
scanf("%d", &n);
```

This statement, similar to the statement calling *printf*, is in a sense its reverse. The conversion specification (%d) within the control string tells the computer that it should expect the user to input an integer (decimal) number. The ampersand symbol (&) with the variable *n* indicates the memory address of the variable *n*. We request data from the user, which the computer places in that particular memory location. If the programmer forgets the ampersand, *n* does not get the value the user enters. To emphasize the difference in their use, compare the following basic calls to *scanf* and *printf:*

```
scanf("%d", &n);     /* ampersand with variable name    */
printf("%d", n);     /* no ampersand with variable name */
```

> *Caution*
>
> For reading integer data (*scanf*), place an ampersand before the variable name. For printing the value of the integer variable (*printf*), do not include an ampersand.

The *scanf* function stops program execution until the user types a value and presses the enter key. If the computer does not tell the user that it is waiting for a value, the user may sit idle for a long time until he or she realizes that the computer needs data. Therefore, the programmer should precede each *scanf* with an appropriate *printf*, which specifies precisely what the user should do. Such a statement is called a **prompt**, and displaying such a message is known as **prompting**.

> **Definition**   In an interactive program, a **prompt** is a request from the computer for the user to enter data.

Example 2.20 _____

Let us write a program to read an integer and return its square. Pseudocode for the program follows:

> *main( )*
>
> Program to read an integer and return its square
>
> *Algorithm:*
>
> print instructions
> read an integer value interactively
> evaluate its square
> print the result

Before reading an input value with *scanf,* we have a call to *printf* prompting the user for integer input. We group these two statements to represent a unit, so that the program is more readable. The call to *scanf* takes the place of the initializing assignment statement we used in earlier programs. Both types of statements store values in the memory locations of variables for later processing. After obtaining an input value, we compute the square of the data and print the original value and its square. The sequence of statements follows that of many short programs—read (or assign), calculate, and print.

```
/*
 * Example 2.20
 * Program to input an integer and print its square
 */

#include <stdio.h>

main()
{   int num,        /* input data */
        square;     /* square of num */

    printf("Please type in an integer: ");
    scanf("%d", &num);

    square = num * num;
    printf("The square of %d is %d.\n", num, square);
}
```

Below is the interactive session during the execution of this program. Input from the user is underlined.

```
Please type in an integer: 5
The square of 5 is 25.
```

Sometimes the program needs to ask the user for more than one input value. The call to *scanf* must have a conversion specification and variable for each required data item. The following segment requests two values at once:

```
printf("Type the length and width, separated by a blank: ");
scanf("%d %d", &length, &width);
```

As the directions indicate, the user should type a length, a space, and a width. An example interactive run might be as follows:

```
Type the length and width, separated by a blank: 12 17
```

We use *scanf* in a number of interactive programs in the following chapters.

Section 2.6 Exercises

1. State if each of the following statements has an error or not. Correct mistakes.

   a. `scanf("%d", x);`   **b.** `scanf("value = %d\n", &x);`
   c. `printf("value = %d", &x);`   **d.** `scanf(&cost);`
   e. `scanf("%d", &x, &y);`   **f.** `scanf("%d", &cost);`
   g. `read(cost);`   **h.** `scanf("%d", &x, "%d", &y);`
   i. `scanf("%d %d", &cost, &price);`

2. Write statement(s) to prompt the user for number of children and to read a value for *NumChildren*.

3. Write statement(s) to prompt the user for his or her age and number of years of schooling and to read values for integer variables *age* and *NumYrsSchool*. Use only one call to *scanf*.

4. Write statement(s) to prompt the user for the month, day, and year of birth and to read values for these with one call to *scanf*.

Section 2.6 Programming Projects

For each of the following programs, label all output and supply ample comments.

1. Develop an interactive program that computes the area of a square from a user-supplied length.

2. Develop an interactive program that computes the perimeter and the area of a rectangle.

3. Develop an interactive program that reads an integer value and computes and prints the value of the variable itself, its square, and its cube.

4. Develop an interactive program that reads three test grades and prints the total of these grades.

Convert the following programming assignments from Section 2.2 Programming Projects to interactive programs:

5. Project 1   6. Project 2

Convert the following programming assignments from Section 2.3 Programming Projects to interactive programs:

7. Project 1   8. Project 2   9. Project 3

10. Project 4   11. Project 5   12. Project 6

13. Project 7

Section 2.7 **Problem Solving with Integer Functions**

Section 1.8 introduced user-defined functions and illustrated some of their important features. However, the functions of that section only printed and did not receive values from or return information to *main*. In this section, we continue the discussion of functions, showing how to communicate between the calling and the called functions.

Preconditions and Post-conditions

We have used the standard I/O library functions *printf* and *scanf,* which accept and return values, respectively. The ANSI C libraries, however, contain many additional functions. For example, the function *abs* in the standard library receives an integer and returns its absolute value. This function is equivalent to the following mathematical function:

$$f(x) = |x|$$

To use *abs,* we must include the *stdlib.h* header file for the ANSI C standard library,

```
#include <stdlib.h>
```

and link the library's object file with our own program. Within the program, to assign the absolute value of -3 to *AbsoluteValue,* we write

```
AbsoluteValue = abs(-3);
```

Accepting the argument or actual parameter (-3), the function returns the integer 3 through its name. Then, that value is assigned to the variable *AbsoluteValue.*

The documentation for the ANSI C library must contain certain information for us to use the absolute value function effectively. We must know the overall task of the function, what the function expects, and, provided we meet those expectations, what the function accomplishes. A black box of the module, shown in Figure 2.7, can be helpful, but it does not explain how *abs* accomplishes its task. Such implementation details are irrelevant to the user of the function, and knowledge of the details may only confuse the user with unnecessary information. Arrows into the black box are labeled with the input data, and arrows coming out are marked with the output. Figure 2.7 presents a procedural abstraction of the absolute value function, in which we consider the module with no concern for implementation details.

Definition   **Procedural abstraction** is a consideration of the input, processing, and output of a module without concern for the details of module implementation.

Documentation often starts with the function's name, a list of arguments, an indication of any returned value, and a statement of the function's task. On the first line of pseudocode, the text uses an arrow pointing to the right ($\rightarrow$) from the function's

Figure 2.7
Black-box
diagram of *abs*

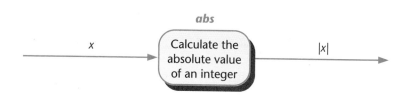

name and argument list to an output to indicate that the function returns a value. The following description is for the function *abs:*

abs(num) → *AbsoluteValue*

    Function to return the absolute value of an integer

The user, however, needs some detail about what must be true for the function to work properly. **Preconditions** describe the situation that exists as the module is to begin execution, any assumptions, and the information the module needs to meet its objectives. We use the abbreviation "Pre" for preconditions in the box below. The precondition for *abs* indicates that the input cannot be the most negative integer that the computer can represent. As discussed in Section 2.5, the range of integers a microcomputer represents is usually $-32,768$ to $32,767$. In this situation, the most negative integer, $-32,768$, has an absolute value of $32,768$, which such a computer cannot represent. Thus, the precondition indicates a restriction to the integer input.

Pre:

    num is an integer that is not the most negative integer that the computer can represent.

Documentation for the module also includes postconditions. The **postconditions** describe the state of the system when the module finishes executing, any error conditions, and the information the module returns or otherwise communicates. We use the abbreviation "Post" for postconditions in the following documentation:

Post:

    The function has returned the absolute value of *num.*

Definitions **Preconditions** describe the situation that exists as the module is to begin execution, any assumptions, and the information the module needs to meet its objectives. **Postconditions** describe the state of the system when the module finishes executing, any error conditions, and the information the module returns or otherwise communicates.

As we perform analysis and design in problem solving, we consider each module with such procedural abstraction. The descriptions developed are carried into the implementation phase. Comments preceding each function should present the function's task, preconditions, and postconditions. Such information enables the reader of the code to obtain an overview of the module immediately.

Analysis and Design of a Function

Suppose we determine that a problem's solution needs a module to return the square of an integer. ANSI C does not specify this function, so we must design and implement the function ourselves. In mathematics, the function has the form

$$f(x) = x^2$$

Figure 2.8 presents a black-box diagram of the function.

As with the description of *abs,* we specify name of the function, the task the function performs, preconditions, and postconditions. For the design phase, we must also develop the algorithm in pseudocode. Following is a design of the function *sqr:*

> *sqr(num)* → *square*
>
> > Function to return the square of *num*
>
> ***Pre:***
>
> > *num* is an integer.*
>
> ***Post:***
>
> > The function has returned the square of *num.*
>
> ***Algorithm:***
>
> > return *num^2*

On the first line of the design, we present the name of the function. The variable *num* in the parentheses is a **parameter** (**formal parameter** or **dummy parameter**). The calling routine passes values into the function through such parameters, and the function uses these variables to perform its task. For example, to assign 97^2 to the variable *area* in *main,* we have the statement

```
area = sqr(97);
```

The argument, 97, is the data item sent to the function's parameter, *num.*

Definition   A function **parameter** (**formal parameter** or **dummy parameter**) is a variable declared in the function's heading that is used to communicate information between the calling routine and the function.

Because *sqr* returns a value, we draw a right-pointing arrow to an identifier, in this case *square.* Sometimes this identifier is a variable that we declare within the function. However, for the short function *sqr, square* is just a name we use to refer to the

---

*More precisely, *num* is an integer whose square can be represented in the computer.

Figure 2.8
Black-box diagram of *sqr*

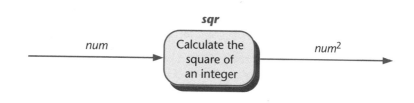

returned value. After a description of the function's task, the *Pre:* section lists the precondition(s); and the *Post:* section describes the postcondition(s).

> On the first line of a pseudocode design of a function, the arrow pointing to the right, as in
>
> `function_name(parameter_list)` → `value`
>
> indicates that the function *function_name* returns a value.

**Implemen-
tation of an
Integer
Function**

Once we design the function, we can implement its definition in C. In the definition of the function *sqr*, we must declare the type of the parameter, *num*, and the type of the returned value. These declarations appear in the first part of the function's definition and use a similar format to other declarations. Because both the returned value and parameter of *sqr* are integers, we preface the names of the function and parameter with the type *int*, as follows:

```
int sqr(int num)
```

This line is called the function's **heading**. Often we refer to the type of a function by the returned value's type, so *sqr* is an **integer function**.

Frequently, a function has more than one parameter. We must declare these independently, with commas separating the declarations, such as

```
int area(int dim1, int dim2)
```

Within a function we can use one *int* to declare several variables, such as

```
int dim1,
    dim2,
    FloorSpace;
```

In parameter declarations, however, a type must appear before each identifier.

Although a function may have no parameter or several, an integer function returns the value of at most one expression. In the case of *sqr*, the function must return the product of *num* with itself:

```
num * num
```

Within the definition of the function, a ***return* statement** contains this expression. This statement consists of the keyword *return* followed by the value to return. This value may be a variable, a constant, a more complex expression, or even another function call. Although unnecessary, parentheses may surround the returned expression. Thus, both of the following statements are syntactically correct:

```
return (num * num);
```

and

```
return num * num;
```

Comments describing the function and its pre- and postconditions precede the C definition of the function *sqr:*

```
/*
 * Function to return the square of an integer
 * Pre:  num is an integer.
 * Post: The function has returned the square of num.
 */

int sqr(int num)
{
    return (num * num);
}
```

For each invocation, the function can return only a single value. As soon as the computer executes a *return* statement, the function terminates, and subsequent statements are meaningless.

The function *sqr* returns a value that the calling routine uses. The first line of the definition and the prototype statement indicate that this value is of type *int.* As with the functions in Section 1.8, the prototype for *sqr* usually is declared at the beginning of the program so the function can be used by *main* and any other functions. The prototype mirrors the first line of the definition, except that it terminates with a semicolon:

```
int sqr(int num);
```

Alternatively, we can write the prototype without parameter names:

```
int sqr(int);
```

Procedures

The next example declares, defines, and uses *sqr* in a program. Another routine in the program, *directions,* prints directions. This module is similar to those in Section 1.8 that do not return values through the names of the functions. Many languages, such as Pascal, would implement such a subprogram as a procedure. Such languages have two kinds of subprograms—functions and procedures—with slightly different syntax for their definitions. In these languages, the procedure does not return a value through the name, and a call to a procedure stands by itself in a program statement, as follows:

```
PrintSalary(salary);
```

By contrast, in such a language, a function returns a value through its name, and the program invokes the function by using it anywhere a value of that type can appear, such as

```
AbsoluteValue = abs(-3);
```

The C language does not distinguish between functions and procedures. All subprograms are functions. In C, a function returns a value if it contains a *return* statement that specifies a value to return. Otherwise, it simply concludes without sending back anything. For clarity in the pseudocode description of a module, we describe the module as a function if it returns a value through a *return* statement and as a procedure if it does not.

Example 2.21

This example develops a program to square the constant 97 and then to prompt the user for an integer, which the computer squares.

In analyzing the problem, we determine that the program must give directions, obtain an integer from the user, and print the square of this input. One top-down design has the main function calling two user-defined routines, *directions,* to print program directions and 97^2, and *sqr,* to return the square of an integer. The structure chart for

Figure 2.9
Structure chart
for program in
Example 2.21

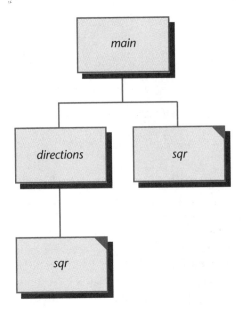

this design is in Figure 2.9. Because both *directions* and *main* call *sqr,* the rectangle for *sqr* appears twice. To emphasize that *sqr* appears more than once in the diagram, we darken the right, top corner of its rectangle.

After designing the overall program with a structure chart, we design each module in pseudocode. In this pseudocode, we use a left-pointing arrow (←), to indicate that the variable on the left gets the value of the expression on the right.

---

main( )

    Program to print 97^2, to prompt user for an integer, and to print the square of that number

Algorithm:

    call *directions* to print program directions
    prompt the user for an integer
    read an integer, *num*
    square ← *sqr(num)*
    print *square*

---

directions( )

    Procedure to print program directions

Pre:

    none

Post:

    Program directions have been printed.

Algorithm:

    print program directions
    print *sqr(97)*

With no parameters or returned value, we use *void* twice in the prototype for *directions,* as follows:

```
void directions(void);
```

In contrast, *sqr* has an integer parameter and returns an integer value, so *int* appears twice in its prototype, as shown:

```
int sqr(int);
```

The code for the program reveals two applications of the function *sqr,* one within the *printf* and one on the right-hand side of an assignment statement. The entire program follows:

```
/*
 * Example 2.21.  Program to print the square of 97 as an
 * example, then to prompt the user for an integer and print
 * its square
 */

#include <stdio.h>

void directions(void);      /* prototypes */
int sqr(int);

main()
{
    int num,                 /* input data    */
        square;              /* square of num */

    directions();            /* call to procedure */

    printf("Please type an integer:  ");
    scanf("%d", &num);

    square = sqr(num);       /* call to function sqr */
    printf("The square of %d is %d.\n", num, square);
}
/*
 * Print directions
 * Pre:  none
 * Post: Program directions have been printed.
 */

void directions(void)
{
    printf("This program will allow you to input an ");
    printf("integer to square.\n");
    printf("For example, if you input 97, ");
    printf("the program will output %d.\n", sqr(97));
}
```

```
/*
 * Function to return the square of an integer
 * Pre:  num is an integer.
 * Post: The square of num has been returned.
 */

int sqr(int num)
{
    return (num * num);
}
```

To test the program, we should run it several times with a variety of input. A sample run of the program follows, with user input underlined:

```
This program will allow you to input an integer to square.
For example, if you input 97, the program will output 9409.
Please type an integer:  43
The square of 43 is 1849.
```

In the invocation of *sqr* from *directions*, we have a constant argument (97) and do not assign the returned value to a variable, but use it directly in the call to *printf*. The function *main* obtains an integer from the user and stores the value in variable *num*. Then, *main* calls *sqr* with this variable as an argument. The value of *num* is copied into *sqr*'s parameter. The value returned through *sqr(num)* is assigned to *square*. Figures 2.10 and 2.11 illustrate the actions during run time of these calls to *sqr*.

In pseudocode,
$$a \leftarrow b$$
means that variable *a* is assigned the value of expression *b*.

Arguments and Parameters

In the last example, the argument and parameter are the same identifier (*num*), but they do not have to be. The program would have worked just as well if we had kept the main program as is but changed the name of the parameter in the definition to *number*, as follows:

```
/* Function to return the square of an integer */

int sqr(int number)
{
    return (number * number);
}
```

Figure 2.12 demonstrates that *sqr* behaves the same way even if the names of the argument and parameter are not the same.

If we call a library function, our argument will probably have a different name than the parameter in the function definition. Moreover, the argument might be an integer

Figure 2.10
Action of call
sqr(97) in
Example 2.21

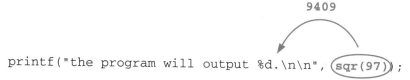

Call to *sqr*

```
printf("the program will output %d.\n\n", sqr(97));
```

                              97

```
int sqr(int num)
{
        return (num * num);
}
```

- -

***sqr* Returns Value**

```
printf("the program will output %d.\n\n", sqr(97)) ;
```

                                   9409

```
int sqr(int num)
{
        return (num * num);
}
```

- -

Print the Returned Value

                              9409

```
printf("the program will output %d.\n\n", sqr(97));
```

constant, such as 97, or an expression, such as *num* + 1. As long as *num* already has a value, the following statements are legal:

```
s = sqr(num + 1);
```

```
t = 5 * sqr(2 * num + 8) + sqr(97);
```

Neither 97 nor *num* + 1 could be a parameter in the function definition. It is certainly acceptable and often necessary to use different argument and parameter identifiers. For instance, we do not know the parameter names in ANSI C library functions. With your own functions, you might find it helpful to employ the same identifiers for corresponding arguments and parameters.

As intimated in the last paragraph, variables can be parameters in the definition of a function, but constants or more complicated expressions cannot. Also, when invoking a function, there should be a match between the types, number, and positions of the arguments and parameters. The function *sqr* is expecting the calling function to

Figure 2.11
Action of *square*
= *sqr(num)*
with *num* = 43
in Example
2.21

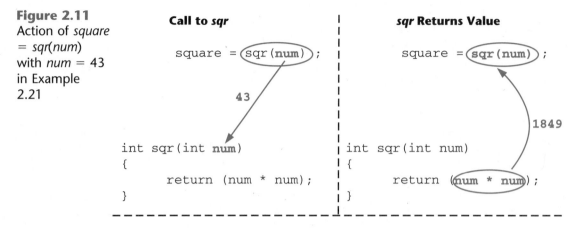

Figure 2.12   Action of *square* = *sqr(num)* with argument *num* = 43 and parameter *number*

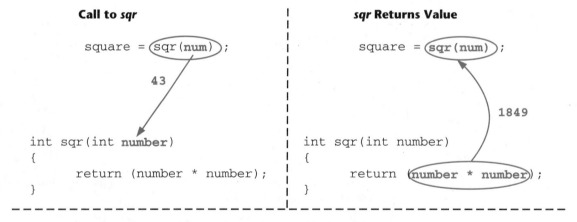

send an integer, so the argument should be of type *int*. Unpredictable results can occur when the types of an argument and corresponding parameter do not agree. Your system may or may not give a compiler warning that the types of the argument and parameter do not match.

Example 2.22

In this example, we develop a program to obtain the dimensions of a room from the user and to calculate and print the room's floor space.

The analysis determines that the program must obtain dimensions from the user, calculate the floor space, and print the value. Thus, we can decompose *main*'s duties into three tasks—print directions; obtain a dimension from the user, which the program does twice; and compute the floor space. The procedure *directions* displays program directions for the user. The function *GetDim* prompts the user for a dimension, then reads and returns the dimension. The function *area* calculates the floor space. Figure 2.13 contains a structure chart for this program.

The pseudocode for *main, GetDim,* and *area* follow:

main( )

    Program to obtain dimensions of a room from the user and to calculate the floor space

Algorithm:

    directions()
    dim1 ← GetDim()
    dim2 ← GetDim()
    FloorSpace ← area(dim1, dim2)
    print *FloorSpace*

Figure 2.13
Structure chart
for program in
Example 2.22

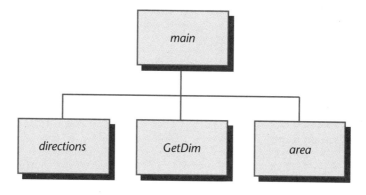

GetDim( ) → dimension

Function to read and return a room dimension

Pre:

The user enters an integer dimension, *dimension*.

Post:

The function returned that integer room dimension.

Algorithm:

prompt the user for a room dimension
read *dimension*
return *dimension*

area(dim1, dim2) → FloorSpace

Function to compute the floor space given the room dimensions

Pre:

dim1 and *dim2* are positive integer dimensions of a room.

Post:

The function has returned the integer floor space of the room.

Algorithm:

return the product of the room dimensions, *dim1* and *dim2*.

C code for the program follows:

```
/*
 * Example 2.22. Program to return the floor space for a room
 */

#include <stdio.h>

void directions(void);
int  GetDim(void);
int  area(int, int);

main()
{
    int dim1,         /* one dimension of the room      */
        dim2,         /* another dimension of the room */
        FloorSpace;   /* area of floor in room          */
```

```
        directions();

        dim1 = GetDim();
        dim2 = GetDim();

        FloorSpace = area(dim1, dim2);

        printf("\nThe floor space is %d square feet.\n",
               FloorSpace);
}

/*
 * Function to print program directions
 * Pre:  none
 * Post: Program directions have been printed.
 */

void directions(void)
{
        printf("This program will give you the floor space ");
        printf("in square feet\n");
        printf("for a room of your choosing.\n\n");
}

/*
 * Function to prompt the user for one dimension
 * of a floor and to return that dimension
 * Pre:  The user enters an integer dimension.
 * Post: The function has returned that dimension.
 */

int GetDim(void)
{
        int dimension;      /* one dimension of floor */

        printf("Type one dimension of the floor in feet:  ");
        scanf("%d", &dimension);
        return (dimension);
}

/*
 * Function to calculate the floor space (area of the floor)
 * given two dimensions (length and width).
 * Pre:  dim1 and dim2 are integer dimensions.
 * Post: The function has returned the integer floor space.
 */

int area(int dim1, int dim2)
{
        return (dim1 * dim2);
}
```

A sample run is as follows:

```
This program will give you the floor space in square feet
for a room of your choosing.

Type one dimension of the floor in feet:  8
Type one dimension of the floor in feet:  10

The floor space is 80 square feet.
```

The function *GetDim* reads an integer and returns this value to the *main* function by way of the *return* statement. We use the variable *dimension* merely to receive the value read before returning that value to *main; dimension* has nothing to do with the variable (*dim1* or *dim2*) that finally receives this value. We must declare *dimension* in the function where we use it.

The function does save effort by allowing us to write the prompt and read statements once. If we decide to change the prompt, we only need to adjust one call to *printf*. Moreover, the function enables the program to obtain values for the variables *dim1* and *dim2* by placing them on the left side of an assignment operator. This format is shorter and clearer than having two identical calls to *printf* and placing the identifiers within the parentheses of a call to *scanf*.

After obtaining the dimensions, the program calculates the area of the floor by calling the function *area*. The function *area* receives the arguments *dim1* and *dim2*, and assigns these values to corresponding parameters in *area* with the same names.

After executing the *return* statement in *area,* the computer assigns the returned value to *FloorSpace* and then prints this result. As an alternative, we could omit reference to the variable *FloorSpace* and call *area* from *printf*.

```
printf("\nThe floor space is %d square feet.\n",
        area(dim1, dim2));
```

Default Type Declarations for Functions

We have carefully declared the type of all functions in this section, but the programs would still run correctly if we omitted *int* at the first of their definitions and prototypes, as follows:

```
area(int dim1, int dim2)
```

The type *int* is the default type for all functions. If we do not declare a type, the compiler assumes its type is *int*. If the function does not return a value, the *int* is irrelevant. This dependence on the default can be misleading, however. Does a function that resorts to the default type return a value or not? We cannot tell without looking in the definition for a *return* statement. Therefore, we should declare *void* or a type for all user-defined functions other than *main*. If the function returns an integer value, we should declare the function to be of type *int*. If the function does not return a value, we should use *void*.

By not specifying a type for *main,* we are by default declaring it to be an integer function; *main* can return a value of type *int.* Some operating systems expect to receive a value from *main* that indicates the possible existence of a run-time error. A returned value of 0 indicates normal termination of a program. To accommodate such expectations, *main* has a final statement of

```
return 0;
```

Because we have not had a *return* statement in *main,* it seems reasonable that we would put *void* before its name. However, some versions of C do not allow such a declaration. Unfortunately, the expectation of a returned value is system dependent. For simplicity, we have opted to omit the declaration when we are not returning a value from *main.*

As we discuss in Chapter 12, *main* can have parameters. In this case, we type a command using arguments to run the program. With no parameters, we can follow the name *main* with parentheses containing *void.* For consistency, we have omitted the declaration of type, the *void* parameter list, and a *return* statement for *main.* Using these options, the definition of *main* has the following structure:

```
int main(void)
{
    ⋮
      return 0;
}
```

Should you desire or should your system demand, this form of the definition of *main* is certainly acceptable in any version of ANSI C.

Section 2.7 Exercises

1. Consider the following function definition:

```
int fun(int x)
{
    return (3 * x + 1);
}
```

What value is assigned to *y* in Parts a–e?

a. `y = fun(2);`

b. `y = 2 + fun(7);`

c. `z = 1;`
  `y = 2 + fun(3 * z + 1);`

d. `z = 5;`
  `fun(z);`
  `y = z;`

e. y = fun(fun(2));

f. Write a statement to print the value of *fun* with argument 9.

g. Write statements to prompt the user for a number, read the number, and print *fun* of the input.

h. Write a function prototype for the function.

2. Find the error(s) in the following function prototype statement:

```
int erfun(int x, y, z)
```

3. Find the error(s) in the following function definition:

```
int erfun2(x);
{
    returns(3x)
    x = x + 1
}
```

4. Write the body of the following function definition to return the double of parameter *x*.

```
int TwoTimes(int x)
{
    ⋮
}
```

5. Write a function *even* to return 0 if an integer is even and 1 otherwise (use %).

6. Write a function *sum2* to return the sum of two integer parameters.

Section 2.7 Programming Projects

1. Develop an interactive program to read the dimensions of a box in inches and calculate and print the volume of a box in cubic inches. (The volume of a box is the product of its length, width, and height.) Use a function to read a dimension and another function to calculate the volume.

2. Convert Programming Project 7 from Section 2.3 to an interactive program that uses a function to calculate the day of the week.

3. Develop an interactive program to read four integer grades between 0 and 100 and print their integer average. Use one function to prompt for, read, and return an integer grade and another function to compute and return the average.

Section 2.8 Problem Solving Revisited

A systematic approach to solving problems can be helpful whether or not a computer system is part of the process. An organized strategy is particularly important when programming is part of the solution. If we begin coding before properly analyzing the problem, the result can be a disaster. A beautiful program that does not satisfy the needs of users may be of little or no use. One systematic approach to problem solving that involves programming is to follow the four basic steps of analysis, design, implementation, and testing. We can apply these steps to each subproblem or module in a top-down design. An enhancement of these steps from Section 1.1 follows:

Steps for Solving a Problem with a Computer:

1. Analysis

    a. Carefully state objectives of the module.

    b. Determine the postconditions, including the output desired.

    c. Determine the preconditions, including the input needed.

    d. Identify the processing needed, including formulas. Perform sample calculations.

    e. Establish input format (if appropriate).

    f. Establish output format (if appropriate).

2. Design

    a. Diagram a structure chart.

    b. Select appropriate data structures.

    c. Develop the logic of each module.

3. Implementation

    a. Code the solution.

    b. Provide documentation.

4. Testing

    a. Select test data.

    b. Perform unit testing of each module.

    c. Perform top-down testing.

    d. Perform prototype testing.

    e. Test the program as a whole.

These steps are flexible. In short examples, we might perform the analysis mentally. The steps may overlap, with coding and testing of some modules starting before completing the design of other modules. We might develop and test a prototype, or partial solution, to help analyze and design the final solution.

Definition   A **prototype** is a trial version that demonstrates some of the functionality and "user friendliness" of the developing system.

You may not understand all the details in the outline at this time, but you should appreciate the four basic steps. Throughout the text, we discuss and illustrate the details of the problem-solving steps.The longer examples in Chapters 1 and 2 followed the problem-solving steps. The objectives of the problem were carefully stated (analysis); a structure chart and a chart of the logic (pseudocode) were developed (design); the code was written (implementation); and finally the program was executed and results observed (testing).

Analysis

The next example considers the analysis of another problem. The design, implementation, and testing of this system are requested in the Exercises.

Example 2.23

A new process for protecting wood floors involves covering the floor with a plastic coating. We need to develop a module to calculate the number of gallons of the new plastic needed to coat a wood floor with given dimensions. The purpose of the module is to calculate the number of gallons of the plastic to sell to the customer. Data

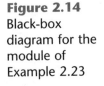

Figure 2.14
Black-box
diagram for the
module of
Example 2.23

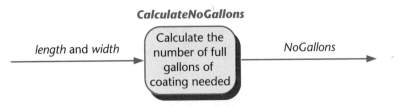

provided are the length and width of the floor in whole number feet. Information returned is the number of full gallons needed. Each gallon covers 50 square feet of floor. The black-box analysis appears in Figure 2.14.

Pre:

   length and *width* are nonnegative integer measurements in feet.

Post:

   The function has returned the number of gallons. Any part of a gallon is a full gallon needed.

Formulas:

   *area = length * width*
   NoGallons = (area − 1) / 50 + 1

Sample Calculations:

   For *length* = 15 and *width* = 10, *area* = 15 * 10 = 150
   NoGallons = 149 / 50 + 1 = 2 + 1 = 3
   For *length* = 16 and *width* = 12, *area* = 16 * 12 = 192
   NoGallons = 191 / 50 + 1 = 3 + 1 = 4

Section 2.8 Exercises

Provide a black-box analysis, preconditions, postconditions, and sample calculations in Exercises 1–3. Although some values are floating point numbers, the analysis should be the same as for integer functions with integer parameters.

1. Calculate the surface area of a closed can, given the radius of the base and the height of the can in inches ($S = 2\pi rh + 2\pi r^2$).

2. Calculate the net pay of day workers paid at the rate of $5.25 per hour with 16% deducted for taxes.

3. Calculate the time in minutes it takes to fill a rectangular swimming pool of uniform depth, given the dimensions in feet (length, width, and height). Assume water flows in at the rate of 20 gallons per minute. A cubic foot of water has 7.8 gallons.

4. Design, implement, and test the module posed in Example 2.23. Write a test program.

Section 2.9 **Scope of Variables**

Local Variables and Scope

A feature introduced in the program of Example 2.22 in Section 2.7 is the declaration of a variable within a function other than *main*. We call a variable declared within a function a **local variable**—in other words, it is **local** to that function. The name of a local variable has meaning only within the declaring function. The **scope** of a variable is the range within a program over which that variable has meaning. Statements within the *GetDim* function can include the variable *dimension*, but statements in *main* cannot. If *main* makes a reference to *dimension*, the compiler flags it as an error. We say that the scope of *dimension* is throughout *GetDim*. Similarly, because *main* contains the declarations of *dim1* and *dim2*, *GetDim* cannot refer directly to these variables. Their scope is *main*.

Definitions A variable is **local** to a function if the function contains a declaration of the variable. The name of a local variable has meaning only within the declaring function. The **scope** of a variable is the range within a program over which that variable has meaning.

The storage of a local variable exists only while the function that contains it is executing. For example, the variable *dimension* does not even exist until *main* calls the function *GetDim*. When the function finishes executing, the variable passes into oblivion. (Space for the routine is released to be used again.)

Pass by Value

The function *area* declares two variables *dim1* and *dim2* in its parameter list. As Figure 2.15 illustrates, these variables are different from those of *main*—they exist only during execution of *area*. When *area* is called, the values of the arguments (*main*'s *dim1* and *dim2*) are copied into the parameters (*area*'s *dim1* and *dim2*). Then, communication between these variables is severed. What *area* does with its *dim1* and *dim2* has no effect on those of *main*, because they have different locations in memory. The computer suspends the ability to reference *main*'s local variables during execution of *area*. In Figure 2.15, the inaccessible portion of memory is shaded. This method of copying the argument's value to the parameter is called **pass by value**.

Definition **Pass by value** is a method of passing information to a function whereby the parameter receives a copy of the value of the argument.

On termination of *area*, the computer releases the memory locations of *area*'s local variables, and again we can use *main*'s *dim1* and *dim2*. Before *main* calls *area* and after execution returns from *area*, locations for its variables do not exist in memory. Figure 2.16 depicts the scope of the variables in this program.

When using pass by value, a called function cannot alter the value of an argument in the calling function. As the next example demonstrates, the computer only copies the value of the argument into the parameter.

Figure 2.15 Memory during execution of program in Example 2.22

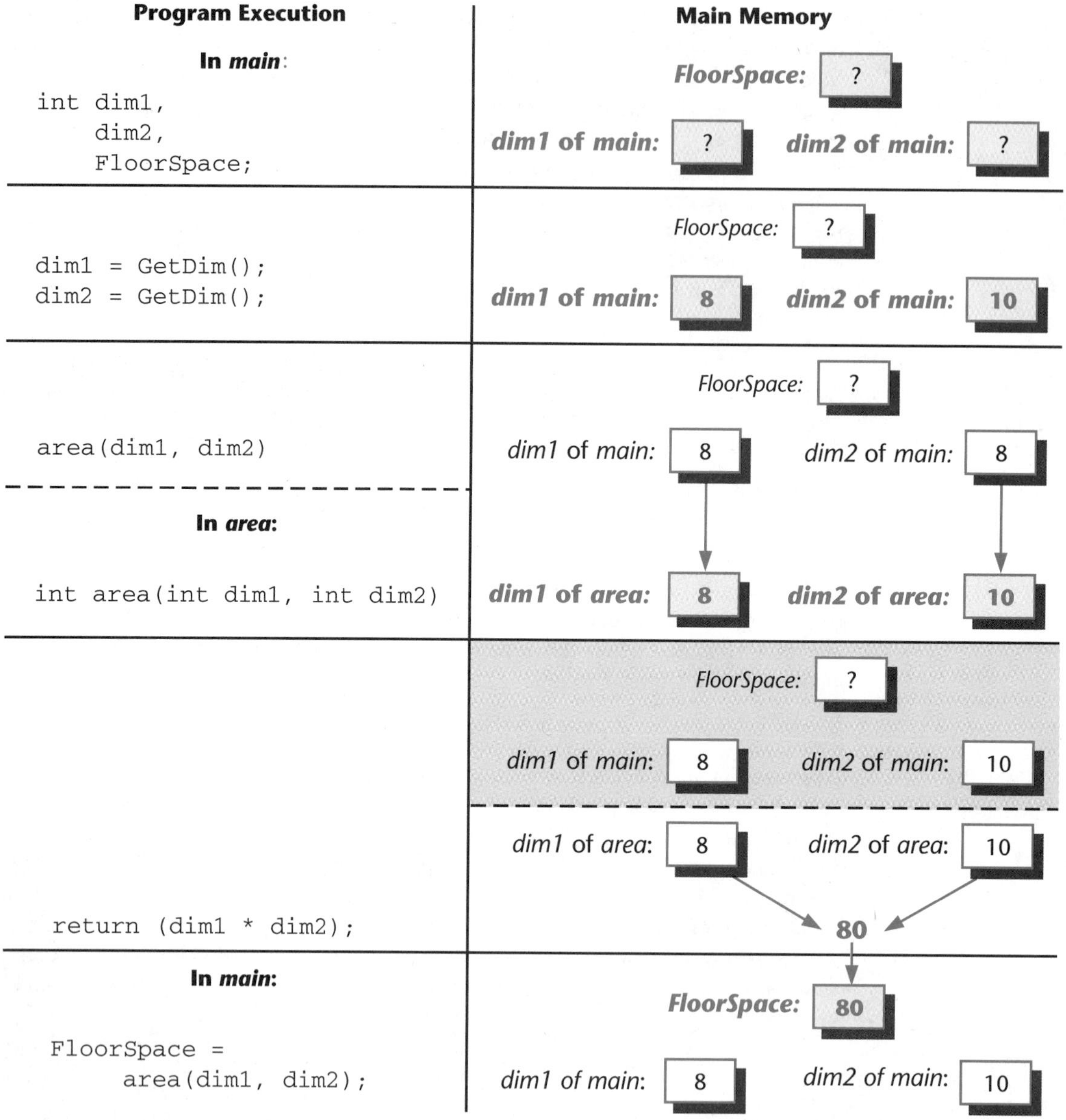

Program Execution	Main Memory

In *main*:
 	
`int dim1,`
`    dim2,`
`    FloorSpace;`
	FloorSpace: `?`
	
	dim1 of main: `?` *dim2 of main:* `?`

`dim1 = GetDim();` `dim2 = GetDim();`	*FloorSpace:* `?` *dim1 of main:* `8` *dim2 of main:* `10`

`area(dim1, dim2)`
- - - - - - - - - - - - - - - - - -
In *area*:
 	
`int area(int dim1, int dim2)`
	FloorSpace: `?`
	
	dim1 of main: `8` *dim2 of main:* `8`
	
	dim1 of area: `8` *dim2 of area:* `10`

`return (dim1 * dim2);`	*FloorSpace:* `?` *dim1 of main:* `8` *dim2 of main:* `10` - - - - - - - - - - - - - - - - - - *dim1 of area:* `8` *dim2 of area:* `10` `80`

In *main*:
 	
`FloorSpace =`
`    area(dim1, dim2);`
	FloorSpace: `80`
	
	dim1 of main: `8` *dim2 of main:* `10`

Example 2.24

The following program emphasizes that in pass by value, changing the value of a parameter does not alter the value of the corresponding argument:

```
/*
 * Demonstration of how a function cannot change
 * the contents of a variable passed as a parameter
 * using pass by value
 */
```

Figure 2.16
Scope of the
variables in the
program of
Example 2.22

Scope of Variables	Program

Scope of Variables

dim1 **and** ***dim2***
of *main:*
—exist from declaration
   throughout
   execution of program
—accessible only during
   execution of *main*

dimension:
—exists only during
   execution of *GetDim*

dim1 **and** ***dim2***
of *area:*
—exist only during
   execution of *area*

Program

```
main()
{
     int  dim1,
          dim2;
          ⋮
}
```

```
/**************************/

int GetDim(void)
{
     int dimension;
          ⋮
}
```

```
/**************************/

int area(int dim1, int dim2)
{
          ⋮
}
```

```
#include <stdio.h>

void modify_i(int i);
main()
{
     int i;          /* local to main */

     i = 1;          /* local variable is assigned 1 */

     printf ("Before calling modify_i, i equals %d\n", i);
     modify_i(i);
     printf ("After  calling modify_i, i equals %d\n", i);
}

/*
 * Function modifies parameter i
 * Pre:    none
 * Post:   none
 */

void modify_i(int i)      /* local to modify_i   */
{
     i = 3;               /* parameter is assigned 3 */
}
```

Figure 2.17
Scope of the
variables in the
program of
Example 2.24

Scope of Variables

Program

```
main()
{       ...
        int i;
          ⋮
}
```

***i* of *main*:**
—exists from declaration
 throughout
 execution of program
—accessible only during
 execution of *main*

```
/ * * * * * * * * * * * * * * * * * * * * * * * * /
```

***i* of *modify_i*:**
—exists only during
 execution of *modify_i*

```
void modify_i(int i)
{
          ⋮
}
```

The call to *modify_i* **did not** change the value of the *i* that is local to *main*.

```
Before calling modify_i, i equals 1
After  calling modify_i, i equals 1
```

This program assigns the value 1 to the variable *i* in *main*. It then copies this value into *modify_i*'s formal parameter, *i*, which is not the same variable as the local variable *i* in *main*.

At this point, parameter *i* contains the value 1. Afterwards, the function's assignment statement stores the value 3 in *i*. The function has no more statements to execute, so the formal parameter *i* disappears. Control returns to the main function, and *main*'s local variable *i* still contains the value 1. Figure 2.17 illustrates the scope of these variables.

Local Variables with the Same Name

When we declare a variable of the same name in each of the two functions, we cannot use that variable to communicate between functions. The following example illustrates this principle.

Example 2.25

In the program below, both *main* and *modify_i* have a variable *i*. Because each function declares *i*, they represent different memory locations.

```
/*
 * An attempt at communication between functions
 */

#include <stdio.h>

main()
```

```
{
    void modify_i(void);      /* local to main */
    int i;                    /* local to main */

    i = 1;      /* local i is assigned 1 */

    printf ("Before calling modify_i, i equals %d\n", i);
    modify_i();
    printf ("After  calling modify_i, i equals %d\n", i);
}


/*
 * Function with local variable i
 * Pre:     none
 * Post:    Local variable i is assigned 3.
 */

void modify_i(void)
{
    int i;      /* local to modify_i */

    i = 3;      /* local i is assigned 3 */
}
```

The output demonstrates that the call to *modify_i* **did not** change the value of the *i* in *main*.

```
Before calling modify_i, i equals 1
After  calling modify_i, i equals 1
```

The function *main* declares a variable named *i,* assigns to it the value 1, and calls the function *modify_i*. This function creates its own local variable *i,* and assigns the value 3 to it. This assignment does not affect the variable *i* of *main*. Figure 2.18 emphasizes the scopes of the two *i*'s.

When control returns to the *main* function, the variable *i*—the one local to *main*—still contains the value 1. A function does not terminate, but only suspends, its execution when calling another function. Therefore, the variable *i* local to the *main* function remains in existence while the function *modify_i* is executing. The variable *i* in the function *main* disappears only when *main* finishes execution, which is at the end of the entire program's execution. The variables named *i* in this program behave in a manner similar to the variables *dim1* and *dim2* of the program in Example 2.22. The names of variables may be the same in the calling and called function, but the computer treats them as separate variables.

In this program, we have placed the prototype of the function *modify_i* within, instead of before, *main* as in earlier examples. Consequently, *modify_i* is local to *main;* *main* can call *modify_i*. No other function can call *modify_i* unless it too declares *modify_i* with a prototype. Because no other functions exist, placement of the prototype before or inside *main* is irrelevant for this program.

Figure 2.18
Scope of the
variables in the
program of
Example 2.25

Scope of Variables

Program

i **of** *main:*
—exists from declaration
   throughout
   execution of program
—accessible only during
   execution of *main*

```
main()
{        ...
         int i;
             ⋮
}
```

```
/*************************/
```

```
void modify_i(void)
{
         int i;
             ⋮
}
```

i **of** *modify_i:*
—exists only during
   execution of *modify_i*

Global Variables

One way of implementing communication among functions is with global variables. The program does not declare these variables in a specific function, so they are accessible to all functions after their declarations. If we declare a global variable *i,* then any function can refer to it unless it defines a local variable *i.* A function can assign a value to *i,* and then call another function, which uses the value contained in the same variable *i* to produce a result. Similarly, functions declared before *main* are available to (or global to) *main* and any functions defined after that declaration.

Definition A **global variable** is not declared within a function. Any function defined after the declaration can access that variable as long as the function does not declare its own variable with that name.

Example 2.26

The following program uses a global variable.

```
/*
 * Example of functions using a global variable
 */

#include <stdio.h>

int i;                      /* global */

main()
{
    void modify_i(void);

    i = 1;                      /* global i is assigned 1 */

    printf ("Before calling modify_i, i equals %d\n", i);
```

```
      modify_i();
      printf ("After  calling modify_i, i equals %d\n", i);
}


/*
 * Function modifies global i
 * Pre:     none
 * Post:    Global variable i has been assigned 3.
 */

void modify_i(void)
{
    i = 3;                          /* global i is assigned 3 */
}
```

In this case, the call to *modify_i* **did** change the value of the global i, as shown:

```
Before calling modify_i, i equals 1
After  calling modify_i, i equals 3
```

Figure 2.19 presents the scope of the variable *i*. Because we use a global variable, the logic of this program is less clear than that of the previous example. In the program of Example 2.25, we could look at the function *main* and see all the changes of *i*'s value. In this example, however, when we look at *main,* we see an assignment and a call to the function *modify_i,* with no indication that the function changes the value of *i.* The problem is not the use of a function, but the difficulty of seeing what is happening. Unless we look directly at the definition of *modify_i,* we could never guess that *modify_i* alters the global variable *i.* One rule of good programming is that we should be able to figure out what a function does without having to look elsewhere. For example, when we see the following statement:

```
printf("Hello.\n");
```

we know that the function *printf* prints the contents of the control string and does nothing else.

Figure 2.19
Scope of the global variable *i* in the program of Example 2.26

Scope of Variables
global *i*:

—exists throughout execution of program
—accessible from anywhere in program

Program

```
int i;

main()
{
    ⋮
}

/******************/

void modify_i(void)
{
    ⋮
}
```

A function should be a self-contained entity with a name that describes what the function does.

The function *modify_i* causes **side effects**. The function affects the state of the program as a whole in a way that is not evident from how the calling function uses the called function. Because the function *modify_i* relies on side effects to operate, sound programming methodologies discourage the use of them.

Definition   A **side effect** occurs when a function affects the state of the program as a whole in a way that is not evident from how the calling function uses the called function.

Sound programming practice frowns on the overuse or abuse of global variables. So far as possible, we should avoid the use of global variables. Any global variable should be carefully documented when it is declared and in the functions in which it is referenced.

Example 2.27

The previous example contains only one declaration of *i*. This declaration before *main* makes *i* globally accessible. However, if *modify_i* declares a local variable also with the name *i*, the global variable would no longer be accessible to that function. The following program presents this situation:

```
/*
 * Example of a global variable and local variable
 * with the same name
 */

#include <stdio.h>

int i;                          /* global */

main()
{
    void modify_i(void);

    i = 1;                      /* global i is assigned 1 */

    printf ("Before calling modify_i, i equals %d\n", i);
    modify_i();
    printf ("After  calling modify_i, i equals %d\n", i);
}

/*
 * Function modifies local i
 * Pre:    none
 * Post:   none
 */
```

Figure 2.20
Scope of the global variable *i* and local variable *i* in the program of Example 2.27

Scope of Variables
global *i*:
—exists from declaration throughout execution of program
—accessible anywhere a local *i* is not declared

Program

```
  int i;

  main()
  {
          ⋮
  }
```

```
/ * * * * * * * * * * * * * * * * * * * * * * * /
```

***i* of *modify_i*:**
—exists only during execution of *modify_i*
—makes global *i* inaccessible

```
void modify_i(void)
{
    int i;
        ⋮
}
```

```
void modify_i(void)
{
    int i;            /* local i */
    i = 3;            /* local i is assigned 3 */
}
```

In this case, the call to *modify_i* **did not** change the value of the global *i*.

```
Before calling modify_i, i equals 1
After  calling modify_i, i equals 1
```

Figure 2.20 illustrates the scope of the global *i* and the local *i*.

Section 2.9   Exercises

1. For Example 2.21 of Section 2.7, give the scope of all variables and the function *sqr*.

2. **a.** Give the output of the following program:

```
/ *
 * Exercise program to illustrate scope
 */

#include <stdio.h>

int fnc(int z);
int y;

main()
```

```
{
    int x = 3;

    y = x;
    printf("In main before calling fnc x = %d, y = %d\n",
            x, y);
    x = fnc(4);
    printf("In main after calling fnc x = %d, y = %d\n",
            x, y);
}

/*
 * Function called by main
 */

int fnc(int z)
{
    int x = 10;

    printf("In fnc x = %d, y = %d, z = %d\n", x, y, z);
    y = z;
    return 50;
}
```

b. Give the scopes of the variables and of *fnc*.

c. Which variables are local and which are global?

d. Are there side effects?

3. Repeat Exercise 2 for the following program:

```
/*
 * Exercise program to illustrate scope
 */

#include <stdio.h>

void fnc(int x);

main()
{
    int x = 8,
        y = 12;

    printf("In main before calling fnc x = %d, y = %d\n",
            x, y);
    fnc(y);
    printf("In main after calling fnc x = %d, y = %d\n",
            x, y);
}
```

```
/*
 * Function called by main
 */

void fnc(int x)
{
    int y = 30;

    x = 2 * x;
    printf("In fnc x = %d, y = %d\n", x, y);
}
```

Programming and Debugging Hints

Clarity of Comments

The need for clear, understandable programs cannot be overstressed. Clarity is essential both for the internal documentation that helps a reader understand the program logic and for the manner in which the program communicates with the user. We should use comments generously and arrange them to catch the eye of the reader. Comments should be

- intelligent
- well placed
- uncluttered
- not obvious

For example,

```
/* add 1 to NumCopies */
```

is an unnecessary comment, because the reader understands the meaning of the code from the statement itself. If such an explanation is necessary, a more useful comment would describe the significance of adding 1 to *NumCopies,* such as the following:

```
/* extra copy for president */
```

The header comment for a function is especially important. Descriptive header comments can help the programmer to correct his or her own code or to maintain the code of another. A header comment should contain the following components:

- a description of the task the function performs
- preconditions or the conditions that must hold for the function to perform its task, including a description of all input parameters
- postconditions or the state of the program after execution of the function, including error conditions and the information the function returns or otherwise communicates to the calling routine

The following header comment is for a function that returns the square of an integer parameter:

```
/*
 * Function to return the square of an integer
 * Pre:  num is an integer.
 * Post: The function has returned the square of num.
 */
```

Today's computers have storage capacities that can easily handle this extra text. The compiled program does not include comments, so they do not affect the efficiency of the program. Badly conceived comments can mislead and confuse the reader, so all documentation should be appropriate and to the point.

Clarity of Code

The programmer should choose identifiers to describe their purposes clearly. Fortunately, the length of names is not limited. A variable name should not take up an entire line, but we should also avoid excessive abbreviation. For example, it is difficult to determine the nature of the variables *v* and *nbk* or of function *calc*. By contrast, the identifiers *volume, NumberOfBooks,* and *CalculateTax* are much more descriptive.

Clarity of User Interface

We should program messages for the user as carefully as we do internal documentation. Some users may have little or no experience in computer programming. Even for a seasoned programmer, a message such as

```
Enter a value for variable pdq
```

is not helpful. The prompt should describe the required data and not give the name of a variable.

A program should explain its purpose, expected input, planned output, and other pertinent information. For example, an opening description for a program might read as follows:

```
This program will allow you to input an integer to square.
For example, if you input 97, the program will output
9409.
```

A prompt should clearly specify the nature of the desired input and, where applicable, the allowable values. For example, the following are descriptive prompts:

```
Enter the length of the road in miles:
Give the number of children:
What is your aunt's name?
Are you registered to vote? (y/n)
```

When necessary, the program should also specify the format of the input, such as

```
Type the amount of purchase
   (Omit $ and comma, such as 4247.56):
Enter your 7-digit ATM number.
```

We should clearly label output from the program, because the results of the computations are useless if the user does not know what the results mean. Consequently, output of

```
1849
```

can be perplexing to the user. The following statement is far more meaningful:

```
The square of 43 is 1849.
```

Attention to descriptive and readable directions, prompts, and output is part of effective human-computer interface.

≈≈≈ **Key Terms**

% 71
%% 74
%d 57
& 94
* 68
+ 68
− 68
/ 68
= 62
abs 97
addition 68
ampersand 94
assignment operator 62
assignment statement 62
batch program 94
binary operator 69
conversion specification 57
debugger 74
diagnostic print 74
division 68

dummy parameter 99
executable statement 61
expression 69
floating point number 57
formal parameter 99
global variable 120
heading 100
increment 66
initialize 67
int 57
integer 56
integer function 100
interactive program 93
local variable 115
lvalue 62
modulus operator 71
multiplication 68
operator precedence 75
parameter 99
pass by value 115

postcondition 98
precondition 98
priority of operators 75
procedural abstraction 97
procedure 101
prompt 94
prototype 113
return statement 100
rvalue 62
scanf 94
scope 115
self-documenting 60
side effect 122
subtraction 68
truncate 69
type 57
unary minus 75
variable 57
variable declaration 57
white space 63

≈≈≈ **Summary**

This chapter considers how C handles integer constants, variables, and functions. In mathematics, the set of integers is {..., −3, −2, −1, 0, 1, 2, 3, ...}. We declare a variable to be of the integer type *int* by writing

```
int variable;
```

The rules for naming a variable in C are the same as those for naming a function. The identifier can contain any combination of letters, digits, and underscores, but must begin with a letter or underscore (_) and cannot be a keyword. The compiler is case sensitive, and at least the first 31 characters in a name are significant. To enhance readability, a programmer should use descriptive variable names.

The assignment statement, which is one of the basic building blocks of C, has the following general format:

```
variable = expression;
```

When executing an assignment statement, the computer evaluates the expression and places its value in the memory location for the variable. An assignment statement is not an algebraic statement. For example, execution of

```
variable = variable + 1;
```

increments the value of the variable by 1. We can initialize a variable while declaring it, such as:

```
int variable = value;
```

or in a separate assignment statement, such as:

```
int variable;
variable = value;
```

Five binary arithmetic operations are addition (+), subtraction (−), multiplication (*), division (/), and modulus (%). In C, the result of *n* / *m*, where *n* and *m* are integers, is the integer quotient. The result of *n* % *m* is the remainder in the division of integer *m* into integer *n*. The unary minus operation (−*n*) produces a value with the same magnitude but the opposite sign of *n*. By operator precedence in C, unary minus is evaluated first. Multiplication, division, and modulus have the next highest priority. Addition and subtraction have a lower priority.

An interactive program converses with the user during program execution. To read interactively in C, we use the function *scanf*. In *scanf*, the ampersand symbol precedes any integer variable, such as &*num*, which is the memory address of the variable *num*. Before reading, the program should prompt or request the user to enter data. The following segment prompts the user for an integer, reads the user's response into a variable *num*, and prints the value.

```
printf("Type an integer: ");
scanf("%d", &num);
printf("You entered %d\n", num);
```

To read values for several variables, the control string of *scanf* has a conversion specification for each variable and commas separate the variable addresses, as follows:

```
scanf("%d %d %d", &month, &day, &year);
```

In the analysis and design of a program, we should develop its preconditions and postconditions. Preconditions describe the situation that exists as the module is to begin execution, any assumptions, and the information the module needs to meet its objectives. Postconditions describe the state of the system when the module finishes executing, any error conditions, and the information the module returns or otherwise communicates. The definition of an integer function with two integer parameters has the form

```
/*
 * description of function's task
 * Pre:  preconditions
 * Post: postconditions
 */

int function_name(int parm1, int parm2)
{
    ⋮
    return (expression);
}
```

The *return* statement can also take the following form:

```
return expression;
```

An argument and its corresponding parameter do not have to have the same name. Arguments and parameters for a function, however, must agree in number, type, and position. C uses the pass by value method of passing information to a function. In this method, the parameter receives a copy of the value of the argument.

The scope of a variable is the range within a program over which that variable has meaning. A variable is local to a function if that function contains a declaration of the variable. The name of a local variable has meaning only within the declaring function from the point of declaration. The scope of a parameter is only the function that declares it. If we declare a variable of the same name in each of two functions, we cannot use that variable to communicate between functions. A global variable is not declared within a function. Any function defined after the declaration of the global variable can access that variable as long as the function does not declare its own variable with that name. When a function alters the value of a global variable, it creates a side effect. We should avoid the use of global variables.

Review Questions

1. What is an integer?

2. What is a variable?

3. What is the form of the assignment statement?

4. In order to store the result of a computation, what kind of statement must be used?

5. Why is the assignment statement regarded as dynamic?

6. How many variables may appear on the left of the equal sign in an assignment statement?

7. Which of the following variable names are valid in C?

   a. *bingo*   **b.** *accts_payable*   **c.** *total-revenue*

   d. *ANNUAL REPORT*   **e.** *acc'ts*

8. What are the rules for naming variables?

9. What purpose is served by including white space in a program?

10. Comment briefly on the following assignment statement:

    ```
    x + y = z;
    ```

11. Which of the two operators, multiplication or division, has the higher precedence?

12. Distinguish between the binary and the unary minus.

13. How may the variable x be declared to be of type *int* and at the same time have the value 456 assigned to it?

14. What is meant by truncation?

15. What role is played by parentheses in evaluating expressions?

16. What is the modulus operator, and how does it work?

17. How would you print the % symbol?

18. Find the results of the following expressions:

    a. 17 % 3   **b.** 20 % 4   **c.** 15 % 15

    d. 6 % 5   **e.** −(9 % 4)   **f.** −9 % 4

19. What function enables a user to input information while the program is executing?

20. What statement should precede every interactive call with the *scanf* function, and why?

21. If a number is entered by means of the *scanf* function, what symbol must precede the corresponding variable name?

22. When is the execution of a function terminated?

23. Describe the role played by the *sizeof* operator (see Section 2.4).

24. Does the *sizeof* operator return the same values on all computers (see Section 2.4)?

25. What are the two different kinds of operands that *sizeof* can take (see Section 2.4)?

26. What is the essential difference between a function call written as a solitary statement and one that is part of an expression or statement?

27. How many values can a function return?

28. Name some primary features of good programming.

29. What is a side effect? Give an example.

30. How is a function invoked?

31. What role does the *return* statement play?

32. Where are declarations of global variables placed within a program?

33. Distinguish between local and global variables.

34. What is a parameter?

35. What is the difference between an argument and a parameter?

36. How many arguments can be passed to a function?

37. What are the rules regarding the relationship between the arguments passed to a function and its parameters?

38. Name two keywords.

39. For the statement

    ```
    scanf("%d %d", &x, &y);
    ```

    how must the user enter the values?

40. What are preconditions?

41. What are postconditions?

Laboratory

Copy all the files (LAB021.c, LAB022.c, LAB023.c, and LAB024.c) *mentioned in this laboratory from the disk that came with your text to your own disk. By working with copies, you preserve the originals for future reference.*

1. The purpose of this laboratory exercise is to improve understanding of the declaration of integers, the assignment statement, arithmetic operations, the *scanf* function, and user-defined integer functions. We develop various versions of the program, considering new features with each version.

   The program takes integer values for speed (rate of travel) and time elapsed and calculates distance covered. The algebraic formula for the computation is as follows:

   $$d = rt$$

   where r = rate, t = time, and d = distance. For example, if we drive for 2 hours at exactly (or at an average) 55 miles per hour, then we cover

   $$\frac{55 \text{ miles}}{\text{hour}} \times 2 \text{ hours} = 110 \text{ miles}$$

a. The first version of this program assigns values to rate and time variables, calculates distance, and prints all three values. Write pseudocode for the program.

b. Below is a shell of the C program in file *LAB021.c*. Replace the comments with statements. Use descriptive variable names, not just single letters. Have the program print values of the three variables embedded in a sentence. After the program runs successfully, print the listing and output.

```
/* Opening comment that describes the program */
/* Preprocessor directive to include header file stdio.h */

main()
{
    /* Declarations of 3 variables with comments for each */

    /* Initialization of speed and time elapsed */
    /* Calculation of distance covered */
    /* Print values of 3 variables */
}
```

c. Change the program to use declaration-initialization statements instead of separate declarations and assignments. Make these changes in your program and test it. What change(s) did you make from Part b?

d. Change the program to prompt the user and to read values for the speed and time. Remember to type an ampersand before each variable name in the call to *scanf*. Make these changes in your program and debug it.

e. Starting with the version from Part d, place the computation of the distance traveled in a function that receives the speed and time and returns the distance. Be sure to have a comment that explains the function's purpose and gives pre- and postconditions. Omit the variable for distance in *main* and have the call to your function in the *printf*. After the program runs successfully, print the listing and the output from several executions.

2. The goal of this exercise is to examine *scanf* and *printf* and to make some observations about integers. We use file *LAB022.c,* which is an interactive program to read and print an integer.

```
/*
 * This program tests the arguments of scanf and printf
 */

#include <stdio.h>

main()
{
    int num;    /* stores an input value */

    printf("Type an integer:  ");
    scanf("%d", &num);
    printf("        You typed %d\n", num);
}
```

a. Run the program to ensure you understand its actions.

b. Test the program with an integer larger than those that your computer can store, perhaps 5000000000. Do not type commas in your input data. What number does the computer print? Execute again with a negative integer smaller than those your computer can store. Explain the discrepancies.

c. Test the program using an integer with a comma, such as 12,345. What answer does the computer print and why?

d. Execute the program again and enter a decimal number that is not an integer, such as 34.85. What answer does the computer print and why?

e. Remove the ampersand in front of *num* in *scanf*, and explain the results.

```
scanf("%d", num);
```

f. Remove the conversion specification in the call to *scanf*, and explain the results.

```
scanf(&num);
```

g. Remove *num* from the call to *scanf*, and explain the results.

```
scanf("%d");
```

h. Restore the *scanf*, but type an ampersand before *num* in the *printf*. Explain the results.

```
scanf("%d", &num);
printf("           You typed %d\n", &num);
```

i. Remove the conversion specification and the incorrect ampersand from the call to *printf*, and explain the results.

```
printf("                You typed \n", num);
```

3. The goal of this exercise is to study operator precedence and the truncation effect of integer division. The following formulas convert a temperature in Fahrenheit (F) to its equivalent in Celsius (C) and vice versa:

$$C = \frac{5}{9}(F - 32)$$

$$F = \frac{9}{5}C + 32$$

For example, 77° F is 25° C, as shown:

$$C = \frac{5}{9}(77 - 32) = \frac{5}{9}(45) = 25$$

Using the second formula, we see that 25° C is 77° F:

$$F = \frac{9}{5}(25) + 32 = 45 + 32 = 77$$

a. Write code on paper for the first formula as given, performing the division first.

b. In integer arithmetic, what is 5/9?

c. Suppose variables in the assignment statement in Part a are integer variables. Using your answer from Part b, what do we always get for the Celsius temperature?

d. To minimize the effect of division truncation, rearrange the expression so that multiplication occurs before division.

e. The C program below is in file *LAB023.c* of your laboratory disk. The program reads a temperature in Fahrenheit and calculates the corresponding integer Celsius temperature. Fill in the body of the function that has a parameter of *Fahrenheit* and returns the desired value. Remember to have your function send a value back to the calling routine. Test the program with several values and check the answers.

```
/*
 * This program reads a temperature in Fahrenheit and
 * calculates the equivalent Celsius temperature.
 */


#include <stdio.h>

int F_to_C(int Fahrenheit);

main()
{
    int Fahrenheit,    /* temperature in Fahrenheit */
        Celsius;       /* temperature in Celsius    */

    printf("This program converts a temperature in\n");
    printf("Fahrenheit to Celsius and vice versa.\n");
    printf("All measurements are in whole numbers.\n\n");
    printf("Please enter a Fahrenheit temperature:  ");
    scanf("%d", &Fahrenheit);

    Celsius = F_to_C(Fahrenheit);
    printf("%d degrees Fahrenheit = %d degrees Celsius\n",
            Fahrenheit, Celsius);
}

/*
 * Given an integer Fahrenheit degree measurement, this
 * function returns the corresponding integer Celsius
 * measurement.
 * Pre:  Fahrenheit is an integer.
 * Post: The function has returned the corresponding
 *       integer Celsius measurement.
 */

int F_to_C(int Fahrenheit)
{
    /*** Fill in ***/
}
```

f. Discuss how to write the second formula to minimize the effect of division truncation.

g. Add to the program a prototype and definition for a function *C_to_F* with parameter *Celsius*. Given an integer Celsius degree measurement, this function returns the corresponding integer Fahrenheit measurement. Be careful of the order of the operations. Add statements in *main* to read a measurement in Celsius, call this function to make the conversion, and print the corresponding Fahrenheit temperature. Test the program, checking your answers. Print the listing and several runs.

h. For several executions of the program from Part g, enter a number for the Fahrenheit measurement and the corresponding temperature for the Celsius measurement. One sample run might appear as follows:

```
This program converts a temperature in
Fahrenheit to Celsius and vice versa.
All measurements are in whole numbers.

Please enter a Fahrenheit temperature:  73
73 degrees Fahrenheit = 22 degrees Celsius

Please enter a Celsius temperature:  22
22 degrees Celsius = 71 degrees Fahrenheit
```

Explain the discrepancy in the Fahrenheit temperatures.

4. The goal of this exercise is to study the scope of variables and functions. The following program is in file *LAB024.c* on your disk.

```
/*
 * This program illustrates global variables
 */

#include <stdio.h>

void print_var(void);
int var;            /* a global variable */

main()
{
    var = 300;

    printf("main before print_global: var = %d\n", var);
    print_var();
    printf("main after print_global: var = %d\n", var);
}


/*
 * This function produces a side effect
 */
```

```
void print_var(void)
{
    printf("print_var before assignment:  var = %d\n",
           var);
    var = 2 * var + 7;
    printf("print_var after  assignment:  var = %d\n",
           var);
}
```

a. Run the program and explain the results. What is the side effect?

b. Move the declaration of *var* into *main*. Change the comment accompanying *var*, because it is now a local variable. Attempt to compile the program. Describe the compilation problem.

c. Overcome this problem by passing *var* as a parameter to *print_var*. Be sure to change the first line of the definition, the prototype of *print_var*, and the call to *print_var* to reflect this improvement. Why is it an improvement?

d. Suppose we want to return this adjusted value of *var* to *main* so that the output matches Part a's output. Make the following adjustments for this new version:

(1) Change the prototype of *print_var*.

(2) Change the first line of the definition of *print_var*.

(3) Add a *return* statement to *print_var*.

(4) Change the statement in *main* that calls *print_var* to an assignment statement.

After debugging the program, print the listing and a sample run. Why is this version better than the original version?

Making Decisions

Introduction

Computers are renowned not only for their ability to execute a large number of instructions at lightning speed, but also for their ability to make decisions. The easy-to-use decision-making constructs in the C language enable us to employ the computer as a tool to make sophisticated judgments.

The computer's decisions, performed during execution time, may involve comparison of values. For example, we might compare the value of a variable *GPA* with a certain grade point average, say 3.00. One statement for making decisions, the *if* statement, causes the computer to perform a task if a condition holds. For example, if a student's grade point average is greater than or equal to 3.00, we can have the computer print that the student is on the Dean's List.

The *if-else* statement makes a two-way comparison. For example, if the number of semester hours the student has earned, *hours,* is less than 60, we might want to print that he or she is in a lower class. Otherwise, we want the computer to display that the student is in an upper class.

For selecting one of several choices, we can use the *switch* statement. For example, we might want to print the day of the week, based on the value (0–6) of an integer variable *day.* As another example, suppose we have the computer display a menu on the screen asking if the user wants directions to the library, bookstore, student center,

137

cafeteria, administration building, or a dorm. The *switch* statement can process the user's answer, to display an appropriate map.

The condition tested by each decision statement can involve a combination of several comparisons. For example, if a student has a grade point average of at least 3.00 and more than 60 semester hours, then we could have the computer deduct $50 from his or her tuition.

After a discussion of various decision-making constructs and applications in C, this chapter contains a breadth section on logic. Logic provides the theoretical basis for the design of computers and of programs.

With additional features, such as the ability to make decisions, the programs we develop gradually become more involved. In the last section of this chapter, we consider two methods of implementing and testing code. The top-down scheme parallels the top-down approach of program design, whereas the bottom-up scheme implements and tests low-level functions before proceeding to higher-level ones. Regardless of the approach, we should test modules in an organized fashion, one at a time, so that errors are easier to find and correct.

Goals

To study

- Relational operators that compare values
- Logical operators that combine and negate conditions that are true or false
- The *if* statement for making decisions
- The *if-else* statement for making two-way decisions
- The *switch* statement for making multiple-way decisions
- Logic, which is the foundation of computer and program design
- Top-down and bottom-up testing

Section 3.1 **Relational and Logical Operators**

As its name implies, the *if* statement is used to make decisions. If a certain condition is true, we direct the computer to take one course of action. If the condition is false, we instruct the computer to do something else. This abstraction is a fundamental concept in computer science.

The most basic form of an *if* statement is as follows:

```
if (expression)
    statement
```

For example,

```
if (x < y)
    printf("%d is smaller than %d\n", x, y);
```

If *x* is less than *y*, then the computer prints a statement to that effect. Otherwise, the computer skips the *printf*.

Before we continue with a detailed discussion of the *if* statement, we explain the relational (such as <) and logical operators that we use in defining the conditions in the *if* statement. In this explanation, we use a few *if* statements as examples, but they are simple and largely self-explanatory. The subsequent discussion of the *if* statement clarifies the material further.

Relational Operators

A **relational operator** is a symbol that we use to test the relationship between two expressions, such as two variables. For example, we make the test for equality employing two adjacent equal signs with no space separating them (==). C has six relational operators, defined in the following table:

Relational Operator	Meaning
==	equal to
>	greater than
<	less than
!=	not equal to
>=	greater than or equal to
<=	less than or equal to

Definition A **relational operator** is a symbol that we use to test the relationship between two expressions. The relational operators in C are == (equal to), > (greater than), < (less than), != (not equal to), >= (greater than or equal to), and <= (less than or equal to).

Operators with two characters must not contain spaces. The expression ($n == 7$) means, "Is the value of the variable n equal to 7?" The answer to this question obviously is either yes or no. In programming logic, however, we use the terms *TRUE* and *FALSE* instead. C encodes *FALSE* as zero and *TRUE* as a nonzero integer.

A common error in C is to forget that the *if* statement's test for equality requires two consecutive equal signs, rather than the single one for assignments. A single equal sign in an *if* statement is not a syntax error, but the symbol's incorrect application produces the wrong results.

Example 3.1

Suppose we use the assignment operator (=) instead of the relational operator (==) in a test. For example, we have

```
if (x = y)                          /* ERROR */
    printf("Values are equal\n");
```

Two rules of the language cause this application of the assignment equal not to be a syntax error. First, when the computer executes ($x = y$), it not only assigns y's value to x, but gives the assignment expression the same value. For instance, suppose we have

```
x = 5;
y = 8;
```

After execution of ($x = y$), both the variable x and the expression ($x = y$) have the value 8. Now, the computer executes

```
if (8)                              /* ERROR */
    printf("Values are equal\n");
```

The second feature of C that contributes to the error is that C does not have a separate type for *TRUE* and *FALSE* but employs *int*. In other words, it interprets zero as *FALSE* and any nonzero integer as *TRUE*. Because 8 is not zero, the condition is true, and the computer prints

```
Values are equal.
```

Only when *y* has the value 0,

```
y = 0;
```

is the condition (*x* = *y*) zero, meaning *FALSE*. In this case, the computer changes *x*'s value so that *x* and *y* are both 0, but it does not execute the call to *printf*.

> When unpredictable results occur, the programmer should carefully check all tests for equality to make sure the correct operator, ==, is present.

If the left-hand side of the assignment operator contains a constant, we obtain a syntax error.

```
if (8 = y)                    /* ERROR */
   printf("Values are equal\n");
```

In this case, the compiler detects an attempt to assign the value of *y* to the constant 8 and issues an error message, such as

```
lvalue required
```

This message does not indicate the real problem—an incorrect operator—but notifies the programmer of an attempt to change the value of a constant. An rvalue, 8, was used when an lvalue, such as a variable, is required. The computer interprets our instructions as best it can, but sometimes a computer's message does not reveal the real root of the problem.

___

Logical Operators

Logical operators are symbols that we use to combine or negate expressions containing relational operators. For example, we might want a program to perform certain steps if *n* is equal to 7 AND *x* is greater than 5. To code this type of expression, we employ the logical operator **AND** in conjunction with the relational operators == and >. C represents the AND operator by a symbol, **&&**. (Do not confuse this operator with the single ampersand, which we use with the *scanf* function.) Thus, to code "if *n* is equal to y and *x* is greater than 5" we write

```
if ((n == 7) && (x > 5))
```

The **compound condition** (*n* == 7) && (*x* > 5) is true only when both (*n* == 7) and (*x* > 5) are true. In every other circumstance, the condition is false. Table 3.1 summarizes this rule in a **truth table** with "T" indicating *TRUE* and "F" replacing *FALSE*. With *p* representing (*n* == 7) and *q* representing (*x* > 5), we read the first line of this table as, "When *p* is false and *q* is false, then *p* && *q* is false." Notice that the only way to get a *TRUE* from an AND is for both (or all) conditions to be true.

Table 3.1   Truth table for p && q

p	q	p && q	Interpretation
F	F	F	*FALSE* AND *FALSE* is *FALSE*
F	T	F	*FALSE* AND *TRUE* is *FALSE*
T	F	F	*TRUE* AND *FALSE* is *FALSE*
T	T	T	*TRUE* AND *TRUE* is *TRUE*

As Table 3.1 indicates, if either p or q (or both) is *FALSE,* so is p && q. If the first condition, $p,$ is *FALSE,* we need not determine the truth or falsity of the second, q. In C, the computer stops evaluation of a logical expression as soon as it can determine the value, *TRUE* or *FALSE,* of the expression.

When at least one of two conditions must be true in order for the compound condition to be true, we use the logical operator **OR**. For example, the compound condition ($n == 7$) OR ($x > 5$) is true in every situation, except when both ($n == 7$) and ($x > 5$) are false. Two consecutive vertical bars (||) represent the OR operator in C. On most keyboards, the vertical bar is on the same key as the backslash character. Table 3.2 has the truth table for p || q. We read the second line of the table as, "If p is false or q is true, then p || q is true." As that and the remaining lines reveal, if p or q or both are true, then p || q is true.

The last two lines of Table 3.2 show that, regardless of the value of q, a value of *TRUE* for p results in the expression p || q being *TRUE*. Thus, if p is *TRUE*, without evaluating q, the computer immediately returns a value of *TRUE* for the expression p || q.

A third logical operator, **NOT**, is represented by a single exclamation point (!). As Table 3.3 indicates, this operator reverses the truth value of the expression to its immediate right. We can do the same thing by changing an expression so that it uses the inverse relational operator. For example,

```
if (!(n <= 4))
```

is equivalent to

```
if (n > 4)
```

In many cases, this latter notation is preferable because it is simpler.

Definition   A **logical operator** is a symbol that we use to combine or negate expressions that are true or false. The logical operators in C are ! (NOT), && (AND), and || (OR).

Table 3.2   Truth table for p || q

p	q	p || q	Interpretation
F	F	F	*FALSE* OR *FALSE* is *FALSE*
F	T	T	*FALSE* OR *TRUE* is *TRUE*
T	F	T	*TRUE* OR *FALSE* is *TRUE*
T	T	T	*TRUE* OR *TRUE* is *TRUE*

Table 3.3 Truth table for !*p*

p	!*p*	Interpretation
F	T	NOT *FALSE* is *TRUE*
T	F	NOT *TRUE* is *FALSE*

Boolean Constants, Expressions, and Variables

A condition having the value *TRUE* or *FALSE*, such as ($x > 3$), is called a **logical** or **boolean expression**, and *TRUE* and *FALSE* are the **boolean constants** or **boolean values**. C has a data type for integer variables and constants, *int*, but the language has no special data type for boolean expressions or values. In C, integers represent these boolean constants. In the context of relational or logical operators, C interprets zero as *FALSE* and any other integer as *TRUE*. For example, to test if a **boolean variable** *n* is *TRUE*, we could start the *if* statement

```
if (n != 0)
```

or we could use the equivalent

```
if (n)
```

Testing for truth corresponds to testing for a nonzero value.

Definitions A **logical** or **boolean expression** is a condition having the value *TRUE* or *FALSE*, and a **boolean variable** is a variable that can have the value *TRUE* or *FALSE*. The **boolean constants** or **boolean values** are *TRUE* and *FALSE*. For a boolean expression, C interprets zero as *FALSE* and any nonzero number as *TRUE*.

For more readable code, we can use the *#define* preprocessor directive to give meaningful aliases to 0 and 1, as follows:

```
#define FALSE 0
#define TRUE  1
```

Thus, for boolean (*int*) variable *n*, instead of writing

```
if (n != 0)
```

we use

```
if (n == TRUE)
```

We can assign a boolean constant or expression to a boolean variable. Thus, we can have the following:

```
int cont,    /* boolean variable, TRUE if should continue */
    IsSenior; /* boolean variable, TRUE if senior status */

cont    = TRUE;
IsSenior = (hours > 100);
```

The first assignment gives the boolean variable *cont* the value *TRUE* (nonzero). The second assigns the value of (*hours* > 100) to *IsSenior*. Thus, if *hours* is greater than 100, the expression is *TRUE*, and *IsSenior* gets the value *TRUE*. If *hours* is less than or equal to 100, the expression (*hours* > 100) is *FALSE*, and *IsSenior* becomes *FALSE*.

Table 3.4 Precedence of operators in descending order

( )	highest
! − (unary)	
* / %	
+ − (binary)	
< <= > >=	
== !=	
&&	
||	
=	lowest

Operator Precedence

In C, every operator has its place in the order of precedence. We have already discussed the precedence of various mathematical operators. For example, multiplication and division take precedence over addition and subtraction. In the same way, the computer performs mathematical operations before the relational operators, and these relational operators take precedence over the binary logical operators. Other than the assignment operator (=), the computer executes binary operators that have the same precedence from left to right in the expression. Table 3.4 lists the operators in descending order of precedence. We add to this table as we cover additional operators. Appendix C contains a complete list of the operators in order of precedence.

Example 3.2

Among the logical operators, NOT has the highest priority, whereas AND takes precedence over OR. As with mathematical operators, expressions within parentheses are evaluated before anything outside the parentheses. Thus, for boolean variables p, q, and r, which are true or false, the following code segment

```
if (p && !q || r)
```

is equivalent to

```
if ((p && (!q)) || r)
```

The computer first evaluates $!q$, then $(p \&\& (!q))$, and then ORs the result with r.

In Table 3.4, the computer evaluates the assignment operator after all the others. Thus,

```
x = y + 3;
```

indicates to evaluate $y + 3$ first and assign the resulting value to x.

Example 3.3

Because of C's storage of boolean values as integers, we must be especially careful in using relational and logical operators. In mathematics, we often write statements with two relational operators, such as

$$2 < x < 5$$

which asserts that x is between 2 and 5. Unfortunately, if we use the same arrangement in C code, we obtain unpredictable results.

```
if (2 < x < 5)                        /* ERROR */
    printf("x is between 2 and 5\n");
```

The *if* statement contains two binary operators (<) with the same precedence. The computer evaluates these from left to right, as follows:

```
if ((2 < x) < 5)                      /* ERROR */
    printf("x is between 2 and 5\n");
```

If the relational expression $(2 < x)$ is true, it produces a value of 1. If false, it gives a value of 0. Thus, for the compound condition, the computer tests $(1 < 5)$ or $(0 < 5)$. Because both are true, the condition is always true. Regardless of the value of x, the computer prints that x is between 2 and 5. Thus, to correctly check if x is between the two numbers, we must use two relational expressions connected with a logical operator.

```
if ((2 < x) && (x < 5))               /* This is CORRECT */
    printf("x is between 2 and 5\n");
```

Example 3.4

Sometimes we might not remember the rules of precedence, but we can always use parentheses to express our intentions explicitly. Moreover, an expression with parentheses is often clearer than an equivalent one that depends on the priority of operators. For example,

```
if (x < y && z + 3 == w)
```

is confusing, while the equivalent

```
if ((x < y) && (z + 3 == w))
```

or even

```
if ((x < y) && ((z + 3) == w)))
```

is far more understandable. The computer evaluates the truth or falsity of $(x < y)$. After the evaluation of $z + 3$ is the test for that value being equal to w. The entire compound expression is true only if both relational expressions are true.

Clarify the operator precedence in an expression by using parentheses.

Section 3.1 Exercises

Write an English phrase corresponding to the C code in Exercises 1–6.

1. `if (x >= y)...`   **2.** `if (x < 3 || y == 3)...`

3. `if (x % 3 == 0)...`   **4.** `cont = count < 50`

5. `if ((x <= 80) && (x > 0))...`   **6.** `if (!(x > 0))...`

Write the C expression that would appear in an if *statement to test each condition in Exercises 7–19.*

   7. x is greater than 56   **8.** the sum of x and y is negative

   9. z is not 9   **10.** y has the value 73

11. y is at most 100   **12.** half of z is at least 20

13. x is evenly divisible by 2   **14.** both x and y are positive

15. x is between 0 and 10 inclusively   **16.** x is greater than 5 or less than -5

17. x or y is 20   **18.** x is not equal to 0 and y is nonnegative

19. x is larger than y, which is larger than z

For Exercises 20–25 place parentheses to indicate the order of execution of the operations.

20. `x % 10 == 5`   **21.** `x != z <= 3`   **22.** `x = y > 0`

23. `x < 15 || !y > 0`   **24.** `x >= y && z == 3`   **25.** `x || y && !z`

Evaluate the expressions in Exercises 26–34, assuming $x = 5$, $y = 3$, and $z = 8$.

26. `x == 5`   **27.** `x = 7`   **28.** `x == z`   **29.** `x = z`

30. `x < y < z`   **31.** `z < x < y`   **32.** `x = y < z`   **33.** `!(x > y)`

34. `x > z < y`

Section 3.2 Selection

Flow of Control

The **flow of control** of a program is the order in which the computer executes statements. Much of the time, the flow of control is sequential, the computer executing statements one after another in sequence. We refer to such segments of code as a **sequential control structure**. A **control structure** consists of statements that determine the flow of control of a program or algorithm.

Definitions   The **flow of control** of a program is the order in which the computer executes statements. A **control structure** consists of statements that determine the flow of control of a program or an algorithm. With a **sequential control structure**, the computer executes statements one after another in sequence.

The sequential flow can be altered by the call to a function. With modular programming, we decompose the solution to a problem into separate tasks, which we can implement as functions. Thus, another control structure is the **modular control structure**.

Definition With a **modular control structure**, the computer suspends execution of the current module to execute another module. When execution of the called module finishes, execution continues in the calling module.

The flow of control can also be altered by a **selection control structure**. With such a control structure, the computer makes a decision by evaluating a logical expression. Depending on the outcome of the decision, program execution continues in one direction or another. C can implement the selection control structure with the *if* statement. The logical expression used in making the decision involves boolean variables, relational operators, and logical operators, which we discussed in the preceding section.

Definition With a **selection control structure**, the computer decides which statement to execute next depending on the value of a logical expression.

The *if* Statement

The simplest form of the *if* statement is as follows:

```
if (expression)
    statement
```

We must follow the keyword *if* with a set of parentheses containing the expression that we are testing. A single C statement follows the parentheses. As Figure 3.1 illustrates, this statement is only executed if the expression evaluates as *TRUE*. If the programmer wants more than one statement at this point, he or she can surround the segment with

Figure 3.1
Diagram of choices in the *if* statement

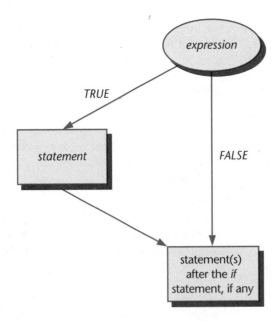

braces to form a **compound statement** or **block**. In the following format, we line up the braces and indent the statements within the braces to make the structure easy to read.

```
if (expression)
{
    statement
        ⋮
    statement
}
```

For example, we can write the following:

```
if ((2 < x) && (x < 5))
{
    printf("x is greater than 2 and \n");
    printf("x is less than 5.\n");
}
```

Some people prefer alternative arrangements, but regardless of the format, the programmer should strive for consistency and readability. We can also enclose a single statement within braces, which is a compound statement with one statement. For example, we can have

```
if ((2 < x) && (x < 5))
{
    printf("x is between 2 and 5\n");
}
```

Definition   A **compound statement** or **block** in C has the following form
```
{
    statement
        ⋮
    statement
}
```

Example 3.5 _____

The program in this example asks the user to choose a positive integer less than 10, and then determines whether the number selected was 7. Pseudocode for the problem reveals use of the *if* statement.

> *main( )*
>   Interactive program to determine if input is 7
>
> *Algorithm:*
>   prompt the user for a number less than 10
>   read the number
>   if the number is 7
>   indicate the number is 7
>   print a good-bye

C code follows the pseudocode closely, as shown:

```
/*
 * Example 3.5.  Program to read a number less than
 * 10 and determine if the number is 7
 */

#include <stdio.h>

main()
{
    int num;

    printf("Enter a positive integer under 10: ");
    scanf("%d", &num);

    if (num == 7)
        printf("I knew you'd select 7!\n");

    printf("Thank you for your cooperation.\n");
}
```

In the following sample run the user enters 7. Because *num* contains the value 7, the expression (*num* == 7) is true. Therefore, the computer prints the message in the first *printf,* "I knew you'd select 7!"

```
Enter a positive integer under 10: 7
I knew you'd select 7!
Thank you for your cooperation.
```

Because program execution can follow one of two different paths, we should see the output from a different input value. In the second test run, *num* contains a value other than 7. Therefore, the expression is false, and the computer only calls the second *printf.*

```
Enter a positive integer under 10: 3
Thank you for your cooperation.
```

The *if-else* Statement

The last program prints only the general good-bye message if the user selects a number other than 7. Suppose we wished to respond with a message like "Why didn't you pick 7?" We could add this option by inserting the following *if* statement after the first one:

```
if (num != 7)
    printf("Why didn't you pick 7?\n");
```

With this method, only one *if* statement would be true for any number the user enters. The computer would print only one of the two messages along with the unconditional message, "Thank you for your cooperation."

It is wasteful, however, to make two comparisons each time, knowing that only one expression is true for any value of *num.* A better way to code the program is to use an optional feature of the *if* statement, the *else* clause. As Figure 3.2 depicts, the programmer writes a single comparison. Based on whether the test condition is true or false, the computer executes one of two statements.

The *if-else* **statement** with two keywords, *if* and *else,* has the following structure:

```
if (expression)
    statement1
else
    statement2
```

Either *statement1* or *statement2* can be a compound statement. The *if* **clause** is

```
if (expression)
    statement1
```

and the *else* **clause** is

```
else
    statement2
```

Even though these two clauses seem like two separate entities, no other statements may appear between them. Only one statement—which can be a compound statement—may appear between *if* and *else.*

Figure 3.2
Diagram of
choices in the
if-else statement

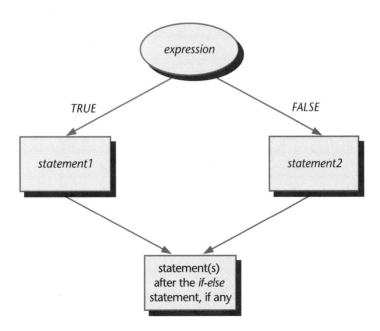

Example 3.6 _____

This example emphasizes the correct structure for the *if-else* statement. An example of an *if-else* statement follows:

```
if (a == b)
   printf("Values are equal.\n");
else                 /* Print warning message; make equal */
{
   printf("Values are not equal, but they will be.\n");
   b = a;            /* Make them equal by assigning a to b */
}
```

As illustrated, the statements in the *if* and *else* clauses can be simple or compound.
   The following example of an *if-else* statement is invalid and causes a syntax error.

```
/* This segment is INCORRECT */

if (a != b)
   printf("Values are not equal, but they will be.\n");
b = a;            /* ERROR--statement intervenes */
else              /* between if and else clauses */
   printf("Values are equal.\n");
```

A typical compiler message indicates the syntax error of a misplaced else.

```
Error ..\SOURCE\TESTEQL.C 10: Misplaced else
```

This segment is invalid because a statement intervenes between the *if* and *else* clauses. The first call to *printf* is part of the *if* clause, and the second one is part of the *else* clause, but the assignment statement (*b = a;*) belongs to neither.
   The indentation has no meaning in C syntax. Even though it might look correct to the unsuspecting programmer, indenting the assignment statement to line up with the first *printf* has no effect. The following segment is still wrong:

```
/* This segment is INCORRECT */

if (a != b)
   printf("Values are not equal, but they will be.\n");
   b = a;            /* ERROR—statement still intervenes */
else              /* between if and else clauses       */
   printf("Values are equal.\n");
```

To correct the segment, we place the first call to *printf* and the assignment statement in braces to form a compound statement. We also indent to aid readability, as shown:

```
/* This segment is CORRECT */

if (a != b)
{               /* braces group the next two statements */
    printf("Values are not equal, but they will be.\n");
    b = a;      /* assignment now part of if clause */
}
else
    printf("Values are equal.\n");
```

This segment is correct and is equivalent to the first segment that tested if ($a == b$). Regardless of the input, the two segments now produce the same output. The latest version, however, is harder for people to understand because it tests on a negation: If it is **true** that a is **not** equal to b, then print they are not equal and make them so; otherwise print that they are equal. We should try to turn around a negative test and make an equivalent positive test.

Example 3.7

The *if* statement can be useful in verifying user input. Regardless of the prompts, unless we check, we can never be sure that the user followed our instructions or typed a correct response. Invalid data can lead to meaningless or disastrous results.

The program in Example 2.22 of Section 2.7 reads the dimensions for a room and prints the floor space. If the user mistakenly types one negative and one positive dimension, the computer multiplies the two dimensions together and prints a negative floor area. The following is an example of such an interactive session:

```
This program will give you the floor space in square feet
for a room of your choosing.

Type one dimension of the floor in feet: -8
Type one dimension of the floor in feet: 10

The floor space is -80 square feet.
```

In this short program, we can easily discern the problem, but in longer programs the invalid data could lead to a long string of incorrect results. The root of the problem could be difficult to trace. It is much better to catch the input error as soon as it occurs. An improved version checks for negative input after obtaining values for *dim1* and *dim2*. If either value is negative, the program prints a message explaining the error and does not compute the floor space. The *if-else* statement is ideal for such a test. It is important to describe the problem to the user; nothing is quite so frustrating to the user as a program that stops without a clue as to the cause. Below is the function *main* from Example 2.22 with a check for valid input data. The other functions are unaltered.

```
/*
 * Example 3.7. Program to return the floor space for a room
 */
     :
main()
{
    int dim1,          /* one dimension of the room      */
        dim2,          /* another dimension of the room */
        FloorSpace;    /* area of floor in room          */

    printf("This program will give you the floor space ");
    printf("in square feet\n");
    printf("for a room of your choosing.\n\n");

    dim1 = GetDim();
    dim2 = GetDim();

    /* only process positive floor dimensions */
    if ( (dim1 <= 0) || (dim2 <= 0) )      /* invalid data */
    {
    /* user types a nonpositive value for dim1 or dim2 */

        printf("\nSorry, only positive dimensions are ");
        printf("allowed.\n");
        printf("Please reexecute the program.\n");
    }
    else                                    /* valid data */
    {
        FloorSpace = area(dim1, dim2);
        printf("\nThe floor space is %d square feet.\n",
               FloorSpace);
    }
}
     :
```

Now if the user enters a negative or zero dimension, he or she sees a session similar to the following:

```
This program will give you the floor space in square feet
for a room of your choosing.

Type one dimension of the floor in feet: -8
Type one dimension of the floor in feet: 10

Sorry, only positive dimensions are allowed.
Please reexecute the program.
```

Positive input data results in a session that has the same appearance as that in Example 2.22.

In coding, we should be especially careful of the logical operator in the compound test condition ((*dim1* <= 0) || (*dim2* <= 0)). Is OR correct, or should it be AND? If either one or both of the two dimensions are nonpositive, the program must stop. Therefore, the OR operator is correct. If we had used the AND operator ((*dim1* <= 0) && (*dim2* <= 0)), then one negative dimension would not abort execution. They would **both** have to be negative.

The program would be better if the code performed the error check immediately after the user entered a dimension and, in the case of an invalid response, allowed the user to retype the data item. In Chapter 5, we see how to code such a disaster recovery.

Example 3.8

This example illustrates the use of the *if-else* structure and the logical operators AND (&&) and OR (||). After a prompt, the user types any year, and the program determines whether it is a leap year or not. A leap year is one that is evenly divisible by 4, other than a century year (such as 1900). However, a century year that is evenly divisible by 400 (such as 2000) is also a leap year.

> *main( )*
>
> Interactive program to determine if an input year is a leap year
>
> *Algorithm:*
>
> prompt the user for a year
> read the year
> if the year is a leap year
>   print that the year is a leap year
> else
>   print that the year is not a leap year

This pseudocode seems straightforward, but using structured programming in this first pass of the design, we have glossed over the details of the *if* statement. Let us carefully examine the definition of a leap year, which includes the following two conditions:

> Condition 1. The year is evenly divisible by 4, other than a century year
> Condition 2. The year is a century year that is evenly divisible by 400

When two cases exist for which something is true, we use an OR to combine the boolean expressions. Thus, we test if Condition 1 is true OR if Condition 2 is true.

For Condition 1, we can rephrase "other than a century year" to "but the year is not a century year." Now we have the following two conditions that must both be true to have a leap year:

> Condition 1a. The year is evenly divisible by 4
> but Condition 1b. The year is not a century year

The word "and" is equivalent to "but" in Condition 1. Therefore, Condition 1 is true if and only if Condition 1a AND Condition 1b are true. With the entire condition put together, the test should read as follows:

if ((Condition 1a AND Condition 1b) OR Condition 2)

Because AND has a higher priority than OR, the inner set of parentheses is unnecessary. For clarity, however, we use parentheses around the compound condition involving AND.

Now that we have the overall structure of the test, we need to convert each simple condition into C. For Condition 1a, we can determine if a number is evenly divisible by 4 by testing if the remainder is zero. The modulus operator performs such a test. Thus, we can write the condition in C as

```
((year % 4) == 0)
```

Because $==$ has a lower precedence than %, we can drop the inner parentheses for Condition 1a, as shown:

```
(year % 4 == 0)
```

Condition 1b tests if the year is **not** a century year. If it were a century year, the remainder of the division of 100 into the year would be 0—(*year* % 100 $==$ 0). For example, 100 divides into 1900 with a remainder of 0. Because we are checking that the year is **not** divisible by 100, Condition 1b reads

```
(year % 100 != 0)
```

Finally, Condition 2 tests if the year is evenly divisible by 400. Using the same logic as the other conditions, we have

```
(year % 400 == 0)
```

Putting the code for the conditions together with the overall structure, the test reads

```
if ( ((year % 4 == 0) && (year % 100 != 0))
           || (year % 400 == 0))
```

The complete program follows:

```
/* Example 3.8.  Program to test for leap year */

#include <stdio.h>

main()
{   int year;  /* year to test */

    printf("Please enter a year: ");
    scanf("%d", &year);
```

```
/*
 * if year is divisible by 4 AND not divisible by 100
 * OR is divisible by 400, then it is a leap year
 */

if ( ((year % 4 == 0) && (year % 100 != 0))
              || (year % 400 == 0))
    printf("%d is a leap year.\n", year);
else
    printf("%d is not a leap year.\n", year);
}
```

The following represent four test runs of the program.

```
Please enter a year: 1986
1986 is not a leap year.

Please enter a year: 1948
1948 is a leap year.

Please enter a year: 1900
1900 is not a leap year.

Please enter a year: 2000
2000 is a leap year.
```

We can use boolean variables to simplify the *if* statement in the program, as follows:

```
int DivBy4Not100,  /* boolean variable */
    DivBy400;      /* boolean variable */
    ⋮
    DivBy4Not100 = (year % 4 == 0) && (year % 100 != 0);
    DivBy400     = (year % 400 == 0);

    if (DivBy4Not100 || DivBy400)
        printf("%d is a leap year.\n", year);
    else
        printf("%d is not a leap year.\n", year);
```

Section 3.2 **Exercises**

Write if *or* if-else *statements in C for Exercises 1–10.*

1. If x is positive, then assign 5 to y.
2. If x is 100, then print x and assign x to y.
3. If x is greater than y or less than z, then print x, y, and z.
4. If *salary* is greater than 20,000, then print an error message and read a new value.

5. If x is between -10 and 10, then double x; otherwise, halve x.

6. If x is odd, then increment x by 1.

7. If neither x nor y is 0, then print a message to that effect.

8. If *price* is at most 1000, then subtract 5 from *price*; otherwise, indicate that the price is too large and request a new value.

9. If the least significant digit of x is 3, then change x so that digit is 5.

10. If *guess* is equal to *correct,* then congratulate the user on a correct guess; otherwise, prompt the user for another guess and read this guess.

11. Find the error(s) in the following segment:

```
if (x > 2) && (y == 3) then
    printf("Found\n");
```

12. Find the error(s) in the following segment:

```
if (x =< 5)
    printf("less or equal\n")
else;
    printf("greater\n");
```

13. Find the error(s) in the following segment:

```
if (x < y)
    min = x;
    printf("%d is smaller\n", x);
else
    min = y;
    printf("%d is smaller\n", y);
```

14. Write a function *minimum* that returns the smaller of two integer parameters.

15. Write a function *even* that returns *TRUE*(1) if the integer parameter is even and returns *FALSE*(0) otherwise.

16. Write a function *absolute* that returns the absolute value of an integer parameter. The definition of the absolute value of x, $|x|$, follows:

$$|x| = \begin{cases} x & \text{if } x > 0 \\ -x & \text{if } x \leq 0 \end{cases}$$

Thus, $|3| = 3$ and $|-3| = -(-3) = 3$. Develop your own function, but the function *abs* in the math library performs the same task as *absolute*.

Section 3.2 Programming Projects

1. Develop a program that prints the higher of two grades on a test.

2. Develop a program that enables a user to enter an integer. The program should then state whether the integer is evenly divisible by 5.

3. Develop a program that asks the user to enter two positive integers, a and b, and then states whether or not one integer is a factor of the other. In other words, state if a is evenly divisible by b or if b is evenly divisible by a. Terminate execution if either integer is not positive.

4. Develop a program that reads two integers, a and b, and then determines whether the product of the two numbers is greater than one-half of a.

5. Develop a program that reads an integer and determines whether it is evenly divisible by both 6 and 7.

6. Develop a program that reads an integer and determines whether it is within a given range (for example, between 1 and 10). The low and high values of the range should be entered by the user rather than fixed by the program.

7. Develop a program that reads three positive integers representing the sides of a triangle and determines whether they form a valid triangle. (Hint: In a triangle, the sum of any two sides must always be greater than the third side.)

8. Develop an interactive program that accepts two integers, *total* and *count,* and prints the quotient *total / count.* Before dividing, the program should check that the denominator is not zero.

In Exercises 9–11, revise the programs in Section 2.6 Programming Projects to include validation of input. If input is not valid, the program should print an error message and terminate execution.

   9. Project 1   **10.** Project 2   **11.** Project 4

In Exercises 12–14, revise the programs in Section 2.7 Programming Projects to include validation of input. If input is not valid, the program should print an error message and terminate execution.

   12. Project 1   **13.** Project 2   **14.** Project 3

Section 3.3 **Nesting**

The ability of the *if* and *else* clauses to contain compound statements provides us with a flexible programming tool. Moreover, either clause may contain another *if* statement. The following segment illustrates this construct, known as a **nested** *if* statement:

```
if (n < 3)
    printf("%d is less than 3\n", n);
else
    if (n > 10)
        printf("%d is greater than 10\n", n);
    else
        printf("%d is between 3 and 10\n", n);
```

Figure 3.3 diagrams this statement. If *n* is less than 3, then execution follows the path to the left. If it is not, the path leads to the box at the right, which contains another selection control structure. One selection control structure contains another. For the innermost selection statement, the computer checks if *n* is greater than 10. Depending on whether the condition is true or not, the computer prints different messages.

Although the indentation mimics the structure in the picture, usually programmers write the code with fewer lines and less deep indentation. They line up all the *else* clauses with the first *if* and place any additional *if* on the same line as an *else* to read *else if* ....

```
if (n < 3)
    printf("%d is less than 3\n", n);
else if (n > 10)
    printf("%d is greater than 10\n", n);
else
    printf("%d is between 3 and 10\n", n);
```

Figure 3.3 Diagram of a nested *if* statement

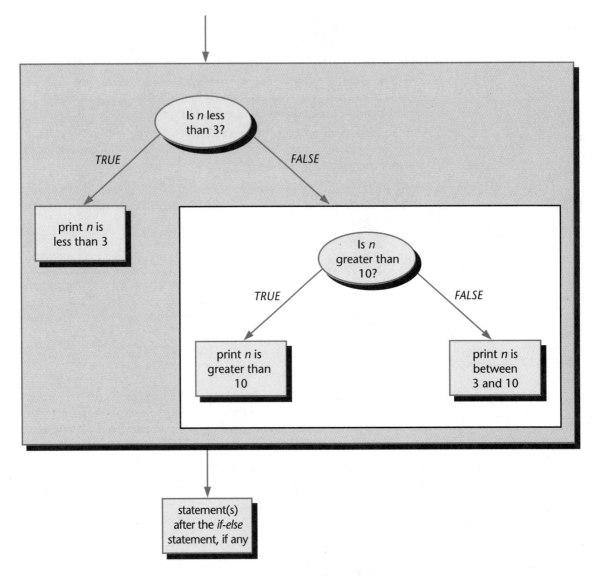

This nested *if* structure has the following syntax:

```
if (expression1)
    statement1
else if (expression2)
    statement2
else if (expression3)
    statement3
⋮
else
    statementn
```

As with an unnested decision control structure, the statements (*statement1, statement2, . . . , statementn*) can be single or compound. Indentation of these statements greatly aids the clarity of the code for a human reader. As previously mentioned, however, lining up the clauses does not determine the connection between them for the compiler. Regardless of the format, an *else* matches the nearest unmatched *if* that precedes it. As Figure 3.3 emphasizes for this example, the first *else* goes with the first *if,* and the second *else* corresponds to the second *if.*

Example 3.9

In Example 3.8 of Section 3.2, we used the logical operators AND (&&) and OR (||) to determine whether an input year was a leap year or not, as shown in the following segment:

```
if ( ((year % 4 == 0) && (year % 100 != 0))
           || (year % 400 == 0))
   printf("%d is a leap year.\n", year);
else
   printf("%d is not a leap year.\n", year);
```

We could rewrite the *if* statement in the program using nested *if-else* statements. Comments in the following segment match each *else* clause with its corresponding *if* clause:

```
if (year % 4 == 0)                    /* #1 if */
   if (year % 100 != 0)               /* #2 if */
      printf("%d is a leap year.\n", year);
   else if (year % 400 == 0)          /* #2 else, #3 if */
      printf("%d is a leap year.\n", year);
   else                               /* #3 else */
      printf("%d is not a leap year.\n", year);
else                                  /* #1 else */
   printf("%d is not a leap year.\n", year);
```

This revised version illustrates two rules that pertain to the use of nested *if-else* statements.

1. An AND (&&) operation can be replaced with an *if* statement nested within an *if* clause.

With &&	With nested if
`if (a && b)`	`if (a)`
`   statement`	`   if (b)`
	`      statement`

2. An OR (||) operation can be replaced with an *if* statement nested within an *else* clause.

With ||	With nested if
`if (a || b)`	`if (a)`
`   statement`	`   statement`
	`else if (b)`
	`   statement`

Example 3.10

This example considers the correspondence of *if*s and *else*s. The following code segment displays indentation that emphasizes the appropriate matches:

```
if (n <= 10)
    if (n >= 3)                    /* (n <= 10) AND (n >= 3) */
        printf("%d is between 3 and 10\n", n);
    else                          /* (n <= 10) AND (n < 3) */
        printf("%d is less than 3\n", n);
```

Using the rule stated earlier, the *else* clause matches the second *if*. Should *n* be 7, both ($n <= 10$) and ($n >= 3$) are true. In this case, the computer executes the first *printf* and prints the following:

```
7 is between 3 and 10
```

If *n* is 2, ($n <= 10$) is true, but ($n >= 3$) is false. Consequently, the computer executes the second *printf*:

```
2 is less than 3
```

If *n* is 15, ($n <= 10$) is false, and the computer skips the rest of the segment.

Suppose we want to print a message when *n* is greater than 10, but we do not need to print a message if *n* is less than 3. The indentation in the following pseudocode indicates that we want to pair *else* with the first *if*.

```
if n is less than or equal to 10
    if n is greater than or equal to 3
        print n is between 3 and 10
else
    print n is greater than 10
```

However, the normal *if-else* pairing would couple the *else* with the second *if*. To override this pairing, we must use braces around an inner *if* statement to cause the pairing of the *else* and the first *if*.

```
if (n <= 10)
{
    if (n >= 3)                   /* (n <= 10) AND (n >= 3) */
        printf("%d is between 3 and 10\n", n);
}
else                              /* (n > 10) */
    printf("%d is greater than 10\n", n);
```

Thus, the *if* clause contains a compound statement. The syntax of this structure is as follows:

```
if (expression1)
{
    if (expression2)
        statement2
}
else
    statement3
```

Braces prevent any association between the *if* statement within the braces and the *else* clause outside them. Even when unnecessary, braces make a program clearer for the human reader.

In this segment, if *n* is 7, both ($n <= 10$) and ($n >= 3$). As in the first segment, the computer uses the first *printf:*

```
7 is between 3 and 10
```

If *n* is 2, ($n <= 10$) is true, but ($n >= 3$) is false, and the program contains no instructions for this situation. If *n* is 15, ($n <= 10$) is false, so the computer calls the second *printf.*

```
15 is greater than 10
```

Example 3.11

A company is giving raises to all its salaried employees. Someone who earns less than $2000 per month receives a raise of $150 a month, and an employee with a monthly salary between $2000 and $5000 earns an additional $250 per month. We want to write a program to read a person's current monthly salary and to print the new salary.

Through analysis, we determine four major tasks—print the instructions, read a salary, discover if a salary is out of range, and compute the new salary. We use a different function for each program task. The function *instructions* prints the opening instructions to the user. *ReadSalary* prompts the user for a salary and returns the data item. *OutOfRange* returns *TRUE* (1) if the salary is negative or greater than $5000. Given the current monthly salary, *NewSalary* returns the new salary. Figure 3.4 contains the structure chart for the design. Using this design, we develop pseudocode for *main*.

Figure 3.4
Structure chart for the program in Example 3.11

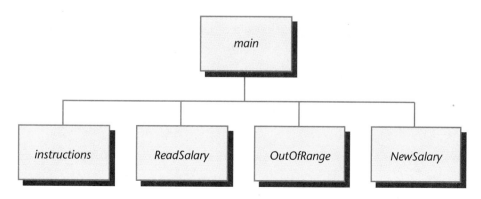

main()

Program to read current salaries and to print new salaries for salaried employees

Algorithm:

read a salary from the user
if the salary is out of range
    print an error message
else
    print the new salary

The functions *instructions* and *ReadSalary* are routine. If *salary* is negative or greater than 5000, *OutOfRange* returns *TRUE*. Thus, it sends back the value of the boolean expression

```
(salary < 0) || (salary > 5000)
```

NewSalary computes the raise in an *if-else* statement with the following design:

if the salary is less than 2000 then
    raise ← 150
else
    raise ← 250

The function then returns the sum of this raise and the current salary. The code displays one *return* statement at the end of the definition, as shown:

```
int NewSalary(int salary)
{
    int raise;                    /* monthly raise in salary */

    if (salary < 2000)
        raise = 150;
    else
        raise = 250;
    return (salary + raise);
}
```

The function would certainly behave correctly if we replace the two assignments with separate returns of *salary* + 150 and *salary* + 250, as shown:

```
/* This version is NOT AS SOUND as the one above */

int NewSalary(int salary)
{
    if (salary < 2000)
        return (salary + 150); /* NOT modular programming */
    else
        return (salary + 250); /* NOT modular programming */
}
```

However, having two or more returns from a function violates a principle of modular programming. Multiple returns make debugging more difficult because, without careful consideration, we do not know how the function finished. Particularly when we call a long function several times, the presence of several returns increases the complexity of reading and debugging the function.

> There should be only one entry point and one exit point for a module.

Bringing together all the functions, we have the following program:

```c
/*
 * Example 3.11
 * Interactive program to compute the raise of a salaried
 * employee. Those that earn less than $2000 a month
 * get a raise of $150 a month, and those with salaries
 * between $2000 and $5000 a month receive a raise of
 * $250 a month.
 */

#include <stdio.h>

void instructions(void);
int ReadSalary(void);
int OutOfRange(int salary);
int NewSalary(int salary);

main()
{
    int salary;              /* monthly salary */

    instructions();
    salary = ReadSalary();
    if (OutOfRange(salary))
        printf("\nThat salary is out of range\n");
    else
        printf("\nThe new salary is %d\n", NewSalary(salary));
}

/*
 * Function to print instructions on what the program does
 * Pre:     none
 * Post:    Instructions have been displayed.
 */

void instructions(void)
{
    printf("This program interactively reads a monthly salary\n");
    printf("and computes a new monthly salary.  If the salary\n");
    printf("is less than $2000 a month, the raise is $150 a month.\n");
```

```
      printf("If the salary is between $2000 and $5000 a month, \n");
      printf("the raise is $250 a month.\n\n");
}

/*
 * Function to read a salary interactively
 * Pre:    none
 * Post:   The salary the user entered has been returned.
 */

int ReadSalary(void)
{
   int salary;              /* monthly salary */

   printf("Type a monthly salary between $0 and $5000.\n");
   printf("Do not use the dollar sign or commas.   ");
   scanf("%d", &salary);
   return salary;
}

/*
 * Function to return TRUE(1) if salary is out of range
 * Range:  $0 - $5000
 * Pre:    salary is an integer.
 * Post:   A nonzero number (TRUE) has been returned if salary
 *         is not in range; 0 (FALSE) if it is.
 */

int OutOfRange(int salary)
{
   return ((salary < 0) || (salary > 5000));
}

/*
 * Function to return new salary.  For salaries < $2000,
 * raise is $150; for salaries between $2000 and $5000,
 * raise is $250
 * Pre:    salary is an integer between 0 and 5000.
 * Post:   The modified salary (previous salary + raise)
 *         has been returned.
 */

int NewSalary(int salary)
{
   int raise;                 /* monthly raise in salary */

   if (salary < 2000)
      raise = 150;
   else
      raise = 250;
   return (salary + raise);
}
```

Output from one interactive run follows:

```
This program interactively reads a monthly salary
and computes a new monthly salary.  If the salary
is less than $2000 a month, the raise is $150 a month.
If the salary is between $2000 and $5000 a month,
the raise is $250 a month.

Type a monthly salary between $0 and $5000.
Do not use the dollar sign or commas. 1800

The new salary is 1950
```

Testing a salary between $2000 and $5000, the output contains the following:

```
Type a monthly salary between $0 and $5000.
Do not use the dollar sign or commas. 4900

The new salary is 5150
```

Verifying the boundary value 2000, we have the following output:

```
Type a monthly salary between $0 and $5000.
Do not use the dollar sign or commas. 2000

The new salary is 2250
```

Testing should also include boundary values 0 and 5000 and some out-of-range values. One such test is as follows:

```
Type a monthly salary between $0 and $5000.
Do not use the dollar sign or commas. 6000

That salary is out of range
```

Using the principles of structured programming, we separate several of the more difficult parts of the code into functions. For example, *OutOfRange* handles the compound logical expression testing for *salary* being out of range, whereas *main* uses the following self-explanatory test:

```
if (OutOfRange(salary))....
```

As the name implies, *NewSalary* returns the new salary. Certainly, *main* could perform this computation, but then we would need a nested *if* statement to test for valid data and calculate the new salary. With *NewSalary*, we have buried the inner *if-else* statement in a function and simplified program development and readability.

Several C statements other than the *if* statement use relational and logical operators. All these statements involve decision making of some sort. Chapters 5 and 6 introduce statements that repeat a sequence of steps as long as a certain condition is true. Such constructs, known as loops, are among the most important, fundamental constructs in computer programming.

Section 3.3 Exercises

Write nested if *or* if-else *statements in C for Exercises 1–3.*

1. If *x* and *y* are both positive, then print the smaller of the two values.

2. If *x* is between −20 and 20, assign its absolute value to *y*.

3. If *x* is greater than 30, then if *y* is positive, print *z*. However, if *x* is less than or equal to 30, then print *y*.

4. For each value of *n*, give the output from execution of the following segment:

```
if (n > 50)
    printf("A");
else if (n > 20)
    printf("B");
else
    printf("C");
```

  a. 15   b. 20   c. 300   d. −7   e. 45

5. For each value of *n*, give the output from execution of the following segment:

```
if (n > 50)
{
    if (n <= 200)
        printf("A");
}
else if (n > 20)
    if (n % 2 == 0)
        printf("B");
    else
        printf("C");
```

  a. 100   b. 300   c. 34   d. 35   e. 15   f. 20

6. For each value of *n*, give the output from execution of the following segment:

```
if (n < 60)
    printf("A");
else if (n < 80)
{
    if (n % 5 == 0)
        printf("B");
}
else
    printf("C");
```

  a. 15   b. 75   c. 76   d. 60   e. 95

7. The indentation and syntax of the following segment do not agree. By placing braces appropriately, correct the syntax to agree with the indentation.

```
if (x == 50)
    if (y < 30)
        printf("A");
else if (x < 50)
    if (y == 30)
        printf("B");
else
    printf("C");
```

8. Use a nested *if* (*not* logical operators) to write C code for the following: If *x* and *y* are both divisible by 30, then print "Both divisible by 30."

9. Use a nested *if* (*not* logical operators) to write C code for the following: If *x* or *y* is divisible by 30, then print "At least one number is divisible by 30."

Section 3.3 Programming Projects

In the following projects, continue to use structured programming methods. Draw a structure chart; use functions; have good prompts and comments; if a data item is not valid, stop the program with an error message.

1. Develop a program to read two test scores, each between 0 and 100 points, and to print the higher of the two scores.

2. Develop a program to read three integer test scores, each between 0 and 100 points, and to print the integer average of the three.

3. A company is giving raises to all its salaried employees. Those who earn less than $1000 a month get raises of $100 a month; those with salaries greater than or equal to $1000 but less than $3000 a month receive raises of $200 a month; and those with higher salaries get $300 a month. Read a person's current monthly salary and print the new salary. Be sure to check for a valid input salary.

Section 3.4 Multiple-Way Selection

The *switch* Statement

An alternative to a nested *if-else* statement is the *switch* **statement**, which permits virtually any number of branches. In this selection control structure, the value of any *int* (or *int*-compatible) variable or expression determines which branch the *switch* statement takes. As in the *if* statement, the variable or expression in parentheses follows a keyword—*switch*.

For example, suppose by using calls to the function *printf* we present the user of an automated library catalogue with the following menu of choices:

```
Please type the number of your selection:

    1  Search for a title
    2  Search for an author
    3  Search for a subject
    4  Get help
    5  Quit

Number:
```

Once the user enters a choice, the program must call one of several functions to process the request. If the variable *choice* holds the user's selection, the following *switch* statement could control the next action of the computer:

```
switch (choice)
{
    case 1:
        Title();
        break;
    case 2:
        Author();
        break;
    case 3:
        Subject();
        break;
    case 4:
        Help();
        break;
    case 5:
        Quit();
        break;
    default:
        InvalidResponse();
}
```

This example has five tests of the equality of *choice* and a constant value. The alternatives in the *switch* statement are more easily discernible than in the following equivalent nested *if* statement:

```
if (choice == 1)
    Title();
else if (choice == 2)
    Author();
else if (choice == 3)
    Subject();
else if (choice == 4)
    Help();
else if (choice == 5)
    Quit();
else
    InvalidResponse();
```

When the computer encounters the *switch* statement, it evaluates the *switch* expression (*choice*). The computer then transfers control to the statement immediately following the *case* label for the appropriate value of *choice*. For example, should the value of *choice* be 3, the program calls *Subject()*.

This example also has a special *default* label, which is a "catch-all" label. If the value of the *switch* expression does not match a case label and if the *default* label is present, control passes to the statement after *default*. If *default* is not present and no match exists, the computer skips the entire body of the *switch* statement. In the above example, if the user types an invalid choice like 6, the program calls the error-handling routine *InvalidResponse()*.

After returning from a function call, the computer executes the next statement, which in the first five cases is a *break* statement. The keyword *break* causes the *switch* to terminate, and execution resumes with the next statement (if any) following the *switch* statement. We do not need a *break* in the default case, because the program has no further instructions to execute in the *switch* statement.

The general syntax of the *switch* statement with an optional *default* is as follows:

```
switch (expression)
{
    case c1:
        any_number_of_statements1
    case c2:
        any_number_of_statements2
      :
    default:
        any_number_of_statementsn
}
```

Braces enclose the body of a *switch* statement, which has *case* labels in the form of the keyword *case* and a constant value. This value should have the same type as the *switch* variable (or expression) and must be *int* or *int*-compatible. (In Chapter 4, we discuss several *int*-compatible types, such as *long* and *char*.) A colon follows the case label. The constants in the *case* labels need not be consecutive, nor must they be in any particular order. For example, a *switch* statement can have the following sequence of labels:

```
case 4:
case 95:
case -3:
case 0:
```

Moreover, the *default* label need not be the last label but can be anywhere in the body of the *switch* statement. The code, however, is usually easier to read if the labels are in order, with *default* last. In C, any number of statements can appear between two labels, and we need not group these statements with braces.

In the above example, the objective was to call a function corresponding to a value of *choice* and to skip all other statements in the *switch* body. To complete this nested *if*-statement action, we use the *break* statement. When the *break* statement is encountered, the *switch* statement is terminated immediately, and any remaining statements in the body are ignored. If we did not include *break* statements, the computer would execute all the statements that follow in the *switch* statement.

Example 3.12 _____

In this example, we write a function that accepts a positive integer parameter (*CountFrom*) less than or equal to 5 and counts down from that number to 1, printing "Ignition" and "Blast off!" at the end. For example, if *CountFrom* is 3, the output contains the following:

```
3
2
1
Ignition
Blast off!
```

We can program this task using a *switch* statement without accompanying *break* statements. After printing the value of *CountFrom*, we do not want to leave the *switch* statement. We want to execute the remaining calls to *printf*. The definition of the function follows:

```
/*
 * Function to count down from parameter CountFrom
 * to 1, and then to print Ignition, Blast off!
 * Pre:    Integer CountFrom has a value between 5 an 1.
 * Post:   A countdown from CountFrom has been displayed.
 */

void CountDown(int CountFrom)
{
   switch (CountFrom)
   {
      case 5:  printf("5\n");
      case 4:  printf("4\n");
      case 3:  printf("3\n");
      case 2:  printf("2\n");
      case 1:
         printf("1\n");
         printf("Ignition\n");
         printf("Blast off!\n");
   }
}
```

Labels are not executable, so a *case* label coming between two *printf* calls has no effect on program execution. As Figure 3.5 illustrates, the *case* or *default* label does not prevent control from falling through to the remaining statements. After control branches to a label, unless a *break* statement intervenes, the computer executes all statements that follow the label.

We assume that another function has checked that the data item is in the range from 1–5. *CountDown* has no *default* label, however. Thus, if the parameter is less than one, *CountDown* returns without printing anything.

Because the nested *if* statement executes only one option, to produce the same output, each alternative must include several calls to *printf*.

```
if (CountFrom == 5)
{
      printf("5\n");
      printf("4\n");
      printf("3\n");
```

Figure 3.5
Execution of
switch
statement in
Example 3.12

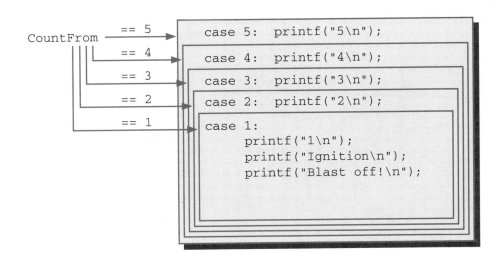

```
        printf("2\n");
        printf("1\n");
        printf("Ignition\n");
        printf("Blast off!\n");
}
else if (CountFrom == 4)
{
        printf("4\n");
        printf("3\n");
        printf("2\n");
        printf("1\n");
        printf("Ignition\n");
        printf("Blast off!\n");
}
    :
```

We can also code this program using loops, which we discuss in Chapters 5 and 6.

Example 3.13

In this example, we develop procedure *PrintNumber* to print a positive one- or two-digit integer using words. For example, an input of 25 results in an output of "twenty-five."

A test program can have *main* prompt the user and read an integer. If the input is positive and less than 100, *main* calls *PrintNumber* to print the number in words. Otherwise, *main* displays an error message.

The following are several sample runs:

```
Enter a positive integer less than 100: 25
twenty-five
```

```
Enter a positive integer less than 100: 345
Sorry, your number is out of range.


Enter a positive integer less than 100: 16
sixteen


Enter a positive integer less than 100: 6
six
```

The procedure *PrintNumber* calls other routines to display words for the units digits, the teens, and the tens digits. *PrintUnits* prints a word for the units digit, which is an integer from 1 to 9. *PrintTeens* displays a word for a teen. *PrintTens* displays a word for a tens digit greater than 1 and a dash, such as "twenty-." Thus, for the integer 21, *PrintNumber* calls *PrintTens* to display "twenty-" and *PrintUnits* to display "one." Figure 3.6 gives the structure chart for the procedure *PrintNumber* and the routines it calls. Pseudocode for *main* follows:

> *main*()
>
> Program to obtain a positive integer less than 100 and display the number in words
>
> *Algorithm:*
>
> prompt and read an integer
> if the number is out of range
>   print an error message
> else
>   call *PrintNumber*

The *PrintNumber* routine first extracts the tens and units digits. If the tens digit is one, *PrintNumber* calls *PrintTeens* to print numbers in the teens using a *switch* statement. If the tens digit is zero, *PrintNumber* calls *PrintUnits* to print single-digit

Figure 3.6
Structure chart for Example 3.13

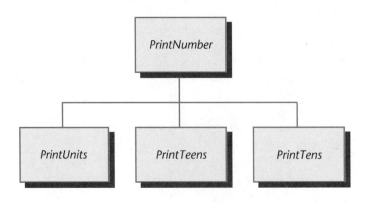

numbers using a *switch* statement. For a tens digit greater than one, we call *PrintTens*
to print the tens digit and then check the units digit. If *UnitsDigit* is greater than zero,
we print a hyphen and call the routine *PrintUnits*. Pseudocode for *PrintNumber* and
PrintUnits appears below (*PrintTens* and *PrintTeens* are similar to *PrintUnits*). The
implementation follows the pseudocode.

PrintNumber(n)

Procedure to print a positive integer less than 100 in words

Pre:

n is an integer satisfying $0 < n < 100$.

Post:

The value of *n* has been displayed in words.

Algorithm:

determine the tens digit (*TensDigit*) and the units digit (*UnitsDigit*)
if (*TensDigit* is 0)
    PrintUnits(*UnitsDigit*)
else if (*TensDigit* is 1)
    PrintTeens(*UnitsDigit*)
else
    PrintTens(*TensDigit*)
    if (*UnitsDigit* is greater than 0)
        print hyphen
        PrintUnits(*UnitsDigit*)

PrintUnits(UnitsDigit)

Procedure to print a single nonzero digit in words

Pre:

UnitsDigit is an integer satisfying $0 < n < 10$.

Post:

The value of *UnitsDigit* has been displayed in words.

Algorithm:

for each possible digit, display the appropriate word

```
/*
 * Example 3.13
 * Program to print a one- or two-digit positive integer in words
 */

#include <stdio.h>

void PrintNumber(int n);
```

```c
void PrintUnits(int UnitsDigit);
void PrintTens(int TensDigit);
void PrintTeens(int UnitsDigit);

main()
{
    int n;

    printf("Enter a positive integer less than 100: ");
    scanf("%d", &n);
    if ((n < 1) || (n > 99))
        printf("Sorry, your number is out of range.");
    else
        PrintNumber(n);
    printf("\n");
}

/*
 * Function to print a positive integer < 100 in words
 * Pre:  n is an integer satisfying 0 < n < 100.
 * Post: n has been printed in words.
 */

void PrintNumber(int n)
{
    int UnitsDigit,        /* units digit */
        TensDigit;         /* tens digit */

    UnitsDigit = n % 10;
    TensDigit  = n / 10;

    if (TensDigit == 0)
        PrintUnits(UnitsDigit);
    else if (TensDigit == 1)
        PrintTeens(UnitsDigit);
    else
        {
            PrintTens(TensDigit);
            if (UnitsDigit > 0)
            {
                printf("-");
                PrintUnits(UnitsDigit);
            }
        }
}

/*
 * Function to print a word for the units digit
 * Pre:  UnitsDigit is an integer with 0 < UnitsDigit < 10.
 * Post: UnitsDigit has been printed in a word.
 */
```

```c
void PrintUnits(int UnitsDigit)
{
   switch (UnitsDigit)
   {
      case 1:     printf("one");
                  break;
      case 2:     printf("two");
                  break;
      case 3:     printf("three");
                  break;
      case 4:     printf("four");
                  break;
      case 5:     printf("five");
                  break;
      case 6:     printf("six");
                  break;
      case 7:     printf("seven");
                  break;
      case 8:     printf("eight");
                  break;
      case 9:     printf("nine");
   }
}

/*
 * Function to print a word for the tens digit
 * Pre:  TensDigit is an integer with 1 < TensDigit < 10.
 * Post: TensDigit has been printed in a word.
 */

void PrintTens(int TensDigit)
{
   switch (TensDigit)
   {
      case 2:     printf("twenty");
                  break;
      case 3:     printf("thirty");
                  break;
      case 4:     printf("forty");
                  break;
      case 5:     printf("fifty");
                  break;
      case 6:     printf("sixty");
                  break;
      case 7:     printf("seventy");
                  break;
      case 8:     printf("eighty");
                  break;
      case 9:     printf("ninety");
   }
}
```

```c
/*
 * Function to print a number in the teens using words
 * Pre:  UnitsDigit is an integer with 0 <= UnitsDigit < 10.
 * Post: Corresponding teen has been printed in a word.
 */

void PrintTeens(int UnitsDigit)
{
    switch (UnitsDigit)
    {
        case 0:    printf("ten");
                   break;
        case 1:    printf("eleven");
                   break;
        case 2:    printf("twelve");
                   break;
        case 3:    printf("thirteen");
                   break;
        case 4:    printf("fourteen");
                   break;
        case 5:    printf("fifteen");
                   break;
        case 6:    printf("sixteen");
                   break;
        case 7:    printf("seventeen");
                   break;
        case 8:    printf("eighteen");
                   break;
        case 9:    printf("nineteen");
    }
}
```

Branching to the Same Point

We might want several different values of the *switch* expression to cause execution of the same set of statements. We can accomplish this branching to the same point by including several labels in succession with no intervening statements, as in the following example:

```c
switch (digit)
{
    case 0:
    case 1:
    case 2:
    case 3:
    case 4:
        printf("Round down\n");
        break;
    case 5:
    case 6:
    case 7:
    case 8:
```

```
    case 9:
        printf("Round up\n");
}
```

In this example, if *digit* has the value 0, 1, 2, 3, or 4, the computer executes the first call to *printf.* Due to the *break* statement, the rest of the *switch* statement is ignored. If, however, the value of *digit* is 5, 6, 7, 8, or 9, the computer prints "Round up" and terminates the *switch* statement. Because this *switch* statement does not include a *default* label, earlier code should have validated the value of *digit.* As in the other examples, we do not include a *break* at the end, because execution of the *switch* statement is complete.

Section 3.4 **Exercises**

1. For each value of *n,* give the output from execution of the following segment:

```
switch (n)
{
    case 24:
        printf("A");
    case 6:
        printf("B");
        break;
    case 7:
        printf("C");
    case 5:
        printf("D");
    default:
        printf("E");
}
```

   a. 24   **b.** 7   **c.** 12   **d.** 6   **e.** -3

2. Determine the syntax errors in the following *switch statement:*

```
switch 3 * n + 7;
    case 1;
        printf("A");
    case 10;
    {
        printf("B");
        break;
    }
    case 5 * n - 17;
        printf("C");
    case 10:
        printf("D");
    case default;
        printf("E");
```

3. Write the following nested *if* statement as a *switch* statement:

```
if (n == 1)
    printf("A");
```

```
        else if ((n == 2) || (n == 3))
            printf("B");
        else
            printf("C");
```

4. Write the following *switch* statement as a nested *if* statement:

```
switch (n + 3)
{
    case 1:
        printf("A");
        break;
    case 2:
        printf("B");
        break;
    case 3:
    case 4:
        printf("D");
    default:
        printf("E");
}
```

For Exercises 5–7, write switch *statements to perform the indicated tasks. Do not write statements before* switch *or code any functions. Be sure to have defaults to check for a valid input data item.*

5. Process the response from a cash register menu by executing the appropriate function. Make up names for these functions. The menu reads as follows:

```
What would you like to do?

    1   Process a charge
    2   Process a return
    3   Void a transaction
    4   Quit

Your choice?
```

6. Process the response from an ATM (automatic teller machine) menu by executing the appropriate function. Make up names for these functions. The menu reads as follows:

```
What would you like to do?

    1   Make a withdrawal
    2   Make a deposit
    3   Transfer funds
    4   Obtain your balance
    5   Quit

Your choice?
```

7. Process the response from a school directory menu. If a person types 1, 2, or 3, a function should display a map of north campus; if a user enters 4 or 5, east campus should display; a choice of 6 presents a map of south campus; and 7 exhibits a west campus map. Make up names for these functions. The menu reads as follows:

```
We will show you a map of various parts of campus.
The map should include which building?  Please type
the appropriate number.

    1  Main Bldg.
    2  Admissions Bldg.
    3  Library
    4  Smith Hall
    5  Athletic Facilities
    6  Science Hall
    7  Fine Arts Bldg.

Building number:
```

Section 3.4 **Programming Projects**

1. Develop a program to present the user with the following menu of choices:

```
This program will perform an integer arithmetic problem for
you.  Please choose the kind of problem by typing the
corresponding number.

    1  addition
    2  subtraction
    3  multiplication
    4  division
    5  modulo
    6  absolute value

Your choice:
```

Depending on the user's choice, the program should obtain one or two operands and perform the appropriate arithmetic. Have a separate function for each task.

2. Develop a program to determine the day of the week for a particular date. The program should read the day in the month, such as 9 for July 9. It should also present a menu of the days of the week and ask the day of the week for the first day in the month. A sample session follows:

```
This program can tell you the day of the week
for any day in a month.

What is the number of today's date (1-31):  9

The first of the month was on which day?

    1   Sunday
    2   Monday
    3   Tuesday
    4   Wednesday
    5   Thursday
    6   Friday
    7   Saturday

Please give the day (1-7):  4

Day 9 of the month is on a Thursday.
```

Check for valid data.

Section 3.5 Breadth: Logic

George Boole and Edmund Berkeley

George Boole

The design of a computer, the manipulation of data and programs in the computer, and the logic of programs are all based on an algebra that has three basic operations and as few as two elements. It is surprising that so much depends on a system that may contain so few elements. When **George Boole** wrote of the algebra that now bears his name in *The Mathematical Analysis of Logic* in 1847, he was presenting an algebraic foundation for logic. Few people appreciated Boole's genius. Born the son of a poor shoemaker in England, George Boole was self-taught. Because of his work in logic, he was given the position of professor of mathematics at Queens College, an honorable, but not particularly respected, position. Little did he or anyone else suspect that 100 years later his work would provide the theoretical basis for the design of electronic circuitry and ultimately of the computer.

Symbolic logic was first applied to business in 1936 by **Edmund Berkeley**. In examination of certain rearrangements of insurance premium payments, he discovered contradictory company rules. The maze of special situations was quite complicated. However, by converting statements to symbols and applying symbolic logic, he discovered conflicts that no one else had detected.

Basic Components of Logic

Propositional calculus or **logic** is the study of the **algebra of propositions**. An element of the algebra of propositions is a **proposition** or **statement** that is true or false. For example, in this chapter we have discussed instructions like the following:

```
if (x > 3)...
```

A condition having the value *TRUE* or *FALSE*, such as $(x > 3)$, is called a logical or boolean expression in a programming context and a proposition or statement in logic. Recall that in the logic context of C, zero represents *FALSE*, and any nonzero integer indicates *TRUE*. We have also combined logical expressions using logical operators (||, &&, and !) to form **compound statements** that themselves are *TRUE* or *FALSE*. For example, in

```
if (((x > 3) && (y == 7)) || !found)...
```

each expression—$(x > 3)$, $(y == 7)$, and *found*—can be true or false, as can the entire compound expression. Notice that the two possible values of a logical expression are *TRUE* and *FALSE*, and we have used the three basic operators OR (||), AND (&&), and NOT (!).

Definitions A **proposition** or **statement** is a declarative sentence that is either true or false. **Propositional calculus** or **logic** is the study of the algebra of propositions.

In the language of logic, statements are often represented by the small letters p, q, and r. In C, we use logical operators ||, &&, and !, whereas in logic, these notations are $\vee$, $\wedge$, and $\sim$, respectively. In the language of logic, $\vee$ (OR) denotes the logical operator of **disjunction**, $\wedge$ (AND) is the symbol for **conjunction**, and $\sim$ (NOT) is **negation**.

Definitions In logic, a **logical operator** is a symbol that we use to combine or negate statements that are true or false. Some logical operators are as follows: **disjunction** ($\vee$) means "or"; **conjunction** ($\wedge$) means "and"; and **negation**, ($\sim$) means "not." A **compound statement** or **compound proposition** is a statement or statements combined with logical operators to form a sentence that is either true or false.

Example 3.14

The following are examples of statements:

p: George Boole developed the algebraic foundation for logic.
q: The electronic computer was invented in 1500 AD.

Both sentences are statements, although the second is clearly false. Using these sentences, the compound statement $p \wedge \sim q$ is as follows: "George Boole developed the algebraic foundation for logic, and the electronic computer was not invented in 1500 AD."

Truth Tables Truth tables provide a concise way of indicating under what conditions a compound statement is true. Using Table 3.5, we note that the basic truth tables for conjunction, disjunction, and negation are identical to Table 3.2 for OR (||), Table 3.1 for AND (&&), and Table 3.3 for NOT (!), respectively.

Table 3.5   Truth tables for $p \vee q$, $p \wedge q$, and $\sim p$

p	q	$p \vee q$
F	F	F
F	T	T
T	F	T
T	T	T

p	q	$p \wedge q$
F	F	F
F	T	F
T	F	F
T	T	T

p	$\sim p$
F	T
T	F

Example 3.15

Let us draw the truth table for the statement in the last example, $p \wedge \sim q$.

p	q	$\sim q$	$p \wedge \sim q$
F	F	T	F
F	T	F	F
T	F	T	T
T	T	F	F

The proposition $p \wedge \sim q$ is true only when p is true and q is false. The sentence of the previous example is true because the statement p, "George Boole developed the algebraic foundation for logic" is true and the sentence q, "The electronic computer was invented in 1500 AD," is false.

Example 3.16

Let us find the truth table for $\sim(\sim p \vee q)$, and compose an English sentence using the corresponding statements from the first example.

p	q	$\sim p$	$\sim p \vee q$	$\sim(\sim p \vee q)$
F	F	T	T	F
F	T	T	T	F
T	F	F	F	T
T	T	F	T	F

The compound statement derived from the first example is as follows: "It is not true that George Boole did not develop the algebraic foundation for logic, and/or the electronic computer was invented in 1500 AD." To emphasize that $\vee$ indicates that one or both statements are true, we sometimes use "and/or" instead of just "or" for its English equivalent.

Notice that $p \wedge \sim q$ of Example 3.15 and $\sim(\sim p \vee q)$ of Example 3.16 have the same values in their truth tables. These two statements are **equivalent** or mean the same thing. We write

$$p \wedge \sim q \equiv \sim(\sim p \vee q)$$

Definition   Two propositions, p and q, are **logically equivalent** or **equivalent** or **equal**, written $p \equiv q$, provided they have identical values in their truth tables.

Algebra of Propositions

By showing with a truth table that $p \wedge \sim q \equiv \sim(\sim p \vee q)$, we have proved a property of algebra of propositions. Other basic properties that we can verify with truth tables are as follows:

For all statements p, q, and r, the following properties are true in the algebra of propositions:

1. **Commutative** properties for disjunction and conjunction
   a. $p \vee q \equiv q \vee p$ **b.** $p \wedge q \equiv q \wedge p$

2. **Associative** properties for disjunction and conjunction
   a. $p \vee (q \vee r) \equiv (q \vee p) \vee r$ **b.** $p \wedge (q \wedge r) \equiv (q \wedge p) \wedge r$

3. **Distributive** properties
   a. $p \vee (q \wedge r) \equiv (p \vee q) \wedge (p \vee r)$ **b.** $p \wedge (q \vee r) \equiv (p \wedge q) \vee (p \wedge r)$

4. **Identities** for disjunction (F) and conjunction (T)
   a. $p \vee \text{F} \equiv p$ **b.** $p \wedge \text{T} \equiv p$

5. **Complement** properties
   a. $p \vee \sim p \equiv \text{T}$ **b.** $p \wedge \sim p \equiv \text{F}$

The commutative property states that the order in which we combine propositions with disjunction or conjunction does not matter. For example, the statement "I like to swim, and I run every day" is equivalent to "I run every day, and I like to swim."

The associative property indicates that in a statement with disjunctions (or conjunctions), the order of evaluation of the proposition is irrelevant. These properties have their counterparts in the arithmetic properties. For example, when adding three numbers together, it does not matter whether we add the last two or the first two numbers together initially.

$$5 + (2 + 4) = 5 + 6 = 11$$
$$(5 + 2) + 4 = 7 + 4 = 11$$

Similarly, in an expression with two products,

$$5 \cdot (2 \cdot 4) = 5 \cdot 8 = 40$$
$$(5 \cdot 2) \cdot 4 = 10 \cdot 4 = 40$$

we get the same answer evaluating $(2 \cdot 4)$ and then multiplying by 5 as we do calculating $(5 \cdot 2)$ and multiplying the result by 4.

The distributive property shows how to distribute $\vee$ through the conjunction of two statements, or vice versa. To illustrate, the statement "I will go bowling, **and** I will go to dinner **or** a movie" is equivalent to "I will go bowling **and** to dinner, **or** I will go bowling **and** to a movie."

F (*FALSE*) is the identity for disjunction. If p is false, so is $p \lor$ F (p OR *FALSE*). If p is true, then $p \lor$ F is true. Because p and $p \lor$ F always agree, they are equivalent. Similarly, T (*TRUE*) is the identity for conjunction. Thus, $p \land$ T (p AND *TRUE*) is equivalent to p.

The complement properties give the results of combining p and $\sim p$. The proposition $p \lor \sim p$ is always true. For example, the statement "I made an 'A' on the test **or** I didn't" is certainly true. In contrast, $p \land \sim p$ is always false. For example, "I made an 'A' on the test **and** I didn't" must be false.

DeMorgan's Laws

DeMorgan's Laws, illustrated below, are also significant in logic:

> **DeMorgan's Laws:** For all statements p and q,
>
> **a.** $\sim(p \lor q) \equiv \sim p \land \sim q$ **b.** $\sim(p \land q) \equiv \sim p \lor \sim q$

We can prove each property in two ways, from the definitions with truth tables or from the properties presented earlier.

For some involved tests in C, we can use these properties to find an equivalent condition that is more understandable and maintainable. For instance, employing DeMorgan's law for the boolean variables *found* and *cont,* we see that the statement

```
if (!(found || cont)) . . .
```

is equivalent to the statement

```
if (!found && !cont) . . . .
```

In English, we might emphatically state, "I did **not** lie or cheat! To repeat, I did **not** lie, **and** I did **not** cheat!" Notice the use of "not," "or," and "and" in these statements.

Section 3.5 Exercises

Let p be "It is cloudy" and q be "It is rainy." Assume the opposite of "cloudy" is "clear." Write each of the statements of Exercises 1–4 in symbolic logic.

1. It is cloudy and rainy.

2. It is cloudy but not rainy.

3. It is neither cloudy nor rainy.

4. It is false that it is clear or rainy.

Consider the following statements:
  p: I go to dinner.   q: I eat spahetti.   r: I eat salad.

Write English equivalents to the compound propositions in Exercises 5–10. Notice the relationship between your two answers in each exercise, and give the name of the illustrated property.

5. $q \land r$, $r \land q$

6. $p \land (q \lor r)$, $(p \land q) \lor (p \land r)$

7. $p \land \sim p$. Is this situation possible?

8. $p \lor \sim p$. Can this situation ever be false?

9. $\sim(q \lor r)$, $\sim q \land \sim r$

10. $\sim(q \land r)$, $\sim q \lor \sim r$

Negate the statements in Exercises 11–14. Then, by DeMorgan's Laws, simplify each using the symbols $<, \leq, >, \geq, =, \neq$ *and the connectives "or" and "and."*

11. $x \leq y$ and $x \leq z$ **12.** $x > y$ or $y = z$

13. $x \neq y$ and $x \geq y$ **14.** $x \neq y$ and $(y \geq z$ or $z < u)$

Using a truth table, verify each equivalence in Exercises 15–19.

15. $p \lor T \equiv T$

16. $p \land F \equiv F$

17. $p \land (q \land r) \equiv (p \land q) \land r$

18. $p \lor (q \land r) \equiv (p \lor q) \land (p \lor r)$

19. $p \lor (p \land q) \equiv p$

20. The problem below appeared in the sample questions of *The Graduate Record Examinations Descriptive Booklet 1991–93*. The binary-coded-decimal (BCD) representation mentioned in the problem is a method of encoding numbers so that each number is encoded separately in base 2. For example, 92 is encoded as 1001 0010 (where $9_{10} = 1001_2$ and $2_{10} = 0010_2$). You need not be familiar with this encoding scheme to answer the problem. According to directions in the booklet

    $\lor$ denotes "inclusive or"

Juxtaposition of statements denotes "and," e.g., *PQ* denotes "*P* and *Q*."

Digits	A	B	C	D
0	0	0	0	0
1	0	0	0	1
2	0	0	1	0
.	.	.	.	.
.	.	.	.	.
9	1	0	0	1
	1	0	1	0
Invalid Codes				
	.	.	.	.
	1	1	1	1

The table in the figure above shows the binary-coded-decimal (BCD) representation of the digits 0 through 9. The Boolean expression that represents the set of invalid codes is

  (A) $A \lor BC$ (B) $ABCD$ (C) $AB \lor AD$ (D) $AB \lor CD$ (E) $AB \lor AC$

Section 3.6 **Testing Schemes**

From the first chapter, we have emphasized the importance of top-down design in problem solving. This method of stepwise refinement involves breaking down complex modules into simpler ones, each performing one task, until each module is manageable. We begin by defining the task of the main function, which consists primarily of a series of function calls. We perform stepwise refinement on each function until the low-level functions are simple enough to code without the use of other functions. By that time, implementation of the functions should not pose any difficulty. In this section, we consider methods of implementing and testing the modular program.

Top-Down Testing

Implementation and testing of the program can also use **top-down strategy**. Instead of entering the entire program before beginning testing, we write and debug functions one at a time, starting with the highest-level functions and proceeding to the lowest. We can more easily determine the location of an error in one function than in a program that has five or ten such functions. With modern computers, it only takes a short time to compile, link, and run programs. Testing units one at a time can save the programmer hours of frustrating debugging.

Testing higher-level functions first is somewhat problematic, because their functioning depends on yet unwritten lower-level functions. To perform the higher-level tests, we use fake lower-level functions, called **stubs**. These functions simulate the operations of the actual functions.

Definitions   A **stub** is a version of a routine that is used for top-down testing of a program. The stub does not implement the routine's algorithm and does not necessarily return correct results. However, the results are sufficient to test the routines that call the stub. The **top-down strategy** of program implementation and testing starts with the highest-level functions and proceeds to the lowest, with debugging occurring one function at a time. Stubs are used in place of lower-level routines.

For example, suppose we are developing the program of Example 3.11 (Section 3.3) to read an employee's salary and return a salary reflecting a raise. We can easily write *main* from the structure chart, which we repeat in Figure 3.7.

```
main()
{
    int salary;              /* monthly salary */

    instructions();
    salary = ReadSalary();
    if (OutOfRange(salary))
        printf("\nThat salary is out of range\n");
    else
        printf("\nThe new salary is %d\n", NewSalary(salary));
}
```

Figure 3.7
Structure chart for the program in Example 3.11, repeated from Figure 3.4

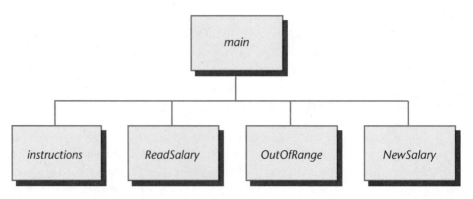

Figure 3.8
Black-box
analysis of
instructions

To test *main,* we must provide prototypes and stubs for the four functions *main* invokes. The function *instructions* only prints the purpose of the program and instructions on its use. Thus, a call to *printf* is sufficient for the body of that stub. The stub provides a preliminary implementation for the black-box analysis of this procedure, which Figure 3.8 presents.

```
/*
 * Function to print instructions on what the program does
 * Pre:     none
 * Post:    Instructions have been displayed.
 */

void instructions(void)
{
    printf("Entering stub for function instructions\n");
}
```

The listing should include an opening comment for the function. A clear statement of purpose, along with pre- and postconditions, can aid our understanding during debugging and development of that segment of code. We can easily write down ideas as they occur, as opposed to rethinking the goals every time we consider the function. The stub and its prototype should contain parameters and appropriate type declarations for the parameters, any known local variables, and the return value. Thus, we establish the structure of the program and enable the compiler to detect syntax errors in our coding of that structure.

The second function that *main* invokes, *ReadSalary,* prompts the user for a salary and reads and returns that salary. Because *main* expects this function to return a value, the stub must provide such a number. Figure 3.9 contains the black-box analysis of *ReadSalary.* An appropriate stub appears in the following code:

```
/*
 * Function to read a salary interactively
 * Pre:     none
 * Post:    The salary the user entered has been returned.
 */

int ReadSalary(void)
{
    int salary;                  /* monthly salary */

    printf("Entering stub for function ReadSalary\n");
    return 1800;
}
```

We declare *ReadSalary* to be of type *int* and return a value to contribute to the processing of *main.* For further testing, we could adjust this returned number to

Figure 3.9
Black-box
analysis of
ReadSalary

Figure 3.10
Black-box
analysis of
OutOfRange

represent a salary with a different raise, such as 4900, or an inappropriate salary, such
as −700.

OutOfRange discovers if the salary is out of an allowable range. The value it returns
is *TRUE*(1) or *FALSE*(0). Figure 3.10 presents a black-box analysis of the routine. We
return the value indicating no range error in the following stub:

```
/* OutOfRange stub version #1 */
/*
 * Function to return TRUE(1) if salary is out of range
 * Range:  $0 - $5000
 * Pre:    salary is an integer.
 * Post:   A nonzero number (TRUE) has been returned if salary
 *         is not in range; 0 (FALSE) if it is.
 */

int OutOfRange(int salary)
{
   printf("Entering stub for function OutOfRange\n");
   return 0;
}
```

Later, we could change the return value to 1 to test another branch in *main.*

An alternative way to write the stub is to code return values for each salary we are
testing.

```
/* OutOfRange stub version #2 */
/*
 * Function to return TRUE(1) if salary is out of range
 * Range:  $0 - $5000
 * Pre:    salary is an integer.
 * Post:   A nonzero number (TRUE) has been returned if salary
 *         is not in range; 0 (FALSE) if it is.
 */
```

```
int OutOfRange(int salary)
{
   int stubReturn;      /* holds value for stub to return */

   printf("Entering stub for function OutOfRange\n");

   if (salary == 1800) stubReturn = 0;
   if (salary == 4900) stubReturn = 0;
   if (salary == -700) stubReturn = 1;
   return stubReturn;
}
```

Another method of obtaining a value for *stubReturn* is for the stub function to print its argument and ask the programmer to enter a return value.

```
/* OutOfRange stub version #3 */
/*
 * Function to return TRUE(1) if salary is out of range
 * Range:   $0 - $5000
 * Pre:     salary is an integer.
 * Post:    A nonzero number (TRUE) has been returned if salary
 *          is not in range; 0 (FALSE) if it is.
 */

int OutOfRange(int salary)
{
   int stubReturn;      /* holds value for stub to return */

   printf("Entering stub for function OutOfRange\n");
   printf("Old salary = %d\n", salary);
   printf("Enter 1 (TRUE) for out of range or 0 (FALSE):  ");
   scanf("%d", &stubReturn);
   return stubReturn;
}
```

As the black-box analysis in Figure 3.11 indicates, the last stub, *NewSalary,* must return some value for *main* to use during execution. The input parameter *salary* is acceptable.

```
   /*
    * Function to return new salary.  For salaries < $2000
    * raise is $150; for salaries between $2000 and $5000,
    * raise is $250
    * Pre:     salary is an integer between 0 and 5000.
    * Post:    The modified salary (previous salary + raise)
    *          has been returned.
    */

   int NewSalary(int salary)
   {
      printf("Entering stub for function NewSalary\n");
      return salary;
   }
```

Figure 3.11
Black-box
analysis of
NewSalary

The use of stubs is valid because we are only testing the higher-level functions. Once we have tested each higher-level function, one at a time, we replace lower-level stubs with the actual functions and test them. If a problem exists, it probably occurs in the new function. This process continues until we have added and tested the lowest-level functions.

Bottom-Up Testing

Another scheme for testing, the **bottom-up strategy**, implements the lower-level functions first and then proceeds to higher-level functions. The design is still top-down, and we still implement and debug functions one at a time. Before testing a function, however, we implement and test all routines beneath it in the structure chart.

For testing, we now have the opposite problem of top-down strategy. The module above the one being tested in the structure chart and *main* have not been implemented. The program file certainly needs a *main*, and often the function under consideration requires input data from a calling routine. To handle these requirements, we design and implement a **test program**. For example, in Example 3.13 of Section 3.4, we developed a procedure, *PrintNumber*, to print a positive one- or two-digit integer using words. To test the procedure, we designed a *main* to read an integer and to call *PrintNumber* using data in the proper range. Once thoroughly tested, the function *PrintNumber* is available for use in any program we desire. The only purpose of *main*, which follows, is to serve as a **driver** for the execution of *PrintNumber*.

```
    :
main()
{
    int n;

    printf("Enter a positive integer less than 100: ");
    scanf("%d", &n);
    if ((n < 1) || (n > 99))
        printf("Sorry, your number is out of range.");
    else
        PrintNumber(n);
    printf("\n");
}
    :
```

In Chapters 5 and 6, we consider looping, in which the computer executes the same segment more than once. With looping, we can repeatedly ask the user for a one- or two-digit number and call *PrintNumber* to display that number in words.

Definitions   The **bottom-up strategy** of program implementation and testing starts with the lowest-level functions and proceeds to the highest, with debugging occurring one function at a time. Before testing a function, we implement and test all routines beneath it in the structure chart. A driver is used in place of the routine that calls the function being tested. A **driver** is a module that exercises a system or part of a system. A **test program** includes a driver and the module or modules it is exercising.

Combined Top-Down and Bottom-Up Testing

Sometimes programmers use a combination of top-down and bottom-up testing. Even though the design is top-down, the overall implementation of a commercial project is usually bottom-up. Such projects often involve a team of programmers, with different members responsible for different components. Each member designs his or her module and performs **unit testing**, or testing of the individual module. Unit testing is often done in a top-down fashion. The modules are gradually assembled into larger portions with **integrated testing** at each phase. Finally, the complete project is assembled, and additional integrated testing occurs.

Definitions   **Unit testing** is the testing of an individual module. **Integrated testing** is the testing of all or part of a system in which programmers have already performed unit testing of modules.

Another situation in which we do not use a strict top-down testing scheme is in the implementation of a prototype. A **prototype**, or partial version of the program, demonstrates some of the functionality and "user friendliness" of the developing system. For example, the credit card verification program from Section 1.1 has the structure chart in Figure 3.12. A prototype might involve reading the card identification record and finding that number in the credit file. For the developing prototype, we implement *main* with stubs for all modules it calls. After testing *main*, we replace the stub for the Read-credit-card-identification-data module with an implementation of its algorithm. After thoroughly testing, we next implement the Update-customer's-credit-file module with stubs for the three routines it calls. Instead of implementing and testing the other modules *main* calls next, however, we implement and test a module at the lowest level, Find-card-number-in-file. When this phase is complete, we have a working program that reads a card number and finds the corresponding record. Thus, we can demonstrate part of the functionality of our program.

Definition   A **prototype** is partial version of a program that demonstrates some of the functionality and "user friendliness" of the developing system.

Regardless of the implementation and testing scheme, obtaining a modular program is extremely important. Implementing and testing the modules one at a time allows us to locate errors more easily. Should we discover an error in the design during implementation, we must return to the analysis phase and then the design phase for revision. Usually, we discover such problems before implementing and testing every module. Thus, we do not waste time implementing code that does not appear in the final, revised version.

Figure 3.12
Structure chart
for a credit card
verification
program from
Figure 1.2

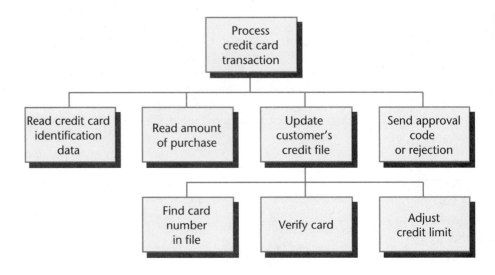

Modular programs are easy to maintain. Often, we do not detect all the bugs during the initial testing. If an error is discovered after the program is supposedly fully tested, then the module concerned can be isolated and retested by itself. After unit testing of the revised module, we repeat the integrated testing of the whole program to ensure that all the modules work together properly.

Section 3.6 Exercises

1. Assume the program in Example 3.13 in Section 3.4 has not been implemented.
   a. Using a top-down scheme, describe how to implement and test the program.
   b. Use a bottom-up scheme.
2. For Exercise 5 of Section 3.4, write a stub for the procedure to process a charge.
3. Write a stub for *CalculateNoGallons* of Example 2.23 of Section 2.8 to calculate the number of gallons of plastic needed to coat a wood floor with given dimensions.
4. Write a test program for the function *minimum* of Exercise 14 in Section 3.2 that returns the smaller of two integer parameters.
5. Write a test program for the function *even* of Exercise 15 in Section 3.2 that returns *TRUE*(1) if the integer parameter is even and returns *FALSE*(0) otherwise.

≋ Programming and Debugging Hints

**Decision
Control
Structures**

The following cautions involve implementation of the decision control structures in C:

1. Always surround with parentheses the logical expression of an *if, else-if,* or *switch* statement.

   ```
   if (x < y)
   ```

2. The mathematical statement $2 < x < 7$ is not valid in C. We must use a compound logical expression.

   ```
   if ((2 < x) && (x < 7))
   ```

3. If in doubt about the operator precedence, use parentheses to clarify the expression.

```
if (((x < y) && (y < 5)) || found)
```

4. Be careful not to confuse the assignment and relational equals operators.

```
if (x == y)
```

5. The relational operators $<=$ and $>=$ cannot be written with $=$ first.

```
if (x <= y)
```

6. The logical operator for AND has two ampersands (&&) not one. The logical operator for OR has two bars (||) not one.

```
if (found && cont || (x < 50))
```

7. A semicolon ends each statement, including any simple statement before *else*.

```
if (x < y)
    printf("less\n");
else
    printf("not less\n");
```

8. For several statements to appear in an *if* or *else* clause, group the statements into a compound statement, which has braces surrounding the group.

```
if (x < y)
{
    printf("less\n");
    z = x;
}
else
{
    printf("not less\n");
    z = y;
}
```

9. Unless the next segment should be executed, too, end the list of statements for a *case* label with a *break* statement.

```
    ⋮
case 5:
    printf("%d\n", x);
    break;
case 6:
    ⋮
```

10. Usually, include a *default* label in a *switch* statement to catch invalid values of the logical expression for the statement.

```
    ⋮
case 5:
    printf("%d\n", x);
    break;
default:
    printf("Invalid data\n");
```

11. The value in the *case* label must be a constant integer expression, not a variable.

```
case i:              /*** ERROR ***/
```

Testing

In Section 3.6, we considered two strategies for modular testing of programs—top-down and bottom-up. The following are some hints for testing a module:

1. During testing, **echo-print** or display what was just read. We should verify that the value the computer obtains is what it should be. For instance, a common error is to forget the ampersand in reading a value for an integer variable. When the ampersand is omitted, unpredictable results occur.

```
scanf("%d", &IdNum);
printf("IdNum = %d\n", IdNum); /* echo print for testing */
```

2. Use test data for which the output can be easily determined by hand or calculator. Check that the output is correct.

3. Type comments, including header comments and pre- and postconditions, when entering a routine. We can more easily remember the purpose of a module at this time. Moreover, during debugging, comments help us to determine the nature of a module more quickly.

4. As much as possible, choose test data to check every branch of a program. For example, suppose the program contains the following *if-else* statement:

```
if (x < y)
    printf("less\n");
else
    printf("not less\n");
```

We should test the program for data with $x < y$, $x > y$, and x equal to y, such as 2 and 6, 8 and 3, and 5 and 5, respectively. As the statements become more involved, we need to check more branches.

```
if (x < y)
    if (y < 5)
        printf("Branch 1");
    else
        printf("Branch 2");
else
    printf("Branch 3");
```

Possible test data for testing this segment are as follows:

x	y	*Branch*
2	3	Branch 1
2	6	Branch 2
2	1	Branch 3

Key Terms

! 141	‖ 141	*break* statement 169
!= 139	AND 141	*case* label 168
&& 141	block 147	compound condition 140
< 139	boolean constant 142	compound statement 147
<= 139	boolean expression 142	control structure 145
== 139	boolean value 142	*default* label 168
> 139	boolean variable 142	driver 191
>= 139	bottom-up strategy 191	echo-print 194

Summary

In this chapter, we discuss several C constructs for decision making and applications involving these constructs. Frequently, a decision is made based on the truth or falsity of a relational expression. A relational operator is a symbol that we use to test the relationship between two expressions. The relational operators in C are == (equal to), > (greater than), < (less than), != (not equal to), >= (greater than or equal to), and <= (less than or equal to). We can create compound boolean expressions using logical operators, which are symbols that we use to combine or negate logical expressions, such as those containing relational operators. The logical operators in C are ! (NOT), && (AND), and || (OR). Boolean constants are *TRUE* and *FALSE*. The operator precedence in C is as follows:

```
()                                          highest
!        − (unary)
*        /        %
+        - (binary)
<        <=       >        >=
==       !=
&&
||
=                                           lowest
```

We clarify the operator precedence in an expression by using parentheses.

The flow of control, or the order in which the computer executes statements, can be altered by a selection control structure. With such a control structure, the computer makes a decision about the next statement to execute by evaluating a logical expression. One implementation of the selection control structure in C is the *if* statement, which has the following form:

```
if (expression)
    statement1
```

If the value of *expression* is *TRUE,* then the computer executes *statement1*. Another selection control structure is the *if-else* statement, which has the following form:

```
if (expression)
    statement1
else
    statement2
```

If the value of *expression* is *TRUE,* then the computer executes *statement1.* Otherwise, the computer executes *statement2.* Either *statement1* or *statement2* can be a compound statement with the form

```
{
    statement
       ⋮
    statement
}
```

We can have an *if* or *if-else* statement as a statement inside an *if* or *if-else* statement. The general form of such nesting is

```
if (expression1)
    statement1
else if (expression2)
    statement2
else if (expression3)
    statement3
⋮
else
    statementn
```

An *else* matches the nearest unmatched *if* that precedes it.

The *switch* statement is a selection control structure that permits virtually any number of branches. Its general format with an optional *default* is as follows:

```
switch (expression)
{
    case c1:
        any_number_of_statements1
    case c2:
        any_number_of_statements2
    ⋮
    default:
        any_number_of_statementsn
}
```

The computer evaluates the *switch* expression and transfers control to the statement immediately following the *case* label for the appropriate value of *expression.* If the value of the *switch* expression does not match any case label and if the *default* label is present, control passes to the statement after *default.* The keyword *break* causes the *switch* to terminate, and execution resumes with the next statement (if any) following the *switch* statement. Often, statements for a case label end in *break.*

This chapter also continues the discussion of problem solving by considering methods for implementing and testing a modular program. The top-down strategy of program implementation and testing starts with the highest-level functions and proceeds to the lowest, with debugging occurring one function at a time. Stubs are used in place of lower-level routines. The stub does not implement the routine's algorithm and does not necessarily return correct results. However, the results are sufficient to test the routines that call the stub. The bottom-up strategy of program implementation and testing starts with the lowest-level functions and proceeds to the highest, with debugging occurring one function at a time. With this strategy, before testing a function, we implement and test all routines beneath it in the structure chart. A driver, which is a module that exercises a system or part of a system, replaces the routine that calls the function being tested.

Review Questions

1. What statements in C permit decisions to be made?

2. What keywords are part of the *if-else* statement?

3. How many relational operators are there? Name them.

4. What symbols are used for the logical operators AND and OR?

5. If two values are compared using a relational operator, what possible answers can be produced?

6. Give the order of precedence, from highest to lowest, of the operators <, &&, =, ||, !, and *.

7. Name three types of control structures.

8. In an *if* statement, if two separate statements are to be executed when a comparison is true, what must be done with them?

9. What is the function of the *else* clause in an *if* statement?

10. Which of the following statements are true, and which are false?

    a. An *if* statement must always include an *else* clause.

    b. An *if* statement may contain only an *else* clause.

    c. An *if* statement may include only simple statements.

    d. An *if* statement may contain compound statements only in the *else* clause.

    e. A semicolon may follow an *if* statement only if a compound statement is used.

    f. The *else* clause must always be indented to line up under the *if* clause.

11. What is a nested *if* statement?

12. How many semicolons must be included in an *if* statement that contains a single statement in the *if* clause and a single statement in the *else* clause?

13. When two *if* statements are nested, what rule determines which *else* clause matches which *if?*

14. Is the following statement correct? If not, explain why.

    ```
    if (q >= r)
        printf("q is greater than or equal to r");
        a = b;
    else
        printf("r is less than q");
        c = d;
    ```

15. What is the difference between the two operators = and ==?

16. Name the logical operator that negates the truth value of the expression to its immediate right.

17. What integer value is equivalent to *FALSE?*

18. What is the maximum number of labels permissible in a *switch* statement?

19. Explain the purpose of the *switch* statement.

20. What role is played by the *break* statement within a *switch* statement?

21. What keywords are always used in a *switch* statement?

22. What other keyword is often used in a *switch* statement?

23. What is the connection between the *switch* variable or expression and the constants in the *case* labels?

24. What role is played by the *default* label in a *switch* statement?

25. In what order can *case* labels be specified?

26. If a particular *case* label has several statements associated with it, how must the statements be grouped?

27. Explain the action of the *switch* statement.

28. How can it be arranged that different values of the *switch* variable or expression cause the same set of statements to be executed?

29. What is a simplified version of a routine that is used for top-down testing of a program?

Laboratory

Copy the files (LAB031.c and LAB032.c) mentioned in this laboratory from the disk that came with your text to your own disk. By working with copies, you preserve the originals for future reference.

1. The purpose of this laboratory exercise is to study the *if-else* statement, nested *if* statement, stubs, validation of input data, and top-down design. We also develop an important function to find the maximum of two values.

   The verbal part of the SAT test counts 800 points. Students can take the test several times, and colleges evaluate a prospective student based on the largest score for each part of the test. The program in this exercise reads two SAT verbal scores for a student and prints the larger of the two scores. A sample run follows:

   ```
   This program interactively reads two SAT
   verbal scores and prints the larger.

   Type an SAT verbal score between 0 and 800:   550
   Type an SAT verbal score between 0 and 800:   600


   Your maximum score is 600
   ```

   The structure of this program is similar to that in Example 3.11 of Section 3.3, which reads a salary and computes and prints a new salary. However, in this SAT program, we read two scores instead of one salary, and we must verify that both are valid. We could read both scores and then alert the user to any problems, but a better design would be to check the validity of a score as soon as the program reads it. If the first score is out of range, the program should indicate the problem and refrain from reading the second score. (When we discuss loops, we can allow the

Figure 3.13
Structure chart
for the program
in Laboratory
Exercise 1

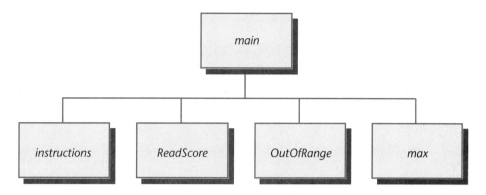

user to correct a mistake, but now we must settle for aborting the program with an error message.)

Figure 3.13 displays the structure chart with five functions:

main	Driver for program
instructions	Prints instructions on what the program does
ReadScore	Reads a score interactively and returns this score
OutOfRange	Returns *TRUE*(1) if the SAT score is out of range (not between 0 and 800) and *FALSE*(0) otherwise
max	Returns the maximum of two integer parameters

Pseudocode for the function *main* follows:

main( )

Program to read two SAT verbal scores for a student and print the larger of the two scores

Algorithm:

call *instructions* to print instructions
read the first score from the user by calling *ReadScore*
if the score is out of range (determined with *OutOfRange*)
    print an error message
else
    read the second score from the user by calling *ReadScore*
    if the score is out of range (determined with *OutOfRange*)
        print an error message
    else
        print the larger of the two scores by calling *max*

The file *LAB031.c* on your disk contains a shell of this program. The function *main* has the pseudocode listed in comments; *instructions* appears in its entirety; and the bodies are missing from the other functions. A listing of the file follows with color marking the parts we replace in this laboratory:

```
/*
 * This program reads two SAT verbal scores (between 0
 * and 800) for a student and prints the larger
 */
```

```c
#include <stdio.h>

void instructions(void);
int ReadScore(void);
int OutOfRange(int score);
int max(int x, int y);

main()
{
    int score1,          /* SAT verbal score #1 */
        score2;          /* SAT verbal score #2 */

    /* call function instructions to print instructions */
    /* obtain a value for score1 by calling ReadScore */
    /* if score1 is out of range
          print an error message
       else
          obtain a value for score2 by calling ReadScore
          if score2 is out of range
             print an error message
          else
             using function max print larger score */
}

/*
 * Function to print instructions on what the program does
 */

void instructions(void)
{
    printf("This program interactively reads two SAT\n");
    printf("verbal scores and prints the larger\n\n");
}

/*
 * Function to read a score interactively
 */

int ReadScore(void)
{
    /* stub for ReadScore */
}

/*
 * Function to return TRUE (1) if the SAT score is out of
 * range.  Range:  0-800
 */

int OutOfRange(int score)
{
    /* stub for OutOfRange */
}
```

```
/*
 * Function to return maximum of two integer parameters
 */

int max(int x, int y)
{
    /* stub for max */
}
```

a. Convert *main* into C code, calling functions when appropriate. Be careful to group the statements in the first *else* clause with braces to form a compound statement.

b. Replace the comment in the body of *ReadScore* with statements to convert it to a stub. Print that the program is entering this stub, and return some integer constant.

c. Replace the comment in the body of *OutOfRange* with statements to convert it to a stub. Print that the program is entering this stub, and return 0 (*FALSE*).

d. Replace the comment in the body of *max* with statements to convert it to a stub. Print that the program is entering this stub, and return the first parameter.

e. Compile and run this program. Debug your work before continuing. The output of your program with stubs should read something like the following:

```
This program interactively reads two SAT
verbal scores and prints the larger

Entering stub ReadScore
Entering stub OutOfRange
Entering stub ReadScore
Entering stub OutOfRange
Entering stub max

Your maximum score is 550
```

Print a listing of your program.

f. Change the returned value of *ReadScore* to 900 and the returned value of *OutOfRange* to 1 (*TRUE*). Execute the program to obtain output similar to the following:

```
This program interactively reads two SAT
verbal scores and prints the larger

Entering stub ReadScore
Entering stub OutOfRange
900 is not between 0 and 800
```

Does your program only call *ReadScore* and *OutOfRange* once and then print an error message? If it does not, you probably need to enclose the statements after the first *else* clause in braces. After the program behaves properly, change the returned value of *OutOfRange* back to 0 (*FALSE*).

g. Replace the stub body of *ReadScore* with the actual code and debug your program. If *max* prints a number you did not type, you probably need an ampersand before *score* in the call to *scanf.*

h. Replace the stub body of *OutOfRange* with the actual code and debug your program.

i. For *max,* we use an *if-else* statement to test which parameter is larger. Store the larger of these in a temporary variable, which the function returns. Replace the stub body of *max* with the actual code and debug your program.

j. Add pre- and postconditions for all routines.

k. Print a listing of the program with several test runs.

2. The purpose of this laboratory exercise is to study the *switch* and *break* statements. We use these statements to develop a program that presents a menu of choices for a vending machine and prints the cost of the user's selection. The menu reads as follows:

```
The vending machine contains

1     chocolate candy bar
2     peppermints
3     crackers

Please make your selection by number:
```

The first item costs 75¢, the second 55¢, and the third 65¢. Selection of 1 results in

```
Please make your selection by number:   1

The cost is 75 cents
```

An out-of-range selection yields an error message, as shown:

```
Please make your selection by number:   7

Invalid selection number
```

File *LAB032.c* contains the shell of this program. Its listing is below with parts we will change in color:

```
/*
 *   This interactive program prints the cost of a vending
 *   machine selection
 */
```

```c
#include <stdio.h>

int menu(void);
void output(int selection);

main()
{
   int selection;          /* menu selection */

   selection = menu();
   output(selection);
}

/*
 * Function to print menu and return user's selection
 * Pre:   none
 * Post: The user's selection was returned.
 */

int menu(void)
{
   int selection;      /* menu selection */

   printf("The vending machine contains\n\n");
   printf("1  chocolate candy bar\n");
   printf("2  peppermints\n");
   printf("3  crackers\n");
   printf("\nPlease make your selection by number:  ");

   scanf(/*** read a value for selection ***/);

   return /*** returned value ***/;
}

/*
 * Function to print the cost of the user's selection
 * Pre:   selection is an integer.
 * Post: The cost of the corresponding item has been printed.
 */

void output(int selection)
{
   if (selection == 1)
     printf("\nThe cost is 75 cents\n");
   else if (selection == 2)
     printf("\nThe cost is 55 cents\n");
   else if (selection == 3)
     printf("\nThe cost is 65 cents\n");
   else
     printf("\nInvalid selection number\n");
}
```

a. Replace the comments in color in *menu* so that the function reads and returns a value for *selection*. Test the resulting program. If the output is "Invalid selection number" regardless of your choice, be sure you have an ampersand before *selection* in the *scanf* statement.

b. Replace the nested *if* statement in the function *output* with an equivalent *switch* statement. Be careful of the syntax. Have *selection* in parentheses; place braces around the body; have *case* labels that start with the word *case* and contain a number and a colon; and include *break* statements for each case other than the *default* case. Debug the program.

c. Add a fourth menu selection for gum in *menu,* and assume it costs 55¢. In *output,* add the following *case* label after the *case* label for the cost of peppermints:

```
case 4:
```

Do not add another *printf.*

d. Print a listing of the program with several test runs.

e. Remove the *break* statements and run the program. Describe and explain the output.

4

Additional Numeric Types

Introduction

In Chapter 2, we covered the integer data type *int*. We considered *int* variables, arithmetic with integers, interactive programs with integer input, storage of integers, and modular programming with emphasis on integer functions. In this chapter, we expand the discussion of data types to other numeric types.

Certainly, integers are important in such situations as counting and recording the number of whole items. Frequently, however, we must deal with numbers that have decimals—floating point numbers. For example, a movie ticket might cost $6.75. Sales tax for a state might be 6% = 0.06. A grade point average for a student might be 3.24.

The first section of this chapter covers two types for numbers that contain a decimal—*float* and *double*. Although *float* is the most common data type for floating point numbers, a variable of type *double* takes up twice the amount of space as one of type *float* and, consequently, can store a larger range of numbers. Building on our knowledge of type *int*, we discuss arithmetic expressions with floating point constants and variables and the printing of numbers of type *float* or *double*. The second section, which contains breadth material, indicates how the computer stores and performs arithmetic involving floating point numbers.

Although storage for integers and floating point numbers differs, many times we must perform arithmetic involving both kinds of numbers. For example, when we buy two movie tickets costing $6.75 each, we must be able to compute the total price as the integer 2 times the floating point number 6.75. The third section of the chapter shows how to handle expressions involving integers and floating point numbers. It also includes a discussion of conversion from one type to another and the implications of this feature.

In Section 4.4, we consider other integer types. The data type *long* is the integer counterpart of *double*. On many computers, a variable of type *long* has twice the storage of one of type *int*. The type *unsigned int* is useful when we have a variable that must only store nonnegative integers, such as the number of tickets a theater sells in a day.

The last section of the chapter discusses various numeric constants and functions that are available in the ANSI C library. So far, we have included the ANSI C header file *stdio.h* in each program and have accessed the standard I/O library containing *printf* and *scanf*. Two other ANSI C libraries define constants that give us the range of integers and floating point numbers on the computer we are using. Another library contains mathematical functions that enable us to perform such computations as taking the square root of a number (for example, $\sqrt{x}$), calculating a value raised to a power (for example, x^4), or finding the sine of a number (for example, $\sin(x)$).

Goals

To study

- Floating point arithmetic
- The printing of floating point numbers
- Storage and manipulation of floating point numbers in the computer
- Mixed-mode arithmetic
- Strong and weak typing in programming languages
- The integer data types *short, long*, and *unsigned int*
- Numeric constants and functions available in ANSI C libraries

Section 4.1 **Floating Point Numbers**

Distinctions between Integers and Floating Point Numbers

Integers are excellent for counting. For example, the number of pages in this book is an integer. The type *int*, however, is not the best data type for describing the cost of a pair of slacks, such as $49.95, or the distance between the library and administration building, such as 0.75 miles. For such numbers, a floating point data type is best.

Floating point numbers have a decimal point. In mathematics, we refer to these as **real numbers** expressed with a decimal point. Some examples are 1.234, −5746.8, 15. and 128.0. The compiler differentiates between floating point numbers and integers because the computer stores them differently. In the next section, we discuss storage of floating point numbers in the computer.

> **Definition**   A **floating point number** is a number stored in the computer with a decimal reference point.

The major distinctions between integers and floating point numbers are as follows:

1. Integers include only whole numbers, such as 27 or −8, but floating point numbers must have a decimal, such as 27., −8.0, or 53.24.

2. Floating point numbers usually have a wider range of numbers than integers. For example, on many microcomputers, the range of integers is from −32,768 to 32,767, whereas floating point numbers range from -10^{37} to 10^{37} (1 with 37 zeros following). The range depends on the particular computer.

3. Floating point numbers sometimes can lead to loss of mathematical **precision**. The result of an arithmetic computation may be slightly "off," such as 4.199999 representing 4.2. Integer arithmetic always produces an exact answer.

4. On most computers, floating point operations execute more slowly and the values occupy more memory than integer operations and numbers, respectively. For example, many microcomputers store an integer in two bytes (16 bits) and a floating point number in four (32 bits).

5. Declarations of integers use the keyword *int*, whereas floating point declarations employ the keyword *float*. The following segment declares *HoursAttempted* to be an integer variable and *GPA* to be a floating point variable:

```
int   HoursAttempted;   /* integer variable */
float GPA;              /* floating point variable */
```

6. As we saw in Chapter 2, the computer stores integers as binary numbers. (The computer might use two's complement notation to represent negative integers, but the result is still a binary number.) In the next section, we detail how the computer splits a floating point number into a fractional portion, the **mantissa**, and an **exponent** and stores each part in binary form.

7. We use the conversion specification %d to print an integer, and %f or %e to display a floating point number. For instance, suppose the integer variable *HoursAttempted* and the floating point variable *GPA* have values. We can print their values with

```
printf("Hours attempted = %d, grade point average = %f\n",
       HoursAttempted, GPA);
```

8. We can determine if two integers are equal using ==, as shown:

```
if (i == j)
```

We should not, however, compare floating point numbers using a relational operator equal. In this chapter, we discuss the reason for this restriction and an alternative method of comparison.

Floating Point Arithmetic

As with integer constants, we can declare and initialize floating point variables in a single statement. We can write these two statements

```
float a;
a = 123.45;
```

as the following single statement:

```
float a = 123.45;
```

Example 4.1

This example illustrates declarations, assignments, computations, and printing involving *float* variables. The program prints the result of addition, subtraction, multiplication, and division of 246.8 and 135.79. Although the computer uses different algorithms for the *float* computations than the *int* arithmetic, C has the same basic integer and floating point operators (+, −, *, and /).

```
/*
 * An illustration of the use of floating point numbers
 */

#include <stdio.h>

main()
{
    float   operand1 = 246.8,   /* first operand */
            operand2 = 135.79,  /* second operand */
            answer;             /* result of computation */

    answer = operand1 + operand2;
    printf("%f + %f = %f\n", operand1, operand2, answer);

    answer = operand1 - operand2;
    printf("%f - %f = %f\n", operand1, operand2, answer);

    answer = operand1 * operand2;
    printf("%f * %f = %f\n", operand1, operand2, answer);

    printf("%f / %f = %f\n",
            operand1, operand2, operand1 / operand2);
}
```

The output may vary among computers due to differences in their storage of floating point numbers. Execution on one computer produces the following results:

```
246.800003 + 135.789993 = 382.589996
246.800003 - 135.789993 = 111.010010
246.800003 * 135.789993 = 33512.972656
246.800003 / 135.789993 = 1.817512
```

This output illustrates the loss of precision, which we mentioned previously. For example, the value of *operand1*, 246.8, appears as 246.800003, and the value of *operand2*, 135.79, prints as 135.789993. The results of the calculations are also not exact. For most nonscientific and many scientific applications, **truncation errors** resulting from floating point calculations are tolerable.

Exponential Notation

C allows the programmer to read and print real numbers in **exponential notation** as a decimal fraction times a power of 10. For instance, with e standing for "exponent," an output of 9.843600e+02 means $9.843600 \times 10^2 = 984.3600$. The computer stores this number in two parts, a **fractional part** or **mantissa**, such as 98436, and an **exponent**, such as 2.

Definition **Exponential notation** represents a floating point number as a decimal fraction times a power of 10. With *a* being a decimal fraction and *n* a nonnegative integer, the exponential notation *a*e*n* represents $a \times 10^n$. The integer formed by dropping the decimal point from *a* is the **fractional part** or **mantissa**, and *n* is the **exponent**.

A normalized number in exponential notation has the decimal point immediately preceding the first nonzero digit, as in 0.594368×10^3 or 0.594368×10^{-3}. The positive exponent of 3 moves the decimal to the right 3 places, as shown:

$$0.594368 \times 10^3 = 594.368$$

The negative exponent, −3, moves the decimal to the left the same number of places, as shown:

$$0.594368 \times 10^{-3} = 0.000594368$$

Definition A **normalized** number in exponential notation has the decimal point immediately preceding the first nonzero digit.

Printing Numbers

Exponential notation is particularly convenient in scientific applications for expressing very large or very small numbers. For example, Avogadro's number, 6.023×10^{23}, is the number of molecules in one gram-molecule of an element. We can assign this value using exponential notation and print it in that notation using the conversion specification %e, as follows:

```
Avogadro = 6.023e23;
printf("Avogadro's number = %e or\n%f\n\n",
       Avogadro, Avogadro);
```

The following output of this segment reveals that the exponential notation is far more readable than the floating point notation for such a large number:

```
Avogadro's number = 6.023000e+23 or
602299993035875123400000.000000
```

Using the conversion specification %e, the number prints in standard exponential notation with one nonzero digit before the decimal and a lowercase e. We can also use an uppercase E in the exponential notation

```
Avogadro = 6.023E23;
```

or in the conversion specification. The statement

```
printf("Avogadro's number = %E\n", Avogadro);
```

produces

```
Avogadro's number = 6.023000E+23
```

Definition **Standard exponential notation** in C has the form *d*e*n*, where *d* is a number with one nonzero digit before the decimal and *n* is an integer.

Between the percent sign and the letter in any conversion specification, we can insert a number specifying the minimum **field width**. For example, %5d indicates to use at least five places to display the integer. Ordinarily, the number is **right-justified** or written on the far right of the output field. If the conversion specification includes a minus sign immediately after the %, however, the number is **left-justified**.

Definitions   A number is **right-justified** if it is written on the far right of the output field. A number is **left-justified** if it is written on the far left of the output field.

Example 4.2 _____

The code segment in this example illustrates the field width with the conversion specification %d. Colons before and after each conversion specification show the exact limits of the number field in the output.

```
printf("Case 1 :%d:\n", 123);
printf("Case 2 :%0d:\n", 123);
printf("Case 3 :%8d:\n", 123);
printf("Case 4 :%-8d:\n", 123);
printf("Case 5 :%8d:\n", -123);
```

Execution yields the following output:

```
Case 1 :123:
Case 2 :123:
Case 3 :     123:
Case 4 :123     :
Case 5 :    -123:
```

The first case is quite familiar to us. The three-digit integer is printed in a field width of three positions, because that is how many are needed to display the full number. In other words, the field width defaults to the width of the number. We obtain the same result in the second case using a specification of %0d. Zero spaces are not sufficient to accommodate a three-digit number. If the minimum field width is not adequate to handle the number, the effect is the same as having no width at all.

In Case 3, the conversion specification %8d supplies eight columns and right-justifies 123 within the field. When the specification is %-8d, as in Case 4, the number is left-justified in the field.

Case 5 prints the negative number −123 using a specification %8d. Thus, the number is right-justified in a field eight columns wide. Because the minus sign also occupies a position, −123 requires at least four print positions.

_____

After the e or f format, we can follow the field width number (if any) with a decimal point and a number that specifies how many digits to display on the right of the decimal point. For example, the conversion specification %9.3f indicates to print the number in a 9-character field with 3 digits after the decimal. The percent sign usually signals the beginning of a conversion specification. Therefore, to print %, we must use % % in the control string.

Example 4.3

Execution of the following segment of code demonstrates conversion specifications of the form *%m.n*f:

```
printf("Case  6 :%f:\n", 123.456);
printf("Case  7 :%f:\n", 123.4567776);
printf("Case  8 :%f:\n", 1.23456E+02);
printf("Case  9 :%4.2f:\n", 123.486);
printf("Case 10 :%8.2f:\n", 123.486);
printf("Case 11 :%.2f%%:\n", .06);
```

The output is

```
Case  6 :123.456000:
Case  7 :123.456778:
Case  8 :123.456000:
Case  9 :123.49:
Case 10 :  123.49:
Case 11 :0.06%:
```

Case 6 uses the %f conversion specification to print 123.456. When no decimal place count is specified, the default is six places. Consequently, the output has three trailing zeroes. Case 7 also employs %f, but the number contains more than six digits after the decimal. In this case, C uses six places and rounds the output to 123.456778.

Case 8 illustrates that we can convert a number from e format to standard notation by using a conversion specification %f.

In Case 9, the specification %4.2f indicates to display the number with two decimal places. Thus, the number 123.486 rounds to 123.49. Because this number requires six positions, rather than the four of the indicated minimum field width, the total field width defaults to six positions.

A similar situation arises in Case 10, in which the computer converts 123.486 using the specification %8.2f. Again, the number is rounded to 2 decimal places, yielding the value 123.49, and the result is right-justified in a field width of 8 positions. Even though eight positions is wide enough to hold the original number 123.486, the conversion specification permits only two decimal places. Consequently, the computer prints the rounded value 123.49.

In Case 11, %.2f indicates to print two places after the decimal. The absence of a value for field width causes .06 to print in a minimum field width. At least one digit, in this case zero, appears before the decimal. We use %% to display %.

Example 4.4

Similar to the last example, execution of the following segment shows the effect of conversion specifications of the form *%m.n*e.

```
printf("Case 12 :%e:\n", 123.486);
printf("Case 13 :%14.3e:\n", 123.486);
```

Running this code produces

```
Case 12 :1.234860e+02:
Case 13 :     1.235e+02:
```

The conversion specification %e in Case 12 prints the number 123.486 in exponential notation as 1.234860e+02. The e format has exactly one nonzero digit to the left of the decimal point. The default is six digits to the right of the decimal point. A minus or plus sign and an exponent of exactly two digits follow the lowercase letter e.

In Case 13, the number is right-justified in a field width of 14 positions. Because of the 3 in %14.3, the computer keeps only three places to the right of the decimal point and rounds the output to 1.235e+02. The original number having three digits to the right of the decimal point is inconsequential. The minimum number of positions needed for a number in exponential form includes four positions for the exponent (the letter e or E, a sign, and two digits), plus two positions for the leading digit and the decimal point, plus the specified or default number of decimal places. If the number is negative, we must also allow one position for a minus sign.

Type *double* If the application requires greater precision than that available with *float*, we can declare a variable to be of type *double*. The computer stores a *double* variable in double the space of a *float* variable, providing about twice the number of **significant digits** for the result. For floating point numbers, all digits are significant except the leading zeros. The exact number of significant digits varies from system to system. Usually, if a *float* variable has seven significant digits, a *double* variable has 16 or 17. Thus, declaring *doubleVar* with the keyword *double*, we obtain greater accuracy than with a variable of type *float*.

```
double doubleVar = 12345.67890123456;
```

Definition The **significant digits** of a floating point number are all the digits except the leading zeros.

In a calculation involving *float* and *double* values, the computer automatically converts the floating point number to *double* before applying the operation. Moreover, we can assign a *float* value to a *double* and vice versa. The computer handles the conversion for us. As with type *float*, we display a *double* value using the format characters %f (for standard floating point notation) or %e (for scientific or exponential notation). Thus, the types *double* and *float* are **compatible** with one another for printing and assignments.

Definition Two types are **assignment-compatible** if we can assign a variable of one type to a variable of the other.

Section 4.1 Exercises

In Exercises 1–8, express the numbers in decimal notation.

1. 0.701e4   **2.** 0.701e–4   **3.** –0.701e4   **4.** 0.35e2

5. 0.35 e–2   **6.** 0.0061e6   **7.** 9807.6e–7   **8.** 78.32e–3

In Exercises 9–16, write the numbers in normalized and standard exponential notation.

9. 63.850   **10.** 29.748   **11.** 0.00032   **12.** 53.7e3

13. 0.0000017   **14.** 0.009e–3   **15.** –8.2   **16.** –0.00082

In Exercises 17–19, give the number of significant digits in the numbers.

17. 29.004   **18.** 0.00074   **19.** 0.0300500

20. Declare a variable x to be of type *float* and y to be of type *double*.

21. How would the number 9876 be printed with the following conversion specifications?

     a. %0d   **b.** %3d   **c.** %4d   **d.** %10d   **e.** % –10d

22. How would the number –456 be printed with the following conversion specifications?

     a. %0d   **b.** %3d   **c.** %5d   **d.** %–5d

23. How would the number 987.65 be printed with the following conversion specifications?

     a. %f   **b.** %8.3f   **c.** %5.3f   **d.** % .1f   **e.** %l0.1f

24. How would the number 0.394820329 be printed with the following conversion specifications?

     a. %f   **b.** %8.3f   **c.** %5.2e   **d.** %10.4e   **e.** %8.1e

25. How would the number 987.65e–1 be printed with the following conversion specifications?

     a. %f   **b.** %8.3f   **c.** %5.2e   **d.** %10.1e   **e.** %.5e

Section 4.1 Programming Projects

1. Write a C program that evaluates the following arithmetic expression and prints the result in exponential notation:

$$\frac{1.234 \times 10^7 + 3.2 \times 10^7}{9.81 \times 10^5 - 2.746 \times 10^7}$$

2. Given that 39.37 inches is equivalent to 1 meter, write a program that converts a given number of inches to the equivalent length in centimeters. Be sure to check for valid input.

3. Write a program to read the cost of an item; compute a 5% sales tax; and print the cost, the tax, and the total cost with dollar signs and two decimal places. For example, if the user enters a cost of 10, the program should print that the cost is $10.00, the tax is $0.50 and the total cost is $10.50. Be sure to check for valid input.

Write programs for the indicated exercises in Section 2.8.

4. Exercise 1 to calculate the surface area of a closed can, given the radius of the base and the height of the can in inches ($S = 2\pi rh + 2\pi r^2$).

5. Exercise 2 to calculate the net pay of day workers paid at the rate of $5.25 per hour with 16% deducted for taxes.

6. Exercise 3 to calculate the time in minutes to fill a rectangular swimming pool of uniform depth, given the floating point dimensions in feet (length, width, and height). Assume water flows in at the rate of 20 gallons per minute. A cubic foot of water contains 7.48 gallons.

Section 4.2   Breadth: Storage of Floating Point Numbers

In Sections 2.4 and 2.5, we considered the representation of integers in the binary number system of the computer. In this section, we continue that discussion by examining floating point number representations. We first consider the conversion of a binary floating point number to an equivalent decimal number.

Conversion from Base 2 to Base 10

Example 4.5

To convert the number with binary floating point representation 101.1101_2 to its decimal representation, we expand by powers of two. We use negative powers for those bits to the right of the decimal place, as shown:

$$101.1101_2 = 1 \cdot 2^2 + 0 \cdot 2^1 + 1 \cdot 2^0 + 1 \cdot 2^{-1} + 1 \cdot 2^{-2} + 0 \cdot 2^{-3} + 1 \cdot 2^{-4}$$
$$= 4 + 1 + 0.5 + 0.25 + 0.0625$$
$$= 5.8125$$

Conversion from Base 10 to Base 2

Example 4.6

We now convert 0.75 in decimal representation to binary representation. Here, we try to find the number of 2^{-1}s, 2^{-2}s, 2^{-3}s, and so on, in 0.75. To find the number of each nonnegative power of 2 in a number, we divide by 2. To find the number of each negative power of 2 in a number, we multiply by 2, as follows:

$$0.75 \cdot 2 = 1.5 = 1 + 0.5 \qquad (1)$$

The first bit after the binary point is 1. We repeat the process with the fractional part, 0.5, of the number from equation (1):

$$0.5 \cdot 2 = 1 \qquad (2)$$

Using these computations, we can justify that 0.75_{10} is equivalent to the binary number 0.11_2. First, we multiply equation (2) by 2^{-1}.

$$0.5 = 1 \cdot 2^{-1}$$

Then substituting $1 \cdot 2^{-1}$ for 0.5 in equation (1), we have

$$0.75 \cdot 2 = 1 + 1 \cdot 2^{-1}$$

Multiplying by 2^{-1} we have

$$0.75 = (1 + 1 \cdot 2^{-1}) \cdot 2^{-1} = 1 \cdot 2^{-1} + 1 \cdot 2^{-2} = 0.11_2$$

Thus, $0.75_{10} = 0.11_2$.

> ### Algorithm 4.1. Algorithm for Converting a Base 10 Representation, F, of a Fractional Number, 0 < F < 1, to a Base 2 Representation:
>
> write down a binary point to start recording the answer
> repeat the following until we have the desired number of places:
>   calculate $F \cdot 2$
>   Write the integer part of the product on the right of the developing answer
>   make F the fractional part of this product

Example 4.7

To convert 26.625_{10} to binary, we deal with the integer and fractional parts separately. As we did in Section 2.4, we repeatedly divide by 2 to obtain $26_{10} = 11010_2$.

```
2 | 26
    | 13      0   ↑
    |  6      1   |
    |  3      0   |
    |  1      1   |
       0      1   |
```

To convert 0.6 to binary notation, we find the number of 2^{-1}s, 2^{-2}s, 2^{-3}s, and so on, in 0.6 by repeatedly multiplying by 2.

$$0.625 \cdot 2 = 1.25 = 1 + 0.25$$

Because one 2^{-1} is in 0.625, 1 is the first binary number after the binary point. We repeat the process with 0.25:

$$0.25 \cdot 2 = 0.5 = 0 + 0.5$$

There is no 2^{-2} in 0.625, yielding a 0 in the second position. Continuing one more time, we obtain

$$0.5 \cdot 2 = 1.0 = 1 + 0.0$$

Thus, 0.625_{10} is 0.101_2, and 26.625 is 11010.101_2. We should always check our work, because careless mistakes are so easy to make:

$$11010.101_2 = 1 \cdot 2^4 + 1 \cdot 2^3 + 1 \cdot 2^1 + 1 \cdot 2^{-1} + 1 \cdot 2^{-3} = 26.625_{10}$$

Multiplication and Division by 2

Example 4.8

In this example, we examine what happens to the binary expansion as we multiply and divide the number by a power of 2. Consider

$$10.11_2 = 1 \cdot 2^1 + 1 \cdot 2^{-1} + 1 \cdot 2^{-2} = 2.75_{10}$$

Notice that when we multiply the binary expansion by 2, we distribute the 2 through the sum and increase each exponent by 1. Thus, we move the binary point one place to the right:

$$2(1 \cdot 2^1 + 1 \cdot 2^{-1} + 1 \cdot 2^{-2}) = 1 \cdot 2^2 + 1 \cdot 2^0 + 1 \cdot 2^{-1}$$
$$= 101.1_2$$
$$= 5.50_{10}$$

If we divide the original number 10.11_2 by 2, we are really multiplying by $1/2 = 2^{-1}$. The result is to move the binary point one place to the left:

$$2^{-1}(1 \cdot 2^1 + 1 \cdot 2^{-1} + 1 \cdot 2^{-2}) = 1 \cdot 2^0 + 1 \cdot 2^{-2} + 1 \cdot 2^{-3}$$
$$= 1.011_2$$
$$= 1.375_{10}$$

> When we multiply a positive integer n by a binary number by 2^n, we move the binary point n places to the right. Division by 2^n, or multiplication by 2^{-n}, moves the binary point n places to the left. This result is an exact parallel to what happens when we multiply or divide a decimal number by 10^n.

Storage of Floating Point Numbers

We are now ready to consider how the computer stores floating point numbers by presenting a form similar to the IEEE standard for single-precision floating point numbers. Recall from the second example in this section that $26.625_{10} = 11010.101_2$. The computer normalizes the number so that the binary point is to the left of the most significant bit—$0.11010101_2 \cdot 2^5$. The fractional part, 11010101, is the mantissa. Because **normalization** places the binary point immediately to the left of the leading 1, for a nonzero number the first bit of the mantissa is 1. Consequently, we can save a bit position by omitting this leading 1, leaving the code 1010101 for storage. The IEEE standard indicates that a *float* number should be stored in 4 bytes or 32 bits. The leftmost bit, bit 31, stores the sign of the number—0 for a positive number and 1 for a negative. The next 8 bits contain the exponent, and the remaining 23 bits store the mantissa. Figure 4.1 pictures such an arrangement.

The exponent, as well as the number, can be positive or negative. Because of considerations in circuitry design, one method for storing this signed exponent in 8 bits is **excess-128 notation**. As we discussed in the section on storage of integers, with 8 bits and two's complement notation we can store integers with values from -128 (1111 1111_2) to 127 (0111 1111_2). In excess-128 notation for the exponent, we add 128 to the exponent before storage.

Figure 4.1   Storage for a floating point number

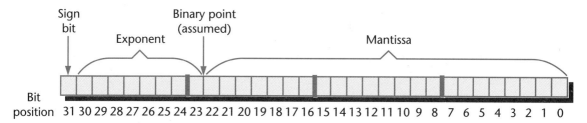

Figure 4.2   Storage for floating point number 26.625

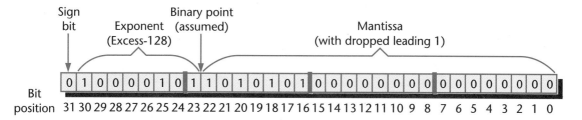

$$
\begin{array}{rcr}
0000\ 0101 & = & 5 \\
+1000\ 0000 & = & +128 \\
\hline
1000\ 0101 & = & 133
\end{array}
$$

Thus, exponents from -128 to 127 are stored as the binary representation of the unsigned integers $0-255$, respectively. Figure 4.2 shows the resulting representation of 26.625 in the computer.

One problem arises with this representation—the storage of 0.0. Because the mantissa has no ones, there is no leading 1 to drop. As a result, floating point zero is stored as the smallest possible positive number. Thus, for the configuration in Figure 4.2, $0.1_2 \cdot 2^{-128}$ represents 0.0. This representation has the desirable characteristic of being all zeros. The storage for the mantissa drops the 1, leaving only zeros, and the excess-128 representation for -128 is zero.

Example 4.9

Let us find the largest positive floating point number that we can store using the above representation. With the understood leading 1, the largest mantissa has 24 ones. However, let us consider a simpler problem first. Suppose our computer only uses 3 bits to store the mantissa. In this case with the assumed leading 1, the largest mantissa is 1111. When we add 2^{-4} to our original number, we obtain 1.0:

$$
\begin{array}{l}
0.1111 \\
+0.0001 = 2^{-4} \\
\hline
1.0000
\end{array}
$$

Thus, our original 4-bit number, 0.1111, is $1 - 2^{-4} = 0.9375$. In this representation, we cannot discern $1 - 2^{-4} = 0.1111_2 = 0.9375$ from $1 - 2^{-5} = 0.11111_2 = 0.96875$, because we can only represent a 4-bit mantissa. This computer could not tell the difference between any two floating point numbers that differ by $2^{-5} = 0.03125$ or less. We can only be confident that the number is correct to the first decimal place. We say these small floating point numbers with a 3-bit mantissa format have a **precision** of 1 digit.

> **Definition**   **Precision** is the number of significant digits in a number.

> For a mantissa of n bits with an assumed leading 1 ($n - 1$ bits stored), the precision is the number of zeros after the decimal place in the expansion of $2^{-(n + 1)}$.

Let us consider the analogous situation in which we use 23 bits to store the mantissa with the understood leading 1. The largest fractional part is $1 - 2^{-24}$, a number very close to 1. Moreover, with 8 bits for the signed exponent, the largest positive exponent of 2 is $111\ 1111_2 = 2^7 - 1 = 127$. Thus, the largest floating point number we can store with this representation is approximately $1 \cdot 2^{127}$ or $3.4 \cdot 10^{38}$.

> For an exponent of m bits in excess–2^{m-1} notation, the largest floating point number is approximately 2 raised to the power $2^{m-1} - 1$.

Using this representation, we see that we cannot distinguish between two floating point numbers that differ by 2^{-25} or less. Because 2^{-25} is about $2.98 \cdot 10^{-8}$, we can trust the number for 7 decimal places, and we say these 32-bit floating point numbers have a precision of 7.

Truncation Error

Example 4.10

This example illustrates the difficulty of expressing exact decimal floating point numbers in the computer. Suppose we make the following assignment in C:

```
x = 0.6;
```

The computer stores the representation of 0.6 in the location for x. For the mantissa, we repeatedly multiply by 2, each time stripping off the integer part for our answer, as shown:

Multiplication	Developing Answer
$0.6 \cdot 2 = 1.2$	0.1
$0.2 \cdot 2 = 0.4$	0.10
$0.4 \cdot 2 = 0.8$	0.100
$0.8 \cdot 2 = 1.6$	0.1001

Notice that we are now back to 0.6. The process continues forever in this repeating binary expansion. Thus, with the line over the 1001 indicating an infinite repetition, we have the following:

$$0.6_{10} = 0.1001\overline{1001}_2$$

If our computer uses five bits to store the mantissa, it truncates or chops off the answer to 0.10011_2. Thus, if we had the statement

```
printf("x = %.5f\n", x);
```

the printout would show

```
x = 0.59375
```

Truncation error involves not having enough bits to store the entire floating point number. If the computer used a greater number of bits to store the number, the truncation error would not be as serious. For example, if we store the mantissa in 23 bits, the printout displays the following:

```
x = 0.60000
```

Example 4.11

Another situation involving truncation error arises when adding floating point numbers that have different magnitudes. Suppose that a computer uses only 5 bits to store the mantissa. Consider the sum of $0.1_2 \cdot 2^3 = 100.0_2 = 8.0$ and $0.1_2 \cdot 2^{-2} = 0.001_2 = 0.125$. As we do in adding by hand, the computer must first line up the binary points.

$$
\begin{array}{rcl}
100.000 & = & 8.0 \\
+0.001 & = & +0.125 \\
\hline
100.001_2 & = & 8.125
\end{array}
$$

Normalizing, we obtain $100.001_2 = 0.100001_2 \cdot 2^3$. The mantissa, 100001, contains six bits, which the computer must truncate to five. Consequently, the computer stores the sum as $0.10000_2 \cdot 2^3 = 8.0$, the same value as one of summands.

Example 4.12

This conversion between bases with a finite amount of storage and error propagation are the very reasons that for floating point variables, we should **NOT** make a test like the following:

```
if (x == y) /* Do NOT make test for floating point variables */
```

For ease of computation, let us again consider a computer that only allows 5 bits for the mantissa. Suppose we made the following assignment:

```
x = 0.53125;
```

In the binary number system, x's value is 0.10001_2. Now, suppose we multiply and divide x by 10, assigning the result to y.

```
y = 10 * x;
y = y / 10;
```

In mathematics x and y are identical, but when we multiply $x = 0.10001_2$ by 10, we have

$$
\begin{array}{rcrr}
0.10001_2 & = & 0.53125 \\
* \quad 1010_2 & = & * \quad 10 \\
\hline
100010 & & \\
100010 \quad\;\; & & \\
\hline
101.01010_2 & = & 5.3125
\end{array}
$$

Because we only have 5 bits in which to store the mantissa, we truncate y to 101.01_2 = 5.25, not 5.3125. When we divide y by 10, we get further truncation error, because $0.525_{10} = 0.1000011\ldots$ in the binary system. Once the computer truncates this value to 5 significant digits, y contains the value $0.10000_2 = 0.5_{10}$, not at all the value of x = 0.53125. We have exaggerated the problem by using only 5 bits for the mantissa, but the idea is the same for a 23-bit mantissa.

Section 4.2 Exercises

Convert the binary numbers in Exercises 1–7 to equivalent decimal numbers.

1. 0.11   **2.** 0.001   **3.** 0.1001   **4.** 101.101

5. 1001.1001   **6.** 11101.011   **7.** 11111.11111

Convert the decimal numbers in Exercises 8–13 to equivalent binary numbers.

8. 0.8125   **9.** 56.75   **10.** 87.8   **11.** 0.45

12. 224.9   **13.** 28.015625

14. By moving the binary point, double and halve the binary number 101110.01.

Fill in the power of 2 or binary number to complete each equality for Exercises 15–18.

15. $110.1111_2 = 0.1101111_2 \cdot 2^{—}$ **16.** $0.001001_2 = 0.1001_2 \cdot 2^{—}$

17. _____ $= 0.11_2 \cdot 2^{-4}$ **18.** _____ $= 0.11_2 \cdot 2^4$

Suppose the decimal numbers in Exercises 19–23 are stored normalized in binary with 8 bits for the fractional part. Write the mantissa after truncation, along with the exponent of 2 in excess-128 notation.

19. 0.82   **20.** 0.23   **21.** 0.0129   **22.** 7.1   **23.** 501.0

24. Give the range of the negative floating point numbers that can be stored with a mantissa of 23 bits and an exponent of 8 bits.

25. A type *double* floating point number is often represented with 64 bits—a sign bit, 11 bits for the excess-notation exponent, and 52 for the mantissa with an understood leading 1.

     a. What excess notation should we use for the exponent?

     b. Give the largest positive *double* number.

     c. What is the precision of such numbers?

26. Suppose a type *long double* floating point number is represented with 80 bits—a sign bit, 15 bits for the exponent, and 64 for the mantissa with an understood leading 1.

a. What excess notation should we use for the exponent?

b. Give the largest positive *long double* number.

c. What is the precision of such numbers?

Compute the answers for the operations on binary numbers in Exercises 27–30.

27. 1101.101 + 11.11   **28.** 10111.0011 + 0.1110111
29. 100110.1 * 11   **30.** 110.001101 * 0.101

Section 4.3 **Coercion**

Implicit Coercion

C permits us to store an integer value into a floating point variable. If enough significant digits are available, the computer converts the number to its floating point equivalent without changing its value. Similarly, C enables the programmer to place a floating point value into an integer variable. In this case, however, the computer truncates the number (it loses the fractional portion), because integer variables do not store a fractional part. For example, the program segment

```
int     intVar;
float   floatVar;


intVar   = 987.654;
floatVar = 3;
printf("intVar = %d, floatVar = %f\n",
        intVar, floatVar);
```

prints the line

```
intVar = 987, floatVar = 3.000000
```

The program assigns the floating point number 987.654 to the integer variable *intVar*, and the computer must truncate this value to 987. The *float* variable *floatVar* accepts the integer 3 but converts it to the floating point equivalent, 3.0.

Clearly, C allows a certain degree of flexibility. Consider the following statement:

```
x = 5 * 6.7;
```

This **mixed-mode expression**, which is not in error, contains one operand of type *int* and another of type *float*. The integer value is automatically converted to type *float* for the calculation in what is known as an **implicit conversion** or **implicit coercion**. We say that 5 is coerced to *float*.

Definitions   A **mixed-mode expression** is an expression that contains operands of different types. **Implicit conversion** or **implicit coercion** occurs when the compiler automatically converts a value from one type to another.

Example 4.13 _____

The following program illustrates mixed-mode calculations:

```
/*
 * Illustration of mixed-mode expressions
 */
```

```
#include <stdio.h>

main()
{
    int intVar = 2,        /* integer operand */
        intAnswer;         /* integer answer */

    float floatVar = 12.34,    /* float operand */
          floatAnswer;         /* float answer */

    floatAnswer = intVar * floatVar;
    printf("%d * %f = %f\n", intVar, floatVar, floatAnswer);
    printf("%f in exponential notation is %e\n\n",
           floatAnswer, floatAnswer);


    intAnswer = intVar * floatVar;
    printf("%d * %f = %d\n\n", intVar, floatVar, intAnswer);

    floatAnswer = intVar / 3 * floatVar;
    printf("%d / 3 * %f = %f\n", intVar, floatVar, floatAnswer);
}
```

Execution on one computer produces the following output:

```
2 * 12.340000 = 24.680000
24.680000 in exponential notation is 2.468000e+01

2 * 12.340000 = 24

2 / 3 * 12.340000 = 0.000000
```

In the first two products, mixed-mode arithmetic with integer and floating point operands converts the *int* operands to *float* numbers and performs the computations. Storage of the result in a *float* or *int* variable changes the representation to floating point or integer, respectively.

In the last computation, priority of operations dictates that the computer first perform the integer division 2 / 3 (*intVar* / 3). Only after obtaining the integer quotient 0 is the mixed-mode computation (0 * 12.34) performed. The intermediate integer value 0 changes to *float* 0.0, but the conversion is too late to retrieve the lost information.

Explicit Coercion

Through **coercion**, the C programmer can explicitly indicate how to convert the values in a mixed-mode expression. To coerce a value of one type into another, we use a **cast operator** in front of the value. For example, suppose *x* is an *int* variable, and we want the corresponding *float* value in an expression. By using the cast operator (*float*) in front of *x*, we can use

```
(float) x
```

as a floating point number without changing the type of *x*. The cast operator is the name of the new data type in parentheses. We place the cast operator directly to the left of the value that we are converting but never use the word "cast."

Definition	**Coercion** or **explicit coercion** occurs when the program explicitly instructs the computer to convert a value from one type to another. In C, a **cast operator** consists of parentheses enclosing a type name in front of a value. The cast operator coerces the value to the indicated type.

Example 4.14

This example illustrates coercion of an expression using *int* variables *numerator* and *denominator* and *float* variable *quotient*.

```
quotient = (float) numerator / denominator;
```

The cast operator (*float*) has the precedence of the unary minus operator, higher than any other binary operator. Therefore, this casting applies to *numerator*. Once the computer converts the value of *numerator* to *float*, the expression becomes mixed-mode, and both quantities change to type *float* for the computation. As the following program shows, without explicit coercion, the integer division truncates the result before the assignment to the *float* variable takes effect.

```
/*
 * Program to illustrate coercion to type float
 */

#include <stdio.h>

main()
{
    int numerator   = 15,
        denominator = 4;
    float  quotient;

    /* integer arithmetic */
    quotient = numerator / denominator;
    printf("With integer division %d / %d = %f\n",
            numerator, denominator, quotient);

    /* floating point arithmetic */
    quotient = (float) numerator / denominator;
    printf("With floating point division %d / %d = %f\n",
            numerator, denominator, quotient);
}
```

The following output affirms that casting *numerator* to *float* avoids the truncation of integer division:

```
With integer division        15 / 4 = 3.000000
With floating point division 15 / 4 = 3.750000
```

We would obtain an identical result to the first computation, 3.000000, if we applied the cast operator to the entire division expression.

```
quotient = (float) (numerator / denominator);
```

Because the parentheses override the usual precedence, the computer performs the integer division first. Truncation occurs and the fractional part is lost before application of the cast operator occurs. Consequently, the value of *quotient* becomes 3.0.

Strong and Weak Typing

Most programming languages allow mixed-mode expressions involving integers and floating point numbers in which the computer converts integers to floating point values for computations. Many also allow the assignment of an integer to a floating point variable, such as

```
float InterestRate;
InterestRate = 6;
```

which gives *InterestRate* the value 6.0. The implicit conversion involved with storing a floating point number in an integer variable, however, dramatically changes the character of the data. In the following example,

```
int time;
time = 5.94;
```

information is lost as *time* obtains the value 5.

We say that C is a **weakly typed language**, because it allows such implicit conversions from one type to another, even when the coercion is not meaningful. Dependence on this implicit coercion often indicates a logic error in the program.

> Sound programming practices discourage the use of mixed-mode expressions and assignments.

Programming languages such as C++ enforce the type abstractions of the language. The compiler issues a syntax error when a statement involves implicit coercion. These **strongly typed languages** hinder us from performing meaningless operations on data. Coercions can still be made, but they must be done explicitly. Explicit conversion indicates that the programmer really wants the conversion to occur.

Definitions   A language is **weakly typed** if it sometimes allows data of one type to be used when another type is expected only because the conversion is possible, not because it is meaningful. If a language does not permit such coercion, the language is **strongly typed**.

Although C is weakly typed, we should avoid implicit conversion. When a meaningful reason exists to perform the coercion, we should include a cast operator, such as

```
int time;
time = (int) 5.94;
```

Thus, we document our specific intention to have the type conversion.

Section 4.3 **Exercises**

1. Assuming the following declarations, give the type of each expression.

   ```
   int    i, j;
   float  x, y;
   double d;
   ```
   a. i / j   **b.** i / x   **c.** i / d   **d.** x * d

2. Assuming the following declaration-initializations, give the value of each expression.

   ```
   int    i = 10;
   float  x = 3.8;
   double d = 4.2e1;
   ```
   a. i / 3   **b.** i / 3 * 3.0   **c.** i * 3.0 / 3
   d. d / 3   **e.** x * i + d

3. Assuming the following declaration-initializations, give the value of each variable on the left-hand side.

   ```
   int    i = 10,
          j = 4,
          k;
   float  x = 3.8,
          y;
   double d = 4.2e1;
   ```
   a. y = i / j;   **b.** y = (float) i / j;
   c. y = i / (float) j;   **d.** y = (float) (i / j);
   e. k = x * i;   **f.** k = (int) x * i;

4. Suppose an interactive program prompts the user for a *float* value for variable *price*, and the user enters the integer 37. Does a run-time error occur? If not, what value does the computer store in *price*? Explain your answers.

5. Write an assignment statement with explicit coercion to store the following:

   a. The value of *float* variable *tax* in *int* variable *WholeTax*

   b. The value of *double* variable *energy* in *float* variable *LowEnergy*

   c. The value of *int* variable *num* in *float* variable *PartNum*

6. Suppose *num* and *val* are *int* variables. In the following, write an expression with explicit coercion so that all arithmetic involves floating point numbers.

   a. $5.7 \times \dfrac{num + 3}{val}$

   b. $\dfrac{1}{val} \times \dfrac{9}{num^2 + 4}$

Section 4.3 **Programming Projects**

1. Write a program that reads four integer test scores in the range 0–100 and prints the floating point average with one decimal place. Be sure to test your program for invalid data and for scores whose sum is not evenly divisible by 4.

2. Some cash registers have the user enter amounts as whole numbers, without a decimal point. For example, a charge of $52.38 would be entered as 5238, and a $10 purchase is recorded as 1000. Write a program to accept this kind of input, positive and of type *int*, and to print the value with a dollar sign and a decimal point. For instance, if the user enters 5238, the program should print $52.38.

Section 4.4 **Additional Integer Types**

Different Sizes of Integers

Just as the programmer can extend the precision of a floating point variable by declaring it to be of type *double*, so can the precision of an integer variable be changed. On many computers the type *short* (or *short int*) provides less precision, whereas on other computers the type *long* (or *long int*) designates more. The following ANSI standard specifies the sizes in bytes for these types:

Type	Size in Bytes
short (or *short int*)	2
int	2 or 4, depending on the implementation
long (or *long int*)	4

As indicated, in every version of ANSI C, the type *int* is synonymous with either *short* or *long*. For control over the size of the integer and portability of the code, the programmer should specify *short* or *long* explicitly.

To display a *short* integer, we type the conversion specification %**hd** in the *printf* statement. For *long*, the specification uses a lowercase letter l, %**ld**.

Example 4.15

The following segment employs the correct conversion specifications for *short* and *long* types:

```
short shortVar = 25000;
long  longVar  = 123456789;

printf("value of short integer = %hd\n", shortVar);
printf("value of long  integer = %ld\n", longVar);
```

The following output reveals that with *long* we can store larger integers than typically available through type *int* on most microcomputers.

```
value of short integer = 25000
value of long  integer = 123456789
```

Table 4.1   Summary of conversion specifications

Type	Conversion Specification
short (or *short int*)	%hd
int	%d
long (or *long int*)	%ld
unsigned (or *unsigned int*)	%u
float	%f, %e, or %E
double	%f, %e, or %E

Unsigned Integers

Another type, *unsigned* (or *unsigned int*), has the conversion specification %u. We use this type for variables that take only nonnegative values, such as those that count.

```
unsigned int count;
```

By prefixing the *int*, *short*, or *long* declaration with the word *unsigned*, we can double the range of the positive numbers. For example, the range for a *short* integer is at least $-32,767$ to $32,767 = 2^{15} - 1$, whereas that of an *unsigned short* is 0 to $65,535 = 2^{16} - 1$. ANSI C guarantees that a *long* variable can have values from $-2,147,483,647$ to $2,147,483,647 = 2^{31} - 1$, and an *unsigned long* extends from 0 to $4,294,967,295 = 2^{32} - 1$. For a particular computer, the range of an *unsigned int* variable matches that of either an *unsigned short* or *unsigned long* variable. Table 4.1 summarizes the conversion specifications for types discussed so far. Appendix D provides a more detailed list.

Mixed-Mode Arithmetic

In mixed-mode calculations involving integers with different sizes, the computer converts all integers to the largest designated size. With operations involving both a *signed* and an *unsigned* value, the computer considers the *signed* value to be *unsigned*.*

Example 4.16

This example demonstrates the automatic upward conversion of integers. The following segment contains variables of types *short*, *int*, and *long*:

```
short    shortVar = 25000;
int      intVar   = 3;
long     longVar  = 123456789;

printf("Case 1:  %d\n",    shortVar + intVar);
printf("Case 2:  %ld\n",   shortVar + longVar);
printf("Case 3:  %ld\n",   longVar  + intVar);
```

---

*In two's complement representation (see Section 2.5), the conversion to unsigned does not change the bit pattern. For example, suppose *UnNum* is *unsigned* and *SignNum* is signed with the value -1. The assignment *UnNum = UnNum + SignNum* still decrements *UnNum* by 1.

This segment generates the following output:

```
Case 1:   25003
Case 2:   123481789
Case 3:   123456792
```

In Case 1, the computer converts the *short* value to type *int* and prints the integer sum. The mixed-mode expression in Case 2 implicitly converts the *short* value to *long*. Similarly, Case 3 implicitly changes the *int* value to a *long* value for the computation.

Section 4.4 Exercises

For Exercises 1–3, write statements to print the values of the variables, assuming the following declaration-initializations:

```
short gauge = 123;
long debt = 839263400;
unsigned int counter = 65000;
```

1. *gauge*   **2.** *debt*   **3.** *counter*

4. Find the error(s) in the following segment:

```
short if = 0;
long Double = 45,000;
unsigned notint = 3;

printf("A value of a short integer is %d\n", if);
printf(" while the long integer is %d\n", Double);
printf(" and the value of the unsigned is %f\n", notint);
```

5. On a particular computer, if a *short* variable has the same amount of storage as an *int* variable, what is the largest possible *int* value?

6. **a.** Write a declaration of a variable *LightYears* to hold a very large integer.

   b. Write a statement to print the value of *LightYears*.

7. **a.** Write a prototype for function *ClubDues* that has a parameter *NumMembers* of the number of club members, which is an unsigned integer.

   b. Write a statement to print the value of *NumMembers*.

8. Assuming the declarations below, give the type of each expression.

```
short       shortVar;
int         intVar;
unsigned    unsignedVar;
float       floatVar;
```

   a. `shortVar + intVar`

   b. `floatVar + unsignedVar`

   c. `unsignedVar + intVar`

Section 4.5 **ANSI C Header Files and *#define***

Compared with other languages, C is small. ANSI C, however, extends the language through its standard libraries. For example, the standard input/output (I/O) source file, *stdio.c*, contains the definitions of *printf* and *scanf*. This file is compiled separately from the user's program. To access its functions, a program links with the standard I/O library and contains the following preprocessor directive:

```
#include <stdio.h>
```

When the preprocessor detects this directive, it inserts the contents of *stdio.h* into the program at that point. The *.h* suffix indicates that the file is a **header file** to appear at the head of the program. Header files contain prototypes of the functions in the corresponding source file and define certain values and symbols related to the purpose of this library. For example, the header file *stdio.h* contains the prototype for *printf*, while the corresponding source file, *stdio.c*, contains its definition. Moreover, *stdio.h* defines certain constants that pertain to input and output facilities. Having such definitions and declarations in the header file saves the programmer time when writing and debugging the code.

Numerical Constants

Some header files, such as *limits.h* and *float.h*, do not have associated source files of function definitions. These header files only contain definitions of constants. The files *limits.h* and *float.h* consist of useful information related to the types *int* and *float*, respectively. The former defines the constant *INT_MAX* as the maximum *int* value (32767 or greater) on the computer on which that version of C is running. Similarly, *INT_MIN* is the minimum integer value (−32767 or less).

Example 4.17

To discover the range of integers on our computer, we execute the following program:

```
/*
 * Program to display range of integers on this machine
 */

#include <stdio.h>
#include <limits.h>   /* contains definitions of limits */

main()
{
    printf("The smallest int on this computer is %d.\n",
           INT_MIN);
    printf("The largest int on this computer is %d.\n",
           INT_MAX);
}
```

On a microcomputer, the output might be as follows:

```
The smallest int on this computer is -32768.
The largest int on this computer is 32767.
```

Table 4.2   Some constants in *limits.h*

Constant	Meaning
INT_MAX	Maximum *int* value (+32767 or greater)
INT_MIN	Minimum *int* value (−32767 or less)
LONG_MAX	Maximum *long* value (+2147483647 or greater)
LONG_MIN	Minimum *long* value (−2147483647 or less)
SHRT_MAX	Maximum *short* value (+32767 or greater)
SHRT_MIN	Minimum *short* value (−32767 or less)

Table 4.3   Some constants in *float.h*

Constant	Meaning
FLT_DIG	Number of decimal digits of precision for a *float* value (at least 6)
FLT_EPSILON	Smallest *float* number x, such that $1.0 + x \neq 1.0$ (at most 10^{-5})
FLT_MAX	Maximum *float* value (at least 10^{37})
FLT_MIN	Minimum positive normalized *float* value (at most 10^{-37})
DBL_DIG	Number of decimal digits of precision for a *double* value (at least 10)
DBL_EPSILON	Smallest *double* number x, such that $1.0 + x \neq 1.0$ (at most 10^{-9})
DBL_MAX	Maximum *double* value (at least 10^{37})
DBL_MIN	Minimum positive normalized *double* value (at most 10^{-37})

By convention, identifiers for such **constants** as *INT_MIN* and *INT_MAX* are in all capital letters. We can use constants in computations, tests, or printing, but we cannot change their values. They are constant throughout the program. The header file might define the constant *INT_MAX* using the following preprocessor directive:

```
#define INT_MAX  32767
```

When the preprocessor encounters this directive, it replaces every occurrence of *INT_MAX*, which is not within a string constant, with 32767. Consequently, before compilation the preprocessor alters the second *printf* in Example 4.17 to be

```
printf("The largest int on this computer is %d.\n",
       32767);
```

When we include *limits.h* in our program, the preprocessor inserts the contents of this header file at the location of the *#include*. Then, as specified by the *#define* directives, the preprocessor replaces all references to the constant identifiers (such as *INT_MAX*) with their values (such as +32787). Table 4.2 contains a list of some constants in *limits.h*. As Table 4.3 indicates, the header file *float.h* contains similar information for types *float* and *double*.

Example 4.18

In Example 4.12 of Section 4.2 we discussed the danger of testing equality of *float* values, such as

```
if (x == y)    /* Do NOT make test for float variables x, y */
    . . .
if (z == 3.5)  /* Do NOT make test for float variable z */
    . . .
```

Because of conversion between bases 2 and 10 and round-off error, two values that that are equal with infinite precision might not be equal with the finite precision of a computer. Instead of testing for equality, we should test if *float* variables x and y (or *float* variable z and 3.5) are within 10 * *FLT_EPSILON* of each other. Numbers that are closer than *FLT_EPSILON* to each other are too close to be accurately distinguishable by the computer. If x and y are within 10 * *FLT_EPSILON* of each other, they agree in all but possibly the least significant digit. Thus, mathematically we should test the truth of the following:

$$-10 * FLT\_EPSILON < (x - y) < 10 * FLT\_EPSILON$$

In C, we write

```
if ((-10 * FLT_EPSILON < (x - y)) &&
       ((x - y) < 10 * FLT_EPSILON))
    printf("The values are equal.\n");
```

Defining Preprocessor Constants

When dealing with logical expressions, we have already found it useful to define symbolic constants *TRUE* and *FALSE*.

```
#define FALSE 0
#define TRUE  1
```

In programs in which we use the same number many times or in which the value should not change, we should define a constant. For example, a program that calculates the area and circumference of a circle uses the value of π, which is approximately 3.1416. It is good programming practice to define such a value as a constant, giving it a name, as follows:

```
#define PI 3.1416
```

This method eliminates the need to rewrite the constant value each time we use it. Defining constants saves time if the value contains many digits or is difficult to remember. Moreover, as the following illustrates, the identifier is more meaningful in the code than a number.

```
circumference = 2.0 * PI * radius;
```

This statement is self-documenting. Clearly, the formula uses the number π and the value of the radius to compute the circumference. If we need to change the value of the constant, we adjust one statement instead of searching the program for every occurrence of the number. For example, should we desire more precision for π, we simply change the preprocessor directive

```
#define PI 3.141593
```

The convention in C of writing constant names in uppercase letters helps the reader easily distinguish constants from variables. The name of a constant, like that of a variable, should be descriptive of its purpose. Like variable names, constant names must begin with a letter (or underscore) and contain only letters, digits, or underscores. In the preprocessor directive, the value of the constant follows its name. The preprocessor directive does not contain an equal sign or semicolon. No type is specified for a constant. Type is determined automatically by the nature of the constant's value.

Absolute Value Function

Instead of constant definitions, the **math library** contains definitions of several mathematical functions. If we link to this library and include the preprocessor directive

```
#include <math.h>
```

we can use various trigonometric, logarithmic, exponential, and absolute value functions.

Use of the math library function *fabs*—the **absolute value function**—can improve the readability of the condition in Example 4.18. In mathematics, the effect of the absolute value of a number is to drop its sign and return a nonnegative number. Thus, the absolute value of -3, $|-3|$, is 3, and $|3|$ is 3. A number z is between -3 and $+3$,

$$-3 < z < 3$$

if and only if its absolute value is less than 3, or

$$|z| < 3$$

Thus, the condition

$$-10\varepsilon < (x - y) < 10\varepsilon$$

is equivalent to

$$|x - y| < 10\varepsilon$$

The function *fabs* takes a *double* argument and returns its absolute value as a *double*. Thus, for $z = -3.0$, the following statement

```
printf("The absolute value of %f is %f.\n", z, fabs(z));
```

prints the sentence

```
The absolute value of -3.000000 is 3.000000.
```

Because of implicit conversion, the argument can be of type *int*, *float*, or *double*. With this powerful addition to the language, we can write the test for equality of x and y, $|x - y| < 10\varepsilon$, as

```
#include <math.h>
#include <float.h>
    ⋮
if (fabs(x - y) < 10 * FLT_EPSILON)
    printf("The values are equal.\n");
```

Square Root Function

The math library also contains the **square root function**, *sqrt*, which returns the square root of a number. The C function *sqrt* is equivalent to the mathematical function

$$f(x) = \sqrt{x}$$

where

$$f(36.0) = \sqrt{36.0} = 6.0$$

For example,

```
y = sqrt(36.0);
```

determines the square root of the argument (36. 0) and assigns the result (6.0) to *y*.

Additional Math Library Functions

With the function *pow*, we can evaluate various **powers**. For example, to print x^5 we code

```
printf("x raised to the 5th power is %f\n", pow(x, 5));
```

The math library also contains the **exponential** and **logarithmic functions**. The invocation *exp*(*x*) returns e^e, and *log*(*x*) gives the **natural logarithm** of *x*.

When we need to convert a floating point value to a whole number, we use the **floor** (*floor* in C; $\lfloor\ \rfloor$ in mathematics) or **ceiling** (**ceil** in C; $\lceil\ \rceil$ in mathematics) func- tions. The former goes down to the nearest integer, and the latter goes up. For example,

$$\lfloor 5.9 \rfloor = 5 \quad \lfloor 5.3 \rfloor = 5 \quad \lfloor -5.9 \rfloor = -6 \quad \lfloor -5.3 \rfloor = -6$$

$$\lceil 5.9 \rceil = 6 \quad \lceil 5.3 \rceil = 6 \quad \lceil -5.9 \rceil = -5 \quad \lceil -5.3 \rceil = -5$$

As Table 4.4 shows, the math library also contains several trigonometric functions.

Example 4.19

In this example, we develop a savings program. The user wants to make a one-time deposit (principal) in an account that pays interest, compounded once a year. In this program, the user can ask how much will be in the bank after a certain number of years

Table 4.4 Some function prototypes in *math.h*

Prototype	Function Returns
double pow(double x, double y)	x^y, *x* to the **power** *y*
double sqrt(double x)	$\sqrt{x}$, the **square root** of *x*
double fabs(double x)	$\|x\|$, the **absolute value** of *x*
double floor(double x)	$\lfloor x \rfloor$, the **floor** of *x*, the largest integer less than or equal to *x*
double ceil(double x)	$\lceil x \rceil$, the **ceiling** of *x*, the smallest integer greater than or equal to *x*
double exp(double x)	e^x, the **exponential function** of *x* ($e = 2.71828\ldots$)
double log(double x)	log(*x*), the **natural logarithm** of *x*
double log10(double x)	$\log_{10}(x)$, the **common logarithm** of *x*
double sin(double x)	sin(*x*), the **sine** of *x*
double cos(double x)	cos(*x*), the **cosine** of *x*
double tan(double x)	tan(*x*), the **tangent** of *x*
double asin(double x)	arcsin(*x*), the **arcsine** of *x*
double acos(double x)	arccos(*x*), the **arccosine** of *x*
double atan(double x)	arctan(*x*), the **arctangent** of *x*, which is between $-\pi/2$ and $\pi/2$
double atan2(double y, double x)	arctan(*y* / *x*), the **arctangent** of *y* / *x*, which is between $-\pi$ and π

or how many years it will take the deposit to grow to a desired amount. The formula for amount (A) in terms of principal (P), rate (r), and time in years (n) is as follows:

$$A = P(1 + r)^n$$

In C, the computation involves the power function *pow,* as shown:

```
amount = principal * pow(1 + rate, years);
```

Given P, r, and A, we can calculate n using a formula that employs a logarithm and the ceiling function, $\lceil\ \rceil$.

$$n = \left\lceil \frac{\log\left(\frac{A}{P}\right)}{\log(1 + r)} \right\rceil$$

We use the ceiling function because the answer must be in whole years. If we used the floor, the deposit would not be in the bank quite long enough. The assignment statement in C translates this formula directly, as shown:

```
years = ceil(log(amount/principal) / log(1 + rate));
```

Figure 4.3 displays the three levels of the structure chart—*main* at the top level and the four functions it calls at the next level. The boxes for *ReadPrincipal* and *ReadRate* have darkened corners to indicate that they appear more than once in the chart.

We present pseudocode for the more interesting functions.

main( )

    Computes the amount of money in the bank after a certain number of years and computes how many years it would take to arrive at a given amount

Algorithm:

    call *menu* to return *choice*
    if *choice* is 1
        compute amount with *FindAmount*
    else if *choice* is 2
        compute years with *FindYears*
    else
        call error-handling routine *error*

menu( ) $\longrightarrow$ *choice*

    Prints menu and returns user's choice

Pre:

    none

Post:

    Function has returned user's choice from the menu.

Figure 4.3   Structure chart for program in Example 4.19

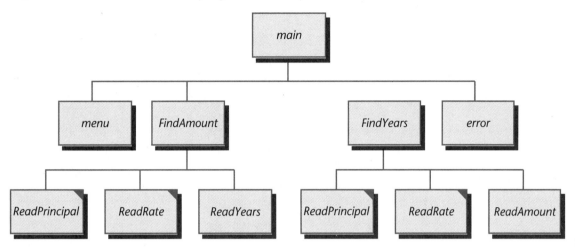

Printing an error message, *error* is a straightforward function. *FindAmount* and *FindYears* have similar designs to each other.

FindAmount ( )

Obtains principal, interest rate, years of deposit; determines if an input error occurs; and if not, calculates and prints final amount

Pre:

Post:

If no errors occur, the final amount has been displayed.

Algorithm:

    principal ←*ReadPrincipal*()
    rate ← *ReadRate*()
    years ← *ReadYears*()
    if any value is not positive
        print an error message
    else
        calculate *amount*

FindYears( )

Obtains principal, interest rate, amount desired; determines if an input error occurs; and if not, calculates and prints number of years needed

Pre:

Post:

The number of years needed or an error message has been displayed.

Algorithm:

principal ⟵ *ReadPrincipal( )*
rate ⟵ *ReadRate( )*
amount ⟵ *ReadAmount( )*
if *amount* is less than *principal* or if *principal* or *rate* is not positive
    print an error message
else
    calculate *years*

The functions *ReadPrincipal*, *ReadYears*, and *ReadAmount* just prompt the user for a value and then read and return that value. If any function returns a value that is not positive, the calling function catches the error, prints an error message, and stops execution.

The function *ReadRate* has a similar design, but we must be more careful about the user's input. Suppose the user wants to indicate an annual interest rate of 5%. Regardless of the directions, the user could erroneously type 5 or 0.5 instead of the correct 0.05. *ReadRate* catches such data errors and returns −1, which the calling program intercepts and processes as an error.

ReadRate ( ) ⟵ *rate*

Reads and returns interest rate, −1 in case of error

Pre:

Post:

Floating point interest rate or error value of -1 has been returned.

Algorithm:

prompt user for an annual interest rate
read *rate*
if the *rate* is not between 0 and 20%
    rate ⟵ −1 as an error code
return *rate*

The code for the program must include *math.h*, so that we have access to the functions *pow*, *ceil*, and *log*.

```
/*
 * Example 4.19
 * This program computes the amount of money in the bank
 * after a certain number of years. It also computes how
 * many years it would take to arrive at a given amount.
 * main calls menu, FindAmount, FindYears, and error
 */

#include <stdio.h>
#include <math.h>

int    menu(void);
void   FindAmount(void);
void   FindYears(void);
void   error(int choice);
float  ReadPrincipal(void);
float  ReadRate(void);

main()
{
    int    choice;          /* menu choice */

    choice = menu();

    switch (choice)
    {
       case 1:   FindAmount();
                 break;
       case 2:   FindYears();
                 break;
       default:  error(choice);
    }
}

/*
 * This function prints a menu of choices, reads and
 * returns the user's integer choice, 1 or 2; all other
 * choices are in error.
 * Pre:     none
 * Post:    Function has returned user's choice from the menu.
 */

int menu(void)
{
    int choice;             /* menu choice */

    printf("This program makes savings computations\n");
    printf("for an account with interest compounded annually.\n");
```

```c
    printf("It will ask you the one-time deposit amount\n");
    printf("and the annual interest rate.\n\n");
    printf("You have two choices: Given a number of years,\n");
    printf("the program will return the final amount;\n");
    printf("given a final amount, the program will tell\n");
    printf("the number of years you must leave the money\n");
    printf("in the bank.\n\n");
    printf("Choose from the following:\n\n");
    printf("1. Given a number of years, calculate amount\n");
    printf("2. Given a desired amount, calculate years\n\n");
    printf("Your choice: ");

    scanf("%d", &choice);
    return choice;
}


/*
 * This function obtains principal, interest rate, and years of
 * deposit; determines if an input error occurs; and if
 * not, calculates and prints final amount.
 *    amount = principal * (1 + rate)^years
 * Function calls:  ReadPrincipal, ReadRate, ReadYears
 * Pre:    none
 * Post:   If no errors, final amount has been displayed.
 */

void FindAmount(void)
{
    int     ReadYears(void);
    float   amount,           /* final amount in bank    */
            principal,        /* original deposit        */
            rate;             /* interest rate           */
    int     years;            /* number of years in bank */
    principal = ReadPrincipal();
    rate      = ReadRate();
    years     = ReadYears();

    if ((principal <= 0)||(rate <= 0)||(years <= 0)) /*error*/
        printf("\nInvalid input. Run program again.\n");
    else
    {
        amount = principal * pow(1 + rate, years);
        printf("\nYou will have $%0.2f in the bank.\n",
                amount);
    }
}


/*
 * This function obtains principal, interest rate, and amount
 * desired; determines if an input error occurs; and if
 * not, calculates and prints number of years needed.
```

```
 *      years = smallest integer greater than or equal to
 *          log(amount/principal)/log(1 + rate)
 * Function calls:  ReadPrincipal, ReadRate, ReadAmount
 * Pre:    none
 * Post:   The number of years needed or an error message
 *         has been displayed.
 */

void FindYears(void)
{
    float   ReadAmount(void);
    float   amount,            /* final amount in bank    */
    principal,                 /* original deposit        */
    rate;                      /* interest rate           */
    int years;                 /* number of years in bank */

    principal  = ReadPrincipal();
    rate       = ReadRate();
    amount     = ReadAmount();

    if ((amount <= principal)||(principal <= 0)||(rate <= 0))
        printf("\nInvalid input. Run program again\n");
    else
    {
        years = ceil(log(amount/principal) / log(1 + rate));
        printf("\nYou will need the account for %d years.\n",
            years);
    }
}


/*
 * This function reads and returns principal
 * Pre:    none
 * Post:   The principal has been returned.
 */

float ReadPrincipal(void)
{
    float principal;              /* original deposit  */

    printf("\nAmount of original deposit (no commas):  $");
    scanf("%f", &principal);
    return principal;
}

/*
 * This function reads and returns interest rate, -1 in
 * case of error
 * Pre:    none
 * Post:   Floating point interest rate has been returned, -1
 *         in case of error.
 */
```

```
float ReadRate(void)
{
    float rate;                  /* interest rate */

    printf("Give the interest rate ");
    printf("as a decimal number\n");
    printf("      For example type 0.0625 for 6.25%%:   ");
    scanf("%f", &rate);
    if ((rate <= 0.0) || (rate >= 0.2))    /* error */
             rate = -1;
    return rate;
}


/*
 * This function reads and returns years of deposit
 * Pre:    none
 * Post:   Years of deposit have been returned.
 */

int ReadYears(void)
{
    int years;               /* number of years in bank  */

    printf("Number of years to leave in bank:          ");
    scanf("%d", &years);
    return years;
}


/*
 * This function reads and returns the amount desired
 * Pre:    none
 * Post:   The amount desired has been returned.
 */

float ReadAmount(void)
{
    float amount;               /* final amount in bank   */

    printf("Amount desired:                          $");
    scanf("%f", &amount);
    return amount;
}


/*
 * This function prints an error message for an invalid
 * menu choice
 * Pre:    choice has an invalid value.
 * Post:   Error message is displayed.
 */
```

```
void error(int choice)
{
    printf("%d is an invalid choice.   Please run again.\n",
        choice);
}
```

We perform several runs to illustrate the program. In the first trial, the user makes menu choice number 1.

```
This program makes savings computations
for an account with interest compounded annually.
It will ask you the one-time deposit amount
and the annual interest rate.

You have two choices: Given a number of years,
the program will return the final amount;
given a final amount, the program will tell
the number of years you must leave the money
in the bank.

Choose from the following:

1. Given a number of years, calculate amount
2. Given a desired amount,  calculate years

Your choice: 1

Amount of original deposit (no commas):  $2000
Give the interest rate as a decimal number
     For example type 0.0625 for 6.25%:    .07
Number of years to leave in bank:          10

You will have $3934.30 in the bank.
```

To illustrate other executions of the program, we omit the opening directions and menu. The following output illustrates a menu choice of 2:

```
Your choice: 2

Amount of original deposit (no commas):  $5000
Give the interest rate as a decimal number
     For example type 0.0625 for 6.25%:    .06
Amount desired:                         $20000

You will need the account for 24 years.
```

In the next run, the user makes an invalid menu choice.

```
Your choice: 3
3 is an invalid choice. Please run again.
```

In the next execution, we test the program with an interest rate of 50% (0.5), which is outside the expected range. This input generates an error message and program termination. We should also test the program for other out-of-range values. Such runs behave in a similar manner to the one below.

```
Your choice: 1

Amount of original deposit (no commas):  $100
Give the interest rate as a decimal number
     For example type 0.0625 for 6.25%:   .5
Number of years to leave in bank:          3

Invalid input. Run program again.
```

Section 4.5 Exercises

1. Write C code to test if *float* variable x equals 3.5.

2. Find the error(s) in the following preprocessor directive:

   ```
   #define value = 50;
   ```

3. Write a preprocessor directive to define *MAXNUM* as the constant 100.

4. Write a preprocessor directive to define *AVOGADRO* as the constant $6.023 \cdot 10^{23}$.

5. Write a statement to print the largest double value.

6. Write a statement to compute the number of bits used to store an integer on your computer.

In Exercises 7–13, write C assignment statements for the equations.

7. $y = \sqrt{x^5 - 8}$

8. $y = e^{3x} + 2$

9. $y = \lfloor 5x + \log(x) \rfloor$

10. $y = \sin(\sqrt{x})$

11. $y = \lceil (2x)^3 \rceil$

12. $y = |\tan(x)|$

13. $y = \arctan(e^x)$

14. The following appeared in the sample questions of *The Graduate Record Examinations Descriptive Booklet 1991–93*:

Which of the following statements must be true?

I. $\lfloor x \rfloor = \lceil x \rceil$ if and only if x is an integer.
II. $\lfloor x \rfloor + 1 = \lceil x \rceil$ if and only if x is not an integer.
III. $\lfloor x \rfloor \lceil y \rceil = \lceil x \rceil \lfloor y \rfloor$ for all x, y
IV. $-\lfloor x \rfloor = \lceil -x \rceil$ for all x

(A) IV only   (B) I and IV only   (C) I, II, and III only
(D) I, II, and IV only   (E) I, II, III, and IV

Section 4.5 Programming Projects

1. Develop a C program that calculates the circumference ($C = 2\pi r$) and area ($A = \pi r^2$) of a circle from its radius. Define π as a constant using the floating point approximation 3.141593.

2. Develop a program to calculate the volume $\left(V = \dfrac{4}{3} \pi r^3\right)$ and surface area ($S = 4\pi r^2$) of a sphere, given the radius. Define π as a constant using the floating point approximation 3.141593.

3. In a right triangle with sides of lengths a and b, the length of the hypotenuse, c, is as follows:

$$c = \sqrt{a^2 + b^2}$$

Develop a program to read positive values for the lengths of the sides and to print the length of the hypotenuse.

4. Develop a program to read three positive floating point numbers and to determine if the three numbers form a Pythagorean triple. With a Pythagorean triple, one number is the length of the hypotenuse of a right triangle having the other two numbers as lengths of the sides (see Programming Project 3).

5. Develop a program to give the user the choice of converting Cartesian coordinates (x, y) to polar coordinates (r, θ), or vice versa (r is the radius or distance from the origin, and θ is the angle of the point off the horizontal axis). The formulas are as follows:

$$r = \sqrt{x^2 + y^2}$$
$$\theta = \arctan\left(\frac{y}{x}\right)$$
$$x = r\cos(\theta)$$
$$y = r\sin(\theta)$$

Because the angle should be between $-\pi$ and π, use *atan2* for the evaluation of θ.

6. For a given quadratic equation $ax^2 + bx + c = 0$ with real numbers a, b, and c and $a \neq 0$, the quadratic formula finds the real number solutions, provided $b^2 - 4ac$ is nonnegative.

$$x = \frac{-b \pm \sqrt{b^2 - 4ac}}{2a}$$

Develop a program that reads floating point values for a, b, and c and prints the solution(s) or a message indicating that no real number solutions exist. If the solutions are equal ($b^2 - 4ac$ is zero), print only one.

≋ **Programming and Debugging Hints**

Interfaces between Functions: Global Variables

A necessary feature of modular programming is the use of good interfaces between functions. Among other things, we should avoid the use of global variables for communication between functions. The side effects created are nonobvious effects that may be purposeful, but they leave the program open to undesired bugs.

For example, suppose a programmer uses global variable *GlobalVar* for communication between two functions, such as *main* and *TripleGlobalVar,* but inadvertently allows a third function, *DisplayGlobalVarTensDigit*, to use that variable as temporary storage. The three functions interfere with each other's communication, and disaster results. If we do not use global variables, we automatically eliminate a whole class of errors, and the program is a lot clearer to the reader.

In the example below, *main* assigns 125 to global variable *GlobalVar*, calls *DisplayGlobalVarTensDigit* to print the tens digit of the value, calls *TripleGlobalVar* to triple the value, and calls *DisplayGlobalVarTensDigit* to print the new tens digit. The routine *DisplayGlobalVarTensDigit*, however, has the side effect of assigning the tens digit to *GlobalVar*. The output, which appears after the program, illustrates the unfortunate result of the side effect.

```
/*
 * Side effects with a global variable
 */

#include <stdio.h>

void TripleGlobalVar(void);
void DisplayGlobalVarTensDigit(void);

int GlobalVar;            /* POOR DESIGN:  a global variable */

main()
{
    GlobalVar = 125;
    printf("The tens digit is ");
    DisplayGlobalVarTensDigit();
    TripleGlobalVar();
    printf(" but the tens digit of the triple is ");
    DisplayGlobalVarTensDigit();
    printf(".\n");

}


/*
 * This routine triples the global variable GlobalVar
 */

void TripleGlobalVar(void)
{
    GlobalVar = 3 * GlobalVar;
}
```

```
/*
 * This routine displays the tens digit of GlobalVar and
 * produces a side effect
 */

void DisplayGlobalVarTensDigit(void)
{
    GlobalVar = (GlobalVar / 10) % 10;   /* SIDE EFFECT */
    printf("%d", GlobalVar);
}
```

> The tens digit is **2** but the tens digit of the triple is **0**.

Because of the side effect in *DisplayGlobalVarTensDigit*, the value of *GlobalVar* is inadvertently changed to 2. Instead of 7 (3 * 125 = 375), 0 is displayed (3 * 2 = 8) for the tens digit of the triple.

Preprocessor Constants

Preprocessor constants are global by nature, but the program cannot change their values. Usually, a preprocessor directive defining a constant, such as

```
#define PI 3.141593
```

appears in a header file or before *main*. We should not use a constant if a parameter would be clearer. Because we pass an argument to a function rather than have the function refer to the value directly, use of the argument makes the function more general. We can place the function in another program without having to include the preprocessor constant. When a value does not change throughout the program or is a mathematical constant, such as π, a preprocessor constant is often desirable. To distinguish it from a variable, we should follow the convention of using all capital letters for the constant name.

Reader's Understanding of the Interface

To aid the reader of the program in understanding the interface, each function should begin with a comment that describes exactly what the function does, the parameters and conditions required for proper execution (preconditions), and the state of the system when the function terminates (postconditions). Typical preconditions are the values that are permissible as arguments, whereas frequent postconditions are the values that the function displays or returns. This last item should include values returned as indications of an error condition. For instance, function *ReadRate* of Example 4.19 returns −1 if the interest rate is not in an acceptable range, as shown:

```
/*
 * This function reads and returns interest rate, -1 in
 * case of error
 * Pre:   none
 * Post:  Floating point interest rate has been returned, -1 in
 *        case of error.
 */
```

The calling routines *FindAmount* and *FindYears* assign the value that *ReadRate* returns to a variable *rate*

```
rate = ReadRate();
```

FindAmount and *FindYears* check the value of *rate*. If either routine detects a value of −1 for *rate*, it prints an error message and does not process the input, as shown:

```
if  ((principal <= 0)||(rate <= 0)||(years <= 0))        /*error*/
    printf("\nInvalid input. Run program again.\n");
else
    ⋮
```

If a function returns error codes, the calling function should always test for these codes.

Key Terms

Summary

In this chapter, we considered other numeric types besides *int*. A floating point number is a number that is stored in the computer with a decimal reference point. The type for a such a number is *float* or *double*. The computer stores a *double* variable in double the space of a *float* variable, providing about twice the number of significant digits for the result. To print a floating point number, we can use the conversion specification %f or %e. Printing a number with the conversion specification of the form %*m.n*f displays a *float* or a *double* number in a field of width *m* with *n* digits after the decimal point. The conversion specification %*m.n*e results in standard exponential notation in a field width of *m*, including a minus if the number is negative, one digit before the decimal point, *n* digits after, e indicating 10, and a signed exponent. For %f or %e, the number is right-justified in the field unless *m* is negative, in which case the number is left-justified. For example,

```
printf(":%10.3e::%-10.3f:\n", 83.4173, 83.4173);
```

displays

```
: 8.342e+01::83.417    :
```

A mixed-mode expression contains operands of different types. In an expression involving *int* and *float* values, an integer value is automatically converted to type *float* for the calculation in a process called implicit coercion. Coercion or explicit coercion occurs when the program explicitly instructs the computer to convert a value from one type to another. In C, a cast operator (parentheses enclosing a type name) in front of a value coerces the value to the indicated type. For example, we can perform floating point division using *int* variables *numerator* and *denominator* with the cast operator (*float*) as follows:

```
(float) numerator / denominator
```

C is weakly typed because the language sometimes allows data of one type to be used when another type is expected simply because the conversion is possible, not because it is meaningful. A strongly typed language does not permit such coercion.

Type *short* (or *short int*) with storage of 2 bytes for a variable provides less precision than type *long* (or *long int*) with 4 bytes of storage for a variable. Depending on the computer, a variable of type *int* has the same precision as *short* or *long*. The conversion specification for *short* is %hd, and the specification for *long* is %ld. A variable of type *unsigned* (or *unsigned int*) only takes on nonnegative values and has the conversion specification %u. In mixed-mode calculations involving integers with different sizes, the computer converts all integers to the largest designated size. With operations involving both a *signed* and an *unsigned* value, the computer considers the *signed* value to be *unsigned*.

The files *limits.h* and *float.h* consist of useful information related to the types *int* and *float*, respectively. Tables 4.2 and 4.3 in Section 4.5 contain lists of the constants in *limits.h* and *float.h*.

If a program links to the ANSI C math library and contains the following compiler directive

```
#include <math.h>
```

the program has access to a number of mathematical functions (see Table 4.4 in Section 4.5). The math library absolute value function is *fabs*. To test if two floating point values, *x* and *y*, are equal, we use *fabs* and *FLT_ELSILON* from *float.h* in

```
if (fabs(x - y) < (10 * FLT_EPSILON))
```

The math library also contains the square root function *sqrt*, which returns the square root of a number. The function call *pow(x, n)* returns x^n. The invocation *exp(x)* returns e^x, and *log(x)* gives the natural logarithm of *x*. To convert a floating point value to a whole number, we use the floor function (*floor(x)* in C; $\lfloor x \rfloor$ in mathematics), which returns the largest integer less than or equal to *x*, or the ceiling function (*ceil(x)* in C; $\lceil x \rceil$ in mathematics), which returns the smallest integer greater than or equal to *x*.

Review Questions

1. Which of the following is not a floating point number?
   a. **125**   b. **987.0**   c. **−425.7**   d. **92.45e12**   e. **10.23E−9**

2. Name the keyword that is used to declare floating point variables.

3. What distinguishes floating point numbers from integers?

4. Write the following numbers in exponential notation, using a mantissa with a single nonzero digit to the left of the decimal point.

    a. 123.456   **b.** 0.000125   **c.** 1230000

5. With what kind of number is the *double* declaration associated?

6. What is the effect of dividing an integer by a real quantity? What is this effect called?

7. What is meant by the term "coercion"?

8. Explain how a language is weakly typed.

9. Is C strongly or weakly typed?

10. How would you use the cast operator to convert 7 * 9 / 11 to *double* before the integer division?

11. What conversion specifications are used to print the following?

    a. an integer   **b.** a floating point number in decimal form

    c. a floating point number in exponential notation

12. What is the minimum field width specifier, and where is it located?

13. What is the effect of a negative number in a field width specifier?

14. Is it wrong to omit a field width specifier entirely? If not, what is the effect?

15. How would the number 9876 appear if printed with the following conversion specifications?

    a. %0d   **b.** %3d   **c.** %4d   **d.** %10d

16. What general statement can be made about the conversion specifications %e and %f?

17. How many decimal places are displayed when a number has a conversion specification of %f?

18. What happens if a number being printed by a conversion specification of %f has more than six decimal places?

19. How would the number 987.65 be printed with a conversion specification of %10.1?

20. What conversion specification ensures that a long integer is printed correctly?

21. What is the difference between the conversion specification letters used in *printf* and those used in *scanf*?

22. List all keywords associated with the types that we have covered.

23. How can an integer be printed right-justified within a six-position field?

24. What happens if the field width specifier is too small for the number being printed?

25. Can more than one field width specifier be included in a single *printf*?

26. What symbolic constant represents the maximum *int* value, and which library contains the function?

27. Write a logical expression in C that is true if floating point variables x and y contain the same value.

28. Call an ANSI C library function to compute x^6.

29. What is the ANSI C library function to compute the square root, and which library contains the function?

Laboratory

1. The purpose of this exercise is to show the importance of matching conversion specifications and types. For example, printing a floating point number with a decimal conversion specification, %d, can produce some puzzling output.

   Copy the file *LAB041.c* from the text disk to one of yours. The main function in the file calls several functions to illustrate problems that can arise in using incorrect conversion specifications. The program follows:

```
/*
 * Program to show problems with using the wrong
 * conversion specification
 */

#include <stdio.h>
void intWrong(void);
void scanfWrong(void);
void shortWrong(void);
void unsignedWrong(void);

main()
{
    intWrong();
/*
    scanfWrong();
/*
    shortWrong();
/*
    unsignedWrong();
*/
}

/*
 * Function to show problem with using the wrong
 * conversion specifications for int and float in printf
 */

void intWrong(void)
{
    int intVar = 75;           /* integer variable */
    float floatVar = 82.6;     /* floating point variable */

    printf("integer value = %f, floating point value = %d\n",
           intVar, floatVar);
    printf("integer value = %e\n", intVar);
}

/*
 * Function to show problem with using the wrong
 * conversion specifications for int and float in scanf
 */
```

```
void scanfWrong(void)
{
    int intVar;                      /* integer variable */
    float floatVar;                  /* floating point variable */;

    printf("Type an integer and a floating point number:  ");
    scanf("%f %d", &intVar, &floatVar);

    printf("integer value = %d, floating point value = %f\n\n",
        intVar, floatVar);
}

/*
 * Function to show problem with using the wrong
 * conversion specifications for short and long in printf
 */

void shortWrong(void)
{
    short shortVar = 234;            /* short int variable */
    long longVar = 1234567890;       /* long int variable */

    printf("short value (%%d) = %d, long value (%%d) = %d\n\n",
        shortVar, longVar);
    printf("short value (%%ld) = %ld ", shortVar);
    printf("long value (%%hd) = %hd\n\n", longVar);
}

/*
 * Function to show problem with using the wrong
 * conversion specification for int in printf
 */

void unsignedWrong(void)
{
    printf("int value (%%u) = %u, int value (%%d) = %d\n\n",
        -1, -1);
}
```

    a. Execute the program. As written, *main* only calls *intWrong*; the other calls are in comments. What is wrong with the output and why? Correct the conversion specifications.

    b. Change the comments so that *main* only calls *scanfWrong*. What is wrong with the output and why? Correct the conversion specifications.

    c. Change the comments so that *main* only calls *shortWrong*. This function uses %% in the control string of *printf* to display %. What is wrong with the output and why? Is any output correct? If so, why? Correct the conversion specifications.

    d. Change the comments so that *main* only calls *unsignedWrong*. What is wrong with the output and why? Correct the call to *printf*.

e. Remove all comments in *main* so that *main* invokes all four functions. Check that all functions are now working properly. Print a listing of the program and of a run.

2. The goal of this exercise is to study implementation-dependent information about types *short*, *int*, *long*, *float*, and *double*. For your computer, you discover the amount of room a variable consumes and the range of numbers for each type. For type *int*, you perform arithmetic to demonstrate overflow. You discover the precision of types *float* and *double* and the epsilon for *float* numbers.

Execution of the completed program in file *LAB042.c* might generate the following output on your computer:

```
*********** Integer Information ***********

size of short  = 2 bytes
size of int    = 2 bytes
size of long   = 4 bytes

The range of short and int is -32768 to 32767
The range of long is -2147483648 to 2147483647

Demonstration of underflow and overflow in int:
For integers: minimum - 1 is 32767, maximum + 1 is -32768

******** Floating Point Information ********

size of float   = 4 bytes
size of double  = 12 bytes

precision of float   = 6
precision of double  = 18

The range of float is 1.175494e-38 to 3.402823e+38
The range of double is 1.000000000000000000e-4914
       to 1.189731495357231765e+4932

float epsilon = 1.192093e-07
```

In the program in *LAB042.c,* three asterisks (***) indicate a place to add information. The code comments out most statements so that you can add them one-by-one. Copy the file *LAB042.c*, listed below, onto your disk.

```
/*
 * Program to display information on storage size and
 * ranges of various types.
 */

#include <stdio.h>
/*** Part a:  Include 2 header files of integer ***/
/*** and floating point information               ***/
```

```
void floatingInfo(void);
void integerInfo(void);

main()
{
    integerInfo();
    floatingInfo();
}

/*
 * Function to display information on storage size and
 * ranges of integer types.
 * Pre:   none
 * Post:  Integer information has been displayed.
 */

void integerInfo(void)
{
    int shortSize,        /* size of short  */
        intSize,          /* size of int    */
        longSize;         /* size of long   */

    printf("********** Integer Information **********\n\n");

    /* Assign sizes of types short, int, long to variables */
/** Part b:
    shortSize = ***;
    intSize = ***;
    longSize = ***;
**/
    /* Print sizes of types */
/** Part c:
    printf("size of short  = %*** bytes\n", shortSize);
    printf("size of int    = %*** bytes\n", intSize);
    printf("size of long   = %*** bytes\n\n", longSize);
**/
    /* Print ranges of types */
    /*** Part d: add "and int" to the appropriate printf ***/
/** Part e:
    printf("The range of short is %*** to %***\n", ***, ***);
    printf("The range of long is %*** to %***\n\n", ***, ***);
**/
    /* Demonstrate integer underflow and overflow by */
    /* printing minimum - 1 and maximum + 1            */
/** Part f:
    printf("Demonstration of underflow and overflow in int:");
    printf("\nFor integers: minimum - 1 is %d, maximum + 1 ");
    printf("is %d\n\n", *** - 1, *** + 1);
**/
}
```

```
/*
 * Function to display information on storage size and
 * ranges of floating point types.
 * Pre:   none
 * Post:  Floating point information has been displayed.
 */

void floatingInfo(void)
{
    int  floatSize,        /* size of float */
         doubleSize;       /* size of double */

    printf("****** Floating Point Information ******\n\n");
    /* Assign sizes of types float and double to variables */
/** Part g:
    floatSize = ***;
    doubleSize = ***;
**/
    /* Print sizes of types */
/** Part h:
    printf("size of float   = %*** bytes\n", floatSize);
    printf("size of double  = %*** bytes\n\n", doubleSize);
**/
    /* Print precision of types */
/** Part i:
    printf("precision of float  = %***\n", FLT_DIG);
    printf("precision of double = %***\n\n", ***);
**/
    /* Print ranges of types using e notation       */
    /* and specifying the number of decimal places  */
/** Part j:
    printf("The range of float is %.***e to %.***e\n",
           ***, ***);
    printf("The range of double is %.***e\n", ***);
    printf("    to %.***e\n\n", ***);
**/
    /* Print the float epsilon */
/** Part k:
    printf("float epsilon = %e \n", ***);
**/
}
```

Execute the program. It should compile and run correctly but produce only heading output, because almost everything is in comments. Each part below corresponds to a part in the program, indicated with a comment, such as

```
/*** Part a: ...
```

For each part, replace any sequence of three asterisks with code, and remove the corresponding comments for that segment. After the changes in each part, make sure the program still works correctly. Answer any questions for a part.

a. In place of the indicated comments immediately below the inclusion of *stdio.h*, include the header files of integer and floating point information.

b. Use the *sizeof* operator to assign values to *shortSize*, *intSize*, and *longSize* (see subsection "Range of Unsigned Integers in a Computer" in Section 2.4). Of what type is each size? Do you need different kinds of conversion specifications for each variable?

c. Fill in the appropriate conversion specifications to print these sizes. On your computer, is *int* equivalent to *short* or *long*?

d. On the basis of your answer to Part c, add the phrase "and int" to the appropriate call to *printf*. The range of *int* should agree with that of *short* or *long*.

e. Be careful to add the appropriate conversion specifications for the ranges in the calls to *printf*. Otherwise, the range for the type that is different from *int* will be wrong.

f. Fill in the constants. Explain the answers.

g. Use the *sizeof* operator to assign values to *floatSize* and *doubleSize*.

h. Fill in the appropriate conversion specifications to print these sizes. The size gives the number of bytes needed to store a value of that type. What is the type of *floatSize*? Should we use the conversion specification %f to print it? Why or why not?

i. The constant *FLT_DIG* gives the number of decimal digits for *float*. Complete the calls to *printf* to discover the precision of *float* and *double*.

j. Use the precisions from Part i as the number of decimal places to print the ranges in exponential notation.

k. Fill in the constant that we use to test if two real numbers are equal.

l. Print a listing and a run of the program.

3. The goal of this exercise is to use floating point variables and design and test solutions with different preconditions. Write a program that reads the lengths of the three sides of a triangle and prints the area. Calculate the area of the triangle by Heron's formula, which defines the semiperimeter, *s*, as half of the sum of the sides of the triangle. By the formula, the area of a triangle is:

$$Area = \sqrt{s(s - a)(s - b)(s - c)}$$

where *a*, *b*, and *c* are the sides of the triangle. Write a function that has the sides of a triangle as parameters and returns the area using Heron's formula.

The program in file *LAB043.c* contains an outline of the solution with the precondition that *a*, *b*, and *c* form a triangle. The listing follows:

```
/*
 * Program to test TriArea function
 */

#include <stdio.h>
#include <math.h>

float TriArea(float a, float b, float c);

main()
{
    float a, b, c;  /* sides of triangle */
```

```
     /* display instructions here */
     printf("Enter side a: ");
     scanf("%f", &a);
     printf("Enter side b: ");
     scanf("%f", &b);
     printf("Enter side c: ");
     scanf("%f", &c);
     printf("Area of Triangle is: %4.3f\n", TriArea(a, b, c));
}


/*
 * Function to calculate the area of a triangle given three
 * sides
 * Pre:  Sides, a, b, c, form a triangle.
 * Post: The function has returned the area of the triangle.
 */

float TriArea(float a, float b, float c)
{
     float s,      /* semiperimeter */
           temp;   /* square of area of triangle */

     /* calculate s */
     /* calculate temp = s(s-a)(s-b)(s-c) */
     /* change stub return below to return area */
     return (0);
}
```

a. Replace the comments "display instructions here" with appropriate calls to *printf* to inform the user of the purpose of the program and the data that are required. Execute the program. You should get 0.000 for an answer.

b. Replace the comments in *TriArea* with appropriate commands to find the area of the triangle. Run the program and provide the values 5, 4, and 3 for the sides of the triangle. What value is displayed? Verify that this is the correct answer and debug if necessary.

c. Run the program with 9, 4, and 3 for the sides of the triangle. What happens when these data are used? Are the preconditions violated?

d. Change the initial comment for the function *TriArea* so that the precondition is *a*, *b*, and *c* are positive floating point numbers with $a > b > c$. Add postconditions: Function has returned area of the triangle; 0 if data do not form a triangle. Use the fact that three sides form a triangle if the sum of the two shorter sides is greater than or equal to the third to rewrite *TriArea* to meet new pre- and postconditions. What happens when 9, 4, and 3 are entered? What happens when 5, 4, and 3 are entered? What happens when 4, 3, and 9 are entered? Are the preconditions violated?

e. Change the initial comments for the function *TriArea* so that the precondition is *a*, *b*, and *c* are positive floating point numbers. Sides *a*, *b*, and *c* form a triangle if $s(s − a)(s − b)(s − c)$ is greater than or equal to zero. Use this fact to rewrite *TriArea* to meet the new precondition. Return an area of zero if the sides do not form a triangle. Test *TriArea* with the three sets of data suggested in Part d above. What happens?

f. Try a negative value for a, b, or c. What happens? Can we relax the precondition and postcondition as follows?

Pre: a, b, and c are floating point numbers.
Post: The function has returned the area of the triangle with lengths of sides represented by absolute value of parameters; zero if no triangle is formed.

g. Print a listing of the program and of sample output.

5

Looping

Introduction

One of the most valuable characteristics of a computer is its ability to execute a series of instructions repeatedly. For example, at the end of each payroll period, a company with 1000 employees executes a program to process everyone's paycheck. For each employee, the program computes wages, Social Security and income tax withholdings, insurance, and other fees. With similar computations for each person, the program uses a loop for generating the checks. Without a loop to process the checks, the program would be much longer. This chapter introduces loop structures, which permit the programmer to control how many times the computer executes a series of C statements, such as producing a paycheck.

Another application of loops is in error recovery. Suppose a program asks the user a question, expecting an answer of Y or N. If the user inadvertently presses a different key, we can detect the error using an *if* statement. Instead of aborting, the program with a loop can allow the user to answer again until he or she types an appropriate response.

Section 5.4 discusses looping in interactive programs. For example, a program may repeatedly allow the user to make moves in a computer game. To create the element of chance, the program generates a sequence of pseudorandom numbers, or numbers that appear to occur at random. For instance, a game might simulate the throw of a pair of dice or the toss of a coin. We discuss how to generate such random numbers and illustrate their application in the repeated playing of a game.

The chapter contains two breadth sections. One section considers various measurements of time within the computer. The other illustrates the seriousness of truncation error within a loop.

The last section continues the discussion of sound programming techniques, especially the importance of structured programming. In all algorithm development and implementation, the programmer should strive to employ structured programming, which includes the use of modules and sequential, selection, and looping constructs.

Goals

To study

- Updating assignment operators
- Loops that test at the beginning of the loop whether to execute
- Loops that test at the end of the loop whether to execute again
- Validation of input
- Looping and interactive programs
- Random number generation
- Measurements of time in the computer
- Propagation of truncation errors in loops
- Structured programming

Section 5.1 Updating Assignment Operators

We have encountered several statements that increment or decrement a variable by 1, such as the following:

```
count = count + 1;    /* increment count by 1 */
count = count - 1;    /* decrement count by 1 */
```

Such counting statements are a useful feature of all programming languages. C has a number of ways of abbreviating these common operations. One method is to use **updating assignment operators**. For example, the following C statements are equivalent:

```
count = count + 1;    /* These statements are equivalent */
count += 1;
```

The operator += (with no space between the + and the =) means, "Add the expression on the right (the rvalue) to the variable named on the left (the lvalue)." Similarly,

```
count = count - 1;
```

is equivalent to

```
count -= 1;
```

where the −=; operator means, "Subtract the expression on the right from the variable on the left." The rvalue can be any arithmetic expression. The computer evaluates this expression and then adds it to or subtracts it from the lvalue. Updating assignment operators also perform multiplication, division, modulus, and the other binary operations in C. The more compact abbreviated version may compile faster. Some examples follow:

Statement	Is Equivalent to
a += b;	a = a + b;
c -= d;	c = c - d;
e *= f;	e = e * f;
g /= h;	g = g / h;
i %= j;	i = i % j;

The updating assignment operator is similar to human thought processes. For example, for the operation x += 5, we customarily say "add five to x" rather than "take the value x, add five to it, and store the result in x."

The computer evaluates the expression to the right of the updating assignment operator before updating. Updating assignment operators have the same low precedence as the assignment operator (=). For example, the statement

    a *= b + c;

is equivalent to

    a = a * (b + c);

The values b and c are added first, as if the variables were enclosed in parentheses. Then the computer performs the multiplication update.

If the lvalue appears more than once on the right-hand side of the assignment operator, then the programmer can eliminate only one occurrence by using the updating assignment operator. For example, we can write the statement

    a = a + a + 3;

as

    a += a + 3;

Even with the updating assignment operator, a still appears on the right side of the statement.

Increment and Decrement Operators

Because the operation of adding 1 to or subtracting 1 from a variable occurs so frequently in programming, C provides a concise way of accomplishing this task. For example, if we wish to add 1 to the variable *count*, we can use the **increment operator** (++). The following statements are equivalent to one another:

```
count = count + 1;   /* These statements are equivalent */
count += 1;
count++;
++count;
```

To subtract 1 from *count* (decrement it by 1), we use the **decrement operator** (--), as shown:

```
count = count - 1;   /* These statements are equivalent */
count -= 1;
count--;
--count;
```

No spaces should appear between the adjacent plus or minus symbols.

Table 5.1   Precedence of operators in descending order

()	highest
! – (unary) sizeof (*type*) ++ --	
* / %	
+ – (binary)	
< <= > >=	
== !=	
&&	
‖	
= += -= *= /= %=	lowest

In contrast to other operators, the increment and decrement operators are the only operators present in their respective statements. Not even the assignment operator appears in the same statement with them. The position of the increment and decrement operators before or after the identifier in these examples does not make a difference. As we see shortly, however, in some cases the position is important.

Being unary operators, the increment and decrement operators have the same priority as other operators that apply to one argument, such as the unary minus (–), NOT (!), type casting, and *sizeof*. Table 5.1 places all these operators in their relative positions in the precedence of operators.

Pre- and Post-increment and Decrement

We can now consider the effect of placing ++ and -- before or after a variable. For an expression with the increment or decrement operator occurring after the variable name—as in (3 * *count*++)—the computer evaluates the expression (3 * *count*) and increments the variable afterwards. Here, the statement indicates to multiply 3 times the current value of *count* and then add 1 to *count*. Thus,

```
triple = 3 * count++;
```

is equivalent to

```
triple = 3 * count;
count += 1;
```

This order of operation is known as **post-increment**, because the increment operator is written **after** the variable name, and the operation is performed **after** the variable's value is used.

If the increment or decrement operator appears **before** the variable—such as (3 * ++*count*)—the computer adds 1 to *count* and uses this new value in the expression. Thus,

```
triple = 3 * ++count;
```

is equivalent to

```
count += 1;
triple = 3 * count;
```

The order of this operation is **pre-increment**.

Example 5.1

This example demonstrates the effect of the placement of the increment operator. Consider the following program:

```
/*
 * Program to illustrate effect of placement of ++
 */

#include <stdio.h>

main()
{
    int x,      /* initially 5 for each case */
        y;      /* final result for each case */

    x = 5;
    y = 3 * x++;
    printf("Case 1: Incrementing after, x = %d, y = %d\n",
            x, y);
    x = 5;
    y = 3 * ++x;
    printf("Case 2: Incrementing before, x = %d, y = %d\n",
            x, y);
}
```

The output follows:

```
Case 1: Incrementing after,  x = 6, y = 15
Case 2: Incrementing before, x = 6, y = 18
```

Figure 5.1 shows memory during execution of the post-increment of Case 1. Because the increment operator follows x, the computer multiplies 3 times the unincremented value of x. After the assignment of the product 15 to y, x's value becomes 6.

By contrast, in Case 2 we increment x to 6 before computing the product. Thus, as Figure 5.2 illustrates, y contains the result 3 * 6 = 18.

Figure 5.1
Case 1 of
Example 5.1, a
post-increment

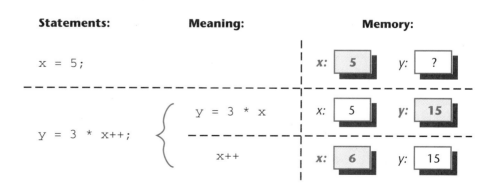

Figure 5.2
Case 2 of
Example 5.1, a
pre-increment

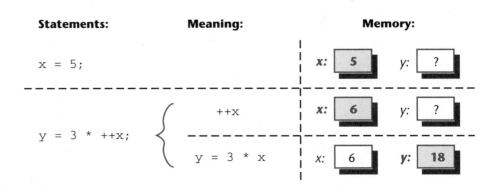

Example 5.2

In this similar example, we consider the placement of the decrement operator in the conditional expression of an *if-else* statement. The following program has two such statements.

```
/*
 * Program to illustrate effect of placement of --
 * in an if-else statement
 */

#include <stdio.h>
main()
{
    int x;        /* initially 5 for each case */

    x = 5;
    if (x-- == 5)
        printf("Case 3: Decrementing after,  x = %d\n", x);
    else
        printf("Case 3: Decrementing before, x = %d\n", x);


    x = 5;
    if (--x == 5)
        printf("Case 4: Decrementing after,  x = %d\n", x);
    else
        printf("Case 4: Decrementing before, x = %d\n", x);
}
```

The output gives x = 4 in both cases, but the action is different.

```
Case 3: Decrementing after,  x = 4
Case 4: Decrementing before, x = 4
```

In the **post-decrementing** of Case 3, we evaluate the condition (x == 5) before changing the value of x. Prior to the subtraction of 1, x is equal to 5, and the expression is true. The computer completes the expression by decrementing *x* before executing the first *printf*. This *if-else* statement is equivalent to the following segment in which decrementing of *x* occurs as the first statement in the *if* and *else* clauses:

```
if (x == 5)
{
    x--;
    printf("Case 3: Decrementing after, x = %d\n", x);
}
else
{
    x--;
    printf("Case 3: Decrementing before, x = %d\n", x);
}
```

We reverse decrementing and evaluating the boolean expression in **pre-decrementing** of Case 4. Before testing, the computer subtracts 1 from *x* to obtain 4. Consequently, the expression (*x* == 5) is false, and the second *printf* becomes active. The following equivalent segment shows an assignment to *x* before execution of the *if-else* statement:

```
--x;
if (x == 5)
    printf("Case 4: Decrementing after,  x = %d\n", x);
else
    printf("Case 4: Decrementing before, x = %d\n", x);
```

Many C programmers prefer this use of the increment and decrement operators to make programs concise. For the novice, however, such techniques can make a program difficult to understand. One solution is to use clear comments describing what each statement or critical section of code does. A better solution is to avoid complicated code until becoming more experienced.

Use of the increment and decrement operators involves some practical considerations. The programmer must carefully determine whether to place the operator before or after the variable in question. This decision can be hard in such situations as Example 5.2, in which the variable appears more than once in the statement.

Section 5.1 Exercises

1. Assuming the following assignments for integer variables *x*, *y*, and *z*, evaluate *x* after execution of each statement.

    ```
    x = 10; y = 5; z = -3;
    ```

    a. x += 7;   **b.** x *= z - y;   **c.** x %= 3;
    d. x /= y;   **e.** x /= 20;   **f.** x -= z - y;

2. Assuming the following assignments for integer variables *x*, *y*, and *z*, evaluate *x* and *y* after execution of each statement.

    ```
    x = 10; y = 5; z = -3;
    ```

a. `y = x++ * z;`   **b.** `y = --x * z;`   **c.** `y = (x++ > 10);`
d. `y = !(x-- == 9);`   **e.** `y += ++x;`   **f.** `y += x++;`

3. For each part, place parentheses to indicate the order in which the computer performs operations.

a. `y += x * ++z;`   **b.** `y *= x >= 3 + z;`   **c.** `y %= x / z;`
d. `a++ * -b`   **e.** `x <= ++y && z != x`   **f.** `x += y - z;`

4. Can we replace the following statement

   ```
   n = n * 3 + 1;
   ```

   with

   ```
   n *= 3 + 1;
   ```

   Why or why not?

In Exercises 5–8, write two equivalent statements for

5. Adding 50 to *NumStudents*

6. Dividing *halve* by 2

7. Assigning *left* the remainder of *left* divided by 10

8. Multiplying *tax* by *rate* plus 0.01

In Exercises 9–13, write equivalent statements that do not use updating assignment, increment, or decrement operators.

9. ```
   if (x++ == 3)
       printf ("%d\n", x);
   ```

10. ```
    if (--x != 3)
        y = x;
    ```

11. `y = ++x + 2;`

12. `y %= x++;`

13. `y -= --x * 5;`

Section 5.2 **Looping with a Pretest**

It is often advantageous to be able to execute all or part of a program a number of times. For example, an automated library catalogue would be inconvenient if the user had to restart the program with each new search for an author, title, or subject. Similarly, to test the procedure *PrintNumber* from Example 3.13 of Section 3.4, we must run the program several times. A less time-consuming solution is for the program itself to allow such repeated testing. In Example 3.12, we developed a procedure, *CountDown*, which used the *switch* statement to print a countdown of values from an integer between 5 and 1. A more flexible alternative employs a control structure that enables such repeated printing of a counter, where the counter varies from any positive integer down to 1. In this chapter and the next, we consider three implementations in C of a control structure that allows the flow of control of a program to repeat a segment.

The *while* Loop

We have considered three major types of control structures—modular, sequential, and selection. A fourth way of altering a program's flow of control is the **looping control structure**, which enables the computer to execute a segment of code several times. A segment of code that is executed repeatedly is called a **loop**. The loop concept is fundamental to programming. The programs in the text so far have not contained loops, but most subsequent ones do.

One implementation in C of the looping control structure is the *while* loop, which has the following general form:

```
while (expression)
    statement
```

As long as the expression is true when execution is at the top of the loop, the computer performs the statement. We say the *while* statement employs a loop **pretest**. The loop condition is tested **before** each **iteration** (loop) and therefore before the loop is entered at all. If the condition initially fails, the computer skips the loop entirely. Figure 5.3 illustrates the action of a loop that has a pretest.

The *while* statement employs a loop pretest, testing the loop condition before each loop iteration.

Example 5.3

The following program prints integers from 1–5 using a *while* loop:

```
/* Program with while loop to print line numbers */

#include <stdio.h>

main()
{
    int i = 1;              /* loop variable */

    while (i < 6)
        printf("Line number %d\n", i++);
}
```

The output displays the action of this loop.

```
Line number 1
Line number 2
Line number 3
Line number 4
Line number 5
```

The declaration-initialization gives integer variable *i* the value 1. Similar to an *if* statement, the computer evaluates the conditional expression in parentheses after *while*. Because *i* is 1 initially, the expression ($i < 6$) is true, and the computer executes the body of the *while* statement. The body can be a compound statement, but in this

Figure 5.3
Action of a
while loop

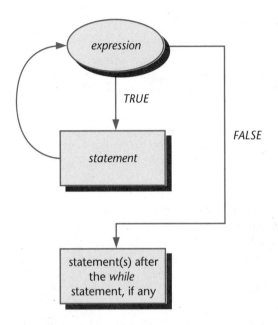

case it is only a call to the *printf* function. With the post-increment *i++*, *printf* produces
the following output:

```
This is line number 1
```

before incrementing *i* to the value 2. Thus, the initial behavior of the *while* statement
is similar to that of the *if* statement, as shown:

```
if (i < 6)
    printf("This is line number %d\n", i++);
```

Instead of proceeding to the next statement, with a *while* loop we go back to the top of
the loop and repeat the entire process. The computer evaluates the test expression
again, which may be just as complex as any found in *if* statements. In the example,
with *i* now 2, (*i* < 6) is still true. Consequently, the *printf* executes once more, printing

```
This is line number 2
```

and incrementing *i* to 3.

This process continues until *i* increments to 6 and the test expression (*i* < 6) becomes
false. At that point, the loop terminates immediately, and program execution continues
with the statement (if any) following the *while* loop. If no more statements exist, the
program stops. Figure 5.4 shows the action of this *while* loop in memory and output.

Suppose in the program, we initialize *i* to a value of 6 or more, as follows:

```
int i = 6;                 /* loop variable */

while (i < 6)
    printf("Line number %d\n", i++);
```

In this case, the condition in the loop initially is false. Consequently, the body of the
loop does not execute at all, and the segment produces no output.

Figure 5.4 Action of *while* loop in Example 5.3

Code:	Meaning:	Output:	Memory:
`int i = 1;`	i ← 1		*i:* 1
`While (1 < 6)`	Is (1 < 6)?		*i:* 1
`printf("Line number %d\n", i++);`	print	Line number 1	*i:* 1
	i++		*i:* 2
`While (i < 6)`	Is (2 < 6)?		*i:* 2
`printf("Line number %d\n", i++);`	print	Line number 2	*i:* 2
	i++		*i:* 3
`While (i < 6)`	Is (3 < 6)?		*i:* 3
`printf("Line number %d\n", i++);`	print	Line number 3	*i:* 3
	i++		*i:* 4
`While (i < 6)`	Is (4 < 6)?		*i:* 4
`printf("Line number% d\n", i++);`	print	Line number 4	*i:* 4
	i++		*i:* 5
`While (i < 6)`	Is (5 < 6)?		*i:* 5
`printf("Line number %d\n", i++);`	print	Line number 5	*i:* 5
	i++		*i:* 6
`While (i < 6)`	Is (6 < 6)?		*i:* 6
	exit		

**Infinite
Loop**

In the above examples, we must initialize all variables in the test expression before the *while* loop. In addition, the body of the loop must change the value of at least one variable in the boolean expression, so that eventually the condition becomes false. Otherwise, the condition remains true, and the loop never stops. We illustrate such an **infinite loop** in the next example.

Definition   An **infinite loop** is a looping control structure that never stops unless an external interrupt of the program occurs.

Example 5.4 _____

As mentioned in the last example, an alternative way of writing the *while* loop uses a compound statement for the body, as shown:

```
int i = 1;              /* loop variable */

while (i < 6)
{
    printf("Line number %d\n", i);
    i++;
}
```

Writing *i*++ on a separate line increases the likelihood that the reader will notice the increment operation.

As with any compound statement, we must be careful to enclose its statements (the call to *printf* and the increment) in braces. If we omit the braces, then the increment would not be part of the loop, and the loop would be infinite, as shown:

```
int i = 1;              /* loop variable */

/*** ERROR:  Infinite loop.  Braces needed. ***/
while (i < 6)

    printf("Line number %d\n", i);
    i++;                 /* ERROR: Not part of loop */
```

The loop in this program is infinite because the value of *i* never changes. The test expression (*i* < 6) starts out being true and remains true forever. Thus, the same message fills the screen and continues printing, as follows:

```
Line number 1
Line number 1
Line number 1
    ⋮
```

For just such errors, we should know how to abort a running program.

On a VAX computer or a computer running the UNIX operating system, **ctrl-c** (press the c key while holding down the control key) interrupts a process; on an IBM-compatible microcomputer, **ctrl-break** aborts a program; and on a Macintosh, **command-period** halts execution.

Nature of the Pretest

Example 5.5

In this example, we show that the computer performs the *while* loop pretest only at the top of the loop. If the condition is false during the test, the loop does not execute. Should the condition become false in the body of the loop, however, execution of the control structure continues through the body. To illustrate this behavior, we add two statements to the body of the loop in Example 5.3—one to make *i* greater than 6 and another to reverse the process.

```
/*
 * Program with while loop to print line numbers
 * and to change i's value back and forth
 */

#include <stdio.h>

main()
{
    int i = 1;              /* loop variable */

    while (i < 6)
    {
        printf("Line number %d\n", i++);
        i += 20;
        i -= 20;
    }
}
```

Because the loop body now contains three statements, we group them with braces to form a compound statement. This loop, however, behaves exactly like the one in Example 5.3. The two new statements have no effect on the value of *i* that the *while* uses in its test. Even though the first assignment adds 20 to *i*, the second subtracts 20 and leaves the value as it was. Between these two statements, *i* has a value greater than 6. The loop does not stop, however, because the computer does not test here. It tests before executing or re-executing the first statement of the loop. At that point, the last assignment statement has restored the sequential value of *i*.

If the test expression becomes false within the body of the loop, execution still continues for the entire body of the loop.

Example 5.6

In the following *while* loop, the test expression involves not only *i* but also the integer variable *a*. The loop executes only while *i* is less than 6 AND *a* is greater than 3. If at least one of these conditions becomes false, the loop terminates. If at least one of the conditions is false when execution comes to the loop, the computer skips the loop entirely.

```
while ((i < 6) && (a > 3))
    printf("Line number %d\n", i++);
```

The value of *a* does not change in the loop, but the value of *i* increments in a way that makes the loop terminate eventually. Therefore, we could rewrite the loop with an *if* and a *while* statement.

```
if( a > 3)
   while (i < 6)
       printf("Line number %d\n", i++);
```

In either form of the loop, if the value of *a* is less than or equal to 3, then the initial test fails, and the computer skips the *while* loop. The version with the *if* statement is more efficient, however, because it does not have a test of *a* at the top of every loop.

Manipulation of Loop Variable

Example 5.7

Just as the condition in the *while* loop may be as complex as desired, the body can change the variables used in the condition in any way that eventually causes the condition to become false. In Example 5.3, we could increment *i* by 2 instead of 1, as follows:

```
int i = 1;            /* loop variable */

    while (i < 6)
    {
        printf("Line number %d\n", i);
        i += 2;
    }
```

This segment prints odd numbers, as *i* takes on values 1, 3, and 5, as shown:

```
Line number 1
Line number 3
Line number 5
```

After *i* becomes 7, the loop terminates.

Example 5.8

In Example 3.12 of Section 3.4, we wrote a function, *CountDown*, that accepted a positive integer argument (to match parameter *CountFrom*) less than or equal to 5, and counted down from that number to 1, printing "Ignition" and "Blast off!" at the end. We limited the argument to some artificial upper bound, such as 5, because we were using a *switch* statement. In the present example, we write a new version without such a restriction. We still verify that the argument is positive. Pseudocode for *CountDown* follows:

> ### CountDown(CountFrom)
>
> Count down from *CountFrom* to 1, and then print Ignition, Blast off!
>
> ### Pre:
>
> *CountFrom* is a positive integer.
>
> ### Post:
>
> The countdown or an error message has been printed.
>
> ### Algorithm:
>
> if *CountFrom* is not positive
>   print an error message
> else
>   while *CountFrom* is positive
>   print *CountFrom*
>   decrement *CountFrom* by 1
>   print "Ignition" and "Blast off!"

```c
/*
 * Function to count down from positive parameter
 * CountFrom to 1, and then to print Ignition, Blast off!
 * Pre:    CountFrom is a positive integer.
 * Post:   The countdown or an error message has been printed.
 */

void CountDown(int CountFrom)
{
    if (CountFrom <= 0)                    /* invalid argument */
        printf("ERROR:  Counting down from %d <= 0\n",
                CountFrom);
    else                                   /* valid argument */
    {
        while (CountFrom > 0)
            printf("%5d\n", CountFrom--);
        printf("Ignition\n");
        printf("Blast off!\n");
    }
}
```

For a *CountFrom* equal to 6, the function generates the following:

```
    6
    5
    4
    3
    2
    1
 Ignition
 Blast off!
```

Formatting with %5d causes the numbers to be right-justified in a field that lines up on the right with the t in "Ignition." The loop can count down from any number between 1 and *INT_MAX*, the largest *int* value. Should the argument be a nonpositive value like −3, the *if* statement intercepts the error and delivers the message

```
ERROR:  Counting down from -3 <= 0
```

Example 5.9

The next program illustrates another way to manipulate the loop variable.* A hypothesis states that any positive integer *n* goes to 1 if we treat it in the following fashion: If *n* is even, we divide *n* by 2. If odd, we multiply *n* by 3 and increment the result by 1. This process continues with the generated number as the new value of *n*. It ceases only when *n* finally reaches 1 (if ever). No one has found an integer that does not go to 1 using this process, but no mathematician has proved that such a number does not exist.

In this example, we develop a program that reads an integer. If that integer is positive, the program prints the step and the next number in the sequence. When the sequence arrives at 1 (presuming that it does so), we print the original input and the number of steps to 1. Figure 5.5 presents the structure chart for the program, in which *main* calls *readn* to return the starting number in the sequence and calls *hailstones* to generate the sequence.

---

*An article, "Hailstones," in *Scientific American* (January 1984) is the basis for this example.

Figure 5.5
Structure chart
for Example 5.9

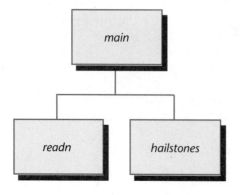

In *main*, we use an *if* statement to verify that the input is valid. The *while* loop is ideally suited to the sequence generation in the function *hailstones*. The execution of the loop continues as long as *n* is greater than 1, and the body of the loop modifies the value of *n* as the problem specifies. Because we must generate each new *n* from the previous *n*, we must save the original *n* in a separate variable, *nsave*. Another variable, *step*, keeps track of the step number.

The function *readn* is fairly routine. Pseudocode for the other two functions and code for the program follow:

main()

Hailstones problem

Algorithm:

call *readn* to obtain the original number, *n*, in the sequence

if (*n* is nonpositive)
    print an error message
else
    call *hailstones* to generate the sequence

hailstones(*n*)

Prints the hailstone sequence for *n* with step numbers

Pre:

n is a positive integer.

Post:

The hailstone sequence for *n* has been printed.

Algorithm:

initialize *step* to 0
save the value of *n* in *nsave*
while *n* is greater than 1
    if *n* is even
        $n \leftarrow n/2$
    else
        $n \leftarrow 3 * n + 1$
    increment *step*
    print *step* and *n*
print *nsave* and the final *step*

```
/*
 * Example 5.9
 * Hailstones problem: For positive input integer n, do the
 * following until n is 1: If n is even, change n to n/2
 * else change n to 3 * n + 1
 */
```

```
#include <stdio.h>

int readn(void);
void hailstones(int n);

main()
{

    int n;

    n = readn();
    if (n <= 0)
        printf("%d is not positive. Please run again.\n", n);
    else
        hailstones(n);
}

/*
 * Function to print directions and read a value for n
 * Pre:     none
 * Post:    Directions have been displayed and
 *          the user input has been returned.
 */

int readn(void)
{
    int n;

    printf("This program prints the hailstone sequence.\n");
    printf("Please enter a positive integer: ");
    scanf("%d", &n);

    return n;
}

/*
 * Given a positive integer n, this function prints the
 * hailstone sequence with step numbers. When the sequence
 * arrives at 1, it prints the original n and the number of
 * steps.
 * Pre:     n is a positive integer.
 * Post:    Hailstone sequence has been displayed.
 */

void hailstones(int n)
{
    int nsave,          /* original n */
        step = 0;       /* step number */

    nsave = n;          /* save original n */
```

```
    /* Generate hailstone sequence */
    while (n > 1)
    {
        if (n % 2 == 0)      /* n even */
            n /= 2;
        else                 /* n odd */
            n = 3 * n + 1;
        step++;
        printf("Step %4d: n = %5d\n", step, n);
    }

    printf("\n%d went to 1 in %d steps.\n", nsave, step);
}
```

If the user provides input of 58, the sequence arrives at 1 in 19 steps. We allocate four column positions to print the intermediate values of *step* and *n*, and within these four positions the numbers print neatly right-justified in columns.

```
This program prints the hailstone sequence.
Please enter a positive integer: 58
Step    1: n =    29
Step    2: n =    88
Step    3: n =    44
Step    4: n =    22
Step    5: n =    11
Step    6: n =    34
Step    7: n =    17
Step    8: n =    52
Step    9: n =    26
Step   10: n =    13
Step   11: n =    40
Step   12: n =    20
Step   13: n =    10
Step   14: n =     5
Step   15: n =    16
Step   16: n =     8
Step   17: n =     4
Step   18: n =     2
Step   19: n =     1

58 went to 1 in 19 steps.
```

An invalid input data item like −58 generates an error message, as shown:

```
This program prints the hailstone sequence.
Please enter a positive integer: -58
-58 is not positive.  Please run again.
```

Because nobody has determined how many steps it takes for any given number to go to 1, we cannot predict how many iterations the loop will have. This situation contrasts sharply with previous loops, in which we increment or decrement the loop variable and can easily determine the number of iterations.

Section 5.2 Exercises

Give the output for the segments in Exercises 1–5.

1.
```
int i = 2;
while (i < 10)
    printf("%d ", ++i);
```

2.
```
int i = 3;
while (i >= 0)
    printf("%d ", i--);
```

3.
```
int i = 10;
while (i != 0)
{
    printf("%d ", i);
    i -=3;
}
```

4.
```
int i = 4,
    j = 0;
while (i >= 0)
    printf("%d %d\n", i--, j++);
```

5.
```
int i = 5,
    j = 5;
while ((i > 0) && (--j > 0))
    if (i-- % 5 == 0)
        printf("Case 1: i = %d, j = %d\n", i, j);
    else
        printf("Case 2: i = %d, j = %d\n", --i, j);
```

6. Find the error(s) in the following program:

```
#include <stdio.h>
main()
{
    int i;              /* loop variable */

    while i < 100
        printf("%d\n", i);
}
```

7. Find the error(s) in the following program:

```
#include <stdio.h>
main()
{
    int i = 1;                /* loop variable */

    while (i < 100)
        printf("%d\n", i);
        i -= 5;
}
```

8. Give the output for the program in Example 5.9 with user input 3.

In Exercises 9–13, write the indicated program segments.

9. To print your name 10 times

10. To print the even positive integers less than 20

11. To print the powers of 2 from 1 to 2^{12} in a loop that doubles the previous result

12. To read and print integers until there is an input of 0. Print the zero, but do not ask for any more numbers.

13. To increment by ones a loop variable from 1 to 1000, but to print the value every hundred iterations (i.e., the output should be 100, 200, and so on.)

14. How can you protect against integer overflow in Example 5.9?

Section 5.2 Programming Project

A **prime** is an integer greater than 1 that can only be divided evenly by 1 or itself. Thus, 2, 3, 5, 7, 11, 13, and 17 are examples of primes, whereas $6 = 2 \times 3$ is not. Prime numbers are an essential ingredient of most encryption schemes.

Develop a program to input a positive integer and determine whether it is a prime or a **composite** (nonprime). Perhaps the easiest (though not the fastest) way of checking is to test whether the number is evenly divisible by all integers between 2 and itself. We can shorten the procedure appreciably by not testing the number against any even numbers above 2. Moreover, we should test the candidate only against integers less than or equal to the square root of its own value.

Section 5.3 Looping with a PostTest

The *do-while* Loop

The *do-while* loop (or *do* loop) differs from its counterpart, the *while* loop, in that the former makes a loop **posttest**. The condition is not tested until the body of the loop has been executed once. By contrast, the test for a *while* loop is on entry. Even if the condition is initially false, the body of the *do-while* loop executes at least once. If the condition is false after the first loop iteration, the loop terminates. If the first iteration makes or leaves the condition true, however, the loop continues. The general form of the *do-while* loop is as follows:

```
do
     statement
while (expression);
```

The placement of the *while* clause after the body of the *do-while* implies that the testing occurs after execution of the body. Figure 5.6 diagrams the action of this looping control structure.

If the body of the loop is a simple statement, it ends with a semicolon. In the following segment, the first semicolon marks the end of the inner statement only, not of the entire loop construct:

```
do
     a += 7;
while (a < b);
```

The loop increments *a* by 7 as long as *a* is less than *b*. Thus, if initially $a = 3$ and $b = 12$, after termination of the loop, *a* is 17. Because the segment loops at least once, if *a* is initially 5000 and *b* is 12, the loop ends after one iteration with *a* being 5007.

Figure 5.6
Diagram of
action of
do-while
statement

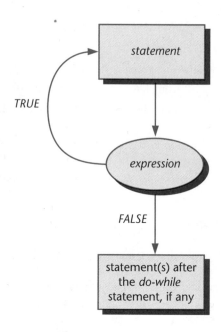

Applications In every situation that requires a loop, we can use either the *while* or *do-while* loop. Some types of problems suggest one loop or the other as a more natural solution.

Example 5.10

In this example, we write an interactive program that adds the digits of a nonnegative integer. For instance, if the user enters the number 456, the computer adds 4 + 5 + 6 and prints the sum, 15.

Like several earlier programs, two functions are under *main* in the structure chart. Unlike these programs, we enable the user to correct an invalid data entry. *ReadNum* performs this task and returns a nonnegative integer. *FindDigitSum* computes and returns the sum of the digits of a nonnegative integer. Because we use pass by value to *FindDigitSum*, regardless of what that function does to the parameter, it has no effect on the *num* in *main*. We can with confidence use *num*'s value without saving it in another variable. Because *ReadNum* performs the error checking, *main* consists almost entirely of calls to functions.

> **main()**
>   Program to add the digits of a nonnegative input integer
>
> **Algorithm:**
>   call *ReadNum* to obtain a nonnegative integer value for *num*
>   print *num* and *FindDigitSum(num)*

In *ReadNum*, we print directions, prompt for input, and read a value. If the value is negative, the data item is invalid, and we repeat the request for and the reading of a value. Because the computer prompts and reads at least once, the situation is ideal for a *do-while* loop. Similar to the code, in the pseudocode we introduce this repeating loop with *do* and close it with *while*.

ReadNum() → *num*

Function to read and return a nonnegative integer

Pre:

Post:

A nonnegative integer has been returned.

Algorithm:

print instructions
do the following
    prompt the user
    read a number, *num*
while *num* is negative
return *num*

Several important actions occur in *FindDigitSum*. One useful process is summation. In the function, we must accumulate the sum of the digits in a variable, *sum*. The method we use is similar to adding a sequence of numbers on a traditional calculator. We first turn on the calculator or press the clear key to remove any previous value and start the summation with zero. Similarly with the computer, we must initialize *sum* to zero. Otherwise we would be using the value that happened to be in the location for *sum*, and the result would probably be wrong. With a calculator, we enter a number and press the + key. This action adds the number to the previous calculator value, 0. We mimic this manipulation with the computer statement

```
sum += RightmostDigit;
```

which adds the value of *RightmostDigit* to *sum*. With the calculator, we continue the process by entering another number and pressing + again. The repetitive action is duplicated in our program with a *do-while* loop. Upon completion of the loop, *sum* holds the total of all the values of *RightmostDigit*.

In *FindDigitSum*, we strip off the rightmost digit using the % operator. Because the remainder in division by 10 is this digit, we have the following assignment statement:

```
RightmostDigit = num % 10;
```

For example, 456 % 10 yields a remainder of 6, which is the rightmost digit.

Once the rightmost digit is extracted, how does the program get at the next digit? The solution is to make the next one the rightmost digit by dividing the value of *num* by 10.

```
num = num / 10;
```

For example, the integer division 456 / 10 yields 45. We can extract the second digit in the same way as the first one, using % 10, and add this digit to the accumulator *sum*. This process concludes when the value of *num* becomes 0 and we have no more digits to add. The entire program follows the pseudocode for *FindDigitSum*. Figure 5.7 illustrates the action of this function for argument 456.

Figure 5.7 Action of the function *FindDigitSum* for argument 456

Code:		Memory:

Code:	Memory:
`FindDigitSum(456);`	num: **456**
`int sum = 0,` `    RightmostDigit;`	num: 456 sum: **0** ***RightmostDigit:*** **?**
`    RightmostDigit = num % 10;`	num: 456 sum: 0 ***RightmostDigit:*** **6**
`    sum += RightmostDigit;`	num: 456 sum: **6** *RightmostDigit:* 6
`    num /= 10;`	***num:*** **45** sum: 6 *RightmostDigit:* 6
`while (num > 0);`	num: 45 sum: 6 *RightmostDigit:* 6
`    RightmostDigit = num % 10;`	num: 45 sum: 6 ***RightmostDigit:*** **5**
`    sum += RightmostDigit;`	num: 45 sum: **11** *RightmostDigit:* 5
`    num /= 10;`	***num:*** **4** sum: 11 *RightmostDigit:* 5
`while (num > 0);`	num: 4 sum: 11 *RightmostDigit:* 5
`    RightmostDigit = num % 10;`	num: 4 sum: 11 ***RightmostDigit:*** **4**
`    sum += RightmostDigit;`	num: 4 sum: **15** *RightmostDigit:* 4
`    num /= 10;`	***num:*** **0** sum: 15 *RightmostDigit:* 4
`while (num > 0);`	num: 0 sum: 15 *RightmostDigit:* 4

FindDigitSum(num) → *sum*

Function to return the sum of the digits of *num*

Pre:

num is a nonnegative integer.

Post:

The sum of digits of *num* has been returned.

Algorithm:

sum ← 0
do the following
    place the rightmost digit of *num* into *RightmostDigit*
    add *RightmostDigit* to *sum*
    strip away the rightmost digit of *num*
while *num* is positive
return *num*

```c
/*
 * Example 5.10
 * Program to add up the digits of a nonnegative input integer
 */

#include <stdio.h>

int ReadNum (void);
int FindDigitSum (int num);

main ()
{
    int num;        /* nonnegative input integer */

    num = ReadNum ();
    printf("The sum of the digits of %d is %d.\n",
            num, FindDigitSum(num));
}

/*
 * Function to print instructions and repeatedly read
 * integers until the user enters a nonnegative integer,
 * which the function returns
 * Pre:    none
 * Post:   A nonnegative integer has been returned.
 */
```

```c
int ReadNum(void)
{
    int num;                    /* nonnegative input integer */

    printf("This program returns the sum of the digits\n");
    printf("of a nonnegative integer.\n\n");

    do
    {
        printf("Enter a nonnegative integer: ");
        scanf("%d", &num);
    }
    while (num < 0);

    return num;
}

/*
 * Function to return the sum of the digits of a positive
 * integer argument
 * Pre:    The argument, num, is a positive integer.
 * Post:   The function has returned the sum of the
 *         digits of num.
 */

int FindDigitSum(int num)
{
    int sum = 0,                /* sum of digits */
        RightmostDigit;         /* rightmost digit of num */

    do
    {
        RightmostDigit = num % 10;      /* extract rightmost digit */
        sum += RightmostDigit;          /* add digit to ongoing sum */
        num /= 10;          /* move next digit into rightmost position */
    }
    while (num > 0);    /* when num is 0, no more digits to extract */

    return sum;
}
```

The following session uses input of a positive integer:

```
This program returns the sum of the digits
of a nonnegative integer.

Enter a nonnegative integer: 1776
The sum of the digits of 1776 is 21
```

If the user enters a negative integer, the program prompts again and waits for another value to use in the computation, as shown:

```
This program returns the sum of the digits
of a nonnegative integer.

Enter a nonnegative integer: -7
Enter a nonnegative integer: -736
Enter a nonnegative integer: 4
The sum of the digits of 4 is 4.
```

The program also works correctly with a data entry of zero, as follows:

```
This program returns the sum of the digits
of a nonnegative integer.

Enter a nonnegative integer: 0
The sum of the digits of 0 is 0.
```

With *num* being 0, the loop body assigns 0 to *RightmostDigit*, *sum*, and *num*. The loop terminates after the first iteration.

In *FindDigitSum*, we could have used a *while* loop instead of a *do-while* loop, as shown:

```
while (num > 0)
{
    RightmostDigit = num % 10;
    sum += RightmostDigit;
    num /= 10;
}
```

The difference in action would occur only with data entry of 0. If we used a *while* loop, the body of the loop would never execute, because the condition (*num* > 0) would be false from the beginning. Thus, *sum* would return its initial value of 0, which is correct. In the next example, we develop a program in which the choice of a *do-while* loop has a clear advantage over the *while* loop.

The following recommendations may be used for determining **which loop to employ**, a *while* loop or a *do-while* loop:

1. If the statements of the loop may not be executed at all, use a *while* loop.

2. If the loop is to execute at least once, we can use either kind of loop, but the *do-while* loop is preferable.

Example 5.11

In this example, we read a nonnegative integer, such as 1234, and print its digits in reverse order—4321. This program is similar to the last one, with *main* calling two functions—*ReadNum* and *PrintReverse*. Other than printing different instructions, *ReadNum* is identical to that function in Example 5.10. *PrintReverse* is similar to *FindDigitSum*. In this program, *main* does not print but assigns that task to *PrintReverse*. The code for *main* is as follows:

```
main()
{
    int num;            /* nonnegative input integer */

    num = ReadNum();
    PrintReverse(num);
}
```

Moreover, *PrintReverse* does not return a value, so we adjust its type to *void*.

```
void PrintReverse(int num);
```

We use a technique to extract the digits that requires us to remove them from right to left. As we strip off a least significant digit, we print the value instead of accumulating it in a sum. The following pseudocode and code for *PrintReverse* are similar to those of *FindDigitSum* in the last program:

> *PrintReverse:*
> > do the following
> > > place the rightmost digit of *num* into *RightmostDigit*
> > > print *RightmostDigit*
> > > strip away the rightmost digit of *num*
> > while *num* is positive

```
/*
 * Function to print the digits of a positive integer
 * argument in reverse order
 * Pre:    The argument, num, is a positive integer.
 * Post:   The procedure has displayed the digits.
 *         of num in reverse order.
 */

void PrintReverse(int num)
{
    int RightmostDigit;     /* rightmost digit of num */

    printf("%d backwards is ", num);
```

```
    do
    {
        RightmostDigit = num % 10;
        printf("%d", RightmostDigit);
        num /= 10; /* move next digit into rightmost position */
    }
    while (num > 0);

    printf("\n");
}
```

One run of the program produces the following:

```
This program prints a nonnegative integer backwards.

Enter a nonnegative integer: 1234
1234 backwards is 4321
```

Another run has the following output:

```
This program prints a nonnegative integer backwards.

Enter a nonnegative integer: 0
0 backwards is 0
```

If we used a *while* loop in *PrintReverse*,

```
while (num > 0)
{
    RightmostDigit = num % 10;
    printf("%d", RightmostDigit);
    num /= 10;   /* move next digit into rightmost position */
}
```

an input of 0 would cause the loop never to execute. The last line of the printout would be incomplete, as shown:

```
0 backwards is
```

Complying with stepwise refinement, the pseudocode for *PrintReverse* does not detail the actions of the calls to *printf*. The *printf* immediately preceding the *do-while* loop not only echoes the input but also prints the first part of the solution line. This literal does not end with \n, because the program prints the reversed number on the same line. The *printf* in the loop does not contain \n either, because each digit would be on a separate line. The program ends with a *printf* that simply ends the output line with a newline character.

Section 5.3 Exercises

Give the output for the segments in Exercises 1–4.

1.
```
int i = 2;
do
    printf("%d ", ++i);
while (i < 10);
```

2.
```
int i = -3;
do
    printf("%d ", i--);
while (i >= 0);
```

3.
```
int i = 3;
do
{
    printf("%d ", i);
    i = (2 * i + 1) % 5;
}
while (i != 3);
```

4.
```
int i = 4,
    j = 0;
do
    printf("%d %d\n", i--, j++)
while (i >= 0);
```

5. Find the error(s) in the following program:

```
#include <stdio.h>
main()
{
    int i;          /* loop variable */

    do
        printf("%d\n", i);
    while i < 100 && j > 0;
}
```

In each of Exercises 6–11, write a program segment to keep prompting and reading the indicated items:

6. The (floating point) cost of an item as long as the user types a nonpositive value

7. The (floating point) salary until the user enters a number in the proper range ($0–$200,000)

8. A (floating point) gauge value until the user enters a number in the proper range (between −5 and 5, inclusively)

9. An integer until the user enters 0. Print the square of each nonzero input value.

10. An integer until the user enters zero. Accumulate and print the sum of the data. Be sure to initialize the accumulator.

11. A floating point number until the user enters a negative number. Accumulate and print the product of the data. Be sure to initialize the accumulator.

12. **a.** Write a *while* loop to replace the *do-while* loop in *FindDigitSum* of Example 5.10.

    b. Which loop is better for that application?

13. **a.** Write a *do-while* loop to replace the *while* loop in *hailstones* of Example 5.9 of Section 5.2.

    b. Which loop is better for that application?

Section 5.3 **Programming Projects**

1. To calculate the grade point average (GPA) of a student, we divide the total quality points earned by the total number of hours attempted. Develop a program that reads such totals and computes the GPA. Repeatedly request total hours until the input is between 0 and 200 exclusively. Repeatedly request total quality points until the input is between 0 and 4 times the total hours inclusively.

2. Develop a program to read a nonnegative integer of up to five digits in length and print its expansion in reverse order in base 10. For example, for the number 4937, the output would be

```
4937 = 7 * 1 + 3 * 10 + 9 * 100 + 4 * 1000
```

3. Develop a program that examines all the numbers from 1 to 999, displaying all those for which the sum of the cubes of the digits equals the number itself. For example, given the number 563, $5^3 + 6^3 + 3^3 = 125 + 216 + 27 = 368$, which is not equal to 563. On the other hand, given 371, $3^3 + 7^3 + 1^3 = 27 + 343 + 1 = 371$.

4. Revise Example 5.11, replacing the function *PrintReverse* with *reverse*. Instead of printing, *reverse* returns the reversed integer to *main* for printing. To do this reversal, initialize an integer variable, *ReverseNum*, to 0. With each iteration of the loop, add the least significant digit of *num* to the product of *ReverseNum* and 10. For example, suppose *num* is originally 945. The following gives the values of the variables after each iteration:

Iteration	num	RightmostDigit	ReverseNum
	945		0
1	94	5	0 * 10 + 5 = 5
2	9	4	5 * 10 + 4 = 54
3	0	9	54 * 10 + 9 = 549

For each of Projects 5–16, revise the Programming Project from the given section to allow the user to correct invalid input.

5. Section 3.3, Project 1   6. Section 3.3, Project 2

7. Section 3.3, Project 3   8. Section 3.4, Project 2

9. Section 4.1, Project 2   10. Section 4.1, Project 3

11. Section 4.3, Project 1   12. Section 4.3, Project 2

13. Section 4.5, Project 1   14. Section 4.5, Project 2

15. Section 4.5, Project 3   16. Section 4.5, Project 4

Section 5.4 **Looping and Interactive Programs**

The Sentinel Technique

One of the most common uses of loops is to input a number repeatedly and perform some operation on it. For example, we might want to read a series of radius values of circles and compute the corresponding circumferences and areas. As another example, we could place the statements of Example 5.11's *main* in a *while* loop, which would make it possible to print several numbers backwards without having to rerun the program for each number.

We must, however, provide the user with a way to tell the computer that there are no further problems to solve. Moreover, we must designate a suitable test condition that terminates the loop when it becomes false. One way to conclude the loop is to choose a number that the user normally would never ask the program to process. For example, if the program requires the user to type a radius, then entering a negative number is a suitable way to indicate the desire to stop processing. Because this special end-of-data value trails all the meaningful data, this method is the **sentinel** or **trailer technique**.

Definition The **sentinel** or **trailer technique** uses a special end-of-data value to indicate the end of meaningful data.

Example 5.12

In this example, we create an interactive program to read nonnegative integers and print their squares. A sentinel of a negative number terminates the program. The program invokes only one function, *ReadNum*, that prompts the user for a value and returns the user's input. The function *main* contains the loop that drives the program.

When the user enters a negative value, we want the program to stop immediately and not square that input. Therefore, we need to read the number just before making the loop test. To accomplish reading immediately before testing, we call *ReadNum* twice. The first invocation reads the first number. If that value is negative, the loop does not execute. Otherwise, the program performs the calculation and produces output. This first exercise of *scanf* before the *while* loop is a **priming read** or **priming** *scanf*. It primes the loop variable with a value. The last action taken in the body of the loop and the one immediately before another check of the loop condition is to read the next number. If this value is still not a sentinel item, the body of the *while* loop executes again, using that number. The general form of the *while* loop with a priming *scanf* is as follows:

```
printf(prompt);
scanf(control_string, loop_variable);
while (test_loop_variable)
{
    :
    printf(prompt);
    scanf(control_string, loop_variable);
}
```

The program follows the pseudocode for *main* and *ReadNum*.

Definition A **priming read** or **priming** *scanf* is an input statement that appears before a *while* loop and that obtains a value for the loop variable.

main( )

Program to read numbers and print their squares

Algorithm:

> $n \leftarrow ReadNum()$
> while *n* is nonnegative
>   print the square of *n*
> $n \leftarrow ReadNum()$

ReadNum( ) → ***num***

> Function to read and return an integer

Pre:

> none

Post:

> The integer entered by the user has been returned.

Algorithm:

> prompt for a nonnegative integer to square or a negative integer to quit
> read the integer
> return the integer

```c
/*
 * Example 5.12
 * A program to read numbers and print their squares
 */

#include <stdio.h>

int ReadNum(void);

main()
{
    int n;              /* number to be squared */

    n = ReadNum();   /* get first number ("priming scanf") */
    while (n >= 0)
    {
        printf("%d squared is %d\n\n", n, n * n);
        n = ReadNum();              /* get next number */
    }
}

/*
 * Function to prompt for and read an integer to return
 * Pre:     none
 * Post:    The integer entered by the user has been returned.
 */

int ReadNum(void)
{
    int num;                            /* input number */

    printf("Enter an integer to be squared (negative to quit): ");
    scanf("%d", &num);
    return num;
}
```

Execution of the program demonstrates that we can process more than one data item. The condition in the *while* loop ensures that the loop runs as long as the value of *n* is nonnegative.

```
Enter an integer to be squared (negative to quit): 5
5 squared is 25

Enter an integer to be squared (negative to quit): 47
47 squared is 2209

Enter an integer to be squared (negative to quit): -1
```

Random Numbers in Interactive Programs

One useful application involving looping is the **simulation** of real-life events that we consider to be random. An example is the simulation of the flow of customers in a bank to help determine the number of tellers needed at peak times. Such a program would model the random flow of customers and compile statistics about the flow. The use of simulation frees bank representatives from having to observe the flow and keep track of exactly when each customer arrives and leaves. The simulation also allows bankers to observe the effects of different plans without actual implementation.

Definition   A **simulation** is a model using a program of a real-life event.

Other examples of simulation are computer games, which are by nature interactive. If the events in a game were predetermined, the player would quickly learn the sequence and become bored. The usual solution is for the game program to choose its own moves at random. In most games, the total number of possible combinations of events or moves is so astronomically large that this method results in each game being unique. To pick the moves, the computer generates a sequence of numbers, called **random numbers** or **pseudorandom numbers**. An algorithm actually produces the numbers, so they are not really random, but they appear to be random. Often, a random number generator must produce numbers in a **uniform distribution**, with each number having an equal likelihood of being anywhere within a specified range. For example, suppose we wish to generate a sequence of uniformly distributed, four-digit random numbers. The algorithm used to accomplish this should, in the long run, produce approximately as many numbers between, say, 1000 and 2000 as it does between 8000 and 9000.

Definitions   **Pseudorandom numbers** (also called **random numbers**) are a sequence of numbers that an algorithm produces but which appear to be randomly generated. The sequence of random numbers is **uniformly distributed** if each random number has an equal likelihood of being anywhere within a specified range.

ANSI C's standard library has a random number generator, *rand*, which returns a uniformly distributed pseudorandom integer in the range from 0–*RAND_MAX*. The header file *stdlib.h* contains the prototype for *rand* and the definition of *RAND_MAX*, which must be at least 32767. We can assign a pseudorandom integer to variable *num* with the following statement:

```
num = rand();
```

Seeding the Random Number Generator

A random number generator starts with a number, which we call a **seed** because all subsequent random numbers sprout from it. The generator uses the seed in a computation to produce a pseudorandom number. The algorithm employs that value as the seed in the computation of the next random number, and so on.

If our random number generator always starts with the same seed, it always produces the same sequence of numbers. A program using this generator performs the same steps with each execution. The ability to reproduce detected errors is useful when debugging a program. However, this replication is not desirable when we are using the program. We do not want a computer game to repeat exactly the same moves each time, nor do we want the same questions to appear in a computerized quiz.

By default, *rand* uses a seed of 1. ANSI C provides another function, *srand*, that allows the programmer to specify a different seed or initial value for the generator. The function *srand* in the standard library accepts an unsigned integer argument and seeds *rand* with that number. For example,

```
srand(23421);
```

forces *rand* to use 23421 instead of 1 as the seed.

Unfortunately, with each execution we still generate the same random number sequence because we start with the same seed, 23421, each time. Alternatively, we could request a seed from the user.

```
unsigned seed;

printf("Enter a seed for the random number generator: ");
scanf("%d", &seed);
srand(seed);
```

The user, however, can enter the same seed each time.

To avoid this problem, we can seed the random number generator with a number that varies, such as the time. The ANSI C time library with header file *time.h* contains the function *time* that returns a value indicating the time, day, month, and year. To seed *rand* with this value, we can use the call

```
srand((unsigned) time((time_t *)NULL));
```

We explain the time argument in Section 11.2. For now, we can use this call to start sequences of random numbers based on time.

Example 5.13

In this example, we write a program to print a sequence of 10 random integers between 0 and *RAND_MAX* using the function *rand*. We must be careful to include the header file *stdlib.h*. After debugging, we should seed the generator with the time, so we must also include the header file *time.h*.

```
/*
 * Program to print a different sequence of random numbers each
 * time in the range 0 - RAND_MAX with seed based on time
 */
```

```
#include <stdio.h>
#include <stdlib.h>
#include <time.h>

main()
{
    int i = 0;

    srand((unsigned) time((time_t *)NULL));

    printf("Random integers between 0 and %d:\n\n", RAND_MAX);
    while (i++ < 10)
        printf("%6d", rand());
}
```

The field width with the conversion specification %9d causes the numbers to appear in a neat column, as shown:

```
Random integers between 0 and 32767:

 29175 17647 29737   926 27943 24694 19753 23874  3432 28555
```

We call *srand* only once, because this function just establishes the seed. If we place this call to *srand* in the loop, the computation of each number would start with its seed and would not appear random.

Ranges of Random Numbers

Some compilers provide extensions to the ANSI C random number generator that allow the programmer to specify a range. The documentation should indicate how to access these extensions. In the next two examples, we develop our own functions to specify the range that only depend on the functions and constants that are in ANSI C libraries.

Example 5.14

Many simulations require a sequence of floating point numbers between 0 and 1. In this example, we develop a function, *random_float*, that generates such numbers. Because *rand()* produces an integer between 0 and *RAND_MAX*, dividing *rand()* by *RAND_MAX* with floating point division generates a floating point number between 0 and 1. Because the value *rand* returns and *RAND_MAX* are both integers, we must cast the numerator (or denominator) to type *float* to avoid integer division. Thus, we define the function as follows:

```
/*
 * Function to return a random float between 0 and 1
 * Pre:    The generator is seeded.
 * Post:   A random floating point number between 0 and 1
 *         has been returned.
 */
```

```
float random_float(void)
{    return ( (float) rand() / RAND_MAX );
}
```

Calling this function from within a *printf*, such as

```
printf("%f\n", random_float());
```

might display 0.697623. If we assign

```
random_0_1 = random_float();
```

then *random_0_1* contains a random floating point number between 0.0 and 1.0.

Suppose, however, we need a random floating point number between 0.0 and 5.0. Because the length of this interval is 5.0, we multiply by this value (5.0 * *random_0_1*) to stretch the interval of numbers. Mathematically we have the following:

$$0.0 \leq random\_0\_1 \leq 1.0$$

Thus, multiplying by 5.0 throughout, we obtain the correct interval, as shown:

$$0.0 \leq 5.0 \cdot random\_0\_1 \leq 5.0$$

If the lower bound of the range is different from 0, we must also add that value. For example, if we need a random floating point number between 2.0 and 7.0, we multiply by the length of the interval, $7.0 - 2.0 = 5.0$, to expand the range. We then add the lower bound, 2.0, to shift or translate the result.

$$2.0 \leq (7.0 - 2.0) \cdot random\_0\_1 + 2.0 \leq 7.0$$

Generalizing, we can define a function (*random_float_range*) that returns a floating point random number in the range from parameter *LowerBound* to parameter *UpperBound*. The function has a local variable (*random_0_1*), which stores a random floating point number between 0 and 1. Because the computation of such a number involves only one expression, (*float*)*rand*() / *RAND_MAX*, we assign this expression to *random_0_1* instead of calling *random_float*.

```
/*
 * Function to generate a random floating point number
 * between LowerBound and UpperBound
 * Pre:    LowerBound and UpperBound are of type float with
 *         LowerBound < UpperBound. The generator is seeded.
 * Post:   A random float between LowerBound and
 *         UpperBound has been returned.
 */

float random_float_range(float LowerBound, float UpperBound)
{
    float random_0_1;   /* random number between 0 and 1 */

    random_0_1 = (float)rand() / RAND_MAX;
    return ((UpperBound - LowerBound) * random_0_1
            + LowerBound);
}
```

Example 5.15

Frequently, we need a more restricted range of random integers than 0 to *RAND_MAX*. A computerized guessing game would certainly be challenging if we had to guess a number between 0 and at least 32,767. One method of restricting the range—such as between 0 and 99—is to multiply a floating point random number between 0 and 1 by 100 (the number of integers from 0 through 99) and then return the integer part. For example, suppose *rand*() returns 22,704 and *RAND_MAX* is 32,767. The floating point quotient is between 0 and 1, as shown:

$$(\textit{float})\ 22704\ /\ 32767 = 0.692892$$

Multiplying by 100, we obtain the following:

$$100 * 0.692892 = 69.2892$$

Truncating, we get an integer (69) between 0 and 99.

In the program below, we define a function *random* that returns a random integer between 0 and one less than argument *UpperBound*. We should also hide the details of seeding the random number generator in another routine, *SeedRand*. The program follows:

```c
/*
 * Example 5.15
 * Program to print a different sequence of random numbers each
 * time in the range 0 - (UpperBound - 1) with seed based on
 * time
 */

void SeedRand(void);
int random(int UpperBound);

#include <stdio.h>
#include <stdlib.h>
#include <time.h>

#define HIGH 100

main()
{
    int i = 0;

    SeedRand();

    printf("Random integers between 0 & %d, inclusively:\n",
            HIGH - 1);
    while (i++ < 10)
        printf("%5d", random(HIGH));
}

/*
 * Function to seed the random number generator
 * Pre:     none
 * Post:    Random number generator has been seeded.
 */
```

```
void SeedRand(void)
{
    srand((unsigned) time((time_t *)NULL));
}


/*
 * Function to generate a random integer
 * between 0 and UpperBound - 1
 * Pre:    UpperBound is a positive integer. The generator is seeded.
 * Post:   A random integer between 0 and UpperBound - 1
 *         has been returned.
 */

int random(int UpperBound)
{
    float random_0_1;  /* random number between 0 and 1 */

    random_0_1 = (float) rand() / RAND_MAX;
    return ( (int)(UpperBound * random_0_1 ) );
}
```

One run of this program might produce the following output:

```
Random integers between 0 & 99, inclusively:
    15    6   89    0    4   13    8   36   92   19
```

Other executions produce different results.

Sometimes we want the range of random integers to have a lower bound other than 0, for example from 100 to 499 (or 500 − 1). As with *random_float_range* of the last example, we add 100 to the length of the interval (500 − 100 = 400).

```
(int)((500 - 100) * random_0_1) + 100
```

Suppose we want a function *random_range* to return a random integer between *LowerBound* and *UpperBound* − 1, inclusively. The definition of the function is identical to that of *random_float_range*, except for casting the return value to *int*, as shown:

```
/*
 * Function to generate a random integer
 * between LowerBound and UpperBound - 1
 * Pre:    LowerBound and UpperBound are integers with
 *         LowerBound < UpperBound. The generator is seeded.
 * Post:   A random integer between LowerBound and
 *         UpperBound - 1 has been returned.
 */
```

```
int random_range(int LowerBound, int UpperBound)
{
    float random_0_1;   /* random number between 0 and 1 */

    random_0_1 = (float) rand() / RAND_MAX;
    return ( (int)( (UpperBound - LowerBound) * random_0_1 )
            + LowerBound );
}
```

It would be useful to have the random number generators *random_float*, *random_float_range*, *random*, and *random_range* in our own library so that we can use them in different programs. In Chapter 12, we discuss placing related functions we develop in a separately compiled file and their prototypes in a corresponding header file. If you wish to use such a library, the header file, *RandDef.h*, and source file of definitions, *RandDef.c*, are on the text disk. To access these random number functions, include *RandDef.h* with the name in quotes before *main*, as shown:

```
#include "RandDef.h"
```

Compile *RandDef.c* and the application program and link the two object files. Because this header file contains prototypes for the functions and includes *stdlib.h* and *time.h*, the application program does not need to do so.

Example 5.16

The program in this example plays a game in which the computer "thinks" of a number between 0 and 99, inclusively, and the user repeatedly tries to guess it. As Figure 5.8 shows, the function *main* calls a function *initialization* to initialize the game, *random* to "think" of a number, and *PlayGame* to do as the name describes. The function *initialization* calls *SeedRand* to seed the random number generator, and *PlayGame* calls *ReadGuess* to prompt the user and read the guess.

> ### main()
> Program to play a guessing game
>
> ### Algorithm:
> call *initialize*
> *target* ← a random number between 0 and 99
> play the game with *target* as the number to guess

After *initialization* calls *SeedRand* to seed the random number generator, it prints the game instructions. The function *PlayGame* has a loop to allow the user to make multiple guesses. As described in Section 3.1, we use the *#define* compiler directive to define *TRUE* and *FALSE*.

```
#define FALSE 0
#define TRUE  1
```

With these definitions at the head of the program, we use a descriptive boolean variable, *GuessAgain*, in *PlayGame* to indicate whether the user needs to guess again or not.

Figure 5.8
Structure chart
for program in
Example 5.16

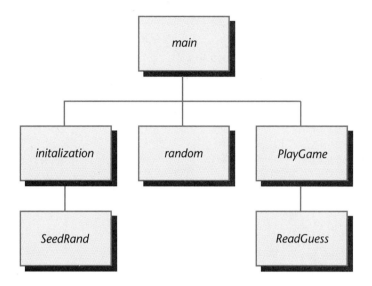

PlayGame(target)

Function to allow the user to play the game

Pre:

target is an integer between 0 and 99.

Post:

The game has been played.

Algorithm:

GuessAgain ← *TRUE*
do
    call *ReadGuess* to return the user's guess, *guess*
    if *guess* is less than the computer's number, *target*
        tell the user to guess higher
    else if *guess* is greater than *target*
        tell the user to guess lower
    else
        congratulate the user
        GuessAgain ← *FALSE*
while *GuessAgain* is *TRUE*

We link the program file below with the source file for the random number generators, *RandDef.c*, and include the corresponding header file, *RandDef.h*.

```
/*
 * Example 5.16
 * Program to play a guessing game.  The computer selects a
 * number at random in the range from 0 through HIGH (100) -
 * 1 and the user repeatedly tries to guess the number
 */
```

```
#include <stdio.h>
#include "RandDef.h"

void initialize(void);
int ReadGuess(void);
void PlayGame(int target);

#define HIGH 100
#define FALSE 0
#define TRUE 1

main()
{
    int target;               /* computer's number */

    initialize();
    target = random(HIGH);
    PlayGame(target);
}

/*
 * Function to print game instructions and seed the random
 * number generator
 * Pre:     none
 * Post:    The game's instructions have been displayed and
 *          the random number generator has been seeded.
 */

void initialize(void)
{
    SeedRand();

    printf("Welcome to the GUESSING GAME!\n\n");
    printf("I'm thinking of a number between 0 and %d.\n", HIGH - 1);
    printf("Enter your guess.\n");
    printf("I'll tell you whether to guess higher or lower.\n\n");
}

/*
 * Function to allow the user to play the game
 * Pre:     target is an integer between 0 and HIGH - 1.
 * Post:    target has been guessed by the user.
 */

void PlayGame(int target)
{
    int ReadGuess(void);
    int guess,                          /* user's guess */
        GuessAgain = TRUE;
```

```
    do
    {
        guess = ReadGuess();
        if (guess < target)
            printf("Guess higher\n\n");
        else if (guess > target)
            printf("Guess lower\n\n");
        else
        {
            printf("Congratulations! You guessed it!\n");
            GuessAgain = FALSE;
        }
    }
    while (GuessAgain);    /* continue while GuessAgain is TRUE */
}


/*
 * Function to prompt for and read an integer to return to main
 * Pre:     none
 * Post:    User's guess has been returned.
 */

int ReadGuess(void)
{
    int guess;                 /* user's guess */

    printf("Enter a guess: ");
    scanf("%d", &guess);
    return guess;
}
```

One execution of the program follows:

```
Welcome to the GUESSING GAME!

I'm thinking of a number between 0 and 99.
Enter your guess.
I'll tell you whether to guess higher or lower.

Enter a guess: 49
Guess higher

Enter a guess: 75
Guess lower

Enter a guess: 63
Guess higher
```

```
Enter a guess: 69
Guess higher

Enter a guess: 72
Guess higher

Enter a guess: 73
Congratulations! You guessed it!
```

Section 5.4 Exercises

1. Find the error(s) in the following code to find the square root of numbers as long as the numbers are nonnegative.

```
#include <stdio.h>
#include <math.h>

main()
{
    float n;                    /* number for sqrt */

    while (n >= 0)
    {
        printf("Type a number: ");
        scanf("%d", n);
        printf("The square root of %d is %d\n", n, sqrt(n));
    }
}
```

2. Write a function to read numbers, computing their ongoing sum and count, until the user types a sentinel value of 0. The function should return their average.

3. Add statements to the function *PlayGame* in Example 5.16 to count and print the number of guesses.

4. Add statements to the function *main* in Example 5.11 of Section 5.3 to print several numbers backwards without having to rerun the program for each number.

Only using rand *and not the functions we have developed in the text, write a segment to generate a random number on the given interval for each of Exercises 5–12.*

5. random integer between 0 and 20, inclusively

6. random floating point number between 0 and 20

7. random integer between 6 and 26, inclusively

8. random floating point number between 6 and 26

9. random integer between 35 and 73, inclusively

10. random floating point number between 35 and 73

11. random integer between −8 and 4, inclusively

12. random floating point number between −8 and 4

Section 5.4 Programming Projects

1. Develop a cash register program that reads (*float*) prices until the user types a negative number. The program should print the total of the prices, a 5% tax, and the total cost with tax.

2. Develop a program to find the average of a set of integer test scores worth 100 points each. The program should read test scores until the user types a negative number.

For each of Projects 3–10, revise the programming project from the given section to allow the user to run the program until entering a trailer value.

3. Section 5.3, Project 1   4. Section 5.3, Project 2

5. Section 5.3, Project 3   6. Section 5.3, Project 4

7. Section 3.4, Project 2   8. Section 3.3, Project 1

9. Section 3.3, Project 2   10. Section 3.3, Project 3

11. Develop an ATM (automatic teller machine) program to present the user with the menu below and to process his or her responses. Initialize the starting balance in the declaration section.

```
What would you like to do?

    1   Make a withdrawal
    2   Make a deposit
    3   Obtain your balance
    4   Quit

Your choice?
```

For example, if the user chooses 1, the ATM prompts and reads the amount of a withdrawal, subtracts that amount from the balance, displays the balance, and asks the user if he or she has another transaction. For menu choice 2, the amount of deposit is added to the balance. Of course, validation of input data should check that the user does not attempt to withdraw more money than is in the account. Withdrawals and deposits should be positive.

12. Some computer services charge people to use their systems. Usually, this is done by tracking the times a person uses the computer and charging based on variable rates. Write a program to simulate this situation. Your program should ask the user what the rate is for using the service during the following time periods: midnight to 6:00 AM, 6:00 to 12:00 PM (noon), 12:00 to 6:00 PM, and 6:00 to midnight. These values are in units of dollars/minute. You must then ask for a series of starting and ending times from the user, continuing until the starting and ending times entered are both zero. The program will compute the total charge and print it out and should be aware that the starting time may be before midnight and ending time after midnight (that is, in the next day).

The program should expect time values to be in military time format. In military format, times range from 0000 to 2359, where times after noon have 12 added to them. For example, 1:15 PM is 1315 in military time. A sample run follows:

```
Enter rate for use of system from 0000 to 0600: 1.00
Enter rate for use of system from 0600 to 1200: 1.10
Enter rate for use of system from 1200 to 1800: 1.25
Enter rate for use of system from 1800 to 0000: 0.95

Enter starting and ending times of use below, ending with
times of 0.
700 825
1405 1435
1130 1500
2350 0010
0 0

Total charge is $408.50
```

Section 5.5 Structured Programming

Having discussed looping, we have covered the following major control structures of a **structured program** or a **structured algorithm**:

1. modular
2. sequential
3. selection
4. looping

We should only use these control structures to modify the order in which the computer executes statements.

In problem solving, we employ top-down design to decompose the problem into a hierarchy of modules. Each module should be a cohesive unit performing one major task. Modules at the lowest level of the structure chart for a program perform relatively simple tasks that the higher-level functions use. Communication between functions should be through the argument-parameter lists, not through a reliance on global variables and side effects.

The design and implementation of each module should involve the four control structures of structured programming. A module may call other modules to perform subtasks. We should only enter a function at the beginning and exit at the end.

Usually, many statements in the module are executed sequentially, one after another. For example, after the following simple assignment statement,

variable = expression;

the computer executes the next statement in the listing.

The selection control structure enables a decision to be made over what is to be executed next at execution time. For example, depending on the value of a logical expression in an *if-else* statement, program execution continues in one direction or another.

The looping control structure allows the computer to execute a segment of code repeatedly. So far, we have considered two implementations in C of this control structure—the *while* loop and the *do-while* loop. The *while* loop performs a test on the loop condition before each iteration and, therefore, before the loop is entered at all. The *do-while* loop tests at the end of each iteration.

Any program can be designed and implemented using these four control structures. Their use can help the program to be organized. A statement available in many high-level languages that is contrary to the ideals of structured programming is the *goto* statement. With this statement, the programmer can alter the flow of control to any place in the program. When *goto* statements are used, the reader cannot be confident about what was executed before a statement. Any part of the program can dictate that execution jump to another place in the program. Such unstructured programs are hard to comprehend. Consequently, they are hard to correct and modify.

Early high-level languages did not fully implement the four control structures. For example, initial versions of BASIC had an *if* statement but not an *if-else* statement. To implement the *if-else* construct, one could use the *goto* statement. Thus, suppose the programmer wanted the computer to execute an *if-else*-type statement, such as the following:

```
if (expression)
    statement1
else
    statement2
```

Without benefit of this type of statement, the programmer often would create the construct using *goto* statements, as shown:

```
           if (expression)
               goto label1
           statement2          /* for else clause */
           goto label2
label1:    statement1          /* for if clause */
label2:    ...
```

This segment is certainly confusing. A more serious problem, however, was that many programmers employed the *goto* statement not to create constructs like the *if-else* statement, but to jump around the program in an unbridled fashion.

In 1968, Edsgar Dijkstra wrote a letter to the editor of the *Communications of the Association for Computing Machinery* entitled "Go To Statement Considered Harmful." In the letter, Dijkstra said, "The **go to** statement as it stands is just too primitive; it is too much an invitation to make a mess of one's program." Dijkstra not only derided the use of *goto* but advocated the use of the modular, sequential, selection, and looping control structures. This letter was a catalyst for the revolution in the design and implementation of programs.

In 1993, Dijkstra wrote of the letter, "This little, innocent, article was intended to explain a phenomenon I thought most of us knew. Instead, it evoked a violent storm that raged for more than a decade." When the storm subsided, computer scientists had come to realize that the organized approach of structured programming results in programs that are easier to design, read, debug, and maintain.

Section 5.6 Breadth: Computer Time

Because of the speed and large memory size of modern digital computers, we should consider small and large numbers. The metric prefixes listed in Table 5.2 help to

Table 5.2 The Metric System

Prefix	Abbreviation	Meaning	
tera	t	$10^{12} = 1{,}000{,}000{,}000{,}000$	trillion
giga	g	$10^9 = 1{,}000{,}000{,}000$	billion
mega	M	$10^6 = 1{,}000{,}000$	million
kilo	K	$10^3 = 1{,}000$	thousand
milli	m	$10^{-3} = 1/1{,}000$	thousandth
micro	μ	$10^{-6} = 1/1{,}000{,}000$	millionth
nano	n	$10^{-9} = 1/1{,}000{,}000{,}000$	billionth
pico	p	$10^{-12} = 1/1{,}000{,}000{,}000{,}000$	trillionth

indicate the magnitudes of numbers. For example, computer scientists measure the time (in nanoseconds) it takes to execute an instruction on a **supercomputer**, the fastest type of computer. One nanosecond is one billionth of a second, a very short period of time. If an average person could take one step each nanosecond, that person could circle the earth about 20 times a second!

Definition   A **supercomputer** is the fastest, largest, and most expensive type of mainframe computer.

Example 5.17

Electrical voltage pulses travel at almost the speed of light, about 186,300 miles per second. Thus, by being conscious of the cancellation of units, we can calculate that in 1 nsec (nanosecond) voltage travels about 11.8 inches:

$$\frac{186{,}300 \text{ mi}}{\text{sec}} \cdot \frac{5280 \text{ ft}}{\text{mi}} \cdot \frac{12 \text{ in}}{\text{ft}} \cdot \frac{\text{sec}}{10^9 \text{ nsec}} = 11.8 \text{ in / nsec}$$

The speed of light is a limiting factor for the speed of a serial computer. With such an enormous speed, this limit may seem inconsequential, but for the designers of supercomputers it is not. To improve speed they place electronic components as close as possible to each other, but then they must design ways to overcome the heat buildup. Some designers have resorted to architectures different from the von Neumann model to make computation faster. **Parallel computers** have several processors that can execute different parts of a program simultaneously, thus speeding up the overall execution time.

Definition   A **parallel computer** has several processors that communicate with one another and that can work concurrently on the same or different programs.

Clock Cycle   Because we are dealing with time, we should consider the internal clock of the computer. This clock, unlike the one on the wall, ticks at astronomical speeds. All activities in the central processing unit (CPU) of a computer are regulated by the clock, and no work is done between ticks. Having this regulator allows all voltages to reach their destinations, whether near or far, before the CPU performs another operation. The length of time between ticks of the CPU clock is a **clock cycle**, which is usually in microseconds (μsec) or nanoseconds (nsec).

Definition   A **clock cycle** is the length of time between ticks of the CPU clock.

Example 5.18

The PDP-8, a **minicomputer** or medium-size computer built in the early 1960s, measured 9.5 cubic feet, weighed 250 pounds, and had a cycle time of 1.6 μsec. Only 15 years after introduction of the PDP-8, a tiny silicon chip, small enough to fit on the tip of a finger, could top the PDP-8's computing power and speed. The CRAY-1 supercomputer developed in the 1970s had a cycle time of 12.5 nsec. A smaller cycle time results in a faster computer. The CRAY-1, in fact, has a clock cycle 128 times faster than the PDP-8, as shown:

$$\frac{1.6 \text{ μsec}}{12.5 \text{ nsec}} \cdot \frac{1000 \text{ nsec}}{\text{μsec}} = 128$$

Definition   A **minicomputer** is a mid-level computer with power usually between that of a microcomputer and a supercomputer.

Clock Frequency

A relative measure of speed is **clock rate** or **frequency**, which is simply the reciprocal of cycle time. Cycle time is the time for one cycle, while clock frequency is the number of cycles per unit of time. Often the latter measurement is expressed in **megahertz (MHz)**, or a million cycles per second.

Definition   The **clock frequency** or **rate** is the number of cycles per unit of time. A **megahertz (MHz)** is a million cycles per second.

Example 5.19

The CRAY-1 with a cycle time of 12.5 nsec has a clock frequency of 80 MHz, as shown:

$$\text{clock frequency} = \frac{1}{12.5 \text{ nsec/cycle}} = 0.08 \text{ cycles/nsec}$$

$$= \frac{0.08 \text{ cycles}}{\text{nsec}} \cdot \frac{10^9 \text{ nsec}}{\text{sec}} \cdot \frac{1 \text{ Mcycle}}{10^6 \text{ cycles}}$$

$$= 80 \text{ Mcycles/sec} = 80 \text{ MHz}$$

Flops

Still another way of measuring performance is to give the number of floating point operations that can be executed in a second, called by the amusing acronym **flops**.

> **Definition**   **Flops** is floating point operations per second. A **megaflops** or **Mflops** is a million floating point operations per second.

Example 5.20

For computer simulation of aerodynamic flow, weather, or other activities in continuous space, a three-dimensional grid is established with several measurements stored for each grid point. For a designated time interval, new values are repeatedly computed at the grid points by performing perhaps 500 operations per data item using previous values. Suppose that a 50-MHz machine can perform one floating point operation per clock cycle,* and that 10^{13} arithmetic operations are required to complete a problem. On this computer,

$$50 \text{ MHz} = 50 \text{ Mflops} = 50 \cdot 10^6 \text{ ops/sec}$$

The computer time needed for the problem is calculated as follows:

$$\frac{10^{13} \text{ ops}}{50 \cdot 10^6 \text{ ops/sec}} = 2 \cdot 10^5 \text{ sec}$$

$$= 2 \cdot 10^5 \text{ sec} \cdot \frac{1 \text{ min}}{60 \text{ sec}} \cdot \frac{1 \text{ hr}}{60 \text{ min}} \cdot \frac{1 \text{ day}}{24 \text{ hr}} = 2.315 \text{ days}$$

Section 5.6   Exercises

For Exercises 1–4, express the times in picoseconds, nanoseconds, and microseconds.

1. 0.00045 sec   2. 892 psec   3. 3×10^5 μsec   4. 14.75 nsec

5. Compare the add times (the times to add pairs of numbers) for the following early computers. For each pair, determine how many times faster the second computer is in performing addition.

    a. PILOT ACE, 0.54 msec; Whirlwind, 0.05 msec

    b. Harvard Mark I, 0.3 sec; ENIAC, 0.2 msec

    c. Zuse Z3, 2 sec; EDSAC, 1.4 msec

6. A particular algorithm when coded into a language takes about 5×10^4 computer clock cycles to run. Two programming teams have a contest to see which can best improve the speed of this algorithm. Team A reduces the number of cycles by a factor of 10, while Team B reduces the number by 7500 cycles. Which team is the winner?

7. In "Mathematics and Computer Science: Coping with Finiteness" (*Science* 194 (4271): 1235–1242, December 17, 1976), Donald E. Knuth compared the changes in transportation and computation speeds. The following questions are based on Dr. Knuth's figures.

---

*One MHz is not necessarily equal to one Mflops. For example, a CRAY-1 computer can perform two floating point operations in one clock cycle. A microcomputer might take several clock cycles to perform a floating point operation.

a. A typical walking speed is 4 miles/hour, and a car's highway speed might be 55 miles/hour. How many times faster is such a car than a human?

b. How many times faster is a supersonic jet flying 600 miles/hour than a snail traveling 0.006 mile/hour?

c. A medium-speed computer (vintage 1976) could complete 200,000 additions of 10-digit numbers in a second. With pencil and paper, a human can only perform 0.2 additions/second. How many times faster is this computer than a human?

Note: Knuth asks us to "consider how much a mere factor of 10 in speed provided by the automobile, has changed our lives. . . . Computers [of that era] have increased our calculation speeds by . . . more than the ratio of the fastest airplane velocity to a snail's pace."

8. The earth has a diameter, d, of about 7918 miles.

   a. Find an approximate value in miles for its circumference, which is πd.

   b. A mile has 1760 yards. Find the approximate circumference in yards.

   c. Suppose the length of a person's step is 1 yard. If this person could take one step each nanosecond, how long would it take to circle the earth?

   d. Compute how many times this hypothetical person could circle the earth in 1 second.

   e. If someone could take a step every picosecond, how many times could this person circle the earth in a second?

9. A Cray X-MP computer has a 9.5-nsec clock cycle. Give its clock frequency in megahertz.

10. a. Suppose computer A has a longer cycle time than computer B, and both computers perform one floating point operation in a clock cycle. Which is faster?

    b. Suppose computer C has a larger clock frequency than computer D, and both computers perform one floating point operation in a clock cycle. Which is faster?

11. Suppose a microcomputer has a 50-MHz clock frequency. Find its clock cycle.

12. The Whirlwind computer project was started in 1945 as an aircraft flight simulator/trainer for the U.S. Navy. With a 1-MHz clock rate, what was its cycle time?

13. The ENIAC's frequency ranged from 60 to 125 KHz. What was its clock rate range?

14. The STAR-100 computer, built in the early 1970s, was designed to produce 10^8 32-bit floating point results per second. Express this quantity in megaflops (millions of flops).

Section 5.7 Breadth: Truncation Error in Loops

The potential for truncation error in a loop is much greater than in sequential code. To understand the magnitude of the problem, we need ways to measure error. The **absolute error** is the difference between the exact answer and the computer answer. The **relative error** is this difference divided by the exact answer.

Definitions If *correct* is the exact answer and *result* is the result of a computation, then

absolute error = *correct – result*

relative error = (*correct – result*) / *correct*

Example 5.21

Suppose a computer has a precision of 3, allowing only three digits in the fractional part. (No computer has such a limited precision. For example, ANSI C specifies at least six decimal digits. Limiting the precision to 3, however, simplifies our computations and still illustrates the problem.) We calculate the absolute and relative errors in the computation $(0.356 \times 10^8)(0.228 \times 10^{-3})$.

The exact answer is as follows:

$$(0.356 \times 10^8)(0.228 \times 10^{-3}) = 0.356 \times 0.228 \times 10^8 \times 10^{-3} = 0.081168 \times 10^5$$

Normalizing, we obtain 0.81168×10^4.

For a computer with a precision of 3, the result of this computation is 0.811×10^4. Thus, an error has been introduced. The absolute error is as follows:

$$correct - result = 0.81168 \times 10^4 - 0.811 \times 10^4 = 0.00068 \times 10^4 = 6.8$$

The relative error is the ratio of the absolute error and the correct answer, as shown:

$$0.00068 \times 10^4 / (0.81168 \times 10^4) = 0.0008378 = 0.08378\%$$

The error is about eight-hundredths of a percent of the exact answer.

Example 5.22

Suppose the machine for this example allows four significant digits. Let us calculate the absolute and relative errors for x for each iteration of the loop, which assigns $0.9389i$ to x.

```
x = 0.0;
i = 1;
while (i <= 108)
{
    x += 0.9389;
    i++;
}
```

Table 5.3 enumerates the absolute and relative errors after several iterations.

As the table illustrates, truncation error increases with the number of loop executions. After the eleventh iteration ($i = 11$), x should contain $11 \times 0.9389 = 10.3279$. For a computer with a precision of 4, however, the value is 10.31. The subsequent absolute error is 0.0179, and the relative error is about two-tenths of a percent (0.1733%). After the last iteration ($i = 108$), the relative error is almost 1% (0.8887%), more than 20 times the original relative error (0.0426%).

To avoid the cumulative error of this loop, we should compute

```
x = i * 0.9389;
```

Table 5.3 Loop errors for Example 5.22

Value of i	Correct x	Computer x	Absolute Error	Relative Error
1	0.9389	0.9389	0	0
2	0.9389 +0.9389 ⎯⎯⎯ 1.8778	0.9389 +0.9389 ⎯⎯⎯ 1.8778	1.8778 −1.8770 ⎯⎯⎯ 0.0008	0.0008/1.8778 =0.000426 =0.0426%
3	0.9389 +1.8778 ⎯⎯⎯ 2.8167	0.9389 +1.8770 ⎯⎯⎯ 2.8159	2.8167 −2.8150 ⎯⎯⎯ 0.0017	0.0017/2.8167 =0.0006035 =0.06035%
4	0.9389 +2.8167 ⎯⎯⎯ 3.7556	0.9389 +2.8150 ⎯⎯⎯ 3.7539	3.7556 −3.7530 ⎯⎯⎯ 0.0026	0.0026/3.7556 =0.0006923 =0.06923%
5	0.9389 +3.7556 ⎯⎯⎯ 4.6945	0.9389 +3.7530 ⎯⎯⎯ 4.6919	4.6945 −4.6910 ⎯⎯⎯ 0.0035	0.0035/4.6945 =0.0007456 =0.07456%
11	10.3279	10.31	0.0179	0.0179/10.3279 =0.001733 =0.1733%
108	101.4012	100.5	0.9012	0.9012/101.4012 =0.008887 =0.8887%

instead of having a loop with

```
x += 0.9389;
```

We still have error, but its effect is minimized because accumulation does not occur. For example, in the evaluation of $11 \times 0.9389 = 10.3279$, the computer would store four significant digits, 10.32. The absolute error is $10.3279 - 10.32 = 0.0079$, while the relative error is $0.0079 / 10.3279 = 0.000765 = 0.0765\%$. These errors using $i * 0.9389$ are less than half the corresponding errors of the accumulated value.

> In looping, avoid accumulating floating point values through repeated addition or subtraction.

Section 5.7 Exercises

For Exercises 1–4 find the absolute error and the relative error of each number as it is truncated to two decimal places.

1. 6.239   **2.** 6.231   **3.** 6.235

4. 1.0/3.0 stored with 5 significant digits

5. Suppose the following segment is executed:

```
x = 6.239;
x = x + x;
```

If the computer's precision is 3, find the value stored in x after execution of each statement and the relative error for the value of x after the last statement. Assume x is truncated, not rounded. Compare this error with your answer in Exercise 1.

6. Suppose a computer's precision is 4. After execution of each statement below, give the value stored in x and the absolute and relative errors.

```
x = 6.239;
x = x + x;
x = x + x;
x = x + x;
```

7. In Example 5.22, change the statement

```
x += 0.9389;
```

to

```
x = i * 0.9389;
```

Using the computer described in Example 5.22, evaluate the computer's value for x, the absolute error, and the relative error for $i = 1, 2, 3, 4, 5, 11$, and 108. Compare your results with those of Table 5.3.

8. In mathematics, the number $1.0 = 0.\overline{99} = 0.\overline{999}$. Suppose this value is assigned to x and y as a series of 9s truncated to 4 significant digits.

   a. If

   ```
   x = x + y;
   ```

   is executed four times in a loop, give the value of x and the absolute and relative errors for the original assignment and each iteration of the loop.

   b. By observing the results of Part a, give the value of x and the absolute and relative errors after the tenth iteration of the loop.

Programming and Debugging Hints

Unfortunately, a compiler is as error-prone as any other program. Companies that write compilers continually find and correct such errors, but compilers still contain bugs. A word of warning is in order, however. When faced with a seemingly unexplainable error, we should not simply throw up our hands and declare that the bug is the fault of the compiler. The vast majority of program errors are the fault of the programmer. Before accusing the compiler, we should have ample evidence to back up the claim.

Updating Assignment Operators

In the early versions of C, updating assignment operators had the equal sign before the associated operator rather than after. For example, to add 7 to the variable x, one would write

```
x =+ 7;
```

This led to ambiguity in a statement such as

```
x=-7;
```

Using the old form of the updating assignment operators, this statement could be interpreted to mean either "subtract 7 from *x*" or "assign −7 to *x*." Some C compilers still recognize the old form and choose the first interpretation. Therefore, when assigning a negative number, the programmer should either place parentheses around the number or spaces on either side of the assignment operator, as shown:

```
x=(-7);
```

or

```
x = -7;
```

Use of spaces around operators in particular helps to make the code more readable for humans, too. The expression below is syntactically correct but difficult for a person to interpret. Moreover, some compilers consider the following expression to contain an updating assignment operator:

```
x=-b+sqrt(b*b-4*a*c)/2*a;
```

The form with spaces and parentheses to emphasize priority of operators is more understandable and portable. All compilers should interpret the following as a simple assignment statement:

```
x = -b + sqrt(b * b - 4 * a * c) / 2 * a;
```

Thus, in mathematics notation, we write the assignment as follows:

$$x = -b + \frac{\sqrt{b^2 - 4ac}}{2} a$$

If the programmer intends to write one solution in the quadratic formula, as shown:

$$x = \frac{-b + \sqrt{b^2 - 4ac}}{2a}$$

then the correct form in C must employ parentheses to override the priority of the division operator, as follows:

```
x = (-b + sqrt(b * b - 4 * a * c)) / (2 * a);
```

Assignment and Relational Equals Operators

One of the tradeoffs inherent in the C language is that the programmer is granted great freedom and power at the price of comprehensive error detection. In other words, C is very permissive. It accepts certain programming mistakes, which it does not consider to be faulty. An example is the inadvertent use of the assignment operator (=) in place of the relational equals operator (==). Because C allows assignment to occur in any expression, the compiler accepts an *if* statement whose condition reads as follows:

```
if (num = 0)
```

The compiler does not treat this operation as a relational test, but rather as an assignment of the value 0 to *num*. The test fails, because an assignment returns the assigned value, and 0 represents *FALSE*.

Key Terms

Summary

In preparation for looping, the first section of the chapter deals with the updating assignment, increment, and decrement operators. The updating assignment operators are as follows:

Statement	Is Equivalent to
a += b;	a = a + b;
c -= d;	c = c - d;
e *= f;	e = e * f;
g /= h;	g = g / h;
i %= j;	i = i % j;

The post-increment operator, which is written after the variable name (x++) uses the variable and then increments its value by one. The pre-increment operator applied to a variable (++x) increments and then uses the new value of the variable in the statement. The post-decrement of x (x--) and pre-decrement of x (--x) decrement x after or before, respectively, using x in a statement. The increment and decrement operators have the same priority as other unary operators, and the updating assignment operators have the same precedence as the assignment operator.

With a looping control structure, the computer can repeatedly execute a segment of code. One implementation in C of the looping control structure is the *while* loop, which has the general form

```
while (expression)
    statement
```

The *while* loop uses a pretest. As long as the expression is true when the execution is at the top of the loop, the computer performs the statement. If the condition is true initially, the body of the loop must change the value of at least one variable in the boolean expression so that eventually the condition becomes false. Otherwise, the condition remains true, and the loop is infinite.

Another implementation in C of the looping control structure is the *do-while* loop, which has the following general form:

```
do
    statement
while (expression);
```

This loop differs from the *while* loop in that the *do-while* loop makes a loop posttest. Consequently, the condition is not tested until the body of the loop has been executed once.

The sentinel or trailer technique uses a special end-of-data value to indicate the end of the meaningful data. For an interactive program to read and process values with a *while* loop, a priming read or priming *scanf* should prime the loop variable with a value before executing the loop. Another *scanf* appears at the end of the loop to obtain an additional value for the loop variable. The general form is as follows:

```
printf(prompt);
scanf(control_string, loop_variable);
while (test_loop_variable)
{
    ⋮
    printf(prompt);
    scanf(control_string, loop_variable);
}
```

One useful application involving looping is the simulation of real-life events that we consider to be random. For simulations, we use a sequence of pseudorandom numbers (often called random numbers). An algorithm produces the numbers, but the sequence appears random. The sequence of random numbers is uniformly distributed if a random number has an equal likelihood of being anywhere within a specified range. ANSI C's standard library has a random number generator, *rand*, which returns a uniformly distributed pseudorandom integer in the range from 0 through *RAND-_MAX*. The header file *stdlib.h* contains the prototype for *rand* and the definition of *RAND_MAX*, which must be at least 32767. ANSI C provides another function, *srand*, that allows the programmer to specify a different seed or initial value for the generator. Section 5.4 develops several functions to generate integers and floating point numbers in various ranges. The source file of their definitions, *RandDef.c*, and the associated header file, *RandDef.h*, are on the text disk.

Having discussed looping, we have covered all the major control structures of a structured program or a structured algorithm:

1. modular
2. sequential
3. selection
4. looping

To modify the order in which the computer executes statements, we should only use these control structures.

Review Questions

1. Show two different ways to multiply the variable *x* by *y*, placing the result in *x*.
2. Which operations can be used with the updating assignment operator?
3. Write equivalent but more concise statements for the following:

   a. `s = s + x;`   **b.** `s = s - x;`   **c.** `s = s / x;`
   d. `s = s * x;`   **e.** `s = s % x;`

4. Write the C equivalents of the following:

   a. Double the value of *v*   **b.** Halve the value of *x*
   c. Triple the value of *b*   **d.** Increment the value of *r* by 9

5. What is the output from the following program?

```
main()
{
    int i, j;

    i = 7;
    j = ++i;
    printf("i = %d, j = %d\n", i, j);
}
```

6. Write an abbreviated form of:

```
total = total - 1;
```

7. What is the difference between a pre-decrement and a post-decrement operation?

8. Which operator has the higher precedence, ++ or +=?

9. What is the essential difference between a *while* and a *do-while* loop?

10. What happens if the condition in a *while* loop is initially false?

11. What is the minimum number of times the body of a *do-while* loop is executed?

12. What control structure is best to use in validating interactive input data?

13. If the sentinel technique is used in a program, how many calls to *scanf* are necessary?

14. Name the ANSI C random number generator?

15. What is the range of random integers generated by this function?

16. What is the ANSI C function to seed the random number generator?

17. What keywords are associated with *while* and *do-while* loops?

18. Name the major control structures of structured programming.

≈≈≈ **Laboratory**

In the exercises in this laboratory, we add improvements to the program in Example 5.16 of Section 5.4. That program employed the function PlayGame *to play a guessing game. After each addition, be sure to test the program. To make debugging easier, the program, which is in file* LAB051.c *on your disk, has a guessing range of 0 through 9. Copy this file onto your disk.*

1. This exercise examines two techniques for making guesses. Play the game several times to get a feel for its action. Try each of the following two methods for playing the game:

   a. Guess the numbers in order, 0, 1, 2, ..., until hitting the target.

   b. Guess the middle number of the range each time until hitting the target. For example, for a range 0–9 with an even number of choices, the first guess would be 4 or 5. Suppose we type 4, and the computer responds "Guess higher." Then our range is 5–9. With an odd number of choices, the middle number is 7. The process continues until you find the number.

   The first method is called a **sequential search**, and the second is called a **binary search**. For each method, what is the least number of guesses you have to make? What is the most? Try the method you like best several times on the range from

0–99. What is the most number of guesses for each method? What is the most number of guesses for each method for the range 0–1022? Which method is faster for playing the game? Explain your answer, giving several examples.

2. In this exercise, we use the increment operator (++).

   Revise *PlayGame* to count and print the number of guesses the user makes. Declare-initialize a counting variable, *NumGuesses*. Immediately after obtaining a guess, use the increment operator to add 1 to *NumGuesses*. After printing "Congratulations," print the number of guesses.

3. In this exercise, we use constants and *random_range* to specify a different range.

   Redesign the program to allow the guesses between constant *LOW* and *HIGH* - 1. Before *main*, define a new constant, *LOW*, that has the value 0. Instead of invoking *random* in *main*, call *random_range* with arguments *LOW* and *HIGH*. The source file *RandDef.c* defines the function *random_range*, and the header file *RandDef.h* contains its prototype. Adjust the program's instructions and comments to reflect the redesign.

   Because we are using the same range, 0–9, as with *random*, the program should behave in the same manner. Change the values of *LOW* and *HIGH*, and play the game again.

4. In this exercise, we use loops to allow the user to play the game more than once.

   Because we need a priming read and another read at the end of the loop, define a function *AskPlay* that prompts the user about playing the game and then reads and returns the answer. (Remember to include & in the *scanf* and to have a prototype.) Later in the text, we see how to accept word responses from the user, such as "yes" and "no," but for now accept 1 for "yes" or "true" and 0 for "no" or "false."

   Using a *while* loop in *main*, allow the user to play the game more than once. Which statements in *main* should you enclose in this loop? Should the loop contain *initialize*? Why or why not? Call *AskPlay* immediately before the loop for a priming read and at the end of the loop. Store the returned value in a variable with a meaningful name. Use the value of this variable as the condition in the *while* loop.

   After the revised program is working properly, enter an invalid response like 3 to the question about playing again. How does the program behave and why? Why is this action not desirable? Adjust *AskPlay* to have a *do-while* loop that makes sure the user types a valid response of 0 or 1 before continuing.

   Put your name and the date in an opening comment. Print the program listing and a sample run.

5. In this exercise, we make some observations about seeding the random number generator.

   Comment out the call to *SeedRand* in *initialize*. Run the program several times. Describe and explain the action of the program.

   In *main*, place the call to *initialize* in the *while* loop. Describe and explain the action of the program.

Counter-Controlled Loops

Introduction

So far we have discussed in detail two commonly used loops—the *while* loop, which performs a pretest, and the *do-while* loop, which performs a posttest. A third versatile looping control structure, the *for* loop is used primarily in counting situations, in which we increment or decrement a loop variable. Like the *while* loop, the *for* loop tests a logical expression before the first iteration. Moreover, we can replace a *while* loop with a *for* loop, and vice versa. When we know exactly how many times to execute the loop, however, the *for* loop is clearer to read. In the second section of this chapter, we see how to nest looping control structures. This nesting is similar to the nesting of selection control structures.

In a breadth section on numerical computing, we employ loops to estimate the area between a curve and the (horizontal) *x*-axis over a certain interval. For many functions, this important problem is impossible to solve in calculus exactly. Computer simulation provides a good estimate of the area.

Another breadth section, Section 6.4, discusses computer software as intellectual property. Intellectual property involves someone's ideas and the expressions of those thoughts. In the section, we consider various legal means of protecting the expressions of ideas.

Goals   To study

- Loops that count

- Nesting of loops
- One technique of numerical computation
- Intellectual property rights

Section 6.1 The *for* Loop

Several *while* loops in the last chapter increment or decrement a variable by 1 until reaching some limit, such as the following:

```
i = 1;
while (i <= 10)
{
    ⋮
    i++;
}
```

In this situation, we know that we want to execute the loop precisely 10 times, for *i* from 1 to 10. Such a loop is called a **counter-controlled loop** or a **counting loop**. Because this looping method is so common, C provides a shorter version of this construct, called the *for* loop, as follows:

```
for (i = 1; i <= 10; i++)
{
    ⋮
}
```

Its general form is as follows:

```
for (expression1; expression2; expression3)
    statement
```

The **initialization expression**, *expression1*, is usually an assignment of the **index** or **loop variable**, which the computer performs once before the loop begins execution. The **test expression**, *expression2*, evaluates before each iteration of the loop and determines whether the loop should continue or stop. Finally, *expression3* is the **modifier statement**, which changes the value of the test variable and perhaps other associated variables. The computer executes this expression at the end of each iteration, after the body of the loop. The **body** of the loop, *statement*, may be compound. Semicolons separate the three loop expressions, but no semicolon appears after the right parenthesis.

> **Definition** A **counter-controlled loop** or a **counting loop** is a looping control structure in which a loop variable manages the repetition through counting.

We can omit the first expression of the *for* loop if we initialize the variable outside the loop, as follows:

```
i = 1;
for ( ; i <= 10; i++)
{
    ⋮
}
```

Although the situation occurs infrequently, we can also omit the third expression, as shown:

```
for (i = 1; i <= 10; )
{
    ⋮
    i++;
}
```

Even if we omit an expression, the two semicolons still must appear.

Example 6.1

To observe in context the loop skeleton above, let us write a program that prints line numbers from 1 through 10.

```
/* Program to print line numbers with a for loop */

#include <stdio.h>

#define MAX_INDEX 10

main()
{
    int i;      /* index */

    for (i = 1; i <= MAX_INDEX; i++)
        printf("This is line %2d\n", i);
}
```

Execution produces the following output:

```
This is line  1
This is line  2
This is line  3
This is line  4
This is line  5
This is line  6
This is line  7
This is line  8
This is line  9
This is line 10
```

As always, we must declare any variable, including the index *i*. When the loop begins, the loop initializes *i* to 1. The computer then determines whether the current value of *i* is less than or equal to *MAX_INDEX*. We define this symbolic constant as 10 in the *#define* preprocessor directive. Consequently, should we decide to have a different upper bound for *i*, such as 100, we do not search the program for numbers to change. We simply adjust this directive at the top of the code. If the condition (*i* <= *MAX_INDEX*) is true, the computer executes the body of the loop and then increments by 1 the value of *i*.

We could write the same program with a *while* loop, as follows:

```
/* Program to print line numbers with a while loop*/

#include <stdio.h>

#define MAX_INDEX 10

main()
{
    int i = 1;      /* index */

    while (i <= MAX_INDEX)
    {
        printf("This is line %2d\n", i);
        i++;
    }
}
```

An advantage of the *for* loop is that it gathers the important parts of the loop construct—the initialization expression, the test expression, and the modifier statement—into one place. We are not tempted to place a declaration-initialization of the index far from the loop. Moreover, we are less likely to forget to increment or decrement the index, resulting in an infinite loop.

Loop Choice

The form of loop to use is largely a matter of personal choice. Any loop that can be written as a *while* loop can be rewritten easily as a *for* loop, and vice versa. We can also rewrite a *do-while* loop as either of the other two loops. However, this change is slightly more complicated, because the *do-while* loop makes one test fewer than the *while* and *for* loops.

> We can consider the following recommendations concerning which loop to employ:
>
> 1. If we know exactly how many times to execute the loop, use *for*.
> 2. Otherwise, if we need to test before the first iteration, use *while*.
> 3. If not testing before the first iteration, we use *do-while*.

Counting Down

We need not restrict ourselves to counting from 1 to 10. We could just as easily specify that the values of i go from −4 to 5.

```
for (i = -4; i <= 5; i++)
```

Moreover, the *for* loop can count down as well as up.

Example 6.2

Using a *for* loop, we can rewrite the function *CountDown* from Example 5.8 of Section 5.2. That function accepts a positive integer argument for parameter *CountFrom* and counts down from that number to 1, printing "Ignition" and "Blast off!" afterwards.

```
/*
 * Function to count down from positive parameter
 * CountFrom to 1, and then to print Ignition, Blast off!
 * Pre:     CountFrom is a positive integer.
 * Post:    The countdown was displayed.
 */

void CountDown(int CountFrom)
{
    if (CountFrom <= 0)                 /* invalid parameter */
        printf("ERROR: Counting down from %d <= 0\n", CountFrom);
    else                               /* valid parameter */
    {
        for (; CountFrom > 0; CountFrom--)
            printf("%5d\n", CountFrom);

        printf("Ignition\n");
        printf("Blast off!\n");
    }
}
```

In the program, the pass by value initializes the index *CountFrom*, so the initialization expression in the *for* loop is empty. Because we are counting down, the test expression is *CountFrom* > 0, and the modifier expression is a post-decrement. A pre-decrement (*--CountFrom*) would work just as well, because the computer does not subtract 1 until after the last statement in the loop body, *printf*.

Tables

Example 6.3

The program in this example takes advantage of the *for* loop to print a table of positive integers and their squares. Because we want to print the table title and the column headings only once, calls to *printf* to display these appear before the loop.

main( )

Program to print a table of positive integers and their squares

Algorithm:

print title and column headings
for *i* from 1 to 10 do the following:
    print i and its square

```
/* Calculate the squares of the integers 1 through 10 */

#include <stdio.h>

#define MAX_INDEX 10

main()
{
    int num;          /* index */

    printf("Table of Squares of Integers\n");
    printf("  Integer  Integer Squared\n");
    printf("  -------  ---------------\n\n");

    for (num = 1; num <= MAX_INDEX; num++)
        printf("%6d %14d\n", num, num * num);
}
```

Field widths in the conversion specifications produce aligned columns of numbers. The program also demonstrates how to underline a word using *printf* and dashes. Sample output follows:

```
Table of Squares of Integers
  Integer  Integer Squared
  -------  ---------------

     1               1
     2               4
     3               9
     4              16
     5              25
     6              36
     7              49
     8              64
     9              81
    10             100
```

In the next example, we write code for the **factorial function**, which has many applications in such areas as probability theory. The factorial of 4, written 4!, is

$$4! = 4 \cdot 3 \cdot 2 \cdot 1 = 24$$

Thus, for a positive integer n, n-factorial ($n!$) is the product of all the positive integers from 1 through n. For consistency in various formulas, the factorial of zero (0!) is 1.

Definition Let n be a nonnegative integer. Then **n-factorial** is
$$n! = n (n - 1) \cdots 3 \cdot 2 \cdot 1$$
Also, define $0! = 1$

In the early 1800s, ⌊*n* was the notation for *n*-factorial, but *n*! evolved because it was easier to print. Some even suggested changing the name to "*n*-admiration" because "!" is a "note of admiration."

Example 6.4

In this example, we write a program to print *n*-factorial for the integers 0 through 16. Because we want the factorials for integers 0–16, the *for* loop is an excellent choice for generating the table. In the loop, we print *n* and *n*!, and *main* obtains the value of *n*! through the invocation *factorial*(*n*). As in the last example, we print headings before the loop and use preprocessor constant *MAX_INDEX* for the upper bound of the loop (16).

> ### *main*( )
>
> Program to print a table of nonnegative integers and their factorials
>
> ### *Algorithm:*
>
> print headings
> for *n* from 0 to *MAX_INDEX* do the following:
>   print *n* and *factorial*(*n*)

The programming definition of the function *factorial* closely resembles the mathematical definition. A local variable, *fact*, which accumulates the developing factorial, obtains an initial value of 1. Through looping, we multiply the integers from *n* down to 2 by *fact*. Multiplication by 1 is unnecessary. We know precisely how many times to loop, so we use a *for* loop.

> ### *factorial*(*n*) ⟶ *fact*
>
> Function to return the factorial of parameter *n*
>
> ### *Pre:*
>
> *n* is a nonnegative integer.
>
> ### *Post:*
>
> *n*! of type *double* has been returned.
>
> ### *Algorithm:*
>
> *fact* ← 1
> for *i* from *n* down to 2 do the following:
>   *fact* ← *fact* * *i*
> return *fact*

When *main* invokes *factorial* with an argument of *n* = 0 or *n* = 1, which is less than the limit 2, the *for* loop in *factorial* does not execute. Thus, for 0! or 1!, *factorial* returns the initial value of *fact*, 1.

As we see in the output, the factorials get very large, very fast. Therefore, we declare the type of the function and the local variable *fact* to be *double*. Even with a type of *double*, many computers cannot accurately store 17!. Thus, we limit display from 0! to 16!.

```
/*
 * Example 6.4
 * Program to print the factorials for integers 0-16
 */

#include <stdio.h>

#define MAX_INDEX 16

double factorial(int n);

main()
{
    int n;       /* number of which we will evaluate n! */

     printf(" Table of Factorials\n\n");
     printf("Number          Factorial\n");
     printf("------          ---------\n\n");

     for (n = 0; n <= MAX_INDEX; n++)
         printf("%4d %18.0f\n", n, factorial(n));
}

/*
 * Function to return the factorial of parameter n as a
 * double
 * Pre:    n is a nonnegative integer.
 * Post:   n! was returned.
 */

double factorial(int n)
{
    int i;               /* index */
    double fact;         /* n! */

    fact = 1;            /* 0! = 1! = 1 */

    for (i = n; i > 1; i--)
        fact *= i;

    return fact;
}
```

The output displays the following table of factorials:

```
      Table of Factorials

   Number          Factorial
   ------          ---------

      0                   1
      1                   1
      2                   2
      3                   6
      4                  24
      5                 120
      6                 720
      7                5040
      8               40320
      9              362880
     10             3628800
     11            39916800
     12           479001600
     13          6227020800
     14         87178291200
     15       1307674368000
     16      20922789888000
```

The values of *n*! increase rapidly, from 0! equaling 1 to 16! being over 20 trillion. The factorial grows so large that if we declare *factorial* to be of type *long int* instead of the floating point *double* and we attempt to compute 13!, we may obtain an overflow error.

Section 6.1 Exercises

Give the output for the segments in Exercises 1–3.

1. ```c
   for (i = 7; i > 3; i--)
       printf("%d", i);
   ```

2. ```c
   for (i = 0; i < 5; printf("%d\n", i++));
   ```

3. ```c
   sum = 0;
   for (i = 1; i < 6; i++)
   {
       sum += i;
       printf("Sum of 1 through %d = %d\n", i, sum);
   }
   ```

Find the errors in the segments in Exercises 4–6.

4. ```c
   for (i == 0, i < n, i++) ...
   ```

5.
```
for (i < n; i--);
    printf("%d\n", i);
```

6.
```
for (i = 7; i > 3; i--)
    j += i;
    printf("%d %d \n", i, j);
```

In Exercises 7–12, write for *loops.*

7. To print "Hello" 100 times

8. To print the even integers from 50 down to 20

9. To print the powers of 3 from 1 to 3^{10} in a loop that triples the previous result

10. To read 10 numbers, one at a time, and to print their squares

11. To print the result of $i \cdot 3^j$ for j going from 1 to 5 and i going from −10 to −6 together

12. To print $i \% j$, where i goes from 3 to 30 with an increment of 3 and j simultaneously goes from 2 up with an increment of 2. Thus, print the results of $3 \% 2, 6 \% 4, \ldots$.

13. Convert *main* in Example 5.13 of Section 5.4 to use a *for* loop.

Section 6.1 **Programming Projects**

1. Design a program to calculate the average of n numbers, with the user entering the value of n and the numbers themselves.

2. Design a program to find the sum of the integers $1-100$ using a *for* loop. Use a preprocessor constant for the upper bound of 100. This method, however, is not the most efficient. Legend has it that when the famous German mathematician **Karl Friedrich Gauss** was only seven years old, his teacher gave the class this problem as punishment. Rather than using the above brute force method, he discovered the following formula:

$$sum = \frac{n(n + 1)}{2}$$

In your program, use this formula to verify the result using the *for* loop.

3. A library has 8000 books on the first floor and 10,000 on the second. The librarians plan to transfer 100 books a week for 10 weeks from the second floor to the first. Write a program that prints the number of books on each floor initially and at the end of each of the 10 weeks.

4. Write a program to print a nonnegative decimal fraction less than 1.0 in binary representation. For example, $0.625_{10} = 0.101_2$. Display 40 bits after the binary point. (See Algorithm 4.1 and Examples 4.6, 4.7, and 4.10 of Section 4.2).

5. The Gregorian calendar was adopted in the British dominions (including Britain's American colonies) in September 1752. It provides that years divisible by four are leap years, except for years divisible by 100 but not by 400. Given that May 1, 1988 was a Sunday, we can calculate the starting day of the week of May 1 of any year by determining the number of days that date is shifted from Sunday. Since 365 = 52 * 7+1, each ordinary year shifts the starting day of May 1 by one. That means

that we can calculate the shift of the starting day of May 1 for year x by means of the following calculation:

$$s = x - 1988 + \text{(adjustment for leap years)}$$
$$\qquad - \text{(adjustment for century years)}$$
$$\qquad + \text{(adjustment for 4-century years)}$$
$$= x - 1988 + (\lfloor x/4 \rfloor - \lfloor 1988/4 \rfloor)$$
$$\qquad - (\lfloor x/100 \rfloor - \lfloor 1988/100 \rfloor)$$
$$\qquad + (\lfloor x/400 \rfloor - \lfloor 1988/400 \rfloor)$$
$$= x + \lfloor x/4 \rfloor - \lfloor x/100 \rfloor + \lfloor x/400 \rfloor - 2470$$

Here $\lfloor y \rfloor$ means the greatest integer $\leq y$. Since multiples of 7 can be ignored, we can write the formula as

$$s = x + \lfloor x/4 \rfloor - \lfloor x/100 \rfloor + \lfloor x/400 \rfloor - 6$$

To shift to the beginning of any other month, add the following values to s:

0 for May (31 days)

1 for August (31)

2 for February, March, or November (28 or 29, 31, 30)

3 for June (30)

4 for September or December (30, 31)

5 for April or July (30, 31)

6 for January or October (31, 31)

(To arrive at these numbers, count the number of days from May 1 to the beginning of the respective month, and take the remainder after dividing by 7. For instance, there are 61 days between May 1 and July 1. Therefore, the number to be added is $5 = 61 - 7 * 8$.) Finally, for January or February, subtract 1 if the year is a leap year.

Throwing out multiples of 7 and considering Sunday as day 1 of the week, we can now calculate the starting day of the week of any month of any year as

$$D = 1 + s - 7* \lfloor s/7 \rfloor$$

Use the foregoing calculation to write a program that will accept input of any month (by number) and year (after 1752) and will print the calendar for that month. Sample output:

```
ENTER NUMBER OF MONTH: 10
ENTER NUMBER OF YEAR: 1999

          October, 1999
Sun  Mon  Tue  Wed  Thu  Fri  Sat
                              1    2
  3    4    5    6    7    8    9
 10   11   12   13   14   15   16
 17   18   19   20   21   22   23
 24   25   26   27   28   29   30
 31
```

Section 6.2 **Nesting of Loops**

As with *while* and *do-while* loops, we may find it necessary to nest *for* loops. This section provides several examples of **nesting of loops.**

Example 6.5

In this example, we display a multiplication table with 10 rows and 12 columns. An element in the row *row* and column *column* is the product *row · column*. For example, the value in the sixth row and fourth column is 6 · 4 = 24. The table is as follows:

```
              Multiplication Table

  1    2    3    4    5    6    7    8    9   10   11   12
  2    4    6    8   10   12   14   16   18   20   22   24
  3    6    9   12   15   18   21   24   27   30   33   36
  4    8   12   16   20   24   28   32   36   40   44   48
  5   10   15   20   25   30   35   40   45   50   55   60
  6   12   18   24   30   36   42   48   54   60   66   72
  7   14   21   28   35   42   49   56   63   70   77   84
  8   16   24   32   40   48   56   64   72   80   88   96
  9   18   27   36   45   54   63   72   81   90   99  108
 10   20   30   40   50   60   70   80   90  100  110  120
```

To produce rows and columns of output, we need a loop within a loop. Because we know the number of rows and columns, *for* loops are advisable. Suppose we only want to print row 6, as shown:

```
6   12   18   24   30   36   42   48   54   60   66   72
```

Holding the row fixed, we would employ a *for* loop to multiply 6 times each integer from 1 to 12, as follows:

```
for (column = 1; column <= 12; column++)
    printf("%4d", 6 * column);
```

The call to *printf* does not contain \n because we need to print all values on one line. We can advance to a new line after the loop with

```
printf("\n");
```

To print 10 rows, we use another *for* loop that begins as follows:

```
for (row = 1; row <= 10; row++)
```

For each row, we print the numbers across with a loop that has index *column* and the computation *row · column*. Thus, to print the table we need nested *for* loops. We use braces around the statements in the outer loop to make a compound statement for the body, as follows:

```
for (row = 1; row <= 10; row++)
{
    for (column = 1; column <= 12; column++)
        printf("%4d", row * column);

    printf("\n");
}
```

The inner loop changes fastest. For a fixed *row*, *column* goes through all the integers between 1 and 12. Figure 6.1 enumerates the action of these nested loops for the first few values of *row*.

In nested loops, the inner loop variable changes the fastest.

Figure 6.1
Action of
nested *for* loops
in Example 6.5

Loop that Changes	*row*	*column*	*row * column*
Outer	1		
Inner		1	1· 1 = 1
Inner		2	1· 2 = 2
Inner		3	1· 3 = 3
Inner		4	1· 4 = 4
Inner		5	1· 5 = 5
Inner		6	1· 6 = 6
Inner		7	1· 7 = 7
Inner		8	1· 8 = 8
Inner		9	1· 9 = 9
Inner		10	1·10 = 10
Inner		11	1·11 = 11
Inner		12	1·12 = 12
Outer	2		
Inner		1	2· 1 = 2
Inner		2	2· 2 = 4
Inner		3	2· 3 = 6
Inner		4	2· 4 = 8
Inner		5	2· 5 = 10
Inner		6	2· 6 = 12
Inner		7	2· 7 = 14
Inner		8	2· 8 = 16
Inner		9	2· 9 = 18
Inner		10	2·10 = 20
Inner		11	2·11 = 22
Inner		12	2·12 = 24
Outer	3		
Inner		1	3· 1 = 3
Inner		2	3· 2 = 6
⋮	⋮	⋮	⋮

In the program, we should use symbolic constants for the upper bounds. The code for the entire program follows:

```
/*
 * Example 6.5.  Program to print a multiplication table
 */

#include <stdio.h>

#define ROW_MAX 10
#define COLUMN_MAX 12

main()
{
    int row,         /* index */
        column;      /* index */

    printf("                 Multiplication Table\n\n");

    for (row = 1; row <= ROW_MAX; row++)
    {
        for (column = 1; column <= COLUMN_MAX; column++)
            printf("%4d", row * column);

        printf("\n");
    }
}
```

Example 6.6

In this example, we develop an interactive program to compute the grade average for each student in a class. Assignments vary in credit. For example, a test might count 100 points, whereas a homework might be worth 10 points. The program reads the number of students

```
How many students are in the class? 25
```

and the number of grades for each student.

```
How many grades are there? 3
```

Using the latter number, the program reads the possible points for each grade

```
Enter the value of each grade.
Enter the nonnegative value of grade 1: 100
Enter the nonnegative value of grade 2: 20
Enter the nonnegative value of grade 3: 100
```

and computes the total, such as 220. Using the values for number of students and grades, the program reads each student's grades

```
Enter the grades for student 1.
Enter the nonnegative value of grade 1: 80
Enter the nonnegative value of grade 2: 15
Enter the nonnegative value of grade 3: 89
```

and calculates the average, such as 184 / 220 = 83.6%.

```
Average for student 1 = 83.6%
```

As the structure chart in Figure 6.2 depicts, the function *main* calls four functions. *ReadNumStudents, ReadNumGrades, GetMaxTotalPoints,* and *ClassGrades* all do as their names indicate. Both *GetMaxTotalPoints* and *ClassGrades* must ask for individual grades and total the responses. Thus, we isolate this task in another function, *ReadAddGrades.* *ReadAddGrades* calls *ReadGrade* to read and return an individual, nonnegative grade.

Pseudocode for *main* follows:

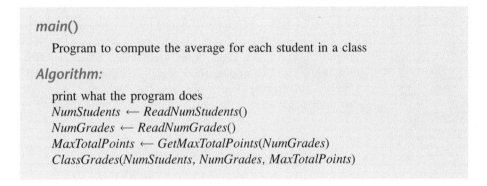

main()

Program to compute the average for each student in a class

Algorithm:

print what the program does
NumStudents ← *ReadNumStudents*()
NumGrades ← *ReadNumGrades*()
MaxTotalPoints ← *GetMaxTotalPoints*(*NumGrades*)
ClassGrades(*NumStudents, NumGrades, MaxTotalPoints*)

Figure 6.2   Structure chart for Example 6.6

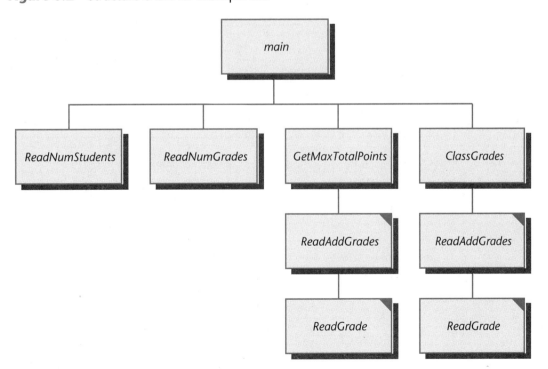

In *ReadNumStudents, ReadNumGrades*, and *GetMaxTotalPoints*, we should verify that the return values are positive. One method, which we have used to this point, employs a *do-while* loop. We continue prompting and obtaining a value as long as that value is not positive, as follows:

```
do
{
    printf("How many students are in the class? ");
    scanf("%d", &NumStudents);
}
while (NumStudents <= 0);
```

Unfortunately, if the user types invalid input repeatedly and does not understand the problem, he or she just keeps seeing the following prompt:

```
How many students are in the class?
```

A clearer method is to prompt and read once in this manner. If the data item is invalid, describe the problem and then prompt and read again. This solution indicates a *while* loop with a priming read. *ReadNumStudents, ReadNumGrades*, and *GetMaxTotalPoints* use this technique. The first two functions are identical in structure. The third is very similar, except that it calls *ReadAddGrades* to obtain *MaxTotalPoints*, a value that must be positive.

ReadNumStudents() ⟶ *NumStudents*

Function to read and return the number of students

Pre:

Post:

A positive integer number of students has been returned.

Algorithm:

prompt for and read number of students, *NumStudents*
while *NumStudents* is not positive
   describe the problem
   prompt for and read number of students, *NumStudents*
return *NumStudents*

ReadNumGrades() ⟶ *NumGrades*

Function to read and return the number of grades

Pre:

Post:

A positive integer number of grades has been returned.

Algorithm:

prompt for and read number of grades, *NumGrades*
while *NumGrades* is not positive
    describe the problem
    prompt for and read number of grades, *NumGrades*
return *NumGrades*

GetMaxTotalPoints(NumGrades) → *MaxTotalPoints*

Function to obtain and return the total number of possible points

Pre:

NumGrades is the positive integer number of grades.

Post:

A positive integer total number of possible points has been returned.

Algorithm:

prompt for the values of the grades
MaxTotalPoints ← *ReadAddGrades(NumGrades)*
while *MaxTotalPoints* is not positive
    describe the problem
    prompt for the values of the grades
    MaxTotalPoints ← *ReadAddGrades(NumGrades)*
return *MaxTotalPoints*

Because *main* obtains the exact number of students in the class, *ClassGrades* can use a *for* loop to process the class members. This function, which computes and prints the average of each student, calls *ReadAddGrades* to obtain the grade total for an individual student.

ClassGrades(NumStudents, NumGrades, MaxTotalPoints)

Procedure to compute and print the average of each student

Pre:

NumStudents is the positive integer number of students.
NumGrades is the positive integer number of grades.
MaxTotalPoints is the positive integer total possible points.

Post:

The average of each student has been printed.

Algorithm:

> for *student* going from 1 through *NumStudents* do the following:
> prompt for grades for *student*
> *TotalPoints* ← *ReadAddGrades(NumGrades)*
> *average* ← 100 * *TotalPoints* / *MaxTotalPoints* as a *float*
> print *student* and *average*

Both *GetMaxTotalPoints* and *ClassGrades* call *ReadAddGrades*. After calling *ReadNumGrades, main* knows the number of grades, so *ReadAddGrades* can use a *for* loop to obtain each grade and accumulate the value in an ongoing total, *TotalPoints*. Because we are summing the point values of the grades, we initialize an accumulator, *TotalPoints*, to be 0.

ReadAddGrades(NumGrades) ⟶ TotalPoints

Function to read and total grade points and to return the total

Pre:

NumGrades is the positive integer number of grades.

Post:

The nonnegative integer point total has been returned.

Algorithm:

> *TotalPoints* ← 0
> for *student* going from 1 through *NumStudents* do the following:
>   add *ReadGrade(grade)* to *TotalPoints*
> return *TotalPoints*

ReadAddGrades calls *ReadGrade* to read and validate an individual grade. To aid the user, we specify which grade we are requesting. We must still verify that each grade is nonnegative. (A grade can be 0.) Thus, *ReadGrade* has a *do-while* loop to obtain a point value repeatedly until the user enters a nonnegative number.

ReadGrade(grade) ⟶ points

Function to read and return a grade

Pre:

grade is the number of the grade.

Post:

The function has returned a nonnegative integer grade.

Algorithm:
> do the following:
>> prompt for the number of points for grade *grade*
>> read the number of points, *points*
> while *points* is negative
>
> return *points*

```
/*
 * Example 6.6
 * Program to compute the average for each student in a class
 */

#include <stdio.h>

main()
{
    int ReadNumStudents(void);
    int ReadNumGrades(void);
    int GetMaxTotalPoints(int NumGrades);
    void ClassGrades(int NumStudents, int NumGrades,
            int MaxTotalPoints);

    int NumStudents,      /* number of students in class      */
        NumGrades,        /* number of grades for each student */
        MaxTotalPoints;   /* total number of possible points   */

    printf("This program finds the average for each student.\n\n");
    NumStudents = ReadNumStudents();
    NumGrades = ReadNumGrades();
    MaxTotalPoints = GetMaxTotalPoints(NumGrades);
    ClassGrades(NumStudents, NumGrades, MaxTotalPoints);
}


/*
 * Function to read and return the number of students
 * Pre: none
 * Post: The (positive) number of students was returned.
 */

int ReadNumStudents(void)
}
    int NumStudents;        /* number of students in class */

    printf("How many students are in the class? ");
    scanf("%d", &NumStudents);
```

```
    while (NumStudents <= 0)
    {
        printf("The number of students must be positive.\n");
        printf("How many students are there? ");
        scanf("%d", &NumStudents);
    }
    return NumStudents;
}


/*
 * Function to read and return the number of grades
 * Pre:     none
 * Post:    The (positive) number of grades was returned.
 */

int ReadNumGrades(void)
{
    int NumGrades;       /* number of grades for each student */

    printf("How many grades are there? ");
    scanf("%d", &NumGrades);
    while (NumGrades <= 0)
    {
        printf("The number of grades must be positive.\n");
        printf("How many grades are there? ");
        scanf("%d", &NumGrades);
    }
    return NumGrades;
}


/*
 * Function to return the maximum total number of points
 * possible for a student to earn
 * Pre:   NumGrades is the (positive) number of grades.
 * Post:  The (positive) maximum possible points was returned.
 */

int GetMaxTotalPoints(int NumGrades)
{
    int ReadAddGrades(int NumGrades);
    int MaxTotalPoints;    /* total number of possible points */

    printf("\nEnter the value of each grade.\n");
    MaxTotalPoints = ReadAddGrades(NumGrades);
    while (MaxTotalPoints <= 0)
    {
        printf("The grade total must be positive.\n");
        printf("Please enter grades again.\n\n");
        MaxTotalPoints = ReadAddGrades(NumGrades);
    }
    return MaxTotalPoints;
}
```

```
/*
 * Function to compute and print the average of each student
 * Pre:    NumStudents is the (positive) number of students.
 *         NumGrades is the (positive) number of grades.
 *         MaxTotalPoints is the (positive) total worth of grades.
 * Post:   Each student's average was displayed.
 */

void ClassGrades(int NumStudents, int NumGrades, int MaxTotalPoints)
{
    int ReadAddGrades(int NumGrades);
    int student,        /* index - which student */
        TotalPoints;    /* total number of points */
    float average;      /* student's average */

    for (student = 1; student <= NumStudents; student++)
    {
        printf("\nEnter the grades for student %d.\n", student);

        TotalPoints = ReadAddGrades(NumGrades);
        average = (float)100 * TotalPoints / MaxTotalPoints;

        printf("\nAverage for student %d = %.1f%%\n",
                student, average);
    }
}


/*
 * Function to read and total grades and to return total
 * Pre:    NumGrades is the (positive) number of grades.
 * Post:   The nonnegative total grade points was returned.
 */

int ReadAddGrades(int NumGrades)
{
    int ReadGrade(int);
    int TotalPoints,        /* total number of points   */
        grade;              /* index - which grade      */

    TotalPoints = 0;

    for (grade = 1; grade <= NumGrades; grade++)
        TotalPoints += ReadGrade(grade);

    return TotalPoints;
}

/*
 * Function to read and return an integer grade
 * Pre:    grade is the number of the grade.
 * Post:   A nonnegative grade was returned.
 */
```

```
int ReadGrade(int grade)
{
    int points;                     /* points for one test*/

    do
    {
        printf("Enter the nonnegative value of grade %d: ",
                grade);
        scanf("%d", &points);
    }
    while (points < 0);

    return points;
}
```

The following is the start of a normal interactive session:

```
This program finds the average for each student.

How many students are in the class? 25
How many grades are there? 3

Enter the value of each grade.
Enter the nonnegative value of grade 1: 100
Enter the nonnegative value of grade 2: 20
Enter the nonnegative value of grade 3: 100

Enter the grades for student 1.
Enter the nonnegative value of grade 1: 80
Enter the nonnegative value of grade 2: 15
Enter the nonnegative value of grade 3: 89

Average for student 1 = 83.6%

Enter the grades for student 2.
Enter the nonnegative value of grade 1: 95
Enter the nonnegative value of grade 2: 17
Enter the nonnegative value of grade 3: 78

Average for student 2 = 86.4%

Enter the grades for student 3.
Enter the nonnegative value of grade 1:
   ⋮
```

Below is the start of a session that illustrates the checking that the program does for valid data:

```
This program finds the average for each student.

How many students are in the class? 0
The number of students must be positive.
How many students are there? 20
How many grades are there? -3
The number of grades must be positive.
How many grades are there? 0
The number of grades must be positive.
How many grades are there? 3

Enter the value of each grade.
Enter the nonnegative value of grade 1: -10
Enter the nonnegative value of grade 1: 100
Enter the nonnegative value of grade 2: 0
Enter the nonnegative value of grade 3: 100
:
```

The computation of the average,

```
average = (float)100 * TotalPoints / MaxTotalPoints;
```

involves a coercion from type *int* for 100, *TotalPoints*, and *MaxTotalPoints* to type *float*. Had we used an integer arithmetic, the computation would have resulted in truncation. We print that average with one decimal place and a percent sign by having *%.1f%%* in the *printf*.

For clarity and structured programming, we place the acquiring and summing of grades in *ReadAddGrades* and the reading of an individual grade in *ReadGrade*. Without these functions, we would have a nesting of three loops.

```
/* BAD DESIGN */

for (student = 1; student <= NumStudents; student++)
{
    printf("\nEnter the grades for student %d.\n", student);

    TotalPoints = 0;
    for (grade = 1; grade <= NumGrades; grade++)
    {
        do
        {
            printf("Enter the nonnegative value of grade %d: ",
                    grade);
            scanf("%d", &points);
        }
        while (points < 0);
        TotalPoints += points;
    }
}
```

```
        average = (float)100 * TotalPoints / MaxTotalPoints;

        printf("\nAverage for student %d = %.1f%%\n",
            student, average);
    }
```

This version is certainly harder to understand. In the code, we must also be careful to reassign 0 to *TotalPoints* for each new student. Had we in error placed that assignment statement before the first *for*, the points would continue totaling, and *TotalPoints* for the second student would be the sum of the first and second students' points. By having *ReadAddGrades*, with an initialization of *TotalPoints* = 0, the placement of this assignment statement is not nearly as puzzling as in the triple-nested version.

Section 6.2 Exercises

Give the output for the segments in Exercises 1–3.

1. ```
   for (i = 7; i > 3; i--)
       for (j = 1; j <= 2; j++)
           printf("%d %d\n", i, j);
   ```

2. ```
   for (i = 2; i < 5; i++)
   {
       sum = 0;
       for (j = 7; j >= 6; j--)
           sum += i * j;
       printf("Sum of products = %d\n", sum);
   }
   ```

3. ```
   sum = 0;
   for (i = 2; i < 5; i++)
       for (j = 7; j >= 6; j--)
           sum += i * j;
   printf("Sum of products = %d\n", sum);
   ```

Find the errors in the segments in Exercises 4–6.

4. ```
   sum = 0;
   for (i = 0, i < n, i++)
       for (j = 1, j < 6, j++)
           sum += i * j;
       printf("For i = %d and j = 1 to 6, ", i);
       printf("sum of products = %d\n", sum);
   ```

5. ```
   for (i = 0; i < 3; i++)
       for (j = 7; j >= 6; j--)
       {
           sum = 0;
           sum += i * j;
       }
   ```
   ```

6.
```
printf("How many numbers do you want to process? ");
scanf("%d", n);
printf("Type number ");
scanf("%d", num);
for (i = 1; i <= n; i++)
{
      printf("Type number ");
      scanf("%d", num);
      Process(num);
}
```

In Exercises 7 and 8, write nested for *loops.*

7. To produce a table of sums with 5 rows and 7 columns similar to the table of products in Example 6.5

8. To read *NumPrices* number of prices for *NumStores* number of stores, printing the total of the prices for each store

Section 6.2 Programming Projects

1. Design a program that reads a minimum and maximum value for a radius, along with an increment factor, and generates a series of radii by repeatedly adding the increment to the minimum until reaching the maximum. For each value of the radius, compute and print the circumference ($C = 2\pi r$), area ($S = 4\pi r^2$), and volume ($V = \frac{4}{3}\pi r^3$) of the sphere. Validate each input value to be sure it is positive. If the user types the minimum in place of the maximum, have the program print an appropriate message and give the user the opportunity to correct the error. Produce a table of the desired results, suitably formatted and with headings.

2. Design a program that reads a positive integer, *MaxNum*. For each integer from 1 through *MaxNum*, the program should count how many times it doubles the number to reach 1 million.

3. Design a program that reads a number and then reads a single digit and determines whether the first number contains the digit. If it does, the program should display how many times the digit occurs in the number.

4. The **Fibonacci sequence** is an infinite list of numbers which starts as follows:

    1, 1, 2, 3, 5, 8, 13, 21, . . .

    After 1, 1, each number in the sequence is the sum of the preceding two numbers. Write a program to generate the sequence to a requested length.

5. Write a program that creates the design below. (To print the backslash (\), the *printf* control string must contain two backslashes (\\).)

```
\/////////
\\////////
\\\///////
\\\\//////
\\\\\/////
\\\\\\////
\\\\\\\///
\\\\\\\\//
\\\\\\\\\/
```

We can modify programs that require input validation to limit the number of chances the user gets to correct errors, for example, 3. If the user does not enter a valid input after three tries, the program terminates. For Exercises 6–9, use such a limit.

6. Section 3.3, Project 1   **7.** Section 3.3, Project 3

8. Section 3.4, Project 2   **9.** Section 4.5, Project 3

Section 6.3 Breadth: A Technique of Numerical Computing

Mathematical modeling is the application of methods to analyze complex, real-world problems in order to make predictions about what might happen with various actions. When performing experiments is too difficult, time-consuming, costly, or dangerous, the modeler might resort to computer simulation, or having a computer program imitate reality. Simulating a process or an object, he or she can consider various scenarios and test the effects of each. For example, a scientist might simulate the effects of ozone depletion on global warming. Flight simulators allow pilots to practice emergency situations under safe conditions. The president of a grocery store chain might use simulation to make a decision on the optimal number of checkout lanes. A political scientist might simulate the actions of voters.

Definition	**Mathematical modeling** is the application of methods to analyze complex, real-world problems in order to make predictions about what might happen with various actions.

At the core of simulation is random number generation. Computer random number generators have been available since some of the earliest days in the development of computers. **John von Neumann**, who introduced the idea of storing programs as well as data in computer memory (see Section 1.4), also introduced the first algorithm for generating random numbers with the computer. In Section 5.4, we discussed the ANSI C standard library function *rand*, which returns a random integer in the range 0 to

Flight Simulator

RAND_MAX. We also developed a function, *random_float_range(LowerBound, UpperBound)* that returns a random floating point number between *LowerBound* and *UpperBound.* The definition of this function is in file *RandDef.c,* and the prototype is in header file *RandDef.h* on the text disk. (Several C compilers have their own random number generators that are extensions to ANSI C.)

Example 6.7

A fundamental problem of calculus is to find the area between a curve and the (horizontal) *x*-axis over a certain interval. In this example, we use computer simulation to estimate this area for functions that are above the *x*-axis. With integration, we can compute the exact area of many, but not all, functions. The graph of the function

$$f(x) = \sqrt{cos(x)^2 + 1}$$

on the interval between $x = 0$ and $x = 2$ in Figure 6.3 is entirely above the *x*-axis. Unfortunately, we cannot use integration to find the pictured area exactly.

One method to estimate the area is to enclose it in a rectangle as in Figure 6.4. We have picked a rectangle of an arbitrary height (1.5) higher than *f.* We hypothetically

Figure 6.3
Graph of
$f(x) =$
$\sqrt{cos(x)^2 + 1}$
on the interval
between $x = 0$
and $x = 2$.

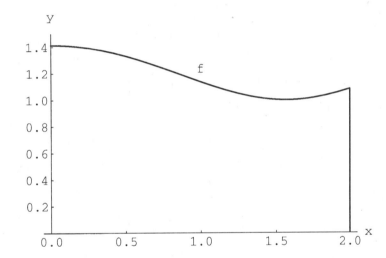

Figure 6.4
Area depicted
in Figure 6.3
enclosed in a
rectangle

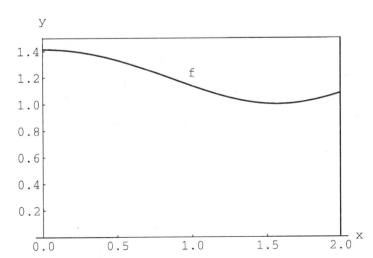

throw darts at the rectangle, counting the total number of darts thrown and the number of darts that hit below *f*. To estimate the desired area, we take that fraction of the total area of the rectangle.

area ≈ (area of enclosing rectangle) * (#darts below) / (#darts)

We can easily compute the area of the rectangle as length times width—in this case, it is 2 · 1.5 = 3.0. If we throw 1000 darts and 778 of them hit below the graph, then 778 / 1000 = 0.778 of the total lands below *f*. This fraction is a good estimate of the portion of the rectangle that is below *f*. In other words, about 77.8% of the rectangle's area rests between *f* and the *x*-axis. Thus, we estimate this smaller area by taking 77.8% of the total area, as follows:

area ≈ 3.0 * 778/1000 = 2.334

We can use the random number generator *random_float_range* of Example 5.14 to help us simulate throwing the darts. In the program, we establish symbolic constants *SMALLEST_X* and *LARGEST_X* as the limits of *x*'s interval—in this case 0.0 and 2.0, respectively. With 0.0 as the lower bound for *y*, we define the preprocessor constant *MAX_Y* as an upper bound. Any number greater than or equal to the largest *y* value on the interval is acceptable. In this program, we use *MAX_Y* = 1.5. As Figure 6.5 pictures, these constants establish the bounds for our "dart board," from *SMALL-EST_X* to *LARGEST_X* horizontally and from 0.0 to *MAX_Y* vertically. Thus, using these constants we can generalize the computation of the area of the rectangle as

area of rectangle = (*LARGEST_X* – *SMALLEST_X*) * *MAX_Y*

For our example,

area of rectangle = (2.0 – 0.0) * 1.5 = 3.0

For the overall structure of the program, *main* calls *SeedRand* to seed the random number generator and *CountHitsBelow* to throw darts and count and return the number that hit below the curve. Then, *main* uses this number to print the estimated area. *CountHitsBelow* calls the random number generator *random_float_range* and the particular mathematical function, *f*. Figure 6.6 presents this structure chart for the program.

Figure 6.5
Bounds of "dart board" for area in Figure 6.4

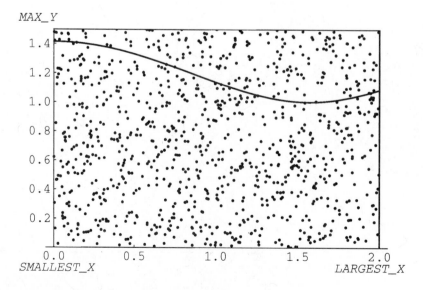

Figure 6.6
Structure chart
for program in
Example 6.7

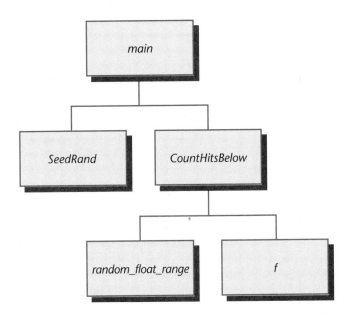

We define constant *NUMDARTS* as the total number of "darts" we throw. We use this value in *main*'s computation of the area below the curve and in *CountHitsBelow*'s loop. The pseudocode for *main* follows:

---

main()

　Program to find the area under a curve using the dartboard method

Algorithm:

　call *SeedRand*() to seed the random number generator
　NumHitsBelow ← *CountHitsBelow*()
　calculate *AreaOfRectangle*
　EstimatedArea ← *AreaOfRectangle* * *NumHitsBelow* / *NUMDARTS*
　print *EstimatedArea*

Because we know the exact number of darts to throw (*NUMDARTS*), a *for* loop is ideal in *CountHitsBelow*. Each time through the loop, we use *random_float_range* to generate a random *x* value (*randomX*) between *SMALLEST_X* and *LARGEST_X*. We also generate a random *y* value (*randomY*) between 0 and *MAX_Y*. Thus, (*randomX*, *randomY*) are the coordinates of where a dart hits the rectangular board. We also must determine where the dart hits in relation to the curve. If the dart hit exactly on the curve, then its *y* coordinate would be *f(randomX)*. For example, *random_float_range* might return 1.434065 for *randomX* and 0.715644 for *randomY*. Substituting the *x* value into the function *f*, we have

$$f(1.434065) = \sqrt{\cos(1.434065)^2 + 1} = 1.009247$$

Because *randomY* = 0.715644 is less than *f*(1.434065) = 1.009247, as Figure 6.7 shows, the dart hits below the curve.

Figure 6.7
Dart hit at
(1.434065,
0.715644) is
below the
curve

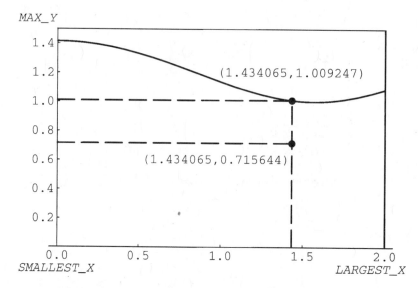

CountHitsBelow simulates throwing *NUMDARTS* number of darts by generating random coordinates of the "hit." For each simulated hit, the computer checks the position of the strike in relation to the function. If the hit is below the graph, the function increments a counter by 1.

CountHitsBelow( ) ⟶ *NumHitsBelow*

Function to throw darts at board and return number of hits below curve

Pre:

Post:

The nonnegative number of darts hitting below curve was returned.

Algorithm:

NumHitsBelow ← 0
do the following *NUMDARTS* times:
    randomX ← random *float* between *SMALLEST_X* and *LARGEST_X*
    randomY ← random *float* between 0 and *MAX_Y*
    f_of_x ← f(*randomX*)
    if *randomY* is smaller than *f_of_x*
        increment *NumHitsBelow* by 1
return *NumHitsBelow*

```
/*
 * Example 6.7
 * Program to estimate the area under a curve using the
 * dartboard method
 */
```

```
#include <stdio.h>
#include <math.h>
#include "RandDef.h"

float f(float x);

#define NUMDARTS 1000        /* number of darts to throw */
#define SMALLEST_X 0.0       /* smallest x value          */
#define LARGEST_X 2.0        /* largest x value           */
#define MAX_Y 1.5            /* upper bound of y values   */

main()
{
    int CountHitsBelow(void);

    int    NumHitsBelow;       /* number of darts below curve   */
    float  AreaOfRectangle,    /* area of rectangular dart board */
           EstimatedArea;      /* estimated area under curve     */

    SeedRand();

    NumHitsBelow    = CountHitsBelow();

    AreaOfRectangle = (LARGEST_X - SMALLEST_X) * MAX_Y;
    EstimatedArea   = AreaOfRectangle * NumHitsBelow / NUMDARTS;

    printf("Estimated area under curve from %.1f to %.1f is %.4f\n",
            SMALLEST_X, LARGEST_X, EstimatedArea);
}

/*
 * Function to throw darts at board and return number of hits
 * below curve
 * Pre:     none
 * Post:    The number of darts hitting below curve was returned.
 */

int CountHitsBelow(void)
{
    int  i,                    /* index                          */
         NumHitsBelow = 0;     /* number of darts below curve */

    float randomX,         /* random x between SMALLEST_X & LARGEST_X */
          randomY,         /* random y between 0 & MaxY               */
          f_of_x;          /* f(x) */
```

```
    for(i = 0; i < NUMDARTS; i++)
    {
        randomX = random_float_range(SMALLEST_X, LARGEST_X);
        randomY = random_float_range(0, MAX_Y);
        f_of_x  = f(randomX);
        if (randomY < f_of_x)
            NumHitsBelow++;
    }

    return NumHitsBelow;
}

/*
 * A mathematical function
 * Pre:    x is a floating point number.
 * Post:   The square root of ((cos(x))^2 + 1) was returned.
 */

float f(float x)
{
    return (sqrt(cos(x) * cos(x) + 1));
}
```

Because we use random numbers to estimate the area, we would expect most runs to produce different results. The output below from three program executions demonstrates this variation:

```
Estimated area under curve from 0.0 to 2.0 is 2.3640
```

```
Estimated area under curve from 0.0 to 2.0 is 2.3490
```

```
Estimated area under curve from 0.0 to 2.0 is 2.3340
```

We can obtain a better estimate by designating a larger number of darts. In this case, we would define *NUMDARTS* to be bigger or run the simulation several more times, taking the average of all runs.

Section 6.3 Programming Projects

1. Revise the program in Example 6.7 to run the simulation several times, taking the average of all the results for the final answer.

2. Develop a program to estimate the area under the curve x^2 on the interval from 2 to 5.

3. Develop a program to estimate the area under the curve e^{x^2} on the interval from 0 to 1.

4. Using the techniques of this section, develop a program to estimate π. The area of a circle is πr^2, where r is the radius. The equation of a circle of radius r with center at the origin is

$$x^2 + y^2 = r^2$$

Use a circle of radius 1. Consider the quarter of the circle in the first quadrant with $0 \leq x \leq 1$ and $0 \leq y \leq 1$. Multiply your result by 4.

5. Develop a program to estimate the volume of a sphere of radius 1 whose equation is

$$x^2 + y^2 + z^2 \leq 1$$

Consider the portion of the sphere with $x \geq 0$, $y \geq 0$, and $z \geq 0$. Multiply your result by 8.

Section 6.4 Breadth: Intellectual Property

Copyright Law

"Copyright © 1990–1994
Deneba Systems, Inc.
All Rights Reserved Worldwide"

So reads the pop-up About Canvas™. . . menu for the graphics application package Canvas. Deneba is proclaiming that the copyright law legally protects its product from unauthorized copying and that the company plans to exercise its rights to this protection. Even if such a notice is not explicitly stated, the **copyright law** says that the author owns his or her work and that others should not copy the material without permission for up to 50 years after the author's death. The law originally applied to written works, but in 1980 Congress amended it to cover software as well. Computer programs fall in the category of **intellectual property**, which involves someone's ideas and the expressions of those thoughts. The copyright law applies to the expressions of the ideas, but not to the ideas themselves. Thus, it protects the text of a book and the code of a piece of software but not a theory an author espouses or the algorithm behind the code. Another person could independently arrive at the same algorithm and legally use it. That person could not, however, take someone else's code, make superficial changes, and present it as his or her own.

Definitions The **copyright law** says that the author owns his or her work and that others should not copy the material without permission for up to 50 years after the author's death. **Intellectual property** is someone's idea and the expression of that thought.

Software vendors take many precautions to guard their intellectual property besides depending on the copyright law. For example, they usually distribute the software in object code form so that others cannot readily discern their methods. Some companies require the user to type the serial number from the original disks when first using the software. With this precaution, they hope to make it difficult for someone to use an illegal copy of their product.

The companies and individuals who create and sell software have a tremendous investment in development time and money for salaries, marketing, and distribution. People who steal a developer's work are also stealing their money. Moreover, unauthorized copying and use of software leads to higher prices for the products. Some gifted people are even reluctant to write software, having had a distasteful experience with others copying their programs.

The copyright law has been applied to the **user interface**, the way by which we interact with a product. In 1987, Lotus Development Corporation brought a suit against Mosaic Software, saying that Mosaic had copied the **look and feel** of the Lotus 1-2-3 spreadsheet's user interface. The courts ruled in favor of Lotus. The next year, Apple Computer Corporation sued Microsoft Corporation, claiming that Microsoft Windows infringed on Apple's copyright by mimicking the look and feel of Apple's graphical user interface. In 1993, the court threw out Apple's suit, primarily because much of the interface appeared in a Xerox computer from the early 1980s. The ideas were not original with Apple.

Definition **User interface** is the way by which the user interacts with a product.

When a customer buys a piece of software, the owner of the copyright gives a **license** to that person for the use of the software. Usually, a single-user license allows that person to make backup copies, but not to distribute the program to others. For much software, organizations can buy some form of **site license** to allow use of an unlimited or a fixed number of copies at the place of business. **Public domain software** and **freeware** are available at no charge over a computer network or through the mails for the cost of disks and postage. The copyright law still applies to freeware, and any new works developed using a freeware package must be freeware, too. The original developer must explicitly relinquish all rights to the software for the package to be public domain. In this case, others can freely use the software without restrictions. **Shareware** is also distributed liberally, although an adopter is asked to send a nominal amount of money to the author. Regardless of the cost, the author still has a copyright to the code.

Definitions A **software license** is authorization to use software. A **site license** allows use of an unlimited or a fixed number of copies at the place of business. Because the developer has explicitly relinquished all rights to **public domain software**, the copyright law does not apply. **Freeware** is available at no charge over a computer network or through the mails for the cost of disks and postage, but the copyright law still applies. Moreover, any new works developed using a freeware package must be freeware, too. **Shareware** is distributed liberally, although an adopter is asked to send a nominal amount of money to the author. The copyright law still applies to shareware.

Patents

A **patent** on software or hardware affords a greater degree of protection for truly unique ideas. Unlike a copyright, one must apply for a patent. If the U.S. Patent and Trademark Office awards a patent, the applicant has exclusive rights to the invention and use of the ideas behind it for 17 years. Although we cannot obtain a copyright on an algorithm, we can obtain a patent on an original, truly innovative method. For example, Narendra Karmarkar developed a fast method of solving linear programming problems that occur in many business decision-making situations. Karmarkar's algorithm is much faster and very different from the simplex algorithm, which is the usual solution technique. Thus, he could obtain a patent for his ideas. Anyone using his algorithm for up to 17 years after the patent must obtain permission and pay a royalty to him.

Definition	A **patent** is exclusive rights for 17 years to an original, truly innovative invention and use of the ideas behind it. The creator must apply to the U.S. Patent and Trademark Office.

One famous patent case dragged on in the courts for years and had a significant impact on the computer industry. As discussed in Chapter 1, John Atanasoff with his assistant Clifford Berry built the first electronic digital computer in the early 1940s to solve a special class of problems. Apparently, no one realized the true significance of the ABC, and with the serious distractions of World War II, neither Atanasoff nor his school applied for a patent. In 1946, John Mauchly and J. Presper Eckert invented a general-purpose electronic digital computer, the ENIAC. They formed their own company, and applied for and received a patent for their invention. Eventually, Sperry Rand bought their company and charged royalties to other computer manufacturers for the use of the ideas on how a computer works. In 1967, Honeywell sued Sperry Rand, saying that the ideas originated with Atanasoff, not Mauchly and Eckert. Early in the development of the ENIAC, one of the inventors had visited Atanasoff for several days, presumably to discuss ideas. After seven years of litigation, the court agreed with Honeywell, invalidated the patent, and declared Atanasoff the inventor of the first computer. Companies were free to use the ideas involved in computer architecture without paying royalties or making intellectual property agreements.

The Company Perspective

Though in many academic situations a free flow of ideas exists, companies have a different perspective. Often, their employees must sign **nondisclosure agreements**, contracts in which an employee promises not to reveal any company trade secrets. A **trade secret** is some proprietary information about a product that a company does not want the competition to know. Theft of trade secrets is a felony. An organization does not apply for a trade secret, but it is very difficult for a company to prove that someone has revealed such a secret. Recently, a large software company accused a former employee of revealing trade secrets about marketing plans and product-release dates to a major competitor before that person went to work for the competition. The company discovered e-mail messages from the then employee to the competitor, allegedly containing trade secrets. The courts may spend years arguing an employee's right to privacy when using commercial e-mail to write someone outside the company, especially a competitor.

Definitions	A **nondisclosure agreement** is a contract in which an employee promises not to reveal any company trade secrets. A **trade secret** is some proprietary information about a product that a company does not want the competition to know.

Companies carefully guard their **trademarks**, which provide name recognition for their products. The trademark can appear in the software and on the documentation. The U.S. Patent and Trademark Office grants trademarks, such as Canvas™.

Definition	A **trademark** is something that provides name recognition for a product or an organization. The U.S. Patent and Trademark Office grants exclusive rights for a trademark.

With these legal means—trademarks, trade secrets, patents, and copyrights—companies try to protect their tremendous investments in product ideas, development, marketing, and distribution.

Section 6.4 Exercises

1. Write a paper with at least three references on the Honeywell lawsuit against Sperry Rand.

2. Write a paper with at least three references on Apple's lawsuit against Microsoft.

3. What does your school do to discourage illegal copying of software? Does your campus have a formal policy on software piracy? If so, obtain a copy of the policy, and write a discussion of what you consider to be its most important aspects.

4. Should someone who publishes an algorithm expect to get royalties when others use it? Justify your answer.

5. Write a paper with at least three references on Atari's lawsuit against North American Consumer Electronics Corporation (NACEC) in 1982 over the similarities between Atari's PAC-MAN and NACECs game K.C. Munchkin.

≋ Programming and Debugging Hints

Debugging Techniques

The C compiler detects a program's syntax errors, which usually are easy to correct. When detecting **run-time errors**, we can print suitably labeled intermediate results to identify the areas in which the errors begin to appear. Once the program is debugged, these redundant *printf* statements are removed.

Many versions of C have an associated **debugger** that helps the programmer to find run-time errors. Appendix H contains an overview of the dbx debugger for the UNIX operating system and the debuggers for Turbo C and Symantec C++ (THINK C). Each debugger has its own facilities and activation method explained in the online (on the computer) or external (written) documentation. Features that are available in many debuggers include the ability to observe the sequence of statements that the computer is executing, to inspect and change intermediate results, and to stop the program at certain points to examine values.

Definition A **debugger** is a program that helps the programmer to find run-time errors.

A **trace** allows us to follow the flow of execution or sequence of program statements as they execute. With some versions of C, when we embed a trace command in the code, the computer prints a message each time execution enters and exits a function. Thus, if *main* does not invoke a function as it should, the trace reveals the problem. More sophisticated debuggers allow interactive control of the trace. Often, a window presents debugging options and displays messages from the debugger. One method of tracing is to **step** through a program, or trace execution one statement at a time. When the programmer presses the return key or clicks a mouse button, the computer executes the next statement. The programmer can carefully examine execution flow and values of variables. Usually, a debugger contains the option of **stepping into** a called function, tracing its execution, or **stepping over** such a call. If a function call is in a loop or if we are confident the function works, the ability to step over such a call saves time.

Definitions   A **trace** is a debugger tool that allows the user to follow the flow of execution or sequence of program statements as they execute. One method of tracing is to **step** through the program, or trace execution one statement at a time.

During a trace, we often need to **inspect intermediate results**. Using this feature, we might detect that a variable unexpectedly becomes zero because of truncation in integer division; or we might discover that a compound condition should contain the AND logical operator instead of OR. Some debuggers allow us to change such values and continue the trace. Often, we can establish a **watch** of an expression, so that when the computer updates the expression during execution, it prints the new value in a watch window.

Definition   The ability to **watch** an expression during execution of the program is a debugger feature that allows the programmer to view any change in the value of the expression.

If we use stubs and add functions one at a time, usually we can quickly narrow down the problem to a particular segment of code. To avoid tracing needlessly before that segment of code, we can set a **breakpoint** at the beginning of the segment. The program executes normally until immediately before the breakpoint. The computer then lets us use debugger options, such as a step-by-step trace or inspection of variable values. After debugging the code, we can remove breakpoints and watches.

Definition   A **breakpoint**, which the programmer establishes using a debugger, is a program location where execution pauses so that the programmer can use other debugging features, such as examining values of variables or commencing stepping through the program.

Figure 6.8 contains a snapshot of the screen during a debugging session in THINK C. A breakpoint is set at the assignment statement for *NumHitsBelow* (indicated by the solid diamond). At this point, the programmer is stepping through the program. Options are available to continue execution (Go), to step into (In) or out of (Out) a routine, or to trace (Trace) execution. The data menu on the right contains values of certain variables, *NumHitsBelow* and *AreaOfRectangle*, that the programmer is watching.

≋ **Key Terms**

Figure 6.8   Snapshot of the screen during a debugging session in THINK C

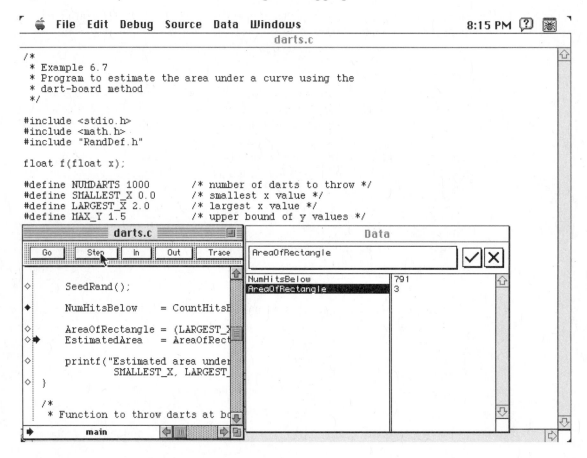

Summary

A counting-controlled or counting loop is a looping control structure in which a loop variable manages the repetition through counting. The *for* loop is often a counting loop with the following general structure:

```
for (expression1; expression2; expression3)
    statement
```

The initialization expression, *expression1*, is usually an assignment of the index or loop variable, which the computer performs once before the loop begins execution. The test expression, *expression2*, evaluates before each iteration of the loop and determines whether the loop should continue or stop. Finally, *expression3* is the modifier statement, which changes the value of the test variable and perhaps other associated variables. The computer executes this expression at the end of each iteration, after the body of the loop. The body of the loop, *statement*, may be compound.

The following recommendations cover which kind of loop to employ:

1. If we know exactly how many times to execute the loop, use *for*.

2. Otherwise, if we need to test before the first iteration, use *while*.

3. If not testing before the first iteration, use *do-while*.

We can use a *for* loop to evaluate *n*-factorial or *n*! for a nonnegative integer *n*. By definition, $0! = 1$, and $n! = n (n - 1) \cdots 2 \cdot 1$ for $n > 0$.

At times, we might find it necessary to nest loops. For example, to generate a multiplication table, we nest a *for* loop that changes the column index inside a loop that increments the row index.

```
for (row = 1; row <= 10; row++)
{
    for (column = 1; column <= 12; column++)
        printf("%4d", row * column);

    printf("\n");
}
```

In nesting of loops, the inner loop variable changes the fastest.

Many versions of C have an associated debugger that helps the programmer to find run-time errors. A trace is a debugger tool that allows the user to follow the flow of execution or sequence of program statements as they execute. One method of tracing is to step through the program, or trace execution one statement at a time. Another debugger feature is the ability to watch an expression during execution of the program. This feature allows the programmer to view any change in the value of the watched expression. With a debugger, the programmer can also establish breakpoints. A breakpoint is a program location where execution pauses so that the programmer can use other debugging features, such as examining values of variables or stepping through the program.

Review Questions

1. What is another name for a loop variable?

2. Which is the better loop to use, the *for* loop or the *while* loop?

3. If you know exactly how many times to execute a loop, which loop would probably be best to use?

4. If you do not know exactly how many times to execute a loop, but you know the loop should execute at least once, which loop would probably be best to use?

5. What is a special advantage of the *for* loop?

6. What separates the three expressions of a *for* statement?

7. Explain the operation of the *for* loop.

8. Under what condition can the first expression of the *for* loop be omitted?

9. Evaluate 0!, 1!, and 5!.

10. What is meant by nested *for* loops?

11. Why is it a good idea to validate input data?

12. In nesting of loops, does the inner or outer loop variable change faster?

13. Name the built-in function for finding a square root.

14. Name some of the features available with debuggers.

Laboratory

Copy file LAB061.c to your own disk. This file contains the program from Example 6.6 in Section 6.2 on averaging grades interactively. In this laboratory, we make modifications to the program to aid understanding of error protection, debugging, loops, and type casting.

1. This exercise provides practice for using the debugger, that should be available with your version of C. If not, you can still perform this exercise by inserting extra output statements. Directions for continuing without a debugger are in parentheses.

   a. Execute the program in the file *LAB061.c*, at times purposefully entering invalid data. If your version of C has a debugger, find out how to activate it from your instructor or laboratory supervisor. Trace through *main* one line at a time without stepping into any other function. Execute a trace, stepping into *ReadNumStudents*. Enter an invalid data item to observe execution of the loop. Write a description of how to access the debugger and use the trace. (Without a debugger, add calls to *printf* at the beginning and end of each routine indicating that execution is entering or leaving the particular module.)

   b. Change the computation of *average* in *ClassGrades* to eliminate the type cast and to have multiplication by the integer 100 after the division, as shown:

   ```
   average = TotalPoints / MaxTotalPoints * 100;
   ```

   Re-execute the program using one student and one grade less than the maximum possible. What is the average? Why?

   c. Put a breakpoint at the assignment of *TotalPoints* in *ClassGrades*. Set a watch of the local variables *TotalPoints* and *MaxTotalPoints* and the expression *TotalPoints / MaxTotalPoints* in that function. (Without a debugger, add *printf* calls to display changes in the values of these expressions. Ignore all comments about breakpoints.) Execute the program using the debugger and enter data for three students. Notice how the computer stops at the assignment of *TotalPoints*, displaying the watched values. Step over the call to *ReadAddGrades* and observe the change in the watched values. Then, let the computer continue executing without stepping. The computer executes until hitting the breakpoint again. Repeat the tracing process. Remove the breakpoint and watches.

   Write a description of how you set and removed the breakpoint and observed values of the variables and expression local to *ClassGrades*. How does observing intermediate values help in debugging?

2. This exercise examines type casting with *float*.

   a. Using the revised computation for *average* in *ClassGrades* (see above assignment), place the *float* type cast before *TotalPoints*, as shown:

   ```
   average = (float)TotalPoints / MaxTotalPoints * 100;
   ```

   Does the expression properly compute the average now? Why or why not?

   Answer the same questions for the following situations:

   b. Move (*float*) before *MaxTotalPoints*.

   c. Place the division *TotalPoints / MaxTotalPoints* in parentheses with the type cast before the parentheses.

   d. Place the entire expression in parentheses with the type cast before the parentheses.

Change the expression to the original version before continuing, as shown:

```
average = (float)100 * TotalPoints / MaxTotalPoints;
```

3. In this exercise, we examine the division-by-zero error and why the programmer must provide ample protection against this run-time error.

   a. In the function *GetMaxTotalPoints*, change the boolean expression in the *while* loop to contain a strict inequality (*MaxTotalPoints* < 0). Run the program entering 0 as the maximum possible points for each grade. Thus, *MaxTotalPoints* is 0. What happens?

   b. Within the loop of *ClassGrades*, add an *if* statement to check if *MaxTotalPoints* is 0. If it is, print out a message to that effect and the total number of points entered for the student. Output should appear as follows:

```
This program finds the average for each student.

How many students are in the class? 4
How many grades are there? 2

Enter the value of each grade.
Enter the nonnegative value of grade 1: 0
Enter the nonnegative value of grade 2: 0

Enter the grades for student 1.
Enter the nonnegative value of grade 1: 89
Enter the nonnegative value of grade 2: 93

The maximum possible points is 0
but the total points for this student is 182
    ⋮
```

The program continues processing for three additional students.

Change the check in *GetMaxTotalPoints* back to (*MaxTotalPoints* <= 0), but leave the additional error checking in *ClassGrades*. It does not hurt to have another audit. Moreover, a programmer might not realize the importance of the less-than-or-equal check and change it to less-than, creating the potential for an error. He or she might also decide to use the *ClassGrades* in another program without considering the possibility of division by zero.

4. In this exercise, we consider the *for* loop and error correction. We use the *for* loop with a compound condition to give the user a maximum number of tries at answering a question.

   a. In *ReadNumStudents*, change the *while* loop to a *for* loop with index *tries*, giving the user at most three attempts to type a positive number. The test expression should check the number of tries and the value read. Be sure to declare your new index. Execute the program.

   b. Clearly, we must also change *main* not to continue processing when *ReadNumStudents* returns zero or a negative integer. Have an *if-else* statement in *main* do the following: If the returned value is not valid (<= 0), print an explanation and stop processing; otherwise, continue execution. A sample run with an invalid number of students follows:

```
This program finds the average for each student.

How many students are in the class? -25
The number of students must be positive.
How many students are there? -3
The number of students must be positive.
How many students are there? -4

Sorry, the input is not correct
and you have exceeded the number of tries.
```

5. We use the *for* loop of the last exercise to improve the information given to the user.

   a. Define a preprocessor constant *NUMTRIES* to be 3 to make the code more readable and adjustable. Place the *#define* preprocessor directive immediately before the definition of the function. Adjust the *for* loop to use this symbolic constant.

   b. Change the *for* loop in *ReadNumStudents* to print the number of attempts remaining, as shown below. Use a new index, *left*, with a decrement.

```
This program finds the average for each student.

How many students are in the class? -25
The number of students must be positive.
Your response is incorrect. You have 2 attempt(s) left.

How many students are there? -3
The number of students must be positive.
Your response is incorrect. You have 1 attempt(s) left.

How many students are there? -4

Sorry, the input is not correct
and you have exceeded the number of tries.
```

Characters

Introduction

In this chapter, we study how to manipulate individual characters, such as y or n for yes–no responses to a question. In doing so, we introduce variable type *char,* which can store a single character. When reading from the keyboard or writing to the screen, the computer places the input or output, respectively, in special locations in memory, called buffers. With an emphasis on character transfer, we discuss the effect of these buffers.

The computer must represent everything in memory with strings of zeros and ones. We studied how the computer represents integers and floating point numbers in Chapters 2 and 4, respectively. In Section 7.2, we see that the machine must encode characters, too.

Certain special characters, such as the newline character (\n), are represented in C with an escape sequence—a backslash followed by another character. In Section 7.2, we present other escape sequences that help us display information in an attractive way.

ANSI C has a number of character manipulation functions in a standard library. For example, a function to change a character to lowercase can simplify programming of the user interface. All input data can be converted to lowercase and compared with expected values. Using loops, we have checked that input numbers are in appropriate ranges. When the program expects numeric data, however, the user could enter a value that is not a number at all, such as 123r.5. With certain character functions, we can validate that the input data item is a number and, if so, convert the string of characters to the appropriate value.

In breadth Section 7.4, we discuss two number systems that are important in computer science—the octal and hexadecimal systems. We use the decimal number system with its ten digits (0–9) every day. The computer employs the binary system containing the binary digits 0 and 1. The octal and hexadecimal number systems, employing 8 and 16 digits, respectively, provide abbreviations for binary numbers.

Before now, we have obtained data by assignments or reading interactively and have presented information on the screen or printer. For large amounts, however, we can more easily store and retrieve the data in a file on disk. In the last section of this chapter, we introduce basic text file (file of characters) manipulation.

Goals

To study

- Character input and output
- Buffering of input and output data
- The ASCII encoding scheme
- Escape sequences that help us display information in an attractive way
- Character functions
- Data validation, such as validation of y/n answers and of numbers
- Octal and hexadecimal number systems
- Basic file manipulation

Section 7.1 **Character Input and Output**

We have considered several data types for numbers, including *int, float, long, double,* and *unsigned int*. Another important data type is *char*, which designates a variable that can store a single character of information. A character constant is one character between two apostrophes, such as 'a', 'R', '*', ':', '#', '{', and even '\n' (as mentioned previously, the latter represents the single newline character). We must use apostrophes, not the quotation marks found with *printf* control strings. A string constant, such as a control string, is simply a sequence of characters between quotation marks. Such a string can contain only one character, but as we see in Chapter 10, the computer represents this string differently than a single character constant. Quotation marks always enclose string constants. Thus, 'a' refers to a character constant, and "a" refers to a string constant. To read or display a character constant, a call to *scanf* or *printf* contains the conversion specification %c.

Example 7.1

The following segment prints several single characters:

```
char letterW = 'W',
     letterO = 'O',
     exclamation = '!',
     newline = '\n';

printf("%c%c%c%c%c%c%c", letterW, letterO, letterW,
       exclamation, newline, exclamation, newline);
```

The code produces the following output:

```
WOW!
!
```

Of course, we can accomplish the same output more easily using the following string constant:

```
printf("WOW!\n!\n");
```

However, it is often desirable to process a string one character at a time.

---

putchar

For displaying an individual character on a video display, programmers usually employ the standard input/output (I/O) library function *putchar*. This function takes a character argument and returns this character to the standard output file, *stdout*, as its result. The file *stdout* is the default output file, which is usually the screen. For example, we can output the value of a *char* variable, *ch*, to the screen with

```
putchar(ch);
```

If an error occurs, *putchar* sends back an error value.

ANSI C implements *putchar* as a **macro** by defining it with a #*define* preprocessor directive instead of a function definition. We study macros in Section 12.1. Macros execute faster than functions. The macro *putchar* is faster for displaying a character than the more general *printf* function, which has a larger code. Although strictly speaking *putchar* is a macro, we use *putchar* like a function. Therefore, we sometimes refer to macros as functions.

Example 7.2 _____

Assuming the *char* declaration-initializations of Example 7.1, we can rewrite the code with *putchar* statements.

```
putchar(letterW);
putchar(letterO);
putchar(letterW);
putchar(exclamation);
putchar(newline);
putchar(exclamation);
putchar(newline);
```

---

getchar

Just as we can use *printf* to print a character, we can use *scanf* to read one. The statement

```
scanf("%c", &ch);
```

causes the computer to read the next character into the properly declared variable *ch*. More commonly, however, we use the specialized *getchar* macro. With no parameters, *getchar* reads a single character from the standard input file *stdin* (usually the keyboard) and returns that character. Thus, we can replace the above *scanf* with the more readable and faster

```
ch = getchar();
```

Buffers

When we read from standard input or write to standard output, the computer buffers the data. A **buffer** is a special location in memory that can hold a fixed number of characters, such as 256 characters. Separate buffers exist for the standard input file *stdin* and the standard output file *stdout*. When we write to standard output with such functions as *printf* or *putchar*, the computer first transfers the characters to a buffer. When the buffer fills or we write a newline character or we attempt to read, the machine empties the buffer, displaying the output. Access to such peripheral devices as the screen or printer is typically much slower than main memory access. One advantage of buffered output is that the computer can quickly accumulate several characters in memory. When the buffer fills, the computer **flushes the buffer**, sending the buffer's contents all at once to the peripheral device. Reducing the number of references to external devices speeds the entire system. Methods exist for using unbuffered output so that the user does not need to press return after a response. However, such methods are machine specific and not part of ANSI C.

Definition	A **buffer** is a special location in main memory, a fixed number of characters in length, that can temporarily hold data being transferred from main memory to secondary storage, or vice versa.

When the program interactively requests input from the user, the data transfers from the keyboard to the buffer. The *scanf* and *getchar* functions also obtain their values from this area of memory. On input, when the user presses the return or enter key or types the **end-of-file (EOF)** character, the program uses the information in the buffer. For input from the keyboard, the EOF character is specific to the operating system. With UNIX or THINK C on the Macintosh, we indicate the end of a file from the keyboard with the control character **ctrl-d** (we press the control and d keys together). For VAX/VMS, MS-DOS, and Turbo C, the signal is **ctrl-z**. The header file *stdio.h* defines the symbolic constant *EOF* usually to be −1. Its definition is irrelevant to us as long as we use the symbolic constant. Both *scanf* and *getchar* return *EOF* if an input failure occurs. The same return would occur if the user indicates end-of-file.

Buffered input has two main advantages. As with buffered output, it is faster to access a memory buffer than an external device, such as a keyboard. The input buffer can accumulate the result of a number of keystrokes and process them all at once. Another advantage of buffered input is that we can backspace to correct errors before entering a line.

Example 7.3

This example explores buffered input. Consider the following program to read and print a character:

```
/* Program to read and print a character */

#include <stdio.h>

main()
{
    char in_char;        /* I/O character */

    printf("Enter a character: ");
    in_char = getchar();
    printf("The character is %c.\n", in_char);
}
```

Figure 7.1 An interactive session with the program in Example 7.3

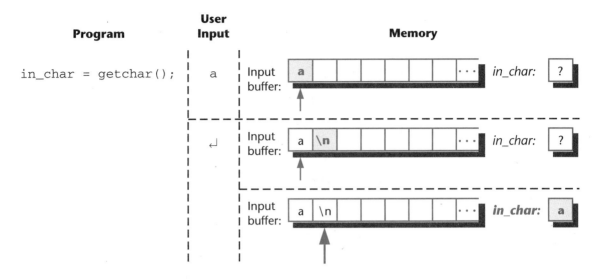

Figure 7.1 illustrates the action of the assignment statement in the following interactive session:

```
Enter a character: a
The character is a.
```

The *printf* statement displays "Enter a character: ". The user types the character 'a', and the computer transfers the character to the input buffer. When the return key (↵) is pressed, the newline character is sent to the input buffer; character 'a', indicated by the input buffer pointer, is copied to the variable *in_char*; and the buffer pointer is advanced to the next position. As we emphasized previously with the *printf*, the newline character is itself a character that takes up a position in the buffer. Consequently, if another *getchar* occurs, it will read the newline character from the buffer.

Example 7.4 _____

This example further illustrates buffering. The following program prompts, reads, and prints two characters, one character at a time:

```
/* Program to read and print two characters */

#include <stdio.h>

main()
{
    char in_char;        /* I/O character */

    printf("Enter a character: ");
    in_char = getchar();
    printf("The character is %c.\n\n", in_char);
```

```
        printf("Enter another character: ");
        in_char = getchar();
        printf("The character is %c.\n", in_char);
    }
```

Suppose the user decides to be funny and, instead of behaving as requested, types the word "char." The output would be as follows:

```
Enter a character: char
The character is c.

Enter another character: The character is h.
```

As Figure 7.2 demonstrates, after the prompt, the computer dutifully waits for the user to press return or the EOF control character. Meanwhile, the machine stores the input stream in the input buffer. When the user presses return, five characters are in the buffer, the word "char" and \n. The computer can then copy the first character ('c'), from the buffer to the memory location for *in_char* and advance the **input buffer**

Figure 7.2 An interactive session with the character program in Example 7.4

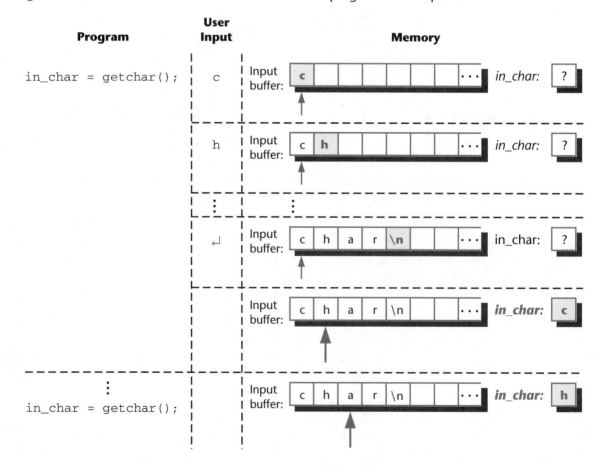

pointer. This buffer pointer indicates the next character to process. When the second *getchar* occurs, four unprocessed characters ('h', 'a', 'r', '\n') remain in the buffer. The computer does not need to get another character from the keyboard. It can grab one from the buffer. The computer copies 'h' into *in_char*, advances the buffer pointer, and proceeds to the next statement. The *printf* prints the value of *in_char*, 'h', and the program ends. The user may wonder why the computer did not obtain more input from the keyboard.

The same problem arises if we have numbers in the buffer, as in the following program:

```
/* Program to read and print two integers */

#include <stdio.h>

main()
{
    int in_int;            /* I/O integer */

    printf("Enter an integer: ");
    scanf("%d", &in_int);
    printf("The integer is %d.\n\n", in_int);

    printf("Enter another integer: ");
    scanf("%d", &in_int);
    printf("The integer is %d.\n", in_int);
}
```

In the first run below, the user enters data as expected:

```
Enter an integer: 98
The integer is 98.

Enter another integer: 473
The integer is 473.
```

The user types 98 and presses return. The buffer contains '9', '8', and '\n'. The computer converts the characters before the newline character into internal format in *in_int*. For a number, **white space**—such as a blank or newline—or a nonnumeric character—such as a comma—terminates the value. When processing the second *scanf*, the computer first advances the buffer pointer, looking for a number. When that search fails, it waits for the buffer to obtain a new data item (473) from the keyboard.

Suppose, however, the user types two numbers instead of one after the first prompt.

```
Enter an integer: 245 57
The integer is 245.

Enter another integer: The integer is 57.
```

Figure 7.3   An interactive session with the integer program in Example 7.4

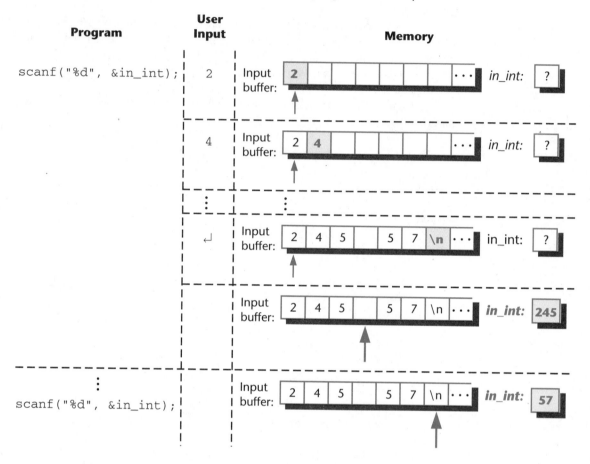

After the first *scanf*, Figure 7.3 shows that the buffer contains both 245 and 57. The input buffer pointer advances past all the digits of the first number as the computer assembles the individual characters into the number 245 for storage in *in_int*. When the second request for data arrives, the pointer moves past all white space and finds the characters of the number 57 before additional white space, \n. Consequently, the user is not given the opportunity to type additional data. The computer has all it needs in the buffer.

When reading character data interactively, we should flush the buffer after obtaining the desired character. As a result, a future *getchar* cannot use the newline character or other unprocessed characters in the buffer. The ANSI C standard I/O library function *fflush* flushes the input buffer with the following:

```
fflush(stdin);
```

This function continues to call *getchar* as long as *getchar* returns a character other than the newline character. The action is equivalent to the following loop:

```
while (getchar() != '\n');
```

ORDER DATE	ORDER NO.
06-12-95	2083009

RETURNS TO:
545 WESCOTT RD
EAGAN, MN 55123

BATCH	OP NO.	P.O. NO.
7647	999-999-950	

SPECIAL INSTRUCTIONS

SHIP TO:

EMBRY-RIDDLE AERON UNIV
DR JANUSZ ZALEWSKI
COMPUTER SCIENCE DEPT
CLYDE MORRIS BLVD
DAYTONA BEACH FL 32014

PAGE	ATTENTION
1	106711518-002083009

PACKING SLIP

ISBN	ORDERED	SHIPPED	AUTHOR/DESCRIPTION	QUANTITY BACKORDERED	RETAIL PRICE
0-314-04554-6	1	1	SHIFLET PROBLEM SOLVING C		0.00
0-000-00000-0	1	1	IM LETTER		0.00
					0.00

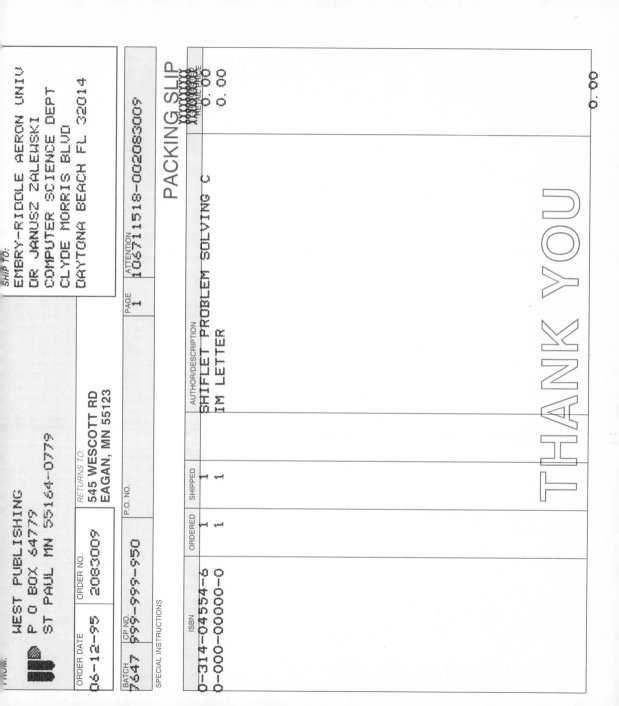

THANK YOU

We need not store the value *getchar* returns in a variable. The macro is only testing that the value is not the newline character and advancing the buffer pointer. Once the function returns the newline character, no more characters are available in the buffer.

Y/N Responses

Example 7.5

We have used the sentinel technique to stop looping when processing an indeterminate amount of user input. Unfortunately, that method forces us to have a value that we cannot process, such as zero for a particular application. Moreover, the resulting loop condition (such as *n* != 0) is not descriptive. An alternative is to ask the user the number of data items and use a *for* loop. However, the user may not know the exact number of items to process. Now that we can read character data, we can ask the user, "Do you want to continue," and can manage responses of 'y' or 'n'.

Example 5.12 of Section 5.4 presents an interactive program to square nonnegative integer input. When the user types a negative number, the loop stops. The version in Chapter 5 has *main* and an additional function, *ReadNum*, to read and return the value to square, *n*. In the structure chart of Figure 7.4, we expand the design to include function, *GetAnswer* to ask the user if he or she wants to square a number and to return the response.

Similar to the program of Example 5.12, *main* determines if the user has a data item to process before executing the loop. In this *while* loop, an initial call to *GetAnswer* provides a priming read, and another call to that function at the end of the loop obtains another answer from the user. Because we are not using a negative number as a sentinel value, the program can now process any integer.

---

main()
   Interactive program to square numbers

Algorithm:
   call *GetAnswer* to determine if the user wants to process a number
   while the user wants to process, do the following:
      call *ReadNum* to obtain a number *n* from the user
      print *n* and its square
      call *GetAnswer* to determine if the user wants to process a number
   print a closing message

The function *GetAnswer* asks if the user wants to square a number, verifying the answer to be 'y' or 'n'. The function then calls *fflush* to move the input buffer pointer past the newline character. Finally, it returns the user's answer.

GetAnswer() ⟶ *answer*
   Function to ask if user wishes to continue and to return the user's response

Pre:
   none

Figure 7.4
Structure chart
for program in
Example 7.5

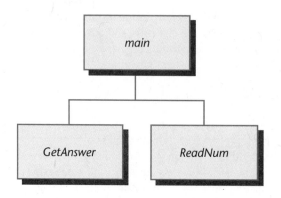

Post:

A 'y' or 'n' user response was returned.

Algorithm:

do the following repeatedly:
  ask if the user wants to square a number
  answer ← *getchar*( )
  fflush(*stdin*) to flush the input buffer
while *answer* is not one of the following: 'y', 'n'
return *answer*

The function *ReadNum* prompts for and reads an integer *n*, calls *fflush* to empty the input buffer, and returns the number. Should the user press return without typing an integer, the computer waits for the number. When reading a character, the computer reads the next character; when reading a number, it advances past white space (including a return) until it finds the number or EOF marker.

ReadNum( ) ⟶ *n*

Function to prompt for and read an integer to return to main

Pre:

Post:

An integer input was returned.

Algorithm:

prompt for and read an integer, *n*
fflush(*stdin*) to flush the input buffer
return *n*

ReadNum and *main* have local variables called *n*. In this program, we have several n's indicating different things—\n is the newline character, 'n' indicates a user response of "no"; and *n* is the variable name. We can employ symbolic constants (*YES* and *NO*) to make the code more readable.

```
/*
 * Interactive program to square numbers.  The user is asked
 * if he or she wishes to square a number and responds with y/n.
 */

#include <stdio.h>

#define YES 'y'
#define NO 'n'

char GetAnswer(void);
int ReadNum(void);

main()
{
    int n;                      /* number to be squared */
    char answer;                /* answer for wanting to square */

    answer = GetAnswer();                    /* ask if want to square */
    while (answer == YES)
    {
        n = ReadNum();                       /* get next number */
        printf("%d squared is %d\n\n", n, n * n);
        answer = GetAnswer();                /* ask if want to square */
    }
    printf("Thank you.\n");
}

/*
 * Function to ask if user wishes to continue and to return
 * the user's response after flushing the input buffer
 * Pre:    none
 * Post:   A 'y' or 'n' user response was returned.
 */

char GetAnswer(void)
{
    char answer; .              /* answer for wanting to square */

    do
    {
        printf("Do you want to square a number? (y/n) ");
        answer = getchar();
        fflush(stdin); /* advance buffer pointer past newline */
    }
    while (answer != YES && answer != NO);

    return answer;
}
```

```
/*
 * Function to prompt for and read an integer to return
 * Pre:    none
 * Post:   An integer input was returned.
 */

int ReadNum(void)
{
    int n;                      /* input number */

    printf("Enter an integer to be squared: ");
    scanf("%d", &n);
    fflush(stdin);              /* advance buffer pointer past newline */

    return n;
}
```

The following is a sample run:

```
Do you want to square a number? (y/n) y
Enter an integer to be squared: 34
34 squared is 1156

Do you want to square a number? (y/n) b
Do you want to square a number? (y/n) 57
Do you want to square a number? (y/n)
Do you want to square a number? (y/n) y
Enter an integer to be squared: 57
57 squared is 3249

Do you want to square a number? (y/n) n
Thank you.
```

After processing the first number (34) the user types 'b' by mistake. Not looking up to read the question, the user types 57 and return. Still in a daze, the user presses return. With each invalid response, the computer prompts again. Finally, with a valid answer, the computer continues processing.

Asking the user if he or she wants to square a number avoids having a sentinel value or an exact count of the number of values to process. When there is much data to enter, however, requiring the user to type y or n after every value does place an unnecessary burden on the user. The programmer must determine which method provides the best user interface for the particular problem.

Before ending this example, we should comment on the following *do-while* test condition in *GetAnswer:*

```
(answer != YES && answer != NO)
```

The loop continues as long as the user does not type a correct response, y/n. In other words, every time the variable *answer* is **not** 'y' **and** is **not** 'n', the loop executes again. An alternative way to say this condition in English is "*answer* is **not** 'y' or 'n'." Similarly, in the code we could write the following condition*:

```
(!(answer == YES || answer == NO))
```

Because the compound conditions are equivalent, the programmer can write the form of the boolean condition that is more understandable to him or her.

Section 7.1 Exercises

1. Assume the following declaration-initialization:

   ```
   char lang = 'C';
   ```

   a. Write a call to *printf* to print the value of *lang*.

   b. Use *putchar* to print the value.

2. Find the error(s) in the following segment:

   ```
   char ch = "A";

   printf("'%c' value is 3.\n", ch);
   printf("The character is ");
   putchar();
   ```

3. Find the error(s) in the following segment:

   ```
   character ch;

   printf("Type a character: ");
   scanf('%c', ch);
   fflush(stdout);
   printf("Type another character: ");
   getchar(ch);
   ```

4. Using *putchar* and the following declaration-initializations

   ```
   char    colon = ':',
           minus = '-',
           RightParen = ')',
   ```

   print the electronic-mail "smiley face"

   ```
   :-)
   ```

---

*DeMorgan's Law in logic provides the justification for this variation. As presented in Section 3.5, with $\sim$ meaning NOT, $\vee$ OR, and $\wedge$ AND, one of the forms of this law is

$$\sim(p \vee q) \equiv \sim p \wedge \sim q$$

For boolean conditions p and q that are *TRUE* or *FALSE*, such as (*answer* == *YES*) and (*answer* == *NO*), we can translate this rule into C as the equivalence of the following conditions:

```
!(p || q)
!p && !q
```

5. Using the %c conversion specification in a call to *printf*, print your first name followed by a newline character.

6. Suppose in the program to read and print two characters of Example 7.4, the user types the word "yes" and return after the first prompt. What is the output?

7. Suppose in the second program of Example 7.4 (to read and print two integers), the user types

    4996   43.9785

and return after the first prompt. What is the output?

8. Write a segment of code to ask the user for a character, to read and print the character, and to flush the appropriate buffer. Use *getchar* and *putchar*.

Section 7.1 Programming Projects

Rewrite any of the first 10 projects in Section 5.4 to obtain y/n character responses from the user about processing more data instead of using the sentinel technique.

Section 7.2 The ASCII Encoding Scheme

Numeric Code

When we type a character at the keyboard, the computer does not record the character itself but a numeric code that represents the typed character. Each brand of computer has a system of assigning a number to a character, but the most widely used is the ASCII (pronounced "ass-kee") encoding scheme. ASCII is an abbreviation for American Standard Code for Information Interchange. (A complete list of the ASCII encoding scheme appears in Appendix A.)

Definition   The **American Standard Code for Information Interchange** (**ASCII**) encoding scheme is a system of assigning a number to a character. Many computers store characters as binary numbers using their ASCII code representations.

The ASCII system represents the capital letters 'A' through 'Z' by the numbers 65–90 and the lowercase letters by 97–122. Single digits can be stored as characters by enclosing them in apostrophes, such as '1', '6', and '9'. We must not confuse these character constants with the numeric values 1, 6, and 9. We use the character digits in apostrophes to store values on which we do not normally plan to perform arithmetic, such as digits of a telephone number or a ZIP code. ASCII internally represents the character digits '0'–'9' by the values 48–57. The intervening values from 32–126 are various punctuation symbols. The values 0–31, and 127 (the highest ASCII number) represent **control characters**, or nonprintable characters (such as the newline character) that perform special functions. We discuss control characters in greater detail later in this section.

As defined in Section 2.4, a **byte** is a sequence of **binary digits** or **bits** (zeros and ones) to encode a character. On most computers, a byte has 8 bits. Because the computer stores characters as binary numbers (their ASCII code representations), the programmer must keep track of the intended use of a particular variable. We have discussed that a variable of type *char* can hold a single character. Inside the computer, however, such a variable simply holds a binary number. We can use a variable of type *char*, another integer type, in almost the same way as a variable of type *int*. In Sections 2.4 and 2.5, we discussed how a sequence of 8 bits can represent $2^8 = 256$ different symbols. Type *char* can be implemented as type *signed char* with a range of values from −128 to 127 or, less commonly, as type *unsigned char* with values from 0 to 255. This range is sufficient to hold the $2^7 = 128$ ASCII values.

Example 7.6

This example illustrates how the computer can interpret a particular value in more than one way. The following program prints the character 'V' with various conversion specifications:

```
/* A printf demonstration of interpretation of values */

#include <stdio.h>

main()
{
    char ch = 'V';

    printf("A character: %c\n", ch);
    printf("Its ASCII value: %d\n", ch);
    printf("Using the ASCII value to print the character: %c\n", 86);
}
```

Execution on one computer yields the following:

```
A character: V
Its ASCII value: 86
Using the ASCII value to print the character: V
```

With the initialization of *ch* as 'V', the computer stores the ASCII code for 'V' in *ch*. This code is the decimal number 86, which is 0101 0110 in binary. The first *printf* displays the *char* variable *ch* in c format producing the expected letter V without the apostrophes. The second uses the %d conversion specification to print the contents of this variable. This time, the computer interprets the value as an integer rather than a character and prints the ASCII equivalent of 'V' as the decimal number 86. The last statement prints the value 86 using the %c conversion specification. Because 86 is the ASCII code for the character 'V', the computer displays the letter rather than a number.

The last section introduced the macro *getchar*, which reads and returns a character from standard input. If there is no character to read, *getchar* returns the constant *EOF*. To avoid confusion with valid data, this constant must not be any possible *char* value. The header file *stdio.h* usually defines *EOF* to be −1. Thus, to return a value like −1, a prototype has *getchar* of type *int*, as shown:

```
int getchar(void);
```

For a character variable *ch*, we still can have the following assignment:

```
ch = getchar();
```

Suppose the user enters an uppercase V. Because input is normal, *getchar* returns the ASCII representation for 'V'—the decimal integer 86—which *ch* receives. As the last example illustrates, however, the programmer must interpret the string of bits for 86 (0101 0110) correctly. Using *ch* as character information, we can continue without error.

Example 7.7

This program enables a user to type a character and see its equivalent ASCII code. The function *main* handles most of the processing. It calls *GetCharNewline* to obtain a character to encode and *GetAnswer* to return whether the user wishes to obtain more codes or not. As Figure 7.5 shows, the structure chart for this program is similar to the one for Example 7.5 in the last section.

The pseudocode for *main* follows:

> *main( )*
>
>   Program repeatedly to ask the user for a character and print its ASCII code
>
> *Algorithm:*
>   print directions
>   do the following repeatedly:
>   prompt for a character
>   *in_char* ← *GetCharNewline*()
>   ask if the user wants to see another code
>   while the user wants to see another code

The design of the other functions is similar to the corresponding functions in Example 7.5. The only variation in *GetAnswer* is the prompt and the ending of the *do-while* loop. In the present treatment, we use the following:

```
while ( !(answer == YES || answer == NO) );
```

As discussed at the end of Example 7.5, this close to the loop is equivalent to the version in that example:

```
while ( (answer != YES && answer != NO) );
```

Figure 7.5
Structure chart
for Example 7.7

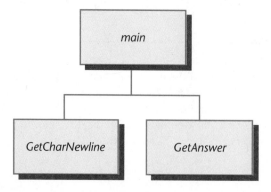

The entire program follows:

```
/*
 * Example 7.7.  This interactive program repeatedly asks
 * the user for a character and prints its ASCII code.
 */

#include <stdio.h>

#define YES 'y'
#define NO 'n'

int GetCharNewline(void);
char GetAnswer(void);

main()
{
    char in_char,    /* input character to encode */
         answer;     /* answer to continue? */

    printf("Given a character, this program prints its ASCII code.\n");
    do
    {
        printf("Enter a character: ");
        in_char = GetCharNewline();

        printf("The ASCII value of %c is %d.\n", in_char, in_char);
        answer = GetAnswer();
    }
    while (answer == YES);
}

/*
 * Function to read and return a character and to move the
 * input buffer pointer past the newline character
 * Pre:    none
 * Post:   An input character was returned and the buffer flushed.
 */

int GetCharNewline(void)
{
    char in_char;

    in_char = getchar();
    fflush(stdin);

    return in_char;
}
```

```
/*
 * Function to ask if user wishes to continue and to return
 * the user's response after flushing the input buffer
 * Pre:     none
 * Post:    A y or an n was returned and the buffer flushed.
 */

char GetAnswer(void)
{
    char answer;                /* answer for wanting another code */

    do
    {
        printf("\nDo you want to find another ASCII code? (y/n) ");
        answer = getchar();
        fflush(stdin);
    }
    while ( !(answer == YES || answer == NO) );

    return answer;
}
```

An interactive session follows:

```
Given a character, this program prints its ASCII code.
Enter a character: {
The ASCII value of { is 123.

Do you want to find another ASCII code? (y/n) y
Enter a character: ?
The ASCII value of ? is 63.

Do you want to find another ASCII code? (y/n) y
Enter a character: 7
The ASCII value of 7 is 55.

Do you want to find another ASCII code? (y/n) y
Enter a character:
The ASCII value of
 is 10.

Do you want to find another ASCII code? (y/n) y
Enter a character:
The ASCII value of is 127.

Do you want to find another ASCII code? (y/n) n
```

The most surprising results are the last two. In the next-to-the-last iteration, the user pressed the return key. The computer assigned the newline character with ASCII decimal representation 10 to *answer*. Thus, after printing "The ASCII value of," the computer printed the newline character and the subsequent output on the next line.

For the next character request, the user pressed the delete key. The delete is an unprintable character, but we use it often to correct mistakes before pressing return. Output reveals that the delete character has an ASCII code of 127.

Integer Equivalent of Character Digit

In the execution of the last program, we discover that the ASCII code of the character '7' is 55, not 7. In many situations, we may need to take numeric character input and derive the corresponding number on which we can perform normal arithmetic. Fortunately, the codes for the character digits '0'–'9' are sequential in virtually all encoding schemes; and ASCII's sequence is 48–57. Thus, to obtain the integer equivalent of a character digit, we subtract the code for '0' from that of its own. For example, to obtain the number corresponding to character '7', we perform the subtraction

$$
\begin{array}{rl}
55 = & \text{ASCII code for '7'} \\
-48 = & - \text{ASCII code for '0'} \\
\hline
7 = & \text{numeric equivalent of '7'}
\end{array}
$$

Suppose *char* variable *ch* has the value '7', and *digit* is a variable of type *int*. Because the computer stores characters as their integer codes and C requires that the programmer keep track of the meaning of a memory location, we can perform the following subtraction in C:

```
digit = ch - '0';
```

or emphasize the coercion to *int*, as follows:

```
digit = (int)ch - (int)'0';
```

Either form of the computation is more meaningful and less prone to error than the following:

```
digit = ch - 48;
```

which contains the ASCII code for '0'. Moreover, not all computers use the ASCII system. IBM mainframe computers use **EBCDIC (Extended Binary Coded Decimal Interchange Code)**, even though IBM microcomputers employ ASCII. By writing the generic *ch* – '0', we leave our code portable to any machine.

Escape Sequences

As demonstrated in the last example, certain ASCII characters, such as newline and delete, are unprintable. In other words, we cannot display them on the screen or printer. These characters perform special functions other than producing text, such as tabbing or ringing a bell. We have frequently used one of these control characters—the newline character—which C represents with the **escape sequence** \n. In C, we call the backslash character the **escape character**, because any character immediately following it takes on a special meaning. A character constant specified in a program is shown within apostrophes. As part of a control string, characters appear inside the quotation marks of the string. Table 7.1 lists some commonly used escape sequences.

Table 7.1   Some escape sequences in C

Escape Sequence in C	Meaning
\0	null character
\a or \007	audible alert (bell)
\b	backspace
\f	form feed
\n	newline, go to first of next line
\r	carriage return, go to first of current line
\t	horizontal tab
\v	vertical tab
\"	quotation mark
\'	apostrophe
\?	question mark
\\	backslash
\ooo	up to 3-digit octal (base 8) number
\x$hh$	up to 2-digit hexadecimal (base 16) number

The tab character '\t', moves to the next tab stop, which is user-determined on some computers, terminals, or printers. The backspace (not delete) character '\b' performs the same task as that key on your computer or typewriter. After backspacing on a screen, new input usually overwrites the old. However, most printers are like typewriters, with both new and old text appearing. The carriage return character '\r' returns to the beginning of the current line, but a printer may not perform this task correctly unless specially set. The form feed character '\f' advances the printer to the next new page, or in the case of video display, clears the screen on some computers.

On some systems, particularly in Europe, the question mark character has a special meaning. To print the symbol on those systems, the programmer must use '\?'. The quotation mark and backslash have special meanings in *printf* control strings, and the apostrophe delimits a character constant. In ambiguous situations, we use a backslash before each to indicate that we really do want to print the next character.

The null character '\0' is important in the context of strings and pointers, which we discuss later. By printing '\a' or '\007' or '\7', a bell alert sounds at a microcomputer or terminal and sometimes at a printer. Both \0 and \007 are special cases of the \ooo control sequence, where ooo indicates any octal or base 8 number of up to 3 digits. The ASCII encoding scheme in Appendix A presents the characters with their representations in the decimal, octal, and hexadecimal systems. Breadth Section 7.4 discusses the octal and hexadecimal number systems.

Example 7.8

In this example, we write code to print the following:

```
Hamlet said, "To be, or not to be...
     That is the question."
```

We print the quotation marks with the escape sequence \″. The second line begins with a tab. After printing "That," we backspace and print four underscores to produce the underlined word. Unfortunately, output on the printer is different from what appears on the screen, because after backspacing on the screen, a new character overwrites the character that was in that position. Thus, on the screen, we see

```
Hamlet said, "To be, or not to be...
        ____ is the question."
```

The code to produce these lines follows, with escape sequences in color:

```
printf("Hamlet said, \"To be, or not to be...\n");
printf("\tthat\b\b\b\b____ is the question.\"\n");
```

Example 7.9

This example illustrates when we must use the backslash before the apostrophe and quotation marks. We should use the escape sequences \″ and \′ in ambiguous situations. Because quotation marks are string delimiters, we must be careful when printing a quotation mark with a *printf*.

```
printf("This is a quotation mark: \" ");
```

Ambiguity does not exist if we define a symbolic constant to be the quotation mark character. In the following case, the escape sequence is unnecessary:

```
#define QUOTATION_MARK '"'
```

The opposite situation occurs with the apostrophe, which demarcates a character constant. To avoid ambiguity, we use the escape sequence \′ in the declaration-initialization, as shown:

```
char apostrophe = '\'';
```

We do not have ambiguity in a string, so its control sequence is unnecessary in the *printf*, as shown:

```
printf("This is an apostrophe: ' ");
```

Table 7.2 summarizes the situations in which it is necessary to use the escape sequences or not. When a backslash is followed by a letter or punctuation mark, the character is printed as is.

Table 7.2 How to indicate a quotation mark or apostrophe

	String constant use	Character constant use
Quotation mark	\"	"
Apostrophe	'	\'

Section 7.2 Exercises

1. Using Appendix A, give the ASCII code for the following:

   a. '#'   b. 'R'   c. 'r'   d. ESCAPE   e. space

2. Encode each character string into ASCII.

   a. LISP   b. 3:25 P.M.

3. The contents of a part of memory are given in hexadecimal representation as 52 45 41 44 20 41 5B 36 5D. Assuming we have characters, decode this part of memory using the ASCII encoding scheme.

4. Give the output of the following segment:

   ```
   char ch = '$';
   int n = 119;

   printf("%c %d\n", ch, ch);
   printf("%c %d\n", n, n);
   ```

5. Consider the segment:

   ```
   char op1 = '8',
        op2 = '5';

   printf("%u times %f is %d\n", op1, op2, op1 * op2);
   ```

   It is supposed to print the following:

   ```
   5 times 8 is 40
   ```

   a. Find the errors.

   b. Describe what the segment prints without correction to the errors.

In Exercises 6–8, determine what is printed (or done) by the statements.

6. `printf("\a\a\a\"Stop! Stop!\" they yelled\n);`
7. `printf("\tCost\b\b\b\b_____\tTax\b\b\b___\n");`
8. `printf("Mark out\b\b\b\\\\\\\\\n");`

In Exercises 9–11, write segments to do the following:

9. Print "Ding Dong" 10 times with a bell after each one.
10. Define *char* constant *APOSTROPHE*.
11. With tabs around the equal mark, print

    ```
    f'(x)   =   2x
    ```

Section 7.2 Programming Projects

1. Develop a program that repeatedly asks the user for a digit, reads the digit as a character, and prints the digit squared. Write a function to convert the character digit to a numeric digit. Have it return −1 if the argument is not a character digit.

2. Develop a program to print all the uppercase letters and the codes for those characters.

3. Develop a program that repeatedly reads an integer in the appropriate range and prints the character it encodes. Find out how to clear the screen on your system, through \f or a function call. Clear the screen between requests.

4. In some situations, it is necessary to have text not plainly readable, so it is encrypted. In one encryption scheme, called "Rot-13," each input alphabetic character is "rotated" 13 places in the alphabet. For example, 'A' becomes 'N', 'B' becomes 'O', and so on. Letters in the last half of the alphabet are rotated to fall within the first half of the alphabet, for example 'p' becomes 'c'. Both upper- and lowercase are rotated, but digits, symbols, and other characters are not.

Develop a program to accept lines of text from the user, and output them in Rot-13 format. There will be at most 10 lines of 80 characters entered, and the input is ended by a $ on its own line, or after 10 lines.

Sample Run (input from the user is <u>underlined</u>):

```
Enter lines of text to be encrypted below.   End with a $.
To be, or not to be.   That is the question.
4 score and 7 years ago.
$
Gb or, be abg gb or.  Gung vf gur dhrfgvba.
4 fpber naq 7 lrnef ntb.
```

Section 7.3 **Character Functions**

Changing Case

ANSI C has a number of functions that deal with characters in its standard library. To access these functions, we must link our program with the library and include the *ctype.h* header file, as shown:

```
#include <ctype.h>
```

One function, *tolower*, returns the lowercase letter corresponding to its character argument. If the argument is not an uppercase letter, the function returns the character argument. For example,

```
printf("%c %c %c\n", tolower('H'), tolower('h'), tolower('3'));
```

prints

```
h h 3
```

Similarly, the function *toupper* accepts a lowercase letter argument and returns the corresponding uppercase letter. It sends back all other arguments without change. Thus, the statement

```
printf("%c %c %c\n", toupper('H'), toupper('h'), toupper('3'));
```

produces

```
H H 3
```

Example 7.10

Example 7.7 in the last section presents a program to enable the user to type a character and see its ASCII equivalent. The function *GetAnswer* prompts, "Do you

want to find another ASCII code? (y/n)." Using symbolic constants YES for 'y' and NO for 'n', a *do-while* loop continues asking for values as long as the user does not type a lowercase y or n.

```
do
{
    printf("\nDo you want to find another ASCII code? (y/n) ");
    answer = getchar();
    fflush(stdin);
}
while ( !(answer == YES || answer == NO) );
```

Some users may prefer to use uppercase letters, such as Y and N. The program would be more user friendly if it accepted such responses. To accomplish this, we must expand the boolean expression in the loop test to accommodate the additional choices, as shown:

```
do
    ⋮
while (!(answer == 'y' || answer == 'Y'
        || answer == 'n' || answer == 'N'));
```

With this change, the program continues requesting characters and printing their ASCII code as long as the user types an uppercase or lowercase y. We must also alter the looping condition in *main* to adjust to the added flexibility, as follows:

```
do
{
    printf("Enter a character: ");
    in_char = GetCharNewline();

    printf("The ASCII value of %c is %d.\n", in_char, in_char);
    answer = GetAnswer();
}
while (answer == 'y' || answer == 'Y');
```

With four possible correct answers—'y', 'Y', 'n', 'N'—we abandon the more readable symbolic constants YES and NO.

Another alternative is to convert the answer to a lowercase (or uppercase) letter before we test in the function *GetAnswer.*

```
answer = getchar();
answer = tolower(answer);
```

A more succinct form of this segment applies *tolower* to the value that *getchar* returns before storage in *answer*, as shown:

```
answer = tolower(getchar());
```

With the conversion, we reinstate the original test for only two legal values of *answer*—'y' and 'n'—and use the symbolic constants YES and NO. Moreover, because we return only one of these possible answers, we restore the test in *main* to its original form. The revised program using *tolower* follows:

```
/*
 * Example 7.10. This interactive program repeatedly asks the user for a
 * character and prints its ASCII code.
 */

#include <stdio.h>
#include <ctype.h>

#define YES 'y'
#define NO 'n'

int GetCharNewline(void);
char GetAnswer(void);

main()
{
    char in_char,    /* input character to encode */
         answer;     /* answer to continue? */

    printf("Given a character, this program prints its ASCII code.\n");
    do
    {
        printf("Enter a character: ");
        in_char = GetCharNewline();

        printf("The ASCII value of %c is %d.\n", in_char, in_char);
        answer = GetAnswer();
    }
    while (answer == YES);
}

/*
 * Function to read and return a character and to move the
 * input buffer pointer past the newline character
 * Pre:    none
 * Post:   An input character was returned and the buffer flushed.
 */

int GetCharNewline(void)
{
    char in_char;

    in_char = getchar();
    fflush(stdin);

    return in_char;
}
```

```
/*
 * Function to ask if user wishes to continue and to return
 * the user's response
 * Pre:     none
 * Post:    A y or an n was returned and the buffer flushed.
 */

char GetAnswer(void)
{
    char answer;            /* answer for wanting another code */

    do
    {
        printf("\nDo you want to find another ASCII code? (y/n) ");
        answer = tolower(getchar());
        fflush(stdin);
    }
    while (!(answer == YES || answer == NO));

    return answer;
}
```

Execution reveals the added flexibility and user friendliness of the revised program, as shown in the following output:

```
Given a character, this program prints its ASCII code.
Enter a character: +
The ASCII value of + is 43.

Do you want to find another ASCII code? (y/n) Y
Enter a character: >
The ASCII value of > is 62.

Do you want to find another ASCII code? (y/n) N
```

Example 7.11

It is instructive to write our own version of the function *toupper* without use of the functions described in *ctype.h*. We first determine if the argument is a lowercase letter. Recall from the last section that each character has a numeric code, and C expects us to determine if the value in a variable is a character or an integer. We used this fact to our advantage in that section to obtain a numeric digit from a character digit through subtraction. Similarly, using the numeric codes in *char* variables, we can compare characters using relational operators. If a character is a lowercase letter, its encoded value is between those for 'a' and 'z'. To determine if *char* variable *ch* stores a lowercase letter, we can use the following logical test:

```
if (('a' <= ch) && (ch <= 'z'))...
```

If the character is not in the range, *toupper* returns the character without change.

If the character is in the appropriate range, however, we can obtain an uppercase version using arithmetic similar to that in which we found the numeric equivalent of a character digit. For example, the expression 'c' – 'a' is 2; c is the second lowercase letter after a. Moreover, 2 + 'A' is 'C'; C is the second uppercase letter after A. Putting these expressions together, 'c' – 'a' + 'A' is 'C'. Extending the computation for any lowercase letter, *ch*, we have the following:

```
ch - 'a' + 'A'
```

is the uppercase equivalent of *ch*. Pseudocode code for the function follows:

OurToUpper(ch) ⟶ *c*

Function to return the uppercase equivalent of lowercase letter *ch*. If *ch* is not a lowercase letter, the function returns *ch*.

Pre:

  ch is a character.

Post:

  The uppercase equivalent of *ch* was returned; if *ch* is not a lowercase letter, *ch* was returned.

Algorithm:

  if *ch* is less than 'a' or greater than 'z'
    c ← ch
  else
    c ← ch – 'a' + 'A'
  return *c*

```c
/*
 * Function to return uppercase equivalent of lowercase
 * letter ch. If ch is not a lowercase letter, return ch.
 * Pre:    ch is a character.
 * Post:   The uppercase equivalent of ch was returned.
 *         If ch was not a lowercase letter, ch was returned.
 */

char OurToUpper(char ch)
{
    char c;

    if ((ch < 'a') || ('z' < ch))
        c = ch;
    else
        c = ch - 'a' + 'A';

    return c;
}
```

Boolean Character Functions

Besides *toupper* and *tolower* that return characters, the header file *ctype.h* contains prototypes of a number of boolean functions that determine if a character argument is of a certain class or not. For example, *isdigit* returns *TRUE* (a nonzero integer) if the argument is a character digit and returns *FALSE* (0) otherwise. Thus, *isdigit*('3') is *TRUE*, while *isdigit*('z') is *FALSE*. The function *isspace* returns *TRUE* if the argument is a white space character—space (' '), newline ('\n'), tab ('\t'), form feed ('\f'), carriage return ('\r'), or vertical tab ('\v'). We use both functions in the next example.

Example 7.12

The goal of this example is to write a function that reads a nonnegative integer without a sign, one character at a time, accumulating the number to return. Other than white space, the input line should only contain one integer, such as

```
7459
```

The function skips over initial and trailing white space. Moreover, it verifies that no nondigit characters are embedded in the number and that only one value appears on the line. The following entries are invalid:

```
74r9
7459     944
```

If the line contains an invalid nonnegative integer or if a character other than white space follows the integer, the function prints a descriptive error message and returns −1 as an error code. The function also flushes the input buffer. Thus, we are writing a specialized function for reading a nonnegative integer that has better diagnostics than the more general *scanf*.

The function *main* is only a driver for this reading function, *GetNonnegative*. Certainly, we could place the call to *GetNonnegative* in a loop, but we choose to call the function only once.

---

main( )

  Program to read a nonnegative integer (without +) one character at a time and to print the integer or an error message

Algorithm:

  prompt for one nonnegative integer, *nonneg_int*
  nonneg_int ← *GetNonnegative*()
  if *nonneg_int* is negative
      print an error message
  else
      print *nonneg_int*

In *GetNonnegative*, we skip over any initial white space (such as blanks and newlines) by continuing to read a character *ch* as long as it is a white space character. We can accomplish this task with the following *while* loop:

```
ch = getchar();
while (isspace(ch))
    ch = getchar();
```

The character read by *getchar* is placed in the variable *ch*. The function *isspace* determines if this character is a white space character or not. If *isspace* returns *TRUE*, then *ch* obtains another character and the process continues.*

When this loop stops, *ch* should contain the first digit of the number, and we can start accumulating the integer in a variable *nonneg_int*. We initialize *nonneg_int* to be 0 and a boolean loop variable, *InputOK*, to be *TRUE*. If the computer reads a nondigit character in the subsequent loop, it prints an error message, changes the value of *InputOK* to *FALSE*, and stops the loop. Looping continues as long as *ch* is not a white space character and *InputOK* is *TRUE*.

Within the loop, we use *isdigit* to check if *ch* is a digit or not. If it is, we obtain *ch*'s number equivalent with *ch* − '0' and add the result to 10 times *nonneg_int*.

```
nonneg_int = nonneg_int * 10 + ch - '0';
```

The variable *nonneg_int* stores the developing integer. Each new character represents the units digit, while the previous value of *nonneg_int* contains the digits to its left. The following iteration illustrates the accumulation of the characters '7', '2', and '4' into the number 724:

ch	*nonneg_int*
	0
7	0 * 10 + 7 = 7
2	7 * 10 + 2 = 70 + 2 = 72
4	72 * 10 + 4 = 720 + 4 = 724

If this loop to accumulate the number terminates normally, *ch* contains a white space character, and *InputOK* is still *TRUE*. Even with valid input so far, we must verify that no other values are on the line. Simultaneously, for valid input data, we are moving the input buffer pointer past the newline character. We continue looping as long as the character read, *ch*, is not the newline character and *InputOK* remains *TRUE*. If the program detects any nonwhite space characters, it changes *InputOK* to *FALSE* and stops looping.

Two error situations can cause the computer to change the value of *InputOK* to *FALSE:*

1. Nondigits are embedded in the input number. This error is detected by the accumulating loop.

2. Nonwhite space characters appear after the number. This error is detected by the loop that processes trailing characters.

After all the looping, if *InputOK* is *FALSE*, the program assigns the error value of -1 to *nonneg_int* and flushes the input buffer. If all goes well in the loop to process trailing characters, *InputOK* is still *TRUE*, the input buffer is empty, and *nonneg_int* has the correct value. The pseudocode for this function and the code for the program follow:

---

*Some programmers prefer a more succinct way of skipping over white space that uses an empty *while* loop body.

```
while (isspace(ch = getchar()));
```

GetNonnegative( ) ⟶ *nonneg_int*

Function to read characters, verifying that they are digits, and to accumulate the digits into a nonnegative integer. The input line should contain only one number and no sign. It returns the nonnegative integer or, in the case of an error, −1

Pre:

Post:

A nonnegative integer was returned, or in the case of an error, −1 was returned.

Algorithm:

read past opening white space, so *ch* contains first nonwhite space character
nonneg_int ← 0
InputOK ← *TRUE*
while in the number do the following:
   if *ch* is a digit
     nonneg_int ← *nonneg_int* * 10 + *ch* − '0'
     ch ← *getchar*()
   else
     print an error message
     InputOK ← *FALSE*
if a valid number was read
   while not at the end of the line and *InputOK* is *TRUE*:
     if *ch* is a white space character
       ch ← *getchar*()
     else
       print an error message
       InputOK ← *FALSE*
if an error was detected
   nonneg_int ← −1
   flush the input buffer
return *nonneg_int*

```
/*
 * Example 7.12
 * Program to read a nonnegative integer one character at a
 * time and to print the integer or an error message
 */

#include <stdio.h>
#include <ctype.h>

int GetNonnegative(void);

#define NEWLINE '\n'
#define TRUE 1
#define FALSE 0
```

```
main()
{
    int nonneg_int;            /* nonnegative integer user enters */

    printf("Enter a nonnegative integer and press return.\n");
    printf("Do not use a sign and only type digits.\n\n");
    printf("Your nonnegative integer: ");
    nonneg_int = GetNonnegative();
    if (nonneg_int < 0)
        printf("\nSorry, input line is invalid.\n");
    else
        printf("\nYour nonnegative integer is %d.\n", nonneg_int);
}


/*
 * Function to read characters, verifying that they are
 * digits, and to accumulate the digits into a nonnegative
 * integer.
 * Pre:    none
 * Post:   A nonnegative integer was returned, or in the case
 *         of an error, -1 was returned.
 */

int GetNonnegative(void)
{
    int nonneg_int,        /* nonnegative integer user enters */
        InputOK;           /* boolean value for continuing loop */
    char ch;               /* character input from user */

    /* skip over white space at beginning of line */
    ch = getchar();
    while (isspace(ch))
        ch = getchar();

    /* Verify each character input is a digit and accumulate */
    nonneg_int = 0;
    InputOK = TRUE;

    while (!isspace(ch) && InputOK)
    {
        if (isdigit(ch))  /* in number, accumulate and cont. */
        {
            nonneg_int = nonneg_int * 10 + ch - '0';
            ch = getchar();
        }
        else                 /* Error: character not a digit */
        {
            printf("\%c is not a digit.", ch);
            InputOK = FALSE;
        }
    }
```

```
    /* Number valid. Make sure nothing else on line. */
    if (InputOK)
        while (ch != NEWLINE && InputOK)
        {
            if (isspace(ch))
                ch = getchar();
            else                /* Error: additional values on line */
            {
                printf("\Have only one integer per line.\");
                InputOK = FALSE;
            }
        }

    /* Error detected.  Last processed character not NEWLINE */
    if (!InputOK)
    {
        nonneg_int = -1;
        fflush(stdin);
    }

    return nonneg_int;
}
```

Several runs of the program demonstrate its capabilities. The following execution shows valid input data:

```
Enter a nonnegative integer and press return.
Do not use a sign and only type digits.

Your nonnegative integer: 5839

Your nonnegative integer is 5839.
```

In the following execution, the user enters a floating point number in error:

```
Enter a nonnegative integer and press return.
Do not use a sign and only type digits.

Your nonnegative integer: 728.3

. is not a digit.
Sorry, input line is invalid.
```

Although *GetNonnegative* checks for invalid nonnegative integers, the function does not inspect for overflow. Nothing prevents the accumulator *nonneg_int* from exceeding *INT_MAX*. One alternative is to declare this accumulator to be of type *float*. Immediately after assigning a value to *nonneg_int*, we check if the value is greater than the integer *INT_MAX*. If so, the program prints an overflow message and assigns *FALSE* to *InputOK*. We should cast *nonneg_int* to *int* for the return value of the function *GetNonnegative*. One of the exercises in this section explores this enhancement to the function.

Instead of using *GetNonnegative*, suppose we use a *scanf* to read the data item, as shown:

```
scanf("%d", &nonneg_int);
```

A *scanf* of the value 728.3 would report no error and would assign 728 to *nonneg_int*. Similarly, our program reports an error with an input value of 90e5, as shown below. Either the user was trying to enter a floating point number in exponential notation, or the person hit the e key by mistake. A *scanf* does not detect the problem and places the number before the e, 90, into *nonneg_int*.

```
Enter a nonnegative integer and press return.
Do not use a sign and only type digits.

Your nonnegative integer: 90e5

e is not a digit.
Sorry, input line is invalid.
```

The input below shows an example of the user mistakenly entering two numbers. Perhaps he or she pressed the space bar by mistake or anticipated a future request for data. The *scanf* function would process the first number (843) and leave the input buffer pointer indicating the blank, while *GetNonnegative* alerts the user to the problem and flushes the buffer.

```
Enter a nonnegative integer and press return.
Do not use a sign and only type digits.

Your nonnegative integer: 843 42

Have only one integer per line.

Sorry, input line is invalid.
```

The last example used *ctype.h* functions *isspace* and *isdigit*. Table 7.3 lists other boolean functions.

Table 7.3 Boolean functions in *ctype.h*

Function	returns *TRUE* ($\neq$ 0) if argument is a(an)
isalnum	letter or digit
isalpha	letter
iscntrl	control character
isdigit	decimal digit
isgraph	printable character, but not white space
islower	lowercase letter
isprint	printable character, including blank
ispunct	printable character other than letter, digit, or white space
isspace	space, newline, tab, form feed, carriage return, vertical tab
isupper	uppercase letter
isxdigit	hexadecimal digit

Section 7.3 Exercises

1. What is printed by the following segment?

```
char littleb = 'b',
     bigB = 'B',
     apostrophe = '\'';
int  n1 = 77,
     n2 = 33;

putchar(toupper(littleb));
if (isalpha(bigB))
   putchar(apostrophe);
if (ispunct(n2))
   putchar(n2);
if (isalpha(n1))
   putchar(bigB);
```

2. Write a segment to read a line, one character at a time, and to print the line with uppercase letters printed as lowercase, and vice versa.

3. Write your own version of the function *tolower*, which is similar to the function in Example 7.11.

4. Change Example 7.12 so that it reads a number one character at a time, skipping over a leading dollar sign and commas within the number.

Write your own versions of the functions in Exercises 5–8.

    5. *isdigit*   **6.** *islower*   **7.** *isalpha*   **8.** *isspace*

9. As described after the program in Example 7.12, have *GetNonnegative* check for integer overflow.

Section 7.3 Programming Projects

1. Develop a program to display all printable characters and their codes from 0 through 127.

2. Develop a program to count each of the following: digits, letters, uppercase letters, lowercase letters, white space characters, and punctuation on an input line.

3. Develop a program that repeatedly reads a nonnegative binary integer one character at a time and converts the number to a decimal integer (see Section 2.4).

4. Develop a program that repeatedly reads a line and prints whether the sequence of characters on a line is in the date format *mm/dd/yy* or not. The month, day, and year should be two digits and should be appropriate ranges. For example, 04/03/97 is a proper date; 4/3/97 is not in the appropriate format; and 02/30/97 is not a proper date because February cannot have 30 days.

5. Develop a program to count the number of words on a line. Consider a word to be a sequence of letters. Ignore all other characters.

6. Develop a program that repeatedly asks for a sentence with a return at the end and prints the sentence without numbers and punctuation marks.

7. Convert the program in Example 7.12 to handle a sign in front of the number.

8. Convert the program in Example 7.12 to handle a floating point number. Make sure the number contains exactly one decimal point.

9. Develop a program to read lines until the user enters the EOF character. Reprint each line in title-case, with the first character in each word in uppercase and all other characters in lowercase.

10. Write a program to find all possible ways in which the ten distinct letters B, L, A, C, K, W, H, I, T, E can be replaced by the digits 0, 1, 2, 3, 4, 5, 6, 7, 8, 9, so as to make the equation

   BLACK * 7 = WHITE

   true. Numbers are allowed to have a leading zero. For example, one solution would be

   BLACK = 05418
   WHITE = 37926 (05418 * 7 = 37926)

   There is one stipulation: The program must be able to solve the problem in less than five minutes. Hint: You can narrow down the search by first asking what the smallest possible value and the largest possible value of BLACK could be.

Section 7.4 Breadth: Octal and Hexadecimal Number Systems

The long strings of bits in the binary number system of the computer are difficult for people to read. Imagine writing programs with only zeros and ones in the days before high-level languages! To keep insanity from setting in, we use the octal and hexadecimal number representations as abbreviations.

Conversion to Decimal Numbers

Example 2.11 of Section 2.4 presented the binary representations for decimal numbers 0–20. We saw that we can represent 16 numbers in 4 bits, from 0 to $1111_2 = 2^4 - 1 = 15_{10}$. In the binary or base 2 system, we have 2 digits—0 and 1. The decimal or base 10 system has 10 digits—0 through 9. Similarly, the **octal** or **base 8 system** has 8 octal digits,—0 through 7—whereas in the **hexadecimal** or **base 16 system**, we must use new symbols to arrive at the 16 hexadecimal (**hex**) digits—0, 1, 2, 3, 4, 5, 6, 7, 8, 9, A, B, C, D, E, F. Conversion from hexadecimal or octal to decimal involves the same procedure as conversion from binary to decimal, except the expansion is in powers of the base (16 or 8) instead of powers of 2.

Definitions   The **octal** or **base 8 system** has 8 octal digits—0 through 7. The **hexadecimal** or **base 16 system** has 16 hexadecimal (**hex**) digits—0, 1, 2, 3, 4, 5, 6, 7, 8, 9, A, B, C, D, E, F.

Example 7.13

To express F5C.4A with the equivalent decimal number, we must convert the hexadecimal digits to decimal numbers (A $\rightarrow$ 10, B $\rightarrow$ 11, C $\rightarrow$ 12, D $\rightarrow$ 13, E $\rightarrow$ 14, F $\rightarrow$ 15) as well as expand the expression. Thus,

$$F5C.4A = 15 \cdot 16^2 + 5 \cdot 16^1 + 12 \cdot 16^0 + 4 \cdot 16^{-1} + 10 \cdot 16^{-2}$$
$$= 15 \cdot 256 + 5 \cdot 16 + 12 \cdot 1 + 4/16 + 10/256 = 3932.2890625$$

We also count in a similar manner as we do in the decimal and binary number systems, incrementing by 1. When we run out of digits in the rightmost position, we put a 0 there and increment the number to the left. Thus, the number after F is $10_{16} = 16_{10}$. Decrementing in base 16 proceeds as presented in Algorithm 2.1 of Section 2.4.

Example 7.14

We count from 14_{10} to 33_{10} in base 16 as follows:

Dec.	Hex.	Dec.	Hex.	Dec.	Hex.	Dec.	Hex.
14	E	19	13	24	18	29	1D
15	F	20	14	25	19	30	1E
16	10	21	15	26	1A	31	1F
17	11	22	16	27	1B	32	20
18	12	23	17	28	1C	33	21

Example 7.15

The largest unsigned integer that can be expressed in two hexadecimal digits is

$$FF_{16} = 100_{16} - 1 = 16^2 - 1 = 255_{10}$$

The octal number 377_8 is also 255_{10}, as shown:

$$377_8 = 3 \cdot 8^2 + 7 \cdot 8^1 + 7 \cdot 8^0 = 3 \cdot 64 + 7 \cdot 8 + 7 = 255_{10}$$

Conversion Between Binary and Hexadecimal Number Systems

We have seen that a hexadecimal digit can represent a group of 4 binary digits, or bits. A complete conversion to hexadecimal consists of splitting the binary number into groups of 4 bits, starting from the binary point and padding with zeros if necessary, and expressing each set in hexadecimal. For example, $1011100.101 = 0101\ 1100.1010 = 5C.A$, because $0101_2 = 4 + 1 = 5_{10} = 5_{16}$; $1100_2 = 8 + 4 = 12_{10} = C_{16}$; and $1010_2 = 8 + 2 = 10_{10} = A_{16}$. Let us examine the following expansion of this number more closely:

$$01011100.1010 = 1{\cdot}2^6 + 1{\cdot}2^4 + (1{\cdot}2^3 + 1{\cdot}2^2) + 1{\cdot}2^{-1} + 1{\cdot}2^{-3}$$
$$= 2^2{\cdot}2^4 + 1{\cdot}2^4 + (8 + 4) + 2^{-1}{\cdot}2^4{\cdot}2^{-4} + 2^{-3}{\cdot}2^4{\cdot}2^{-4}$$
$$= (2^2 + 1)2^4 + 12 + (2^3 + 2^1)2^{-4}$$
$$= (4 + 1)16 + 12 + (8 + 2)\ 1/16$$
$$= 5{\cdot}16 + 12 + 10{\cdot}16^{-1} = 5C.A_{16}$$

Example 7.16

Remembering to group from the binary point, we express the binary number 1101110.1 in hexadecimal as follows:

$110\ 1110.1000 = 6E.8_{16}$ because $1110 = 8 + 4 + 2 = 14_{10} = E_{16}$

Example 7.17

Conversion from hexadecimal to binary notation is just as easy. We simply express each hexadecimal digit in 4 bits. Because $F = 15_{10}$, $D = 13_{10}$, and $C = 12_{10}$

$F8D47.C = 1111\ 1000\ 1101\ 0100\ 0111.1100$

Constants and Conversion Specifications in C

In Section 7.2, we presented forms of the escape sequence that use octal and hexadecimal numbers. Referring to the Appendix A ASCII code table, in C we represent the lowercase character 'z', which has ASCII decimal value 122, with the octal escape sequence '\172' or the hexadecimal escape sequence '\x7A'. Thus, each of the following displays the letter z:

```
putchar('z');
printf("z");
printf("%c", 122);
putchar('\172');
putchar('\x7A');
```

A variable of type *char* can take on 256 possible values, from 0 to 255 (or −128 to 127). As Example 7.15 shows, we only need three octal or two hexadecimal digits for an escape sequence.

The C compiler assumes that a number beginning with one of the digits 1 through 9 is in decimal (base 10). To indicate an octal constant in a program, the number begins with a **leading 0**, as shown:

```
int base8 = 0172;
```

A number beginning with **0x** or **0X** (a zero and a lowercase or an uppercase letter x) is in base 16, as shown:

```
int base16 = 0x7A;
```

Hex digits may be either uppercase (A–F) or lowercase (a–f). The conversion specification for an octal integer is %o, and the specification for a hexadecimal integer is %x for lowercase and %X for uppercase.

Example 7.18

The program in this example stores in variables the ASCII code for 'z' in bases 8 (172_8), 10 (122_{10}), and 16 ($7A_{16}$). To assign 172_8 to a variable, we must precede the number with a zero. For $7A_{16}$, we use 0x7a or 0x7A. After the three assignments, we print each variable with four conversion specifications—%o, %d, %x, and %X.

```c
/*
 * Program to assign & print decimal, octal, and hex numbers
 */

#include <stdio.h>

main()
{
    int base8  = 0172,      /* octal number */
        base10 = 122,       /* decimal number */
        base16 = 0x7a;      /* hexadecimal number */

    printf("ASCII code for 'z' in bases 8, 10, and 16\n\n");
    printf("Printed with conversion specifications:\n");
    printf("Number\t %%o \t %%d \t %%x \t %%X \n\n");

    printf(" 0172\t %o \t %d \t %x \t %X\n",
            base8, base8, base8, base8);
    printf(" 122\t %o \t %d \t %x \t %X\",
            base10, base10, base10, base10);
    printf(" 0x7a\t %o \t %d \t %x \t %X\n",
            base16, base16, base16, base16);
}
```

Output follows:

```
ASCII code for 'z' in bases 8, 10, and 16

Printed with conversion specifications:
Number    %o        %d        %x        %X

    0172      172       122       7a        7A
     122      172       122       7a        7A
    0x7a      172       122       7a        7A
```

The numbers in the assignment statements indicate their bases. The declaration-initialization of *base10* has a typical assignment of a decimal number to a variable. The leading zero in the number 0172 indicates an octal number in the first assignment.

The 0x prefix in the third assignment indicates a hexadecimal number. In an assignment, the representation for the number has nothing to do with the type of the variable. The variables *base8*, *base10*, and *base16* are all of type *int*.

Although the three representations appear quite different, the computer stores them as identical binary (base 2) numbers (111 1010). The equivalence of all three representations is demonstrated when the values of the three variables are printed in octal notation, then in decimal, and finally in hex. Each column displays the same output, because all three variables contain the same number, and the program displays them with identical conversion specifications. Although the program must contain the appropriate prefixes for the different bases, the computer does not print the 0 (for octal) and 0x or 0X (for hex) before the numbers.

Example 7.19

This program demonstrates how to read octal and hexadecimal integers. Like *printf*, the *scanf* function uses %o for an octal integer and %x for hex.

```
/* Program to read and print decimal, octal, and hex integers */

#include <stdio.h>

main()
{
    int num;

    printf("Enter an integer. in decimal: ");
    scanf("%d", &num);
    printf("You entered %d\n", num);

    printf("\nEnter an integer in octal. ");
    scanf("%o", &num);
    printf("You entered %o, or %d in decimal\n", num, num);

    printf("\nEnter an integer in hex: ");
    scanf("%x", &num);
    printf("You entered %x, or %d in decimal\n", num, num);
}
```

The interactive session requires that the user enter numbers in three bases, as shown:

```
Enter an integer in decimal: 27
You entered 27

Enter an integer in octal: 33
You entered 33, or 27 in decimal

Enter an integer in hex: 1B
You entered 1b, or 27 in decimal
```

We need not enter the octal value with a leading 0 or the hex value with 0x, because the conversion specification determines how to interpret the input digits. Even though the user entered the hex integer with an uppercase letter, the number prints in lowercase. The *scanf* function permits the user to type the digits A through F of a hex integer in uppercase or lowercase. However, the %x conversion specification always prints them in lowercase, whereas %X produces uppercase.

The computer only accepts input digits that are legal for the particular base. For example, *scanf* receives the letter b as part of a hexadecimal integer, but only understands the digits 0–7 for an octal integer. Conversion stops when an input character does not match the specification.

Applications   As mentioned at the beginning of this section, hexadecimal numbers are used extensively as an abbreviation for binary numbers. For example, a **memory dump**, or printout of the contents of an area of memory, from an aborted program is displayed in hexadecimal as opposed to binary. A table indicating how characters are encoded in a computer, such as ASCII, is generally written in hexadecimal and decimal. A knowledge of the hexadecimal system is essential for an understanding of programming and debugging in assembler language, which we consider in Chapter 12.

Definition   A **memory dump** is a printout of the contents of an area of memory.

Example 7.20

By looking up each character in the ASCII conversion table in Appendix A, we can write in hexadecimal notation the name "UNIVAC 1" as follows:

55 4E 49 56 41 43 20 31

Notice that blank is a character as well as '1' in this case. Actual storage in the computer is in base 2, which is much more difficult for people to read and interpret:

0101 0101 0100 1110 0100 1001 0101 0110 0100 0001 0100 0011 0010 0000 0011 0001

The assembler language of the CRAY supercomputer uses the base 8, or octal number system, to abbreviate binary numbers. Emanuel Swedberg proposed in the early 1700s that Sweden change from the decimal to the octal system for arithmetic, weights, and measures. King Charles XII was won over to the idea of a number system based on some power of 2. They even considered base 64, but rejected the idea because this system requires 64 different digits. A cannon ball killed the king before Sweden could convert to the octal system.

In the UNIX operating system, which we consider in greater detail in Section 12.4, we can assign read (r), write (w), and execute (x) permission on each file for the owner, for his or her group, and for all others. Nine on/off switches exist, with a 1 bit indicating that the user grants permission to use the corresponding resource. With the following format:

rwx	**rwx**	**rwx**
owner	group	public

King Charles XII

111101100_2 or 754_8 indicates rwxr-xr--. Everyone has permission to read the file; both the owner and group can execute; but only the owner can write to the file. To change a file (*myfile*) to have this protection, we could use the following change mode command:

```
chmod  754  myfile
```

Conversion of Decimal Numbers to Hexadecimal

In Sections 2.4, 2.5, and 4.2, we covered algorithms for the conversion of decimal numbers to binary. For the integer part, we repeatedly divide by 2, taking the remainders in reverse order. For the fractional part, we repeatedly multiply by 2, taking the integral parts in order. For conversion from base 10 to base 8 or 16, we just change the base 2 of the algorithm to the appropriate base. From base 10 to base 16, however, we must be careful to express the digits in the hexadecimal number system.

Example 7.21

We start converting the decimal number 64,462.75 to hexadecimal by separating the number into the integer and fractional parts. For the integer part, we repeatedly divide by the base, 16, as follows:

```
16 | 64462
   |  4028    14
   |   251    12
   |    15    11
   |     0    15
```

Because $15_{10} = F$, $11_{10} = B$, $12_{10} = C$, and $14_{10} = E$, $64,462_{10} = FBCE_{16}$.

Continuing in a similar manner to Example 4.6, to convert 0.75 to hexadecimal, we have $0.75 \cdot 16 = 12$, so $0.75_{10} = 0.C_{16}$. The final answer is $FBCE.C_{16}$.

We check our answer as follows:

$$FBCE.C = 15 \cdot 16^3 + 11 \cdot 16^2 + 12 \cdot 16 + 14 + 12 \cdot 16^{-1}$$
$$= 15 \cdot 4096 + 11 \cdot 256 + 12 \cdot 16 + 14 + 12/16$$
$$= 64,462.75$$

Section 7.4 Exercises

Express the hexadecimal numbers of Exercises 1–6 in decimal notation.

1. E2　　　**2.** 987　　　**3.** FFF
4. A.4　　　**5** CD.D3　　　**6.** 4E.8

7. Express the hexadecimal numbers from Exercises 1–6 in binary notation.

Express the octal numbers in Exercises 8–10 with decimal representation.

8. 25　　**9.** 604　　**10.** 7136

Start with the hexadecimal numbers in Exercises 11–13 and give the next 4 hexadecimal integers in order.

11. B8　　**12.** FD　　**13.** FFF

Start with the octal numbers in Exercises 14–16 and give the next 4 octal integers in order.

14. 6　　**15.** 37　　**16.** 7704

17. Increment by 1 each hexadecimal number.

   a. 9999　　**b.** 60BF

18. Increment by 1 each octal number.

   a. 777　　**b.** 7577

19. Give the largest unsigned hexadecimal number, written in hexadecimal and decimal notation, that can be expressed in

   a. 3 hexadecimal digits　　**b.** 4 hexadecimal digits

Express each binary number in Exercises 20–22 as a hexadecimal number.

20. 1001.0011　　**21.** 1100.11　　**22.** 100000.00111

23. Write a declaration-initialization statement in C that

   a. Assigns the octal number 64 to variable *oct*

   b. Assigns the hexadecimal number 64 to variable *hex*

24. **a.** Write a statement to print *oct* and *hex* of the last exercise.

   b. What is the output?

25. **a.** Write a statement to read values in base 8 for *oct* and in base 16 for *hex*.

   b. Suppose the user wishes the octal integer to be 4253 and the hexadecimal to be 3AC. What is the format of the input?

26. Suppose a computer works with 8 bits in a byte and 4 bytes in a word.

   a. How many hexadecimal digits are there in a byte?

   b. How many hexadecimal digits are there in a word?

   c. In how many bytes can 6 hexadecimal digits be expressed?

Express the decimal numbers of Exercises 27–32 in hexadecimal notation.

27. 24　　　　**28.** 33　　　　**29.** 125
30. 0.28125　　**31.** 186.4　　**32.** 2692.625

Express the decimal numbers of Exercises 33–35 with octal representation.

33. 13　　**34.** 33　　**35.** 3038

36. Give the largest octal number, written in octal and decimal notation, that can be expressed in 4 octal digits.

37. Write a change mode UNIX command to provide the following permissions:

   a. rwx--x---   **b.** r-x--xr--

Section 7.5 **A Brief Introduction to Files**

We have obtained data by assignments or by reading interactively and have presented information on the screen or printer. We can easily store and retrieve large amounts of data in a file on disk. In this section, we introduce basic manipulation of text files. In Chapter 14, we discuss this material in detail.

A **text file** is a file of characters. We can create and look at such a file with a text editor or word processor. Header files and source files for programs are examples of text files. The header file *stdio.h* defines a new data type, *FILE*. (Chapter 11 describes how to define new data types in C.) The word *FILE* must always be in capitals.

Definition   A **text file** is a file of characters.

The data type *FILE* describes various features of a file. Each file used by a program must have an associated **file pointer**. The pointer is an identifier that holds an address, in this case, the address of the file information. A file pointer has type *FILE **. In Chapter 9, we explain the asterisk notation, but for now, we use the syntax as a requirement of C. The header file *stdio.h* defines *stdin* (standard input) and *stdout* (standard output), which are constants of type *FILE **. Suppose a program employs user-defined input and output files. We can declare pointers to these files, *infile_ptr* and *outfile_ptr*, as follows:

```
FILE *infile_ptr,
     *outfile_ptr;
```

Opening a File

Before a program can read from or write to a file, the program must **open** the file. This process establishes a connection between the file and the program dictated by the requirements of the operating system and the C library functions. Once we open the file, the program can perform input/output (I/O) processes on the file. In C, the *fopen* (file open) function opens a file and returns a *FILE* pointer, which all I/O functions that operate on the file must access.

The *fopen* function requires two arguments, both strings, which may be literals or variables. The first string is the name of the file that the program is to open. The second string specifies the file's **mode**, which determines how to operate upon the file. The two most common mode strings are "r" and "w", which stand for read and write, respectively. Suppose the input file is disk file *price.dat*, and the output disk file is *tax.dat*. We can open the former for reading and the latter for writing as follows:

```
infile_ptr  = fopen("price.dat", "r");
outfile_ptr = fopen("tax.dat", "w");
```

The program uses the name of the file on disk (like *price.dat*) in the *fopen* statement. From then on, the program references the file through its pointer (*infile_ptr*).

Once the program executes correctly, the file *tax.dat* exists on disk. If necessary, we can use it as an input file for another program. Another method of creating an input text file like *price.dat* is with a text editor. We can write a text file in the same way we write the source code for a program. We can use an editor to enter the file. We type the data for *price.dat* perhaps down the page or separated by blanks, and save the file.

For program execution, an open disk file in mode r must already exist, because something to read must exist. If the file is not there, *fopen* returns a special constant, *NULL*. We should verify that the computer successfully opened the file before continuing, or unpredictable results can occur. We start verification with the following:*

```
if (infile_ptr == NULL)...
```

If the file does not open, the program should print an error message and terminate. The standard library function *exit* aborts the program and returns its argument to the operating system. Because the function's prototype is in *stdlib.h*, we should include that header file and link to the library, as follows:

```
#include <stdlib.h>
```

An argument of 1 for *exit*, as shown,

```
exit(1);    /* abnormal program termination */
```

indicates an abnormal end to the program. Thus, a complete *if* statement to check if the file opens properly is as follows:

```
if (infile_ptr == NULL)
{
    printf("price.dat does not exist.\n");
    exit(1);
}
```

One rule of structured programming is to have only one exit from a function. An exit from the program under conditions that make it impossible to continue is one exception to this rule. We can engineer a **soft crash** of the program—in other words, an execution-time error occurs, but the program prints a descriptive error message and ends. With a **hard crash**, the computer detects a serious error, perhaps well past where the error occurs. Program execution terminates with a potentially misleading or cryptic error message. Particularly after opening a file for reading, we should check that the file exists and stop execution if it does not.

Definition With a **soft crash** of a program, an execution-time error occurs. The program prints a descriptive error message and ends. With a **hard crash**, the computer detects a serious error, perhaps well past where the error occurs. Program execution terminates with a potentially misleading or cryptic error message.

If we open a disk file with mode w, either the file must already exist or it must be possible to create the file. If the file already exists, opening in mode w erases its former contents. Otherwise, opening creates the file. If for some reason the computer cannot create the file, *fopen* returns *NULL*. In Chapter 14, we discuss several other modes with which to open the file.

NULL is treated as *FALSE* in conditions. Thus, an equivalent verification is

```
if (!infile_ptr)...
```

Closing a File

We use the function *fclose* (file close) to close a file when the program is to perform no further I/O on it. The computer closes all files automatically when a program terminates, so if a programmer forgets to close a file, no harm occurs. However, there is a restriction on how many files can be open at any one time. Because we can reach this limit in a large program, we should close files when the program no longer needs them. Closing is an indication that we require no further I/O on those files. The parameter to *fclose* is the file pointer representing the file (the value that *fopen* returns). For example, we can close the above files as follows:

```
fclose(infile_ptr);
fclose(outfile_ptr);
```

A pointer to a closed file cannot be an argument to *fclose*.

File I/O

The library function *fprintf* (file *printf*) behaves almost the same as *printf*. However, it sends its output to a specified file, rather than to the standard output. The parameters to this function are the same as for *printf*, except for one additional parameter—the *FILE* pointer associated with its output file. This parameter appears immediately before the control string. Thus, we can write the formatted value of a variable *price* and an expression to the output file as follows:

```
fprintf(outfile_ptr, "For price = $%.2f, tax = $%.2f\n",
                price, price * TAX_RATE);
```

After execution, we can use the text editor or a word processor to view the output file that the program identified as *tax.dat*. If the value of *price* is 89.45, execution of the above call to *fprintf* produces the following:

```
For price = $89.45, tax = $4.47
```

This line is exactly what we would see on the screen with the following *printf*:

```
printf("For price = $%.2f, tax = $%.2f\n",
                price, price * TAX_RATE);
```

The header file *stdio.h* also declares a file reading function, *fscanf*, which takes input from the file specified by a *FILE* pointer as the first parameter. Thus, to read a *float* value from the input file to which *infile_ptr* points and to store that value in *price*, we write

```
fscanf(infile_ptr, "%f", &price);
```

As with *scanf*, we must include the ampersand with the variable name (*price*). Both *scanf* and *fscanf* return the number of items read and stored in variables. If either function cannot read because it encounters the end of the file or an error, then it returns *EOF*.

We often want the computer to read and process data from an input file sequentially until encountering the end of the file. We can use the standard library function *feof*, which indicates the existence of additional data in the file or not. With an argument of a pointer to a file, *feof* returns a nonnegative integer (*TRUE*) after an attempt to read past the end of the file. If more data are in the file, *feof* returns zero (*FALSE*). Thus, for

```
if (feof(infile_ptr))...
```

the computer executes the body of the *if* statement with the EOF for the corresponding input file.

Usually, for continuous processing of a file we employ a *while* statement. Within the *while* condition, we read data and test for the proper amount of input, such as the following segment to read two integers:

```
while (fscanf(infile_ptr, "%d %d", &id, &quantity) == 2)
{
    ⋮
}
```

As long as the computer can read values for *id* and *quantity*, the loop continues. With any attempt to read past the end of the file, *fscanf* returns *EOF* (−1), which is not 2, so the loop terminates. Moreover, for invalid data in the file, such as the following:

34 **xxx**

fscanf returns 1 or 0, and the loop terminates. If we do not check for the reason the loop ends, we do not know if the cause is EOF or invalid data. Thus, after the loop, we use an *if* statement to print an error message if *feof* does not return *TRUE*, as shown:

```
if  (!feof(infile_ptr))
        printf("There was an error reading the file.\n");
```

Example 7.22 _____

This example brings together all the pieces of reading from an input file and writing to an output file. The input file contains a list of prices. The output file should contain those prices and a 5% tax. The program's header comment should document that *price.dat* is the input file and *tax.dat* is the output file. The program follows:

```
/*
 * Program to read a file of prices and to write a file of
 * prices with tax
 *        Input file:    price.dat
 *        Output file:   tax.dat
 */

#include <stdio.h>
#include <stdlib.h>

#define TAX_RATE 0.05

main()
{
    FILE *infile_ptr,    /* pointer to input file */
         *outfile_ptr;   /* pointer to output file */
    float price;

    /* open the files */
    infile_ptr = fopen("price.dat", "r");
    if (infile_ptr == NULL)
    {
        printf("price.dat does not exist.\n");
        exit(1);
    }
```

```
outfile_ptr = fopen("tax.dat", "w");
if (outfile_ptr == NULL)
{
    printf("cannot write to tax.dat.\n");
    exit(1);
}

/* read from input file, calculate, write to output file */
while (fscanf(infile_ptr, "%f", &price) == 1)
{
    fprintf(outfile_ptr, "For price = $%6.2f, tax = $%5.2f\n",
            price, price * TAX_RATE);
}

if (!feof(infile_ptr))
    printf("There was an error reading the file. \n");

fclose(infile_ptr);
fclose(outfile_ptr);
}
```

Suppose before program execution, we created the text file *price.dat* as follows:

```
89.45
298.00
36.95
766.66
```

After program execution with this input file, we can open the output file *tax.dat* to view the following results:

```
For price = $ 89.45, tax = $ 4.47
For price = $298.00, tax = $14.90
For price = $ 36.95, tax = $ 1.85
For price = $766.66, tax = $38.33
```

This file contains exactly the output that repeated execution of the following call to *printf* would yield:

```
printf("For price = $%.2f, tax = $%.2f\n",
        price, price * TAX_RATE);
```

Sometimes, the programmer wishes to see some output on the screen while sending information to a file or files. We can *printf* values to the screen as we *fprintf* that information to a file.

Character I/O with Files

Besides the general file I/O functions *fscanf* and *fprintf*, specialized macros exist for character input from and output to files. The macro **getc**, which is analogous to *getchar*, reads the next character from an input file. Its one argument is a *FILE* pointer representing this file. Thus, the following segment

```
ch = getc(infile_ptr);
```

stores the next character from the file into the variable *ch*. Like *fscanf*, if no more characters are in the file or if a reading error occurs, then *getc* returns *EOF*. Sometimes we must examine the next character to realize that it should not be part of the present processing. In this case, we may want to return the character to the input stream and read it at a later time. The macro **ungetc** returns the first argument, a character, to the stream that is the second argument. Thus,

```
ungetc(ch, infile_ptr);
```

makes *ch* the next character available from the file to which *infile_ptr* points.

The header file *stdio.h* also defines the file character writing macro **putc**, which is analogous to *putchar*. However, a second argument is a *FILE* pointer. Therefore,

```
putc(ch, outfile_ptr);
```

writes the value of *ch* to the file to which *outfile_ptr* points. With both *putc* and *ungetc*, we must be careful to have the file pointer as the second argument.

Tables 7.4 and 7.5 summarize the C I/O functions and macros we have discussed.

Table 7.4 Functions and macros to manipulate an input text file

Example Function Call	Read from	Read What	Error Return
`ch = getchar();`	*stdin*	character	*EOF*
`scanf("%d %f", &i, &x);`	*stdin*	anything	*EOF*
`ch = getc(infile_ptr);`	input file	character	*EOF*
`ungetc(ch, infile_ptr);`	input file	(return character to file)	*EOF*
`fscanf(infile_ptr, "%d %f", &i, &x);`	input file	anything	*EOF*

Table 7.5 Functions and macros to manipulate an output text file

Example Function Call	Write to	Write What	Error Return
`putchar(ch);`	*stdout*	character	*EOF*
`printf("%d %f\n", i, x);`	*stdout*	anything	negative
`putc(ch, outfile_ptr);`	output file	character	*EOF*
`fprintf(outfile_ptr, "%d %f", i, x);`	output file	anything	negative

Section 7.5 Exercises

In Exercises 1–8, write a statement or statements to do the following:

1. Declare *EmpFile_ptr*, *ScaleFile_ptr*, and *WageFile_ptr* as file pointers.

2. Open the file to which *EmpFile_ptr* points for input and the file to which *WageFile_ptr* points for output. On disk, these files are *employee.dat* and *wage.dat*.

3. Check if the input file to which *EmpFile_ptr* points opened properly. If it did not, print an error message and terminate execution of the program.

4. Read an integer and a floating point number from the file to which *EmpFile_ptr* points into variables *EmpNum* and *salary*, respectively.

5. Write the *int* value of *EmpNum* and the *float* values of *salary* and *raise* into the file to which *WageFile_ptr* points.

6. While there is more data in the input file to which *EmpFile_ptr* points (as in Exercise 4), compute the raise as 10% of *salary* and write as in Exercise 5.

7. If there is more data in the file to which *ScaleFile_ptr* points, read an integer from the file into *quantity*.

8. Close the files that were opened in Exercise 1.

9. Find the error(s) in the following segment:

```
file in_ptr;

in_ptr = open(ratefile.dat);
if (ratefile.dat == null)
    exit;
fscanf("%f", x);
close(ratefile.dat);
```

Section 7.5 Programming Projects

1. Develop a program to make a backup copy of a file of *int* values.

2. Develop a program to read nonnegative integers from a file and write their expansions in base 10 to the screen and an output file. For example, for the number 4937, the expansion would be as follows:

$$4937 = 7 * 1 + 3 * 10 + 9 * 100 + 4 * 1000$$

3. Develop a program to find the average of a set of integer scores from a file. The program should validate that all data are between 0 and 800 and print an error message for any out-of-range value. The program should print the average of all in-range data.

≋ Programming and Debugging Hints

Defensive Programming: Detection and Recovery

Interactive programs require user input. Unlike computers, however, humans are prone to making errors. A well-written program must be able to deal with invalid input in a way that benefits the user (in terms of informing him or her of the nature of the error) and perhaps even prevents the premature termination of the program.

The major criterion by which a program is judged is whether it produces the correct results. So, what degree of confidence can we place in the results?

Careful analysis, design, and review are all important steps in the prevention of errors. The debugging process described so far is also significant in the elimination of errors. Once the program is up and running, however, we may not avoid several potential sources of error. One source is the possibility of the user entering unacceptable data. When feasible, we should design a program so that invalid input does not cause it to crash (come to a halt). Through looping, we verify input data and allow the user to correct mistakes.

Defensive Programming: Read Data as Strings

One effective debugging technique that is available in C is to input all data as character strings and examine the format of the input. This step prevents the errors that occur when, say, the program expects an integer but is given a floating point number. Once the data have been verified in the correct format, they can be converted to the desired form for storage. For example, we can verify that input is an unsigned integer and place the number in *nonneg_int* with this segment from Example 7.12 (Section 7.3):

```
InputOK = TRUE;
while (!isspace(ch) && InputOK)
{
    if (isdigit(ch))    /* in number, accumulate and cont. */
    {
        nonneg_int = nonneg_int * 10 + ch - '0';
        ch = getchar();
    }
    else                    /* Error: character not a digit */
    {
        printf("\n%c is not a digit.", ch);
        InputOK = FALSE;
    }
}
```

Defensive Programming: "Bullet-Proof" All Levels

Just because the computer has successfully read a value does not mean a data item is harmless. We may still need to verify that the value is within the acceptable range for the algorithm. Sometimes the separation between acceptable and unacceptable data is not always apparent until the computer performs some elementary computation. The programmer should "bullet-proof" all levels of the program, not just the input functions, against bad data.

Bad data may not only lead to incorrect results, but also can cause the program to crash. For example, suppose a program contains the following expression:

```
a / b
```

This division looks innocent enough to the programmer and even to the compiler. If the executing program uses a value of 0 for *b*, however, then a division-by-zero error occurs and the program crashes. Because the error is common and causes a crash, the programmer should examine every segment involving division to ensure adequate protection against division by zero.

A program that detects a data error should be able to recover. If an input function discovers the error, that routine should inform the user of an error in the data. The erroneous data item should be clearly identified, along with the reason it is considered erroneous. The user should then be given an opportunity to reenter some or all of the data. The function can contain a *while* or *do-while* loop that continues to request input until the data are valid, such as with the following segment from Example 7.10 of Section 7.3:

```
do
{
    printf("Do you want to find another ASCII code? (y/n) ");
    answer = tolower(getchar());
    fflush(stdin);
}
while (!(answer == YES || answer == NO));
```

A programmer might impose a limit on how many chances the user has to reenter data with a *for* loop. If the user exceeds that number of chances, the program terminates.

If the program detects an error farther along in execution, the situation is more problematic. The program must undo the effects that the erroneous data have produced, and then allow the user to reenter the data. Sometimes it is not possible to recover, and the best thing the program can do is terminate after displaying a clear explanation of the cause of the error.

The time to decide where to insert error-detecting functions is during the initial writing of the program. Including this additional code makes the program longer, necessitates more time to complete the project, and might even result in a less efficient program. The computer must execute all the error-detecting techniques, regardless of whether any errors appear. Nevertheless, the extra effort and expense involved in defensive programming may help to avoid disastrous results.

≋ **Key Terms**

%c 360	form feed 378	read mode 401
ASCII 372	*fprintf* 403	return 378
audible alert 378	*fscanf* 403	soft crash 402
backslash 378	*getc* 406	*stdin* 361
backspace 378	*getchar* 361	*stdout* 361
binary digit 372	hard crash 402	text file 401
bit 372	horizontal tab 378	*tolower* 381
buffer 362	input buffer pointer 364–365	*toupper* 381
byte 372	*isalnum* 392	*ungetc* 406
char 360	*isalpha* 392	vertical tab 378
control character 372	*iscntrl* 392	write mode 401
crash 408	*isdigit* 386	white space character 365
ctrl-d 362	*isgraph* 392	\" 378
ctrl-z 362	*islower* 392	\n 378
ctype.h 381	*isprint* 392	\007 378
EBCDIC 377	*ispunct* 392	\? 378
end-of-file 362	*isspace* 386	\a 378
EOF 362	*isupper* 392	\b 378
escape character 377	*isxdigit* 392	\f 378
escape sequence 377	macro 361	\ 378
exit 402	mode 401	\ooo 378
fclose 403	newline 378	\r 378
feof 403	*NULL* 402	\t 378
fflush 366	null character 378	\v 378
FILE * 401	open 401	\xhh 378
file pointer 401	pointer 401	\\ 378
flush the buffer 362	*putc* 406	
fopen 401	*putchar* 361	

Summary

This chapter deals with the handling of character information. Type *char* designates a variable that can store a single character. A character constant is one character between two apostrophes, such as 'A', and the conversion specification is %c.

For printing an individual character to the standard output file (ordinarily a video display), programmers usually employ the standard I/O library function *putchar*. To display the value of a *char* variable, *ch*, to the screen, we use

```
putchar(ch);
```

With no parameters, *getchar* reads a single character from the standard input file *stdin* (usually the keyboard) and returns that character. Thus, to read a value for *ch*, we write

```
ch = getchar();
```

Input or output passes through an input or output buffer, respectively. A buffer is a special location in main memory, a fixed number of characters in length, that can temporarily hold data being transferred from main memory to secondary storage, or vice versa. The ANSI C standard I/O library function *fflush* flushes the input buffer, as shown:

```
fflush(stdin);
```

After execution of this call, the input buffer is empty.

When we type a character at the keyboard, the computer does not record the item itself but a numeric code that represents the typed character. The most widely used encoding scheme is ASCII. Type *char* can be implemented as type *signed char* with a range of values from −128 to 127 or, less commonly, as type *unsigned char* with values from 0 to 255. To find the *int* equivalent, *digit*, of character digit *ch*, we use

```
digit = ch - '0';
```

In C, we call the backslash character (\) the escape character, because any character immediately following it takes on a special meaning. Some escape sequences in C are as follows: \0, null character; \a or \007, audible alert (bell); \b, backspace; \f, form feed; \n, newline, go to first of next line; \r, carriage return, go to first of current line; \t, horizontal tab; \v, vertical tab; \", quotation mark; \', apostrophe; \?, question mark; \\, backslash; \\ooo, up to 3-digit octal (base 8) number; and \xhh, up to 2-digit hexadecimal (base 16) number.

ANSI C has a number of functions that deal with characters in its library with header file *ctype.h*. The function *tolower* returns the lowercase letter corresponding to its character argument, and *toupper* returns the corresponding uppercase letter. The function *isdigit* returns *TRUE* (a nonzero integer) if the argument is a character digit and returns *FALSE* (0) otherwise. Another boolean function, *isspace*, returns *TRUE* if the argument is a white space character—space (' '), newline ('\n'), tab ('\t'), form feed ('\f'), carriage return ('\r'), or vertical tab ('\v'). Using character functions, we developed a function that reads a nonnegative integer without a sign, one character at a time, accumulating the number to return. The function verifies that no nondigit characters are embedded in the number and that only one value is on the line. Other boolean functions in *ctype.h* are as follows (where the kind of argument that causes the function to return *TRUE* (≠ 0) is in parentheses): *isalnum* (letter or digit); *isalpha* (letter); *iscntrl* (control character); *isdigit* (decimal digit); *isgraph* (printable character, but not white space); *islower* (lowercase letter); *isprint* (printable character, including blank); *ispunct* (printable character other than letter, digit, or white space); *isspace*

(space, newline, tab, form feed, carriage return, or vertical tab); *isupper* (uppercase letter); and *isxdigit* (hexadecimal digit).

A text file is a file of characters. The data type *FILE* describes various features of a file. Each file in a program must have an associated pointer to this type. We can declare a pointer to file, *file_ptr*, as follows:

```
FILE *file_ptr;
```

We can open a file for reading (input) and a file for writing (output) as follows:

```
infile_ptr  = fopen("price.dat", "r"); /* input file */
outfile_ptr = fopen("tax.dat", "w");   /* output file */
```

If the file does not exist, *fopen* returns a special constant, *NULL*. We should verify that the computer successfully opened the file before continuing, as follows:

```
if (infile_ptr == NULL)
{
    printf("price.dat does not exist.\n");
    exit(1);
}
```

The standard library with header file *stdlib.h* contains *exit*, which aborts the program and returns its argument to the operating system. To close the file with pointer *file_ptr*, we write

```
fclose(file_ptr);
```

The standard I/O library function *fprintf*, which behaves almost the same as *printf*, sends its output to a specified file. An example call to this function follows:

```
fprintf(outfile_ptr, "%d\n", amt);
```

The header file *stdio.h* declares a file input function, *fscanf*, which reads from the file specified by a *FILE* pointer as the first parameter. An example call to this function follows:

```
fscanf(infile_ptr, "%d", &amt);
```

One method to accomplish continuous processing is to read and test for the correct amount of input in a *while* condition. Afterwards, we use the *feof* in an *if* statement to check for EOF, as shown:

```
while (fscanf(infile_ptr, "%f", &price) == 1)
{
    ⋮
}
if (!feof(infile_ptr))
    printf("There was an error reading the file.\n");
```

The macro *getc*, which is analogous to *getchar*, reads the next character from an input file, such as

```
ch = getc(infile_ptr);
```

The macro *ungetc* returns the first argument, a character, to the stream that is the second argument, such as

```
ungetc(ch, infile_ptr);
```

The file macro *putc* is analogous to *putchar*, as shown:

```
putc(ch, outfile_ptr);
```

This call writes the value of *ch* to the file to which *outfile_ptr* points.

Review Questions

1. What is a character constant?
2. What maximum number of characters can a variable of type *char* hold?
3. What conversion specifications are used to print a single character?
4. What is the critical difference between 'x' and "x"?
5. Give the keyword associated with the type that we covered in this chapter.
6. What function call flushes the input buffer?
7. Name the files that are normally associated with the *printf* and *scanf* functions.
8. What restrictions are related to the *putchar* function?
9. Name the function that reads a single character from the standard input and is counterpart to *putchar*.
10. Name a possible advantage of the function *getchar* over *scanf*.
11. What is *EOF*?
12. What does ASCII stand for?
13. How is a character (printable or otherwise) stored in the memory of the computer?
14. Write an expression that returns the integer equivalent to a character digit stored in the variable *digit*. For example, if *digit* is '8', the value of the expression is 8.
15. What are control characters?
16. Give some examples of control characters.
17. What significance does a backslash character have when placed immediately before a one-, two-, or three-digit number?
18. If the following *scanf* statement is executed:

    ```
    scanf("%d%c", &n, &c);
    ```

    where *n* is of type *int* and *c* is of type *char*, and the input is

    ```
    23
    x
    ```

    what values are read for *n* and *c*?
19. How could the call to *scanf* in the previous problem be rewritten so that the letter x is read into the variable *c*?
20. What header file must the programmer include to obtain access to the ANSI C standard library character functions.
21. What function converts an uppercase letter to lowercase?
22. Write an expression with one ! equivalent to the following:

    ```
    answer != YES && answer != NO
    ```

23. What function returns *TRUE* ($\neq$ 0) if the argument is a white space character?
24. What is the value of *isalnum*('B')?

25. What function returns *TRUE* (≠ 0) if the argument is a printable character other than letter, digit, or white space?

26. What function returns *TRUE* (≠ 0) if the argument is a letter?

27. What conversion specifications are used for the printing of octal and hexadecimal numbers?

28. True or false: C ignores leading zeros, so that 123 is the same as 0123.

29. True or false: When specifying a hexadecimal number in C, the letters A through F and also X may be written in uppercase or lowercase as desired.

30. True or false: The conversion specification %h is used to read values in hexadecimal format.

31. On what medium is a file generally stored?

32. What must each file have associated with it?

33. What must be done to a file before it can be used?

34. What is a file of characters called?

35. What two functions were covered for writing to a file?

36. Write two statements using different functions to read a character from the file pointed to by *file_ptr* into the character variable *ch*.

37. What function is used to detect the end of a file?

≋ **Laboratory**

This laboratory uses files *LAB071.c*, *RandDef.c*, and *RandDef.h* on the text disk. As described in Section 5.4, *RandDef.c* is a source file of definitions of functions for seeding and generating random numbers. *RandDef.h* is the associated header file. Please copy these three files to your own disk. The file *LAB071.c* contains a program to help children practice integer arithmetic problems. After introductory remarks, the user is given a menu of choices: To perform a random addition (integers between −50 and 50), subtraction (integers between −50 and 50), multiplication (integers between −12 and 12), or division (dividend—integers between 2 and 144; divisor—integers between 2 and 12) or quit. When the user makes a choice, the computer presents the student with a corresponding random problem and indicates whether the user's answer is correct. The process repeats until the user chooses to quit. The program contains the functions listed in Table 7.6, and Figure 7.6 presents the structure chart.

The function *main* drives the program with a *while* loop that has a priming read of the user's choice preceding it. Within the loop, a *switch* statement processes the choice by calling the appropriate function. The functions *add*, *subtract*, and *multiply* are similar. Two operands are picked at random, and the user is presented with the corresponding problem. Each function congratulates the user for a correct response or gives the right answer for an incorrect one. For the division question to have a whole number answer, the program works the problem backwards. The computer picks the divisor and the answer (the quotient) at random and computes the dividend as the product of the divisor and the answer, as shown:

```
divisor = random_range(2, 13);
CorrectAnswer = random_range(1, 13);
dividend = divisor * CorrectAnswer;
```

Table 7.6 List of functions in *LAB071.c*

Prototype	Description
`main()`	driver for system
`void welcome(void);`	prints introductory remarks
`int menu(void);`	prints menu, returns user's selection
`void add(void);`	does an addition problem interactively
`void subtract(void);`	does a subtraction problem interactively
`void multiply(void);`	does a multiplication problem interactively
`void divide(void);`	does a division problem interactively
`void SeedRand(void);`	seeds random number generator
`int random_range(` `    int LowerBound, int UpperBound);`	returns a random integer between *LowerBound* and *UpperBound* − 1

Figure 7.6 Structure chart for program in *LAB071.c*

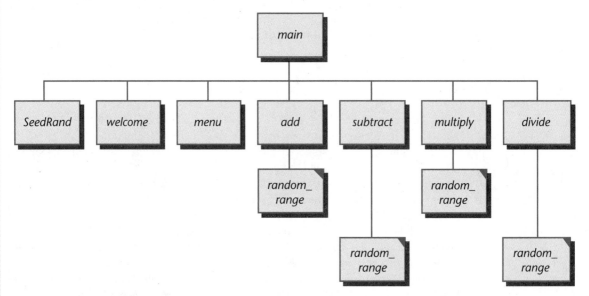

The program then presents the user with the dividend and divisor and asks for the quotient.

```
printf("\n%d / %d = ", dividend, divisor);
```

For example, if the computer generates 6 for *divisor* and 5 for *CorrectAnswer*, it calculates 6·5 = 30 for *dividend*. The user, however, sees the problem as follows:

```
30 / 6 =
```

The functions *SeedRand* to seed the random number generator and *random_range* to return a random integer are as in Example 5.15 of Section 5.4. Their prototypes are in *RandDef.h*, and their definitions are in *RandDef.c*. The following call:

```
random_range(LowerBound, UpperBound)
```

returns a random integer between *LowerBound* and *UpperBound* − 1. Thus, to assign to *op1* a random integer between −50 and 50, inclusively, we must call the function with arguments −50 and 51.

```
op1 = random_range(-50, 51);
```

The code for the program on the disk is as follows:

```
/*
 * Program to help children practice arithmetic problems
 */

#include <stdio.h>
#include <time.h>
#include <stdlib.h>
#include "RandDef.h"

main()
{
    void welcome(void);
    int menu(void);
    void add(void);
    void subtract(void);
    void multiply(void);
    void divide(void);

    int choice;        /* menu choice */

    SeedRand();
    welcome();

    choice = menu();
    while (choice != 5)
    {
        switch (choice)
        {
            case 1:    add();
                       break;

            case 2:    subtract();
                       break;

            case 3:    multiply();
                       break;

            case 4:    divide();
                       break;

            case 5:    break;

            default:  printf("Sorry, that is not a valid choice.\n\n");
        }
        choice = menu();
    }
    printf("\nHave a nice day.\n");}
```

```c
/*
 * Function to explain program
 * Pre:     none
 * Post:    Directions have been printed.
 */

void welcome(void)
{
    printf("Welcome to Arithmetic Practice\n\n");
    printf("You can practice:\");
    printf("Addition with two integers between -50 and 50\n");
    printf("Subtraction with two integers between -50 and 50\n");
    printf("Multiplication with two integers between -12 and 12\n");
    printf("Division with two integers. The dividend is between 2\n");
    printf("and 144, and the divisor is between 2 and 12\n\n");
}

/*
 * Function to print menu of choices
 * Pre:     none
 * Post:    The user's menu choice has been returned.
 */

int menu(void)
{
    int choice;          /* menu choice */

    printf("Please choose a type of problem:\n\n");
    printf("\t1 Addition\n");
    printf("\t2 Subtraction\n");
    printf("\t3 Multiplication\n");
    printf("\t4 Division\n");
    printf("\t5 Quit\n");

    printf("\n\tYour choice: ");
    scanf("%d", &choice);
    return choice;
}

/*
 * Function to do an addition problem interactively
 * Pre:     none
 * Post:    An interactive addition problem has been done.
 */
```

```
void add(void)
{
    int op1,                   /* first operand */
        op2,                   /* second operand */
        CorrectAnswer,         /* correct answer to problem */
        UserAnswer;            /* user's answer to problem */

    op1 = random_range(-50, 51);
    op2 = random_range(-50, 51);
    CorrectAnswer = op1 + op2;

    printf("\%d + %d = ", op1, op2);
    scanf("n%d", &UserAnswer);

    if (UserAnswer == CorrectAnswer)
        printf("Congratulations! You got it right!\n\n");
    else
        printf("Sorry, %d + %d = %d\n\n", op1, op2, CorrectAnswer);
}

/*
 * Function to do a subtraction problem interactively
 * Pre:     none
 * Post:    An interactive subtraction problem has been done.
 */

void subtract(void)
{
    int op1,                   /* first operand */
        op2,                   /* second operand */
        CorrectAnswer,         /* correct answer to problem */
        UserAnswer;            /* user's answer to problem */

    op1 = random_range(-50, 51);
    op2 = random_range(-50, 51);
    CorrectAnswer = op1 - op2;

     printf("\n%d - %d = ", op1, op2);
    scanf("%d", &UserAnswer);

    if (UserAnswer == CorrectAnswer)
        printf("Congratulations! You got it right!\n\n");
    else
        printf("Sorry, %d - %d = %d\n\n", op1, op2, CorrectAnswer);
}

/*
 * Function to do a multiplication problem interactively
 * Pre:     none
 * Post:    An interactive multiplication problem has been done.
 */
```

```c
void multiply(void)
{
    int op1,                 /* first operand */
        op2,                 /* second operand */
        CorrectAnswer,       /* correct answer to problem */
        UserAnswer;          /* user's answer to problem */

    op1 = random_range(-12, 13);
    op2 = random_range(-12, 13);
    CorrectAnswer = op1 * op2;

    printf("\n%d * %d = ", op1, op2);
    scanf("%d", &UserAnswer);

    if (UserAnswer == CorrectAnswer)
        printf("Congratulations! You got it right!\n\n");
    else
        printf("Sorry, %d * %d = %d\\", op1, op2, CorrectAnswer);
}

/*
 * Function to do a division problem interactively
 * Pre:     none
 * Post:    An interactive division problem has been done.
 */

void divide(void)
{
    int divisor,             /* denominator in division */
        dividend,            /* numerator in division */
        CorrectAnswer,       /* correct answer to problem */
        UserAnswer;          /* user's answer to problem */

    divisor = random_range(2,  13);
    CorrectAnswer = random_range(1,  13);
    dividend = divisor * CorrectAnswer;

    printf("\n%d / %d = ", dividend, divisor);
    scanf("%d", &UserAnswer);

    if (UserAnswer == CorrectAnswer)
        printf("Congratulations! You got it right!\n\n");
    else
        printf("Sorry, %d / %d = %d\n\n",
                dividend, divisor, CorrectAnswer);
}
```

To get a feel for the program's actions, compile the files *LAB071.c* and *RandDef.c*; link them; and execute the program trying every problem and attempting an invalid choice.

1. This exercise makes the program more user friendly by having character responses. The goals of this exercise are to study processing of character data, flushing of the input buffer, and use of the character function *tolower*.

   a. In *main* and *menu*, change the type of *choice* to *char*. Use *getchar* to obtain a value for *choice*. The program now reads the choice as a character digit instead of a numeric digit. Why is it unnecessary to change the type that *menu* returns?

   b. Run the program, typing a choice of 1. Explain why the computer says that this is not a valid choice. Why does it tell us that it is invalid twice when we type but one value?

   c. Change the test condition in the *while* loop and the *case* labels in the *switch* statement in *main* to reflect that *choice* is of type *char*. What must we write instead of (*choice* != 5)? What must we write instead of *case 1*?

   d. We can process choices now, but why do we see a new menu and

   ```
   Your choice:  Sorry, that is not a valid choice.
   ```

   after completion of each problem? To overcome this problem, we flush the input buffer in the appropriate place(s) with

   ```
   fflush(stdin);
   ```

   We can put this statement in just one location in *main*. Where would that be? Another alternative is to flush the buffer immediately after each read in the four arithmetic functions and *menu*. Discuss the advantages and disadvantages of the two alternatives. Correct the program so that it behaves properly.

   e. We can now make the program more user friendly by having menu choices be the letters a, s, m, d, and q instead of the numbers 1, 2, 3, 4, and 5, respectively. Change *menu* and *main* to reflect this change. Make sure the program still runs properly.

   f. We should be able to type character responses in uppercase as well as lowercase. How do we change *menu* with the function *tolower* to allow such choices? Include the header file *ctype.h*, make the change to *menu*, and test the program.

2. This exercise examines the application of some control characters.

   a. Output of the program would look more professional if the screen cleared after the initial instructions and between problems. We do not, however, want to clear the screen prematurely, before the user has examined its contents. Handle this situation by requiring that the user press return to continue. For example, initially the user sees the following display:

   ```
   Welcome to Arithmetic Practice

   You can practice:
   Addition with two integers between -50 and 50
   Subtraction with two integers between -50 and 50
   Multiplication with two integers between -12 and 12
   Division with two integers. The dividend is between 2
   and 144, and the divisor is between 2 and 12

   Press return to continue.
   ```

Once the user presses return, the menu appears and processing continues, as shown:

```
Please choose a type of problem:

        a Addition
        s Subtraction
        m Multiplication
        d Division
        q Quit

        Your choice: a

12 + 25 = 37
Congratulations!  You got it right!

Press return to continue.
```

Accomplish this feature through statements in *menu*. First, have a call to *printf* instructing the user to press return. Then read a character with *getchar*. Because we do not need this character, we need not store the value in a variable. Be sure to flush the buffer after the *getchar*. To clear the screen, we add the form feed control character ('\f') to the first *printf* for displaying the menu. If the form feed does not clear the screen in your version of C, check your documentation for a function that performs this operation or write your own. A scrolling-type method involves a *for* loop that prints the newline character a sufficient number of times.

b. Make the introduction more attractive by using the tab control character ('\t') in the call to *printf* that displays "Welcome to Arithmetic Practice." During execution, this welcome should appear more centered.

c. If the user makes an invalid menu choice, ring the bell. Do so by printing the bell (alarm) control character after the *default* label in *main*.

3. In this problem, we consider prototypes and counting.

a. Why are the prototypes for the functions located as they are? Are there other choices for their locations? If so, where?

b. It would be nice to tell the user how many problems he or she attempted. Declare and initialize a variable in *main* to count the number of problems. Have it count the number of problems attempted using an incrementing operator. Do not count 'q' and invalid menu choices. Before the closing statement in *main*, print the number of problems attempted.

c. We can also count how many answers are correct. Because the functions are similar, we first concentrate on how we count the number of correct addition problems. We have *add* (and eventually each function) return *CORRECT* (1) or *INCORRECT* (0) depending on whether the answer is right or not. In *main*, we accumulate and print the number of correct answers. Make the following modifications:

(1) In *main*, declare and initialize a variable *NumCorrect* to count the number of correct (addition) problems.

(2) Have the prototype and definition of *add* be of type *int.*

(3) Have an updating assignment add the value *add* returns to *NumCorrect.*

(4) Have *main* print the number of correct additions along with the total number of problems.

(5) Using a preprocessor *#define*, define constants *CORRECT* (1) and *INCOR-RECT* (0).

(6) Change the function *add* to return *CORRECT* for a correct answer and *INCORRECT* for an incorrect answer. Have a local variable store this value, so that only one *return* is necessary. Be sure to use braces as needed to group statements in the *if-else* statement.

d. If time allows, make similar changes to the other three arithmetic functions. In *main*, have *NumCorrect* compute the total number of correct responses. After the program runs properly, print a listing and an interactive session.

Arrays

Introduction

We have seen in previous chapters that variables are the entities in C that the computer uses to hold data in memory. So far, we have needed to know how many items to store and to declare a variable for each one. This method has several disadvantages. First, using separate variables does not allow for the common case in which we must store and operate on an indeterminate number of related values of the same type. Second, assuming a large amount of data, we face a tedious task of naming and declaring separate variables. Third, if we must perform the same sequence of operations using these different variable names, we do not have the power of looping. We must type practically the same statements repeatedly.

Arrays are the solution to these problems. Arrays are an important part of programming included in virtually every high-level language. In the first section of the chapter, we study how to declare, read values into, and retrieve values from an array. We illustrate an array *score* that stores the golf scores for players in a tournament. In the next section, we see how to pass an array reference to a function. For example, we can have functions to compute the average, maximum, and minimum values of an array.

Another common task is to search an array for one item, such as a particular golf score. If the array is not in ascending or descending order, we employ a sequential search, in which we methodically go through each element until locating the item. If the array is sorted, we can also use a binary search. For sorted arrays of 20 elements or more, the binary search is more efficient. Often, the array should be arranged in order anyway. For example, in the golf tournament, we may want to list the scores from lowest (the winner) to highest. Section 8.4 covers one method of sorting an array—the selection sort.

Multidimensional arrays can store a table of information, such as the golf scores for each player over several days of a tournament. A breadth section discusses another example of such an array—a color lookup table, which stores the intensity levels to produce color on a graphics video display.

Goals

To study

- Manipulation of one-dimensional arrays
- Functions with array parameters, such as one to find the maximum in an array
- Sequential and binary searches for an element in an array
- Selection sort of an array to order its elements
- Manipulation of multidimensional arrays
- The role of arrays in generating color for computer graphics

Section 8.1 **What Is An Array?**

In C, as in other computer languages, we can assign a single name to a whole group of similar data. For example, if we are interested in a large number of recorded Celsius temperatures, we can assign a common name—such as *CTemp*—to all the data. We can then reference each element by position within the list of items. Mathematics calls such a structure a **vector**, but its name in computer science is an "array." A large number of computer programs use arrays to store data. Some computers, such as the CRAY-2™ pictured on the next page, operate most efficiently on arrays of numbers instead of on individual data items.

An **array** is a sequence of elements of the same type that share a common name and that are distinguishable by their positions within the array. For example, suppose we have a list of five related numbers—58, 63, 49, 18, 7. In mathematics, we can refer to the list by the name x and indicate individual elements using a **subscript**, for example, $x_0 = 58$, $x_1 = 63$, $x_2 = 49$, $x_3 = 18$, $x_4 = 7$. The subscript indicates the position of the particular element in the list.

Because it is impossible to display subscripts on a standard computer terminal, C encloses the numbers in square brackets. Thus, we refer to elements $x[0]$, $x[1]$, $x[2]$, $x[3]$, and $x[4]$. In computer science, we often call the subscript the **index**. For example, in array x, element $x[3]$ has index 3.

Definition

An **array** is a sequence of elements of the same type that share a common name and that are distinguishable by their positions within the array. A **subscript** or **index** indicates the position in the array.

Declaration

Because an array is a collection of variables, a program must declare each array. We declare an array x containing five elements, all of which are integers, as follows:

The CRAY-2 supercomputer, designed by **Seymour Cray,** has four processors working in parallel along with another processor an an overseer. It usually operates fastest on data that are arranged in one-dimensional arrays of 64 elements each. The CRAY-2 has 65 million words, a 4.1 nsec clock cycle, and originally cost about $15 million. The dense circuitry is cooled by direct contact with Fluorinert, a fluid that looks much like water. This inert liquid, however, does not conduct electricity and is so rich in oxygen that it can be used as a blood substitute. The CRAY-2 supercomputer was delivered to Lawrence Livermore National Laboratory in 1985. A Cray engineer is pictured standing inside the hollow center of the CRAY-2.

```
int x[5];
```

The same rules for naming an identifier apply to naming arrays, and the name of the array cannot be the same as that of any other variable in the function. We specify the size of the array—the number of elements—with the subscript notation. Using the above declaration, at compile time the computer allocates space for five integers under the array name x. As with scalar variables, which can hold only one value, the declaration of an array does not assign values, but simply sets aside memory. Figure 8.1 illustrates such an allocation.

The subscript in the declaration (5) is the dimension or size of the array. This dimension must always be a positive integer constant or an expression that evaluates to a constant at compile time. For example, with the following preprocessor directive:

```
#define MAX_NUM_ELS 5
```

we can declare the array x with

```
int x[MAX_NUM_ELS];
```

Use of a symbolic constant makes the code more readable and easier to change if we later decide we need more elements in the array.

Figure 8.1
Memory allocation after declaration *int x*[5];

x: | ? | ? | ? | ? | ? |

index: 0 1 2 3 4

Assigning Values

The method of assigning subscripts or indexing arrays in C is different from that in many other programming languages. In C, the numbering always starts with 0, not with 1 or some other choice. The reason for this unusual numbering scheme is that C models the operation of the computer at a level lower than that dealt with by most programming languages. The calculation of the memory location corresponding to a subscript is simpler when the first array element has index 0. Figure 8.2 depicts memory after the following assignment statements for this example:

```
x[0] = 58;
x[1] = 63;
x[2] = 49;
x[3] = 18;
x[4] = 7;
```

This example has no element $x[5]$.

Most C compilers do not consider it an error if the programmer attempts to access an element outside the legal subscript range of an array—for example, $x[8]$. The program may even run without crashing because of C's flexibility, which we discuss further in the next chapter. Referencing an index out of range, however, is almost always a logical error, so the programmer should ensure that all subscripts are within the correct limits.

All elements of an array are of the same type. In other words, if we declare an array to be of type *int*, it can only contain elements that are of type *int*. We can use each element of an array anywhere that it is legal to use a scalar variable. With a few exceptions, a program does not use unsubscripted array names, such as x. The following assignment statements are all valid in C:

```
x[0] = 4;
x[0] += 7;
x[1] = x[0] - 2;
x[2] = x[1] * 5 + x[0];
```

Array Index

The feature that makes arrays such powerful tools is that the index can be any integer expression. For example, if the integer variable i has the value 3, $x[i]$ refers to array element number 3—the fourth array element. All index variables must be of type *int* or a compatible type, such as *short, char,* or *unsigned.*

Because we can use a variable as an index, the ideal construct to manipulate an array is usually the *for* loop. The following loop reads five Celsius temperatures into an array *CTemp*, which consists of at least five elements (assuming we have properly declared all variables):

```
for (i = 0; i < 5; i++)
    scanf("%d", &CTemp[i]);
```

The body of the loop executes five times. The first time, i has the value 0, and the program reads a value for element *CTemp*[0]. The second time, i has the value 1. The fifth and last time the loop executes, i has the value 4, and *CTemp*[4] obtains a value. When i increments to 5, the loop test fails, and the loop terminates.

This loop illustrates an important fact about arrays. We cannot read an entire array at once. (One exception to this rule is described later.) We must read each element of

Figure 8.2
Memory after assignment

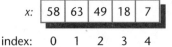

x: | 58 | 63 | 49 | 18 | 7 |

index: 0   1   2   3   4

an array separately. We cannot assign an entire array to another array. Even if both *x* and *y* are arrays of the same type and size and all the elements of *x* have values, the following statement is illegal in C:

```
y = x;      /* ERROR for arrays x and y */
```

Such an assignment would cause the compiler to signal an error. We discuss the reason for this error in the next chapter.

Example 8.1

This example contains a program to read scores from one round of an amateur golf tournament. In this version, we first call a function, *GetNumPlayers*, to ask for the number of players. After reading the scores, we print them in a table format.

```c
/*
 * Example 8.1. Program to read the number of golf scores
 * and then to read and print those scores
 */

#include <stdio.h>

#define MAX_NUM_PLAYERS 100

main()
{
    int GetNumPlayers(void);

    int score[MAX_NUM_PLAYERS],    /* array of scores */
        player,                    /* index for array */
        NumPlayers;                /* actual number of players */

    NumPlayers = GetNumPlayers();


    /* read values for array score */
    printf("\nPlease enter %d scores ", NumPlayers);
    printf("with blanks separating scores:\n");

    for (player = 0; player < NumPlayers; player++)
        scanf("%d", &score[player]);


    /* Print the scores */
    printf("\n\tGolf Scores for Round:\n\n");
    printf("\tPlayer #\tScore\n");
    printf("\t_____\t_____\n");

    for (player = 0; player < NumPlayers; player++)
        printf("\t %3d \t\t %3d \n", player + 1, score[player]);
}
```

```
/*
 * Function to read and return number of players
 * Pre:    none
 * Post:   The number of players, an integer between
 *         1 and MAX_NUM_PLAYERS was returned.
 */

int GetNumPlayers(void)
{
    int NumPlayers;       /* actual number of players */

    printf("How many players are in the golf tournament? ");
    scanf("%d", &NumPlayers);

    while ((NumPlayers <= 0) || (MAX_NUM_PLAYERS < NumPlayers))
    {
        printf("The number of players must be between 1 and %d\n",
            MAX_NUM_PLAYERS);
        printf("Please enter the number of players again. ");
        scanf("%d", &NumPlayers);
    }

    return NumPlayers;
}
```

A sample run follows:

```
How many players are in the golf tournament? 4

Please enter 4 scores with blanks separating scores:
79 88 94 76

        Golf Scores for Round:

        Player #          Score
        _____          _____
           1                79
           2                88
           3                94
           4                76
```

We declare the integer array *score* to contain *MAX_NUM_PLAYERS* (100) elements. The variable *NumPlayers* is to hold the actual number of scores in the array, which is a nonnegative number less than or equal to *MAX_NUM_PLAYERS*. We must have enough room in the array for all the scores, but we do not need to fill the structure completely. As an index to *score*, the variable *player* helps us process the different elements.

Figure 8.3
Memory after
the reading of
data for
Example 8.1

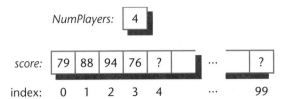

The function *main* calls *GetNumPlayers* to ask and return the number of players; *NumPlayers* stores this answer. After prompting the user to enter all the scores, the program has a *for* loop that reads the elements one at a time. The loop executes for values of *player* from 0 through *NumPlayers* − 1. With each new value of *player*, the computer reads an integer value for another element, *score[player]*. In our example, the user designated *NumPlayers* to be 4. Thus, reading with the *for* loop is equivalent to

```
scanf("%d", &score[0]);
scanf("%d", &score[1]);
scanf("%d", &score[2]);
scanf("%d", &score[3]);
```

The user must enter the scores with white space separating the items. The number of scores must correspond to the number that the user specifies at the beginning of the program. If the person enters too few scores, the program waits for him or her to type the remaining values. If the user provides too many, the program ignores the extra ones.

Figure 8.3 depicts memory after completion of the loop with user input of 79, 88, 94, and 76. Had the user entered 100 instead of 4 for the number of players, the segment would have worked just as well. This flexibility in processing a varying number of items with loops is a powerful feature of arrays.

Because the array stores the input values, we can print them in a table format with another *for* loop. Again, we use the variable *player* as an index into the array and have the loop print *score[player]* for *player* taking on values from 0 through 3. We also print *player* + 1, rather than *player*, as the player's number, as shown:

```
printf("\t %3d \t\t %3d \n", player + 1, score[player]);
```

This approach enables the user to see the numbering of the elements in the natural way, starting with 1 rather than 0.

We could have used this numbering to prompt the user for scores in the first *for* loop. Instead of requiring that the user remember the players' numbers on entering their scores, we could have a *printf* in the reading *for* loop as follows:

```
for (player = 0; player < NumPlayers; player++)
{
    printf("Enter score for player #%d: ", player + 1);
    scanf("%d", &score[player]);
}
```

With this change, the first part of the interactive session appears as follows:

```
How many players are in the golf tournament? 4
Enter score for player #1: 79
Enter score for player #2: 88
Enter score for player #3: 94
Enter score for player #4: 76
```

Another improvement would be for the program to verify that the user enters a reasonable score, such as one between 50 and 200.

Example 8.2

This program takes a different approach from Example 8.1 to determine how many elements to store in the array of golf scores. A user may have a large amount of data to enter into an array and may not want to count the values. Besides setting a maximum number of array elements, the program can establish an arbitrary trailer or sentinel number, such as −9999. The best way to do so is with a preprocessor *#define*.

```
#define TRAILER -9999
```

As the user enters each element, the program tests to see whether the data item is equal to the trailer item. If it is not, the program enters the item into the array, and reads the next number.

The program must keep a running count of the number of items currently in the array. This information is readily available, because it is necessary to maintain the index of the next available array element. In the program, the variable *player* serves as an index for the loops and a subscript for the array *score*. As soon as the program detects the trailer item, reading ceases, and the loop index *player* contains the number of elements read. When the reading loop ends, we store the value of this index in a variable, *NumPlayers*. In later processing of this array, we can use *NumPlayers* as an upper bound and again use *player* as an index.

Reading must stop, not only when the user enters the trailer value, but if the array fills. For example, if we declare an array *score* to have size 100 and we read values into *score*[100] and beyond, the computer usually does not issue an error message, but unpredictable results are likely to occur. The computer stores the 101st value in the next memory location after the array, overwriting whatever is there.

We do not want to place the trailer value into the array. Therefore, we read each value into a temporary variable and compare the value to *TRAILER*. If they are not equal and the array has room, we store the value in the next available array element. Because the user might type the trailer immediately, we should have a priming read and another read at the end of the loop.

We should also alert the user if he or she entered more data than the array can hold. The following pseudocode is for reading items into an array using the trailer technique:

> *Segment to read values into an array (*score*) using the trailer technique*
>
> This segment reads values interactively, placing them into an array as long as the array has room and as long as the data item is not *TRAILER*. On completion, the array contains *NumPlayers* number of items.
>
> *Algorithm:*
>
> read a value for *OneScore*
> *player* ← 0
> while *player* < *MAX_NUM_PLAYERS* and *OneScore* is not *TRAILER*
>   *score[player]* ← *OneScore*
>   read a value for *OneScore*
>   increment *player* by 1
> if *player* is equal to *MAX_NUM_PLAYERS* and *OneScore* is not *TRAILER*
>   print an error message
> *NumPlayers* ← *player*

The following is a revision of the program in Example 8.1, in which the user enters scores ending with a trailer of –9999:

```
/*
 * Example 8.2. Program to read golf scores until the user
 * types a trailer value and then to print those scores
 */

#include <stdio.h>

#define MAX_NUM_PLAYERS 100
#define TRAILER -9999

main()
{
    int score[MAX_NUM_PLAYERS],   /* array of scores */
        player,                    /* index for array */
        NumPlayers,                /* actual number of players */
        OneScore;                  /* used to read a score */

    /* read values for array score until trailer */
    printf("\nPlease enter up to %d scores. ", MAX_NUM_PLAYERS);
    printf("Enter %d to signal end of data.\n", TRAILER );

    player = 0;
    scanf("%d", &OneScore);
    while (player < MAX_NUM_PLAYERS && OneScore != TRAILER)
    {
        score[player] = OneScore;
        player++;
        scanf("%d", &OneScore);
    }
```

```
/* print error message if too much data for array */
if (player == MAX_NUM_PLAYERS && OneScore != TRAILER)
{
    printf("\nYou have entered more than %d scores.\n",
            MAX_NUM_PLAYERS);
    printf("Only the first %d scores will be processed.\n",
            MAX_NUM_PLAYERS);
}

/* last value of player is actual number of scores */
NumPlayers = player;


/* Print the scores */
printf("\n\tGolf Scores for Round:\n\n");
printf("\tPlayer #\tScore\n");
printf("\t_____\t_____\n");

for (player = 0; player < NumPlayers; player++)
    printf("\t %3d \t\t %3d \n", player + 1, score[player]);
}
```

The following output shows an execution of the program with *MAX_NUM_PLAY-ERS* set equal to the low number of 3, where the user attempts to enter more than 3 values:

```
Please enter up to 3 scores. Enter -9999 to signal end of data.
88
95
77
83


You have entered more than 3 scores.
Only the first 3 scores will be processed.

        Golf Scores for Round:

        Player #        Score
        _____        _____
            1             88
            2             95
            3             77
```

If, however, the user enters 3 scores or less before typing the trailer, processing continues normally, as shown:

```
Please enter up to 3 scores, using -9999 as a trailer:
76
88
92
-9999

        Golf Scores for Round:

        Player #          Score
        _____          _____
           1                76
           2                88
           3                92
```

Example 8.3

In this example, we modify the program from the last example so that the golf scores are read from a text file, *golf.dat*. A text file is convenient with a large amount of data. The design is similar to Example 8.2. We open and close the file. As usually occurs, we read values into the array sequentially. Instead of using a trailer, input terminates when the program detects the end of the file. Because we read within the *while* test, we do not use a priming read. The code for this version of the program follows:

```c
/*
 * Example 8.3.  Program to read golf scores from the file golf.dat
 * and then to print those scores
 */

#include <stdio.h>
#include <stdlib.h>

#define MAX_NUM_PLAYERS 100

main()
{
    int score[MAX_NUM_PLAYERS], /* array of scores */
        player,                 /* index for array */
        NumPlayers;             /* actual number of players*/
    FILE *golffile_ptr;         /* pointer to input file */

    /* open the file */
    golffile_ptr = fopen("golf.dat", "r");
    if (golffile_ptr == NULL)
    {
        printf("golf.dat does not exist.\n");
        exit(1);
    }
```

```
/* read values for array score until end of file */
player = 0;
while (player < MAX_NUM_PLAYERS &&
        fscanf(golffile_ptr, "%d", &score[player]) > 0)
{
    player++;
}

/* print error message if too much data for array */
if (player == MAX_NUM_PLAYERS && !feof(golffile_ptr))
{
    printf("\nFile contained more than %d scores.\n",
            MAX_NUM_PLAYERS);
    printf("Only the first %d scores will be processed.\n",
            MAX_NUM_PLAYERS);
}

/* last value of player is actual number of scores */
NumPlayers = player;


/* Print the scores */
printf("\n\tGolf Scores for Round:\n\n");
printf("\tPlayer #\tScore\n");
printf("\t_____\t_____\n");

for (player = 0; player < NumPlayers; player++)
    printf("\t %3d \t\t %3d \n", player + 1, score[player]);

fclose(golffile_ptr);
}
```

Declaration-Initialization

We have read data into an array and assigned values to array elements. An array can also obtain values through a array declaration-initialization. To do this, we follow the type, array name, and dimension position with an assignment equal and a pair of braces containing a list of constants separated by commas. For example, to initialize an integer array *x* with five values—58, 63, 49, 18, and 7—we write the following:

```
int x[5] = {58, 63, 49, 18, 7};
```

The values used to initialize an array must be constants, never variables or function calls.

When initializing, we need not specify the dimension of the array. For example, the following is an equivalent declaration-initialization in C:

```
int x[] = {58, 63, 49, 18, 7};
```

Because the square brackets following the array name are empty, the compiler determines how many elements to allocate for the array by counting the number of values within the braces. This approach can help avoid errors. If the program specifies the dimension explicitly and the braces contain more initialization values than the size, the compiler indicates a syntax error.

Many arrays exist throughout execution of the program, such as global arrays declared before *main* and arrays declared within *main*. (Later, we see that *static* arrays, as with all *static* variables, also remain in memory throughout execution.) In a declaration-initialization of such an array, if we do not explicitly initialize an element, the compiler sets it to 0 automatically.

In an array local to a function other than *main*, uninitialized elements contain unpredictable values, which depend on the particular compiler. For this reason, we must be careful not to use an uninitialized element in an expression. The C compiler does not regard the use of an uninitialized variable as an error. (This situation is also true for uninitialized scalar variables.)

Section 8.1 Exercises

1. Write a declaration for an array *flt* of 20 elements of type *float*.

2. Define a constant *ARRAY_SIZE* to be 50, and declare an array *dbl* of that size with elements of type *double*.

3. Find the error(s) in the following segment:

```
#define SIZE 40;
main()
{
    char CharArray(SIZE);
    int i;

    for(i = 1; i <= SIZE; i++)
        CharArray(i) = 0;
```

4. Suppose an array *amount* has the following values: 56, 24, 67, 87, and 99. What is the value of *amount* [2]?

5. Suppose *a* is an array with size 50. Write a segment to assign its own index to each element. That is, assign 0 to a[0], 1 to a[1], and so on.

6. Suppose *a* is a *float* array with *NumEls* number of elements. Write a segment to add these values.

7. Suppose array elements *chairs*[0] through *chairs*[49] hold the number of chairs in Rooms 101 through 150, respectively. Write a loop to print the room number and number of chairs for each room.

8. Write a segment to delete the value at location *loc* of a sorted array *a* of *n* elements. Move larger values down to delete the element. For example, if *a* contains 14, 25, 47, 57, and 88, then *n* = 5. Suppose we wish to delete the element at location *loc* = 2 (47). After the deletion, *a* should contain 14, 25, 57, and 88, and *n* should be 4. Use an incrementing *for* loop to move values down.

9. Write a segment to insert a value, *x*, into location *loc* of a sorted array *a* of *n* elements. Do not remove any elements, but move up larger values to make room for the new element. For example, if *a* contains 14, 25, 47, 57, and 88, then *n* = 5. Suppose we wish to insert *x* = 30 in location *loc* = 2, so that a[2] is 30. After the insertion, *a* should contain 14, 25, 30, 47, 57, and 88, and *n* should be 6. Use a decrementing *for* loop to move values up.

10. Write a segment to write the first *NumPlayers* number of values from array *score* into output file with file pointer *FinalFile_ ptr*.

11. Improve the program in Example 8.1 by verifying that the user enters a reasonable score, such as one between 50 and 200.

12. Write a declaration-initialization to fill 5-element array *a* with ones. Do not explicitly give a dimension for *a*.

13. Write a declaration-initialization to place 44, 53, and 68 in an array *a* of size 3.

14. Write a declaration-initialization to place 0 in every element of array *a* of size 500, where *a* is in *main*.

Section 8.1 Programming Projects

1. Read a collection of integers and print it forwards and backwards. For example, for an input of the following four integers:

    23 34 123 7

    display them as entered and as follows:

    7 123 34 23

2. The standard telephone associates each of the digits 2 through 9 with a group of three letters. For example, the number 2 is associated with the letters A, B, and C; 3 with D, E, and F; and 9 with W, X, and Y. The letters Q and Z are not generally used, but a new standard has Q on the 7 key and Z on the 9 key. Therefore, we can translate telephone numbers into words. Some companies use such a mnemonic to help customers remember their numbers. For example, the word PROGRAM stands for the number 776-4726. Write a program to read 7 characters (excluding Q and Z) and translate them into a telephone number. Have an array of 26 elements corresponding to the letters of the alphabet. Each array element should store the phone digit for that character.

Section 8.2 Functions with Array Parameters

As programs become larger, it is preferable to separate tasks into different functions. In the examples of Section 8.1, it would have been clearer to have functions for reading values into the array and for printing the table. The prototype for a function, *ReadScores*, to read the first *NumPlayers* number of elements of an integer array *score* is

```
void ReadScores(int [], int);
```

or

```
void ReadScores(int score[], int NumPlayers);
```

We will study in greater detail in the next chapter, that the name of an array, such as *score*, evaluates to the memory location of the first array element. Hence, we are not passing a copy of the entire array to *ReadScores*, but where to find the array. Such a mechanism saves time and space, since the computer does not take the time to copy the elements into another array that is active only while the function executes. Moreover, even while *ReadScores* is executing, there is only one copy of the array in memory. Particularly for large arrays, such economy of time and space is advantageous.

Before now, we have only been able to send one value back to the calling function through the return statement. The calling function, however, passes the reference to the array and not the individual array values. Therefore, when the called function changes a value in the array, it is changing the element in the array of the calling function. In the next chapter on pointers, we will see how a called function can make similar changes to other calling function variables.

In the above prototype, we used empty square brackets to declare that the first parameter is an array. Consequently, we could call the function several times with different arrays of different dimensions. The prototype has a second parameter, which is of type *int* and holds the number of elements in the array. We call the function without using brackets after the array name.

```
ReadScores(score, NumPlayers);
```

Read, Average, and Print

Example 8.4

In this program, we find the average golf score for the situation in Example 8.1 of Section 8.1. Because in a golf tournament the low score wins, we also print those scores that are below average. Using top-down design, we have *main* call functions to perform the various tasks. No routine needs to call another user-defined function, so the structure chart of Figure 8.4 has only two levels.

> **main()**
>
> Program to read the number of golf scores, to read scores, to print the average score, and to print the number of scores below the average
>
> **Algorithm:**
>
> obtain number of players: *NumPlayers* ← *GetNumPlayers()*
> read scores into array *score* by calling *ReadScores*
> compute the average score, *AverageScore*, by calling *average*
> print the scores below this average by calling *PrintBelowAverage*

Figure 8.4 Structure chart for program in Example 8.4

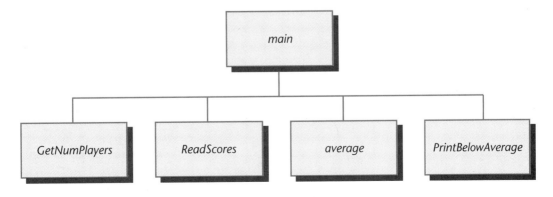

The function *GetNumPlayers* is as in Example 8.1. *ReadScores* displays the prompt from Example 8.1 and reads array values using the *for* loop from that example. The function *average* is sent the location of the first element of the array *score*, and the number of elements that have values, *NumPlayers*. Using a local variable (*total*) with an initial value of 0, the function sums the scores in a loop, as shown:

```
total = 0;
for (player = 0; player < NumPlayers; player++)
    total += score[player];
```

Figure 8.5 pictures the first couple of iterations of this loop.

The pseudocode for *average* shows the computation of the average after accumulation of the sum. Although another function (*GetNumPlayers*) ensures that the divisor *NumPlayers* is not 0, we should check for a potential division-by-zero error. In the future, someone could change *GetNumPlayers*, not realizing the implications elsewhere in the program, or we could decide to use *average* in another program that does not guarantee *NumPlayers* to be positive.

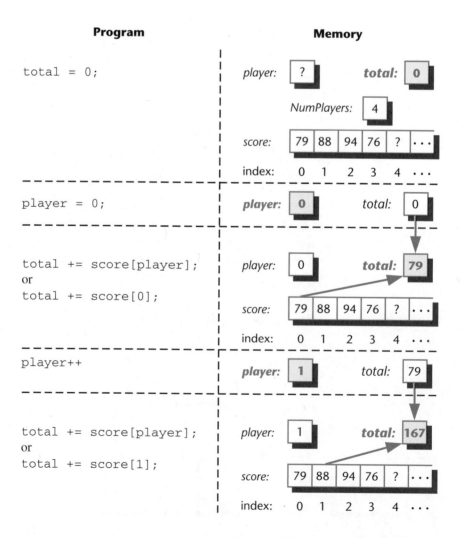

Figure 8.5
Initialization of *total* and two iterations of loop to add scores

average(score, NumPlayers) ⟶ *AverageScore*

Function to return the average of elements 0 through *NumPlayers* − 1 in *int* array *score*

Pre:

score is an array of integers.
NumPlayers a positive integer indicating the number of values in *score*.

Post:

The floating point average score has been returned. If *NumPlayers* was 0, an error message was printed and 0.0 returned.

Algorithm:

if *NumPlayers* is 0
   print an error message—cannot divide by 0
   AverageScore ← 0.0
else
   total ← 0
   for *player* from 0 through *NumPlayers* − 1 do the following:
      total ← *total* + *score*[*player*]
   AverageScore ← floating point quotient *total* / *NumPlayers*
return *AverageScore*

The function *PrintBelowAverage* contains a similar segment to that of the programs in Examples 8.1–8.3, which printed a table of the players' scores. In the current loop, however, we only print a score (*score*[*player*]) if it is less than the average (*AverageScore*). The code for the program appears after the following pseudocode for *PrintBelowAverage:*

PrintBelowAverage(score, NumPlayers, AverageScore)

Function to print the average, *AverageScore*, and those elements in array *score* that are below the average

Pre:

score is an array of integers.
NumPlayers is an integer indicating number of values in *score*.
AverageScore is a floating point number indicating the average score.

Post:

Below average scores were displayed.

Algorithm:

print headings and *AverageScore*
for *player* from 0 through *NumPlayers* − 1 do the following:
   if (*score*[*player*] is less than *AverageScore*)
      print *player* + 1 and *score*[*player*]

```c
/*
 * Example 8.4
 * Program to read the number of golf scores, to read
 * scores, to print the average score, and to print
 * the scores below the average
 */

#include <stdio.h>

#define MAX_NUM_PLAYERS 100

main()
{
    int GetNumPlayers(void);
    void ReadScores(int [], int );
    float average(int [], int );
    void PrintBelowAverage(int [], int, float);


    int score[MAX_NUM_PLAYERS],   /* array of scores */
        NumPlayers;        /* actual number of players */
    float AverageScore; /* average of the scores */

    NumPlayers = GetNumPlayers();
    ReadScores(score, NumPlayers);
    AverageScore = average(score, NumPlayers);
    PrintBelowAverage(score, NumPlayers, AverageScore);
}

/*
 * Function to read and return number of players
 * Pre:    none
 * Post:   The number of players, an integer between
 *         1 and MAX_NUM_PLAYERS, was returned.
 */

int GetNumPlayers(void)
{
    int NumPlayers;        /* actual number of players */
    printf("How many players are in the golf tournament? ");
    scanf("%d", &NumPlayers);

    while ((NumPlayers <= 0) || (MAX_NUM_PLAYERS < NumPlayers))
    {
        printf("The number of players must be between 1 and %d\n",
                MAX_NUM_PLAYERS);
        printf("Please enter the number of players again. ");
        scanf("%d", &NumPlayers);
    }

    return NumPlayers;
}
```

```c
/*
 * Function to read NumPlayers number of values for
 * array score
 * Pre:    NumPlayers is a positive integer.
 * Post:   NumPlayers number of integers has been read
 *         into array scores
 */

void ReadScores(int score[],  int NumPlayers)
{
    int player;          /* index for array */

    printf("\nPlease enter %d scores ", NumPlayers);
    printf("with blanks separating scores:\n");

    for (player = 0; player < NumPlayers; player++)
        scanf("%d", &score[player]);
}


/*
 * Function to return the average of elements 0 through
 * NumPlayers - 1 in array score
 * Pre:    score is an array of integers.
 *         NumPlayers is a positive number of values in score.
 * Post:   The floating point average score has been returned.
 *         If NumPlayers was 0, an error message was printed
 *         and 0.0 returned.
 */

float average(int score[], int NumPlayers)
{
    int player,              /* index for array */
        total = 0;           /* sum of scores */
    float AverageScore;      /* average of the scores */

    if (NumPlayers == 0)
    {
        printf("0 number of players. Returning 0 for average\n");
        AverageScore = 0.0;
    }
    else
    {
        for (player = 0; player < NumPlayers; player++)
            total += score[player];
        AverageScore = (float)total / NumPlayers;
    }

    return AverageScore;
}
```

```
/*
 * Function to print average of NumPlayers number of
 * scores. Also, print player number and score for those
 * players with a below average score.
 * Pre:     score is an array of integers.
 *          NumPlayers is an integer; the number of values in score.
 *          AverageScore is a float; the average score.
 * Post:    Below average scores were displayed.
 */

void PrintBelowAverage(int score[], int NumPlayers,
        float AverageScore)
{
    int player;         /* index for array */

    printf("\nThe average score is %.2f\n", AverageScore);

    printf("\n\tBelow Average Golf Scores for Round:\n\n");
    printf("\tPlayer #\tScore\n");
    printf("\t_____\t_____\n");

    for (player = 0; player < NumPlayers; player++)
        if (score[player] < AverageScore)
            printf("\t %3d \t\t %3d \n", player + 1, score[player]);
}
```

The following printout from an execution of this program contains the average and a table of the numbers of the leading players with their scores.

```
How many players are in the golf tournament? 4

Please enter 4 scores with blanks separating scores:
79 88 94 76

The average score is 84.25

        Below Average Golf Scores for Round:

    Player #        Score
    _____        _____
        1               79
        4               76
```

Minimum and Maximum

Often it is necessary to find the minimum or maximum of a set of values. For instance, the winner of the golf tournament has the low, or minimum, score.

To find the minimum value in a nonempty array, we copy the first value of the array to another variable (say *min*), which represents a temporary minimum. We then compare *min*'s value successively with each remaining element of the array, beginning with the second and ending with the last element. Each element that is smaller than the current value of *min* replaces the current minimum, and the comparison continues from that point in the array. When we reach the end of the array, *min* contains the array's minimum value. We can find the maximum in a similar way. Instead of searching for smaller elements, the loop searches for elements larger than the temporary maximum.

Example 8.5

Let us revise the last program, adding a function, *winner*, to print the score of the winner. When *main* calls *winner* with

```
winner(score, NumPlayers);
```

the program performs the actions of Figure 8.6. For that data, the function prints

```
The winning score is 76.
```

The code for the function follows.

```
/*
 * Function to find and print score of
 * golf tournament winner (lowest score)
 * Pre:    score is a nonempty array of integers.
 *         NumPlayers is an integer; the number of values in score.
 * Post:   Tournament winning score was displayed.
 */

void winner(int score[], int NumPlayers)
{
    int player,         /* index for array */
        min;            /* ongoing minimum in array */

    min = score[0];
    for (player = 1; player < NumPlayers; player++)
        if (score[player] < min)
            min = score[player];

    printf("\nThe winning score is %d.\n", min);
}
```

We could also implement this function as one that does not print, but instead returns the minimum value for processing by the calling function. To do this, we change the first line of the prototype and definition to reflect a function type of *int*.

If we want to print the number of the player who wins, we must have another variable (*MinPlayer*) to store the index of the minimum value. As *min* is initialized to *score*[0], *MinPlayer* is initialized to 0. On the last iteration of the loop, when *min* gets the value of *score*[3], *MinPlayer* gets the value 3. The answer prints the value of *MinPlayer* + 1 (or 4) to match the player numbers. This approach assumes that no tie for the winner occurs. In the exercises, we examine how to print all players who score the minimum. The revised function follows:

Figure 8.6
Action of
segment to find
minimum
element in
array *score*

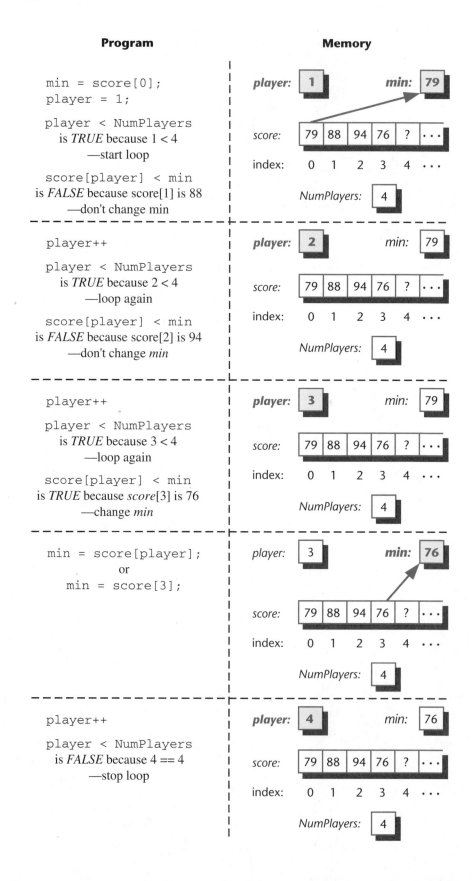

Program

```
min = score[0];
player = 1;
```

player < NumPlayers
    is *TRUE* because 1 < 4
        —start loop

```
score[player] < min
```
is *FALSE* because score[1] is 88
        —don't change min

```
player++
```

player < NumPlayers
    is *TRUE* because 2 < 4
        —loop again

```
score[player] < min
```
is *FALSE* because score[2] is 94
        —don't change *min*

```
player++
```

player < NumPlayers
    is *TRUE* because 3 < 4
        —loop again

```
score[player] < min
```
is *TRUE* because *score*[3] is 76
        —change *min*

```
min = score[player];
            or
min = score[3];
```

```
player++
```

player < NumPlayers
    is *FALSE* because 4 == 4
        —stop loop

Memory

player: 1   *min:* 79

score: | 79 | 88 | 94 | 76 | ? | · · ·

index: 0   1   2   3   4 · · ·

NumPlayers: 4

---

player: 2   *min:* 79

score: | 79 | 88 | 94 | 76 | ? | · · ·

index: 0   1   2   3   4 · · ·

NumPlayers: 4

---

player: 3   *min:* 79

score: | 79 | 88 | 94 | 76 | ? | · · ·

index: 0   1   2   3   4 · · ·

NumPlayers: 4

---

player: 3   *min:* 76

score: | 79 | 88 | 94 | 76 | ? | · · ·

index: 0   1   2   3   4 · · ·

NumPlayers: 4

---

player: 4   *min:* 76

score: | 79 | 88 | 94 | 76 | ? | · · ·

index: 0   1   2   3   4 · · ·

NumPlayers: 4

```
/*
 * Function to find and print player number and score of
 * golf tournament winner (with lowest score) assuming no tie
 * Pre:     score is a nonempty array of integers with the minimum
 *          occurring only once.
 *          NumPlayers is an integer; the number of values in score.
 * Post:    Tournament winning score and player number were displayed.
 */

void winner(int score[], int NumPlayers)
{
    int player,     /* index for array */
        min,        /* ongoing minimum in array */
        MinPlayer;  /* index of minimum */

    min = score[0];
    MinPlayer = 0;

    for (player = 1; player < NumPlayers; player++)
        if (score[player] < min)
        {
            min = score[player];
            MinPlayer = player;
        }

    printf("\nThe winner is Player #%d with a score of %d.\n",
           MinPlayer + 1, min);
}
```

This new version produces the following output:

> The winner is Player #4 with a score of 76.

Frequency

Example 8.6

The function in this example has two parameters—*ar*, an array, and *NumEls*, the number of elements that occupy the array. This function, *frequency*, displays how many array elements are equal to each integer in a particular range. It plays the role of a frequency counter. For example, suppose the lower bound for the range is *RANGE_LOW* = 80, the upper bound is *RANGE_HIGH* = 89, and the array *ar* contains the following 20 elements:

88 83 88 79 85 94 88 82 87 76 87 83 89 90 80 86 86 89 87 88

In this case, the function should print the following:

```
        Frequency Distribution

        Value    Frequency
        -----    ---------

         80          1
         81          0
         82          1
         83          2
         84          0
         85          1
         86          2
         87          3
         88          4
         89          2
```

There is one 80 in *ar* and no 81s, while 88 has a frequency of 4. Four array elements—79, 94, 76, and 90—are out of the range from 80 to 89 entirely.

To compute the frequencies, we have an integer array, *tally*, which contains one element for each number in the range. Therefore, we determine its *SIZE* using the difference between *RANGE_HIGH* and *RANGE_LOW*. We add an extra 1 to make the range inclusive, as shown:

```
#define RANGE_LOW 80
#define RANGE_HIGH 89
#define SIZE (RANGE_HIGH - RANGE_LOW + 1)
    ⋮
    int tally[SIZE];
```

For the range from 80 through 89, *tally* has 89 − 80 + 1 = 10 elements, *tally*[0] through *tally*[9].

Each element of *tally* is a counter, which, as with all counters, must be initialized to 0. We use a bodiless *for* loop with index *bin* going from 0 to *SIZE* − 1 for the initialization, as shown:

```
for (bin = 0; bin < SIZE; tally[bin++] = 0);
```

Figure 8.7 pictures *tally* after execution of this loop. As the figure indicates, *tally*[0] stores the number of 80s in array *ar*; *tally*[1], the frequency of 81; and so on.

Another *for* loop with index *i* processes each element of *ar*, determining to which "bin," if any, it belongs. This loop begins as follows:

```
for (i = 0; i < NumEls; i++)...
```

Within the loop, we must first check if the array element *ar*[*i*] is in the range between *RANGE_LOW* and *RANGE_HIGH*, as shown:

```
if (RANGE_LOW <= ar[i] && ar[i] <= RANGE_HIGH)...
```

Figure 8.7
Array *tally* after
initialization in
Example 8.6

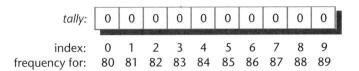

For instance, the values 79, 94, 76, and 90 are not between 80 and 89—no counters exist for them. If the value is in the proper range, we use the value itself (*ar*[*i*]) to locate an element of the array *tally*. We determine the index, or subscript, of this element by *ar*[*i*] – *RANGE_LOW*, so that 0 represents the lowest value in the range. For example, if *ar*[*i*] is 87 and *RANGE_LOW* is 80, then *ar*[*i*] – *RANGE_LOW* is 87 – 80 = 7. The element *tally*[7] stores how frequently 87 occurs in *ar*. Consequently, we must increment this counter by 1, *tally*[7]++. In the program, the post-increment is as follows:

```
tally[ar[i] - RANGE_LOW]++;
```

Figure 8.8 depicts the first three iterations of this loop to tally the values.

In the final segment of the function, we use a *for* loop to print the various frequencies, the elements of *tally*, as follows:

```
for (bin = 0; bin < SIZE; bin++)...
```

We add the value *RANGE_LOW* to the index *bin* to display the actual range, rather than the indices of *tally*, as shown:

```
printf("\t%3d\t%3d\n", bin + RANGE_LOW, tally[bin]);
```

For example, when *bin* is 7, we are printing the frequency of 7 + 80 = 87. The element *tally*[7] contains this frequency, which is 3—87 occurs 3 times in array *ar*. Thus, the output from this iteration is as follows:

```
87          3
```

The entire code for the function is as follows:

```
/*
 * Example 8.6. Tally numbers between RANGE_LOW and RANGE_HIGH
 */

#define RANGE_LOW 80
#define RANGE_HIGH 89
#define SIZE (RANGE_HIGH - RANGE_LOW + 1)

/*
 * Function to compute and print the frequency of values
 * between RANGE_LOW and RANGE_HIGH in array ar from ar[0]
 * to ar[NumEls - 1]
 * Pre:    ar is an array of integers.
 *
 *         NumEls is the number of elements in ar.
 * Post:   The frequency of values from ar between
 *         RANGE_LOW and RANGE_HIGH was displayed.
 */
```

Figure 8.8 First three iterations of this loop to tally in Example 8.6

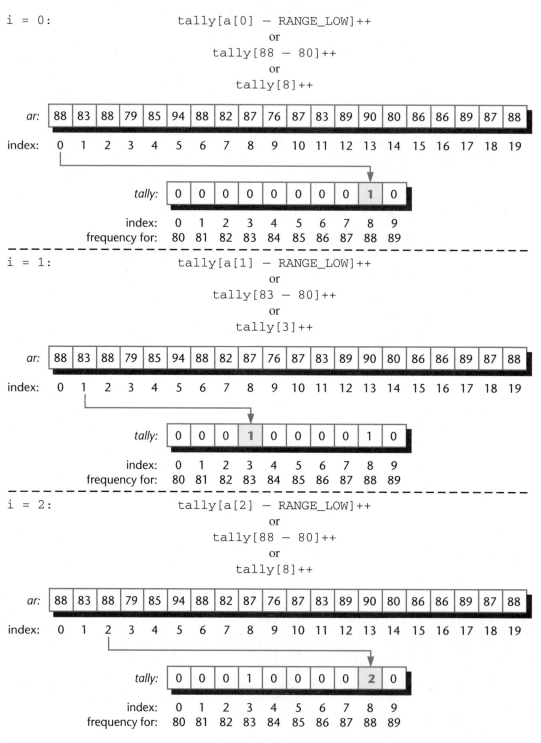

```
void frequency(int ar[], int NumEls)
{
    int tally[SIZE],    /* one bin for each number in the range */
        bin,            /* index for tally */
        i;              /* index for ar */

    /* initialize array tally to zero */
    for (bin = 0; bin < SIZE; tally[bin++] = 0);

    /* tally elements of array ar */
    for (i = 0; i < NumEls; i++)
        if (RANGE_LOW <= ar[i] && ar[i] <= RANGE_HIGH)
            tally[ar[i] - RANGE_LOW]++;

    /* print tally results */
    printf("\n         Frequency Distribution\n\n");
    printf("\tValue\tFrequency\n");
    printf("\t-----\t---------\n\n");

    for (bin = 0; bin < SIZE; bin++)
        printf("\t%3d\t%3d\n", bin + RANGE_LOW, tally[bin]);
}
```

Section 8.2 Exercises

1. Write a function *sum* that returns the sum of the first *n* elements of *float* array *a*.

2. Write a function *maximum* that returns the maximum of the first *n* elements of *float* array *a*.

3. Write a function *copy* that copies the first *n* elements of array *a* into array *b*, where the elements of both *a* and *b* are of type *int*.

4. Write a function *ReplaceNeg* that replaces each negative value in the first *n* elements of array *A* of integers with zero.

5. Revise the function *winner* in Example 8.5 to print the minimum score and the numbers of all the players who score the minimum. We now include the possibility of a tie.

Section 8.2 Programming Projects

1. Develop a program to read grades with values of type *float* using interactive input and the trailer method. Then, print a table of the students' numbers and grades, and print the high and low grades.

2. Modify Project 1 to print the numbers of students with the highest and lowest grades.

3. Modify Project 1 and/or 2 so they read the grades from text file *grades.dat* with grades entered one per line.

4. Develop a program to generate 500 random integers between 1 and 20 and to print the frequency distribution (that is, the number of ones, the number of twos, and so on). Use the files *RandDef.c* and *RandDef.h* on your text disk (see Appendix F).

5. Example 8.6 shows how to use bins to tally values in a range. The lower and upper bounds of the range could be changed, but not the size of the bins. For example, suppose we wish to accept numbers between 1 and 50, using only 10 bins. The first bin records how many of the numbers are between 1 and 5, the second tallies the numbers are between 6 and 10, and so on, up to the tenth bin, which counts the numbers 46 through 50. The "width" of each bin, in this case 5, is the total number of values in the range divided by the number of bins.

Develop a program similar to Example 8.6, which uses 10 bins and permits the user to input the lower and upper bounds of the range. The number of values in the range should be a multiple of 10, so that all 10 bins can have the same width. Generate data with a random number generator (see Appendix F).

6. Develop a program to do the following:

a. Give a prompt and accept input of a sentence of up to 80 characters.

b. Give a prompt and accept input of a single letter.

c. Use the letter from Part b to encode the sentence of Part a as follows: Replace each letter of the sentence by another letter of the alphabet in such a way that the distance within the alphabet from the original letter to its replacement is the same as the distance from the letter A to the letter obtained in Part b. For this exercise, assume that the letters following Z are A, B, C, etc. For example, if the letter obtained in Part b were an H, then any A would be replaced by H, any B by I, any C by J, etc. The letter Z would be replaced by G. Characters other than letters should not be affected by the encoding, and you can assume that only capital letters are used. The program should print out the encoded sentence.

d. Count the number of occurrences of each letter in the original sentence and print a list of the frequency counts.

Sample Dialogue:

```
PLEASE TYPE IN THE SENTENCE:
FDU PROGRAMMING CONTEST

PLEASE TYPE IN THE ENCODING CHARACTER:
K

PNE ZBYQBKWWSXQ MYXDOCD

THE LETTER FREQUENCIES ARE:

A - 1   B - 0   C - 1   D - 1   E - 1   F - 1   G - 2
H - 0   I - 1   J - 0   K - 0   L - 0   M - 2   N - 2
O - 2   P - 1   Q - 0   R - 2   S - 1   T - 2   U - 1
V - 0   W - 0   X - 0   Y - 0   Z - 0
```

7. The bar codes used on most products include a check digit (the last digit in the bar code), which allows error checking by the bar code reader. The bar code reader compares it to a digit calculated by the following method:

1. Add up all the odd-numbered digits in the bar code (counting from the left, with the leftmost digit being number 0), excluding the check digit.

2. Multiply each even-numbered digit, excluding the check digit, by 2. If the result of the multiplication exceeds 9, add its two digits. Add the sum of these results to the sum calculated in Step 1.

3. Divide the result of Step 2 by 10 and subtract the remainder from 10. If the result is less than 10, it should equal the check digit. Otherwise, the check digit should be zero.

Develop a program that accepts input of a bar code (as a string of decimal digits) and checks it for correctness using the algorithm given above. The program should check the individual characters of the input string to verify that they are decimal digits.

Here are two sample runs of such a program with the input underlined.

```
Bar Code: 1347830
Correct!
Bar Code: 78147791
Wrong!
```

8. When trying to identify the author of an unknown manuscript, experts compare the writing style to that of known authors and look for similarities. People searching for these "hidden signatures" may look at things like average length of words and sentences, common words, or known grammatical styles such as alliteration. In our case, the Signature Function of a text is given by this formula:

$$SF = \sum_{i=1}^{26} \frac{f_i 2^i}{10000}$$

That is, the Signature Function (SF) for the text is the sum of the relative frequency of each letter f_i (frequency/(number of letters), a value between 0 and 1) multiplied by 2 raised to the power of the letter's position in the alphabet (that is, 'a' is in position 1 and 'z' is in position 26) divided by ten thousand. When counting letters, case is ignored.

Develop a program that prompts for the names and signature functions of 5 known authors. Next, you accept up to 20 lines of 80 characters from the user as the unknown text. Input should end automatically after 20 lines or if a dollar sign is entered on a line by itself. (Alternatively, use text input from a file.) Your program should determine the signature function for this unknown text and return the name of the author whose signature function most closely matches that of the text.

Sample run:

```
Enter name of author number 1: Peter
Enter is person's signature function value: 1306
Enter name of author number 2: Kathy
Enter is person's signature function value: 830
Enter name of author number 3: Neal
Enter is person's signature function value: 492
Enter name of author number 4: John
Enter is person's signature function value: 729
Enter name of author number 5: Carol
Enter is person's signature function value: 239

Enter lines of text below. End input with a $ on its own
line.

It used to seem to me,
that my life went on too fast.
And I had to take it slowly,
just to make the good parts last.
$
This person's SF value is 127.08121 and most closely
matches Carol.
```

9. Develop a program to score a bowling game, which consists of ten frames. In each frame, the objective is to knock down all or most of the ten pins using one or two throws of the ball. If all ten pins are knocked down on the first throw in a frame, a strike is scored, and the score for that frame is 10 plus the total number of pins knocked down in the next two throws. In the case of a strike, there is no second throw of the ball in the same frame. If only some of the pins are knocked down in the first throw of a frame but the remaining pins are knocked down in the second throw, a spare is scored. The score for a spare is 10 plus the number of pins knocked down in the next throw. If the total number of pins knocked down in the two throws of a frame is less than ten, then that total number is the score for the frame. If a strike is scored in the tenth frame, two more balls are thrown to determine the score for that frame. A spare in the tenth frame allows the player to throw one more ball to complete the scoring for the tenth frame.

   The input to the program will be a list of numbers indicating the number of pins knocked down on each throw. The program must check that the input is valid. There must be enough numbers to score all ten frames, and the total number of pins knocked down in any frame can never exceed 10. If the input is valid, the program should produce an output like the example below.

   A typical input might be the following:

   8   1   6   4   10   10   3   5   9   1   10   6   4   10   7   3   9

   It would result in the following scoring, where an X indicates a strike and a / indicates a spare:

```
Frame |  1  |  2  |  3  |  4  |  5  |  6  |  7  |  8  | ·9  | 10  |  Extra
      ------------------------------------------------------------------
Ball 1|  8  |  6. |  X  |  X  |  3  |  9  |  X  |  6  |  X  |  7  |    9
      ------------------------------------------------------------------
Ball 2|  1  |  /  |     |     |  5  |  /  |     |  /  |     |  /  |
      ------------------------------------------------------------------
Score |  9  | 29  | 52  | 70  | 78  | 98  |118  |138  |158  |177  |
```

The score at the bottom is cumulative. For instance, the score for frame 2 is 10 (for the spare) plus the 10 on the next ball. That is added to the frame 1 score of 9 to yield a total score of 29 through the second frame. Similarly, the score for the third frame is 10 (for the strike) plus the 10 on the next ball, plus the 3 on the next ball, for a total of 23. That added to the previous score of 29 yields a total of 52 through the third frame.

The following would be an invalid input list, because there are not enough scores:

10   3   4   5   5   10   10   8   2   7   3   10   10   10

The following would be invalid, because of an excessive number of pins in the third frame:

2 `7 10   6   6   9   1   10   8   2   10   10   9   1   10   2   4

Section 8.3 **Sequential and Binary Searches**

Sequential Search

Probably the first method most people use to look for an item in an array is a **sequential** or **linear search**. The technique is like looking through a notebook for the answer to a question. We are sure the solution is there but we have no idea exactly where it is. We start at the beginning of the notebook, thumbing through every page looking for the answer. When we find it, we may jot down the answer or the page number on which it occurs. If we get to the end of the notebook without locating the answer, we might throw the notes down in frustration. If we had some recollection of where the answer was, we might have stopped searching well before the final page.

Let us consider this sequential search of an array a for a value x. If we find x, we return the index where the value occurs. Otherwise, we return a value that is not a possible index, such as -1, to indicate that the search has failed. Suppose the array is not sorted into ascending (elements arranged from smallest to largest) or descending order (elements arranged from largest to smallest). With such an unordered array, we must examine the entire array before we are certain x is not there. If the data in the array are ordered, however, we halt as soon as we are past the point in the array where x should be. Figure 8.9 pictures a character array in ascending order. If we are searching for $x = $ 'G', we know we have failed when we compare $x = $ 'G' with $a[3] = $

Figure 8.9
Character array
a in ascending
order

```
a:   'B' | 'E' | 'F' | 'H' | 'K' | 'N' | 'S'
index:  0    1     2     3     4     5     6
```

'H'. Because 'G' appears before 'H' in the alphabet, we are beyond the point where 'G' could occur. The algorithm for a sequential search of an array *a*, sorted into ascending order, is in Algorithm 8.1.

Algorithm 8.1.   Sequential search of a sorted array

SeqSearch(a, n, x) → i

> Function to perform sequential search for *x* in the first *n* elements of array *a*. Function returns index of the first element found equaling *x* or −1 if not found.

Pre:

> *a* is an array and the elements *a*[0] through *a*[*n* − 1] are in ascending order.
> *n* is the number of elements in *a*.
> *x* is an item for which to search. It has the same type as an element of *a*.

Post:

> The index of *a* where *x* is found (or −1 if not found) has been returned.

Algorithm:

> $i \leftarrow 0$
> *done* ← *FALSE*
> while (*i* is less than *n* and not *done*) do the following:
>   if (*x* is less than or equal to *a*[*i*])
>   *done* ← *TRUE*
>   else
> $i \leftarrow i + 1$
>
> if (*i* is equal to *n* or *x* is not equal to *a*[*i*])
> $i \leftarrow -1$
> return *i*

The index *i* gets an initial value of 0. When the loop terminates, *i* is *n* or the index of the array element that the last iteration examined. The loop could stop because *i* had exceeded the largest index (*n* − 1) without our finding the element. In this case, *i* equals *n*, and the function must return −1. The loop could also terminate because *x* ≤ *a*[*i*], causing *done* to become *TRUE*. If *x* equals *a*[*i*], the search is successful, and the function returns the index *i*. If not, we again return −1.

Example 8.7 _____

In this example, we code a function, *SeqSearchUnordered*, to perform a sequential search for an item (*x*) in an unordered array (*a*) of *n* elements. The design is similar to that of *SeqSearch*. However, because the array is not sorted, we test for equality of *x* and each array element until the item is found or we have exhausted the array. If *x* equals *a*[*i*] for any *i*, then the boolean variable *found* becomes *TRUE*. After a search of the array, if *found* remains *FALSE*, we return −1.

```
/*
 * Example 8.7
 * Function to search an unordered array sequentially
 * Pre:     a is a char array with n elements.
 *          x is a char.
 * Post:    The index of the first occurrence of x in a has been
 *          returned or, if not found, -1.
 */

int SeqSearchUnordered(char a[], int n, char x)
{
    int i = 0,                  /* index */
        found = FALSE;          /* indicates if x has been found */

    while (i < n && !found)
    {
        if (x == a[i])
            found = TRUE;
        else
            i++;
    }

    if (!found)
        i = -1;
    return i;
}
```

Number of Elements to Search

In a sequential search, what is the largest number of iterations of the loop? Under what condition does this worst case scenario occur? In a sequential search of the sorted array in Figure 8.9, if $x = $ 'S', we must examine every element to deduce that *SeqSearch* or *SeqSearchUnordered* should return 6. If the value of x is beyond 'S', say 'T' or 'Z', then we must make 7 comparisons and terminate, returning -1. For an array of n elements, the worst case occurs when we must search all n elements. Even on the average, we must search about half of the n elements.

Searching through n elements does not really seem so bad, but suppose a million elements are in the array ($n = 1,000,000$). Would we really want to look through a phone book sequentially for the telephone number of J. Zwen? Of course, we would have to do so if the phone book or the array is not sorted. However, a better way exists for searching a large array arranged in ascending or descending order.

Binary Search

A **binary search** is close to how we would look for someone's name in the sorted phone book. We open the book to the middle and see if the name is there. If not, we decide which part of the book should contain the name. Then we repeat the process with that part of the book. The search stops when we find the name or when we have subdivided the book so much that there is nothing left and we know the name must not be present. Although we may not open the phone directory exactly in the middle, in a binary search we cut the problem in half with each iteration. Division by 2 is built into the hardware of many computers and, consequently, is very fast.

Figure 8.10
Picture of the
binary search of
array *a* for *x* =
'K'

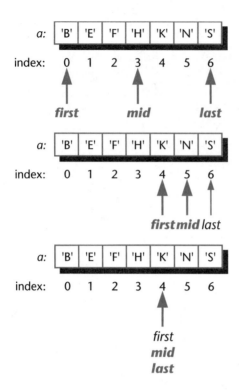

Figure 8.10 shows a picture of the binary search of array *a* for *x* = 'K'. The variables *first* and *last* are the indices of the first and last elements, respectively, of the part of the array under consideration. The middle index of that subarray is *mid*. Initially, *first* = 0 and *last* = 6. To calculate the index of the middle element, we add the first and last indices and divide the result by 2. In this situation, *mid* = (0 + 6)/2 = 3. Suppose *last* had been 7. With integer division, we also obtain *mid* = (0 + 7) / 2 = 3. Our formula for the middle index is as follows:

mid = (*first* + *last*) / 2

Since *x*'s value, 'K', is larger than that of this middle element, *a*[3] ='H', we no longer need to consider the left half of the array. We continue the search from just beyond the *a*[3] element to the end of the array. In this subarray, *first* = 4 and *last* still is 6 with the resulting *mid* = 5. Now, *x* = 'K' is less than *a*[5] = 'N', so we must take the left half of the subarray and change the value of *last* to 4. With *first* = *last* = *mid* = 4, *x* must be in that position if it is there at all. In this case, *x* does equal *a*[4]. As shown in Figure 8.11, had *x* been 'L' instead of 'K', on the last step we would have assigned *first* a value of 5. Then *first* = 5 would have been larger than *last* = 4, and the search would have terminated with the realization that *x*'s value was not in the array. Algorithm 8.2 presents the method for a binary search.

Figure 8.11
Picture of the
binary search of
array *a* for *x =*
'L'

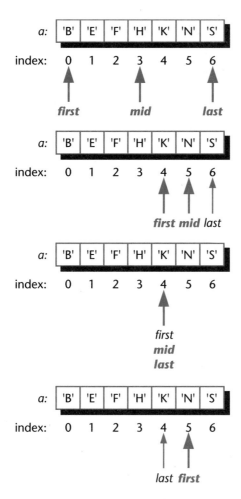

Algorithm 8.2. Binary search of a sorted array

BiSearch(a, n, x) → i

> Function to perform binary search for *x* in the first *n* elements of array *a*.
> Function returns index of the first element found equaling *x* or −1 if not
> found.

Pre:

> *a* is an array, and the elements *a*[0] through *a*[*n* − 1] are in ascending order.
> *n* is the number of elements in *a*.
> *x* is an item for which to search. It has the same type as an element of *a*.

Post:

> The index of *a* where *x* is found (or −1 if not found) has been returned.

Algorithm:

> *first* ← 0
> *last* ← *n* − 1
> *found* ← FALSE
> while (*first* is less than or equal to *last* and not *found*) do the following:
> > *mid* ← (*first* + *last*) / 2
> > if (*x* is less than *a*[*mid*])
> > > *last* ← *mid* − 1
> > else if (*x* is greater than *a*[*mid*])
> > > *first* ← *mid* + 1
> > else
> > > *found* ← TRUE
> if not *found* then
> > *mid* ← −1
> return *mid*

Number of Elements to Search

In the binary search for x = 'K' or 'L', we initially examine an array of 7 elements. On the next iteration, we search a subarray of 7 / 2 = 3 elements, and lastly an array of 3 / 2 = 1 element. Thus, for $7 = 2^3 - 1$ elements, we need at most 3 iterations. Even for $15 = 2^4 - 1$ elements, more than double the size, we only need to check at most 4 elements, because if the middle element is not x, we cut the problem in half and consider a subarray of 15 / 2 = 7 elements. With an array of $255 = 2^8 - 1$ elements, what is the maximum number of iterations? Table 8.1 shows the number of elements in the subarray for each iteration. Each time the subarray under consideration is cut in half. In general, for $2^m - 1$ elements, at most m elements must be checked because each time the problem is halved.

Figure 8.12 shows the search for x = 'S' or 'T' in an array of 20 elements—a search that requires 5 iterations. Observe for each iteration in Table 8.2, we have a subarray half or less the size of the previous array. During the fourth iteration, we consider a subarray with two elements, so in the worst case we must divide the problem one more time. Because 20 is between $2^4 - 1 = 15$ and $2^5 - 1 = 31$, we take the larger exponent of 2. For 20 elements, *BiSearch* needs at most 5 iterations.

Suppose the number of elements n, such as 20, is not of the form $2^m - 1$. How many iterations must be made in a binary search? Before continuing, we should review

Table 8.1   Number of elements in subarray of a, an array of 255 elements, used in successive iterations of the loop in *BiSearch*

Iteration	Size of Subarray		
1		255 =	$2^8 - 1$
2	255/2 =	127 =	$2^7 - 1$
3	127 / 2 =	63 =	$2^6 - 1$
4	63 / 2 =	31 =	$2^5 - 1$
5	31 / 2 =	15 =	$2^4 - 1$
6	15 / 2 =	7 =	$2^3 - 1$
7	7 / 2 =	3 =	$2^2 - 1$
8	3 / 2 =	1 =	$2^1 - 1$

Figure 8.12   Binary search for *x* = 'S' or 'T' in an array of 20 elements

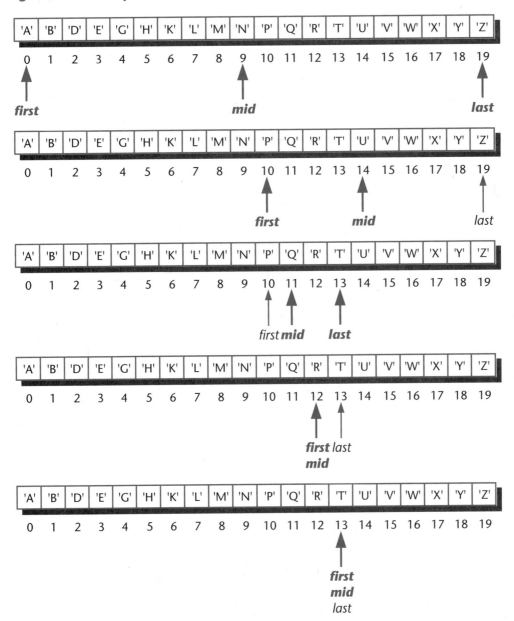

Table 8.2   Maximum size of subarray of an array *a* of 20 elements on each successive iteration of *BiSearch*

Iteration	Size of Subarray
1	20
2	10
3	5
4	2
5	1

logarithms. By definition, m is the **logarithm to the base 2 of n**, $\log_2 n = m$, provided m is the exponent of 2 such that 2^m is n or

> $\log_2 n = m$ **if and only if $n = 2^m$**

A logarithm is an exponent. Thus,

$\log_2 8 = 3$	because	$8 = 2^3$
$\log_2 32 = 5$	because	$32 = 2^5$
$\log_2 1024 = 10$	because	$1024 = 2^{10}$
$\log_2 2^m = m$	because	$2^m = 2^m$

Definition   The **logarithm to the base 2 of n**, written **$\log_2 n$**, is m if and only if $n = 2^m$.

In general, suppose we have a sorted n-element array. The maximum number of iterations in *BiSearch* is m, which is the smallest number of the form $2^m - 1$ greater than or equal to n.

> $n \le 2^m - 1$.

The most number of iterations is m, the exponent of 2. Following through the arithmetic, we have the following:

> $n + 1 \le 2^m$

Because $\log_2(2^m) = m$, the exponent of 2 that yields 2^m, we have

> $\log_2(n + 1) \le \log_2(2^m)$

or

> $\log_2(n + 1) \le m$.

Taking the ceiling function to obtain the next integer greater than or equal to $\log_2(n + 1)$, we obtain

> $\lceil \log_2(n + 1) \rceil = m$

For example, with $n = 7$ elements, $\log_2(7 + 1) = \log_2(8) = \log_2(2^3) = 3$. With $n = 20$ elements, we have $\lceil \log_2(20 + 1) \rceil = \lceil \log_2(21) \rceil = 5$ since $2^4 < 21 \le 2^5$.

Even in the worst case, a binary search algorithm of a sorted array of n elements takes roughly $\log_2 n$ iterations, whereas a sequential search takes n iterations. Because $\log_2 n < n$, the binary search is more efficient than the sequential one. Displaying the continuous forms of the curves, Figure 8.13 illustrates how much larger n can grow than $\log_2 n$. There is some overhead, however, in the binary search, such as the calculation of *mid* and the possibility of more than one comparison in the *if-else* statement. For about 20 or more sorted elements, the binary search is better. Because we can only perform this technique on a sorted array, the overhead of sorting first might tip the scales in favor of a sequential method. If we must search frequently, sorting is worth the effort so that we can use the binary search. In the next section, we examine a sorting method.

Figure 8.13
As x becomes larger, x grows much larger than $\log_2 x$.

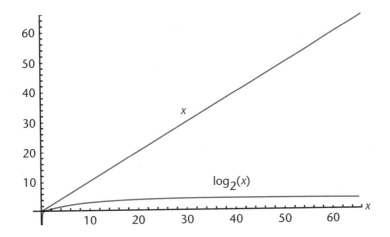

Section 8.3 Exercises

1. Code in C the sequential search function *SeqSearch* of Algorithm 8.1.

2. Apply the sequential search function *SeqSearchUnordered* from Example 8.7 to find each of the following characters in array a of Figure 8.9. Give the returned value and the number of comparisons in each case.

   a. 'E' **b.** 'N' **c.** 'D'
   d. 'S' **e.** 'W' **f.** 'F'

3. Apply the binary search algorithm to find each of the following characters in array a of Figure 8.9. Give the index i for each comparison.

   a. 'E' **b.** 'N' **c.** 'D'
   d. 'S' **e.** 'W' **f.** 'F'

4. Apply the binary search algorithm to find each of the following characters in array a of Figure 8.12. Give the index i for each comparison.

   a. 'G' **b.** 'C' **c.** 'R' **d.** 'Z'

5. **a.** Consider the array in Figure 8.9. In the binary search for x = 'K' or 'L', we compared x with $a[3]$, $a[5]$, and $a[4]$. List the other possible search orders of length 3.

   b. Are any search sequences longer than 3?

6. **a.** In what situation(s) is only one iteration necessary in a sequential search?

   b. At most two iterations?

   c. At most three iterations?

7. Repeat Exercise 6 for a binary search.

8. Fill in the following chart for the worst case number of comparisons needed for a search of a sorted array with n elements using sequential and binary searches.

n	1	$2^7 - 1 = 127$	$2^8 - 1 = 255$	$2^{10} - 1 = 1023$	$2^{20} - 1 = 1048575$	$2^{24} - 1 = 16{,}777{,}215$
SeqSearch						
BiSearch						

9. Repeat Exercise 8 for the following chart.

n	10	100	200	300	1000	5000	10,000	20,000	30,000	100,000	400,000	500,000
SeqSearch												
BiSearch												

10. a. Code in C the *BiSearch* function of Algorithm 8.2.

b. Test this function for a large array with various values for *n* and *x*. Print the index and array element value in each comparison.

11. a. Suppose array *SAT* contains a sorted list of SAT scores for students in a school. Write a segment using a sequential search to return the indices, *MinRange* and *MaxRange*, for the high and low grades, respectively, in the range from 550 to 650. This procedure is a **range search**.

b. Repeat Part a using two binary searches.

Section 8.3 Programming Projects

1. Declare an array to have dimension 50, and read a sorted list of 20 different integers between 1 and 50 from a text file into the array. Print the array. Repeatedly, ask the user for numbers in this range. If the number is in the array, delete it by moving larger elements down. If the number is not in the array, insert it. In other words, move larger elements up to make room and insert the new element. Be sure to have a variable that stores the number of elements in the array, and adjust its value with each insertion and deletion. The process ends when the user types a sentinel value. Print the revised array.

2. Develop a program to read values for two sorted *n*-dimensional arrays *g* and *h* from a text file. Then repeatedly read interactively a value and indicate whether or not the value is in both arrays.

Section 8.4 Selection Sort

To make sense of large amounts of data, we should arrange the values in some specified way. Moreover, an efficient binary search requires that the array be sorted. In many industrial computing centers, as much as 30 percent of total computer time is devoted to sorting data. Many approaches have been adopted to expedite sorting. Unfortunately, the most efficient sorting techniques are rather subtle and beyond the scope of this text. In this section, we demonstrate a sorting technique that is satisfactory for modest jobs, although it may not be efficient for large amounts of data. The method we describe is the **selection sort**.

As an illustration of the selection sort, suppose you are working for the school library to organize the volumes of an old encyclopedia. Unfortunately, some volumes are missing, some are duplicates of others, shelf space is limited, and each book is heavy to move. You look through all the books, selecting the one with the smallest volume number. Once found, you swap that book with the first one. Then, starting with the next book, you look for the smallest volume number in the remaining books and exchange that book with the one in the second position. We repeat the process until only one book remains in the unsorted section of books. Of course, that book must have the largest volume number and, consequently, must already be in place.

The general idea of the selection sort is to find the element that belongs in each slot.

Selection Sort Algorithm

Figure 8.14 illustrates the selection sort for a small array a of n characters. On each step the sorted subarray appears in color. As the last step shows, once the first $n - 1$ least items are in place, the last element must contain the maximum value. Thus, we repeat the process $n - 1$ times as stated in Algorithm 8.3. In the postcondition, we use the notation $a[0 .. n - 1]$ to indicate the subarray of elements $a[0], a[1], \ldots, a[n - 1]$.

Algorithm 8.3.   Selection sort of an array

SelectionSort(a, n)

  Procedure to perform a selection sort of array a from $a[0]$ through $a[n - 1]$

Pre:

  a is an array with n elements.

Figure 8.14
Action of selection sort on an array

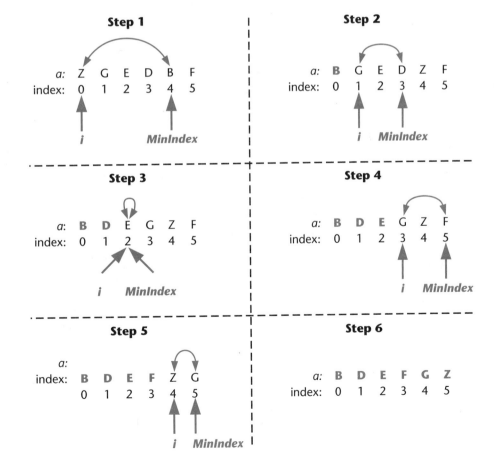

Post:

a[0 .. n − 1] has been sorted.

Algorithm:

for *i* from 0 through *n* − 2 do
    MinIndex ← *IndexOfMin*(*a*, *i*, *n*)
    swap *a*[*i*] and *a*[*MinIndex*]

Index of Minimum Element

In this design, a function invocation returns the index of the smallest element that is in the unsorted subarray, from the *i*th index to the end of the array. A segment swaps that element and the *i*th one. As shown below, the *IndexOfMin* function has three parameters, the array, the low index, and one plus the high index of the subarray under consideration. Should the minimum element be repeated, the index of its first occurrence is returned.

IndexOfMin(a, i, n) ⟶ *MinIndex*

Function to return the index of the first occurrence of the minimum element in the subarray from *a*[*i*] through *a*[*n* − 1]

Pre:

a is an array with at least *n* elements.
i and *n* are indices, and *i* < *n*.

Post:

The function returns the index of the first occurrence of the minimum element in the subarray from *a*[*i*] through *a*[*n* − 1].

Algorithm:

MinIndex ← *i*
for *j* from *i* + 1 through *n* − 1 do
    if *a*[*j*] is less than *a*[*MinIndex*] then
        MinIndex ← *j*
return *MinIndex*

Swapping Values

After we obtain *MinIndex*, we must swap two array elements. In general, how can we swap the values in variables *x* and *y*? At first glance, the following two statements seem to accomplish the task:

```
x = y;     /* This segment does NOT swap x and y */
y = x;
```

Suppose *x* is 3, and *y* is 5 before execution of these two statements. After the first assignment (*x* = *y*), *x* gets *y*'s value—5. Both variables are now 5, and the 3 is lost. When the second assignment executes (*y* = *x*), nothing changes because both variables already hold 5.

Figure 8.15
Swap of the
values in *x* and
y

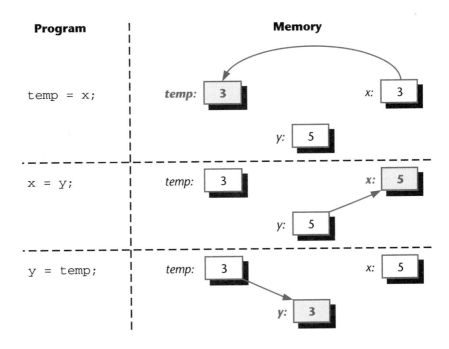

```
temp = x;
```

```
x = y;
```

```
y = temp;
```

The segment to swap values in variables *x* and *y* must use a temporary variable to handle the proper exchange of elements. Suppose two people, *x* and *y*, are holding large presents for each other, and each person can hold only one present at a time. To make the exchange, one person, say *x*, temporarily hands the present to a third person, *temp*. Then *x* can receive the gift from *y*. After this handoff, *y* gets the present from *temp*, although that gift is really from *x*. Figure 8.15 pictures this exchange.

Segment to swap the values stored in variables *x* and *y*

Algorithm:

$temp \leftarrow x$
$x \qquad \leftarrow y$
$y \qquad \leftarrow temp$

We would accomplish the same results by first copying *y* into *temp*. Notice the cyclical pattern in either approach:

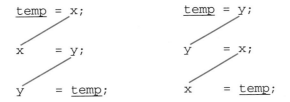

As we have emphasized throughout the text, we should place a task like swapping into its own function. We are, however, changing values in two variables, not just returning one value. In the next chapter, we study how to accomplish such communication between functions. For now, we must settle on using inline code for the swap. The swap is inside a loop, and for sorting a large array, the swap can occur many times. Because of the overhead with a function call, inline code is faster. Therefore, for faster sorting, we have the three assignments inside the loop instead of a call to a swapping function.

Returning to the selection sort, we always swap the values of $a[i]$ and the minimum element in the subarray from $a[i]$ through $a[n - 1]$, even if that minimum element is $a[i]$. We could switch only if i and $MinIndex$ are not equal. However, this test would be performed every time for a condition that may never occur. Therefore, it is more efficient not to test for equality of i and $MinIndex$ and swap on each iteration.

The code for swapping $a[j]$ and $a[MinIndex]$ follows the algorithm, as shown:

```
temp        = a[j];
a[j]        = a[MinIndex];
a[MinIndex] = temp;
```

Section 8.4 Exercises

1. Similar to Figure 8.14, show the steps of a selection sort on the following data:
   M S C R T F P

2. Repeat Exercise 1 for the following data:
   C D F M R S T

3. Repeat Exercise 1 for the following data:
   T S R M F D C

4. Deal hands of 13 cards and perform the selection sort method of arranging the hands.

5. a. Code the procedure *SelectionSort* in C for an array of characters.

   b. Code the procedure *IndexOfMin* in C for an array of characters.

   c. Revise the procedure in Part a to have embedded code instead of a separate routine for finding the index of the minimum element.

6. Suppose the order of the first two statements for the swap of $a[j]$ and $a[MinIndex]$ was reversed to read as follows:

```
a[j]        = a[MinIndex];   /* ERROR - out of order */
temp        = a[j];          /* ERROR - out of order */
a[MinIndex] = temp;
```

   What would be the contents of the array from Figure 8.14 after performing *SelectionSort* with the incorrect swap?

7. Suppose 10,000 student records, each record with a Social Security Number key and a total size of 300 characters, are stored in a file. In the worst case, what is the total number of characters that would be moved in a selection sort?

Section 8.4 Programming Projects

1. Develop a program to read grades interactively and print the top five. Hint: One way to do this is to sort the grades and choose the top five.

2. Develop a program that reads up to 100 numbers from a text file into an array and sorts the array of numbers using *SelectionSort*. Print the array before and after the sort. Print the maximum, minimum, and median. For an odd number of elements, the median is the middle value. For an even number of elements, the median is the average of the two middle values.

3. Develop a function that reverses an array in memory by reversing the elements in place (within the original array).

4. Revise Project 1 from Section 8.3 to read a file of unsorted data into an array and to sort the array before continuing with the problem.

Section 8.5 Multidimensional Arrays

The arrays discussed so far have been one-dimensional. We can represent the elements of the array as a single row or column. Many applications, however, revolve around arrays that have more than one dimension.

A typical example of a **two-dimensional array** is a driving timetable. To determine the driving time between two cities, we find the row for one city and the column for another, and then read the number where they meet. In the same way, a two-dimensional array is a grid containing rows and columns, in which row and column coordinates uniquely specify each element.

Figure 8.16 is a representation of a two-dimensional array or **matrix**, *a*, of type *int*, with 3 rows and 4 columns. Because numbering starts with 0 for the row and column, position (row 1, column 2) of *a* stores the number 9.

Indices

When dealing with one-dimensional arrays, we specify a single subscript or index to locate an element. Because elements of two-dimensional arrays are located by means of a row and a column, two subscripts or indices are required. The row subscript generally appears before the column subscript. Thus, C refers to the element containing the value 9 in Figure 8.16 as $a[1][2]$. Unlike most other languages, C requires that each subscript be within its own separate pair of brackets.

In C, a two-dimensional array actually is an array of arrays. In other words, we can think of *a* as being an array of 3 elements, each of which is an array of 4 integers, as in Figure 8.17. In array notation, $a[1]$ represents row 1, and $a[1][2]$ represents column 2 within that row. This definition of a two-dimensional array is more significant in the next chapter.

Figure 8.16
Matrix or two-dimensional array *a* of numbers

```
        0   1  2   3   column
   0  ⎡ 4   5  1   0 ⎤
   1  ⎢ 2   6  9   1 ⎥
   2  ⎣ 5  -2  6   7 ⎦
      row
```

Figure 8.17
Matrix *a* from Figure 8.16 as an array of arrays

```
      row 0        row 1        row2
  [[4   5   1   0][2   6   9   1][5   -2   6   7]]
```

Example 8.8

Suppose a 3 by 4 array *a* already has values. Let us write a segment to print the array in the rectangular format. To do this, we print the three rows, one row at a time, using a *for* loop with index *row*. We print the elements (columns) in a row as we did a one-dimensional array, and we use another *for* loop with index *column*. Therefore, this problem uses nested *for* loops. The inner loop changes most rapidly and, thus, must print the row. After printing the values in a row, we print a newline character to advance to the next row.

```
for (row = 0; row < 3; row++)
{
    for (column = 0; column < 4; column++)      /* print a row */
        printf("%3d", a[row][column]);
    printf("\n");
}
```

The order of the indices is important. For example, in Figure 8.16, *a*[2][1] is not the same element as *a*[1][2]. The former is −2, the element in the third row (row 2) and second column (column 1). The latter is 9, the element in the second row (row 1), third column (column 2).

Declaration

Consistent with the declaration of one-dimensional arrays, we declare the two-dimensional array *a* of Figure 8.16 as follows:

```
int a[3][4];
```

A declaration-initialization of this matrix is as follows:

```
int a[3][4] = { { 4,   5, 1, 0 },
                { 2,   6, 9, 1 },
                { 5, -2, 6, 7 } };
```

This initialization is somewhat more involved than the initialization of a one-dimensional array, partly because it contains much data and partly because it is two-dimensional. Because each row is a separate array, a pair of braces must enclose the values for each row. Then all the rows, separated by commas, are enclosed within an outer pair of braces.

When using a multidimensional array as a parameter, we can have empty brackets for the first dimension, but we must explicitly state all other dimensions. For example, the following prototype is illegal:

```
void PrintArray(int a[][], int NumEls); /* ERROR */
```

Instead, we must use one of the following forms of the prototype:

```
void PrintArray(int a[][4], int NumEls);

void PrintArray(int [][4], int);

void PrintArray(int a[3][4], int NumEls);

void PrintArray(int [3][4], int);
```

To declare arrays of more than two dimensions in C, we add more subscripts. Such multidimensional arrays are used less frequently than one- or two-dimensional arrays.

We can extend the principles in this section to arrays of many dimensions. Usually, only the amount of memory available to the program limits the number of dimensions.

Example 8.9

The program in this example illustrates the use of a two-dimensional array. The matrix consists of 4 rows and 12 columns, in which each row represents a particular make of car, and each column indicates a year between 1985 and 1996. Each element contains the fictitious price in dollars of the car that its row and column represent.

To find the price of a 1985 Ford, for example, we look in row 0 (representing Ford) and column 0 (representing 1985). The value is 4775, so a 1985 Ford costs $4775. The program in this example repeatedly reads the make and year from the user and then prints the price.

The function *main* contains a declaration-initialization for the matrix of information. Using the sentinel technique, it continues to obtain the make and year of car and to print the price. The function *main* calls the following routines:

instructions to print instructions on the program's use

GetMake to read and return the make as a character

GetYear to read and return the year

PrintMake to print the car's make from its character representation

price to return the matrix price of the particular make and year car

Figure 8.18 contains the structure chart. Pseudocode for most of the routines and the program are below.

---

main()

Interactive program to print price of a particular make and year car

Algorithm:

initialize *NUMMAKES* by *NUMYEARS* array of prices, *PriceList*
print instructions by calling *instructions*
get a character, *make*, representing the make of car by calling *GetMake*
while *make* is not equal to *TRAILER* do the following:
    get year, *year*, of car by calling *GetYear*
    print the make of car with *PrintMake(make)*
    print the price of the car with *price(make, year, PriceList)*
    get a character, *make*, representing the make of car by calling *GetMake*
print closing

Figure 8.18
Structure chart for the program in Example 8.9

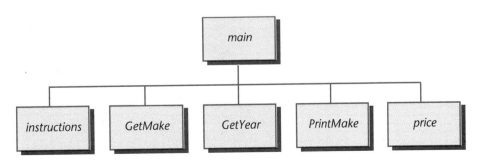

GetMake( ) ⟶ *make*

Function to read and return a character representing the make of car

Pre:

Post:

The function returned a character representing the make of car or *TRAILER*.

Algorithm:

print the choice characters and names
repeatedly do the following
    prompt for make character
    make ← *tolower(getchar())*
    flush the input buffer
while the character, *make*, is not a legal one

return *make*

GetYear( ) ⟶ *year*

Read and return the year of the desired car

Pre:

Post:

The function returned an integer between *FIRSTYEAR* and *LASTYEAR*.

Algorithm:

repeatedly do the following:
    prompt for a year
    read a year, *year*
    flush the input buffer
while *year* is not between *FIRSTYEAR* and *LASTYEAR*

return *year*

price(make, year, PriceList) ⟶ *price*

Return price of car based on make and year

Pre:

make is a character representing the make of car or *TRAILER*.
year is an integer between *FIRSTYEAR* and *LASTYEAR*.
PriceList is a *NUMMAKES* by *NUMYEARS* array of prices.

Post:

> The function returned an integer price of the particular make and year of the
> car.

Algorithm:

> *row* ← row of matrix corresponding to *make*
> return *PriceList*[*row*][*year* − *FIRSTYEAR*]

```c
/*
 * Example 8.9. Program to report car prices. User enters
 * car make by character and car year. Program reports
 * prices. All data are fictitious.
 */

#include <stdio.h>
#include <ctype.h>

#define NUMMAKES   4
#define NUMYEARS   12
#define FIRSTYEAR  1985
#define LASTYEAR   (FIRSTYEAR + NUMYEARS - 1)
#define TRAILER    '*'
#define FORD       'f'
#define CHEVY      'c'
#define DODGE      'd'
#define HONDA      'h'

main()
{
    void instructions(void);
    char GetMake(void);
    int GetYear(void);
    void PrintMake(char);
    int price(char, int, int [NUMMAKES][NUMYEARS]);

int PriceList[NUMMAKES][NUMYEARS] =  /* 2-D array of prices.    */
                                     /* row = make, column = year. */
    {
    /* Ford */    { 4775, 4980, 5222, 5305, 5483, 5547,    /* 85-90 */
                    5596, 5713, 5842, 5903, 5043, 6230 },  /* 91-96 */

    /* Chevy */   { 4853, 5140, 5413, 5590, 5723, 5848,    /* 85-90 */
                    5762, 5944, 6104, 6255, 6370, 6526 },  /* 91-96 */

    /* Dodge */   { 5627, 5772, 5973, 6210, 6539, 6720,    /* 85-90 */
                    6792, 6930, 7054, 7202, 7365, 7562 },  /* 91-96 */

    /* Honda */   { 1576, 1738, 1970, 2161, 2205, 2280,    /* 85-90 */
                    2442, 2580, 2814, 2953, 3078, 3201 }   /* 91-96 */
    };
```

```
    char make;    /* make of the car as a character (f, c, d, h, *) */
    int year;     /* year of the car, FIRSTYEAR to LASTYEAR */

    instructions();
    make = GetMake();            /* priming read */
    while (make != TRAILER)
    {
        year = GetYear();
        printf("The price of a %d ", year);
        PrintMake(make);
        printf(" is $%d.\n\n", price(make, year, PriceList));
        make = GetMake();        /* for the next time around */
    }
    printf("\nThank you for buying all those cars!\n");
}

/*
 * Function to print program instructions
 * Pre:     none
 * Post:    Instructions were displayed.
 */

void instructions(void)
{
    printf("Welcome to CAR PRICES!\n");
    printf("When you choose a car make and year,\n");
    printf("we print the car's price.\n\n");
}

/*
 * Read and return the character (make) of the desired car
 * Pre:     none
 * Post:    The function returned a character representing the make
 *          of car or TRAILER.
 */

char GetMake(void)
{
    int i;          /* index */
    char make;      /* make of the car as a character */

    /* Print the choice characters and names */
    printf("f=Ford, c=Chevy, d=Dodge, h=Honda, *=END\n");

    /* Read in the selection by number */
    do
    {
        printf("    Which car do you want? ");
        make = tolower(getchar());
        fflush(stdin);
    }
```

```
    while (!(make == FORD || make == CHEVY || make == DODGE
              || make == HONDA || make == TRAILER));

    return(make);
}


/*
 * Read and return the year of the desired car
 * Pre:    none
 * Post:   The function returned an integer between
 *         FIRSTYEAR and LASTYEAR.
 */

int GetYear(void)
{
    int year;        /* year of the desired car */

    do
    {
        printf("   What year (%d-%d)? ", FIRSTYEAR, LASTYEAR);
        scanf("%d", &year);
        fflush(stdin);
    }
    while (year < FIRSTYEAR || year > LASTYEAR);

    return(year);
}


/*
 * Return price of car based on make and year
 * Pre:    make is a character representing the make of car or TRAILER.
 *         year is an integer between FIRSTYEAR and LASTYEAR.
 *         PriceList is a NUMMAKES by NUMYEARS array of prices.
 * Post:   The function returned an integer price of the particular
 *         make and year of the car.
 */

int price(char make, int year, int PriceList[NUMMAKES][NUMYEARS])
{
    int row;   /* row of matrix corresponding to make */

    switch (make)
    {
        case FORD:  row = 0;
                    break;
        case CHEVY: row = 1;
                    break;
        case DODGE: row = 2;
                    break;
        case HONDA: row = 3;
    }
```

```
        return( PriceList[row][year - FIRSTYEAR] );
}


/*
 * Print the make according to its character value
 * Pre:     make is a character representing the make of car or TRAILER.
 * Post:    The make of the car was displayed.
 */

void PrintMake(char make)
{
    switch (make)
    {
        case FORD:   printf("Ford");
                     break;
        case CHEVY:  printf("Chevy");
                     break;
        case DODGE:  printf("Dodge");
                     break;
        case HONDA:  printf("Honda");
    }
}
```

The following is an interactive session:

```
Welcome to CAR PRICES!
When you choose a car make and year,
we print the car's price.

f=Ford, c=Chevy, d=Dodge, h=Honda, *=END
    Which car do you want? c
    What year (1985-1996)? 1990
The price of a 1990 Chevy is $5848.

f=Ford, c=Chevy, d=Dodge, h=Honda, *=END
    Which car do you want? d
    What year (1985-1996)? 1984
    What year (1985-1996)? 1986
The price of a 1986 Dodge is $5772.

f=Ford, c=Chevy, d=Dodge, h=Honda, *=END
    Which car do you want? 4
    Which car do you want? h
    What year (1985-1996)? 1992
The price of a 1992 Honda is $2580.

f=Ford, c=Chevy, d=Dodge, h=Honda, *=END
    Which car do you want? f
    What year (1985-1996)? 1992
The price of a 1992 Ford is $5713.
```

```
f=Ford, c=Chevy, d=Dodge, h=Honda, *=END
    Which car do you want? h
    What year (1985-1996)? 1996
The price of a 1996 Honda is $3201.


f=Ford, c=Chevy, d=Dodge, h=Honda, *=END
    Which car do you want? *

Thank you for buying all those cars!
```

Because each row of the array *PriceList* is too long to fit on a single line, the program presents each on two lines. For the sake of clarity, comments indicating the years each line represents follow the data for the row. A comment specifying the make that particular row represents precedes each row.

Because we are using character input in *GetMake*, we must be careful in that function and the function *GetYear* to purge the input buffer after reading data.

The function *price* returns the price of the car based on its two parameters, *make* and *year*, which represent the make of the car and the year, respectively. The function converts these two parameters to valid subscripts of the matrix *PriceList*. Because *make* is one of four nonconsecutive characters—'f', 'c', 'd', or 'h'—we use a *switch* statement to assign a make's row number to *row*. The year is decremented by the value *FIRSTYEAR* (1985) so that *FIRSTYEAR* corresponds to column 0, *FIRSTYEAR* + 1 (1986) corresponds to column 1, and so forth. This function does not validate its parameters, assuming that the functions *GetMake* and *GetYear* have done so.

Even though it might not be apparent to the casual observer, arrays depend to a considerable extent on the class of C data types known as pointers. Values and variables of these types make it possible to manipulate memory addresses, thereby giving the C programmer low-level access that is not present in most other languages. Pointers are the subject of the next chapter.

Section 8.5 Exercises

1. Write a declaration for a two-dimensional *float* array, *d*, of 20 rows and 50 columns.

2. Suppose an array *a* has the following values:

6	2	3
4	8	7
1	5	0

   What is the value of

   a. $a[1][2]$ b. $a[2][1]$ c. $a[0][1]$ d. $a[1][3]$

   Give the array element for

   e. 6   f. 3   g. 1   h. 8

3. Give a declaration-initialization of the matrix in Exercise 2.

4. Write nested *for* loops to read values into the array of Exercise 1.

5. Write nested *for* loops to initialize to 0 each element of the array in Exercise 1.

6. Suppose *a* is an array with size 15 by 10. Write a segment to assign the product of the coordinates to each element. For example, assign 20 to *a*[4][5].

7. Write a function to return the sum of the values in the array of Exercise 2. Pass the array and its dimensions to the function.

8. Write a function, *copy*, that copies the elements of two-dimensional array *a* into array *b*, where *a* and *b* have the same dimensions and type (*int*). Parameters for the function include *a*, *b*, and dimensions *n* and *m*.

Section 8.5 Programming Projects

1. The transpose of a two-dimensional array is a second array containing the same elements as the first, but in which the rows become columns and vice versa. For example, given the array

1	5	7
9	6	3
52	11	9

the transpose would be:

1	9	52
5	6	11
7	3	9

Develop a program to read the size of a square, two-dimensional array and read its values. Then display the matrix and its transpose.

2. Develop a program that reads an array (not necessarily square) of numbers, and calculates and displays the row and column sums, as well as the grand total. Place the sums next to their respective rows and columns. For example, an output might look like the following:

							Sums
5	3	4	8	2	6	|	28
1	0	7	7	4	3	|	22
6	9	2	5	1	3	|	26
3	8	4	9	2	1	|	27
15	20	17	29	9	13	|	103

3. This project produces a picture called **Sierpinski's Triangle**. Simulate a rectangular section of a plane with a two-dimensional boolean array. The pair of indices for an array element correspond to the *x* and *y* coordinates in the plane. The value of the array element is *TRUE* when the point (*x*, *y*) is to appear on the graph, so initialize the elements of this array to be *FALSE*. Take three points forming a triangle—two at the extreme ends of the base of the rectangle and the third in the middle of the opposite side—and change the corresponding elements in the two-dimensional array to be *TRUE*. Randomly select a point in the plane. Then, randomly pick one of the three vertices of the triangle. Find the integer coordinates of the point half way between the point and the vertex. Change the corresponding array element to be *TRUE*. At random, select a triangle vertex again. Once more, find the coordinates of the midpoint between the point and the vertex. Continue for some

designated number of times. Then, for every point on the "plane," print a nonblank character if the array element is *TRUE* and a blank otherwise.

Refer to Appendix F about random number generation. If your version of C has graphics, you may choose to employ its built-in features instead of using the two-dimensional array.

4. Slot machines were once simple: a single coin was dropped in, the handle pulled, and a single row of pictures was checked for a winner. Today, they are more complicated. You are to write a program to simulate one of these newer slot machines.

The slot machine has 3 "wheels." Each wheel has 7 positions, each holding one of 4 pictures on it. The symbols on each wheel are as follows:

First Wheel: Cherry, Cherry, Cherry, Plum, Plum, Bell, Bar

Second Wheel: Cherry, Cherry, Plum, Plum, Plum, Bell, Bar

Third Wheel: Cherry, Cherry, Plum, Plum, Bell, Bell, Bar

The program must ask the user how many coins are being inserted: a number from 1 to 5 inclusive. Entering a number outside that range should end the program.

You start the program with 10 coins. The number of coins entered is subtracted from this amount, and any winnings (described below) are added in. At the end of the program, the final number of coins should be printed. The balance may go negative during play.

The wheels are "spun" and a 3 by 3 table is displayed on the screen. The first column should correspond to the first wheel, and the symbols shown must be three symbols that appear next to each other on the wheels. Of course, the two end symbols for each wheel in the listing above are next to each other on the wheel. The second and third columns correspond to the other two wheels. Each wheel spins independently of the others.

Determine payout based on the following information:

If only one coin was entered, the middle row is evaluated.

If 2 were entered, the top two rows are evaluated.

If 3 were entered, all three rows are evaluated.

If 4 coins, then check all three rows, and the diagonal going from the upper left to the lower right.

If 5 coins, then check all three rows and both diagonals.

```
                    /--5 coins
2 coins--   A1--B1--C1
                 \     /
1 coin--    A2--B2--C2
                 /     \
3 coins--   A3--B3--C3
                    \--4 coins
```

For each row or diagonal to be evaluated, the payout is as follows:

Plum in first position:	5 coins
Plum in first 2 positions:	10 coins
Plum in all three positions:	20 coins
Bell in first position:	10 coins

Bell in first 2 positions:	20 coins
Bell in all three positions:	40 coins
Bar in first position:	50 coins
Bar in first 2 positions:	100 coins
Bar in all three positions:	200 coins

Only the highest payout per row or diagonal is accumulated. Play continues until an invalid number of coins is entered.

Sample run:

```
How many coins are entered? 3
The wheels spin.  They show the following:
     Bar    Plum    Bell
   Cherry   Plum    Bell
   Cherry   Plum    Bar
You win 50 coin(s).

How many coins are entered? 2
The wheels spin.  They show the following:
     Plum Cherry   Plum
     Bell   Plum   Plum
     Bar    Plum   Bell
You win 15 coin(s).

How many coins are entered? 5
The wheels spin.  They show the following:
     Bell   Plum    Bar
     Bar    Plum  Cherry
   Cherry   Plum  Cherry
You win 70 coin(s).

How many coins are entered? 1
The wheels spin.  They show the following:
     Plum   Bell   Bell
     Bell   Bar    Bar
     Bar  Cherry Cherry
You win 10 coin(s).

How many coins are entered? 4
The wheels spin.  They show the following:
   Cherry   Plum Cherry
     Plum   Bell   Plum
     Plum   Bar    Plum
You win 10 coin(s).
```

```
How many coins are entered? 2
The wheels spin.  They show the following:
   Cherry   Bell     Bar
      Plum     Bar Cherry
      Plum Cherry Cherry
You win 5 coin(s).

How many coins are entered? 0

Your final balance is 153.
```

5. A standard crossword puzzle consists of a large grid where each box is either white and holds a letter, or is shaded black to indicate that no letter may be placed there. In addition, some of the white boxes also have numbers assigned to them, indicating the first letter of a word going across and/or down.

You are to develop a program to generate a 15 by 15 crossword, then help the user to find where a list of words would fit in the puzzle.

First, your program must ask the user for the positions of the black squares in the grid. These will be given as pairs of numbers, indicating a row and a column. You should ask for pairs until values of zero are entered for both.

At this point, your program should print the crossword grid with the black squares shaded in as "##" characters and with numbers in appropriate squares. Numbers are assigned sequentially, starting with 1. To determine if a box should get a number, a given square must be white and pass one or both of the following tests:

If the square above the current square is black or off the grid, and the square below the current square is not black or off the grid, then the box is assigned a number.

If the square to the left of the current square is black or off the grid, and the square to the right of the current square is not black or off the grid, then the box is assigned a number.

Third, your program will ask the user for words, and for each word, tell which positions in the crossword puzzle the word will fit. A word fits only if the length of the word exactly matches the number of white squares between two black squares or the borders. Ask for words until a dollar sign is entered.

Sample run:

```
Enter row and column values below, enter 0 0 when finished.
5 5   3 10   1 7   6 1   8 10   2 9   8 8   0 0

      1  2  3  4  5  6  7  8  9 10 11 12 13 14 15
    ----------------------------------------------
 1|  1  2  3  4  5  6 ##  7     8  9 10 11 12 13
 2| 14             15     ## 16
 3| 17                    18 ## 19
 4| 20                       21
 5| 22          ## 23
 6| ## 24       25
 7| 26
 8| 27                 ##     ## 28
 9| 29                 30     31
10| 32
11| 33
12| 34
13| 35
14| 36
15| 37

Enter word. Enter $ when finished   compute
    7 down.
   27 across.
   30 down.
   31 down.
Enter word. Enter $ when finished   encyclopedia
Enter word. Enter $ when finished   possessiveness
   15 down.
   24 across.
Enter word. Enter $ when finished   hi
    8 down
Enter word. Enter $ when finished   $
```

6. Sometimes, storing an image is easier if you store the steps taken to draw the image rather than the image itself. In such a situation, a sequence of directed lines are concatenated to form the image. For example, a simple drawing program might allow eight simple directions of movement:

For this example, a "picture" composed of the sequence "1, 3, 4, 3" would draw a line segment up, to the right, down on an angle, then right again, and yield something similar to the following figure:

Develop a program to take an encoding sequence of numbers and create a drawing based on the sequence, using the arrow directions displayed in the first figure. Your program should use the text screen for the drawing surface and should allow for a figure up to 20 characters tall and 70 characters wide. Your drawings on this grid should be made with the asterisk (*) character. Each drawing must start in the lower left corner and if a command would have the figure move "off the page," you should ignore that command and proceed on to the next command in the sequence.

Each encoded sequence entered will be a list of numbers, positive and/or negative, ending with a 0 as the indicator that the drawing is finished. If the number is positive, you should take this number as meaning "move in the direction indicated, then output an asterisk to the position currently occupied." If the number is negative, you should move in the direction you would if the value were positive, but you do not put an asterisk in the position when done moving. Sequences may be of any length. After inputting the zero value, your program will display the final image.

Sample run:

```
Enter drawing sequence below.
1 1 1 2 2 4 4 5 5 7 7 0

Your picture:




    *
   *  *
  *     *
  *     *
  *****
```

Section 8.6 Breadth: Color in Computer Graphics

Computer graphics is used extensively today in movies, commercials, business and scientific reports, newspaper articles, user interfaces for some computers and languages, and computer-aided software engineering tools, to name a few examples. A properly created picture can catch our attention and impart its message more clearly than pages of words and numbers. People drawn to the profession of computer graphics range from computer scientists, who develop graphics algorithms, to artists, who do not program but use sophisticated packages to create elaborate three-dimensional images.

Display Devices

Arrays are an essential data structure for computer scientists exploring the area of graphics. Most display media, such as a screen or paper, use a two-dimensional array of dots, called **pixels** or picture elements. A microcomputer screen might display an array of 680 pixels across and 480 down the monitor. Televisions and most microcomputers have the most common display device, the **cathode ray tube (CRT)** screen. An electron gun emits a beam of electrons that passes through a focusing system, hitting the phosphor-coated screen. When the beam strikes the screen at a point, the phosphor crystal there emits a small spot of light. The number of electrons striking the point determines the intensity there. In a **raster-scan video monitor**, like the CRT for televisions and most microcomputers, the beam passes over the screen a row at a time, from top to bottom, adjusting the intensity at each point.

Definitions   A **pixel**, which stands for picture element, is a dot on a two-dimensional array of dots on a display medium. A **cathode ray tube** (**CRT**) screen is a display device used with televisions and most microcomputers. In a CRT, at least one electron gun emits a beam of electrons that passes through a focusing system, hitting the phosphor-coated screen. In a **raster-scan video monitor**, a beam of electrons passes over the screen a row at a time, from top to bottom, adjusting the intensity at each point.

A **monochrome CRT**, which is usually black and white, has one gun, whereas a color CRT has three—red, green, and blue. Combinations of various intensities of these three primary colors create all the colors. For example, red and green lights produce yellow. Equal intensities of all three electron beams generate white and various shades of gray. In a raster-scan system, an area of memory called the **frame buffer** stores information for each pixel in a two-dimensional array.

Definitions   A **monochrome CRT** has one electron gun, whereas a **color CRT** has three—red, green, and blue. A **frame buffer** is an area of memory that stores information for each pixel in a two-dimensional array.

The simplest monochrome system uses one bit to store the intensity of a pixel. Thus, a pixel can only be on (1) or off (0). If two bits control the electron gun, then 2^2 = 4 intensity levels exist—00 (off), 01 (one-third of full intensity), 10 (two-thirds of full intensity), 11 (full on); 3 bits yield 2^3 = 8 intensities. In a color CRT, a certain number of pixels control each electron gun. A system that has 6 bits to control the guns uses 2 bits for each gun and can produce 2^6 = 64 different colors.

Color Lookup Table

A common method for storing color information utilizes another two-dimensional array, a **color lookup table** (LUT). The frame buffer does not hold the actual intensity values but an index into the LUT, which stores the intensity levels. For example, suppose for each pixel a frame buffer stores a 6-bit index into the LUT. Thus, the table can have 2^6 = 64 entries and 64 possible colors for the picture. The entries in the table can have any number of bits, not just 6. Suppose each entry has 12 bits, 4 bits of intensity information for each gun. If we listed every possible 12-bit string, we would have 2^{12} = 4096 possibilities. Our **palette** has 4096 colors from which to choose in the color lookup table, but only 64 are available at any one time. Without making any other changes, the artist can produce dramatic effects by varying the colors in the table. Figure 8.19 shows a situation in which the frame buffer stores $100011_2 = 35_{10}$ at a pixel position. Thus, the color for this pixel is in position 35 of the color lookup table, $LUT[35]$. That table entry has the 12-bit pattern $0110\ 0101\ 0001_2$. Because each gun has 4 bits, 16 possible intensities (zero plus 15 steps to full intensity) exist for each. The pattern $0110_2 = 6_{10}$ controls the red electron gun and produces 6/15 th of full intensity. Similarly, the $0101_2 = 5_{10}$ indicates the green gun is at 5/15 th of full power. The blue gun does not emit many electrons at 1/15 th its maximum strength. The resulting color is a shade of brown.

Definitions	A **color lookup table** (**LUT**) is a two-dimensional array where each value represents intensity levels for the three electron guns of a raster-scan video monitor. These intensity levels correspond to a color. A **palette** is the set of colors from which to choose colors in the color lookup table.

After we have covered pointers and structures, we can develop and use a computer graphics package to create images.

Figure 8.19
The value for a pixel in the frame buffer is an index into the color lookup table, which stores intensity values for the red, green, and blue electron guns of a color CRT

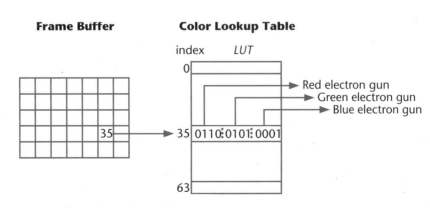

Section 8.6 Exercises

1. Suppose a monochrome CRT has 4 bits per pixel to store the intensity. How many intensities exist? Generalize your answer by giving the number of intensity levels for n bits per pixel.

2. **a.** Suppose a frame buffer stores the intensity levels instead of indices into a color lookup table. Assuming 12 bits of information for each pixel in a 640×480 display, how much memory does the frame buffer use?

   b. If the frame buffer stores LUT indices using 6 bits, how much memory do the frame buffer and LUT use together?

3. Suppose a color system has a frame buffer that stores 9 bits per pixel and 24 bits for each position in the LUT.

   a. How many entries does the LUT have?

   b. How many colors are possible in a picture?

   c. How many colors does the palette contain?

4. A graphics system that uses a color lookup table specifies a resolution of $1024 = 2^{10}$ by $512 = 2^9$ with $16 = 2^4$ colors available at any time from a selection of $4096 = 2^{12}$ colors. Assume $8 = 2^3$ bits in a byte.

   a. How many bits are in each LUT entry?

   b. How many bits are required for each pixel?

   c. How many bytes of memory are required in the frame buffer?

   d. How many bytes of memory are required in the LUT?

≈≈≈ Programming and Debugging Hints

Selecting Test Data: Edge Data

The most obvious way to check a program is to use ordinary, reasonable data as input. We should check the output against previously known results. (A calculator might be useful here.) Once we know the program works with ordinary data, then we should use more maliciously contrived data, including data close to the edges of the allowable ranges. The program should be able to detect and reject out-of-range data before further errors occur.

The **edge data** are perhaps the most important, because the programmer is likely to neglect those values. Input to a program, either in actual use or during testing, usually consists of either ordinary or erroneous data. Yet the data on the edges of the ranges are just as important in testing as any other data.

As an example, the factorial function of Example 6.4 in Section 6.1 does not work for negative integers, because $n!$ is undefined for values less than zero. For a positive integer n, the factorial is the product of the positive integers from 1 through n. A special case is $0! = 1$. To make sure *factorial* works for this edge value, we should test the function with an input value of 0.

Data to Test Branches

At first glance, it might appear a simple matter to develop a limited set of test data that verifies a program's correctness for all inputs. For all but the most trivial programs, however, testing every combination of branches is virtually impossible. The number of combinations of possible inputs to a program can be astronomical. For example, in Example 6.6 of Section 6.2, we wrote a program to read the number of class members and grades and the maximum possible points on each assignment. The program then

Figure 8.20 Exponential growth of number of combinations of data that should be checked

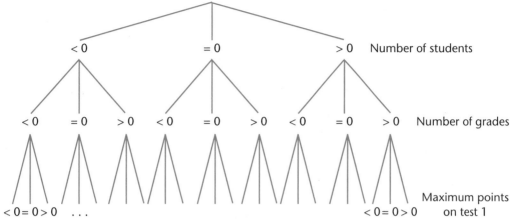

reads students' grades and computes their averages. With computation of the average as (*float*) 100 * *TotalPoints* / *MaxTotalPoints*, we must be especially careful of division by zero. This situation could arise if the user enters that no (0) grades exist or if the user enters that each assignment counts 0 points. A number of other situations should be checked as well. Suppose we check for negative, zero, and positive quantities of number of students, number of tests, value of a test, and a student's score on that test. With three choices for each of the four kinds of data, $3 \cdot 3 \cdot 3 \cdot 3 = 3^4 = 81$ different possibilities should be checked. If we modify the program to need another data item with three possible values, we triple the number of branches to check. Figure 8.20 illustrates this exponential growth. As noted at the end of Example 6.6, the program should also take precautions against any of the data being too large. For instance, we would not want to allow 3000 grades or 5000 students in the class. If we took such precautions, four possibilities would exist for each value and a total of $4^4 = 256$ combinations of different kinds of data.

Testing by Novices or with Random Data

Before a project goes into production, novice users should try the system. After months or years of working on a system, a programmer may have a preconceived idea of what the user will do. Users unfamiliar with the programming might attempt things the programmer never envisioned. Such users can help the programmer to answer some important questions. Do the directions and user's manual explain what to do for someone not acquainted with the inner workings of the system? Is the system user friendly? Does the program recover from whatever the user enters?

Another testing technique is to generate test data at random using a random number generator. Often, the program reads such data from a file.

Key Terms

≋ Summary

An array is a sequence of elements of the same type that share a common name and that are distinguishable by their positions within the array. A subscript or index indicates the position. In C, indices start with 0. We declare an array x containing five elements, all of which are integers, as follows:

```
int x[5];
```

Thus, we refer to elements $x[0]$, $x[1]$, $x[2]$, $x[3]$, $x[4]$. The dimension of an array is its number of elements or size, in this case, 5. The index of an array can be an expression, so we can read values into array x interactively with the following:

```
for (i = 0; i < 5; i++)
    scanf("%d", &x[i]);
```

To initialize an integer array x with five values—58, 63, 49, 18, 7—during the declaration, we write the following:

```
int x[5] = {58, 63, 49, 18, 7};
```

We can have an array as a function parameter. Usually, the number of actual elements in the array is also a parameter. Below are two alternatives of a prototype having an array parameter with no explicit dimension. The array parameter uses the dimension of the array argument from a function call.

```
float maximum(float ar[], int NumEls);
```

or

```
float maximum(float [], int);
```

The computer does not pass a copy of the entire array to the function, only its address. Therefore, when the called function changes a value in the array, it is changing the element in the array of the calling function. With a function call, we do not use the dimension of an array, as shown for array *grades*:

```
MaxGrade = maximum(grades, NumGrades);
```

In Section 8.2, we considered functions that performed tasks of reading values into an array, computing the average or minimum value in an array, printing the values in an array, and computing their frequencies.

In the next section, we covered two methods of searching an array for an item. The sequential method (Algorithm 8.1 and Example 8.7 in Section 8.3) starts at the first element of the array and examines the elements in sequence. For an array with n elements, a sequential search inspects at most all n elements. When an array of about 20 elements or more is sorted, a binary search (Algorithm 8.2) is more efficient. This technique checks if the value for which we are searching is the middle element. If the value is less than that element, we repeat the process on the subarray of elements less than the middle element. Otherwise, we perform the process on the subarray of those greater than the middle value. The process continues until we find the element or there are no more elements to search. For a sorted n-element array, the maximum number of iterations in a binary search is $\lceil \log_2(n + 1) \rceil$.

To perform a binary search, we must sort the data first. Moreover, to make sense of large amounts of data, we should arrange the values in some specified way. The selection sort (Algorithm 8.3 in Section 8.4), which sorts an array of n elements, has the following algorithm:

> for *i* from 0 through *n* − 2 do
>   *MinIndex* ← *IndexOfMin*(*a*, *i*, *n*)
>   swap *a*[*i*] and *a*[*MinIndex*]

IndexOfMin returns the index of the minimum element in the unsorted subarray, *a*[*i* .. *n* − 1]. The segment to swap the values stored in variables *a*[*i*] and *a*[*MinIndex*] is as follows:

> *temp*   ←   *a*[*i*]
> *a*[*i*]   ←   *a*[*MinIndex*]
> *a*[*MinIndex*] ←   *temp*

After an iteration, *a*[0 .. *i*] has been sorted and *a*[*i* + 1 .. *n* − 1] has not.

In Section 8.5, we discussed two-dimensional arrays. In C, a two-dimensional array is an array of arrays. We can picture a two-dimensional array as a rectangular grid containing rows and columns, in which row and column coordinates uniquely specify each element. We declare an array *a* containing three rows (0 through 2) and four columns (0 through 3), all of which are floating point numbers, as

```
float a[3][4];
```

In array notation, *a*[2] represents row 2, and *a*[2][1] represents column 1 within that row. A declaration-initialization of this matrix is

```
float a[3][4] = { { 4,   5, 1, 0 },
                  { 2,   6, 9, 1 },
                  { 5, -2, 6, 7 } };
```

To declare arrays of more than two dimensions in C, we add more subscripts. When using such a multidimensional array as a parameter, we can have empty brackets for the first dimension, but we must explicitly state all other dimensions, as shown:

```
void PrintArray(float a[][4], int NumEls);
```

or

```
void PrintArray(float [][4], int);
```

Review Questions

1. What is an array?
2. How is the integer array *a*, containing 100 elements, declared in C?
3. What is the subscript of the first element of an array in C?
4. What are the rules for naming arrays?
5. How would you declare an array *x* containing 50 integer elements followed immediately by 50 real elements?
6. What is the purpose of initializing an array?
7. Is it possible to declare and initialize an array in C simultaneously? If so, how?

8. If *array1* and *array2* are dimensioned as follows:

```
char array1[10], array2[10];
```

and *array1* has been initialized, what is the effect of the following?

```
array1 = array2;
```

9. Is it obligatory to use all the elements of an array?

10. When a one-dimensional array is declared, under what condition may the dimension be omitted, with the array name followed by an empty pair of square brackets?

11. Must the elements of an array be accessed in order of subscript?

12. Give a prototype for a function *PrintArray* that prints the first *n* elements of an integer array *ar*, where *ar* and *n* are parameters.

13. Call *PrintArray* to print the values in an array *quantities* that has dimension 100 but only 30 actual values.

14. What method should we use to search for an item in an unsorted array?

15. For a sorted array of 1000 items, is the sequential or binary search more efficient?

16. In the worst case, how many elements are examined in a binary search of a sorted array of *n* elements?

17. When sorting the elements of an array, is it necessary to use another array to store the sorted elements?

18. During the first iteration of the selection sort of array *ar*, the routine swaps what values?

19. Write a segment to exchange the values of *x* and *y*.

20. What is the maximum number of dimensions an array in C may have?

21. True or false: If all the elements of a two-dimensional array are initialized in the declaration of the array, both subscripts may be omitted.

22. What is the meaning of the expression *array*[4][2]?

Laboratory

This laboratory practices several important array manipulations, including printing particular array elements, printing all array elements, adding array elements, inserting an element into an array, deleting another from the same array, and reading values from a file into an array.

Copy the file *LAB081.c* from the text disk onto one of your own. The program contains two stubs and two comments for code in *main*. Figure 8.21 contains the structure chart for the program, whose listing is below. The array is initialized with an array-type constant.

```
/*
 * Lab program to practice with arrays: printing, adding,
 * inserting, deleting
 * Date:
 * Programmer:
 */
```

Figure 8.21
Structure chart
for *LAB081.c*

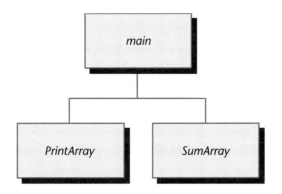

```
#include <stdio.h>

void  PrintArray(int [], int);
int   SumArray(int [], int);

main()
{
    int a[20] = {14, 17, 23, 26, 33, 38, 39, 41, 52, 56,
                  0,  0,  0,  0,  0,  0,  0,  0,  0,  0},
        i,               /* index                           */
        sum,             /* sum of the elements of the array */
        NumEls = 10,     /* number of elements in array     */
        DeleteIndex,     /* index of element to delete      */
        InsertIndex,     /* index of element to insert      */
        x;               /* item to insert                  */

    printf("Array at start of program:\n\n");
    PrintArray(a, NumEls);
    printf("\n\n");

    printf("The sum of these elements is %d.\n\n",
           SumArray(a, NumEls));

    DeleteIndex = 5;
    /* Add statements in Exercise 3 to delete a[DeleteIndex] */
    printf("After deletion of %d:\n", a[DeleteIndex]);
    PrintArray(a, NumEls);
    printf("\n\n");

    /*
     * Add statements in Exercise 4 to insert an element into
     * the array and display the results
     */
}
```

```
/*
 * Function to print the first NumEls elements of array b
 * Pre:    b is an integer array.
 *         NumEls is the number of elements in b.
 * Post:   The elements of b have been printed on a line
 *         separated by spaces.
 */

void PrintArray(int b[], int NumEls)
{
    int i;

    i = 9;
    printf("The element at index %d is %d.", i, b[i]);
}


/*
 * Function to return the sum of the first NumEls elements
 * of array b
 */

int SumArray(int b[], int NumEls)
{
    return 0;
}
```

1. **a.** Add your name and date to the initial comments and execute the program in *LAB081.c.* Modify the procedure *PrintArray* to print the element with index 2, then with 14, and finally with index 25. Describe the results when you use indices that are out of range, such as 25. To what value is *a*[14] initialized?

   b. In this part, finish code to print the values in the array. The execution of the completed procedure should produce the following line of output:

   ```
   Array a has 10 elements: 14 17 23 26 33 38 39 41 52 56
   ```

2. In this exercise, complete the definition of the function *SumArray* to return the sum of the first *n* elements of an array, *b.* Complete appropriate initial comments and replace the stub with a complete definition. Output should appear as follows:

   ```
   The sum of these elements is 339.
   ```

3. In many applications, we have a sorted array, such as *a,* in which we must make insertions and deletions and maintain the ordering. Perhaps the array contains flight information that travel agents must access frequently. Having the array sorted allows the program to use faster searching techniques, such as a binary search. When we remove an element from a sorted array, we want to close the gap by moving higher elements down. Figure 8.22 depicts this manipulation with the arrow from *a*[6] to *a*[5] indicating the first copy.

   Replace the comment for Exercise 3 in *main* with code for deleting *a*[*DeleteIndex*]. What is the index of the first element in the array that should get a new value? What is the last? Recall that no element exists with index *NumEls* (10) and that we are not changing the value of *a*[9]. How will the value of *NumEls* change? The

Figure 8.22
Deletion of an element at index 5 from an array

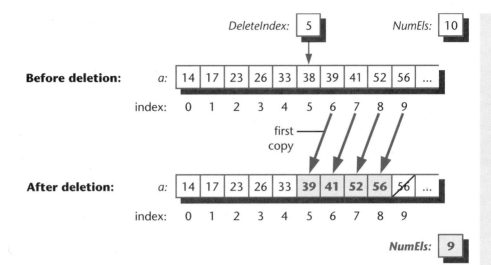

Figure 8.23
Movement of array elements to make room for insertion

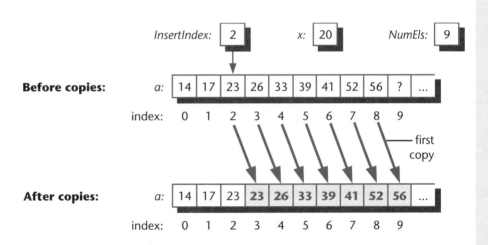

answers to these questions will help with your design. Execution of the corrected program contains the following:

```
After deletion of 38:
Array a has 9 elements: 14 17 23 26 33 39 41 52 56
```

It is better to place a task like this deletion in a function. We must not only change the values in the array *a*, but also reduce *NumEls* by 1. In the next chapter, we see how a function can change the value of a simple variable (such as *NumEls*) in the calling function (such as *main*). For now, we place the entire segment in *main* to avoid having to pass back a new value for *NumEls*.

4. The segment in this exercise inserts a value, *x*, at location *InsertIndex*, while keeping the other elements in the array. As Figure 8.23 shows, for the insertion, we first must move up the elements in the array starting with location *InsertIndex*. The rightmost arrow from *a*[8] to *a*[9] (*a*[*NumEls*]) indicates the first assignment.

```
a[9] = a[8];
```

After this copying, two array elements, *a*[2] and *a*[3], contain 23, and there is room to place the new element. Figure 8.24 shows the assignment of *x*'s value to

Figure 8.24
From Figure 8.23, completion of insertion of *x* (20) at *InsertIndex*(2)

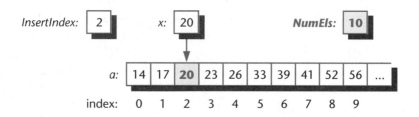

a[2] and the adjustment of *NumEls*. We must be careful that *a* has a large enough dimension to handle the additional element. What is the dimension of *a*?

Replace the comment for Exercise 4 in *main* with statements to perform the insertion. Write necessary code in main to assign *x* the value of 20 and *InsertIndex* the value of 3, along with required calls to *printf*. Proper execution produces the following output:

```
After insertion of 20 at 3:
Array a has 10 elements: 14 17 20 23 26 33 39 41 52 56
```

5. Remove the code that initializes the array. Add a procedure *ReadData* that reads 10 values from a text file *values.dat*, which you create. The procedure should return the array with the first 10 elements initialized.

9

Pointers

Introduction

One major feature that distinguishes the C language from most others is the abundant use of pointers, a data type that we introduce in this chapter. A pointer variable can store a memory address. Through the pointer, we can access a location to store and retrieve information.

Variable names are not sufficient to provide the kinds of manipulations C requires. Local variable names are meaningful only within their declaring functions. However, memory addresses are global to all functions. One function can pass the address of a local variable to another function, and the second function can use this address to access the contents of the first function's local variable. Passing addresses does not violate the rules of modular programming, as the use of global variables does. Addresses are passed only to the functions that need to access those memory locations. Passing a local variable's address is analogous to passing a key. Only the functions possessing the key can access the variable in question.

Access to addresses in C allows a called function to communicate more than one piece of information back to the calling function. With pass by value, the value of an argument is copied into the parameter. Any change in the parameter does not affect the corresponding argument. When we pass an address to a called function, the called function can alter the contents at that location.

Pointers are intimately associated with arrays in C. The unsubscripted name of an array evaluates to the address of the first element. In Section 9.4, we consider the impact of this fact in using arrays as arguments and in accessing various array elements through pointers.

In a program using an array, we declare the dimension of the array to be some maximum size. This technique can waste memory if the amount of data is much less than the maximum. Unfortunately, we cannot always predict the array size. Thus, for some applications, it is desirable to be able to start a program with the smallest amount of memory necessary and then allocate extra space as needed. Through various ANSI C library functions, we can allocate and deallocate space dynamically during program execution.

Sometimes, we do not know until execution time which of several lower-level functions a routine needs to call. In this case, it is useful to be able to pass a reference to the desired function through the argument-parameter list. In Section 9.6, we consider this use of pointers.

With the discussion of memory addresses in this chapter is an accompanying breadth section on memory, which covers sizes and categories of memories.

Goals

To study

- The concept of pointers
- Pointer declaration, the address operator, and indirection
- Memory sizes, RAM, and ROM
- Pass by reference
- Communication between called and calling function
- Accessing array elements through pointers
- Dynamic memory allocation
- Passing a reference to a function through the argument-parameter list

Section 9.1 **The Concept of Pointers**

The computer stores variables in memory, and each memory location has a numeric address, in much the same way that each element of an array has its own subscript. Variable names in C and other high-level languages enable the programmer to refer to memory locations by name, but the compiler must translate these names into addresses. This process is automatic, so we need not concern ourselves with it. However, the kind of problems for which C is particularly noted requires that the user be able to refer to those addresses indirectly in order to manipulate the contents of the corresponding memory locations. In a sense, the address or name of a memory location points to whatever that memory location contains.

Declarations

Variables called **pointers** can store memory addresses. An address is a separate data type in C. In fact, several types of addresses exist. The address of an *int* variable is of a type distinctly different from that of a *char* variable. We declare a variable, *ptr*, that can hold the address of an integer as follows:*

```
int *ptr;
```

---

*The following form of the declaration is also acceptable:
```
int* ptr;
```

The asterisk is not part of the variable name. Rather, *int* * (read "pointer to *int*") is the type of variable *ptr*. If we declare

```
int *ptr,    /* of type int *   */
      v;     /* of type int     */
```

only *ptr* is of type *int* *. The variable *v* is simply of type *int*. In this text, sometimes we refer to the type of item pointed to by a pointer variable as the **target type**. For example, the target type of *int* * is *int*.

Definitions   A **pointer** is a variable that can store a memory address. The type of item pointed to by a pointer variable is the **target type**.

We name pointer variables in the same manner as any other variable. Because the asterisk is not part of the name, the following example is illegal. It is an attempt to declare the variable *num* twice with two different types, *int* and *int* *.

```
int num, *num;     /* ILLEGAL */
```

Address Operator

When a variable is declared as a pointer, it is not automatically initialized to a value. In this respect, it is just like any other variable. Initially, the pointer does not point to anything. To assign an address to a pointer, the programmer must assign it a value. An ampersand (&) immediately preceding a variable name, such as *v*, returns the address of the variable. Thus, execution of the statement

```
ptr = &v;
```

assigns the address of *v* to *ptr*. This **ampersand** or **address operator** applied to a variable of type *int* returns a constant value of type *int* *, which we can assign to a variable of type *int* *. We can use the & operator with any lvalue, such as a variable name or array element, but it can never precede a constant, an expression (other than a scalar variable), or the unsubscripted name of an array. Figure 9.1 pictures memory with addresses after the declaration of *ptr* and *v* and the above assignment statement.

In its declaration, we can initialize a pointer variable to the address of any variable already declared. For example, the following is acceptable in C:

```
int v,
    *ptr = &v;
```

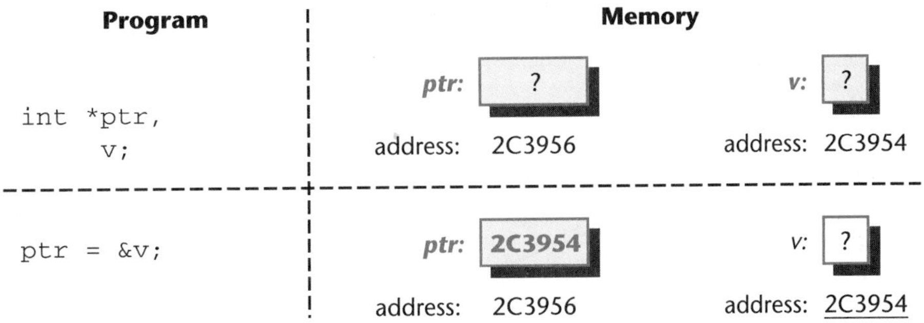

Figure 9.1
Memory after declaration and assignment statements involving a pointer

Program	Memory
`int *ptr,` `      v;`	ptr: `?` address: 2C3956 v: `?` address: 2C3954
`ptr = &v;`	ptr: `2C3954` address: 2C3956 v: `?` address: 2C3954

The statement declares *v* as a variable of type *int*, declares *ptr* as a pointer to target type *int*, and initializes *ptr* to the address of *v*. This declaration-initialization behaves in exactly the same way as the declarations and assignment in Figure 9.1.

Each time the program executes, the locations of the variables and, consequently, the values of pointer variables are likely to change. Most of the time, the actual address that a pointer variable, such as *ptr*, stores is irrelevant. Thus, when a pointer variable stores the address of a variable, as in

```
ptr = &v;
```

we draw an arrow from the pointer to its target location. Figure 9.2 pictures such a situation drawn two ways.

Since first covering the *scanf* function, without explanation, we have been using addresses of variables, such as

```
scanf("%d", &v);
```

In Section 9.3, we discuss in detail passing of such addresses to this and other functions.

Indirection Operator

Once the address of integer variable *v* has been assigned to the pointer variable *ptr*, *ptr* can be used to manipulate the contents of *v*. By placing an asterisk before the pointer, we reference not the pointer, but the location to which *ptr* points. For example,

```
*ptr = 5;
```

is equivalent to

```
v = 5;
```

The first statement contains an **indirection operator** (*). Through the pointer, we indirectly access another memory location. With the indirection operator, we are **dereferencing the pointer**. We are not obtaining the address to which it refers, but the value the computer stores at that memory location. Thus, when we assign 5 to **ptr*, we are changing the value of *v* to 5. Figure 9.3 depicts this assignment involving a dereferenced pointer with an asterisk by *ptr*'s arrow.

We can use **ptr* anywhere we can use the integer variable *v*. For example, after the assignment

```
*ptr = 5;
```

we can print this value with

```
printf("%d\n", *ptr);
```

or

```
printf("%d\n", v);
```

Figure 9.2
Representation of memory after *ptr = &v;*

Figure 9.3
Memory after
execution of
either
statement

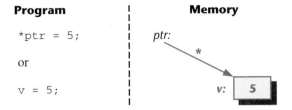

Figure 9.4
Memory after
execution of
ptr = NULL;

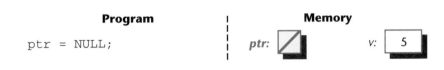

Moreover, blanks can appear between the asterisk and the identifier, as shown:

```
int * ptr;
* ptr = 5;
printf("%d\n", * ptr);
```

We can read the declaration

```
int *ptr;
```

as, "declare *ptr* to be an *int*." However, memory is allocated for *ptr*, not for *ptr*. Thus, the statement

```
ptr = &v;
```

or the declaration-initialization

```
int *ptr = &v;
```

assigns the address of *v* to *ptr*, not to *ptr*, which does not exist before the assignment.

NULL

To have *ptr* no longer store the address of *v*, we can assign a special constant, *NULL*, to *ptr*, as follows:

```
ptr = NULL;
```

Several header files, including *stdio.h*, define *NULL* to be 0. In Figure 9.4, we use a slash in the rectangle for *ptr* to indicate that the pointer has the value *NULL*.

**Printing
Addresses**

We use the %p conversion specification to print a memory address, and the output appears in hexadecimal. Because *&ptr*, *ptr*, and *&v* are all addresses, we print their values with

```
printf("&ptr = %p, ptr = %p, &v = %p\n", &ptr, ptr, &v);
```

Output affirms that *ptr* stores the address of *v*.

```
&ptr = 002C3956, ptr = 002C3954, &v = 002C3954
```

Table 9.1 Summary of meaning of code for declaration-initializations

```
int v = 5,
    *ptr = &v;
```

Code	Meaning	Picture
&ptr	address of variable *ptr*	ptr: 2C3954 → 5 v **address: 2C3956** address: 2C3954
ptr	value of *ptr*; contents of memory location for *ptr*; address of *v*	ptr: **2C3954** → 5 v address: 2C3956 **address: 2C3954**
&v	address of variable *v*	ptr: 2C3954 → 5 v address: 2C3956 **address: 2C3954**
*ptr	dereferenced value of *ptr*; contents of location to which *ptr* points; value of *v*	ptr: 2C3954 → * 5 v address: 2C3956 address: 2C3954
v	value of *v*; contents of memory location for *v*	ptr: 2C3954 → 5 v address: 2C3956 address: 2C3954

Summary

Table 9.1 summarizes the meaning of the various variables with the ampersand and indirection operators. The example provides further practice with pointers.

Example 9.1 _____

The program in this example illustrates manipulations with pointers. We present the code gradually with explanations and figures between segments.

```
/* Practice with pointers */

#include <stdio.h>

main()
{
    int i,          /* integer variable */
        k = 5,      /* integer variable */
        *p,         /* pointer with integer target type */
        *q = NULL;  /* pointer with integer target type */
```

With this declaration, the compiler sets aside enough space for integer variables *i* and *k* and for pointer variables *p* and *q*. Moreover, *k* is initialized to be 5; and *q* is given the value *NULL*. Figure 9.5 depicts memory after these declarations.

Figure 9.5
Memory after
execution of
declaration-
initialization

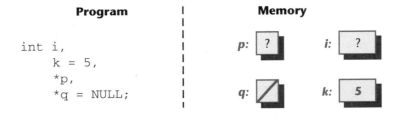

Figure 9.6
Effect on
memory of
p = q;

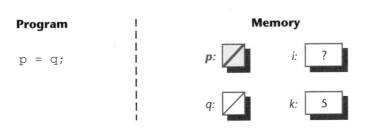

Suppose now we copy *q*'s value into *p* and test equality with an *if* statement, as follows:

```
p = q;
if (p == q)
    printf("Case 1: equal\n");
else
    printf("Case 1: not equal\n");
```

Figure 9.6 illustrates the effect on memory of such an assignment. Because variables *p* and *q* now store the same value (*NULL*), the test (*p == q*) is *TRUE*, and the computer prints

```
Case 1: equal
```

If we now change *q*'s value to the address of *k*, we are not simultaneously changing *p*'s value.

```
q = &k;
```

We do not use the indirection operator (*) with *q*, because we are directly changing *q*'s value. Figure 9.7 shows *q* pointing to the memory location for *k*.

Suppose we again copy the address in *q* into variable *p* and test for equality.

```
p = q;
if (p == q)
    printf("Case 2: equal\n");
else
    printf("Case 2: not equal\n");
```

As Figure 9.8 shows, the pointers *p* and *q* once again store the same value, the address of *k*. With *p* and *q* equal, the output includes the following:

```
Case 2: equal
```

Figure 9.7
Effect on
memory of
q = &k;

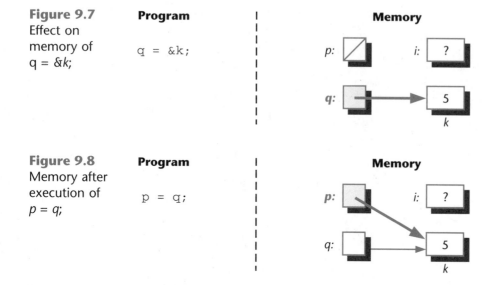

Figure 9.8
Memory after
execution of
p = q;

Suppose now we change *p*'s value to point to *i* and through indirection change *i*'s value.

```
p = &i;
*p = 5;
if (p == q)
    printf("Case 3: equal\n");
else
    printf("Case 3: not equal\n");
```

Figure 9.9 shows that although **p* and **q* now have the same value (5), *p* and *q* do not. The pointer *p* references the location for *i*, and *q* stores the address of *k*. Thus, the segment prints the following:

```
Case 3: not equal
```

Through assigning 7 to the dereferenced *p*, we now change *i*'s value to 7.

```
*p = 7;
```

Figure 9.10 illustrates how the value in the location for *i* is now 7.

Several calls to *printf* close the example. Using the ANSI C conversion specification %p, we can print the addresses of *p* and *q* as follows:

```
printf("p's address (&p) = %p and q's address (&q) = %p\n", &p, &q);
```

Particularly on a mainframe computer, these values are likely to vary with each execution. One run might reveal the following addresses:

```
p's address (&p) = 002C3806 and q's address (&q) = 002C3802
```

In the next two calls to *printf*, we print the addresses which *p* and *q* store and the addresses of *i* and *k*, as follows:

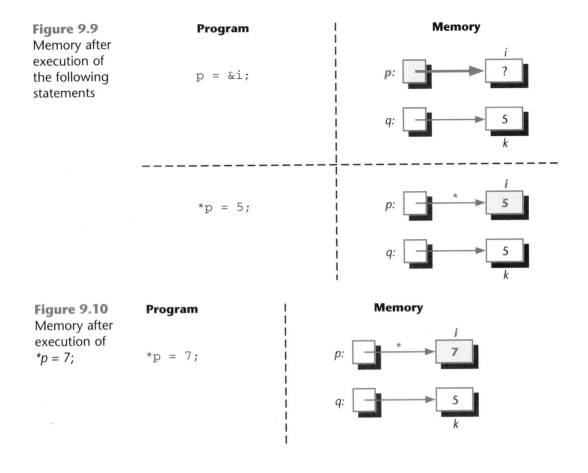

Figure 9.9 Memory after execution of the following statements

Figure 9.10 Memory after execution of *p = 7;*

```
printf("                        p = %p and                        q = %p\n", p, q);
printf("i's address (&i) = %p and k's address (&k) = %p\n", &i, &k);
```

As the output verifies, p and &i are identical, as are q and &k. The value of p is the address of i. Similarly, q contains the address of k, &k, as shown:

```
        p = 002C380C and                        q = 002C380A
i's address (&i) = 002C380C and k's address (&k) = 002C380A
```

Thus, to access i's value, we can use i or the indirection operator with p, *p.

```
printf("Dereferenced value of p (*p) = %d; of q (*q) = %d\n",
        *p, *q);
printf("                        i = %d and        k = %d\n",
        i, k);
```

The output emphasizes that with p pointing to i, dereferencing p (*p) accesses i. Thus, *p equals i. Using the same reasoning, we see that *q equals k, as shown:

```
Dereferenced value of p (*p) = 7; of q (*q) = 5
                i = 7 and        k = 5
```

Point before Dereferencing

One final note of caution: We must assign a location to a pointer variable before dereferencing. For example, the following segment is not correct.

```
int *p,            /* pointer with integer target type */
    *q = NULL;     /* pointer with integer target type */

/* ERROR - The next 3 statements are WRONG!!!        */
/* We have not pointed p or q to memory locations.   */
*p = 7;
printf("p = %p and dereferenced value of p (*p) = %d\n", p, *p);
printf("q = %p and dereferenced value of q (*q) = %d\n", q, *q);
```

One execution might yield

```
p = 0026168C and dereferenced value of p (*p) = 7
q = 00000000 and dereferenced value of q (*q) = 16513
```

We have not assigned p a value, so whatever happens to be in p is the address we use in the dereferencing. In this example, we are accidentally changing the contents of location 0026168C to 7. If that location is used by another variable, its value would be destroyed and unpredictable results would occur. We have assigned q the value *NULL*, a string of 0 bits. By doing so, we are indicating that we do not mean for q to point to a memory location. When we erroneously dereference q with $*q$, we print the contents of address 0, which happens to be 16513.

Section 9.1 Exercises

For Exercises 1–5 show a diagram of memory after execution of each statement, and give the output. Assume the following declarations:

```
float x, y, *p, *q;
```

1.
```
p = &x;
*p = 14.5;
q = &y;
*q = 23.8;
printf("%f %f\n", *p, *q);
p = q;
*p = 36.1;
printf("%f %f\n", *p, *q);
q = NULL;
printf("%f %f\n", x, y);
```

2.
```
p = &x;
*p = 14.5;
q = &y;
*q = 23.8;
printf("%f %f\n", *p, *q);
*p = *q;
printf("%f %f\n", *p, *q);
q = NULL;
printf("%f\n", *p);
printf("%f %f\n", x, y);
```

3.
```
p = &x;
*p = 14.5;
q = p;
printf("%f %f\n", *p, *q);
q = NULL;
printf("%f %f\n", x, y);
```

4.
```
p = &x;
*p = 14.5;
q = p;
if (p == q)
      printf("1. yes\n");
q = &y;
if (p == q)
      printf("2. yes\n");
*q = 14.5;
if (p == q)
      printf("3. yes\n");
```

5.
```
p = &x;
*p = 14.5;
q = p;
if (*p == *q)
    printf("1. yes\n");
q = &y;
*q = 14.5;
if (*p == *q)
    printf("2. yes\n");
```
6. Find the error(s) in the following segment.
```
char ch = 'Y',
     *p,
     *q = ch;

printf("The address of p is %x\n", p);
printf("The contents of q is %c\n", q);
*p = 'Z';
```
7. Find the error(s) in the following segment.
```
int *ptr = &v,
    v;
```
8. Write a declaration-initialization to establish a pointer, *char_ptr*, to a location that stores a character and place the letter B in that location. Declare any other variable necessary.

9. Using *char_ptr* from the last example, write a statement to print the address of *char_ptr*, its contents, and the contents of the location to which it points.

Section 9.2 Breadth: Memory

In Chapter 1, we considered two types of memory—primary and secondary. Secondary memory or storage consists of such items as disks and tapes. Primary or main memory, which holds data and programs, provides fast storage access for the central processing unit (CPU).

The CPU is faster than main memory. When the CPU issues a request for a data item or an instruction, several clock cycles may elapse before the information is available. Very fast memory is possible technologically, but not economically. The cost of a high-speed, large main memory is prohibitively expensive. As an alternative, some computers—such as VAX computers—have a small, fast memory that is a buffer between the CPU and main memory. Such a memory is called a **cache** (pronounced "cash"), a term derived from the French word *cacher*, which means "to hide." Figure 9.11 depicts the flow of information in a system with a cache. Over a short interval of time, the CPU usually needs to access only a small portion of memory. For example, most of the time for program execution occurs in loops. During execution of a loop, the computer executes a few instructions over and over. The computer can copy such a segment into the fast cache memory. The CPU can obtain instructions and data much faster from the cache than from main memory.

Definition   A **cache** is a fast, small memory that is a buffer between the CPU and main memory.

Figure 9.11
Flow of
information in a
system with a
cache

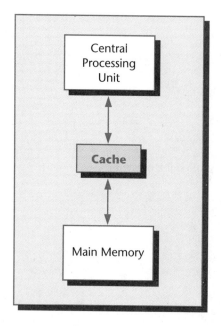

**Memory
Sizes**

The sizes of memories are measured in bytes. Recall that a byte encodes a character and that on most computers one byte contains 8 bits. The memory sizes of early microcomputers and their diskettes were expressed in terms of chunks of $2^{10} = 1024$ bytes. Because 1024 is close to 1000, we use the metric notation **K** for 1000 or kilo. Today, a calculator might have 256 K of memory, which is $256 \cdot 1024 = 262,144$ bytes. A cache memory can be several K in size. A double-density $3\frac{1}{2}''$ diskette has about 800 K = 819,200 bytes of storage space, more than enough to store a 200 page book. We discuss secondary storage, such as with diskettes, in greater detail later in the book.

Definition   A **K** is 2^{10} bytes = 1024 bytes.

Frequently, we must resort to larger units when expressing size of newer disks and computers. As the prefix indicates, a **megabyte (Mbyte)** is about one million bytes. More precisely, 1 Mbyte is meant to represent $1024 \cdot 1024 = 2^{10} \cdot 2^{10} = 2^{20} = 1,048,576$ bytes. A high density $3\frac{1}{2}''$ diskette has about 1.44 Mbyte of storage space. A 32 Mbyte computer has a main memory that can store about 32,000,000 characters (33,554,432 characters to be exact), enough for many books.

Definition   A **megabyte (Mbyte)** is $1024 \cdot 1024 = 2^{10} \cdot 2^{10} = 2^{20} = 1,048,576$ bytes.

Larger memory sizes are helpful with complex applications and graphics. For example, if we use a color scanner to digitize a photograph, we might need several Mbytes of main memory to view that one image on our computer screen. With an increasing number of multimedia applications, computers not only need to process single images but moving sequences of frames with sound. A 15-second movie with sound might take up 40 Mbytes of disk space. Even with larger memories, such demand indicates the need for sophisticated algorithms for compression, which reduce the sizes of such files. For example, compression software might reduce a 3-Mbyte file to 1 Mbyte. Before using this file, the programmer must reverse the process of compression. The increase in network traffic and the need to transmit large graphics files and other data files have encouraged research and development of high-speed computer networks to handle rates, such as 1 **gigabit (Gbyte)** per second (about one billion bits per second).

Definition   A **gigabyte (Gbyte)** is 1024 Mbytes or $2^{10} \cdot 2^{10} \cdot 2^{10} = 2^{30} = 1,073,741,824$ bytes. A **gigabit** is 2^{30} bits.

With any size main memory, the computer must be able to access each byte, and, thus, must be able to determine the address of each word. Recall that a pointer is just a variable that stores an address.

Example 9.2

Suppose the memory of a certain computer is **byte-addressable**, where starting with 0, each byte has a different address. Suppose also that each address is 24 bits long. Thus, the largest address is 1111 1111 1111 1111 1111 1111$_2$, which is $2^{24} - 1$. Because there can be 2^{24} bytes, memory can be of size 2^{14} K = 16,384 K or 2^4 Mbytes = 16 Mbytes.

Definition   A computer is **byte-addressable** if each byte has a different address.

Example 9.3

Suppose a particular computer has 32 Mbytes of memory. How many bits are needed for a pointer? A Mbyte is 2^{10} K or $2^{10} \cdot 2^{10} = 2^{20}$ bytes. Also, $32 = 2^5$. Thus, 32 Mbytes is $2^5 \cdot 2^{20} = 2^{25}$ bytes. To access 2^{25} different locations, we need a string of 25 bits. Comparing this answer to that of the last example, we see that when we have one more bit in the address, we can double the amount of addressable memory. A pointer of 24 bits can address $2^{24} = 16,777,216$ cells, whereas a pointer of 25 bits can address $2^{25} = 2 \cdot 2^{24} = 33,554,432$ different locations.

RAM and ROM

Although all of memory is addressable, actually two types of main memory chips exist—RAM and ROM. **Random access memory (RAM)** is the part of memory that can change. We use it to store much of our software and all of our work—a word processor and our term paper, a C compiler and the source code for our program. What is in this part of memory can change as we turn from working on English homework to a computer science assignment. RAM is generally **volatile**. In other words, if electricity is lost, so is the information in RAM. Anyone who has worked for a couple of hours, forgetting to save, and has lost power understands all too well the meaning of "volatile."

Definition   **Random access memory (RAM)** is the part of main memory that can change. We can read from and write to this type of memory.

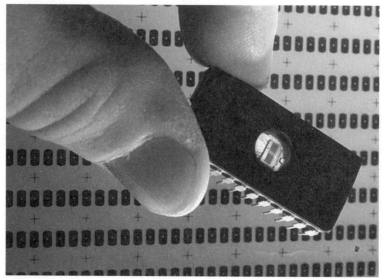

RAM chip

The other type of memory is **read-only memory (ROM)**. ROM chips are **nonvolatile** and store permanent information. Some computers have ROM chips that store a BASIC interpreter or the entire operating system (OS). In many microcomputers, ROM contains the **BIOS** or **Basic Input/Output System**, the primitive functions that are the foundation of the operating system. The advantage of such an arrangement is speed and convenience. Accessing ROM is much faster and easier than accessing a disk. The disadvantage is that its contents cannot change, so we cannot update a version of software without changing the appropriate chip. Because of this disadvantage, ROM is usually very small and often only contains a program that loads the operating system from disk into RAM and starts OS execution. Analogous to the bootstrap, which is only used to help pull on a boot and then is no longer needed, this program is only used to initiate the operating system. Consequently, the program is called a **bootstrap**, and this process of loading and initiating operating system execution is called **bootstrapping** or **booting**. Historically the concept has to do with the impossibility of "lifting yourself by your own bootstraps," or reading a program into a computer that does not yet have a program.

Definitions   The contents of **volatile** memory are lost if electricity is lost, whereas the contents of **nonvolatile** memory persist. **Read-only memory (ROM)** is the part of main memory that **cannot** change. We can read from but not write to this type of memory. A **bootstrap** is a program that is only used to initiate the operating system. The process of loading and initiating operating system execution is called **bootstrapping** or **booting**.

Section 9.2 Exercises

1. A disk pack stores data for a mainframe much as a diskette is a secondary storage medium for a microcomputer. Suppose a disk pack has a capacity of $7 \cdot 10^9$ bytes How many K and Mbytes can it contain?

2. How many bytes are in a 64 K memory? Express your answer as a power of 2.

3. Repeat Exercise 2 using 256 K.

4. How many bytes and Gbytes are in 56 Mbytes?

Express as a power of 2 the number of K in Exercises 5–7.

5. 2^{23} bytes   **6.** 16,384 bytes   **7.** 131,072 bytes

If a memory address is n bits long, how many bytes and how many K are addressable for n equal to each of the numbers in Exercises 8–11? Assume the computer is byte-addressable.

8. 9   **9.** 8   **10.** 22   **11.** 29

How many bits must be in the address for each memory size in Exercises 12–15?

12. 256 K   **13.** 48 K   **14.** 8 Mbytes   **15.** 48 Mbytes

16. Why might a microcomputer manufacturer equip a machine with 131,072 bytes of memory instead of some round number like 130,000?

17. **a.** An Intel 8088 microprocessor has a 20-bit address. What is its maximum possible memory size on a byte-addressable machine?

    b. If 384 K is reserved for video, input/output, and other peripheral address space, how much space is left?

18. How much main memory does your computer have? For a DOS machine, at the DOS prompt, type *chkdsk*. For a Macintosh on the desktop, under the Apple menu, select About this Macintosh. . . . For a VAX/VMS computer, type *show memory*.

19. What is the size of the last program you wrote?

Section 9.2 Programming Projects

1. Write a program to accept the number of bits in an address and to return the memory size in K for a byte-addressable machine. Allow the user to make repeated requests.

2. Write a program to accept a memory size as input and to return the number of bits needed for an address. The program should ask for a number and whether the unit is K or Mbytes. Allow the user to make repeated requests.

Section 9.3 Passing Pointers as Parameters

Functions are an essential ingredient of top-down design and structured programming. We call a function, passing it any number of arguments, and the function returns at most one value. With scalar parameters, we have used pass by value. The computer copies the value of the argument into the corresponding parameter, and then it severs all communication between the two. If the called function changes the value of the parameter, the modification has no effect on the corresponding argument. Only with arrays have we been able to pass a reference to the function. If the called function changes the array elements, it is actually altering the elements of the original array.

Sometimes we need to send back more than one value from a function, but the values are not in an array. For example, in Section 8.4 to perform a selection sort, we needed to swap the contents of two variables. A swap function must accept two arguments and exchange values for the calling function. In Section 8.2, a function read data into an array, but we had to know the number of items before calling the function. A more realistic approach is to use the sentinel technique or to detect end-of-file in the reading function and to communicate the number of items read, as well as the array, to *main*.

To establish such communication, we can have a pointer argument, which is the address of the value we wish to change. The receiving function modifies that value by dereferencing the pointer. For example, a call to the *scanf* function uses the & operator to pass the addresses of the variables, such as

```
scanf("%d", &x);
```

We pass the address of *x* to the function *scanf*. The function *scanf* now knows where the computer stores *x*'s value. When the function obtains a value from standard input, it can store the value in that location. Thus, *scanf* can indirectly alter the value of *x*.

The technique of making a variable accessible to a function by passing its address is **pass by reference**. In true pass by reference available with many computer languages, we do not use pointer notation. In the strictest sense of the terms, C has only one method of passing information between a calling and a called routine—pass by value. With pass by value, the parameter receives a copy of the value of the argument. Thus, even with a pointer argument, the called function cannot change its value in the calling function. When the argument is a pointer, however, the called function can alter the value in the location referenced by the pointer.

Definition **Pass by reference** is the technique of making a variable accessible to a function by passing its address.

Example 9.4 _____

In Examples 2.24–2.27 of Section 2.9, we considered several versions of a function *modify_i*. We saw that assignment to a local variable, *i*, in *modify_i* does not affect a variable with the same name in *main*. Even if we pass the variable as an argument, the function's modifications to the formal parameter do not change the corresponding argument. With call by value, the value is copied from the argument to the parameter, but not back again. Using a global variable *i* is a poor solution, because then any function can change *i*'s value. A function could do so by mistake. Moreover, we cannot readily tell if a function uses the variable or not. In this example, however, the function *main* passes the address of *i* (&*i*) to *modify_i*, and the called function uses that address to assign a new value to *i*.

To accommodate this variation, we must rewrite the function *modify_i* to accept and process an address. Therefore, we declare the parameter *i_ptr* in *modify_i* as a pointer to an *int*. Now, *modify_i* can change the value of *main*'s local variable *i* by dereferencing the pointer *i_ptr*. In the text, we use a suffix of *_ptr* for a variable name to indicate a pointer to that variable.

```
/*
 * Example 9.4
 * Communication between functions through pass by reference
 */
```

```
#include <stdio.h>

main()
{
    void modify_i(int *);     /* local to main */
    int i;                    /* local to main */

    i = 1;     /* local i is assigned 1 */

    printf ("Before calling modify_i, i equals %d\n", i);
    modify_i(&i);
    printf ("After  calling modify_i, i equals %d\n", i);
}

/*
 * Function to modify a value in main
 * Pre:    i_ptr points to an integer.
 * Post:   *i_ptr was modified.
 */

void modify_i(int *i_ptr)
{
    *i_ptr = 3;

}
```

The following output affirms that *modify_i* can change the value of *i*:

```
Before calling modify_i, i equals 1
After  calling modify_i, i equals 3
```

The function *main* assigns the address of *i* (*&i*) to the pointer variable *i_ptr* in *modify_i*. Through indirection, *i_ptr* updates the contents of that location. Because *main* associates the identifier *i* with that location, *modify_i* changes *i*. Figure 9.12 shows the actions of the program.

Example 9.5

As a further illustration of passing a reference, this program includes the function *swap* to exchange the values of two variables. In Section 8.4, we developed a segment in *main* to switch the values of *x* and *y* using a temporary variable, *temp*. Figure 8.15 presents a diagram of memory during execution of the code.

In this program, we send the addresses of *x* and *y* (*&x* and *&y*, respectively) to pointer parameters (*x_ptr* and *y_ptr*, respectively) in the function *swap*. Through indirection, *swap* can manipulate the contents of the memory locations for *x* and *y*.

Figure 9.12
Action of a pass
by reference in
Example 9.4

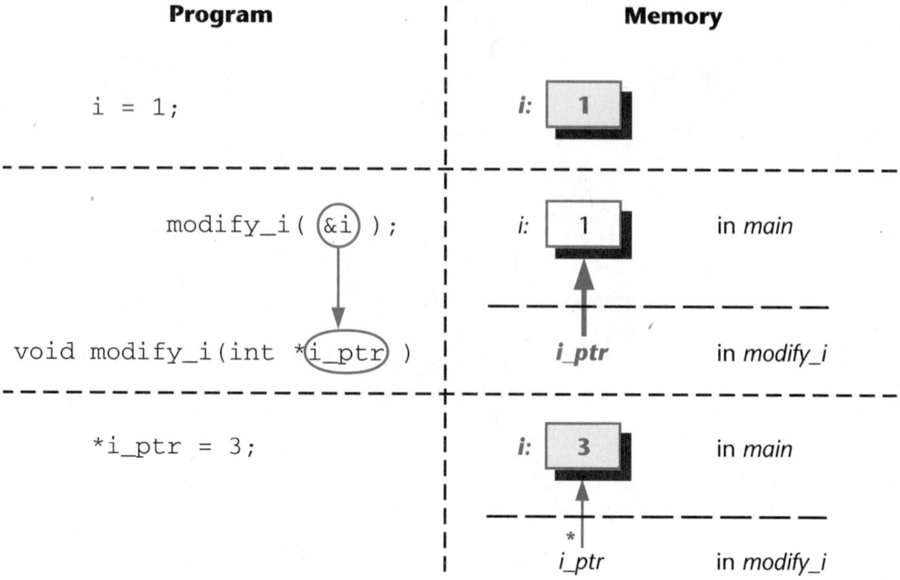

	Program		Memory

```
/*
 * Example 9.5
 * Illustration of swap of values of two variables
 */

#include <stdio.h>

void swap(int *, int *);

main()
{
    int x = 3,      /* values to exchange */
        y = 5;

    printf("Before swap: x = %d and y = %d\n", x, y);
    swap(&x, &y);
    printf("After swap:  x = %d and y = %d\n", x, y);
}

/*
 * Swap *x_ptr and *y_ptr
 * Pre:    *x_ptr and *y_ptr have integer values.
 * Post:   *x_ptr and *y_ptr were swapped.
 */

void swap(int *x_ptr, int *y_ptr)
{
    int temp;     /* temporary variable for swap */

    temp  = *x_ptr;
    *x_ptr = *y_ptr;
    *y_ptr = temp;
}
```

The following output verifies that the function exchanges the values of *x* and *y*:

```
Before swap: x = 3 and y = 5
After swap:  x = 5 and y = 3
```

With dotted arrows indicating copying of values, Figure 9.13 illustrates this manipulation of *x* and *y* through pointers.

If we declare the formal parameters of *swap* to be of type *int* and *main* passes only *x* and *y* rather than their addresses, the exchange in *swap* would have no effect on the variables *x* and *y* in *main*. We would be using pass by value. Consequently, we pass

Figure 9.13   Action of call to *swap* in Example 9.5

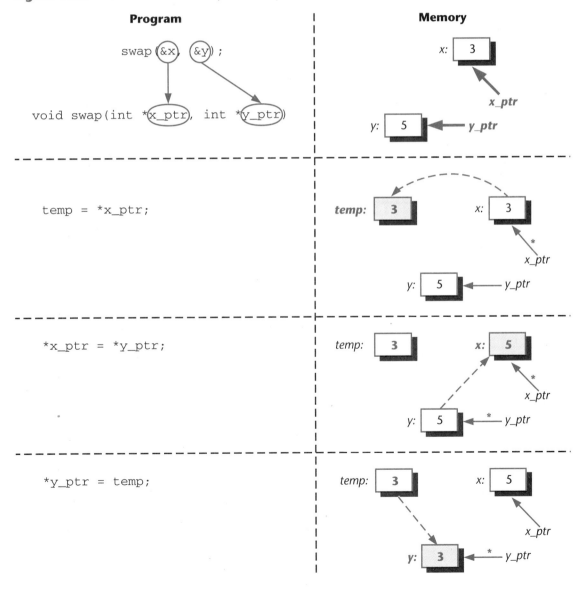

addresses and access the contents of those addresses by dereferencing pointers. Although we are passing the addresses &x and &y by value—the function cannot change the addresses—we are passing x and y by reference. The function can and does alter the values in those locations.

The variable *temp* in *swap* is of type *int*, not *int **. The values being exchanged are not the pointers, but the integers being pointed to by them.

Example 9.6

In this example, we write a function, *ReadGRE*, to read scores on the three parts (verbal, mathematical, and analytical) of the Graduate Record Exam (GRE). The function should verify that each score is between 200 and 800. The function *main* is a driver to test *ReadGRE*. It calls this function and prints the scores. The design is straightforward, but we should pay special attention to how the function deals with the pointer parameters.

```
/*
 * Example 9.6
 * Function to read scores on the three parts of the GRE
 * Pre:  none
 * Post: Values have been read for *verbal_ptr, *math_ptr, and
 *       *analytical_ptr, the verbal, mathematical, and analytical
 *       scores, respectively, of the GRE
 */

void ReadGRE(int *verbal_ptr, int *math_ptr, int *analytical_ptr)
{
    printf("Type the verbal, mathematical, and analytical\n");
    printf("scores, separated by blanks.\n");
    scanf("%d %d %d", verbal_ptr, math_ptr, analytical_ptr);

    while( *verbal_ptr     < 200 || *verbal_ptr     > 800 ||
           *math_ptr       < 200 || *math_ptr       > 800 ||
           *analytical_ptr < 200 || *analytical_ptr > 800)
    {
        printf("Each score must be between 200 and 800\n");
        printf("Please re-enter the three scores: ");
        scanf("%d %d %d", verbal_ptr, math_ptr, analytical_ptr);
    }
}
```

Because *main* must obtain the values using pass by reference, the formal parameters of *ReadGRE* are pointers to integers of type *int **. These variables already point to the locations where the computer is to store the values. Therefore, we do not use the address operator (&) before the parameters to *scanf*. The value of *verbal_ptr* already stores an address of an integer location; *&verbal_ptr* would be the address of the pointer. The C compiler does not give an error message if we inadvertently use an address operator here, because the form is syntactically acceptable. The results would be incorrect, however, because the computer would assign the value to the pointer, such as *verbal_ptr*, instead of storing it in the location for the integer, such as *verbal_ptr*. Using an address operator here would be as disastrous as omitting it in the *scanf* calls of earlier examples. Once the function reads the values, it must verify that each is in the appropriate range. To do so, we need the score, not the address of the score. Consequently, for the conditional expression in the *while* loop, we dereference each pointer, such as *verbal_ptr*.

The following illustrates a *main* function that calls *ReadGRE* and prints the scores:

```
main()
{
    int verbal,      /* scores on the various parts of the GRE */
        math,
        analytical;

    ReadGRE(&verbal, &math, &analytical);
    printf("\nverbal score       = %d\n", verbal);
    printf("mathematical score = %d\n", math);
    printf("analytical score   = %d\n", analytical);
}
```

We declare the three variables that hold the scores of type *int*, as we normally do. Moreover, the calls to *printf* again use the identifiers. When we call *ReadGRE*, however, the arguments must be the addresses of these variables. These locations are copied into the corresponding pointers in *ReadGRE*. The printout from an interactive session follows:

```
Type the verbal, mathematical, and analytical
scores, separated by blanks.
100 600 650
Each score must be between 200 and 800
Please re-enter the three scores: 500 600 650

verbal score       = 500
mathematical score = 600
analytical score   = 650
```

Section 9.3 **Exercises**

1. Suppose variable *ch* is of type *char*, *num* is of type *int*, and *val* is a *float* variable. Assuming the following invocation of function *compute*, give the prototype of the function:

   ```
   compute(&ch, num, &val);
   ```

2. Assuming the following prototype, give an example of an invocation of the function:

   ```
   int manipulate(float a[], int *NumEls_ptr,
                  float *x_ptr);
   ```

3. Find and correct the error(s) in the following segment.

```
    float rate, time;

    ReadData(rate, time);
    ⋮
    /*
     * Function to read values for rate and time and to
     * change the appropriate variables in main
     * Pre:    none
     * Post:   Values for rate and time were returned.
     */

    void ReadData(float rate, float time)
    {
        printf("Enter the rate and time: ");
        scanf("%f %f", &rate, &time);
    }
```

4. Convert the segment in Example 8.2 of Section 8.1 into a function definition. The segment uses the trailer technique to read values into an array. Give the call to the function from *main*.

5. Write a function to delete from a sorted array the item at index *DeleteIndex* (see Exercise 3 of Chapter 8's Laboratory). The function must change the array and *NumEls*, the number of elements in the array.

6. Write a function to insert into a sorted array the item *x* at index *InsertIndex* (see Exercise 4 of Chapter 8's Laboratory). The function must change the array and *NumEls*, the number of elements in the array.

Section 9.3 Programming Projects

1. Write a program to read sets of coefficients, *a*, *b*, and *c*, of a quadratic equation, $ax^2 + bx + c = 0$ with $a \neq 0$, and to calculate the roots using the quadratic formula, as follows:

$$x = \frac{-b \pm \sqrt{b^2 - 4ac}}{2a}$$

If $b^2 - 4ac$ is zero, print the single root $-b/(2a)$. If $b^2 - 4ac$ is negative, we cannot take the square root, and the equation has no real roots. A function accepts the coefficients as parameters, and through pass by reference, communicates to *main* the roots of the equation. The function should also return the number of roots.

2. Do Projects 1 and 2 of Section 8.2 using a function to read values into the array and count the number of data items.

3. Do Project 3 of Section 8.2 using a function to read values into the array and count the number of data items.

4. Do Project 1 from Section 8.3. Use functions to delete and insert and to change the variable storing the number of array elements.

5. Do Project 3 from Section 8.4. Use a function to read grades interactively and to change the variable storing the number of array elements.

Section 9.4 **Arrays and Pointers**

Array Name as a Constant Pointer

Pointers are intimately associated with arrays. We do not use the address operator & in passing an array to a function because the unsubscripted name of an array evaluates to a constant pointer, the address of the array element with subscript 0. Therefore, if *a* and *b* are the names of arrays, the assignment statement

```
a = b;    /* ERROR if a and b are arrays */
```

is illegal in C, because a constant, such as *a*, cannot be an lvalue.

> The unsubscripted name of an array evaluates to a constant pointer, the address of the array element with subscript 0.

Because the name of an array points to its first element, the elements of an array are always contiguously (adjacent to one another) in memory, and the elements are all of the same type, the computer only needs the address of the first element to access an entire array. For example, suppose we declare array *ar* as follows:

```
int ar[10];
```

Let us assume that a variable of type *int* takes up 2 bytes of memory on the machine we are using. Suppose, also, that the machine is **byte-addressable**, with each byte having an address, starting with 0. If the address of *ar* is memory location 100, then the address of *ar*[0] is 100. Because *ar*[0] is, like all the other elements of *ar*, a variable of type *int*, it takes up two memory locations, 100 and 101. Thus, *ar*[1] is at memory location 102. By the same reasoning, 104 is the location of *ar*[2]. Figure 9.14 illustrates the storage of this array.

Example 9.7 _____

In this example, we illustrate the idea of an array name being a constant pointer. We start by initializing a two-element integer array, *AnArray*, to contain 3 and 7. The variable *also* is declared as a pointer to an integer and is initialized to the address of *AnArray*, which is also the address of *AnArray*[0].

```
main()
{
    int AnArray[2] = {3, 7},
        *also = AnArray;
```

Figure 9.14
Storage of an integer array in a byte-addressable computer with each integer in two bytes

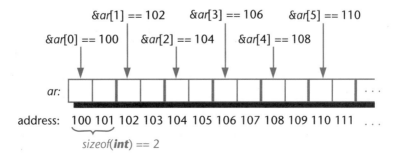

Figure 9.15
Memory after
declaration-
initialization in
Example 9.7

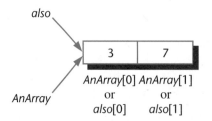

The variable *also* is of type *int* *. No special type for an *int* array exists, so a pointer to an array has as its target type the type of the elements in the array.

The concepts of pointer and array are closely related, but not identical, in C. The name of an array—such as *AnArray*—evaluates to its address in memory, the location of *AnArray*[0] (&*AnArray*[0]). This identifier is a constant, however. Because we cannot change its address, we cannot move an array in memory. The array name can appear on the right side of an assignment, as above, but it is not an lvalue. By contrast, we can change the value of a pointer, such as *also*. Moreover, we can write this pointer identifier on the left (as above) or the right of an assignment equals.

Once we have assigned *AnArray* to *also*, we can use the pointer to manipulate the elements of the array. *AnArray* and *also* both evaluate to the address of the first element of the array, and we can use the identifier *also* in the same way as *AnArray*. Consequently, as Figure 9.15 illustrates, we can have a subscript with *also*, and the element *also*[0] is identical to *AnArray*[0].

In C, we can index any pointer variable. As with arrays, the programmer must be sure that the index is within the proper limits. In the case of a pointer, the programmer must also be sure that the pointer holds the address of an array. By assigning 14 to *also*[0], we are replacing the contents of *AnArray*[0], the first element of *AnArray*.

```
also[0] = 14;
```

Because *also* points to the first location of *AnArray*, we could have written the assignment, *also*[0] = 14, as follows:

```
*also = 14;
```

Finally, the program prints the values of *AnArray* to show that a change has indeed taken place. We must list each element individually in the call to *printf*, as follows:

```
printf("AnArray = {%d %d}\n", AnArray[0], AnArray[1]);
```

The segment generates the following output:

```
AnArray = {14, 7}
```

Parameters

At the beginning of Section 8.2, we presented two forms of the prototype for a function *ReadScores*, which reads the first *NumPlayers* number of elements into an integer array *score*:

```
void ReadScores(int [], int);
```

or

```
void ReadScores(int score[], int NumPlayers);
```

When a formal parameter corresponds to an array, however, we can omit the braces and use pointer notation as follows:

```
void ReadScores(int *, int);
```

or

```
void ReadScores(int *score, int NumPlayers);
```

The address of an array is a pointer to its first element.

Pointer Arithmetic

Because an array name evaluates to the address of the first element, an alternate way exists for addressing individual elements than using an index in brackets. For the 10-element integer array in Figure 9.14, the following statement:

```
scanf("%d", &ar[i]);
```

is equivalent to

```
scanf("%d", ar + i);
```

$ar + i$ is a pointer to the *i*th element beyond *ar*. Its value is &$ar[i]$. The sum of an integer (such as *i*) and a pointer (such as *ar*) of any target type (such as *int*) is a pointer of the same target type as the pointer operand (such as *int*). Thus, $ar + i$ is a pointer of type *int* *. Figure 9.14 has the array *ar* starting at address 100 in a byte-addressable computer, which stores an integer in two bytes. For this situation, $ar + 3$ is 106, the address of $ar[3]$; $ar + 3$ is a pointer to the third *int* element past the location pointed to by array *ar* (see Figure 9.16). The value is the sum of the pointer operand *ar* and as many target units (such as 3) as the integer operand indicates. The *sizeof* operator of the target type, such as *sizeof*(*int*), gives the size of a target unit, the number of bytes to store an element of that type. Because *sizeof*(*int*) for this example is 2, the computation of the address is as follows:

$$ar + 3 = 100 + 3 \cdot 2 = 106$$

For array *ar*, the addresses &$ar[i]$ and $ar + i$ are equal. We can compute this address algebraically as follows:

(**Address of *ar*[0]**) + *i* · *sizeof*(*type*), where *type* is the target type

Figure 9.16
Storage of an integer array in a byte-addressable computer with each integer in two bytes with access through pointers

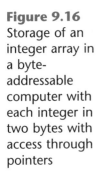
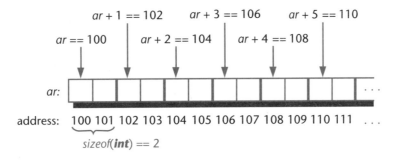

This addition of a pointer and an integer is one of the few arithmetic operations C allows on pointers. It is not a case of mixed-mode arithmetic, because the two operands are supposed to be of different types. There is no casting.

The expression

```
ar + i
```

is equivalent to

```
&ar[i]
```

Both are the address of element i of the array ar. In the above example, $ar + 3$ and $&ar[3]$ are both 106. Therefore, the expression

```
*(ar + i)
```

is equivalent to

```
ar[i]
```

This form of addition works with any array or pointer target type. If ar were an array of type *char*, $ar + 3$ would return the value of ar incremented by 3 *char* lengths, which would still be equivalent to

```
&ar[3]
```

As with regular addition, the operation does not change either operand.

For array ar, the elements $ar[i]$ and $*(ar + i)$ are equal.

Section 9.4 **Exercises**

1. Suppose a computer is byte-addressable with four bytes to a *float*. Array *flt* has address 360 and the following declaration:

   ```
   float flt[100];
   ```

   Give the values of the following addresses:

   a. *flt*   **b.** *&flt*[1]   **c.** *flt* + 8   **d.** *&flt* [20]

2. Consider the array b:

   ```
   int b = { 6, -8, 4, -2, -6, 3,
             9, 5, 0, -3, 7, 1 };
   ```

   Describe the meaning of each of the following:

   a. b **b.** $*b$ **c.** $b + 6$ **d.** $*(b + 6)$

3. Write the following segment using pointer notation instead of subscripts:

   ```
   temp = a[0];
   for (i = 0; i < n - 1; i++)
       a[i] = a[i + 1];
   a[n] = temp;
   ```

4. Consider the declarations

```
float x,
        *x_ptr = &x;
```

Suppose a computer is byte-addressable with four bytes to a *float* and &x = 2000. Evaluate the following:

a. *x_ptr* + 3   **b.** *x_ptr* + 10

Section 9.4 **Programming Projects**

1. Write a program to read an array of integers. Instead of using subscripts, however, employ an integer pointer that points to the element currently being read and that you increment each time.

2. Write a program that reads an integer constant and reads integer values into an array. The program also prints how many elements of the array are less than the constant, equal to it, and greater than it. Write a function that is passed the array and the constant. The function should compute the three counters and send them back to a calling function. For each array reference, use the pointer plus an index instead of a subscript.

3. Write a program to declare-initialize an array of 10 short integers and an array of 10 floating point numbers. Print the size of a *short* and a *float* on your computer. Print the elements of each array along with their addresses using pointer arithmetic.

Section 9.5 **Dynamic Memory Allocation**

In many of the programs in this chapter and the last, we have dimensioned arrays to some maximum size. This technique can waste memory if the amount of data is much less than the maximum. Unfortunately, we cannot always predict what the array size will be. A similar situation occurs with character strings, such as someone's name. In the next chapter, we discuss an application in which it is desirable to change the space allocated for a character string variable. In certain implementations of other structures that hold data, we should be able to activate and free memory locations as needed, or employ **dynamic memory allocation**.

Allocate Memory

For a number of applications, we should be able to start a program with the smallest amount of memory necessary and allocate extra space as needed. The C standard library function *malloc* (memory allocation) provides this capability.

When a computer executes a C function, the CPU must allocate memory for the local variables. It takes this storage from a pool of **free memory**, or memory that the program is not using. When the function finishes execution, the CPU returns this memory to the pool for subsequent use. The *malloc* function permits allocation of memory from a similar pool. The parameter for the *malloc* function is an integer that specifies the number of bytes to allocate. The function returns a pointer to a contiguous block of memory of that size. The pointer is of type *void* *, so that we can assign it to a pointer with any target type. The memory so allocated can be returned to the free pool by passing the pointer to the *free* function.

As an example of the use of the *malloc* function, suppose we need an integer array but will not know its size until execution. We include the standard library header file, *stdlib.h*, and declare a pointer, say *int_array_ptr*, of type *int **, as shown:

```
#include <stdlib.h>
main()
{
    int *int_array_ptr;    /* pointer to an int array */
```

During program execution, when the computer determines the array size, *dim*, we execute the following statement:

```
int_array_ptr = (int *) malloc(dim * sizeof(int));
```

For example, if *dim* is 500 and 2 bytes store an integer, we are requesting use of a contiguous block of 500 · 2 = 1000 bytes. We cast the address that *malloc* returns to a pointer to *int* with (*int **). If all goes well, we can use *int_array_ptr* like an array declared as follows:

```
int int_array_ptr[500];
```

Even though *int_array_ptr* is a pointer variable, we should not change its value, because that would cause the program to lose track of the location of the allocated array. (If we first assign the location of the array to another pointer variable, this restriction does not apply.)

If the requested block of memory is not available, *malloc* returns the null pointer, *NULL*. Therefore, before continuing, the program should check if the computer has been able to allocate the memory.

```
if ((int_array_ptr = (int *)malloc(dim * sizeof(int))) == NULL)
{
    /* Space for array not allocated. Issue error message */
    ⋮
}
else
{
    /* Memory has been allocated. Proceed as normal */
    ⋮
```

The conditional expression assigns the address that *malloc* returns to *int_array_ptr* and then checks if the pointer is *NULL*. If it is, the code should issue an error message and not attempt to manipulate the array. Because the relational equal (==) has a higher priority than the assignment equal (=), we must place the assignment statement in parentheses in the conditional expression.

Deallocate Memory

When the program no longer needs the block of storage, we return the allocated memory to the free pool with the following:

```
free(int_array_ptr);
```

After execution of this statement, we should not use the value of *int_array_ptr*. The memory to which it points no longer belongs to the program. (For the same reason, a function should not return a pointer to a local variable.) At this point, the program can assign a new value to *int_array_ptr*.

**Allocate
Initialized
Memory**

Two other functions related to memory allocation are in the ANSI C standard library. We use the function *calloc* (clear and allocate) both to allocate memory and to initialize each element to 0. Whereas the parameter for *malloc* is the number of bytes requested, *calloc* has two parameters, the size of the array and the number of bytes for each element. Thus, to both allocate and initialize the array, we write

```
if ((int_array_ptr =
        (int*)calloc(dim, sizeof(int))) == NULL)
   ⋮
```

The function *calloc* computes the total amount of storage as we did with *malloc*, as the product *dim* * *sizeof(int)*. Like *malloc*, the function returns the null pointer, *NULL*, when allocation is not possible.

Example 9.8

Each state has congressional voting by district. Suppose a file contains the following data for each district: a number representing the district, the number of candidates, the number of votes cast in the district, and a list of the votes by candidate number. In this example, we develop a program that for each district reads this information, tallies the votes for each candidate, and prints the results. As Figure 9.17 illustrates, *main* calls two routines, *ReadVotes* to read the votes for a district and *PrintTally* to print the results for a district.

In *main*, as long as data are in the file, we read the district number (*district*), the number of candidates (*NumCandidates*), and the number of votes cast (*NumVotes*). With *calloc*, we allocate space for an array of integers to hold a tally for each candidate and initialize each tally to zero. The pointer *candidates* references this area of memory. After the votes have been read, tallied, and printed for a district, the area is freed in preparation for another district's votes. By having the dynamic allocation of space for the array of tallies, we can accommodate any number of candidates.

Within *ReadVotes* and *PrintTally*, we access the individual tallies using array notation, such as *candidates[i]*. Alternatively, we could use pointer notation, such as **(candidates + i)*. Suppose *NumCandidates* is 5, so that we designate the candidates as 0, 1, 2, 3, and 4. Thus, each vote for that district is an integer between 0 and 4. A vote of 3 increments by 1 the tally for candidate #3, *candidate[3]*. The complete program follows:

Figure 9.17
Structure chart
for program of
Example 9.8

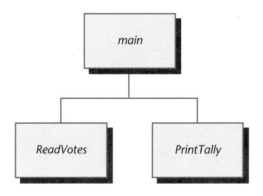

```
/*
 * Example 9.8. Program to read votes for candidates in each
 * district and to tally the votes
 * Input file: vote.dat
 *      For each district, the file contains the district number,
 *      number of candidates, number of votes, and votes
 */

#include <stdio.h>
#include <stdlib.h>

void ReadVotes(FILE *, int *, int, int);
void PrintTally(int *, int);

main()
{
    FILE *infile_ptr;       /* pointer to input file */
    int *candidates,        /* pointer to array of tally information */
        NumCandidates,      /* number of candidates in a district */
        NumVotes,           /* number of votes cast in district */
        district;           /* number of district */

    /* open the file */
    infile_ptr  = fopen("vote.dat", "r");
    if (infile_ptr == NULL)
    { .
        printf("vote.dat does not exist.\n");
        exit(1);
    }
    while (fscanf(infile_ptr, "%d %d %d",
                &district, &NumCandidates, &NumVotes) == 3);
    {
        if ((candidates = (int *)calloc(NumCandidates, sizeof(int)))
                == NULL)
        {
            printf("Space not allocated for array. \n");
            exit(1);
        }
        else
        {
            ReadVotes(infile_ptr,
                    candidates, NumCandidates, NumVotes);
            printf("  District #%d\n", district);
            PrintTally(candidates, NumCandidates);
            free(candidates);
        }
    }

    if(!feof(infile_ptr))
        printf("Error reading file.\n");

    fclose(infile_ptr);
}
```

```
/*
 * Function to read the votes in a district
 * Pre:   infile_ptr is a pointer to a file of votes.
 *        NumVotes is the number of votes cast in district.
 * Post:  candidates is an array that tallies the votes
 *        for candidates.
 */

void ReadVotes(FILE *infile_ptr, int *candidates, int NumVotes)
{
    int i,          /* index */
        vote;       /* number indicating candidate */
                    /* from 0 to NumCandidates - 1 */

    for (i = 0; i < NumVotes; i++)
    {
        fscanf(infile_ptr, "%d", &vote);
        candidates[vote]++;
    }
}


/*
 * Function to print the tallies of votes
 * Pre:   candidate is an array of tallies of votes for candidates.
 *        NumCandidates is the number of candidates.
 * Post: The tally information has been printed.
 */

void PrintTally(int *candidates, int NumCandidates)
{
    int i;              /* index */

    printf("Candidate    Tally\n\n");
    for (i = 0; i < NumCandidates; i++)
    {
        printf("    %d          %d\n", i, candidates[i]);
    }
    printf("\n");
}
```

Suppose the input file, *vote.dat*, is as follows:

```
1 5 10
2 0 2 1 3 1 4 4 3 3
2 7 20
1 1 6 4 6 2 5 4 5 6 0 1 4 0 2 6 5 2 4 2
```

With these data, the program produces the following output:

```
    District #1
 Candidate    Tally

     0           1
     1           2
     2           2
     3           3
     4           2

    District #2
 Candidate    Tally

     0           2
     1           3
     2           4
     3           0
     4           4
     5           3
     6           4
```

In the exercises, we improve the program by validating input. In the next chapter, we discuss how to read and print character string data, such as the candidates' names.

Reallocate Memory

Another standard function is *realloc* (reallocate), which we use to change the size of a previously allocated block. The function takes as parameters the pointer to the original block and the size in bytes of the requested storage (like *malloc*'s parameter) and returns a pointer to the newly allocated memory. Again, if reallocation is not successful, *realloc* returns *NULL*. For example, to expand the array from 500 elements to 700, we write

```
if ( (int_array_ptr =
        (int *)realloc(int_array_ptr, 700 * sizeof(int)) ) == NULL)
```

When the program requests more space than is available immediately after the original block, the computer copies the information to a sufficiently large contiguous storage area. If the computer does not find enough contiguous cells, then *realloc* returns *NULL*. Should the computer request reallocation to a smaller amount of storage, *realloc* frees the unneeded storage at the end of the existing block.

Table 9.2 summaries the memory allocation/deallocation functions in the standard library.

Section 9.5 Exercises

1. Write statements to do the following: Define constant *NUM_ELS* as 30. Declare variable *array_ptr* as a pointer to a *float*. Allocate space for an array of *NUM_ELS*

Table 9.2   Memory allocation/deallocation functions with prototypes in *stdlib.h*
Notation:

> *dim* - dimension of array
> *el_t* - type of an element in the array
> *ElSize* - number of bytes for one element, usually calculated as *sizeof(el_t)*
> *BlockSize* - number of bytes for the block, calculated as *dim * ElSize*
> *ptr, old_ptr* - pointers to a block of memory

Invocation of Function	Action
`ptr = calloc(dim, ElSize);`	Assign to *ptr* a pointer to a block of memory of *dim* * *ElSize* number of bytes or assign *NULL* if allocation unsuccessful. Initialize locations to 0.
`free(ptr);`	Free the block of memory to which *ptr* points
`ptr = malloc(BlockSize);`	Assign to *ptr* a pointer to a block of memory of *BlockSize* number of bytes or assign *NULL* if allocation unsuccessful
`ptr = realloc(old_ptr, BlockSize);`	Change the size of block pointed to by *old_ptr* to *BlockSize* number of bytes. Assign to *ptr* a pointer to this block or *NULL* if reallocation unsuccessful

   float numbers and assign the address of the block to *array_ptr*. If the allocation is unsuccessful, print an error message. Otherwise, read a value for each array element.

2. Reallocate the array of Exercise 1 to an array of 50 elements.

3. Free the space allocated in Exercise 1.

4. Change Exercise 1 to initialize each element to zero. Do not read values into the array, but call a function *tally* that has the array and number of elements as parameters.

5. How would you change Exercises 1–4 to have an array of characters?

6. How would you change Exercises 1–4 to have an array of pointers to integers?

7. Why do you think the parameters for *malloc* and *calloc* are different?

8. Improve the program in Example 9.8 to validate input data. For example, the votes in a district should range between 0 and *NumCandidates* − 1.

Section 9.5 Programming Projects

1. Write a program repeatedly to generate a random integer, *dim*, between 5 and 500 and then to generate an array of *dim* random numbers between 1 and 10. For each array, the program should print the frequency distribution and the average of the numbers. Use memory allocation/deallocation functions to use only the necessary amount of space.

2. Revise Project 1 from Section 8.2 to allocate space for the array at execution time. We could use the program for a small class or for a standardized test given to everyone in a school.

Section 9.6 **Function Pointers**

With structured programming, we have a hierarchy of functions. Sometimes, it is not known until execution time which of several lower-level functions we need to call. In this case, it is useful to be able to pass a reference to the desired function through the argument-parameter list.

The purpose of a **function pointer** is illustrated by the functions *printf, fprintf,* and *sprintf,* all of which operate in basically the same way. They differ only in what they do with the characters the function generates. The *printf* function sends its characters to the standard output, *fprintf* sends them to a specified file, and *sprintf* stores them in a string. All three functions call a common function, say *print* (the name varies from one function library to another). This function is passed a control string, a variable list, and a pointer to a function that is used to output characters to the proper destination. When the *print* function is ready to output a character, it calls the passed function, which sends the character to the appropriate location (standard output, a file, or a string).

As another example, suppose the function *sigma* is to compute the sum

$$f(1) + f(2) + \cdots + f(n)$$

for positive integer n and any function f that accepts an integer argument and returns a *float* value. Thus, for $triple(x) = 3x$ and $n = 5$, *sigma* substitutes the function *triple* for f.

$$triple(1) + triple(2) + triple(3) + triple(4) + triple(5)$$
$$= 3 \cdot 1 + 3 \cdot 2 + 3 \cdot 3 + 3 \cdot 4 + 3 \cdot 5 = 45$$

For $sqr(x) = x^2$ and $n = 4$, *sigma* returns

$$sqr(1) + sqr(2) + sqr(3) + sqr(4) = 1^2 + 2^2 + 3^2 + 4^2 = 30$$

To accomplish such a substitution, we use a pointer to the function *triple* or *sqr* and pass the pointer to *sigma.*

C contains a type that corresponds to a function pointer. Because every function is compiled into a series of instructions in memory, a function can be associated with a pointer to its first instruction. This permits an indirect call to a function, stating in effect: "Call the function to which this variable points."

Declarations and Assignments

To declare a variable called *fun_ptr,* which points to a function that has an *int* parameter and returns a *float*, we write the following:

```
float (*fun_ptr)(int i);
```

If the first pair of parentheses around **fun_ptr* are not present, the declaration would be as follows:

```
float *fun_ptr(int i);

    /* ERROR if function pointer */
```

which would mean: "*fun_ptr* is the name of a function that has an integer parameter and returns a pointer to a floating point number." In the first case, *fun_ptr* is a pointer, and in the second case, *fun_ptr* is a function that returns a pointer.

In order to assign a function's address to a pointer variable, we need to declare the function. For example, suppose we declare the functions *triple* and *sqr* with the following prototypes:

```
float triple(int);
float sqr(int);
```

Because the name of the function evaluates to a constant pointer to the function, we can now assign the address of *triple* to *fun_ptr* with the following:

```
fun_ptr = triple;
```

We only assign a function's address to a variable, never the function itself. Therefore, the address operator & is not used. If we had parentheses, as in

```
fun_ptr = triple();       /* ERROR */
```

then the compiler would consider *triple()* to be an attempt to call *triple* and to assign the returned value to *fun_ptr*. With the presumed invocation to *triple* containing an incorrect number of arguments, the compiler would issue an error message. If no parentheses appear, the computer assigns the address of the function *triple* to the pointer variable *fun_ptr*.

Calling Functions Indirectly

To call *triple* indirectly by way of *fun_ptr* and to have an argument of 5, we write the following:

```
printf("%f\n", (*fun_ptr)(5) );
```

The statement prints *triple*(5) or

```
15.000000
```

ANSI C also permits omission of the indirection operator (*) and the first pair of parentheses, as shown:

```
printf("%f\n", fun_ptr(5) );
```

This syntax is simpler than the first, but it does not document the fact that *fun_ptr* is a pointer to a function instead of the function itself.

Function Pointers as Parameters

We can pass a function address to another function. To do this, we first declare the function that is receiving the pointer, such as *sigma*, with a corresponding formal parameter, such as the following

```
float sigma(float (*f)(int i), int n);
```

The programmer can pass as an argument the value of a function pointer variable or the function name (without parentheses). Thus, in calling *sigma*, we pass it the pointer to *triple*, *fun_ptr*,

```
sum = sigma(fun_ptr, n);
```

or we can use the name of the function directly, as shown:

```
sum = sigma(triple, 5);
```

In either case, *sum* receives the value 45.0, the sum of *triple*(1) through *triple*(5).

Example 9.9

In this example, we put all these ingredients together in a program that uses the function *sigma*. This function evaluates

$$f(1) + f(2) + \cdots + f(n)$$

for positive integer *n* and any function *f* that accepts an integer argument and returns a *float* value. We also print *f*(*n*).

The function *main* calls a function *menu* to print a menu of function choices, to read the choice and the number of summands, and to send back these values. Because *menu* must communicate two values to *main*, we use pass by reference for *main*'s variables, *choice* and *n*. Thus, *main* sends the addresses of these variables to pointer parameters *choice_ptr* and *n_ptr* in *menu*. Because these already are pointer variables, *scanf* uses the variables *choice_ptr* and *n_ptr* instead of their addresses (*&choice_ptr* and *&n_ptr*), as shown:

```
scanf("%d", choice_ptr);
scanf("%d", n_ptr);
```

When *menu* tests if the choice is in the correct range, however, the function must dereference the pointer to obtain the integer choice.

```
do
{
    ⋮
}
while (*choice_ptr < 1 || 4 < *choice_ptr);
```

Similarly, for *menu* to assign a new value to *main*'s *n*, we must dereference the pointer *n_ptr*. We also use **n_ptr* to verify that the number of summands is appropriate, as shown:

```
if (*choice_ptr == QUIT) /* no function, don't pick n */
    *n_ptr = 0;
else                            /* function chosen, pick n */
    do
    {
        ⋮
    }
    while (*n_ptr < 1);
```

One of the *menu* function selections uses *sqrt*. Therefore, we include the header file *math.h*, which has the prototype of *sqrt*. We also define several preprocessor constants to help readability. The complete program follows:

```
/*
 * Example 9.9. Function to evaluate f(1) + f(2) + ... + f(n)
 * for a variety of functions f and values of positive integer n
 */
```

```
#include <stdio.h>
#include <math.h>

#define TRIPLE_FUN  1
#define SQR_FUN     2
#define SQRT_3X_FUN 3
#define QUIT        4

main()
{
    void menu(int *choice_ptr, int *n_ptr);
    float sigma(float (*f)(int i), int n);
    float triple(int i);
    float sqr(int i);
    float sqrt_3x(int i);
    float (*fun_ptr)(int i);

    int choice,     /* menu choice */
        n;          /* number of summands */
    float sum;      /* f(1) + f(2) + ... + f(n) */

    menu(&choice, &n);     /* priming read */
    while (choice != QUIT)
    {
        if (choice == TRIPLE_FUN)
            fun_ptr = triple;
        else if (choice == SQR_FUN)
            fun_ptr = sqr;
        else if (choice == SQRT_3X_FUN)
            fun_ptr = sqrt_3x;

        printf("\nf(%d) = %.2f\n", n, (*fun_ptr)(n));
        sum = sigma(fun_ptr, n);
        printf("f(1) + f(2) + ... + f(%d) = %.2f\n\n", n, sum);

        menu(&choice, &n); /* another choice */
    }
    printf("\nThank you\n");
}

/*
 * Function to give a menu of function choices and to
 * return that choice.  The function also reads and returns
 * n, the number of summands
 * Pre:    none
 * Post:   A menu choice (*choice_ptr) and a number of summands
 *         (*n_ptr) was returned.
 */
```

```
void menu(int *choice_ptr, int *n_ptr)
{

    printf("Program evaluates f(n) & f(1) + f(2) +...+ f(n)\n");

    do
    {
        printf("Choose a function\n");
        printf("\t1 f(x) = 3x\n");
        printf("\t2 f(x) = x^2\n");
        printf("\t3 f(x) = square_root of 3x\n");
        printf("\t4 Quit\n\n");
        printf("Your choice: ");
        scanf("%d", choice_ptr);
    }
    while (*choice_ptr < 1 || 4 < *choice_ptr);

    if (*choice_ptr == QUIT) /* no function, don't pick n */
        *n_ptr = 0;
    else          /* function chosen, pick n */
        do
        {
            printf("Give a positive integer value for n: ");
            scanf("%d", n_ptr);
        }
        while (*n_ptr < 1);
}


/*
 * Function to return f(1) + f(2) + ... + f(n) for
 * a function to which f points and positive integer n
 * Pre:    n is a positive integer.
 * Post:   A floating point sum f(1) + f(2) + ... + f(n)
 *         was returned.
 */

float sigma(float (*f)(int i), int n)
{
    int k;              /* index */
    float sum = 0;      /* f(1) + f(2) + ... + f(n) */

    for (k = 1; k <= n; k++)
        sum += (*f)(k);

    return sum;
}


/*
 * Function to return float 3i for integer i
 * Pre:    i is an integer.
 * Post:   float 3i was returned.
 */
```

```
float triple(int i)
{
    return (float) 3 * i;
}


/*
 * Function to return float i^2 for integer i
 * Pre:     i is an integer.
 * Post:    float i^2 was returned.
 */

float sqr(int i)
{
    return (float) i * i;
}


/*
 * Function to return float sqrt(3x) for integer i
 * Pre:     i is an integer.
 * Post:    float sqrt(3x) was returned.
 */

float sqrt_3x(int i)
{
    return (float) sqrt(3 * i);
}
```

The following printout is from an interactive run of the program:

```
Program evaluates f(n) & f(1) + f(2) +...+ f(n)
Choose a function
        1 f(x) = 3x
        2 f(x) = x^2
        3 f(x) = square_root of 3x
        4 Quit

Your choice: 1
Give a positive integer value for n: 5

f(5) = 15.00
f(1) + f(2) + ... + f(5) = 45.00

Program evaluates f(n) & f(1) + f(2) +...+ f(n)
Choose a function
        1 f(x) = 3x
        2 f(x) = x^2
        3 f(x) = square_root of 3x
        4 Quit
```

```
Your choice: 2
Give a positive integer value for n: -4
Give a positive integer value for n: 4

f(4) = 16.00
f(1) + f(2) + ... + f(4) = 30.00

Program evaluates f(n) & f(1) + f(2) +...+ f(n)
Choose a function
        1 f(x) = 3x
        2 f(x) = x^2
        3 f(x) = square_root of 3x
        4 Quit

Your choice: 3
Give a positive integer value for n: 3

f(3) = 3.00
f(1) + f(2) + ... + f(3) = 7.18

Program evaluates f(n) & f(1) + f(2) +...+ f(n)
Choose a function
        1 f(x) = 3x
        2 f(x) = x^2
        3 f(x) = square_root of 3x
        4 Quit

Your choice: 5
Choose a function
        1 f(x) = 3x
        2 f(x) = x^2
        3 f(x) = square_root of 3x
        4 Quit

Your choice: 4

Thank you
```

Section 9.6 Exercises

For each of Exercises 1–4, declare a variable fun_ptr, *which is a pointer to a function that has*

1. An *int* and a *float* parameter and returns a *double* value
2. No parameters and returns no value, such as a function that only prints
3. Two integer pointer parameters and returns no value
4. An *int* parameter and returns a pointer to a *float*
5. Assign *fun_ptr* of Exercise 1 to the starting address of an appropriate function, *ActualFun.*

6. Assign *fun_ptr* of Exercise 2 to the starting address of an appropriate function, *ErrorFun*.

7. Assume that *fun_ptr* from Exercise 1 has been assigned the starting address of *ActualFun*. Write a statement using *fun_ptr* to print *ActualFun* evaluated at arguments 7 and 23.8.

8. Assume that *fun_ptr* from Exercise 2 has been assigned the starting address of *ErrorFun*. Write a statement using *fun_ptr* to invoke the function.

9. Assume that *fun_ptr* from Exercise 3 has been assigned the starting address of *MenuFun*. Write a statement using *fun_ptr* to invoke the function with arguments that are the addresses of integer variables *var1* and *var2*.

10. **a.** Write a prototype for a function *ExFun1* that has three parameters, an *int*, a *float*, and a pointer to a function like the one described in Exercise 1.

　　b. Invoke function *ExFun1* using the function pointer *fun_ptr* from Exercise 1.

　　c. Invoke function *ExFun1* using the function *ActualFun* from Exercise 7.

11. **a.** Write a prototype for a function *ExFun2* that has one parameter, a pointer to a function like the one described in Exercise 2.

　　b. Invoke function *ExFun2* using the function pointer *fun_ptr* from Exercise 2.

　　c. Invoke function *ExFun2* using the function *ErrorFun* from Exercise 8.

12. **a.** Write a prototype for a function *ExFun3* that has three parameters, two integers and a pointer to a function like the one described in Exercise 3.

　　b. Invoke function *ExFun3* using the function pointer *fun_ptr* from Exercise 3.

　　c. Invoke function *ExFun3* using the function *MenuFun* from Exercise 9.

Section 9.6 **Programming Projects**

1. Develop a program that reads values into a *float* array, *a*. Give the user the option of several functions with which to process each element of the array. Have at least four processing functions, and use *math.h*. The returned floating point values are to be stored in the corresponding element of a second array, *b*. For example, if $a[5]$ is 2.0 and the function is $f(x) = \sin(7x)$, $b[5]$ gets the value $f(a[5]) = \sin(7a[5]) = \sin(7 \cdot 2.0) = \sin(14)$. Create a general function *multi* that can perform this operation, given any function and array. Print the first and second arrays for each processing function.

2. Develop a calculator program to present the following menu to the user repeatedly:

```
This program will perform an integer arithmetic problem for
you. Choose the kind of problem by typing the corresponding
number.

    1  addition
    2  subtraction
    3  multiplication
    4  division
    5  quit

Your choice:
```

Have the program use a special function to do the calculation. The function takes three arguments—the two operands and a pointer to a function that performs the proper operation (addition, subtraction, and so on). Each operation must have a corresponding function that takes two arguments and returns the result of the operation. You may wish to store the pointers to these functions in an array. Constructing your program in this manner allows you to add other binary operations later, such as an operation to raise a number to a power.

3. The derivative of a function f at x can be estimated by the following difference quotient

$$\frac{f(x + d) - f(x)}{d}$$

for a small value of d, such as 0.0001. Develop a program that repeatedly presents the user with a menu of functions. The user chooses a function and enters value for x, and the program returns an estimate of the derivative.

Programming and Debugging Hints

Pointer Post-Increment

The abundance of C operators, each with its own syntax, sometimes can lead to confusion on the part of the programmer. For example, a novice programmer can easily forget whether the expression

```
*p++
```

is evaluated as

```
* (p++)
```

or

```
(*p)++
```

As Appendix C lists, the precedence rules of C specify that the first interpretation, *(p++), is correct. The post-increment applies to the pointer. If a programmer is unsure of the priority, he or she should use parentheses.

*p++ is equivalent to *(p++); the post-increment applies to the pointer.

To emphasize the impact of the placement of the parentheses, we assume a program contains the following segment:

```
int a[2] = {20,30},         /* initialized array */
    *p = &a[0];             /* pointer, point to a[0] */

printf("p = %p\n", p);
printf("*p++ = * (p++) = %d\n", *p++);
printf("a[0] = %d. a[1] = %d\n", a[0], a[1]);
printf("p = %p, *p = %d\n\n", p, *p);
```

Initially, p points to the first element of the array, $a[0]$, which contains 20. On a machine that stores an *int* value in two bytes, one run of the segment produces the following:

```
p = 002C38E6
*p++ = *(p++) = 20
a[0] = 20. a[1] = 30
p = 002C38E8, *p = 30
```

With *p++ or the equivalent *(p++), the dereferenced pointer (*p) in the second call to *printf* is 20. Because we have a post-increment, only after the computer prints this value does it increment the pointer *p* by one *int* unit. Consequently, after execution of *(p++), *p* points to the next integer, *a*[1] or 30. Execution does not affect the contents of the array *a*. Figure 9.18 illustrates the action of this indirection and post-increment of the pointer.

If we put parentheses around *p and then post-increment, as in (*p)++, we still print the value of *p. Then we increment the contents of the location to which *p* points, *a*[0]. Thus, *a*[0] becomes 21. The following segment is the same as the one above, except for the second call to *printf*.

```
int a[2] = {20,30},        /* initialized array */
    *p = &a[0];            /* pointer, point to a[0] */

printf("p = %p\n", p);
printf("(*p)++ = %d\n", (*p)++);
printf("a[0] = %d. a[1] = %d\n", a[0], a[1]);
printf("p = %p, *p = %d\n\n", p, *p);
```

The output is as follows:

```
p = 002C38E6
(*p)++ = 20
a[0] = 21. a[1] = 30
p = 002C38E6, *p = 21
```

Figure 9.18   Action of *p++ or *(p++)

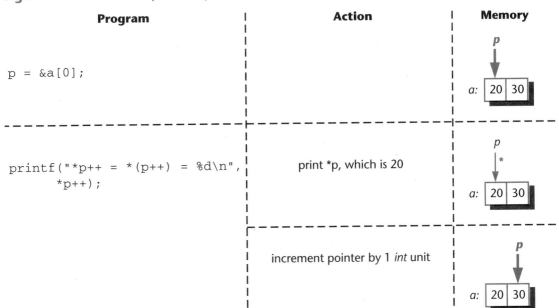

Program	Action	Memory
p = &a[0];		*p* a: 20 30
printf("*p++ = *(p++) = %d\n", *p++);	print *p, which is 20	*p* a: 20 30
	increment pointer by 1 *int* unit	*p* a: 20 30

Figure 9.19   Action of (*p)++

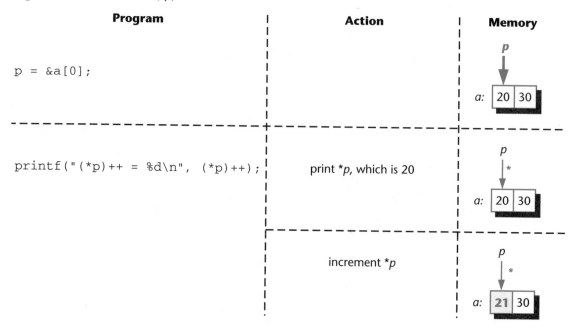

The second call to *printf* prints the contents of the location to which *p* points, which is *a*[0]. Then the post-increment of that location changes *a*[0] to 21. As Figure 9.19 shows, however, the value of the pointer, *p*, does not change.

Pointer Assignment

The forgiving nature of most C compilers often makes it possible for programmers to commit errors they would not make otherwise. For example, suppose *p* is a pointer to an *int* and *i* is an *int* variable, as shown:

```
int i,          /* integer variable  */
    j = 5,      /* integer variable  */
    *p = &j;    /* pointer to an int */
```

Suppose the programmer intends to assign *p to *i*,

```
i = *p;
```

but accidentally omits the * and instead assigns the pointer *p* to the integer variable *i*.

```
i = p;   /* ERROR - don't assign pointer to int variable */
```

C compilers allow this, some without even displaying a warning. As a result, the unfortunate programmer may have to spend a long time tracking down this single mistake.

Allocation of Space

Another common error with pointers is forgetting to allocate space before dereferencing a pointer. For example, this segment is incorrect:

```
int *p;      /* pointer to an int */
*p = 5;      /* ERROR - p does not point to anything */
```

The compiler does not complain, but we have not assigned a value to *p*. It does not point to anything. Whatever happens to be in *p* is taken as the address in which to store 5. Unpredictable results are likely.

~~~ Key Terms

%p 497   dynamic memory allocation 519   *NULL* 497
& 495   *free* 520   pass by reference 508
* 496   free memory 519   pointer 495
*p++ 534   function pointer 526   pointer arithmetic 517–518
address operator 495   function pointer as parameter 527   *realloc* 524
ampersand operator 495   indirection operator 496   *sizeof* 517
byte-addressable 515   *int ** 494   *swap* 510–511
calloc 521   *malloc* 519   target type 495
dereferencing a pointer 496

~~~ Summary

Variables called pointers can store memory addresses. The address of an *int* variable is of a type distinctly different from that of a *char* variable. We declare a variable *ptr* that can hold the address of an integer as follows:

```
int *ptr;
```

The type of item pointed to by a pointer variable is the target type. The ampersand or address operator applied to a variable returns the address of the variable. Thus, execution of the statement

```
ptr = &v;
```

assigns the address of *v* to *ptr*. We can declare-initialize *ptr* with the following:

```
int v,
    *ptr = &v;
```

Using an indirection operator (*) through the pointer, we indirectly access another memory location. Thus, the following:

```
*ptr = 5;
```

is equivalent to

```
v = 5;
```

With the indirection operator, we dereference the pointer. We do not obtain the address to which it refers, but the value the computer stores at that memory location. We can use **ptr* anywhere we can use the integer variable *v*. We must, however, assign a location to a pointer variable before dereferencing. To have *ptr* no longer store the address of *v*, we assign a special constant (*NULL*) to *ptr*, as shown:

```
ptr = NULL;
```

We use the %p conversion specification to print a memory address. The output appears in hexadecimal.

To send back a value from a function, we can have a pointer parameter, which holds the address of the value we wish to change. For example, the function *swap* exchanges the values of two integer variables by employing pointer parameters (*x_ptr* and *y_ptr*) to point to the variables. The definition follows:

```
/*
 * Swap *x_ptr and *y_ptr
 * Pre:     *x_ptr and *y_ptr have integer values.
 * Post:    *x_ptr and *y_ptr were swapped.
 */
```

```
void swap(int *x_ptr, int *y_ptr)
{
    int temp;        /* temporary variable for swap */

    temp  = *x_ptr;
    *x_ptr = *y_ptr;
    *y_ptr = temp;
}
```

To call the function to swap the values in *int* variables *x* and *y*, we use the following:

```
swap(&x, &y);
```

Pass by reference is the technique of making a variable accessible to a function by passing its address. In the strictest sense of the terms, C has only one method of passing information between a calling and a called routine—pass by value.

We do not use the address operator & in passing an array to a function because the unsubscripted name of an array evaluates to a constant pointer—the address of the array element with subscript 0. Thus, changes the called function makes to the array parameter are evident in the array argument of the calling function. After the declarations

```
int ar[MAX_NUM_ELS],
    *ptr = ar;
```

ptr contains &*ar*[0], so **ptr* equals *ar*[0]. When a parameter corresponds to an array, we can omit the braces and use pointer notation as follows:

```
void ReadScores(int *, int);
```

For array *ar*, the addresses &*ar*[i] and *ar* + *i* are equal. We can compute this address algebraically as

(Address of *ar*[0]) + *i* · *sizeof*(*type*), where *type* is the target type

The Hints section cautions that because ++ has a higher precedence than *, the expression **p++* is evaluated as **(p++)*. The post-increment applies to the pointer.

Using pointers and the C standard library function *malloc* (memory allocation), a program can start with the smallest amount of memory necessary and allocate extra space as needed. The segment below declares a pointer to *int* (*int_array_ptr*), allocates space enough for *dim* number of integers, and points *int_array_ptr* to that area. If the requested block of memory is not available, *malloc* returns the null pointer (*NULL*).

```
#include <stdlib.h>
main()
{
    int *int_array_ptr;    /* pointer to start of an integer array */
        :
    if ((int_array_ptr = (int *)malloc(dim * sizeof(int))) == NULL)
    {
        /* Space for array not allocated. Issue error message */
            :
    }
```

When the program no longer needs the block of storage, we return the allocated memory to the free pool with the following:

```
free(int_array_ptr);
```

To both allocate and initialize the array to all zeros, we use the function *calloc*, as shown:

```
if ((int_array_ptr = (int*)calloc(dim, sizeof(int))) == NULL)
```

To expand the allocation of the space to *dim2* number of integers, we use *realloc*, as follows:

```
if ( (int_array_ptr =
      (int *)realloc(int_array_ptr, dim2 * sizeof(int)) ) == NULL)
```

It is useful to be able to pass a reference to the desired function through the argument-parameter list. To declare a variable called *fun_ptr*, which points to a function that has an *int* parameter and returns a *float*, we write the following:

```
float (*fun_ptr)(int i);
```

Suppose we declare the function *triple* with the following prototype:

```
float triple(int);
```

We can now assign the address of *triple* to *fun_ptr* with

```
fun_ptr = triple;
```

To call *triple* indirectly by way of *fun_ptr* and to have an argument of 5, we write

```
printf("%f\n", (*fun_ptr)(5) );
```

or

```
printf("%f\n", fun_ptr(5) );
```

To pass a function address to another function, we first declare the function that is receiving the pointer, such as *sigma*, with a corresponding parameter, such as

```
float sigma(float (*f)(int i), int n);
```

In calling *sigma*, we pass it the pointer *fun_ptr* to a function as shown:

```
sum = sigma(fun_ptr, n);
```

or we can use the name of the function directly, as follows:

```
sum = sigma(triple, 5);
```

Review Questions

1. What numeric value is associated with every memory location?
2. How are variable names translated to their corresponding addresses?
3. Why is it desirable in C to be able to refer to a particular memory location by its address?
4. Why should we distinguish between a variable's address and the contents of that location?

5. Why can a function refer to a local variable in another function only by its address?

6. What must be done to a pointer variable before it can be used?

7. Why is it preferable to pass the address of a local variable for the purpose of communication between functions, as opposed to using a global variable?

8. What is the role played by the & operator in a call to the *scanf* function?

9. What restrictions apply to the use of the & operator?

10. Can addresses be stored? If so, where?

11. What are the effects of the following C declarations?

    a. `int *x;`   **b.** `int z;`
    c. `int p, *p, q, *q;`   **d.** `int x, *y = &x;`

12. What is the meaning of the following assignment statement?

    `q = &r;`

13. Are the following statements legal? If so, explain their meanings.

    a. `m = (char *)&n;`   **b.** `o = (float *)&p;`

14. What is the indirection operator, and what role does it play?

15. Memory addresses are merely integers on most computers, so in what sense are they different from integers?

16. What is meant by pass by reference?

17. What is the fundamental difference between passing by value and passing by reference?

18. When a function is written to swap the values of two variables, what special provisions must be made?

19. In what ways are arrays and pointers involved with each other?

20. Why is the & operator not used with array names in a call to *scanf*?

21. If *ary* is the name of an array, what can be said about the following statement?

    `ary = &x;`

22. Why is only the address of an array's first element necessary in order to access the entire array?

23. In what order must the parameters of a function be declared?

24. What can be said about adding an integer to a pointer?

25. How is the unsubscripted name of a two-dimensional array interpreted in C?

26. If an array is declared as

    `char z[10][12];`

    what is referred to by *z*[5]?

27. Given the following declaration:

    `int a, *b = &a, **c = &b;`

what is the effect of the following statements?

```
a = 4;
**c = 5;
b = (int *)**c;
```

28. What, if anything, is wrong with the following section of code?

```
int *a;  *a -= 7;
```

29. Under what circumstances is the *malloc* function useful?

30. How does the *malloc* function operate?

31. What function is like *malloc*, but also initializes each array element to be 0?

32. What is the purpose of the *free* function?

33. Suppose because of a previous call to *malloc*, *p* points to a block of memory for an array of 100 integers. Write a statement to reallocate room for the array to hold 50 integers.

34. What is a function pointer?

35. Give a declaration for a *void* function, *fnc*, that has as a parameter a pointer to an *int* function which has a *float* parameter.

36. Suppose *sub* is an *int* function that has a *float* parameter. Call *fnc* of the last question with argument *sub*.

Laboratory

1. In this exercise, we examine pointers and indirection by creating our own **memory dump** or a printout of an area of memory. When execution of a program aborts, on some systems we can get a memory dump of the area of memory in which the program and its variables reside. Copy the file *LAB091.c*, which contains the shell of a memory dump program, to your own disk.

Definition   A **memory dump** is a printout of an area of memory.

The program we are developing prints the contents of an allocated area of memory whose address is *start_ptr*. The program has 10 (*NUM_LINES*) lines of printout with each line starting with a new memory address. Beginning with location *start_ptr*, the program prints the contents of memory. On each line, the contents are printed a byte at a time with blank separators. A block of 4 bytes is printed followed by two blanks and another block of 4 bytes. Each line has 5 (*NUM_BLOCKS*) blocks of 4 bytes each, or 20 bytes in all. Thus, we print the contents of $NUM\_LINES \cdot NUM\_BLOCKS \cdot 4 = 10 \cdot 5 \cdot 4 = 200$ bytes of allocated memory. *LAB091.c* reads as follows:

```c
/*
 * Program to print an area of memory
 * Date:
 * Programmer:
 */

#include <stdio.h>
#include <stdlib.h>

void AlphaInit(unsigned char *);

#define NUM_LINES 10
#define NUM_BLOCKS 5

main()
{
    unsigned char *p,            /* pointer to a character */
                  *start_ptr;  /* pointer to allocated area */
    int LineNum,              /* index to line */
        BlockNum,             /* index to block of 4 bytes on line */
        ByteNum,              /* index to byte in block */
        i;                    /* index */

    if ( **1** )
    {
        printf("Memory could not be allocated.\n");
        exit(1);
    }

    /* Part c:  Initialize first 26 bytes to A through Z */
    /* AlphaInit(start_ptr); */

    printf("Address\t\t\t\tMemory\n\n");

    p = start_ptr;               /* starting location */
    for (LineNum = 0; LineNum < NUM_LINES; LineNum++)
    {
        printf("%**2**  ", **2**);    /*address at first of line */

        for (BlockNum = 0; BlockNum < NUM_BLOCKS; BlockNum++)
        {
            for (ByteNum = 0; ByteNum < 4; ByteNum++)
                printf(" %2x", **3**);

            printf(" ");
        }
        printf("\n");
    }
}
```

```
/*
 * Function to initialize 26 bytes starting with start_ptr
 * with A through Z
 * Pre:  start_ptr is the starting address.
 * Post: The first 26 bytes starting with location start_ptr
 *       have been initialized with letters of the alphabet.
 */

/*
void AlphaInit(unsigned char *start_ptr)
{
    unsigned char *p;
    int i;

    p = start_ptr;
    for (i = 0; i < 26; i++)
    {
        **4** = 'A' + i;
        **5**;
    }
}
```

Below is a sample run after replacement of **1**, **2**, and **3** with code. Because the starting address of the memory allocation and the contents of that area vary, your memory dump will be different.

Address				Memory																
0095D8C2	0	0	0	64	ff	ff	ff	ff	ff	fc	0	1	0	0	0	9c	ff	fe	0	0
0095D8D6	0	8c	0	1	0	0	1	6e	ff	ff	0	0	0	0	0	1	0	0	1	6c
0095D8EA	ff	ff	0	0	0	0	0	1	0	0	1	ea	ff	ff	0	0	0	0	0	1
0095D8FE	0	0	1	f0	ff	ff	0	0	0	0	0	1	0	0	2	8	ff	ff	0	0
0095D912	0	0	0	1	0	0	2	e	ff	ff	0	0	0	0	0	1	0	0	2	12
0095D926	ff	ff	0	0	0	0	0	1	0	0	2	16	ff	ff	0	0	0	0	0	1
0095D93A	0	0	2	1e	ff	ff	0	0	0	0	0	1	0	0	2	3a	ff	ff	0	0
0095D94E	0	0	0	1	0	0	2	3e	ff	ff	0	0	0	0	0	1	0	0	2	52
0095D962	ff	ff	0	0	0	0	0	1	0	0	2	56	ff	ff	0	0	0	0	0	1
0095D976	0	0	2	78	ff	ff	0	0	0	0	0	1	0	0	2	fc	ff	ff	ff	ff

a. Enter your name and the date in the opening comment.

In place of **1**, write the code with *malloc* to allocate an area of memory to hold *NUM_LINES · NUM_BLOCKS · 4* unsigned characters and to assign the starting address of this area to *start_ptr*. We use *p* to access each byte of this area.

Replace **2** to print the address at the first of each line. Be sure to use the conversion specification for an address (a pointer). In this call to *printf*, we are printing the contents of *p*, not the contents of the location to which *p* points.

In the call to *printf* with **3**, we print the contents of the byte to which *p* points by dereferencing *p*. We use the conversion specification for hexadecimal

(%x) to display the result in hexadecimal. (See Section 7.4, particularly subsection Conversion to Decimal Numbers, for a discussion of the hexadecimal number system.) We also increment the pointer p to point to the next byte (see Chapter 9 Hints).

Run the program and make sure it is behaving properly.

b. Give the hexadecimal values of the first 4 bytes in the allocated memory area. Give the character values of these 4 bytes (see Appendix A).

c. Remove the comment symbols around the call to *AlphaInit* (at the beginning of the program) and its definition. Complete the definition of the function to initialize the first 26 bytes in memory to the uppercase letters of the alphabet, A through Z.

In the last assignment statement at **4**, we are taking the ASCII value of 'A' and adding the index i which varies from 0 through 25. As the loop increments, the right side of the assignment takes on the ASCII values of 'A' through 'Z'. Replace **4** so that the ASCII value is stored in the memory location pointed to by p. In **5**, post-increment the pointer, so that it advances to point to the next location.

Run the program and observe the contents of memory.

d. Change the memory allocation at **1** to use *calloc* instead of *malloc*. Recall that *calloc* has two parameters instead of one. What changes do you observe in the output?

e. Print the listing and output of the program.

2. In this exercise, we work with pointers as parameters, pointers and arrays, pointer arithmetic, and pass by reference. Copy the file *LAB092.c* to your disk. It contains most of a program to print an array element, to call a function *PrintArray* to print the contents of an array, to call *GetInsert* to read an item to insert and its location, and to call *insert* to insert that item. Figure 9.20 presents the structure chart for the program. The program file follows:

```
/*
 * Lab program to practice with arrays, pointers, and pass by
 * reference
 * Date:
 * Programmer:
 */
```

Figure 9.20
Structure chart for Laboratory Exercise 2

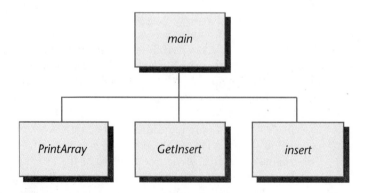

```
#include <stdio.h>

/**3**/
void PrintArray(int a[], int NumEls);
/* void GetInsert(int, int *, int *); */
/* void insert(int a[], **13**, int, int); */

main()
{
    int a[20] = {14, 17, 23, 26, 33, 38, 39, 41, 52, 56},
        i,               /* index */
        NumEls = 10,     /* number of elements in array */
        InsertIndex,     /* index of element to insert */
        item,            /* item to insert */
        **1**;           /* pointer to array */

    /**2**/
    printf("The tenth array element is %d\n\n", a[9]);

    /**6**/
    PrintArray(a, NumEls);

/*  GetInsert(NumEls, **7**item, **8**InsertIndex);
 *
 *  printf("Insertion %d at %d requested :\n", item, InsertIndex);
 *  insert(a, &NumEls, item, InsertIndex);
 *  PrintArray(a, NumEls);
 */

}

/*
 * Function to print the first NumEls elements of array a
 * Pre:  a is an integer array.
 *       NumEls is the number of elements in a.
 * Post: The first NumEls elements of a have been printed.
 */

/**4**/
void PrintArray(int a[], int NumEls)
{
   int i;

   printf("Array a has %d elements: ", NumEls);
   for(i = 0; i < NumEls; i++)
       printf("%3d", a[i]);        /**5**/
   printf("\n\n");
}
```

```
/*
 * Function to read and send back an integer item (through
 * dereferencing item_ptr) to insert in array a and to read and
 * send back the index (through dereferencing InsertIndex_ptr)
 * of where to insert. Verify that the index is less than or
 * equal to NumEls
 * Pre:     NumEls is the number of elements in array a.
 * Post:    item_ptr points to an item to insert into the array.
 *          InsertIndex_ptr references the index of where to insert.
 */


/*
void GetInsert(int NumEls, int *item_ptr, int *InsertIndex_ptr)
{
    printf("What do you want to insert? ");
    scanf("%d", **9**);
    do
    {
        printf("Give the index <= %d where to insert ", NumEls);
        scanf("%d", **10**);
    }
    while (**11** < 0 || NumEls < **12**);
}
*/


/*
 * Function to insert item at index InsertIndex in array
 * leaving the other array elements in order and increasing
 * the number of array elements by 1
 * Pre:  a is an integer array.
 *       item is the element to insert in array a.
 *       InsertIndex is the index of where to insert item in a.
 * Post: NumEls_ptr points to the number of elements in array a.
 */


/*
void insert(int a[], **14**NumEls_ptr, int item, int InsertIndex)
{
    int i;

    for(i = *NumEls_ptr - 1; i >= InsertIndex; i--)
        a[i + 1] = a[i];

    a[InsertIndex] = item;
    **15**;
}
*/
```

a. Add your name and date to the header comment. Replace **1** with the declaration-initialization of *ptr* as a pointer to an *int*, with initial value being the starting address of the array. Verify that the program runs correctly.

b. After comment /**2**/, replace the array reference *a*[9] with the dereferencing of the appropriate pointer sum, that is, the dereferencing of *ptr* plus a number. Be sure to use parentheses appropriately.

c. Change *PrintArray* to operate with pointer arithmetic. Change its prototype (at /**3**/) and first line of definition (at /**4**/) by omitting the brackets after *a*. At /**5**/, use pointer arithmetic and dereferencing instead of *a*[*i*]. After the program is working properly, change the call to *PrintArray* (at /**6**/) to use *ptr*, which points to the first element of the array.

d. In *main*, move the comment so that the call to *GetInsert* and the next *printf* execute. Remove the comment symbols surrounding the prototype and definition of *GetInsert*. In *GetInsert*, *item_ptr* and *InsertIndex_ptr* are declared as pointer parameters. They receive the addresses of *item* and *InsertIndex*, because we are trying to obtain values for those variables in *main*. Replace **7** and **8** appropriately. Within the definition of *GetInsert*, make four replacements(**9** through **12**). Remember that *scanf* needs an address, but a pointer provides an address. Also recall that to access the value that a pointer indicates, we must dereference the pointer.

e. Remove the comment in *main* so that it calls *insert* and *PrintArray* at the end. Remove the comment symbols enclosing the prototype and definition of *insert*. The function *insert* receives the array, its number of elements, an item to insert, and the insertion location (*InsertIndex*). It then moves the array elements from *InsertIndex* up and places the item in that location. Because the number of items in the array changes, using pass by reference, the function must send back a new value for *NumEls*. Replace **13** and **14** with the appropriate type for *int* pointer *NumEls_ptr*. At the end of that function, we must increment by 1 the contents of the location to which *NumEls_ptr* points so that *main*'s *NumEls* obtains the correct number of elements in the array. We must dereference the pointer and increment that value. Replace **15** with the appropriate code, using parentheses as necessary.

f. After the program is working correctly, print the listing and output of the program.

10

Strings and String Functions

Introduction

One feature of computers that makes them so valuable is that they can process entities other than numbers. Since the introduction of low-cost word processing programs, the number of users has increased dramatically. With various C functions, we can accomplish the familiar word processing operations of searching for a sequence of characters, replacing them with another sequence, inserting, and deleting.

In C, an array of characters ending with the null character ('\0') stores a character string, such as a sentence. Using the conversion specification %s with a call to *printf* or *scanf*, we can print or read a string. Some specialized functions exist for reading strings from standard input or from user-defined files. Similarly, other functions are used for writing strings to standard output or to our own files.

In the last chapter, we examined the close relationship between pointers and arrays. Because strings are stored in arrays, that discussion continues in this chapter. We can *malloc* an area for character information and have a pointer reference a string that we place in that location.

Another manipulation of strings is helpful in the detection of erroneous input. We can read the data as a string and check the string character by character. Perhaps the data item should be an integer and, consequently, should not contain any other characters than a leading sign and digits. If this input is valid, then we use an ANSI C function to convert the string to the required data type, such as *int*. Such validation of data is an important feature for interactive programming.

The ANSI C header file *string.h* declares several string functions, such as *strlen* to return the length of a string, *strcpy* to copy strings, *strcat* to concatenate strings, *strchr* to search for a character in a string, *strstr* to search for a substring, and *strcmp* to compare. With these functions, we can consider such applications as the manipulation of words to understand human language.

Many large and significant applications involve strings, such as word processing systems. The breadth section, Section 10.7, considers the software life cycle for large systems. In developing approaches to problem solving, we have discussed various aspects of this topic since the beginning of the text. In this section, we examine techniques used by software development teams to perform the analysis, design, implementation, testing, and maintenance needed for a large project.

Goals

To study

- Storage of character strings
- How to read and write strings
- Manipulation of pointers to character strings
- Data verification
- Functions to return a string's length, to copy strings, and to concatenate strings
- String search and comparison functions
- The software life cycle

Section 10.1 **Character Strings**

Anyone who has used a word processor is aware that computers manipulate text as well as numbers. So far, our programs have used text only in the control strings of *printf* and *scanf* functions, such as

```
printf("The value is %d\n", num);
```

The control string "The value is %d\n" is a special-purpose string. A **string** is any group of characters enclosed in quotation marks, such as "a string".

> **Definition**   A **string** or **character string** is any group of characters enclosed in quotation marks.

Literals

At the lowest level, the computer stores a character as a number. The compiler and the programmer make it possible to treat certain values as characters and to manipulate them accordingly. C has no string type. The language, however, treats an array of type *char* as a string if the ASCII value 0—the null character '\0'—follows its last meaningful character. Thus, in the context of strings, '\0' indicates the end of a string.

Figure 10.1 illustrates the storage of the string constant "computer" in a *char* array with last element '\0'. The quotation marks are not part of the string, but merely serve as delimiters. We sometimes refer to a character string constant, such as "computer", as a **string literal**. The following are valid C literals:

```
"1234"
"So shaken as we are, so wan with care...\n"
"\007"
"\"\n"
" "
```

Definition   A **string literal** is a character string constant.

A quotation mark after a backslash (\") is part of the string literal and not a delimiter. Therefore, the string "\"\n" containing the quotation mark and newline character has length 2. A pair of quotation marks with nothing between them is the **null string**. As Figure 10.2 displays, the computer stores the null string as the null character with nothing preceding it.

The **length of a string** is the number of nonnull characters it contains, so the number of locations needed to store a string is one more than the string's length. Thus, the string "computer" in Figure 10.1 has length 8, and the null string in Figure 10.2 has length 0.

Definition   The **length of a string** is the number of nonnull characters it contains.

When a string literal is in a C program, the computer stores the string somewhere in memory. We are not concerned with its exact location, so long as it is accessible. To access a literal, we simply refer to its pointer. Each time we use the literal in the program, the computer replaces the literal reference by the pointer that has the memory address of that literal. For example, when the *printf* function receives a control string, as in

```
printf("a = %d\n", a);
```

the first parameter is a pointer to the literal, such as "a = %d\n". The type of a string literal is *char **.

Figure 10.1
Character array holding string constant "computer"

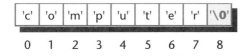

Figure 10.2
Storage of the null string constant in a *char* array

0

We can use a string literal to initialize a *char* array. The declaration

```
char str[] = "computer";
```

is an abbreviation for the declaration

```
char str[] = { 'c', 'o', 'm', 'p', 'u', 't', 'e', 'r', '\0' };
```

We declare *str* as a character array, dimensioned to hold all the characters, including the null character. In this case, *str* has 9 elements. In both forms of the declaration, we can specify an explicit dimension, which must be equal to or greater than the number of characters in the initializer, including the null character. For example, the minimum dimension for *str* is 9, as shown:

```
char str[9] = "computer";
```

Displaying Strings

To print the string that the *char* array *str* stores, we can use the %s conversion specification with *printf* , such as

```
printf("%s\n", str);
```

or equivalently

```
printf("%s\n", "computer");
```

The printing of strings is the only situation in which C displays an entire array at once.

The specification %c is for a single character, not a string. A character of type *char* appears between apostrophes, such as 'p', but quotation marks enclose a string, such as "p". Even though the string "p" contains a single character, as Figure 10.3 shows, its storage has two, 'p' and '\0'.

Example 10.1

The program in this example introduces the printing of string constants with %s.

```
/* Illustration of some ways to print a string */

#include <stdio.h>

main()
{
    printf("Case 1. This is simply a control string.\n");
    printf("%s\n", "Case 2. The control string tells how to print.");
    printf("%s", "Case 3. Newline may be put here, instead!\n");
    printf("%s %s %s\n", "Case 4. This", "is", "valid.");
}
```

The printout contains seven lines.

Figure 10.3
Storage of the string "p"

0   1

```
Case 1. This is simply a control string.
Case 2. The control string tells how to print.
Case 3. Newline may be put here, instead!
Case 4. This is valid.
```

The first *printf* consists of the control string, which contains no conversion specifications, only a line of text. In the second example, the control string, which is the first of the two strings, contains the conversion specification %s and the newline character. The %s means that a string must follow the control string in the *printf*. The only difference between the second and third *printf* statements is that the newline character has moved from the first string to the end of the second. The effect is the same, because in both cases the computer prints the newline last.

Case 4 shows that the control string may specify to print more than one string. A one-to-one correspondence between strings and conversion specifications exists, so the program has three %s conversion specifications with three strings that follow the control string. Because the conversion specifications are separated by spaces, these spaces are printed during execution of the function. Therefore, it is unnecessary (and incorrect) to include spaces in the corresponding strings. Of course, if we omit the spaces in the control string (the first string), we have to include them in the strings containing the text. Like their numeric counterparts, commas separate strings in a call to *printf*.

Like the other specifications, the string conversion specification can have the format %*m*s, where *m* specifies the field width. For example, %20s says to right-justify the string in a field of width 20. A minus sign for the field width specifier, such as %-20s, indicates left justification.

Example 10.2

The following program concentrates on variations of the %s conversion specification:

```
/* %ms conversion specification demonstrated */

#include <stdio.h>

main()
{
    printf("Case 5 :%s:\n", "A string");
    printf("Case 6 :%3s:\n", "A string");
    printf("Case 7 :%12s:\n", "A string");
    printf("Case 8 :%-12s:\n", "A string");
}
```

The subsequent output is as follows:

```
Case 5 :A string:
Case 6 :A string:
Case 7 :    A string:
Case 8 :A string    :
```

In Case 5, the computer prints the string normally, taking as many print positions as necessary to accommodate the string. Because the string in Case 6 requires more than three positions, the computer overrules this width and uses the minimum field necessary to print the entire string.

In Case 7, the field width of 12 is larger than the length of the string, so the computer right-justifies the string in a field of 12 positions. This rule differs from most other languages, in which strings are left-justified. In C, a string is left-justified only if a minus sign precedes the field width, as in Case 8.

Example 10.3

The following program uses a string variable (an array of characters) to store the control string for a *printf* call:

```
/* The control string is just a string */

#include <stdio.h>

main()
{
    char format[]  = "%s\n",      /* control string for printf */
         message[] = "hello";     /* string to be displayed */

    printf(format, message);
}
```

The program prints the following string along with the newline character:

```
hello
```

The program has a declaration-initialization of two strings. The array *format* holds a string, which takes the form of a control string in a call to *printf*. The other array, *message*, holds a string for printing. The *printf*, which uses the string variable *format* instead of a literal control string, is equivalent to the following:

```
printf("%s\n", message);
```

With this statement, we print the contents of the string array *message*, followed by a newline character.

Reading Strings

Suppose we prepare room for storage of a string by declaring a 10-element *char* array *str*, as follows:

```
char str[10];
```

The most obvious way to read a string into *str* is to read the characters into the elements one at a time and then to insert the null character at the end. We skip over leading white space characters—such as newline, tab, and blank—and we stop placing characters into *str* when we encounter a white space character.

This algorithm is somewhat tedious. With the conversion specification %s, we can read a string into *str* using a *scanf* statement, as shown:

```
scanf("%s", str);    /* No & before string variable str */
```

Because the array name is a pointer to the first element in the array, we use *str* without a subscript, and no ampersand (&) appears before the array name.

We should note two restrictions for reading strings. First, *scanf* defines a string as delimited by white space. When reading a string, *scanf* skips over all leading blanks, tabs, and newline characters. Then, *scanf* reads all the characters up to the next blank, tab, or newline character, stopping with the input buffer pointer indicating the subsequent white space character. For this reason, we can only use %s to read a single word (a sequence of characters without any embedded white space) at a time.

The second restriction is that the array of characters must be large enough to hold the longest possible string plus one extra element for the null character. If the array is too small to hold the input string, the string overwrites other locations. The results are unpredictable and certainly undesirable. Fortunately, we can use a maximum field width with the %s specification. For example, for the 10-element *char* array *str*, we use %9s to read no more than 9 characters and ensure against overflow of the array, as shown:

```
scanf("%9s", str);
```

Thus, if the user enters a string of length greater than 9, the computer stores the first 9 characters and stops the input buffer pointer at the tenth character.

Interactive Responses

We can use the ability to read strings to process y/n user responses. When the program prompts the user for y or n and reads a single character, the code must skip over any blanks or other white space before the character. Moreover, the user can only type one character. An alternative is to use the %s conversion specification, which automatically skips over any leading white space. Thus, we can read the y/n response into an array of two characters (one for the response, and one for the null character) using the conversion specification %1s, as shown:

```
char ans[2];
⋮
printf("Do you want to continue? (y/n) ");
scanf("%1s", ans);
fflush(stdin);
```

We should flush the input buffer to prepare for the next response in case the user enters more than one character. For example, suppose the user types "yes." Without the *fflush(stdin)*, the above segment would place "y" in *ans* and leave "es" and the newline character in the input buffer. The next *scanf* would use these leftover characters.

Example 10.4

This program prompts the user for a word of up to 15 characters and prints the word in reverse. After reading the word into an array (*word*), the function *main* calls a user-defined function *StringLength* to return the length of the word, *StringSize*. Using this length, *main* prints the array from one character before the null character to the beginning. We do not want to print the null character, so we print the characters from *word*[*StringSize* − 1] to *word*[0]. For example, with the string "programming" of length 11, *word*[0] through *word*[10] contain the letters; *word*[11] contains '\0', which we do not print.

---

main( )

Program to read a character string and print its reverse

Algorithm:

prompt for word
read the word into *char* array *word*
print word
obtain length of word *StringSize* by calling *StringLength*
for *i* going from *StringSize* - 1 to 0 do the following:
    print element *i* of the word, *word*[*i*]

In a later section, we discuss a library function for determining the length of a string. In this example, we write our own function, *StringLength*, to count the number of characters up to, but not including, the null character at the end of the string.

StringLength(str) → StringSize

Function to return the string length

Pre:

str is a *char* array

Post:

The length of string was returned.

Algorithm:

StringSize ← 0
while *word*[*StringSize*] is not the null character
    increment *StringSize* by 1
return *StringSize*

To read and print the string, we use the conversion specification %s in the *scanf* and *printf*. Because the program has only one *scanf*, we do not need to flush the input buffer. To avoid overflow of the 16-element array *word*, however, we only read the first 15 characters or less of the string with %15s. For printing the string in reverse order, we must print each *char* array element separately. Thus, we use *printf* with the character conversion specification %c, as follows:

```
printf("%c", word[i]);
```

or with *putchar*

```
putchar(word[i]);
```

The program follows:

```
/*
 * Example 10.4
 * Program to read a character string and print its reverse
 */

#include <stdio.h>

int StringLength(char str[]);

main()
{
    char word[16];     /* holds the string */
    int StringSize,    /* holds actual string length */
        i;             /* index */

    printf("Please enter a word of up to 15 letters:\n");
    scanf("%15s", word);

    printf("The word is %s.\n", word);

    StringSize = StringLength(word);

    printf("The reversed word is ");
    for (i = StringSize - 1; i >= 0; i--)
        printf("%c", word[i]);
    printf(".\n");
}

/*
 * Function to return the string length
 * Pre:    str is a char array containing a string
 * Post:   The length of string was returned.
 */

int StringLength(char str[])
{
    int StringSize = 0;    /* holds actual string length */

    while (str[StringSize] != '\0')
        StringSize++;

    return StringSize;
}
```

Execution with an input string of length 11 follows:

```
Please enter a word of up to 15 letters:
programming
The word is programming.
The reversed word is gnimmargorp.
```

The following run shows truncation of the input string to length 15:

```
Please enter a word of up to 15 letters:
ThisIsWayTooLongFor15Chars
The word is ThisIsWayTooLon.
The reversed word is noLooTyaWsIsihT.
```

Section 10.1 Exercises

In Exercises 1–11, give the output resulting from the calls to printf.

1. `printf("%s\n", "Print this line.");`

2. `printf("%s %s %s", "Print", "this", "\n");`

3. `printf("%s", "Print", "this", "\n");`

4. `printf(":%5s:\n", "programming");`

5. `printf(":%15s:\n", "programming");`

6. `printf(":%-15s:\n", "programming");`

In Exercises 7–11, give the length of each string. How many characters are in the string's storage?

7. "Exercise 12"

8. "\007"

9. " "

10. "\fTax\b\b\b____\n"

11. "He said, \"No!\"\n"

12. Give a declaration-initialization of a *char* array *prog* to the string "program".

13. Give a declaration-initialization of a 20-element *char* array *prog* to the string "program".

14. Give two declaration-initializations of the *char* array *name* to the name Johnson. One declaration should use a string and the other characters.

15. **a.** Declare *car* to be a 14-element *char* array.

    b. Write a *scanf* to read no more than the maximum possible length string into *car*.

    c. Write a *printf* to print the string that *car* stores.

16. **a.** Suppose a program reads a string into a 25-character array, *name*, with

    ```
    scanf("%s", name);
    ```

After execution, what is the value of *name* if the user types three blanks and the following name:

    Kim Lee

b. Repeat Part a using the following:

    scanf("%9s", name);

Section 10.1 Programming Projects

1. A palindrome is a word that is spelled the same forward and backward, such as level and radar. Write a program to read five-letter words and determine whether they are palindromes or not.

2. Modify the palindrome program of Project 1 to accept variable-length words, up to a predetermined length. This requires determining how many characters are in the word.

3. Write a program to read a number and print it digit by digit, as a series of words. For example, the number 523 would be printed as "five two three."

4. A harder version of Project 3 involves reading a number and printing it in "true" English. For example, 523 would be displayed as "five hundred twenty-three." This problem is more difficult, because we must take into account the digit's position within the number. Have your program accept numbers into the billions. The digits must be grouped into threes. For example, 1,234,517 would be displayed as "one million, two hundred thirty-four thousand, five hundred seventeen." Hint: One function can be used to convert a set of three digits into words—for example "two hundred thirty-four"—and that function can be called by another that adds the appropriate word ("thousand", "million", and so on), for example "two hundred thirty-four thousand."

5. Write a program to make a backup copy of a file. Interactively ask for the names of the input and output files.

Section 10.2 String I/O Functions

The functions *scanf* and *printf* can perform I/O on many different type values. In the last section, we saw how to read strings with *scanf* and the conversion specification %s. Similarly, we can print a string using %s in the control string for *printf*. In this section, we consider functions that interactively read and print strings only.

For file I/O, we have the general functions *fscanf* and *fprintf*. As we see, however, some functions exist specifically for string input from and output to files.

Writing to Standard Output

The library function *puts* (put string), which *stdio.h* declares, is a specialized function for displaying to standard output a string followed by a carriage return. Thus, for string variable *str*,

    puts(str);

is equivalent to

    printf("%s\n", str);

The function *puts* assumes that its argument is a string. It prints the characters in the argument up to, but not including, '\0' and then prints the newline character.

Example 10.5

Suppose we have

```
char str[15] = "Good morning!";
```

Then

```
puts(str);
puts(str);
```

prints

```
Good morning!
Good morning!
```

and advances to the next line.

For unformatted printing of strings, *puts* is preferable to *printf* because the latter is a generalized printing function. The function *printf* prints three kinds of integers, floating point numbers, characters, and strings in many different formats. Therefore, the code for *printf* is much larger than that for *puts*.

Reading from Standard Input

The read-string function counterpart to *puts* is *gets*. The following call

```
gets(str);
```

reads characters into *str* from the input stream until encountering the newline character. The function does not place '\n' into *str* but replaces it with the null character to terminate the string. With *scanf*, white space delimits the string, but with *gets*, the characters for the string start at the beginning of the input buffer and go past the end of the line. Thus, *scanf* reads a word, but *gets* reads a whole line. The type of *gets* is *char* *. Usually it returns a value equal to its argument, such as *str*; but if end-of-file (EOF) occurs, *gets* returns *NULL*. As with *puts*, *gets* is a specialized function that is much smaller in length than the general *scanf*. When appropriate, we should use *gets* for efficiency.

With both *scanf* and *gets*, the programmer should ensure that enough room is available in the *char* array. For many applications, we are safe declaring the string to be as large as the input buffer. The header file *stdio.h* declares *BUFSIZ* to be the size of the area of memory that holds the input stream. On some systems, *BUFSIZ*. is 512. We can declare *str* to be of that length with the following:

```
char str[BUFSIZ];
```

Example 10.6

This example emphasizes the differences between *scanf* and *gets* through two versions of a program to read string input. The first version prompts the user, reads a string with *scanf*, and prints the string delimited by colons. The program then prompts for another character, reads that character from the input stream, and prints it.

```
/*
 * Example 10.6
 * Program to illustrate string input with scanf
 */

#include <stdio.h>

main()
{
    char str[BUFSIZ],    /* string */
         ch;             /* character */

    printf("Type something:");
    scanf("%s", str);
    printf(":%s:\n", str);

    printf("We need the next character:");
    ch = getchar();
    printf("Next character:");
    putchar(ch);

    printf(":Done\n");
}
```

Suppose after the prompt, the user types several blanks before the sentence, "This is a sentence." The *scanf* with %s conversion specification skips over the blanks and places the string "This" into *str*. Because the input buffer pointer then indicates the blank after the first word, the call to *getchar* returns that blank to *ch*. The user does not have the opportunity to type an additional character, as shown:

```
Type something: This is a sentence.
:This:
We need the next character:Next character: :Done
```

The second version of the program uses *gets* instead of *scanf*.

```
/*
 * Example 10.6
 * Program to illustrate string input with gets
 */

#include <stdio.h>

main()
{
    char str[BUFSIZ],    /* string */
         ch;             /* character */
```

```
    printf("Type something:");
    gets(str);
    printf(":%s:\n", str);

    printf("We need the next character:");
    ch = getchar();
    printf("Next character:");
    putchar(ch);

    printf(":Done\n");
}
```

The *gets* captures the entire user input, except for the newline character, for *str*. Thus, *str* contains the blanks at the beginning and end of the line as well as all the words. The input buffer pointer advances past the newline character. Thus, when the program executes *getchar*, the user must enter another character, as shown:

```
Type something:  This sentence has white space at the end.
_: This sentence has white space at the end. :
We need the next character:a
Next character:a:Done
```

Writing to a File

The specialized functions for file I/O of strings are *fputs* and *fgets*. The function *fputs* writes a string to a file. The first argument is the string, and the second is a pointer to the file. A common error is to switch the positions of these arguments. Suppose that *outfile_ptr* is an output file pointer. The following statement writes the string *str* to the file:

```
fputs(str, outfile_ptr);
```

Unlike *puts*, *fputs* does not add the newline character at the end. If *fputs* cannot write the string to the file, the function returns *EOF*.

Example 10.7

Suppose we have the following declarations:

```
char str[15] = "Good morning!";
FILE *outfile_ptr;
```

After appropriate opening of the file,

```
fputs(str, outfile_ptr);
fputs(str, outfile_ptr);
```

places

```
Good morning!Good morning!
```

in the output file. The function removes the null characters and does not add newline characters to the file.

Example 10.8

Suppose a string contains a line with the newline character at the end, and we do not want to print the extra newline character that *puts* adds. In this case, we can use the general *printf*

```
printf("%s", str);
```

or *fputs*, writing to the standard output stream, as shown:

```
fputs(str, stdout);
```

An example program follows:

```
/*
 * Example 10.8. Program to print a string containing a
 * newline character at the end
 */

#include <stdio.h>

main()
{
    char str[15] = "Good morning!\n";

    /* does not print an extra newline character */
    printf("%s", str);
    printf("%s", str);
    printf("***\n");

    /* does not print an extra newline character */
    fputs(str, stdout);
    fputs(str, stdout);
    printf("***\n");

    /* prints an extra newline character */
    puts(str);
    puts(str);
    printf("***\n");
}
```

The output reflects the fact that the '\n' in *str* and the generation of the newline character by *puts* cause double-spacing of the bottom output. The calls to *printf* and *fputs* only print the newline character that is in *str* and yield single-spacing.

```
Good morning!
Good morning!
***
Good morning!
Good morning!
***
Good morning!

Good morning!

***
```

Reading from a File

The function *fgets*, which reads from a file into a string, accepts three arguments—the string variable, the maximum number of characters (including '\0') to place in the string, and a pointer to the input file. For instance,

```
fgets(str, 15, infile_ptr);
```

In this example, *fgets* places characters in the string *str* until encountering an EOF or the newline character or after reading **14** (or 15 − 1) characters. If the input contains the newline character, the computer copies it to the string. The function then attaches the null character at the end, converting the input into a string. Thus, suppose the input file contains the following:

```
Good day\nGood night\n
```

After execution of the above *fgets* statement, *str* has the value "Good day\n".

Summary

Tables 10.1 and 10.2 summarize I/O with strings.

Section 10.2 Exercises

1. Suppose we have the following segment:

```
char InStr[20];
printf("Type a line: ");
```

If the user types four blanks at the beginning of the line

```
    This is a line.
```

and presses return, what does *InStr* store after execution of

a. `scanf("%s", InStr);`

b. `gets(InStr);`

c. `fscanf(stdin, "%s", InStr);`

d. `fgets(InStr, 7, stdin);`

e. `fgets(InStr, 37, stdin);`

Table 10.1   Functions to write strings up to '\0'

Example Function Call	Write to	Adds '\n'?	Error Return
printf("%s", str);	*stdout*	no	negative
puts(str);	*stdout*	yes	*EOF*
fprintf(outfile_ptr, "%s", str);	output file	no	negative
fputs(str, outfile_ptr);	output file	no	*EOF*

Table 10.2   Functions to read strings, placing '\0' at the end

Example Function Call	Read from	Skip White Space before?	Read	Stop Reading with	Error Return
scanf("%s", str);	*stdin*	yes	word	white space	*EOF*
gets(str);	*stdin*	no	line	'\n' (discard)	*NULL*
fscanf(infile_ptr, [11]"%s", str);	input file	yes	word	white space	*EOF*
fgets (str, n, infile_ptr);	input file	no	line	'\n' (keep), EOF, or $n - 1$ characters	*NULL*

2. Give the output for

   a. printf("%s", ": Before:"); printf("%s", ":After :");

   b. puts(": Before:"); puts(":After :");

3. Give the contents of the output file to which *outfile_ptr* points after execution of

   a. fprintf(outfile_ptr, "%s", ": Before:");
 fprintf(outfile_ptr, "%s", ":After :");

   b. fputs(": Before:", outfile_ptr);
 fputs(":After :", outfile_ptr);

4. Give the contents of *stdout* after execution of

   fputs(": Before:", stdout); fputs(":After :", stdout);

5. **a.** Declare *car* to be a 14-element *char* array.

   b. Write a *gets* statement to read a string into *car*.

   c. Write a *puts* statement to print the string that *car* stores.

6. Suppose a program reads a string into a 25-character array, *name*, with

   gets(name);

   After execution, what is the value of *name* if the user types three blanks and the name

   ```
      Kim Lee
   ```

7. Write a statement to read a line from the keyboard, storing the line and the newline character in a string variable.

Section 10.2 Programming Project

Write a program to read lines from the keyboard and store them in a file. Give the user the option of having the newline characters appear in the file or not.

Section 10.3 Constant and Variable Strings

In the first two sections, we used *char* arrays to hold strings. The name of an array stores the address of the first element of the array. Although the contents of the array can change during execution, this address cannot.

In Section 9.4 on arrays and pointers, we showed how a pointer variable can also store the address of the first element of an array and how we can access those elements through pointer arithmetic and dereferencing the pointer. Unlike an array, the address that the pointer variable stores can change.

As noted earlier, the computer stores a string literal somewhere in memory, accessing this constant through its pointer. We can define our own pointer of type *char* * and can assign a string literal to it. Literals, however, are constant strings that we should not alter through a pointer.

In this section, we examine the similarities and differences between array and pointer access to strings.

Example 10.9

In this example, we start with a segment of a program that declares and initializes a 12-element character array *StringAr* with the string constant "ar hello". An array name, *StringAr* is a constant pointer. The name evaluates to a location in memory that cannot change. It points to a string (character array) whose contents change in the ordinary way. In other words, the string is variable. The initialization places the characters of the string "ar hello" and '\0' into the array.

The program also declares *string_ptr*, a pointer to a *char*. Being a variable pointer, we can set *string_ptr* to point to any string. The initialization assigns a literal to the string pointer. The string "ptr hello" is a constant somewhere in memory. The computer causes the variable *string_ptr* to point to that location, wherever it happens to be. Figure 10.4 illustrates that after execution of this segment, the 12-element array *StringAr* stores a string of length 8, whereas the pointer *string_ptr* contains the address of a literal of length 9.

Figure 10.4 Memory after declaration-initializations in Example 10.9

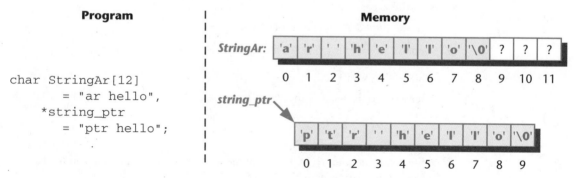

```
/*
 * Example 10.9
 * Program to illustrate pointers to constant strings
 * (literals) vs. constant pointers (array names) to strings
 */

#include <stdio.h>

main()
{
    char StringAr[12] = "ar hello",    /* holds string */
         *string_ptr  = "ptr hello";  /* points to string */
    int  i:                            /* index */

    puts(StringAr);
    puts(string_ptr);
```

The segment produces the following output:

```
ar hello
ptr hello
```

The program continues by assigning the pointer *string_ptr* the address of another literal constant, "ptr How are you?", as shown:

```
string_ptr = "ptr How are you?";
puts(string_ptr);
```

The segment produces the following:

```
ptr How are you?
```

As Figure 10.5 shows, the length of this string is 16.

Figure 10.5 Memory after assignment of literal to *char* pointer in Example 10.9

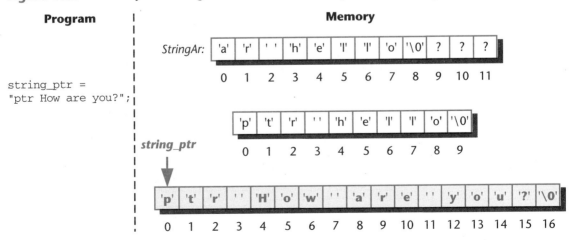

After the assignment, *string_ptr* contains the address of the literal "ptr How are you?". We cannot make a similar assignment to *StringAr*, because its address is constant. We can assign values to individual elements of the array, as the next segment illustrates. Element 2, *StringAr*[2], gets the null character, which ends the string. Thus, the new value of *StringAr* is "ar", a string of length 2.

```
StringAr[2] = '\0';
puts(StringAr);
```

Figure 10.6 shows memory after the assignment. Although the assignment does not destroy the other elements, the earlier occurrence of the null character does truncate the string. The following output affirms that the new value of *StringAr* is a string of length 2:

```
ar
```

We can access the characters that constitute *string_ptr* in the same manner as *StringAr* or any other string. The memory locations pointed to by *string_ptr* should not be modified in any way, because a constant string was assigned to *string_ptr*. Even if the compiler does not explicitly prevent such a modification, unpredictable side effects could occur. We can change the value of pointer variable *string_ptr*, thereby changing the address that it stores. If a literal is assigned to *string_ptr*, however, that string itself should be treated as a constant. For instance, we should not attempt to assign '\0' to *string_ptr*[2]. In contrast, *StringAr* is not an lvalue, but we can alter the string to which it points, or specifically we can change the array containing the string.

The similarities between the two strings outnumber the differences. We can print both strings using the %s conversion specification. Moreover, we can print an element at a time using the subscript or pointer arithmetic notation, as follows:

```
for(i = 0; i < 2; i++)
    putchar(StringAr[i]);
printf("\n");
```

Figure 10.6 Memory after assignment of '\0' to *StringAr*[2] in Example 10.9

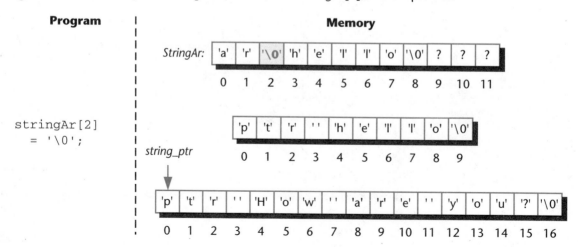

```
for(i = 0; i < 2; i++)
   putchar(*(StringAr + i));
printf("\n");

for(i = 0; i < 16; i++)
   putchar(string_ptr[i]);
printf("\n");

for(i = 0; i < 16; i++)
   putchar(*(string_ptr + i));
printf("\n");
```

Output displays two copies of each variable, as shown:

```
ar
ar
ptr How are you?
ptr How are you?
```

As mentioned, we can assign a new value to *string_ptr*, such as the address of *StringAr*, as shown:

```
string_ptr = StringAr;
puts(StringAr);
puts(string_ptr);
```

As Figure 10.7 and the following output show, after the assignment, *string_ptr* and *StringAr* are the same strings:

```
ar
ar
```

Figure 10.7 Memory after assignment *string_ptr = StringAr* in Example 10.9

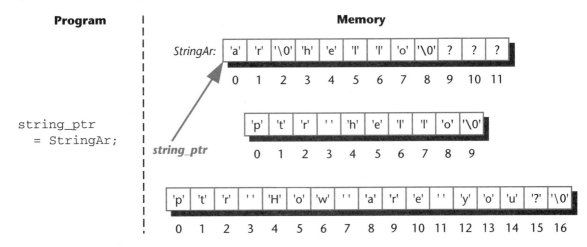

> We can change the value of pointer variable of type *char* *, thereby changing the address that it stores. If a string literal is assigned to that pointer, the string should be treated as a constant. We should not alter the string literal through the pointer.
>
>   We cannot change the location of a *char* array that stores a string. The name of any array evaluates to a location in memory that is constant. For example, we cannot assign (except at declaration-initialization) a string literal to an array. We can, however, alter the string to which an array points. The array contains a variable string.

String Arguments

Example 10.10

Sometimes, we need to prompt for an integer and, if the data item is not within a certain range, to print an error message and prompt again. For instance, in Example 6.6, we had one function to read the number of students in a class and another to read the number of grades. Both functions checked that the user entered a positive value. The only differences in substance between the two functions are the prompt and the help message.

```c
/*
 * Function to read and return the number of students
 * Pre:    none
 * Post:   The (positive) number of students was returned.
 */

int ReadNumStudents(void)
{
    int NumStudents;        /* number of students in class */

    printf("How many students are in the class?  ");
    scanf("%d", &NumStudents);
    while (NumStudents <= 0)
    {
        printf("The number of students must be positive.\n");
        printf("How many students are there?  ");
        scanf("%d", &NumStudents);
    }
    return NumStudents;
}

/*
 * Function to read and return the number of grades
 * Pre:    none
 * Post:   The (positive) number of grades was returned.
 */
```

```c
int ReadNumGrades(void)
{
    int NumGrades;        /* number of grades for each student */

    printf("How many grades are there? ");
    scanf("%d", &NumGrades);
    while (NumGrades <= 0)
    {
        printf("The number of grades must be positive.\n");
        printf("How many grades are there? ");
        scanf("%d", &NumGrades);
    }
    return NumGrades;
}
```

In a similar program, we might also read a grade and verify that it is between 0 and 100. If not in the proper range, the function prints a help message and reads another grade. Only when the user enters an appropriate value does the program return the integer.

```c
/*
 * Function to read and return a grade between 0 and 100
 * Pre:    none
 * Post:   A grade between 0 and 100 was returned.
 */

int ReadGrade(void)
{
    int grade;        /* test grade */

    printf("Type a grade between 0 and 100:  ");
    scanf("%d", &grade);
    while (grade < 0 || 100 < grade)
    {
        printf("\nThe grade must be between 0 and 100.\n");
        printf("Type a grade between 0 and 100:  ");
        scanf("%d", &grade);
    }
    return grade;
}
```

We can construct a general verifying read function that accepts the in-range bounds and strings for the prompt and help message. Because we might use this routine in conjunction with character input, we should flush the input buffer before returning.

```c
/*
 * Function to prompt, read an integer and verify it is in
 * the range LowerBound to UpperBound. If not, it issues a
 * help message and prompts again. When the user enters an
 * in-range integer, the function returns the value.
```

```
 * Pre:   prompt is the string prompt for input data.
 *        help is the string error message for invalid input.
 *        LowerBound and UpperBound are integers with
 *        LowerBound <= UpperBound.
 * Post: An integer between LowerBound to UpperBound
 *        was returned.
 */

int ReadInt(char *prompt, char *help,
                int LowerBound, int UpperBound)
{
    int value;      /* value to read and return */

    printf("%s", prompt);
    scanf("%d", &value);
    while (value < LowerBound || UpperBound < value)
    {
        printf("%s", help);
        printf("%s", prompt);
        scanf("%d", &value);
    }
    fflush(stdin);
    return value;
}
```

Thus, a call to obtain a test grade might be as follows:

```
grade = ReadInt("Type a grade between 0 and 100:  ",
            "\nThe grade must be between 0 and 100.\n",
            0, 100);
```

The string and integer arguments generate the following sample run:

```
Type a grade between 0 and 100:  -4

The grade must be between 0 and 100.
Type a grade between 0 and 100:  105

The grade must be between 0 and 100.
Type a grade between 0 and 100:  98
```

As with *ReadNumStudents* and *ReadNumGrades* above, the valid numbers are often the positive integers, and the smallest such integer is 1. Mathematics has no upper bound to the set of positive integers, but the computer must have one. As discussed in Section 4.5, the header file *limits.h* defines *INT_MAX* as this largest integer value for the particular computer. Thus, the valid range for a positive integer is from 1 through *INT_MAX*. To obtain a positive number of students, we call:

```
#include <limits.h>
    ⋮
NumStudents = ReadInt("How many students are in the class?   ",
          "\nThe number of students must be positive.\n",
          1, INT_MAX);
```

The following interactive execution of the segment illustrates the change of strings on output:

> How many students are in the class? <u>0</u>
>
> The number of students must be positive.
> How many students are in the class? <u>30</u>

Constant Parameters

From the format of the prototypes thus far, when a parameter is a pointer type—such as *char* * for a string—we cannot tell whether the function changes the location that the pointer references or not. For example, consider the following prototype for the function *StringLength* to return the length of a string:

```
int StringLength(char *);
```

Because *s* is a pointer to *char*, the function may change the value to which *s* points through indirection. The value, however, should be input only. The function *String-Length* accepts a string argument and returns its length without changing the string itself. The value to which *s* points, should be held constant.

To clarify that a parameter is for input only and to enforce that the function does not change the string, we use a type qualifier. Besides having a type, a variable can have a **type qualifier** that indicates additional information about the status of the variable. One such qualifier is *const*, which allows us to define constants. Consequently, we can declare *StringLength* with the following prototype:

```
int StringLength(const char *);
```

By using *const*, we make clear that a parameter is for input only. Moreover, the function cannot inadvertently change a value that should be constant.

We can use the type qualifier *const* in other situations, too. Previously, we have defined symbolic constants with the *#define* preprocessor directive. The ANSI C language also includes variables, whose values cannot change. By having the type qualifier *const* before or after the type name in a declaration-initialization, we establish a constant. Because its value cannot change, we must initialize every constant variable, such as

```
const float PI = 3.1415;
```

Two-Dimensional Array of Characters

Quite often, we must store a set of strings in a structure for manipulation. Perhaps we wish to sort a list of names or print the list at a later time. As the next example illustrates, one method of storage is in a two-dimensional array of *char* elements.

Example 10.11

We can initialize a two-dimensional array of characters (an array of pointers to strings) to a list of strings, as the following code shows:

```c
char WordList[10][20] =
{
    "hello",
    "goodbye",
    "nice day",
    "it's cold"
};
```

Because the list specifies four literals, the computer only initializes the first four rows of the array. We could omit the row dimension (10), but not the column. In this case, the number of allocated rows would be equal to the number of initializing strings, 4. As Figure 10.8 illustrates, the preceding statement is equivalent to the following:

```c
char WordList[10][20] =
{
    {'h', 'e', 'l', 'l', '\0'},
    {'g', 'o', 'o', 'd', 'b', 'y', 'e','\0'},
    {'n', 'i', 'c', 'e', ' ', 'd', 'a', 'y', '\0'},
    {'i', 't', '\'', 's', ' ', 'c', 'o', 'l', 'd', '\0'}
};
```

The null ('\0') and apostrophe characters ('\'') use the backslash in C, and a blank is a space between two apostrophes (' ').

Figure 10.8   Storage of *WordList* in Example 10.11

word_list:	'h'	'e'	'l'	'l'	'o'	'\0'	?	?	?	?	?	?	?	?	?	?	?	?	?	?
	'g'	'o'	'o'	'd'	'b'	'y'	'e'	'\0'	?	?	?	?	?	?	?	?	?	?	?	?
	'n'	'i'	'c'	'e'	' '	'd'	'a'	'y'	'\0'	?	?	?	?	?	?	?	?	?	?	?
	'i'	't'	'\''	's'	' '	'c'	'o'	'l'	'd'	'\0'	?	?	?	?	?	?	?	?	?	?
	?	?	?	?	?	?	?	?	?	?	?	?	?	?	?	?	?	?	?	?
	?	?	?	?	?	?	?	?	?	?	?	?	?	?	?	?	?	?	?	?
	?	?	?	?	?	?	?	?	?	?	?	?	?	?	?	?	?	?	?	?
	?	?	?	?	?	?	?	?	?	?	?	?	?	?	?	?	?	?	?	?
	?	?	?	?	?	?	?	?	?	?	?	?	?	?	?	?	?	?	?	?
	?	?	?	?	?	?	?	?	?	?	?	?	?	?	?	?	?	?	?	?

We can use *printf* or *puts* to print the strings that the structure holds, as shown:

```
for(i = 0; i < 4; i++)
    puts(WordList[i]);
```

The output is as follows:

```
hello
goodbye
nice day
it's cold
```

One-Dimensional Array of Strings

Another method of storing a list of strings uses a one-dimensional array of pointers, where each element can point to a string. Example 10.12 illustrates an array of type *char **, with each element having the value of a string literal.

Example 10.12

We can initialize a one-dimensional array of pointers to characters using a set of literals, as shown here:

```
char *word_ptrs[4] =
{
    "hello",
    "goodbye",
    "nice day",
    "it's cold"
};
```

In this case, the initializing strings are constants, and each array element points to its corresponding string constant. Figure 10.9 depicts this situation.

As with the two-dimensional array of characters, we can print the strings using *printf* or *puts*. The pointer to the *i*th literal is *word_ptrs + i* or *word_ptrs[i]*. To obtain

Figure 10.9
Storage of *word_ptrs* in Example 10.12

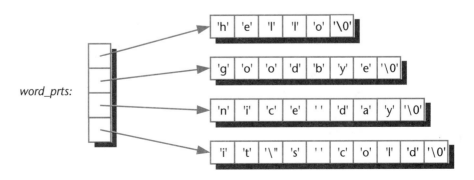

the literal itself, we must use the indirection operator (*), such as *(*word_ptrs* + *i*). Thus, to print all the literals, we can use the following segment:

```
for(i = 0; i < 4; i++)
    puts(*(word_ptrs + i));
```

which produces the same output as in Example 10.11.

Section 10.3 Exercises

1. **a.** Write a declaration-initialization for a 20-element *char* array *title* to store the string "Problem Solving in C".

   b. What is the length of this string?

   c. How many elements of the array have values?

   d. Draw a picture of memory similar to Figure 10.4.

   e. Using *printf*, write a statement to print the string which the array stores.

   f. Using *putchar* and subscript notation, write statements to print the string.

   g. Using the assignment of the null character to an element of *title*, truncate the string to be "Problem".

2. Using the array *title* from Exercise 1, find the error(s) in the following statement:

   ```
   title = "Data Structures";
   ```

3. **a.** Write a declaration-initialization for a *char* pointer *course_ptr* to point to the string literal "Computer Science 1".

   b. Draw a picture of memory similar to Figure 10.4.

   c. Using *printf*, write a statement to print the string to which *course_ptr* points.

   d. Using *putchar*, pointer arithmetic, and dereferencing, write statements to print the string.

   e. Write a statement to assign the string literal "English" to *course_ptr*.

   f. Write a statement to point *course_ptr* to the array *title* of Exercise 1.

4. Using the pointer *course_ptr* from Exercise 3, find the error(s) in the following statement:

   ```
   *course_ptr = 'c';
   ```

5. **a.** Write a function that accepts a name, such as Robin Smith, as an argument and prints a greeting using the name, such as the following:

   ```
   Good morning, Robin Smith! How are you doing today?
   ```

   b. Write a statement to call the function with that name.

6. Give a declaration-initialization of a two-dimensional *char* array *names* of 4 names of 25 characters each, where the names are John L. Smith, Mary Jones, Jeff Lee, and Alice M. Dwight.

7. Give a declaration-initialization of a one-dimensional array of 4 pointers with the four elements pointing to the names listed in Exercise 6.

8. Define a function to accept two strings as arguments and to return 1 if they are identical and 0 otherwise. Declare the parameters to indicate that the function does not change the strings.

Section 10.3 Programming Projects

1. This project provides practice in array storage and pointer reference to strings. Write a function that reads an entire line of input into a string by reading single characters until reading a newline. Include the newline in the string. (Remember to add the terminating null character.) Another function should print the string using a pointer to the array, pointer arithmetic, and the indirection operator. The function *main* should call both the reading and printing functions and pass the string as a parameter.

2. Rewrite *PrintNumber* of Example 3.13 (Section 3.4) to use arrays of strings. This function prints a positive one- or two-digit integer using words.

Section 10.4 Validation of Data

The detection of erroneous input or validation of data is an important feature of interactive programming. We have, for example, checked that the values are within a required range. By reading a character at a time, we have ensured that if (say) input should be an unsigned integer, the user does not enter a floating point number or string literal.

An easier approach is to input all data as strings with the *scanf* or *gets* function, as shown:

```
char input[BUFSIZ];
int  num;
  ⋮
gets(input);
```

We check the string character by character to make sure it is valid. For example, if the required data item is an unsigned integer, we can check the input string to make sure it contains only digits. (The function *StringLength* is from Example 10.4 of Section 10.1.)

```
StringSize = StringLength(input);
valid = TRUE;
i = 0;
while(valid && i < StringLength)
    if (isdigit(input[i]))
        i++;
    else
        valid = FALSE;
```

If input is valid, then we can use the ANSI C standard library function *atoi* (ASCII to *int*) to convert the string to type *int* and store the result in *num,* as shown:

```
#include <stdlib.h>
  ⋮
if (valid)
    num = atoi(input);
```

If the input is not valid, the program can tell the user why and display the nondigits and their positions.

The ANSI C standard library contains two other functions for similar conversions. The function *atol* (ASCII to *long*) returns the *long int* equivalent of the string argument, such as

```
#include <stdlib.h>
    ⋮
long_num = atol(input);
```

To return a *double* number, we use the function *atof* (ASCII to floating point), such as

```
#include <stdlib.h>
    ⋮
double_num = atof(input);
```

Example 10.13

Example 7.13 of Section 7.3 contains a program to read an unsigned integer one character at a time and to print the integer or an error message. This example improves on that program by repeatedly reading the input as a string and determining if the data item is a valid integer or not.

The function *main* calls *GetIntInput* to read the data item as a string until the user enters an integer. Because *GetIntInput* processes each character of the input string, it calls a function, such as *StringLength*, to obtain the length of the string. The function *GetIntInput* returns a validated integer to *main*, which prints the number. Then, *main* calls *GetAnswer* to ask if the user wishes to process additional input and to return an answer of 'y' or 'n'. If the answer is *YES* ('y'), the process continues. Figure 10.10 contains the structure chart for this program, and pseudocode for *main* is below.

---

main( )

    Program to read data, validating that they are integers

Algorithm:

    do the following:
        obtain an integer, *num*, by calling *GetIntInput*
        print *num*
    while *GetAnswer( )* is *YES*

The function *GetIntInput* prompts for an integer. If the input is not valid, it obtains another value. The function allows signed or unsigned input—such as -35, +24, or 15—but does not allow the null string or only a sign—such as + or -. If the first character in the string is a plus or minus sign, the function sets the index *i* to 1. In this case, the loop that scans for digits in the input string should start with character 1, skipping over character 0, which the computer has already validated (it contains a plus or minus sign). Otherwise, the program assigns 0 to *i*, meaning that the first character is neither a plus nor a minus sign and all the characters should be digits. If at this point the length of the string is *i*, the string is empty or only contains a sign. Such an input

Figure 10.10
Structure chart
for the program
in Example
10.13

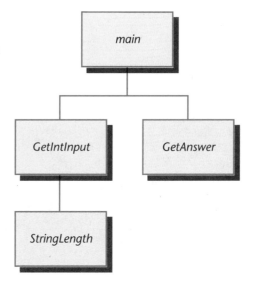

is invalid. Element by element, the program then checks if the remaining characters of the string are digits. After the function determines that the data item is a valid integer, we still must verify that the number is in the integer range. To check for overflow, we use *atof* to convert the string input to a *double* and compare the value with *INT_MIN* and *INT_MAX*. If the input is a valid integer between *INT_MIN* and *INT_MAX*, the routine returns to *main* the string converted to *int* with *atoi*.

GetIntInput( ) ⟶ *num*

Function to read data item as a string, verify it is an integer, and return a valid integer

Pre:

Post:

Valid integer user input has been returned.

Algorithm:

do the following:
  prompt for an integer
  read input as a string into *char* array *input* using *scanf*
  flush the input buffer

  if the first character, *input*[0], is + or −
    $i \leftarrow 1$
  else
    $i \leftarrow 0$
  StringSize ← *StringLength*(*input*)
  valid ← *TRUE*

```
        if i equals StringSize
            valid ←FALSE
        while (valid is TRUE and i is less than StringSize)
            if input[i] is a digit
                increment i by 1
            else ·
                valid ←FALSE

        if input was valid
            if (input converted to double with atof is
                    greater than INT_MAX or less than INT_MIN)
                print overflow error message
                valid ←FALSE
        else
            print invalid integer error message
    while input is not valid

    return input converted to int with atoi
```

The function *GetAnswer*, which *main* calls, asks if the user would like to enter another number and reads the answer into a string (*answer*). The function keeps questioning until the user types a response with a first character (*answer*[0]) of 'y', 'Y', 'n', or 'N'. Therefore, responses such as yes, yup!, Yeah, y, no, n, nope, or any response beginning with y or n are valid. The function returns 'y' or 'n'. Pseudocode for *GetAnswer* follows.

GetAnswer( ) ⟶ ans

Function to ask if the user would like to enter another number and return 'y' or 'n'

Pre:

Post:

A 'y' or 'n' user answer has been returned.

Algorithm:

```
do the following:
    ask if the user would like to enter another number
    read answer into char array answer with gets
while the first element of answer (answer[0]) is not 'y', 'Y', 'n', or 'N'

return the lowercase letter corresponding to the first character of answer
```

We use *scanf* for *GetIntInput*, because it skips over any initial white space, such as blanks. After *scanf*, we must flush the input buffer to prepare for the next input stream. The program uses *gets* for *GetAnswer*, because *gets* takes the whole line and we do not need to flush the buffer after its use. If the user types a leading blank, however, *gets* stores that character in *answer*[0], and *GetAnswer* requires that the user retype a response. The program follows:

```c
/*
 * Example 10.13. Program to read an integer a character at a
 * time and to print the integer or an error message
 */

#include <stdio.h>
#include <stdlib.h>
#include <ctype.h>
#include <limits.h>

#define TRUE 1
#define FALSE 0
#define YES 'y'

int GetIntInput(void);
char GetAnswer(void);

main()
{
    int num;    /* input integer */

    printf("This program validates integer input.\n\n");
    do
    {
        num = GetIntInput();
        printf("You typed the number %d.\n", num);
    }
    while (GetAnswer() == YES);
}

/*
 * Function to read integer input as a string and return a
 * valid integer data item
 * Pre:    none
 * Post:   An integer was returned.
 */

int GetIntInput(void)
{
    int StringLength(const char *);

    int StringSize,       /* size of input string */
        valid,            /* boolean value for string being valid */
        i;                /* index */
    char input[BUFSIZ];   /* input string */
```

```c
        do
        {
            printf("Please enter an integer: ");
            scanf("%s", input);
            fflush(stdin);

            if (input[0] == '+' || input[0] == '-')
                i = 1;
            else
                i = 0;

            StringSize = StringLength(input);
            valid = TRUE;

            if (i == StringSize)   /* empty string or only + or - */
                valid = FALSE;

            while(valid && i < StringSize)
                if (isdigit(input[i]))
                    i++;
                else
                    valid = FALSE;

            if (valid)
            {
                if ((atof(input) < INT_MIN) || (atof(input) > INT_MAX))
                {
                    printf("Invalid data: Integer overflow\n\n");
                    valid = FALSE;
                }
            }
            else
                printf("%s is not an integer!\n\n", input);

        }
        while (!valid);

        /* return integer converted from string */
        return (atoi(input));
}

/*
 * Function to return the length of the string parameter
 * Pre:     str points to a constant string.
 * Post:    The length of the string str was returned.
 */
```

```
int StringLength(const char *str)
{
    int StringSize = 0;      /* holds actual string length */

    while (str[String Size] != '\0')
        StringSize++;

    return StringSize;
}


/*
 * Function to determine if the user wishes to enter more
 * integers and to return a character answer, y or n
 * Pre:     none
 * Post:    A y or n was returned.
 */

char GetAnswer(void)
{
    char answer[BUFSIZ];   /* answer of wanting to continue */

    do
    {
        printf("\nWould you like to enter another number? (y/n) ");
        gets(answer);
    }
    while (answer[0] != 'y' && answer[0] != 'Y' &&
            answer[0] != 'n' && answer[0] != 'N');

    return (tolower(answer[0]));
}
```

The following is an interactive session using the program:

```
This program validates integer input.

Please enter an integer: 7
You typed the number 7.

Would you like to enter another number? (y/n) yes
Please enter an integer: 4*5
4*5 is not an integer!

Please enter an integer: -
- is not an integer!

Please enter an integer: -2
You typed the number -2.
```

```
Would you like to enter another number? (y/n)   y

Would you like to enter another number? (y/n) yup!
Please enter an integer: zero
zero is not an integer!

Please enter an integer: 0
You typed the number 0.

Would you like to enter another number? (y/n) I guess so

Would you like to enter another number? (y/n) Yeah
Please enter an integer: +
+ is not an integer!

Please enter an integer: +4
You typed the number 4.

Would you like to enter another number? (y/n) y
Please enter an integer: 16w
16w is not an integer!

Please enter an integer: 16
You typed the number 16.

Would you like to enter another number? (y/n) y
Please enter an integer: 55000
Invalid data: Integer overflow

Please enter an integer: 25000
You typed the number 25000.

Would you like to enter another number? (y/n) nope
```

Section 10.4 Exercises

1. a. Declare a 20-element character array *long_str* and a *long* variable *lng*.

   b. Write a statement to read *long_str* as a string.

   c. Write a statement to convert *long_str* to a *long*, storing the result in *lng*.

2. a. Declare a 20-element character array *double_str* and a *double* variable *dbl*.

   b. Write a statement to read *double_str* as a string.

   c. Write a statement to convert *double_str* to a *float*, storing the result in *dbl*.

3. Give the changes in the program of Example 10.13 to read a value into *num*, which is of type *long*.

Section 10.4 Programming Projects

1. Convert the program in Example 10.13 to handle floating point numbers that are not in exponential format. Make sure the number contains no more than one decimal point. The user can enter a number without a decimal, such as 493.

2. Convert the program in Example 10.13 to handle floating point numbers that are in exponential (such as 83.455e-6), decimal (such as 734.2), or integer (such as 63) format.

Section 10.5 Several String Functions

The ANSI C header file *string.h* declares several string functions, such as *strlen* to return the length of a string, *strcpy* to copy strings, *strcat* to concatenate strings, *strchr* to search for a character in a string, *strstr* to search for a substring, and *strcmp* to compare. Therefore, to access these functions, we must include the header file, as shown:

```
#include <string.h>
```

This section and the next concentrate on several functions that are helpful in many programs involving string manipulations.

Storage Size
The header file *string.h* includes the definition of the type *size_t*, which is the type of the value that *sizeof* returns. The *sizeof* operator applied to a type or expression gives the number of storage bytes needed for the operand. For example, *sizeof(float)* or *sizeof(x)* for a *float* variable *x* is the number of bytes to store a floating point value in memory. The type *size_t* is compatible with type *int*. For instance, C on a particular machine might define *size_t* as *unsigned long*. (In Section 11.2, we see how to define our own types.)

Suppose we declare-initialize *version* to be a *char* array of 10 elements storing the string "ANSI" and declare *int* variable *size*.

```
char version[10] = "ANSI";
int size;
```

As Figure 10.11 shows, although *version* has 10 elements, only five characters ('A', 'N', 'S', 'I', and '\0') occupy elements. The null character is in element *version*[4], and there are 4 characters until '\0' in the array. The expression *sizeof(version)* is the number of bytes in the *char* array *version*. Dividing the result by the number of bytes in one element, *sizeof(char)*, we obtain the number of elements in *version*.

```
size = sizeof(version) / sizeof(char);
printf("The number of elements in version is %d.\n",
        size);
```

Figure 10.11   *sizeof(version)/sizeof(char)* is 10

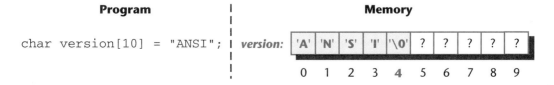

The output is

```
The number of elements in version is 10.
```

(For a *char* array, division by *sizeof*(*char*) is unnecessary, because one byte stores a character. We include the divisor to emphasize that in general we must divide the *sizeof* the array by the *sizeof* an element to obtain the dimension of the array.)

Because *sizeof* returns a value of type *size_t*, on some systems we must store the result in an *int* variable or cast it to an *int* for printing. Thus,

```
printf("The number of elements in version is %d.\n",
        (int)(sizeof(version)/sizeof(char)));
```

produces the same output as the above. Applying *sizeof* to the literal "ANSI"

```
printf("The number of bytes in \"ANSI\" is %d.\n",
        (int)sizeof("ANSI"));
```

we see that the *sizeof* function counts the null character in the string, as follows:

```
The number of bytes in "ANSI" is 5.
```

String Length

In Example 10.4 of Section 10.1, we defined a function *StringLength* that returned the length of its string parameter. The ANSI C library function *strlen* also returns the number of characters (other than '\0') in the string or the position of the null character in its storage as a value of type *size_t*. For example, the following statement with *strlen*(*version*) coerced to an *int*

```
printf("The length of \"%s\" is %d.\n", version,
        (int)strlen(version));
```

prints

```
The length of "ANSI" is 4.
```

Copying Strings

In the above declaration of *version*, we could initialize the array with the string "ANSI". Such an initialization copies the characters of "ANSI" and the null character into the array. As discussed in the chapter on arrays and Section 10.3, however, we cannot assign a string to *version*.

```
version = "Richie"    /* ERROR for char array version */
```

The literal on the right evaluates to an address in memory as does the name of the array. However, the locations of arrays are fixed. We cannot directly copy one string into another with an assignment statement. Similarly, for *char* arrays *source* and *destination* storing strings,

```
char destination[10] = "Richie",
     source[10]       = "ANSI";
```

we cannot copy the contents of *source* to *destination* with a single assignment statement.

```
destination = source;  /* ERROR for arrays */
```

One method is to copy the values one element at a time, as follows:

```
for (i = 0; i <= strlen(source); i++)
    destination[i] = source[i];
```

Figure 10.12   Action of *strcpy*

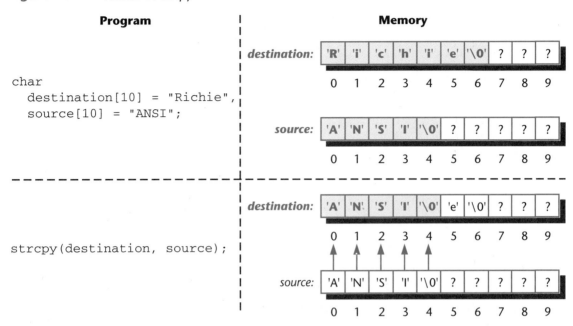

Because we can copy the value of one character variable into another, we can assign a *char* element from *source* to an element of *destination*. So that *destination* receives a string that ends properly, we also copy the null character from the *source* element with index *strlen(source)*.

The function *strcpy* with prototype in *string.h* accomplishes the same task of string copying. Thus, the statement

```
strcpy(destination, source);
```

copies the string in *source* to *destination*. The programmer must ensure that *destination* has enough room for the string. Unpredictable results can occur if *destination* is not sufficiently large. Figure 10.12 shows that after the above call to *strcpy*, the array *destination* stores the string "ANSI".

Example 10.14

In this example, we write a function to read several lines of input from the user, storing the strings in a structure. The structure consists of an array of *NUM_LINES* number of type *char* * pointers.

```
char *line_ptr[NUM_LINES];   /* array of pointers to strings */
```

With *gets*, we read a line into a temporary storage area, *LineTemp*, which is an array of characters. To allow for maximum-length input, the array is the size of the input buffer, *BUFSIZ*.

```
char LineTemp[BUFSIZ];   /* one line */
```

We should not leave each line in such an array. *BUFSIZ* might be 512, and user input might be a string of length 1. Thus, as Figure 10.13 shows, we determine the length of the input string, *strlen(LineTemp)*, and with *malloc* we allocate just enough storage

Figure 10.13 Memory allocation and string copying in Example 10.14

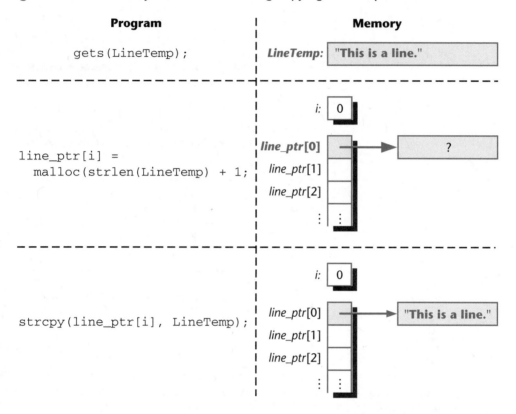

space for the string. Because we must also store the null character, the necessary number of characters is one more than the length of a string. The function *malloc* returns a pointer to this storage area, which we assign to one of the elements of *line_ptr*, as shown:

```
line_ptr[i] = malloc( strlen(LineTemp) + 1 );
```

If *malloc* cannot successfully allocate space, then the function returns *NULL*. Otherwise, with *strcpy* we copy the elements of *LineTemp* into the storage area to which *line_ptr[i]* points.

```
strcpy(line_ptr[i], LineTemp);
```

The program example below obtains the number of lines the user wishes to enter through a call to the function *ReadInt* of Example 10.10 in Section 10.3. After reading all the lines into the structure, the program prints each line with a line-number prefix.

```
/*
 * Example 10.14. Program to read lines into an array of
 * pointers to lines and print them
 */

#include <stdio.h>
#include <limits.h>
#include <string.h>
#include <stdlib.h>
```

```
#define NUM_LINES 20
#define TRUE 1
#define FALSE 0

int ReadInt(const char *, const char *, int, int);

main()
{

    int  i = 0,                       /* index */
         NumLines,                    /* number of lines */
         error = FALSE;               /* memory allocation error */
    char *line_ptr[NUM_LINES],        /* array of pointers to strings */
         LineTemp[BUFSIZ];            /* one line */

    printf("This program reads lines into an array.\n\n");
    NumLines = ReadInt("How many lines will you type?  ",
            "\nThe number of lines must be positive.\n",
            1, INT_MAX);

    while ((i < NumLines) && (!error))
    {
        gets(LineTemp);
        line_ptr[i] = malloc( strlen(LineTemp) + 1 );
        if (line_ptr[i] == NULL)
        {
            error = TRUE;
            NumLines = i;
            printf("Space could not be allocated for line %d\n", i);
        }
        else
        {
            strcpy(line_ptr[i], LineTemp);
            i++;
        }
    }

    printf("\nNumbered Lines:\n");
    for (i = 0; (i < NumLines) && (!error); i++)
    {
        printf("%d: ", i);
        puts(line_ptr[i]);
    }
}

/*** Insert ReadInt (Ex. 10.10, Sec. 10.3) with const/ ***/
/*** type qualifies for prompt and help parameters      ***/
```

A sample run follows:

```
This program reads lines into an array.

How many lines will you type?  3
It is very important to include stdlib.h for malloc.
We also need string.h for strlen and strcpy.
Because we use INT_MAX, we also need limits.h.

Numbered Lines:
0: It is very important to include stdlib.h for malloc.
1: We also need string.h for strlen and strcpy.
2: Because we use INT_MAX, we also need limits.h.
```

**Concatena-
tion**

Another important string operation is **concatenation** or the joining of two strings to form another. The ANSI C library function *strcat* replaces the first string variable argument with the concatenation of the two arguments. For example, suppose we have the following:

```
char str1[10] = "Hi",
      str2[]   = " there";
```

As Figure 10.14 illustrates, after execution of the following statement:

```
strcat(str1, str2);
```

str1 holds the string "Hi there", and *str2* is unchanged. The copying of *str2* onto the end of *str1* starts with *str2*[0] overwriting the null character at the end of the string in

Figure 10.14   Action of *strcat*

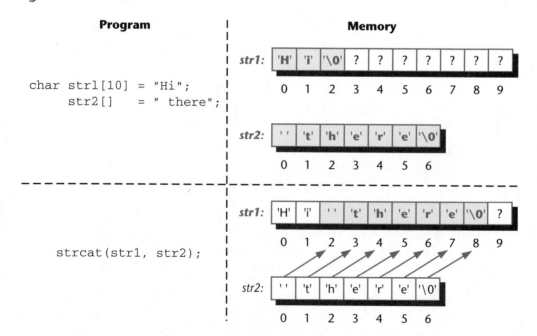

str1. Thus, this concatenation lengthens the string in *str1*. We must be careful that enough room exists in the destination string.

The following two requirements exist for *strcat*:

1. The first parameter to the *strcat* function, such as *str1*, must be a variable string (an array).

2. The array which stores the first string, such as *str1*, must be large enough to hold the concatenated string (that is, both the first and the second string together).

The next section continues the discussion of string functions with two searching functions, *strchr* and *strstr*, and a string-comparison operation, *strcmp*.

Section 10.5 Exercises

For each of Exercises 1–8, start with the following declaration-initializations and give the value of any variable that changes.

```
char s1[20] = "well",
     s2[20] = "come";
int len;
```

1. `len = sizeof(s1);`
2. `len = sizeof("well");`
3. `s1[strlen(s1) - 1] = '\0';`
4. `strcat(s1, s2);`
5. `strcat(s1, ", "); strcat(s1, s2);`
6. `strcpy(s1, s2);`
7. `strcpy(s1 + 3, s2);`
8. `strcpy(s1, s2 + 2);`
9. Explain what the following segment does:
   ```
   char *copy, *original;
   ⋮
   while (*copy++ = *original++);
   ```
10. Using a loop, write your own version of the function *strcat*.
11. Using pointer arithmetic, *strcpy*, and *strlen*, write your own version of *strcat*.

Section 10.5 Programming Project

Write a program to obtain from a file the following information for several people: first name, middle initial, last name, form of address (Mr., Ms., Mrs., Miss, Dr.), street address, apartment (if any), city, state, and ZIP code. For each person, form three strings that are lines of the address label and print the label.

Section 10.6 String Comparisons

Many applications involving strings require some form of string comparison, such as searching for a word in a file or determining if a list of names is in alphabetical order.

Figure 10.15
Action of *loc =
strstr(str, "ear")*
where *str* is
"appearance"

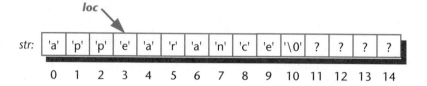

Some functions with prototypes in *string.h* use character comparisons to return the location of a string or a character in another string. Another function compares two strings alphabetically. This section considers three string functions that use comparisons.

Search for a String

One basic operation of word processors is to search for the first occurrence of a string in the text. In C, the function call *strstr(str, substr)* returns a pointer to the first occurrence of the string *substr* in the string *str*. Should *substr* not be a substring of *str*, the function returns *NULL*. Figure 10.15 depicts the result of the search for the string "ear" in "appearance" using the following segment:

```
char str[15] = "appearance",
      *loc;
   ⋮
loc = strstr(str, "ear");
```

Using this pointer information, we can do a number of operations. Perhaps we would like to print the rest of the string ("earance") with

```
puts(loc);
```

With pointer arithmetic, we can advance past the substring, having *loc* point to "ance", to prepare for another search, as shown:

```
loc += 3;
```

Search for a Character

A similar function declared in *string.h*, *strchr*, returns a pointer (or *NULL*) to the first occurrence of a character in a string. Thus, using the above declaration,

```
loc = strchr(str, 'e');
```

returns the same address as the search for "ear" (see Figure 10.15). Because the second argument is a character instead of a string, we use apostrophes around the e.

Example 10.15

Suppose we are interactively reading an expression, such as *x* + *y*. We need to verify that the user has entered a valid operation, say +, −, *, or /. With *ch* storing the relevant character, we could test with the following rather tedious statement:

```
if (ch == '+' || ch == '-' || ch == '*' || ch == or '/')
     /* process valid input */
```

Alternatively, we could search for the character in a string containing all the operations, "+-*/". If the *strchr* finds the character, *ch*, it returns a pointer to that location. Otherwise, the function returns *NULL*. Thus, a replacement for the above *if* condition is the following:

```
if (strchr("+-*/", ch) != NULL)
    /* ch found - process valid input */
```

We are checking if *ch* belongs to the set { '+', '-', '*', '/' }. Using *strchr* to test membership of a character in a set is effective for a number of one-character possibilities.

String Comparison

A number of applications require that an array of strings, such as a list of names, be in alphabetical order. Most sorting algorithms require comparisons. For example, suppose the string pointers *str_ptr1* and *str_ptr2* point to literals "their" and "there", respectively, as shown:

```
char *str_ptr1 = "their",
     *str_ptr2 = "there";
```

The boolean expression *str_ptr1* < *str_ptr2*, which tests if the value of *str_ptr1* is less than the value of *str_ptr2*, does not perform the correct comparison. These variables are pointers, and their values are the addresses of the string literals, not the literals themselves. Moreover, comparing the dereferenced pointers (**str_ptr1* < **str_ptr2*) only compares the first elements of the literals.

The library function *strcmp* (string compare) accomplishes the comparison by returning an integer. If the first string argument is less than the second, *strcmp* returns a value less than zero. If the first argument is equal to the second, the function returns a zero. If the first is greater than the second, *strcmp* returns an integer greater than zero. Thus, the following segment prints the relative lexical (alphabetical) positions of the strings:

```
if (strcmp(str_ptr1, str_ptr2) < 0)
    printf("The string \"%s\" occurs before \"%s\" alphabetically.\n",
            str_ptr1, str_ptr2);
else if (strcmp(str_ptr1, str_ptr2) == 0)
    printf("The string \"%s\" is the same as \"%s\".\n",
            str_ptr1, str_ptr2);
else
    printf("The string \"%s\" occurs after \"%s\" alphabetically.\n",
            str_ptr1, str_ptr2);
```

For *str_ptr1* being "their" and *str_ptr2* "there", *strcmp(str_ptr1, str_ptr2)* is negative and the segment prints

```
The string "their" occurs before "there" alphabetically.
```

The function makes the comparison by moving along the two strings and comparing the characters in corresponding positions. When the two characters differ, the function returns a value specifying that the first string is either greater than or less than the second, depending on which character is greater. If the function reaches the ends of the strings without detecting unequal characters, then the two strings are equal. The null character ('\0') has a smaller ASCII value than any other. Therefore, if the comparison reaches the end of one string before the other—such as with "the" and "there"—the algorithm correctly designates the shorter string as the lexically smaller string. Figures 10.16 through 10.19 depict the various situations that can arise with *strcmp*.

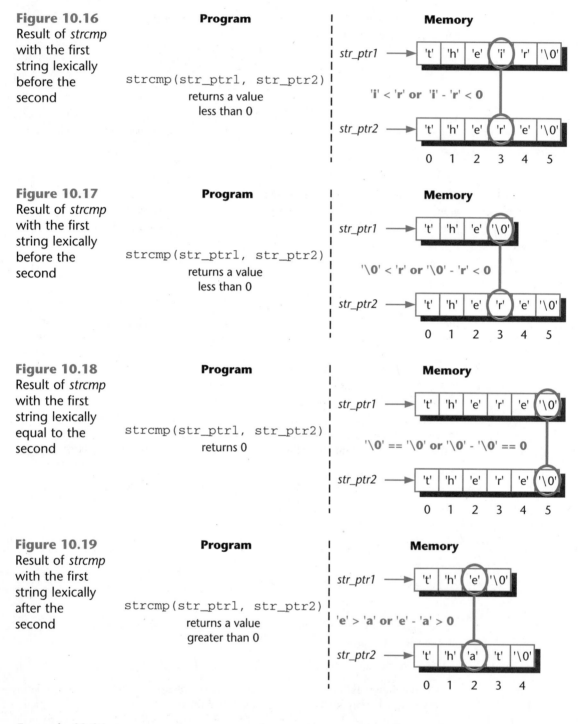

Figure 10.16
Result of *strcmp* with the first string lexically before the second

Figure 10.17
Result of *strcmp* with the first string lexically before the second

Figure 10.18
Result of *strcmp* with the first string lexically equal to the second

Figure 10.19
Result of *strcmp* with the first string lexically after the second

Example 10.16

One string-processing application is the manipulation of words to understand human language. Such programs, which are in the realm of **natural language processing**, are too complex for this book. However, this example presents one mechanism that is useful in the handling of words and sentences.

Figure 10.20   Structure chart for the program in Example 10.16

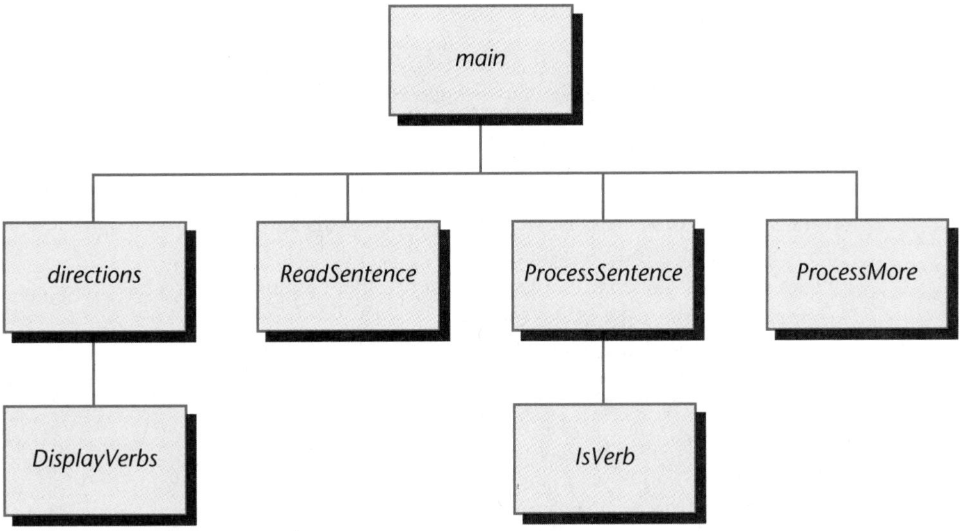

In this program, the user types a sentence, and the program prints subject and predicate on separate lines without punctuation. Normally this task would be very difficult, but we make a few assumptions about the sentences. The verb must be in a list of verbs that the program stores. A sentence must end with a period. The sentence is simple—it has one subject phrase at the beginning and one predicate phrase from the verb to the end. Any punctuation immediately follows a word. For example, suppose the user types the following:

```
The child laughed at the clown.
```

The output would be

```
Subject:    The child
Predicate:  laughed at the clown
```

As the structure chart in Figure 10.20 shows, *main* calls four functions:

- *directions*, which prints program directions and calls *DisplayVerbs* to print the list of verbs
- *ReadSentence*, which reads strings, separates the words from the punctuation, and stores the words as an array of strings. It communicates to *main* the list of words and the number of such words.
- *ProcessSentence*, which receives the array of words, the number of words, the array of verbs, and the number of verbs, and which prints the subject and predicate on separate lines
- *ProcessMore*, which asks if the user wishes to process more sentences and returns *TRUE* or *FALSE* accordingly

The pseudocode for *main* is below.

---

main( )

Program to read sentences and print subject and predicate on separate lines without punctuation

Assumptions:

The verb must be in a list of verbs that the program stores.
A sentence must end in a period.
The sentence has one subject phrase at the beginning and one predicate phrase from the verb to the end.
Any punctuation immediately follows a word.

Algorithm:

initialize array of verbs
VerbCount ⟵ number of verbs in array
call *directions* to print program instructions
do the following:
    call *ReadSentence* to read the sentence and place words in array
    call *ProcessSentence* to print subject and predicate
while the function *ProcessMore* returns *TRUE*

The function *directions* just prints directions for the program's use and calls *DisplayVerbs* to print the list of verbs. The function *DisplayVerbs* prints the verbs five across the page. One index (*i*) controls the element, and another (*j*) monitors the number across the page.

DisplayVerbs(VerbList, VerbCount)

Function to print list of verbs, five across page

Pre:

VerbList is an array of pointers to verbs.
VerbCount is the number of elements in *VerbList*.

Post:

The list of verbs has been printed.

Algorithm:

i ⟵ 0
while *i* is less than *VerbCount*
    for *j* going from 0 to 4 as long as *i* is less than *VerbCount*
        print *VerbList[i]*
        increment *i* by 1
    advance to the next line

The function *ReadSentence* reads a sentence, placing words in the array *WordList* and counting the number of words. Moreover, it strips any punctuation from the end of a word. The function detects the completion of a sentence by a word ending with a period.

ReadSentence(WordList, NumWords_ptr)

Function to read a sentence and to put words in an array, without punctuation

Pre:

Post:

WordList is a two-dimensional *char* array of words.
NumWords_ptr is an *int* pointer to number of words in *WordList*.

Algorithm:

cont ← TRUE
print prompt to type a sentence
i ← 0
do the following
   read the next string into *word*
   if there is a period at the end of *word*, it is the last word, so
     cont ← FALSE
   if there is punctuation at the end of the word
     eliminate it
   WordList[i] ← *word* by using *strcpy*
   increment *i* by 1
while *cont* is TRUE
store *i* in the location to which *NumWords_ptr* points
flush the input buffer

To perform the separation of subject and predicate, *ProcessSentence* first prints the line heading "Subject:" and then starts processing and printing each word in *WordList*. The function calls *IsVerb* to determine if a word is a listed verb or not. When it detects the verb, *ProcessSentence* advances to a new line, prints the line heading "Predicate:", and prints the rest of the words in *WordList* without checking if they are verbs or not.

ProcessSentence(WordList, NumWords, VerbList, VerbCount)

Function to put the subject from *WordList* on one line and the predicate on the next

Pre:

WordList is a two-dimensional *char* array of words.
NumWords is the number of words in *WordList*.
VerbList is an array of pointers to strings.
VerbCount is the number of elements in *VerbList*.

Post:

The subject and predicate from *WordList* have been printed on separate lines.

Algorithm:

    InSubject ← *TRUE*
    print "Subject:"
    for *i* going from 0 up to *NumWords* do the following
        if still in subject (*InSubject* is *TRUE*)
            if *WordList*[*i*] is a verb according to *IsVerb*
                InSubject ← *FALSE* because *WordList*[*i*] no longer in subject
                print "Predicate:" on a new line
        print *WordList*[*i*]
    advance printing to the next line

The function *IsVerb* determines if a word is in the list of verbs (*VerbList*) by doing a sequential search. The function *ProcessMore* keeps asking if the user wishes to process more sentences until he or she enters an appropriate response. If the answer begins with y or Y, the function returns *TRUE*, and a start of n or N causes the function to return *FALSE*.

Before presenting the program, we should comment on several pieces of code. We declare *VerbList* to be an array of pointers to strings. To avoid counting the number of verbs, we use the *sizeof* operator to compute *VerbCount*. The expression *sizeof*(*Verb-List*) is the number of bytes in all the array elements. Because *VerbList* is an array of *char* pointers, each element is an address. To determine the number of elements in *VerbList*, we must divide *sizeof*(*VerbList*) by the size of a *char* pointer, as shown:

```
VerbCount = sizeof(VerbList) / sizeof(char *);
```

To determine if the last character in the string (*word*) is a period or another punctuation, *ReadSentence* must examine the character before '\0'. The length of the string is *strlen*(*word*); *word*[*strlen*(*word*)] contains the null character; and *word*[*strlen*-(*word*) - 1] stores the last character in the string. For example, if *word* were "line.", its length would be 5. As Figure 10.21 shows, *word*[5] contains the null character, and the period is in *word*[4]. If we detect punctuation in *word*[*strlen*(*word*) - 1], we place the null character in that element, as shown:

```
word[strlen(word) - 1] = '\0';
```

This assignment eliminates the punctuation and shortens the string by 1. After removing any punctuation, the function copies the string into the appropriate array

Figure 10.21
Word of length
5 with the
punctuation in
element 4

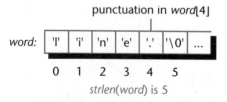

strlen(word) is 5

element, *WordList*[*i*], with *strcpy*. In this implementation, the statement also increments the index *i* by 1 to prepare for the next word, as shown:

```
strcpy(WordList[i++], word);
```

To perform the sequential search for *word* in *VerbList*, *IsVerb* must compare *word*
with each element, *VerbList*[*i*], unitl there is a match. The string comparison *strcmp-*
(*word, VerbList*[*i*]) returns 0 if the strings are the same. Thus, the test for the word being
in a particular element of the verb list is as follows:

```
if (strcmp(word, VerbList[i]) == 0)
```

The complete program follows.

```
/*
 * Example 10.16
 * This program reads sentences, locates their verbs, and
 * displays the subject and predicate (without punctuation)
 * on separate lines. The verb must be in a list of verbs
 * that the program stores. A sentence must end in a period.
 * The sentence is simple--it has one subject and one
 * predicate. Any punctuation immediately follows a word.
 */

#include <stdio.h>
#include <string.h>
#include <ctype.h>

#define PERIOD '.'
#define TRUE   1
#define FALSE  0
#define MAX_NUM_WORDS 50

void directions(char *VerbList[], int VerbCount);
void DisplayVerbs(char *VerbList[], int VerbCount);
void ReadSentence(
        char WordList[MAX_NUM_WORDS][15], int *NumWords_ptr);
void ProcessSentence(char WordList[MAX_NUM_WORDS][15], int NumWords,
        char *VerbList[], int VerbCount);
int ProcessMore(void);

main()
{
    char *VerbList[] =            /* list of verbs */
    {
        "eat", "eats", "ate",
        "run", "runs", "ran",
        "sleep", "sleeps", "slept",
        "laugh", "laughs", "laughed",
        "am", "are", "is", "was", "were"
    };
```

```
    /* number of verbs in VerbList */
    int VerbCount = sizeof(VerbList) / sizeof(char *);
    char WordList[MAX_NUM_WORDS][15]; /* words in sentence */
    int NumWords;              /* number of words in WordList */

    directions(VerbList, VerbCount);
    do
    {
        ReadSentence(WordList, &NumWords);
        ProcessSentence(
            WordList, NumWords, VerbList, VerbCount);
    }
    while (ProcessMore());
}

/*
 * Function to print program directions and verb list
 * Pre:    VerbList is an array of pointers to verbs.
 *         VerbCount is the number of verbs in VerbList.
 * Post:   Directions and a verb list were displayed.
 */

void directions(char *VerbList[], int VerbCount)
{
    printf("This program reads sentences and displays subject\n");
    printf("and predicate on separate lines. The verb must be \n");
    printf("in a list. A sentence must end in a period.\n");
    printf("The sentence has one subject and one predicate.\n");
    printf("Any punctuation immediately follows a word.\n\n");

    DisplayVerbs(VerbList, VerbCount);
}

/*
 * Function to print list of verbs, left-justified, 5 across
 * Pre:    VerbList is an array of pointers to verbs.
 *         VerbCount is the number of verbs in VerbList.
 * Post:   The list of verbs has been printed.
 */

void DisplayVerbs(char *VerbList[], int VerbCount)
{
    int i,        /* index */
        j;        /* index */

    printf("List of verbs:\n");
```

```
    i = 0;
    while(i < VerbCount)
    {
        for(j = 0; j < 5 && i < VerbCount; j++)
            printf("%-12s", VerbList[i++]);
        printf("\n");
    }
}


/*
 * Function to read a sentence and to put words in an array,
 * omitting punctuation. Send the array and number of
 * elements it has to main.
 * Pre:     none
 * Post:    WordList is a two-dimensional char array of words in
 *          the sentence.
 *          NumWords_ptr is an int pointer to number of words
 *          in WordList.
 */

void ReadSentence(
    char WordList[MAX_NUM_WORDS][15], int *NumWords_ptr)
{
    int  cont = TRUE,   /* boolean indicating if still in sentence */
         i;             /* index */
    char word[15];      /* a word in the sentence */

    printf("\nType a sentence:   ");

    i = 0;
    do
    {
        scanf("%s", word);

        /* If period at end of word, it is the last word. */
        if (word[strlen(word) - 1] == PERIOD)
            cont = FALSE;

        /* Eliminate punctuation at the end of a word */
        if (ispunct(word[strlen(word) - 1]))
            word[strlen(word) - 1] = '\0';

        /* Store the word in the array of words */
        strcpy(WordList[i++], word);
    }
    while(cont);
    *NumWords_ptr = i;
    fflush(stdin);
}
```

```
/*
 * Function to receive array of words in sentence and the
 * number of words and to put the subject on one line and the
 * predicate on the next. (See program heading.)
 * Pre:     WordList is a two-dimensional char array of words.
 *          NumWords is the number of words in WordList.
 *          VerbList is an array of pointers to verbs.
 *          VerbCount is the number of verbs in VerbList.
 * Post:    Subject and predicate from WordList have been
 *          displayed on separate lines.
 */

void ProcessSentence(
        char WordList[MAX_NUM_WORDS][15], int NumWords,
        char *VerbList[], int VerbCount)
{
    int IsVerb(char *VerbList[], int VerbCount, char *word);

    int InSubject = TRUE,    /* boolean: TRUE if still in subject */
        i;                   /* index */

     printf("\nSubject:    ");
     for (i = 0; i < NumWords; i++)
     {
         if (InSubject)
             if (IsVerb(VerbList, VerbCount, WordList[i]))
             {
                 InSubject = FALSE;
                 printf("\nPredicate:  ");
             }
         printf("%s ", WordList[i]);
     }
     printf("\n\n");
}

/*
 * Function to return if a word is in the verb list or not
 * Pre:     VerbList is an array of pointers to verbs.
 *          VerbCount is the number of verbs in VerbList.
 *          word is a string.
 * Post:    TRUE was returned if word is in VerbList,
 *          FALSE otherwise.
 */

int IsVerb(char *VerbList[], int VerbCount, char *word)
{
    int i = 0,          /* index */
        verb = FALSE; /* boolean variable for word being a verb */
```

```
    while (i <= VerbCount && !verb)
    {
        if (strcmp(word, VerbList[i]) == 0)
            verb = TRUE;
        else
            i++;
    }
    return verb;
}


/*
 * Function to determine if the user wishes to process more
 * sentences and to return an answer, TRUE or FALSE
 * Pre:    none
 * Post:   TRUE was returned if the user wishes to process
 *         more, FALSE otherwise.
 */

int ProcessMore(void)
{
    char answer[40];    /* answer of wanting to continue or not */

    do
    {
        printf("Would you like to process another sentence? (y/n) ");
        gets(answer);
    }
    while (answer[0] != 'y' && answer[0] != 'Y' &&
           answer[0] != 'n' && answer[0] != 'N');

    return (tolower(answer[0]) == 'y');
}
```

An interactive session shows the elimination of punctuation at the end of words. Moreover, the program correctly splits the sentence into subject and predicate for sentences that have a verb in the list of verbs. If the computer does not find the verb, all the words appear in the subject display.

```
This program reads sentences and displays subject
and predicate on separate lines. The verb must be
in a list. A sentence must end in a period.
The sentence has one subject and one predicate.
Any punctuation immediately follows a word.

List of verbs:
eat          eats         ate          run          runs
ran          sleep        sleeps       slept        laugh
laughs       laughed      am           are          is
was          were
```

```
Type a sentence:   This is a sentence.

Subject:    This
Predicate:  is a sentence

Would you like to process another sentence? (y/n) y

Type a sentence:  Mary and Jim laughed together.

Subject:    Mary and Jim
Predicate:  laughed together

Would you like to process another sentence? (y/n) y

Type a sentence:  She read the book, too.

Subject:    She read the book too

Would you like to process another sentence? (y/n) n
```

Enhancements to the program could involve sorting the list of verbs and performing a binary search of *IsVerb*. Moreover, we could allow the user to enter more or all of the verbs, or the program could read the list of verbs from a file.

Summary

In this section and the last, we discussed six string operations and various applications. The header file *string.h* declares several other string functions, such as searching for the last occurrence of a character (*strchr*) or concatenating at most *n* characters from one string onto the end of another (*strncat*). Consult the documentation for your system for a detailed list. Table 10.3 presents a summary of the functions that we have covered.

Table 10.3 Summary of six string functions

Function	Action	Returns
strcat(ToS, FromS)	Concatenate string *FromS* onto the end of string *ToS*	*ToS*
strchr(s, c)	Find *char c* in string *s*	Pointer to first occurrence of *c* in *s* or *NULL*
strcmp(s1, s2)	Compare lexically strings *s1* and *s2*	If *s1* before *s2*, negative integer; if *s1* the same as *s2*, 0; if *s1* after *s2*, positive integer
strcpy(ToS, FromS)	Copy string *FromS* into string *ToS*	*ToS*
strlen(s)	Length of string *s*	Length of *s*
strstr(s, find)	Find string *find* in string *s*	Pointer to first occurrence of substring in *s* or *NULL*

Section 10.6 Exercises

For each of Exercises 1-3, start with the following declaration-initializations and give the value of any variable that changes.

```
char s1[20] = "well",
     s2[20] = "come",
     *loc;
int comp;
```

1. comp = strcmp(s1, s2);
2. comp = strcmp(s2, s1);
3. comp = strcmp(s1, s1);

Use the declarations from the instructions for Exercises 1–3. Draw a picture of loc and appropriate strings after execution of each statement in Exercises 4–8.

4. loc = strstr(s2, "me");
5. loc = strstr(s1, s2 + 3);
6. loc = strstr(concat(s1, s2), "lco");
7. loc = strchr(s1, 'l');
8. loc = strchr(s1, 'n');
9. Write your own version of *strstr*.
10. Write a function to delete the first occurrence of the string *sub* from the string *str*.
11. Write your own version of *strchr*.
12. Write a segment obtaining a one-character response from the user, and using *strchr*, verify that the answer is 'y', 'Y', 'n', or 'N'.
13. Write a function *ReplaceChr* to replace every occurrence of one character in a string with another. For example, if the string *str* is "appearance", after execution of the following:

    ```
    ReplaceChr(str, 'a', '*');
    ```

    the string is "*ppe*r*nce".
14. Write your own version of the function *strcmp*.
15. Write a routine to perform a selection sort on the list of verbs, *VerbList*, from Example 10.16.
16. Assuming that *VerbList* is sorted, write a binary search version of the function *IsVerb* from Example 10.16.

Section 10.6 Programming Projects

1. Revise Example 10.16 to read the list of verbs from a file with *fscanf*, to allow the user to enter additional verbs, to sort the list *VerbList*, to perform a binary search in *IsVerb*, and to allow the user to view the list of verbs before typing each new sentence.
2. This project is similar to a Free Response question on the *1992 Advanced Placement Examinations in Computer Science*.

Crossword puzzles and some advertisements print two words crossing at a common letter, with one word appearing vertically and the other horizontally. For example, we can print "float" and "double", which share the letter o, as follows:

```
f
l
double
a
t
```

Develop a program that reads pairs of strings that share exactly one letter and print them as described.

3. Develop a program to read a text file that contains several paragraphs of text and to print the file on the screen with appropriate wraparound. In the file, a line return is at the end of each line, and a blank line is between paragraphs. Each line in the file contains exactly 50 characters. Consequently, a word could be split between two lines. The display, however, should not start a new line in the middle of a word. Moreover, the screen display should have up to 80 characters per line.

4. Develop a program to do the following:

   a. Give a prompt and then input a sentence of up to 80 characters.

   b. Reverse the order of the words in the sentence and print out the resulting backwards sentence. You may assume that there is no punctuation in the sentence and that adjacent words are separated by a single space.

   c. Give a prompt and accept a second input string of the form

   ```
   xxxx:yyy:
   ```

   where *xxxx* is a substring of the original sentence and *yyy* is a replacement string. The program should replace the first and the last occurrence of *xxxx* in the original sentence by *yyy*, but leave any other occurrences of *xxxx* unchanged. It should then print the modified sentence.

   Sample Dialogue:

   ```
   PLEASE TYPE IN THE SENTENCE:
   give me some men who are stout hearted men
   men hearted stout are who men some me give

   PLEASE TYPE CHANGE COMMAND:
   me:you:
   give you some men who are stout hearted youn
   ```

5. Develop a program to read in three lines of text without punctuation, and to print out the words of the text in ascending order of their lengths. Words of equal length should be listed in alphabetical order.

6. Develop a program that will accept up to 50 lines of text input and will print out the numbers of lines, words, and characters read. The input should be terminated by a line with three asterisks in the first three columns. For purposes of this problem, a word is considered to be any contiguous string of letters or digits.

Sample run:

```
TYPE INPUT TEXT:
This is the first problem in
the 1988 FDU Programming
Contest. It is easy. The other
ones are probably harder.
***


4 LINES
20 WORDS
108 CHARACTERS
```

7. Pig Latin is an encoding of English words using the following rules:

a. For any word starting with one or more consonants, move the starting consonants to the end of the word and append "ay".

b. For any word starting with a vowel, simply append "way".

Develop a program that will accept up to 10 lines of input from the keyboard, each line being at most 80 characters in length, and translate the input into Pig Latin. Notice that the input may contain such punctuation marks as periods, commas, exclamation points, colons, question marks, apostrophes, and quotation marks. They, as well as spaces and end-of-line characters, should be interpreted as word terminators and should be copied to the output without change. The output lines can be longer than 80 characters. You can assume that all input will be in lower case.

Sample Run of Such a Program:

```
Give input text terminated by a line starting with a car-
riage return:

this is the time for all good men to
come to the aid of their country.
```

```
Pig Latin Translation:

isthay isway ethay imetay orfay allway oodgay enmay otay
omecay otay ethay aidway ofway eirthay ountrycay.
```

Section 10.7   Breadth: Software Life Cycle for Large Systems

Not long ago, the cost of computer hardware was far more significant than that of software. Computers had limited speeds and memories. In this environment, programmers were very conscious of finding tricks to squeeze out every possible cycle and byte. Today, a revolution is occurring, as evidenced by the widespread use of computers, their dramatic increase in memory size and processor speed, and their decrease in cost. Several years ago, experts predicted that about every year-and-a-half the speed and memory size of computers would double, but price ranges would remain about the same. So far this prediction has been fairly accurate. Such increases would involve 20 such doublings over a 30-year period. In this case, speeds and memories would be about $2^{20} = 1,048,576$ times greater than 30 years earlier. If snails could double their speed every year-and-a-half, in 30 years we would have snails that could crawl at 6000 miles per hour!

In this environment, the cost of software production has become far more significant. For example, version 3.0 of Lotus 1-2-3 spreadsheet had 400,000 lines of code, took 263 person-years (the number of years for one person to complete the task), and cost $22,000,000 to complete. More striking are the 25.6 million lines of code in the Space Shuttle software, costing more than a billion dollars and over 22,000 person-years of effort. Some important advancements have occurred in how we approach program development—such as structured programming and object-oriented programming—but these have not occurred as rapidly as those related to hardware. Experts estimated that in 1955 the ratio of software to hardware costs was 15:85. By 1985 this ratio had reversed itself to 85:15. Computer scientists have discovered that application of certain software engineering principles can increase the productivity of programming projects.

A **software engineer** or **systems analyst** is in charge of analysis and preliminary design for a software engineering project. Usually, such a project involves a team of analysts and programmers. The laboratory for this chapter provides some experience of working in teams on a project.

Definition   A **software engineer** or **systems analyst** is in charge of analysis and preliminary design for a software engineering project.

Software engineering encompasses much more than writing code. In fact, the implementation phase is usually only about 10% to 20% of the entire process. On the average, documentation consumes about 30% and correcting errors about 25% of the time. The image of a software engineer or programmer as someone cloistered away in front of a computer screen is incorrect. The systems analyst should have extensive discussions with those who request the project to determine needs and to communicate the team's progress; team members work closely together to develop the project; and the analyst must report to management at critical junctures. Careful investigation of the problem and design of the solution lead to a better system with fewer flaws. Complete documentation increases the likelihood that users can apply the software effectively and programmers can maintain it easily.

The entire process from project inception to product obsolescence is the software life cycle. In earlier chapters, we discussed analysis through the testing phases, with particular emphasis on problem solving for small projects, such as those for a class assignment. In this section, we consider the steps in greater detail as they apply to a large team project. The software life cycle for a large system has the same basic outline as for a small one but includes several more components than discussed earlier:

1. Analysis
   a. Preliminary assessment
   b. Requirements analysis
   c. Requirements specification
2. Design
   a. Preliminary design and planning
   b. Detailed unit design
3. Implementation
   a. Coding
   b. Documentation—internal, user manual, system manual
4. Testing
   a. Unit testing
   b. System testing and integration
5. Maintenance

As the name indicates, the software life cycle is cyclic, not linear. Considerations at one stage often make it necessary to rethink earlier work and cycle back through several steps. Moreover, one phase, such as implementation, might overlap with another, such as testing.

Analysis   Typically, a project begins with a request. The following scenario, which actually occurred, is typical. The Maintenance Department for a college requested that people on campus be able to report maintenance problems through the campus computer system. Members of the department also wanted to view and revise requests, print work orders, and generate reports. Their goals were to shorten the time for successful completion of a maintenance request, to alleviate their paper storage problem, and to obtain better and faster access to information about maintenance problems.

With such a request, **systems analysis** begins, involving preliminary assessment, requirements analysis, and requirements specification. Tasks of systems analysis include investigating the need for the system, determining its feasibility, and specifying its requirements. In the first step of systems analysis, **preliminary assessment**, the data processing manager with the advice of others determines whether the project is feasible. Considering available software, hardware, personnel, prior commitments, and time, is the need for the project sufficient? Of course, the desires of upper-level management can increase the project's priority.

Definitions   **Systems analysis** involves preliminary assessment, requirements analysis, and requirements specification. In **preliminary assessment**, the data processing manager with the advice of others determines whether the project is feasible.

If the organization decides to continue, the manager names a systems analyst to be in charge of the project. In performing a **requirements analysis**, the systems analyst must determine exactly what the users need. More often than not, users do not know their exact needs and do not understand computer jargon. The analyst must communicate effectively to discover the precise requirements of the system and to establish a good working relationship with the clients. He or she must collect, analyze, and organize pertinent information and must determine the precise features and requirements of the system. On the basis of a report from the systems analyst management must again decide whether to continue with the project.

Definition   In performing a **requirements analysis**, the software engineering must determine exactly what the users need.

Assuming management agrees to continue, the software engineer starts on the next part of the software life cycle to produce a **Software Requirements Specification (SRS).** The SRS is a formal document that reviews the needs and gives a detailed, clear description of system requirements. This document is a guide for system design and implementation, but the SRS should not contain algorithms or anything that would prejudice the design. Thus, in producing the SRS, the software engineer should employ one of the basic paradigms of computer science—abstraction.

Definition   The **Software Requirements Specification (SRS)** is a formal document that reviews the needs and gives a detailed, clear description of system requirements.

Several features help clarify the requirements specification. One is a **data flow diagram**, which pictures the flow of information through the system. Figure 10.22 shows the second level of a data flow diagram of the *Maintenance_Supervisor* section of the Maintenance Department's system. The system contains two major sections, one that processes requests for maintenance from students, faculty, and staff across campus and the other (*Maintenance_Supervisor*) that the Maintenance Department uses to manage the requests. The data flow diagram reveals that a member of the Maintenance Department (MD), *User*, can send one of four inquiries to the system:

Figure 10.22   Second level of a data flow diagram of the *Maintenance_ Supervisor*, which is a portion of a system for a college's Maintenance Department

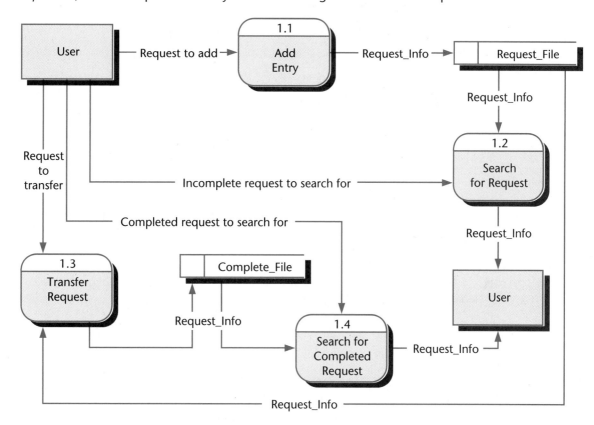

1. Request to add: The MD user may receive a phone call requesting maintenance service. In this case, the MD user wishes to add a request to the file of requests awaiting processing, *Request_File*.

2. Incomplete request to search for: The MD user may need to look at the record, *Request_Info*, of an incomplete job from *Request_File*.

3. Completed request to search for: The MD user may need to refer to the *Request_Info* record of a complete job from *Complete_File*.

4. Request to transfer: Once the MD has serviced the request, the *Request_Info* record should be removed from *Request_File* and copied into the file of completed tasks, *Complete_File*.

The data flow diagram shows the flow of these four inquiries from a *User* block in the top left. Another *User* box receives output of records from the files. The numbered boxes with rounded corners indicate processes or modules that process the inquiries. The two open-ended boxes represent the files—*Request_File* and *Complete_File*. Arrows indicate the flow of the information with which they are labeled. In the same fashion as top-down design of a program, other diagrams show increasing detail on the flow of data through various system parts.

Definition   A **data flow diagram** pictures the flow of information through the system.

Figure 10.23
Part of the data
dictionary for a
system for a
college's
Maintenance
Department

Request_Info
    key_field - array of 23 characters
    Building_Number - integer
    Room_Number
        number - integer
        letter - char
    Priority - integer
    Comment - array of 240 characters
    Time
        year - integer between 1990 and 2050
        month - integer between 1 and 12
        day - integer between 1 and 31
        ⋮

Another feature of an SRS is a **data dictionary**, which contains a list of all data items for the system along with their descriptions. Figure 10.23 shows part of the dictionary entry for the record *Request_Info*, which appears in the data flow diagram of Figure 10.22. In the next chapter, we see how to code such records or structures in C.

> **Definition**   A **data dictionary** contains a list of all data items for the system along with their descriptions.

Other types of diagrams and figures are useful as well. In the 1980s, software engineering teams started using powerful **CASE (Computer-Aided Software Engineering)** tools to help in analysis, design, development, and documentation. Among other features, CASE tools help the team to generate a data flow diagram and to create the data dictionary.

Once the SRS is complete, analysts often conduct a **walkthrough** of the requirements specifications with users and programmers who are not part of the project team. The purpose of this inspection is to find errors in the analysis before starting the design phase. Walkthroughs at this and other stages generally catch about 60% of the errors. Moreover, finding and correcting an error then is likely to be 100 times cheaper than doing so after product delivery. The analyst should return to earlier stages of the software life cycle to correct errors and rethink the analysis.

> **Definition**   A **walkthrough** is a review of the analysis, design, or implementation of all or part of a system. The developer(s) leads the walkthrough, and others ask questions and make suggestions.

Design

The design phase starts with **preliminary design and planning**. We have described and used structure or hierarchy charts in the text. The software engineer employs such charts to depict graphically the system's overall design. Moreover, for each module he or she specifies the output, input, and process. The analyst also names the programmer responsible for a module's development (see Figure 10.24).

At this stage, the systems analyst should enunciate a plan for testing. Next, the analyst must predict the length of time needed to complete each module and the entire project. **Critical path analysis** might be used to determine an order in which the modules must be completed to minimize delays. In the late 1950s the team in charge of building the Polaris missile developed such a method, called **PERT (Program**

Figure 10.24 Module name, description, and programmer as specified in the preliminary design and planning stage.

Module Name: Add_Entry   **Programmer:** Parrott

Module Number: 1.1

Module Description: This module allows the maintenance officials to add an entry to the file of requests that have not been satisfied.

Module Inputs:
Building_Number - integer
Equipment_Number - integer
Room_Number - integer
Priority - integer
Comment - character[80]
Name - character[30]
Time - character[11]
Username - character[30]
Man_Hours - integer
Cost - integer
Type_of_request - integer
Employee_Comment - character[80]

Module Outputs:
Request_File - text file

Evaluation and Review Technique), which resulted in completion of the project two years ahead of schedule. One way of displaying the time table for the components of the system is with a type of bar chart, called a Gantt chart (see Figure 10.25). A system design walkthrough can once again illuminate errors.

Definition   A **Gantt chart** is a time table bar chart.

In the detailed unit design part of the design phase, programmer/analysts might use structure charts and pseudocode to design each module. Frequently, design walkthroughs are conducted for each module.

Implementation and Testing

Only after this point in the project should coding begin. Before starting the implementation and testing phases, each programmer should have a well-documented plan for verifying that the coded module is correct. Thorough testing of each unit in the project is important before integrating all the modules and testing the entire system. For each module, the programmer needs to report carefully on the purpose of the test, the input data, the test results, and the conclusions.

Unit and integrated testing reports are only part of the final documentation for the project. Inevitably, as part of the software life cycle, the SRS changes. Without changing the SRS itself, project members should describe modifications and their rationale so that maintenance programmers do not make the same mistakes. Studies show that about 50% to 70% of professional programming is in maintenance, and probably the greatest difficulties in maintaining systems are the result of poor documentation. The project systems manual for future maintenance programmers should include printouts of well-documented source code for each module. As with our own programs for this course, each module should have a header comment. The comment gives the author; date; a variable dictionary with the name, type, and use of each variable; input and output files; and a narrative description of the module. To help the reader, a comment should accompany each section of code.

Figure 10.25   A Gantt chart

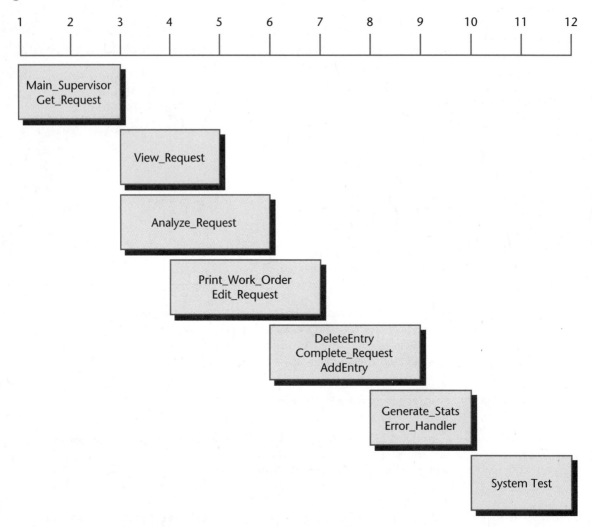

Besides considering maintenance, team members must think about the user if they do not want to waste their extensive amount of work. At every step of the software life cycle, the systems analyst should keep close contacts with those that requested the project. Their input and approval throughout can avert the disaster of development of a system that is not at all what the users want. Moreover, for the customers to learn to use the system quickly, the project team should provide good training and an organized, clear, well-indexed **user's manual**.

Maintenance   At product delivery, the **maintenance** stage begins. Maintenance has three components—correction, adaptation, and improvement. An estimated 20% of maintenance is involved with fixing bugs. Another 25% of the efforts consists of adapting the product to new environments, such as a network or a different computer or operating system. The remaining 55% improves performance or functionality (see Figure 10.26). Frequently, after working with the system, the user realizes that an additional feature

Figure 10.26
Components of maintenance stage

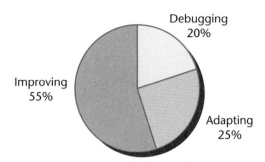

Debugging
20%

Improving
55%

Adapting
25%

would be helpful. The original project team can minimize such requests for user enhancements by obtaining opinions from the user throughout the software life cycle and sometimes by implementing a prototype of the system. A prototype is a trial version that demonstrates some of the functionality and "user friendliness" of the developing system. When the maintenance programmer makes changes, he or she should provide accurate internal and external documentation containing the author and date, as well as the nature of and rationale for the changes.

Definition A prototype is a trial version that demonstrates some of the functionality and "user friendliness" of a developing system.

With careful analysis, sound design, structured development, complete documentation, and a maintenance plan that continues the same quality work, a system should be a valuable product for years.

Section 10.7 Exercises

1. Draw a data flow diagram of the system for class registration at your school.

2. Give a data dictionary for a recent program of yours or of one in the text.

3. As in Figure 10.24, specify the output, input, process, and programmer for a recent function of yours or of one in the text.

4. Draw a Gantt chart for the preparation of a meal.

Programming and Debugging Hints

Verification

In Section 10.4, we presented a powerful validation tool with *atoi*, *atol*, and *atof*. Using one of the string input functions, the program reads input as a string. By examining the individual characters of this string, the computer determines if the input is valid or not. If valid, we use *atoi*, *atol*, or *atof* to convert the data in the string to the required numeric data type.

String Comparison

In Section 10.6, we covered the string comparison function *strcmp*. Suppose two *char* * type variables, *str_ptr1* and *str_ptr2*, point to strings. To test for equality of the strings, we must be very careful not to use the comparison equals. The test

```
if (str_ptr1 == str_ptr2)...
```

compares the values of *str_ptr1* and *str_ptr2*, which are **addresses** of the strings, **not** the strings themselves. Instead, we should use *strcmp*

```
if (strcmp(str_ptr1, str_ptr2) == 0)...
```

to test for equality of the strings to which *str_ptr1* and *str_ptr2* point. We also use *strcmp* to check if one string occurs before the other lexically.

Semicolon and Closing Brace

Perhaps the most frustrating syntax errors that can occur in C are those that take place when we omit a semicolon or closing brace. The compiler flags such errors, but the line identified in the error message might not be the one where the omission occurred. Unfortunately, the compiler cannot detect the missing symbol until one or more lines past the point of error. The error message can also be misleading.

For example, consider the following code, found at the beginning of *main*:

```
int a[] =
{
    "is",
    "are",
    "am"
float b;
```

We can easily spot the error—no closing brace and semicolon that should close the array initializer. Yet the compiler does not detect this omission until encountering the keyword *float*. The compiler is likely to display an error message indicating that an initializer is using an illegal keyword, rather than detecting the true nature of the error.

Another related error, often made by C programmers, is the omission of the semicolon before the *else* clause of an *if* statement. This error is relatively easy to trace. A simple C statement that precedes a closing brace also must end with a semicolon, and an array initializer must have a semicolon **after** the closing brace.

Comment Delimiters

A frequent error involving comments is the omission of the closing delimiter (*/), which can result in unintentionally "commenting out" huge chunks of the program. The compiler indicates an error only when reaching the end of the program and finding no closing to the comment or when detecting the closing delimiter of some other comment. This single error can lead to a cascade of error messages, perhaps none of which refers to a comment at all. Even worse, the compiler may detect no error and merely exclude a series of crucial statements from the program. The omission of the closing delimiter of a comment is harder to trace than the omission of a closing brace, because nested comments do not exist.

Very often, a programmer purposefully places a comment around a series of statements, in order to exclude them temporarily from execution and yet retain the segment for possible use later (simply by removing the comment delimiters). The code can, however, already contain a comment, which interferes. For example, suppose we try to comment out a function *PrintArray* by surrounding it with comment delimiters (/* and */). Unfortunately, if the function contains a comment, the closing delimiter of that comment prematurely terminates the function comment. The following segment shows the function comment with its early end in color.

```
/* ERROR - incorrect attempt to comment out function
void PrintArray(char *text[], int NumEls)
{
    int i;       /* index */

    for (i = 0; i < NumEls; i++)
        :
}
*/
```

The compiler interprets the code following the first opening comment delimiter (/*) as a comment and treats the second opening delimiter (the one to the right of the declaration) as part of the comment. The compiler only recognizes a closing delimiter as a terminator for the comment. Finding one at the end of the line containing the *int i*, the compiler considers subsequent text (the *for* statement) to be part of the program. After the closing brace for the function, the compiler encounters the final closing comment delimiter. Because this delimiter has no match, the compiler flags an error. Depending on the clarity of the compiler's message, the programmer may or may not be able to locate the error quickly.

A better solution is to use the preprocessor directives *#if 0* and *#endif* to begin and end, respectively, a segment we do not want to compile.

```
#if 0
void PrintArray(char *text[], int NumEls)
{
    int i;       /* index */

    for (i = 0; i < NumEls; i++)
        :
}
#endif
```

As with all compiler directives, *#if 0* and *#endif* must appear on lines by themselves. These directives form a structure that is similar to an *if* statement in C. The compiler evaluates the expression after the *#if*, in this case 0. Because the expression is *FALSE* (0), the compiler does not translate into machine language the source code from there to the *#endif* directive. In Chapter 12, we consider these directives in greater detail.

≈≈ **Key Terms**

#endif 617	concatenation 590	*size_t* 585
#if 0 617	*const* 573	strcat 590
%ms 553	*fflush(stdin)* 555	strchr 592
%s 552	fgets 564	strcmp 593
'\0' 550	fputs 562	strcpy 587
atof 578	gets 560	string 550
atoi 577	length of a string 551, 586	string literal 551
atol 578	null character 550	*string.h* 585
BUFSIZ 560	null string 551	strlen 586
*char ** 551	puts 559	strstr 592
character string 550	*sizeof* 585	type qualifier 573

Summary

A string or character string is any group of characters enclosed in quotation marks. C has no string type. The language, however, treats an array of type *char* as a string if the ASCII value 0 (the null character '\0') follows its last meaningful character. We sometimes refer to a character string constant, such as "computer", as a string literal. A quotation mark after a backslash (\") is part of the literal and not a delimiter. A pair of quotation marks with nothing between them is the null string. The length of a string is the number of nonnull characters it contains, so the number of locations needed to store a string is one more than the string's length. The type of a string literal is *char* *. The declaration

```
char str[] = "computer";
```

is an abbreviation for the following declaration:

```
char str[] = {'c', 'o', 'm', 'p', 'u', 't', 'e', 'r', '\0'};
```

To print the string that the *char* array *str* stores, we can use the %s conversion specification with *printf*, such as

```
printf("%s\n", str);
```

Like the other specifications, the string conversion specification can have the format %*m*s, where *m* specifies the field width.

With the conversion specification %s, we can read a string into *str* using a *scanf* statement, as shown:

```
scanf("%s", str);    /* No & before string variable str */
```

Because the array name is a pointer to the first element in the array, we use *str* without a subscript, and no ampersand (&) appears before the array name. We can use a maximum field width with the %s specification in reading a string. For example, for the 10-element *char* array *str*, we use %9s to read no more than 9 characters and ensure against overflow of the array, as shown:

```
scanf("%9s", str);
```

We can read the y/n response into an array of two characters (one for the response, and one for the null character) using the conversion specification %1s, as follows:

```
char ans[2];
⋮
printf("Do you want to continue? (y/n) ");
scanf("%1s", ans);
fflush(stdin);
```

The library function *puts* (put string), which *stdio.h* declares, is a specialized function for printing a string followed by a carriage return to standard output. The following is a call to *puts*:

```
puts(str);
```

The call

```
gets(str);
```

reads characters into *str* from the input stream until encountering the newline character. The function does not place '\n' into *str* but replaces it with the null character to terminate the string. The header file *stdio.h* declares *BUFSIZ* to be the size of the area of memory that holds the input stream. We can declare *str* to be of that length with the following:

```
char str[BUFSIZ];
```

The function *fputs* writes a string to a file, such as

```
fputs(str, outfile_ptr);
```

If *fputs* cannot write the string to the file, the function returns *EOF*. The function *fgets* to read from a file into a string accepts three arguments—the string variable, the maximum number of characters (including '\0') to place in the string, and a pointer to the input file, as shown:

```
fgets(str, 15, infile_ptr);
```

If *fgets* cannot read the string to the file, the function returns *NULL*. Tables 10.1 and 10.2 of Section 10.2 summarize I/O with strings.

We can change the value of pointer variable of type *char **, thereby changing the address that it stores. If a string literal is assigned to that pointer, the string should be treated as a constant. We should not alter the literal through the pointer. We cannot assign (except at declaration-initialization) a string literal to an array. We can, however, alter the string to which an array points. The array contains a variable string.

Besides having a type, a variable can have a type qualifier that indicates additional information about the status of the variable. One such qualifier is *const*, which allows us to define constants. The prototype

```
int stringlength(const char *s);
```

indicates that the function does not change the value to which *s* points.

The detection of erroneous input or validation of data is an important feature of interactive programming. To validate data, we can read an input data item as a string with the *scanf* or *gets* function. We check the string character by character to make sure it is valid. If input is satisfactory, then we can use an ANSI C standard library function—*atoi* (ASCII to *int*), *atol* (ASCII to *long*), or *atof* (ASCII to floating point)—to return the *int*, *long int*, or *double* equivalent, respectively, of the string argument. For example, if *input* is the string containing the user input, which should be an integer, and *num* is of type *int*, we perform the conversion with the following:

```
num = atoi(input);
```

We should also check for overflow. For example, if the input should be an integer, then we should test as follows:

```
if ((atof(input) < INT_MIN) || (atof(input) > INT_MAX))
    /* process overflow error */
```

The ANSI C header file *string.h* includes the definitions of other string functions and of the type *size_t*, which is the type of the value that *sizeof* returns. The *sizeof* operator applied to a type or expression gives the number of storage bytes needed for the operand. For example, *sizeof(float)* or *sizeof(x)* for a *float* variable *x* is the number of bytes to store a floating point value in memory.

The ANSI C string library function *strlen* returns the number of characters (other than '\0') in the string as a value of type *size_t*. Thus, after execution of

```
length = strlen(str);
```

length holds the length of *str*. The function *strcpy* with prototype in *string.h* accomplishes string copying. The statement

```
strcpy(destination, source);
```

copies the string in *source* to *destination*. The function *strcat* replaces the first string variable argument with the concatenation or joining of the two arguments with a call such as

```
strcat(str1, str2);
```

The first parameter to the *strcat* function must be a variable string (an array) and large enough to hold the concatenated string.

One of the basic operations of word processors is to search for the first occurrence of a string in the text. In C, the function call *strstr(str, substr)* returns a pointer to the first occurrence of the string *substr* in the string *str*. Should *substr* not be a substring of *str*, the function returns *NULL*. A similar function call, *strchr(str, ch)*, returns a pointer (or *NULL*) to the first occurrence of a character, *ch*, in a string, *str*. The library function *strcmp* (string compare) accomplishes the comparison of strings by returning an integer. If the first string argument is less than the second, *strcmp* returns a value less than zero. If the first argument is equal to the second, the function returns a zero. If the first is greater than the second, *strcmp* returns an integer greater than zero.

As indicated in the Programming and Debugging Hints section, we can use the preprocessor directives *#if 0* and *#endif* to begin and end, respectively, a segment we do not want to compile, such as

```
#if 0
    ⋮
#endif
```

Review Questions

1. How is a string stored in an array in C?
2. Give the declaration for the array *pref* into which the string "Review Questions" is to be stored.
3. What conversion specification usually is used to read a string?
4. When the conversion specification %s is used in a *scanf* statement to read a string, what is unusual about the way the name of the array is specified?
5. How can one ensure that a *scanf* used to read a string does not read more characters than the corresponding character array can hold?
6. Why is it harder in C to compare strings than numeric values?
7. How can an array of strings be represented in C?
8. When an array of pointers is used to represent a string array, what extra steps must be taken which are not necessary when using a two-dimensional character array?
9. What is another name sometimes given to arrays of type *char*?
10. What type in C corresponds to strings?

11. How is the string "take care" stored in C?

12. How is the end of a string recognized in C?

13. What is the length of the string "take care"?

14. What is another name for a character string expressed as a constant?

15. In what way is a string literal handled differently than an array of type *char*?

16. What is the difference between \" and "\ ?

17. How is a string literal accessed within a program?

18. What is the null string? What is its length?

19. What is a more elaborate way of stating the following?

```
char str[] = "string";
```

20. Describe the purpose of the *strcpy* function.

21. How does the *atoi* function operate?

22. As a general concept, why is the validation of data so important?

23. In what ways are a constant string and a variable string similar?

24. What is meant by concatenation? What function is used to achieve this operation?

25. What is the result of the concatenation of "conca" with "tenation"?

26. What is the restriction regarding the returning of strings by functions?

27. What function returns the length of a string?

28. What is an easy way of locating the end of a string?

29. How can an array of string pointers be initialized? Illustrate your answer with an example.

30. What possible values can the *strcmp* function return, and what do they mean?

31. In ANSI C, how can you declare *E* to be a constant variable with the value 2.71828?

Laboratory

You probably use a text editor, which is a specialized word processor, to create and edit your program source codes. Some text editors provide a **line editing mode** that presents one line at a time and relies on typed line-oriented commands. Most people prefer **screen editing mode**, where they see a screen at a time and can make changes throughout more easily. Because we press return at the end of each line of source code, however, it is feasible to use a line text editor. In this laboratory, we develop some features of a command-driven, line-oriented text editor. In developing these tools, we gain insight into how word processing programs work in general. Because strings of characters make up a program, we rely heavily on the string storage and functions described in the chapter.

The assignment is organized for teams of four members, whom we designate A, B, C, and D. The letter T marks the exercise for the team to do together, and A, B, C, and D designate exercises for the respective team member. Copy file *LAB10.c* onto your disk. This file contains a shell of the program with stubs for all the higher-level modules. The stubs are incomplete. Each team must decide the exact number and order of parameters used by each module.

In this line text editor, the user interactively enters the names of the files to edit and to store the edited results. Possible commands are as follows:

delete line:	d *num*
exit:	e
find string:	f *str*
insert line:	i *num*
	line to insert
list line:	l *num*
substitute:	s/*find*/*replace*

Below is a sample run of a completed program. The program first prompts for an input file. For convenience, the short file *AUX10* is on your disk, but you can edit any file you wish. After loading the file, the program types the line number (1), the first line of the input file, and an asterisk on the next line. The asterisk is a prompt for a command. In this case, the user types the command to find (*f*) a word (*srand*). The program finds the word on line 16, which becomes the current line and the one the computer prints. After another prompt of *, the user types *L* 17 to list line 17 and make it the current line. Then the user lists line 16 and deletes that line with the command *d* 16. The user then inserts a new line 15, whose contents are "/* stub */." With line 15 being the new current line, the user requests to replace "stub" with "STUB." A command of *e* causes the program to display the edited version, to ask for the name of an output file, and to save the revised copy in that file.

```
Give the name of the input file: AUX10

1         /*
*         f srand

16                    srand((unsigned) time((time_t *)NULL));
*         L 17

17          }
*         L 16

16                    srand((unsigned) time((time_t *)NULL));
*         d 16

16          }
*         i 15
/* stub */

15          /* stub */
*         s/stub/STUB
```

```
15        /* STUB */
*        e
  ⋮
void SeedRand(void)
/* STUB */
{
}
  ⋮
Give the name of the output file: temp
```

Figure 10.27 contains the structure diagram for the program. A listing follows.

```
/*
 * This program is a line text editor that is command oriented
 * The user interactively enters the names of the file to edit and
 * where to store the edited results. Possible commands are:
 *
 *      delete line:  d num
 *      exit:         e
 *      find string:  f str
 *      insert line:  i num
 *                    line to be inserted
 *      list line:    l num
 *      substitute:   s/find/replace
 *
```

Figure 10.27 Structure diagram for text editor

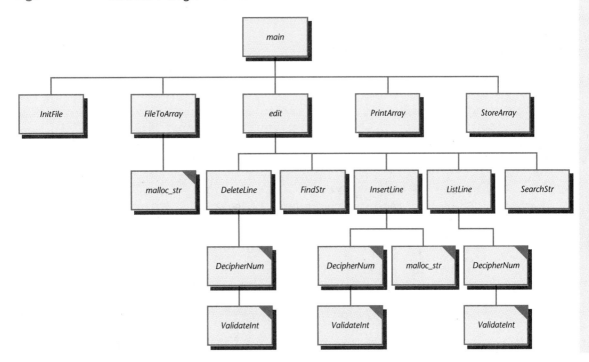

```
 *   Input file of program to edit:   interactively obtained
 *   Output file of edited program:   interactively obtained
 *
 *   Author:
 *   Date:
 */

#include <stdio.h>
#include <string.h>
#include <ctype.h>
#include <stdlib.h>

#define MAX_LINE_CHARS BUFSIZ /* max. num. chars. in string */
#define MAX_NUM_LINES 5 * 24  /* 5 pages of 24 lines each */
#define BLANK ' '
#define TRUE  1
#define FALSE 0

char *malloc_str(void);
int  ValidateInt(void);
void DeleteLine(void);
void DecipherNum(void);
void FindStr(void);
void InsertLine(void);
void ListLine(void);
void SearchStr(void);

main()
{
    FILE *InitFile(void);
    void FileToArray(void);
    void edit(void);
    void PrintArray(void);
    void StoreArray(void);

    FILE *infile_ptr,             /* pointer to input file */
         *outfile_ptr;            /* pointer to output file */
    char *text[MAX_NUM_LINES];    /* array of pointers to lines */
    int NumEls;                   /* number of elements in array */

    /* input file -> array text */
    printf("Give the name of the input file: ");
    infile_ptr = InitFile();
    FileToArray();

    /* edit and print array text */
    edit();
    PrintArray();
```

```
    /* array text -> output file */
    printf("\nGive the name of the output file: ");
    outfile_ptr = InitFile();
    StoreArray();
    fclose(infile_ptr);
    fclose(outfile_ptr);}

/*
 * Function to read name of file and open file in argument mode.
 * If trouble opening, print error message and abort. If not,
 * return file pointer.
 */

FILE *InitFile(void)
{
    printf("\nInitFile is not implemented.\n");
    printf("Press return to continue.\n");
    getchar();
    return NULL;
}

/*
 * Function to read file pointed to by infile_ptr into array text.
 * Send back text and pointer to number of elements, NumEls_ptr.
 */

void FileToArray(void)
{
    printf("\nFileToArray is not implemented.\n");
    printf("Press return to continue.\n");
    getchar();
}

/*
 * Function to malloc space for a string and return a pointer to
 * that area or NULL.
 */

char *malloc_str(void)
{
    printf("\nmalloc_str is not implemented.\n");
    printf("Press return to continue.\n");
    getchar();
    return NULL;
}

/*
 * Function to print array text a page at a time.
 */
```

```c
void PrintArray(void)
{
    printf("\nPrintArray is not implemented.\n");
    printf("Press return to continue.\n");
    getchar();
}

/*
 * Function to edit array with command lines
 */

void edit(void)
{
    int LineNum = 0;   /* current text element number = */
                       /* 1 less than screen line number */
    char command[MAX_LINE_CHARS]; /* line command */

    do
    {
        printf("\nPrint line number and line here\n");
        printf("*\t");
        gets(command);

        switch(command[0])
        {
                        /* delete line */
            case 'd':  /* format: d num */
            case 'D':
                DeleteLine();
                break;

            case 'e':  /* exit */
            case 'E':
                break;
                        /* find string */
            case 'f':  /* format: f str */
            case 'F':
                FindStr();
                break;
                        /* insert line */
            case 'i':  /* format: i num, then line on next line */
            case 'I':
                InsertLine();
                break;
                        /* list line */
            case 'l':  /* format: l num */
            case 'L':
                ListLine();
                break;
                        /* substitute */
            case 's':  /* format: s/findstr/replace */
```

```
                case 'S':
                    SearchStr();
                    break;

                default: printf("Command not valid\n");
            }
        }
    while (command[0] != 'e' && command[0] != 'E');
}

/*
 * Function to find the first occurrence of the string in
 * command line and change the LineNum to that line
 */

void FindStr(void)
{
    printf("\nFindStr is not implemented.\n");
    printf("Press return to continue.\n");
    getchar();
}

/*
 * Function to print line number indicated in command and to change
 * the current line number to be that line.
 */

void ListLine(void)
{
    printf("\nListLine is not implemented.\n");
    printf("Press return to continue.\n");
    getchar();
}

/*
 * Function to determine if RestCommand contains a valid integer
 * which is less than NumEls. If so, make *valid_ptr TRUE and
 * return the number through LineNum_ptr.
 */

void DecipherNum(void)
{
    printf("\nDecipherNum is not implemented.\n");
    printf("Press return to continue.\n");
    getchar();
}

/*
 * Function to validate that integer follows past location *i_ptr
 * in RestCommand
 */
```

```
int ValidateInt(void)
{
    printf("\nValidateInt is not implemented.\n");
    printf("Press return to continue.\n");
    getchar();

    return TRUE;
}

/*
 * Delete function. If RestCommand is empty, delete the present
 * line. Otherwise, delete the indicated line.
 */

void DeleteLine(void)
{
    printf("\nDeleteLine is not implemented.\n");
    printf("Press return to continue.\n");
    getchar();
}

/*
 * Insert function. If RestCommand is empty, insert after present
 * line. Otherwise, insert after the indicated line.
 */

void InsertLine(void)
{
    printf("\nInsertLine is not implemented.\n");
    printf("Press return to continue.\n");
    getchar();
}

/*
 * Function to find the first occurrence of string FindStr in present
 * line and replace it with ReplaceStr. Format in RestCommand
 * should be /FindStr/ReplaceStr
 */

void SearchStr(void)
{
    printf("\nSearchStr is not implemented.\n");
    printf("Press return to continue.\n");
    getchar();
}

/*
 * Function to store array text (without null characters) in file
 * to which outfile_ptr points
 */
```

```
void StoreArray(void)
{
    printf("\nStoreArray is not implemented.\n");
    printf("Press return to continue.\n");
    getchar();
}
```

T. In this exercise, the team develops data structures and black-box analysis of each top-level module.

Notice that *text* is an array of pointers to *char*. After execution of *FileToArray*, each line originally from the input file has an element of *text* pointing to it. For example, *text*[0] points to the first line, *text*[1] to the second, and so on. *NumEls* is the number of elements in *text*.

A description of each module is shown below. As a team, do a black-box analysis of each module and decide the number, type, and order of all parameters. The present listing has *void* for each parameter list in the definition and prototype. Agree on any global constants, types, and variables.

Each team member should properly document his or her modules. Any member who finishes his or her task early should help the rest. All the team members' implementations should be integrated into a working program.

The function *main* of the text editor calls the following functions:

- *InitFile* to read the name of a file interactively and open the file in the mode indicated by the string argument, "r" or "w". If you have trouble opening the file, the function prints an error message and aborts the program. If not, the function returns a file pointer to the file.

- *FileToArray* to place each line of the file in a string and have an element of *text* point to it. The procedure also communicates to the calling function through a pointer, *NumEls_ptr*, the number of elements in *text*.

- *edit* to edit the lines. Edit must send *DeleteLine*, *FindStr*, *InsertLine*, *ListLine*, and *SearchLine* four arguments—*text*, a pointer (*NumEls_ptr*) to *NumEls* from *main* or the dereferenced pointer, the current *text* element number (*LineNum*) or the address of *LineNum*, and a pointer to one or two characters beyond the start of the string *command* containing the user's command.

- *PrintArray* to print the lines to which the array elements of *text* point

- *StoreArray* to save the edited lines of *text* in a file

The functions that *edit* calls are as follows:

- *DeleteLine* to delete a line
- *FindStr* to find a string in the file at or beyond the present line
- *InsertLine* to insert a line
- *ListLine* to change the current line
- *SearchStr* to find and replace a string in the present line
- The functions *FileToArray* and *InsertLine* call *malloc_str* to allocate space for a string parameter, copy the string into that space, and return a pointer to that area.
- The functions *DeleteLine*, *InsertLine*, and *ListLine* call *DecipherNum* to determine if the rest of the command line after d, D, i, I, l, or L contains a valid number and, if valid, to obtain that integer. This function communicates to the calling function

TRUE or *FALSE*, indicating whether the command line contains a valid integer in the proper range of line numbers or not. If the number is valid, *DecipherNum* also communicates the integer to the calling function.

■ *DecipherNum* calls *ValidateInt* to return *TRUE* or *FALSE* indicating whether the command line contains a valid integer or not.

A. This exercise outlines team member A's assignment. You are to write *main*, *ListLine*, *DecipherNum*, and *ValidateInt*.

The other team members need your implementation of *main*.

For testing purposes, you must write a simple version of *DecipherNum* to return the line number in the command. Team members B and D need this version.

The function *ListLine* modifies the current line that the editor displays by changing *LineNum*, the index of the current *text* element.

B. This exercise outlines team member B's assignment. You are to write the modules *InitFile*, *DeleteLine*, and *FindStr*.

The other team members need a preliminary version of *InitFile*, which opens a file for reading or writing. *InitFile* receives a string from the calling function that indicates the mode of the file it will open, such as "r" or "w". Obtaining the name of a file interactively, the function places that name in the *char* array *filename*. After opening the file in the appropriate mode, the code verifies that the *fopen* statement was successful. If not, it prints an error message containing the name of the file and exits the program. If the computer finds the file, the function returns the file pointer.

DeleteLine calls *DecipherNum* to obtain the integer after *i* or *I* in the command line. For example, with the command

```
d 10
```

the user wishes to delete line 10, *text*[9]. Get a preliminary version of *DecipherNum* from team member A. *DeleteLine* moves the values of *text* to eliminate a line and decreases the number of lines that *text* stores. The *int* pointer variable *NumEls_ptr* contains the address of the variable (*NumEls*) in *main* that stores the number of elements in *text*. By decrementing **NumEls_ptr*, the function changes *NumEls* in *main*. Through *edit*, the program reports *NumEls* to *main*.

FindStr searches *text* for the string argument at or beyond the current line. If found, the function changes **LineNum_ptr*.

C. This exercise outlines team member C's assignment. You are to write the modules *FileToArray*, *malloc_ptr*, and *SearchStr*.

The other team members need a preliminary version of *FileToArray*, which copies the lines from the file to the array *text*. Until you receive *InitFile* from team member B, in *main* code opening the input file for reading. Repeatedly, *FileToArray* reads a line from the input file, which we will edit, into variable *line*. The function then calls *malloc_str* to allocate just enough room for the line and to point an element of *text* to that area of memory. Finally, the function copies the line, which *line* contains, into the allocated area of memory. Thus, after execution of the function, each line originally from the input file has an element of *text* pointing to it. For example, *text*[0] points to the first line, *text*[1] to the second, and so on. Figure 10.28 shows the actions of the two functions on the first line from a file. The variable *line* and the area to which *text*[0] points are arrays of characters.

Figure 10.28
Action of
FileToArray and
malloc_str

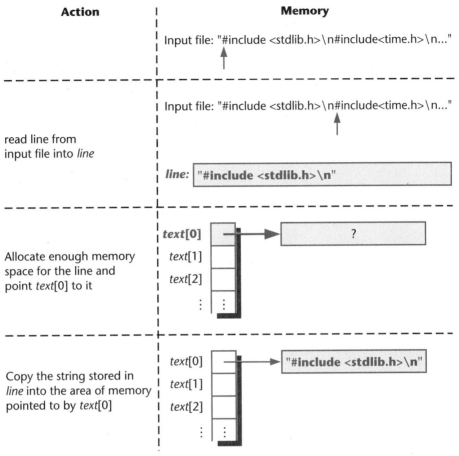

Develop *malloc_ptr* to allocate just enough room for the string parameter, to copy the parameter into that area, and to return a pointer to that area of memory. Team member D needs a copy of this implementation to complete *InsertLine*.

SearchStr is a search-and-replace function. With a command, such as

```
s/stub/STUB
```

SearchStr searches for the first occurrence of the string "stub" in the current line and, if found, replaces the substring with "STUB".

D. This exercise outlines team member D's assignment. You are to finish module *edit* and write the modules *InsertLine*, *StoreArray*, and *PrintArray*.

The other team members need your implementation of *edit*. The function *edit* is the main driver for the editing features. It starts by printing 1 and the first line (to which *text*[0] points) from the input file. On the next line, the function displays * as a prompt for a line command. After reading the command into the *char* array *command*, it determines the command by examining the first character: d or D for delete a line, e or E for exit, f or F for find a string, i or I for insert a line, l or L for list a line, and s or S for find and replace a string in the current line. The program uses a *switch* statement with the first character of the command as the expression to determine which function to execute. Among other arguments, the function *edit* must send each editing routine a pointer to a substring of *command* past the first character. For example, with the command "d 5", *edit* sends *DeleteLine* a pointer to the substring starting one character beyond *d*, " 5". With the command "f srand", *edit* sends *FindStr* a pointer to the substring starting two characters beyond *f*, "srand".

PrintArray and *StoreArray* are for displaying and saving to a file the lines of *text*.

InsertLine calls *DecipherNum* to obtain the integer after *i* or *I* in the command line. For example, with the command

```
i 10
```

the user wishes to insert a new line 10, *text*[9]. Get a preliminary version of *DecipherNum* from team member A. *InsertLine* changes *LineNum*, the index of the current *text* element that the editor displays. The procedure must move subsequent elements of *text* to make room for the new line and must increase the number of lines that *text* stores. The *int* pointer variable *NumEls_ptr* contains the address of the variable (*NumEls*) in *main* that stores the number of elements in *text*. For insertion of the new line in *text*[*LineNum*], *InsertLine* must first call *malloc_ptr* to allocate space for the line and then must perform a string copy to move the text into the allocated area. Get a preliminary version of *malloc_ptr* from team member C.

T. This exercise brings the team members' work together. Copy all modules into a single file and test the system. Correct any errors and note suggestions for improvements.

Structures and User-Defined Types

Introduction

In many real-life situations, it is desirable to store data of different types—say, strings and integers—in one data structure. Perhaps we wish to store a student's name and test grades together. However, we cannot use a single array for this purpose, because elements of an array must be homogeneous, of the same type. This chapter introduces a data structure, called a structure in C, that helps to solve this type of problem. A structure is the implementation of the concept of a record, such as a student's grade record.

Elements of a structure can be heterogeneous, of different types, including arrays and other structures. For example, the name in a student's record is a *char* array. An array can also have elements that are structures. For instance, a gradebook program for a professor might have an array containing student-grade records. When creating a combination of elements to form a structure, it is often useful in a program to define our own type for such a structure.

Files and arrays often contain structures. A record is also a fundamental unit of a database, which is an integrated collection of files. In breadth Section 11.3, we consider traditional file processing and various kinds of databases.

Frequently, we need to pass to a function a reference to a structure instead of the structure itself. Many data structures can be implemented using structures than contain pointers. Thus, we should examine how to manipulate a structure through a pointer.

Several other types are closely related to structures. Enumeration data types allow the manipulation of symbols as new types of constants. The syntax for unions is similar to that for structures, but a union allocates only enough memory to hold the largest member.

In breadth Section 11.7, we develop a computer graphics package, which is an application involving structures. For example, a package might define a structure to hold the coordinates of the top left and bottom right corners of a rectangle.

Goals

To study

- Manipulation of structures
- User-defined types
- Arrays of structures
- Databases
- Pointers to structures
- Parameter passing involving structures
- Enumeration types
- A computer graphics package

Section 11.1 **The Concept of a Structure**

Declaration

Under most circumstances, if all the data elements of a program are of the same type, we can represent them as an array. If the elements are of different types, however, we must use an alternative. In C, we resort to a **structure**, which some languages call a **record**. A structure is a composite type that can represent several different types of data in a single unit. For example, we can represent a single catalog card from a library by the following individual variables:

```
char   title[40];
char   author[20];
float  CatalogNumber;
int    YearPublished;
int    CopyNumber;
```

A single structure can group these variables using the following definition:

```
struct
{
    char   title[40];
    char   author[20];
    float  CatalogNumber;
    int    YearPublished;
    int    CopyNumber;
}
card, PreviousCard;
```

The keyword *struct* specifies a structure definition. After *struct*, braces surround a **template**, which describes the **members** or **elements** of the structure. A member of a structure is a single unit, so the structure here has five members. Some languages or applications call such a member a **field**. Elements *title* and *author* are *char* arrays of 40 and 20 elements, respectively. The member *CatalogNumber* is a *float* variable and the remaining two—*YearPublished* and *CopyNumber*—are *int* variables. Every member of a structure must have its own name and type. We complete the statement by declaring the identifiers *card* and *PreviousCard* to be variables of this type, structure variables with five members. Figure 11.1 pictures the templates and the areas of memory for *card* and *PreviousCard* after compilation.

Reference to Members

Contrary to appearances, the members of a structure—such as *YearPublished*—are not variables. Only when a program declares a structure variable, like *card*, do the members represent locations in memory.

Unlike array indexes, we must name the members of a structure explicitly. To reference a member of a structure variable, we use the variable name with a period and the member name. Thus, to indicate the first integer field in *card*, we use the following:

```
card.YearPublished
```

The period is the **structure member operator** or the **period operator**. We can use each member of the structure like an ordinary variable. For example, after execution of the segment,

```
strcpy(card.title, "The Art of Computer Programming, v. 1");
strcpy(card.author, "Knuth, D. E.");
card.CatalogNumber = 76.6;
card.YearPublished = 1981;
card.CopyNumber = 3;
```

card.author stores "Knuth, D. E.", and the member *CopyNumber* of the structure *card* has the value 3. Once the elements of *card* have values, we can assign the entire structure to *PreviousCard* as a unit with the following:

```
PreviousCard = card;
```

Even if individual members of the structure variable are strings, we can assign the whole variable to another variable of the same type.

Figure 11.1   Memory for variables *card* and *PreviousCard*, structures with five members

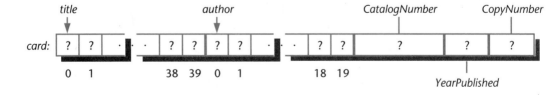

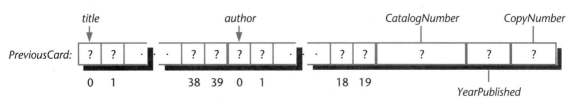

Element by Element

Although we can assign an entire structure at one time, interactively we must read and print the structure variable one element at a time. The period operator has a higher priority than the ampersand operator. Thus, we can read the element &(*card.YearPublished*) as &*card.YearPublished*, as shown:

```
printf("Year published: ");
scanf("%d", &card.YearPublished);
  ⋮
/* printing after reading values for all elements of card */
printf("The structure's values are as follows:");
printf("%s %s %f %d %d\n", card.title, card.author,
        card.CatalogNumber, card.YearPublished,
        card.CopyNumber);
```

We must also perform input and output to a text file element by element.

> The period operator has a higher priority than the ampersand operator.

Just as we cannot read from or write to a text file an entire record, we cannot compare two structures as a unit. Thus, the following two statements are illegal:

```
if (card == PreviousCard) ... /* ERROR - cannot compare records */
if (card <= PreviousCard) ... /* ERROR - cannot compare records */
```

Naming Structures

In any nontrivial program employing structures, we must pass a structure (by reference or value) to a function. Therefore, the function must be able to declare its parameters using the same template as the structure argument. C simplifies this process by allowing a structure template to have a name, the **structure tag**. In subsequent declarations, we can substitute the structure tag for the structure template. This structure name appears between the keyword *struct* and the opening brace of the structure template. The following defines the tag *card_struct* to be a structure template:

```
struct card_struct
{
    char    title[40];
    char    author[20];
    float CatalogNumber;
    int     YearPublished;
    int     CopyNumber;
}
card, PreviousCard;
```

Thus, *struct card_struct* is a new data type, and we can declare a variable, such as *NextCard*, to be of that type, as shown:

```
struct card_struct NextCard;
```

We can use the definition of this new type (*struct card_struct*) in declaring a function parameter. For example, we might declare

```
void PrintRecord(struct card_struct);
```

The function *PrintRecord* expects to receive an argument of type *struct card_struct*. For this call by value, the computer copies the entire structure into the parameter. In Section 11.4, we discuss passing a reference to the structure instead of the structure itself.

The programmer who wishes to use the definition of *struct card_struct* in another function must define the type globally. That is, we must write its definition outside any function body as in the following:

```
#include <stdio.h>

struct card_struct
{
    char  title[40];
    char  author[20];
    float CatalogNumber;
    int   YearPublished;
    int   CopyNumber;
};

main()
{
    struct card_struct card, PreviousCard;
```

The definition of the type *struct card_struct* before *main* does not contain declarations of any variables. Thus, the C syntax demands that we end the structure definition with a semicolon after the closing brace. We can then use type *struct card_struct* in any function of the program, eliminating the need to specify the template again.

Size of a Structure

Because *struct card_struct* is a data type, it can be an operand to the *sizeof* operator. The expression

```
sizeof(struct card_struct)
```

returns the same value as

```
sizeof(card)
```

which in turn is (usually) equal to the sums of the sizes of the individual elements, as shown:

```
40 + 20 + sizeof(float) + sizeof(int) + sizeof(int)
```

The size varies, depending on the number of bytes to store individual members—such as an integer and a floating point number—and storage requirements.

The size of a structure is not always equal to the sum of its parts. A structure may contain unused bytes, which the *sizeof* operator detects. This discrepancy occurs because of a requirement known as **alignment**. For example, some computers require that an integer begin in a byte at a **full word boundary**, or at the start of a new word. A **word** is a unit of storage and transfer in a computer. The computer usually moves information one word at a time. Typical word lengths are one, two, and four bytes. Often in a byte-addressable machine, an address at a full word boundary is divisible by 2. Assume that a structure contains a character followed by an integer, as shown:

```
struct
{
    char c;
    int i;
}
hello;
```

and that the character is at an even address. Assuming the integer must begin at an even address, the compiler inserts an unused byte (with an odd address) between the character and the beginning of the integer so that the integer starts at an even address. Assuming that an integer is 2 bytes long, Figure 11.2 shows memory for this structure.

Definitions A **word** is a unit of storage and transfer in a computer. A computer usually moves information one word at a time. A **full word boundary** is the starting point of a word in memory. **Alignment** on some computers requires that values of certain types begin in certain locations within a word, such as on a full word boundary.

Structure Members

Because a structure can include members of any legal C type, it can also contain other structures. In *struct card_struct*, for example, suppose we wish to record the last date someone borrowed a book. Such a structure might be as follows:

```
struct date_struct
{
    int month;
    int day;
    int year;
};

struct card_struct
{
    char   title[40];
    char   author[20];
    float  CatalogNumber;
    struct date_struct DateBorrowed;
    int    YearPublished;
    int    CopyNumber;
};
```

To access the three members of the *DateBorrowed* member of *card*, we must use the full path, as follows:

```
card.DateBorrowed.month
card.DateBorrowed.day
card.DateBorrowed.year
```

Figure 11.2
Memory for structure with *char c* and *int i*

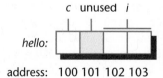

c unused i

hello:

address: 100 101 102 103

When two period operators appear in an expression, we group from right to left. Thus, the first expression is equivalent to

`card.(DateBorrowed.month)`

The field *month* is an element of *DateBorrowed*, which in turn is an element of *card*.

Because of this method of specification, we can have two submembers of the same name if they are part of different substructures. Thus, we could expand *card_struct* to contain the return date, as shown:

```
struct card_struct
{
    char   title[40];
    char   author[20];
    float  CatalogNumber;
    struct date_struct DateBorrowed;
    struct date_struct DateReturned;
    int    YearPublished;
    int    CopyNumber;
};
```

Thus,

`card.DateBorrowed.month`

stores the month in which someone borrowed the book, and

`card.DateReturned.month`

contains the month the person returned the text.

Section 11.1 Exercises

1. a. Define a *struct* type, *address_struct*, that has fields for *name* (30 *char*), *street* (40 *char*), *city* (30 *char*), and *state* (2 *char*).

   b. Declare *OneAddr* and *TwoAddr* to be variables of the type described in Part a.

   c. Write a statement to store a string literal in the *name* element of *OneAddr*.

   d. Write a statement to read interactively a value for the *street* element of *OneAddr*.

   e. Suppose *OneAddr* and *TwoAddr* have values. Write a statement to print "Equal structures" if the variables contain the same information.

2. a. Define a *struct* type, *emp_struct*, that has the following elements: a Social Security Number, *SSN* (string of length 9); *salary* (*float*); *hours* (*float*); and *address* (*struct address_struct* from Exercise 1).

   b. Declare *OneEmp* to be a variable of the type described in Part a.

   c. Assign a value to the *salary* element of *OneEmp*.

   d. Write a statement to read a value for *SSN*.

   e. Write a statement to print the size of variable *OneEmp*.

   f. Suppose the computer requires that floating point and integer numbers begin on full word boundaries and that each word uses 4 bytes. If the storage for *OneEmp* begins at decimal address 1604, what is the location of the salary element?

Section 11.1 Programming Project

Design a structure to store a length in yards, feet and inches (for example, 7 yards, 2 feet, 3 inches). Write a function to find the difference between two measurements as represented by these structures.

Section 11.2 User-Defined Types

C enables the user to define individualized type names with a *typedef* (type definition) statement. If we want *integer_t* be a synonym for *int*, we can write:

```
typedef int integer_t;
```

After this definition, we can use the word *integer_t* anywhere that *int* is legal with the same effect. The *#define* preprocessor directive could perform a similar substitution, except that *typedef* is part of the C language. Furthermore, user-defined types obey the same scope rules as variables. Only the function that defines a type recognizes that type.

Many programmers use the convention of ending a user-defined type, such as *integer_t*, with an underscore and the letter t for "type." Such a naming convention clearly distinguishes user-defined from built-in types.

Example 11.1
_____

In this example, we define *int_ptr_t* to be equivalent to the data type *int ** or pointer to integer. We also declare *a_ptr* and *b_ptr* to be of this type, as shown:

```
typedef int * int_ptr_t;
int_ptr_t a_ptr, b_ptr;
```

The last statement declares *a_ptr* and *b_ptr* as pointers to integer. This declaration is equivalent to the following:

```
int *a_ptr, *b_ptr;
```

The statement

```
int_ptr_t a_ptr, *b_ptr;
```

declares *b_ptr* as a pointer to a pointer to integer. The cast operators associated with these variables are (*int_ptr_t*) and (*int_ptr_t**), respectively.

_____

Example 11.2
_____

Suppose we wish to define *string_t* as a string type. We can use

```
typedef char * string_t;
```

to define *string_t* as a type equivalent to a pointer to *char*, thus making possible the declaration of string pointers as if they were a special data type. Alternately, we could use the following definition:

```
typedef char string_t[10];
```

This definition means that the statement

```
string_t word;
```

declares the variable *word* as a 10-character array. The dimension becomes part of the defined type. The declaration

```
string_t sentence[20];
```

creates a two-dimensional (20 by 10) character array *sentence,* which we can interpret as a 20-element array of type *string_t.*

User-defined types are useful for documentation. A variable of type *char* * could be a pointer to a string or merely to an array of *char*-sized values. A declaration using type *string_t* makes it clear that the variable points to a string.

Example 11.3

Another application of user-defined types gives a single name to a structure. We defined the structure templates *date_struct* and *card_struct* at the end of Section 11.1. In declarations, we must refer to the types *struct date_struct* and *struct card_struct,* as shown:

```
struct date_struct today;
struct card_struct card, PreviousCard;
```

We can define type *card_t* while giving the template and not mention of the structure tag *card_struct.* Similarly, we can define a date type, *date_t,* with the first template and use this definition in the template of *card_t.* Subsequently, we can declare structure variables *card* and *PreviousCard* to be of type *card_t,* which is the same as type *struct card_struct,* as follows:

```
typedef
struct
{
    int month;
    int day;
    int year;
}
date_t;
```

```
typedef
struct
{
    char  title[40];
    char  author[20];
    float CatalogNumber;
    date_t DateBorrowed;
    date_t DateReturned;
    int   YearPublished;
    int   CopyNumber;
}
card_t;

card_t card, PreviousCard;
```

Type Definitions in Header Files

ANSI C specifies that its library header files define several types. For instance, the header file *stdio.h* defines the type *FILE* in a manner similar to the last example. It describes a structure that contains information about an open file.

The header file for time, *time.h*, defines an arithmetic type, *time_t*, to represent calendar time. Some versions of the language define this type as an *unsigned long* integer, as follows:

```
typedef unsigned long time_t;
```

The ANSI C standard specifies the meaning of type *time_t*, but not the implementation. The header file *time.h* for each version of the language defines *time_t* in a *typedef* statement. Thus, programs are more portable. A programmer can use *time_t* in a program developed on one computer knowing that *time.h* defines the type appropriately for the program to run on another computer.

In the same header file is the prototype for *time*, a function that returns the current calendar time, as follows:

```
time_t time(time_t *timer);
```

Besides returning a *time_t* type value, this function also sets the *time_t* type location pointed to by *timer* to the current calendar time. If *timer* is *NULL*, the function only returns a value and does not change a value through its pointer argument.

We have used the function *time* to define *SeedRand*, a function to seed the random number generator with a clock time, as follows:

```
#include <stdlib.h>
#include <time.h>
   ⋮
/*
 * Function to seed the random number generator
 * Pre:    none
 * Post:   Random number generator has been seeded.
 */

void SeedRand(void)
{
    srand((unsigned) time((time_t *)NULL));
}
```

We send *time* the argument *NULL*, type cast to be a pointer to a *time_t* value. Thus, we only expect time to return a value, not to set a value through a pointer. The returned value is the initial seed for *srand*. This function to set the seed for *rand* expects an *unsigned int* argument. Thus, we cast the value that *time* returns to *unsigned*.

Example 11.4

Sometimes we need to delay execution of a program for a certain amount of time. For example, we may wish to leave a page of a report on the screen for a few seconds before displaying the next page, or in computer graphics, we may wish to show one picture for several seconds before presenting another. We can use the function *time* to perform such a delay. We first call *time* and store the value in a variable, *cur_time*. Then we execute a *while* loop with an empty body as long as the present time is less than *cur_time* plus the desired number of delay seconds, *seconds*. We cast the *int* variable *seconds* to *time_t* for the sum, as follows:

```
#include <time.h>
    ⋮
/*
 * Delay seconds number of seconds
 * Pre:      seconds is a positive integer.
 * Post:     Execution was delayed seconds number of seconds.
 */

void DelaySec (int seconds)
{
    time_t cur_time = time((time_t *)NULL);

    while(time((time_t *)NULL) < cur_time + (time_t)seconds);
}
```

Arrays of Structures

The *typedef* can help simplify and clarify code involving composite constructs, such as arrays of structures. In a program using structures to represent a card catalog, it is not sufficient to declare one- or two-structure variables. We need an array, each element of which is a structure of the specified template. Employing the user-defined type *card_t*, we can declare *BookCard* to be an array of 500 structures as follows:

```
card_t BookCard[500];
```

Thus, the fifth element of the array, *BookCard*[4], is a structure. To reference the publication year for this book, we use the name of the array element, the period operator, and the member name of the structure.

```
BookCard[4].YearPublished
```

The title of the fifth book begins with the character

```
BookCard[4].title[0]
```

Example 11.5

This problem is analogous to a supermarket in which a checkout clerk, using a bar code reader, scans each item to access its price. In our program, the user enters the product name and the number of units purchased. The program prints the unit cost of the item and the total cost of the purchase (unit cost times quantity).

The function *main* calls *directions* to print program directions, *InitFile* to obtain a file pointer to an input or an output file, *FileToArray* to copy item prices and names from the file to an array of structures, and *GroceryList* to search for items and print their prices. As Figure 11.3 shows, the structure diagram has only two levels, the one with *main* and the one with the other four functions. Pseudocode for the program follows.

> ### main( )
>
> Program to read grocery items and prices from a file. The user types a sequence of item names and quantities. The program prints the unit price and total price.
>
> ### Algorithm:
>
> call *directions* to print program directions
> prompt for name of input file
> call *InitFile* to read the name of the file, to open it for reading, and to return
>   a file pointer, which *infile_ptr* stores
> call *FileToArray* to copy names and prices from file to array
> close the file
> call *GroceryList* to read items and quantities and print total and unit prices

The function *directions* only prints program directions. *InitFile* declares the variable *filename* to be of type *string_t*; reads the name of a file interactively; opens the file in the mode indicated by the string argument, "r" or "w"; and if no trouble occurs during opening, returns a file pointer to the file.

> ### InitFile(mode) ⟶ file_ptr
>
> Function to read the name of a file and open the file in the argument's mode, "r" or "w". If trouble occurs during opening of the file, the routine prints an error message and aborts program execution. If not, it returns a file pointer.

Figure 11.3
Structure chart for program in Example 11.5

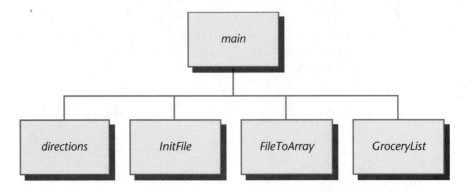

Pre:

mode is a string variable holding "r" or "w".

Post:

The function has returned a file pointer to the input file indicated by the user. If an error opening the file occurred, an error message was printed and program execution was aborted.

Algorithm

read the file name
open the file in mode *mode* and make *file_ptr* the file pointer
if an error opening the file occurred
    print an error message
    abort program execution
return *file_ptr*

Because each line of the input file contains an item price and name, we read these values separately, storing the results in an array element. Each such array element is a structure that can hold this aggregate data.

FileToArray(item, NumEls_ptr, infile_ptr)

Function to read file pointed to by *infile_ptr* into array *item*

Pre:

infile_ptr is a file pointer to the input file.

Post:

item is an array of structures; each element contains name and price.
NumEls_ptr is a pointer to number of elements in *item* (*NumEls* in *main*).

Algorithm:

$i \leftarrow 0$
while not at end of file and enough room exists in the array
    read price from file into *price* member of *item*[i]
    read name from file into *name* member of *item*[i]
    if reading of the name was unsuccessful
        print error message
        abort program execution
    else
        flush input buffer
        increment *i* by 1
if not enough room in array or error reading price
    print error message
    abort program execution
assign *i* to the cell to which *NumEls_ptr* points

The function *GroceryList* repeatedly reads a grocery item name interactively and searches for it sequentially in the *item* array of structures. If the search is successful, the function asks for the quantity and prints the unit and total prices. Pseudocode follows.

GroceryList(*item, NumEls*)

Function to read repeatedly a grocery item and quantity, and search for its name in the item array. If successful, it asks for the quantity and prints the unit and total prices.

Pre:

item is an array of structures; each element contains name and price.
NumEls is the number of elements in array *item*.

Post:

The unit and total prices for each item requested from the item array have been displayed.

Algorithm:

prompt for item name, period to stop
read item name into *SearchName*
while the first character of *SearchName* is not a period
    perform a sequential search for *SearchName* in *item* array
    if *SearchName* is found in the array
        prompt for and read the quantity
        print the unit price from the array
        compute and print the total price
    else
        print that the item was not found
    flush the input buffer
    prompt for item name, period to stop
    read item name into *SearchName*

Before presenting the complete program, we should comment about several details in the function *FileToArray*. The input file has a separate line for each grocery item. A line in the file contains the item's price followed by a blank and the item's name, which may contain blanks, such as

```
2.29 dill pickles
```

The function *fscanf* with %f conversion specification reads a value into the price component of the *i*th *item*, as shown:

```
fscanf(infile_ptr, "%f", &item[i].price)
```

Reading into the *float* variable stops when the computer encounters a character that cannot be part of the number, such as a blank.

We call *getc* to read past the blank, as follows:

```
getc(infile_ptr);
```

The item name, which is next, may contain blanks. Thus, using *fgets*, we read the rest of the line from the file into the *name* component of the *i*th *item*, as shown:

```
fgets(item[i].name, MAX_NUM_CHARS, infile_ptr)
```

Should the last line of the file contain only a price, *fgets* returns *NULL*. We can test for *NULL* and return an error message, should it occur.

This string reading function does have the advantage of reading the rest of a line instead of just one word, but it has the disadvantage of placing the newline character (if present) in the string *item[i].name*. Thus, we should check if the end of the string contains '\n'. If it does, we should replace it with the null character ('\0'). The position in question is one less than the length of the string. For example, suppose, as in Figure 11.4, *item[i].name* contains the word "milk" followed by the newline and null characters. The length of this string is 5, and '\n' is in *item[4].name*. By assigning the null character to *item[4].name*, we shorten the string by one character and, consequently, eliminate the newline character.

```
/*
 * Example 11.5
 * Program to read grocery items and prices from a file. The
 * user types a sequence of item names and quantities, and
 * the program prints the unit price and total price.
 *
 * Input file name read interactively. Each line of the
 * file contains a price and a blank followed immediately
 * by its name
 */

#include <stdio.h>
#include <string.h>
#include <stdlib.h>

#define MAX_NUM_CHARS 21
#define MAX_NUM_ELS 500
#define PERIOD '.'
#define TRUE  1
#define FALSE 0

typedef char string_t[MAX_NUM_CHARS];   /* string type */
```

Figure 11.4
String with newline character at the end

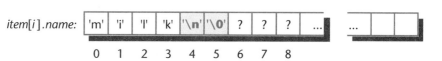

item[i].name:

```
typedef    /* structure type for item name and price */
struct
{
    string_t name;
    float price;
}
el_t;

main()
{
    void directions(void);
    FILE *InitFile(const string_t mode);
    void FileToArray(el_t item[],
            int *NumEls_ptr, FILE *infile_ptr);
    void GroceryList(el_t item[], int NumEls);

    el_t item[MAX_NUM_ELS];   /* array of structures */
                              /* of names and prices */
    int NumEls;               /* number of elements in array item */
    FILE *infile_ptr;         /* pointer to input file */

    directions();
    printf("Give the name of the input file: ");
    infile_ptr = InitFile("r");
    FileToArray(item, &NumEls, infile_ptr);
    fclose(infile_ptr);

    GroceryList(item, NumEls);
}

/*
 * Program directions
 * Pre:    none
 * Post:   Directions were displayed.
 */

void directions(void)
{
    printf("This program reads grocery names and prices\n");
    printf("from a file. The user enters an item name and\n");
    printf("quantity and the program returns the total.\n\n");
}

/*
 * Function to read the name of file and open file in the
 * argument's mode. If trouble opening, print error message
 * and abort. If not, return file pointer.
 * Pre:    mode is a string variable holding "r" or "w".
 * Post:   Error message was displayed or file pointer was
 *         returned.
 */
```

```c
FILE *InitFile(const string_t mode)
{
    FILE *file_ptr;          /* pointer to input file */
    string_t filename;       /* name of file */

    /* read file name and open the file */
    gets(filename);
    file_ptr = fopen(filename, mode);
    if (file_ptr == NULL)
    {
        printf("Error opening file %s.\n", filename);
        exit(1);
    }
    return file_ptr;
}


/*
 * Function to read file pointed to by infile_ptr into array
 * item. Send back item and pointer to number of elements,
 * NumEls_ptr. Data in file assumed to have on each line
 * one price and a blank followed immediately by its name.
 * Pre:    infile_ptr is a file pointer to the input file.
 * Post:   item is an array of structures; each element
 *         contains name and price.
 *         NumEls_ptr is a pointer to number of elements in
 *         item (NumEls in main).
 */

void FileToArray (el_t item[], int *NumEls_ptr,
      FILE *infile_ptr)
{
    int i = 0; /* index */

    /* read price and name from file, store in array */
    while ((i < MAX_NUM_ELS) &&
           (fscanf(infile_ptr, "%f", &item[i].price) == 1))
    {
        getc(infile_ptr); /* read past blank after price */
        if (fgets (item[i].name, MAX_NUM_CHARS, infile_ptr)
              == NULL)
        {
            printf("ERROR: no name for last data item\n");
            exit(1);
        }
        else
        {
            if (item[i].name[strlen(item[i].name) - 1] == '\n')
                item[i].name[strlen(item[i].name) - 1] = '\0';
            fflush(infile_ptr);
            i++;
        }
    }
}
```

```
    if ((i == MAX_NUM_ELS) && !feof(infile_ptr)) /* out of room */
    {
        printf("ERROR: array not large enough\n");
        exit(1);
    }
    else if (!feof(infile_ptr))        /* error reading price */
    {
        printf("ERROR reading price from file\n");
        exit(1);
    }

    *NumEls_ptr = i;
}

/*
 * Function repeatedly to read a grocery item and quantity,
 * search for its name in the item array, retrieve its unit
 * price, read quantity, print unit price and total price.
 * Pre:    item is an array of structures; each element
 *         contains name and price.
 *         NumEls is the number of elements in item.
 * Post:   Quantities and unit prices were printed.
 */

void GroceryList(el_t item[], int NumEls)
{
    string_t SearchName;    /* item name entered by user */
    int i,                  /* index */
        quantity,           /* number of an item */
        found;              /* becomes TRUE if item name in list */

    printf("\nEnter an item name (. to stop): ");
    gets(SearchName);
    while (*SearchName != PERIOD)
    {
        /* sequential search for SearchName in item names */
        found = FALSE;
        i = 0;
        while (!found && i < NumEls)
        {
            if (strcmp(item[i].name, SearchName) == 0)
                found = TRUE;
            else
                i++;
        }
```

```
        if (found)
        {
            printf("Enter quantity: ");
            scanf("%d", &quantity);
            printf("Unit price = $%.2f, ", item[i].price);
            printf("total price = $%.2f.\n",
                    quantity * item[i].price);
        }
        else /* not found */
            printf("\nItem \"%s\" is not in the list.\n",
                    SearchName);

        fflush(stdin);
        printf("\nEnter an item name (. to stop): ");
        gets(SearchName);
    }

    printf("Thank you.\n");
}
```

Suppose the following is the data file grocery.dat:

```
2.29 dill pickles
0.99 soda
0.59 yogurt
1.09 bread
0.69 milk
```

An interactive session might proceed as follows:

```
This program reads grocery names and prices
from a file. The user enters an item name and
quantity and the program returns the total.

Give the name of the input file: grocery.dat

Enter an item name (. to stop): soda
Enter quantity: 4
Unit price = $0.99, total price = $3.96.

Enter an item name (. to stop): bread
Enter quantity: 1
Unit price = $1.09, total price = $1.09.
```

```
Enter an item name (. to stop): yogurt
Enter quantity: 6
Unit price = $0.59, total price = $3.54.

Enter an item name (. to stop): eggs

Item "eggs" is not in the list.

Enter an item name (. to stop): .
Thank you.
```

Section 11.2 Exercises

1. Use *typedef* to define a type, *emp_t*, that is equivalent to a structure containing an array of 30 characters (*name*), a *float* value (*salary*), and an *int* (*age*).

2. Use *typedef* to define a type, *EmpArray_t*, that is an array of *MAX_NUM_ELS* number of structures of type *emp_t* from Exercise 1.

3. **a.** Declare *EmpArray* to be an array of type *EmpArray_t* from Exercise 2.

   b. Write a statement to print the name and salary of the tenth employee in the array.

   c. Give the code for the first letter of that employee's name.

   d. Write a statement to shorten the employee's name by one letter.

   e. Write a statement to increase that employee's salary by 10%.

4. Use *typedef* to define a type that is equivalent to an array of 15 pointers to a structure whose members are promotion exam records—*name*, *age*, *score1*, and *score2*.

5. Write a procedure to wait for the user to press return for no more than the number of seconds that a parameter designates. If the user does not press return in the time limit, display a message that time has expired.

Section 11.2 Programming Projects

1. Revise Example 11.5 to write a report of the item names, unit prices, and total prices to a file instead of to the screen. Print the sum of all the prices, the tax (at 5%), and the final bill. Write messages about an item not being in the list to another file, called an **exceptions report**.

2. Write a program to implement the card catalog system used as an example at the beginning of this chapter. The program should be able to handle browsing through the catalog; searching for a particular title, author, or catalog number; the borrowing and returning of books; charging of late fines; and acquisition of new titles. Use modular programming techniques to add one feature at a time.

3. Revise the program in Example 5.16 of Section 5.4 to require the user to guess the correct number in the guessing game in a certain amount of time.

4. Revise Chapter 7 Laboratory Exercise 1 to require that the user give an answer in a certain amount of time.

5. Revise Project 3 from Section 7.2 to leave the answer on the screen for a fixed amount of time before clearing the screen and asking if the user wishes to process another integer.

6. Write a program that simulates the operation of a vending machine. The machine should sell the following items at the indicated prices:

Mr. Goodbar	$0.65	Hershey Kisses	$0.70
M & Ms	0.60	Kracker Jacks	0.80
Potato Chips	0.40	Oreos	0.55
Chewing Gum	0.20	Fritos	0.45
Pretzels	0.45	Milky Way	0.65

Initially, the machine should ask the user how many items of each type it should hold. The machine should also have a change maker containing nickels, dimes, and quarters. At the beginning, the user should be asked to specify how many of each the change maker should contain. The program should show the list of available items with their prices. If the machine is out of any item, it should show "OUT" for the price of that item. The machine should then ask the user to insert money in the form of a dollar bill or quarters, dimes, and nickels and ask for the number of the item desired. If the money inserted was less than the price of the item requested, the machine cannot dispense the appropriate amount of change, or the user requested an invalid item, the money should be returned with an appropriate error message, and the process should start over from the beginning. Otherwise, the machine should dispense the item together with any appropriate change. In making change, the machine should use as few coins as possible. At the end of the program run, the program should indicate how many of each item being sold remain in the machine and how many dollars, quarters, dimes and nickels are in the change maker.

The following is a sample run of such a program with input underlined:

```
How many of each of the ten items should I start with?
1 1 1 1 1 1 1 1 1 1
How many nickels, dimes, and quarters should I have?
3 3 3

Please type 1 to make a purchase or 0 to stop: 1

1.  Mr. Goodbar      0.65
2.  M & Ms           0.60
3.  Potato Chips      0.40
4.  Chewing Gum       0.20
5.  Pretzels          0.45
6.  Hershey Kisses    0.70
7.  Kracker Jacks     0.80
8.  Oreos             0.55
9.  Fritos            0.45
10. Milky Way         0.65

Indicate how many are being inserted:
Dollar (0 or 1): 1
Quarters: 0
Dimes: 0
Nickels: 0
Indicate number of item to be purchased: 4
```

```
Dispensing one Chewing Gum
Returning 3 quarters
Returning 1 nickels

Please type 1 to make a purchase or 0 to stop: 1

1.  Mr. Goodbar        0.65
2.  M & Ms             0.60
3.  Potato Chips       0.40
4.  Chewing Gum        OUT
5.  Pretzels           0.45
6.  Hershey Kisses     0.70
7.  Kracker Jacks      0.80
8.  Oreos              0.55
9.  Fritos             0.45
10. Milky Way          0.65

Indicate how many are being inserted:
Dollar (0 or 1): 1
Quarters: 0
Dimes: 0
Nickels: 0
Indicate number of item to be purchased: 5
Exact Change Needed. Please try again
Returning 1 dollar

Please type 1 to make a purchase or 0 to stop: 0

Items Remaining:

1.  Mr. Goodbar        1
2.  M & Ms             1
3.  Potato Chips       1
4.  Chewing Gum        0
5.  Pretzels           1
6.  Hershey Kisses     1
7.  Kracker Jacks      1
8.  Oreos              1
9.  Fritos             1
10. Milky Way          1

Money in Change Maker:

1 Dollar
0 Quarters
3 Dimes
2 Nickels
```

Section 11.3 Breadth: Databases

An organization, such as a school, usually needs to access enormous amounts of information about its people, facilities, and inventory. For example the registrar must maintain each student's name, Social Security Number, addresses, phone numbers, advisor, this semester's course work, and general academic record. The housing office wants access to the first four items, along with billing information and meal plan. The financial aid office also requires the four main items and a detailed financial report. The registrar must create rolls with names of the students and the professor for each class. The personnel department has to access information about the professors and staff. Besides catalog information, the library needs the addresses and book acquisitions of each person connected with the school.

If the school stored all of these data in separate files, a change in an address would result in updating several different files. Inevitably, a case would occur in which the address would be correct in one place, but not another. Moreover, the housing office would need to consult three different files to verify that a student is carrying enough hours to live on campus and has a financial aid grant to pay the bills. We do not want to give that office the ability to see or change a student's grades. The solution to this complex interaction of data is to store the information in a database instead of in separate files. A **database** is an integrated collection of files. Data are placed in the database only once with methods of interrelation and retrieval of the information in many different forms.

> **Definition** A **database** is an integrated collection of files.

Traditional File Processing

To appreciate the advantages of databases, we consider in detail some problems associated with traditional file processing. Since Chapter 7, we have retrieved from files to eliminate tedious retyping of data and have stored in files to keep our results in electronic form. When organizations started buying computers in the 1950s and 60s, they appreciated the ability to store huge volumes of information on files and to reduce the cost, time, and errors inherent with manual processing. As computer use grew, however, problems with file processing became apparent. Personnel who could appreciate the power of the computer demanded more processing and different combinations of the data in files. The end user, however, usually did not know how to program and could not add the new features. Requests flooded into already overworked data processing departments.

Realizing the capabilities, the housing office might request a match of information in files from three offices—housing, registrar, and financial aid. Two difficulties can arise in such a situation. Someone must write a program to handle matching data from all the files. Moreover, because programmers create files independently, some fields, which should hold the same information, might have different formats. The lengths could be different, or one field could be of type *float* and another of type *double*. We say that a **data inconsistency** between the files exists.

> **Definition** **Data inconsistency** between files occurs if the same data are stored in different formats in two files or if data must be matched between files.

Some files duplicate some of the data, such as names and addresses. These **redundant data** compromise **data integrity**. In other words, we have the possibility of a value being changed in one file, but not in another. Many times, such inconsistencies are difficult and expensive to rectify.

Definitions   **Redundant data** are duplicated between files. **Data integrity** is the assurance that data are correct.

Related to this need for multiple file access is the problem of **data security** in traditional file processing. Using the registrar's file, personnel in the housing office only need to ascertain the number of hours each student is carrying. They should not have the authority to check or change grades. They may also need to determine if the student has a grant, but they should not be able to view the family's financial history.

Definition   **Data security** refers to data being protected so that only authorized personnel can access them.

Another problem arises from the occasional requirement to change the structure of a file, perhaps to add or adjust a field. For example, a few years ago ZIP codes expanded from five characters to nine. The school's data processing department had to change every program that accessed ZIP codes for students, faculty, or staff. We say that traditional file processing suffers from **data dependence**.

Definition   **Data dependence** occurs if the format of the data storage is dependent on the application program.

We summarize the difficulties with traditional file processing as follows:

1. Necessity of programming to access the data
2. Data inconsistency
3. Redundant data's compromise of data integrity
4. Lack of data security
5. Data dependence

Database Management System

Starting in the late 1960s **database management system** (**DBMS**) software was developed to facilitate formation, manipulation, and maintenance of databases. A DBMS contains two major functional parts—a data manipulation language and a data definition language. End users employ the **data manipulation language** (**DML**) or **query language** to access and update data in the database. This language is usually very high level, so the user does not need to be a programmer to manipulate the data. Database managers, system engineers, and programmers use the **data definition language** (**DDL**) to design and maintain the database. With the DDL, they define the structure of the database; they develop a **data dictionary**, which contains a list of the data names, types, lengths, and locations; and they establish system security. A schema is a description of the overall database structure, and a subschema holds the definition of part of the data described in the schema. Through the use of subschema, the database administrator can control access to the data. If the housing office only needs to access students' housing, billing, and meal plan information, the subschema for the housing office contains only these items. Thus, the housing office staff has a simplified view of the database, and they cannot accidentally or maliciously access or change data outside their purview.

Definitions A **database management system** (**DBMS**) is database software that contains two major functional parts—a **data manipulation language** (**DML**) or **query language** to access and update data in the database and a **data definition language** (**DDL**) to design and maintain the database. A **schema** is a description of the overall database structure, and a **subschema** holds the definition of part of the data described in the schema.

Three major types of DBMS exist—hierarchical, network, and relational. A hierarchical DBMS maintains a tree-like structure of data, much like the hierarchy diagram of a structure chart. A network database has more involved connections, like the view of U.S. airline routes. Both models, developed in the late 1960s, have complex data definition and manipulation languages. Moreover, the database definition establishes relationships among the data. Thus, queries into the database are restricted to those permitted by these relationships. The hierarchical and network databases are not very flexible in allowing new ways of navigating the system. Many organizations still use such DBMSs, but we should wait to consider them further until we cover trees and graphs in data structures.

Relational Database

In the 1970s, the relational database model was developed, based on mathematical principles. Not only are its DDL and DML simple, but relational databases do not restrict queries to prearranged interrelationships of the data. This powerful system had limited use at first because of the insufficient speed and memories of computers. Advances in hardware, however, have now made relational databases attractive for microcomputers and mainframes alike.

The designer of a relational database establishes relations, or two-dimensional tables of data. Various attributes, which correspond to the columns in a table, are like elements or fields in a C structure. The domain of an attribute, as with the domain of a function in mathematics, is the set of all possible values of that attribute. Thus, for a Social Security Number (SSN) attribute, the domain might be the set of all 9-digit character strings. A tuple is like a row in a table or a particular value of a structure variable. For example, suppose the relation *StudentAddr* has the structure

(SSN, *name, address1, address2, city, state, zip, phone*)

with the attributes SSN, *name, address1, address2, city, state, zip,* and *phone*. Figure 11.5 displays part of this relation containing the student address information. In this relation, one tuple is

("123456789", "Mary Smith", "123 Baker Rd.", , "Atlanta", "GA", "30342", "(404)555-2345")

Figure 11.5   Part of the relation *StudentAddr*

SSN	name	address1	address2	city	state	zip	phone
123456789	Mary Smith	123 Baker Rd.		Atlanta	GA	30342	(404)555-2345
946573218	Jim Hodges	847 El Dorado		San Ramone	CA	94583	(510)555-9876
565324884	B.H. Hall	Apt. 12	4424 Center St.	Spartanburg	SC	29303	(803)555-3838
⋮	⋮	⋮	⋮	⋮	⋮	⋮	⋮

Definitions   The **relational database model** is based on mathematical principles. A **relation** is a two-dimensional table of data. An **attribute** corresponds to a column in a relation. The **domain** of an attribute is the set of all possible values of that attribute. A **tuple** corresponds to a row in a relation.

Suppose for each semester there is a relation like *FinancialFall98* for those receiving aid in the fall of 1998. The structure of this relation might be

(*SSN*, *grant*, *income*)

and the relation might be as in Figure 11.6.

Using mathematical operations, we can form new relations from existing ones. The **SELECT** command in the DML takes a subset of the set of tuples (rows) in a relation (table). For example, to obtain a table, *CAStudentAddress*, of the address information for all students from California, we would write a statement similar to the following:

CAStudentAddress ← SELECT FROM *StudentAddr* WHERE *state* = "CA"

The resulting relation would be like that of Figure 11.7.

The **PROJECT** command takes a subset of the attribute values (columns) in a table, which in mathematics is a projection of the relation. For instance, we might be

Figure 11.6
Part of the relation *FinancialFall98*

SSN	grant	income
946573218	$4,000	$56,900
123456789		$120,350
657982253	$10,000	$38,200
⋮	⋮	⋮

Figure 11.7   Part of the relation *CAStudentAddress*

SSN	name	address1	address2	city	state	zip	phone
946573218	Jim Hodges	847 El Dorado		San Ramone	CA	94583	(510)555-9876
⋮	⋮	⋮	⋮	⋮	⋮	⋮	⋮

Figure 11.8
Part of the
relation
NamePhone

name	phone
Mary Smith	(404)555-2345
Jim Hodges	(510)555-9876
B.H. Hall	(803)555-3838
⋮	⋮

Figure 11.9 Part of the relation *AddrFinancialFall98*

SSN	name	address1	address2	city	state	zip	phone	grant	income
123456789	Mary Smith	123 Baker Rd.		Atlanta	GA	30342	(404)555-2345		$120,350
946573218	Jim Hodges	847 El Dorado		San Ramone	CA	94583	(510)555-9876	$4,000	$56,900
565324884	B.H. Hall	Apt. 12	4 Elm St.	Spartanburg	SC	29303	(803)555-3838	$7,000	$63,500
657982253	Ann May	654 Main St.		Richland	WA	94550	(912)555-8329	$10,000	$38,200
⋮	⋮	⋮	⋮	⋮	⋮	⋮	⋮	⋮	⋮

interested in obtaining a report of the names and phone numbers of all students. To do so, we create a *NamePhone* relation, as follows:

> *NamePhone* ← PROJECT *name, phone* FROM *StudentAddr*

Figure 11.8 displays part of the *NamePhone* relation. If we only want the names and phone numbers of students from California, we would perform the projection on *CAStudentAddress* instead of *StudentAddr*.

We can also take the union of the columns from several tables with the **JOIN** operation. For example, we can form a new relation, *AddrFinancialFall98*, with all the information from *StudentAddr* and *FinancialFall98* matched by Social Security Number.

> *AddrFinancialFall98* ← JOIN *StudentAddr* AND *FinancialFall98* WHERE
> *StudentAddr.SSN* = *FinancialFall98.SSN*

Notice we specify to which relation *SSN* belongs by using a syntax similar to that of structures. Figure 11.9 shows the result of such an operation.

With its powerful ability to restructure data in any number of ways and its relative ease of use, relational databases have become popular. Some examples of such databases are DB2 for IBM mainframe computers, Oracle and Sybase for UNIX systems, Paradox for IBM PCs, and 4th Dimension for the Macintosh.

Section 11.3 Exercises

1. Suppose for this semester a relation *Course* stores the courses each student takes with an attribute structure of (*SSN, course*). Give part of this relation, containing information for you and a friend. Note that each *SSN* appears several times with different courses in the relation.

2. For the relations *StudentAddr*, sketch the table that is formed as a result of each of the following commands:

   a. *A* ← SELECT FROM *StudentAddr* WHERE *zip* = "30342"

   b. *B* ← PROJECT *SSN*, *grant* FROM *FinancialFall98*

   c. *C* ← JOIN *A* AND *B* WHERE *A.SSN* = *B.SSN*

3. How is data integrity preserved in a relational database?

4. How is data consistency preserved in a relational database?

5. How is data independence preserved in a relational database?

In the following exercises, write relational database commands to create the relations:

6. A relation with the *name* and *state* columns from *StudentAddr*

7. A relation with the records from *FinancialFall98* of those students having a grant of more than $2000

8. A relation with the *SSN* and *name* attributes from *StudentAddr* and the *grant* attribute from *FinancialFall98*

Section 11.3 Programming Projects

1. Write a program to read from a file that has the data of *StudentAddr* into an array of structures. Write routines that perform the SELECT and PROJECT operations. In a menu, give the user the option of performing any combination of these operations, printing and/or storing the results on disk.

2. Write a program that reads *StudentAddr* information from one file and *FinancialFall98* information from another. The information in the files should be ordered by Social Security Number (SSN). Construct a report having all the information from *StudentAddr* and *FinancialFall98*, matched by SSN. Thus, this report is the join of the information from the two files. Have an exceptions report of SSNs that appear in one file but not the other.

Section 11.4 Pointers and Structures

Passing a Structure Reference

Quite often, a structure is very large, and pass by value to a function requires a great deal of copying. For example, suppose a particular computer stores an integer in two bytes and a floating point number in four, and the variable *card* is of user-defined type *card_t* from Example 11.3 of Section 11.2. To pass *card* as an argument to a function, the computer must copy at least 74 bytes. When an array is in a structure that is an argument to a function, the computer copies the entire array into the function. Some computers may not have enough room for a copy of a structure with large embedded arrays. Some versions of C even restrict the size of such a copy. Moreover, because C uses pass by value, the called function cannot change the value of the structure argument.

Thus, we should pass a reference to the structure instead of the structure itself. For example, the prototype of a function that updates the structure variable might read as follows:

```
void ChangeCard(card_t *card_ptr);
```

In this situation, we pass the starting address of the structure to the function, such as

```
ChangeCard(&card);
```

Dereferencing Suppose in function *ChangeCard* we wish to change the value of the *CopyNumber* member to 5 using the indirection operator on *card_ptr*. The period operator has a higher priority than *, so we must be careful to use parentheses to override this precedence, as follows:

```
(*card_ptr).CopyNumber = 5;
```

Without parentheses

```
*card_ptr.CopyNumber = 5;   /* ERROR */
```

is equivalent to

```
*(card_ptr.CopyNumber) = 5;   /* ERROR */
```

These two statements attempt to change the value to which *card_ptr.CopyNumber* points. The variable *card_ptr*, however, is of pointer type *card_t **, not of the structure type *card_t*, and *card_ptr* has no fields.

> The period operator has a higher priority than the indirection operator (*).

ANSI C provides a clearer way of referencing the fields of the structure to which *card_ptr* points. By using an **arrow operator**, -> (dash and greater than), we can replace

```
(*card_ptr).CopyNumber
```

with

```
card_ptr -> CopyNumber
```

The arrow operator has the same high precedence as the unary operators period, parentheses, and brackets. Moreover, the unary operators associate right to left; if two unary operators are in an expression, the computer performs the right unary operation first. Thus, to reference the month-borrowed field in the *card* structure, we can use

```
card_ptr -> DateBorrowed.month
```

which is equivalent to

```
card_ptr -> (DateBorrowed.month)
```

Table 11.1 presents the precedence of operators we have covered so far.

> The arrow operator has the same high precedence as the unary operators period, parentheses, and brackets.

Table 11.1 Precedence of operators in descending order

()	[]	.	->						
!	– (unary)	+ (unary)	& (address)	++	--	* (indirection)	*sizeof*	*(type)*	
*	/	%							
+	– (binary)								
<	<=	>	>=						
==	!=								
&&									
||									
=	+=	–=	*=	/=	%=				

Example 11.6

We can pass the address of an individual element to a function instead of the address of the structure. For example, suppose the function *read_int* reads a positive integer and communicates the value to the calling function through a pointer, as follows:

```
/*
 * Procedure to read interactively a positive integer and
 * communicate that value to the calling function
 * Pre:    none
 * Post:   *int_ptr is a positive integer
 */

void read_int(int *int_ptr)
{
    do
    {
        printf("Enter a positive integer: ");
        scanf("%d", int_ptr);
    }
    while (*int_ptr <= 0);
}
```

The call to *read_int* to change the value of *card.CopyNumber* is

```
read_int(&card.CopyNumber);
```

Because the period operator has higher priority than the ampersand operator, the call is equivalent to the following:

```
read_int(&(card.CopyNumber));
```

We are sending the address of the *CopyNumber* field of *card* to *read_int*.

In ANSI C, we can pass a pointer to a structure or the structure itself to a function. Moreover, the function can return either type of values. Particularly if the structure is small so that there is little copying in the pass by value, clarity and convenience become more important than efficiency.

Example 11.7

A rational number is a number that we can write in the form *a/b*, where *a* and *b* are integers and *b* is nonzero. For example, 1/2, 3 = 3/1, and −5/4 are rational numbers. To store the numerator and denominator together but as separate integers, we use a structure. With *typedef*, we define *rational_t* as the type of this structure template, as follows:

```
typedef
struct
{
    int numerator;
    int denominator;
}
rational_t;
```

We can define a function *QMult* to return the product of two rational numbers. An arithmetic example of what we do in C follows:

$$\frac{2}{5} \times \frac{3}{7} = \frac{6}{35}$$

Ignoring reducing the fraction, the function multiplies numerator structure elements together and denominators together.

The function *main* is a driver for the function. For illustration purposes, *read_int* from the last example obtains positive integer parts for two rational numbers. Receiving these structures as arguments, *QMult* computes and returns the product, which *main* prints.

```
/*
 * Example 11.7 Program to read 2 rational numbers with positive
 * numerators and denominators. The program then computes and
 * prints their product. The numbers are not necessarily in
 * lowest terms.
 */

#include <stdio.h>

typedef      /* structure type for a rational number*/
struct
{
    int numerator;
    int denominator;
}
rational_t;

void read_int(int *int_ptr);
rational_t QMult(rational_t op1, rational_t op2);
```

```
main()
{
    rational_t a, b, c;

    printf("Enter numerator and denominator of a fraction:\n");
    read_int(&a.numerator);
    read_int(&a.denominator);

    printf("\nEnter numerator and denominator of a fraction:\n");
    read_int(&b.numerator);
    read_int(&b.denominator);

    c = QMult(a, b);
    printf("\nproduct = %d/%d\n", c.numerator, c.denominator);
}

/*
 * Procedure to return the product of two rational numbers.
 * The result is not reduced.
 * Pre:     op1 and op2 represent valid rational numbers.
 * Post:    The product of op1 and op2 has been returned.
 */

rational_t QMult(rational_t op1, rational_t op2)
{
    rational_t result;    /* rational number product */

    result.numerator   = op1.numerator   * op2.numerator;
    result.denominator = op1.denominator * op2.denominator;

    return result;
}

/**** Place read_int definition from last example here ****/
```

An interactive session that mimics the above arithmetic example follows:

```
Enter numerator and denominator of a fraction:
Enter a positive integer: 2
Enter a positive integer: 5

Enter numerator and denominator of a fraction:
Enter a positive integer: 3
Enter a positive integer: 7

product = 6/35
```

Although the computer copies the entire structure for the operands, these arguments are small. Thus, the maneuver consumes very little time and space. The code is also more straightforward than a comparable program using pointers.

QMult is only one function in a package of rational number operations. Such a package could contain a function to accept a rational number argument and return an equivalent number, where the numerator and denominator have no common factor. For example, this function would accept a representation of the number 10/18 and return a structure representing 5/9. One improvement to *QMult* would be for it to call the function to reduce *result* to lowest terms before returning the structure. In the next chapter, we see how to assemble a package, such as one for rational numbers, into a separately compiled file that many functions can access.

Linked Lists

The one restriction on structure nesting is that a structure cannot contain an image of itself. In other words, a structure cannot contain a member defined with the same tag as the outside structure. However, a structure can contain a pointer to a structure of the same type, as shown here in an extension to the grocery problem of Example 11.5 (Section 11.2):

```
typedef     /* structure type for item name and price */
struct
{
    string_t name;
    float price;
}
el_t;
typedef struct node node_t;
typedef node_t * pointer_t;

struct node     /* structure with item and pointer */
{
    el_t el;
    pointer_t next;
};
```

Each *node* structure contains a member, *next*, that is a pointer to another *node* structure. We use the member *next* to point to the *node* structure that logically follows it in the grocery list. That structure in turn points to the one following it, and so forth. The structures that make up the grocery list, therefore, are linked together in a chain. Figure 11.10 pictures such a chain with a pointer *head* pointing to the first node. We call the chain a **linked list** and a single element a **node**.

Figure 11.10 Linked list of nodes with grocery information

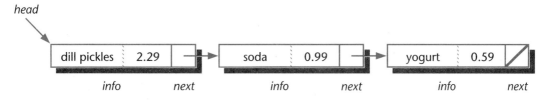

Figure 11.11 Linked list after declaration of *head* and allocation of a first node

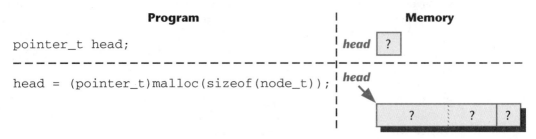

One advantage of a linked list is that it is easier to use than a dynamically allocated array. Whereas we should know the number of elements needed before allocating an array, we can expand a linked list as necessary. We allocate additional structures only as required.

We declare *head* to be a pointer to a node structure.

```
pointer_t head;
```

To start the linked list, we allocate space for a node, pointing *head* to this area.

```
head = (pointer_t)malloc(sizeof(node_t));
```

Figure 11.11 shows memory after declaration of *head* and then after allocation of a first node for the linked list.

Once the computer has allocated a node structure, the program can assign or read values for the *el* portion of the node. To indicate that no more nodes are in the list, we assign the null pointer, *NULL*, to the next field, *head–>next*.

```
strcpy(head -> el.name, "dill pickles");
head -> el.price = 2.29;
head -> next = NULL;
```

Figure 11.12 shows the results of this segment.

If we need another node in the list, we can allocate space for the structure and point the first node's *next* field to the new area. Figure 11.13 shows memory as a result of the following statement:

```
head->next = (pointer_t)malloc(sizeof(node_t));
```

A linked list is a powerful abstraction. Various operations on and applications of linked lists are in the domain of data structures. Chapter 16 considers linked lists in greater detail.

Figure 11.12 Linked list after filling the first node

Figure 11.13
Memory after
allocation of
the second
node in the
linked list

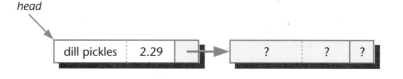

Section 11.4 Exercises

1. **a.** Define a function *ReadDate* that accepts a pointer to a structure of type *date_t* (see example 11.3, section 11.2). The function reads values into the elements of the structure. Use the arrow notation.

   b. Declare *today* to be of type *date_t*.

   c. Write a statement to call *ReadDate* to obtain today's date.

2. **a.** Write a function *ReturnDate* that has no parameters, but reads a date and returns the date in a structure of type *date_t*.

   b. Write a statement to obtain a value for *today* from Exercise 1b by calling *ReturnDate*.

3. Write a function *QDisplay* that accepts an argument of type *rational_t* from Example 11.7 and prints the rational number in the form *a/b* or *a* if *b* is 1. Thus, for a numerator of 23 and denominator of 67 the function prints

       23/67

   For a numerator of 25 and denominator of 1, a call to the function yields output

       25

4. **a.** At the end of this section, we defined types *node_t* and *pointer_t*. Declare *p* and *q* to be pointers to such a node structure.

   b. Write a statement to have *p* point to the first node in the linked list of Figure 11.10. Notice that *head* already points to this node.

   c. Write a statement to have *q* point to the second node in the linked list of Figure 11.10. Notice that the *next* field of the first node already points to this node.

   d. Suppose *q* points to the second node of the linked list of Figure 11.10. How can we reference the *next* element of this node? Using this element, write a statement to free the last node in the linked list.

   e. Suppose *q* points to the second node of the linked list of Figure 11.10. Write a statement to place "eggs" in the *name* field and 0.89 in the *price* field of the *el* portion of that node.

Section 11.4 Programming Project

Complex numbers are important in mathematics, engineering, and physics. One special complex number is $i = \sqrt{-1}$. Any complex number can be written in the form $a + bi$, where a and b are real numbers, and a is called the **real part** and b the

imaginary part. Thus, $3 + 5i$ is a complex number with real part 3 and imaginary part 5. The following are other examples of complex numbers: $4.8 - 2.6i, 34.7, 0$, and $-16i$. We add complex numbers by adding corresponding parts.

$$(a + bi) + (c + di) = (a + c) + (b + d)i$$

Thus,

$$(2 + 5i) + (3 - 7i) = 5 - 2i$$

The product of two complex numbers follows from the fact that $i^2 = (\sqrt{-1})^2 = -1$.

$$(a + bi)(c + di) = (ac - bd) + (ad + bc)i$$

Thus,

$$(2 + 5i)(3 - 7i) = 41 + i$$

One way to store complex numbers is in a structure containing the real and imaginary parts. Develop a program to allow the user to repeatedly enter pairs of complex numbers. For each pair, the program prints their sum and product.

Section 11.5 Enumeration Types

Enumeration data types allow the manipulation of symbols as new types of constants. The definition of such a data type begins with the keyword *enum* and looks like a *struct* definition. For example, we can define the enumeration type *week* to contain symbolic constants indicating the days of the week. In the same statement, we can declare *today* to be of type *enum week* and *day_ptr* to be a pointer to that type, as follows:

```
enum week
{
    MONDAY, TUESDAY, WEDNESDAY, THURSDAY, FRIDAY, SATURDAY, SUNDAY
}
today, *day_ptr;
```

The statement creates the user-defined type, *enum week*, which is the name following *enum*. The pair of braces that follow enclose a list of all the values, expressed as identifiers, which variables of this type can have. These names—like *MONDAY*—must be valid C identifiers and must be unique within the scope of the definition. Moreover, the identifiers in the template are constants. They are rvalues but not lvalues. In this example, two variable names follow the definition of *week*. We declare *today* to be a variable of type *enum week*, whereas *day_ptr* is of type *enum week* *. As with structures, once we have defined the type name, we can use it to declare other variables, as shown:

```
enum week tomorrow;
```

As with *struct*, we can use *typedef* to define a data type that includes the keyword *enum* and the template, as follows:

```
typedef
enum
{
    MONDAY, TUESDAY, WEDNESDAY, THURSDAY, FRIDAY, SATURDAY, SUNDAY
}
week_t;
```

After its definition, we can use *week_t* (instead of *enum week*) in variable declarations, as follows:

```
week_t today, *day_ptr, tomorrow;
```

We can assign the constant *WEDNESDAY* to the variable *today* of type *week_t* as

```
today = WEDNESDAY;
```

As with preprocessor constants, by convention, we use all uppercase to distinguish enumeration constants from variables.

Enumeration data types are useful if we wish to manipulate values that are, at least conceptually, not numbers or characters. Comparable to the declaration of preprocessor constants, enumerated values lend meaning to otherwise anonymous numeric values. The difference is that enumeration types are part of the C language itself.

Implementation

We should treat enumeration types as incompatible with any other data type. We should only assign constants of enumeration types to variables of the same type. C, however, implements an enumeration data type as *int*. The language assigns a sequential nonnegative integer, starting with 0, to each constant identifier in the *enum* definition. In effect, the type definition of *week_t* is equivalent to the following preprocessor definitions:

```
#define week_t     int
#define MONDAY     0
#define TUESDAY    1
#define WEDNESDAY  2
#define THURSDAY   3
#define FRIDAY     4
#define SATURDAY   5
#define SUNDAY     6
```

Boolean Type

Example 11.8

This example defines an enumeration data type, *boolean_t*, that is equivalent to the boolean type. Previously, we have used preprocessor directives to define symbolic constants *TRUE* and *FALSE* as

```
#define FALSE 0
#define TRUE  1
```

Using these same identifier constants, we define *boolean_t* as*

```
typedef enum {FALSE, TRUE} boolean_t;
```

---

*THINK C on the Macintosh defines *boolean_t*. Thus, to use the definition in the text, remove automatic inclusion of the following from the *Edit, Options, Think C..., Prefix* menu:

```
#include <MacHeaders>
```

Because of the order of the identifiers in the template, the constant identifier *FALSE* has the value 0, and *TRUE* is 1. Such a definition of *boolean_t* and its constants has the advantages of being part of the C language and of enabling us to define variables and functions of the type *boolean_t*. Thus, with a global definition of *boolean_t*, we can declare a sequential search routine to have type *boolean_t*, as shown:

```
boolean_t SequentialSearch(int a[], int NumEls,
    int SearchFor, int *loc_ptr);
```

The function definition can have the declaration-initialization statement

```
boolean_t found = FALSE;
```

The function *SequentialSearch* returns the value of *found*—*TRUE* or *FALSE*—to the calling function. If the value of *found* is *TRUE*, then the variable *loc_ptr* points to the index of the array element that is equal to *SearchFor*. Use of *boolean_t* is self-documenting. By using *boolean_t*, it is much clearer that *SequentialSearch* is returning a value to indicate the success or failure of the search than if we had declared the function to be of type *int*.

Coercion

Because the identifier constants in the *enum* template represent integers, without casting, we can assign integers to variables of enumeration types or constants of enumeration types to *int* variables. Some compilers do not even display a warning. We should, however, use a cast to clarify the code. For the following declarations:

```
int     int_var;
week_t today;
```

the assignments

```
int_var = (int)FRIDAY;    /* Avoid these assignments */
today   = (week_t)2;
```

are equivalent to the more straightforward

```
int_var = 4; /* These assignments are preferable */
today   = WEDNESDAY;
```

Because the integer values of enumeration constants of different types all range from the integer 0 up, we can assign a variable of one enumeration data type to that of another. In fact, we may be able to assign a value to an enumeration variable that does not have any constant representation, such as the following:

```
today = 9; /* ERROR, probably not caught by compiler */
```

Extreme caution should be used in mixing data types. Just because the C language allows the programmer to assign variables of different types to one another does not mean that it is logically correct. The compiler probably checks compatibility when a cast operator appears. Thus, if the programmer mixes types, he or she should use casting.

Because enumeration constants are equivalent to integer constants, we can use them in integer constant expressions.

Example 11.9

Suppose the first day of the month occurs on *FirstDay*, which is of type *week_t*. In this example, we develop a program to print the day of the week on which a particular date in the month occurs. For example, if the first day of the month occurs on a Wednesday, then the fourteenth is a Tuesday. An execution of the program to obtain this information follows:

```
This program tells the day of the week on which
a date in the month occurs.

The first day of the month occurred on
         0   MONDAY
         1   TUESDAY
         2   WEDNESDAY
         3   THURSDAY
         4   FRIDAY
         5   SATURDAY
         6   SUNDAY

Day (0-6): 2
Date (1-31) for the day in the month: 14
The day occurs on TUESDAY.
```

As Figure 11.14 shows, the function *main* calls the following three functions:

- *ReadFirstDay* to read and return the day of the week (of type *week_t*) on which the first day of the month occurs
- *ReadDate* to read and return a date in the month, an integer between 1 and 31
- *PrintDay* to print the day of the week on which the date occurs for the particular month

Before the definition of *main*, we define the global enumeration type *week_t* so that the type is available throughout the program. Pseudocode for *main* follows:

Figure 11.14
Structure
diagram for
Example 11.9

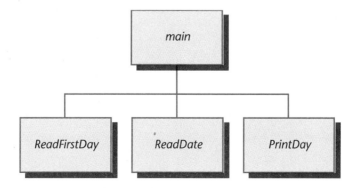

main( )

Program to read the day of the week on which the first day of the month occurs and an integer day of the month and to print the day on which the date occurs

Algorithm:

FirstDay ← *ReadFirstDay*();
int_date ← *ReadDate*();
PrintDay(*FirstDay*, *int_date*);

It is impossible to read a symbolic constant for the value of a *week_t* type variable, but an enumeration type is compatible with *int*. Thus, the function *ReadFirstDay* displays a menu of the days of the week with associated integers (from 0 to 6) and asks the user to type the number for the first day of the month. The program reads this value into an integer variable (*int_FirstDay*), and returns that value cast to *week_t*.

ReadFirstDay( ) ⟶ *FirstDay*

Function to read and return the first day of the month

Pre:

Post:

The first day of the month of type *week_t* was returned.

Algorithm:

display a menu of days of the week and prompt for the first day of the month
read *int_FirstDay*, an integer between 0 and 6, corresponding to the day
return *int_FirstDay* cast to type *week_t*

The function *main* obtains the integer day of the month, *int_date*, from *ReadDate*. Then to complete the program's task, *main* calls *PrintDay* with arguments *FirstDay* and *int_date*.

PrintDay(*FirstDay*, *int_date*)

Procedure to print the day in the week in which the date *int_date* occurs for the month, where the first day of the month occurs on day *FirstDay*.

Pre:

FirstDay of type *week_t* is the first day of the month.
int_date of type *int* is the date of a day of the month.

Post:

The day of the week corresponding to *int_date* was displayed.

Algorithm:

compute *DayOfWeek*, the day of the week on which *int_date* falls
print the day of the week

The function *PrintDay* declares *DayOfWeek*, which stores the day of the week for the date in question, to be of type *week_t*. Because the calculation of this day involves both the *week_t* type variable *FirstDay* and the *int* variable *int_date*, the expression uses casting. To compute the day, we add the first day of the month, *FirstDay*, cast as an integer and the date in the month, *int_date*. We must subtract 1, because calendar dates begin with 1 instead of 0.

```
(int)FirstDay + int_date - 1
```

For example, suppose that the first day of the month is on a Wednesday. Thus, the value of *FirstDay* is *WEDNESDAY*. Because that constant is the third in the template for *week_t*, (*int*)*FirstDay* is 2. Suppose *int_date* is 14, and the user wants to know on which day of the week the fourteenth falls. Numbering for the month starts with day 1, so we subtract 1 from the sum of 2 and 14 to obtain $2 + 14 - 1 = 15$.

We find the remainder from division by 7. The result is an integer between 0 and 6 that corresponds to the day of the week. Casting to *week_t*, we can assign the value to *DayOfWeek*, as shown:

```
DayOfWeek = (week_t)(((int)FirstDay + int_date - 1) % 7);
```

For example, we must take 15 modulo 7. Because the remainder is 1, the second symbolic constant in *week_t*'s definition, *TUESDAY*, corresponds to the day for the fourteenth of the month.

We should be careful to cast the *FirstDay* to *int* for the integer arithmetic. After obtaining an integer value, we should cast the result to *week_t*. The *week_t* type variable *DayOfWeek* now stores the appropriate value. Storage within the computer, however, is as an integer. Consequently, to print meaningful words for the day of the week, we use the *enum* constants in a *switch* expression and print the corresponding string constant, as shown:

```
switch (DayOfWeek)
    {
        case MONDAY:
            printf("MONDAY.\n");
            break;
        case TUESDAY:
    ⋮
```

The entire program follows:

```
/*
 * Example 11.9
 * Program to read the day of the week on which the first day
 * of the month occurs. Then it reads an integer day of the
 * month and prints the day on which it occurs.
 */

#include <stdio.h>

typedef
enum
{
    MONDAY, TUESDAY, WEDNESDAY, THURSDAY, FRIDAY, SATURDAY, SUNDAY
}
week_t;

week_t ReadFirstDay(void);
int    ReadDate(void);
void   PrintDay(week_t, int);

main()
{
    week_t FirstDay;    /* day of first day of month */
    int int_date;       /* date in month */
    printf("This program tells the day of the week on which\n");
    printf("a date in the month occurs.\n\n");

    FirstDay = ReadFirstDay();
    int_date = ReadDate();
    PrintDay(FirstDay, int_date);
}

/*
 * Function to read and return the first day of the month
 * Pre:    none
 * Post:   The first day of the month of type week_t was returned.
 */

week_t ReadFirstDay(void)
{
    int int_FirstDay;   /* int first day of month       */
                        /* 0 == MONDAY, ..., 6 == SUNDAY */

    do
    {
        printf("The first day of the month occurred on \n");
        printf("\t0  MONDAY\n");
        printf("\t1  TUESDAY\n");
```

```
        printf("\t2   WEDNESDAY\n");
        printf("\t3   THURSDAY\n");
        printf("\t4   FRIDAY\n");
        printf("\t5   SATURDAY\n");
        printf("\t6   SUNDAY\n");

        printf("\nDay (0-6): ");
        scanf("%d", &int_FirstDay);
    }
    while (int_FirstDay < 0 || 6 < int_FirstDay);

    return (week_t)int_FirstDay;
}


/*
 * Function to read an integer day of the month, 1 - 31
 * Pre:     none
 * Post:    An integer day of the month was returned.
 */

int ReadDate(void)
{
    int int_date;    /* date in month */

    do
    {
        printf("Date (1-31) for the day in the month: ");
        scanf("%d", &int_date);
    }
    while (int_date < 1 || 31 < int_date);

    return int_date;
}


/*
 * Function to print the day in the week in which the date
 * int_date occurs for the month, where the first day of
 * the month occurs on the day FirstDay.
 * Pre:     FirstDay of type week_t is the first day of the month.
 *          int_date is an integer date.
 * Post:    Day corresponding to int_date was displayed.
 */

void PrintDay(week_t FirstDay, int int_date)
{
    week_t DayOfWeek;   /* day of week on which int_date occurs */

    DayOfWeek = (week_t)(((int)FirstDay + int_date - 1) % 7);

    printf("The day occurs on ");
```

```
        switch (DayOfWeek)
        {
            case MONDAY:
                printf("MONDAY.\n");
                break;
            case TUESDAY:
                printf("TUESDAY.\n");
                break;
            case WEDNESDAY:
                printf("WEDNESDAY.\n");
                break;
            case THURSDAY:
                printf("THURSDAY.\n");
                break;
            case FRIDAY:
                printf("FRIDAY.\n");
                break;
            case SATURDAY:
                printf("SATURDAY.\n");
                break;
            case SUNDAY:
                printf("SUNDAY.\n");
        }
    }
```

Section 11.5 **Exercises**

1. **a.** Define with *typedef* an enumeration data type, *SweatSize_t*, that contains identifier constants for sizes small, medium, and large.

   b. Write a function to ask the user for his or her size sweatshirt. The function should return the corresponding value of type *SweatSize_t*.

   c. Write a procedure with an argument of type *SweatSize_t* that prints the corresponding size.

2. **a.** Define with *typedef* an enumeration data type, *color_t*, that contains identifier constants for five colors.

   b. Write a function to ask the user to choose a favorite color from the list. The function should return the corresponding value of type *color_t*.

   c. Write a procedure with an argument of type *color_t* that prints the corresponding color.

3. Write a function to accept an argument of pointer type *week_t* * (see the first part of this section). The function should change the value to which the argument points to the next day. For example, if the location stores *MONDAY* before execution of the function, it should store *TUESDAY* afterwards. Be sure to use appropriate casting and to account for the fact that Monday follows Sunday.

4. **a.** Define enumerated type for a card suit, *suit_t*, with constants for club, diamond, heart, and spade.

b. Write a function to ask the user to choose a suit from a list. The function should return the corresponding value of type *suit_t*.

c. Write a procedure with a parameter of type *suit_t* that prints the corresponding suit.

Section 11.5 Programming Projects

1. Write a program that simulates shuffling a deck of 52 playing cards and dealing all the cards to four players. Have an array to hold the deck and a structure to represent a card. This structure contains an enumeration value for the suit (*CLUB, DIA-MOND, HEART, SPADE*) and another for its value (*TWO, THREE, FOUR, FIVE, SIX, SEVEN, EIGHT, NINE, TEN, JACK, QUEEN, KING, ACE*). Shuffle the cards by repeatedly picking two random integers in the appropriate range and swapping the corresponding array elements. Print the contents of each hand after the deal. (See Appendix F for random number generators.)

2. Write a program that calculates the pay of day workers. Each worker is paid at the end of the day at a rate of $8.00 per hour, with time and a half for Saturday work and double time for Sunday work. Use *week_t* for the type of a day. Using a menu, the program should read a day and then repeatedly read hours worked and display the worker's pay until all workers are paid.

Section 11.6 Union Type

Sometimes we should be able to treat a single area of memory as if it contains, at different times, values of different types. For example, an employee file might store different information for a manager than a salesperson, but we might want to read each kind of record one-at-a-time into the same area of memory. The *union* construct in C provides a facility for accomplishing this overlay.

The syntax for unions is identical to that for structures, except we replace the keyword *struct* with the keyword *union.* Here is a sample *union* declaration:

```
union sample
{
    int integer;
    float real;
}
example;
```

This statement declares a variable *example* of type *union sample.* The members of *example* are *example.integer* and *example.real.*

Rather than containing enough room for two members, however, *example* contains memory for one value, either an *int* or a *float*, as specified in the body of the union. Assume in a particular computer that an *int* is two bytes long and a *float* is four. Then the variable *example* has the maximum of the two lengths (four bytes). As with a structure, a union can contain as many members as desired, and of any type, but it allocates only enough memory to hold the largest member. Figure 11.15 depicts this situation. We can refer to the area as either a *float* variable, *example.real*, or an *int* variable, *example.integer.*

If a value is assigned to *example.integer*, then the value is placed, in integer format, in the memory locations belonging to *example.* The variable *example.real* can access the resulting bit pattern, interpreted as a floating point number, but the results probably

Figure 11.15
Union structure
containing
elements
integer and *real*

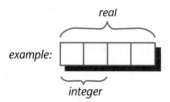

are meaningless because no conversion occurs. Because they share the same memory location, changing *example.real* also changes *example.integer,* and vice versa.

The programmer must keep up with the meaning of the area. One method of doing so is to have a structure with a flag and the union. The value of the flag indicates the format of the rest of the record. Frequently, some common elements in the structure do not appear in the union.

Example 11.10

In this example, we define a structure that can contain information for a manager or a salesperson. For both categories, we store name (*name*) and Social Security Number (*SSN*). For a manager, we also store monthly salary, and for a salesperson, we need hourly wage and the number of hours worked. This variant part is in a union, and a flag indicates which union member is relevant. The flag member *flag* is an enumeration type that contains one of two values—*MANAGER* or *SALESPERSON*. If the value of *flag* is *MANAGER*, then the rest of the structure contains information about a store manager. If *flag*'s value is *SALESPERSON*, the structure contains slightly different information.

```
typedef enum {MANAGER, SALESPERSON} flag_t;
typedef char string_t[31];

typedef          /* type for salesperson's record */
struct
{
    float HourWage;
    float hours;
}
salesperson_t;

typedef          /* type for employee's record */
struct
{
    string_t name;
    char SSN[10];
    flag_t flag;
    union
    {
        float        MonthSalary;
        salesperson_t SalespersonEmp;
    }
    worker;
}
employee_t;

employee_t employee;   /* employee's record */
```

To store the record of a manager in the variable *employee*, we obtain values for the name (*employee.name*) and Social Security Number (*employee.SSN*). These elements, as well as the flag, are common to both a manager's and a salesperson's record. We assign the appropriate value to the flag to indicate a manager's record, as shown:

```
employee.flag = MANAGER;
```

In using the union, we can check the flag to determine whether the subsequent area is for the record of a manager or of a salesperson.

To assign a monthly salary of $3900 to the manager, we start with the name of the variable (*employee*). We reference *worker*, but this element is a union with two members *MonthSalary* and *SalespersonEmp*. For a manager, we use the former.

```
employee.worker.MonthSalary = 3900.00;
```

For a salesperson, we set the flag as

```
employee.flag = SALESPERSON;
```

To assign an hourly wage of $11.50, we must access the *worker* element *Salesperson-Emp*, which is a structure itself with members *HourWage* and *hours*. We use the full path name in the assignment, as follows:

```
employee.worker.SalespersonEmp.HourWage = 11.50;
```

Unions are syntactically the same as structures. We refer to their members in the same manner, and we can apply the address, period, and arrow operators to both in the same way. Moreover, the nesting rules (unions in structures, unions in unions, and so on) are the same. The only difference is that union members occupy the same memory and behave accordingly.

Section 11.6 Exercises

1. a. Define with *typedef* a union type with two elements—one is a structure for a full-time student's record and the other for a part-time student. The full-time student's record contains a boolean value for boarding or not and a character array for interests. The part-time student's record contains a boolean value indicating whether the student already has an undergraduate degree or not and a character array indicating the school granting the degree.

   b. For both full- and part-time students, we store a Social Security Number (*SSN*) and number of semester hours (*hours*). Similar to Example 11.10, set up a structure containing *SSN*, *hours*, a flag, and the union from Part a.

2. Write a procedure that interactively reads student information and communicates a record of the type defined in Exercise 1, Part a to the calling function.

3. Define an array type consisting of up to 100 records of the type defined in Exercise 1, Part a.

4. Write a procedure that accepts an array of student records (Exercise 3) and the number of active records and prints a list of the names of all off-campus students.

Section 11.6 Programming Project

Develop a program that reads a file of employee records into an array of structures and prints two tables. The first table lists the Social Security Number (SSN) and monthly salaries of all managers, including a total salary line. The second table lists the SSN of salespersons, their hourly salaries, the number of hours worked, and the salaries (hours times hourly salary). Include a line with total hours and total salary. Display an appropriate heading for each table and design the tables for screen output pausing for each full screen (20 lines). Ask the user to press return to view an additional screen. The structures should be of the type described in Example 11.10. Each line of the input file consists of a character code (M or S) followed by monthly salary, SSN, and name for managers or hourly salary, hours, SSN, and name for salespersons. All data values are separated by a single space. The following are example input file lines:

```
M 3800.50 548996355 Jim Jones
S 5.50 155 392847584 John Smith
M 4400.75 485937264 Sue Brown
```

Section 11.7 Breadth: A Computer Graphics Package

Interactive programs can involve pictures instead of written and spoken words. For example, video games are interactive. They pose situations, the player responds with various moves, and the game reacts. Popular games are not only exciting but are easily understandable and have good graphics. Many special effects we see in movies and commercials are also created with computer graphics. Computer scientists develop sophisticated graphics packages which artists use to generate realistic images.

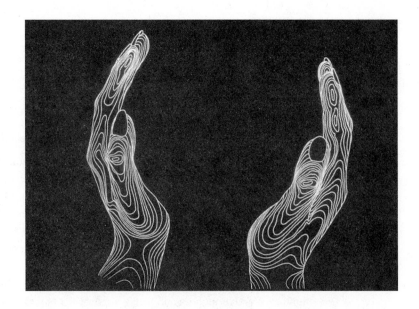

Device Driver

A great deal of variation exists among computer graphics output units that display these images. For example, devices vary widely in dimensions and available colors. One display may have $640 \times 480 = 19,200$ points or **pixels**, whereas another has $1024 \times 768 = 786,452$. Some displays are monochrome, such as black-and-white, and some systems have a palette with millions of colors. Differences exist in software, too. Some compilers, such as Turbo C and THINK C, even contain their own version-specific graphics routines. Moreover, some computers, like the Macintosh, have a toolbox of graphics routines. How can we hope for any degree of portability in a graphics package? One method is to place all device-dependent routines together in a file, called a **device driver**, and to have a different device driver for each display device. Other files contain graphics primitives that do not depend on the system. The programmer uses routines from this package in writing higher-level programs.

Definitions
A **pixel**, which stands for picture element, is a dot on a two-dimensional array of dots on a display medium. A **device driver** for a computer graphics system is a file that contains all the device-dependent routines.

A vendor typically sells such a package in object-code form that hides implementation details. Several standards exist for graphics packages. One is **GKS** or **Graphical Kernel System**, and another is **PHIGS** or **Programmer's Hierarchical Interactive Graphics Standard**, which contains more powerful interactive and 3-dimensional graphics functions. Device drivers for Turbo C and THINK C are on the disk that comes with this text. Moreover, the outline of a generic driver can be used to develop drivers for other systems. If you can plot a point in graphics mode on your system with C, you can implement the rest of the driver fairly easily. (See Appendix G for the exact locations of these files.) The disk also contains files for the device-independent routines of a small graphics package (*graphics.h* and *graphics.c*) that you can use to create pictures with your own C programs. The names of the types, constants, and functions are specific to this package. With the package, we can create images and obtain an understanding of the utility of graphics packages.

Each device driver on the disk has a header file (*driver.h*) and definition file (*driver.c*). Definitions of the higher-level functions are in the file *graphics.c*, which has header file *graphics.h*. The header files contain type and symbolic constant definitions, along with prototypes for the functions in the definition files. The programmer creates another file (or files) with his or her program. Our graphics programs include the header file *graphics.h* by having the preprocessor directive that has the header's name in quotes, as shown:

```
#include "graphics.h"
```

This file already has a directive to include *driver.h*. After writing our program, we compile and link files *driver.c*, *graphics.c*, and our program file to form an executable file. In the next chapter, we discuss the use of several program files and separate compilation in greater detail.

The file *driver.c* contains the following variables and function definitions:

- *MaxX* and *MaxY* are global variables to hold the maximum number of horizontal and vertical pixels, respectively, for the graphics window on the particular device.

- *EnterGraphics*() to initialize *MaxX* and *MaxY* and the graphics window and initiate graphics mode

- *SetPixel(int x, int y)* to draw a pixel at position (x, y). When available, this function calls a system-dependent routine to draw the pixel. For example,

      SetPixel(50, 230)

  plots a point at pixel position (50, 230).

- *DD_Line(int row1, int col1, int row2, int col2)* to draw a line from device position (*row1*, *col1*) to (*row2*, *col2*). When available, this function calls a system-dependent routine to draw the line. For example,

      DD_Line(50, 230, 300, 80)

  draws a line from point (50, 230) to point (300, 80).

- *ExitGraphics()* to end graphics mode

Device Coordinates

The device-independent routines are in *graphics.c*. One routine is *DelaySec* from Example 11.4 in Section 11.2 that produces a delay of a specified number of integer seconds and allows the user to view a picture for that period of time. We develop other device-independent routines in this section.

The device origin for plotting points is in the top left corner with the positive *x*-axis pointing to the right and the positive *y*-axis pointing down. Figure 11.16 illustrates a CRT device with typical **device coordinates (DC)** ranges indicated.

Definition **Device coordinates (DC)** are the integer coordinates used by a graphics display device. Often the origin is in the top left corner, and the positive horizontal axis points to the right, and the positive vertical axis points down.

Example 11.11

This example introduces the necessary details to draw a large X as shown in Figure 11.17. In the program, we initialize the graphics window and enter graphics mode by calling *EnterGraphics*. To draw the X, we call the device-dependent line drawing routine *DD_Line* to draw a line from (0, 0) to (*MaxX*, *MaxY*) and from (0, *MaxY*) to (*MaxX*, 0). After displaying the picture for 2 seconds, we exit graphics mode. The program is as follows:

Figure 11.16
Coordinate system on a particular CRT screen that is a 640 × 480 array of pixels

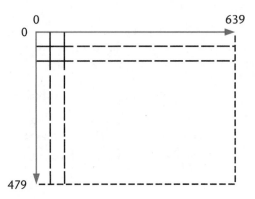

Figure 11.17
Large X display

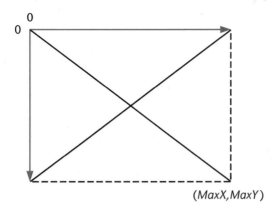

```
/*
 *  Program to draw an X on the screen
 */

#include <stdio.h>
#include "graphics.h"

main()
{
    EnterGraphics();

    DD_Line(0, 0, MaxX, MaxY);
    DD_Line(0, MaxY, MaxX, 0);

    DelaySec(2);
    ExitGraphics();
}
```

In this example and all remaining examples in this introduction, we use the default background and drawing colors. For further information concerning color, you may wish to refer to the reference manual for your version of C.

World and Normalized Device Coordinate Systems

The direct use of device coordinates is inconvenient and often device-dependent. For a device-independent coordinate system, we use **world coordinates (WC)** and/or **normalized device coordinates (NDC)**. World coordinates represent a square region with positive axes pointing in the familiar directions to the right and up. Coordinates are expressed as floating point numbers that range from *WMinX* to *WMaxX* and *WMinY* to *WMaxY*. *WMinX*, *WMaxX*, *WMinY*, and *WMaxY* are values determined in the application's coordinate framework, so the display is contained in the square region. Figure 11.18 pictures such a WC system.

Definition   **World coordinates (WC)** are the floating point coordinates used by an application with the positive horizontal axis pointing to the right and the positive vertical axis pointing up.

Figure 11.18
World
coordinate
(WC) system

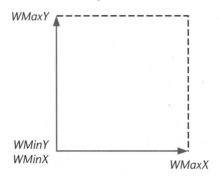

Figure 11.19
Normalized
device
coordinate
(NDC) system

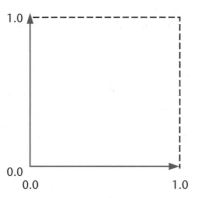

Normalized device coordinates (Figure 11.19) represent a square region with the origin at the bottom left and positive axes pointing to the right and up. Coordinates, however, are expressed as floating point numbers that range from 0.0 to 1.0.

> **Definition**   **Normalized device coordinates (NDC)** are floating point coordinates for a square region with the positive horizontal axis pointing to the right, the vertical axis pointing up, and the origin in the bottom left corner. Each coordinate ranges from 0.0 to 1.0.

Suppose we are interested in drawing a star. First, we draw a star on graph paper using convenient scales and record the coordinates of the end points. Figure 11.20 shows a star with *WMinX* = 0, *WMinY* = 0, *WMaxX* = 100, and *WMaxY* = 100. We could select any range of values for world coordinates.

Next, we transform from world coordinates to normalized device coordinates and finally to device coordinates. Figure 11.21 shows the transformation process for a point (*xw*, *yw*).

The normalized coordinates simply represent the floating point proportion of *xw* to the total *x* scale and proportion of *yw* to the total *y* scale, as follows:

```
xn = (xw - WMinX)/ (WMaxX - WMinX);
yn = (yw - WMinY)/ (WMaxY - WMinY);
```

Knowing the proportion of the total scale, we can multiply *MaxX* by this proportion to obtain the *x* device coordinate. Because device coordinates represent pixel positions, we need to cast the product to *int*, as follows:

Figure 11.20
Star in world
coordinates

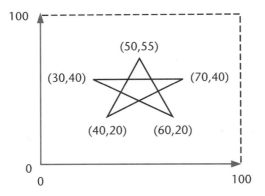

Figure 11.21   Transformation of a point

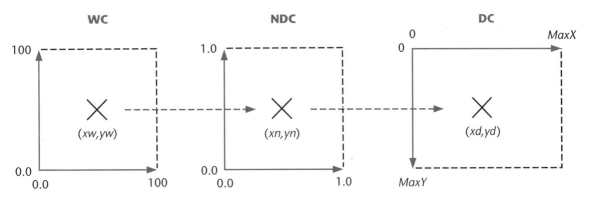

```
(int)(MaxX * xn)
```

The device y-axis points down, so for the y device coordinate, we need to calculate the proportion from the top or $(1 - yn)$, as follows:

```
(int)(MaxY * (1 - yn))
```

One problem with this arrangement is that some devices are not square. Consequently, a mapping from uniform normalized coordinates to display coordinates could generate a distorted picture, elongated in one direction. The ratio of the number of pixels in the y direction to the number of pixels in the x direction is the device's **aspect ratio**, R. A device with 480 pixels in the y direction and 640 pixels in the x direction has an aspect ratio of $R = 480/640 = 0.75$. The trend is toward devices with an aspect ratio of 1, but many devices have an aspect ratio different from 1. Although we can adjust for an aspect ratio different from 1 by multiplying pixel lengths in the y direction by the aspect ratio, we ignore the aspect ratio problem in this brief introduction. We encapsulate the coordinate transformations in two functions *MapXw* and *MapYw* that assume we have defined global variables *WMinX*, *WMinY*, *WMaxX*, and *WMaxY*.

Definition   The ratio of the number of pixels in the y direction to the number of pixels in the x direction is the device's **aspect ratio**.

```
/*
 * Function to convert a world x coordinate to a device coordinate
 * Pre:   Global values WMinX and WMaxX are defined.
 *        xw represents a valid float x world coordinate.
 * Post: The function has returned the device coordinate
 *        corresponding to xw.
 */

int MapXw(float xw)
{
    float xn;

    xn = (xw - WMinX)/ (WMaxX - WMinX);
    return (int)(MaxX * xn);
}


/*
 * Function to convert a world y coordinate to a device coordinate
 * Pre:   Global values WMinY and WMaxY are defined.
 *        yw represents a valid float y world coordinate.
 * Post: The function has returned the device coordinate
 *        corresponding to yw.
 */

int MapYw(float yw)
{
    float yn;

    yn = (yw - WMinY)/ (WMaxY - WMinY);
    return (int)(MaxY * (1 - yn));
}
```

Example 11.12

In this example, we develop a program that sketches the graph of the function $f(x) = x \sin(x)$ near the origin. We consider x values ranging from -8π to 8π and y values from -25 to 25. We can generate graphs of other functions using different world coordinates. This version plots points as x varies from -8π to 8π. We use the device-dependent routine *SetPixel* defined in *device.c* to plot a point at device coordinates (*xd, yd*). The header file *graphics.h* defines the preprocessor constant *PI* (π) and includes the header file for the math library, *math*.

```
/*
 * Example 11.12
 * Program to graph f(x) = x sin(x)
 */

#include "graphics.h"

#define INC 0.05

float xsinx(float);
```

```
main()
{
    float x, y;              /* world coordinates of a point */

    WMinX = -8*PI;           /* PI returns π */
    WMaxX = 8*PI;
    WMinY = -25.0;
    WMaxY = 25.0;

    EnterGraphics();

    x = WMinX;
    while (x <= WMaxX)
    {
        y = xsinx(x);
        SetPixel(MapXw(x), MapYw(y));
        x += INC;
    }

    DelaySec(3);
    ExitGraphics();
}

/*
 * Function to plot
 */

float xsinx(float x)
{
    return (x * sin(x));
}
```

Figure 11.22 shows the result of execution of this program. To obtain a smoother graph, we connect the points by line segments (see Exercise 3).

Figure 11.22
Graph of
$x \sin(x)$
generated by
the program in
Example 11.12

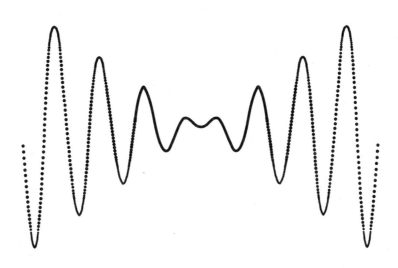

Polylines

We can generate an impressive collection of pictures with only points and lines. As with the star in Figure 11.20, many objects are **polyline**, sequences of line segments in which the end of one segment joins the beginning of another. With only the endpoints, we can repeatedly call a line-drawing routine to "connect the dots." We store the device coordinate endpoints in a structure of type *Dpts_t*, which is an array of points of type *Dpoint_t*.

> **Definition**   A **polyline** is a sequence of line segments in which the end of one segment joins the beginning of another.

```
#define MAXPOINTS 100

typedef
struct
{
    int x, y;
}
Dpoint_t;

typedef Dpoint_t Dpts_t[MAXPOINTS];
```

We can draw similar types with coordinates of type *float* for a point in world coordinates (*Wpoint_t*) and an array of such points (*Wpts_t*). A routine *DrawFigure* draws a polyline with device coordinates.

Example 11.13

In this example, we develop a program that reads a text file of points and draws a figure formed by connecting the points with lines. The first line of the file consists of the world coordinate limits (*WMinX*, *WMaxX*, *WMinY*, *WMaxY*) separated by spaces. The remainder of the file contains a sequence of the coordinates of line segment end points. The file for the star in Figure 11.20 is as follows:

```
0 100 0 100
30 40   70 40   40 20   50 55   60 20   30 40
```

The program should request the name of the text file, read the points into an array of points (*x* and *y* coordinates), and then display the figure on the screen. The function *main* initiates and terminates graphics mode and calls three procedures—*GetData* to read the limits and points from a text file, *ScalePoints* to map the points from WC to DC, and *DrawFigure* to draw the figure. Definitions of the three routines are in *graphics.c*, and *graphics.h* contains their prototypes. The structure to hold the WC points is an array of structures consisting of *float x* and *y* coordinate elements. The structure for the DC is similar, except the fields are of type *int*. Besides prototypes of functions, the header file *graphics.h* contains the definitions of the constant *MAX-POINTS* and the types *Dpoint_t*, *Dpts_t*, *Wpoint_t*, and *Wpts_t*. *GetData*, which we call before entering graphics mode, is similar to previous examples. (So that *MaxX* and *MaxY* from *device.c* are available to *graphics.c* and our program, *graphics.h* also must declare these variables as *extern int*. Similarly, *WMinX*, *WMaxX*, *WMinY*, *WMaxY* from *graphics.c* are declared as *extern float*. In Section 12.2, we explain the meaning of *extern*. For now, ignore the preprocessor directives *#ifndef GKS*, *#define GKS*, and *#endif* in *graphics.h*. We explain their utility in Section 12.3.) Pseudocode for *ScalePoints* and *DrawFigure* are followed by the code in *graphics.h*, *graphics.c*, and the program.

ScalePoints(Wpoints, Dpoints, NumEls)

Procedure to map the first *NumEls* WC points in *Wpoints* to corresponding DC points in *Dpoints*

Pre:

In graphics mode, an array of WC *Wpoints* has the first *NumEls* points defined.

Post:

Dpoints is an array of the DC of the corresponding points in *Wpoints*.

Algorithm:

for each of the first *NumEls* element in *Wpoints*
  convert *xw* to *xd* using *MapXw*
  convert *yw* to *yd* using *MapYw*

DrawFigure(Dpoints, NumEls)

Procedure to draw the figure determined by connecting the points with a sequence of lines

Pre:

In graphic mode, an array of DC, *Dpoints*, has the first *NumEls* points defined.
NumEls is an integer that is at least 2.

Post:

The figure was displayed on the output screen.

Algorithm:

for *i* ranging from 0 to *NumEls* - 2 do the following:
  draw the line connecting the *i* and *i*+1 points

```
/*
 * File:  graphics.h - public interface for graphics.c
 * graphics package
 */

#ifndef GKS
#define GKS

#include <stdio.h>
#include <stdlib.h>
```

```
#include <math.h>
#include "driver.h"

#define MAXPOINTS 100
#define PI 3.14159265

/* type for a point in device coordinates */
typedef
struct
{
    int x, y;
}
Dpoint_t;

/* type for an array of points in device coordinates */
typedef Dpoint_t Dpts_t[MAXPOINTS];

/* type for a point in world coordinates */
typedef
struct
{
    float x, y;
}
Wpoint_t;

/* type for an array of points in world coordinates */
typedef Wpoint_t Wpts_t[MAXPOINTS];

extern int MaxX,    /* Max. number of horizontal pixels */
           MaxY;    /* Max. number of vertical pixels */

extern float WMinX, WMaxX, WMinY, WMaxY;

void DelaySec (int);
int MapXw(float);
int MapYw(float);
void GetData(Wpts_t, int *);
void ScalePoints(Wpts_t, Dpts_t, int);
void DrawFigure(Dpts_t, int);

#endif
```

```
/*
 * File: graphics.c
 * Definitions for device-independent routines of graphics package
 */

#include "graphics.h"
#include <time.h>

    float WMinX, WMaxX, WMinY, WMaxY;
```

```
/* Definition of DelaySec from Example 11.4 of Section 11.2 goes here */

/* Definition of MapXw above goes here */

/* Definition of MapYw above goes here */

/*
 * Procedure to get data for figure from text file.
 * Pre:  The first line of the file contains smallest x
 *       value, largest x value, smallest y value, largest y value
 *       separated by spaces; remaining lines contain x and y
 *       coordinates separated by a space.
 * Post: Wpoints is an array of world coordinate points.
 *       NumEls_ptr points to the number of elements in Wpoints.
 */

void GetData(Wpts_t Wpoints, int *NumEls_ptr)
{
   FILE *infile_ptr,      /* pointer to input file */
        *outfile_ptr;     /* pointer to output file */

   char filename[20];

   printf("Give the name of the input file for your figure:  ");
   gets(filename);

   /* open the files */
   infile_ptr  = fopen(filename, "r");
   if (infile_ptr == NULL)
   {
      printf("%s does not exist.\n", filename);
      exit(1);
   }

   fscanf(infile_ptr, "%f %f %f %f", &WMinX, &WMaxX, &WMinY, &WMaxY);

   *NumEls_ptr = 0;
   while ((*NumEls_ptr < MAXPOINTS) &&
          fscanf(infile_ptr, "%f %f",
                 &Wpoints[*NumEls_ptr].x, &Wpoints[*NumEls_ptr].y)>0)
      (*NumEls_ptr)++;

   if (!feof(infile_ptr) && *NumEls_ptr == MAXPOINTS)
   {
      printf("File contains more than %d points.\n", MAXPOINTS);
      printf("Only the first %d points will be processed.\n",
             MAXPOINTS);
   }

   fclose(infile_ptr);
}
```

```
/*
 * Procedure to map the first NumEls WC points to the
 * corresponding points in DC points
 * Pre:  In graphics mode, the first NumEls points of Wpoints are
 *       defined in WC.
 * Post: Dpoints contains the corresponding DC points.
 */

void ScalePoints(Wpts_t Wpoints, Dpts_t Dpoints, int NumEls)
{
   int i;   /* index */

   for(i = 0; i < NumEls; i++)
   {
      Dpoints[i].x = MapXw(Wpoints[i].x);
      Dpoints[i].y = MapYw(Wpoints[i].y);
   }
}


/*
 * Procedure to draw the figure determined by connecting the points
 * in Dpoints with a sequence of lines.
 * Pre:  In graphics mode, the first NumEls points of Dpoints are
 *       defined with NumEls > 1.
 * Post: The figure was displayed on the output screen.
 */

void DrawFigure(Dpts_t Dpoints, int NumEls)
{
   int i;                  /* index */
   int x1, x2, y1, y2; /* coordinates of points */

   for(i = 0; i < NumEls - 1; i++)
   {
      x1 = Dpoints[i].x;
      y1 = Dpoints[i].y;
      x2 = Dpoints[i + 1].x;
      y2 = Dpoints[i + 1].y;
      DD_Line(x1, y1, x2, y2);
   }
}

/* Example 11.13
 * Program to read world limits and world points for a figure
 * and draw the figure formed by connecting the dots.
 * The name of the text file is supplied by the user.
 * The first line of the file contains smallest x value,
 * largest x value, smallest y value, largest y value
 * separated by spaces; remaining lines contain x and y
 * coordinates separated by a space.
 */
```

```
#include "graphics.h"

main()
{
    Wpts_t Wpoints;      /* points of polyline in world coordinates  */
    Dpts_t Dpoints;      /* points of polyline in device coordinates */
    int NumEls;          /* number of points in polyline */

    GetData(Wpoints, &NumEls);
    EnterGraphics();
    ScalePoints(Wpoints, Dpoints, NumEls);
    DrawFigure(Dpoints, NumEls);
    .DelaySec(2);
    ExitGraphics();
}
```

This discussion represents a brief introduction to a programmer's graphics system. All figures are two dimensional with no windows, text output, or color. Interactive user input to modify, load, or save figures is not discussed. We have only looked at graphics from the application programmer's view. A wide variety of end-user graphics systems require little or no programming. Moreover, the development of graphics systems or the designing of fundamental graphics algorithms is not considered.

Section 11.7 Exercises

1. Calculate the aspect ratio of a device with 1360 pixels in the x direction and 880 pixels in the y direction.

2. A device has 900 pixels in the x direction and 1200 pixels in the y direction. What is the aspect ratio for the device?

3. **a.** Modify Example 11.12 so that it draws line segments connecting the points.

   b. Modify the same example to plot $y = \sin(x)\, e^{-0.5x}$ with x ranging from 0 to 6π.

4. Modify Example 11.12 to display an x-axis.

5. Use graph paper to develop a polyline figure and construct a text file using the specifications in Example 11.13. Use Example 11.13 to draw your figure.

6. Consider an example where the world x coordinates range from -50 to 100 and the world y coordinates range from 0 to 200. If the device has a 640×480 resolution, find the normalized and device coordinates corresponding to the world coordinates (-20, 140).

7. Write a procedure, *PlotGraph*, for *graphics.c* that plots any function. *PlotGraph* has three parameters—a pointer to a *float* function with one *float* parameter, a lower bound, and an upper bound. *PlotGraph* graphs the function for x going from the lower bound to the upper bound in increments of 0.05 (see Example 11.12).

Section 11.7 Programming Projects

1. Write a program that reads several lists of world points from a text file and displays a design by drawing a polyline figure for each list of points. Use 999 as a sentinel

value to separate lists. Assume the world coordinates are between 0 and 100 in each direction. The following is an example text file:

```
20 20    45 67    30 90    999 999    67.5 33.4    28.2 44.6
35.5 88.5    999 999
```

2. The orbit of a point x with respect to a function F is the point x together with the points obtained by successive applications of F—x, $F(x)$, $F(F(x))$, $F(F(F(x)))$,. . . . Consider the function from the xy-plane into the xy-plane defined by $F(x, y) = (1 - y + \text{abs}(x), x)$. Successive points can be obtained from $x_{n+1} = 1 - y_n + \text{abs}(x_n)$ and $y_{n+1} = x_n$. Write a program that plots the first 20,000 points of the orbit of (- 0.1, 0) with respect to F. Generate the points twice. The first time, determine maximum and minimum x and y values to use for world coordinate limits. The second time, plot the points. The orbit should look like a gingerbread man. You might find it interesting to consider the orbit of other points.

Programming and Debugging Hints

Internal Limitations

Run-time errors often result from internal limitations of a program. To increase the reliability of the program, the programmer must give it the ability to survive its own errors as well as the errors of the user.

Consider a program that accepts data from the user or a file and stores them in a linked list. We have seen in the description of the *malloc* function that the amount of memory the computer can allocate is limited. Generally, the program cannot predict how many list nodes the computer can allot before memory fills. The programmer must decide what steps to take when the program attempts to allocate memory for a new node and finds no room. Does the program crash? Does it reject the input and refuse to accept any more? Or does it somehow manage to readjust its data structures to accommodate the new request?

These fundamental questions have no right or wrong answer. The programmer must decide the best course of action for a given situation. Sometimes cost, measured in terms of execution and programming time, is a dominant factor. At other times, available memory may be a more important consideration. We should remember that these sources of error are not the fault of the user or the file and therefore can occur no matter how much validation of input the program performs.

Structures with Array Elements

An array's name evaluates to the address of its first element. Thus, when an array is an argument, the computer copies the address of the first element for the function, not all the elements of the array. We must be particularly careful in communicating a structure of information to a called function. With a structure argument, the computer copies the entire structure. If an array is a member of a structure, the computer copies all the elements of the array as well as the other members of the structure. Thus, the programmer should usually have a pointer to the structure as the parameter instead of the structure.

For example, a team recently developed a differential equations package that uses a structure that includes three two-dimensional arrays to hold floating point coordinates of points. Each array can hold 10,000 points. Thus, the structure holds at least 3 × 10,000 × 2 = 60,000 floating point numbers. On a computer that stores a floating point number in 4 bytes, the structure consumes 4 × 60,000 = 240,000 bytes, which is about 240 K of space. When we pass the structure by value to a function, the computer copies the entire structure, doubling the space requirements to about 2 × 240 K = 480 K or almost 0.5 Mbyte. Moreover, copying the entire structure takes more time than copying a pointer to the structure and results in slower performance for the interactive package. Unless the programmer is confident that a structure is small, he or she should pass a reference to the structure to a called function instead of passing the structure itself.

Key Terms

alignment 638
arrow operator 661
boolean_t 669
element 635
enum 668
field 635
full word boundary 638
linked list 665

member 635
node 665
period operator 635
record 634
struct 635
structure 634
structure member operator 635
structure tag 636

template 635
time 642
time.h 642
time_t 642
typedef 640
union 677
word 638
-> 661

Summary

Structures constitute a sort of super-data type, which can represent several different types of data in a single unit. The keyword *struct* specifies a structure definition. After *struct*, an optional structure tag and braces surround a template, which describes the members or elements of the structure. In the following example of a structure,

```
struct inventory
{
    char  name[20];
    float price;
    int   quantity;
}
item1, item2;
```

struct inventory is a new data type. We can declare a variable—such as *item3*—to be of that type, as shown:

```
struct inventory item3;
```

To reference a member of a structure variable, we use the variable name with the period operator and the member name, such as *item1.price*. Once the elements of *item1* have values, we can assign the entire structure to *item2* as a unit with the following:

```
item2 = item1;
```

With file or interactive I/O, however, we must read and print the structure variable one element at a time, such as

```
scanf("%d", &item1.quantity);
```

The period operator has a higher precedence than the ampersand operator, so *&item1.quantity* is equivalent to *&(item1.quantity)*.

As a data type, *struct inventory* can be an operand to the *sizeof* operator. The expression

```
sizeof(struct inventory)
```

returns the same value as

```
sizeof(item1)
```

which in turn is usually, but not always, equal to the sums of the sizes of the individual elements. The discrepancy occurs because of a requirement known as alignment. Some computers require that values of certain types begin in certain locations within a word, such as on a full word boundary, which is the starting point of a word in memory. A word is a unit of storage and transfer in a computer.

C enables the user to define individualized type names with a *typedef* (type definition) statement, such as

```
typedef int integer_t;
```

or

```
typedef
struct
{
    char  name[20];
    float price;
    int   quantity;
}
inventory_t;
```

Then, we can have the declaration

```
inventory_t item1, item2;
```

and we can declare an array of such structures as

```
inventory_t items[100];
```

The header file for time (*time.h*) uses *typedef* to define an arithmetic type (*time_t*) to represent calendar time.

Frequently it is advisable to pass a reference to the structure, instead of the structure itself, to a function. The following is the prototype of a function that updates the structure variable:

```
void ReadItem(inventory_t *item_ptr);
```

In this situation, we pass the starting address of the structure to the function, such as

```
ReadItem(&item);
```

The period operator has a higher priority than the indirection operator (*). Thus, to reference the *quantity* element in *ReadItem*, we write the following:

```
(*item_ptr).quantity
```

Alternatively, we can use the arrow operator, as shown:

```
item_ptr -> quantity
```

The arrow operator has the same high precedence as the other unary operators. Table 11.1 of Section 11.4 presents a summary of the precedences of operators.

A structure can contain a pointer to a structure of the same type, such as

```
typedef struct node   node_t;
typedef node_t *      pointer_t;

struct node
{
    el_t el;
    pointer_t next;
};
```

Each *node* structure contains a member, *next*, that is a pointer to another *node* structure. That structure in turn points to the one following it, and so forth. The structures are linked together in a chain. We call the chain a linked list, and a single element is a node. We can expand and contract a linked list as necessary. Declaring *head* to be a pointer to a node structure,

```
pointer_t head;
```

we start the linked list by allocating space for a node and pointing *head* to this area, as follows:

```
head = (pointer_t)malloc(sizeof(node_t));
```

If we need another node in the list, we can allocate space for the structure and point the first node's *next* field to the new area, as shown:

```
head->next = (pointer_t)malloc(sizeof(node_t));
```

The chapter considered two other data types besides structures with which we frequently use *typedef*—enumeration and union types. Enumeration types allow the manipulation of symbols as new types of constants. We define the enumeration type *enum week* as follows:

```
enum week
{
    MONDAY, TUESDAY, WEDNESDAY, THURSDAY, FRIDAY, SATURDAY, SUNDAY
};
```

and declare a variable *today* of that type as

```
enum week today;
```

We can use *typedef* to define a data type that includes the keyword *enum* and the template, as shown:

```
typedef
enum
{
    MONDAY, TUESDAY, WEDNESDAY, THURSDAY, FRIDAY, SATURDAY, SUNDAY
}
week_t;
```

and declare *today* as

```
week_t today;
```

We define the boolean type *boolean_t* as

```
typedef enum {FALSE, TRUE} boolean_t;
```

C implements an enumeration data type as *int*, with the first constant corresponding to 0, the second to 1, and so on. In an expression involving values of type *int* and of an enumeration type, we should cast all values to the same type.

We cannot read or print a symbolic constant directly. Consequently, to print meaningful words for the day of the week, we often use the *enum* constants in a *switch* expression and print the corresponding string constant, as follows:

```
switch (today)
{
    case MONDAY:
```

```
        printf("MONDAY.\n");
        break;
    case TUESDAY:
        ⋮
```

Sometimes it is helpful to be able to treat a single area of memory as if it contains, at different times, values of different types. The *union* construct in C provides a facility for accomplishing such an overlay. The syntax for unions is identical to that for structures, except we replace the keyword *struct* with the keyword *union*. Here is a sample *union* declaration:

```
union sample
{
    int    integer;
    float real;
}
example;
```

The variable *example* has the maximum of the lengths of the two elements. It is the programmer's responsibility to keep up with the meaning of the area. One method of doing so is to have a structure with a flag and the union, as follows:

```
typedef
struct
{
    flag_t flag;
    union
    {
        int    integer;
        float real;
    }
    example;
}
number_t;
```

The value of the flag indicates the format of the rest of the record.

Review Questions

1. What is the chief reason for using structures?

2. What distinguishes an array from a structure?

3. Name the special keyword used in defining a structure.

4. What is a template, and how does it relate to a structure?

5. What is a structure tag and what is its purpose?

6. In what two ways can a structure variable be declared?

7. What rules govern the use of the period (.) operator?

8. What is the connection between a structure and a new data type?

9. Suppose you want to define *price_t* to be equivalent to type *float*. How would you accomplish this using the *typedef* declaration?

10. What advantage is there in writing the following?

```
typedef char * string_t;
```

11. Give the name of the function that we can use to return the calendar time along with the type of its returned value and the header file that declares the function.

12. What is meant by an array of structures?

13. What is meant by the nesting of structures?

14. What restriction applies to the nesting of structures?

15. What is the meaning of the arrow (->) operator?

16. Define a linked list.

17. Define enumeration type *class_t* to contain constants for college classes, freshman, sophomore, junior, and senior.

18. What must a structure include if it is to be a node in a linked list?

19. What is the *union* construct?

Laboratory

In this laboratory, we develop a program to maintain a stock portfolio. The program provides a menu of options that allow the user to load and save portfolios, enter stock purchases and sales, update stock prices, and display a portfolio. The assignment is organized for teams of three members, whom we designate A, B, and C. The letter T marks exercises for the team to do together, and A, B, and C designate exercises for each respective team member.

Copy file *LAB11.c* onto your disk. This file contains a shell of the program with stubs for all the top-level modules. The stubs are incomplete. Each team must choose the exact number, order, and type of parameters for each module. Figure 11.23 shows the top-level structure chart for the stock portfolio program. A listing and example output follow.

Figure 11.23 Structure chart for Chapter 11 Laboratory

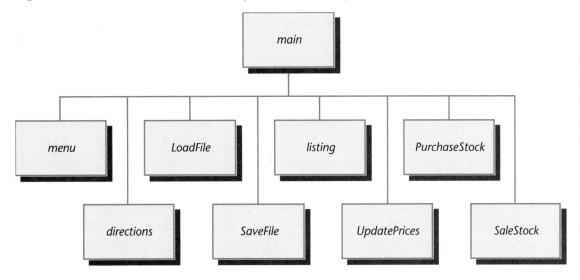

```
 *
 * Program to maintain a stock portfolio.
 */

#include <stdio.h>

#define MAXSTOCKS 100

void directions(void);
void menu(void);
void LoadFile(void);
void SaveFile(void);
void listing(void);
void UpdatePrices(void);
void PurchaseStock(void);
void SaleStock(void);
void error(void);

typedef char string20_t[20];

main()
{
    char choice;
    int NumStocks = 0;
    string20_t FileName = "";

    do
    {
        menu();
        choice = getchar();
        fflush(stdin);

        switch (choice)
        {
            case '1': directions();
                    break;
            case '2': LoadFile();
                    break;
            case '3': SaveFile();
                    break;
            case '4': listing();
                    break;
            case '5': UpdatePrices();
                    break;
            case '6': PurchaseStock();
                    break;
            case '7': SaleStock();
                    break;
            case '8': break;
            default: error();
        }
```

```
    }
    while (choice != '8');
}

void directions(void)
{
    printf("Directions module is not implemented.\n\n");
    printf("Press return to continue ");
    getchar();
}

void menu(void)
{
    printf("           STOCK PORTFOLIO MAINTENANCE\n");
    printf("(1)  Directions\n");
    printf("(2)  Load Portfolio\n");
    printf("(3)  Save Portfolio\n");
    printf("(4)  Portfolio Listing\n");
    printf("(5)  Update Stock Price\n");
    printf("(6)  Enter a Stock Purchase\n");
    printf("(7)  Enter a Stock Sale\n");
    printf("(8)  Quit\n");
    printf("           Enter your Choice: ");
}

void LoadFile(void)
{
    printf("Load Portfolio module is not implemented.\n\n");
    printf("Press return to continue ");
    getchar();
}

void SaveFile(void)
{
    printf("Save Portfolio File module is not implemented.\n\n");
    printf("Press return to continue ");
    getchar();
}

void listing(void)
{
    printf("Portfolio listing module is not implemented.\n\n");
    printf("Press return to continue ");
    getchar();
}

void UpdatePrices(void)
{
    printf("Update Prices module is not implemented.\n\n");
    printf("Press return to continue ");
    getchar();
}
```

```
void PurchaseStock(void)
{
    printf("Purchase Stock module is not implemented.\n\n");
    printf("Press return to continue ");
    getchar();
}

void SaleStock(void)
{
    printf("Sale Stock module is not implemented.\n\n");
    printf("Press return to continue ");
    getchar();
}

void error(void)
{
    printf("Error module is not implemented.\n\n");
    printf("Press return to continue ");
    getchar();
}
```

Sample output follows:

```
                STOCK PORTFOLIO MAINTENANCE
    (1)   Directions
    (2)   Load Portfolio
    (3)   Save Portfolio
    (4)   Portfolio Listing
    (5)   Update Stock Price
    (6)   Enter a Stock Purchase
    (7)   Enter a Stock Sale
    (8)   Quit
                Enter your Choice: 3
    Save Portfolio File module is not implemented.

    Press return to continue
```

T. In this exercise, the team develops data structures and a black-box analysis of each top-level module. The stock portfolio should be maintained in memory as an unordered array of records. *MAXSTOCKS* (100) represents the maximum number of stocks allowed in any portfolio. If no file is loaded from disk, the user is starting a new portfolio.

The format of the text file is as follows:

- columns 1–6: ticker symbol; uppercase; all 6 columns used, pad if necessary
- number, average price, and current price separated by blanks, all *float*
- stock name, up to 20 characters

An example line in text file is

```
CAO    23.500  12.750  13.125  Carolina Freight
```

A description of each module is shown below. As a team, do a black-box analysis of each module and choose the number, type, and order of all parameters. Agree on any global constants, types, and variables.

The following are descriptions of the routines:

- *directions* to provide capabilities and detailed instructions for the use of the program

- *LoadFile* to prompt for the name of a file containing a stock portfolio and return a disk file name, an array of stocks, and the current number of stocks

- *SaveFile* to accept the disk file name, array of stocks, and the current number of stocks. If the file name is the empty string, prompts for disk file name, otherwise uses the current file name. Saves the portfolio in the specified format.

- *listing* to accept an array of stocks and the current number of stocks and list the stocks in the portfolio on the screen

- *UpdatePrices* to accept an array of stocks and the current number of stocks. Provides the user with name of each stock, prompts for current price, then updates the current price.

- *PurchaseStock* to accept an array of stocks and the current number of stocks. Prompts the user for ticker symbol (convert to all uppercase). If not in portfolio, prompts for remaining information and adds stock to portfolio. If already in portfolio, prompts for purchase price per share, number purchased and then updates. Returns updated portfolio.

- *SaleStock* to accept an array of stocks and the current number of stocks. Prompts the user for ticker symbol (convert to all uppercase). If symbol not found, displays error message, otherwise displays number of stocks and prompts for number sold and sale price per share. If all shares are sold, deletes the stock from the portfolio, otherwise updates stock record. Returns updated portfolio.

A. This exercise outlines team member A's assignment. Write the *directions*, *LoadFile*, and *SaveFile* modules. Write a simple version of the *listing* module for testing purposes. The *directions* module simply outlines the available features and provides instructions for the use of the program.

The *LoadFile* module prompts for the name of the disk file containing the stocks, reads each line of the text file into array of records, and closes the file. The file name (disk file name), array of records, and current number of records are returned. Repeatedly prompt the user to reenter the file name until a valid file name is entered. Use the editor to produce an example file for testing purposes.

The *SaveFile* module saves the records to a disk file in the specified format. If *FileName* is empty, prompt the user for the name of the file, otherwise use the file name provided. You can test the *SaveFile* by loading with *LoadFile*. Be sure to properly document each module.

B. This exercise outlines team member B's assignment. Write the *listing* and *UpdatePrices* modules. Write a simple version of *LoadFile* to load or assign stocks for testing purposes. The *listing* module should neatly list all stocks with headings. Sample output follows:

```
Ticker   Stock Name        Avg cost   # Shares    Cur.Price    Stock Valve
CAO      Carolina Freight    12.125    300.234      13.500        4053.16

              Total   Portfolio Value -->            234789.98
```

The *UpdatePrices* module should process all stocks in the portfolio, listing the ticker symbol and the current price stored, and then prompt the user for the new price. Return the portfolio with all current prices updated.

Be sure to properly document each module.

C. This exercise outlines team member C's assignment. Write the *PurchaseStock* and *SaleStock* modules. Write a simple version of the *listing* module for testing purposes. The *StockPurchase* module should prompt the user for the ticker symbol of the stock purchased. Search for the stock in the portfolio. If it is a new stock and the portfolio has room (error message if no room), prompt and enter all fields into a record. Add to the portfolio. If the stock exists, display current number in portfolio and prompt and read number purchased and purchase price. Update the number of stock and average purchase price. Calculate average purchase price using the following formula:

(old avg. price $\times$ old # + purchase price $\times$ # purchased)/(old # + #purchased)

The *SaleStock* module should prompt the user for the ticker symbol of the stock sold and the number sold. If the ticker number is not found or the number sold is more than number available, display an error message. If all the stock is sold, delete the record, otherwise update number of stock. Calculate and display the capital gain or loss for the sale, ignoring broker commissions. Use the following formula for gain:

(avg. purchase - sale price) $\times$ number sold

Be sure to properly document each module.

T. This exercise brings the team members' work together. Copy all modules into a single file and test the system. Correct any errors and note suggestions for improvements.

12

Levels of Programming Abstraction

Introduction

This chapter is substantially about levels of abstraction in programming. Higher levels of abstraction help the program developer to think in terms of larger tasks and to create more error-free programs faster. One feature of C that supports abstraction is libraries.

Since Chapter 1, we have used ANSI C standard libraries. A library includes a collection of implementations of useful and related tasks. Among others, we have used the standard I/O library for reading and printing and the string library for text manipulation. In this chapter, we discuss defining our own libraries of type and function definitions. Libraries often contain macros, too, which we define with the *#define* preprocessor directive. Frequently, we have used this preprocessor directive to define symbolic constants, such as the upper bound of an array index. The definitions can be more extensive and can even include parameters. For example, the standard I/O library defines *getchar,* which reads and returns a character from standard input, as a macro.

After collecting macro, function, and type definitions and variable and function declarations for a library, the developer often compiles the function definition file. An application program file is compiled separately and linked to the library. By separately compiling files containing function definitions, we can hide the implementation details of the library from the user. The user can think on a higher level of abstraction for the problem solving and not get mired in details of function implementation. For example, we have used many ANSI C library functions, such as *printf* or *strcmp*. We do not need to know how a library implements such a function. We only need to know its name, the arguments it expects, the task it performs, what it returns, and where to find the function. Header files containing type definitions and function prototypes provide an interface between a program and the library definitions. We include the header file that contains prototype and macro definitions and link our program to the source file of function definitions from the library.

Many programs include header files for several libraries, and some of these header files include others. If the compiler attempts to process declarations from a header file more than once, it issues an error message about multiple declarations. To avoid accidentally including a header file twice, the header file can contain preprocessor directives to check whether the program has already included the code.

Operating systems (OS) often provide features that help us manage multiple files in a project. In breadth Section 12.4, we consider an overview of operating systems and several features of the UNIX, MS-DOS, and MacOS operating systems. For example, each OS has a directory structure for organizing files. Other helpful utilities available through the OS or OS-type functions are the ability to search for every occurrence of a text pattern in files and facilities for managing projects.

We can use a library to implement a data structure. On a higher level of abstraction, we consider a data structure as an abstract data type (ADT) or a set of data objects and fundamental operations on this set. The ADT encapsulates types and operations of the data structure. The implementation as a library enhances the encapsulation and reusability of code, and separate compilation promotes hiding from the user of the package information he or she does not need to know. Thus, the programmer can use the package to develop programs without concern for the lower-level details of data structure implementation.

This level of abstraction is advanced further by a new programming paradigm or method of programming—object-oriented programming (OOP). An object-oriented language facilitates encapsulation of a data structure and its associated operations into one entity, an object. Moreover, the language can prevent the user from accessing the data structure in unacceptable ways. OOP is more than data abstraction and detail hiding, however. Object-oriented programming allows the designer to work with and direct the objects in a natural way, in the language of the application. It enables a new object to inherit the properties of its ancestor and yet allows the new object to have expanded properties.

In contrast to the high-level of abstraction provided by OOP, in breadth Section 12.7, we consider programming on the machine's level or on the slightly higher level of an assembler language. Assembler languages use English mnemonics as substitutions for the machine instructions. With a machine or assembler language, it is harder for the programmer to think in terms of larger tasks. However, an understanding of programming at that level can enhance our knowledge of the computer and higher-level language features. A laboratory simulates machine-language programming.

Goals

To study

- Macros
- The conditional expression operator
- Separate compilation

- Storage classes
- Conditional compilation
- Some operating system features with a comparison of UNIX, MS-DOS, and MacOS
- The object-oriented paradigm
- Object-oriented programming in C++
- Machine and assembler languages

Section 12.1 Macros

In Chapter 7, we noted that *putchar* and *getchar* from the standard I/O library are macros. As with functions, these macros perform tasks. Macros, however, are defined with a *#define* preprocessor directive, not a function definition. As we consider developing our own libraries, we should understand how to define and use macros.

When we associate a constant with a defined symbol, the preprocessor replaces every occurrence of the symbol with the characters making up the constant, not the numeric value of the constant. For example, the definition

```
#define EOF -1
```

assigns the string "−1" to *EOF*. Thus, constants have no innate type. The preprocessor replaces the symbol *EOF* by the characters "−1" without any consideration of the meaning of the two characters. We can assign any string at all to a preprocessor symbol.

The following is a valid preprocessor directive:

```
#define TEST if (a > b)
```

The statement defines *TEST* to be the entire contents of the directive following the symbol—that is, the following string:

```
if (a > b)
```

The statement

```
TEST printf("It worked\n");
```

translates to

```
if (a > b) printf("It worked\n");
```

A preprocessor symbol that is defined as a segment of code is called a **macro**. Macros are useful in making C code more readable and compact.

Example 12.1

Some programmers include the following definitions in all their programs:

```
#define AND &&
#define OR  ||
```

These definitions enable the programmer to write more readable code, such as the following:

```
if (a < b OR c > d AND e < f) ...
```

Example 12.2

We can use a macro to define descriptive words. For example, the definition

```
#define LOCAL /**/
```

makes possible the declaration of a local variable, such as

```
LOCAL int i;
```

in which the preprocessor replaces the word *LOCAL* with an empty comment, as shown:

```
/**/ int i;
```

Such a definition makes C more wordy but helps clarify the meaning of statements that might otherwise be unclear to the reader of the program.

Continuation of Definitions

If a *#define* directive does not fit on a single line, we can continue it on subsequent lines. All lines of the directive except the last must end with a backslash (\) character. A directive can be split only at a point where a space is legal.

A comment can appear at the end of a macro or constant definition as shown:

```
#define CHECK if (a > b) /* test if a is larger than b */
```

A comment can appear at any point in a C program where white space is legal (except, of course, within a literal). The comment is part of the definition, so if it continues onto the following line, the first line must end with a backslash.

Example 12.3

This example defines a macro containing a long comment:

```
#define VERIFY if (a < 500 || 10000 < a) \
    /* check for value out of range */
```

We can also use macros as abbreviations for lengthy and frequently used statements. Even though macro definitions can occupy more than one line, they cannot include a newline character. When the preprocessor replaces the symbol with the text it represents, the preprocessor places the resulting text on the same line.

Parameters

In some cases, a program uses a certain construct frequently, but the details of the statement vary. As an example, suppose a program contains the statement

```
if (a > 0) a -= 1;
```

and the statement

```
if (b > 0) b -= 1;
```

Other than the different variables, the statements are identical in form. It would be convenient to have a single macro to represent both statements. The preprocessor permits macros to have arguments, just as functions do. The difference is that the arguments are strings rather than values. Consider the following definition:

```
#define   DECREMENT(x) if (x > 0) x -= 1
```

During expansion of the macro, the string passed to the parameter *x* replaces all occurrences of *x* in the symbol's value. That is, the statement

```
DECREMENT(a);
```

expands to

```
if (a > 0) a -= 1;
```

and the statement

```
DECREMENT(b);
```

becomes

```
if (b > 0) b -= 1;
```

The macro definition itself (the line containing the word *#define*) does not include a semicolon. When the program invokes the macro later, a semicolon follows the macro call, as shown:

```
DECREMENT(a);
```

A common oversight is to inadvertently place a semicolon at the end of the macro definition, leading to the possibility of two semicolons in the subsequent preprocessor replacement.

The parameter names in a macro are local to the macro. Thus, no conflict exists between a macro's parameter names and identifiers in the program itself. In the definition of *DECREMENT*, it does not matter if *x* is a variable in the program, because the preprocessor replaces the parameter with the argument. Any symbols in the macro definition that are not parameter names or names of other macros are left unchanged and are assumed to be variable names or other C symbols.

Parentheses   The importance of parentheses in macro definitions cannot be overstressed. Consider the following macro:

```
#define SQR(a) a * a
```

The expansion of

```
SQR(x + 4)
```

is

```
x + 4 * x + 4
```

By operator precedence, this expression is equivalent to

```
x + (4 * x) + 4
```

Instead, the macro definition should read

```
#define SQR(a) ((a) * (a))
```

which would result in the following correct expansion:

```
((x + 4) * (x + 4))
```

The outer set of parentheses is useful in the following case:

```
(char)SQR(x)
```

which, without the outer parentheses, expands to

```
(char)(x) * (x)
```

The cast operator has a higher precedence than multiplication. For example, assume x is an *int*. The expansion casts the first x to a *char* and then multiplies this value by the *int* value of x, producing an *int* result. The outer parentheses in the macro definition result in the multiplication being performed first, with the result cast into a *char* as intended.

The *SQR* macro uses no type-dependent operators, so even if x were of type *float*, the macro invocation

```
SQR(x)
```

still would produce the correct expression, as shown:

```
((x) * (x))
```

> To perform the correct macro substitution, we should surround each parameter appearance and the entire definition with parentheses.

Example 12.4

With macros, we can make meaningful substitutions, such as the following:

```
#define UNTIL(x) while (!(x))
```

Thus, the loop heading

```
UNTIL(a > 7)
```

converts to

```
while (!(a > 7))
```

In the macro value field, parentheses separate the argument from the ! operator. If we had defined the macro without these parentheses, as in

```
/* ERROR - need parentheses around x in definition */
#define UNTIL(x) while (!x)
```

then the statement fragment

```
UNTIL(a > 7)
```

would convert to

```
while (!a > 7)
```

Because the ! operator has a higher precedence than the > operator, the compiler interprets the statement as equivalent to

```
while ((!a) > 7)
```

which is not the intended result.

Speed of Execution

If a program must execute a short task several times, a macro definition is a good substitution for a function. The preprocessor conceptually substitutes the macro's definition into the code at each location where the function calls the macro. (The preprocessor performs this conversion without actually changing the source file.) Thus, during execution, the computer finds code for the task, not the invocation. Execution is faster as the computer executes the segment immediately as opposed to taking the time to call a function.

Conditional Expression Operator

Many macros that substitute for functions need to express a form similar to the *if-then* construct—the **conditional expression operator**—which the symbols ? and : represent. With this operator, the question mark and colon are not adjacent. They constitute an example of a rare entity known as a **ternary operator**, meaning it operates on three values rather than one or two. The form of the conditional expression is as follows:

expression1 ? expression2 : expression3

The expression *expression1* is a boolean expression that is a switch to determine which of the two expressions, *expression2* or *expression3,* is to return. This boolean expression is similar to the condition in an *if* statement that determines which of two statements will execute. As Figure 12.1 diagrams, if the value of *expression1* is *TRUE,* the ?: operator returns the value after the ? symbol but before the : symbol—*expression2.* Otherwise, the ?: operator returns *expression3.*

> **Definition** A **ternary operator** operates upon three values.

For example, suppose we have the following assignment:

```
j = (i > 4) ? 100 : 200;
```

Figure 12.1
Action of
expression1 ?
expression2 :
expression3

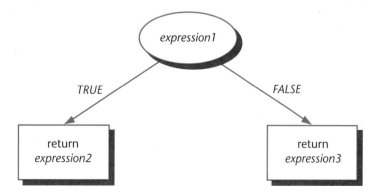

If the value of *i* is 7, then the expression (*i* > 4) evaluates to *TRUE*. In this case, the ?: operator returns the value 100 (the value after the question mark), which *j* receives. If *i* is 3, the expression (*i* > 4) is false, and *j* gets the value 200. The parentheses around the boolean expression are merely for clarity, because the computer evaluates the > operator before ?:. Because the assignment operator has the lowest priority of all, the computer completely evaluates the conditional expression before assigning its value to *j*.

Example 12.5

A frequently defined macro is one to find the smaller of two numbers:

```
#define MIN(a, b)    ((a) < (b) ? (a) : (b))
```

Many programmers consider the operation of returning the minimum too simple to define as a function, but the conditional expression can seem complicated if *a* and *b* are nontrivial expressions. The *MIN* macro makes an expression look like a function call, as shown:

```
printf("Minimum grade = %d\n", MIN(grade1, grade2) );
```

The segment expands to the following:

```
printf("Minimum grade = %d\n",
       ((grade1) < (grade2) ? (grade1) : (grade2)) );
```

The equivalent *if-else* statement is as follows:

```
if (grade1 < grade2)
   printf("Minimum grade = %d\n", grade1);
else
   printf("Minimum grade = %d\n", grade2);
```

We can use the *MIN* macro for arguments of any numeric type, such as two integers, two floating point numbers, or one of each. However, if we define a function to return the minimum, we must declare the parameter types. If the same program must find the minimum of two *float* numbers and later of two *int* values, then we must define two functions, identical except for the parameter declarations. By contrast, we only need one such macro definition.

Incrementing and Decrementing

We should be careful about having a macro argument with post- or pre-incrementing or decrementing. Consider the following use of the *MIN* macro from the last example:

```
z = MIN(++x, y);
```

The intention seems to be to increment the value of *x*, and then to assign *x* or *y*, whichever is smaller, to *z*. The macro expansion, however, is as follows:

```
z = ((++x) < (y) ? (++x) : (y))
```

If *x* is less than *y*, the computer increments the value of *x* twice, because the parameter, *a*, corresponding to the argument ++*x* appears twice in the macro definition. As Figure 12.2 illustrates, if *x* is 2 and *y* is 9, an increment of *x* to 3 precedes evaluation of (*x*)

Figure 12.2
Action of $z = $
$MIN(++x, y);$

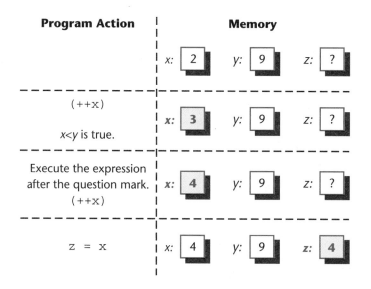

Program Action	Memory
	x: 2 y: 9 z: ?
$(++x)$ $x<y$ is true.	x: **3** y: 9 z: ?
Execute the expression after the question mark. $(++x)$	x: **4** y: 9 z: ?
$z = x$	x: 4 y: 9 z: **4**

$< (y)$. Because 3 is less than 9, the computer increments x to 4 and assigns that value to z. Thus, unexpectedly, for arguments of 2 and 9, z obtains the value 4. Such a problem would not occur with an actual function, because the computer would first increment x and then pass its value to the function. We must be careful in defining and using macros. The programmer should always specify clearly any restrictions on the macro arguments.

> Avoid having a macro argument with post- or pre- incrementing or decrementing.

When to Use

Macros like *UNTIL* can radically alter the syntax used in a program, possibly rendering it unintelligible to a reader other than the original programmer. Macros such as *MIN* do not suffer from this problem because they adhere to the standard function-call syntax.

The advantages of macros versus functions depend on the situation. If a function would consist of only one line of code, to save computing time, we usually should implement the task as a macro. If memory space is the primary consideration, however, a macro may not be the best choice. The computer expands each macro invocation, whereas the code for a function appears only once in a program.

> If a function would consist of only one line of code, to save computing time, we usually should implement the task as a macro.

Although only suitable in certain situations, macros are more powerful than functions in that their arguments can be any strings at all. We can also use macros with arguments of different types. However, we must be careful in supplying adequate parentheses in the macro definition. A post- or pre-incrementing or decrementing argument can cause unexpected results. Moreover, the programmer must not treat macros syntactically like functions. For example, he or she must not declare the type of a macro or take its address.

Section 12.1 Exercises

1. Define a macro *ERROR* to print "An error has been detected."

2. What is the result of the following segment:

```
#define CHK(x)  x > 5 ? 0 : 2 * x
    ⋮
    int i = 7;
    printf("%d\n", CHK(i));
    printf("%d\n", CHK(3));
    printf("%d\n", CHK(++i));
    printf("%d\n", i);
    i = 2;
    printf("%d\n", CHK(++i));
    i = 3;
    printf("%d\n", CHK(i + 1));
```

3. Define a macro to return $5\,x^3$ for parameter x. Be careful about parentheses.

4. Find the error(s) in the following macro definition. The variable z is supposed to get the value of $10((5 + y)^2 - 3(5 + y))$. What is the value of z?

```
#define EQ(x)  x * x - 3 * x;
⋮
    int y = 2,
        a;
    z = 10 * EQ(5 + y);
```

5. Define a macro that accepts a character digit, such as '3', and returns the numeric equivalent, such as 3.

6. Define a macro *ABS* to return the absolute value of a numeric argument, x. (If x is nonnegative, return x; otherwise, return -x.)

7. Define a macro *MAX* to return the maximum of two arguments.

8. **a.** Define the function *random_float* from Example 5.14 of Section 5.4 as a macro.

   b. Define the functions *SeedRand* and *random* from Example 5.15 of Section 5.4 as macros.

Section 12.1 Programming Project

Write a program to simulate the play of a repeated dice game. With each game, the player places a bet and "rolls" a pair of dice. If the player rolls a 7 or 11, he or she wins. If not, the player keeps rolling until getting the first total (a win situation) or 7 or 11 (a loss situation). Define the random number generator to generate a random integer between 1 and 6 and the random seeder as macros. Use any other macros you think appropriate.

Section 12.2 Separate Compilation

Often, a programmer accumulates a collection of useful code, such as symbolic constant and macro definitions, that he or she uses in a number of programs. Conveniently, we can store such code in a separate header file and automatically insert the file into a program with the *#include* preprocessor directive.

Besides preprocessor directives to define constants and macros, a header file can also contain C code for structure template definitions, type definitions, and function declarations. Header files usually do not contain function definitions, however, as it is more efficient to store these in function libraries set up by the user.

A **library** includes a collection of implementations of useful and related tasks. We can thoroughly test these functions and use the library again and again. With a library, we can **encapsulate** these tasks or isolate them with only their inputs, outputs, and actions known to the user and with the behavior of the application program unknown to the library operations. Moreover, by compiling the file of library function definitions, we can hide the details of implementation of the functions. The programmer can use these functions in the development of his or her programs. Moreover, such libraries help the programmer to think on a higher level of abstraction instead of becoming consumed with details of implementation. In this section and the next, we consider features of C that enable us to develop our own libraries. In two breadth sections later in the chapter, we examine how object-oriented programming enables the programmer to solve problems on an even higher level.

Definitions   A **library** includes a collection of implementations of useful and related tasks. **Encapsulated** tasks are isolated so that only their inputs, outputs, and actions are known to the user, and the behavior of the application program is unknown to the encapsulated tasks.

Header Files

In every program, we have included the header file *stdio.h* for standard I/O with

```
#include <stdio.h>
```

ANSI C specifies that *stdio.h* contains, among other things, the *typedef* for *FILE*, the definition of the global variable *EOF*, the macro definition of *getchar*, and the prototype for *printf*. The supporting standard I/O library, which holds the function definitions, is separately compiled. For example, the header file *stdio.h* contains the prototype of *scanf*, and the library contains the object code for this function's definition.

The angle brackets surrounding *stdio.h* in the *#include* directive tell the preprocessor to search for the file in one or more standard directories. These directories contain header files that the system provides and those that several programmers (if the computer is a multiple-user machine) commonly use. When we define our own header file, quotation marks replace the angle brackets, as shown:

```
#include "random.h"
```

In this case, the preprocessor looks first in the programmer's directory that contains the program file. If the file is not there, then the preprocessor searches the standard directories.

Another common use for header files is to provide consistency among several program files. Often a program is so large that it is convenient to break the code into smaller modules, storing each in a separate file. After compiling these separate program files, the linkage editor links the object files to form a single program. By the inclusion of the same header files, separate program files can use the same macros and structure definitions and have access to a common pool of global variables.

A header file can contain other #include directives. It cannot, however, include itself or another file that includes the first file.

Example 12.6

In this example, we assemble a program containing several header files and separately compiled files. The program generates and prints *LOOP_MAX* number of random numbers between 0 and *MAX_NUM* - 1. Finally, the program prints the count of random numbers that were below some *MARK*. One file, say *mainhit.c,* contains the function *main* but no other functions, prototypes, macros, or global variable definitions. (Some operating systems, such as UNIX, require that we name C source files with other extensions, such as *.cc.*) We depend on header files and separately compiled libraries for this information. After assembling the various parts, we compile the program files that contain function definitions and link the various files to form a program.

The function *main* calls *SeedRand* to seed the random number generator and *random* to return a random integer between 0 and *MAX_NUM* - 1. These and several other functions related to random number generation (*random_range, random_float, random_float_range*) were defined in Section 5.4. With the information from the last section, we can now define these short functions as macros. So many applications use these functions, that we group them together in one header file, ***random.h***, which is on the text disk. We can name this header file with any legal file name ending in a period and h. Within this header file, we also place compiler directives to include header files for the time standard library and the standard library, as shown:

```
#include <time.h>
#include <stdlib.h>
```

SeedRand uses *time* and *time_t*, and all the other macros employ standard library function *rand.* By including *random.h* in a program, the programmer does not need to remember to include these header files to access a random number macro.

The function *main* also calls the user-defined function *CountHit*, which increments a counter each time the random number is below *MARK*. We place the definition of *CountHit* in its own file (*count.c*), which we separately compile.

We put the prototype for this function in the header file, *hits.h*. This file contains preprocessor definitions of the global variables *LOOP_MAX, MARK,* and *MAX_NUM*. The file also includes *stdio.h* and our header file *random.h*. Therefore, we only need to include the one header file *hits.h* in *main*. By placing prototypes, symbolic definitions, and inclusions of several other header files in this file, we reduce the amount of source code in *main*.

In all, our program contains the following four user-defined files:

1. *mainhit.c* containing *main* and *#include "hits.h"*. We compile this file.

2. *count.c* containing the definition for *CountHit* and *#include "hits.h"*. We compile this file.

3. *hits.h* containing the prototype for *CountHit,* definitions of global variables, and *#include* directives for *stdio.h* and *random.h*. We do not compile this file.

4. *random.h* containing the definitions of macros related to random number generation. We do not compile this file.

Thus, *mainhit.c* contains the following code:

```
/*
 * File: mainhit.c    Example 12.6
 * Program to generate and print LOOP_MAX number of random integers
 * between 0 and MAX_NUM - 1, then to print the number of these
 * random integers below MARK.
 */

#include "hits.h"

main()
{
    int i,            /* index */
        rand_int,     /* random integer */
        num_hits = 0; /* number of random integers below MARK */

    SeedRand();

    for (i = 0; i < LOOP_MAX; i++)
    {
        printf("random number = %2d\n", rand_int = random(MAX_NUM));

        if (rand_int < MARK)
            CountHit(&num_hits);
    }

    printf("\nThere were %d hits below %d.\n", num_hits, MARK);
}
```

The file *count.c* contains:

```
/* File: count.c */

#include "hits.h"

/*
 * Function to increment a counter
 * Pre:  count_ptr references an integer.
 * Post: *count_ptr has been incremented by 1.
 */

void CountHit(int *count_ptr)
{
    (*count_ptr)++;
}
```

The header file *random.h* is below. In the next section, we explain the meaning of the *#ifndef, #define,* and *#endif* preprocessor directives.

```c
/*
 * File: random.h
 * random.h - header file for user-defined random number generators
 */

#ifndef RANDOM
#define RANDOM

#include <time.h>
#include <stdlib.h>

/*
 * Macro to seed the random number generator srand
 */

#define SeedRand() (srand((unsigned) time((time_t *)NULL)))

/*
 * Macro to return a random float between 0 and 1
 */

#define random_float() ((float) rand() / RAND_MAX)

/*
 * Macro to return a random integer between 0 and UpperBound - 1
 */

#define random_range(UpperBound) ((int)((UpperBound) * random_float()))

/*
 * Macro to generate a random integer between LowerBound
 * and UpperBound - 1
 */

#define random_range(LowerBound, UpperBound)                        \
    ((int)(((int)(UpperBound) - (int)(LowerBound)) * random_float()) \
            + (int)(LowerBound))

/*
 * Macro to generate a random floating point number between
 * LowerBound and UpperBound
 */

#define random_float_range(LowerBound, UpperBound)                  \
    (((float)(UpperBound) - (float)(LowerBound)) * random_float()   \
            + (float)(LowerBound))

#endif
```

The header file *hits.h* follows:

```
/* File: hits.h */
/* header file for main in mainhit.c */

#include <stdio.h>
#include "random.h"

#define LOOP_MAX 10
#define MAX_NUM 100
#define MARK 25

void CountHit(int *count_ptr);
```

A sample run of the program follows:

```
random number = 68
random number = 47
random number = 48
random number = 22
random number = 71
random number =  5
random number = 21
random number = 41
random number = 78
random number = 72

There were 3 hits below 25.
```

**External
Variables**

If we declare a variable globally, any function in the same program file can reference it. A function in another program file, however, cannot use that variable unless the function (or globally, the file containing the function) declares the variable to be *extern*. For example, suppose most functions in a program need to access an array, *price,* and the file containing *main,* say *mainfile.c,* contains its declaration, as shown:

```
int price[MAX_NUM_PRICES];

main()
    ⋮
```

When the compiler encounters the declaration of *price,* the computer sets aside enough space for the array. We define as well as declare the array. Suppose a function, *CalculateTax,* in another file (say *taxfile.c*) wants to access the array, not through an argument-parameter list, but through a global reference. In *taxfile.c,* we must declare *price* to be *extern,* as follows:

```
void CalculateTax(float *tax_ptr)
{
    extern int price[MAX_NUM_PRICES];
```

We do not define *price* in this file, but only declare the array. The computer sets aside space for *price* through its declaration-definition in *mainfile.c,* not because of its declaration here. An *extern* declaration can never include an initialization, because the computer does not create the variable from an *extern* declaration. The *extern* storage class does not create a variable, but merely informs the compiler of its existence.

static and auto Storage Classes

We say that *extern* is a **storage class** because it determines how the computer should allocate storage to the variable. Other storage classes exist, such as *static* and *auto.* Global variables are *static* if they come into existence when the program starts execution and continue to exist until the entire program terminates. Local variables are by default *auto* variables, because the computer automatically allocates them when a function is executing and deallocates when the function terminates. To declare a local variable as *static,* we place the keyword *static* at the head of the declaration, as follows:

```
static int num;
```

If the computer assigns a value to a *static* local variable during the first invocation to the function, that value is still there when the program invokes the function a second time. Consider the following function:

```
void PrintNum(void)
{
    static int num = 1;

    printf(num = %d\n", num);
    num++;
}
```

The first time the program calls *PrintNum,* the function prints *num*'s initial value, 1. Then *num* increments to 2, and *PrintNum* terminates. The second time, *PrintNum* prints the value 2. On the third call, the function prints 3, and so forth. After the first call, the function does not reinitialize *PrintNum.* The computer allocates space for a *static* variable when the program begins and leaves the variable with its value intact throughout execution. Thus, the initialization occurs only once during the entire program, no matter how many times the program calls the function.

A global variable automatically remains in existence throughout program execution. However, if we explicitly declare a global variable to be *static,* such as

```
static int GlobalVar;
```

functions from a different program file cannot access the variable. Global variables that we declare to be *static* are useful when a program file contains a group of functions that share information with one another through global variables, but functions in other program files do not need that information.

In a declaration that starts with the keyword *auto* instead of *static,* the variable is of storage class *auto.* The variable exists only during execution of the function. Because *auto* is the default storage class for local variables, we usually omit that keyword. Table 12.1 presents a summary of the storage classes *extern, static,* and *auto.*

Command-Line Parameters

In order to run, a complete program must have one function that has the name *main.* This function exists throughout program execution. Computer scientists developed the C language under the UNIX operating system in which every command is a program and every program is a command. Under UNIX, when we type the name of a file

Table 12.1   Summary of the storage classes *extern, static,* and *auto*

Storage Class	Example	Meaning
extern	`extern int MaxX;`	Does not allocate memory for variable, but declares it to have been created elsewhere in the program, usually another file.
static	`static int num = 1;`	Default storage class for global variables. Variable remains in existence throughout program execution. When declared explicitly to be *static,* scope of global variable restricted to the file in which it is declared. When local variable declared to be *static,* initialization (if any) only occurs the first time the function is called.
auto	`auto int i;`	Default storage class for local variables, so use of *auto* is unnecessary. Variable created each time the block in which it is declared is entered and destroyed each time the block is exited.

containing a compiled program, the operating system calls *main* to start execution of the program. On the same line, we can follow the program name, like a command, with various arguments that specify how the program is to operate. Virtually all computers with C compilers allow C programs to be executed in this manner and provide a facility whereby the program can access command-line parameters.

To access **command-line arguments**, the function *main* must have two parameters, as shown:

```
main(int argc, char **argv)
```

or

```
main(int argc, char *argv[])
```

Like all parameters, these two parameters of *main* can be any valid names, but the names *argc* and *argv* are conventional and must have the types shown. The computer generates these two arguments whether or not *main* declares them. If *main* does not declare *argc* and *argv,* however, the function need not access them.

The first parameter, which we usually call *argc*, is an integer indicating the number of strings in *argv*, and *argv* contains the command-line arguments. For example, suppose we type the command

```
multiply 7 9
```

to execute the program *multiply.* The operating system automatically spits the command line into strings of non-white space characters delimited by white space. Usually, we can include white space characters in the arguments if we use quotation marks or backslashes. The exact rules vary, depending on the compiler or operating system. The command line above contains three arguments—"multiply", "7", and "9". When we enter the command line, the operating system sends 3, the number of strings in the command line, to *main.* Because we always type the program's name, the minimum value for *argc* is 1. The second parameter, *argv,* is a pointer to an array of pointers, each of which points to a string representing a word in the command line. Figure 12.3 pictures this situation.

If the purpose of the program *multiply* is to multiply its two arguments and print the result, it can accomplish this task by converting *argv*[1] and *argv*[2] into integers,

Figure 12.3
argc and *argv*
for the
command line
"multiply 7 9"

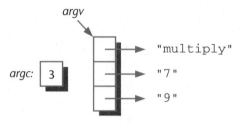

multiplying their values, and printing the result. The program can test the value of *argc* first to determine that the user has entered the correct number of arguments. The program should also make sure that the arguments are strings representing integers.

Example 12.7

In the laboratory for this chapter, we use a CPU simulator written in C. We write "machine language" programs for this simulated CPU, displaying at the user's option "memory" locations, "registers," or both. The command line to run the simulator has the following form:

```
cpusim [-v | -m | -r [-s]] progfile
```

Thus, the command begins with the name of the program (*cpusim*), and ends with the file name. Between the two names, the user can specify one of the options— -v, -m, -r, -v -s, -m -s, or -r -s—where the symbols mean

 -v: verbose output, display memory and CPU registers

 -m: memory output, display memory only

 -r: register output, display CPU registers only

 -s: run output in single-step mode

Thus, to run the program *cpusim,* at the operating system prompt, the user might type

```
cpusim -v myfile
```

In this case, the "machine code" is in the file *myfile,* and the user wants output to be "verbose."

Within the program is a *switch* statement based on the number of arguments, *argc*. Depending on the option, the *switch* statement sets the appropriate flag(s). With four arguments, *argv*[2] should be the option "-s", and *argv*[2][1] should contain the character 's'. If four or three arguments exist, we must check if the second character of the second argument, *argv*[1][1], is 'v', 'm', or 'r'. For two, three, or four arguments, the last argument (*argv*[argc - 1]) should be the name of the input file. The *switch* statement follows:

```
switch(argc) {
case 4: /*
     * Check the -s option (argv[2]) and then
     * fall through to check -v, -m, or -r.
     */
    switch(argv[2][1]) {
    case 's' : SingleStep = TRUE; break;
```

```
        default  : UsageError = TRUE; break;
        }
        /* BREAK OMITTED */

case 3: /*
        * Check for -v, -m, or -r and then fall through
        * to load the program file.
        */
        switch(argv[1][1]) {
        case 'v' : VerboseFlag  = TRUE; break;
        case 'm' : MemoryFlag   = TRUE; break;
        case 'r' : RegisterFlag = TRUE; break;
        default  : UsageError   = TRUE; break;
        }
        /* BREAK OMITTED */

case 2: /* Load the program file argv[ argc - 1 ]. */
        ProgramLoaded = LoadProgram(argv[ argc - 1 ]);
        break;

default: /* Any other argc is a usage error. */
        UsageError = TRUE;
}
```

Section 12.2 **Exercises**

1. Suppose we define *int* variable *count* in one program file. How must we declare it in another?

2. Write a compiler directive to include a user-defined header file, *assem.h*.

3. Write a function, *ErrorProc,* that accepts a string parameter, *error.* The first time *ErrorProc* is called, it should print 1 and the value of *error.* On a subsequent invocation, *ErrorProc* should print the next consecutive integer and the value of *error.*

4. Write a program that prints all of its command-line arguments. For example, if the command line is

   ```
   testing -v -s infile
   ```

   then the output is

   ```
   testing
   -v
   -s
   infile
   ```

5. Write a program *multiply,* which we discussed in this section, that prints the product of its second and third command-line arguments.

6. Explain why variables *MaxX, MaxY, WMinX, WMaxX, WMinY,* and *WMaxY* are declared to be *extern* in *graphics.h* of Example 11.13 (Section 11.7).

Section 12.2 Programming Projects

1. Write a version of the calculator program described below that evaluates only a single expression per program run. The expression is to be specified on the command line. Employ user-defined header file(s) and separate compilation of program files.

   The program can evaluate an expression with any number of binary operators (+, -, *, /) and numbers. You need not handle operator precedence correctly. You may simply perform each operation as it occurs. For example, if the name of the program is *calculate* and the command line is

```
calculate 3 + 2 * 4
```

then the program calculates 3 + 2 for a result of 5 and then multiplies 5 by 4 to yield 20. Write the program so it can handle floating point numbers.

2. Assume you are writing a program, *email,* to handle part of electronic mail. A user sending a message to a foreign country specifies the country as a two-letter code. Every country is represented by exactly two uppercase letters. The program must convert this code into an integer, which is used by the hardware that routes the message. Have the user specify the country code on the command line. The program should look up the integer code in a table, based on the two-letter code. Because the program is to be used for communications, it must be as fast as possible. Assume that memory is not at a premium. Employ user-defined header file(s) and separate compilation of program files.

Section 12.3 Conditional Compilation

Sometimes we need two different versions of a program. For example, suppose we are selling a store inventory system commercially. Some stores may want a version that saves an exceptions report of errors in a disk file, but other stores may want a printed report. The two versions of the program are more alike than they are different, so it would be redundant to maintain both. One solution is to combine the code for both versions into a single program, and then remove the portions not required for a particular version.

#ifdef and *#endif*

Removing statements by hand is tedious and can lead to errors. For this reason, the preprocessor provides directives for removing selective sections of code or for choosing between two possible sections. One form of this **conditional compilation** is similar to the *if* statement.

```
#ifdef preprocessor_symbol
    ⋮
#endif
```

If we define the preprocessor symbol before the segment, the preprocessor includes the code between the two directives (*#ifdef* and *#endif*), in the translated program that it passes to the C compiler. For example, for only the file version of the program to call the function *AddRecord,* we have

```
#ifdef RECORD_FILE
    AddRecord(InvBytes, ErrFile);
#endif
```

If *RECORD_FILE* has a definition, then the compiler receives the statement between the directives. Otherwise, the preprocessor removes the invocation from the program.

The *#ifdef* directive tests whether a particular symbol is defined. It does not matter what value the symbol has or even if the definition includes a value, as in the following:

```
#define RECORD_FILE
```

After this definition, the directive *#ifdef RECORD_FILE* produces a *TRUE* result. However, if the directive

```
#undef RECORD_FILE
```

occurs before the *#ifdef* directive, then *RECORD_FILE* becomes undefined.

If an *#ifdef* returns a true value, all the lines between the *#ifdef* and the corresponding *#endif* directive (or the *#else* directive, as discussed later) remain in the program. The preprocessor processes any directives in those lines, allowing nesting of conditional compilation directives. If the *#ifdef* is false, the preprocessor ignores the associated lines and any preprocessor directives within them.

Even though we talk about conditional compilation directives in the same terms as the C *if* statement, the preprocessor executes the directives before compilation. No overlap can exist between C code and preprocessor directives. For example, we cannot use the *#ifdef* directive to test for the declaration of a variable.

We can use the *#ifdef* and *#endif* directives as many times as necessary. For the file version of our inventory program, we insert the following directive at the beginning of the file or in a header file:

```
#define RECORD_FILE
```

Now the preprocessor passes all the code pertaining to the file version to the compiler.

Command-Line Definitions

On some computers, we may define a preprocessor symbol as part of the command that tells the computer to preprocess and compile a program. In such a case, we need not change the program file. For example, on a computer with a UNIX operating system, we can define *RECORD_FILE* with the **-D option** on the command line that calls the preprocessor and compiler to operate on our program, *ourprog.c,* as follows:

```
cc -DRECORD_FILE ourprog.c
```

To equate a symbol with an explicit value, we use an equals sign, as shown:

```
cc -DVERSION=1 ourprog.c
```

This command is equivalent to beginning the file *ourprog.c* with the following directive:

```
#define VERSION 1
```

#ifndef

The preprocessor also provides the directive *#ifndef*, which produces a *TRUE* result if a symbol is undefined. This directive makes it possible to use a single symbol to switch between two versions. Consider the following:

```
#ifdef RECORD_FILE
    AddRecord(InvBytes, ErrFile);
#endif
#ifndef RECORD_FILE
    PrintRecord(InvBytes);
#endif
```

In this example, if we have defined *RECORD_FILE,* such as for the file version, the program includes the call to *AddRecord.* If we have not defined *RECORD_FILE,* the compiled program calls *PrintRecord* instead.

We need not include a corresponding section of code for every segment in the two versions. Some code may exist in the file version that has no counterpart in the printed report version, or vice versa.

Example 12.8

We can use conditional compilation to select preprocessor directives as well as C code. For example, suppose a program includes a number of header files, which may or may not define the preprocessor symbol *FLAG.* If the programmer never wants *FLAG* defined, then the *#include* directives can be followed by

```
#ifdef FLAG
#undef FLAG
#endif
```

If a header file defined the symbol, we remove its definition. It is not sufficient merely to write

```
#undef FLAG
```

because if *FLAG* is undefined, the directive is erroneous.

By contrast, if FLAG should always be defined, then we write

```
#ifndef FLAG
#define FLAG
#endif
```

An important application of these preprocessor commands is to eliminate the possibility that a program, by including a header file more than once, attempts to redefine a type or redeclare a function. For example, suppose we have developed a library of rational number operations. The header file *rational.h* contains type definitions and function prototypes, and *rational.c* is the source file of function definitions. After a comment, the rest of the file *rational.h* is between preprocessor directives *#ifndef RATIONAL_H* and *#endif,* as shown:

```
/* File:   rational.h */
#ifndef RATIONAL_H
#define RATIONAL_H
  :
#endif
```

If *RATIONAL_H* is not defined, another directive defines the symbolic constant. Thus, even if several program files include this header file, *typedef*s and prototypes should not occur more than once. The first time the header file is included, *RATIONAL_H* is initially undefined. However, with all other inclusions, it is defined and the preprocessor does not pass the subsequent code to the compiler. We should enclose the contents of any header file in such preprocessor directives.

To avoid including a header file more than once, use the following preprocessor directives:

```
#ifndef preprocessor_symbol
#define preprocessor_symbol
    ⋮
#endif
```

#else

Because we often choose between two sections of code with the *#ifdef* and *#ifndef* directives, the preprocessor provides the *#else* directive to operate in much the same way as the *else* clause of an *if* statement. For example, we could write the earlier segment as follows:

```
#ifdef RECORD_FILE
    AddRecord(InvBytes, ErrFile);
#else
    PrintRecord(InvBytes);
#endif
```

If the symbol *RECORD_FILE* is defined, the line before the *#else* directive is included, and the line between the *#else* and the *#endif* is ignored. Otherwise, the preprocessor incorporates the line between the *#else* and the corresponding *#endif*. We can omit the #else directive and the lines that follow, but never the *#endif* directive. Moreover, we can write no other text on the same line as the *#else* or *#endif* directive. We can nest conditional compilation constructs in the same way that *if* and *else* clauses nest.

The *#ifdef* and *#ifndef* directives have two disadvantages. Although we can test whether we have defined a symbol, we cannot test whether that symbol has a specific value. Also, we cannot test if we have defined several symbols or one of several symbols. No connecting logical AND and OR operators exist. The general *#if* directive overcomes these two problems.

#if

The *#if* directive tests an expression. This expression can be of any form that a program uses, with virtually any operators, but it can include only integer constant values. The expression cannot contain variables, function calls, floating point numbers, characters, or string constants.

The *#if* directive is true if the expression evaluates to *TRUE* (nonzero). For example, suppose we wish to select a version of a program as follows:

```
#if VERSION == 1
    AddRecord(InvBytes, ErrFile);
#else
    PrintRecord(InvBytes);
#endif
```

If *VERSION* has the value 1, this code calls *AddRecord*.

If the program has three versions and a segment of code applies to versions 1 and 2, we can write

```
#if VERSION == 1 || VERSION == 2
    ⋮
#endif
```

The preprocessor treats any undefined symbol in the *#if* expression as if it were 0. Using a defined symbol with no value does not work with all preprocessors, and an attempt to do so might result in an error. The same rule applies to a symbol defined to have a nonnumeric or noninteger value, unless the preprocessor can evaluate the symbol's value as a constant integer. For example, with the definitions

```
#define A 4
#define B 5
#define SUM A + B
```

we can use *SUM* in an *#if* expression, because *A* + *B* evaluates to 4 + 5 or 9.

In the Chapter 10 Programming and Debugging Hints, we discussed using the *#if 0* and *#endif* directives to "comment out" a block of code. For example,

```
#if 0
    ⋮
#endif
```

Because 0 is *FALSE,* the preprocessor does not pass the segment to the compiler. Using these directives is better than placing the segment in a comment block (with /* and */), because the close of any comment in the segment with */ would prematurely end the block comment. For example,

```
/* comment out the following segment
    ⋮
    ...        /* ERROR the commented out segment ends here --> */
    ⋮
the commented out segment is supposed to end here */
```

> Comment out large blocks of code with the following:
>
> ```
> #if 0
>     ⋮
> #endif
> ```

Section 12.3 Exercises

1. **a.** Write a segment with conditional compilation—*#ifdef, #ifndef,* and *#endif*—that defines a structure type *AcctRec_t.* The structure contains the element fields *name, AccountCode,* and *balance.* If the preprocessor symbol *LONG_ACCT* is defined, then allow 15 characters for *AccountCode.* Otherwise, allow 8 characters.

   b. Repeat Part a using the preprocessor directives *#ifdef, #else,* and *#endif.*

2. **a.** Write a segment with *#ifdef* and *#ifndef* that defines *INTEGER* as *short int* if the symbol *VAX_COMPUTER* is defined and defines *INTEGER* as *int* otherwise.

   b. Repeat Part a using *#else.*

3. **a.** Write a segment using *#ifdef* and *#endif* that prints

   ```
   C Version running on VAX
   ```

   if the symbol *VAX* is defined. The segment should write similar statements for the symbols *SUN* and *CRAY.*

b. Repeat Part a using the preprocessor directives *#ifdef, #else,* and *#endif.*

4. Write a segment using conditional compilation that undefines *TRUE* and *FALSE* if they are defined.

5. Write a segment using conditional compilation that includes the header file *level1.h* if *LEVEL* is 1, *level2.h* if *LEVEL* is 2, and *level3.h* if *LEVEL* is 3.

6. Explain the utility of the preprocessor directives *#ifndef GKS, #define GKS,* and *#endif* in *graphics.h* of Example 11.13 (Section 11.7).

7. Why are the *#ifndef, #define,* and *#endif* preprocessor directives used in Example 12.6 of Section 12.2?

8. Suppose *stack.h* is a header file for a library. Give preprocessor directives that eliminate the possibility of a program including the contents of the header file more than once.

Section 12.3   Programming Project

Write a program that reads a file of records, where each record contains fields for last name, first name, middle initial, Social Security Number (SSN), and salary. The records should be sorted by SSN. Write a report to a file of the SSNs and salaries of the records that are in order. Write an exceptions report to another file of the records that are out of order, that is, where the SSN on the present record is less than the SSN on the previous record. Using conditional compilation, display the exceptions file on the screen if the symbol *SCREEN* is defined. If your system allows it, define *SCREEN* on the command line. Produce two compiled versions of the program—one that prints the exceptions file to the screen and one that does not.

Section 12.4   Breadth: Some Operating System Features

Even though each one could fill a room, early computers were inefficient and could manage only one program at a time. When an instruction caused the computer to access a peripheral device, the CPU went idle, waiting for the much slower apparatus to complete its work. Typically, a university would have only one expensive, single-user system. Consequently, people signed up to use the computer for an hour, perhaps only once a week, perhaps at 3:00 A.M. Graduate students camped out in the hallway of the computer center, in case someone did not show up for his or her scheduled appointment.

In the 1960s, IBM announced an operating system for their new 360 Series Computer. An **operating system (OS)** is a collection of programs that enables the user to interact with computer system resources efficiently. Some features of operating systems are as follows:

1. In a **time-sharing system**, many users employ terminals to communicate with a larger computer system. **The OS manages the multiuser environment by switching quickly from one job to another,** giving the impression to each user that he or she alone has access to the machine. We say each job gets a **time slice.** People's reactions are so much slower than a computer's execution times, we usually do not notice the time difference. Only in situations with a great number of users or a large program do we observe slow response time. In a **multiprogramming** or **multitasking system,** many programs reside in memory at the same time.

IBM 360 series computer

When an executing program needs to access a peripheral device, such as a printer or disk drive, the OS initiates this slower operation and continues execution of another job. No longer do people have to "camp out" to use the computer at 3:00 A.M. on a Saturday night! Such multitasking systems are available on some single-user computers. In a multitasking environment, when we wish to run a program that takes a long time to execute, we can initiate execution and then use a word processor to write a report. The computer shares the CPU and other resources so that both tasks appear to be working simultaneously.

2. **The OS allocates space in memory for a program and loads it into this space for execution,** being careful that the code does not intrude on another program's designated area. When we perform the steps to initiate use of our word processor, the OS finds the requested program on disk and transfers the word processing program to memory.

3. **When errors occur, the OS may be able to give an error statement and recover.** For example, if we attempt to load our word processor from the wrong disk, the OS tells us to switch disks. If the printer runs out of paper, the OS alerts us to the problem. Lacking such software, the system would freeze up or crash without giving a clue as to the error.

4. **The OS manages I/O.** When we have a *scanf* in a C program, the OS obtains the input data. The OS directs the output for a *printf*. In a time-sharing system, the OS also **spools** the output, so that the printer does not intersperse lines of output from different programs. With spooling, the printer generates all the output for one job before doing another job.

Definitions An **operating system (OS)** is a collection of programs that enables the user to interact with the resources of a computer system efficiently. A **time-sharing system** is a large computer system in which many users employ terminals to communicate with the computer. A **time slice** is a period of time that the OS assigns to a job for execution. When one job is over, the computer executes a time slice for another job.

A **multiprogramming** or **multitasking system** is a computer in which many programs reside in memory at the same time. **Spooling** is a technique of collecting all the output from a program before printing, so that the printer does not intersperse lines of output from different programs.

We now consider some particular features of three major operating systems—UNIX, MS-DOS, and MacOS.

UNIX

The UNIX operating system, which has close associations with C, has been adapted for a larger variety of computers than any other operating system. In 1968, **Ken Thompson** and **Dennis Ritchie** of AT&T's Bell Laboratories wrote the original version of UNIX in assembly language for internal use only. (UNIX® is a registered trademark of UNIX System Laboratories.) Ritchie wrote C in the early 1970s, and later he and others rewrote UNIX so that about 95% of the operating system is in C. Because it is primarily in C, UNIX is portable to different computers, from microcomputers to supercomputers, and provides excellent file-transfer capabilities between systems. UNIX is a flexible multiuser, interactive operating system that supports multitasking.

UNIX files reside in conceptual structures called **directories**, which can be thought of as "boxes" that contain files. These directories in turn can contain files and subdirectories, forming a tree structure as shown in Figure 12.4. In this figure, the directory *ann* contains two files (*data.txt* and *login.com*) and two subdirectories (*sources* and *progs*). The **root directory** is at the top of the tree.

Notice that directory structures are diagrammed as trees rather than as boxes within boxes. A directory does not literally contain other directories or files, but merely points to them. In fact, a UNIX directory is a type of file that lists the names and locations of other files.

Definitions   A **directory** is a tree-like index of files on a disk. The **root directory** is at the top of the tree.

At any given time, a user is **connected** to the **current directory**. When the user refers to a file name in a command without specifying a directory, the system looks for that file in the current directory. (When the file in question is a command name, the system searches several alternate directories.) If the operating system does not find the file, UNIX generates an error message. When the user creates a file, the operating system places it in the current directory by default. Typing the command *ls* alone on a line produces a list of the files and directories in the current directory.

When you log onto a UNIX system, the current directory initially is your **home directory**. In Figure 12.4, *ann* might be the home directory of a user named Ann. This directory contains files and directories belonging to this particular user.

The user can specify the location of a file outside the current directory by identifying the file by its **path name**. For example, suppose our current directory is *users,* and we wish to access the file *prog.c*. In this case, we refer to the file by the path name *ann/sources/prog.c*. Suppose, however, our current directory is *herb,* and Ann has given permission for others to access *prog.c*. The path name now is */users/ann/sources/prog.c* or *../ann/sources/prog.c*. The slash at the beginning of the path name

Figure 12.4 A UNIX directory structure

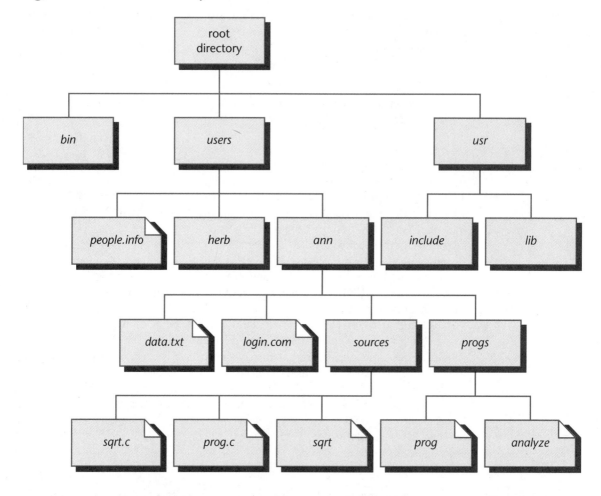

tells the system that the path starts at the root directory. The two consecutive dots indicate a pointer to the parent directory—in *herb's* case, *users.*

We use the *cd* command to change the current directory. For example, Herb in his home directory can make *ann* the current directory by typing the following:

cd /users/ann

Merely typing *cd* connects us to our home directory.

Besides the main operating system programs, UNIX has a number of **utilities** or short programs that provide extra features for the user. Because a C program is usually composed of many separately compiled files, one particularly helpful UNIX utility is *grep* (Global Regular Expression Print). With this command, we can search for every occurrence of a text pattern in a file or files. For example, the following command requests all references to a function called *normalize* in the file *matrix.c:*

grep normalize matrix.c

UNIX lists the line numbers and lines in *matrix.c* that contain "normalize." If we forget where we defined *normalize* in the present directory, we can get a complete list of all references to the function in files with extensions of *.c* or *.h* as follows:

grep normalize *.c *.h

Should we wish to distinguish "normalize" from "vecnormalize" or "normalized," we can surround the name with blanks. In this case, we need to delimit the expression with apostrophes, as shown:

```
grep ' normalize ' *.c *.h
```

Another powerful utility, *make*, helps users to manage projects. For example, suppose in our project we have files *matrix.c, CopyMat.c, MatMult.c,* and *MatSum.c.* With the editor, we create a file called *Makefile* that holds all the instructions for compiling, linking, and executing the project, as follows:

```
matrix.o:  matrix.c
   cc -c matrix.c

CopyMat.o: CopyMat.c
   cc -c CopyMat.c

MatMult.o: MatMult.c
   cc -c MatMult.c

MatSum.o:  MatSum.c
   cc -c MatSum.c


matrix:    matrix.o CopyMat.o MatMult.o MatSum.o
```

The first line states that *matrix.o* should be the name of the object file associated with the source file *matrix.c.* The *cc* line instructs the computer to compile the source file but suppress loading. A similar pair of lines appears for each file. The last line says to create an executable file *matrix* of all the object files and to proceed with execution. To compile, link, and execute, we type *make matrix.* Once we have successfully accomplished this task, we type *matrix* to execute again. Suppose we then decide to change the file *CopyMat.c.* After editing, we type *make matrix,* and the *make* utility only recompiles what is necessary. For large projects, we save time retyping lengthy commands. Moreover, we avoid the problem of forgetting to recompile an altered file or of performing unnecessary compilations.

The UNIX environment is rich with many capabilities. Further study into its commands and utilities can help you become a more efficient programmer on a computer that has a UNIX operating system.

MS-DOS

The **Microsoft Disk Operating System, MS-DOS,** has a similar directory structure to that of UNIX, but is for single-user, IBM-compatible microcomputers. (MS-DOS™ is a registered trademark of Microsoft Corporation.) DOS usually is stored on disk and loaded into memory. Except for syntactic changes, maneuvering through the directory structure is similar to UNIX. Each disk has its own root directory. For example, on a microcomputer with a hard drive (*C*) and two floppy drives (*A* and *B*), to change connection from drive *A* to drive *C* we type *C:.* Suppose the directory structure for drive *C* is as in Figure 12.5. In this case, the root directory is *C: *, and the path from there to *prog.c is C:\sources\prog.c.* Notice the slant of the slash is opposite to that in UNIX. The *cd* command also changes directories. If we are in the *sources* directory, to change to the *progs* directory, we type *cd \progs.* As with UNIX, we type *cd..* to move up a level. To connect to the home directory, however, we must specify the slash, *cd * The command for viewing the contents of the current directory is *dir*, not *ls*.

Figure 12.5   A DOS directory structure

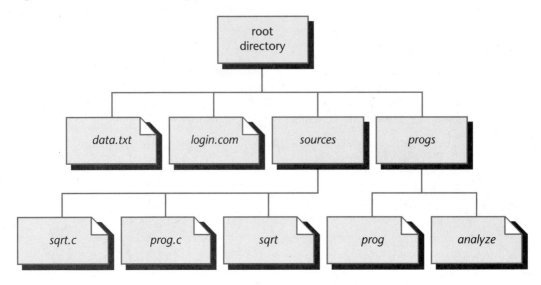

Although *grep* and *make* are not DOS utilities, some C compilers mimic these features. For example, the command file *GREP.COM* is part of Turbo C. Using the same type of command as in UNIX, we can search files for a text pattern. Turbo C supplies *make* capabilities as well. As with UNIX, we build a *Makefile* using the compile command *tcc,* the extension *obj* instead of *o,* and the extension *exe* for the executable file, as follows:

```
matrix.obj:    matrix.c
     tcc -c matrix.c

CopyMat.obj:  CopyMat.c
     tcc -c CopyMat.c

MatMult.obj:  MatMult.c
     tcc -c MatMult.c

MatSum.obj:    MatSum.c
     tcc -c MatSum.c

matrix.exe:    matrix.obj CopyMat.obj MatMult.obj MatSum.obj
```

At the DOS prompt, we type *make. Grep* and *make* can be helpful in managing projects with several files.

MacOS   Instead of typed commands, the operating system for the Apple Macintosh, **MacOS,** has a **graphical user interface** or **GUI** (pronounced gooey). (Macintosh™ is a registered trademark of Apple Corporation.) With a GUI, virtually all actions can be accomplished by making choices with a mouse from menus or visual cues on the screen. A work area on the screen, called a **desktop,** can contain **icons** and overlapping **windows** displaying part of the directory structure. On the Macintosh, a directory is called a **folder** and is so pictured. To see the contents of a folder, disk, or file, we open by double-clicking (clicking twice quickly) its icon. To move from one level to another in the hierarchical structure, we do not type a *cd* command, but click on the appropriate window. Pull-down menus at the top of the screen provide other operating system options. Moreover, the menus are similar from one application to another. For example, whether the application is a word processor or a graphics program, to save we choose *Save* from the *File* menu on the left. To make a copy of a paragraph or a figure, we select the item with the mouse and choose *Copy* from the second menu, which is *Edit*. To place the copy, we click on the desired location and choose *Paste* from the *Edit* menu. We can copy a figure from the graphics package, switch to a word processor from a different vendor with a click of the mouse, and paste in the figure in the middle of the paper.

Definitions   **Graphical user interface** (**GUI**) is a computer interface in which the user can accomplish virtually all actions by making choices with a mouse from menus or visual cues on the screen. **Windows** are overlapping rectangles on a screen display.

Although *grep* and *make* are not standard utilities of MacOS, a popular C compiler for the Macintosh, THINK C, provides similar capabilities. Following the same GUI in THINK C, we can search for a text pattern by selecting *Find* from the *Search* menu. The operating system then presents us with pop-up windows. By making appropriate choices, we can search for the pattern in multiple files, look for whole words only, consider or ignore case, and even use search extensions accessible with *grep*.

The capabilities of *make* are also available through the GUI of THINK C. When we choose *New* from the *Project* menu, THINK C starts making the project. Through menu choices, we can add files to or remove files from the project. When we select *Run* from the *Project* menu, the compiler determines which files, if any, need compilation.

The GUI is a significant departure from the command-line interfaces of UNIX and DOS. Systems designers made definite, distinct choices in designing operating systems to help the user interact with the computer's resources. For DOS machines, Microsoft developed *Windows* software that provides a GUI. The operating system is still MS-DOS, but the interface is more user friendly.

Section 12.4 Exercises

1. Attempt to load a file that is not in your current directory or folder into the memory of the computer. What error message does the operating system give?

2. Issue a command by typing or using mouse clicks to see the files in your current directory or folder.

3. How many files are in your current directory or folder? How many subdirectories or folders? Following one path, go to the deepest level you can.

4. **a.** In one of your recent programming projects, search for all occurrences of *int* in all the files.

   b. Search for the equals operator, surrounded by blanks.

5. In a recent programming project, construct a *Makefile* and make it. (This step is already done for THINK C users.) Edit one or more files by adding some blank lines, remake the project, and describe what happens.

6. Write a one-page paper with references on a separate page on the history of a particular operating system.

Section 12.5 Breadth: The Object-Oriented Paradigm

Abstract Data Type

A big deal was in the making, the biggest ever for the company, and the president was in no mood for the problems and questions of his subordinates. As vice presidents, lawyers, and secretaries listened intently, the boss spoke deliberately, "I don't care how you do it, just do it!" The object of his displeasure stuttered, "Well, I . . . I guess I can . . . " A frown appeared on the president's face as he interrupted, "I really don't want to hear it! I told you I need you to shift our assets, and I've given you all the information you asked for. Now, do your job, and stop bothering me with how you plan to pull it off." He looked around the hushed room to make his point to everyone, "I've got enough on my mind putting this whole glorious mess together without getting bogged down in the minute details of how each of you does your part and without having to keep you informed of my every move." In a calmer and more encouraging tone, the president ended, "This deal is important. I sketched out the plan for it a year ago, and now I'm depending on each of you to somehow get your jobs done so I can do mine. I'm counting on you."

No, you haven't picked up the wrong book. Actually, this scene is an analogy for two important concepts in computer science—high-level program design and abstract data types. The president has designed an overall plan for this important deal, and now he is calling on subordinates to consider specific parts of the scheme in greater detail. Undoubtedly, some individuals will order others to carry out the specifics of their jobs. This hierarchy of command and work is reminiscent of high-level program design, of breaking the project down into smaller and smaller modules. As discussed earlier, programs designed from the top down in a modular fashion are far easier to develop and maintain.

The drama is also an analogy for the concept of an abstract data type. The president knows what tasks need to be done, and he is depending on others to perform these duties correctly. Just as it is easier for the president to create the blueprint of the big deal in terms of objects—such as assets—and definite, larger operations on these objects, it is easier for us to design major programs considering each data structure as a set of data objects and the basic operations performed on them. Moreover, while fitting all the pieces together, the president does not need or want to know the details of implementation. Such details would only muddle his thinking about the larger goal. He does not care how his subordinates solve their tasks. Similarly, if we first consider data structures on a high level without concern for the implementation details, we have a powerful tool that simplifies the process of handling data and extends naturally the concept of structured programming. We often approach a data structure as an **abstract data type (ADT)**, or a set of data items and fundamental operations on this set, before implementing the structure and developing major applications. Not only is it more manageable to design algorithms with the high-level operations of an ADT, it is easier to study each data structure as an ADT before examining how to code the items and operations in a computer language.

Definition	An **abstract data type (ADT)** is a set of data items and fundamental operations on this set.

To illustrate another issue involved in **data abstraction**, the president wanted to remain isolated from the details of the individual tasks he had assigned. He gave each person the information needed, and he expected results. Moreover, he saw no need for subordinates to meddle in his affairs. This situation mirrors the concept of **encapsu-**

lation for data structure operations. Within a program, each operation should be encapsulated or isolated with only its inputs, outputs, and action known to the user and with the behavior of the rest of the program unknown to the operation.

> **Definition**   **Encapsulated** tasks are isolated so that only their inputs, outputs, and actions are known to the user, and the behavior of the application program is unknown to the encapsulated tasks.

As another analogy, a data structure operation is like a soft drink machine whose contents are not visible. You put the correct money in the slot, press the proper button, and get the drink you want. What goes on inside the machine is unknown and unimportant as long as you get your drink. If you do not put in enough money or if you press the wrong button, you do not get the soft drink you want. Similarly, each operation has particular inputs and assumptions that must be met to return the desired results.

An Abstract View of the Integer Type

Several data types are built into C—such as *int*, *float*, and *char*—that encapsulate a data structure and operations. How might we define the data type *int* on the abstract level? We need to give values that variables of that type can hold and the basic operations that can be performed with these variables. We can develop other operations in terms of these basic ones. These basic operations are the axioms by which we define our structure. Just as we can start with a different set of axioms and basic definitions to define the same mathematical structure, so we can have different sets of basic operations to define the same data structure. We choose one set of basic operations for the ADT integer, realizing that we could have legitimately picked a different set or defined an operation in a slightly different way. Figure 12.6 gives one possible description of an ADT integer.

Levels of Implementation

With this ADT, we are not concerned with how the operations are represented in C or how they are implemented in the computer. For instance, C represents *IntegerAddition(i, j)* as $i + j$. In LISP, however, $(+ \ i \ j)$ indicates this addition, and in Forth, $i \ j \ +$ accomplishes the same thing. At this high level of an ADT, we do not need to consider the syntax of a particular language.

In C, the same representation $(x + y)$ is used for the addition of two floating point numbers as well as of two integers. The implementation is in fact very different. Because this operation is built in, we have not worried about these details. We have used the operation with a clear understanding of what + does, if not how the computer performs the addition. The details of how integer addition is accomplished are hidden from us.

An Abstract View of Arrays

Let us consider a one-dimensional array as another example of an ADT. A one-dimensional array is certainly a composite type, made up of at least one element. Moreover, a fixed number of elements of the same type are arranged in a **linear order** or as a **sequence**, such that there is a first element, a second, and so forth. An index, which has type *int* and a smallest value 0, is used in accessing individual array elements. Each index has an associated array element, and vice versa, so we can say that a **one-to-one correspondence** exists between the set of index values and the set of array elements. Having discussed the data objects, what operations do we wish to

Figure 12.6
Definition of
ADT integer

ADT Integer

Data: Scalar elements with values in the set

{ . . . , –3, –2, –1, 0, 1, 2, 3, . . . }

Operations:

Notation:

i, j, k	integers
nzi	nonzero integer
e	integer data item
b	boolean value of *FALSE* or *TRUE*

StoreInteger(i, e)

Procedure to store *e*'s value in variable *i*

IntegerAddition(i, j) ⟶ *k*

Function to return the sum of *i* and *j*

IntegerSubtraction(i, j) ⟶ *k*

Function to return the difference of *j* subtracted from *i*

IntegerMultiplication(i, j) ⟶ *k*

Function to return the product of *i* and *j*

IntegerDivision(i, nzi) ⟶ *k*

Function to return the quotient of *i* divided by *nzi*

Remainder(i, nzi) ⟶ *k*

Function to return the integer remainder of *i* divided by *nzi*

EqualZero(i) ⟶ *b*

Function to return *TRUE* if *i* equals zero, *FALSE* otherwise

GreaterThanZero(i) ⟶ *b*

Function to return *TRUE* if *i* is greater than zero, *FALSE* otherwise

perform on this structure? For the applications, we need to be able to place a value into an element of the array and to get a value from it. The definition of ADT array is displayed in Figure 12.7.

Definitions   A **linear order** or **sequence** is an arrangement of values such that there is a first element, a second, and so forth. A **one-to-one correspondence** exists between sets *A* and *B* if there is a pairing of the elements, such that for each element of *A* there corresponds exactly one element of *B*, and vice versa.

Object-Oriented Programming

Object-oriented programming (OOP) is a method of programming or a **paradigm** that takes the abstract data model to a higher level of abstraction. An object-oriented language facilitates encapsulation of a data structure and its associated operations into one entity—an **object.** Moreover, the language can prevent the user from accessing the

Figure 12.7
Definition of
ADT array

ADT Array

Data: Sequence of elements of the same type. An associated index has type *int* and smallest value 0. A one-to-one correspondence exists between the values of the index and the array elements.

Operations:

Notation:

el_t	type of each element of the array
a	one-dimensional array
i	index
e	item of type *el_t*

StoreArray(a, i, e)

Procedure to store *e*'s value in the element of array *a* with index *i*

RetrieveArray(a, i) $\longrightarrow$ *e*

Function to return the value of the element in array *a* with index *i*

data structure in unacceptable ways. OOP is more than data abstraction and detail hiding. It allows the designer to work with and direct the objects in a natural way, in the language of the application. It enables a new object to inherit the properties of its ancestor and yet allows the new object to have expanded properties. The three main characteristics of OOP are encapsulation, inheritance, and polymorphism.

Encapsulation is combining the data and **methods** or actions that manipulate the data in one place, an object. Details of the data structure and the algorithms used in the methods are hidden from the program that uses the object.

Inheritance is the ability to define an object as a descendant of an existing object. The new object inherits the data structure and methods of its ancestors, but can have additional data structures and methods. An object can be extended and enhanced without considering the details of its ancestors. Many programming environments now provide objects that the programmer can extend and modify to meet his or her needs without knowledge of the details of its ancestors.

Polymorphism occurs when a single method name, used up and down the hierarchy of objects, acts in an appropriate—possibly different—way for each object. The idea of polymorphism is really not new to us. We use the same "+" sign when we add integers or floating point numbers, yet floating point numbers are stored and added differently than integers. The "+" sign exhibits polymorphism, or taking more than one form.

Definitions   **Object-oriented programming (OOP)** is a programming paradigm that takes the abstract data model to a higher level of abstraction. In OOP, an **object** is an entity consisting of a data structure and its associated operations or **methods**. The three main characteristics of OOP are encapsulation, inheritance and polymorphism. **Encapsulation** is combining the data and methods that manipulate the data in one place—an object. **Inheritance** is the ability to define an object as a descendant of an existing object. **Polymorphism** occurs when a single method name, used up and down the hierarchy of objects, acts in an appropriate—possibly different—way for each object.

Objects in the C++ language are like structures that include methods as functions. Objects also have the ability to inherit. Before we look at the implementation of objects in the next section, we consider some examples to illustrate OOP's main characteristics—encapsulation, inheritance, and polymorphism.

Example 12.9

Consider the problem of maintaining and displaying a date. The data structure and the methods are all one object, as follows:

object *date:*
- data structure:
  - *month*
  - *day*
  - *year*
- methods:
  - *AssignDate*
  - *DisplayShort*
  - *DisplayVerbose*
  - *NextDay*

We can create a date by passing the method *AssignDate* integer arguments for the month, day, and year. The actual representation of the date is hidden from the user. If the date is January 23, 1997, *DisplayShort* would print 1/23/97. Calling *DisplayVerbose* would print January 23, 1997. Invoking *NextDay* would change the date to January 24, 1997.

Example 12.10

The set of complex numbers is important in engineering and mathematics. Although you might not be familiar with complex numbers, you do not need to know much to understand this example. The general form of a complex number is $a + bi$, where a and b are real numbers and i is $\sqrt{-1}$. We call a the real part and b the imaginary part of the number. For example, $2 + 3i$ is a complex number with real part 2 and imaginary part 3. The two basic operations we perform on complex numbers are addition and multiplication. (In the next section, we define these operations.) Thus, we can define the object *complex* as follows:

object *complex:*
- data structure:
  - *real*
  - *imag*
- methods:
  - *complex*
  - *display*
  - *add*
  - *multiply*

For real numbers a and b, we can use the method *complex* to construct a complex number, $a + bi$. Suppose we create complex number objects f and g. With f's *add*, we can add g to f, so that f becomes the sum of the two numbers. Similarly, we can multiply f by g, giving f the result of the product. With an object's *display*, we can display the complex number in the usual format, $a + bi$.

Example 12.11

Consider some playing cards. A *PlayingCard* object has a face value (ace, 2–10, jack, queen, king) and suit (club, diamond, heart, spade). We might have methods to assign and display and another method (*WhatFaceValue*) to return the face value of the playing card object. Scoring of the card, however, varies from game to game. Thus, we can develop playing card objects specific to each game that inherit the data structure and methods from *PlayingCard* but have their own functions for scoring. The objects *BJCard* and *BridgeCard* inherit all the attributes of *PlayingCard*, but score the card differently. We picture the objects *PlayingCard*, *BJCard*, and *BridgeCard* as below. The arrow going from *BJCard* to *PlayingCard* indicates *BJCard* inherits from *PlayingCard*. We say that *BJCard* "is a" *PlayingCard*. Similarly, *BridgeCard* "is a" *PlayingCard*.

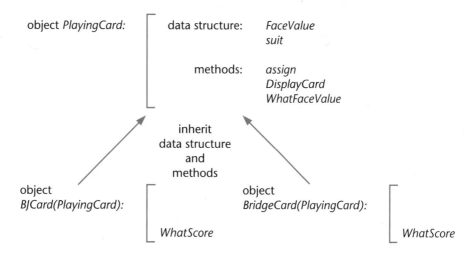

The objects *BJCard* and *BridgeCard* inherit their data structure and methods from *PlayingCard* and add their own method (*WhatScore*). By having the same method name, *WhatScore*, that acts differently and appropriately for each object, *BJCard* and *BridgeCard* exhibit polymorphism.

Example 12.12

Another example of objects that exhibit polymorphism might be *figure* objects like *circle* and *square*. Each *figure* includes a title. Moreover, each can be located by a point. In the case of a circle, the point is its center. We locate a square using one corner, such as the lower left-hand corner. The diagram below with data structure and methods might describe the three objects—*figure*, *circle*, and *square*. Clearly, the action *display* must adapt to the particular object we are drawing—*circle* or *square*. We use the same name but different forms of the operation. This situation exhibits polymorphism.

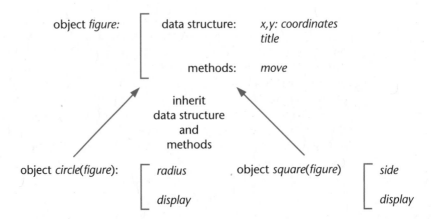

The software design and implementation techniques of data abstraction and OOP enhance reusability, testability, and reliability and reduce software development and implementation time. One goal of object-oriented languages is to provide language support for encapsulation, inheritance, and polymorphism.

Section 12.5 **Exercises**

1. Write a formal definition of ADT floating point with the operations of *StoreFloat*, *FloatAddition*, *FloatSubtraction*, *FloatMultiplication*, *FloatDivision*, *EqualZero*, *GreaterThanZero*, and *trunc* for truncation.

2. Write a formal definition of ADT boolean with the operations of *StoreBoolean*, *And*, *Or*, and *Not*.

3. Give a diagram of an object *time*. Its structure stores the time in hours (0–23), minutes, and seconds. We should be able to display a particular time, such as 2:30 in the afternoon, in standard time (2:30:00 PM) and military time (14:30:00). Have methods to assign a time and increment the time to the next second.

4. Give a diagram of an object *employee*. Its structure stores the employee's name (*name*), Social Security Number (*SSN*), and salary (*salary*). The methods involve assigning and displaying. Have other objects—*manager* and *HourlyWorker*—that inherit the attributes of *employee*. Both should also have methods for returning yearly salary, although the algorithms for doing so are different. (In the case of a manager, the element *salary* is the monthly salary, but *salary* for an hourly employee is the hourly wage.)

5. Many cars have computers. One such computer might keep track of the mileage and time for a trip. Give the diagram for an object *car* with the appropriate data structure and methods (increment and display a mileage and time). Diagram the object *taxi*, which inherits the attributes of *car* and provides an additional method to return the fare.

Section 12.6 Breadth: C++: Object-Oriented Programming

To use a function in an ANSI C or a user-defined library, we only need to know its name, information about its parameters and returned value, and what the function does. The interface information is fully visible in the header file. The user of the package does not need to know the implementation details, and the object code of the library hides most of these well. In ANSI C, sometimes a header file must define a type. Unfortunately, with this knowledge, the user can access the data structure in a way that violates the abstraction of the data structure. In the soft drink machine analogy of the last section, it is like giving the customer enough information and ability to bypass normal operations, break into the machine, and illegally take a drink.

With object-oriented programming, we can prevent the user from accessing a data structure in unacceptable ways by designating certain data and functions as private. Moreover, an OOP language takes the abstract data model to a higher level of abstraction by allowing us to speak in the terms of the application.

Information Hiding

The language C++ (pronounced C plus plus) is a hybrid language that allows OOP and, with a few exceptions, contains ANSI C as a subset. The ++ in the name represents the increment operator in C and indicates the evolution of the language. In C++, a user-defined data structure is a **class**, and its **methods** or **member functions** are the associated functions. Usually, a header file contains the class specification. Such specification includes the prototypes of methods (functions) in a *public* area and declarations of variables—**data members** of the class—in a *private* area. The methods can access the data members, but functions outside the class definition cannot. The class specification usually has the following outline:

```
class class_name
{
public:
    Function prototypes of member functions that are public and can be
    used by statements outside the class definition
private:
    Type definitions and variable declarations of data members that are
    private and can be used only by statements inside the class
    definition
};
```

Such a specification employs **information hiding**. We hide the structure of data members and restrict access to them. Only member functions can manipulate these variables. Thus, if such a variable obtains an illegal value, we know the problem occurs with a member function and not with a function outside the class definition. Moreover, someone wishing to use this class does not need to be concerned with the representation of the data, but only with the methods to manipulate the data members.

The next example has the *date* class specification. Before presenting this header file, we should note C++ has an alternate syntax for **comments**. A double slash (//) indicates that the remainder of the line is a comment, such as

```
// declarations
int i;     // index
```

If the comment continues to the next line, we must repeat // on the new line, as shown:

```
// This comment extends over two lines, so we must begin
// this line with two slashes, too.
```

Example 12.13

In this example, we present an implementation for the *date* class specification in a header file. Example 12.9 of the last section describes this class as having a data structure for a date and having methods for assigning a date, displaying a date in long and short formats, and changing the date to the next day. The public section of the data class specification contains prototypes for these methods, presenting the function names along with the parameter types. The private area declares three data members of type *int*—*month* (1–12), *day* (1–31), and *year* (such as 1922). Because these declarations are in the private section, a program cannot manipulate these variables directly. They are undefined outside the class definition. Only member functions have the privilege of using these data members. The header file follows:

```
//
// File:    dateobj.h
// Content: C++ source code for date class specification.
//

#ifndef DATE_OBJ_H
#define DATE_OBJ_H

class date
{
public:
    void AssignDate(int, int, int); // assign to specified date
    void DisplayShort(void);        // print date in MM/DD/YY format
    void DisplayVerbose(void);      // print date in Month Day, Year
                                    // as in October 31, 1998
    void NextDay(void);             // increment a date by one day
private:
    int month,     // 1-12
        day,       // 1-31
        year;      // such as 1922
};

#endif
```

Another file has the definitions of the methods whose prototypes are in the class specification header file. This file is usually separately compiled from the program file containing *main* and for many compilers ends in the extension *.cpp*. The implementation is hidden from the user. The programmer, who uses this class in his or her program, does not need to know implementation details but only what the methods do and how to access them. These definitions are similar to any function definition in ANSI C, except the class name and a double colon precede the function name, such as

```
void date::AssignDate(int mo, int dy, int yr)
```

This first line of the definition indicates that the function *AssignDate* is a method in the class *date*. A method with the same name may be in another class.

Input/ Output

Two functions in the *date* class display dates. C++ has an improved method of I/O over that found in ANSI C. In every C program, we have included the I/O header file *stdio.h*. C++ can still use this file, but almost always we should include *iostream.h* instead. The iostream library contains an **extraction operator** (>>) for input and an **insertion operator** (<<) for output. These binary operators have an input or output stream as the first operand and an expression as the second. The input stream *cin* corresponds to the standard C input stream *stdin*, and the output stream *cout* is comparable to *stdout*. In place of the newline character ('\n') for advancing to a new line in output, we can use the more descriptive term *endl*. Thus, in C++, we can have

```
cout << "Enter the price: ";
cin  >> price;
cout << "Enter the quantity: ";
cin  >> quantity;
cout << "Quantity = " << quantity <<
        " Total = " << price * quantity << endl;
```

The equivalent segment in C is as follows:

```
printf("%s", "Enter the price: ");
scanf("%f", &price):
printf("%s", "Enter the quantity: ");
scanf("%d", &quantity):
printf("Quantity = %d Total = %f\n", quantity, price * quantity);
```

In C, we must specify the type conversion—such as %s, %f, or %d—and for reading must preface the *float* and *int* variables *price* and *quantity* with an ampersand. The compiler does not detect an incorrect conversion or the omission of &, but either error leads to unpredictable results. In C++, we do not need to specify a type conversion or preface an input variable with an ampersand. In defining << and >>, the iostream library uses **operator overloading**. Based on the type of the expression operand, the extraction or insertion operator makes the proper conversion.

Definition **Operator overloading** is multiple implementations of the actions of an operator, where the particular implementation depends on the type(s) of the operand(s).

Example 12.14

This example presents the source code for the *date* objects. The descriptions of these objects are in Example 12.9, and the associated header file, *dateobj.h*, is in Example 12.13. Because these functions are member functions, they can access the private member variables. They do not redeclare these variables—*month*, *day*, and *year* are part of the object. The function *AssignDate* assigns the parameters to the appropriate variables. Both *DisplayShort* and *DisplayVerbose* print in different formats the date that the member variables represent. Because *year* stores the year in full format (1956), *DisplayShort* must strip off the rightmost two digits (56).

The function *NextDay* adjusts the values of *month*, *day*, and *year* to indicate the next day. If the present day is the last day in the month, instead of incrementing *day*, we assign 1 to that element. In this situation, if the present month is December, instead of incrementing *month*, we change its value to 1 and increment the year.

No value checking occurs in *AssignDate*. The function assumes that the caller passes a legitimate date. Moreover, *NextDay* does not adjust the increment properly in the case of a leap year. The exercises in this section suggest such improvements in the code. Source code follows:

```
//
// File:   date.cpp   C++ source code for date objects.
//


#include <iostream.h>
#include "dateobj.h"


//
// Function to assign a month, day, and year to the date object.
// There is no value checking--the function assumes that the caller
// passes a legitimate date.
// Pre:  mo is an integer between 1 and 12.
//       dy is an integer between 1 and 31.
//       yr is an integer between 0 and 9999.
// Post: The date object has been assigned a date with month mo,
//       day dy, and year yr.
//

void date::AssignDate(int mo, int dy, int yr)
{
    month = mo;
    day   = dy;
    year  = yr;
}


//
// Function to display the date in MM/DD/YY format
// Pre:  The date object has a value.
// Post: The date has been displayed in format MM/DD/YY.
//

void date::DisplayShort( void )
{
    cout << month << '/' << day << '/' << (year % 100);
}


//
// Function to print the date to standard
// output in verbose form, i.e., similar to October 31, 1998.
// Pre:  The date object has a value.
// Post: The date has been displayed in verbose format.
//
```

```cpp
void date::DisplayVerbose( void )
{
    switch (month)
    {
        case 1:  cout << "January ";
                 break;
        case 2:  cout << "February ";
                 break;
        case 3:  cout << "March ";
                 break;
        case 4:  cout << "April ";
                 break;
        case 5:  cout << "May ";
                 break;
        case 6:  cout << "June ";
                 break;
        case 7:  cout << "July ";
                 break;
        case 8:  cout << "August ";
                 break;
        case 9:  cout << "September ";
                 break;
        case 10: cout << "October ";
                 break;
        case 11: cout << "November ";
                 break;
        case 12: cout << "December ";
    }
    cout << day << ", " << year;
}


//
// Function to increment the date to the next day.
// There is no leap year checking.
// Pre:  The date object has a value.
// Post: The date has been incremented to the next day.
//

void date::NextDay( void )
{
    int DaysInMonth;  // number of days in date's month

    switch (month)
    {
        case 4:
        case 6:
        case 9:
        case 11: DaysInMonth = 30;
                 break;
        case 1:
        case 3:
```

```
        case 5:
        case 7:
        case 8:
        case 10:
        case 12: DaysInMonth = 31;
                 break;
        case 2:  DaysInMonth = 28;
    }

if (day < DaysInMonth)      // not a new month
    day++;
else                        // new month
{
    day = 1;
    if (month < 12)
        month++;
    else                    // new year
    {
        month = 1;
        year++;
    }
}
}
```

Another way of defining the *date* class uses the time standard library and two data members—one representing a time structure and the other representing the date as Greenwich Mean Time. With the same public interface to the member functions and same described behavior of the functions, the user of the class is isolated from any changes made by the class developer. Thus, the developer can improve the performance of the routines without the class user having to modify programs employing the class.

Once we have a definition of the data structure (such as *date*), we can declare such variables as *birthday* and *today* to be of that same type, as shown:

```
date birthday, today;
```

We call *birthday* and *today* **objects** in the class *date* or **instances** of that data structure. Suppose in a program we want to establish *birthday* as representing October 6, 1981. The data members for the object *birthday* need to be adjusted. The data structure, however, does not allow direct access to its private variables (*month*, *day*, and *year*). Instead, the program must use the *date* member function *AssignDate*. We indicate that we are giving a date to *birthday*, not *today*, by appending a prefix of the object and a period, as shown:

```
birthday.AssignDate(10, 6, 1981);
```

The segment

```
cout << "Her birthday is ";
birthday.DisplayVerbose();
cout << '.' << endl;
```

displays

```
Her birthday is October 6, 1981.
```

Example 12.15

In this example, we write a short test program to create an instance of a date object, *OneDay*; read values for the month, day, and year; establish the corresponding date for *OneDay*; display that date; change the date to the next day; and print that date. In C++, every function must have a parameter list (even if *void*), a return type, and a return value. Thus, we define *main* as having a *void* parameter. Moreover, *main* returns the *int* 0 upon successful completion of the program, as shown:

```
return 0;
```

The program reads as follows:

```
// File: timpiece.cpp   Test program for date.cpp

#include <iostream.h>
#include "dateobj.h"

int main(void)
{
    date OneDay;        // instance of date object
    int Amonth,         // month--read interactively
        Aday,           // day--read interactively
        Ayear;          // year--read interactively

    cout << "Month (1-12): ";
    cin  >> Amonth;
    cout << "Day (1-31): ";
    cin  >> Aday;
    cout << "Year (0-9999): ";
    cin  >> Ayear;

    OneDay.AssignDate(Amonth, Aday, Ayear);
    OneDay.DisplayShort();
    cout << endl;
    OneDay.DisplayVerbose();
    cout << endl << endl;

    cout << "Next day: ";
    OneDay.NextDay();
    OneDay.DisplayShort();
    cout << endl;
    OneDay.DisplayVerbose();
    cout << endl;

    return 0;
}
```

The display from an interactive session follows:

```
Month (1-12): 10
Day (1-31): 6
Year (0-9999): 1981
10/6/81
October 6, 1981

Next day: 10/7/81
October 7, 1981
```

Constructors

Sometimes a member function has the same name as the class. Such a function, called a **constructor**, is automatically invoked when a variable is declared to be an instance of a class. A constructor, which may or may not have parameters, initializes the object. The program does not explicitly invoke the constructor. By properly defining a data structure with a constructor, we no longer have to remember to initialize the structure.

Example 12.16

In this example, we develop the class *complex* from Example 12.10 of the last section. We use a constructor to initialize the object upon creating an instance of the data structure. Other methods display the complex number, add another complex number to it, and multiply a complex number by it. The addition of complex numbers involves adding corresponding terms, such as

$$(2 + 3i) + (4 + 5i) = (2 + 4) + (3 + 5)i = 6 + 8i$$

In general,

$$(a + bi) + (c + di) = (a + c) + (b + d)i$$

Because $i^2 = -1$, the product of the above numbers can be shown to be

$$(2 + 3i) \cdot (4 + 5i) = (2 \cdot 4 - 3 \cdot 5) + (2 \cdot 5 + 3 \cdot 4)i = -7 + 22i$$

The product formula is

$$(a + bi) \cdot (c + di) = (ac - bd) + (ad + bc)i$$

The header file reveals the prototype of a *complex* constructor with two parameters, one representing the real part and the other representing the imaginary part of the complex number. Thus, the statement

```
complex x(2, 3);
```

creates an object x with data members representing the complex number $2 + 3i$. The private area shows a representation of the data in two variables—*real* and *imag*. We could have stored the data in a structure with real and imaginary elements. The member functions, whose implementations are hidden from the user, would change, but the interface would not. The class specification follows:

```
// File: cmplxobj.h
// Content: Source code for complex number class specification.

#ifndef COMPLEX_OBJ_H
#define COMPLEX_OBJ_H

class complex {
public:
    complex(float, float); // construct from real & imaginary parts
    void add(complex);
    void multiply(complex);
    void display(void);
private:
    float real;
    float imag;
};

#endif
```

The definition of the constructor for *complex* assigns the appropriate parameters to the private variables *real* and *imag*. The function *display* is similar to *DisplayShort* in the *date* class. Both *add* and *multiply* have a constant parameter (z) of type *complex*. We access the data members of z as we would a member function, with the object name, period, and member name. For example, the private data members of z are *z.real* and *z.imag*. We add these values to the corresponding data members of the invoked object, as follows:

```
real += z.real;
imag += z.imag;
```

For example, for complex objects x and y,

```
x.add(y);
```

adds y's *real* to x's *real* and y's *imag* to x's *imag*. If object x represents $2 + 3i$ and object y represents $4 + 5i$, then execution of this function results in x representing $6 + 8i$. The function *multiply* behaves in a similar manner. Because the function changes the real part and we use *real* in the computation of *imag*, we must use a temporary variable, *tmp*, to hold the computation of the real part. The file containing these definitions follows:

```
// File: complex.cpp
// C++ source code for complex number class member functions.

#include <iostream.h>
#include "cmplxobj.h"
```

```
//
// Construct complex number from real and imaginary components
// Pre:   r and i are of type float.
// Post: The complex number object has been assigned a value
//        with real part r and imaginary part i.
//

complex::complex(float r, float i)
{
    real = r;
    imag = i;
}


//
// Function to add a complex number to this complex number
// Pre:   z is a complex number.
// Post: The object's complex number has had z added to it.
//

void complex::add(complex z)
{
    real += z.real;
    imag += z.imag;
}


//
// Function to multiply this complex number by another
// Pre:   z is a complex number.
// Post: The object's complex number has had z multiplied by it.

//

void complex::multiply(complex z)
{
    float tmp = (real * z.real) - (imag * z.imag);
    imag = (real * z.imag) + (imag * z.real);
    real = tmp;
}


//
// Function to print this complex number to standard output
// Pre:   The complex number object has a value.
// Post: The complex number has been displayed.
//

void complex::display(void)
{
    cout << real << " + " << imag << "i";
}
```

A sample test program creating and using objects *x* and *y* follows:

```
// File: cmplxtst.cpp
// Program to test complex.cpp, the complex number class

#include <iostream.h>
#include "cmplxobj.h"

int main( void )
{
    complex x(2, 3);    // construct 2 + 3i
    complex y(1, 2);    // construct 1 + 2i

    // x = x + y
    x.display();
    cout << "  +  ";
    y.display();
    cout << " = ";
    x.add(y);
    x.display();
    cout << endl;

    // y = y * y
    y.display();
    cout << " squared is ";
    y.multiply(y);
    y.display();
    cout << endl;

    return 0;
}
```

The output from this program follows:

```
2 + 3i  +  1 + 2i = 3 + 5i
1 + 2i squared is -3 + 4i
```

Polymorphism and Inheritance

For a *PlayingCard* object from Example 12.11, we have two data members, *FaceValue* and *suit*. These variables are of enumeration types *FaceValue_t* and *suit_t*, respectively. For example, we have

```
enum suit_t {SPADE, HEART, CLUB, DIAMOND};
```

C++ allows us to declare a variable to be of an enumeration type without the prefacing type name with *enum*. For example, in C we would declare *suit* as

```
enum suit_t suit;
```

while in C++ we only must write

```
suit_t suit;
```

The definition of *PlayingCard* is similar to the objects in the last two examples. However, two **derived classes** or **subclasses**—*BJCard* and *BridgeCard*—**inherit** all the (data and function) members of the **parent** or **base class**, *PlayingCard*. A derived class can redefine or create members. For example, we define the class *BJCard* as inheriting the function and data members of the class *PlayingCard*, as well as containing the extra member function *WhatScore*. To indicate that *BJCard* inherits from *PlayingCard* and maintains the same *public* or *private* view of members, we follow *class BJCard* with a colon and *public PlayingCard*. The prototype for function *WhatScore* is *public*. Thus, the definition of class *BJCard* is as follows:

```
class BJCard : public PlayingCard {
public:
    int WhatScore(void); // return card's score
};
```

The derived class *BridgeCard* has its own version of *WhatScore*. Thus, the function *WhatScore* demonstrates polymorphism. The following example contains the code for the class *PlayingCard* and its derived classes.

Example 12.17 _____

The header file *cards.h* has the specifications for the base class, *PlayingCard*, and the derived classes, *BJCard* and *BridgeCard*.

```
// File: cards.h
// Class and type definitions for general-purpose playing card
// (base class) and derived blackjack and bridge playing cards

// Type definitions for playing card face values and suits
enum FaceValue_t {ACE, TWO, THREE, FOUR, FIVE, SIX, SEVEN,
                            EIGHT, NINE, TEN, JACK, QUEEN, KING};

enum suit_t        {SPADE, HEART, CLUB, DIAMOND};

//
// General-purpose playing card class
// Base class for BJCard and BridgeCard
//

class PlayingCard {
public:
    void assign(FaceValue_t, suit_t);   // specify face value and suit
    void DisplayCard(void);             // display card to cout
    FaceValue_t WhatFaceValue(void);    // what is face value?
private:
    FaceValue_t FaceValue;              // card's face value
    suit_t      suit;                   // card's suit
};

//
// Blackjack playing card derived from general-purpose playing card
//
```

```
class BJCard : public PlayingCard {
public:
    int WhatScore(void);      // return card's score
};


//
// A bridge playing card derived from the general-purpose playing card
//

class BridgeCard : public PlayingCard {
public:
    int WhatScore(void);      // return card's score
};
```

The routine, *DisplayCard*, to display the face value and suit of the card uses two arrays of strings, *FaceValueStrings* and *SuitStrings*. The former array is as follows:

```
char *FaceValueStrings[] = { " A", " 2", " 3", " 4", " 5",
                             " 6", " 7", " 8", " 9", "10",
                             " J", " Q", " K" };
```

The latter array is

```
char *SuitStrings[] = { "S", "H", "C", "D" };
```

For example, *FaceValueStrings*[1] is the string " 2"; and *SuitStrings*[1] is the string "H". To print " 2H," representing the two of hearts, we write

```
cout << FaceValueStrings[1] << SuitStrings[1];
```

In general, we print a card with *FaceValue* and *suit* as

```
cout << FaceValueStrings[FaceValue] << SuitStrings[suit];
```

The function *DisplayCard* uses arrays *FaceValueStrings* and *SuitStrings*, but these arrays are inaccessible by functions outside this file of definitions.

To compute the score of a card in their respective *WhatScore* functions, *BJCard* and *BridgeCard* obtain the face value by calling *PlayingCard*'s *WhatFaceValue*. For the bridge card, *WhatScore* returns 4 as the value of an ace, 1 for a jack, 2 for a queen, and 3 for a king. *BJCard*'s *WhatScore* returns 11 for a face value of *ACE*. (Because in blackjack an ace can represent a score of 1 or 11, the program may need to adjust the score for an ace at play time.) Otherwise, if the face value is less than *TEN*, then the function returns one plus the corresponding integer value of the enumeration value. For example, *SEVEN* has an *int* value of 6, so the function must return 6 + 1. For *TEN* through *KING*, the function returns 10.

The source code for the member functions of *PlayingCard*, *BJCard*, and *Bridge-Card* follows:

```
// File:    cards.cpp
// Content: C++ source code for card classes' member functions

#include <iostream.h>
#include "cards.h"
```

```cpp
char *FaceValueStrings[] = { " A", " 2", " 3", " 4", " 5",
                             " 6", " 7", " 8", " 9", "10",
                             " J", " Q", " K" };

char *SuitStrings[] = { "S", "H", "C", "D" };

//
// Function to assign suit and face value to card
// Pre:   f is of type FaceValue_t.
//        s is of type suit_t.
// Post: The playing card object has been assigned a face value of
//        f and a suit of s.
//

void PlayingCard::assign(FaceValue_t f, suit_t s)
{
    FaceValue = f;
    suit = s;
}


//
// Function to return face value of card
// Pre:   The playing card object has a value.
// Post: The face value of a card has been returned.
//

FaceValue_t PlayingCard::WhatFaceValue(void)
{
    return FaceValue;
}


//
// Function to display card
// Pre:   The playing card object has a value.
// Post: The card has been displayed.
//

void PlayingCard::DisplayCard(void)
{
    cout << FaceValueStrings[FaceValue] << SuitStrings[suit];
}


//
// Function to return the score of a blackjack card
// Pre:   The blackjack card object has a value.
// Post: The score of the card in blackjack has been returned:
//        ace -> 11 (application program may need to revise),
//        2 -> 2, ... 9 -> 9, 10 - king -> 10
//
```

```
int BJCard::WhatScore(void)
{
    int ReturnScore;

    FaceValue_t f = WhatFaceValue();
    if (f == ACE)
        ReturnScore = 11;
    else if (f < TEN)
        ReturnScore = f + 1;
    else
        ReturnScore = 10;

    return ReturnScore;
}

//
// Function to return the score of a bridge card
// Pre:  The bridge card object has a value.
// Post: The score of the card in bridge has been returned.
//

int BridgeCard::WhatScore(void)
{
    int r;

    switch( WhatFaceValue() )
    {
        case ACE  : r = 4;
                    break;
        case JACK : r = 1;
                    break;
        case QUEEN: r = 2;
                    break;
        case KING : r = 3;
                    break;
        default   : r = 0;
    }

    return r;
}
```

A program to test these classes is below. The instance *c* of *BJCard* and *d* of *BridgeCard* through inheritance can use the *PlayingCard*'s methods—*assign* and *DisplayCard*. Each object has its own unique version of *WhatScore*.

```
#include <iostream.h>
#include "cards.h"

int main( void )
{
    BJCard c;
```

```
c.assign(KING, SPADE);
c.DisplayCard();
cout << endl << "Blackjack score = " << c.WhatScore() << endl;

BridgeCard d;

d.assign(KING, HEART);
d.DisplayCard();
cout << endl << "Bridge score = " << d.WhatScore() << endl;

return 0;
}
```

The following output of the program shows the different scoring for a king in blackjack than in bridge.

```
 KS
Blackjack score = 10
 KH
Bridge score = 3
```

In this brief introduction, we see that OOP provides a high level of data abstraction, allowing us to encapsulate data and functions into a data structure. We can hide implementations of member data and functions that do not need to be publicly available. Thus, we prevent access to the data structure that is contrary to the definition of the type. Through operator and function overloading, we can allow one operator to process values of different types. Constructors automatically initialize an object, freeing the programmer from this responsibility. Once we have defined a class, through inheritance we can derive other similar classes easily. Thus, we can build class libraries that can provide high-level building blocks for programs.

Section 12.6 Exercises

Write answers to the following exercises in C++.

1. Write statements to prompt the user and to read a value for *int* variable *num*.

2. Write a statement to print the value of *int* variable *SSN* and string variable *name* along with descriptions of the values.

3. Declare *answer* to be of enumeration type *YesOrNo_t*. Write a comment on the same line describing *answer* as the answer to a question about continuing the game or not.

4. For *AssignDate* of Example 12.14, verify that the arguments represent a legitimate date. If they do not, print an error message and assign zeros to the data members.

5. For *NextDay* of Example 12.14, account for leap year. Every year divisible by 4 is a leap year, except those divisible by 100. Years divisible by 400 are leap years.

6. Using *date* of Examples 12.13–12.15, assign your birthday to an instance of *date*, increment the date to one week later using a loop, then print the date in the short and verbose formats.

7. Change *AssignDate* of Examples 12.13 and 12.14 to a constructor.

8. Describe the advantage(s) of the data members of *date* being three variables instead of a structure.

9. Using the *complex* class of Example 12.16, write a C++ program to create objects representing $x = 7 - 4i$ and $y = -9 + 2i$, to generate $x = x^2 + y$, and to print the result.

10. Using the *PlayingCard* class of Example 12.17, declare *hand* to be an array of 5 playing cards.

11. Suppose *BridgeHand* is an array of 13 *BridgeCard* objects that have values. Write statements to calculate and print the face card points of the bridge hand.

In Exercises 12–14, give the header file containing the specifications and the file of member function definitions for the given exercises in Section 12.5.

12. The object *time* of Exercise 3

13. Objects *employee*, *manager*, and *HourlyWorker* of Exercise 4

14. Objects *car* and *taxi* of Exercise 5

Section 12.6 Programming Projects

For Projects 1–3, implement the objects of the Exercises in Section 12.5 and write test programs.

1. The object *time* of Exercise 3

2. The object *employee* of Exercise 4

3. The objects *car* and *taxi* of Exercise 5

Section 12.7 Breadth: Machine and Assembler Languages

In the section "Model of a Computer System" in Chapter 1, we examined a model of a computer having the von Neumann architecture with its input, output, secondary storage, and process units. On a rudimentary level, we also considered the fetch/execute cycle in which the central processing unit (CPU) retrieves an instruction from memory, decodes, and executes it. In this section, we discuss in more detail this cycle and a simplified processor architecture.

Each computer has its own distinctive architecture. We can think of main memory as an array of cells, *Memory*, so that the index of an array element is the address of a cell. For our simplified computer, let us assume only 40 cells in memory, numbered 0–39. Thus, the last cell in memory has address 39 and contents *Memory*[39]. In the computer everything, including an address, is expressed with strings of bits, and printouts are usually presented with hexadecimal notation. To simplify the situation, however, we use the decimal number system instead of the binary or hexadecimal.

Figure 12.8
Architecture of
a processor
with 40 cells in
memory and
registers IR, PC,
and AC

| CPU registers: | PC: | IR: | AC: |

Memory

00		10		20		30	
01		11		21		31	
02		12		22		32	
03		13		23		33	
04		14		24		34	
05		15		25		35	
06		16		26		36	
07		17		27		37	
08		18		28		38	
09		19		29		39	

Machine Architecture

At a minimum, our machine needs three **registers** or high-speed CPU locations—an **instruction register** (**IR**), a **program counter** (**PC**), and an **accumulator** (**AC**). The IR contains the machine language instruction that is under active consideration, and the PC holds the memory address of the next instruction scheduled for execution. The AC is an arithmetic register, which holds intermediate results. Figure 12.8 depicts such an architecture.

Definition   A **register** is a high-speed location in the CPU.

Machine Instructions

Because each type of computer has a different architecture, each has its own instruction set. Although computers store instructions in binary and people abbreviate machine code with hexadecimal, we resort to the decimal system for our illustration. Each operation has its own numeric value, called an **opcode**. For example, the opcode 2 might instruct the computer to **load** the accumulator or copy the value from an indicated memory location into AC. Opcode 3 might indicate the reverse operation, to **store** the accumulator or copy the value from AC into a particular memory location. Suppose opcode 4 instructs the computer to add the contents of AC and the contents of a memory location, placing the sum in AC. Similarly, opcode 5 might direct the computer to subtract a data item at an address from the AC. For each opcode, the corresponding instruction must also indicate a memory address. In our machine instruction, we use the leading one or two digits for the opcode and a two-digit number for the location, as follows:

instruction: opcode location

The instruction to copy the value from memory location 35 into AC is 235, with 2 indicating the load opcode.

People have a difficult time dealing with such numeric representations. As a result, early in the history of computers, assembler languages using English mnemonics were developed. In an assembler language, LDA 35 might symbolize the machine instruction 235. STA, ADD, and SUBT might signify "store the accumulator," "add a value to the AC," and "subtract a value from the AC," respectively. The programmer writes instructions in this assembler language, and another program, called an assembler, translates the instructions into machine language. Even when we write in machine language, we can comment our work with assembler code. Frequently in assembler language, a comment begins with a semicolon and lasts for the remainder of the line. Thus, we would write the following:

```
235  ;LDA 35
```

With *loc* indicating a two-digit address, such as 35, Table 12.2 lists the instructions we have so far.

In a high-level language like C, we might write the following statement:

```
y += z;
```

In this situation, suppose y has an initial value of 3, and z is 5. After execution of this one statement, y is 8. Three machine instructions are needed to accomplish the same task when we deal with low-level operations instead of high-level statements. For example, suppose y's location in memory is at address 20 and z's is 21. To add z to y using machine or assembler code, we must copy y's value into AC, add z's value to it, and copy the result back to y's cell, as follows:

Machine Instruction	Assembler Instruction	Meaning
220	LDA 20	AC $\leftarrow$ *Memory*[20] or AC $\leftarrow y$
421	ADD 21	AC $\leftarrow$ AC + *Memory*[21] or AC $\leftarrow y + z$
320	STA 20	*Memory*[20] $\leftarrow$ AC or $y \leftarrow$ AC $= y + z$

With color emphasis for the changes, Figure 12.9 illustrates this sequence of events involving data movement and arithmetic. Notice the lower the level of the language, the more we become mired in details.

Table 12.2 Some machine and assembler instructions for a simplified computer

Machine Instruction	Assembler Instruction	Meaning
2*loc*	LDA *loc*	AC $\leftarrow$ *Memory*[*loc*]
3*loc*	STA *loc*	*Memory*[*loc*] $\leftarrow$ AC
4*loc*	ADD *loc*	AC $\leftarrow$ AC + *Memory*[*loc*]
5*loc*	SUBT *loc*	AC $\leftarrow$ AC $-$ *Memory*[*loc*]

Figure 12.9
Changes in
memory and
AC to
accomplish
$y = y + z$

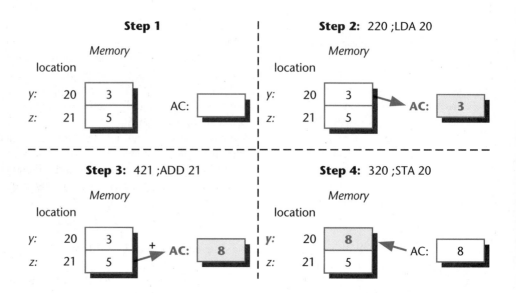

For a complete program to read two values, add them, and print the result, we need additional instructions. We must read the values of y and z from the input unit into their proper memory locations, add as we did above, send y's value to the output unit, and then stop the program. Consequently, we include the instructions from Table 12.3 in our languages.

For the HALT machine instruction, the opcode is 99, but the *loc* field is irrelevant. Consequently, we can use any two digits in place of the xx. For simplicity, we use 9999 for HALT. With the von Neumann architecture, the program and the data are loaded into memory, and for our system, the program is always placed starting at location 0. The following table presents the entire machine language program with memory addresses of instructions, assembler code as comments, and a detailed description of the process to add two values.

Address	Machine Language	Assembler	Description	
0	020	;IN 20	Read y	or *Memory*[20] ← input
1	021	;IN 21	Read z	or *Memory*[21] ← input
2	220	;LDA 20	AC ← *Memory*[20]	or AC ← y
3	421	;ADD 21	AC ← AC + *Memory*[21]	or AC ← $y + z$
4	320	;STA 20	*Memory*[20] ← AC	or y ← AC $= y + z$
5	120	;OUT 20	output ← *Memory*[20]	or output ← y
6	9999	;HALT	Stop	

**Fetch/
Execute
Cycle**

The program counter (PC) and instruction register (IR) also play an essential role in the execution of a program. The fetch/execute cycle for each instruction requires their services. The PC is a place holder that stores the memory location of the next machine instruction the computer anticipates executing. Because our programs start at location 0, the PC has an initial value of 0. As fetching begins, the instruction in the memory

Table 12.3 Some machine and assembler instructions for a simplified computer

Machine Instruction	Assembler Instruction	Meaning
0*loc*	IN *loc*	*Memory*[*loc*] ← input
1*loc*	OUT *loc*	output ← *Memory*[*loc*]
99xx	HALT	Halt execution

location indicated by the PC is loaded into the IR. The CPU increments the PC by 1 to point to the next instruction. In the execution phase, the CPU deciphers the instruction by splitting off the opcode from the location portion and retrieving its meaning from a list of opcodes. Then, using the address as necessary, the computer performs the task. Figure 12.10 shows the changes in the registers and memory locations during execution of the instruction at location 2, 220, or LDA 20. As the cycle begins, IR still contains the previous instruction, and PC contains the address of the forthcoming one.

Using this notation, the fetch/execute cycle is as follows:

1. Fetch Phase:

   a. IR ← *Memory*[PC]

   b. PC ← PC + 1

2. Execute Phase:

   a. Decode IR into opcode and *loc*

   b. Execute instruction with opcode using location *loc* as necessary

Example 12.18

With this instruction set, we cannot copy a value directly from one memory location to another as we would in a high-level language with the following:

```
result = y;
```

Instead, we must load *y*'s value into AC, and store AC's value into the location for *result*. Suppose location 20 holds *y*'s value, and *result* is at address 22. As Figure 12.11 shows, we accomplish the memory move as follows:

```
220        ;LDA 20        AC ← y
322          ;STA 22            result ← AC
```

Branching

We have developed a sequential program using six instructions, but we need additional instructions to accomplish decisions and looping. We can construct these structures using various branch instructions. An **unconditional branch** or a **jump** causes execution to continue, not with the next instruction in sequence, but with an instruction elsewhere in the program. In a high-level language, this unconditional branch is a *goto*. Within a structured programming environment, except under some unusual situations, we should not use a *goto* statement. In machine and assembler languages, however, we do not have built-in *if-else* and *while* statements and the only way to devise these structures is with branches.

Figure 12.10
Fetch/execute
cycle for
machine
instruction 220

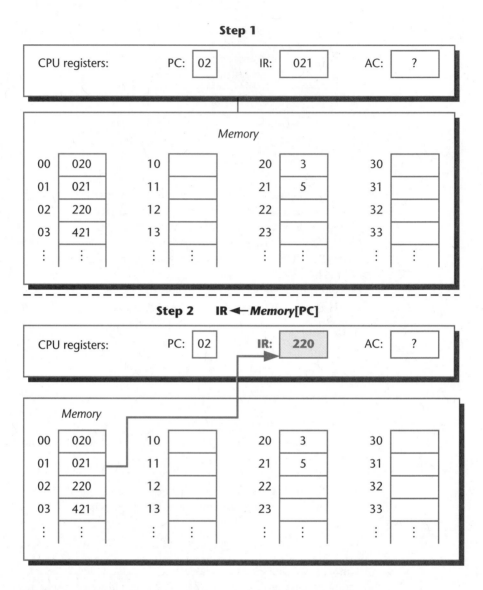

For our simple computer, suppose the jump instruction has the opcode 6 with the assembler mnemonic JUMP. The instruction must include the memory location of the instruction where execution should continue. For example, suppose the instruction

```
619      ;JUMP 19
```

is at address 14. The unconditional jump tells the computer, "Do not execute the instruction at address 15 next, but continue with the one at location 19." How does the computer accomplish such a branch? The PC holds the address of the next instruction scheduled for execution, in this case 15. To perform the jump, the computer copies 19 into PC. Then, when the fetch/execute cycle begins again, the CPU fetches the contents of *Memory*[19].

Assembler codes BRAN and BRAZ indicate conditional branches. The instruction "BRAN *loc*" means, "if the value of AC is negative, then continue execution at location *loc*." The computer tests the contents in the accumulator. If it is less than zero,

Figure 12.10
Continued

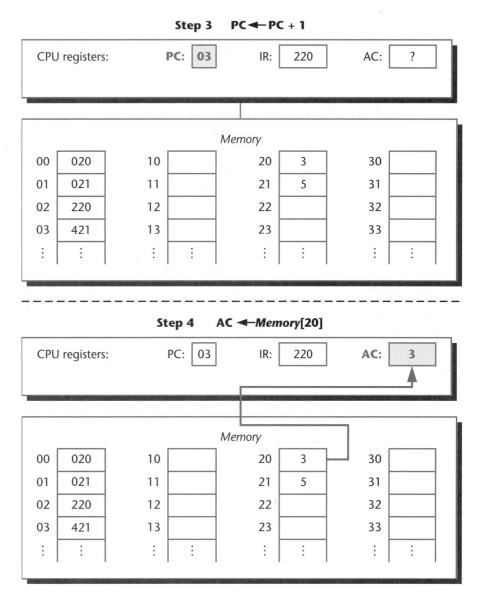

Step 3   PC ← PC + 1

CPU registers: **PC:** 03   IR: 220   AC: ?

Memory

00	020	10		20	3	30	
01	021	11		21	5	31	
02	220	12		22		32	
03	421	13		23		33	

Step 4   AC ← *Memory*[20]

CPU registers: PC: 03   IR: 220   **AC:** 3

Memory

00	020	10		20	3	30	
01	021	11		21	5	31	
02	220	12		22		32	
03	421	13		23		33	

Figure 12.11   Sequence of instructions to accomplish a memory copy

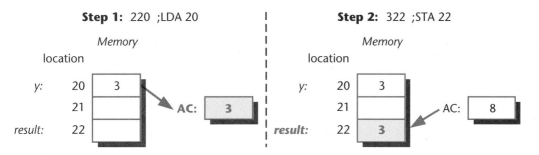

Step 1: 220 ;LDA 20

Memory

location

y: 20 | 3 | → AC: 3

         21 | |

result: 22 | |

Step 2: 322 ;STA 22

Memory

location

y: 20 | 3 | AC: 8

         21 | |

result: 22 | 3 |

Table 12.4   Branch machine and assembler instructions for a simplified computer

Machine Instruction	Assembler Instruction	Meaning
6*loc*	JUMP *loc*	PC ← *loc*
7*loc*	BRAN *loc*	If AC < 0, then PC ← *loc*
8*loc*	BRAZ *loc*	If AC == 0, then PC ← *loc*

the CPU changes the value of the PC to *loc*. Similarly, BRAZ accomplishes the branch when AC is zero. The list in Table 12.4 summarizes the three branches.

Example 12.19

Let us write a program to read two values and print the larger of the two. Using pseudocode, the high-level program design is as follows:

```
read y and z
if y < z then
        print z
else
        print y
```

Although no direct machine instruction tests $y < z$, we can accomplish the same thing by subtracting z and testing $y - z < 0$. Therefore, a redesign shows

```
read y and z
if y − z < 0 then
        print z                         /* then section: y < z */
else
        print y                         /* else section: y ≥ z */
```

Our branch instructions are not *if-else* structures per se. Should the condition be true, a jump occurs. Moreover, we output from a memory location. Therefore, we must take our design to an even lower level using statement labels and *goto* statements.

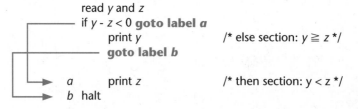

Notice if the condition $y - z < 0$ (or $y < z$) is true, the computer does not execute the next instruction but jumps to the instruction at label *a*. If $y - z < 0$ is false so that $y - z \geq 0$ or $y \geq z$, the computer does not go to label *a*. Instead, execution falls through to the next statement to print *y*. After printing *y*, we do not want to print *z*, so the computer must jump over the next statement to label *b*. This awkward, "leap-frog" construction, unfortunately, is the method of building an *if-else* statement in an unstructured language.

Using our limited instruction set, we read y and z. Then we load y into AC and subtract z. If the result is negative, z is the maximum of the two. We skip to a part of the code that copies $z = Memory[21]$ to output. If the difference $y - z$ is nonnegative, y is larger, and we fall through to code that prints $y = Memory[20]$. We then jump over an instruction that would print z. Color emphasizes the "leap-frog" branching that accomplishes the *if-else* statement in the following program.

Address	Machine Language	Assembler	Description	
0	020	;IN 20	Read y	or $Memory[20] \leftarrow$ input
1	021	;IN 21	Read z	or $Memory[21] \leftarrow$ input
2	220	;LDA 20	$AC \leftarrow Memory[20]$	or $AC \leftarrow y$
3	521	;SUBT 21	$AC \leftarrow AC - Memory[21]$	or $AC \leftarrow y - z$
4	707	;BRAN 07	If $y < z$, then $PC \leftarrow 7$	
5	120	;OUT 20	y is larger, so output $\leftarrow Memory[20] = y$	
6	608	;JUMP 08	$PC \leftarrow 8$	
7	121	;OUT 21	z is larger, so output $\leftarrow Memory[21] = z$	
8	9999	;HALT	Stop	

Several times in this program, we refer to specific memory locations in accessing data and in branching to program statements. Consequently, if we insert a statement or move a data item, we must adjust the address reference.

Example 12.20

In this example, as long as the first data item is not zero, we compare pairs of input values and print the larger. Essentially, this assignment places a loop around much of the program in the last example. Considering the branches at our disposal, we have the following high-level design:

```
          read y and z
       ── if y - z < 0 goto label a
  ┌────
  │         print y              /* else section: y ≧ z */
  │   ──── goto label b
  │
  └─►  a    print z              /* then section: y < z */
  └─►  b halt
```

In this design, we have a priming read for the value of y. So that we can test, we must copy y's value into the accumulator. Should y be zero, there is no need to read z or to execute the loop. At the bottom of the *while* loop, we must read another value for y and load that number into AC to prepare for the test at the top of the loop. The top and bottom of the loop with the appropriate branches are shown in color in the following code:

768 CHAPTER 12 LEVELS OF PROGRAMMING ABSTRACTION

Address	Machine Language	Assembler	Description	
0	020	;IN 20	Read *y*	or *Memory*[20] ← input
1	220	;LDA 20	AC ← *Memory*[20]	or AC ← *y*
2	812	;BRAZ 12	Top of *while* loop; if *y* == 0, jump out of loop	
3	021	;IN 21	Read *z*	or *Memory*[21] ← input
4	521	;SUBT 21	AC ← AC - *Memory*[21]	or AC ← *y* - *z*
5	708	;BRAN 08	If *y* < *z*, then PC ← 8	
6	120	;OUT 20	*y* is larger, so output ← *Memory*[20] = *y*	
7	609	;JUMP 09	PC ← 9	
8	121	;OUT 21	*z* is larger, so output ← *Memory*[21] = *z*	
9	020	;IN 20	Read *y* again	or *Memory*[20] ← input
10	220	;LDA 20	AC ← *Memory*[20]	or AC ← *y*
11	602	;JUMP 02	Bottom of *while* loop; jump to top at address 2	
12	9999	;HALT	Stop	

Certainly, in real computer systems, the architecture is far more complicated than in the hypothetical one of this section. Usually, more registers exist. Some are specialized for counting in loops, others for array references, and others for additional storage of intermediate results. Moreover, usually several addressing techniques and more instructions are available than that which Table 12.5 summarizes. Computer organization and assembler language courses consider such systems in great detail. The material of this section is intended to give a greater understanding of the workings of a computer and an introduction to machine and assembler languages.

Table 12.5 Summary of machine and assembler instructions for a simplified computer

Machine Instruction	Assembler Instruction	Meaning
0*loc*	IN *loc*	*Memory*[*loc*] ← input
1*loc*	OUT *loc*	output ← *Memory*[*loc*]
2*loc*	LDA *loc*	AC ← *Memory*[*loc*]
3*loc*	STA *loc*	*Memory*[*loc*] ← AC
4*loc*	ADD *loc*	AC ← AC + *Memory*[*loc*]
5*loc*	SUBT *loc*	AC ← AC - *Memory*[*loc*]
6*loc*	JUMP *loc*	PC ← *loc*
7*loc*	BRAN *loc*	If AC < 0, then PC ← *loc*
8*loc*	BRAZ *loc*	If AC == 0, then PC ← *loc*
99xx	HALT	Halt execution

CPU Simulator Program *cpusim*

Included on the text disk is the source code for a CPU simulator program, *cpusim*, which executes the example machine language of this section. The source files are as follows:

cpusim.c:	source code file for the main routine
cpu.c:	source code for the CPU and associated operations
mem.c:	source code for simulated memory services
cpusim.h:	header file for the entire simulator
cpu.h:	header file for the CPU source
simem.h:	header file for the memory source

The *.c* files should be compiled and linked.*

The command line for execution of *cpusim* has the format

```
cpusim [-v | -r | -m [-s]] program_file
```

Brackets surround the output options, and the vertical bar means "or". The options are as follows:

- v calls for verbose output; *cpusim* dumps both the registers and memory after each cycle
- r calls for register output only
- m calls for memory output only
- s causes *cpusim* to run in single-step mode; it pauses after each cycle until the user presses the return key
- *program_file* is the file name of the machine language program file

A program file consists of a series of instructions and comments. The text disk also includes three machine language program files—*add2.m*, *max2.m*, and *maxloop.m*, corresponding to those at the beginning of the section and in Examples 12.19 and 12.20.

For example, suppose we wish to perform the simulated CPU operations in the machine language program *add2.m*. To display input and output only, we type the command

```
cpusim add2.m
```

A question mark is the prompt for input. The program *add2.m* prompts for two integers and displays their sum, as follows:

```
? 3
? 9
12
```

To exhibit the contents of registers IR, PC, and AC after execution of each instruction of *add2.m* along with output, we issue the following command:

```
cpusim -r add2.m
```

The resulting display follows:

---

*For THINK C in *cpusim.c*, uncomment the following:

```
#include <console.h>
```
and
```
argc = ccommand(&argv);
```

```
? 5
PC:  0001        IR:  0020  (IN 0020)       AC:  0000
? 3
PC:  0002        IR:  0021  (IN 0021)       AC:  0000
PC:  0003        IR:  0220  (LDA 0020)      AC:  0005
PC:  0004        IR:  0421  (ADD 0021)      AC:  0008
PC:  0005        IR:  0320  (STA 0020)      AC:  0008
8
PC:  0006        IR:  0120  (OUT 0020)      AC:  0008
PC:  0007        IR:  9999  (HALT 0099)     AC:  0008
```

The first instruction of *add2.m*, 0020 (IN 20), is to read a number interactively and place the input into memory location 20. After the user types the input value, in this example 5, the simulator shows the three registers. The program counter (PC) has already advanced to point to the next instruction, the one at memory location 01. The IR contains the input instruction, and the AC has its initialization value of 0. As a result of the third instruction, 0220 (LDA 20), AC obtains a copy of the contents of memory location 20—the value 5. The register displays continue until the HALT instruction, 9999.

Should we desire to see memory instead, we type

```
cpusim -m add2.m
```

In this situation, the computer displays the contents of the 40 memory locations after execution of each command. Thus, as a result of the first machine language command, we can have

```
? 7
Addr      +00     +01     +02     +03     +04     +05     +06     +07     +08     +09
-----------------------------------------------------------------------------------
0000:   00020   00021   00220   00421   00320   00120   09999   00000   00000   00000
0010:   00000   00000   00000   00000   00000   00000   00000   00000   00000   00000
0020:   00007   00000   00000   00000   00000   00000   00000   00000   00000   00000
0030:   00000   00000   00000   00000   00000   00000   00000   00000   00000   00000
-----------------------------------------------------------------------------------
?
```

This display shows the seven instructions of the program in memory locations 0000 through 0006. Moreover, execution of the first instruction, 00020 or IN 20, reads an integer, 7, interactively and places the value in memory location 20. Execution of each subsequent instruction results in a display of memory.

The command

```
cpusim -v add2.m
```

produces a combination of the memory and register display commands. To step through execution, we include the -s option immediately after the -m, -v, or -r option, as shown:

```
cpusim -v -s add2.m
```

After the display of registers and memory for each instruction, the computer pauses for the user to press return.

```
? 193
PC:  0001       IR:   0020   (IN 0020)    AC:  0000
Addr      +00   +01   +02    +03    +04    +05    +06    +07    +08    +09
---------------------------------------------------------------------------
0000:  00020 00021 00220 00421 00320 00120 09999 00000 00000 00000
0010:  00000 00000 00000 00000 00000 00000 00000 00000 00000 00000
0020:  00193 00000 00000 00000 00000 00000 00000 00000 00000 00000
0030:  00000 00000 00000 00000 00000 00000 00000 00000 00000 00000
---------------------------------------------------------------------------

? 54
PC:  0002       IR:   0021   (IN 0021)    AC:  0000
Addr      +00   +01   +02    +03    +04    +05    +06    +07    +08    +09
---------------------------------------------------------------------------
0000:  00020 00021 00220 00421 00320 00120 09999 00000 00000 00000
0010:  00000 00000 00000 00000 00000 00000 00000 00000 00000 00000
0020:  00193 00054 00000 00000 00000 00000 00000 00000 00000 00000
0030:  00000 00000 00000 00000 00000 00000 00000 00000 00000 00000
---------------------------------------------------------------------------
  ⋮
```

We create other machine language program files using any editor. The simulator treats any line that starts with a decimal number string as an instruction. The loader does not verify syntax (like a real loader), but the CPU's execute function checks for invalid opcodes. We write only one instruction to a line, and the simulator considers that any string of characters following the instruction is a comment. Lines that do not start with a decimal string and blank lines are assumed to be comments. The loader reads the file and loads memory until it reaches the end of the file. Another way to think of a program file is as a memory image. Playing the part of the compiler/assembler, we are responsible for coding the memory image (code and data) correctly. Consequently, no address checking occurs in the memory functions.

The exercises below suggest several machine language programs, and the laboratory develops several such programs. A later laboratory also examines the simulation program itself and explores how to expand the simulator to process other machine language instructions.

Section 12.7 Exercises

In each exercise, write the requested machine and assembler language program and execute the program using the CPU simulator on your text disk.

1. Compute the difference of data at locations 30 and 31 and place the result in location 32.

2. Read values into *Memory*[20] and *Memory*[21] and compute the sum. If the result is negative, place the value in *Memory*[22]. Otherwise, place it in *Memory*[23].

3. Calculate the absolute value of *Memory*[25]. By definition, if $x \geq 0$, then $|x| = x$; if $x < 0$, then $|x| = -x$.

4. Output a countdown from 10 to 0.

5. Output the maximum of a collection of input data.

6. The following appeared in the sample questions of *Practicing to Take the GRE Computer Science Test, 2nd Edition:*
A compiler generates code for the following assignment statement.

$$G := (A + B) *C - (D + E) * F$$

The target machine has a single accumulator and a single-address instruction set consisting of instructions load, store, add, subtract, and multiply. For the arithmetic operations, the left operand is taken from the accumulator and the result appears in the accumulator. The smallest possible number of instructions in the resulting code is
(A) 5   (B) 6   (C) 7   (D) 9   (E) 11

Programming and Debugging Hints

Debugging with Conditional Compilation

As previously mentioned, we can use *printf* to examine the values of variables and trace execution for debugging purposes. We should have these statements flush with the left margin so that they are obvious, and we can highlight them by using comments containing asterisks.

After debugging a function, we must remove the calls to *printf*. One way of expediting this process is to place the debugging statements within conditional compilation blocks, as shown:

```
#ifdef DEBUG
printf("***** ListSize = %d\n", ListSize);
#endif
```

The debugging statements are compiled only when earlier code contains

```
#define DEBUG
```

or when the user defines *DEBUG* on the command line. On UNIX systems for the program *taxprog.c*, this command line is as follows:

```
cc -DDEBUG taxprog.c
```

If we do not define *DEBUG*, the preprocessor does not send the debugging statements to the compiler. If the function is modified at a later time and new bugs appear, the debugging statements can be activated merely by defining *DEBUG*.

Levels of Debugging

We can activate different levels of debugging output by using several symbolic constants. For example, suppose definition of *DEBUG_LOW* should result in the most basic level of debugging output. Defining *DEBUG_MEDIUM* signals an intermediate level, and *DEBUG_HIGH* indicates the need for detailed debugging. Any level of debugging should contain the calls to *printf* at a more elementary level. Thus, a header file would contain the following:

```
#ifdef DEBUG_HIGH
#define DEBUG_MEDIUM
#endif

#ifdef DEBUG_MEDIUM
#define DEBUG_LOW
#endif
```

Definition of *DEBUG_HIGH* results in our defining *DEBUG_MEDIUM* and *DEBUG_LOW* as well. By defining *DEBUG_MEDIUM*, we also define *DEBUG_LOW*, but not *DEBUG_HIGH*. A function might contain the following:

```
#ifdef DEBUG_LOW
printf("***** Entering function SortList\n");
printf("***** ListSize = %d\n", ListSize);
#endif
    .
    .
    .
#ifdef DEBUG_HIGH
{
    int debug_i;

    for (debug_i = 0; debug_i < ListSize; debug_i++)
        printf("***** list[%d] = %d\n",
                debug_i, list[debug_i]);
}
#endif
    .
    .
    .
#ifdef DEBUG_MEDIUM
printf("***** mid = %d\n", mid);
#endif
```

If we define *DEBUG_LOW*, then output contains

```
***** Entering function SortList
```

and the size of the list. Definition of *DEBUG_MEDIUM* causes the printout to contain those two lines and the value of *mid*. Defining *DEBUG_HIGH* simultaneously defines *DEBUG_MEDIUM* and *DEBUG_LOW* and triggers the greatest level of debugging. In this case, the program declares *debug_i* within a block that prints the elements of the array *list* and produces debugging output from the *DEBUG_MEDIUM* and *DEBUG_LOW* levels. Thus, the programmer has control over the amount of debugging he or she desires.

Key Terms

#else 727	?: 711	encapsulate 715
#endif 724	*argc* 721	*extern* 719
#if 0 728	*argv* 721	library 715
#if 727	*auto* 720	macro 707
#ifdef 724	command-line arguments 721	*static* 720
#ifndef 725	conditional compilation 724	storage class 720
#undef 725	conditional expression operator 711	ternary operator 711

Summary

This chapter covers three levels of abstraction in programming. The first three sections cover material that enables us to develop our own libraries of type, function, macro, and symbolic constant definitions. A library includes a collection of implementations of useful and related tasks. We encapsulate related material into a library. Moreover, we can hide many details of implementation by compiling the file of function definitions. The user can think on a higher level of abstraction without getting "bogged down" in details of implementation of the library functions. Object-oriented programming (OOP) provides built-in language features that help the programmer to think on a higher level of abstraction. By contrast, programming on the machine level makes it more difficult for the programmer to perform problem solving. Because OOP and machine language programming are in breadth sections, we concentrate on the first three sections of the chapter for this summary.

When a preprocessor symbol is defined as a segment of code, it is called a macro. The preprocessor replaces the symbol by its string definition without any consideration of the meaning. If a *#define* directive does not fit on a single line, we can continue it on subsequent lines by using a backslash (\) character at the end of the line, such as

```
#define VERIFY if (a < 500 || 10000 < a)   \
    /* check for value out of range */
```

The preprocessor permits macros to have arguments, just as functions do, such as

```
#define   DECREMENT(x)    if (x > 0) x -= 1
```

The difference is that the arguments are strings rather than values. During expansion of the macro, the string passed to the argument x replaces all occurrences of x in the symbol's value. That is, the statement

```
DECREMENT(a);
```

expands to

```
if (a > 0) a -= 1;
```

Many macros that substitute for functions use the conditional expression operator (?:), which yields an expression similar to the *if-then* construct. The form of the conditional expression is as follows:

```
expression1 ? expression2 : expression3
```

If the value of the boolean *expression1* is *TRUE*, the ?: operator returns *expression2*. Otherwise, the ?: operator returns *expression3*. The following is a macro to find the smaller of two numbers:

```
#define   MIN(a, b)    ((a) < (b) ? (a) : (b))
```

If a function would consist of only one line of code, to save computing time, we should usually implement the task as a macro. We should observe some cautions, however. A common oversight is to inadvertently place a semicolon at the end of the macro definition, leading to the possibility of two semicolons in the subsequent preprocessor replacement. To perform the correct substitution, we should surround each parameter appearance and the entire definition with parentheses. We should be very careful about having a macro argument with post- or pre-incrementing or decrementing. If the corresponding parameter appears twice in the macro definition, the expansion increments or decrements the argument twice.

Besides preprocessor directives to define constants and macros, a header file can also contain C code for structure template definitions, type definitions, and function declarations. When we include our own header file, quotation marks replace the angle brackets, as shown:

```
#include "random.h"
```

Storage classes, which determine how the computer allocates storage to variables, are important in the development and use of libraries. The text discussed three storage classes—*extern*, *static*, and *auto*. A function cannot use a global variable in another program file unless the function (or globally, the file containing the function) declares the variable to be *extern*, such as

```
extern int MaxX;
```

We are not defining *MaxX* here, but only declaring the variable.

Global variables are *static*. They come into existence when the program starts execution and continue to exist until the entire program terminates. However, if we explicitly declare a global variable to be *static*, such as

```
static int GlobalVar;
```

functions from a different program file cannot access the variable. If a program assigns a value to a *static* local variable during the first invocation to a function, that value still exists when the program invokes the function a second time. Initialization of the variable occurs only once.

An *auto* variable exists only during execution of the function. Because *auto* is the default storage class for local variables, we usually omit that keyword.

Virtually all computers with C compilers allow execution of C programs using a command line with arguments and provide a facility whereby the program can access command-line parameters. In order to access command-line arguments, the function *main* must have two parameters, as shown:

```
main(int argc, char **argv)
```

The first parameter, which we usually call *argc*, is an integer indicating the number of strings in *argv*, and *argv* contains the command-line arguments. For example, suppose we type the command

```
multiply 7 9
```

to execute the program *multiply*. In this case, *argc* gets the value 3, and *argv* is a pointer to an array of pointers, each of which points to a string representing one of the words in the command line—"multiply", "7", and "9".

The preprocessor provides directives for removing selective sections of code or for choosing between two possible sections. One form of this conditional compilation is similar to the *if*-statement, as shown:

```
#ifdef preprocessor_symbol
      ⋮
#endif
```

If we define the preprocessor symbol before the segment, the preprocessor includes the code between the two directives (*#ifdef* and *#endif*) in the translated program that it passes to the C compiler.

After the definition,

```
#define RECORD_FILE
```

the directive *#ifdef RECORD_FILE* produces a *TRUE* result. However, if the directive

```
#undef RECORD_FILE
```

occurs before the *#ifdef* directive, then *RECORD_FILE* becomes undefined. The directive *#ifndef* produces a *TRUE* result if a symbol is undefined.

We should enclose the contents of any header file in preprocessor directives, such as

```
#ifndef preprocessor_symbol
#define preprocessor_symbol
    ⋮
#endif
```

to avoid including a header file more than once.

The preprocessor provides the *#else* directive to operate in much the same way as the *else* clause of an *if* statement. For example, we could write

```
#ifdef RECORD_FILE
    AddRecord(InvBytes, ErrFile);
#else
    PrintRecord(InvBytes);
#endif
```

The *#if* directive tests an expression. This expression can be of any form that a program uses, with virtually any operators, except that it can include only integer constant values. We can use the *#if 0* and *#endif* directives to "comment out" a block of code, such as

```
#if 0
    ⋮
#endif
```

∼∼∼ Review Questions

1. How can a *#define* directive be continued to a new line?
2. Where can a preprocessor directive be written?
3. Where can a preprocessor directive be split?
4. What is a macro, and for what is it used?
5. What symbol is used to separate the arguments of a macro?
6. What can a macro argument be?
7. What role is played by the *#undef* directive?
8. What are common uses of a header file?
9. What is conditional compilation?
10. State the reason for using the *#ifdef* directive.
11. How is the *#ifndef* directive used?
12. When a C program is compiled, at what point are the preprocessor directives processed?
13. What directive is used to terminate the scope of an *#ifdef*, *#ifndef*, or *#if* directive?
14. How is the *#else* directive used?
15. What is characteristic of the *#else* and the *#endif* directives?
16. How does the *#if* directive operate?
17. What happens if a preprocessor symbol in the *#if* expression is undefined?
18. What preprocessor symbols, if any, cannot be used in the expression of an *#if* directive?

19. What is the name of the construct used in the following statement, and how does it operate?

```
a = (b > c) ? b: c;
```

20. What does the *extern* storage class accomplish?

21. What are *static* variables? Compare them with standard local variables.

22. Explain the meaning of an *auto* variable.

23. Why is the keyword *auto* generally omitted from a C program?

24. Why are global variables sometimes declared as *static*?

25. How are command-line arguments accessed?

26. What is always the first string in *argv*?

27. Give the keywords associated with storage classes that we have discussed so far.

28. What compiler directives accomplish "commenting out" a segment of code that contains comments?

≋ **Laboratory**

Note: This chapter has a choice of two different laboratories, one involving a CPU simulator and the other a stock portfolio program.

CPU Simulator

This laboratory works with the CPU simulator program, *cpusim*, which executes the example machine language of Section 12.7. Please read this section before coming to lab.

1. The goal of this exercise is to become acquainted with the machine and assembler languages of Section 12.7 and the CPU simulator, *cpusim*.

   a. Compile and link the program as described in the "CPU Simulator Program *cpusim*" subsection of Section 12.7. Then execute *cpusim* using no options and the machine language program file *max2.m*. Example 12.19 presents this program, which displays the maximum of two input numbers. How does the simulator prompt for input?

   b. Step through the simulation with the program file *max2.m* and a verbose display. Be sure to enter a data item only at the ? prompt. Enter the larger of the two integers first. On each step, describe register(s) and memory changes.

   c. Run the simulation with the program file *max2.m*, displaying the registers. Input the smaller of the two integers first. Explain why the PC changes from 004 to 007.

   d. Copy the file *max2.m* to a file named *min2.m*. Change machine instructions and assembler comments to output the minimum of two input integers. What did you change?

   e. In this part, we examine the difficulties of making changes in this low-level language. Copy the file *max2.m* to a file named *max2data.m*.

      We make alterations to print the maximum of two data items that appear in memory immediately after the program listing. Because we no longer need to read two values, we omit the first two lines. Consequently, the addresses and address references for the other instructions must change. Fill in the blanks below to print the maximum of the numbers at locations 7 and 8. Perform the simulation with your program.

Address	Machine Language	Assembler	Description
0	2__	;LDA __	AC ← *Memory*[__] or AC ← *y*
1	5__	;SUBT __	AC ← AC - *Memory*[__] or AC ← *y* - *z*
2	7__	;BRAN __	If *y* < *z*, then PC ← __
3	1__	;OUT __	*y* is larger, so output ← *Memory*[__] = *y*
4	6__	;JUMP __	PC ← __
5	1__	;OUT __	*z* is larger, so output ← *Memory*[__] = *z*
6	9999	;HALT	Stop
7	56	data item	
8	34	data item	

2. This exercise illustrates looping in machine language. We develop a machine language program file to multiply one memory location (the multiplier) by another (multiplicand) through repeated additions. For example, 5 * 10 = 10 + 10 + 10 + 10 + 10. The program also prints the result (50). Assume that the multiplier, such as 5, is nonnegative. Immediately after the HALT instruction are locations for the multiplier; the multiplicand; the ongoing sum, which we initialize to 0; and 1. We use 1 to decrement the multiplier. Thus, for data of 5 and 10, the locations from the HALT instruction on are as follows:

```
9999      ;HALT
5         ;multiplier
10        ;multiplicand
0         ;on-going sum
1         ;used to decrement counter
```

Pseudocode for the program follows:

load the multiplier (counter) into AC   /*top of *while* loop */
if the value in AC is zero, branch to display answer
    decrement AC by 1 by subtracting data item 1 from AC
    store AC in memory location for the multiplier (counter)
    load the ongoing sum into AC
    add the multiplicand to AC
    store AC in the memory location for the ongoing sum
    jump to the beginning, which is top of *while* loop
display the ongoing sum
halt

Fill in the machine instructions and assembler code comments for this program.

Address	Machine Language	Assembler	Description
0			Load multiplier (counter). Start of *while* loop
1			If 0, branch to display answer
2			Subtract 1 from counter in AC
3			Store counter
4			Load ongoing sum
5			Add multiplicand
6			Store ongoing sum
7			Go to top of *while* loop
8			Print product
9	9999	;HALT	Stop
10	5	;multiplier	
11	10	;multiplicand	
12	0	;ongoing sum	
13	1	;used to decrement counter	

Execute the program. If errors occur, step through the execution.

~~~ Alternative Laboratory

Stock Portfolio Program

This laboratory provides practice in separate compilation, macros, and conditional compilation. Separate the program file from Laboratory 11 into three files—a file containing *main* (*LAB12.c*), a function definitions file (*portfolio.c*), and a header file (*portfolio.h*). A stub may be used for any function that has not been implemented. The header file should contain definitions of symbolic constants, type definitions, *#include* directives, and function prototypes. Define a macro for gain (see team member C's assignment from Laboratory 11). As described after Example 12.8 in Section 12.3, have preprocessor directives in the header file to eliminate the possibility of including a header file more than once. You can test that this feature is working properly by attempting to include the header file twice in *LAB12.c*. Be sure to include the header file in *portfolio.c*. Compile *portfolio.c* and *LAB12.c*. Link the files and execute the program. Once the program is working properly, print listings of each program file and a sample session.

Recursion

Introduction

In this chapter, we examine recursion, or the process of a task calling itself. With each invocation, the problem is reduced to a smaller problem until it arrives at some condition that stops the process. For a number of algorithms, it is more natural to think of a recursive solution that an iterative one, and it may be extremely difficult to arrive initially at a nonrecursive solution. Recursion is a powerful tool in computer science and in other disciplines.

We may find it necessary or desirable to convert the recursive process to one that uses looping. In the second section, we discuss why an iterative solution may be better in some cases and how to make this conversion.

In breadth Section 13.3, we examine a notation, BNF, that uses recursion to define formally the syntax of computer languages. The BNF description of a particular language is an example of the use of a formal grammar. A formal grammar is an effective tool for describing and analyzing natural languages (such as English) and programming languages (such as C). Using a formal grammar, a compiler can recognize programs that follow the syntax of a language.

Goals

To study

- Recursion
- Comparisons of recursion and iteration
- Finding iterative solutions
- Formal grammars

Section 13.1 **Recursive Functions**

Recursion is an important feature of many programming languages like C, Pascal, Ada, and LISP, but not of standard FORTRAN, COBOL, or BASIC. This powerful approach is used to develop a number of algorithms, functions, and even definitions in an elegant, top-down fashion. A **recursive task** is one that calls itself. With each invocation, the problem is reduced to a smaller problem (**reducing case**) until the task arrives at some **terminal** or **base case**, which stops the process. The condition that must be true to achieve the terminal case is the **terminal condition**.

For example, suppose everyone in a company must become familiar with a new government policy. The company's organizational chart is hierarchical. Vice presidents, who are leaders of their divisions, report directly to the president. Divisions have subdivisions, each with a leader, and so forth. The president decides to use the following recursive algorithm to accomplish the task of having everyone in the company become familiar with the new policy:

inform(*group*)

Method of having everyone in a company become familiar with a new government policy

Algorithm:

if there is only one person in the group
    have that person become familiar with the new policy
else
    have the leader of the group become familiar with the new policy
    for each subgroup
        inform(*subgroup*)

Initiating the algorithm with *inform*(*company*), the president becomes familiar with the new policy and calls a meeting of the vice presidents. Each vice president is told that everyone in his or her division must become familiar with the new policy. Thus, for each division, *inform*(*division*) must be executed.

Each vice president follows the same algorithm. The vice president becomes familiar with the new policy and calls a meeting of the subdivision managers reporting directly to him or her. As a result, *inform*(*subdivision*) is executed for each subdivision of the division.

The process continues until arriving at the lowest level of the company's hierarchy, the individual worker, whom we consider to form a one-person group. Thus, the terminal condition of only one person in the group is achieved. The terminal or base case indicates that this worker, too, must become familiar with the policy.

Every recursive task has the following two characteristics:

1. The task is defined in terms of itself, with each invocation working on a smaller version of the problem.

2. The task has a terminal case that is nonrecursive.

Definitions   A **recursive task** is one that calls itself. With each invocation, the problem is reduced to a smaller task (**reducing case**) until the task arrives at some **terminal** or **base case**, which stops the process. The condition that must be true to achieve the terminal case is the **terminal condition**.

Example 13.1

Many definitions in computer science and mathematics are expressed recursively. The factorial function has important applications in such topics as analyzing the efficiency of algorithms and probability. As presented in Section 6.1, one definition of n-factorial is

$$n! = n \cdot (n - 1) \cdot \cdots \cdot 3 \cdot 2 \cdot 1 \text{ for } n > 0$$

Thus,

$$4! = 4 \cdot 3 \cdot 2 \cdot 1 = 4 \cdot (3 \cdot 2 \cdot 1) = 4 \cdot 3!$$

By convention, zero-factorial is defined as one, as shown:

$$0! = 1$$

These equalities motivate a recursive form of the definition:

$$n! = \begin{cases} 1 & \text{if } n=0 \\ n(n-1)! & \text{if } n > 0 \end{cases}$$

For a terminal condition of $n = 0$, the terminal case is $0! = 1$.

Definition n-factorial or $n!$ is defined recusively as

$$n! = \begin{cases} 1 & \text{if } n=0 \\ n(n-1)! & \text{if } n > 0 \end{cases}$$

Using the recursive definition, we can calculate $n!$ as n times $(n - 1)!$, but we must know the value of $(n - 1)!$. The definition is recursive because n-factorial is itself defined in terms of a factorial. For example, 4! is $4 \cdot 3!$, where the factorial function of 3 (3!) is evaluated before the multiplication by 4. Notice the recursion—4-factorial is defined in terms of 3-factorial. However, we must evaluate 3! before multiplying. At least we have a smaller problem with which to work. Using the definition once more, we see that 3! is $3 \cdot 2!$, which involves another factorial. We continue, however, because each time we get a smaller problem. Eventually, we must compute $n!$ for the smallest possible value of n ($n = 0$). When this condition is met, we can stop the recursive process of having the factorial function call itself and use the assignment in the first line of the definition ($n! = 0! = 1$). Because the recursive process terminates when the expression ($n = 0$) becomes true, this equality is called the terminal condition, and the assignment for that condition ($0! = 1$) is called the terminal case. After achieving the terminal condition, we can then trace backwards, substituting, and eventually arrive at the value of 4!.

Figure 13.1 shows the steps to the terminal case in the evaluation of 4-factorial. When the terminal condition of $n = 0$ is encountered, we can substitute the terminal case, $0! = 1$, and evaluate $1! = 1 \cdot 0!$ as $1 \cdot 1 = 1$. Knowing the value of 1!, we can compute 2! as $2 \cdot 1! = 2 \cdot 1 = 2$. Similarly, $3! = 3 \cdot 2! = 3 \cdot 2 = 6$, and so $4! = 4 \cdot 3! = 4 \cdot 6 = 24$. Figure 13.2 shows the steps involved in substituting values in reverse order.

Figure 13.1
Steps to arrive
at the terminal
case of
evaluating 4!
recursively

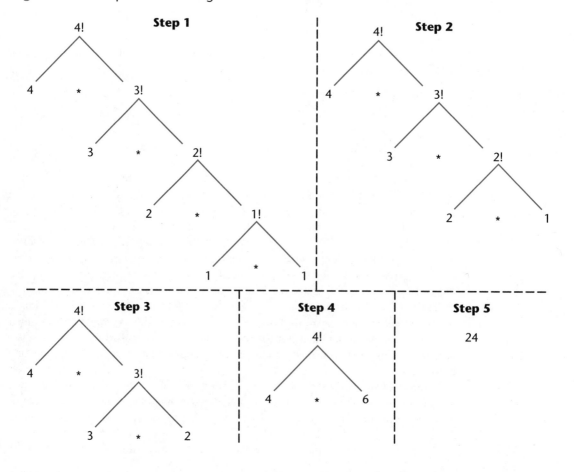

Figure 13.2   Steps in substituting values to evaluate 4!

This recursive definition has the ingredients of any recursive task:

1. The task is defined in terms of itself, working on a smaller version of the problem. Here, $n! = n \, (n - 1)!$ for $n > 0$, but $(n - 1)!$ is a smaller problem than $n!$.

2. The task has a terminal case that is nonrecursive—in this example, $0! = 1$. As we see in Example 13.4, the terminal case might be to do nothing.

This mathematical function can be translated into C as below. The predefined constant *INT_MAX* is the largest integer that our computer can use. On many microcomputers, its value is 32,767. The value of $n!$, however, can get very large quite rapidly. For example, 16! is 20,922,789,888,000. Because such a large integer is greater than *INT_MAX* on most computers, in this implementation we declare that the function *factorial* returns a double precision floating point number, as shown:

```
/*
 * Example 13.1. Recursive function to return n!
 * Pre:     n is a nonnegative integer.
 * Post:    The return value is n!, a double so
 *          numbers larger than INT_MAX can be returned.
 */

double factorial(int n)
{
    double Afactorial; /* n-factorial */

    if (n == 0)
        Afactorial = 1;
    else
        Afactorial = n * factorial(n - 1);
    return Afactorial;
}
```

Because a recursive invocation is not a loop, we must use an *if* statement as opposed to a *while*. The *if* tests to see whether the terminal situation has been achieved. A recursive task should always have a terminal condition and should always work on a smaller problem with each recursive call.

Instead of a looping control structure, recursive functions use an *if* or *if-else* statement, such as

```
if (terminal_condition)
    terminal_case
else
    reducing_case
```
or
```
if (!terminal_condition)
    reducing_case
```

When a function is invoked, an **activation record** comes into existence. This record contains information about the routine, such as parameter values, local variables, and the return location after execution of the routine. With a statement such as

```
printf("%f\n", factorial(4) );
```

the function references in the form of activation records are stacked as illustrated in Figure 13.3. (An activation record holds more information than Figure 13.3 shows, but the purpose of this figure is to explain the evaluation of a recursive call.) Once the terminal case (*factorial*(0) ← 1) is encountered in Step 5, each value of the function can be substituted in the expression from last to first. With each value returned through the function name, a corresponding activation record is removed from the stack. In the **stack** data structure, data can only be added to or removed from one end—the top. The last item placed on the stack must be the first item taken from the stack. At a salad bar, we typically take the top plate from a stack of salad plates. If the plates are recessed into a spring-loaded receptacle, we only have access to the top plate. For example, we cannot get to the third plate from the top without removing the two above it, one at a time. If we put a plate back, it also goes on top of the stack.

Definition A **stack** is a data structure in which data can only be added to or removed from one end—the top.

Figure 13.3
Stack of function references and returns for *factorial*(4)

Step 1

| *factorial*(4) ← 4 * *factorial*(3) |

Step 2

| *factorial*(3) ← 3 * *factorial*(2) |
| *factorial*(4) ← 4 * *factorial*(3) |

Step 3

| *factorial*(2) ← 2 * *factorial*(1) |
| *factorial*(3) ← 3 * *factorial*(2) |
| *factorial*(4) ← 4 * *factorial*(3) |

Step 4

| *factorial*(1) ← 1 * *factorial*(0) |
| *factorial*(2) ← 2 * *factorial*(1) |
| *factorial*(3) ← 3 * *factorial*(2) |
| *factorial*(4) ← 4 * *factorial*(3) |

Step 5

| *factorial*(0) ← 1 |
| *factorial*(1) ← 1 * factorial(0) |
| *factorial*(2) ← 2 * *factorial*(1) |
| *factorial*(3) ← 3 * *factorial*(2) |
| *factorial*(4) ← 4 * *factorial*(3) |

Step 6

| *factorial*(1) ← 1 * 1 = 1 |
| *factorial*(2) ← 2 * *factorial*(1) |
| *factorial*(3) ← 3 * *factorial*(2) |
| *factorial*(4) ← 4 * *factorial*(3) |

Step 7

| *factorial*(2) ← 2 * 1 = 2 |
| *factorial*(3) ← 3 * *factorial*(2) |
| *factorial*(4) ← 4 * *factorial*(3) |

Step 8

| *factorial*(3) ← 3 * 2 = 6 |
| *factorial*(4) ← 4 * *factorial*(3) |

Step 9

| *factorial*(4) ← 4 * 6 = 24 |

We should make one note of caution about the argument to *factorial*. The preconditions state that this value must be nonnegative. Thus, the function that calls *factorial* must ensure that the argument is not negative. Should the invocation to *factorial* have a negative argument, *factorial* would never meet the terminal condition. In this case, n is initially negative, and the function keeps decrementing n until no more room exists on the activation stack. Such a situation is called a **stack overflow**.

Definition **Stack overflow** occurs with an attempt to put something on a stack that has no more room.

Example 13.2

In this example, we develop a recursive function to find the minimum of elements 0 through n in an array of integers. Because the iterative solution is straightforward, we would usually implement this function with a loop. However, the version in this example is instructive in how we process an array recursively.

Whether we use a recursive or iterative solution to find the minimum value in an array, a macro to return the minimum of two integers is useful.

```
#define MIN(a, b) ((a) < (b) ? (a) : (b))
```

To determine the terminal case of the recursive function to find the minimum of elements 0–n in an array of integers, we consider the smallest problem. This situation occurs when we have n being 0 and we are finding the minimum of the one-element subarray, $a[0]$. Clearly, in this situation, the minimum is that element. Thus, the terminal case reads as follows:

```
if (n == 0)
    MinA = a[n];
```

where *MinA* is the value that the function returns.

If n is greater than 0, then the recursive step consists of finding the smaller of $a[n]$ and the minimum of the array elements before $a[n]$. To obtain the minimum of the subarray $a[0]$ through $a[n - 1]$, we invoke *MinInArray* with arguments a and $n - 1$, (*MinInArray*($a, n - 1$)). Figure 13.4 illustrates the process for an array a with elements 24, 12, 27, and 15 and with $n = 3$. The result is *MIN*(*MinInArray*(a, 2), $a[3]$). Because *MinInArray*(a, 2), the minimum of the subarray from $a[0]$ through $a[2]$, is 12, the answer is *MIN*(12, 15) = 12.

Figure 13.4
Action of
MinInArray(a, 3)

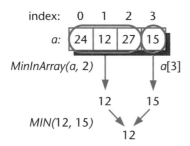

Figure 13.5
Stack of function references for *MinInArray(a, 3)* for array, *a*, with elements 24, 12, 27, 15

Step 1

MinInArray(a, 3) ⟵ *MIN(**MinInArray(a, 2**), a[3])* = *MIN(**MinInArray(a, 2**),* 15)

Step 2

MinInArray(a, 2) ⟵ *MIN(**MinInArray(a, 1**), a[2])* = *MIN(**MinInArray(a, 1**),* 27)
MinInArray(a, 3) ⟵ *MIN(MinInArray(a, 2), a[3])* = *MIN(MinInArray(a, 2),* 15)

Step 3

MinInArray(a, 1) ⟵ *MIN(**MinInArray(a, 0**), a[1]* = *MIN(**MinInArray(a, 0**),* 12)
MinInArray(a, 2) ⟵ *MIN(MinInArray(a,1), a[2])* = *MIN(MinInArray(a, 1),* 27)
MinInArray(a, 3) ⟵ *MIN(MinInArray(a, 2), a[3])* = *MIN(MinInArray(a, 2),* 15)

Step 4

MinInArray(a, 0) ⟵ *a[0]* = **24**
MinInArray(a, 1) ⟵ *MIN(MinInArray(a, 0), a[1])* = *MIN(MinInArray(a, 0),* 12)
MinInArray(a, 2) ⟵ *MIN(MinInArray(a, 1), a[2])* = *MIN(MinInArray(a, 1),* 27)
MinInArray(a, 3) ⟵ *MIN(MinInArray(a, 2), a[3])* = *MIN(MinInArray(a, 2),* 15)

Figure 13.6
Stack of returns continued from Figure 13.5

Step 5

MinInArray(a, 1) ⟵ *MIN(**24**, 12)* = **12**
MinInArray(a, 2) ⟵ *MIN(MinInArray(a, 1), a[2])* = *MIN(MinInArray(a, 1),* 27)
MinInArray(a, 3) ⟵ *MIN(MinInArray(a, 2), a[3])* = *MIN(MinInArray(a, 2),* 15)

Step 6

MinInArray(a, 2) ⟵ *MIN(**12**, 27)* = **12**
MinInArray(a, 3) ⟵ *MIN(MinInArray(a, 2), a[3])* = *MIN(MinInArray(a, 2),* 15)

Step 7

MinInArray(a, 3) ⟵ *MIN(**12**, 15)* = **12**

Figures 13.5 and 13.6 show the stack of function references and returns for *MinInArray(a, 3)*. Below is the definition of the function.

```
/*
 * Example 13.2. Function to return the minimum of
 * elements a[0] through a[n]
 * Pre:   n is a nonnegative integer.
 *        a is an integer array with values for
 *        elements a[0] through a[n].
 * Post:  The return value is the smallest value of
 *        elements a[0] through a[n].
 */
```

```
int MinInArray(int a[], int n)
{
   int MinA;   /* return value of the minimum array element */

      if (n == 0)
          MinA = a[n];
      else
          MinA = MIN(MinInArray(a, n - 1), a[n]);

      return MinA;
}
```

Following is a function *main* along with an *#include* directive and prototypes to test *MinInArray*:

```
/* Example 13.2. Test program for function MinInArray. */

#include <stdio.h>

int MinInArray(int a[], int n);

main()
{
    int a[] = {24, 12, 27, 15};

    printf("The minimum array element is %d.\n",
        MinInArray(a, 3));
}
```

The output from execution of this program confirms the minimum value 12, as shown:

```
The minimum array element is 12.
```

**Example 13.3
Power
Function**

Exponentiation is implemented in C with the *pow* function, which is defined in the math library. As another example of recursion, we consider two versions of our own function to evaluate x^n, where n is a nonnegative integer and x is a floating point number. (Because 0^0 is undefined, both n and x cannot be zero.) In developing our own versions, we show that one version is more efficient than the other.

As a mathematical function, x^n could be defined as follows:

$$x^n = \begin{cases} 1 & \text{if } n = 0 \\ x \cdot x^{n-1} & \text{if } n > 0 \end{cases} \qquad (1)$$

For instance, $5^0 = 1$, while

$$5^3 = 5 \cdot 5^2$$
$$5^2 = 5 \cdot 5^1$$
$$5^1 = 5 \cdot 5^0$$
$$5^0 = 1$$

Thus, substituting in reverse order, we have

$$5^1 = 5 \cdot 5^0 = 5 \cdot 1 = 5$$
$$5^2 = 5 \cdot 5^1 = 5 \cdot 5 = 25$$
$$5^3 = 5 \cdot 5^2 = 5 \cdot 25 = 125$$

Thus, for $n = 3$, this recursive function is called four times—for exponents of 3, 2, 1, and 0. In general, to evaluate x^n the function at (1) must be called about n times (to be exact, $n + 1$ times).

We certainly could implement this definition in C, but a better algorithm involves cutting the problem in half with each recursive reference. To write the mathematical definition, we use the floor function $\lfloor n \rfloor$, which is the largest integer less than or equal to n. Thus, $\lfloor 2.9 \rfloor = 2$, $\lfloor 5.1 \rfloor = 5$, and $\lfloor 7 \rfloor = 7$.

Suppose we want to evaluate x^{14}. By one of the properties of exponents,

$$x^{14} = (x^7)^2$$

We have reduced the problem of evaluating x^{14} to a problem half its size, that of computing x^7. But what is x^7?

$$x^7 = x(x^3)^2$$

where the exponent 3 is $\lfloor 7/2 \rfloor$. We can now write a better algorithm for evaluating x^n, as follows:

$$x^n = \begin{cases} 1 & \text{if } n = 0 \\ x \, (x^{\lfloor n/2 \rfloor})^2 & \text{if } n \text{ is odd} \\ (x^{\lfloor n/2 \rfloor})^2 & \text{otherwise} \end{cases} \qquad (2)$$

The call $Power(x, n/2)$ with integer division $n/2$ returns $x^{\lfloor n/2 \rfloor}$. To avoid calling $Power$ twice to square $x^{\lfloor n/2 \rfloor}$, we store the result of one invocation in a temporary variable, $HalfPower$, and calculate the product $HalfPower * HalfPower$. In C, this function reads as follows:

```
/*
 * Example 13.3. A function to evaluate x^n in a binary fashion.
 * Pre:   x is a floating point number.
 *        n is a nonnegative integer.
 *        x and n cannot both be 0.
 * Post: The return value is x^n.
 */

float Power(float x, int n)
{
    float ReturnPower,    /* x^n              */
          HalfPower;      /* Power(x, n/2) */

    if (n == 0)
       ReturnPower = 1;
    else if (n % 2 == 1)          /* n odd */
    {
        HalfPower    = Power(x, n/2);
        ReturnPower  = x * HalfPower * HalfPower;
    }
```

```
    else                                    /* n even */
    {
        HalfPower    = Power(x, n/2);
        ReturnPower  = HalfPower * HalfPower;
    }

    return ReturnPower;

}
```

Figure 13.7 shows the function references to $f(x) = x^n$ and the corresponding *Power* function placed on the top of the stack. To simplify the diagram, we use *sqr(Power(x, n/2))* in place of *HalfPower * HalfPower*, where *HalfPower = Power(x, n/2)*. The overhead of the calls to *sqr* makes this version less efficient in the implementation of the function. Figure 13.8 illustrates the values of *Power* taken from the stack in reverse order after the terminal condition has been achieved.

Figure 13.7
The stack of recursive function calls to the mathematical function $f(x) = x^n$ and the corresponding *Power* function

Step 1

$5^{14} = (5^7)^2$

or

$Power(5,14) \leftarrow sqr(Power(5, 7))$

Step 2

$5^7 = 5(5^3)^2$
$5^{14} = (5^7)^2$

or

$Power(5, 7) \leftarrow 5 * sqr(Power(5, 3))$
$Power(5,14) \leftarrow sqr(Power (5, 7))$

Step 3

$5^3 = 5(5^1)^2$
$5^7 = 5(5^3)^2$
$5^{14} = (5^7)^2$

or

$Power(5, 3) \leftarrow 5 * sqr(Power(5, 1))$
$Power(5, 7) \leftarrow 5 * sqr(Power(5, 3))$
$Power(5,14) \leftarrow sqr(Power(5,7))$

Step 4

$5^1 = 5(5^0)^2$
$5^3 = 5(5^1)^2$
$5^7 = 5(5^3)^2$
$5^{14} = (5^7)^2$

or

$Power(5, 1) \leftarrow 5 * sqr(Power(5, 0))$
$Power(5, 3) \leftarrow 5 * sqr(Power(5, 1))$
$Power(5, 7) \leftarrow 5 *sqr(Power(5, 3))$
$Power(5,14) \leftarrow sqr(Power(5, 7))$

Step 5

$5^0 = 1$
$5^1 = 5(5^0)^2$
$5^3 = 5(5^1)^2$
$5^7 = 5(5^3)^2$
$5^{14} = (5^7)^2$

or

$Power(5, 0) \leftarrow 1$
$Power(5, 1) \leftarrow 5 * sqr(Power(5, 0))$
$Power(5, 3) \leftarrow 5 * sqr(Power(5, 1))$
$Power(5, 7) \leftarrow 5 * sqr(Power(5, 3))$
$Power(5,14) \leftarrow sqr(Power(5, 7))$

Figure 13.8
The stack of recursive function values for the mathematical function $f(x) = x^n$ or the corresponding *Power* function after the terminal condition has been achieved (Note: The integer answer here would be stored and returned as a floating point number by the function *Power*)

Step 6

$$5^1 = 5(\ 1\ )^2 = 5$$
$$5^3 = 5(5^1)^2$$
$$5^7 = 5(5^3)^2$$
$$5^{14} = (5^7)^2$$

or

$$Power(5, 1) \leftarrow 5 * sqr(\ 1\ ) = 5$$
$$Power(5, 3) \leftarrow 5 * sqr(Power(5, 1)\ )$$
$$Power(5, 7) \leftarrow 5 * sqr(Power(5, 3)\ )$$
$$Power(5,14) \leftarrow sqr(Power(5, 7)\ )$$

Step 7

$$5^3 = 5(\ 5)^2 = 125$$
$$5^7 = 5(5^3)^2$$
$$5^{14} = (5^7)^2$$

or

$$Power(5, 3) \leftarrow 5 * sqr(\ 5\ ) = 125$$
$$Power(5, 7) \leftarrow 5 * sqr(Power\ (5, 3)\ )$$
$$Power(5,14) \leftarrow sqr(Power\ (5, 7)\ )$$

Step 8

$$5^7 = 5(125)^2 = 78125$$
$$5^{14} = (5^7)^2$$

or

$$Power(5, 7) \leftarrow 5 * sqr(\ 125\ ) = 78125$$
$$Power(5,14) \leftarrow sqr(Power\ (5, 7))$$

Step 9

$$5^{14} = (78125)^2$$
$$= 6103515625$$

or

$$Power(5,14) \leftarrow sqr(\ 78125\ )$$
$$= 6,103,515,625$$

This second version of the power function is more efficient than the first. With each recursive call, we cut the problem in half. As Figure 13.7 shows, to evaluate x^n for $n = 14$, we only need to call the function 5 times, for exponents of 14, 7, 3, 1, and 0. The evaluation of x^{28} has only one additional call to the function. The binary search algorithm, which we discussed in Section 8.3, repeatedly cuts the problem in half. We saw that a binary search algorithm of a sorted array of n elements takes roughly $\log_2 n$ iterations. Similarly, the power algorithm at (2) requires about $\log_2 n$ calls to the function. Figure 8.16 illustrates that as n becomes large, the graph of $\log_2 n$ is significantly below that of n. Thus, the power definition at (2) is more much efficient than the definition at (1).

Example 13.4

A computer graphics image is composed of rectangular points or pixels on the computer screen. In a black-and-white picture, we can use 0 to represent white and 1 for black. We can store a representation of the picture in a two-dimensional array, as follows:

```
#define SIZE 5

typedef int pic_t[SIZE][SIZE];
⋮
pic_t pic =
    {{1, 1, 0, 1, 0},
     {1, 0, 0, 1, 1},
     {1, 0, 1, 1, 1},
     {0, 1, 1, 0, 1},
     {0, 0, 1, 0, 0}}};
```

With *pic*[0][0] indicating the color for the pixel in the top left corner, *pic* represents the image in Figure 13.9.

Two black pixels are part of the same object if we can get from one to the other with horizontal and vertical moves. Thus, Figure 13.9 contains two objects.

Given coordinates (indices) for a particular black pixel, (*row*, *col*), we can design a function (*ErasePic*) to erase or white-out the object of which the pixel is part. First, we change the representation for that point to white, as follows:

```
pic[row][col] = 0;
```

Then we call the erasing function for the points above, below, to the left, and to the right of (*row*, *col*). Thus, we spread out within the object from the initial point and erase as we go. The terminal condition arises if a point is outside the 5 × 5 square containing the image or if the point is white and consequently not part of the object. In the terminal case, we do nothing with the point and immediately exit the function.

Invoking the function for the point (3, 2)

```
ErasePic(pic, 3, 2);
```

results in erasing a representation of the rightmost object of Figure 13.9 (see Figure 13.10). The definition of the recursive function is below.

```
/*
 * Example 13.4
 * Function to erase an object containing point (row, col)
 * Two pixels are part of the same object if we can get from
 * one to the other with horizontal and vertical moves.
 * Pre: pic is a two-dimensional array of zeros and ones, with
 *      0 representing white and 1 black in an image.
 *      row and col are integers.
 *
```

Figure 13.9
Initial image for
Example 13.4

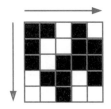

Figure 13.10
Image from
Figure 13.9
after execution
of *ErasePic(pic,
3, 2);*

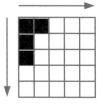

```
 *  Post:If (row, col) was in an object, then the object has
 *        been erased (whited-out).
 */

void ErasePic(pic_t pic, int row, int col)
{
    if ((0 <= row) && (row < SIZE) &&
        (0 <= col) && (col < SIZE) &&
        (pic[row][col] == 1))
    {
        pic[row][col] = 0;
        ErasePic(pic, row + 1, col      );
        ErasePic(pic, row,     col + 1 );
        ErasePic(pic, row - 1, col      );
        ErasePic(pic, row,     col - 1 );
    }
}
```

Example 13.5

The Towers of Hanoi game can be solved nicely with recursion. The game involves three pegs (A, B, C) and N disks of varying sizes that can be stacked on a peg. The object is to move the disks from one peg to another by moving one disk at a time, never placing a larger disk on top of a smaller one.

To simulate moving *Disk* 1 from *Peg A* to *Peg C*, we write

```
Move Disk 1 from Peg A to Peg C.
```

Suppose we are moving two disks, the top disk numbered 1 and the bottom numbered 2, from *Peg A* to *Peg C*.

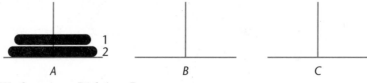

We first move *Disk* 1 to *B*.

Then we move *Disk* 2 to *C*.

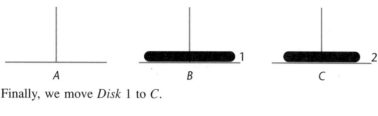

Finally, we move *Disk* 1 to *C*.

Similarly, suppose we want to move *N* disks from *A* to *C*, and we know how to move *N* − 1 disks from any one peg to any other.

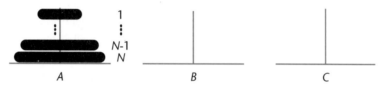

To move the *N* disks from *A* to *C*, we first move the top *N* − 1 disks by a series of legal moves from peg *A* to *B*.

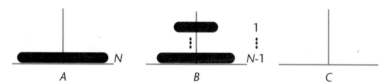

We then move *Disk N* from *A* to *C*.

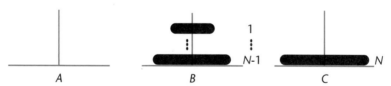

Finally, using our knowledge of how to legally move *N* − 1 disks, we move the *N* − 1 disks from *B* to *C*.

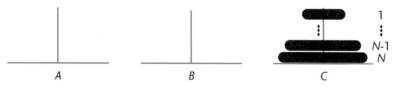

We use the variables *FromPeg*, *AuxPeg*, and *ToPeg* to represent the peg from which we start, the auxiliary peg, and the peg to which we are moving the *N* disks, respectively. Following the above description, we design the function *Hanoi* to play the game as follows:

Hanoi Algorithm to move N *disks from FromPeg to ToPeg:*

if *N* is 1 then
    move Disk 1 from *FromPeg* to *ToPeg*
else
    call *Hanoi* to move *N* − 1 disks from *FromPeg* to *AuxPeg*
    move Disk *N* from *FromPeg* to *ToPeg*
    call *Hanoi* to move *N* − 1 disks from *AuxPeg* to *ToPeg*

Section 13.1 Exercises

1. **a.** Using the fact that 4! = 24, evaluate 5!
   b. Give the stacks for *factorial*(5) as in Figure 13.3.
   c. Write a driver function, *main*, and test the *factorial* function on the computer.
   d. Using the computer, add diagnostic statements to the *factorial* function to print the values of appropriate variables when entering and leaving this function, or perform a trace with a debugger.

2. **a.** Write the first 5 terms of the sequence, $f(0)$ through $f(4)$, defined by the following function:

$$f(n) = \begin{cases} 3 & \text{if } n = 0 \\ 2f(n-1)+1 & \text{if } n > 0 \end{cases}$$

   b. Write this function in C.

3. The following question is similar to one found in the sample questions of the *1984 AP Course Description in Computer Science:*

```c
#include <stdio.h>
int f(int x);

main()
{
    int z;
    z = f(f(2) + f(5));
}

int f(int x)
{
    int ReturnValue;

    if ((x == 1) || (x == 3))
        ReturnValue = x;
    else
        ReturnValue = x * f(x - 1);
    return ReturnValue;
}
```

If *INT_MAX* is large enough for the computer to execute the program above, what is the value of *z* when the program ends?

a. 62   **b.** $5! + 2!$ **c.** $(5! + 2!)!$ **d.** $(7!)!$ **e.** $(62!) \div (2!)$

4. A principal P of \$3000 is deposited in a bank that compounds interest at a yearly rate of $R = 10\%$. If A_n is the amount present after n years, we have

$$A_0 = P = 3000$$
$$A_1 = A_0 + A_0 R = A_0(1 + R) = A_0(1 + 0.10) = 3300$$
$$A_2 = A_1 + A_1 R = A_1(1 + R) = A_1(1 + 0.10) = 3630$$

    a. Find A_3, A_4, and A_5.

    b. Write a recursive function *amount* with parameters P, R, and n in C to calculate the amount in the bank after n years.

5. **a.** Using the first definition of x^n as given in the text at (1) of Example 13.3, write a function *PowerLin* to calculate x^n.

    b. Using that definition, give the stack to evaluate 3^4 or *PowerLin*(3,4).

    c. Determine the most number of elements that would be on the stack to evaluate 3^{42} or *PowerLin*(3,42).

    d. Test this function on the computer with appropriate diagnostic statements.

6. **a.** Using the second definition of x^n as given in the text at (2) of Example 13.3, give the stack to evaluate 3^4 or *Power*(3,4).

    b. Determine the most number of elements that would be on the stack to evaluate 3^{42} or *Power*(3,42).

    c. Which is the better algorithm, *PowerLin* of Exercise 5 or *Power*?

7. In about 1200 A.D., mathematician Leonardo **Fibonacci** presented a sequence of numbers that has several applications to natural events. The terminal case defines the first two terms of the sequence, and any subsequent term is the sum of the two immediately preceding numbers. Thus, for $x_0 = x_1 = 1$, we have

$$x_2 = x_1 + x_0 = 1 + 1 = 2$$
$$x_3 = x_2 + x_1 = 2 + 1 = 3$$
$$x_4 = x_3 + x_2 = 3 + 2 = 5$$

    a. Define this sequence with a recursive mathematical function.

    b. Find x_{10}.

    c. Write a recursive function to find the nth Fibonacci number.

8. The following algorithm, developed by Euclid, finds the greatest common divisor, *gcd*, of two positive integers. For example, $gcd(18,12) = 6$.

gcd(x, y) ⟶ *d*

    Function to return the greatest common divisor of x and y

Pre:

    x and y are positive integers

Post:

    The greatest common divisor of x and y has been returned.

> *Algorithm:*
>
> if $x > y$ then
> $\quad d \leftarrow gcd(x - y, y)$
> else if $y > x$ then
> $\quad d \leftarrow gcd(x, y - x)$
> else $d \leftarrow x$
> return d

    a. Verify that the algorithm works for $x = 18$ and $y = 12$ by showing the development of the stack.

    b. Write *gcd* as a C function.

   9. Write a recursive function to find the product of elements 0 through n of an array of integers. The recursive step is to multiply element n of the array by the product of elements 0 through $n - 1$. The terminal condition is true when $n == 0$.

10. a. Implement a recursive version of the sequential search *SeqSearchUnordered* from Example 8.7 of Section 8.3.

    b. Implement a recursive version of the binary search from Section 8.3.

11. Write a recursive function to find the maximum of elements 0 through n of an array of floating point numbers.

12. a. Write a recursive function to print elements 0 through n of a character array in reverse order. Let $n < 0$ be the terminal condition.

    b. Write a recursive function to print elements 0 through n of a character array in normal order.

13. Write a recursive boolean function to return *TRUE* (1) if the character string is a **palindrome**, that is, the string reads the same backwards as forwards. Examples of some palindromes are "dad" and "ABLE WAS I ERE I SAW ELBA". Parameters for the function are an array for the character string and *first* and *last,* indices of the first and last elements of the part of the string being checked, respectively. If the *first* and *last* elements are not equal, return *FALSE* (0). If they are equal, however, repeat the process with the substring having indices *first* + 1 and *last* − 1. Do not neglect the terminal condition.

14. Write a recursive function to evaluate *na*

$$na = \underbrace{a + a + \dots + a,}_{n \text{ summands}}$$

where n is a nonnegative integer and a is a floating point number. For example,

$$7 \cdot 3.1 = 3.1 + 3.1 + 3.1 + 3.1 + 3.1 + 3.1 + 3.1 = 21.7$$

n and a should be the parameters for the function.

15. a. Give the moves for moving three disks from *Peg A* to *C* in the Towers of Hanoi game of Example 13.5.

    b. Code in C the function *Hanoi* from Example 13.5 to simulate the Towers of Hanoi game.

    c. Write a recursive function to calculate the number of moves for N disks.

    d. Suppose $N + 1$ pegs are available for the N disks in the game. How many moves are necessary?

16. The number of combinations or subsets of r distinct objects chosen from n objects is

$$C(n,r) = \frac{n!}{r!(n-r)!}, \quad 0 \le r \le n$$

For example, a 5-element set, such as $S = \{0, 3, 5, 8, 9\}$, has 10 2-element subsets or

$$C(5,2) = \frac{5!}{2!3!} = \frac{5 \cdot 4 \cdot 3 \cdot 2 \cdot 1}{2 \cdot 1 \cdot 3 \cdot 2 \cdot 1} = 10$$

a. Complete the following recursive mathematics formula for $C(n, r)$:

$$C(n,r) = \begin{cases} \underline{\hspace{5cm}} & \text{if } n = r \\ \underline{\hspace{5cm}} & \text{if } r = 0 \\ C(n-1, r-1) + C(n-1, r) & \text{if } n > r > 1 \end{cases}$$

b. Write a C function to implement this formula.

17. Write a recursive function to merge two sorted arrays of the same type into a third array.

18. Write a recursive function to convert a character string of n digits to the corresponding integer number. For example, for the input string "5274", return the number 5274. Recall that (int)'5' $- (int)$'0' is the number 5. The following calculations demonstrate the idea of the recursion:

5274 = (527)10 + 4
527 = (52)10 + 7
52 = (5)10 + 2

19. The decimal or base 10 number system, which we use every day, has 10 digits, and the binary or base 2 number system, which is used in the computer, has only the digits 0 and 1. The decimal number 5274 can be expanded in powers of 10 as follows:

$$5 \cdot 10^3 + 2 \cdot 10^2 + 7 \cdot 10^1 + 4 \cdot 10^0 = 5 \cdot 1000 + 2 \cdot 100 + 7 \cdot 10 + 4 \cdot 1$$

The binary number 111001, expressed in powers of 2, yields the following decimal equivalent:

$$\begin{aligned} 111001 &= 1 \cdot 2^5 + 1 \cdot 2^4 + 1 \cdot 2^3 + 0 \cdot 2^2 + 0 \cdot 2^1 + 1 \cdot 2^0 \\ &= 1 \cdot 32 + 1 \cdot 16 + 1 \cdot 8 + 0 \cdot 4 + 0 \cdot 2 + 1 \cdot 1 \\ &= 32 + 16 + 8 + 0 + 0 + 1 \\ &= 57 \end{aligned}$$

Thus, 57 is the decimal equivalent of the binary number 111001. Modify the function from Exercise 18 to convert a binary number to a decimal one.

20. To convert a positive decimal integer num to a binary number, repeatedly perform integer division of successive quotients. The remainders, written in reverse order, are num expressed in the base 2 number system. For example, consider the following conversion of 19:

$$\begin{array}{ccccc} 9 & 4 & 2 & 1 & 0 \\ 2\overline{)19} & 2\overline{)9} & 2\overline{)4} & 2\overline{)2} & 2\overline{)1} \\ \underline{18} & \underline{8} & \underline{4} & \underline{2} & \underline{0} \\ 1 & 1 & 0 & 0 & 1 \end{array}$$

Taking the remainders in reverse order, we see that 19 is 10011 in the binary number system. Write a recursive function to print a nonnegative decimal integer in the binary number system.

21. a. Write a recursive function *primes* to print all the prime factors of an integer, *num,* which is greater than 1. A prime is an integer greater than 1 whose only positive factors are 1 and itself. Thus, the prime factorizations of 40 and 126 are as follows:

$$40 = 2 \cdot 2 \cdot 2 \cdot 5$$
$$126 = 2 \cdot 3 \cdot 3 \cdot 7$$

Use the function *PrimeFactor* below, whose only purpose is to call the recursive function *primes.* This calling function passes *primes* the arguments *num* and 2, the first prime. With recursive calls to *primes,* we have arguments of a revised number and *n* or *n* + 1.

```
void PrimeFactor (int num)
{
    primes(num, 2)
}

void primes (int num, int n)
{
    ⋮
}
```

b. Test *primes* with *num* = 40.

c. Test *primes* with *num* = 126.

22. The following is similar to a sample question in *Practicing to Take the GRE Computer Science Test, 2nd Edition:* For $x \geq 0$, $y \geq 0$, define $f(x,y)$ by

$f(0, y) = y + 1,$
$f(x + 1, 0) = f(x, 1),$ and
$f(x + 1, y + 1) = f(x, f(x + 1, y)).$

For nonnegative integer y, evaluate $f(1, y)$.

Section 13.1 Programming Projects

1. One root of the polynomial function $f(x) = 2x^3 - 14x^2 + 31x - 22$ is $x = 2$ because $f(2) = 2 \cdot 2^3 - 14 \cdot 2^2 + 31 \cdot 2 - 22 = 0$. Thus, the graph of f crosses the x-axis at $x = 2$. We know another root is between $x = 3$ and $x = 4$ because $f(3) = 2 \cdot 3^3 - 14 \cdot 3^2 + 31 \cdot 3 - 22 = -1$ is negative and $f(4) = 2 \cdot 4^3 - 14 \cdot 4^2 + 31 \cdot 4 - 22 = 6$ is positive. Because f is continuous, having an unbroken graph, the graph crosses the x-axis—or f has a root—between $x = 3$ and $x = 4$. Cutting the interval in half, we find at $x = 3.5$, $f(3.5) = 2 \cdot 3.5^3 - 14 \cdot 3.5^2 + 31 \cdot 3.5 - 22 = 0.75$ is also positive. Therefore, the root must be between $x = 3$ and $x = 3.5$. We continue cutting the interval in half and testing the midpoint. We stop the function and return x as soon as the value of $f(x)$ is within some designated distance, say 0.001, of 0.

Write a program to read the representation for a polynomial, a distance (*distance*), and two x values (*first* and *last*). The program should print an approximation for a root, x, between those two points so that $f(x)$ is within *distance* of 0. Represent the polynomial by a list of its coefficients with their corresponding exponents. Print an error message if evaluations of the function at the two end points do not have opposite signs. Your program should define two recursive functions—one to calculate exponentiation efficiently and the other to return an approximation for a root of f between *first* and *last*.

2. The number of combinations of r distinct objects chosen from n, $C(n, r)$, is also called a binary coefficient (see Exercise 16). These coefficients are in the following binomial expansion:

$$(x + y)^n = C(n, 0)x^n + C(n, 1)x^{n-1}y + C(n, 2)x^{n-2}y^2 + \ldots +$$
$$C(n, n - 2)x^2y^{n-2} + C(n, n - 1)xy^{n-1} + C(n, n)y^n$$

where n is a nonnegative integer. Using this formula, we have

$$(x + y)^2 = x^2 + 2xy + y^2$$
$$(x + y)^3 = x^3 + 3x^2y + 3xy^2 + y^3$$
$$(x + y)^4 = x^4 + 4x^3y + 6x^2y^2 + 4xy^3 + y^4$$

Write a program to read a nonnegative integer exponent, n, and to write the binomial expansion of $(x + y)^n$. Use ^ to indicate exponentiation. For example, write x^2 as x^2. Use a recursive function to evaluate $C(n, r)$.

3. Exercise 19 of this section describes how to convert a nonnegative binary (base 2) number to its decimal (base 10) equivalent, and Exercise 20 presents the reverse process. Create a menu-driven program that repeatedly gives the user the options of converting a nonnegative number in a base less than 10 to a decimal number, of performing the opposite maneuver, or of quitting. After selection, prompt the user for the other base and then for the number to be used in the conversion. Have error checking to verify that the user types an integer from 2 to 9 for the other base. When a number is entered in another base, an error message should be issued if any digit not in the appropriate base is used. For example, a base 2 number has only 2 possible digits, 0 and 1. A base 8 number has digits 0, 1, 2, 3, 4, 5, 6, and 7. Your conversion routines should be recursive.

In Projects 4–10 develop a program to test the recursive routine in the indicated exercise or example.

4. *Hanoi* from Example 13.5 to play Towers of Hanoi

5. Function from Exercise 7 to find the nth Fibonacci number

6. Sequential and binary search functions from Exercise 10

7. Function from Exercise 11 to print elements 0 through n of a character array in reverse order

8. Boolean function from Exercise 13 to return *TRUE* (1) if a character string is a palindrome

9. Function from Exercise 17 to merge two sorted arrays of the same type into a third array

10. *primes* from Exercise 21 to print all the prime factors of an integer, *num,* which is greater than 1

11. Develop a program that, for any value of N between 1 and 10 inclusive, will print a list of all the subsets of the set $\{1, 2, \ldots, N\}$.

Sample run:

```
GIVE SET SIZE: 3
THE SUBSETS OF {1,2,3} ARE:
{}
{1}
{2}
{1,2}
{3}
{1,3}
{2,3}
{1,2,3}
```

12. Numbers can be represented in factorial notation by considering each digit as being multiplied by an appropriate factorial. Working from the right side of the number, the first digit is multiplied by 1!, the second by 2!, and so on. The largest digit that can appear in any position is the digit corresponding to the factorial multiplier of that position. In other words, the rightmost digit can be either 0 or 1. The second digit from the right can be 0, 1, or 2, and so on. As an example, consider the factorial notation number 52311. It represents

$$5 * 5! + 2 * 4! + 3 * 3! + 1 * 2! + 1 * 1! = 5 * 120 + 2 * 24 + 3 * 6 + 1 * 2 + 1 * 1$$
$$= 669 \text{ decimal}$$

Here is a conversion of the decimal number 3257 to factorial notation:

$$3257 = 4 * 720 + 377$$
$$= 4 * 6! + 3 * 120 + 17$$
$$= 4 * 6! + 3 * 5! + 2 * 6 + 5$$
$$= 4 * 6! + 3 * 5! + 0 * 4! + 2 * 3! + 2 * 2! + 1 * 1!$$
$$= 430221 \text{ in factorial notation.}$$

Develop a program to convert decimal numbers to factorial notation and vice versa. The program should ask the user to indicate whether he or she wants to convert a factorial number or decimal number. It should then accept input of the number and print the value of the number in the other notation. Note that, when writing factorial notation, digits greater than 9 are represented by letters—A = 10, B = 11, C = 12, and so on. For the purposes of this problem you may assume that all numbers are less than 2**31, which is less than 13!, and no invalid input is given.

Here is a sample run of such a program, with input underlined:

```
Is input (F)actorial or (D)ecimal? d
> 3257
The factorial number is 430221
Is input (F)actorial or (D)ecimal? f
> 430221
The decimal number is 3257
```

```
Is input (F)actorial or (D)ecimal? d
> 333333321
The factorial number is 83851353111
Is input (F)actorial or (D)ecimal? f
> 83851353111
The decimal number is 333333321
Is input (F)actorial or (D)ecimal? d
> 1234567890
The factorial number is 26A211633300
Is input (F)actorial or (D)ecimal? f
> 26A211633300
The decimal number is 1234567890
Is input (F)actorial or (D)ecimal? x
```

13. The partition of a positive whole number N is a set $\{a_1, a_2, ... a_k\}$ of integers between 1 and N inclusive whose sum is N. Write a program that accepts input of an integer N, $1 \le N \le 50$ and prints all distinct partitions of N. It should also indicate how many such partitions there are.

Sample output follows:

```
WHAT IS THE VALUE OF N?   5
THE PARTITIONS OF 5 ARE:
{5}
{4,1}
{3,2}
{3,1,1,}
{2,2,1}
{2,1,1,1}
{1,1,1,1,1}


THERE ARE 7 DISTINCT PARTITIONS OF THE NUMBER 5.
```

Section 13.2 Recursion vs. Iteration

In the text and exercises, we have considered a number of problems that can be solved recursively. However, such a solution is not always the most efficient.

The stack in Figure 13.3 clarifies the behavior of the recursive function *factorial*, but in reality a more extensive **run-time stack** of activation records exists during execution. Each activation record contains the values of all local variables and parameters, such as n and *Afactorial*, and the return location for reentry to that instance of the routine. This run-time stack is only allotted a certain amount of space in memory, which itself is finite. For instance, a reference to *factorial* with argument 100 to evaluate 100! results in a stack that has at least 300 items—100 values of n, 100 values for *Afactorial*, and 100 return locations. The run-time stack on a particular machine might not be able to handle the load, resulting in a run-time error message of STACK OVERFLOW.

Figure 13.11 Summary of points about iterative and recursive solutions

Iteration	Recursion
If we can readily develop an iterative algorithm, we should do so. There is always an equivalent iterative solution to a recursive one.	Many times, the most natural and understandable solution to a problem is a recursive one.

Argument against Using Recursion	Counterarguments
The potential exists for run-time stack overflow for large problems. Because of the function calls, a recursive routine often consumes more time.	Memories are larger. Some compilers allow the user to allocate more memory to the stack. Computers are faster. The architectures of some computers enable fast execution of recursive routines. Some compilers can convert many recursive routines to iterative ones automatically.

Not only does a recursive solution usually gobble up more space than a nonrecursive one, but often the recursive routine consumes more time. Generally, a function call takes more time than a sequential execution of statements.

You might reasonably be wondering why we use recursion at all. Many times, the most natural and understandable solution to a problem is a recursive one. For example, it is much easier to develop recursive solutions to the problems from Example 13.4 of erasing a graphics object and from Example 13.5 of playing Towers of Hanoi. Similarly, many data structures operations have straightforward recursive algorithms, whereas their iterative counterparts are difficult. As computers have become faster with larger memories, the programmer's time is now a more important consideration than it was in the early days of the computer industry. Furthermore, with some modern computers and compilers, a recursive routine can actually execute faster than a nonrecursive counterpart. Some compilers can convert many recursive routines to iterative ones automatically. With some compilers, we can increase the space that the computer allocates for the run-time stack. However, if we can readily develop a nonrecursive algorithm, we should do so. Moreover, we might be forced to consider a nonrecursive solution after designing a recursive one because of stack overflow or speed considerations. In these cases, we must convert the recursive idea to an iterative one. There is always an equivalent iterative solution to a recursive one. Figure 13.11 summarizes these points about iterative versus recursive solutions.

Solving a Recursive Routine

Recursion takes a problem from its highest level, for instance the evaluation of *factorial*(4), to its lowest, as in the terminal case of *factorial*(0). In contrast, an iterative solution can proceed from the bottom up—for example, from *factorial*(0) to *factorial*(4). Iteration is implemented in structured C with a *for*, *while*, or *do-while* loop.

Let us **solve** the recursive routine *factorial* or, in other words, find a nonrecursive definition for this function. The terminal case in the recursive definition now becomes the initial case, as shown:

$0! = 1$ or *factorial*(0) = 1

Using the recursive part, $n! = n (n - 1)!$ and proceeding from the lowest terms up to the nth case, we hope to discover how to program the function nonrecursively.

$$1! = 1 \cdot 0! = 1 \cdot 1 = 1$$
$$2! = 2 \cdot 1! = 2 \cdot 1 = 2$$
$$3! = 3 \cdot 2! = 3 \cdot 2 = 6$$
$$4! = 4 \cdot 3! = 4 \cdot 6 = 24$$

We start with $0! = 1$ as an initial value of the local variable *Afactorial*. The previous factorial, stored in *Afactorial*, is multiplied by the index at each iteration of the loop. The nonrecursive definition of *factorial* follows:

```
/*
 * Nonrecursive version of the factorial function.
 * Pre:    n is a nonnegative integer.
 * Post:   The return value is n!, a double so
 *         numbers larger than INT_MAX can be returned.
 */

double NRfactorial (int n)
{
    double Afactorial = 1;   /* ongoing value of factorial */
    int i;                   /* index */

    for (i = 1; i <= n; i++)
        Afactorial = i * Afactorial;

    return Afactorial;
}
```

Because the nonrecursive *NRfactorial* is at least as easy to understand as the recursive *factorial*, the former is the more desirable implementation of the factorial function.

Definition To **solve** a recursive routine means to find an equivalent nonrecursive definition.

Section 13.2 **Exercises**

In Exercises 1–16, find an iterative solution to the indicated problems from Section 13.1.

1. Example 13.2, a function to return the minimum of array elements 0 through n
2. Example 13.3, Equation (1), for x^n
3. Exercise 12b, a function to print the elements 0 through n of an array in normal order
4. Exercise 2, the function f, where

$$f(n) = \begin{cases} 3 & \text{if } n = 0 \\ 2f(n - 1) + 1 & \text{if } n > 0 \end{cases}$$

5. Exercise 4b, a function *amount* with parameters P, R, and n to calculate the amount compounded in the bank after n years

6. Exercise 7, a function to find the *n*th Fibonacci number

7. Exercise 8, the greatest common divisor function (*gcd*)

8. Exercise 9, a function to find the product of elements 0 through *n* of an array of integers

9. Exercise 21, a function *primes* to print all the prime factors of an integer, *num*, which is greater than 1

10. Exercise 11, a function to find the maximum of elements 0 through *n* of an array of floating point numbers

11. Example 13.3, Equation (2) for x^n

12. Exercise 13, a boolean function to return *TRUE* if a character string is a palindrome

13. Exercise 17, a function to merge two sorted arrays into a third array

14. Exercise 18, a function to convert a character string of *n* digits to the corresponding integer number

15. Exercise 19, a function to convert a binary number to a decimal one

16. Exercise 20, a function to print the binary equivalent of a nonnegative decimal number

Section 13.2 Programming Projects

For the following projects, produce a nonrecursive version of the corresponding project in Section 13.1.

1. Project 1, to find the root of a polynomial

2. Project 2, to produce a binomial expansion

3. Project 3, for conversion from a base *b* ($2 \leq b \leq 9$) number to the base 10 equivalent and vice versa

Section 13.3 Breadth: Formal Grammars

BNF

We can use recursion to define formally the syntax of a computer language. Languages defined in **Backus-Naur Form** or **BNF**, which employs recursion, can be recognized and translated easily by a compiler. (Backus-Naur Form is sometimes called **Backus-Normal Form**.) **John Backus**, who headed the team that created FORTRAN, developed BNF and used it to give an exact definition of the language ALGOL in the late 1950s. Many language manuals and texts today use BNF to display their syntax precisely. In BNF, the symbol ::= is similar to a C assignment symbol, that is, what appears on the right of the symbol defines the term on the left. A **nonterminal symbol** is in angle brackets (< >) and can appear on either side in a definition. **Terminal symbols**, such as the letter B or the digit 5, cannot be defined and, hence, can only be listed on the right-hand side of a definition. Adjacent symbols are concatenated or glued together, and a vertical bar (|) represents "or."

Definition **Backus-Naur Form** or **BNF** is a method of defining formally the syntax of a computer language.

Figure 13.12
Parse tree for
variable name
t_2a

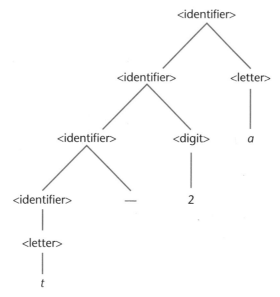

The BNF description of a C identifier shows that such a name must begin with a letter or an underscore. Any number of letters, digits, or underscores can follow. Because C is case sensitive, we must include both upper- and lower-case letters in the description, as shown:

```
<identifier> ::= <letter> | _ | <identifier><letter> | <identifier><digit> | <identifier>_
<letter>     ::= a | b | c | . . . | z | A | B | C | . . . | Z
<digit>      ::= 0 | 1 | 2 | . . . | 9
```

Using this definition, Figure 13.12 demonstrates that the language description can recognize *t_2a* as a C identifier. **Parsing** is the process of recognizing that an item is part of a language. The tree in Figure 13.12 is a **parse tree**.

Definition **Parsing** is the process of recognizing that an item is part of a language.

The definition of *identifier* is recursive because we use <identifier> to define <identifier>. However, recursive tasks cannot continue forever. We have terminal cases, which are nonrecursive, of defining <identifier> as a <letter> or underscore (_).

Parsing

The BNF description of C is a particular example of the use of a **formal grammar**,* the study of which is part of **automata theory**. A grammar has four parts, a **vocabulary** or set of symbols (V), a nonempty subset of **terminal symbols** (V_T), the **start symbol** (S), and a finite set of **productions** or rules (P). A **word** is a finite-length string of terminals. (In this section, "string" means a list of characters. We do not mean a C string, which ends in the null character.) A **language** is the set of all words generated using the vocabulary and the productions. The vocabulary of C consists of the start symbol, letters, digits, some special symbols (such as an underscore) reserved words (such as *while*) and other words (such as *t_2a*). The above definition of *identifier* could be written with the following productions:

---

*Specifically, a context-free grammar.

$$S \longrightarrow identifier$$
$$identifier \longrightarrow letter \mid \_ \mid identifier\ letter \mid identifier\ digit \mid identifier\ \_$$
$$letter \longrightarrow a \mid b \mid c \mid \ldots \mid z \mid A \mid B \mid C \mid \ldots \mid Z$$
$$digit \longrightarrow 0 \mid 1 \mid 2 \mid \ldots \mid 9$$

Definitions   A **formal grammar** has four parts—a **vocabulary** or set of symbols (V), a nonempty subset of **terminal symbols** (V_T), the **start symbol** (S), and a finite set of **productions** or **rules** (P). A **word** is a finite-length string of terminals. A **language** is the set of all words generated using the vocabulary and the productions of a formal grammar.

Example 13.6

Suppose a language has vocabulary $V = \{0, 1, S\}$ with a set of terminals $V_T = \{0, 1\}$ and the following productions:

1. $S \longrightarrow 0S$

2. $S \longrightarrow 1S$

3. $S \longrightarrow 0$

4. $S \longrightarrow 1$

The language contains all finite strings of zeros and ones, such as in the contents of a computer's memory. Moreover, the next sequence with the indicated productions shows the formation of the string 10011, as follows:

$$\begin{array}{ccccccccc} & 2 & & 1 & & 1 & & 2 & & 4 \\ S & \longrightarrow & 1S & \longrightarrow & 1\ 0S & \longrightarrow & 10\ 0S & \longrightarrow & 100\ 1S & \longrightarrow & 10011 \end{array}$$

Notice the recursive nature of the definition, as S appears on the left and right of productions 1 and 2. The productions define S in terms of S. Productions 3 and 4 give a way to stop the process. Thus, productions 1 and 2 give the reducing cases, and productions 3 and 4 are comparable to the terminal cases. Figure 13.13 displays the parse tree for 10011.

A formal grammar is an effective tool for describing and analyzing both natural and programming languages. The area of computer science called artificial intelligence uses grammars to interpret natural languages like English. Moreover, a component of each compiler is a parser. The **parser** uses the programming language's grammar to recognize valid programs in the language.

Example 13.7

In this example, we develop a recursive boolean function to recognize valid words in the language having the grammar of the last example. The function returns *TRUE* if a string is in the language and *FALSE* otherwise. Recall that the grammar of that example has the following productions:

1. $S \longrightarrow 0S$

2. $S \longrightarrow 1S$

3. $S \longrightarrow 0$

4. $S \longrightarrow 1$

According to the last two productions of the grammar, two terminal conditions exist—the string parameter is only "0" or "1". The first two productions indicate two

Figure 13.13
Parse tree for 10011 using the grammar in Example 13.6

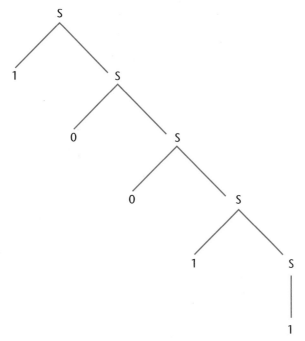

reducing cases—If the string parameter starts with 0 or 1, we strip off the prefix and apply the function to the remaining string. Closely following the recursion of the productions, we develop the following boolean function:

```c
#include <string.h>

typedef enum {FALSE, TRUE} boolean_t;
  ⋮
/*
 * Example 13.7
 * Boolean function to return TRUE if a string parameter is in
 * the language which has the following grammar rules:
 * S -> 0, S -> 1, S -> 0S, S -> 1S
 * Pre:   S is a string of characters.
 * Post:  TRUE has been returned if S is in the language,
 *        FALSE otherwise.
 */

boolean_t InLanguage(char *S)
{
    boolean_t recognize;       /* boolean return value */

    if (strlen(S) == 1)
        recognize = (S[0] == '0' || S[0] == '1') ? TRUE : FALSE;
    else if (S[0] == '0' || S[0] == '1')
        recognize = InLanguage(S + 1);
    else
        recognize = FALSE;

    return recognize;
}
```

If string S has length 1, we verify using the conditional expression operator that $S[0]$ is '0' or '1'. If the length is greater than 1 and the first character, $S[0]$, is '0' or '1', we call *InLanguage* to process the rest of the string $(S + 1)$. Because S is the address of $S[0]$, the pointer sum $S + 1$ is the address of $S[1]$. If the leading character is not '0' or '1', the string is not in the language.

Example 13.8

In this example, we use recursion to develop the grammar for the language L, containing all finite nonempty strings of bits that do **not** contain 11. This language has a vocabulary $\{0, 1, S\}$, a set of terminal symbols $\{0, 1\}$, and a start symbol S. A string in the language can begin with 0 or 1. If the string contains more than one bit and commences with 0, another string in the language must follow:

$$\underbrace{0x\ldots x}_{\epsilon\, L}$$

If the string begins with 1, another 1 cannot immediately follow. Thus, a word of length greater than two must start with 10 and then have another string from the language:

$$\underbrace{10x\ldots x}_{\epsilon\, L}$$

Thus, the reducing cases for the words in the language are as follows:

1. $S \longrightarrow 0S$

2. $S \longrightarrow 10S$

For the terminal cases, we must generate strings of length one or two. There are two strings of length one—0 and 1. Bit strings 0 and 1 are both in the language, so we have the following productions:

3. $S \longrightarrow 0$

4. $S \longrightarrow 1$

The words of length two are 00, 01, and 10, but not 11, because it contains adjacent ones. Thus, to form the 2-bit words 00, 01, 10, we have the following rules:

5. $S \longrightarrow 00$

6. $S \longrightarrow 01$

7. $S \longrightarrow 10$

We can generate the strings starting with 0 in productions 5 and 6 using productions 1, 3, and 4 as follows:

$$S \overset{1}{\longrightarrow} 0S \overset{3}{\longrightarrow} 00$$
$$S \overset{1}{\longrightarrow} 0S \overset{4}{\longrightarrow} 01$$

Thus, the minimum set of productions is as follows:

$$\begin{cases} S \longrightarrow 0 \\ S \longrightarrow 1 \\ S \longrightarrow 10 \\ S \longrightarrow 0S \\ S \longrightarrow 10S \end{cases}$$

Figure 13.14
Parse tree for
the word 1001
in the language
of bit strings
that do not
contain 11

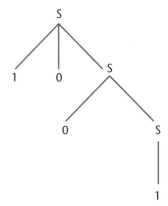

Figure 13.14 displays the parse tree for the word 1001 in *L*.

Example 13.9

The start symbol does not need to be on either end, as we demonstrate in this example. Starting with a vocabulary of {0, 1, *S*}, we find the productions to generate the language containing all palindromes, strings that read the same left to right as right to left. For example, 1001001 and 011110 are both in the language.

The reducing cases need to produce the same bit on both ends and to have a way of continuing the process. Because two possibilities exist for the end bits, 0 and 1, there are two generating productions:

1. $S \rightarrow 0S0$

2. $S \rightarrow 1S1$

For the terminal cases, we need to consider two situations—odd- and even-length palindromes. The shortest palindromes are of length one—0 and 1. To generate odd-length palindromes, we must end with a production replacing *S* with a bit. Thus, we have the following productions:

3. $S \rightarrow 0$

4. $S \rightarrow 1$

We still do not have a way of completing the parsing of an even-length palindrome. Consequently, we must include productions that replace *S* with the palindromes of length two—00 and 11—as shown:

5. $S \rightarrow 00$

6. $S \rightarrow 11$

To demonstrate that 1001001 and 011110 are in the language with this grammar, we use the parse trees in Figure 13.15 or the following applications of the productions:

$$
\begin{array}{ccccc}
2 & 1 & 1 & 4 \\
S \rightarrow 1S1 & \rightarrow 10S01 & \rightarrow 100S001 & \rightarrow 1001001
\end{array}
$$

$$
\begin{array}{cccc}
1 & 2 & 6 \\
S \rightarrow 0S0 & \rightarrow 01S10 & \rightarrow 011110
\end{array}
$$

Figure 13.15
Parse trees
for the
palindromes
1001001 and
011110

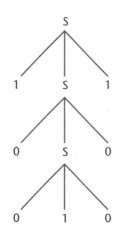

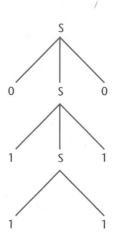

Section 13.3 Exercises

1. a. Write a recursive definition for <signed integer> using <digit>, <signed integer>, and terminals "+", "−", and the digits.

b. Using the definition in Part a, give a parse tree for +52; 42; −795

In each of the Exercises 2–5, do the following:

a. *Describe the language that the productions generate on the vocabulary {0, 1, S}.*

b. *Show how to generate the string.*

c. *Write a recursive boolean function to return* TRUE *(1) if a particular string is in this language.*

2. a. $S \rightarrow 0S$ **3. a.** $S \rightarrow 01S$ **4. a.** $S \rightarrow 0S0$ **5. a.** $S \rightarrow 0S0$
     $S \rightarrow 0$ $S \rightarrow 01$ $S \rightarrow 1$ $S \rightarrow 1S1$
  b. 000   **b.** 0101   **b.** 0001000 $S \rightarrow 1$
                                                              b. 0011100

Consider the vocabulary {0, 1, S}. Write productions to generate the languages in Exercises 6–8. Then write a recursive boolean function to return TRUE *(1) if a particular string is in this language.*

6. The set of all nonempty strings (strings that contain at least one character) of ones

7. The set of all nonempty strings of an even number of zeros and no ones

8. The set of all even-length palindromes of length at least 2

For each of the languages in Exercises 9–11, give the productions to generate the language. Then write a recursive boolean function to return TRUE *(1) if a particular string is in this language.*

9. The set of all bit strings that do not contain 00

10. The set of all bit strings that do not contain 001

11. The set of all bit strings that do not contain 10

12. Using the grammar of Example 13.6, parse the word 0010.

13. Using the following productions:

$$S \rightarrow S0, \ S \rightarrow 1S, \ S \rightarrow 1$$

of a grammar, draw the parse tree for 11000.

14. Using the following productions:

$$S \rightarrow S0S, S \rightarrow 1S1, S \rightarrow 0$$

of a grammar, draw the parse tree for

a. 10100   **b.** 1110111

15. Consider the grammar with vocabulary $V = \{0, 1, S, A\}$, terminals $V_T = \{0, 1\}$, start symbol S and productions

$$S \rightarrow 0SA, A \rightarrow A1, S \rightarrow 0, A \rightarrow 1$$

a. Draw a parse tree for 001.

b. Draw two parse trees for 000111.

16. Consider the following simplified structure of an English sentence:

sentence $\rightarrow$ *subject predicate*

predicate $\rightarrow$ *verb direct-object*

subject $\rightarrow$ *noun* | *adjective-phrase noun*

direct-object $\rightarrow$ *noun* | *adjective-phrase noun*

adjective-phrase $\rightarrow$ *adjective* | *article adjective*

article $\rightarrow$ a | an | the

Productions would also send each nonterminal—such as *noun*, *verb*, and *adjective*—to all appropriate English words. Artificial intelligence studies use a similar structure as part of a natural language interpreter. Parse the following sentence:

IDLE HANDS ARE THE DEVIL'S WORKSHOP.

17. Repeat Exercise 16 using the following sentence:

WILLFUL WASTE MAKES WOEFUL WANT.

18. a. What words written with zeros and ones are in the language defined by the following BNF description?

$$<S> ::= <S>0 \mid 1$$

b. By drawing a parse tree, show that 1000 is in the language.

c. Write a recursive boolean function to return *TRUE* (1) if a particular string is in this language.

d. Find an iterative solution to the problem.

19. a. What words written with zeros and ones are in the language defined by the following BNF description?

$$<S> ::= <S>0 \mid <S>1 \mid 00$$

b. By drawing a parse tree, show that 0001 is in the language.

c. Write a recursive boolean function to return *TRUE* (1) if a particular string of $n + 1$ characters is in this language.

d. Find an iterative solution to the problem.

20. The following appeared in the sample questions of *Practicing to Take the GRE Computer Scienct Test, 2nd Edition:*

Let the syntactic category $<S>$ be defined by the Backus-Naur form description:

$$<S> ::= r\ell \mid r <S> \ell \mid <S> <S>$$

Which of the following strings can be generated from *<S>* according to this definition?

I.   rrℓℓrℓ
II.   rℓℓrrrℓ ℓ
III.   rrℓrℓrℓℓrℓrrℓ
(A) I only   (B) II only   (C) III only   (D) I and III   (E) II and III

Section 13.3 Programming Projects

1. Write a test program and a recursive boolean function to return *TRUE*(1) if a particular string is in the language of Example 13.8.

2. Write a test program and a recursive boolean function to return *TRUE*(1) if a particular string is in the language of Example 13.9.

〰 Programming and Debugging Hints

The *lint* Program

Most C compilers are forgiving in an effort to provide maximum flexibility. Consequently, these compilers do not flag code that we usually would consider incorrect. The program *lint*, which is on most computers running the UNIX operating system, does not compile a C source program, but rather examines it for strict adherence to the semantic rules of C. It "picks lint" out of the program. For example, *lint* requires cast operators when mixing data types, such as when we assign pointers to integer variables or integers to floating point variables. When *lint* detects a violation of its rules, it displays a message describing the location and nature of the problem. The *lint* program encourages the programmer to use pristine code that is easier for the human reader to understand. Unfortunately, not many C compilers for microcomputers come with the *lint* program.

Error C Compilers Do Not Flag: Number of Arguments

The C compiler does not automatically check whether the correct number of arguments is passed to a function, even if the calling and called functions are defined in the same program file. It is therefore easier to pass the wrong number of arguments to a C function than to make the same error in many modern languages, such as Pascal, in which the compilers perform argument-parameter checks. We are more likely to detect this error when it occurs with the *printf* function, because we can clearly see the results of the mistake. For example, the following program has two errors in the number of arguments to *printf*:

```
/*
 * Program to illustrate errors in number of arguments
 * passed to printf
 */

#include <stdio.h>

main()
{
```

```
        int NumStu = 5;      /* number of students */

        /* ERROR 1 - no %d */
        printf("Number of students = d\n", NumStu);

        /* ERROR 2 - no variable */
        printf("Number of students = %d\n");
    }
```

A sample output is

```
Number of students = d
Number of students = 33
```

At ERROR 1, the *printf* contains d instead of the conversion specification %d. Thus, the *printf* function expects only one argument, the control string, and the output does not contain the value of *NumStu*. The *printf* at ERROR 2 contains %d but does not contain a corresponding value. Consequently, the output contains the unexpected number 33.

Another Error: Types of Arguments

The C compiler also does not automatically check the data types of arguments. Thus, a common error that the compiler does not flag is the omission of the address operator (&) before a variable name in a call to *scanf*, such as

```
    scanf("%d", NumStu);   /* ERROR - need & before NumStu */
```

To the compiler, *scanf* is just another function, so any sort of argument is acceptable. Especially on larger computers, the omission of the address operator or of an entire argument to *scanf* can result in the function attempting to store a value at a nonexistent address. This omission can lead to the operating system generating a run-time error, which usually says something about an illegal address or a segmentation error, but is never clear in terms of the cause of the error. This message also occurs when a program inadvertently stores a value other than a true address in a pointer variable.

It is also an error to use the address operator when a pointer variable is an argument to *scanf*, as in the following:

```
    int *NumStu_ptr = &NumStu;

    scanf("%d", &NumStu_ptr); /* ERROR - should omit & */
```

Even with the address operator before the pointer variable, the program does not crash immediately. The computer stores the input value in the pointer variable (here *NumStu_ptr*) rather than in the location to which the variable points (*NumStu_ptr*). This error may later cause the program to crash when we use the pointer variable. When we should use indirection, a similar problem can arise with the omission of the indirection operator (*) before a pointer variable, such as follows:

```
    /* ERROR - need indirection operator - *NumStu_ptr */
    printf("%d\n", NumStu_ptr);
```

≋ **Key Terms**

≋ **Summary**

A recursive task is one that calls itself. With each invocation, the problem is reduced to a smaller task (reducing case) until it arrives at some terminal or base case, which stops the process. The condition that must be true to achieve the terminal case is the terminal condition. Recursive functions use an *if* or *if-else* statement instead of a looping control structure, such as

```
if (terminal_condition)
    terminal_case
else
    reducing_case
```

or

```
if (!terminal_condition)
    reducing_case
```

The two characteristics of every recursive task are as follows:

1. The task is defined in terms of itself, with each invocation working on a smaller version of the problem.

2. The task has a terminal case that is nonrecursive.

When a function is invoked, an activation record comes into existence. This record contains information about the routine, such as parameter values, local variables, and the return location after execution of the routine. This activation record is placed on the top of a run-time stack. After the terminal case is encountered with a recursive function, the corresponding activation records are removed from the stack in the reverse order in which they were added. Stack overflow occurs with an attempt to put something on a stack when no more room exists.

If we can readily develop an iterative algorithm, we should do so. However, many times the most natural and understandable solution to a problem is a recursive one. One disadvantage of a recursive routine is the potential for run-time stack overflow for large problems. However, memories are larger today, and some compilers allow the user to allocate more memory to the stack. Another disadvantage of recursion is that a recursive routine consumes more time because of the function calls. However, computers are faster today; the architectures of some computers enable fast execution of recursive routine; and some compilers can convert many recursive routines to iterative ones automatically.

There is always an equivalent iterative solution to a recursive one. To solve the recursive routine means to find an equivalent nonrecursive definition.

≋ **Review Questions**

1. What is meant by recursion?

2. How is a C function declared to be recursive?

3. What is a terminal case for a recursive function?

4. What is an activation record?

5. What structure holds the activation records?

6. What run-time error can occur with many recursive calls to a function?

7. What does it mean to solve a recursive routine?

Laboratory

1. In this exercise, we develop a nonrecursive function, *sum,* to find the sum of elements 0 through *n* of an array of integers, *a.*

Copy the files for this laboratory from the text disk to your own. For this exercise and the next two, we use program files *summainL.c,* containing *main,* and *sumfncsL.c,* containing three incomplete versions of the summation function. There is one header file, *sumfncs.h.* Assemble these files into a project, perhaps with a *Makefile.*

The function *main* only calls the three versions of the summation function and prints the results. Preprocessor directives surround the calls to the recursive versions, so that *main* only invokes the nonrecursive *sum.* For simplicity, array *a* has five elements with indices from 0 through *n* = 4. Figure 13.16 displays a picture of the array *a,* whose initialization is in *main.* The definition of the function *main* follows.

```
/*
 * Program to drive 3 functions (one nonrecursive and
 * two recursive) to return the sum of elements a[0]
 * through a[n] of an integer array
 */

#include "sumfncs.h"

main()
{
    int a[] = {9, 10, -2, 25, -3},    /* array to sum */
        n = 4;                         /* high index in array a */

    printf("sum    of the elements in a = %d\n", sum(a, n));

#if 0
    printf("rsum    of the elements in a = %d\n", rsum(a, n));
    printf("DivSum of the elements in a = %d\n", DivSum(a, 0, n));
#endif
}
```

Figure 13.16
Array *a* of five
elements

a: | 9 | 10 | -2 | 25 | -3 | n: | 4 |

index: 0   1   2   3   4

For this exercise, the relevant parts of the header file *sumfncs.h* are the inclusion of *stdio.h* and the prototype for *sum,* as shown:

```
#include <stdio.h>
  ⋮
int sum(int a[], int n);
```

Most of our work is in the program file *sumfncsL.c.* For this exercise, complete the code for *sum* using a *for* loop to add each element from a[0] through a[n] into *total.* Be sure to include the element with index *n* in the sum.

```
/*
 * Nonrecursive algorithm for returning the sum of
 * elements a[0] through a[n]
 * Pre:   a is an int array with elements a[0] through a[n] defined.
 * Post:  The function has returned the sum of a[0] through a[n].
 */

int sum(int a[], int n)
{
    int total = 0,   /* sum of a[0] through a[n] */
        i;           /* index */

    /*** 1 ***/

    return total;
}
```

Once the function is working properly, the program produces the following output:

```
sum     of the elements in a = 39
```

2. The goal of this exercise is to develop a recursive counterpart, *rsum,* to *sum* of Exercise 1.

The outline of this function is in *sumfncsL.c.* Move the preprocessor directive

```
#if 0
```

to after the definition of *rsum,* so that it compiles. In *main,* move this directive down one statement so that *main* calls *rsum.* The prototype for this function is already in the header file *sumfncs.h.* The incomplete function *rsum* is below. For now, ignore the preprocessor directives and diagnostic print statements about entering and leaving *rsum.*

```
/*
 * Recursive algorithm for returning the sum of elements
 * a[0] through a[n]
 * Pre:   a is an int array with elements a[0] through a[n] defined.
 * Post:  The function has returned the sum of a[0] through a[n].
 */

int rsum(int a[], int n)
{
    int total; /* sum of a[0] through a[n] */
```

```
#ifdef PRINT_STACK1
printf("Entering rsum: n = %d \n", n);
#endif

    if (/*** a ***/)
        total = /*** b ***/;
    else
        total = rsum(/*** c ***/) + /*** c ***/;

#ifdef PRINT_STACK1
printf("Leaving rsum:  n = %d, a[%d] = %d, total = %d\n",
        n, n, a[n], total);
#endif

    return total;
}
```

a. Notice that the nonrecursive function *sum* from Exercise 1 contains a *for* loop. The recursive version, *rsum,* however, contains an *if-else* statement instead. The expression at /*** a ***/ is the terminal condition. This condition is true for the smallest possible case—for an array (or subarray) of one element having index 0. Figure 13.17 displays such an array with the resulting value for *total.* Fill in the condition at /*** a ***/. Be careful to use the relational equal (==) and not the assignment equal (=).

b. Complete the *if* clause by assigning the appropriate value to *total.* Do NOT write *total* = 9, because the code should work for any 1-element subarray.

c. In a sense, at /*** c ***/, we want to strip off element *n* of *a* and add it to the sum of the subarray, *a*[0] through *a*[*n* − 1]. Figure 13.18 depicts the action of *rsum* at the top level. To compute the sum of the subarray (such as *a*[0] through *a*[3]), we again call *rsum,* but with the maximum index being one less to accommodate the subarray.

Replace the /*** c ***/ comments with the appropriate code. Run the program. The output should be as follows:

```
sum   of the elements in a = 39
rsum  of the elements in a = 39
```

If your output is not correct, you might want to go on to the next part before completely debugging.

d. To observe the action of the run-time stack of function calls, let us activate the printing of the statements about entering and leaving *rsum. PRINT_STACK1* is undefined, so these calls to *printf* are not sent to the compiler. The header file *sumfncs.h* contains the following:

```
#ifdef PRINT_STACK1
#undefine PRINT_STACK1
#endif
```

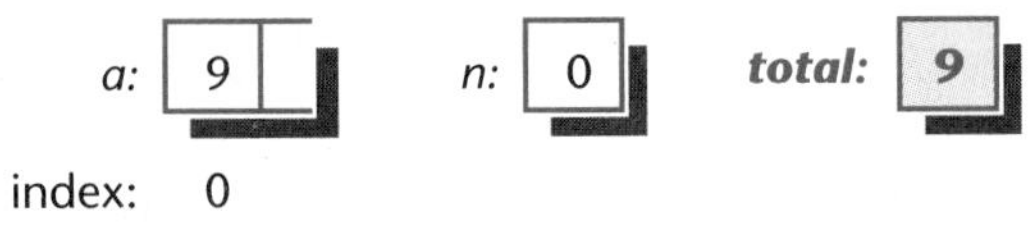

Figure 13.17
Array *a* of one element

a: [9]   n: [0]   *total:* [9]

index: 0

Figure 13.18
Top level of
action of *rsum*
on array *a*

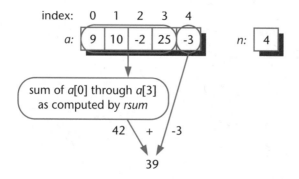

To define *PRINT_STACK1*, we change the directives to

```
#ifndef PRINT_STACK1
#define PRINT_STACK1
#endif
```

We do not want to define *PRINT_STACK1* twice. Thus, we define this symbolic constant only if it has not already been defined (*#ifndef*). Once you have adjusted these directives, the output of the program should be as follows:

```
sum     of the elements in a = 39
Entering rsum: n = 4
Entering rsum: n = 3
Entering rsum: n = 2
Entering rsum: n = 1
Entering rsum: n = 0
Leaving rsum:  n = 0, a[0] = 9, total = 9
Leaving rsum:  n = 1, a[1] = 10, total = 19
Leaving rsum:  n = 2, a[2] = -2, total = 17
Leaving rsum:  n = 3, a[3] = 25, total = 42
Leaving rsum:  n = 4, a[4] = -3, total = 39
rsum  of the elements in a = 39
```

Notice that the program indicates that the computer pushes *rsum*'s activation records onto the run-time stack with *n* from 4 down to 0. The condition *n == 0* is the terminal condition. Once the terminal condition is reached, the activation records are popped from the stack in reverse order, for *n* from 0 up to 4. At the terminal case, the function *rsum* only returns *total = a[0]*. Upon leaving *rsum* with *n* being 1, why is *total* equal to 19? Explain each value that *rsum* returns.

3. In this exercise, we develop another recursive solution to the summation problem using a technique called divide-and-conquer.

Remove the *#if 0* preprocessor directive and its matching *#endif* (at the end) from the program files *summainL.c* and *sumfncsL.c* to expose the definition of and invocation to *DivSum*, respectively. In *sumfncs.h*, change the preprocessor directives to undefine *PRINT_STACK1*.

Instead of adding one element to the sum of the rest in a subarray, *DivSum* uses the **divide-and-conquer technique**. This function divides the array into two halves, computes the sum of each subarray by recursively calling *DivSum*, and adds

Figure 13.19
Divide-and-conquer to add the elements in an array

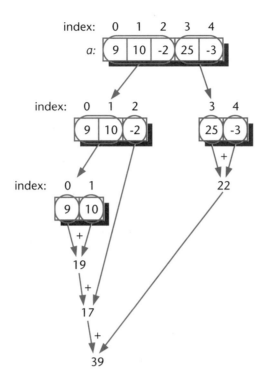

the two results to find the overall total. With each call to *DivSum,* the array is divided in two until only one element remains. In this terminal case, the function returns that element. Figure 13.19 illustrates this division and recombination.

To manage the division of a subarray into smaller subarrays, we must have variables, *first* and *last,* to store the first and last indices of the subarray, respectively. For the array in Figure 13.19, initially we call *DivSum* with arguments of the array (*a*) and first and last indices (0 and 4). The function adds the sum of the first half of the array and the sum of the second half of the array. For the first sum, the function recursively calls itself with arguments of the array and indices 0 (*first*) and 2 (*last*). Similarly, to obtain the sum of the second half of the array, *DivSum* invokes itself with arguments of *a,* 3 (*first*), and 4 (*last*). The function computes the sum of each subarray in a like manner. When *DivSum* receives a subarray of only one element, such as when *first* and *last* are both 4, the function returns that array element, in this case −3. Eventually, all the sums of the subarrays are combined to find the overall total.

If in *sumfncs.h,* we change preprocessor directives to define *PRINT_STACK2* and we complete the definition of *DivSum,* the program produces the output below. Because we are using a sequential machine, the computer processes the calls to *rsum* one at a time. Following Figure 13.19, the computer completely processes each left subarray before computing the sum of the corresponding right subarray. The following output reveals this depth-first approach:

```
sum     of the elements in a = 39
rsum    of the elements in a = 39
Entering DivSum: first = 0, last = 4
Entering DivSum: first = 0, last = 2
```

```
Entering DivSum: first = 0, last = 1
Entering DivSum: first = 0, last = 0
Leaving DivSum:  first = 0, last = 0, total = 9
Entering DivSum: first = 1, last = 1
Leaving DivSum:  first = 1, last = 1, total = 10
Leaving DivSum:  first = 0, last = 1, total = 19
Entering DivSum: first = 2, last = 2
Leaving DivSum:  first = 2, last = 2, total = -2
Leaving DivSum:  first = 0, last = 2, total = 17
Entering DivSum: first = 3, last = 4
Entering DivSum: first = 3, last = 3
Leaving DivSum:  first = 3, last = 3, total = 25
Entering DivSum: first = 4, last = 4
Leaving DivSum:  first = 4, last = 4, total = -3
Leaving DivSum:  first = 3, last = 4, total = 22
Leaving DivSum:  first = 0, last = 4, total = 39
DivSum of the elements in a = 39
```

The following is the incomplete code for the definition of *DivSum:*

```
/*
 * Divide-and-conquer recursive algorithm for returning
 * the sum of elements a[first] through a[last]
 * Pre:    a is an int array with elements a[first]
 *         through a[last] defined.
 * Post:   The function has returned the sum of a[first]
 *         through a[last].
 */

int DivSum(int a[], int first, int last)
{
    int total, /* sum of a[0] through a[n] */
        mid;   /* index halfway between first & last */

#ifdef PRINT_STACK2
printf("Entering DivSum: first = %d, last = %d \n",
      first, last);
#endif

    if (/*** a ***/)
        total = /*** b ***/;
    else
    {
        mid = /*** c ***/;
        total = DivSum(/*** d ***/) + DivSum(/*** d ***/);
    }
```

```
#ifdef PRINT_STACK2
printf("Leaving DivSum:  first = %d, last = %d, total = %d\n",
       first, last, total);
#endif

    return total;
}
```

    a. Replace /*** a ***/ with the terminal condition. This condition occurs when the subarray has only one element. What is the relationship between *first* and *last* in this case?

    b. When the subarray only contains one element, there is nothing more to add. Thus, we want to return that element. Replace /*** b ***/ with the element, so that *DivSum* can return it through *total*.

    c. To divide the array in two, we must compute its middle index. For the initial array with *first* being 0 and *last* 4, the value of *mid* is $(0 + 4)/2 = 2$. For the subarray with indices 3 and 4, the computation of *mid* depends on integer division—$(3 + 4)/2 = 3$. Replace /*** c ***/ with the evaluation of *mid*.

    d. For the computation of *total*, we call *DivSum* twice, once for each half of the array. The array *a* is the first argument for both calls, but the arguments for the indices are different. For the first half, the indices go from the first index to *mid*. In the second sum, the indices start just beyond *mid* (one more than *mid*) and continue through *last*. Complete this code and execute the program. To print information related to the stack of activation records, define *PRINT_STACK2* in *sumfncs.h*.

4. In this exercise, we replace *main* with code to generate larger random arrays. We perform an experiment to compare the efficiency of the three summation algorithms, encounter a stack-overflow situation, and consider the approach best suited to parallel processing. Copy files *ranmain.c* and *random.h* from the text disk to your own.

    In *sumfncs.h,* change the preprocessor directives so that neither *PRINT_STACK1* nor *PRINT_STACK2* has a definition. Thus, we will not print information on entering and leaving *rsum* and *DivSum*. In your project, replace the file *summainL.c* with *ranmain.c*. The new *main* calls a function, *init*, to initialize array *a* with *n* = *MAX_NUM_ELS* number of random integers between −*BOUND* and +*BOUND* − 1. The header file *sumfncs.h* defines these symbolic constants as 10 and 20, respectively.

```
#ifndef MAX_NUM_ELS
#define MAX_NUM_ELS 10
#endif
    ⋮
#ifndef BOUND
#define BOUND 20
#endif
```

    The file *ranmain.c* includes the header file *random.h* from Example 12.6 of Section 12.2. The file *random.h* contains macro *SeedRand* to seed the random number generator, macro *random_range* to return a pseudorandom integer in a specified range, and includes *stdlib.h* and *time.h*.

The code for the file *ranmain.c* follows:

```
/*
 * File:   ranmain.c
 * Program to generate a random array and sum the array
 * with three different functions
 */

#include "sumfncs.h"
#include "random.h"

void init(int a[], int n);

main()
{
    int a[MAX_NUM_ELS],         /* array to be summed */
        n = MAX_NUM_ELS - 1;    /* largest index */

    init(a, n);

    printf("sum    of the elements in a = %d\n", sum(a, n));
    printf("rsum   of the elements in a = %d\n", rsum(a, n));
    printf("DivSum of the elements in a = %d\n", DivSum(a, 0, n));
}


/*
 * Function to initialize the array a with integers between
 * -BOUND and +BOUND - 1
 */

void init(int a[], int n)
{
    int i; /* index */

    SeedRand();

    for (i = 0; i <= n; i++)
        a[i] = random_range(-BOUND, BOUND);
}
```

a. Run the program several times with *MAX_NUM_ELS* equal to various values from 10 through 1000 until a stack overflow error occurs. What is the smallest size array that causes a stack overflow on your computer? What indication of the problem does it give?

b. To compare the efficiency of the three functions, define two global variables *NuCalls* to count the number of times the program calls a function and *NuOperations* to count the number of numeric operations. In each function, include a statement that adds one to *NuCalls* each time the program calls the function and a statement that adds one to *NuOperations* each time the function performs a numeric operation. In *main*, initialize *NuCalls* and *NuOperations* to zero just before each function call and display the results upon returning from each call. Design the output to have the format shown below. Which recursive function do you think is more efficient?

```
sum     of the elements in a = xx
sum used xx function calls and xx operations

rsum    of the elements in a = xx
rsum used xx function calls and xx operations

DivSum of the elements in a = xx
DivSum used xx function calls and xx operations
```

c. With a parallel processing computer, several processors can work simultaneously on a program. For such a computer, which recursive routine do you think would perform faster? Why?

Input/Output and Files

Introduction

Data stored on a medium, such as a disk, are called a file. A computer file is analogous to the customary office file, which stores related information according to title or some other convenient label. In many programming situations, it is easier to access a file than to enter a succession of individual data items from the keyboard.

Since the end of Chapter 7, we have read from and written to text files. In C, a text file is a stream of characters, analogous to an array of characters. In this present chapter, we discuss in greater detail the ANSI C library functions that assist the programmer in handling input and output (I/O) in a simple, device-independent manner. We also consider several modes of data transfer to and from files.

A file resides on a storage medium, not in memory. The computer reads one or more bytes from a file, and after processing them, the machine can discard that data from memory and read more. Thus, we can process an entire file without having to store it all in memory at one time.

In C jargon, the term "file" often refers to the I/O device. For example, we can think of a keyboard as a file, because it provides a stream of characters to the program. We can read characters from a keyboard, but it would be meaningless to try to send output to the keyboard. In the same way, the computer screen can receive a stream of characters as output, but most screens cannot be input devices. (An exception is the so-called touchscreen available on some computers, which serves as both an input and an output device.) We can both read from and write to a file on disk.

In breadth Section 14.2, we discuss various external storage media. With one such medium, magnetic tape, we access information sequentially, one record at a time. Magnetic disks, however, are direct access storage media. Any record can be accessed directly without processing all those that appear before it.

Direct access files are almost always binary files. Information is stored in a binary file exactly as it is in the computer. Thus, because there is no conversion between the computer and file storage, processing of information on a binary file is faster than on a text file. A record can usually be stored in less space in a binary file. Moreover, it is easier to read and write large structures in a binary file than in a text file. The method of storage requires that we create such a file through programming instead of with a text editor. Because of the ability to access records directly, to process them faster, to read and write large structures easily, and to store them in less space, binary files are widely used commercially.

Goals

To study

- Standard text files
- External storage
- File-handling modes, including reading, writing, appending, and updating
- Binary file storage and sequential access
- Random access files

Section 14.1 Basic File Manipulation

Standard Files

When a C program begins execution, it has access to three standard files—*stdin, stdout,* and *stderr.* Because these files are always available, we do not declare or open them. The **standard input** or *stdin* is the file from which the program receives input by default. This file usually is the keyboard, but with many operating systems, we can also redirect *stdin* to obtain input from a disk file or other device.

The second file, the **standard output** or *stdout,* is the default output file. Although usually the screen, on many systems we can also redirect standard output to another device, such as a disk file.

The third file available to the program is **standard error** or *stderr.* Its purpose is to keep error messages separate from other program output. For example, if standard output is going to a disk file, the standard error file can be the screen, so that the user sees error messages immediately.

We have used standard input and standard output extensively throughout this book. The *printf* function sends its results to standard output, whereas *scanf* receives its characters from standard input. Because files in C are streams of characters, the *scanf* function serves to decode the input characters into the various internal representations that the program needs. The *printf* function encodes the data into character format before sending the characters to the standard output file. Some additional operations that give the programmer more direct access to standard input and output are *getchar* and *putchar* for character input and output, receptively, and *gets* and *puts* for string I/O.

Summary

Section 7.5 introduced how to create and read user-defined text files. The functions *fscanf* and *fprintf* provide general file input and output; *getc* and *putc* are for character I/O with files; and *fgets* and *fputs* transfer strings between the computer memory and files. Tables 14.1 and 14.2 summarize the C I/O functions and macros.

Table 14.1 Functions and macros to manipulate an input text file. Assume the following declarations:

```
char ch, *str;
int i, n;
float x;
FILE *infile_ptr;
```

Example Function Call	Read from	Read What	Error Return
ch = getchar;();	*stdin*	character	*EOF*
gets (str);	*stdin*	string	*NULL*
scanf("%d %f %s", &i, &x, str);	*stdin*	anything	*EOF*
infile_ptr = fopen("f.dat", "r");	input file	(open file for reading)	*NULL*
ch = getc(infile_ptr);	input file	character	*EOF*
ungetc(ch, infile_ptr);	input file	(return character to file)	*EOF*
fgets(str, n, infile_ptr);	input file	line	*NULL*
fscanf(infile_ptr, "%d %f %s", &i, &x, str);	input file	anything	*EOF*
if (feof(infile_ptr)) ...	input file	(*TRUE* if there was attempt to read past end of file, *FALSE* otherwise)	(none)
fclose(infile_ptr);	input file	(close file)	*EOF*

Table 14.2 Functions and macros to manipulate an output text file. Assume the following declarations:

```
char ch, *str;
int i;
float x;
FILE *outfile_ptr;
```

Example Function Call	Write to	Write What	Error Return
putchar(ch);	*stdout*	character	*EOF*
puts(str);	*stdout*	string	*EOF*
printf("%d %f %s\n", i, x, str);	*stdout*	anything	negative
outfile_ptr = fopen("f.dat", "w");	output file	(open file for writing)	*NULL*
putc(ch, outfile_ptr);	output file	character	*EOF*
fputs(str, outfile_ptr);	output file	string	*EOF*
fprintf(outfile_ptr, "%d %f %s", i, x, str);	output file	anything	negative
fclose(outfile_ptr);	output file	(close file)	*EOF*

Example 14.1

Suppose a company has two files of data about its products. The price file, *price.dat,* contains an identification number, name, and price for each product. The *onhand.dat* file contains the identification number, warehouse code (a character), and quantity on hand. Both files are sorted on the identification number field. The president wants a file of merged information. An exceptions report in a file should indicate records in the two files that do not match.

The price file consists of lines of text, with each line containing an identification number (4 characters), price (*float*), and description (up to 40 characters) separated by single blanks. The on-hand file consists of lines of text with each line containing an identification number (4 characters), a warehouse code (*char*), and a quantity (*int*) separated by single blanks. The files are in order by identification number. (For simplicity, we assume that another program has already verified that records from the price and on-hand files are sorted by identification number.) For a production program, however, the present program should also do such verification.

To open the file and trap errors in opening, the function *main* calls the function *OpenFile* for each file. Then *main* reads identification numbers of a record from each file. If they match, the function reads the rest of both records and stores the data in another record for the file that combines the data. Should the identification numbers not match, the program determines which number is smaller and calls an appropriate advance function, *AdvancePrice* or *AdvanceOnHand,* to store the number in an exceptions file and to retrieve the next record. If we complete reading one file before the other, we must also store identification numbers from the extra records in this exceptions report file. Figure 14.1 has the structure chart for the program, and the pseudocode follows.

---

main( )

Program to merge data from a price and on-hand file into another file and to have an exceptions report file. Records are assumed to be sorted.

Algorithm:

open files
print header for exceptions file
read identification (ID) numbers from both input files
while more data are in both files
    if the ID numbers are equal
        read the rest of the data for record from both files
        store a record with this data in the merged file
        if the price file is not empty, read another ID number
        if the on-hand file is not empty, read another ID number
    else if ID number from the price file < ID number from the on-hand file
        call *AdvancePrice* to process the unmatched price record
    else
        call *AdvanceOnHand* to process the unmatched on-hand record
while more data are in the price file
    call *AdvancePrice* to process the unmatched price record
while more data are in the on-hand file
    call *AdvanceOnHand* to process the unmatched on-hand record

Figure 14.1
Structure chart for the program in Example 14.1

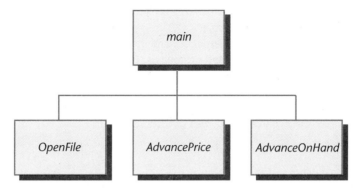

OpenFile(name, mode) ⟶ *file_ptr*

Function to open file *name* in mode *mode* and return a file pointer

Pre:

name is the name of a file.
mode is a file mode, such as "r" or "w".

Post:

file_ptr points to the file *name,* which is opened in *mode,* or in case of error, an error message is printed and execution ends.

Algorithm:

call *fopen* to open the file with pointer *file_ptr*
if *file_ptr* is *NULL*
    print an error message
    exit from execution of the program

AdvancePrice(exceptions_ptr, price_ptr, PriceRec_ptr)

Function to write "price.dat" and ID number from price file in exceptions file, to read and discard the rest of the price record, and to read the next ID number.

Pre:

exceptions_ptr points to the exceptions file, which is open for writing.
price_ptr points to the price file, which is open for reading and positioned to read rest of price record.
PriceRec_ptr points to a price record, which contains an unmatched ID number.

Post:

price_ptr is empty or **PriceRec_ptr* contains an unmatched ID number, and *price_ptr* is positioned to read the rest of the price record.

Algorithm:

store "price.dat" and the price ID number in the exceptions file
read the price and name from the price file, but do not use
if the price file is not empty, read the next ID number into the price record

The function *AdvanceOnHand* has exactly the same structure as *AdvancePrice*, but with a different record format.

The program file is *mergefil.c*, and its header file is *mergefil.h*. The header file contains type definitions and prototypes. Code from these files follows:

```
/*
 * File: mergefil.h
 * Header file for mergefil.c
 */

#include <stdio.h>
#include <string.h>
#include <stdlib.h>

typedef    /* type for price record */
struct
{
   char  id[5];
   float price;
   char  name[41];
}
price_struct_t;

typedef     /* type for on-hand record */
struct
{
   char id[5];
   char warehouse;
   int  quantity;
}
OnHand_struct_t;

typedef     /* type for merged record */
struct
{
   char  id[5];
   int   quantity;
   char  warehouse;
   float price;
   char  name[41];
}
merge_struct_t;

FILE *OpenFile(char name[], char mode[]);
void AdvancePrice(FILE *exceptions_ptr, FILE *price_ptr,
        price_struct_t *PriceRec_ptr);
void AdvanceOnHand(FILE *exceptions_ptr, FILE *OnHand_ptr,
        OnHand_struct_t *OnHandRec_ptr);
```

```c
/*
 * File: mergefil.c
 * Program to merge data from files price.dat and onhand.dat
 * into file pricquan.dat.(Exceptions report file = except.dat).
 * It is assumed that both files are sorted properly by ID.
 *    Input files:  price.dat, onhand.dat
 *    Output files: pricquan.dat, except.dat
 */

#include "mergefil.h"

main()
{
    FILE *price_ptr,        /* input price file pointer      */
         *OnHand_ptr,       /* input on-hand file pointer    */
         *merge_ptr,        /* output merged file pointer    */
         *exceptions_ptr;   /* exceptions file pointer       */

    price_struct_t  PriceRec;    /* record in price file     */
    OnHand_struct_t OnHandRec;   /* record in on-hand file   */
    merge_struct_t  MergeRec;    /* record in merged file    */

    /* open the files */
    price_ptr      = OpenFile("price.dat", "r");
    OnHand_ptr     = OpenFile("onhand.dat", "r");
    merge_ptr      = OpenFile("pricquan.dat", "w");
    exceptions_ptr = OpenFile("except.dat", "w");

    fprintf(exceptions_ptr, "\t\tExceptions Report\n\n");
    fprintf(exceptions_ptr, "\tRecords not in both files\n");
    fprintf(exceptions_ptr, "File\t\tId\n\n");

    /* read from input files, merge, write to output file */
    fscanf(price_ptr, "%4s", &PriceRec.id);
    fscanf(OnHand_ptr, "%4s", &OnHandRec.id);
    while (!feof(price_ptr) && !feof(OnHand_ptr))
    {
        /* price and on-hand records have same id */
        if (strcmp(PriceRec.id, OnHandRec.id) == 0)
        {
            strcpy(MergeRec.id, PriceRec.id);
            fscanf(price_ptr, "%f", &MergeRec.price);
            fgets(MergeRec.name, 40, price_ptr);
            getc(OnHand_ptr);  /* discard next character */
            fscanf(OnHand_ptr, "%c %d", &MergeRec.warehouse,
                    &MergeRec.quantity);
            fprintf(merge_ptr, "%-4s %3d %c %6.2f %s",
                    MergeRec.id, MergeRec.quantity,
                    MergeRec.warehouse, MergeRec.price,
                    MergeRec.name);
```

```
            if (!feof(price_ptr))
                fscanf(price_ptr, "%4s", &PriceRec.id);
            if (!feof(OnHand_ptr))
                fscanf(OnHand_ptr, "%4s", &OnHandRec.id);
        }
        /* price record not in on-hand file */
        else if (strcmp(PriceRec.id, OnHandRec.id) < 0)
            AdvancePrice(exceptions_ptr, price_ptr,
                    &PriceRec);
        /* on-hand record not in price file */
        else
            AdvanceOnHand(exceptions_ptr, OnHand_ptr,
                    &OnHandRec);
    }

    while (!feof(price_ptr))
        AdvancePrice(exceptions_ptr, price_ptr,
                &PriceRec);
    while (!feof(OnHand_ptr))
        AdvanceOnHand(exceptions_ptr, OnHand_ptr,
                &OnHandRec);

    fclose(price_ptr);
    fclose(OnHand_ptr);
    fclose(merge_ptr);
    fclose(exceptions_ptr);
}


/*
 * Function to open the file named "name" in mode "mode" and
 * to return a file pointer
 * Pre:   name is the name of a file.
 *        mode is a file mode.
 * Post:  The file name is opened in mode and a pointer is
 *        returned to the file.  In case of error, an error
 *        message is printed and execution ends.
 */

FILE *OpenFile(char name[], char mode[])
{
    FILE *file_ptr; /* pointer to file */

    file_ptr = fopen(name, mode);
    if (file_ptr == NULL)
    {
        printf("Error opening file %s.\n", name);
        exit(1);
    }

    return file_ptr;
}
```

```
/*
 * Put ID from price.dat in exceptions report. Read and discard
 *    rest of the price record.  Read ID of the next record.
 * Pre:  exceptions_ptr points to the exceptions file,
 *       which is open for writing.
 *       price_ptr points to the price file, which is open for
 *       reading and positioned to read rest of price record.
 *       PriceRec_ptr points to a price record, which contains
 *       an unmatched ID.
 * Post: price_ptr is empty or *PriceRec_ptr contains an unmatched
 *       ID and price_ptr is positioned to read the rest of the
 *       price record.
 */

void AdvancePrice(FILE *exceptions_ptr, FILE *price_ptr,
      price_struct_t *PriceRec_ptr)
{
   float discard_price;       /* price to read and discard */
   char  discard_name[41];    /* name to read and discard */

   /* read and discard rest of record */
   fprintf(exceptions_ptr, "price.dat\t%-4s\n",
         (*PriceRec_ptr).id);
   fscanf(price_ptr, "%f", &discard_price);
   fgets(discard_name, 40, price_ptr);

   /* read ID of next record */
   if (!feof(price_ptr))
      fscanf(price_ptr, "%4s", (*PriceRec_ptr).id);
}

/*
 * Put ID from onhand.dat in exceptions report.  Read and discard
 *    rest of the on-hand record.  Read ID of the next record.
 * Pre:  exceptions_ptr points to the exceptions file,
 *       which is open for writing.
 *       OnHand_ptr points to the on-hand file, which is open for
 *       reading and positioned to read rest of on-hand record.
 *       OnHandRec_ptr points to an on-hand record, which contains
 *       an unmatched ID.
 * Post: OnHand_ptr is empty or *OnHandRec_ptr contains an unmatched
 *       ID and OnHand_ptr is positioned to read the rest of the
 *       On-Hand record.
 */

void AdvanceOnHand(FILE *exceptions_ptr, FILE *OnHand_ptr,
         OnHand_struct_t *OnHandRec_ptr)
{
   char DiscardWarehouse,      /* warehouse-read and discard */
        DiscardBlank;          /* read and discard blank */
   int DiscardQuantity;        /* quantity-read and discard */
```

```
        /* read and discard rest of record */
        fprintf(exceptions_ptr,"onhand.dat\t%-4s\n", (*OnHandRec_ptr).id);

        fscanf(OnHand_ptr, "%c%c%d", &DiscardBlank, &DiscardWarehouse,
                &DiscardQuantity);

        /* read ID of next record */
        if (!feof(OnHand_ptr))
                fscanf(OnHand_ptr, "%4s", (*OnHandRec_ptr).id);
}
```

Suppose the file *price.dat* is as follows:

```
1234 78.99flat-back rocker
1235 415.75desk
1236 18.99pot stand
1237 120.90file cabinet
1239 289.79end table
```

The corresponding *onhand.dat* file might be:

```
1234 A 34
1235 A 62
1237 B 100
1239 A 44
```

With these files, the program generates the following *pricquan.dat* file:

```
1234    34 A    78.99 flat-back rocker
1235    62 A   415.75 desk
1237   100 B   120.90 file cabinet
1239    44 A   289.79 end table
```

Moreover, because one unmatched record exists, the program produces the following exceptions file, *except.dat:*

```
            Exceptions Report

      Records not in both files
    File        Id

    price.dat    1236
```

Section 14.1 **Exercises**

In Exercises 1–4, give a statement to read the requested data from an input file, infile.dat.

1. A name into variable *name,* where the name is on a line by itself
2. An age into *int* variable *age*
3. A middle initial into *char* variable *initial*
4. A salary and initial year of employment into variables *salary* and *EmpYear,* respectively.

In Exercises 5–8, give a statement to write the requested data to an output file, outfile.dat.

5. The name in variable, *name* (use *fputs*)
6. The age in *int* variable *age*
7. The middle initial in *char* variable *initial*
8. The salary and initial year of employment in variables *salary* and *EmpYear,* respectively.
9. In this exercise, we assemble the body of a function *main* to make a backup file, character by character.
   a. Declare *source_ptr* and *destination_ptr* to be pointers to the source and destination files. Declare *ch* to be of type *char.*
   b. Open both files. Abort execution with an error message if a file does not open properly.
   c. Character by character, copy the source file to the destination.
   d. Close both files.
10. Using the standard input file *stdin* with *fscanf,* write a statement equivalent to the following:

    ```
    scanf("%d\n", &i);
    ```

11. Using the standard output file *stdout* with *fprintf,* write a statement equivalent to the following:

    ```
    printf("%d\n", i);
    ```

12. Implement your own version of the function *fgets* using *getc.*
13. Implement your own version of the function *fputs* using *putc.*

Section 14.1 **Programming Projects**

1. Develop a program to change all uppercase characters in a file to lowercase, and vice versa. (Make the actual modifications to the stored file.)
2. The sorting technique we have seen so far has required that all data to be sorted be kept in memory. It is frequently necessary, however, to sort files that are so large that they cannot be stored in their entirety in the computer's memory. One solution to this problem is the mergesort technique. The data are read from the file in

chunks of a fixed size, sorted, and stored in temporary files. For example, suppose we have a file called *data.dat* containing the following data:

data: 7 3 14 22 9 16 3 17 2 14 9 27

We can divide the file *data.dat* conceptually into chunks, each containing three numbers, as shown:

data: 7 3 14   22 9 16   3 17 2   14 9 27

Now, the computer reads the first three numbers of the file and sorts them. This sorted chunk is stored in a file called *data1*. A similar process is performed on the second, third, and fourth 3-number chunks of the file *data.dat,* resulting in the following four files:

data1: 3 7 14   *data2:* 9 16 22   *data3:* 2 3 17   *data4:* 9 14 27

Each file has been sorted, but if the four files were merely joined together, they would not form a sorted sequence. We must merge the files into a single, sorted file.

   First, all four files need to be open at the same time. We also open an output file, called *sorted.dat,* to hold the fully sorted data. The first numbers in each file are read. We show the contents of all files, with arrows indicating the numbers that are in memory:

data1	*data2*	*data3*	*data4*
→3	→9	→2	→9
7	16	3	14
14	22	17	27

Because 2 (from file *data3*) is the smallest value, it is written first into the file *sorted.dat* (We know that no other file contains a smaller value, because they are all sorted and begin with values greater than 2.) Because the first value came from *data3,* we read the next number from that file.

data1	*data2*	*data3*	*data4*	*sorted.dat:* 2
→3	→9	2	→9	
7	16	→3	14	
14	22	17	27	

The smallest values in memory are the two threes, so they are written to *sorted*. Because the two numbers were from files *data1* and *data3,* the next values are read from those two files, and the value 7 is smallest, as shown:.

data1	*data2*	*data3*	*data4*
3	→9	2	→9
→7	16	3	14
14	22	→17	27

sorted.dat: 2 3 3

This process continues until all files are depleted. The subsequent steps are as follows:

data1	*data2*	*data3*	*data4*		*data1*	*data2*	*data3*	*data4*
3	→9	2	→9		3	9	2	9
7	16	3	14		7	→16	3	→14
→14	22	→17	27		→14	22	→17	27

sorted.dat: 2 3 3 7

sorted.dat: 2 3 3 7 9 9

data1	data2	data3	data4	data1	data2	data3	data4
(end	9	2	9	(end	9	2	9
of	→16	3	14	of	16	3	14
file)	22	→17	→27	file)	→22	→17	→27

sorted.dat: 2 3 3 7 9 9 14 14   *sorted.dat:* 2 3 3 7 9 9 14 14 16

The last three numbers are 17, 22, and 27, resulting in the file *sorted* as follows:

> 2 3 3 7 9 9 14 14 16 17 22 27

In summary, the steps of sorting and merging are as follows:

1. Divide the unsorted file into small chunks that fit in memory. Sort each chunk and store it in a separate file.

2. Read the first value from each file into memory.

3. Select the smallest value(s) in memory and write it (them) to the sorted file.

4. Read the next value from each file for which a value was just written to the sorted file. If the end of a file is reached, make sure to indicate this so its last value is not reused.

5. Repeat Steps 3 and 4 until the end of all input files has been reached. At this point, the output file is the sorted version of the unsorted file.

Write a program to implement this external sort for text files of integers. Use chunks of *CHUNKSIZE* integers with at most *MAXCHUNK* chunks.

Section 14.2 Breadth: Secondary Storage

Tape Storage

A file structure provides a unique link between computer memory and a secondary storage medium such as a diskette, disk pack, compact disk, or tape. Magnetic tape was introduced in the early 1950s as an external storage medium for the UNIVAC, the first commercially produced computer. Some people would not believe that information was recorded on the tape, because they could not see holes as they did on punched cards. One plant worker, who did not know about computer tape, received a delivery of tape he thought was no good because it had no adhesive back! Today, enormous amounts of information are stored for backup or additional processing. A bank's records, an airline's reservations, a pollster's voting surveys, a scientist's research data—the list is endless—all are saved outside the computer.

As depicted in Figure 14.2, data are usually stored on a tape as magnetized spots on nine parallel **tracks** running the length of the tape. Across the tape, there is a byte of information plus an extra bit, called a **parity bit**, to help check that the information is correctly recorded. For **odd parity**, there should be an odd number of ones in a byte and the accompanying parity bit. An even number of ones indicates an error. For example, the byte 1011 1110 contains six ones. The computer writes a parity bit of 1 to yield an odd number of ones. Similarly, in reading this byte with odd parity, if the number of ones is even, the computer knows that one of the bits is incorrect. At least one 0 should be a 1, or vice versa.

Figure 14.2
Magnetic tape
with 9 tracks

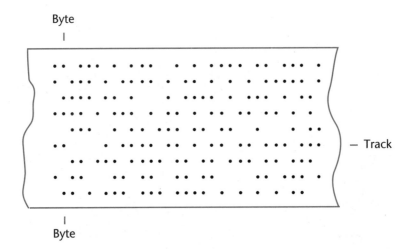

Definitions On magnetic tape, a **track** is a sequence of bits running the length of the tape. A **parity bit** is an extra bit associated with a byte and used for error checking. With **odd parity**, the total number of ones in the byte and accompanying parity bit should be odd.

Several measurements associated with tapes are as follows:

1. **storage density** expressed in bytes/inch or bits/inch (**bpi**), the number of bits in one track of length 1 inch
2. **tape speed** expressed in inches/second
3. **data transfer rate** expressed in bytes/second

Given any two quantities, we can calculate the third.

Definition **Storage density** of a tape is the number of bits in one track of length 1 inch. This measurement is expressed in bytes/inch or bits/inch (**bpi**).

Example 14.2

Suppose a tape with density of 1600 bytes/inch transfers data to and from the computer at a rate of 30,000 bytes/second. Thus, when transferring data, the speed of the tape in inches/second is as follows:

$$\frac{30{,}000 \text{ bytes/second}}{1600 \text{ bytes/inch}} = 18.75 \text{ inches/second}$$

Information is stored on tape in chunks called **records**, which are comparable to C structures. For instance, in a tape file containing inventory for a company, each record might contain all the information about a particular item, such as inventory number, description, cost, and quantity on hand.

The tape must reach the proper speed before writing or reading occurs. If the computer stores and accesses records one at a time from the tape, a gap of about one-half to one inch occurs between records. Figure 14.3 pictures such an **interrecord**

Figure 14.3
Unblocked
records on a
tape

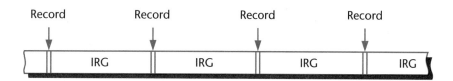

Figure 14.4
Blocked records
on a tape

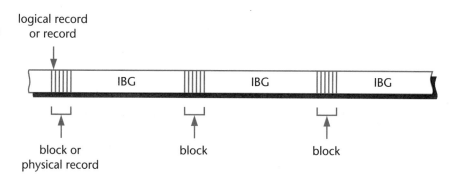

gap (**IRG**). To avoid so much wasted space, the computer often **blocks** or groups records together, as in Figure 14.4. The computer reads and writes a fixed number of records (a **block** or a **physical record**) at a time. With a block in memory, the computer can then access individual records or **logical records**. Because the computer does not need to speed up and slow down for individual records in a block, much less room is consumed by gaps with only an **interblock gap** (**IBG**) between blocks.

Definitions A **block** or a **physical record** is a fixed number of records the computer reads from or writes to secondary storage media as a group. A **logical record** is an individual record. An **interrecord gap** (**IRG**) is wasted space between records stored individually on a tape. An **interblock gap** (**IBG**) is wasted space between blocks stored on a tape.

Example 14.3

Suppose a standard 2400-ft tape is recorded at 1600 bpi with 80-byte records unblocked and an IRG of 0.75 inch. Without all the gaps, we could store the following number of records:

$$\frac{2400 \text{ ft}}{\text{tape}} \cdot \frac{12 \text{ in}}{\text{ft}} \cdot \frac{1600 \text{ bytes}}{\text{inch}} \cdot \frac{\text{rec}}{80 \text{ bytes}} = \frac{576{,}000 \text{ rec}}{\text{tape}}$$

In a 0.75-inch interrecord gap, we could have recorded 15 records, as shown:

$$0.75 \cdot \frac{1600 \text{ bytes}}{\text{inch}} \cdot \frac{1 \text{ rec}}{80 \text{ bytes}} = 15 \text{ rec}$$

Thus, 15 out of every 16 record positions are wasted. Consequently, the actual amount of data in unblocked 80-byte records that we can store on the tape is about 2.88 megabytes, as shown:

$$\frac{576{,}000 \text{ rec}}{16} \cdot \frac{80 \text{ bytes}}{\text{rec}} = 2{,}880{,}000 \text{ bytes} \approx 2.88 \text{ megabytes}$$

With five records in a block, the fraction of tape wasted is as follows:

$$\frac{15}{15+5} = \frac{15}{20} = \frac{3}{4}$$

The one-fourth of the tape in blocked 80-byte records stores about 11.52 megabytes of actual data, as shown:

$$\frac{576,000 \text{ rec}}{4} \cdot \frac{80 \text{ bytes}}{\text{rec}} = 11,520,000 \text{ bytes} \approx 11.52 \text{ megabytes}$$

A main characteristic of storage on tape is that it is **sequential**. Records are read or written one after another. To access the data in the three-thousandth record, we must read through each of the 2999 records before the desired one. Such access is like access on a tape of music. If we want to hear the fifth song, we must advance the tape past earlier ones. If we wish to update a file by adding, changing, or deleting records, we must read each record, make appropriate alterations, and re-record the entire file on a tape. Because of their capacity and cost, however, tapes are an excellent medium for long-term storage and backup.

Definition In **sequential access** to data, records are read or written one after another in sequence.

Disk Storage Data on magnetic disk storage is much faster to access than on magnetic tape. IBM first introduced magnetic disks in 1955. Mainframe computer disks, which look much like old phonograph records, are arranged into packs of perhaps 12 disks, and each can have data stored on both sides. This stack might rotate at a speed of 3600 revolutions per minute. An **access arm** has a **read/write head** for each surface. Amazingly, each read/write head floats on a cushion of air about a half-a-millionth of an inch from the surface. On a disk, as in Figure 14.5, data are recorded not in spirals but in concentric circles, called **tracks**. Each track usually contains eight equal-length, arc-shaped **sectors**. Each sector contains a **block** of records. As with tape storage, records are read and written a block at a time. As illustrated in Figure 14.6, a **cylinder** in a disk pack is a set of tracks that are all the same radius from the center and thus are directly under or above each other. When recording sequentially to a disk pack, the disk drive records

Figure 14.5
Surface of a disk

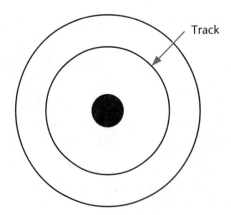

Track

Figure 14.6
Cylinder in a
disk pack

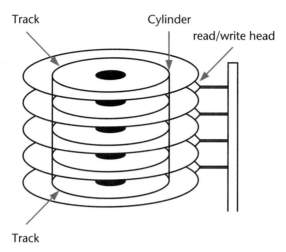

Track   Cylinder
                        read/write head

Track

on one track and then switches electronically to another track in the same cylinder. The drive completely fills the cylinder before adjusting the access arm to another. Using this arrangement, the disk drive minimizes the relatively slow mechanical movement of the access arm.

Definitions   On magnetic disk, data are stored in concentric circles, called **tracks**. Each track usually contains eight equal-length, arc-shaped areas, called **sectors**. In a disk pack, a set of tracks that are all the same radius from the center and thus are directly under or above each other is a **cylinder**.

Example 14.4

Suppose we are writing a program for a college registrar's office to store a data set consisting of student records. Each record contains 324 characters (bytes) of information, and the school has at most 6000 students. If a disk contains 47,480 bytes per track and 8 sectors per track, we compute the number of records a sector can store as follows:

$$\frac{47{,}480 \text{ bytes / track}}{8 \text{ sectors / track}} \cdot \frac{1}{324 \text{ bytes / record}} \approx 18.3 \text{ records / sector}$$

We cannot store a fraction of a record on a sector, however, so a sector contains a block of 18 records, and a track has $8 \cdot 18 = 144$ records. For the entire data set we have the following:

$$\frac{6000 \text{ records / data set}}{144 \text{ records / track}} = 41.\overline{66} \text{ tracks / data set.}$$

Thus, if a cylinder has 15 tracks, we must have at least 42 tracks and most of 3 cylinders, as shown:

$$\frac{42 \text{ tracks}}{15 \text{ tracks / cylinder}} = 2.8 \text{ cylinders}$$

A disk for a microcomputer, often called a **diskette** or **floppy disk**, is comparable to one platter of the disk pack. A magnetically chargeable substance, similar to the coating on an audio tape, covers the surface, and the read/write head of the disk drive records data by magnetizing certain sections of the disk.

Disks connected to any size computer are **direct access storage** media. If we need to access the three-thousandth record in a file, the disk drive can go directly to it, without processing all the earlier records. Moreover, we can update records in a disk file of fixed-length records without processing the entire file. For online services such as airline reservations, disk access is essential. Thus, even though disk storage is more expensive than tape, its speed and direct access capabilities make it an attractive medium for many applications.

Definition   **Direct access storage** is a secondary storage media in which a record can be accessed directly without processing all the data that appear before the desired item.

CD-ROM   Another direct access storage medium is **CD-ROM**, which first appeared in 1985. A **compact disk** or **CD** has a shiny surface with data stored as variations in the reflective material. As the disk rotates, a laser beam reflects these variations so that the mechanism can detect the information. As the name indicates, CD-ROM is a read-only medium. It can store several gigabytes of data, such as an audio/video encyclopedia or the entire works of Shakespeare.

Section 14.2 Exercises

1. Suppose a 2400-ft tape reel can move at a speed of 75 inches/second and store a maximum of 560 K of information.

    a. What is its storage density?

    b. What is the data transfer rate?

2. For a tape with density of 1600 bpi, how many inches are used by one record of 120 bytes?

3. Repeat Exercise 2 for a tape density of 6250 bpi.

4. a. How much room in feet on the tape in Example 14.3 was wasted in gaps?

    b. What percentage was wasted?

5. Suppose a 3600-ft tape is recorded at 1600 bpi with 100-byte records that are unblocked and an IRG of 0.75 inch.

    a. How many megabytes of information can be stored on the tape?

    b. How many gigabytes of information can be stored on the tape?

    c. How many feet are wasted in gaps?

6. Suppose on the tape in Exercise 5, 80-byte records are grouped into blocks of 8 records each. A gap of 0.75 inch appears between blocks.

    a. How many megabytes can be stored on the tape?

    b. How many feet are wasted in gaps?

7. Repeat Exercise 6 with 100-byte records and blocks of 12 records each.

8. Suppose a 3600-ft tape is recorded at 1600 bpi with 160-byte records, grouped into blocks of 10 records each, and an interblock gap of 0.6 inch. How many megabytes of information can be stored on the tape?

9. With a data transfer rate of 1170 K/sec for a tape, how long does it take to read a block of 32,768 bytes?

10. If a block of size 16,384 bytes on a tape can be read in 54.6 msec, what is the data transfer rate in K/sec?

11. The tape used with the UNIVAC was thin electroplated magnetic film with a tape speed of 100 inches/second and a density of 120 bpi.

    a. What was its data transfer rate?

    b. A 720-character block could be stored in what amount of space?

12. Suppose 100-byte records from a data set of 11,250 records are stored in a disk pack that can hold 13,030 bytes/track and has 19 tracks/cylinder and 200 cylinders.

    a. How many records can be stored in a block on a track?

    b. How many tracks are needed?

    c. How many cylinders are needed?

    d. What is the maximum storage in megabytes in the disk pack?

    e. What is the maximum storage in gigabytes in the disk pack?

13. Consider Exercise 12 assuming we want to place three blocks on each track with each block using at most 4253 bytes.

    a. How many records are in a block?

    b. In a track?

    c. How many tracks are needed?

    d. How many cylinders?

Section 14.3 **File Handling Modes**

Since Chapter 7, we have used two handling modes—read and write. The second argument in the file opening statement specifies these modes with the strings "r" and "w", respectively. For example, the statement

```
infile_ptr = fopen("price.dat", "r");
```

opens the file *price.dat* in reading mode and establishes *infile_ptr* as the file pointer. Similarly,

```
outfile_ptr = fopen("tax.dat", "w");
```

opens the file *tax.dat* for writing, destroying anything that was in the file.

Append Mode

Another useful mode is append, which has corresponding string "a". In append mode, the computer opens the file for writing, as with write mode. If the file does not exist, the computer creates the file. Unlike write mode, however, if a file opened under append mode already exists, the computer does not erase the previous contents. Instead, new characters written to the file are appended to the end of the text that is already in the file.

Example 14.5

In this example, we compare the effects of opening files in append and write modes. The program opens the two files *writefil.dat* and *appndfil.dat,* which contain identical text. With the function *OpenFile* (Example 14.1, Section 14.1), which also traps errors, we open the file *writefil.dat* in write mode and *appndfil.dat* in append mode. Using the *fprintf* function twice, the program then writes the same string to each file. After closing both files, the program calls the function *FileDisplay* twice, once with each file. This function opens the file argument, displays the contents character by character, and then closes the file. The program follows:

```
/*
 * Example 14.5. Program to illustrate the difference between
 * append and write modes
 * Output files: writefil.dat and appndfil.dat
 */

#include <stdio.h>
#include <stdlib.h>

FILE *OpenFile(char name[], char mode[]);
void FileDisplay(char name[]);

main()
{
    FILE *WriteFile_ptr,  /* pointer to first file  */
         *AppendFile_ptr; /* pointer to second file */

    /* Open the first file for writing (it already exists) */
    WriteFile_ptr = OpenFile("writefil.dat", "w");

    /* Open the second file for appending (it already exists) */
    AppendFile_ptr = OpenFile("appndfil.dat", "a");

    /* Write line to both files */
    fprintf(WriteFile_ptr,  "\n    Bacon--Of Studies\n");
    fprintf(AppendFile_ptr, "\n    Bacon--Of Studies\n");

    fclose(WriteFile_ptr);
    fclose(AppendFile_ptr);

    /* Display contents of the files */
    printf("AFTER WRITE, writefil.dat CONTAINS:\n");
    FileDisplay("writefil.dat");
    printf("*********************************************\n");
    printf("AFTER APPEND, appndfil.dat CONTAINS:\n");
    FileDisplay("appndfil.dat");
}

/*
 * Function to display the contents of the file named "name"
 * Pre:  name is the name of a file that already exists on disk.
 * Post: The contents of that file have been displayed.
 */
```

```
void FileDisplay(char name[])
{
    FILE *file_ptr; /* pointer to file */
    char c;         /* receives one character of input */

    file_ptr = OpenFile(name, "r");

    while ((c = getc(file_ptr)) != EOF)
        putchar(c);

    fclose(file_ptr);
}

/*
 * Insert function OpenFile from Example 14.1 in Section 14.1 here.
 */
```

Suppose before execution of the program *writefil.dat* and *appndfil.dat*, both contain the following quote from Bacon's *Of Studies*:

```
Histories make men wise; poets, witty;
the mathematics, subtile; natural philosophy, deep;
morals, grave; logic and rhetoric, able to contend.
```

Execution of the program overwrites *writefil.dat* but appends the reference to *appndfil.dat*, resulting in the following output:

```
AFTER WRITE, writefil.dat CONTAINS:

    Bacon--Of Studies
*************************************************
AFTER APPEND, appndfil.dat CONTAINS:
Histories make men wise; poets, witty;
the mathematics, subtile; natural philosophy, deep;
morals, grave; logic and rhetoric, able to contend.

    Bacon--Of Studies
```

Combining Modes

We can use a combination of modes, such as write/read, read/update, and append/update. To do so, we should manipulate the **file position marker**, which determines the byte or location upon which the next read or write acts. For example, we might want to point the file position marker to the first byte without destroying the file's contents and without closing and reopening the file. The ANSI C standard I/O function *rewind* accomplishes this task by rewinding the file to which its argument points with a statement such as

```
rewind(fp);
```

This operation allows us to read and reread a file. We can also use *rewind* with the proper mode to write a file and then read it back.

If a file is opened with the mode string "w+", the file can be written to and read from without the need to close and reopen the file. The mode w+ signifies "**writing plus (reading).**" As with write mode, if the file does not exist, the computer creates it. If the file already exists, the computer erases the contents. When a file is open for writing and reading, the computer uses a single marker for both. After writing to the file, we can use the *rewind* function to reposition the file position marker to the first of the file for reading. In Section 14.5, we see how we can use the function *fseek* to move the marker to other locations in the file. The program can intersperse reading and writing, but a change in the file position marker must occur between the two actions. For example, after writing new data to the file, rewinding, and reading that data, we can reposition to the end of the file (with *fseek* in Section 14.5) and continue adding characters, or even write over characters. We can perform these tasks without closing and reopening the file.

Similarly, the mode **appending plus (reading)**, with designation "a+", allows us to append data on the end of a file, then perform any mixture of reading and updating other data in the file. The *fseek* function of Section 14.5 enables us to position the marker to any character, and *rewind* is specifically for starting at the beginning. As with w+, we cannot have a read immediately after a write or vice versa without first changing the file position marker.

Example 14.6

We can now revise Example 14.5 to open each file only once, *writefil.dat* for writing and reading, *appndfil.dat* for appending and reading. The adjustment occurs in *main* and in *FileDisplay*, which no longer needs to open the file, but should rewind it. Thus, the argument to the revised *OpenedFileDisplay* becomes the pointer to the file, instead of the name of the file on disk. The revised program is below. The function *OpenFile* does not change from the previous example, so we do not include it in this listing. The output is also identical to that of Example 14.1.

```c
/*
 * Example 14.6. Program to illustrate the difference
 * between append + read and write + read modes
 * Output files: writefil.dat and appndfil.dat
 */

#include <stdio.h>
#include <stdlib.h>

FILE *OpenFile(char name[], char mode[]);
void OpenedFileDisplay(FILE *file_ptr);

main()
{
    FILE *WriteFile_ptr,  /* pointer to first file  */
         *AppendFile_ptr; /* pointer to second file */
```

```
    /*
     * Open the first file for writing (it already exists)
     * and reading
     */
    WriteFile_ptr = OpenFile("writefil.dat", "w+");

    /*
     * Open the second file for appending (it already exists)
     * and reading
     */
    AppendFile_ptr = OpenFile("appndfil.dat", "a+");

    /* Write line to both files */
    fprintf(WriteFile_ptr,  "\n    Bacon--Of Studies\n");
    fprintf(AppendFile_ptr, "\n    Bacon--Of Studies\n");

    /* Display contents of the files */
    printf("AFTER WRITE, writefil.dat CONTAINS:\n");
    OpenedFileDisplay(WriteFile_ptr);
    fclose(WriteFile_ptr);

    printf("*********************************************\n");
    printf("AFTER APPEND, appndfil.dat CONTAINS:\n");
    OpenedFileDisplay(AppendFile_ptr);
    fclose(AppendFile_ptr);
}


/*
 * Function to display the contents of the file pointed to by
 * file_ptr
 * Pre:  The file pointed to by file_ptr is opened for reading.
 * Post: The contents of that file have been displayed.
 */

void OpenedFileDisplay(FILE *file_ptr)
{
    char c;            /* receives one character of input */

    rewind(file_ptr);
    while ((c = getc(file_ptr)) != EOF)
        putchar(c);
}


/*
 * Insert function OpenFile from Example 14.1 here
 */
```

Another file mode is **r+ (reading plus (writing))**. This mode allows a file to be read from or written to without closing and reopening. The letter r signifies that this mode operates like the read mode, in that the file must already exist and the computer does

Table 14.3 File modes

Mode String	New/Existing File	Action
"a"	New or Existing	Append data to end
"a+"	New or Existing	Append, read, and update data (reposition marker between different actions)
"r"	Existing	Read data
"r+"	Existing	Read and update data (reposition marker between different actions)
"w"	New (erases existing)	Write data
"w+"	New (erases existing)	Write, read, and update data (reposition marker between different actions)

not erase its contents. After opening the file, however, we can operate on it as in the w+ mode. We can even extend the file by positioning the file position marker at the end and writing. Because this mode is useful in modifying or adding to a file that already exists, it sometimes is called **update mode**. In the next section, we see additional examples of these modes and cover another mode. Table 14.3 summarizes the modes we have covered so far.

In "w+", "a+", or "r+" mode, the program can intersperse reading from and writing to the file, but a change in the file position marker must occur between the two actions.

Section 14.3 Exercises

1. a. Suppose the file *product.dat* contains product data. Give the statement to open the file to add information about a new product.

   b. Adjust the open statement to be able to display the adjusted file.

   c. Write a statement to rewind the file.

2. Find the error(s) in the following segment:

```
FILE *tree.dat;

open("tree.dat", "a+r"); /* open file for append and read */
if (tree.dat == EOF)
{
   printf("Error opening file tree.dat");
   abort;
}

fprintf("tree.dat", " dogwood");   /* append a tree */

while ((c = getc(tree.dat)) != NULL) /* display the file */
   putchar(c);
```

3. Suppose the file *book.dat* contains information about books in the library. We want to add information about several other books and then display the file. Why is it incorrect to open the file with w+ mode?

4. **a.** Declare *file_ptr* to be a pointer to a file.

   b. Open the existing file, *class.dat,* for reading and updating with pointer *file_ptr.*

   c. Read the first "word." If that word is CS100 (no space), rewind the file and overwrite the information with CS101.

Section 14.3 **Programming Project**

Develop a program to record information about stock received at a store. The user enters information about each product received—the item name, the price per unit (jar of jelly, can of tuna, and so on), the quantity and date received, and the supplier. Each product is represented by a structure that is stored as a record in a file called *inventory.dat*. The structure also contains a member named *count,* which records the number of product units in the store at any time. This member is initialized to *QuantityReceived* and is decremented by 1 each time a unit of the product is sold. This latter process is not performed by this program. After entering and storing all the data, display the contents of the file.

Section 14.4 **Binary Files**

Before now, we have considered only text files, which are streams of characters. C also provides a different form of storage with a binary file. In a text file, each character is translated separately into the encoding scheme—such as ASCII or EBCDIC—of that particular computer. Because the ASCII system encodes the character "3" as 0011 0011, "7" as 0011 0111, and "2" as 0011 0010, a text file in ASCII stores the number 372 with the three bytes for the individual characters concatenated as follows:

   0011 0011 0011 0111 0011 0010

In reading a number from a text file, the computer must convert the number from its character stream form to the number encoding of the computer. Similarly, on output the computer translates the binary number into a stream of characters. In a **binary file**, however, the number 372 is stored in a binary form, such as 0000 0001 0111 0100, exactly as it is in the computer. For input and output no, conversion is necessary between the external file and main memory, so processing is faster. Information usually takes less space in a binary file than in a text file. Because of its method of storage, a binary file might not be portable to a different machine. Moreover, the programmer cannot use a text editor to create a binary file but must resort to programming. The program would read the data from the keyboard interactively or from an existing text file or compute the data in some way and then write that data to the binary file. Text files, however, can be generated and viewed with a text editor. To open a C file in **binary mode**, we add **b** to the mode string—"rb", "wb", "ab", "r+b", "w+b", or "a+b". For example,

```
file_ptr = fopen("employ.dat", "r+b");
```

opens existing binary file *employ.dat* for reading and updating.

Definition   A **binary file** stores information in binary form, exactly as it is in the computer.

Reading from a Binary File

In professional situations, programmers use binary files frequently because of the economy of space, the elimination of conversion between internal and character coding, and the ease of reading and writing large structures. With a text file, we must read or write each element of a structure separately. For example, suppose we have a structure for an employee's record with Social Security Number, name, salary, and 30 more fields, as follows:

```
typedef
struct
{
    char SSN[10];
    char name[31];
    float salary;
        ⋮
}
employee_t;
    ⋮
employee_t EmployeeRec;
```

If the information for each employee is in a text file and we need to read the data to print a report, we must specify each element individually. Thus, if *employ_ptr* is the file pointer, the read statement must contain 30 conversion specifications and 30 element names.

```
fscanf(employ_ptr, "%s %s %f ... ", EmployeeRec.SSN,
    EmployeeRec.name, &EmployeeRec.salary, ...);
```

If the information is in a binary file, however, we can read one record or an array of records all at once with a call to *fread*. The corresponding *fread* statement to the above *fscanf* is

```
fread(&EmployeeRec, sizeof(employee_t), 1, employ_ptr);
```

The four arguments are as follows:

1. The starting address of the area of memory to receive the data
2. The number of bytes in an item, such as the number of bytes in a structure, to be read
3. The number of data, such as the number of records, to be read
4. The file pointer

The function returns the number of items it successfully reads. Thus, we can use a positive return value as a condition to continue executing a *while* loop that is processing an entire binary file.

```
while(fread(&EmployeeRec, sizeof(employee_t), 1, employ_ptr)) ...
```

To illustrate with specific numbers, suppose *sizeof(employee_t)* is 240, so that an employee's record consumes 240 bytes in the binary file. The *fread* statement causes the computer to copy 240 bytes starting at the file marker position from the file into *EmployeeRec*. Should the read be successful in this case, *fread* returns 1.

Suppose instead of reading one record at a time, we read an entire array of records. If declaration of the array is

```
employee_t EmployeeArray[MAX_NUM_ELS];
```

and we wish to read *NumEls* = 100 number of elements from the file into the array, then the *fread* statement is

```
fread(EmployeeArray, sizeof(employee_t), NumEls, employ_ptr);
```

Thus, for *sizeof(employee_t)* being 240, the computer reads 100 items of size 240 or 24,000 bytes in all from the file pointed to by *employ_ptr* into elements *EmployeeArray*[0] through *EmployeeArray*[99]. The *fread* statement returns the number of elements it successfully reads, here a value between 0 and 100.

Writing to a Binary File

To store information from the computer's memory into the binary file, we use *fwrite* and arguments that correspond to those of *fread*. Thus, we could write an employee record to this file with

```
fwrite(&EmployeeRec, sizeof(employee_t), 1, employ_ptr);
```

or an array with

```
fwrite(EmployeeArray, sizeof(employee_t), NumEls, employ_ptr);
```

The arguments are:

1. The starting address of the area of memory that contains the data

2. The number of bytes in an item, such as the number of bytes in a structure, to be written

3. The number of data, such as the number of records, to be written

4. The file pointer

The first argument for *fread* and *fwrite* is the memory address of the variable that sends or obtains the data. With text files, however, *fprintf* uses the variable name, as shown:

```
fprintf(TextFile_ptr, "%d\n", x);
```

As with *fread*, *fwrite* returns the number of items it successfully processes.

Example 14.7

Suppose we wish to store in a binary file data on Social Security Number, grade point average, and hours earned for a group of students. Because the file stores information in the internal format of the computer, we cannot create the binary file with an editor. The program reads the data interactively, stores the data in a binary file, and prints a report of all the data at the end.

As Figure 14.7 indicates, *main* calls the following three functions:

1. *OpenFile* to open the binary file for writing and reading

2. *ReadData* to read the data interactively and store it a record at a time in the file

3. *DisplayStuFile* to read records from the file and print their elements in a report

The function *OpenFile* is identical to that of Example 14.1 in Section 14.1, so we do not include its pseudocode or code here. The designs and implementations of the other functions follow:

Figure 14.7
Structure chart
for Example
14.7

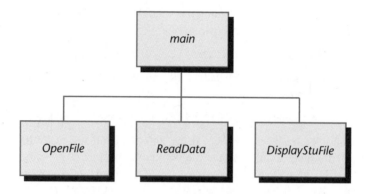

main( )

Program to read interactively Social Security Number (SSN), grade point average (GPA), and hours earned for students and to store this data in a binary file, *student.dat*

Algorithm:

call *OpenFile* to open *student.dat* as a binary file for writing and reading
call *ReadData* to interactively read data and store it in the file
call *DisplayStuFile* to print a report of the data in the file

ReadData(file_ptr)

Function to read data interactively and store the data in the file pointed to by *file_ptr*

Pre:

The file pointed to by *file_ptr* is open for writing.

Post:

The file contains the data read interactively.

Algorithm:

do the following:
    prompt for and read SSN, GPA, and hours earned
    write the record of this information to the file
    ask if the user wishes to add another record
while user wishes to add another record

DisplayStuFile(file_ptr)

Function to display the contents of the binary file pointed to by *file_ptr*

Pre:

The file pointed to by *file_ptr* is open for reading.

Post:

The contents of that file have been printed in a report.

Algorithm:

rewind the file
print headings
while a record was successfully read from the file
print the data in that report

```c
/*
 * Example 14.7
 * Program to read interactively Social Security Number,
 * grade point average, and hours earned for a group of
 * students and to store this data in a binary file
 * Output binary file: student.dat
 */

#include <stdio.h>
#include <stdlib.h>
#include <ctype.h>

FILE *OpenFile(char name[], char mode[]);
void ReadData(FILE *file_ptr);
void DisplayStuFile(FILE *file_ptr);

typedef
struct
{
    char SSN[10];   /* Social Security Number */
    float GPA;      /* grade point average    */
    int hours;      /* hours earned           */
}
record_t;

main()
{
    FILE *file_ptr; /* pointer to student file */

    /* Open the binary file for writing and reading */
    file_ptr = OpenFile("student.dat", "w+b");

    ReadData(file_ptr);
    DisplayStuFile(file_ptr);

    fclose(file_ptr);
}
```

```
/*
 * Insert function OpenFile from Example 14.1 here
 */
  ⋮
/*
 * Function to read data interactively and store the data in the
 * file pointed to by file_ptr
 * Pre:  The file pointed to by file_ptr is open for writing.
 * Post: The file contains the data read.
 */

void ReadData(FILE *file_ptr)
{
    record_t StuRec;        /* record of student information */
    char ans[BUFSIZ];       /* answer of whether to continue or not */

    printf("Enter student data:\n");
    do
    {
        printf("\nSSN: ");
        scanf("%9s", StuRec.SSN);
        fflush(stdin);
        printf("GPA: ");
        scanf("%f", &StuRec.GPA);
        printf("Number of hours earned: ");
        scanf("%d", &StuRec.hours);
        fflush(stdin);

        fwrite(&StuRec, sizeof(record_t), 1, file_ptr);

        do
        {
            printf("\nDo you want to add another record? (y/n) ");
            gets(ans);
        }
        while ((tolower(ans[0]) != 'y') && (tolower(ans[0]) != 'n'));
    }
    while (tolower(ans[0]) == 'y');
}

/*
 * Function to display the contents of the binary file pointed to
 * by file_ptr with records of type record_t
 * Pre:  The binary file pointed to by file_ptr is open for reading.
 * Post: The contents of that file have been printed in a report.
 */
```

```
void DisplayStuFile(FILE *file_ptr)
{
    record_t StuRec;        /* receives one record of input */

    rewind(file_ptr);

    printf("\n\n**************************************************\n");
    printf("\t\tStudent file:\n");
    printf("SSN\t\tGPA\tHours Earned\n\n");

    while (fread(&StuRec, sizeof(record_t), 1, file_ptr))
    {
        printf("%s\t%.2f\t%4d\n", StuRec.SSN, StuRec.GPA,
               StuRec.hours);
    }
}
```

Section 14.4 **Exercises**

1. Find the error(s) in the following segment that processes a binary file, *my.dat:*

```
int int_array[] = {16,7,23,65,312},
    i = 45,
    j;
FILE *file_ptr;

file_ptr = fopen("my.dat", "w");
fwrite(i,         45, 1, file_ptr);
fwrite(int_array,  5, 1, file_ptr);
rewind(file_ptr);
fscanf(file_ptr, &j);
```

2. a. Suppose a computer stores an integer in two bytes and a floating point number in four. For a record of type *record_t* from Example 14.7, how many bytes are consumed in memory?

b. In a binary file?

c. Suppose the GPA is 3.427 and the number of hours earned is 5. If SSN, GPA, and hours are written to a text file with a blank between each value, how many bytes would the information consume in the text file?

3. Write a statement to open a binary file, *binprod.dat,* for adding data at the end.

4. a. Write a statement to open a binary file, *binplant.dat,* for creating and then printing it. Have *PlantFile_ptr* be the file pointer.

b. Define a type *plant_t* that contains a plant name (string of 20 characters plus another character for the null character); enumeration value of *TREE, SHRUB, GRASS, BULB,* or *OTHER*; quantity on hand; and price.

c. Declare *PlantRec* to be of type *plant_t.*

d. Write statements to interactively read values for the record elements.

    e. Write a statement to write this record to the binary file pointed to by *PlantFile_ptr.*

    f. Write a statement to read a record from the binary file pointed to by *PlantFile_ptr* into *PlantRec.*

    g. If a floating point number is stored in four bytes and an integer in two, how much room does this record consume in the computer and in the file?

5. a. Declare *TimeArray* to be an array of *MAX_NUM_ELS* floating point numbers and *NumEls* to be an integer.

    b. Declare *TimeFile_ptr* to be a pointer to a file.

    c. Write a segment to open an existing binary file, *timer.dat,* for reading and establish *TimeFile_ptr* as a pointer to this file.

    d. Write a statement to read a value for *NumEls* from the first of this file.

    e. Write a statement then to read *NumEls* number of elements from the file into the array *TimeArray* provided *NumEls* is less than or equal to *MAX_NUM_ELS.*

Section 14.4 Programming Projects

1. Redo Project 1 of Section 14.3 so that the file is a binary one.

2. Write a program to generate a random integer *NumEls* between 200 and 300 and to store the value in a binary file. Generate *NumEls* number of random integers between 150 and 850, storing them one at a time in the binary file. These numbers could simulate SAT verbal scores. Write another program to read *NumEls* from this file and then to read the remainder of the file all at once into an array, *verbal.* This second program should produce a text report file with the average of the scores that are between 200 and 800. The file should also include a list of out-of-range scores.

Section 14.5 Random Access Files

One advantage of disk files over files on most other devices (such as printers and tapes) is that a disk is a **random access** or **direct access** device. We can write to or read from a disk file by specifying the exact location where this operation is to occur. For example, we can read the fifth byte in a disk file without having to read the first four bytes. A disk file is much like an array in that the computer can index this random access file directly. In C, the analogy between files and arrays is further reinforced by numbering the bytes of a file consecutively from 0.

Definition   **Random access** or **direct access** storage media can be written to or read from by specifying the exact location where the operation is to occur.

Because of these disk file features, if an array is too large to fit in memory, we can write the data to a disk file and access elements selectively as needed. Admittedly, it takes longer to access a character from a disk file than it does to access an array element in memory. This is another example of how programming involves tradeoffs between speed and memory usage.

Random access files are almost always binary files. Thus, we use b with the other mode designations to open such a file and *fread* and *fwrite* to access the file. The function *rewind* moves the file position marker to the first byte of a text or a binary file, but *fseek* provides an even greater degree of specificity.

Seeking a File Position

We use the C library function, *fseek*, to seek a specific position or location in a file. This function manipulates the file position marker. A read or write of a single byte increments the marker by 1. With *fseek*, we can increment or decrement the marker by any amount or reposition the marker relative to the beginning or end of the file. The *fseek* function only repositions the file marker. It does not perform any I/O.

The *fseek* function takes three arguments. The first is the *FILE* pointer of an open file, and the second is a long integer. The third is one of three integers–0, 1, or 2. The file *stdio.h* defines the symbolic constants *SEEK_SET* (0), *SEEK_CUR* (1), and *SEEK_END* (2) to represent these values. The second and third parameters specify the repositioning according to the following rules:

1. If the third argument is 0 (*SEEK_SET*), then the second argument specifies the byte position relative to the beginning of the file for the file position marker. The second argument in this case must be equal to or greater than 0. As Figure 14.8 illustrates, the statement

   ```
   fseek(fp, 5L, SEEK_SET);
   ```

   positions the file associated with *fp* to the sixth byte of the file (the first byte is at position 0). In C, we usually speak of "positioning a file," without referring to the concept of a marker. When the third argument is 0, the behavior of *fseek* is close to array indexing.

2. If the third argument is 1 (*SEEK_CUR*), the second argument specifies an increment or decrement to the current position of the file. For example, starting at position 5, the statement

   ```
   fseek(fp, 2L, SEEK_CUR);
   ```

   skips ahead two bytes in the file to position 7, whereas

   ```
   fseek(fp, -2L, SEEK_CUR);
   ```

   moves back two bytes (see Figures 14.9 and 14.10).

3. If the third argument is 2 (*SEEK_END*), the second argument specifies how many bytes the file is to be positioned from the end. The second argument must be equal to or greater than 0. As Figure 14.11 shows,

   ```
   fseek(fp, 4L, SEEK_END);
   ```

   positions the file to the fourth byte from the end of the file. The statement

   ```
   fseek(fp, 0L, SEEK_END);
   ```

   in which the second argument is equal to zero, positions the file to the end, past the last byte of the file (in other words, to the point where the *EOF* would be if it were in the file). Figure 14.12 depicts the action of this statement.

Figure 14.8
Action of
fseek(fp, 5L, SEEK_SET)

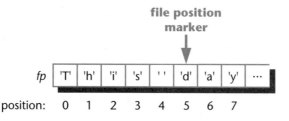

Figure 14.9
Starting at
position 5,
action of
*fseek(fp, 2L,
SEEK_CUR)*

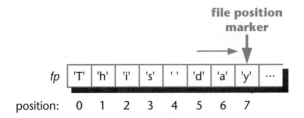

Figure 14.10
Starting at
position 5,
action of
*fseek(fp, -2L,
SEEK_CUR)*

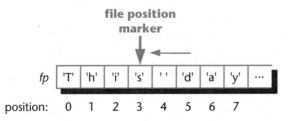

Figure 14.11
Action of
*fseek(fp, 4L,
SEEK_END)*

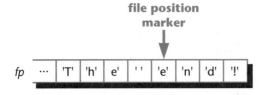

Figure 14.12
Action of
*fseek(fp, 0L,
SEEK_END)*

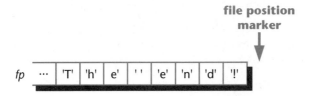

The second and third arguments may both be variables, but the third argument rarely is. A variable used for the second argument must be a *long int* or must be cast explicitly into one.

If *fseek* finds the file location, the function returns 0. Otherwise, it returns a nonzero value. Thus, we should couple error-handling with each *fseek*, as shown:

```
if (fseek(fp, 5L, SEEK_SET))
{
    printf("Error calling fseek\n");
    exit(1);
}
```

When an error occurs, *fseek* returns a nonzero value. In this case, the conditional expression evaluates to *TRUE,* and the body of the *if* statement executes.

Obtaining the Current Position

With a file pointer as an argument, the standard I/O library contains the function *ftell*, which returns the current position of the file. For example, suppose *fp* is a *FILE* pointer for an open file. Then the statement

```
WhichByte = ftell(fp);
```

assigns the value of the file position marker to *WhichByte*. The function returns a *long int,* just as a *long int* positions the file with *fseek*.

Perhaps the most common use of *ftell* is to determine the size of a file. If *size* is a *long int,* the statements

```
fseek(fp, 0L, SEEK_END);
size = ftell(fp);
```

result in *size* containing the number of bytes in the file. The call to *fseek* positions the file past the last character, and *ftell* returns this position. For example, if the file contains 100 characters, the last character is numbered 99. This call to *fseek,* however, positions past the last character, at byte position 100. Thus, *ftell* returns the value 100.

Example 14.8

Suppose a small social club on campus, which never has more than 50 members, wishes to keep information on its members in a random access file. They assign to each member an identification (ID) number from 0–49 that serves as an index to the member's record. Because the membership is small, the file contains 50 record positions, one for each possible ID number. As members graduate, their numbers are assigned to new members. Undoubtedly, some record positions do not contain active records. Such a **relative file organization** only works well for data sets that have small ID numbers.

For the sake of simplicity, suppose that each record contains the member's name and graduation year. We can compute the ID number from the record's position.

A program similar to that of Example 14.7 initializes the file. The variations include definition of *MAX_NUM_RECS* and a change in the record structure, as follows:

```
#define MAX_NUM_RECS 50

typedef
struct
{
    char name[41];
    int year;
}
record_t;
```

The functions *main* and *OpenFile* do not change. In *ReadData,* however, we adjust prompts and use *gets* to read the person's name. We also count the number of records being initialized, and indicate that the remaining records do not contain data by placing the null character in the first character of the name.

```
/*
 * Function to read data interactively and store the data in
 * the direct access binary file pointed to by file_ptr.
 * There are exactly MAX_NUM_RECS number of record
 * positions in the file. An empty position is indicated by
 * the null character in the first byte of the record.
 * Pre:  The file pointed to by file_ptr is open for writing.
 * Post: The file contains the data read to a maximum of
 *       MAX_NUM_RECS number of records.  Other records
 *       have a first byte of the null character.
 */

void ReadData(FILE *file_ptr)
{
    record_t MemberRec;    /* record for member            */
    char ans[BUFSIZ];      /* y/n answer                   */
    int count = 0;         /* number of records entered    */

    printf("Enter member data:\n");
    do
    {
        count++;

        printf("Name: ");
        gets(MemberRec.name);
        printf("Graduation year: ");
        scanf("%d", &MemberRec.year);
        fflush(stdin);

        fwrite(&MemberRec, sizeof(record_t), 1, file_ptr);

        if (count < MAX_NUM_RECS)
            do
            {
                printf("\nDo you want to add another record?");
                printf(" (y/n) ");
                gets(ans);
            }
            while ((tolower(ans[0]) != 'y') &&
                    (tolower(ans[0]) != 'n'));
    }
    while ((tolower(ans[0]) == 'y') &&
            (count < MAX_NUM_RECS));

    MemberRec.name[0] = '\0';
    for (; count < MAX_NUM_RECS; count++)
        fwrite(&MemberRec, sizeof(record_t), 1, file_ptr);
}
```

To display the file, we must be careful to skip any records that have a leading null character. Through a counter, *id*, we can derive the ID number for each valid member. The code for the display module, *DisplayFile*, follows:

```
/*
 * Function to display the contents of the binary file
 * pointed to by file_ptr with records of type record_t
 * Pre:  The binary file pointed to by file_ptr is open for
 *       reading.  Empty record positions are indicated by
 *       a null character in the first byte.
 * Post: The contents of that file have been displayed.
 */

void DisplayFile(FILE *file_ptr)
{
    record_t MemberRec;    /* record for member */
    int id = 0;            /* member id number */

    rewind(file_ptr);

printf("***********************************************\n");
    printf("\t\tMember file:\n");
    printf("%s%24s%22s\n\n", "Id", "Name", "Year");

    while (fread(&MemberRec, sizeof(record_t), 1, file_ptr))
    {
        if (MemberRec.name[0] != '\0')
            printf("%2d  %-40s%4d\n", id, MemberRec.name,
                   MemberRec.year);

        id++;
    }
}
```

After interactively entering names, *DisplayFile* prints the member's ID number, name, and graduation year, such as follows:

```
**************************************************
                Member file:
    Id                      Name                Year


     0  Adams, Keith                            2001
     1  Blackwell, Henry                        1999
     2  Davis, Susan                            1999
     3  Kirk, Chris                             2000
     4  Jordan, Ann                             2002
     5  Patterson, Lynn                         1999
     6  Suarez, Rosa                            2001
     7  Williams, George                        2001
```

Example 14.9

This example contains a program to update and display the file created in Example 14.8. Thus, we open this binary file in mode "r+b". The function *main* calls *OpenFile* of Example 14.1 to open the file before invoking *choice* to present a menu of choices to the user. Through this menu, the user can add, change, or delete a record; display member information with ID numbers; or quit. In the routines to add, change, and delete, we must perform an *fseek* to find the proper record location. Thus, in case of an *fseek* error, each function calls an error handling function, *fseek_error*. Figure 14.13 presents the structure diagram for the program.

The pseudocode for *AddMember* follows:

AddMember(*file_ptr*)

Procedure to read data interactively and store the data in a record of the direct access binary file pointed to by file_ptr.

Pre:

The file pointed to by file_ptr is open for writing.

Post:

The file contains a new record, or an error message has been printed saying the file is full

Algorithm:

move the file position pointer to the first of the file
id ← 0

do the following:
    read a record
    increment *id*
while the initial character is not null and *id* is less than *MAX_NUM_RECS*

if *id* is *MAX_NUM_RECS*
    print that the file is full
else
    decrement *id* by 1
    move the file position marker back one record
    interactively read the data
    write the record to the file

Of significance in this routine is the fact that after reading to discover a vacant position, we must back up to that record position. The following *fread*

```
fread(&MemberRec, sizeof(record_t), 1, file_ptr);
```

reads a record and advances the file position marker. If *MemberRec.name*[0] is the null character, we have found an empty record slot. The *id*, however, is one greater than the ID number for this record, and the file position marker is past the record position. Thus, before writing a new record to that location, we must decrement *id* and the file position marker, as follows:

Figure 14.13   Structure chart for Example 14.9

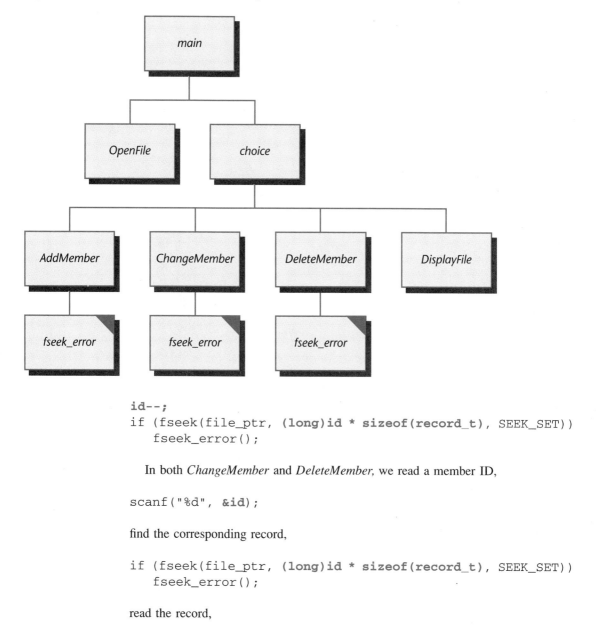

```
id--;
if (fseek(file_ptr, (long)id * sizeof(record_t), SEEK_SET))
    fseek_error();
```

In both *ChangeMember* and *DeleteMember*, we read a member ID,

```
scanf("%d", &id);
```

find the corresponding record,

```
if (fseek(file_ptr, (long)id * sizeof(record_t), SEEK_SET))
    fseek_error();
```

read the record,

```
fread(&MemberRec, sizeof(record_t), 1, file_ptr);
```

and display the record. Both functions make sure that the record is not empty by checking that the first character is not null. Then, upon obtaining verification from the user, the program again returns the file position marker to the proper record

```
if (fseek(file_ptr, (long)id * sizeof(record_t), SEEK_SET))
    fseek_error();
```

and proceeds with changing or deleting the record. The code for the program follows:

```
/*
 * Example 14.9
 * Program to update and display a binary random access file
 * Input/output binary file: member.dat
 */

#include <stdio.h>
#include <stdlib.h>
#include <ctype.d>

#define MAX_NUM_RECS 50

FILE *OpenFile(char name[], char mode[]);
void choice(FILE *file_ptr);
void AddMember(FILE *file_ptr);
void ChangeMember(FILE *file_ptr);
void DeleteMember(FILE *file_ptr);
void DisplayFile(FILE *file_ptr);
void fseek_error(void);

typedef
struct
{
    char name[41];    /* member's name */
    int year;         /* year of graduation */
}
record_t;

main()
{
    FILE *file_ptr; /* pointer to student file */

    /* Open the binary file for writing and reading */
    file_ptr = OpenFile("member.dat", "r+b");

    choice(file_ptr);
    fclose(file_ptr);
}

/*
 * Insert function OpenFile from Example 14.1
 */
    ⋮
/*
 * Function to drive additions, changes, deletions to the
 * binary file.
 * Pre:  The file pointed to by file_ptr is open for reading
 *       + updating.
 * Post: The file contains the data read to a maximum of
 *       MAX_NUM_RECS number of records. Other records (up
 *       to exactly MAX_NUM_RECS in number) have a first
```

```
 *         byte of the null character.  Additions, changes, and
 *         deletions may have occurred.  The file may have been
 *         printed.
 */

void choice(FILE *file_ptr)
{
    char ans[BUFSIZ];   /* answer or a, c, d, s, or q */

    do
    {
        printf("\nOptions:\n");
        printf("a  Add\n");
        printf("c  Change\n");
        printf("d  Delete\n");
        printf("s  Show file\n");
        printf("q  Quit\n");
        printf("\nYour choice:  ");
        gets(ans);
        ans[0] = tolower(ans[0]);

        switch (ans[0])
        {
            case 'a':
                AddMember(file_ptr);
                break;
            case 'c':
                ChangeMember(file_ptr);
                break;
            case 'd':
                DeleteMember(file_ptr);
                break;
            case 's':
            case 'q':
                DisplayFile(file_ptr);
                break;
            default:
                printf("Please type a, c, d, s, or q\n");
        }
    }
    while (ans[0] != 'q');
}

/*
 * Function to read data interactively and store the data in
 * a record of the direct access binary file pointed to by
 * file_ptr.  The record cannot be added if there are
 * MAX_NUM_RECS number of records in the file.  The record
 * is added in the first empty position.  An empty position
 * is indicated by the null character in the first byte of
 * the record.
```

```
 * Pre:    The file pointed to by file_ptr is open for writing.
 * Post:   The file contains a new record or the function
 *         printed an error message saying the file is full.
 */

void AddMember(FILE *file_ptr)
{
    record_t MemberRec;        /* one record */
    int id = 0;                /* member id number */

    rewind(file_ptr);

    do
    {
        fread(&MemberRec, sizeof(record_t), 1, file_ptr);
        id++;
    }
    while ((MemberRec.name[0] != '\0') &&
           (id < MAX_NUM_RECS));

    if (id == MAX_NUM_RECS)
        printf("There is no more room in the file.\n");
    else
    {
        id--;
        if (fseek(file_ptr, (long)id * sizeof(record_t),
                  SEEK_SET))
            fseek_error();
        printf("member id = %d\n", id);
        printf("Enter student data:\n");
        printf("Name: ");
        gets(MemberRec.name);
        printf("Graduation year: ");
        scanf("%d", &MemberRec.year);
        fflush(stdin);

        fwrite(&MemberRec, sizeof(record_t), 1, file_ptr);
    }
}

/*
 * Function to change the information in a record.
 * Pre:    The file pointed to by file_ptr is open for updating.
 * Post:   The file possibly has one updated record.
 */

void ChangeMember(FILE *file_ptr)
{
    record_t MemberRec;        /* one record         */
    int id;                    /* member id number   */
    char ans[BUFSIZ];          /* y/n answer         */
```

```c
printf("Give the id of the member information to change: ");
scanf("%d", &id);
fflush(stdin);

if (fseek(file_ptr, (long)id * sizeof(record_t), SEEK_SET))
    fseek_error();
fread(&MemberRec, sizeof(record_t), 1, file_ptr);
if (MemberRec.name[0] == '\0')
    printf("That is not the id of a present member.\n");
else
{
    printf("%s%24s%23s\n\n", "Id", "Name", "Year");
    printf("%2d %-40s %4d\n", id, MemberRec.name,
                    MemberRec.year);
    do
    {
        printf("Do you want to change this information?");
        printf(" (y/n): ");
        gets(ans);
        ans[0] = tolower(ans[0]);
    }
    while ((ans[0] != 'y') && (ans[0] != 'n'));
    if (ans[0] == 'y')
    {
        if (fseek(file_ptr, (long)id * sizeof(record_t),
                SEEK_SET))
            fseek_error();
        do
        {
            printf("Do you want to change the name? (y/n): ");
            gets(ans);
            ans[0] = tolower(ans[0]);
        }
        while ((ans[0] != 'y') && (ans[0] != 'n'));
        if (ans[0] == 'y')
        {
            printf("Name: ");
            gets(MemberRec.name);
        }

        do
        {
            printf("Do you want to change the year? (y/n): ");
            gets(ans);
            ans[0] = tolower(ans[0]);
        }
        while ((ans[0] != 'y') && (ans[0] != 'n'));
        if (ans[0] == 'y')
        {
            printf("Graduation year: ");
            scanf("%d", &MemberRec.year);
```

```
                fflush(stdin);
            }

            fwrite(&MemberRec, sizeof(record_t), 1, file_ptr);
        }
    }
}

/*
 * Function to delete a record.
 * Pre:   The file pointed to by file_ptr is open for updating.
 * Post:  The file possibly has one deleted record.
 */

void DeleteMember(FILE *file_ptr)
{
    record_t MemberRec;         /* one record        */
    int id;                     /* member id number  */
    char ans[BUFSIZ];           /* y/n answer        */

    printf("Give the id of the member information to delete: " );
    scanf("%d", &id);
    fflush(stdin);
    if (fseek(file_ptr, (long)id * sizeof(record_t), SEEK_SET))
        fseek_error();
    fread(&MemberRec, sizeof(record_t), 1, file_ptr);
    if (MemberRec.name[0] == '\0')
        printf("That is not the id of a present member.\n");
    else
    {
        printf("%s%24s%23s\n\n", "Id", "Name", "Year");
        printf("%2d %-40s %4d\n", id, MemberRec.name,
                        MemberRec.year);
        do
        {
            printf("Do you want to delete this record? (y/n): ");
            gets(ans);
            ans[0] = tolower(ans[0]);
        }
        while ((ans[0] != 'y') && (ans[0] != 'n'));

        if (ans[0] == 'y')
        {
            if (fseek(file_ptr, (long)id * sizeof(record_t),
                        SEEK_SET))
                fseek_error();
            MemberRec.name[0] = '\0';
            fwrite(&MemberRec, sizeof(record_t), 1, file_ptr);
        }
    }
}
```

```
/*
 * Insert function DisplayFile from Example 14.8
 */
  ⋮

/*
 * Function to print fseek error message and abort program
 * Pre:    A fseek error is detected.
 * Post:   An error message has been printed and
 *         execution has stopped.
 */

void fseek_error(void)
{
    printf("Error calling fseek\n");
    exit(1);
}
```

An interactive session follows with some of the menus omitted to save space:

```
Options:
a   Add
c   Change
d   Delete
s   Show file
q   Quit

Your choice:  s
**************************************************
              Member file:
Id                    Name                   Year

  0  Adams, Keith                            2001
  1  Blackwell, Henry                        1999
  2  Davis, Susan                            1999
  3  Kirk, Chris                             2000
  4  Jordan, Ann                             2002
  5  Patterson, Lynn                         1999
  6  Suarez, Rosa                            2001
  7  Williams, George                        2001

Options:
a   Add
c   Change
d   Delete
s   Show file
q   Quit
```

```
Your choice:  d
Give the id of the member information to delete: 3
Id                      Name                    Year

 3  Kirk, Chris                                 2000
Do you want to delete this record? (y/n): y
⋮
Your choice:  d
Give the id of the member information to delete: 7
Id                      Name                    Year

 7  Williams, George                            2001
Do you want to delete this record? (y/n): n
⋮
Your choice:  d
Give the id of the member information to delete: 9
That is not the id of a present member.
⋮
Your choice:  d
Give the id of the member information to delete: 6
Id                      Name                    Year

 6  Suarez, Rosa                                2001
Do you want to delete this record? (y/n): y
⋮
Your choice:  c
Give the id of the member information to change: 7
Id                      Name                    Year

 7  Williams, George                            2001
Do you want to change this information? (y/n): y
Do you want to change the name? (y/n): n
Do you want to change the year? (y/n): y
Graduation year: 2002
⋮
Your choice:  a
member id = 3
Enter student data:
Name: Norton, Ralph
Graduation year: 2002
⋮
Your choice:  q
```

```
**************************************************
              Member file:
Id                    Name                Year

 0   Adams, Keith                         2001
 1   Blackwell, Henry                     1999
 2   Davis, Susan                         1999
 3   Norton, Ralph                        2002
 4   Jordan, Ann                          2002
 5   Patterson, Lynn                      1999
 7   Williams, George                     2002
```

Section 14.5 Exercises

Suppose fp *points to a file. In Exercises 1–8, write statements to place the file position marker at the*

1. Beginning of the file

2. End of the file

3. Tenth byte

4. Tenth byte forward from the current position

5. Tenth byte backward from the current position

6. Tenth byte from the end of the file

7. Tenth record, where each record is of type *employee_t*

8. One record back from the current position, where each record is of type *employee_t*

9. Write statements to print the number of bytes in a file.

10. Write statements to print the number of records in a file, where each record is of type *employee_t.*

11. Write statements to print the number of the current record in a file, where each record is of type *employee_t.*

12. Suppose *SalesRec* is of type *sales_t,* where

```
typedef
struct
{
    char name[41];
    float amount;
    char MakeQuota;
}
sales_t;
```

Write statements to read a record, *SalesRec,* from the binary file to which *SalesFile_ptr* points. If the *amount* element is greater than or equal to $100,000, then have *MakeQuota* be 'y', otherwise, 'n'. Store this adjusted record in the file.

13. Suppose *alum.dat* is a random access binary data file of integers. Write statements to update each record. If the integer is greater than 10, add 1 to its value, and if it is less than 0, subtract 2.

14. Rewrite *AddMember* of Example 14.9 not to have a variable *id,* but to compute the ID number from the file position. Use *SEEK_CUR* with *fseek* to back up one record position.

Section 14.5 Programming Projects

1. Develop a program that uses the inventory file produced by Project 1 of Section 14.4. Consider the record position of an item to be its ID number. The user presents the program with a shopping list of items (by ID number) to be purchased. The program inputs the stored inventory file, and then it decrements the count for each item on the shopping list and charges the customer appropriately. The program must check for the presence of the item and for sufficient quantities in stock. Before terminating the program, it must update the inventory file to reflect the depletion in stock, and print a list of items that need to be restocked.

2. Space can be saved in a file if numbers are stored in their internal form rather than as displayable numbers. Write a function that stores integers on disk in their internal form and one that reads in those numbers. Use *fseek* in these functions in order to access the file like an array. The function is passed an index, which is then converted into a byte address in the file. Design a driver program to test these functions.

〰 Programming and Debugging Hints

Run-Time Errors and Buffering

Sometimes a program contains a run-time or execution error, which is an error that occurs when the program runs, making continued execution impossible. In such an instance, we can use a debugger or tracing *printf*s to determine the point of the program crash. The *printf*s can tell where the program terminates with an error condition and the values of key variables. In order for this method to be reliable in C, we must follow each call to *printf* with a call to the *fflush* function. Often the standard output file is buffered, meaning that the output to those files is collected in memory but not displayed until the buffer becomes full. If the program suddenly crashes, some undisplayed characters may still be in the buffer. The result is that the program appears to stop earlier than it actually does. The *fflush* function, as its name suggests, flushes out the buffer. The function argument is a *FILE* pointer, such as *stdout* or *stderr.* For example,

```
fflush(stdout);
```

flushes the output buffer.

Often the standard error file is not buffered. If you know this to be the case with your compiler, you can output tracing messages through *stderr* using the *fprintf* function, without the need to call *fflush.* For example, we might have

```
fprintf(stderr, "Entering DisplayEl with id = %d\n", id);
```

Sometimes the standard error file is only line buffered. It stores characters only until a newline is output and then displays the line.

≋ **Key Terms**

≋ **Summary**

In C, a text file is a stream of characters. When a C program begins execution, it has access to three standard files—*stdin, stdout,* and *stderr.* The standard input or *stdin* is the file from which the program receives input by default. This file usually is the keyboard. The second file, the standard output or *stdout*, is the default output file, which is usually the screen. The file standard error or *stderr* keeps error messages separate from other program output. Tables 14.1 and 14.2 summarize the functions and macros to manipulate input and output text files.

In Section 7.5, we studied the read and write modes with mode strings "r" and "w", respectively. In the append mode, with corresponding string "a", the computer opens the file for writing. If the file does not exist, the computer creates the file. If the file already exists, new characters written to the file are appended to the end of the text that is already in the file.

The ANSI C standard I/O function *rewind* rewinds the file to which its argument points with a statement such as

```
rewind(fp);
```

If a file is opened with the mode string "w+", signifying "writing plus (reading)," the file can be written to and read from without the need to close and reopen the file. The mode "appending plus (reading)," with designation "a+", allows us to append data on the end of a file and then to perform any mixture of reading and updating data in the file. The mode r+ (reading plus (writing)), called the update mode, allows a file to be read from or written to without closing and reopening. When a file is open for writing and reading, the computer uses a file position marker, which determines the byte or location upon which the next read or write acts. In "w+", "a+", or "r+" mode, the program can intersperse reading from and writing to the file, but a change in the file position marker must occur between the two actions.

A binary file stores information in binary form, exactly as it is in the computer. In professional situations, programmers use binary files frequently because of the economy of space, the elimination of conversion between internal and character coding, the ability to access records directly, and the ease of reading and writing large structures. To open a C file in binary mode, we add b to the mode string—"rb", "wb", "ab", "r+b", "w+b", or "a+b". With a binary file, we can read one record or an array of records all at once with a call to *fread*, such as

```
fread(&EmployeeRec, sizeof(employee_t), 1, employ_ptr);
```

or

```
fread(EmployeeArray, sizeof(employee_t), NumEls, employ_ptr);
```

The arguments are the starting address of the area of memory to receive the data, the number of bytes in the item to be read, the number of data to be read, and the file pointer. The function returns the number of items it successfully reads. Thus, we can use a positive return value as a condition to continue executing a *while* loop that is processing an entire binary file as follows:

```
while(fread(&EmployeeRec, sizeof(employee_t), 1, employ_ptr))...
```

To store information from the computer's memory into the binary file, we use *fwrite* and arguments that correspond to those of *fread*. Thus, we could write an employee record to this file with

```
fwrite(&EmployeeRec, sizeof(employee_t), 1, employ_ptr);
```

or an array with

```
fwrite(EmployeeArray, sizeof(employee_t), NumEls, employ_ptr);
```

Random access or direct access files, which are almost always binary files, can be written to or read from by specifying the exact location where the operation is to occur. We use the C library function *fseek* to seek a specific position or location in the file. This function manipulates the file position marker. The *fseek* function takes the following three arguments: The *FILE* pointer of an (open) file; a long integer indicating the position in number of bytes from a specific location; and one of three integers indicating the specific location—0 (*SEEK_SET*) for the beginning of the file, 1 (*SEEK_CUR*) for the current position, or 2 (*SEEK_END*) for the end of the file. The statement

```
fseek(fp, 5L, SEEK_SET);
```

positions the file associated with *fp* to the sixth byte of the file. The statement

```
fseek(fp, 2L, SEEK_CUR);
```

skips ahead two bytes in the file to position 7, whereas

```
fseek(fp, -2L, SEEK_CUR);
```

moves back two bytes. The statement

```
fseek(fp, 4L, SEEK_END);
```

positions the file to the fourth byte from the end of the file. The statement

```
fseek(file_ptr, (long)id * sizeof(record_t), SEEK_SET)
```

moves the file position marker to record number *id*, where *file_ptr* is the file pointer for a binary file of records of type *record_t*. If *fseek* finds the file location, the function returns 0. Otherwise, it returns a nonzero value.

The function *ftell* returns the current *long int* position of the file, such as

```
WhichByte = ftell(fp);
```

If *size* is a *long int,* the statements

```
fseek(fp, 0L, SEEK_END);
size = ftell(fp);
```

result in *size* containing the number of bytes in the file.

Review Questions

1. Under what circumstances is a file more useful than an array?
2. What kind of information is generally associated with the screen? With the keyboard?
3. What three files are automatically associated with every C program?
4. What is the major difference between the end of a string and the end of a file?
5. Are the words "input" and "output" keywords in C?
6. What is the effect of trying to write to the keyboard, an input device?
7. What is append mode, and what letter is used to specify it?
8. How does write mode differ from append mode when an existing file is being written to?
9. How do you indicate a binary file?
10. In what sense is a disk a direct access device?
11. What role does the *fseek* function play, and how many arguments does it have?
12. If the ANSI C library did not contain a *rewind* function, how could we implement it?
13. What is the significance of the "w+" mode string?
14. Give a statement to read a record, *rec,* of type *record_t* from a random access file pointed to by *fp.*
15. Give a statement to write a record, *rec,* of type *record_t* from a random access file pointed to by *fp.*
16. What does the *ftell* function do, and what is one of its most common uses?
17. What does the "r+" mode string accomplish, and how does it work?
18. What is special about "a+" mode?

Laboratory

The purpose of this laboratory is to give experience in maintaining a program and working in teams. The laboratory has two versions—one that extends the CPU simulator from Chapter 12's Laboratory, and one that extends the stock portfolio program from Chapter 11's Laboratory.

Quite often after working with a program, such as the simulator or stock portfolio program, users request additional features and improvements. You should generate a new version of one of these programs. Form a three- or four-person team to perform the desired modifications. Carefully design each modification, document accurately, and test thoroughly. Internal documentation should include the date and author of each modification or addition, a precise description of the change, and the reason(s) for the alteration. After unit testing each module, perform system testing. Keep careful records of all unit and system tests and their results. (We use this material in Chapter 15's Laboratory.)

CPU Simulator

Section 12.7 presented a hypothetical CPU with a corresponding machine language. The exercises of Section 12.7 and the Laboratory from Chapter 12 covered writing machine language programs for this simulator.

Your text disk contains C program and header files that simulate the actions of such a computer. These source files are as follows:

cpusim.c: source code file for the main routine

cpu.c: source code for the CPU and associated operations

mem.c: source code for simulated memory services

cpusim.h: header file for the entire simulator

cpu.h: header file for the CPU source

simem.h: header file for the memory source

The program is organized as follows:

1. *main* parses the command-line options and calls the program loader. It checks for invalid options and the return code from the program loader. Options specify the program's output. If everything is valid, it runs the program, dumping output according to the specified options.

2. *mem.c* declares the memory segment and contains the memory operations. It has two basic operations—*MemoryFetch,* to get a word from memory, and *Memory-Write,* to place a word into memory. This file also contains the program loader, *LoadProgram,* and an output routine, *DumpMemory,* to dump the contents of memory to standard output.

3. *cpu.c* declares the CPU itself and the related CPU operations, including routines like *LoadIR* to load the instruction register; *AddToAC,* one of the CPU operations; and *GetOpcode,* one of the two instruction decoders. It also contains a procedure to dump the registers to standard output.

Figure 14.14 contains the structure chart for the program. The code appears after the exercises. Modify the simulator as follows:

1. Extend the instruction set to include a No-op instruction (NOP) with opcode 9 that does not do anything. Such an instruction is useful as filler when revising a program. For example, suppose we have a machine language program that contains the following statements at memory addresses 1 and 2:

```
220    ;LDA 20     AC <- Memory[20]
704    ;BRAN 4     if AC < 0, then PC <- 4
```

Should we revise this program and eliminate the 220 instruction, we probably need to change the branch address to 3. To avoid adjusting this and other address references, we can replace the LDA instruction with a NOP, such as

```
900    ;NOP        no operation
704    ;BRAN 4     if AC < 0, then PC <- 4
```

Any integer can follow the opcode of 9, so that the machine and assembler instructions and meaning are as follows:

   9xx   **;NOP**   **no operation**

2. Extend the instruction set to include a multiply operation (MULT) with opcode 10 to multiply a value from memory times the AC. The machine and assembler instructions and meaning are as follows:

   10*loc*   **;MULT *loc*** $AC \leftarrow AC * Memory[loc]$

Figure 14.14   Structure chart for CPU simulator

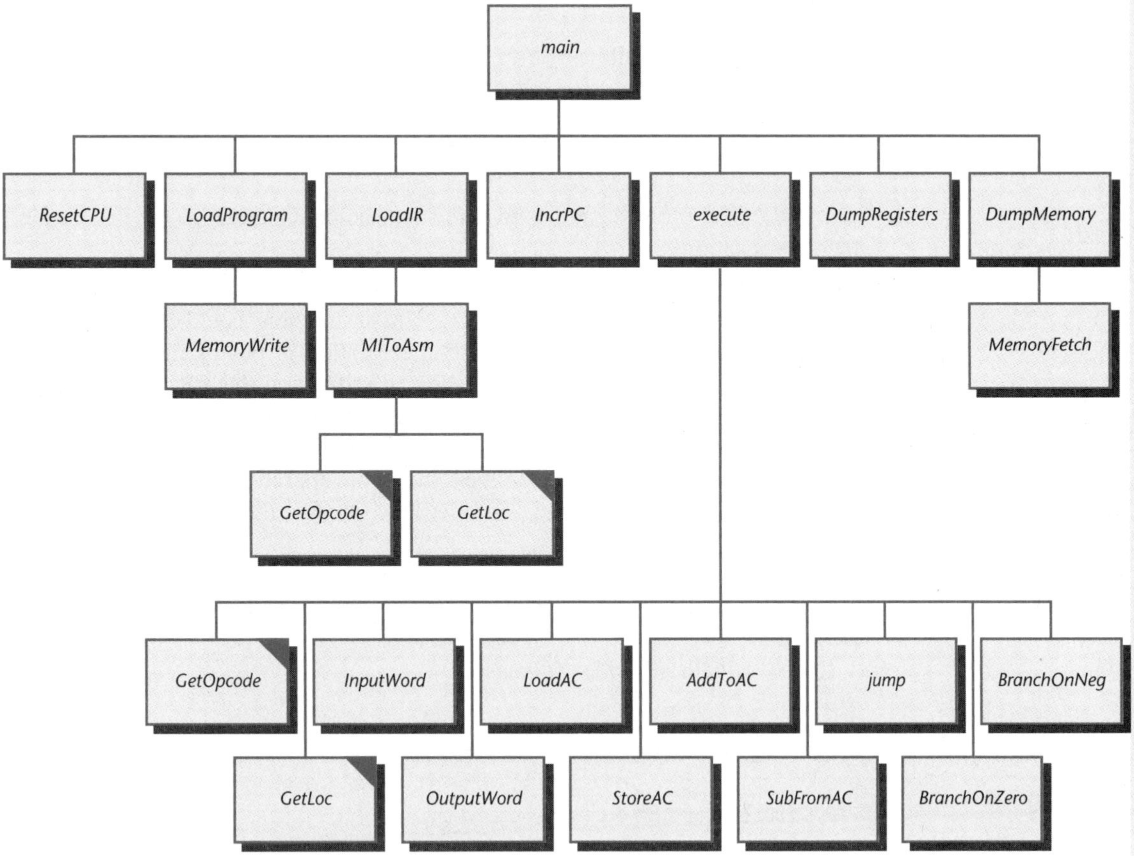

For example, suppose AC contains 845 and memory location 21 contains 5. After execution of

```
1021
```

AC contains 845 * 5 or 4225.

3. Extend the instruction set to include an integer division operation (DIV) with opcode 11 to divide a value from memory into the AC, yielding the integer quotient. The machine and assembler instructions and meaning are as follows:

11*loc*   **;DIV** *loc*   **AC** ← **AC** / *Memory*[*loc*]

For example, suppose AC contains 845 and memory location 21 contains 10. After execution of

```
1121
```

AC contains 845 / 10 or 84.

4. Extend the instruction set to include a load immediate operation (LDI) with opcode 12. The integer to the right of the opcode is the data word to be loaded into the AC. The machine and assembler instructions and meaning are as follows:

12*data*   **;LDI** *data*   **AC** ← *data*

For example, the instruction

```
1237
```

loads the constant 37 into AC.

5. Extend the instruction set to include a branch positive instruction (BRAP) with opcode 13. If the AC is positive, then the simulator continues execution at the memory location listed after the opcode. The machine and assembler instructions and meaning are as follows:

   13*loc*   ;**BRAP** *loc*   if $AC \geq 0$, then $PC \leftarrow loc$

   For example, the instruction

   ```
   1308
   ```

   tests the AC. If the value is positive, then execution continues at the instruction in memory location 8.

6. Add an error register (ER) to the CPU and implement address range checking in the memory routines. That is, each fetch and write instruction should check the location and set (make 1) the error register if the location is out of range. Extend the instruction set to include an On-Error Branch instruction (ONER) with opcode 14. The machine and assembler instructions and meaning are as follows:

   14*loc*   ;**ONER** *loc*   if $ER == 1$, then $PC \leftarrow loc$

   If the error register contains 1, then the simulator continues execution at the memory location listed after the opcode. For example, the instruction

   ```
   1408
   ```

   tests the ER. If the value is 1, then execution continues at the instruction in memory location 8.

   Code for the header files follows:

```
/*
 * File:       cpusim.h
 * Content:    type definitions, constants, and so forth for the
 *      CPU Simulator program--cpusim.
 */

#ifndef CPUSIM_H
#define CPUSIM_H

typedef enum {FALSE = 0, TRUE} boolean_t;
typedef unsigned int  addr_t;         /* address data type    */
typedef int           word_t;         /* word data type       */
typedef int           register_t;     /* register data type   */

typedef struct {
    register_t PC;      /* program counter      */
    register_t IR;      /* instruction register */
    register_t AC;      /* accumulator          */
} CPU_t;

#endif
```

```
/*
 * File:       simem.h
 * Content:    type definitions, constants, and so forth for the
 *      CPU Simulator program's memory operations.
 */

#include "cpusim.h"
```

```
#ifndef MEMORY_H
#define MEMORY_H

#define SEG_SIZE    10
#define MEM_SIZE    (4 * SEG_SIZE)

void      DumpMemory (   void           );
boolean_t LoadProgram(   char*          );
void      MemoryFetch(   addr_t, word_t* );
void      MemoryWrite(   word_t, addr_t  );

#endif
```

```
/*
 * File:       cpu.h
 * Content:    function prototypes and symbolic constant definitions
 *      for CPU operations.
 */

#ifndef CPU_H
#define CPU_H

#define IN     0
#define OUT    1
#define LDA    2
#define STA    3
#define ADD    4
#define SUBT   5
#define JUMP   6
#define BRAN   7
#define BRAZ   8
#define HALT  99

void   AddToAC       ( addr_t );
void   BranchOnNeg   ( addr_t );
void   BranchOnZero  ( addr_t );
void   DumpRegisters ( void );
void   execute       ( boolean_t* );
word_t GetLoc        ( word_t );
word_t GetOpcode     ( word_t );
void   IncrPC        ( void );
void   MlToAsm       ( word_t, char* );
void   jump          ( addr_t );
void   LoadAC        ( addr_t );
void   LoadIR        ( void );
void   ResetCPU      ( void );
void   StoreAC       ( addr_t );
void   SubFromAC     ( addr_t );
void   InputWord     ( addr_t );
void   OutputWord    ( addr_t );

#endif
```

The program files containing function definitions follow:*

```
/*
 * File:       cpusim.c
 * Content:    ANSI C source code for CPU Simulator--cpusim.
 * Usage:      cpusim [-v | -m | -r [-s]] progfile
 *      -v: verbose output, display memory and CPU registers.
 *      -m: memory output, display memory only.
 *      -r: register output, display CPU registers only.
 *      -s: run output in single-step mode.
 *      progfile: name of program file
 * Logic:
 *   initialize output flags
 *   load program into memory
 *   reset CPU
 *   set run flag to true
 *   while run flag is true
 *       load instruction register
 *       increment program counter
 *       execute
 */

#include <stdio.h>
#include "cpusim.h"
#include "cpu.h"
#include "simem.h"
/*
 * for THINK C uncomment the following #include
 * #include <console.h>
 */
int main( int argc, char *argv[] )
{
    /*
     * The following flags determine the simulator's output
     * mode and indicate the occurrence of certain errors:
     * MemoryFlag is TRUE if the user wants memory dumped,
     * ProgramLoaded is TRUE if the program loads OK,
     * RegisterFlag is TRUE if the user wants the registers dumped,
     * SingleStep is TRUE if the user wants single-step mode,
     * UsageError is TRUE if a usage error is detected,
     * VerboseFlag is TRUE if the user wants memory and registers
     * dumped.
     */
    boolean_t  MemoryFlag    = FALSE;
    boolean_t  ProgramLoaded = FALSE;
    boolean_t  RegisterFlag  = FALSE;
```

---

*For THINK C, uncomment the preprocessor directive *#include <console.h>* and the assignment *argc = ccommand (&argv);*

```
boolean_t  SingleStep    = FALSE;
boolean_t  UsageError     = FALSE;
boolean_t  VerboseFlag    = FALSE;
/* for THINK C uncomment the following assignment */
/* argc = ccommand(&argv);                        */
/*
 * Parse the command line. argv[0] is always the program
 * name. argv[ argc - 1 ] is always the program filename
 * (according to the program's syntax). If the argc is > 2,
 * the user provided one or two options. In this case, argv[1]
 * is always "-m", "-r", or "-v". If the argc is 4, then argv[2]
 * is "-s".
 */
switch( argc ) {
case 4: /*
        * Check the -s option (argv[2]) and then
        * fall through to check -v, -m, or -r.
        */
    switch( argv[2][1] ) {
    case 's' : SingleStep = TRUE; break;
    default  : UsageError = TRUE; break;
    }
    /* BREAK OMITTED */

case 3: /*
        * Check for -v, -m, or -r and then fall through
        * to load the program file.
        */
    switch( argv[1][1] ) {
    case 'v' : VerboseFlag =  TRUE; break;
    case 'm' : MemoryFlag =   TRUE; break;
    case 'r' : RegisterFlag = TRUE; break;
    default  : UsageError =   TRUE; break;
    }
    /* BREAK OMITTED */
case 2: /* Load the program file argv[argc - 1]. */
        ProgramLoaded = LoadProgram( argv[ argc - 1 ] );
        break;
default: /* Any other argc is a usage error. */
        UsageError = TRUE;
}

if( !UsageError && ProgramLoaded )
{
    /*
     * There is no usage error and the program loaded
     * OK. Set the run flag to TRUE, reset the CPU and
     * run the program flag.
     */
```

```
            boolean_t RunFlag = TRUE;
            ResetCPU();

            while( RunFlag )
            {
                /*
                 * Load the next instruction, increment the program counter,
                 * execute the loaded instruction.
                 */
                LoadIR();
                IncrPC();
                execute( &RunFlag );

                /* Check the output flags and print appropriate stuff. */
                if( RegisterFlag || VerboseFlag )
                    DumpRegisters();
                if( MemoryFlag || VerboseFlag )
                    DumpMemory();

                /* If user wants single step, wait for user input. */
                if( SingleStep )
                {
                    char InputLine[ BUFSIZ ];
                    gets( InputLine );
                }
            }
        }
        else
        {
            /* Usage error or error loading program file. */
            if( UsageError )
            {
                printf( "usage: %s [-v|-m|-r [-s]] progfile\n",
                    argv[0] );
            }
            else
            {
                printf("%s: error loading program file, halt.\n",
                    argv[0] );
            }
        }
        return 0;
    }

/*
 * File:    mem.c
 * Content:ANSI C source code for the CPU simulator's memory
 *      operations. This includes the program loader procedure
 *      since programs are loaded directly into (simulated) memory.
 */
```

```c
#include <stdio.h>
#include <stdlib.h>
#include <string.h>
#include <ctype.h>
#include "cpusim.h"
#include "simem.h"

/*
 * The simulated memory segment.
 */

static word_t memory[ MEM_SIZE ];

/*
 * Print the contents of the memory segment.
 */

void DumpMemory( void )
{
    register i, j;
    word_t tmp;
    printf( "Addr     +00     +01     +02     +03     +04     +05     " );
    printf( "+06     +07     +08     +09\n" );
    printf( "----------------------------------------------------------" );
    printf( "--------------------\n" );

    /* Loop through memory in 10 word segments. */
    for( i = 0; i < (MEM_SIZE / SEG_SIZE); ++i )
    {
        /*
         * Print the current segment's base address and then
         * loop through the segment printing the contents of
         * each word.   (%4.4d to print leading zeros.)
         */
        printf( "%4.4d:  ", i * 10 );
        for( j = 0; j < SEG_SIZE; ++j )
        {
            MemoryFetch( (addr_t) (i * SEG_SIZE + j), &tmp );
            printf( "%5.5d ", tmp );
        }
        printf( "\n" );
    }
    printf( "----------------------------------------------------------" );
    printf( "--------------------\n" );
}

/*
 * Read a program from the specified file directly into memory.
 * Pre:   ProgFilename is the name of the program file on disk.
 * Post:  Program has been read into memory and TRUE returned
 *        or FALSE if unsuccessful.
 */
```

```
boolean_t LoadProgram( char* ProgFilename )
{
    addr_t      loc;
    word_t      data;
    char        InputLine[ BUFSIZ ]; /* buffer for program lines   */
    FILE        *ProgFile;           /* program file pointer        */
    boolean_t rc = TRUE;             /* return code: TRUE by default */

    ProgFile = fopen( ProgFilename , "r" );
    if( ProgFile )
    {
        /*
         * Opened the file--set the starting address to
         * 0 and process each line in the file. The format
         * of a program line is INSTR [COMMENT]
         * where INSTR is a decimal number string and COMMENT
         * (optional) is any string following INSTR. Any line
         * that is blank or that starts with something other
         * than a decimal number string is treated as a comment.
         */
        loc = (addr_t) 0;
        while( fgets(InputLine, (BUFSIZ, ProgFile) )
        {
            /*
             * atoi is called to convert the decimal
             * number string into a word (integer) value.
             * If the line is empty or if the line starts with
             * something other than a decimal number string,
             * the line is skipped
             */
            if( strlen(InputLine) > 0 && isdigit(InputLine[0]) )
            {
                data = atoi(InputLine);
                MemoryWrite( data, loc );
                ++loc;
            }
        }
    }
    else /* Failed to open the program file. */
        rc = FALSE;

    return rc;
}

/*
 * Fetch the word from memory at address and store it in destination.
 * Pre:    loc is the address of a word in memory.
 *         memory is a global array.
 * Post:   destination, the contents of that location, has been returned.
 */
```

```c
void MemoryFetch( addr_t loc, word_t* destination )
{
    *destination = memory[ loc ];
}

/*
 * Store data in memory at address.
 * Pre:    data is of type word_t.
 *         word is the address of a word in memory.
 *         memory is a global array.
 * Post:   Location loc in memory contains data.
 */

void MemoryWrite( word_t data, addr_t loc )
{
    memory[ loc ] = data;
}
```

```c
/*
 * File:    cpu.c
 * Content:    ANSI C source code for CPU Simulator's CPU and associated
 *       operations.
 */

#include <stdio.h>
#include <stdlib.h>
#include <string.h>
#include <ctype.h>
#include "cpusim.h"
#include "cpu.h"
#include "simem.h"

/*
 * The strings contained in the following array correspond to
 * the instructions themselves--an instruction value is used as
 * an index into the array in order to access the appropriate
 * assembler string. The instruction values are defined in the
 * header file cpu.h.
 */

static char *AsmStrings[] = {
    "IN","OUT","LDA","STA","ADD","SUBT","JUMP","BRAN","BRAZ"
};

/*
 * The CPU data structure.
 */

static CPU_t CPU;
```

```
/*
 * Add contents of location to accumulator.
 * Pre:    loc is the address of a word in memory.
 *         CPU is a global structure with member AC.
 * Post:   The contents of memory location loc has been added to AC.
 */

void AddToAC( addr_t loc )
{
    word_t tmp;
    MemoryFetch( loc, &tmp );
    CPU.AC += tmp;
}


/*
 * Branch to location if accumulator less than zero.
 * Pre:    loc is the address of a word in memory.
 *         CPU is a global structure with members AC and PC.
 * Post:   If AC is negative, PC has been changed to loc.
 */

void BranchOnNeg( addr_t loc )
{
    if( CPU.AC < (word_t) 0 )
        CPU.PC = loc;
}


/*
 * Branch to location if accumulator equals zero.
 * Pre:    loc is the address of a word in memory.
 *         CPU is a global structure with members AC and PC.
 * Post:   If AC is zero, PC has been changed to loc.
 */

void BranchOnZero( addr_t loc )
{
    if( CPU.AC == (word_t) 0 )
        CPU.PC = loc;
}


/*
 * Print contents of CPU registers.
 * Pre:    CPU is a global structure with members AC, IR, and PC.
 * Post:   The contents of AC, IR, and PC have been printed.
 */

void DumpRegisters( void )
{
    char AsmString[ BUFSIZ ];

    MlToAsm( CPU.IR, AsmString );
```

```
        printf( "PC:  %4.4d\tIR:  %4.4d  (%s)\tAC:  %4.4d\n",
            CPU.PC, CPU.IR, AsmString, CPU.AC );
}


/*
 * Execute the instruction contained in the instruction register.
 * Pre:  CPU is a global structure with member IR.
 * Post: The instruction in IR has been executed.
 *       RunFlag has been set to FALSE if the instruction is halt.
 */

void execute( boolean_t* RunFlag )
{
    word_t opcode = GetOpcode( CPU.IR );
    addr_t loc    = GetLoc( CPU.IR );

    /*
     * Select the appropriate operation based on the op code.
     * There is no halt operation, so set the
     * run flag to FALSE when the halt instruction is reached.
     * If the op code is invalid, output an error message and halt.
     */
    switch( opcode ) {
    case IN    : InputWord( loc );      break;
    case OUT   : OutputWord( loc );     break;
    case LDA   : LoadAC( loc );         break;
    case STA   : StoreAC( loc );        break;
    case ADD   : AddToAC( loc );        break;
    case SUBT  : SubFromAC( loc );      break;
    case JUMP  : jump( loc );           break;
    case BRAN  : BranchOnNeg( loc );    break;
    case BRAZ  : BranchOnZero( loc );   break;
    case HALT  : *RunFlag = FALSE;      break;
    default    : printf( "Invalid opcode, execution halted.\n" );
                 *RunFlag = FALSE;
    }
}


/*
 * Decode the location (address) portion of an instruction.
 * Pre:   instr is an instruction.
 * Post:  The location portion has been returned.
 */

word_t GetLoc( word_t instr )
{
    return instr % 100;
}
```

```
/*
 * Decode the opcode portion of an instruction.
 * Pre:    instr is an instruction.
 * Post:   The opcode portion has been returned.
 */

word_t GetOpcode( word_t instr )
{
    return instr / 100;
}

/*
 * Increment the program counter.
 * Pre:    CPU is a global structure with member PC.
 * Post:   PC has been incremented.
 */

void IncrPC( void )
{
    ++CPU.PC;
}

/*
 * Decode a machine language instruction
 * and produce the assembler language representation.
 * Pre:    instr is an instruction.
 *         AsmStrings is a global array of assembler mnemonics.
 * Post:   AsmString is the assembler language representation of
 *         the instruction.
 */

void MlToAsm( word_t instr, char* AsmString )
{
    word_t opcode = GetOpcode( instr );
    addr_t loc    = GetLoc( instr );

    /*
     * sprintf is C print-to-string instruction. The result of the
     * "print" is stored in AsmString instead of being displayed.
     */
    sprintf( AsmString,
        "%s %4.4d",
        opcode == HALT ? "HALT" : AsmStrings[ opcode ],
        loc );
}

/*
 * Unconditional branch to location.
 * Pre:    loc is the address of a word in memory.
 *         CPU is a global structure with member PC.
 * Post:   PC has been changed to loc.
 */
```

```
void jump( addr_t loc )
{
    CPU.PC = loc;
}


/*
 * Load accumulator with contents of location.
 * Pre:   loc is the address of a word in memory.
 *        CPU is a global structure with member AC.
 * Post:  AC has the contents of memory location loc.
 */

void LoadAC( addr_t loc )
{
    MemoryFetch( loc, &CPU.AC );
}


/*
 * Load instruction register with contents of the
 * location indicated by the program counter.
 * Pre:   CPU is a global structure with members PC and IR.
 * Post:  IR has the instruction at memory location PC.
 */

void LoadIR( void )
{
    MemoryFetch( CPU.PC, &CPU.IR );
}

/*
 * Reset the CPU.
 * Pre:   CPU is a global structure with members AC, PC, and IR.
 * Post:  AC, PC, and IR are 0.
 */

void ResetCPU( void )
{
    CPU.PC = (addr_t) 0;
    CPU.IR = (word_t) 0;
    CPU.AC = (word_t) 0;
}

/*
 * Store contents of AC to location.
 * Pre:   loc is the address of a word in memory.
 *        CPU is a global structure with member AC.
 * Post:  Memory location loc contains AC.
 */
```

```
void StoreAC( addr_t loc )
{
    MemoryWrite( CPU.AC, loc );
}


/*
 * Subtract contents at location from accumulator.
 * Pre:  loc is the address of a word in memory.
 *       CPU is a global structure with member AC.
 * Post: The contents of memory location loc were subtracted from AC.
 */

void SubFromAC( addr_t loc )
{
    word_t tmp;
    MemoryFetch( loc, &tmp );
    CPU.AC -= tmp;
}


/*
 * Input word from keyboard and store at location.
 * Pre:  loc is the address of a word in memory.
 * Post: The keyboard input has been stored in memory location loc.
 */

void InputWord( addr_t loc )
{
    char   InString[ BUFSIZ ];
    word_t tmp = (word_t) 0;
    /*
     * Prompt with a question mark and read a string from standard
     * input. Convert the string to an integer value and store it
     * in tmp--tmp is 0 by default so any string that does not start
     * with a decimal number string is effectively converted to 0.
     * Store tmp into memory.
     */

    printf( "? " );
    gets( InString );
    tmp = atoi( InString );
    MemoryWrite( tmp, loc );
}


/*
 * Output word at address to screen.
 * Pre:   loc is the address of a word in memory.
 * Post:  The contents of memory location loc has been printed.
 */
```

```
void OutputWord( addr_t loc )
{
    word_t tmp;
    MemoryFetch( loc, &tmp );
    printf( "%d\n", tmp );
}
```

Stock Portfolio Program

Use a completed copy of Laboratory 11 as a starting point. Modify the stock portfolio as follows:

1. Change the disk file format from text file to binary file. Modify the *SaveFile* routine to save a binary file of stock records. Then modify *LoadFile* to read a binary file of stock records.

2. Modify *LoadFile* and *Quit* so the program warns the user that the current portfolio will be lost if it has changed since the last save. Allow the user to continue or return to the main menu. Maintain a global boolean variable *modified* that is initially set to *FALSE* and set to *FALSE* each time a new file is loaded or saved. Each time the portfolio is changed, set *modified* to *TRUE*.

3. Modify the *listing* routine for screen control. Pause for each 20 lines of output and display the message "Press return to continue".

4. Add a sort routine that sorts the array of records alphabetically on ticker symbol. The *listing* routine should sort the array of records each time before listing to provide a sorted display.

5. Make the program "crash proof." Write a function *GetFloat* repeatedly to prompt and read a floating point number as a string until a valid input is obtained (see Section 10.4).

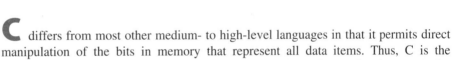

Binary Operations

Introduction

C differs from most other medium- to high-level languages in that it permits direct manipulation of the bits in memory that represent all data items. Thus, C is the preferred language of systems programmers who write software for the users of a computer system. Systems programmers develop the operating systems, compilers, and utilities for computers. They frequently need to manipulate data on the bit level.

C provides a full range of operators for this purpose. For example, bitwise logical operators correspond to the logical operators, OR (||), AND (&&), and NOT (!). The bitwise operators, however, perform their operations on each individual bit of their operand(s). With a technique called masking, we can change any particular bit in a byte. The shift operators move bit patterns to the right or to the left, allowing us to extract particular bits or to perform certain computations quickly.

In the breadth sections, we connect these low-level operations with the hardware logic components of the computer. Corresponding to the three bitwise logical operators are the three basic parts to a logic circuit—the OR gate, the AND gate, and the inverter. These three gates are the building blocks of electronic circuitry. For example, using these gates, we can build a circuit that performs addition or computes the parity bit.

Goals

To study

- Bitwise operators
- Logic gates
- Logic circuits

895

Section 15.1 **Bitwise Operators**

The computer represents all values in memory as binary numbers. In the binary representation of integers, the rightmost bit represents the ones place, the next represents twos, the next fours, then eights, and so forth. From right to left, each bit represents a successively higher power of 2 (see Section 2.4). For example, the binary number 1101 represents the following in decimal:

$$1 \cdot 2^3 + 1 \cdot 2^2 + 0 \cdot 2^1 + 1 \cdot 2^0 = 1 \cdot 8 + 1 \cdot 4 + 0 \cdot 2 + 1 \cdot 1$$

which equals 13. In bit parlance, a **set bit** is one that has the value 1, whereas a **clear bit** has the value 0.

Definitions   A **set bit** is a bit that has the value 1. A **clear bit** is a bit that has the value 0.

In some previous programs, we have used variables as flags that store the value *TRUE* or *FALSE* as a nonzero integer or zero, respectively. We can also represent a truth value by a single bit, rather than by the eight (or more) bits that make up a C variable. If the bit is 0, it indicates a value of *FALSE,* and if it is 1, it represents *TRUE.* Even if a *char* variable is used as a boolean flag, all but one of the bits making up that variable are wasted. Programs that use many flags usually pack these flags economically eight per byte. Structures make use of this facility to minimize their size. For example, in the *FILE* structure that represents an open file, one member contains flag bits that represent various features or states of the file. Among the flags, one flag indicates whether the file is binary or not, and another determines if *EOF* is true. A bit set to 1 means that the feature or state applies to the file.

Bitwise AND and OR Operators

If eight flags are packed into a byte, we should be able to manipulate one bit without affecting the others. To do this, we use the bitwise logical operators. Two of these operators have symbols & and |, which represent the **bitwise AND** and **OR** operations, respectively. The same symbols are used in the logical operators (&& and ||) of conditional expressions, but their roles are different. The logical operators test the truth values of two variables and produce a value of *TRUE* or *FALSE,* whereas the bitwise operators perform their operations on each individual bit of their operands.

We can use the bitwise operators on any integer-compatible scalar variable, but for ease of explanation we confine ourselves to eight-bit *char* variables. Suppose the variables *a* and *b* have the values 7 and 12, respectively. The binary representations of these variables are as follows:

```
a:  0 0 0 0 0 1 1 1
b:  0 0 0 0 1 1 0 0
```

If we then execute the statement

```
c = a & b;
```

each bit in *c* is the result of ANDing the corresponding bits of *a* and *b*. As with &&, an AND operation returns a true result only if both of its operands are true. Table 15.1 presents the truth table for &, which is analogous to Table 3.1 for && with 0 substituting for F and 1 for T. Therefore, a bit in *c* has the value 1 only if the corresponding bits of both *a* and *b* are 1. The bit patterns are as follows:

Table 15.1
Truth table for
p & q, where p
and q are bits

p	q	p & q
0	0	0
0	1	0
1	0	0
1	1	1

Table 15.2
Truth table for
$p \mid q$, for bits p
and q

p	q	$p \mid q$
0	0	0
0	1	1
1	0	1
1	1	1

```
a:         0 0 0 0 0 1 1 1
b:         0 0 0 0 1 1 0 0
_____
a & b:     0 0 0 0 0 1 0 0
```

In the calculation, all the bits in a single column are corresponding bits. Only one column, the third from the right, contains bits with the value 1 for both a and b. Therefore, only one bit of c, the third from the right, has the value 1. If we interpret c as an integer, it has the decimal value 4, but on that level, no apparent connection exists between the values of a (7) and b (12) and the result, c (4). The bitwise AND operation has meaning only on the bit level.

The rules for the bitwise OR operation state that the result is 1 if either operand is 1 (or if both are 1). Thus, Table 15.2 for the bitwise OR operation coincides with Table 3.2 for the logical OR operation with the correspondences F $\leftrightarrow$ 0 and T $\leftrightarrow$ 1.

Therefore, suppose we execute the statement

```
c = a | b;
```

The result is

```
a:         0 0 0 0 0 1 1 1
b:         0 0 0 0 1 1 0 0
_____
a | b:     0 0 0 0 1 1 1 1
```

A bit in c becomes 1 if either of the corresponding bits of a and b is set. Any column that has a 1 bit for a or b also has a 1 bit for c. The integer representation for c in this case is 15.

Masks

We can now approach the question of how to set a single bit in a variable. Suppose our goal is to assign to c the bit pattern in a (0000 0111), but with the fourth bit from the right set (0000 1111). We do this by using b, whose bits are all clear except for the fourth from the right, which is set (0000 1000). When we OR this variable with the value of a, the clear bits in b have no effect on the result. The result of ORing any value with zero is the original value. For example, 0 | 0 = 0 and 1 | 0 = 1. The set bit in b, however, ensures that the corresponding bit in c is always set. Thus, to set the fourth bit from the right in a, we perform the following bitwise operation:

```
a:         0 0 0 0 0 1 1 1
b:         0 0 0 0 1 0 0 0
_____
a | b:     0 0 0 0 1 1 1 1
```

If the bit in *a* corresponding to the set bit in *b* is already 1, then no change takes place. For example, 0 | 1 == 1 and 1 | 1 == 1. Thus, with *a* being 0010 1101, we have

```
a:        0 0 1 0 1 1 0 1
b:        0 0 0 0 1 0 0 0
        _____

a | b:    0 0 1 0 1 1 0 1
```

In this case, *a* | *b* == *a*.

Variables such as *b* are **masks**, because they selectively mask or filter the bits of another variable, allowing some of the bits to remain unaffected while changing others. Usually the mask is a constant value, because the programmer knows which bits to set. Consider the following statement:

```
a |= 0x08;
```

where the number to the right of the |= operator is in hexadecimal notation (see Section 7.4). This statement is equivalent to

```
a = a | 0x08;
```

because |= is an updating assignment operator. (Notice that logical operators are commutative, meaning that *a* | 0x08 is the same as 0x08 | *a*.) The mask 0x08 is the same value (0000 1000) as in *b* from the previous computation, only represented as a hexadecimal constant. The statement sets the fourth bit from the right in *a*. If *a* contains eight flags, then this operation sets the fourth flag from the right to the value *TRUE* (regardless of its original value).

C programmers use hexadecimal or octal notation for masks more frequently than decimal because they more directly reflect bit patterns than does decimal notation. For example, if we start with the bit pattern

```
10011010
```

and then divide it into two groups, each containing four bits, we can readily convert the result to hexadecimal as follows:

```
1001 1010
  9    A
```

This bit pattern is 0x9A in hex. To represent the pattern in octal, we split the bits into groups of three instead. The octal equivalent is assigned to each group, as shown:

```
10 011 010
2   3   2
```

We start the grouping from the right, so the leftmost group only contains two bits. The result is the octal representation 0232. By the reverse process, we can convert the octal and hexadecimal representations into binary much more easily than converting the decimal representation, which is 154 (or -66 if the byte represents a signed value).

Another disadvantage of decimal notation for bit patterns is that the sign must be specified. If we assign a bit pattern to a *char* variable, for example, any pattern in which the leftmost bit is set represents a negative number, unless we declare the variable to be an *unsigned char*. If decimal notation is used, the signed representation must be employed. When the constant is specified in octal or hex notation, however, a sign is never needed, and this complication is avoided.

Example 15.1

We can easily extend the method of setting a single bit to setting several bits at once. For example, to set both the fourth bit from the right and the rightmost bit in *a,* leaving the remaining bits intact, we OR *a* with the bit pattern 0000 1001, 0x09. Thus, if *a* is 0010 0101, we have

```
a:           0 0 1 0 0 1 0 1
mask:        0 0 0 0 1 0 0 1
```

```
a | mask:    0 0 1 0 1 1 0 1
```

The statement in C is

```
a |= 0x09;
```

To clear a single bit, we use the bitwise & operator. When we AND any bit with a zero bit, the result is zero (because the AND operation is true only when both operands are true). Thus, $0 \And 0 == 0$ and $1 \And 0 == 0$. When we AND a bit with 1, the result is the value of the original bit—$0 \And 1 == 0$ and $1 \And 1 == 1$.

> To set a bit, we use the bitwise | operator with a mask containing 1 in the corresponding position and zeros elsewhere. To clear a bit, we use the bitwise & operator with a mask containing 0 in the corresponding position and ones elsewhere.

Example 15.2

We again make use of the variable *a,* which contains the bit pattern 0010 1101. Suppose we wish to clear the third bit from the left, obtaining 0000 1101. Thus, we AND *a* with a mask that has 1 in every position, except the third from the left.

```
a:           0 0 1 0   1 1 0 1
mask:        1 1 0 1   1 1 1 1
```

```
a & mask:    0 0 0 0   1 1 0 1
```

The bit pattern 1101 1111 is the hexadecimal constant 0xDF. Thus, we use the operation

```
a &= 0xDF;
```

If the third bit from the left in *a* is already clear, no change occurs, and the new value of *a* is the same as the old one.

If we wish to clear more than one bit, the mask must contain clear bits in all positions corresponding to the ones to clear.

Bitwise NOT Operator

The mask used to clear bits with the bitwise & operator may be somewhat confusing, because it requires a 1 bit for each position that is not to change. We can easily see that the mask 0x20 sets the third bit from the left in a *char* variable using the | operation. It is less obvious, however, that 0xDF contains a clear bit in the third position from the left. To help clarify and expedite matters, we can use the bitwise NOT operator.

The **bitwise NOT operator** or the **one's complement operator** is analogous to the logical NOT (!) operator. This bitwise ~, a tilde, also is a unary operator. When we apply ~ to a value, it flips or complements each bit. In other words, each set bit is cleared, and each clear bit is set. Table 15.3 for ~ corresponds to Table 3.3 for !.

For example, if *a* has the value

```
a:        0 0 1 0  1 1 0 1
```

then the value of ~*a* is

```
~a:       1 1 0 1  0 0 1 0
```

We can complement the bit pattern of *a* with the statement

```
a = ~a;
```

We cannot use the bitwise ~, like the unary negation operator, within an updating assignment operator. The operator ~= does not exist. Updating assignment operators are available only for binary operators.

To make use of the bitwise ~ operator in conjunction with clearing a bit, the programmer first develops a mask with a set bit in each position to be cleared. For example, to clear the first and fourth bits from the left, we use the mask

```
1 0 0 1  0 0 0 0
```

or 0x90. When we apply the bitwise ~ operator to this mask, as in

```
~0x90
```

the resulting bit pattern is as follows:

```
0 1 1 0  1 1 1 1
```

Each bit position we wish to clear contains a 0, and every other position contains a 1. This is the proper mask to use in clearing the first and fourth bits, as in the following statement:

```
a &= ~0x90;
```

> To clear a bit, we use the bitwise & operator with the complement (bitwise ~) of a mask containing 1 in the corresponding position and zeros elsewhere.

EXCLUSIVE OR Operator

The ~ operator can operate only on entire constants or variables, not on individual bits. To complement an individual bit in a variable, we use the **bitwise EXCLUSIVE OR operator**. The EXCLUSIVE OR operation yields *TRUE* if either of its operands is *TRUE*, but not both. We sometimes call the | operator the **inclusive OR**. The bitwise EXCLUSIVE OR operator in C is the caret (^). The truth table for the ^ operation is in Table 15.4. The result of the ^ operation is a 1 bit if and only if the two operand bits

Table 15.3
Truth table for
~*p*, where *p* is
a bit

p	~*p*
0	1
1	0

Table 15.4
Truth table for
p ^ *q*, for bits *p*
and *q*

p	*q*	*p* ^ *q*
0	0	0
0	1	1
1	0	1
1	1	0

are different. Thus, EXCLUSIVE ORing with the bit 1 yields the opposite sign: 0 ^ 1 == 1 and 1 ^ 1 == 0.

Example 15.3

To complement individual bits of a bit pattern, we use the EXCLUSIVE OR operation with a mask containing a set bit in each bit position to be flipped. As an example, let us say *a* has the value 1001 0011, and we wish to flip the first and fifth bits from the left to obtain 0001 1011. The mask is 1000 1000, which in hexadecimal is 0x88. The resulting operation is

```
a:          1 0 0 1   0 0 1 1
mask:       1 0 0 0   1 0 0 0

a ^ mask:   0 0 0 1   1 0 1 1
```

The C statement is

```
a ^= 0x88;
```

> To complement a bit, we use the EXCLUSIVE OR operation (^) with a mask containing 1 in the corresponding position and zeros elsewhere.

Shifting

Two more operations facilitate the manipulation of bit patterns—the **left** and **right** **shift operator**, << and >>, respectively. Sometimes we need to move bit patterns either to the right or to the left for computational purposes or to extract a single bit. Each shift operator has two operands. The left operand is the value to shift (always an integer-compatible type), and the right operand is the number of bit positions by which to shift the value. As an example, suppose *a* has the following value:

```
a:  0 0 1 1   0 1 0 0
```

and we execute the statement

```
b = a >> 1;
```

Each bit of *a* shifts to the right by one bit position. After the leftmost bit shifts right, zero fills its former position. The rightmost bit shifts out completely and vanishes. The result is stored in *b*, and *a* remains unaffected. Thus, *b* gets the value

```
b:  0 0 0 1   1 0 1 0
```

With

```
b = a >> 3;
```

a set bit is lost with *b* obtaining the value

b: **0 0 0** 0   0 1 1 0

Different versions of C handle right shifts differently. Some compilers implement a **logical shift**, in which zeros move into the leftmost positions as in the above example. On other computers, the shift is an **arithmetic shift**. If the variable or constant is a signed integer, the sign bit in the leftmost position propagates to the vacated positions. For example, shifting the pattern

0 1 0 0   1 0 1 0

one bit to the right in an arithmetic shift, yields the same result as a logical shift.

0 0 1 0   0 1 0 1

However, an arithmetic shift one bit to the right in the following pattern:

1 1 0 0   1 0 1 0

copies the 1 bit instead of the 0 bit of the logical shift, as shown:

1 1 1 0   0 1 0 1

Shifting a bit pattern to the left shifts the leftmost bit out the left side, and always shifts a zero bit in from the right. Therefore, with *a* being

a: 0 0 1 1   0 1 0 0

the C statement

```
b = a << 3;
```

gives *b* the value

b: 1 0 1 0   0 **0 0 0**

Either operand of the shift operators can be a constant or a variable. The shift count must be an integer, and the results of the shift are undefined if the shift count is equal to or greater than the number of bits in the value.

Example 15.4

Suppose we wish to extract the third bit from the right from variable *a*, and store it as a 1 or 0 value in another variable, *c*. We are unpacking a flag and storing it in its own individual variable. The statement

```
c = a & 0x4;
```

extracts the correct bit. Because this bit in *c* is the third bit from the right, however, the value of *c* is either 0 or 4, rather than 0 or 1. One solution would be to use an *if* test, but a more elegant (and sometimes faster) method is to shift the value two positions to the right, making the extracted bit the rightmost bit. Thus, we rewrite the preceding statement as

```
c = (a & 0x4) >> 2;
```

In this statement, the shift count, 2, is related to the bit position being extracted.

Example 15.5

To unpack all eight bits of a *char* variable into, say, an array of eight *char* elements, we could perform a series of operations eight times. Extract the rightmost bit by ANDing the variable with 1 (*a* & 0x1), then shift the number right one bit. Performing this manipulation in a loop, the loop index also indexes the destination array. If we extract the bits right-to-left, the loop should count down, as follows:

```
for (i = 7; i >= 0; i--)
{
    c[i] = a & 0x1;
    a >>= 1;
}
```

Thus, if *a* is

a: 0 0 1 1   0 1 0 0

c[7] becomes 0 (0000 0000), and *a* shifts right one position to become

a: 0 0 0 1   1 0 1 0

On the next iteration, *c*[6] also gets the value 0 (0000 0000), and *a* shifts to

a: 0 0 0 0   1 1 0 1

Then *c*[5] becomes 1 (0000 0001), while *a* shifts right again

a: 0 0 0 0   0 1 1 0

This process continues for five more iterations, giving each element of *c* the value 0 or 1. Later, we see how to store such flags in variables that are only one bit in length. In the exercises, we consider extracting the bits from left to right.

> To extract a bit, we shift the value right (>>) so that the bit is in the rightmost position and perform a bitwise & with the mask 0x1.

Example 15.6

Shift operators often are used for multiplication and division by powers of two. Suppose a particular computer stores an integer in two bytes, and *int* variable *n* has the decimal value 76, which in binary is as follows:

num: 0000 0000 0100 1100

To divide this integer by two and obtain 38, we shift the variable right by one bit (*num* >> 1), as shown:

num >> 1:   0000 0000 0010 0110

To divide by four to get 19, we shift *num* right by two bit positions, as follows:

num >> 2:   0000 0000 0001 0011

Another shift right truncates the integer to 9, as follows:

num >> 3:   0000 0000 0000 1001

If the compiler implements the right shift as a logical shift, however, we obtain correct results only if the value is unsigned or positive.

To multiply integers by powers of two, we use the left shift. Thus, *num* (76) times 2 is 152.

num << 1:   0000 0000 1001 1000

This operation produces correct results only if the shift never causes a bit with a value of 1 to shift out the left side creating an overflow situation.

To multiply a positive integer by 2^n, shift the number to the left n positions. To divide a positive integer by 2^n, (logical) shift the number to the right n positions.

The new bitwise operations complete our ongoing precedence of operators in Table 15.5.

Bit Fields

Structures can contain special members, bit fields, whose type is *int* (or *unsigned int*), but whose length is in bits rather than bytes. We specify the number of bits in a structure element by following the name of the element with a colon and a nonnegative integer, which is the bit count. For example, within a structure declaration,

```
unsigned ThreeBits : 3;
```

proclaims *ThreeBits* as a variable of only three bits. The size of a field cannot exceed the number of bits in an *int* variable.

Table 15.5   Precedence of operators in descending order

```
()  []  .   ->
!  ~  -(unary) +(unary) &(address) ++ -- * (indirection) sizeof (type)
*   /   %
+   -   (binary)
<<  >>
<   <=  >   >=
==  !=
&
^
|
&&
||
?:
=   +=  -=  *=  /=  %=  &=  |=  ^=  <<=  >>=
```

We can access and manipulate bit fields in almost the same way as integers. Often, several bit fields are in the same byte. Because individual bits within a byte do not have separate addresses, however, we cannot apply the address (&) operator to bit fields.

The advantage of bit fields is that they force the computer to perform bit packing and unpacking automatically. For example, we can define eight flags as eight one-bit fields in a structure, as follows:

```
struct
{
    unsigned    FirstFlag   : 1,
                SecondFlag  : 1,
                ThirdFlag   : 1,
                FourthFlag  : 1,
                FifthFlag   : 1,
                SixthFlag   : 1,
                SeventhFlag : 1,
                EighthFlag  : 1;
}
pack;
```

Most computers store the eight fields as individual bits of a byte. If we assign an individual field value to a *int* variable, as in

```
c = pack.ThirdFlag;
```

then the accessed value is always either 0 or 1. This operation avoids the need for shifting. Depending on the implementation, in a sequence of bit fields such as in this byte, the first bit can be either the leftmost or rightmost bit of the byte. Bit fields cannot be members of unions, but they can be members of structures that are themselves members of unions.

As mentioned in Chapter 11, the size of a structure often is greater than the total size of its members. With bit fields, the difference can take the form of unused bits. Suppose that a structure contains, among other members, a bit field of size 5. If we follow that bit field by an integer member, the integer must start at the beginning of a new byte. Thus, the three bits left over in the byte occupied by the bit field of size 5 must go unused. Furthermore, fields cannot cross *int* boundaries. Thus, if we follow a field of 10 bits by a field of 8 bits (on a machine where an *int* has 16 bits), the second field begins on the next *int* boundary, leaving 6 unused bits after the first field.

Section 15.1 Exercises

For Exercises 1–24, assume the following declaration-initializations:

```
unsigned char   a = 0xB8,
                b = 0x16,
                c = 0xC3;
```

Evaluate the expressions, giving the answer in binary and hexadecimal.

1. a & b	**2.** a & c	**3.** $a \mid b$	**4.** $a \mid c$
5. $\sim a$	**6.** $\sim b$	**7.** $a \wedge b$	**8.** $a >> 6$ (logical shift)
9. $b >> 3$	**10.** $a << 4$	**11.** $c << 5$	**12.** $\sim a \mid c$
13. $\sim (a \mid c)$	**14.** $c \mid b$ & $\sim a$	**15.** $b \mid 0x40$	**16.** $a \mid 0x22$
17. b & 0xEF	**18.** c & 0xF0	**19.** a & $\sim 0x10$	**20.** b & $\sim 0x44$
21. $b \wedge 0x80$	**22.** $a \wedge 0x0D$	**23.** $a \mid c << 3$	**24.** $a \wedge \sim a$

In Exercises 25–37, assume a *is an* unsigned char *variable. Give the assignment statement with the appropriate bitwise operation to*

25. Set the rightmost bit of *a*

26. Set the fourth and fifth bits from the left in *a*

27. Clear the rightmost bit of *a*

28. Clear the fourth and fifth bits from the left in *a*

29. Complement all the bits of *a*

30. Flip the first and second bits from the right in *a*

31. Flip the first and second bits from the left in *a*

32. Shift *a* to the right 4 bits

33. Shift *a* to the left 4 bits

34. Divide *a* by 8

35. Divide *a* by 32

36. Multiply *a* by 8

37. Multiply *a* by 32

38. Declare a variable *TwoBits* to be two bits in length.

39. Declare a structure that has elements for name, age, and bit fields to indicate whether the person has paid dues or not, whether the member has completed requirements or not, and whether the person is an officer or not.

40. Revise the function *Power* of Example 13.3 in Section 13.1 to use shifting instead of division by 2.

41. Redo the loop in Example 15.5, extracting the bits from left to right.

Section 15.1 Programming Projects

1. Using bitwise operations, write a program to convert a nonnegative binary (base 2) number to its decimal (base 10) equivalent. Display the number in bases 2 and 10.

2. Develop a program that accepts input of two sets of integers and finds the union and intersection of the two sets, eliminating any duplicates. The program should allow each set to have up to 200 integers between 0 and 199.

   Here is a sample run of such a program:

```
Number of entries for first set:   3
 :  2
 :  125
 :  60
Number of entries for second set:  4
 :  2
 :  60
 :  9
 :  9

The union of the sets is:  {2, 9, 60, 125}
The intersection of the sets is:  {2, 60}
```

Section 15.2 **Breadth: Logic Gates**

**Boolean
Algebra**

A boolean algebra is a structure with a set of elements and three operations. The set can contain just two elements, such as 0 and 1. Although this situation seems too simple, the only possible value of a logical expression in the algebra of propositions is *TRUE* or *FALSE;* a switch in a computer has just two states, off and on; and a condition in a program has but one of two values, *TRUE* or *FALSE*. The mathematical model for these structures is a boolean algebra. There can, however, be more than two elements in the algebra. In Section 3.5, we considered the algebra of propositions [*S*, $\vee$, $\wedge$, $\sim$, F, T] with its 2^n statements; three operations of disjunction ($\vee$), conjunction ($\wedge$), and negation ($\sim$); and special elements F (*FALSE*) and T (*TRUE*). The collection of all subsets of a set, *U*, along with union, intersection, complement, and the special elements ø and *U* is also a boolean algebra.

The formal definition of boolean algebra is below. In reading through it, consider how [*S*, $\vee$, $\wedge$, $\sim$, F, T] is such an algebra with + interpreted as $\vee$, · as $\wedge$, $\sim$ as ', 0 as F , and 1 as T. One note of caution—+ and · do not mean regular addition and multiplication, and 0 and 1 do not necessarily stand for the numbers 0 and 1. Some notation has to be used, and these symbols are convenient. However, they are just symbols with different meanings in different contexts.

Definition   A **boolean algebra**, [*A*, +, ·, ', 0, 1] is a set *A* with two binary operations (+ and ·), a unary operation ('), and two distinct elements (0 and 1), satisfying the following properties for all *x*, *y*, *z* ∈ *A*:

1. **Commutative Properties**
   a. $x + y = y + x$ **b.** $x \cdot y = y \cdot x$

2. **Associative Properties**
   a. $x + (y + z) = (x + y) + z$ **b.** $x \cdot (y \cdot z) = (x \cdot y) \cdot z$

3. **Distributive Properties**
   a. $x + (y \cdot z) = (x + y) \cdot (x + z)$ **b.** $x \cdot (y + z) = (x \cdot y) + (x \cdot z)$

4. **Identities**
   a. $x + 0 = x$ **b.** $x \cdot 1 = x$

5. **Complement**
   a. $x + x' = 1$ **b.** $x \cdot x' = 0$

A boolean algebra containing only 0 and 1 is important to computer science, in part because the three fundamental circuit components of a computer obey the properties of this algebra. We can interpret the elements 0 and 1 as bits or as the two states of a switch—off and on.

Example 15.7

Consider the set **B** = {0, 1} with Table 15.6 defining the three operations +, ·, and '.

Let us compare Table 15.6 with Table 3.5 of Section 3.5, which contains truth tables for $p \vee q$, $p \wedge q$, and $\sim p$ in the algebra of propositions. Making some symbol substitutions (+ $\leftrightarrow$ $\vee$, · $\leftrightarrow$ $\wedge$, ' $\leftrightarrow$ $\sim$, 0 $\leftrightarrow$ F, 1 $\leftrightarrow$ T), we see that the corresponding tables behave in exactly the same way. Just as the algebra of propositions is a boolean algebra, so is [**B**, +, ·, ' , 0, 1].

Table 15.6 Tables for +, ·, and '

x	y	x + y
0	0	0
0	1	1
1	0	1
1	1	1

x	y	x · y
0	0	0
0	1	0
1	0	0
1	1	1

x	x'
0	1
1	0

As we did in Section 3.5 on logic, we can prove many additional properties that hold in any boolean algebra from the 10 basic properties in the definition. Some significant ones follow.

Properties true for all x, y, z in any boolean algebra:

6. Idempotent Properties
    a. $x + x = x$ **b.** $x \cdot x = x$

7. DeMorgan's Laws
    a. $(x + y)' = x' \cdot y'$ **b.** $(x \cdot y)' = x' + y'$

8. · with 0; + with 1
    a. $x \cdot 0 = 0$ **b.** $x + 1 = 1$

9. Double Complement Property
    a. $x'' = x$

Gates

In 1938, a paper titled "A Symbolic Analysis of Relay and Switching Circuits" by Claude Shannon gave an electronic circuitry interpretation of boolean algebra. In a truly important masters thesis, Shannon showed how people can use boolean algebras to create, study, and simplify relay circuits. His paper changed circuit design from an art to a science and prepared the way for the use of electronic circuits in computers, calculators, and telephone systems.

We have seen that a boolean algebra has three basic operations—+, ·, and '. Corresponding to these are three basic parts to a **logic circuit**—**OR gate, AND gate,** and **inverter,** respectively. In a **logic circuit,** only two possible values, 0 and 1, are present. The gates are the building blocks of this electronic circuitry. Given two binary inputs x and y, the OR gate yields an output of $x + y$, while the AND gate produces an output of $x \cdot y$. The inverter complements an input of x, giving x'. Thus, these logic gates are the physical realization of the operations in a two-element boolean algebra. Figure 15.1 gives the engineering symbols for these gates. These tables correspond to those for [**B**, +, ·, ', 0, 1] in the above example. In this figure and from now on, we use the abbreviation xy for $x \cdot y$.

Figure 15.1
Three basic gates

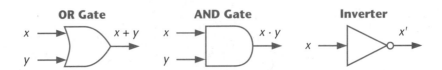

Definitions   A **logic circuit** is a circuit where voltage on each line is interpreted as 0 or 1. The three basic parts to a logic circuit are the **OR gate**, the **AND gate**, and the **inverter**. Given two binary inputs x and y, the **OR gate** yields an output of the boolean algebra $x + y$, and the **AND gate** produces an output of the boolean algebra $x \cdot y$. The **inverter** complements an input of x, giving x'.

An **integrated circuit chip** has a logic circuit on a small piece of semiconductor material, such as silicon. Chip technology has advanced from small-scale integration (**SSI**) with 10 or fewer gates on a chip to very-large-scale integration (**VLSI**) with hundreds of thousands of gates per chip. The **microprocessor** or CPU on a chip has enabled the development of microcomputers and fueled a computer revolution. In 1970, Intel developed the first microprocessor for a Japanese calculator manufacturer. The calculator company was not sure the chip met its needs adequately or cheaply enough, so Intel was stuck with the product. Not realizing its potential, the young Intel Company hesitantly introduced the chip to the public in 1971. When engineers grasped the importance of the invention, sales soared as did microprocessor technology.

Definitions   An **integrated circuit chip** has a logic circuit on a small piece of semiconductor material, such as silicon. A **microprocessor** is a CPU on a chip.

UNIVAC I computer; chip compared to the eye of a needle inset in upper, left corner. The UNIVAC I, built in the early 1950s using vacuum tubes, was the first commercial computer. Within 15 years, the chip had even greater computing power. *NOTE:* This computer was used in the November 4, 1952, CBS News Broadcast with Walter Cronkite, "Eisenhower vs. Stevenson," to predict the outcome of the presidential election. Both the computer and television were in their infancy. With but a few million votes counted, at 8:30 P.M., the computer correctly predicted a landslide for Eisenhower. Because polls had indicated a close race, nervous computer officials changed the values of some of the variables and had the computer recalculate to predict a closer election. Only when the landslide was evident was the original prediction revealed to the TV audience.

Figure 15.2
Circuit for
$u = xy + z'$

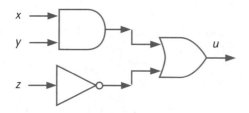

Table15.7 Truth table for $u = xy + z'$

x	y	z	xy	z'	$u = xy + z'$
0	0	0	0	1	1
0	0	1	0	0	0
0	1	0	0	1	1
0	1	1	0	0	0
1	0	0	0	1	1
1	0	1	0	0	0
1	1	0	1	1	1
1	1	1	1	0	1

Combinational Circuits

We can combine logic gates to create any number of logic circuits on a chip, such as the logic network in Figure 15.2. With three boolean or binary inputs of x, y, and z, the circuit produces one output of u. By ANDing x and y, NOTing z, and ORing the two results, we obtain u. The boolean algebra notation $u = xy + z'$ represents this logic circuit.

A truth table in Table 15.7 indicates exactly when u is 1. We have columns of values for the inputs x, y, and z and the output u. To make computation of u easier, intermediate results, xy and z', also have columns. Because there are three inputs and each input has two possible values, 0 and 1, the truth table has $2^3 = 8$ rows. For consistency in listing the inputs, we start with 000 and count in binary. Observation of the table tells us that the circuit has an output of 1 provided x and y are both 1 or z is 0.

The expression $xy + z'$ is an example of a **boolean expression**. Using the basic boolean operations, we combine the boolean variables x, y, and z with the boolean constants of 0 or 1. Notice that the definition of boolean expression below is recursive.

Definitions A variable x that can only have a value of 0 or 1 in the two-element boolean algebra on $\mathbf{B} = \{0, 1\}$ is called a **boolean variable**. Let $x_1, x_2, \ldots, x_n$ be boolean variables. A **boolean expression** is
1. $0, 1, x_1, x_2, \ldots,$ or x_n
2. $A + B, A \cdot B,$ or A' if A and B are boolean expressions

In $u = xy + z'$, output u is actually a function of inputs x, y, and z so that we can write

$$u = f(x, y, z) = xy + z'.$$

The function f is called a **switching** or **combinational function** from the set of all triples of boolean values, $\mathbf{B}^3$, to $\mathbf{B}$. For example, the fifth row of its truth table in Table

15.7 tells us that $f(1, 0, 0) = 1$. That is, input values of $x = 1$, $y = 0$, and $z = 0$ result in an output value of $u = 1$. For this function, we write $f: \mathbf{B}^3 \rightarrow \mathbf{B}$.

Definitions

A **combinational circuit** is a circuit where outputs are uniquely determined by the inputs. Function f is a **switching** or **combinational function**, provided f is a mapping from $\mathbf{B}^n$, the set of all boolean n-tuples, to $\mathbf{B}$ ($f: \mathbf{B}^n \rightarrow \mathbf{B}$) for some positive integer n. A combinational function is a mathematical model of a combinational circuit.

Example 15.8

Using the properties of a boolean algebra, we can find another combinational function, g, equivalent to $f(x, y, z) = xy + z'$. By Property 3a of boolean algebras we can distribute z' through the product, as follows:

$$xy + z' = (x + z')(y + z')$$

Thus, one answer for g is

$$g(x, y, z) = (x + z')(y + z')$$

By boolean algebra properties, we can find other such functions. Figure 15.4 depicts the circuit corresponding to g. Although this circuit is equivalent to that in Figure 15.2, Figure 15.3 is more complicated, using 4 gates instead of 3. Functions f and g are equivalent, having the same output for the same input, but the circuit for f is more efficient than that for g.

Definition

Two combinational functions $f: \mathbf{B}^n \rightarrow \mathbf{B}$ and $g: \mathbf{B}^n \rightarrow \mathbf{B}$ are **equivalent** (or **equal**), written $f = g$, if $f(x_1, x_2, \ldots, x_n) = g(x_1, x_2, \ldots, x_n)$ for all $(x_1, x_2, \ldots, x_n) \in \mathbf{B}^n$.

To use the value on a line in two places, we connect another line to that line. A solid dot on a diagram indicates a connection. When lines cross in the diagram without a solid dot, no connection occurs (see Figure 15.4).

Figure 15.3
Combinational circuit for
$g(x, y, z) = (x + z')(y + z')$

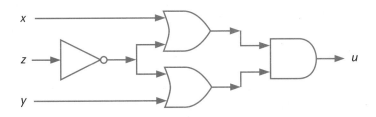

Figure 15.4
Connection indicated by solid dot

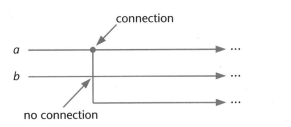

Figure 15.5
Symbol for OR gate with three inputs along with two implementations for this OR gate

Symbol for OR gate

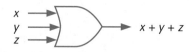

Two implementations for this OR gate

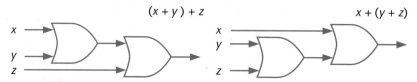

On a diagram, we can also draw three lines entering an OR gate. Because the associative property for + holds in a boolean algebra, grouping is irrelevant, that is,

$$(x + y) + z = x + (y + z) = x + y + z$$

We could draw the OR gate with three inputs in any of the ways shown in Figure 15.5. Similarly, we can draw three lines going into an AND gate.

Example 15.9

In this example, we write the combinational function f corresponding to the circuit in Figure 15.6. Then, using the techniques of boolean algebra, we find a simpler, equivalent function g. We draw the truth tables for both f and g to observe the equality of output.

The top AND gate of the diagram in Figure 15.6 has inputs a and b', causing an output of ab'. The middle AND gate operates on b' and b to produce $b'b$, and the bottom gate ANDs a and b, or ab. The output from these three gates are ORed together to give c:

$$c = f(a, b) = ab' + b'b + ab$$

Using boolean algebra, we simplify $f(a, b)$, as follows:

$$
\begin{aligned}
ab' + b'b + ab &= ab' + 0 + ab &&\text{(complement)} \\
&= ab' + ab &&\text{(identity)} \\
&= a(b' + b) &&\text{(distributive)} \\
&= a(1) &&\text{(complement)} \\
&= a &&\text{(identity)}
\end{aligned}
$$

Thus, the projection function onto the first coordinate, $g(a, b) = a$ is equivalent to f, and the circuit does not need any gates at all.

$$a \rightarrow a$$
$$b \rightarrow$$

The truth table for f is in Table 15.8, and that of g is in Table 15.9. With two inputs, we need $2^2 = 4$ rows. Notice the last columns of the two tables are equal, reaffirming that f and g are equivalent.

Figure 15.6
Circuit for
Example 15.9

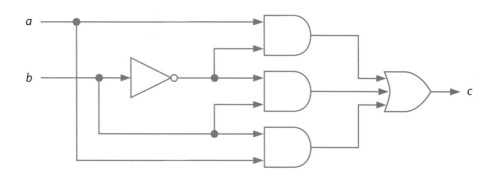

Table 15.8 Truth table for $f(a, b) = ab' + b'b + ab$

a	b	b'	ab'	b'b	ab	ab' + b'b + ab
0	0	1	0	0	0	0
0	1	0	0	0	0	0
1	0	1	1	0	0	1
1	1	0	0	0	1	1

Table 15.9
Truth table for
$g(a, b) = a$

a	b	a
0	0	0
0	1	0
1	0	1
1	1	1

Section 15.2 Exercises

For each of the circuits in Exercises 1–4, give

    a. *The combinational function*

    b. *The truth table*

    c. *For each circuit, describe in English the conditions that cause an output of 1.
For instance, in Figure 15.3 "xy + z' is 1 if both x and y are 1 or if z is 0."*

1.

2.
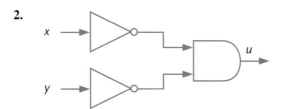

3.
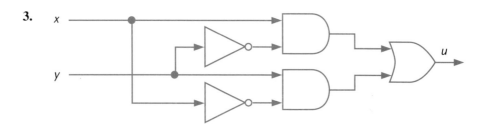

4.

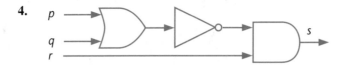

5. Using the properties of boolean algebra, find an equivalent function to that of Exercise 1.

6. Using the properties of boolean algebra, find an equivalent function to that of Exercise 2.

Simplify the combinational circuits in Exercises 7–9 using boolean algebra. NOTE: A label of 1 or 0 on a line means that constant value is on the line.

7.

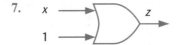

8.

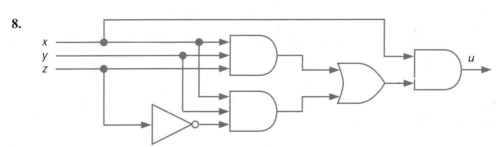

9.

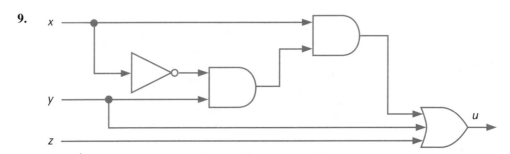

For each of the combinational functions in Exercises 10–13, sketch the corresponding combinational circuit.

10. $h(x, y) = (x + y)'$ **12.** $f(x, y, z) = x' + y' + z$

11. $f(p, q) = pq'$ **13.** $g(a, b, c) = ab'c + a'bc$

14. Suppose a combinational circuit has eight input lines. How many rows are in the corresponding truth table?

Section 15.3 Breadth: Logic Circuits

In the section on logic gates, we saw how to generate a circuit from a boolean expression and vice versa. But how do you start with an application, generate the truth table, and then find the boolean expression and logic circuit?

Canonical Sum-of-Products

We start with a particular example. One task that the computer certainly needs to perform is to add two bits. Recall that in the binary number system we have the following sums:

$$0 + 0 = 0$$
$$0 + 1 = 1$$
$$1 + 0 = 1$$
$$1 + 1 = 10_2$$

For two inputs x and y, we really desire two outputs, the least significant bit, which we call the sum (s), and the carry (c). The truth table in Table 15.10 follows the above addition with two inputs and two outputs.

We consider the circuits for c and s separately. In some situations, we might be able to look at the truth table and figure out the boolean expression. For instance, c is 1 only in the case where both x and y are 1. Does any basic gate perform this function? Sending x and y through the AND gate produces c. Thus, $c = xy$.

Generating output s is more challenging. This output is 1 when exactly one of x and y is 1. The method we use for generating the boolean expression for s is the **canonical sum-of-products**. From the table, we see that either the second or the third row generates an output of 1. Because of the "or" in the last sentence, the expression has the following overall structure:

$$(\ ) + (\ )$$

Multiplication (ab) in the two-element boolean algebra yields 1 in exactly one situation—when both a and b are 1. Consequently, given values for x and y, exactly one of the following products is 1—xy, xy', $x'y$, $x'y'$. Table 15.11 shows all these products in truth table form, and exactly one 1 appears in each product row. We derive the following cases from this table:

1. If $x = 1$ and $y = 1$, then only xy is 1.

2. If $x = 1$ and $y = 0$, then only xy' is 1.

Table 15.10 Truth table for computing $x + y$

x	y	c	s
0	0	0	0
0	1	0	1
1	0	0	1
1	1	1	0

Table 15.11 Truth table for xy, xy', $x'y$, and $x'y'$

x	y	x'	y'	xy	xy'	$x'y$	$x'y'$
0	0	1	1	0	0	0	1
0	1	1	0	0	0	1	0
1	0	0	1	0	1	0	0
1	1	0	0	1	0	0	0

Figure 15.7
Circuit for a
half adder

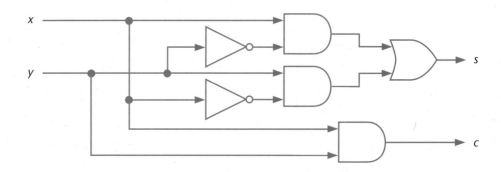

3. If $x = 0$ and $y = 1$, then only $x'y$ is 1.

4. If $x = 0$ and $y = 0$, then only $x'y'$ is 1.

We want an output of $s = 1$ when exactly one of x and y is 1. Thus, for inputs of $x = 0$ and $y = 1$, we need the product $x'y$. For inputs of $x = 1$ and $y = 0$, the product xy' gives an output of 1. ORing the results, we have the following:

$s = x'y + xy'$

For the other inputs, s is 0, as shown:

$x = 0, y = 0: s = 0' \cdot 0 + 0 \cdot 0' = 1 \cdot 0 + 0 \cdot 1 = 0 + 0 = 0$
$x = 1, y = 1: s = 1' \cdot 1 + 1 \cdot 1' = 0 \cdot 1 + 1 \cdot 0 = 0 + 0 = 0$

We can use a shortcut to obtain each term of the expression without resorting to Table 15.11. If an input is 1, use the variable as is. If the input is 0, complement the variable. Thus, for the second row with $x = 0$ and $y = 1$, we use $x'y$, and for the third row with $x = 1$ and $y = 0$, we use xy'. The complete circuit, which is called a **half adder**, is shown in Figure 15.7.

> *Algorithm 15.1. Creating a Canonical Sum-of-Products Form of a Boolean Expression from a Truth Table:*
>
> **1.** A term is added for each row of the truth table with an output of 1.
>
> **2.** For each term corresponding to a row, write down the input variables in order, complementing any variable whose value on that row is 0.

Example 15.10

Consider a combinational function *op:* $\mathbf{B}^7 \rightarrow \mathbf{B}$ that takes a 7-bit string (or ordered 7-tuple) and returns 1 when an even number of ones is in the string. The 7-bit string s with $op(s)$ appended is then assured of having an odd number of ones. For example, $op(1001000) = 1$ so that 1001000 1 has three ones, and $op(1001010) = 0$ so that 1001010 0 also has an odd number of ones. The value of $op(s)$ is the **parity bit** when we are generating **odd parity**. A computer transmitting information often attaches a parity bit to every n bits of information. Here, $n = 7$. At the receiving end, if the 8 bits (7 bits of information with the parity bit) contain an even number of ones instead of an odd number, an error in transmission has occurred.

Table 15.12 Truth table for function *op* of Example 15.10

x	y	z	op(x, y, z)
0	0	0	1
0	0	1	0
0	1	0	0
0	1	1	1
1	0	0	0
1	0	1	1
1	1	0	1
1	1	1	0

Let us develop the boolean expression to generate odd parity. From such an expression, we can create a circuit. The first step is to build the truth table. With an input string of 7 bits, we need $2^7 = 128$ rows. To make the problem more manageable for this example, we suppose that input strings are only 3 bits long. The same procedure would be used for 7 bits. We write down all possible selections of input bits. For any row with an even number of ones, we put a 1 in the output column, so that the completed row now has an odd number of ones. The final truth table is in Table 15.12.

We can now apply the canonical sum-of-products method. Because we have 4 rows with an output of 1, the expression has 4 terms.

$$( ) + ( ) + ( ) + ( )$$

In the first row, all input values are 0, so each variable is complemented before multiplication—$x'y'z'$. The fourth row indicates that only x is complemented—$x'yz$. Continuing in the same fashion for the sixth and seventh rows, we generate the canonical sum-of-products form of the boolean expression as follows:

$$x'y'z' + x'yz + xy'z + xyz'$$

The canonical sum-of-products form is not necessarily the most efficient boolean expression for a truth table. We saw in the last section how we can use properties of boolean algebra to simplify such expressions. We can use other methods based on boolean algebra to minimize a circuit. These methods are left for you to explore in future courses.

Section 15.3 Exercises

1. Consider the mapping f to take a 6-tuple of bits and return 0 if any input bit is 0.

   a. What situation(s) causes an output of 1?

   b. Without drawing the truth table, give the boolean expression and circuit for this function.

Give the truth table, canonical sum-of-products form, simplified boolean expression, and resulting circuit diagram for each of the combinational functions in Exercises 2–5.

2. $f(x\ y) = \begin{cases} 1, \text{if } y = 0 \\ 0, \text{otherwise} \end{cases}$

3. $f(x, y, z) = \begin{cases} 1, \text{if exactly two of } x, y, \text{and } z \text{ are } 1 \\ 0, \text{otherwise} \end{cases}$

4. $f(x, y, z) = \begin{cases} 1, \text{if } x = z \\ 0, \text{otherwise} \end{cases}$

5. $f(x, y, z) = \begin{cases} 1, \text{if } x = 1 \text{ or } y \neq z \\ 0, \text{otherwise} \end{cases}$

6. A committee has three members, two regular members and a chairperson. Members vote electronically on motions with yes ≡ 1 and no ≡ 0. The one output of the circuit indicates if the motion passes (yes) or not (no). The chairperson has veto power over any motion.

   a. Give the truth table.

   b. Find the canonical sum-of-products form of the boolean expression.

   c. Simplify the boolean expression.

   d. Draw the simplified circuit.

7. Figure 15.8 illustrates the circuit for a half-adder given in this section as a block diagram.

   A **full-adder** adds three inputs—x, y, and a previous carry—and produces a sum (s) and carry (c_i). Therefore, a full-adder can be used to add two n-bit numbers, two bits and a carry at a time. We can use half-adders to design the full-adder. Besides the sums listed at the first of this section, we need the following equality in the binary number system:

   $$1 + 1 + 1 = 11_2$$

   To construct a full-adder, we first add x and the previous carry (c_{i-1}) with a half-adder and generate a sum z and a carry u. Now add z and y with another half-adder, getting the final sum s and a carry v. We have a final sum s, but two carries u and v. If either carry is 1, the carry out of the full-adder should be 1. Thus, we OR u and v together to get the carry out at the ith step c_i. (u and v could not both be 1 because we are adding at most three ones for the three inputs x, y, and c_{i-1}.) Figure 15.9 gives the block diagram for the full adder.

   a. Draw the truth table for inputs x, y, c_{i-1} and outputs c_i and s.

   b. Give values of z, u, s, v, and c_i with inputs of $c_{i-1} = x = 1$ and $y = 0$.

   c. Repeat Part b for all inputs equal to 1.

   d. Apply the full-adder to add 1011 and 0011. In other words, the least significant bits are processed first as x and y. This circuit is a **serial adder.** What should c_0 be on this first step? Give x, y, c_{i-1}, s, and c_i at every step by filling in the table below. Notice the carry out at step 1, $c_1 = 1$, is the carry in for step 2, $c_{2-1} = c_1$ = 1.

Figure 15.8
Block diagram
of a half-adder

Figure 15.9
A full-adder
circuit

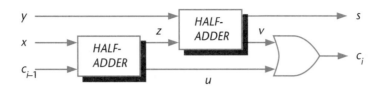

Figure 15.10
Block diagram
of an n-to-2^n
decoder

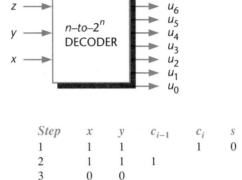

Step	x	y	c_{i-1}	c_i	s
1	1	1		1	0
2	1	1	1		
3	0	0			
4	1	0			

8. The n-to-2^n **decoder** (see Figure 15.10) has n input lines and 2^n output lines. The device decodes an n-bit binary input as one of 2^n numbers. Recall that the $2^3 = 8$ integers from 0 to 7 are represented by 3-bit binary numbers as follows:

Binary Number	Decimal Number	Binary Number	Decimal Number
000	0	100	4
001	1	101	5
010	2	110	6
011	3	111	7

If, for instance, the binary number 011 ($x = 0$, $y = 1$, $z = 1$) is input, then the fourth output line, u_3, and no other, becomes active.

a. Give the boolean expressions for each of $u_0, u_1, \ldots$, and u_7.

b. Draw the circuit diagram for u_0.

c. Draw the circuit diagram for u_3.

9. Use a block diagram of a full-adder (Exercise 7) to design an incrementer, which generates an output of $x + 1$ upon input of x.

10. A Gray code encodes integers so that in going from one integer to the next only one bit is changed. Below is one example of a Gray code, along with the corresponding numbers in the decimal and binary number systems:

Decimal N	Binary $wxyz$	Gray $abcd$	Decimal N	Binary $wxyz$	Gray $abcd$
0	0000	0000	8	1000	1100
1	0001	0001	9	1001	1101
2	0010	0011	10	1010	1111
3	0011	0010	11	1011	1110
4	0100	0110	12	1100	1010
5	0101	0111	13	1101	1011
6	0110	0101	14	1110	1001
7	0111	0100	15	1111	1000

The four input lines—w, x, y, z—have four output lines—a, b, c, d.

a. Find and simplify the boolean expressions for a, b, c, and d.

b. Suppose a, b, c, and d are the input lines and w, x, y, and z are the output lines. Give the simplified boolean expressions for w, x, y, and z to convert a number from a Gray code representation to the corresponding binary number.

11. Consider a combinational circuit that accepts a 2-bit number and returns the square of that number.

   a. How many input variables are needed?

   b. How many output variables are needed?

   c. Give the truth table.

   d. Find the boolean expression for each output variable.

   e. Design the simplified circuits.

Programming and Debugging Hints

Mistaken Operator Symbols

The C language uses a small set of symbols to perform many different roles. For this reason, several C operators can be mistaken for other operators without causing a syntax error. These operators include the logical and bitwise AND (&&, &) and OR (||, |) operators, which are syntactically interchangeable but operate differently. We have already mentioned of the notorious confusion between the = and == operators.

Program Correctness

Every programmer should be aware of the following fact: No matter how much debugging and testing we do and no matter how thoroughly we perform these tasks, the best that we can say at any time is that we have eliminated all known bugs. We are never 100% certain, except in the most trivial programs, that the program is completely error-free. In other words, we can always prove the presence of errors, but never their absence. That is why programmers say that there is no such thing as a debugged program. Yet a diligent programmer, through concentrated effort, can produce a program almost totally devoid of errors.

To reduce errors, computer scientists have developed techniques of **program verification**, which means proving mathematically that a program is correct as we are writing it. Thus, the time spent debugging can be decreased dramatically. The same techniques can also be used in creating a more efficient, and correct, program.

Key Terms

~ 900	bit field 904	left shift operator 901
^ 900	bitwise logical operators 896	logical shift 902
& 896	bitwise AND operator 896	mask 898
<< 901	bitwise EXCLUSIVE OR operator 900	one's complement operator 900
>> 901	bitwise NOT operator 900	right shift operator 901
	896	bitwise OR operator 896	set bit 896
arithmetic shift 902	clear bit 896	

Summary

The computer represents all values in memory as binary numbers. In the binary representation of integers, the rightmost bit represents the ones place, the next represents twos, the next fours, then eights, and so forth. For example, the binary number 1100 represents the following in decimal:

$$1 \cdot 2^3 + 1 \cdot 2^2 + 0 \cdot 2^1 + 0 \cdot 2^0 = 1 \cdot 8 + 1 \cdot 4 + 0 \cdot 2 + 0 \cdot 1$$

which equals 12. In bit parlance, a set bit is one that has the value 1, whereas a clear bit has the value 0.

The bitwise logical operators (&, |, ~) perform their operations on each individual bit of their operand(s). If we execute the statement

```
c = a & b;
```

each bit in *c* is set to the result of ANDing the corresponding bits of *a* and *b*. Therefore, a bit in *c* has the value 1 if and only if the corresponding bits of both *a* and *b* are 1.

Suppose we execute the following statement to compute the bitwise OR operation on *a* and *b*:

```
c = a | b;
```

A bit in *c* becomes 1 if either of the corresponding bits of *a* and *b* is set, whereas the ORing of two zeros is 0.

The bitwise NOT operator or the one's complement operator (~) is analogous to the logical NOT (!) operator. When we apply ~ to a value, such as ~*a*, the operation flips or complements each bit.

With bit operations and bit configurations called masks, we can set or clear a single bit in a variable. To set a bit, we use the bitwise | operator with a mask containing 1 in the corresponding position and zeros elsewhere. For example,

```
a |= 0x08;
```

sets the fourth bit from the right in *a*. To clear a bit, we use the bitwise & operator with a mask containing 0 in the corresponding position and ones elsewhere. Alternatively, we use the bitwise & operator with the complement (bitwise ~) of a mask containing 1 in the corresponding position and zeros elsewhere. Therefore, to clear the third bit from the left, we use

```
a &= 0xDF;
```

or

```
a &= ~0x20;
```

The bitwise EXCLUSIVE OR operator in C is the caret (^). The result of the ^ operation is a 1 bit if and only if the two operand bits are different. To complement individual bits of a bit pattern, we use the EXCLUSIVE OR operation with a mask containing a set bit in each bit position to be flipped. Therefore, to flip the first and fifth bits from the left, we write

```
a ^= 0x88;
```

The right and left shift operators (>> and <<) move bit patterns either to the right or to the left, respectively. For example,

```
a = a >> 2;
```

shifts each bit of *a* the right by two bit positions. Different versions of C handle right shifts differently. Some compilers implement a logical shift, in which zeros move into the leftmost positions. On other computers, the shift is an arithmetic shift. If the variable or constant is a signed integer, the sign bit in the leftmost position propagates to the vacated positions.

Structures can contain special members called bit fields, whose type is *int* (or *unsigned int*), but whose length is in bits rather than bytes. For example, in a structure declaration,

```
unsigned ThreeBits : 3;
```

proclaims *ThreeBits* as a member of only three bits.

Review Questions

1. Why is it sometimes useful to manipulate bits rather than bytes?
2. If x contains the bit pattern 1001 and y contains the pattern 1110, determine the results of the following bit operations.

   a. $x \& y$ **b.** $x \mid y$

3. What logical operation is associated with the $\sim$ operator, and what is the name of the symbol used?
4. Distinguish between the inclusive and EXCLUSIVE OR operations.
5. What symbols are used in C for the following operation?

   a. left shift   **b.** right shift

6. Distinguish between a logical and an arithmetic right shift.
7. How are the shift operators used in computation?
8. What are bit fields?
9. What is the meaning of the following definition?

   ```
   int FourBits : 4;
   ```

Laboratory

This laboratory is a continuation of the one from the last chapter. Its purpose is to cover the documentation needed with system maintenance, as well as to provide further teamwork experience.

Internal and external documentation are extremely important for any system. Imagine trying to use the CPU simulator without the documentation in Section 12.7, or attempting to modify a program with no internal comments. Any time we update a system, we must update the documentation. While making changes, programmers should carefully write internal comments to include the author, date, description of the modification(s), and justification for the change(s). The external documentation must also be updated.

For a large system, external documentation should be extensive. The bound reference contains the following material:

1. Software Requirement Specification with a Preliminary User's Manual
   This document is the culmination of the analysis phase of the software life cycle. It contains, among other things, a description of the need for and scope of the system, its functions, and functional and performance requirements.

2. System Plan
   This document is part of the preliminary design phase. It contains the system development plan; structure charts; a list of named modules with inputs, outputs, process, and the name of the person responsible for it; and schedule of code and test completion.

3. Test Specification Document

   Part of the preliminary design phase, this document identifies test cases, including input data and expected results, for each module and for the entire system.

4. Test Reporting Document

   This document presents a list of the tests, including the data, and their results.

5. User's Manual

   This manual gives instructions to the user on system access, its features, command formats, necessary inputs, expected outputs, examples of its use, and error messages.

6. System Design

   This part of the final documentation contains a finalized structure chart, well-documented source code for all modules, and information on how to run the system.

An update to the system must include an update to the documentation as well. In this laboratory, you and your team members should provide documentation for the changes you made to the CPU simulator or the stock portfolio program in the Chapter 14 Laboratory. Your documentation should contain a title page, table of contents, and sections for updates to the Test Reporting Document, User's Manual, and System Design. The material should be typed using a word processor. Divide the work among the team members.

The Test Reporting Document update should describe all module and system tests, who performed each test, the input and output, and the results of each test. This material should be gathered from your records from the last laboratory.

The User's Manual must contain detailed instructions to the user on the revised system. It must document each new feature, describe the format for each new instruction, expected input and output, examples, and error handling.

Because your team added modules, the System Design must include revisions to the structure chart. This section should also contain source code for each new and revised function.

Data Structures

Introduction ≋

Structures that hold data, operations that manipulate these structures, and algorithms that use these operations are the essence of data structures. One data structure, the list, has a chain of nodes that we can expand and contract as needed. The implementation of a list that we discuss is a dynamic linked list, where pointers chain one node to the next. With links, we can easily insert new nodes into the linked list and remove others that we no longer need.

Another data structure, the stack, is appropriate when the last data placed into the structure should be the first processed. All activity occurs at the top of the stack. We add a new value to or remove an old value from the top of the stack. In Section 13.1, we discussed how to implement recursion by use of a run-time stack. An activation record for each invocation of a recursive function to itself is placed onto the top of the stack until the terminal condition is met. Then, one-by-one and in reverse order, the references are taken from the top of the stack with appropriate values substituted. Breadth Section 16.4 examines this run-time stack in greater detail. Besides employing stacks when executing functions, many computers and some calculators use stacks to perform arithmetic.

After discussing stacks on the abstract data type level, we consider an implementation of this important data structure. We can implement all stack operations easily and efficiently with dynamic linked lists.

Goals   To study

- Linked list configuration and operations and their implementations
- Abstract data type stack

- Stack applications
- Linked list implementation of the abstract data type stack
- The run-time stack

Section 16.1 **Linked Lists**

Data structures involve a study of the various frameworks for storing data and the algorithms that implement and perform operations on these structures. As discussed in the first subsection of Section 12.5, we often approach a data structure as an **abstract data type (ADT)** or a set of data items and fundamental operations on this set, before implementing the structure and developing major applications.

Definition An **abstract data type (ADT)** is a set of data items and fundamental operations on this set.

One data structure is a **list**, which provides a linking configuration of **nodes** of information that we can expand and contract as needed. Moreover, we can insert and delete nodes easily. An analogy is a line of children who are holding hands in a game of Snake with the leader at one end. A new child, running up to play, can quickly join hands with others at an end or somewhere in the middle. If the child goes to the head of the line, he or she is the new leader. Another child can leave the line, and the friends easily reform the "snake." If the leader must go home, the second in line becomes the new leader.

An abstract data type list is often called a **linked list** at the implementation level. Two major implementations of lists exist—one using arrays and the other using pointers. In this section, we do not give the formal definition of an ADT list, but concentrate on its implementation as a dynamic linked list with pointers. We call a "dynamic linked list" a "linked list" for brevity.

For the linked list, we need the structure discussed in Section 11.4, which uses pointers to nodes. The information portion of the node can be as small as a bit or as large as a record with numerous fields. The pointer portion holds the location of yet another node, which is a structure of the same type. The type definitions and variable declarations below create a list *L*. Nodes of type *node_t* have an information field (*el*) of type *el_t* and a link field (*next*) of type *pointer_t*, the type of a pointer to a node. Defining pointer type *pointer_t* in terms of *node_t*, which has an element of type *pointer_t*, is the only situation in C when we can use a type before its definition. The list maintains *head*, a pointer to the first node, and *cur*, a pointer to a current node. Thus, we define type *list* as a structure containing elements *head* and *cur*. In various operations in this section, we also need a variable *e* of type *el_t* and *target* of type *pointer_t*, as shown:

```
typedef .........   el_t;      /* any reasonable type */
typedef struct node  node_t;
typedef node_t*      pointer_t;
struct node {
   el_t       el;
   pointer_t next;
};
```

Figure 16.1
Result of *InitList*

head   *cur*

```
typedef
struct {
   pointer_t head;
   pointer_t cur;
} list;
   ⋮
list L;
el_t e;
pointer_t target;
```

Initialize List

The special constant *NULL* indicates a null pointer in this dynamic allocation of lists. Thus, as Figure 16.1 shows, to initialize the list, *InitList* assigns *NULL* to *head* and *cur*. Because *InitList* changes the values of elements *head* and *cur* of *L*, the function has a parameter *l_ptr*, which is a pointer to an element of type *list*. Many list operations change *head* or *cur*. Therefore, for consistency, we use *l_ptr* as a parameter throughout the implementation. To reference the individual fields of *L*, we use the arrow operator, such as *l_ptr->head* for the *head* element.

```
/*
 * Function to initialize a list to an empty condition
 * Pre:  none
 * Post: The head and current pointers are null.
 */

void InitList(list *l_ptr)
{
   l_ptr->head = NULL;
   l_ptr->cur  = NULL;
}
```

We invoke the function by sending it the address of a list variable as an argument, as follows:

```
InitList(&L);
```

Make a Node

To generate a linked list of nodes, we develop a procedure *MakeNode* to return the address of a new node and to place a data item *e* into the information portion and *NULL* into the link field of that node. To create a node pointed to by *target* storing the information *e*, we call the function *MakeNode*, as shown:

```
target = MakeNode(e);
```

Figure 16.2 diagrams the steps of the action of this function. The function allocates space for the node dynamically with *calloc* and points *P* to this area. If *calloc* cannot allocate space, we abort the program. If *calloc* is successful, we store *e*'s value in the

Figure 16.2
Action of
MakeNode

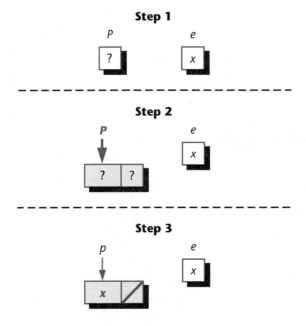

information portion of the new node, *P->el,* and *NULL* in the link portion, *P->next.*
The definition of *MakeNode* as follows:

```c
#include <stdlib.h>
    :
/*
 * Function to return a pointer to a new node with fields for
 * information and a link and with data item  e  in the
 * information portion and NULL in the link portion
 * Pre:  e is an item having type of information portion of a node.
 * Post: The function has returned a pointer to a new node
 *       that contains an information portion with the
 *       value of e and link portion with value NULL.
 */

pointer_t MakeNode(el_t e)
{
    pointer_t P = calloc(1, sizeof(node_t));   /* Step 2 */

    if(P == NULL)
    {
        printf("Error making node\n");
        exit(1);
    }
    else
    {
        P->el   = e;          /* Step 3 */
        P->next = NULL;
    }
    return(P);
}
```

Insert at the First of a List

Inserting at the first of a list with *InsertFirst* causes *head* to point to a new first node with information from a parameter. If initially empty, after insertion, the list has one node. Figures 16.3 and 16.4 present these two situations of inserting a node with information *e* at the beginning of the list. In both cases, the value of *head* changes.

Insertion at the beginning of the list requires adjustment of *head* to point to a new first node. We must be careful to link this node to the list before changing the value of *head,* because we may lose all reference to the rest of the list. Figures 16.5 and 16.6 illustrate a wrong and right sequence of events, respectively, of attaching a node pointed to by *target* to the first of the list.

As Figure 16.5 shows, when we change the value of *head* before we attach *target*'s node, we lose the reference to the linked list. No pointer contains the address of the list. Thus, *InsertFirst* must be implemented in the following order:

Figure 16.3
Action of *InsertFirst* to insert a node at the first of a nonempty list

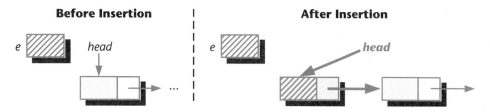

Figure 16.4
Action of *InsertFirst* to insert into an empty list

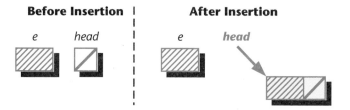

Figure 16.5
Wrong way to insert node at first of a list

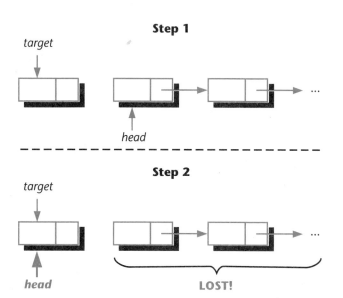

Figure 16.6
Correct way to
insert node at
first of a list

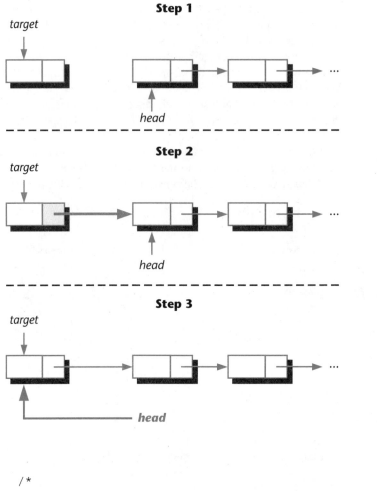

```
/*
 * Function to insert a node at the head of the list
 * Pre:  *l_ptr is a list.
 *       e is the value for the node to be inserted.
 * Post: The list has a new first node with e's value.
 */

void InsertFirst(list *l_ptr, el_t e)
{
    pointer_t target = MakeNode(e);

    target->next = l_ptr->head;
    l_ptr->head = target;
}
```

Because the operation does not change the value of *e*, the second parameter is of type *el_t* and an invocation has the following form:

```
InsertFirst(&L, e);
```

Figure 16.7
Action of
InsertAfter to
insert in the
middle of a list

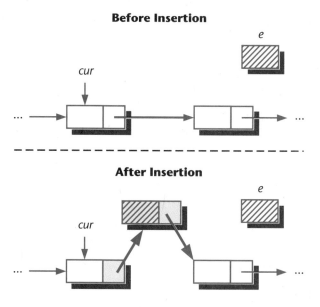

Before Insertion

e

cur

...

After Insertion

cur

e

...

Figure 16.8
Action of
InsertAfter to
insert at the
end of a list

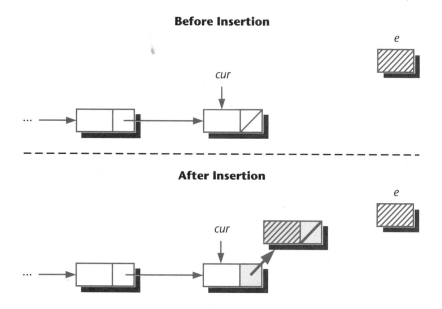

Before Insertion

e

cur

...

After Insertion

e

cur

...

**Insert Later
in a List**

To insert later in the list (in the middle or at the end), we use the *InsertAfter* procedure. In this case, the insertion occurs after the node to which *cur* points. We need not involve *head* because its value does not change and because *cur* marks the location for the insertion (see Figures 16.7 and 16.8).

Figures 16.9 and 16.10 detail how we first change the pointer field of *target*'s node and then the pointer field of the *cur* node to link in the new node. The *next* field of *cur*'s node continues to point to the next node. As the following code shows, we should verify that *cur* points to a node. If it does not, we call a procedure, *NodeReferenceError*, to print an error message and abort program execution.

Figure 16.9
Insert a node
within a list

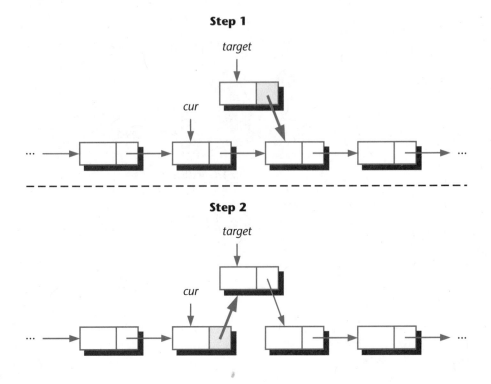

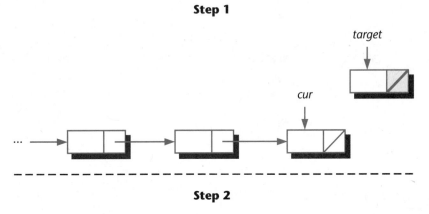

Figure 16.10
Insert a node at
the end of a list

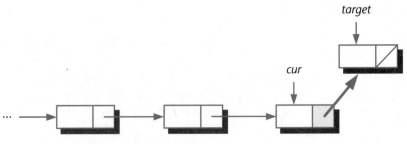

```
/*
 * Function to insert new node after current node
 * Pre:  cur points to a node.
 *       e is the value for the node to be inserted.
 * Post: The list has a new node after the current one with e's value
 *       or NodeReferenceError was called.
 */

void InsertAfter(list *l_ptr, el_t e)
{
   pointer_t target = MakeNode(e);
   if (l_ptr->cur == NULL)
      NodeReferenceError();
   else
   {
      target->next = (l_ptr->cur)->next;
      (l_ptr->cur)->next = target;
   }
}


/*
 * Error routine for no current node or an improper node
 * Pre:  A node reference error condition exists.
 * Post: An error message has been printed and the program aborted.
 */

void NodeReferenceError(void)
{
   printf("ERROR:  No current node or an improper node\n");
   exit(1);
}
```

Even if insertion is to take place at the end of the linked list, with the value of (*l_ptr->cur*)->*next* being *NULL,* the procedure assigns *target* ->*next* the appropriate terminal value of *NULL.*

Advance the Current Pointer

Advancing the pointer *cur* with *Advance* changes its value to the address of the following node. As shown in Figure 16.11, *cur*'s *next* field already points to this node. Even when *cur* references the last node in a list, as in Figure 16.12, the *next* field has the proper value (*NULL*) for *cur* to fall off the end of the list. Before attempting to advance *cur* to the next node, however, we verify that *cur* points to a node.

Figure 16.11
The *next* field of *cur* points to the next node

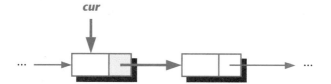

Figure 16.12
cur->next is
NULL.

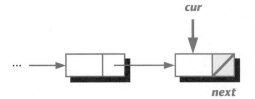

```
/*
 * Function to advance the current node to the next node in the list
 * Pre:   *l_ptr is a list.
 * Post:  l_ptr->cur points to the next node or is NULL in
 *        case l_ptr->cur initially pointed to the last node.
 */

void Advance(list *l_ptr)
{
    if (l_ptr->cur == NULL)
        NodeReferenceError();
    else
        l_ptr->cur = (l_ptr->cur)->next;
}
```

**Delete the
First Node**

Just as insertion at the first of the list is different from adding a node inside the list, so deletion of the first node is distinctive. Figure 16.13 illustrates this special case for deletion. When we remove the first node, we not only want to advance *head* to point to the second node, but we also want to release the memory occupied by the abandoned node. To accomplish this removal, we use a temporary pointer *tmp* to hold the position of the first node. Then after advancing *head*, we dispose of the extra node using *free*.

Before attempting removal of the first node, we verify that the list is not empty. If it is empty, we call the procedure *NodeReferenceError* to print an error message and abort program execution. We must also be careful of another situation—*cur* pointing to the first node. When we delete the first node, we do not want *cur* pointing to that freed node. Unpredictable results can then occur when we reference the current node. Thus, when *cur* is at the first of the list, we advance the pointer before completing the deletion. The *DeleteFirst* procedure reads as follows:

```
/*
 * Function to delete the head node of the list
 * Pre:   *l_ptr is a nonempty list.
 * Post:  *l_ptr is a revised list where the first node
 *        has been deleted.
 */

void DeleteFirst(list *l_ptr)
{
    pointer_t tmp;
```

Figure 16.13
Deletion at the
head of a list

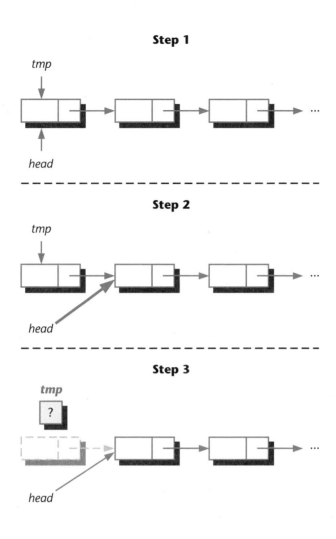

```
if(l_ptr->head == NULL)
   NodeReferenceError();
else
{
   if (l_ptr->cur == l_ptr->head)
      Advance(l_ptr);

   tmp = l_ptr->head;
   l_ptr->head = (l_ptr->head)->next;
   free(tmp);
}
}
```

It is important to hold the position of the first node in *tmp* before advancing *head,*
because the reference to the former head node may be lost. The error of forgetting to
free memory space does not immediately (or perhaps ever) affect the performance of
the linked list. If, however, a number of deletions occur without nodes being released
for further use, we may eventually obtain an OUT OF MEMORY error.

**Delete a
Later Node**

The *DeleteAfter* operation generates a deletion of the node following the one *cur* references. We again use a local pointer variable *tmp* to indicate the node after the current node. We break the existing link of *cur*'s node by advancing its *next* field to reference the node after the one indicated by *tmp*. Then we free the node to which *tmp* points. Figures 16.14 and 16.15 illustrate this process. Before attempting a removal, we must verify that *cur* is not *NULL* and that a node really exists after the current node. If either situation occurs, we call *NodeReferenceError* to handle the error condition. Code for *DeleteAfter* follows:

```
/*
 * Function to delete a node after the current node
 * Pre:  l_ptr->cur points to the node before the one to be deleted.
 * Post: The node originally after the current one has been deleted.
 */

void DeleteAfter(list *l_ptr)
{
    pointer_t tmp;

    if(l_ptr->cur == NULL || (l_ptr->cur)->next == NULL)
        NodeReferenceError();
    else
    {
        tmp = (l_ptr->cur)->next;
        (l_ptr->cur)->next = tmp->next;
        free(tmp);
    }
}
```

Example 16.1

This example creates a list of grocery items and displays all items with a price over one dollar. As with Example 11.5 from Section 11.2, grocery prices and item names are read from a file, such as follows:

```
2.29 dill pickles
0.99 soda
0.59 yogurt
1.09 bread
0.69 milk
```

The function *main* displays a title line and calls the two procedures *CreateList* and *DisplayOverDollar*. *CreateList* invokes *InitFile* of Example 11.5 (Section 11.2) to obtain a file pointer to an input file; reads items from the text file with the routine *ReadRec,* which is similar to *FileToArray* of that same example; and generates a list with this information by calling the appropriate linked list routines. To simplify the problem, we assume the file is not empty and '\n' does not follow the last name. *DisplayOverDollar* traverses the list, displaying all items whose prices exceed one dollar. Figure 16.16 presents the structure chart for the program. Pseudocode designs for *CreateList* and *DisplayOverDollar* are below.

Figure 16.14
Deletion of a
node inside the
list

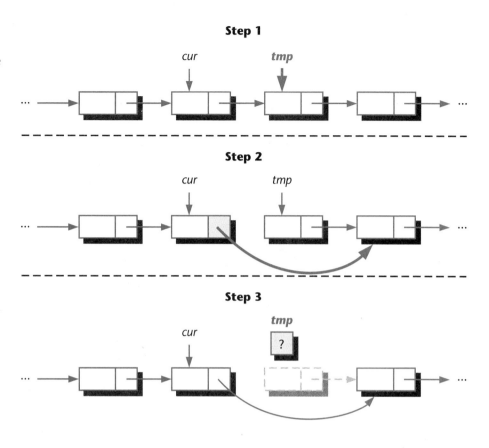

Figure 16.15
Deletion of the
last node in a
list

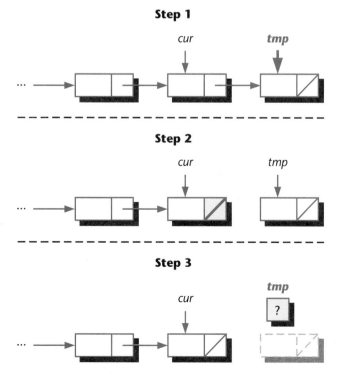

Figure 16.16   Structure chart for Example 16.1

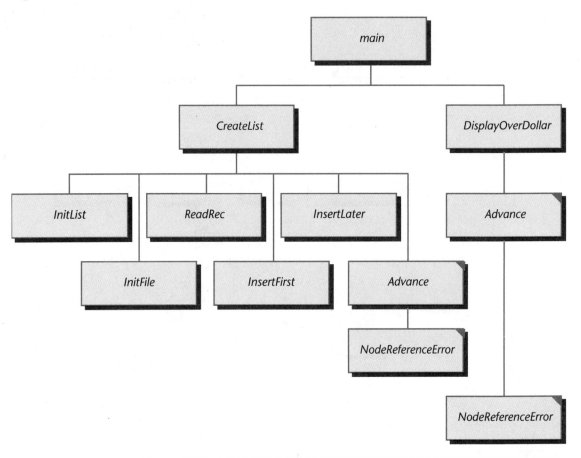

CreateList(l_ptr)

Procedure to read file into a linked list

Pre:

Each line of the price file consists of an item price followed by a single space and an item name. The file is not empty, and '\n' does not follow the last name.

Post:

l_ptr references a list of information from the file.

Algorithm:

InitList(l_ptr)
prompt and read name of file
open file for input
read first record, *e*
InsertFirst(l_ptr, e)
while not at end of file
   read next record
   InsertAfter(l_ptr, e)
   Advance(l_ptr)

DisplayOverDollar(L)

Procedure to display item name and price of all items over one dollar

Pre:

L is a linked list of grocery item names and prices.

Post:

All items with prices over one dollar in the list have been displayed.

Algorithm:

> *L.cur* ← *L.head*
> while (*L.cur* is not *NULL*)
>   get information part of node
>   if price greater than one dollar
>   print item name and price
>   *Advance(L)*

Below are the listings for the program files. The source file *list.c* contains the definitions of the linked list routines that the program uses. The header file *list.h* contains #*include* and #*define* preprocessor directives, type definitions for the list, and function prototypes. The file *grocery.c* has the definitions of *main, CreateList, DisplayOverDollar, ReadRec,* and *InitFile.* The header file, *grocery.h* includes *list.h* and contains the prototypes for the program routines in *grocery.c.*

```
/*
 * File: list.h
 * Header file for list.c of linked list routines
 */

#ifndef LIST_H
#define LIST_H

#include <stdio.h>
#include <stdlib.h>
#include <string.h>

#define MAX_NUM_CHARS 21

typedef char string_t[MAX_NUM_CHARS];    /* string type */

typedef    /* structure type for item name and price */
struct
{
    string_t name;
    float price;
} el_t;

typedef struct node node_t;
typedef node_t*    pointer_t;
```

```
struct node
{
   el_t el;
   pointer_t next;
};
typedef
struct {
   pointer_t head;
   pointer_t cur;
} list;

void InitList(list *l_ptr);
pointer_t MakeNode(el_t e);
void InsertFirst(list *l_ptr, el_t e);
void InsertAfter(list *l_ptr, el_t e);
void Advance(list *l_ptr);
void NodeReferenceError(void);

#endif
```

_____

```
/*
 * File: list.c
 * Source file of some linked list routines
 */

#include "list.h"

/* Place InitList here          */
/* Place MakeNode here          */
/* Place InsertFirst here       */
/* Place InsertAfter here       */
/* Place Advance here           */
/* Place NodeReferenceError here */
```

_____

```
/*
 * File: grocery.h
 * Header file for grocery.c
 */

#ifndef GROCERY_H
#define GROCERY_H

#include "list.h"

void CreateList(list *l_ptr);
void DisplayOverDollar (list L);
FILE *InitFile(char mode[]);
void ReadRec(FILE *infile_ptr, el_t *e_ptr);

#endif
```

_____

```
/*
 * Example 16.1                     File: grocery.c
 * Program to read grocery items and prices from a file into
 * a linked list and display items with prices over $1.00
 */

#include "grocery.h"

main()
{
   list L;

   CreateList(&L);
   printf("\nList of items over one dollar\n\n");
   DisplayOverDollar(L);
}


/*
 * Function to read item prices and names into linked list
 * Pre:  Each line of the price file consists of an item price
 *       followed by a single space and an item name.
 *       The file is not empty, and the last line does not have '\n'.
 * Post: l_ptr references a list of information from the file.
 */

void CreateList(list *l_ptr)
{

   FILE *infile_ptr;      /* pointer to input file */
   string_t filename;     /* name of file          */
   el_t e;                /* input record          */

   InitList(l_ptr);
   printf("Give the name of the input file: ");
   infile_ptr = InitFile("r");

   /* read price and name from file, put in list */
   ReadRec(infile_ptr, &e);
   InsertFirst(l_ptr, e);
   l_ptr->cur = l_ptr->head;
   while (!feof(infile_ptr))
   {
      ReadRec(infile_ptr, &e);
      InsertAfter(l_ptr, e);
      Advance(l_ptr);
   }
   fclose(infile_ptr);
}
```

```
/*
 * Function to display item name and price of all items
 * over one dollar.
 * Pre:  L is a linked list of grocery item names and prices.
 * Post: All items with price over $1.00 have been displayed.
 */

void DisplayOverDollar(list L)
{
    el_t e;

    L.cur = L.head;
    while (L.cur != NULL)
    {
        e = (L.cur)->el;
        if (e.price > 1)
            printf("%-20s $%3.2f\n", e.name, e.price);
        Advance(&L);
    }
}


/*
 * Function to read a record
 * Pre:  infile_ptr points to a file open for reading containing
 *       price, a blank, and product name on each line.
 * Post: infile_ptr has advanced one record.
 *       *e_ptr contains a record from the file.
 */

void ReadRec(FILE *infile_ptr, el_t *e_ptr)
{
    char filler;

    if (fscanf(infile_ptr, "%f%c", &(e_ptr->price), &filler) == 2)
        {
            fgets(e_ptr->name, MAX_NUM_CHARS, infile_ptr);
            if (e_ptr->name[strlen(e_ptr->name) - 1] == '\n')
                e_ptr->name[strlen(e_ptr->name) - 1] = '\0';
            fflush(infile_ptr);
        }
}

/*** Place InitFile (Example 11.5, Section 11.2) here ***/
```

The reader may find it educational to trace the action of this example, drawing the list as the program processes it.

Section 16.1 **Exercises**

1. Give the value of each expression by referring to Figure 16.17.

   a. `P->el`

   b. `(P->next)->el`

   c. `R->next`

For each of Exercises 2–5 starting with Figure 16.17, draw the list after execution of the sequence of statements.

2.
```
R->next  = Q;
head->el = 1;
P        = P->next;
```

3.
```
P->el = head->el;
Q     = NULL;
P     = (P->next) -> next;
head  = R;
```

4.
```
Q->next = NULL;
R->next = head;
head    = R;
```

5.
```
Q = MakeNode(10);
R->next = Q;
```

In Exercises 6 and 7, the subfields of the el *portion of a node are given. Define the types and declare the* list *variable* L *to create a dynamic memory allocation implementation of a linked list structure.*

6. *Count* of type *int*

7. *SSN, name, salary*

In Exercises 8–16, code each routine.

8. Procedure to install a node with the information from the first node of *L1* as the first node in a list *L2* and to remove the first node from a list *L1*

9. Procedure to form a list with two nodes, the first with the value of *x* and the second with the value of *y*

10. a. Nonrecursive function *size* to return the number of nodes in a list pointed to by *head*

    b. Find a recursive version of the function in Part a.

11. a. Nonrecursive procedure to print the values in the information fields of the nodes of a list

    b. Find a recursive version of the procedure in Part a.

12. Procedure to read records from a file and insert each data item in turn at the beginning of a list

Figure 16.17 Linked list for Exercises 1–5

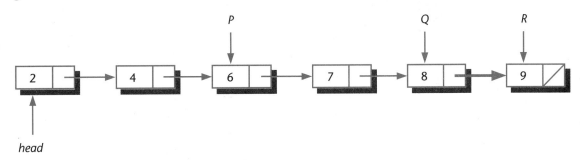

13. **a.** Nonrecursive function to return the sum of the values stored in a list

    b. Find a recursive version of the function in Part a.

14. Recursive version of *DestroyList* to delete all the nodes in a list by repeatedly deleting the first node

15. *SearchDelete* to search for *e*'s value in an ordered list and to delete that node

16. *DeleteValues* to read records from a file and delete nodes with that information from a list arranged in ascending order with no two nodes containing the same information

Section 16.1 Programming Projects

Note: The text disk contains linked list routines in list.h *and* list.c.

1. Revise the program in Example 16.1 to allow the user to insert or delete items in the grocery list. Repeatedly ask the user if he or she wishes to insert, delete, update, or quit. Unless quitting, the user enters the name of a grocery item. For an insertion, if the item is found in the linked list, a message is issued that the item is already in the list. If the item is not found, a node with that information is inserted at the first of the list. For a deletion or an update, search for the item. If found, delete or update the item. Otherwise, issue an error message. Print the list immediately after creation and at the end of program execution.

2. Revise the program in Example 16.1 so that the list of grocery items is developed with the items in order from least expensive to most expensive.

3. Revise the program in Example 16.1 so that the list of grocery items is developed with the items in alphabetical order.

Section 16.2 Stack Abstraction

A stack is an appropriate data structure when the last data placed into the structure is the first processed. The acronym **LIFO** symbolizes the situation—*Last In First Out*, and the name "stack" is itself descriptive. At a salad bar, we typically take the top plate from a stack of salad plates. If the plates are recessed into a spring-loaded receptacle, we only have access to the top plate. We cannot get to the third plate from the top without removing the two above it, one at a time. If we put a plate back, it goes on top of the stack. The operation to place a data item on top of the stack is push, and the pop operation removes a data item from the stack. These pop-and-push operations are illustrated with a stack of plates in Figure 16.18. The ADT stack definition projects the basic characteristic illustrated with the plates. All activity occurs at the top of the stack. The following examples define additional stack operations.

ADT Stack

Data:

    A sequence of elements of the same type (*el_t*). Associated with each element is the order in which the item entered the stack.

Figure 16.18
Pushing onto
and popping
from a stack of
plates

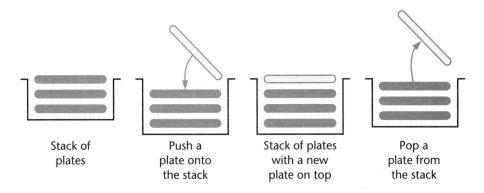

| Stack of plates | Push a plate onto the stack | Stack of plates with a new plate on top | Pop a plate from the stack |

Operations:

Notation	Meaning
el_t	type of an element in the stack
s	stack
e	item of type el_t
b	boolean value

InitStack(s)

Procedure to initialize *s* to an empty stack

StackIsEmpty(s) ⟶ b

Boolean function to return *TRUE* if *s* is empty

StackIsFull(s) ⟶ b

Boolean function to return *TRUE* if *s* is full

Push(s, e)

Procedure to place an item with *e*'s value into *s* (assume room is in *s* for this new item)

Pop(s, e)

Procedure to take the top item or the last item placed into nonempty *s* out of *s* and give its value to *e* (assume *s* is not empty initially)

Example 16.2

Applications exist in which we wish to know the element on the top of the stack (perhaps for comparison or assignment), but we do not want to pop this item from the stack. This *RetrieveStack* function involves popping the top item from the stack, assigning that value to a variable, and then pushing the same item once more onto the stack.

Even though *RetrieveStack* can be defined in terms of *Pop* and *Push,* if the operation is to be used frequently in an application, we should consider *RetrieveStack* as a basic ADT stack operations. The list of abstract data type operations is not absolute for any data structure and can be logically expanded or contracted to meet the needs of a particular application. Figure 16.19 shows the action of this operation, which is designed below using *Pop* and *Push.*

Figure 16.19
The action of
RetrieveStack(s)

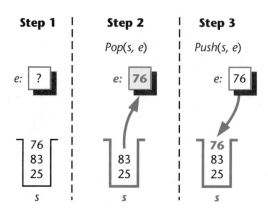

Figure 16.20
Action of
AddTop
procedure on a
stack of at least
two numbers

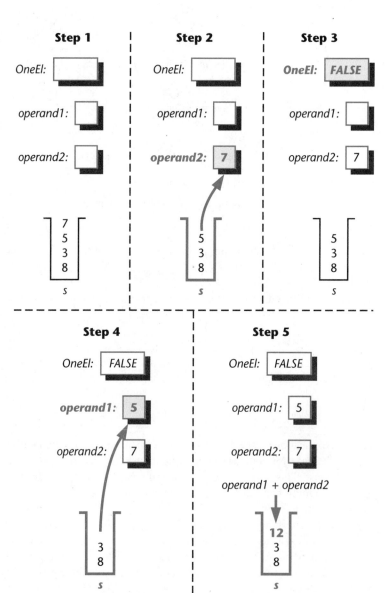

RetrieveStack(s) ⟶ *e*

>   Function to return the value at the top of the stack, leaving the stack
>   unchanged. Assume *s* is not empty

Pre:

>   *s* is a nonempty stack.

Post:

>   The value of item at the top of *s* has been returned.

Algorithm:

>   *Pop(s, e)*
>   *Push(s, e)*
>   return *e*

Example 16.3

Suppose the data in a stack *s* are numbers. Design a procedure that replaces the top two
elements with their sum. Figure 16.20 illustrates the action of this *AddTop* procedure.
We pop the top two elements and then push their sum onto the stack.

   We assume that *s* is nonempty before calling *AddTop,* but we can only be sure that
the stack contains one element. With the basic ADT stack operations, reference is only
made to the top of the stack. *StackIsEmpty(s)* being *FALSE* does not give us a clue as
to whether *s* has one or 1000 elements. Thus, the routine *AddTop* must handle the
situation where the stack contains exactly one number. In this case, shown in Figure
16.21, we pop the top and only element; discover that now the stack is empty; and,
consequently, replace the element and change a flag, *OneEl,* to be *TRUE.* In Figure
16.20, we have more than one element, so *OneEl* gets the value *FALSE.*

   The pseudocode and ADT stack operations for *AddTop* follow:

AddTop(s, OneEl)

>   Procedure to replace the top two elements of a nonempty stack, *s,* of numbers
>   with their sum. If *s* contains only one number, we leave the stack unchanged.

Pre:

>   *s* is a nonempty stack of numbers.

Post:

>   *s* is a nonempty stack of numbers, where the top element is the sum of the top
>   two elements on the original stack.
>   *OneEl* is a boolean variable that becomes true when *s* has only one element
>   initially.

Figure 16.21
Action of
AddTop from
Example 16.3,
where the stack
has one
element

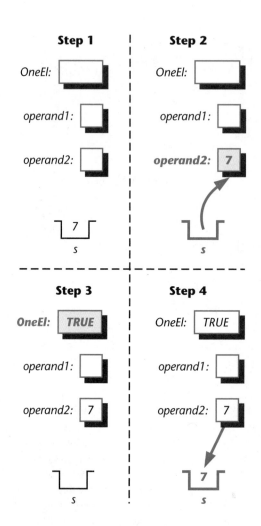

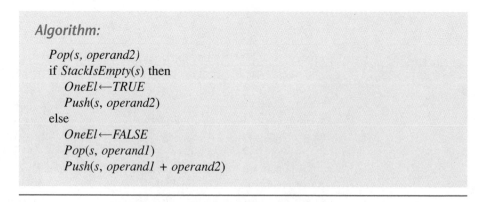

Algorithm:

Pop(s, operand2)
if *StackIsEmpty(s)* then
　　OneEl←TRUE
　　Push(s, operand2)
else
　　OneEl←FALSE
　　Pop(s, operand1)
　　Push(s, operand1 + operand2)

Example 16.4

Using *AddTop*, we can design an operation, *AddStack*, to replace all the elements in a nonempty stack of numbers with their sum. This procedure repeatedly calls *AddTop* until *OneEl* is *TRUE*. Figure 16.22 shows an example of the action of *AddStack* whose design follows:

Figure 16.22 Action of *AddStack*

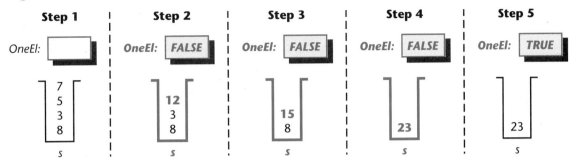

AddStack(s)

Procedure to replace the elements of a nonempty stack, *s*, of numbers with their sum

Pre:

s is a nonempty stack of numbers.

Post:

s is a stack of one number, the sum of elements on the original stack.

Algorithm:

repeat the following
    AddTop(s, OneEl)
until *OneEl* is *TRUE*

Example 16.5

In this example, we design a recursive procedure *PrintStackUp* to print the elements of a stack from bottom to top, leaving the stack unchanged when execution is complete. *StackIsEmpty(s)* is our terminal condition, because there is nothing to print in an empty stack. When the stack has at least one element, we pop the top element, *e*. Before proceeding, we recursively call *PrintStackUp* to print the remainder of the stack from bottom to top. With those elements written in the desired order, we can now print the value of *e* and push *e* back onto the stack. The value of this top element is recorded only after all the elements beneath it have been printed. Thus, the output lists the elements of the stack from bottom to top. Figure 16.23 demonstrates the action of the *PrintStackUp* procedure, the design of which follows:

PrintStackUp(s)

Procedure to print the elements of a stack from bottom to top, leaving the stack unchanged

Figure 16.23
Action of
PrintStackUp(s)
from Example
16.5

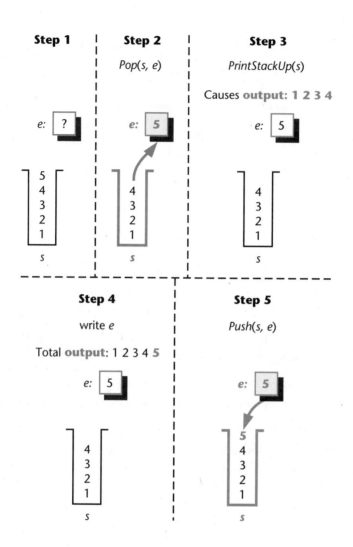

Pre:

   s is a stack.

Post:

   Elements of *s* are printed from bottom to top.

Algorithm:

   if not *StackIsEmpty(s)* then
       Pop(s, e)
       PrintStackUp(s)
       write *e*
       Push(s, e)

Section 16.2 **Exercises**

Starting with the stack and variable in Figure 16.24, draw a picture of s *and* e *and give any output after execution of each segment in Exercises 1–7.*

1. *Push(s, e)*
  Push(s, e)
3. *AddTop(s, OneEl)*
6. *product ← 1*
  while (not *StackIsEmpty(s)*)
    Pop(s, e)
    *product ← product * e*
  Push(s, product)

2. *RetrieveStack(s, e)*
4. *AddStack(s)*
5. *PrintStackUp(s))*
7. *InitStack(u)*
  Push(u, e)
  Pop(s, e)
  *Push(u, e *e)*

8. Suppose input, consisting of the integers 1, 2, and 3, in that order, is pushed onto a stack *s*. Only when a number is popped from the stack is it written. If possible, with appropriate pushes and pops, show how to print each of the following permutations of the input stream.

    a. 1 2 3   **b.** 1 3 2   **c.** 2 1 3
    d. 2 3 1   **e.** 3 1 2   **f.** 3 2 1

Using pseudocode and ADT stack operations and notation, define the operations in Exercises 9–25. Answer any other questions about the operations.

9. Procedure *SwapStack* to exchange the top two elements on a stack

10. Procedure *dup* to duplicate the top element on a nonempty stack

11. Procedure *ClearStack* to remove all the elements from a stack

12. Procedure *FileToStack* to read from a line of a file of integers and place each data item in a stack

13. Procedure *PrintStack* to print the elements in a stack from top to bottom, leaving the stack empty

14. Procedure to print data from a file of integers, with each line printed in reverse order. Use *FileToStack* and *PrintStack* from Exercises 12 and 13, respectively.

15. Recursive procedure *append(s, u)* to append a stack *u* on the top of stack *s* so that *u*'s top element is on the top. The procedure should cause *u* to be empty.

16. Nonrecursive procedure *PrintStackUp* from Example 16.5 to print the elements of a stack from bottom to top

17. a. Nonrecursive procedure *NRCopyStack* to make a copy of a stack

    b. Design a recursive version of *NRCopyStack* from Part a.

Figure 16.24
Stack *s* and
variable *e* for
Exercises 1–7

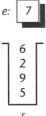

18. Procedure *bottom* to place the bottom element of the stack, *s,* into *e,* making *s* empty

19. Recursive version of *AddStack* from Example 16.4

20. a. Procedure *AddStack2* that is a revision of *AddStack* of Example 16.4. *AddStack2* initializes *sum* to be 0; pops the elements from the stack, accumulating their sum in *sum;* and then pushes the value of *sum* onto the stack.

   b. What is the total number of statements executed with *AddStack* for a stack of *n* elements?

   c. What is the total number of statements executed with *AddStack2* for a stack of *n* elements?

21. Procedure *AddStack3* that first checks that the stack is nonempty before calling *AddStack2* of Exercise 20. An error message should be printed for an empty initial stack.

22. Procedure *AddStack4,* a recursive version of *AddStack2* from Exercise 20.

23. a. Procedure *DeleteStack* to delete the topmost occurrence of an item, *e,* from a stack, *s,* leaving the stack otherwise unchanged. Assume *e* is in the stack.

   b. Revise the procedure in Part a to handle the situation of *e* not being in *s.*

24. Procedure *RemoveBlanks* to remove all blanks from a stack of characters, leaving the stack otherwise unchanged

25. a. Nonrecursive boolean function *EqualStack* to return *TRUE* if two stacks are identical, ordered in the same way. The procedure should leave the stacks unchanged.

   b. Recursive version of *EqualStack* from Part a

Section 16.3 Linked List Implementation of Stacks

A major goal of data abstraction is to encapsulate the structure so that details of implementation are hidden from the user. With such information hidden, the programmer can consider applications on a higher plane with major operations as opposed to a lower level where a programmer can become lost in a sea of details.

For example, two major ways exist to implement an ADT stack—statically with arrays and dynamically with lists. Using the specifications for the operations, the user of the package should be able to develop an application without knowing the specific implementation that the stack programmer chose. For each stack operation, the developer of an application program must know the input the operation needs, what the operation does, the values it returns, and how to access the package. In C, such an ADT package usually has two files, a separately compiled file of operation definitions and a header file of *#include* preprocessor directives; symbolic constant, macro, and type definitions; and function prototypes. The application program that uses the package should be able to run without change to the C statements regardless of the implementation. Thus, if the package developer discovers a better algorithm for an operation, he or she should be able to make the improvement without affecting the application program. Moreover, if several ADT stack implementations are available, the user of the package should be able to switch the implementation to improve overall performance by only including a different header file and linking with a different separately compiled definitions file.

The array and linked list implementations of ADT stack have advantages and disadvantages. The main difference involves the static nature of arrays and the dynamic nature of linked lists using pointers. Usually, the size of the array is established at compile time and is not changed throughout program execution. Thus, with an array implementation of ADT stack, the stack may fill during execution of a particular program. For example, most computers implement the run-time stack, which holds activation records for each function invocation and procedure call, as an array. Consequently, we may obtain a **STACK OVERFLOW error** while using recursion. With a dynamic linked list implementation of stacks in C, as long as enough memory exists, the stack never fills. Moreover, space for stack elements is allocated only as needed. We do have the overhead of the room for pointers. For each array element, 100% of the element is used to store data. Each node in a linked list, however, has a pointer field that contains no information but references the next node. On many computers, a pointer consumes twice as much space as an integer. As the information field becomes larger, the space efficiency of a node approaches that of an array element—100%. It is faster to access an array element directly through an index instead of accessing a linked list node through a pointer. The dynamic nature of the linked list, however, still makes it very attractive for implementation of an abstract data type. A linked list implementation of an ADT stack can accommodate any size stack that an application program needs (up to the limitations of memory size). For the remainder of the section, we consider such an implementation, leaving an array implementation for the exercises.

Stack Creation

The creation of the stack follows the typical linked list structure, as shown:

```
typedef ......... el_t;

typedef struct node node_t;
typedef node_t* stack;

struct node {
   el_t el;
   struct node* next;
};
   ⋮
stack s;
```

Here, *stack* is the identifier for the pointer type *node_t**; and the pointer variable *s* is the variable we have often called *head*. Because we already maintain a pointer at the first of the list, we consider the top of the stack to be there. Figure 16.25 shows a stack along with its storage in a linked list.

Figure 16.25
Stack with linked list representation

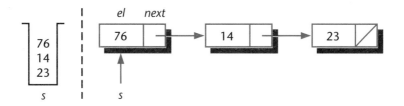

Initialize Stack

As pictured in Figure 16.26, the *InitStack* operation reduces to the linked list operation *InitList* without *cur*. The dynamic implementation follows:

```
/*
 * Function to initialize the stack pointed to by s_ptr
 * Pre:  s_ptr is a pointer to a stack.
 * Post: The stack is initialized to be empty.
 */

void InitStack(stack *s_ptr)
{
    *s_ptr = NULL;
}
```

Similarly, *StackIsEmpty* tests if *s* is *NULL*. To avoid copying an entire structure containing an array, the static implementation of *StackIsEmpty* employs a parameter of type *stack**. So that the application program can switch implementations without changing code, we use the same parameter declarations for the dynamic version, as follows:

```
/*
 * Boolean function to return TRUE if the stack to which
 * s_ptr points is empty
 * Pre:  s_ptr points to a stack that has been initialized.
 * Post: The function returns TRUE if the stack is empty,
 *       FALSE otherwise.
 */

boolean_t StackIsEmpty(stack *s_ptr)
{
    return(*s_ptr == NULL ? TRUE : FALSE);
}
```

Never Fills

As mentioned earlier, one major advantage of a dynamic linked list implementation of ADT stack is that the stack can grow virtually indefinitely. Therefore, the operation *StackIsFull* can degenerate to always being *FALSE*. Although unnecessary with the dynamic implementation, we again use a parameter of type *stack** for consistency with the static implementation, as follows:

```
/*
 * Boolean function to return TRUE if the stack is full
 * Pre:  s_ptr points to a stack.
 * Post: The function returns FALSE.
 */

boolean_t StackIsFull(stack *s_ptr)
{
    return(FALSE);
}
```

Figure 16.26
Empty stack
with linked list
implementation

Figure 16.27 Action of *Push* operation along with the implementation with a linked list

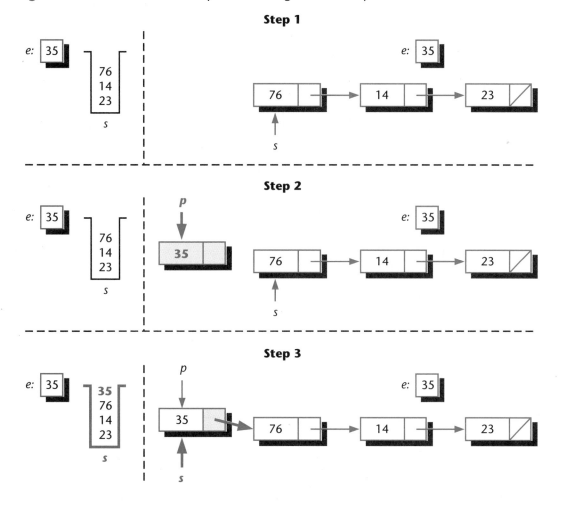

Push

Because we maintain the top at the first of the list, *Push(s, e)* inserts that node at the first of the linked list. As Figure 16.27 demonstrates, the code parallels that of *InsertFirst*. Because the stack never fills, however, we do not need to check *StackIsFull* as we do with the static implementation. For creation of a stack node, we use the same definition of *MakeNode* as in Section 16.1, except we tailor the function to return a value of type *stack*. The definition of *Push* follows:

```
/*
 * Function to push an element, e, onto a stack pointed
 * to by s_ptr
 *    Pre:  e is a data element.
 *          s_ptr is a pointer to a stack.
 *    Post: s_ptr is a pointer to a stack with e at the top.
 */

void Push(stack *s_ptr, el_t e)
{                                          /* Figure 16.27 */
    stack p = MakeNode(e);                 /* Step 2 */
    p->next = *s_ptr;                       /* Step 3 */
    *s_ptr = p;
}
```

Pop

As Figure 16.28 illustrates for the *Pop* procedure, we store the information in the first node into *e* before executing a *DeleteFirst* operation. With the linked list or array implementation, we should verify that the stack is not empty before attempting to access the top item. The code for *Pop* follows:

```
/*
 * Function to pop an element from a stack pointed to by
 * s_ptr and place the value in the location pointed
 * to by e_ptr
 * Pre:  s_ptr points to a stack.
 * Post: s_ptr points to a stack with the top element popped.
 *       e_ptr points to an element with the former top.
 *       If the stack was initially empty, execution was aborted.
 */

void Pop(stack *s_ptr, el_t *e)
{
    stack p;

    if (StackIsEmpty(s_ptr))
    {
        printf("ERROR:  Stack is empty\n");
        exit(1);
    }
    else                              /* Figure 16.28 */
    {
        *e  =  (*s_ptr)->el;          /* Step 2 - Retrieve info */
                                      /* Step 3 - DeleteFirst */
        p  =  *s_ptr;
        *s_ptr  =  (*s_ptr)->next;
        free(p);
    }
}
```

Figure 16.28   Action of *Pop* operation along with a linked list implementation

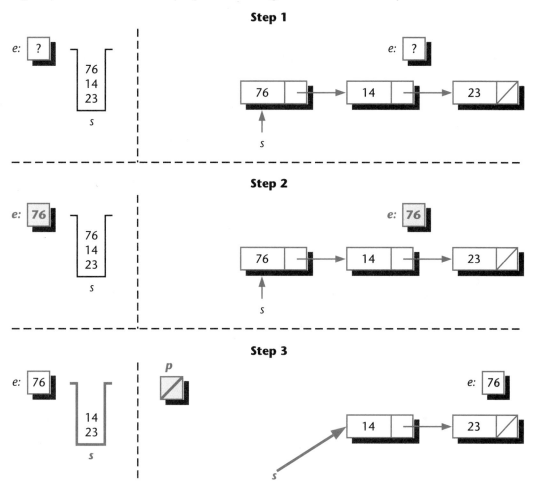

Summary   Figure 16.29 summarizes this linked list implementation of ADT stack in C.

Example 16.6

In this example, we implement the recursive procedure *PrintStackUp* of Example 16.5 (Section 16.2) to print the elements of a stack from bottom to top, leaving the stack unchanged when execution is complete. The code consists of a straightforward translation of the design into C. For *s* of type *stack*, we must pass the address of *s* (&*s*) to the ADT stack operations. Similarly, *Pop* also requires the address of a data variable. Assume that the *el_t* is *int*. The code follows:

```
/*
 * Example 16.6
 * Recursive function to print the elements of a stack
 * from bottom to top, leaving the stack unchanged
 * Pre:  s is a stack of integers.
 * Post: The elements of s have been printed, bottom to top.
 */
```

```
void PrintStackUp(stack s)
{
   el_t e;

   if (!StackIsEmpty(&s))
   {
      Pop(&s, &e);
      PrintStackUp(s);
      printf("%d\n", e);
      Push(&s, e);
   }
}
```

Figure 16.29
Dynamic
linked list
implementation
of ADT stack

Header File

```
/*
 * File: stackd.h —- type definitions, symbolic constants,
 * and function prototypes for dynamic linked list
 * implementation of stack ADT.
 */

#ifndef STACKD_H
#define STACKD_H

#include <stdlib.h>
#include <stdio.h>

typedef enum {FALSE, TRUE} boolean_t;
typedef ...... el_t;    /* type varies with application */

typedef struct node node_t;
typedef node_t* stack;

struct node {
    el_t el;
    struct node* next;
};

/* Function prototypes for the stack operations */

stack     MakeNode(el_t);
void      InitStack(stack*);
boolean_t StackIsEmpty(stack*);
boolean_t StackIsFull(stack*);
void      Push(stack*, el_t);
void      Pop(stack*, el_t*);

#endif
```

In Calling Routine
```
   #include "stackd.h"
   :
   stack s;
   el_t e;
```

Figure 16.29
Continued

File of Operation Definitions

```
/*
 * File: stackd.c -- ANSI C source code for linked list
 * implementation of ADT stack
 */

#include "stackd.h"

/*
 * Function to initialize the stack pointed to by s_ptr
 * Pre:  s_ptr is a pointer to a stack.
 * Post: The stack is initialized to be empty.
 */

void InitStack(stack *s_ptr)
{
   *s_ptr = NULL;
}

/*
 * Boolean function to return TRUE if the stack to which
 * s_ptr points is empty
 * Pre:  s_ptr points to a stack that has been initialized.
 * Post: The function returns TRUE if the stack is empty,
 *       FALSE otherwise.
 */

boolean_t StackIsEmpty(stack *s_ptr)
{
   return(*s_ptr == NULL ? TRUE : FALSE);
}

/*
 * Boolean function to return TRUE if the stack is full
 * Pre:  s_ptr points to a stack.
 * Post: The function returns FALSE.
 */

boolean_t StackIsFull(stack *s_ptr)
{
   return(FALSE);
}

/*
 * Function to push an element, e, onto a stack pointed
 * to by s_ptr
 *  Pre:  e is a data element.
 *        s_ptr is a pointer to a stack.
 *  Post: s_ptr is a pointer to a stack with e at the top.
 */

void Push(stack *s_ptr, el_t e)
{
   stack p = MakeNode(e);
   p->next = *s_ptr;
   *s_ptr = p;
}
```

Figure 16.29
Continued

```
/*
 * Function to pop an element from a stack pointed to by
 * s_ptr and place the value in the location pointed
 * to by e_ptr
 * Pre:  s_ptr points to a stack.
 * Post: s_ptr points to a stack with the top element popped.
 *       e_ptr points to an element with the former top.
 *       If the stack was empty, execution was aborted.
 */

void Pop(stack *s_ptr, el_t *e)
{
   stack p;

   if (StackIsEmpty(s_ptr))
   {
      printf("ERROR: Stack is empty\n");
      exit(1);
   }
   else
   {
      *e = (*s_ptr)->el;

      p = *s_ptr;
      *s_ptr = (*s_ptr)->next;
      free(p);
   }
}

/*
 * Function to place information into a new node
 * and return a pointer to that node
 * Pre:  e is an item having the type of the information
 *       portion of a list node.
 * Post: Function returns pointer to a node that contains an
 *       information portion with the value of e.
 */

stack MakeNode(el_t e)
{
   stack s = calloc(1, sizeof(node_t));

   if(s == NULL)
   {
      printf("Error making node\n");
      exit(1);
   }
```

Figure 16.29
Continued

```
                          else
                          {
                                  s->el    = e;
                                  s->next = NULL;
                          }

                          return(s);
          }
```

Section 16.3 **Exercises**

For Exercises 1–20, code each routine from the referenced exercise or example in Section 16.2 using an implementation with linked lists.

1. **a.** Procedure *RetrieveStack* of Example 16.2 to obtain the top value on the stack

   b. Add *RetrieveStack* to the ADT stack package by implementing the procedure without a push and a pop but with an assignment statement.

2. Procedure *AddTop* of Example 16.3 to pop the top two elements and push their sum onto the stack

3. Procedure *SwapStack* from Exercise 9 to exchange the top two elements on a stack

4. Procedure *dup* from Exercise 10 to duplicate the top element on a nonempty stack

5. Procedure *ClearStack* from Exercise 11 to remove all the elements from a stack

6. Procedure *FileToStack* from Exercise 12 to read from a line of a text file and place each character in a stack

7. Procedure *PrintStack* from Exercise 13 to print the elements in a stack from top to bottom

8. Procedure from Exercise 14 to print data from a file with each line printed in reverse order

9. Recursive procedure *append* (*s, u*) from Exercise 15 to append a stack *u* on the top of stack *s* so that *u*'s top element is on the top. The procedure should cause *u* to be empty.

10. Nonrecursive version of *PrintStackUp* from Exercise 16

11. **a.** Nonrecursive procedure *NRCopyStack* from Exercise 17a to make a copy of a stack

    b. Nonrecursive version of *NRCopyStack* from Exercise 17b

12. Procedure *bottom* from Exercise 18 to place the bottom element of the stack, *s,* into *e,* making *s* empty

13. Recursive version of *AddStack* from Exercise 19

14. Procedure *AddStack2* from Exercise 20 that initializes *sum* to be 0; pops the elements from the stack, accumulating their sum in *sum;* and then pushes the value of *sum* onto the stack.

15. Procedure *AddStack3* from Exercise 21, which first checks that the stack is nonempty before calling *AddStack2*

16. Procedure *AddStack4* from Exercise 22 that is a recursive version of *AddStack2*

17. Procedure *DeleteStack* from Exercise 23a to delete the topmost occurrence of an item, *e,* from a stack, *s,* leaving the stack otherwise unchanged (assume *e* is in the stack).

18. Procedure *RemoveBlanks* from Exercise 24 to remove all blanks from a stack of characters

19. a. Boolean function *EqualStack* from Exercise 25a to return *TRUE* if two stacks are identical, ordered in the same way. The procedure should leave the stacks unchanged.

   b. Nonrecursive version of *EqualStack* from Exercise 25b

20. Summarize the advantages and disadvantages of the array and dynamic linked list implementations of ADT stack. What conclusions do you draw about each?

In Exercises 21–26, implement the requested ADT stack operation using an array implementation, where

```
#define MAX_NUM_ELS 256

typedef ........ el_t;
typedef int       index_t;

typedef struct {
    index_t    top;
    el_t       el[ MAX_NUM_ELS ];
} stack;
```

Figure 16.30 pictures a stack along with its storage in such a structure.

21. *InitStack*

22. *StackIsEmpty*

23. *StackIsFull*

24. *Push*

25. *Pop*

26. *RetrieveStack*

Figure 16.30
Stack along with its implementation with an array

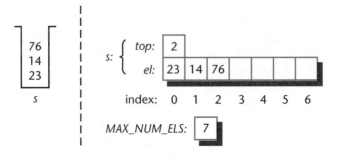

Section 16.3 Programming Project

Note: The text disk contains the stack package in files stackd.h *and* stackd.c.
Write a program to read a text file and print whether or not a line is a palindrome. Use stacks to implement the program. As a line is read, push each character onto stack *s* and stack *u*. Then, transfer the information from stack *u* to stack *r* so that *r* is in reverse order. Repeatedly popping elements from *s* and *r*, test for equality.

Section 16.4 Breadth: Run-Time Stack during Program Execution

An operating system (OS) is a collection of programs that help the user to interact efficiently with the resources of a computer system. The OS manages memory, input/output, and processing (see Section 12.4).

For each running program, the OS must know the next statement to execute. The computer has a register or high-speed memory location, called the program counter (PC), that holds the address of this statement (see Section 12.7). When *main* calls a function *A,* the computer must store the value of the PC to know where to return on completion of the function. An activation record or stack frame is formulated with this return location, the list of arguments, room for a return value (if any), and an area for the function's local variables. If function *A* calls another function *B,* the computer must store the same information for *B* without losing the activation record for *A.* When *B* finishes execution, the computer no longer needs *B*'s activation record, and execution continues at the return location in *A.* Eventually, *A* terminates, and the computer returns to *main.* Figure 16.31 shows the progression of function calls and returns in the opposite order.

Definition	An **activation record** or **stack frame** is a record that comes into existence when a function is called. It contains the return location, the list of arguments, room for a return value (if any), and an area for the function's local variables.

This LIFO character of function calls and returns is ideal for a stack data structure. Many compilers maintain a run-time stack of activation records for each executing program. This stack stores the activation records of the current and all suspended

Figure 16.31 Progression of function calls and returns in the opposite order

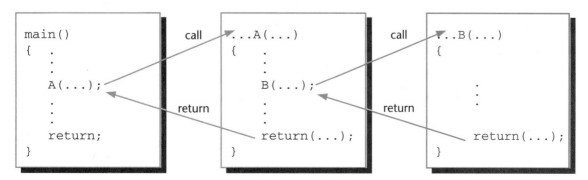

Figure 16.32 Changing run-time stack during program execution

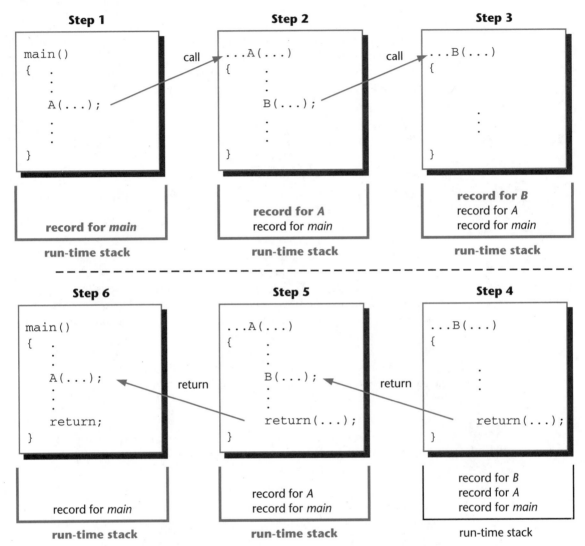

routines. As Figure 16.32 shows, with the run-time stack, the computer can back out of these subprograms in the reverse order of the calling sequence. At any time, the run-time stack represents the state of the program by showing information about all functions that are in the midst of execution.

Definition A **run-time stack** is a stack of activation records that exists during execution of a program.

As Figure 16.32 indicates, the function *main* has an activation record. The operating system calls *main* and can pass arguments to this function. When execution of the program ends, *main* can return an error value to the operating system. As noted in Section 12.2, most C compilers allow the user to send command-line arguments to *main.* Besides accepting arguments, *main* can also return a value to the operating system. Many C programmers end *main* with

```
return 0;
```

and end error-handling routines with

```
return error_value;
```

A return value of zero indicates normal termination, and *error_value* is an error number that the operating system uses to process the error.

When writing in an assembly language as opposed to a high-level language, the programmer is responsible for saving a "snapshot" of the system—including register values—with each function call. On this low level, the programmer maintains the run-time stack.

In Section 13.1, we discussed this stack of activation records relative to recursion. With a run-time stack, the computer need not be aware that a function is calling itself. The system merely stacks the activation record with the return address and other information, whether the function is different or the same as the calling function. Thus, the stack data structure facilitates the implementation of recursion.

The information stored on many run-time stacks is as follows:

1. Function return value
2. Pointer to the previous activation record, called a **dynamic link**
3. Return address
4. Parameters
5. Local variables

Because functions have different numbers and types of parameters and local variables, the dynamic link is useful in determining where one activation record ends and another begins. Sometimes the computer does not maintain the local variables in the activation record, but instead has a pointer to another area of memory with these values. Figure 16.33 depicts the activation record for a function *A* on the run-time stack.

Definition   A **dynamic link** in an activation record is a pointer to the previous activation record.

In many computers, the run-time stack is a stack of computer words. Thus, items within the activation record are pushed onto the run-time stack, and after execution of the function, the values are popped in reverse order.

Section 16.4 **Exercises**

1. **a.** Using pseudocode and ADT stack operations and notation, define the procedure *SaveVariables* to save the values of *int* variables *x, y,* and *z* by placing them onto an existing stack, *s.*
   b. Code the routine in Part a.

2. **a.** Using pseudocode and ADT stack operations and notation, define the procedure *RestoreVariables* to recover the values saved by *SaveVariables* of Exercise 1.
   b. Code the routine in Part a.

Figure 16.33
Activation
record of
function *A* on
run-time stack

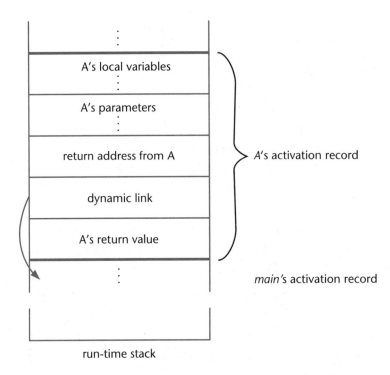

run-time stack

Section 16.4 **Programming Project**

This project involves a program to simulate some duties of the run-time stack. Write a program with several functions that have integer parameters and return values. Then, define a global stack to store arguments and return values. The calling function is responsible for pushing arguments for a function call onto the stack. The called function pushes the value to return onto the stack. Upon return, the calling function pops the arguments and return value. Print the stack on entering and leaving each function.

〰 **Programming and Debugging Hints**

Freeing Pointers

In the linked list operations of *DeleteFirst* and *DeleteAfter* and the stack operation of *Pop*, we carefully returned the deleted node to available memory space with a statement, such as

```
free(tmp);
```

Without such freeing and with frequent insertions and deletions, memory could fill with inaccessible nodes.

Destroying Linked Structures

If we declare locally a linked list or stack implemented as a linked list, we should remove all the elements before the structure goes out of scope. For example, consider the following routine that declares a local stack, *TempStack:*

```
void example(stack s)
{
    stack TempStack;
    ⋮
}
```

Suppose that during execution of *example, TempStack* grows to 100 records of 50 bytes each. When the function returns, the space allocated for *TempStack* is freed for other use. However, *TempStack* is only a pointer. The node to which *TempStack* points and the remainder of the stack members are not freed. Each time the function returns from a call, the routine abandons another 100 nodes in memory. Each node contains 50 bytes of information and several bytes (say 4) for a pointer. Thus, each abandoned stack consumes 5400 bytes or about 5.27 K. If the program calls the routine enough, the computer will run out of memory.

To avoid this problem, before leaving *example,* we should call a routine to destroy the local stack by popping every element. The definition of *DestroyStack* follows:

```
/*
 * Function to remove all the nodes from a stack
 * Pre:  s_ptr points to a stack.
 * Post: The stack has been emptied.
 */

void DestroyStack(stack *s_ptr)
{
    while (!StackIsEmpty(s_ptr))
        Pop(s_ptr);
}
```

Thus, the amended *example* should read

```
void example(stack s)
{
    stack TempStack;
    ⋮
    DestroyStack(&TempStack);
}
```

Key Terms

Summary

Data structures involve a study of the various frameworks for storing data and the algorithms that implement and perform operations on these structures. One data structure is a list, which provides a linking configuration of nodes of information that we can expand and contract as needed. The data type list is often called a linked list at the implementation level. In Section 16.1, we implement linked list operations dynamically with pointers. We create the structure as follows:

```
typedef .......... el_t;
typedef struct node node_t;
typedef node_t* pointer_t;

struct node {
    el_t    el;
    pointer_t next;
};

typedef
struct {
    pointer_t head;
    pointer_t cur;
} list;
```

We developed several list operations—*InitList, MakeNode, Advance, InsertFirst, InsertAfter, DeleteFirst,* and *DeleteAfter.* Each has at least one parameter—*l_ptr,* of type *list *.* To initialize the list, we assign *NULL* to *head* and *cur. MakeNode* returns the address of a new node and places a data item *e* into the information portion and *NULL* into the link field of that node. Inserting at the first of a list with *InsertFirst(L, e)* causes *head* to point to a new first node with information *e.* Its definition is as follows:

```
void InsertFirst(list *l_ptr, el_t e)
{
    pointer_t target = MakeNode(e);

    target->next = l_ptr->head;
    l_ptr->head = target;
}
```

To insert later in the list, after the node to which *cur* points, we use the *InsertAfter* procedure. We first change the pointer field of *target*'s node and then the pointer field of the *cur* node to link in the new node, as shown:

```
target->next = (l_ptr->cur)->next;
(l_ptr->cur)->next = target;
```

Advancing *cur* to point to the next node employs the following assignment:

```
l_ptr->cur = (l_ptr->cur)->next;
```

Just as insertion at the first of the list is different from adding a node inside the list, so deletion of the first node is distinctive. Along with checking that *head* points to a node, *DeleteFirst* contains the following segment:

```
if (l_ptr->cur == l_ptr->head)
    Advance(l_ptr);

tmp = l_ptr->head;
l_ptr->head = (l_ptr->head)->next;
free(tmp);
```

The *DeleteAfter* operation generates a deletion of the node following the one *cur* references. After checking that *cur* points to a node and a next node exists, the function definition contains the following:

```
tmp = (l_ptr->cur)->next;
(l_ptr->cur)->next = tmp->next;
free(tmp);
```

A stack is an appropriate data structure when the last data placed into the structure is the first processed. The acronym LIFO symbolizes the situation—*Last In First Out.* All activity occurs at the top of the stack. Two major ways exist to implement ADT stack—statically with arrays and dynamically with lists. The application program that uses the package should be able to run without change to its C statements regardless of the implementation.

In Sections 16.2 and 16.3, we discussed the ADT stack and its linked list implementation, respectively. The creation of the stack as a linked list structure follows:

```
typedef ......... el_t;

typedef struct node node_t;
typedef node_t* stack;

struct node {
   el_t el;
   struct node* next;
};
   ⋮
stack s;
```

InitStack, which initializes a stack *s* to be empty, has the following definition:

```
void InitStack(stack *s_ptr)
{
   *s_ptr = NULL;
}
```

StackIsEmpty, which is a boolean function to return *TRUE* if *s* is empty, tests if *s* is *NULL,* as shown:

```
return(*s_ptr == NULL ? TRUE : FALSE);
```

One major advantage of a dynamic linked list implementation of an ADT stack is that the stack can grow virtually indefinitely. Therefore, the operation *StackIsFull,* which returns *TRUE* if the stack is full, can degenerate to always being *FALSE.*

The procedure *Push* places an item with *e*'s value into *s.* Because we maintain the top at the first of the list, the implementation for *Push* follows that of *InsertFirst. Pop* takes the top item or the last item placed into nonempty *s* out of *s* and gives its value to *e.* For the implementation, we store the information of the first node into *e* before executing a *DeleteFirst* operation. Its definition follows:

```
void Pop(stack *s_ptr, el_t *e)
{
   stack p;

   if (StackIsEmpty(s_ptr))
   {
      printf("ERROR:  Stack is empty\n");
      exit(1);
   }
```

```
        else
        {
            *e = (*s_ptr)->el;

            p = *s_ptr;
            *s_ptr = (*s_ptr)->next;
            free(p);
        }
    }
```

Review Questions

1. What is an abstract data type?

2. Characterize a dynamic linked list.

3. Can insertions into a linked list be handled with the same algorithm anywhere?

4. Suppose *target* points to a node to be inserted at the first of a linked list pointed to by *head*. Which link should change first?

5. Suppose *P* points to a node in a linked list. Write a statement to cause *P* to point to the next node.

6. When deleting a node from a linked list, after changing the links, what must be done?

7. What acronym characterizes the stack data structure?

8. Where does all activity occur in a stack?

9. What term means to place an item on the top of a stack?

10. What term means to take an item from the top of a stack?

11. Determine the output from the following segment, where *s* is a stack:

```
Push(s, 1); Push(s, 2);
Pop(s, x); printf("%d ", x);
Push(s, 3);
Pop(s, x); printf("%d ", x);
Pop(s, x); printf("%d ", x);
```

12. Does a stack ever fill?

13. Suppose *s_ptr* is of type *stack *, as defined with the linked list implementation of this chapter. Write a *return* statement for the *StackIsEmpty* routine.

14. The operation *Push* can be implemented with what list operation?

15. What should we check before attempting to pop from a stack?

Laboratory

1. In this exercise, we develop and use a tool to practice with stacks. In the development, we access the files containing the linked list implementation of the ADT stack and practice calling various stack routines. Copy the ADT stack files *stackD.c* and *stackD.h* and the laboratory file *LAB161.c* onto your own disk.

In the program, we initialize an integer variable *e* to 1. Three possible actions can occur:

CopyInput   Display and increment *e*

PushInput   Push the *e* onto stack *s* and increment *e*

PopDisplay Pop and display a value from *s*

All three functions have a pointer to a stack as a parameter. Because *CopyInput* and *PushInput* also change the value of *e,* they include as a parameter a pointer to a type *el_t* item. Starting with a value of 1, through calls to *CopyInput* and *PushInput, e* progresses sequentially through the integers, 1, 2, 3, ...

To produce the output of 2, 1, 3, we have the following segment in ANSI C:

```
el_t e = 1;
    ⋮
/* output 2 1 3 */
PushInput(&s, &e);   /* push 1 and e = 2  */
CopyInput(&e);       /* print 2 and e = 3 */
PopDisplay(&s);      /* pop and print 1   */
CopyInput(&e);       /* print 3 and e = 4 */
```

The program file *LAB161.c* is as follows:

```
/*
 * Program to produce various output from input e, initialized to be 1
 * with only the following operations:
 * 1.  print the next integer and increment e
 * 2.  push e onto stack s and increment e
 * 3.  pop and display a value from s
 */

#include <stdio.h>
#include /*** a ***/

void CopyInput(el_t *);
void PushInput(stack *, el_t *);
void PopDisplay(stack *);

main()
{
   el_t e = 1;
   /*** b ***/;

   /*** c ***/;

   /* output 2 1 3 */
   PushInput(&s, &e); /* push 1 and e = 2  */
   CopyInput(&e);     /* print 2 and e = 3 */
```

```
    PopDisplay(&s);      /* pop and print 1    */
    CopyInput(&e);       /* print 3 and e = 4 */
}


/*
 * Function to print the integer pointed to by input_ptr
 * and increment the integer
 * Pre:  input_ptr points to an integer.
 * Post: *input_ptr has been displayed and incremented.
 */

void CopyInput(el_t *input_ptr)
{
    printf("%d ", *input_ptr);
    (*input_ptr)++;
}


/*
 * Function to push the integer pointed to by input_ptr onto
 * the stack pointed to by s_ptr and to increment the integer
 * Pre:  s_ptr points to a stack.
 *       input_ptr points to an integer.
 * Post: *input_ptr has been pushed onto s and incremented.
 */

void PushInput(stack *s_ptr, el_t *input_ptr)
{
    Push(/*** d ***/);
    (*input_ptr)++;
}


/*
 * Function to pop the top element from the stack pointed
 * to by s_ptr and to print that value
 * Pre:  s_ptr points to a stack.
 * Post: The top element of the stack has been popped and displayed.
 */

void PopDisplay(stack *s_ptr)
{
    el_t e;

    Pop(/*** e ***/);
    printf("%d ", e);
}
```

a. In *stackD.h* change the definition of *el_t* to be *int,* as shown:

```
    typedef int el_t;
```

Include the proper header file for the stack ADT at /*** a ***/ in *LAB161.c.*

b. Declare *s* to be *stack* at /*** b ***/.

c. Initialize stack *s* by calling the appropriate ADT stack operation at /*** c ***/.

d. In *PushInput,* complete the call to push the integer pointed to by *input_ptr* onto the stack pointed to by *s_ptr.*

e. In *PopDisplay,* complete the call to pop an integer *e* from the stack pointed to by *s_ptr.*

f. Compile and link *LAB161.c* and *stackD.c.* Execute the program to obtain the following output:

    2 1 3

g. Place the preprocessor directives *#if 0* and *#endif* around the four statements in *main* that generate this output. These statements are not sent to the compiler. Write calls to *CopyInput, PushInput,* and *PopDisplay* to produce the following output:

    2 4 5 3 1

h. Place the preprocessor directives *#if 0* and *#endif* around your answer to Part g. Create your own permutation of the integers 1 through 7 using calls to *CopyInput, PushInput,* and *PopDisplay.* Turn in a printout of your program and output on separate pages with your name on both pages. Pick up someone else's output and determine the sequence of calls to the three routines that produces the results.

2. This exercise provides further practice with the stack ADT. We develop and test a function that determines if a string contains properly balanced enclosure symbols—(,), {, }, [, and]. For example, $((a + b) - \{c - d\})$ and $[c + d * (x - y)]$ are balanced, but $(a - d\}(c + d)$ and $(a - d))[x + 3]$ are not.

a. The general approach is to scan the string from left to right, ignoring all characters that are not enclosure characters. Each left symbol is pushed onto a stack. We check to see if each right symbol matches the left symbol on the stack. If the stack is empty or the symbols do not match, then the string is not balanced. If all left and right symbols match, the string is balanced. An algorithm is shown below:

Algorithm:

> initialize a stack of characters
> *Balanced* ← *TRUE*
> *index* ← 0
> while (the string is balanced and more characters are in the string)
>   if (the next character is a left symbol)
>   push the character onto the stack
>   else if (the next character is a right symbol)
>   if (the stack is empty)
>   *Balanced* ← *FALSE*
>   else
>   pop the top element from the stack
>   if (the popped character does not match the current character)
>   *Balanced* ← *FALSE*
>   increment *index* by 1
> if (the stack is not empty)
>   *Balanced* ← *FALSE*

Write a function *EnclosureBalanced* that accepts a string as a parameter and returns *TRUE* if the string has balanced enclosure symbols and *FALSE* otherwise.

b. Write a test program for *EnclosureBalanced* that prompts and reads a string and displays whether the string has balanced enclosure symbols. In *stackd.h,* if necessary, change the definition of *el_t* to *char.*

The ASCII Character Code

Note: The caret (^) represents the control key. That is, ^A is the key combination control-A, whereas ^^ is control caret.

Decimal	Octal	Hexadecimal	Symbol	Name
0	000	00	^@	(null)
1	001	01	^A	
2	002	02	^B	
3	003	03	^C	
4	004	04	^D	
5	005	05	^E	
6	006	06	^F	
7	007	07	^G	(bell)
8	010	08	^H	(backspace)
9	011	09	^I	(tab)
10	012	0A	^J	(newline)
11	013	0B	^K	
12	014	0C	^L	(form feed)
13	015	0D	^M	(RETURN)
14	016	0E	^N	
15	017	0F	^O	
16	020	10	^P	
17	021	11	^Q	
18	022	12	^R	
19	023	13	^S	
20	024	14	^T	
21	025	15	^U	
22	026	16	^V	
23	027	17	^W	
24	030	18	^X	
25	031	19	^Y	
26	032	1A	^Z	
27	033	1B	^[	(ESCAPE)
28	034	1C	^\	
29	035	1D	^]	
30	036	1E	^^	
31	037	1F	^_	
32	040	20	space	
33	041	21	!	

Decimal	Octal	Hexadecimal	Symbol	Name
34	042	22	"	
35	043	23	#	
36	044	24	$	
37	045	25	%	
38	046	26	&	
39	047	27	'	(apostrophe)
40	050	28	(	
41	051	29	)	
42	052	2A	*	
43	053	2B	+	
44	054	2C	,	(comma)
45	055	2D	-	
46	056	2E	.	(period)
47	057	2F	/	
48	060	30	0	
49	061	31	1	
50	062	32	2	
51	063	33	3	
52	064	34	4	
53	065	35	5	
54	066	36	6	
55	067	37	7	
56	070	38	8	
57	071	39	9	
58	072	3A	:	
59	073	3B	;	
60	074	3C	<	
61	075	3D	=	
62	076	3E	>	
63	077	3F	?	
64	100	40	@	
65	101	41	A	
66	102	42	B	
67	103	43	C	
68	104	44	D	
69	105	45	E	
70	106	46	F	
71	107	47	G	
72	110	48	H	
73	111	49	I	
74	112	4A	J	
75	113	4B	K	
76	114	4C	L	
77	115	4D	M	
78	116	4E	N	
79	117	4F	O	
80	120	50	P	
81	121	51	Q	
82	122	52	R	
83	123	53	S	
84	124	54	T	

Decimal	Octal	Hexadecimal	Symbol	Name
85	125	55	U	
86	126	56	V	
87	127	57	W	
88	130	58	X	
89	131	59	Y	
90	132	5A	Z	
91	133	5B	[	
92	134	5C	\	
93	135	5D	]	
94	136	5E	^	
95	137	5F	_	(underscore)
96	140	60	`	(grave accent)
97	141	61	a	
98	142	62	b	
99	143	63	c	
100	144	64	d	
101	145	65	e	
102	146	66	f	
103	147	67	g	
104	150	68	h	
105	151	69	i	
106	152	6A	j	
107	153	6B	k	
108	154	6C	l	
109	155	6D	m	
110	156	6E	n	
111	157	6F	o	
112	160	70	p	
113	161	71	q	
114	162	72	r	
115	163	73	s	
116	164	74	t	
117	165	75	u	
118	166	76	v	
119	167	77	w	
120	170	78	x	
121	171	79	y	
122	172	7A	z	
123	173	7B	{	
124	174	7C			
125	175	7D	}	
126	176	7E	~	
127	177	7F	DELETE	

Keywords in C

The following identifiers, written as shown without embedded blanks and in lower-case, are reserved by the compiler and cannot be used for any purpose other than those for which they are defined:

auto	*break*	*case*	*char*	*const*	*continue*	*default*
do	*double*	*else*	*enum*	*extern*	*float*	*for*
goto	*if*	*int*	*long*	*register*	*return*	*short*
signed	*sizeof*	*static*	*struct*	*switch*	*typedef*	*union*
unsigned	*void*	*volatile*	*while*			

Precedence of Operators

In the following table, the precedence of the operators in C appears in descending order.

```
()   []   .   ->
!   ~   - (unary)   + (unary)   & (address)   ++   --   * (indirection)   sizeof   (type)
*   /   %
+   - (binary)
<<   >>
<   <=   >   >=
==   !=
&
^
|
&&
||
?:
=   +=   -=   *=   /=   %=   &=   |=   ^=   <<=   >>=
```

Conversion Specifications

Type	Representation	Conversion Specification
char	character	%c
char *	string	%s
double	decimal	%f
double	scientific notation	%e or %E
float	decimal	%f
float	scientific notation	%e or %E
int	decimal	%d
int	hexadecimal	%x or %X
int	octal	%o
long (or *long int*)	decimal	%ld
pointer	hexadecimal	%p
short (or *short int*)	decimal	%hd
unsigned (or *unsigned int*)	unsigned decimal	%u

File I/O

Input Text File Manipulation

Assume the following declarations:

```
char ch, *str;
int i, n;
float x;
FILE *infile_ptr;
```

Example Function Call	Read from	Read What	Error Return
ch = getchar();	*stdin*	character	*EOF*
gets(str);	*stdin*	string	*NULL*
scanf("%d %f %s", &i, &x, str);	*stdin*	anything	*EOF*
infile_ptr = fopen("f.dat", "r");	input file	(open file for reading)	*NULL*
ch = getc(infile_ptr);	input file	character	*EOF*
ungetc(ch, infile_ptr);	input file	(return character to file)	*EOF*
fgets(str, n, infile_ptr);	input file	line	*NULL*
fscanf(infile_ptr, "%d %f %s", &i, &x, str);	input file	anything	*EOF*
if (feof (infile_ptr)). . .	input file	(*TRUE* if there was attempt to read past end of file, *FALSE* otherwise)	(none)
fclose(infile_ptr);	input file	(close file)	*EOF*

Output Text File Manipulation

Assume the following declarations:

```
char ch, *str;
int i;
float x;
FILE *outfile_ptr;
```

Example Function Call	Write to	Write What	Error Return
`putchar(ch);`	*stdout*	character	*EOF*
`puts(str);`	*stdout*	string	*EOF*
`printf("%d %f %s", i, x,` `    str);`	*stdout*	anything	negative
`outfile_ptr = fopen("f.dat",` `    "w");`	output file	(open file for writing)	*NULL*
`outfile_ptr = fopen("f.dat",` `    "a");`	output file	(open file for appending)	*NULL*
`putc(ch, outfile_ptr);`	output file	character	*EOF*
`fputs(str, outfile_ptr);`	output file	string	*EOF*

`fprintf(outfile_ptr,`
`    "%d %f %s",`
`    i, x, str);`
	output file	anything	negative

`fclose(outfile_ptr);`	output file	(close file)	*EOF*

Binary File Manipulation

Assume the following declarations:

```
typedef struct {...} rec_t;
rec_t rec;
FILE *fp;
long WhichByte;
```

Example Function Call	Description	Error Return
`fp = fopen("f.dat", "rb");`	Open binary file for reading	*NULL*
`rewind(fp);`	Rewind file	
`fread(&rec, sizeof(rec_t), 1, fp);`	Read a record	0
`fwrite(&rec, sizeof(rec_t), 1, fp);`	Write a record	0
`fseek(fp, 5L, SEEK_SET);`	Seek location 5 bytes from beginning of file	nonzero
`fseek(fp, 5L, SEEK_CUR);`	Seek location 5 bytes from current position	nonzero
`fseek(fp, 5L, SEEK_END);`	Seek location 5 bytes from end of file	nonzero
`WhichByte = ftell(fp);`	Return current position of file	−1L

Mode Strings

The letter b in a mode string indicates a binary file.

Mode Sting	New/Existing File	Action
"a" or "ab"	New or Existing	Append data to end
"a+" or "a+b"	New or Existing	Append, read, and update data (reposition marker between different actions)
"r" or "rb"	Existing	Read data
"r+" or "r+b"	Existing	Read and update data (reposition marker between different actions)
"w" or "wb"	New (erases existing)	Write data
"w+" or "w+b"	New (erases existing)	Write, read, and update data (reposition marker between different actions)

Random Number Generation

Besides the ANSI C standard library function *rand,* many compilers have their own random number generators. Three files for random number generation are on the disk accompanying the text—*RandDef.c, RandDef.h,* and *random.h. RandDef.c* contains function definitions, and *random.h* has macro definitions for the generators. *RandDef.c* and *RandDef.h* are explained in Section 5.4 (Examples 5.14 and 5.15). Section 12.2 (Example 12.6) contains *random.h.**

To access the random number functions in *RandDef.c,* we include *RandDef.h* with the name in quotes before *main,* as follows:

```
#include "RandDef.h"
```

We then compile *RandDef.c* and the application program and link the two object files. The definitions of these files follow:

```
/*
 * File: RandDef.h
 * Header file for RandDef.c, source file of definitions of
 * random number generating functions
 */

#include <stdlib.h>
#include <time.h>

#ifndef RANDOM
#define RANDOM

void SeedRand(void);
float random_float(void);
float random_float_range(float LowerBound, float UpperBound);
int random(int UpperBound);
int random_range(int LowerBound, int UpperBound);

#endif
```

---

*Some compilers contain their own versions of a function *random,* which *RandDef.c* and *random.h* define. Should a conflict exist, change the identifier *random* to another name, such as *Random,* in the files on the disk.

```c
/*
 * File: RandDef.c
 * Source file of definitions of random number generating functions
 */

#include "RandDef.h"

/*
 * Function to seed the random number generator
 * Pre:    none
 * Post:   Random number generator has been seeded.
 */

void SeedRand(void)
{
    srand((unsigned) time((time_t *)NULL));
}

/*
 * Function to return a random float between 0 and 1
 * Pre:    The generator is seeded.
 * Post:   A random floating point number between 0 and 1
 *         has been returned
 */

float random_float(void)
{
    return((float) rand() / RAND_MAX);
}

/*
 * Function to generate a random floating point number
 * between LowerBound and UpperBound
 * Pre:    LowerBound and UpperBound are of type float with
 *         LowerBound < UpperBound. The generator is seeded.
 * Post:   A random float between LowerBound and
 *         UpperBound has been returned.
 */

float random_float_range(float LowerBound, float UpperBound)
{
    float random_0_1;    /* random number between 0 and 1 */

    random_0_1 = (float)rand() / RAND_MAX;
    return ((UpperBound - LowerBound) * random_0_1
                    + LowerBound);
}
```

```
/*
 * Function to generate a random integer
 * between 0 and UpperBound - 1
 * Pre:    UpperBound is a positive integer. The generator is seeded.
 * Post:   A random integer between 0 and UpperBound - 1
 *         has been returned.
 */

int random(int UpperBound)
{
    float random_0_1;    /* random number between 0 and 1 */

    random_0_1 = (float) rand() / RAND_MAX;
    return ((int)(UpperBound * random_0_1));
}

/*
 * Function to generate a random integer
 * between LowerBound and UpperBound - 1
 * Pre:    LowerBound and UpperBound are integers with
 *         LowerBound < UpperBound. The generator is seeded.
 * Post:   A random integer between LowerBound and
 *         UpperBound - 1 has been returned.
 */

int random_range(int LowerBound, int UpperBound)
{
    float random_0_1;   /* random number between 0 and 1 */

    random_0_1 = (float) rand() / RAND_MAX;
    return ((int)((UpperBound - LowerBound) * random_0_1)
                      + LowerBound);
}
```

To have access to the macro version of these functions, we include *random.h* in our program with the following:

```
#include "random.h"
```

The listing for this file follows:

```
/*
 * File: random.h
 * random.h - header file for user-defined random number generators
 */

#ifndef RANDOM
#define RANDOM

#include <time.h>
#include <stdlib.h>
```

```c
/*
 * Macro to seed the random number generator srand
 */

#define SeedRand() (srand((unsigned) time((time_t *)NULL)))

/*
 * Macro to return a random float between 0 and 1
 */

#define random_float() ((float) rand() / RAND_MAX)

/*
 * Macro to return a random integer between 0 and UpperBound - 1
 */

#define random(UpperBound) ((int)((UpperBound) * random_float()))

/*
 * Macro to generate a random integer between LowerBound
 * and UpperBound - 1
 */

#define random_range(LowerBound, UpperBound)                          \
    ((int)(((int)(UpperBound) - (int)(LowerBound)) * random_float()) \
           + (int)(LowerBound))

/*
 * Macro to generate a random floating point number between
 * LowerBound and UpperBound
 */

#define random_float_range(LowerBound, UpperBound)                   \
    (((float)(UpperBound) - (float)(LowerBound)) * random_float() \
           + (float)(LowerBound))

#endif
```

Contents of Text Disk

The disk accompanying the text contains the laboratory templates. Most of the time, the name contains *LAB*, the chapter number, the exercise number, and *.c*. For example, *LAB042.c* is the laboratory file for Chapter 4, Exercise 2. See the *README* file on the text disk for a list of laboratory files.

The disk has three files for random number generation. *RandDef.c* contains the definitions of seeding function *SeedRand* and random number generators *random_float*, *random_float_range*, *random*, and *random_range*. Header file *RandDef.h* has the functions' prototypes. Examples 5.14 and 5.15 of Section 5.4 define these functions. After the discussion of macros in Chapter 12, we introduce the header file *random.h* with macro definitions for these random number generators. Appendix F presents listings for *RandDef.c*, *RandDef.h*, and *random.h*.

The file *AUX10* is a data file for Laboratory 10.

The breadth section on "A Computer Graphics Package," Section 11.7, has an accompanying computer graphics package. Definitions of device independent functions are in the file *graphics.c*, which has header file *graphics.h*. Example 11.13 presents the code for these two files. The device-dependent routines are grouped in a file called a device driver. Subsection "Device Driver" describes the global variables and functions that the package's device driver defines. Three such files are on the disk:

Definitions File	Header File	Machine/Compiler
driveibm.c	*driveibm.h*	IBM compatible/Turbo C
drivemac.c	*drivemac.h*	Macintosh/THINK C or Symantec C++
drivegen.c	*drivegen.h*	generic

Copy the appropriate files to your own disk, and name them *driver.h* and *driver.c*. *MaxX* and *MaxY* of the *EnterGraphics* routine may need to be adjusted to match your screen size. The drivers for Turbo C and THINK C call line drawing routines that are available with the compilers. The generic driver uses Bresenham's algorithm for line drawing. To use the generic driver, you must define the functions *EnterGraphics*, *SetPixel*, and *ExitGraphics* for your system. See the *README* file for further details.

Laboratories in Chapters 12 and 14 use the CPU simulator that Section 12.7 describes. (An alternative laboratory is available for each.) Subsection "CPU Simulator Program *cpusim*" describes the six files for this program—*cpusim.c*, *cpu.c*, *mem.c*, *cpusim.h*, *cpu.h*, *simem.h*. The text disk also includes three machine language program files—*add2.m, max2.m,* and *maxloop.m*.

The Chapter 13 Laboratory employs the following files—*summainL.c*, *sumfncsL.c*, *sumfncs.h*, *ranmain.c* and *random.h*.

The file *listd.c* includes the linked list function definitions that we discuss in Section 16.1. The associated header file is *listd.h*.

The file *stackd.c* with header file *stackd.h* contains the abstract data type (ADT) definition for stack. Figure 16.29 of Section 16.3 gives this linked list implementation of ADT stack.

The disk also contains source code for all of the example programs in the text. Usually, the name of such a file begins with *EX*. Two digits for the chapter and two digits for the example number follow. Thus, file *EX0712.c* contains the program from Example 7.12. When an example contains several files, opening comments specify file names. The *README* file on the text disk contains a list of such source code and data files by chapter.

Debuggers

This appendix contains short tutorials on Borland's Turbo Debugger (TD) for DOS, Symantec's THINK C Debugger, and the UNIX dbx debugger. Chapter 6's Programming and Debugging Hints introduces debugging. Students are encouraged to read the product documentation and online help in order to take full advantage of this product as well as to enhance their debugging skills. This tutorial assumes that the student is familiar with the operating system on his or her computer and how to edit and execute a program with the compiler. The appropriate debugger software must also be available.

Borland's Turbo Debugger (TD) for DOS

Starting TD

TD may be launched from DOS or Windows—if launched from Windows, it runs in a DOS shell. To launch TD from Windows, choose the *Turbo Debugger for DOS* icon from the Borland C++ program group. To launch TD from DOS, change to the appropriate directory and type TD. TD can be launched from any directory if the appropriate directory is listed in the PATH variable.

To load a program for debugging, choose *open* from the *file* menu and select a DOS executable file (*.exe*). If the target executable is not in the current directory, choose *browse* to look through the DOS directories and locate the desired file. By default, TD executes the startup code when the program is loaded so that the debugging session is ready to start with *main* immediately.

If the source code is contained in the same directory as the target program, TD displays the source for the main function immediately. Otherwise, TD displays the CPU window. To access source code in another directory, choose *Path for source...* from the *Options* menu, enter the necessary path name or names, and then choose *Module...* from the *View* menu. On choosing *Module...*, TD displays a list of available source modules. Choose the appropriate module. Once the source is on display, TD indicates the current source line with a triangle character in the left margin. Initially, this character is positioned at the first line (declaration) of the *main* function.

Tracing Execution with TD

To start the debugging session, choose *Trace into* from the *Run* menu, press F7, or click on *Trace* (displayed in the last line of the screen). TD advances to the first executable source line. *Trace* or *Trace into* executes single lines of source. If the line is a simple statement, TD executes the line and advances to the next source line. If the line contains a function call and the source code is accessible, TD "traces into" the function—TD advances to the first line (declaration) of the called function. *Trace* can then be used to execute source lines in the called function, including accessing (tracing into) additional called functions.

Choosing *Step over* from the *Run* menu (pressing F8 or clicking on *Step* from the lower menu) is similar to *Trace*, except that it "steps over" function calls. *Step* executes all source lines as simple statements without entering called functions.

Inspecting Intermediate Results with TD

Choosing *Watches* from the *View* menu opens the *Watches* window. This window displays and constantly updates the value of various C expressions—including variables, pointers, dereferenced pointers, arrays, structures, and so on—as source lines are executed. To inspect the value of a variable during execution, open the *Watches* window, click on the window, and type the desired expression or press return. TD opens a dialog window, allowing the user to complete the expression. On completing the expression, press return or click OK. TD adds the expression to the *Watches* window. The *Watches* window can be scrolled and resized to display any number of expressions during execution. The dialog box also allows the user to update existing expressions. To update an existing expression, position the cursor on the desired expression and press return.

Breakpoints with TD

To set a breakpoint, position the cursor on the desired source line and choose *Toggle* from the *Breakpoints* menu, press F2, or click on *Bkpt* in the lower menu. TD highlights the line with a red background indicating that a breakpoint is set on that line. Choosing *Toggle* again releases the breakpoint. To execute the program up to the breakpoint, choose *Run* from the *Run* menu, press F9, or click on *Run* in the lower menu. TD executes all source lines, including called functions, from the current line up to the breakpoint.

Symantec's THINK C Debugger for the Macintosh

Starting

To start the debugger on an open project, choose *Use Debugger* from the *Project* menu. A "bug" column then appears to the left of the project window. We start execution as we normally do. The debugger is launched, however, instead of the program. The debugger controls execution of the program. Two debugger windows and a debugger menu bar appear at the top of the screen. The larger source window, which is on the left, contains the program and a debugger status panel. The smaller *Data* window is used for watching and changing values of variables.

The debugger indicates the current statement, which is the statement about to execute, with a black arrow in the left margin. Diamonds in the left column indicate executable statements. The name of the function that is currently executing appears in the lower left of the source window.

Tracing Execution with THINK C Debugger

To trace through the program a statement at a time, click the *Trace* button in the status panel at the top of the source window. With each click on that button, the debugger executes a program statement. A click of the *Step In* button causes the computer to execute until falling into a function. Clicking the *Step Out* button causes execution to continue until leaving the present function.

Inspecting Intermediate Results with THINK C Debugger

With the *Data* window, we can watch the values of expressions as they change. We enter an expression at the top of the *Data* window. The expression is in the context of the current statement in the source window. After pressing return, the expression appears in the left column. During execution, the debugger displays the value of this expression in the right column. We can cut, copy, paste, and edit the expression as we would any text with the Macintosh. To remove an expression from the *Data* window, select the expression and choose *Clear* from the *Edit* menu.

Breakpoints with THINK C Debugger

To set a breakpoint at a statement, click its diamond marker. The diamond becomes black. Pressing the *Go* button in the status panel causes the program to execute until it hits a break point, ends, or aborts. Click on the black diamond to clear a breakpoint. To clear all breakpoints, choose *Clear All Breakpoints* from the *Source* menu.

UNIX's dbx Debugger

Starting dbx

We can run the dbx debugger using our executable *a.out* with the command

```
dbx a.out
```

A (dbx) prompt appears. Once in dbx, we can list the commands by typing *help*. We obtain some of the following commands:

```
run                        - begin execution of the program
print <exp>                - print the value of the expression
where                      - print currently active functions
stop at <line#>            - suspend execution at the line
stop in <func>             - suspend execution when <func> is called
stop <var>                 - suspend execution if variable <var> changes
cont                       - continue execution
step                       - single-step one line
next                       - step to next line (skip over calls)
trace <line#>              - trace execution of the line
trace <func>               - trace calls to the function
trace <var>                - trace changes to the variable
trace <exp> at <line#>     - print <exp> when <line#> is reached
status                     - print trace/stop's in effect
delete <number>            - remove trace or stop of given number
call <func>                - call a function in program
whatis <name>              - print the declaration of the name
list <line#>, <line#>      - list source lines
quit                       - exit dbx
```

For a detailed explanation of a command, type *help* and the name of the command. To list the first 20 lines, we type

```
list 1,20
```

To exit the debugger, we type *quit*. We start execution of our program by typing *run*. After a pause in execution, we continue execution with *cont*.

Tracing Execution with dbx

To execute one statement, we type *step*. We can step over a function call by typing *next*.

Inspecting Intermediate Results with dbx

To watch the value of a variable, *x*, we type the following:

```
trace x
```

Similarly, we can obtain the value of an expression at a particular line number, such as

```
trace (x + y) at 29
```

Once execution is suspended, we can inspect the value of a variable *y* by typing

```
print y
```

Breakpoints with dbx

To set a breakpoint at an executable statement at line 17, we type

```
stop at 17
```

To delete this breakpoint, we type

```
delete 17
```

To stop when a function, *ComputeAverage*, begins execution, we enter

```
stop in ComputeAverage
```

The command

```
stop x
```

suspends execution if *x* changes.

Glossary of Computer Science Terms

abstract data type An abstract data type (ADT) is a set of data items and fundamental operations on this set.

activation record An activation record or stack frame is a record that comes into existence when a function is called. It contains the return location, the list of arguments, room for a return value (if any), and an area for the function's local variables.

address The address of a memory location is a number associated with that location. Addresses are sequential (0, 1, 2,. . .).

algorithm An algorithm is a precise, unambiguous, step-by-step method of doing a task in a finite amount of time.

alignment Alignment is a requirement of some computers that values of certain types begin in certain locations within a word, such as on a full word boundary.

AND gate An AND gate is a basic part of a logic circuit. Given two binary inputs, x and y, the AND gate produces an output of the boolean algebra $x \cdot y$.

argument An argument or actual parameter to a function is a data item passed to the function at the time the function is used.

arithmetic/logic unit The arithmetic/logic unit, a major component of the CPU, performs all arithmetic and logic.

array An array is a sequence of elements of the same type that share a common name and that are distinguishable by their positions within the array. A subscript or index indicates the position.

ASCII The American Standard Code for Information Interchange (ASCII) encoding scheme is a system of assigning a number to a character. Many computers store characters as binary numbers using their ASCII code representations.

aspect ratio The ratio of the number of pixels in the y direction to the number of pixels in the x direction is a device's aspect ratio.

assembler language An assembler language is a computer language that provides mnemonic abbreviations for machine language instructions.

assignment-compatible Two types are assignment-compatible if we can assign a variable of one type to a variable of the other.

associative properties The associative properties in a boolean algebra are $x + (y + z) = (x + y) + z$ and $x \cdot (y \cdot z) = (x \cdot y) \cdot z$

attribute An attribute corresponds to a column in a relation.

Backus-Naur Form Backus-Naur Form or BNF is a method of defining formally the syntax of a computer language.

base 2 number system The binary or base 2 number system has two digits—0 and 1.

base 8 number system The octal or base 8 system has 8 octal digits, 0–7.

base 16 number system The hexadecimal or base 16 system has 16 hexadecimal (hex) digits—0, 1, 2, 3, 4, 5, 6, 7, 8, 9, A, B, C, D, E, F.

base case A terminal or base case in a recursive task stops the recursion process.

batch program A batch program does not converse with the user during program execution. Instead, data are obtained from files.

binary digit The binary digits or bits are 0 and 1.

binary file A binary file stores information in binary form, exactly as it is in the computer.

binary number system The binary or base 2 number system has two digits—0 and 1.

binary operator A binary operator performs operations on two operands (terms).

bit The binary digits or bits are 0 and 1.

block A block or a physical record is a fixed number of records the computer reads from or writes to secondary storage media as a group.

BNF Backus-Naur Form or BNF is a method of defining formally the syntax of a computer language.

boolean algebra A boolean algebra, $[A, +, \cdot, ', 0, 1]$ is a set A with two binary operations (+ and $\cdot$), a unary operation, ('), and two distinct elements (0 and 1), satisfying the following properties for all $x, y, z \in A$—commutative, associative, distributive, identity, and complement properties.

boolean constants The boolean constants or boolean values are *TRUE* and *FALSE*.

boolean expression A logical or boolean expression is a condition that is true or false. Alternatively, let $x_1, x_2, \ldots, x_n$ be boolean variables. A boolean expression is 0, 1, $x_1, x_2, \ldots$, or x_n; and $A + B, A \cdot B$, or A' if A and B are boolean expressions.

boolean values The boolean constants or boolean values are *TRUE* and *FALSE*.

boolean variable A boolean variable is a variable that can have a true or false value. Alternatively, a variable x that can only have a value of 0 or 1 in the two-element boolean algebra on **B** = {0, 1} is called a boolean variable.

booting The process of loading and initiating operating system execution is called bootstrapping or booting.

bootstrap A bootstrap is a program that is only used to initiate the operating system.

bottom-up strategy The bottom-up strategy of program implementation and testing starts with the lowest-level functions and proceeds to the highest, with debugging occurring one function at a time. Before testing a function, we implement and test all routines beneath it in the structure chart. A driver is used in place of the routine that calls the function being tested.

breakpoint A breakpoint, which the programmer establishes using a debugger, is a program location where execution pauses so that the programmer can use other debugging features, such as examining values of variables or commencing stepping through the program.

buffer A buffer is a special location in main memory, a fixed number of characters in length, that can temporarily hold data being transferred from main memory to secondary storage, or vice versa.

byte A byte is a sequence of bits that can encode a character.

byte-addressable A computer is byte-addressable if each byte has a different address.

cache A cache is a fast, small memory that is a buffer between the CPU and main memory.

call To call or invoke a function means to use it. A call or invocation of a function in a program causes the computer to interrupt execution of the routine containing the call in order to execute the function.

case sensitive A programming language is case sensitive if it considers two identifiers different because they consist of the same characters in the same order except for variations in upper- and lowercase.

cathode ray tube A cathode ray tube (CRT) screen is a display device used with televisions and most microcomputers. In a CRT, at least one electron gun emits a beam of electrons that passes through a focusing system, hitting the phosphor-coated screen.

central processing unit The central processing unit (CPU), which is a major hardware component of a computer system, is in charge of processing for the computer.

clear bit A clear bit is a bit that has the value 0.

clock cycle A clock cycle is the length of time between ticks of the CPU clock.

clock frequency The clock frequency or rate is the number of cycles per unit of time.

code All or part of a program is called code.

coding The process of writing instructions to the computer in a programming language is called coding.

coercion Coercion or explicit coercion occurs when the program explicitly instructs the computer to convert a value from one type to another.

color lookup table A color lookup table (LUT) is a two-dimensional array where each value represents intensity levels for the three electron guns of a raster-scan video monitor. These intensity levels correspond to a color.

combinational circuit A combinational circuit is a circuit where outputs are uniquely determined by the inputs.

combinational function Function f is a switching or combinational function provided f is a mapping from $\mathbf{B}^n$, the set of all boolean n-tuples, to $\mathbf{B} = \{0, 1\}$ for some positive integer n. A combinational function is a mathematical model of a combinational circuit.

comment A comment inside a program is documentation for people. The compiler ignores comments.

commutative properties The commutative properties in a boolean algebra are $x + y = y + x$ and $x \cdot y = y \cdot x$

compile-time error A syntax error (compile-time error) violates the syntax of a language.

compiler A compiler is a program that translates preprocessed source code into machine language.

complement The complement of a bit is its opposite value—0 or 1.

complement properties The complement properties in a boolean algebra are $x + x' = 1$ and $x \cdot x' = 0$

compound proposition (compound statement) in logic A compound statement or compound proposition in logic is a statement or statements combined with logical operators to form a sentence that is either true or false.

computer system A computer system consists of both software and hardware.

computing, discipline of The discipline of computing is the systematic study of algorithmic processes that describe and transform information: their theory, analysis, design, efficiency, implementation, and application. The fundamental question underlying all of computing is, "What can be (efficiently) automated?"

conjunction Conjunction, denoted $\wedge$, is a logical operator meaning "and."

control structure A control structure consists of statements that determine the flow of control of a program or of an algorithm.

control unit The arithmetic/logic unit, a major component of the CPU, is in charge of directing all the devices in the computer system.

copyright law The copyright law says that the author owns his or her work and that others should not copy the material without permission for up to 50 years after the author's death.

counter-controlled loop (or counting loop) A counter-controlled loop or a counting loop is a looping control structure in which a loop variable manages the repetition through counting.

CRT A cathode ray tube (CRT) screen is a display device used with televisions and most microcomputers. In a CRT, at least one electron gun emits a beam of electrons that passes through a focusing system, hitting the phosphor-coated screen.

cylinder In a disk pack, a set of tracks that are all the same radius from the center and thus are directly under or above each other is a cylinder.

data Data are values in a form that the computer can use for processing.

data definition language A data definition language (DDL) is used to design and maintain a database management system.

data dependence Data dependence exists if the format of the data storage is dependent on the application program.

data dictionary A data dictionary contains a list of all data items for the system along with their descriptions.

data flow diagram A data flow diagram pictures the flow of information through the system.

data inconsistency Data inconsistency between the files exists if the same data are stored in different formats in two files or if data must be matched between files.

data integrity Data integrity is the assurance that data are correct.

data manipulation language A data manipulation language (DML) or query language is used to access and update data in a database management system.

data security Data security refers to data being protected so that only authorized personnel can access them.

data structure A data structure is a framework for storing data and the algorithms that implement and perform operations on the structure.

database A database is an integrated collection of files.

database management system A database management system (DBMS) is database software that contains two major functional parts—a data manipulation language (DML) or query language to access and update data in the database and a data definition language (DDL) to design and maintain the database.

debugger A debugger is a program that helps the programmer to find run-time errors.

device coordinates Device coordinates (DC) are the integer coordinates used by a graphics display device. Often the origin is in the top left corner and the positive horizontal axis points to the right and the positive vertical axis points down.

device driver A device driver for a computer graphics system is a file that contains all the device-dependent routines.

direct access storage Direct access storage media are secondary storage media in which a record can be accessed directly without processing all the data that appear before the desired item.

directory A directory is a tree-like index of files in on a disk.

disjunction Disjunction, denoted $\vee$, is a logical operator meaning "or."

distributive properties The distributive properties in a boolean algebra are $x + (y \cdot z) = (x + y) \cdot (x + z)$ and $x \cdot (y + z) = (x \cdot y) + (x \cdot z)$

domain The domain of an attribute is the set of all possible values of that attribute.

driver A driver is a module that exercises a system or part of a system.

dummy parameter A function parameter (formal parameter or dummy parameter) is a variable declared in the function's heading that is used to communicate information between the calling routine and the function.

dynamic link A dynamic link in an activation record is a pointer to the previous activation record.

editor An editor is a specialized word processor to create and edit source code and data.

encapsulated Encapsulated tasks are isolated so that only their inputs, outputs, and actions are known to the user and so that the behavior of the application program is unknown to the encapsulated tasks.

encapsulation Encapsulation is combining the data and methods that manipulate the data in one place.

equivalent Two propositions p and q are logically equivalent or equal, written $p \equiv q$, provided they have identical values in their truth tables.

executable statement An executable statement is an instruction for the computer to follow during execution.

execute A computer executes or runs a program when the machine is following the instructions in the program.

explicit coercion Coercion or explicit coercion occurs when the program explicitly instructs the computer to convert a value from one type to another.

exponential notation Exponential notation represents a floating point number as a decimal fraction times a power of 10. With a being a decimal fraction and n a nonnegative integer, the exponential notation represents $a \times 10^n$. The integer formed by dropping the decimal point from a is the fractional part or mantissa and n is the exponent.

fetch/execute cycle The fetch/execute cycle is the process performed by the computer while executing a program. As long as instructions remain, the control unit fetches or retrieves the next instruction from main memory; CPU decodes the instruction; and the control unit commands the appropriate unit to execute the instruction.

file A file, which is stored by name, is a collection of information.

floating point number A floating point number is a number stored in the computer with a decimal reference point.

flops Flops is floating point operations per second.

flow of control The flow of control of a program is the order in which the computer executes statements.

formal grammar A formal grammar has four parts—a vocabulary or set of symbols (V), a nonempty subset of terminal symbols (V_T), the start symbol (S), and a finite set of productions or rules (P).

formal parameter A function parameter (formal parameter or dummy parameter) is a variable declared in the function's heading that is used to communicate information between the calling routine and the function.

frame buffer A frame buffer is an area of memory that stores information for each pixel in a two-dimensional array.

free format A language has free format if statements may appear anywhere on one or several lines.

freeware Freeware is available at no charge over a computer network or through the mails for the cost of disks and postage, but the copyright law still applies. Moreover, any new works developed using a freeware package must be freeware, too.

full word boundary A full word boundary is the starting point of a word in memory.

function A function is a subprogram that implements a task.

Gantt chart A Gantt chart is a time table bar chart.

gigabit A gigabit is 2^{30} bits.

gigabyte A gigabyte (Gbyte) is 1024 megabytes or $2^{30} = 1,073,741,824$ bytes.

global variable A global variable is a variable that has meaning anywhere in a program.

graphical user interface Graphical user interface (GUI) is a computer interface in which the user can accomplish virtually all actions by making choices with a mouse from menus or visual cues on the screen.

hard crash With a hard crash, the computer detects a serious error, perhaps well past where the error occurs. Program execution terminates with a potentially misleading or cryptic error message.

hardware The equipment or physical components of a computer system are hardware.

header file A header file or header defines certain values, symbols, and operations. Typically, files include such a header file to obtain access to its contents.

hexadecimal number system The hexadecimal or base 16 system has 16 hexadecimal (hex) digits—0, 1, 2, 3, 4, 5, 6, 7, 8, 9, A, B, C, D, E, F.

hierarchy diagram A structure chart or hierarchy diagram is a tree diagram of the major tasks of a program and their relation to one another.

high-level language A high-level language, such as FORTRAN or C, can express algorithms on a higher level of abstraction.

identifier An identifier is the name of something in a program.

identity properties The identity properties in a boolean algebra are $x + 0 = x$ and $x \cdot 1 = x$

implicit coercion (or implicit conversion) Implicit conversion or implicit coercion occurs when the compiler automatically converts a value from one type to another.

infinite loop An infinite loop is a looping control structure that never stops unless an external interrupt of the program occurs.

inheritance Inheritance is the ability to define an object as a descendant of an existing object.

input The data that a program requires to produce its results are called input.

integers, set of In mathematics, the set of integers is $\{\ldots,-3, -2, -1, 0, 1, 2, 3, \ldots\}$.

integrated circuit chip An integrated circuit chip has a logic circuit on a small piece of semiconductor material, such as silicon.

integrated testing Integrated testing is the testing of all or part of a system in which programmers have already performed unit testing of modules.

intellectual property Intellectual property is someone's idea and the expression of that thought.

interactive program An interactive program converses with the user during program execution.

interblock gap An interblock gap (IBG) is wasted space between blocks stored on a tape.

interrecord gap An interrecord gap (IRG) is wasted space between records stored individually on a tape.

inverter An inverter is a basic part of a logic circuit. The inverter complements an input of x, giving x'.

invoke To call or invoke a function means to use it. A call or invocation of a function in a program causes the computer to interrupt execution of the routine containing the call in order to execute the function.

K A K is 2^{10} bytes = 1024 bytes.

keyword A keyword in C is a reserved name that cannot be used for a user-defined identifier.

language A language is the set of all words generated using the vocabulary and the productions of a formal grammar.

left-justified A value is left-justified if it is written on the far left of the output field.

library   A library includes a collection of implementations of useful and related tasks.

linear order   A linear order or sequence is an arrangement of values such that there is a first element, a second, and so forth.

linker   A linker or linkage editor is a program that combines all the object code of a program with necessary external items to form an executable program.

local variable   A local variable is a variable that has meaning only within a certain function.

logarithm to the base 2   The logarithm to the base 2 of n, written $\log_2 n$, is m if and only if $n = 2^m$.

logic   Propositional calculus or logic is the study of the algebra of propositions.

logic circuit   A logic circuit is a circuit where voltage on each line is interpreted as 0 or 1. The three basic parts to a logic circuit are the OR gate, the AND gate, and the inverter.

logical expression   A logical or boolean expression is a condition that is true or false.

logical operator   A logical operator is a symbol that we use to combine or negate expressions that are true or false, such as NOT, AND, and OR.

logical record   A logical record is an individual record.

logically equivalent   Two propositions p and q are logically equivalent or equal, written $p \equiv q$, provided they have identical values in their truth tables.

loop   A loop is a segment of code that is executed repeatedly.

looping control structure   With a looping control structure, the computer can execute a segment of code repeatedly.

low-level language   A low-level language, such as an assembler language or machine language, is closely associated with the underlying machine.

machine dependent   Machine dependent code varies depending on the particular machine on which it runs.

maintenance   The activities after a software product has been delivered in which it is corrected, adapted, and improved are called maintenance.

mathematical modeling   Mathematical modeling is the application of methods to analyze complex, real-world problems in order to make predictions about what might happen with various actions.

megabyte   A megabyte (Mbyte) is $1024 \cdot 1024 = 2^{10} \cdot 2^{10} = 2^{20} = 1,048,576$ bytes.

megaflops   A megaflops or Mflops is a million floating point operations per second.

megahertz   A megahertz (MHz) is a million cycles per second.

memory dump   A memory dump is a printout of the contents of an area of memory.

method   In OOP, a method is an operation in an object.

microprocessor   A microprocessor is a CPU on a chip.

minicomputer   A minicomputer is a midlevel computer with power usually between that of a microcomputer and a supercomputer.

mixed-mode expression   A mixed-mode expression is an expression that contains operands of different types.

modular control structure   With a modular control structure, the computer suspends execution of the current module to execute another module. When execution of the called module finishes, execution continues in the calling module.

modular programming   Modular programming is a process of developing programs in terms of subprograms or modules.

module   A module is a major task of a program or process.

multiprogramming system (or multitasking system)   A multiprogramming or multitasking system is a computer in which many programs reside in memory at the same time.

negation   Negation, denoted $\sim$, is a logical operator meaning "not."

nondisclosure agreement   A nondisclosure agreement is a contract in which an employee promises not to reveal any company trade secrets.

nonexecutable statement   A nonexecutable statement gives instructions to the compiler.

nonvolatile memory   The contents of nonvolatile memory persist even if electricity is lost.

normalized device coordinates   Normalized device coordinates (NDC) are floating point coordinates for a square region with the positive horizontal axis pointing to the right, the vertical axis pointing up, and the origin in the bottom left corner. Each coordinate ranges from 0.0 to 1.0.

normalized number A normalized number in exponential notation has the decimal point immediately preceding the first nonzero digit.

object In OOP, an object is an entity consisting of a data structure and its associated operations or methods.

object-oriented programming Object-oriented programming (OOP) is a programming paradigm that takes the abstract data model to a higher level of abstraction. The three main characteristics of object-oriented programming are encapsulation, inheritance, and polymorphism.

octal number system The octal or base 8 system has 8 octal digits, 0–7.

odd parity With odd parity, the total number of ones in the byte and accompanying parity bit should be odd.

one's complement The one's complement of a binary number is the number with each bit complemented.

one-to-one correspondence One-to-one correspondence exists between sets A and B if there is a pairing of the elements, such that for each element of A there corresponds exactly one element of B, and vice versa.

operating system An operating system (OS) is a collection of programs that enables the user to interact with the resources of a computer system efficiently.

operator overloading Operator overloading is multiple implementations of the actions of an operator, where the particular implementation depends on the type(s) of the operand(s).

operator precedence Operator precedence or priority of operators designates the order in which to perform operations in an expression.

OR gate An OR gate is a basic part of a logic circuit. Given two binary inputs, x and y, the OR gate yields an output of the boolean algebra $x + y$.

output The information that a computer program produces is output.

overflow Overflow is an error condition that occurs when not enough bits exist to express a value.

palette A palette is the set of colors from which to choose in the color lookup table.

paradigm A paradigm is a working methodology, a process, or a technique for approaching a subject

parallel computer A parallel computer has several processors that communicate with one another and that can work concurrently on the same or different programs.

parameter A function parameter (formal parameter or dummy parameter) is a variable declared in the function's heading that is used to communicate information between the calling routine and the function.

parity bit A parity bit is an extra bit associated with a byte and used for error checking.

parsing Parsing is the process of recognizing that an item is part of a language.

pass by reference Pass by reference is the technique of making a variable accessible to a function by passing its address.

pass by value Pass by value is a method of passing information to a function whereby the parameter receives a copy of the value of the argument.

patent A patent is exclusive rights for 17 years to an original, truly innovative invention and use of the ideas behind it. The creator must apply to the U.S. Patent and Trademark Office, which awards patents.

peripheral equipment The input, output, and secondary storage devices attached to the computer are called peripheral equipment.

physical record A block or a physical record is a fixed number of records the computer reads from or writes to secondary storage media as a group.

pixel A pixel, which stands for picture element, is a dot on a two-dimensional array of dots on a display medium.

pointer A pointer is a variable that can store a memory address.

polyline A polyline is a sequence of line segments with the end of one segment joining the beginning of another.

polymorphism In OOP, polymorphism occurs when a single method name, used up and down the hierarchy of objects, acts in an appropriate, possibly different, way for each object.

portable A program is portable if it can run without modification on different machines just by compiling it with the appropriate compilers.

postconditions Postconditions describe the state of the system when the module finishes executing, any error conditions, and the information the module returns or otherwise communicates.

precision   Precision is the number of significant digits in a number.

preconditions   Preconditions describe the situation that exists as the module is to begin execution, any assumptions, and the information the module needs to meet its objectives.

preliminary assessment   In preliminary assessment, the data processing manager with the advice of others determines whether it is feasible for the department to embark upon the project.

preprocessor   A preprocessor is a program that removes all comments and modifies source code according to directives supplied in the program.

preprocessor directive   A preprocessor directive, which begins with #, is an instruction to the preprocessor.

priming read   A priming read is an input statement that appears before a pretesting loop and that obtains a value for the loop variable.

priority of operators   Operator precedence or priority of operators designates the order in which to perform operations in an expression.

procedural abstraction   Procedural abstraction is a consideration of the input, processing, and output of a module. There is, however, no concern for the details of module implementation.

process   A process is a mechanism for converting input to output.

program   A program is a sequence of instructions to the computer.

prompt   In an interactive program, a prompt is a request from the computer for the user to enter data.

proposition   A statement or proposition in logic is a declarative sentence that is either true or false.

propositional calculus   Propositional calculus or logic is the study of the algebra of propositions.

prototype   A prototype is a trial version that demonstrates the functionality and "user friendliness" of the developing system.

pseudocode   Pseudocode is a sequence of statements that are close to those of a programming language, but more English-like, sometimes more general, and without the syntax requirements of a formal computer language.

pseudorandom number   A sequence of pseudorandom numbers (often called random numbers for short) is a sequence of numbers that an algorithm produces but has the appearance of being randomly generated.

public domain software   Public domain software is software in which the developer has explicitly relinquished all rights to the software. Thus, the copyright law does not apply to this software.

query language   A data manipulation language (DML) or query language is used to access and update data in a database management system.

random access memory (RAM)   RAM is the part of main memory that can change. We can read from and write to this type of memory.

random access storage media   Random access or direct access storage media can be written to or read from by specifying the exact location where the operation is to occur.

random number   A sequence of pseudorandom numbers (often called random numbers for short) is a sequence of numbers that an algorithm produces but has the appearance of being randomly generated.

raster-scan video monitor   In a raster-scan video monitor, a beam of electrons passes over the screen a row at a time, from top to bottom, adjusting the intensity at each point.

read-only memory (ROM)   ROM is the part of main memory that cannot change. We can read from but not write to this type of memory.

recursive task   A recursive task is one that calls itself. With each invocation, the problem is reduced to a smaller task (reducing case) until arriving at some terminal or base case, which stops the process.

reducing case   A reducing case is a smaller task in a recursive process.

redundant data   Redundant data are data that are duplicated between files.

register   A register is a high-speed location in the CPU.

relation   In a relational database, a relation is a two-dimensional table of data.

relational database model   The relational database model is based on mathematical principles.

relational operator   A relational operator is a symbol that we use to test the relationship between two expressions—such as equal, greater than, less than, not equal, greater than or equal, and less than or equal.

requirements analysis In performing a requirements analysis, the software engineer must determine exactly what the users need.

right-justified A value is right-justified if it is written on the far right of the output field.

root directory The root directory is at the top of the directory structure.

run-time stack A run-time stack is a stack of activation records that exists during execution of a program.

schema A schema is a description of the overall database structure.

scope The scope of a variable is the range within a program over which that variable has meaning.

sector Each track of a disk usually contains eight equal-length, arc-shaped areas called sectors.

secondary storage unit The secondary storage unit, which is a major hardware component of a computer system, stores information on a semi-permanent basis.

selection control structure With a selection control structure, the computer decides which statement to execute next depending on the value of a logical expression.

self-documenting An identifier is self-documenting if the name is descriptive of the role of the item.

sentinel technique The sentinel or trailer technique uses a special end-of-data value to indicate the end of the meaningful data.

sequence A linear order or sequence is an arrangement of values such that there is a first element, a second, and so forth.

sequential access In sequential access to data, records are read or written one after another in sequence.

sequential control structure With a sequential control structure, the computer executes statements one after another in sequence.

set bit A set bit is a bit that has the value 1.

shareware Shareware is distributed liberally, and an adopter is asked to send a nominal amount of money to the author. The copyright law applies to shareware.

side effect A side effect occurs when a function affects the state of the program as a whole in a way that is not evident from how the calling function uses the called function.

signed-magnitude representation The signed-magnitude representation of signed integers expresses the number in binary in a fixed number of bits, and the most significant (leftmost) bit indicates the sign—0 for positive and 1 for negative.

significant digits The significant digits of a floating point number are all the digits except the leading zeros.

simulation A simulation is a model using a program of a real-life event.

site license A site license allows use of an unlimited or a fixed number of copies at the place of business.

soft crash A soft crash of a program involves an execution-time error, but the program prints a descriptive error message and ends.

software Programs and data are software.

software engineer A software engineer or systems analyst is in charge of analysis and preliminary design for a software engineering project.

software license A software license is authorization to use software.

software requirements specification The Software Requirements Specification (SRS) is a formal document that reviews the need and gives a detailed, clear description of the requirements of a system.

solve To solve a recursive routine means to find an equivalent nonrecursive definition.

source code (or source program) A program typed into the computer is called source code or a source program.

spooling Spooling is a technique of collecting all the output from a program before printing, so that the printer does not intersperse lines of output from different programs.

stack A stack is a data structure in which data can only be added to or removed from one end—the top.

stack frame An activation record or stack frame is a record that comes into existence when a function is called. It contains the return location, the list of arguments, room for a return value (if any), and an area for the function's local variables.

stack overflow Stack overflow occurs with an attempt to put something on a stack but no more room exists.

statement A statement in a program is a programming language instruction to the computer. A statement or proposition in logic is a declarative sentence that is either true or false.

step To step through a program is to trace execution one statement at a time for debugging.

stepwise refinement Stepwise refinement is a method of problem solving whereby we start with the most general and work our way to the specific.

storage density Storage density of a tape is the number of bits in one track of length 1 inch. This measurement is expressed in bytes/inch or bits/inch (bpi).

strongly typed A language is strongly typed if it does not allow data of one type to be used where another type is expected.

structure chart A structure chart or hierarchy diagram is a tree diagram of the major tasks of the program and their relation to one another.

stub A stub is a version of a routine that is used for top-down testing of a program. The stub does not implement the routine's algorithm and does not necessarily return correct results. The results, however, are sufficient to test the routines that call the stub.

subschema A subschema holds the definition of part of the data described in the schema.

supercomputer A supercomputer is the fastest, largest, and most expensive type of mainframe computer.

switching function Function f is a switching or combinational function provided f is a mapping from $\mathbf{B}^n$, the set of all boolean n-tuples, to $\mathbf{B} = \{0, 1\}$ for some positive integer n. A combinational function is a mathematical model of a combinational circuit.

syntax The syntax of a programming language is the set of rules for forming valid instructions.

syntax error A syntax error (compile-time error) violates the syntax of a language.

systems analysis Systems analysis involves preliminary assessment, requirements analysis, and requirements specification.

systems analyst A software engineer or systems analyst is in charge of analysis and preliminary design for a software engineering project.

terminal case A terminal or base case in a recursive task stops the recursion process.

terminal condition The condition that must be true to achieve the terminal case is the terminal condition.

ternary operator A ternary operator operates upon three values.

test program A test program includes a driver and the module or modules it is exercising.

text file A text file is a file of characters.

time-sharing system A time-sharing system is a large computer system in which many users employ terminals to communicate with the computer.

time-slice A time-slice is a period of time that the OS assigns to a job for execution. When one time-slice is over, the computer executes a time-slice for another job.

top The top is the end of a stack to which a data item is added and from which a data item is removed.

top-down design Top-down design (with modular programming and stepwise refinement) is a design technique whereby we decompose a problem into manageable subproblems (modules). We can then subdivide each subproblem in the same manner.

top-down strategy The top-down strategy of program implementation and testing starts with the highest-level functions and proceeds to the lowest, with debugging occurring one function at a time. Stubs are used in place of lower-level routines.

trace A trace is a debugger tool that allows the user to follow the flow of execution or sequence of program statements as they execute.

track On a magnetic disk, data are stored in concentric circles called tracks. On magnetic tape, a track is a sequence of bits running the length of the tape.

trademark A trademark is something that provides name recognition for a product or an organization. The U.S. Patent and Trademark Office grants exclusive rights for a trademark.

trade secret A trade secret is some proprietary information about a product that a company does not want the competition to know.

trailer technique The sentinel or trailer technique uses a special end-of-data value to indicate the end of the meaningful data.

truncate To truncate a real number means to chop off the value to the integer part.

tuple A tuple corresponds to a row in a relation.

type The type of a variable is the kind of data it can store.

uniformly distributed A sequence of random numbers is uniformly distributed if a random number has an equal likelihood of being anywhere within a specified range.

unit testing Unit testing is the testing of an individual module.

user interface User interface is how the user interacts with a product.

variable A variable is a program's name for a memory location

variable declaration A variable declaration is a statement that indicates the variable's name and type.

volatile memory The contents of volatile memory are lost if electricity is lost.

walkthrough A walkthrough is a review of the analysis, design, or implementation of all or part of a system. The developer(s) leads the walkthrough, and others ask questions and make suggestions.

warning message A warning message from a compiler advises the programmer that a statement is technically acceptable but is unusual enough to constitute a potential error.

watch The ability to watch an expression during execution of the program is a debugger feature that allows the programmer to view any change in the value of the expression.

weakly typed A language is weakly typed if it sometimes allows data of one type to be used where another type is expected only because the conversion is possible, not because it is meaningful.

windows Windows are overlapping rectangles on a screen display.

word A word is a unit of storage and transfer in a computer. A computer usually moves information one word at a time. A word in a formal grammar is a finite-length string of terminals.

world coordinates In computer graphics, world coordinates (WC) are the floating point coordinates used by an application, with the positive horizontal axis pointing to the right and the positive vertical axis pointing up.

APPENDIX
J

Answers to Selected Exercises

Chapter 1

Section 1.1
6. a, d, e

Section 1.5
1. `tax = 50 * .06 * price;`

Section 1.7
1. Change the first *printf* to

```
printf("Give me land, lots of land\n\n");
```

3. Opening comment does not have */; *main* has semicolon instead of (); body of *main* begins and ends with () instead of {}; calls to *printf* have ' instead of "; last *printf* does not have semicolon

5.
```
He who
laughs last
lasts
last.
```

Section 1.8
3. [] should be (); semicolon omitted from end

Chapter 2

Section 2.1
1. b. no   2. a. not legal, contains a exclamation mark

Section 2.2
1. a. `int tax;`   b. `printf("%d",tax);`
5. 3 3 3   7. `int month = 1;`   11. `tax = 2 * tax;`

Section 2.3
1. 9   7. 3   17. 4   21. 0
25. `ans = x * x / (y + 3) * z;`

Section 2.4
1. 7   10. 100   19. 11010, 11000   23. 0, 15
27. 10111   31. D

Section 2.5
1. 0101 1011   9. 0000 0000 0101 1011   13. 0111 1100
19. 1000 1000, overflow: 43 + 93 ≠ −120
23. 157; doubled: 0011 1010, overflow: 2 * 156 ≠ 58; halved: 0100 1110, 78
24. D

Section 2.6
1. e. error, `scanf("%d %d", &x, &y);`
3. `printf("Enter your age and number of years of schooling: ");`
`scanf("%d %d",&age, &NumYrsSchool);`

Section 2.7
1. a. 7
5.
```
int even(int x)
{
    return(x % 2);
}
```

Section 2.9
1. Variables *num* and *square* of *main* exist from declaration throughout execution of program. They are accessible in *main* only. Variable *num* of *sqr* exists only during execution of *sqr*. It is accessible in *sqr* only. Function *sqr* is global and is accessible throughout.

Chapter 3

Section 3.1
1. if *x* is greater than or equal to *y*   7. `if (x > 56)`
13. `if ( x % 2 == 0)`   21. `(x != (z <= 3))`   27. 7

Section 3.2
1.
```
if (x > 0)
    y = 5;
```
5.
```
if ((-10 <= x) && (x <= 10))
    x = 2 * x;
else
    x = x / 2;
```
8.
```
if (price <= 1000)
    price = price - 5;
else
{
    printf("The price is too large.\n");
    printf("Please enter a new value: ");
    scanf("%d", &price);
}
```

Section 3.3
1.
```
if ((x > 0) && (y > 0))
    if (x < y)
        printf("%d", x);
    else
        printf("%d", y);
```

4. a. C   5. a. A   6. a. A

Section 3.4

1. a. AB

```
5. switch (choice)
   {
       case 1:   ProcessCharge();
                 break;
       case 2:   ProcessReturn();
                 break;
       case 3:   VoidTransaction();
                 break;
       case 4:   Quit();
                 break;
       default:  InvalidResponse();
   }
```

Section 3.5

1. $p \wedge q$

5. I eat spaghetti, and I eat salad. I eat salad, and I eat spaghetti. Same meaning. Commutative Property.

11. not ($x \leq y$ and $x \leq z$); $x > y$ or $x > z$ 20. E

Section 3.6

```
2. void ProcessCharge(void)
   {
       printf("Entering stub for ProcessCharge\n");
   }
```

Chapter 4

Section 4.1

1. 7010   5. 0.0035   9. 0.6385e2, 6.385e1   17. 5
21. a. 9876   e. 9876 followed by 6 blanks
23. c. 987.650   25. a. 98.765000

Section 4.2

1. 0.75   8. 0.1101   15. 3
19. mantissa: 1101 0000, exponent: 128_{10} 27. 10001.011

Section 4.3

2. b. 9.0   3. b. 2.500000

Section 4.4

2. printf("%ld", debt);   5. 32767

Section 4.5

1. if (fabs(x - 3.5) < 10 * FLT_EPSILON)
5. printf("%f", DBL_MAX);
7. y = sqrt(pow(x,5) - 8);   14. D

Chapter 5

Section 5.1   1. a. 17   2. a. 11, -30   3. a. (y += (x * (++z)));
5. NumStudents = NumStudents + 50; NumStudents += 50;

Section 5.2   1. 3 4 5 6 7 8 9 10
10.
```c
int i = 2;
while (i < 20)
{
    printf("%d ", i);
    i += 2;
}
```

Section 5.3   1. 3 4 5 6 7 8 9 10
6.
```c
do
{
    printf("Enter the cost of the item: ");
    scanf("%f", &cost);
}
while (cost <= 0);
```

Section 5.4   2.
```c
float average(void)
{
    float num,
          sum = 0.0,
          ReturnAverage;
    int count = 0;

    printf("\nPlease enter a number (0 to stop): ");
    scanf("%f", &num);
    while (fabs(num) >= 10 * FLT_EPSILON)
    {
        sum += num;
        count++;
        printf("\nPlease enter a number (0 to stop): ");
        scanf("%f",&num);
    }

    if (count == 0)
        ReturnAverage = 0.0;
    else
        ReturnAverage = sum / count;
    return( ReturnAverage );
}
```
7. num = (int)(20 * (float) rand() / RAND_MAX + 6);

Section 5.6   1. 450,000,000 psec = 450,000 nsec = 450 μsec

5. a. 10.8   6. A   9. 105.26 MHz   14. 100 Mflops

Section 5.7   1. 0.009, 0.016%   5. 6.23, 12.4, 0.625%

Chapter 6

Section 6.1   1. 7654

7.
```
for (i = 0; i < 100; i++)
    printf("Hello\n");
```

Section 6.2   1.
```
7 1
7 2
6 1
6 2
5 1
5 2
4 1
4 2
```

7.
```
for (row = 1; row <= 5; row++)
{
    for (column = 1; column <= 7; column++)
        printf("%4d", row + column);
    printf("\n");
}
```

Chapter 7

Section 7.1   1. a. `printf("%c", lang);`   b. `putchar(lang);`

6. Enter another character: <u>yes</u>
The character is y.

Enter another character:
The character is e.

Section 7.2   1. a. 35   11. `printf("f'(x)\t=\t2x");`

Section 7.3   1. B'!B

5.
```
int isdigit(char c)
{
    return( ('0' <= c) && (c <= '9') );
}
```

Section 7.4   1. 226   8. 21   11. B9, BA, BB, BC   20. 9.3
             23. `int oct = 064;`   27. 18   30. 0.48

Section 7.5   1. `FILE *EmpFile_ptr,`
                 `*ScaleFile_ptr,`
                 `*WageFile_ptr;`
             4. `fscanf(EmpFile_ptr, "%d %f", &EmpNum, &salary);`

Chapter 8

Section 8.1   1. `float flt[20];`
             5. `for ( i = 0; i < 50; i++)`
                 `a[i] = i;`
             10. `for ( i= 0; i < NumPlayers; i++)`
                  `fprintf(FinalFile_ptr,"%d\n", score[i]);`
             12. `int a[] = {1, 1, 1, 1, 1};`

Section 8.2   1. `float sum(float a[], int n)`
                 `{`
                      `float TempSum = 0.0;`
                      `int i:`

                      `for (i = 0; i < n; i++)`
                          `TempSum += a[i];`
                      `return(TempSum);`
                 `}`

Section 8.3   3. a. 3, 1; 2 comparisons
             11. b. `/* search from the low scores up */`
                  `found = FALSE;`
                  `MinRange = 0;`
                  `while ( !found && MinRange < MAX_NUM)`
                      `if SAT[MinRange] >= 550 if SAT`
                          `found = TRUE;`
                      `else`
                          `MinRange++;`

                  `/* search from the high scores down */`
                  `found = FALSE;`
                  `MaxRange = MAX_NUM - 1;`
                  `while ( !found && MaxRange >= 0)`
                      `if SAT[MaxRange] <= 650 if SAT`
                          `found = TRUE;`
                      `else`
                          `MaxRange--;`

Section 8.4

1. Sorted array in color, swaps underlined:

C S M R T F P
C F M R T S P
C F M R T S P
C F M P T S R
C F M P R S T
C F M P R S T

5. a.
```
void SelectionSort(char a[], int n)
{
    char temp;
    int i;

    for (i = 0; i < n - 1; i++)
    {
        MinIndex = IndexOfMin(a, i, n);
        temp = a[i];
        a[i] = a[MinIndex];
        a[MinIndex] = temp;
    }
}
```

Section 8.5

1. `float d[20][50];`   2. a. 7

7.
```
int ArraySum(int a[MAX_ROWS][MAX_COL],
             int rows, int columns)
{
    int i;
    int j;
    int sum = 0;

    for (i = 0; i < rows; i++)
        for (j = 0; j < columns; j++)
            sum += a[i][j];
    return (sum);
}
```

Section 8.6

1. 16, 2^n

Chapter 9

Section 9.1

1. `p = &x;   *p=14.5;   q = &y;   *q=23.8;   printf("%f %f\n", *p, *q);`

output:
14.500000 23.800000

p → x: ?
p → x: 14.5
q → y: ?
q → y: 23.8

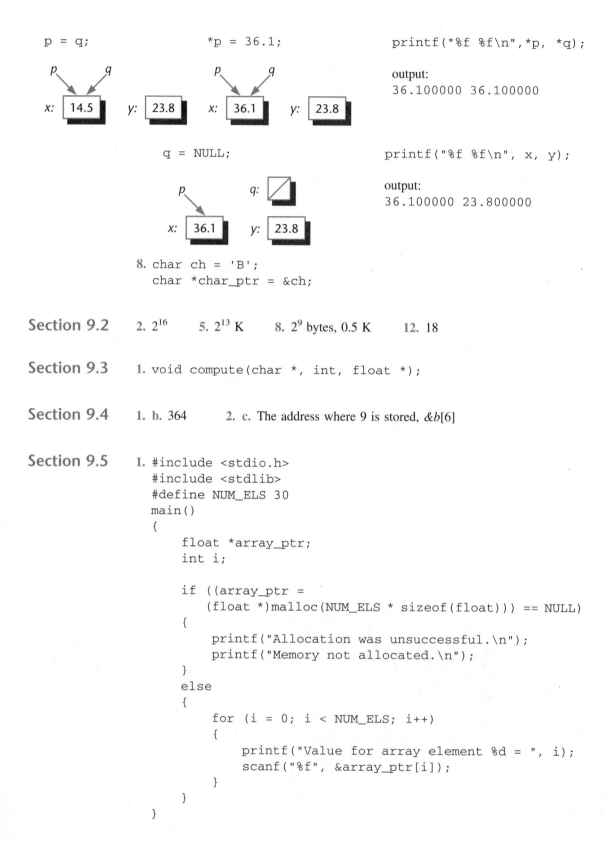

```
      p = q;                   *p = 36.1;                  printf("%f %f\n",*p, *q);
```

output:
36.100000 36.100000

```
                   q = NULL;                          printf("%f %f\n", x, y);
```

output:
36.100000 23.800000

```
8. char ch = 'B';
   char *char_ptr = &ch;
```

Section 9.2   2. 2^{16} 5. 2^{13} K   8. 2^9 bytes, 0.5 K   12. 18

Section 9.3   1. `void compute(char *, int, float *);`

Section 9.4   1. b. 364   2. c. The address where 9 is stored, &*b*[6]

Section 9.5
```
1. #include <stdio.h>
   #include <stdlib>
   #define NUM_ELS 30
   main()
   {
       float *array_ptr;
       int i;

       if ((array_ptr =
          (float *)malloc(NUM_ELS * sizeof(float))) == NULL)
       {
           printf("Allocation was unsuccessful.\n");
           printf("Memory not allocated.\n");
       }
       else
       {
           for (i = 0; i < NUM_ELS; i++)
           {
               printf("Value for array element %d = ", i);
               scanf("%f", &array_ptr[i]);
           }
       }
   }
```

Section 9.6   1. `double (*fun_ptr)(int, float);`   **5.** `fun_ptr = ActualFun;`

7. `printf("%f",(*fun_ptr)(7, 23.8));`

10. **a.** `void ExFun1(int, float, double (*)(int, float));`

b. `ExFun1(7, 23.8, fun_ptr);`

Chapter 10

Section 10.1   1. `Print this line.`   **7.** `11, 12`

12. `char prog[] = "program";`

Section 10.2   1. **a.** "This"   **b.** " This is a line."

2. **b.** `: Before:`
   `:After :`

3. **b.** `: Before::After :`

Section 10.3   1. **a.** `char title[20] = "Problem Solving in C";`

e. `printf("%s", title);`

3. **a.** `char *course_ptr = "Computer Science 1";`

Section 10.4   1. **a.** `char long_str[20];`   **c.** `lng = atol(long_str);`
   `long lng;`

Section 10.5   1. *len* is 20   3. *s1* is "wel"   4. *s1* is "wellcome"
   6. *s1* is "come"

Section 10.6   1. *comp* is positive

10.
```c
void delete(char str[], char sub[])
{
    char *temp;

    if ((temp = strstr(str, sub)) == NULL)
        printf("\"%s\" did not occur in \"%s\"",
                sub, str);
    else
    {
        *temp = '\0';
        strcat(str, temp + strlen(sub));
    }
}
```

Chapter 11

Section 11.1   1. a.
```
struct address_struct
    {
        char name[30];
        char street[40];
        char city[30];
        char state[2];
    };
```
b. `struct address_struct OneAddr, TwoAddr;`

d. `scanf("%39s", OneAddr.street);`

e.
```
if ( strcmp(OneAddr.name, TwoAddr.name) == 0 &&
        strcmp(OneAddr.street, TwoAddr.street) == 0 &&
        strcmp(OneAddr.city, TwoAddr.city) == 0 &&
        strcmp(OneAddr.state, TwoAddr.state) == 0 )
    printf("Equal structures\n");
```

Section 11.2   1.
```
typedef
struct
{
    char name[30];
    float salary;
    int age;
}
emp_t;
```
3. b.
```
printf("Name: %s    Salary: %.2f",
        EmpArray[9].name, EmpArray[9].salary);
```
c. `EmpArray[9].name[0]`

Section 11.3   6. NameState ← **PROJECT** *name, state* **FROM** *StudentAddr*

Section 11.4   1. a.
```
void ReadDate(date_t *date)
    {
        printf("Enter the month, day, and year");
scanf("%d %d %d",
        &date->month, &date->day, &date->year);
    }
```
4. b. `p = head;`   c. `q = head->next;`

d. `free(q->next);`

Section 11.5   1. a.
```
typedef
enum
{
    SMALL, MEDIUM, LARGE
}
SweatSize_t;
```

b.
```
SweatSize_t AskSize(void)
{
    int int_size;

    do
    {
        printf(" What is your sweatshirt size?\n");
        printf("\t0 SMALL\n");
        printf("\t1 MEDIUM\n");
        printf("\t2 LARGE\n");
        printf("\nSize (0-2): ");
        scanf("%d",&int_size);
    }
    while (int_size < 0 || 2 < int_size);

    return (SweatSize_t)int_size;
}
```

c.
```
void PrintSize(SweatSize_t size)
{
    printf("Your sweatshirt size is ");
    switch (size)
    {
        case SMALL:
            printf("SMALL.\n");
            break;
        case MEDIUM:
            printf("MEDIUM.\n");
            break;
        case LARGE:
            printf("LARGE.\n");
    }
}
```

Section 11.6 1. a.
```
typedef
struct
{
    boolean_t boarding;
    char interests[100];
}
full_t;

typedef
struct
{
    boolean_t degree;
    char school[40];
}
part_t;
```

```
typedef
union
{
    full_t FullTime;
    part_t PartTime;
}
StudentsUnion_t;
```

b.
```
typedef enum {FULLTIME, PARTTIME} flag_t;
typedef
struct
{
    char SSN[10];
    int hours;
    flag_t flag;
    StudentsUnion_t students;
}
student_t
```

Section 11.7

1. 0.65

Chapter 12

Section 12.1

1. `#define ERROR printf("An error has been detected.\n")`

3. `#define MULT_CUBE(x)  (5*(x)*(x)*(x))`

Section 12.2

1. `extern int count;`

4.
```
#include <stdio.h>
main (int argc, char *argv[])
{
    int loop;

    for (loop = 0; loop < argc; loop++)
        printf("%s\n", argv[loop]);
}
```

Section 12.3

2. b.
```
#ifdef VAX_COMPUTER
    short int INTEGER;
#else
    int INTEGER;
#endif
```

4.
```
#ifdef TRUE
#undef TRUE
#endif

#ifdef FALSE
#undef FALSE
#endif
```

Section 12.5   3.   object *time:*

data structure:	*minutes*
	seconds
methods:	*DisplayStd*
	DisplayMil
	SetTime
	IncrementTime

Section 12.6   1.
```
cout << "Please enter an integer: ";
cin >> num;
```
7.
```
date::date(int mo, int dy, int yr)
{
    month = mo;
    day   = dy;
    year  = yr;
}
```
11.
```
int totalScore = 0;
for(int i = 0; i < 13; ++i)
{
    switch(BridgeHand[i].whatFaceValue())
    {
    case Jack:   // NO BREAK
    case Queen:  // NO BREAK
    case King:   // NO BREAK
    case Ace:    totalScore += BridgeHand[i].whatScore();
    }
}
cout << "Total score for face cards is " << totalScore << ".\n";
```

Section 12.7   1.
```
0    0230 ; LDA   30 AC <- Memory[30]
1    0531 ; SUBT  31 AC <- AC - Memory[31]
2    0332 ; STA   32 Memory[32] <- AC
3    9999 ; HALT
```
3.
```
0    0225 ; LDA   25 AC <- Memory[25]
1    0703 ; BRAN  03 if AC < 0 PC <- 03
2    0606 ; JUMP  06 PC <- 06
3    0525 ; SUBT  25 AC <- AC - Memory[25]
4    0525 ; SUBT  25 AC <- AC - Memory[25]
5    0325 ; STA   25 Memory[25] <- AC
6    0125 ; OUT   25 Output <- Memory[25]
7    9999 ; HALT
```
6. D

Chapter 13

Section 13.1   2. a. 3, 7, 15, 31, 63

```
b. int pattern (int n)
   {
       int num;       /* Number in the sequence */

       if (n == 0)
           num = 3;
       else
           num = (2 * pattern(n -1)) + 1;
       return (num);
   }
```

```
4. b. float  amount (float P, float R, int n)
      {
          float temp;       /* Temporary storage for Amount */

          if (n == 0)
              temp = P;
          else
              temp = amount(n - 1) * (1 + R);
          return (temp)P, R,;
      }
```

```
9. int product(int a[], int n)
   {
       int prod;       /* Product of numbers */

       if (n == 0)
           prod = a[0];
       else
           prod = a[n] * product a(n - 1);

       return (prod);
   }
```

Section 13.2   1. int MinAr(int a[], int n)

```
   {
       int i,       /* loop control */
           temp;   /* Temporary storage of Min */

       temp = a[0];
       for (i = 1; i <= n; i++)
           if (a[i] < temp)
               temp = a[i];
       return (temp);
   }
```

4.
```
int f(int n)
{
    int num, i;

    num = 3;
    for     (i = 1; i <= n; i++)
            num = 2 * num + 1;
    return (num);
}
```

5.
```
float amount (float P, float R, int n)
{
    float amt;
    int i;      /* Loop control */

    amt = P;
    for (i = 0; i < n; i++)
        amt += amt * (1 + R);
    return (amt);
}
```

10.
```
float max (float a[], int n)
{
    float temp;       /* Temporary storage of Max */
    int i;            /* Loop control */

    temp = a[0];
    for (i = 1; i <= n; i++)
        if (a[i] > temp)
            temp = a[i];
    return (temp);
}
```

Section 13.3

3. a. $\{01, 0101, 010101, \ldots\}$ **b.** $S \to 01S \to 0101$

7. $S \to 00S, S \to 00$

```
boolean_t InLanguage(char *S)
{
    boolean_t recognize;      /* return value */

    if (strlen(S) == 2)
        recognize = (S[0] == '0' && S[1] == '0') ? TRUE : FALSE;
    else if (strlen(S) > 2 && S[0] == '0' && S[1] == '0')
        recognize = InLanguage(S + 2);
    else
        recognize = FALSE;

    return recognize;
}
```

9. $S \to 1S, S \to 01S, S \to 0, S \to 1, S \to 01$

Chapter 14

Section 14.1
1. `fgets(name, 40, infile_ptr);`
5. `fputs(name, outfile_ptr);`
10. `fscanf(stdin, "%d\n", &i);`

Section 14.2
1. a. 20 bpi   b. 1500 bytes/sec   5. a. 5.071 Mbytes
9. 28.01 msec   12. a. 130 records/track

Section 14.3
1. a. `appfile_ptr = fopen("product.dat","a");`
b. `appfile_ptr = fopen("product.dat","a+");`
c. `rewind(appfile_ptr);`

Section 14.4
3. `binprod_ptr = fopen("binprod.dat","ab");`
4. e. `fwritee(&PlantRec, sizeof(plant_t), 1, PlantFile_ptr);`
f. `fread(&PlantRec, sizeof(plant_t), 1, PlantFile_ptr);`

Section 14.5
2. `fseek(fp, 0L, SEEK_END);`   3. `fseek(fp, 9L, SEEK_SET);`
9. `fseek (fp, 0L, SEEK_END);`
```
printf("The number of bytes in the file is %ld.\n",
        ftell(fp));
```
12.
```
fread(&SalesRec, sizeof(sales_t), 1, SalesFile_ptr);
if (SalesRec.amount >= 100000)
    SalesRec.MakeQuota = 'y';
else
    SalesRec.MakeQuota = 'n';
fseek(SalesFile_ptr, (long) -1 * sizeof(sales_t), SEEK_CUR);
fwrite(&SalesRec, sizeof(sales_t), 1, SalesFile_ptr);
```

Chapter 15

Section 15.1
1. 0001 0000, 0x10   3. 1011 1110, 0xBE
5. 0100 0111, 0x47   7. 1010 1110 , 0xAE
9. 0000 0010, 0x02   25. `a |= 0x01;`   27. `a &= 0xFE;`
31. `a ^= 0xC0;`   35. `a >>= 5;`

Section 15.2   1. a. $u = (xy)'$

b.

x	y	xy	(xy)'
0	0	0	1
0	1	0	1
1	0	0	1
1	1	1	0

c. u is 1 if x or y or both are 0

5. $u = x' + y'$ 7. $z = 1$

Section 15.3   2.

x	y	f(x, y)
0	0	1
0	1	0
1	0	1
1	1	0

$f(x, y) = x'y' + xy' = y'$

6. b. $u = cx'y + cxy' + cxy$ 11. a. 2   b. 4

Chapter 16

Section 16.1   1. a. 6.   b. 7   c. *NULL*

9.
```
void TwoNodes(list* l_ptr, el_t x, el_t y)
{
    l_ptr->head = MakeNode(x);
    l_ptr->head->next = MakeNode(y);
}
```

11. a.
```
void PrintList(list L)
{
    L.cur = L.head;
    while (L.cur != NULL)
    {
        PrintEl((L.cur)->el);
        Advance(&L);
    }
}
```

11. b.
```
void CallRPrintList(list L)
{
    L.cur = L.head;
    RPrintList(L);
}
```

```
void RPrintList(list L)
{
    if (L.cur != NULL)
    {
        PrintEl((L.cur)->el);
        Advance(&L);
        RPrintList(L);
    }
}
```

Section 16.2

8. b. *Push(s, 1); Pop(s, e)*, write *e*, which is 1; *Push(s, 2); Push(s, 3); Pop(s, e)*, write *e*, which is 3; *Pop(s, e)*, write *e*, which is 2

9. *SwapStack(s)*
   Pre: *s* is a stack.
   Post: If *s* has at least two elements, its top two elements were exchanged.
   Algorithm:
   if (not *StackIsEmpty(s)*)
       Pop(s, first)
       if(*StackIsEmpty(s)*)
           Push(s, first)
       else
           Pop(s, second)
           Push(s, first)
           Push(s, second)

15. *append(s, u)*
    Pre: *s* and *u* are stacks.
    Post: *u* has been appended on top of *s* so that *u*'s top element is on top.
        u has been made empty.
    Algorithm:
    if not *StackIsEmpty(u)* then
        Pop(u, e)
        append(s, u)
        if *StackIsFull(s)* then
            StackIsFullError(e)
        else
            Push(s, e)

Section 16.3

3.
```
void StackSwap(stack s)
{
    el_t first;
    el_t second;

    if (!StackIsEmpty(&s))
    {
        Pop(&s, &first);
        if (StackIsEmpty(&s))
            Push(&s, first);
        else
```

```
            {
                Pop(&s, &second);
                Push(&s, first);
                Push(&s, second);
            }
        }
    }
9. void append(stack* s_ptr, stack* u_ptr)
   {
   el_t e;

        if (!StackIsEmpty(u_ptr))
        {
            Pop(u_ptr, &e);
            append(s_ptr, u_ptr);
            if (StackIsFull(s_ptr))
                StackIsFullError(e);
            else
                Push(s_ptr, e);
        }
   }
21. void InitStack( stack *s_ptr )
    {
        s_ptr->top = -1;
    }
24. void Push( stack *s_ptr, el_t e )
    {
        if( StackIsFull(s_ptr) )
        {
            printf("Stack is full\n");
            exit(1);
        }
        else
        {
            ++(s_ptr->top);
            s_ptr->el[ s_ptr->top ] = e;
        }
    }
```

Answers to Review Questions

Chapter 1

1. Analysis, design, implementation, and testing
2. A diagram of the major tasks or functions of a program and their relation to one another
3. A precise, step-by-step method of doing a task in a finite amount of time
4. Input unit, output unit, secondary storage, CPU, and main memory
5. ALU and control unit
6. The fetch/execute cycle
7. The name of something in a program
8. A number associated with a particular location (addresses are sequential, 0, 1, 2, etc.)
9. Editor or text editor
10. The preprocessor converts the source code to preprocessed source code. The compiler converts this code to object code. The linker combines this code with necessary external items to form executable code.
11. It is the first step in the compilation of a C program, which performs several initial tasks, including the processing of constant definitions.
12. #define PI 3.14159
13. Quotation marks
14. The control string
15. The semicolon
16. The left and right braces, { and }
17. By the two adjacent symbols \ and n
18. The /* symbol pair, followed by the comment and then terminated with */
19. The *printf* function
20. To enhance readability and to enable the reader to understand the code
21. Yes; they may be as long as you like.
22. A datum passed to the function at the time the function is used
23. The statements of a user-defined function are written as part of the program according to the programmer's requirements. Functions in the C library are written by those who develop the compiler.
24. A function may be designed to carry out some frequently used task and called upon when needed merely by specifying the name of the function.
25. *printf*

26. A prototype gives vital information about how to invoke a function and what type of value to expect in return.

27. `chorus();`

28. Functions enable you to divide the program into more understandable segments, each performing a single task.

29. The finding and eliminating of errors in programs

30. A section of code that performs its own subtask. In C, modules are written as functions.

31. **a.** The name must begin with a letter or an underscore.

    b. The name can contain only letters, digits, or underscores.

    c. The name should not be a keyword.

    d. The name should not be in all capitals, to avoid confusion with constants.

    e. The name should not begin with an underscore, to avoid conflict with system names.

32. As many times as needed

33. The process of breaking a problem into subtasks, which in turn may be broken down again, so that the lowest level functions are straightforward

34. Braces, { and }

35. The position of *main* makes no difference, as long as it is not inside another function.

36. This is done automatically by the operating system when the program is executed.

Chapter 2

1. It is a whole number without a decimal point.

2. It is a symbolic name for a memory location in which a value is stored.

3. *variable = expression;*

4. The assignment statement

5. During execution of the program, the expression to the right of the equal sign is reduced to a single value, which is then stored in the variable specified on the left.

6. Only one

7. a and b only

8. They must begin with a letter (including the underscore); may contain only letters, digits, and underscores; and may not be a keyword.

9. It highlights program statements and output, and makes the program listing easier to read.

10. It is invalid, because only one variable may appear to the left of the equal sign.

11. Neither; they have the same priority. If they are both present, the computer evaluates the operations from left to right.

12. The binary minus has an operand before and after the minus sign, and it indicates subtraction. The unary minus has only one operand—to its right—and converts a positive value into its corresponding negative value and vice versa.

13. `int x = 456;`

14. It is chopping off, such as the chopping off of a decimal number to its integer part.

15. They override the normal priorities. The computer evaluates first what is within the parentheses in the normal order.

16. The modulus operator (%) finds the remainder when dividing one integer by another integer.

17. By including two adjacent % signs in the *printf* control string

18. a. 2   **b.** 0   **c.** 0   **d.** 1   **e.** −1
   f. This answer depends on the particular machine, but would be either 3 or −1.

19. The *scanf* function

20. A *printf* advising the user that input is required and specifying of what type it should be

21. The ampersand (&) symbol

22. When it executes the *return* statement or when the last statement in the body of the function is executed

23. It returns the size in bytes (or, more generally, character-sized units) of its operand.

24. No. The *sizeof* operator is machine-dependent, because different computers or compilers assign different sizes to various data types. However, by definition, the *sizeof* operator always returns 1 as the size of a character operand.

25. The name of a data type and an expression, such as a variable or a constant

26. When a function call is written as a statement, any value returned is discarded.

27. One

28. Modular programming; avoidance of side effects and global variables; well-chosen comments; intelligently selected and descriptive variable and function names

29. This term describes the situation that results when a function performs an operation that is not evident from the use of the function. An example is placing a value into a global variable.

30. Its name is specified, followed by a pair of parentheses, which contain the arguments, if needed.

31. It specifies the value for the function to return and terminates execution of the function.

32. Outside all function definitions, usually at the beginning of the program

33. Local variables are declared within the body of a function, and they can be referenced only within the function. They disappear when the function finishes execution. Global variables are declared outside the function definitions and can be referenced from any function defined after their declaration. They remain in existence for the entire execution of the program.

34. It is like a local variable but holds a value passed from the calling function to the called function.

35. A parameter is the local variable that holds the value of the argument.

36. As many parameters as are specified in the function definition

37. A one-to-one correspondence must exist between the arguments and parameters. Corresponding arguments and parameters must be of the same type.

38. *int, return,* and *sizeof* from Section 2.4

39. Separated by at least one blank (or tab or carriage return)

40. Preconditions describe the situation that exists as the module is to begin execution, any assumptions, and the information the module needs to meet its objectives.

41. Postconditions describe the state of the system when the module finishes executing, any error conditions, and the information the module returns or otherwise communicates.2

Chapter 3

1. The *if, if-else,* and *switch* statements

2. *if* and *else*

3. Six, as follows:
== equal to
!= not equal to
< less than
> greater than
<= less than or equal to
>= greater than or equal to

4. && for AND, || for OR

5. *TRUE* and *FALSE*

6. !, *, <, &&, ||, =

7. Sequential, modular, and selection

8. They must be combined into a compound statement using braces.

9. If present, it is followed by a statement that is executed only if the condition being tested proves to be false.

10. All the statements are false.

11. An *if* (or *if-else*) statement in which the *if* clause or the *else* clause contains another *if* (or *if-else*) statement

12. Two

13. Each *else* matches the nearest *if* before it which has not already been matched by a previous *else*.

14. The statement contains only one syntactical error. The first assignment statement ($a = b$;) is not part of the *if* clause, and therefore intervenes between the *if* and *else* clauses. This error can be corrected by joining the first call to *printf* and the first assignment statement within braces to form a compound statement.

In addition, the statement apparently has logical errors. The indentation has no effect on the compiler, but evidently the programmer intended both the second call to *printf* and the second assignment statement to be part of the *else* clause. Therefore, they should be joined in a compound statement. Both calls to *printf* should probably contain the newline character (\n) at the end of their control strings. Finally, the second *printf* should have "q is less than r".

15. The single equal sign means assignment, whereas the double equal sign is a relational operator used for testing equality.

16. The NOT operator, symbolized by !

17. 0 (zero)

18. There is virtually no limit.

19. The *switch* statement allows execution of its body to begin at one of several points, based on the value of an *int* (or *int*-compatible) variable or expression.

20. It causes the remaining statements in the body of the *switch* statement to be skipped.

21. *switch* and *case*

22. *break*

23. Program control is transferred to the statement immediately following the *case* label whose constant equals the value of the *switch* variable or expression.

24. If it is present, control transfers to the statement immediately following that label if the value of the *switch* variable or expression does not match any *case* labels.

25. In any order that suits the logic of the program

26. The statements just have to follow each other; they need not be placed within a compound statement.

27. When the *switch* statement is encountered, the *switch* variable or expression is evaluated. Program execution then continues at the *case* label whose constant is equal to the value of the *switch* variable or expression. If no such *case* label exists and the *default* label is present, execution continues there. If neither a matching *case* label nor a *default* label is present, the computer skips the statements in the *switch* statement body and continues execution at the statement following the *switch*. If a *break* statement is encountered during execution of the *switch* body, the rest of the statements in the body are skipped, and the statement after the *switch* statement is executed.

28. The *case* labels of all the values involved must be placed one after the other, with no intervening statements, before the statements to be executed.

29. Stub

Chapter 4

1. a is not

2. *float* (or *double*)

3. Floating point numbers have a broader range; may have a fractional portion; are stored differently; use the %e, %E, or %f conversion specification rather than %d; and on most computers, occupy more memory.

4.   **a.** 1.23456e2   **b.** 1.23e–4   **c.** 1.23e6

5. With a floating point number

6. The integer is temporarily converted to its floating point equivalent before the calculation is performed. This automatic operation is known as implicit conversion.

7. Coercion refers to the use of the cast operator by the programmer to specify explicitly to what type a value (or value of an expression) is to be converted.

8. A language is weakly typed if it sometimes allows data of one type to be used when another type is expected simply because the conversion is possible, not because it is meaningful.

9. Weakly typed

10. (*double*) 7 * 9 / 11

11. **a.** %d   **b.** %f   **c.** %e or %E

12. It specifies the smallest field in which a value is to be printed. It is used in a conversion specification, and if present, is placed immediately following the % sign.

13. The displayed value is left-justified instead of right-justified within the field.

14. It is perfectly acceptable. The effect is as if 0 is specified, which means the value is displayed in as many columns as necessary (and no more).

15. **a.** 9876   **b.** 9876   **c.** 9876
    d. 9876 preceded by six spaces

16. Either one may be used to read or print a floating point number, regardless of how that number is written in the program or entered by the user.

17. Six places are displayed, even if they are all zero.

18. It is rounded to the sixth decimal place.

19. It would not be printed, because %10.1 is an invalid specification. It does not end with e or f (or any other letter).

20. %ld

21. Generally, the set of letters used is not different. However, some difference in operation exists. For example, %f used in *printf* always displays a floating point number in decimal notation, but when it is used in *scanf* it is equivalent to %e. Both accept a number in either decimal or exponential notation.

22. *int, float, double, short, long, unsigned*

23. By using a conversion specification of %6d

24. The computer uses as many columns (or print positions) as necessary to display the full number.

25. Yes

26. *INT_MAX* in *limits.h*

27. fabs(x - y) < 10 * FLT_EPSILON

28. pow(x, 6)

29. *sqrt* in the math library

Chapter 5

1. x = x * y; x *= y;

2. All binary operators (+, −, *, /, %, and others yet to be described)

3. **a.** s +=x;   **b.** s -= x;   **c.** s /= x;
   d. s *= x;   **e.** s %= x;

4. **a.** v *= 2;   or v += v;   **b.** x /= 2;
   c. b *= 3;   **d.** r += 9;

5. i = 8, j = 8

6. total -= 1;   or   --total;   or   total--;

7. A pre-decrement operation, such as --*a*, decrements the value of *a* by 1 before *a* is used in a computation. A post-decrement, like *a*--, uses the current value of *a* in a calculation, and then decrements it.

8. ++

9. A *while* loop performs its test before the body of the loop is executed, whereas a *do-while* loop makes the test after the body is executed.

10. The whole loop is skipped.

11. One

12. The looping control structure

13. Two are necessary—one right before the *while* loop (the priming *scanf*) and one at the end of the body of the loop.

14. *rand*

15. 0–*RAND_MAX*

16. *srand*

17. *do, while*

18. Modular, sequential, selection, and looping control structures

Chapter 6

1. Index

2. It depends on the nature of the problem to be solved and on the preference of the programmer.

3. The *for* loop

4. The *do-while* loop

5. The initialization, testing, and modifier expressions of the loop are all specified within a single set of parentheses.

6. Semicolons

7. The first expression is executed once. The second expression is then tested, and if it evaluates as true, the body of the loop is executed. Then the third expression is executed, usually to change the value of the test variable.The second expression is evaluated again. As long as the second expression is true, the body of the loop is executed, followed by the third expression. When the second expression evaluates as false, the loop terminates.

8. If the initialization for the loop is done before the loop is reached

9. 0! = 1, 1! = 1, 5! = 120

10. The body of one *for* loop contains another *for* loop.

11. Bad data may create havoc with the program.

12. Inner

13. C has no built-in funcions, but its math library contains a square root function, *sqrt*.

14. Tracing, stepping through the code, stepping into a routine, stepping over a routine, watching the changing values of expressions, and establishing break-points

Chapter 7

1. It is a single character enclosed by apostrophes.

2. One

3. *%c*

4. The first is a single character, whereas the second is a string.

5. *char*

6. `fflush(stdin);`

7. Standard output, *stdout*, and standard input, *stdin*

8. It can output only one character at a time and only to the standard output.

9. The *getchar* function

10. The *getchar* function is specialized for character input, so its code is smaller than that of *scanf*. Moreover, *getchar* is implemented as a macro, while *scanf* has a function definition. Thus, *getchar* is more efficient and runs faster than *scanf*.

11. *EOF* is a constant returned by many I/O functions to indicate that the end of an input file has been reached.

12. American Standard Code for Information Interchange, which is the most popular character encoding scheme used on microcomputers

13. It is stored as a number.

14. *digit* – '0'

15. They are unprintable characters that play a special role of some kind.

16. Backspace, tab, newline, carriage return, form feed, and audible alert

17. It refers to the ASCII character with that particular value, when the three digits are interpreted as an octal number.

18. The variable *n* gets the value 23, whereas *x* gets the value '\n' (or ASCII code 10 or '\012'), because that is the character immediately following the integer 23 in the input.

19. `scanf("%d %c %c", &n, &c, &c);`
    `/* The blanks in the control string may be omitted */`

20. *ctype.h*

21. *tolower*

22. `!(answer == YES || answer == NO)`

23. *isspace*

24. *TRUE* ($\neq$ 0)

25. *ispunct*

26. *isalpha*

27. %o for octal and %x or %X for hexadecimal.

28. False; the leading zero indicates that the number is expressed in octal. The number 0123 is interpreted as an octal number whose value is equal to 85 in decimal. (This does not apply to input.)

29. True

30. False; %h is used to read in short integers, whereas %x is used to read hexadecimal values.

31. A file generally is stored on a disk.

32. A pointer of target type *FILE*

33. It must be opened by the program.

34. A text file

35. *fprintf* and *putc*

36. ```
ch = getc(file_ptr);
fscanf(file_ptr, "%c", ch);
```

**37.** *feof*

## Chapter 8

**1.** An array is a sequence of elements that share the same name and type.

**2.** `int a[100];`

**3.** 0 (zero)

**4.** The same as for naming regular variables or functions. An array cannot have the same name as a variable or function within the same program.

**5.** It cannot be done. (All elements of a single array must be of the same type.)

**6.** Before an element of an array can be used, it must have a value. Initializing an array gives a value to each of its elements.

**7.** Yes. The array declaration is followed immediately by an equal sign. This is followed by the list of values to be assigned (separated by commas) enclosed in braces.

**8.** A syntax error is flagged by the compiler. One array cannot be assigned to another using the assignment operator. Each element must be assigned individually.

**9.** No, but the program must keep track of how many elements are being used and which ones.

**10.** If the entire array is being initialized within the declaration

**11.** No. The elements of an array may be accessed in any order.

**12.** `PrintArray(int [], int);`     or
`PrintArray(int ar[], int n);`

**13.** `PrintArray(quantities, 30);`

**14.** Sequential search

**15.** Binary search

**16.** $\lceil \log_2(n + 1) \rceil$

**17.** Not always. In this chapter, the selection sort employed did not use another array. The advantage to using another array is that the original array is retained. Its disadvantage is that it uses extra memory.

**18.** The first element of the array, *ar*[0], and the array element with the minimum value

**19.** `temp = x;   x = y;   y = temp;`

**20.** Theoretically, there is no limit. The only practical limits are memory size and the restrictions imposed by the compiler being used.

**21.** False. Only the first (row) subscript can be omitted, with the first pair of square brackets left empty. The second subscript must always be specified.

**22.** The third entry of the fifth row of a two-dimensional array *array*
```

Chapter 9

1. Its address

2. With the & (address) operator

3. That is the only way one function can reference another function's local variables.

4. A variable's contents may change during execution of the function, but its address cannot be changed.

5. The name of a local variable is meaningful only within the function in which it is declared.

6. After it has been declared, it must be initialized.

7. The local variable can be accessed only by the function that contains it and the function that receives its address.

8. It passes the address of the variable being input, making it possible for the contents of that location to be changed.

9. It can be used only before the name of a scalar variable or a subscripted array element, not before an unsubscripted array name or an expression (other than a scalar variable).

10. Addresses can be stored in pointer variables.

11. **a.** Declares variable x as a pointer to *int*

    b. Declares variable z as an *int*

    c. Illegal, because the * is not part of a pointer variable's name, and therefore this statement tries to declare p and q twice

    d. Declares variable x as an *int*, declares variable y as a pointer to *int*, and initializes y to the address of x

12. Assign the address of r to q.

13. They are both legal.

    a. Takes the address of n, casts it into a pointer to *char*, and assigns this pointer to m.

    b. Takes the address of p, casts it into a pointer to *float*, and assigns this pointer to o.

14. The indirection operator is the asterisk (*). When placed before the name of a pointer variable, it means that the location being referred to is not the pointer variable, but the location pointed to by the pointer variable.

15. C treats addresses (pointers) and integers as different data types.

16. Pass by reference is the term used to refer to the passing of a variable's address to a function.

17. When a variable is passed by value to a function, only its value is passed. The function cannot change the contents of the variable. Passing by reference means that the variable's address is passed, giving the function the power to change the contents of that variable.

18. The parameters must be the addresses of the variables, and the contents of the locations pointed to by the addresses must be exchanged.

19. The unsubscripted name of an array is interpreted as a constant pointer, and any pointer variable can be subscripted.

20. Because the name of an array is already a constant pointer, the & would be both illegal (you cannot take the address of a constant) and redundant.

21. It is illegal; *ary* is a constant pointer, and therefore cannot have its value redefined.

22. Because all the elements of an array are of the same type and all the elements are stored contiguously in memory, the location of the first element can be used to find the second element, the third element, and so forth.

23. They may be declared in any order.

24. It is perfectly legal and returns a pointer, which is the original pointer incremented by the number of target units specified by the integer.

25. The same as a one-dimensional array name—as a constant pointer to the array's first element

26. *z*[5] is a pointer to the sixth row (row #5) of the array.

27. The first statement assigns 4 to *a*. The second statement assigns 5 to the location pointed to by the location pointed to by *c*. Because *c* points to *b*, this is the same as assigning 5 to the location pointed to by *b*. Because *b* points to *a*, this statement is equivalent to assigning 5 to *a*. The third statement casts **c*, which is the value of *a*, into type *int* *, and assigns this value to *b*. The result is probably meaningless, because location 5 (5 is the value of *a*) has no significance.

28. Because *a* is not initialized, **a* does not refer to any location, and so the value 7 has nowhere to go.

29. When we want to start a program with the smallest amount of memory necessary and to allocate extra space as needed. For example, we may not know in advance how large an array will be, and we may need to conserve memory.

30. Its parameter is the number of bytes to be allocated. It returns a pointer to a vacant area of memory of the specified size or *NULL* if the specified amount of memory cannot be allocated.

31. *calloc*

32. It returns the memory allocated by the *malloc, calloc,* or *realloc* functions to the pool of free memory. It is especially important to use this function in programs that place heavy emphasis on memory allocation.

33. `p = realloc(p, 50 * sizeof(int));`

34. A function pointer points to the location of a function in memory in much the same way that other pointers point to data in memory.

35. `void fnc(int (*f)(float x));`

36. `fnc(sub);`

Chapter 10

1. It is stored as an array of characters terminated by the null character, which has the ASCII value 0 and is written in C as '\0'.

2. `char pref[17];`
`/* one element reserved for null character, '\0' */`

3. %s

4. The ampersand (&) is not used, and the array is not subscripted.

5. A maximum field width specifier should be used with the %s conversion specification, for example, %10s.

6. Strings cannot be compared in a single operation. Each character must be compared to its corresponding element in the other array. The ANSI C standard library function *strcmp* accomplishes a comparison.

7. As a two-dimensional array of characters, in which each row is a separate string, or as an array of *char* pointers

8. Space must be allocated to hold the actual strings. The pointer array must be initialized so that its elements point to the allocated areas.

9. Strings (if they are used to store data in string format)

10. Type *char* *

11.

't'	"a"	'k'	'e'	' '	'c"	'a"	'r"	'e'	'\0'
0	1	2	3	4	5	6	7	8	9

12. By the null character ('\0')

13. 9—The null character is not included in a string's length; spaces, on the other hand, always are

14. A string literal

15. A literal string should not be modified in any way, but an array can be modified.

16. In C, \" is used to include a quotation mark as part of a literal. There is no such thing as "\ in C.

17. By a pointer to the literal

18. The null string is an empty pair of quotation marks (""). It is stored as a null character with no preceding characters. Its length is zero.

19. `char str[] = {'s', 't', 'r', 'i', 'n', 'g', '\0'};`

20. It stores one string, its second argument, into the array which is its first argument.

21. It returns the integer equivalent of the string argument, provided the string has the appearance of a valid integer.

22. When implemented to the fullest, it assists the user in preventing errors from occurring in the input, alerts the user to the nature of the error, and also enables recovery from the error to take place.

23. They are stored in exactly the same format and are both accessed by pointers.

24. Concatenation is the joining together of two or more strings so that one begins where the other ends. The *strcat* function concatenates its second argument to the end of its first argument, which must be a variable string (an array).

25. "concatenation"

26. A function can only return a pointer to a string. Because a string is an array, the function cannot directly return the body of the string.

27. The *strlen* function

28. Add the value returned by *strlen* to the pointer to the string. For example, if *string_ptr* points to the beginning of a string, *string_ptr + strlen(string_ptr)* points to the null character, the character that terminates the string. This is equivalent to *string_ptr[strlen(string_ptr)]*.

29.
```
char *array[4] =
{
    "hello",
    "there",
    "y'all",
    "have a nice day."
};
```

30. If *strcmp* returns zero, its two arguments are identical. A negative value indicates that the first argument is alphabetically (lexically) less than the second. A positive value means the first argument is lexically greater than the second.

31. `const float E = 2.71828;`

Chapter 11

1. In everyday applications, it is helpful to group together nonhomogeneous data into a single entity.

2. Whereas the elements of an array are always of the same data type, the members of a structure can be of different types. We reference elements of an array through an index, but we use the period operator and member name for a structure element.

3. *struct*

4. A template is a list of the members of a structure, along with their type specifications, enclosed in braces.

5. A structure tag is a name associated with a structure template. The tag allows us to declare other variables of the same structure type without having to rewrite the template itself.

6. By preceding the variable name with the keyword *struct* and either a previously defined structure tag or a template (optionally preceded by a tag not previously defined) or by preceding the variable name with a type name for the structure

7. An individual member of a structure is accessed by following the name of the structure variable with the period operator and the member name. The member name must be explicitly specified.

8. Associating a tag with a template makes it possible to use the tag (preceded by the keyword *struct*) in the same way a type keyword is used, for example, to declare variables or the types returned by functions.

9. `typedef float price_t;`

10. It aids in program documentation, because it is clear to the reader that a variable declared as type *string_t* is in fact a string pointer (as opposed to, say, just a pointer to a character).

11. The function *time* returns a value of type *time_t*. Its prototype is in *time.h*.

12. An array in which each element is a structure

13. A situation in which a structure contains another structure as a member

14. A structure cannot contain a member that is itself a structure of the same type (defined with the same tag) as the outer structure.

15. The notation $a\text{->}b$ means $(*a).b$, that is, "the member named b of the structure pointed to by a."

16. A linked list is a group of structures in which the first structure points to the second, the second points to the third, and so forth.

17. `typedef enum {FRESHMAN, SOPHOMORE, JUNIOR, SENIOR} class_t;`

18. It must include a member that is a pointer to another structure of the same type.

19. The *union* construct allows the same portion of memory to be accessed as different data types.

≋ Chapter 12

1. The line that is to be continued is ended with a backslash.

2. Anywhere in a program, so long as it is not on the same line as another directive or C statement

3. Wherever a blank space could safely be placed

4. A macro is an abbreviation for a segment of code. It is useful when a sequence of code is repeated often (with few if any modifications), but is too small to warrant the creation of a function. In such a case, a macro saves the programmer typing effort.

5. The comma

6. Any series of characters (except that the comma can be used only within quotation marks or parentheses)

7. It undefines a preprocessor symbol. In other words, it makes the preprocessor forget that the symbol was defined. It is necessary if we wish to change the value of a preprocessor symbol.

8. To include various definitions that the programmer uses often; to include definitions needed for certain operations, such as I/O; and to facilitate communication between program files through the use of shared global variables and function prototypes

9. The including or excluding of certain program lines, depending on the values of specified preprocessor symbols

10. The *#ifdef* directive is used in order to pass certain lines of code to the compiler only if the specified preprocessor symbol is defined before the *#ifdef* directive is encountered.

11. It passes lines of code to the compiler only if the specified preprocessor symbol is not defined.

12. The preprocessor runs first, before the program reaches the C language compiler.

13. The *#endif* directive

14. If an *#ifdef*, *#ifndef*, or *#if* directive returns a *FALSE* result, the *#else* directive specifies lines to be passed to the compiler in place of those following the *#ifdef*, *#ifndef*, or *#if* directive. The *#else* directive and its associated lines must follow the lines associated with the *#ifdef*, *#ifndef*, or *#if* directive and must precede the *#endif* directive.

15. They are the only text permitted on the lines they occupy.

16. The *#if* directive is followed by an integer constant expression. If the expression evaluates to a *TRUE* (nonzero) value, the lines following the directive are passed on to the compiler. Otherwise (if the expression evaluates to zero, or *FALSE),* the lines are omitted.

17. It is treated as having the value zero.

18. Symbols defined to be anything other than integer constants or expressions that evaluate to integer constants

19. The statement makes use of the conditional expression. If b is greater than c, the conditional expression returns the value of b (the value following the ?). Otherwise, it returns the value of c (the value following the :). The returned value is assigned to a. The overall effect is that the larger of the two variables b and c is assigned to a.

20. When used in declarations outside any function, *extern* indicates that the variable in question is declared (has memory allocated to it) in another program file. When *extern* is used within a function, it specifies that the named variable is a global variable.

21. A *static* variable is created when a program begins execution and remains in existence until the program terminates. A local variable declared as *static* does not disappear when the function in which it is declared terminates. A standard local variable, by contrast, disappears when the function terminates.

22. An *auto* variable comes into existence when the function in which it is declared is executed. It disappears (along with its contents) when the function returns. The next time the function is called, it is recreated.

23. The default class for local variables is *auto*. Global variables can never be of that class. Therefore, we need not specify *auto* as a storage class.

24. When this is done, the global variable cannot be accessed outside the program file in which it is declared. This allows the variable to be used for communication between functions in the same file, while preventing it from being global to the entire program.

25. Through the *argc* and *argv* parameters of the *main* function

26. The name used to execute the program, usually the name of the file containing the compiled and linked program

27. *auto*, *static*, *extern*

28. *#if 0* before the segment and *#endif* after

Chapter 13

1. Recursion is a technique whereby a function calls itself. It is useful in problems that can be defined in terms of smaller versions of the same problem.

2. No such declaration is needed in C.

3. The terminal case is the stopping situation for a recursive function. In such a case, the function does not invoke itself.

4. This record contains information about the routine, such as parameter values, local variables, and the return location after execution of the routine. The activation record comes into existence when we call a function.

5. A run-time stack

6. Stack overflow

7. Find a nonrecursive definition for the function

Chapter 14

1. A file not only can store more data than an array but retains its contents even when the computer is turned off.

2. The screen normally is used for output, and the keyboard is used for input.

3. Standard input, standard output, and standard error

4. The end of a string is always indicated by a null character, whereas the manner in which the end of a file is indicated depends on the storage device and the computer.

5. The words "input" and "output" are not keywords in C.

6. An error code probably would be returned by the I/O function.

7. Append mode is used to add characters to the end of a file that already exists. It is specified by using the mode string "a" as the second parameter to *fopen*.

8. When write mode is used, the former contents of the file are erased. With append mode, the contents of the file are retained, and new information is added to the end of the file.

9. By including b in the mode string, such as "r+b" or "rb"

10. A program can read a byte or record from any point in a file without having to read all preceding characters. The same statement applies to writing information to the file.

11. The *fseek* function is used to position the file (or the file's marker) to a specified location. The three arguments are the *FILE* pointer of an (open) file; a long integer indicating the position in number of bytes from a specific location; and one of three integers indicating the specific location—0 (*SEEK_SET*) for the beginning of the file, 1 (*SEEK_CUR*) for the current position, or 2 (*SEEK_END*) for the end of the file.

12. A file can be rewound by the statement

```
fseek(fp, 0L, SEEK_SET);
```

where *fp* is the file pointer.

13. A file opened with "w+" mode is opened in the same manner as with w mode (it is erased or created), except that the file can be both read from and written to without the necessity of closing and reopening it.

14. `fread(&rec, sizeof(record_t), 1, fp);`

15. `fwrite(&rec, sizeof(record_t), 1, fp);`

16. The *ftell* function returns the current position in the file. It is useful in determining the size of a file.

17. In "r+" mode, a file is expected to exist already. Its contents are retained, and it is opened for both reading and writing.

18. It is used to open a file for appending, but also permits the file to be read without the need to close and reopen the file.

Chapter 15

1. A byte or variable might contain individual bits or bit fields, each of which represents a different flag or value. In such a case, we want to be able to manipulate the bits individually.

2. a. 1000   **b.** 1111

3. The tilde (~) represents the logical NOT (or one's complement) operation.

4. In the inclusive OR operation, the result is *TRUE* (1) when one or both operands are *TRUE*. In the EXCLUSIVE OR, the result is *TRUE* when one of the operands is *TRUE*, but not both.

5. a. <<   **b.** >>

6. In the logical right shift, zeros always are shifted in from the left. In the arithmetic shift, the bit value shifted in from the left is the same as that which formerly was the leftmost bit (in other words, the leftmost bit is propagated).

7. The left shift can be used for multiplication by powers of 2, and the right shift can be used for division by powers of 2.

8. Bit fields are structure members whose sizes, in bits, are explicitly specified and are less than the size of a word or *int*.

9. This definition can be used only in a structure template. It defines a bit field named *FourBits,* which is four bits in length. Because the field is not explicitly defined as unsigned, some compilers treat it as an unsigned variable and others treat it as signed.

Chapter 16

1. A set of data items and fundamental operations on this set

2. A dynamic linked list provides a linking configuration of nodes of information that can expand or contract as needed.

3. No, insertions at the head of the list are different from those made later in the list.

4. *target->next*

5. `P = P->next;`

6. The deleted node must be freed so that its memory space can be reused.

7. LIFO—*Last In First Out*

8. The top

9. Push

10. Pop

11. 2 3 1

12. The meaning of filling depends on the implementation. In an array implementation, which is static, the stack can fill. In a linked list implementation, which is dynamic, the stack never fills within the limits of the size of the computer's memory.

13. `return(*s_ptr == NULL ? TRUE : FALSE);`

14. *InsertFirst*

15. We should make sure the stack is not empty.

Index